Computer Service and Repair

A Guide to Upgrading, Configuring, Troubleshooting, and Networking Personal Computers

Third Edition

Richard M. Roberts

Publisher
The Goodheart-Willcox Company, Inc.
Tinley Park, Illinois
www.g-w.com

Manufactured in the United States of America.

Library of Congress Catalog Card Number 2007036135

ISBN 978-1-59070-857-6

1 2 3 4 5 6 7 8 9 – 08 – 12 11 10 09 08

The Goodheart-Willcox Company, Inc., Brand Disclaimer: Brand names, company names, and illustrations for products and services included in this text are provided for educational purposes only and do not represent or imply endorsement or recommendation by the author or the publisher.

The Goodheart-Willcox Company, Inc., Safety Notice: The reader is expressly advised to carefully read, understand, and apply all safety precautions and warnings described in this book or that might also be indicated in undertaking the activities and exercises described herein to minimize risk of personal injury or injury to others. Common sense and good judgment should also be exercised and applied to help avoid all potential hazards. The reader should always refer to the appropriate manufacturer's technical information, directions, and recommendations; then proceed with care to follow specific equipment operating instructions. The reader should understand these notices and cautions are not exhaustive.

The publisher makes no warranty or representation whatsoever, either expressed or implied, including but not limited to equipment, procedures, and applications described or referred to herein, their quality, performance, merchantability, or fitness for a particular purpose. The publisher assumes no responsibility for any changes, errors, or omissions in this book. The publisher specifically disclaims any liability whatsoever, including any direct, indirect, incidental, consequential, special, or exemplary damages resulting, in whole or in part, from the reader's use or reliance upon the information, instructions, procedures, warnings, cautions, applications, or other matter contained in this book. The publisher assumes no responsibility for the activities of the reader.

Library of Congress Cataloging-in-Publication Data

Roberts, Richard M.
Computer service and repair: a guide to upgrading, configuring, troubleshooting, and networking personal computers/ Richard M. Roberts. — [3rd ed.].
p. cm.
Includes index.
ISBN 978-1-59070-857-6
1. Microcomputers—Maintenance and repair. I. Title.
TK7887.R62 2008
004. 16—dc22 2007036135

Introduction

Personal computer (PC) support has evolved into one of the largest service industries in the world. The demand for skilled technicians to maintain, support, and upgrade PCs is ever growing. It is a rewarding and challenging career that can take you anywhere in the world. If you enjoy tinkering with PCs or have ever wondered how they work and what it takes to repair them, this course is for you. If you wish to learn computer networking, programming, administration, or any of the computer sciences, then this is the perfect place to start. A good foundation in PC technology will provide you with a base of knowledge that will make learning the other technical areas much easier.

Most computer troubleshooting is performed at the keyboard using knowledge about the PC system. You need to have a good understanding of how the components work hand-in-hand with the operating system software rather than knowing how the electronic parts (transistors, resistors, and capacitors) function. PC repair started out as a domain dominated by electronic technicians with thousands of hours of training. It has evolved into a specialized field of PC technicians requiring little to no electronics background at all.

The actual concepts and mechanics of computer repair are quite easy. You can show someone how to change the major components inside a PC very quickly with very few tools. For example, the mechanics of replacing a hard drive are extremely easy. Problems arise, however, if the hard drive doesn't work as expected and you start to read the technical manual specifications for help. Questions and answers are filled with unfamiliar terms such as *format, fdisk, partition, active partition, sectors, block allocation units, boot sector, system files, FAT16, FAT32, NTFS, HPFS, OS/2, MB, boot disk, system recovery disk, system disk, cable select, IDE, ATA, EIDE,* and *SCSI*. This can prove very confusing to the novice. However, with a little effort, soon you will be talking "techie talk" like the rest of the technicians.

Computer systems are built better than ever before. The constant problems caused by failing components encountered 30 years ago are seldom found today. Computers still do fail because of bad components, but now the majority of failures are due to software problems or they are caused by the computer users themselves. Only a small percentage of computer failures require component replacement. What is needed is someone who can diagnose the problem and determine if it is hardware related, software related, or user generated. This is the job of the PC technician. Remember that with PC repair, it is important to complete all lab activities. They are designed to give you valuable computer experiences and enhance the skills you are being taught. This will better prepare you for the CompTIA A+ exams if you choose to take them, and better prepare you for a career as a PC technician.

I wish you much success in your future.

Sincerely,

Richard M. Roberts

The Author

For the past 35 years, Richard Roberts has been designing curriculum, teaching Electricity and Electronics as well as Computer Technology, and supervising technical teachers. Mr. Roberts is an accomplished programmer and computer technician. He has experience as the system administrator for Novell NetWare, Microsoft NT, and IBM Token Ring networking systems. He possesses a Bachelor's degree in Technical Education and a Master's degree in Administration/ Supervision. He also has CompTIA A+, Network+, iNet+, and Security+ certifications and is a certified IT technician, remote desktop support technician, and depot technician.

His computer experiences started as early as 1974 when he began programming and teaching the Motorola 6800, which eventually evolved into the Motorola 68000, once the core processor of the Apple Macintosh computer system. Since then, Mr. Roberts has maintained his teaching status to both instructors and students as the technology has evolved, and he has remained at a state-of-the-art technical level through research, teaching, and applications. He is currently an adjunct instructor at South Florida Community College where he teaches PC repair, A+ Certification, Network Fundamentals, Network+ Certification, and many short workshops in various Microsoft business applications. He also coauthored the textbook *Electricity and Electronics* as well as designed and programmed the accompanying interactive CD-ROM.

In addition to his current position, Mr. Roberts has taught at Erwin Technical Center and Tampa Bay Technical High School, and he has taught adults in the military service. His time is now divided between computer consulting and applications, teaching students and instructors, and writing textbooks and other ancillary instructional materials. Occasionally, he goes fishing, but not too often.

Using This Text

Each chapter begins with a number of learning objectives. These are the goals you should set to accomplish while working through the chapter. In addition to your objectives, each chapter begins with a list of these new terms, which are important for you to learn as you move through the chapter. When these words are introduced in the text, they are printed in a bold italic typeface. At that point in the text, you will find these terms defined in the margin.

As you read this text, you will also notice some other words or phrases that stand out. File names that you encounter will appear like notepad.exe, student.txt, or io.sys. Any data you must enter, be it by typing at the command and Run prompts or button/tabs/menus that you will click on with your mouse are set out like **dir C:** or **Start | All Programs | Accessories | System Tools**. Any Internet addresses within the text are in the traditional Web style and in blue, such as www.g-w.com. Internet address listed under Interesting Web Sites for More Information at the end of each chapter are in the traditional Web style, underlined, and in blue, such as www.g-w.com. Be sure to read any A+ Notes, Tech Tips, Warnings, Cautions, and Dangers that you encounter. A+ Notes contain tips that will help you study for the CompTIA A+ Certification exams. Tech Tips are useful tidbits that might come in handy in the field. Take heed when you see Warnings, Cautions, and Dangers. Warnings alert you of minor injury that may occur to yourself or to others. Cautions alert you when an act may damage your computer and incur minor injury to yourself. Losing all of your data is the most common act to be cautious of. Dangers alert you of possible serious or fatal injury to yourself or others. For example, you may encounter some dangerous voltages, especially when dealing with monitors. Most of those repairs should be left to special technicians.

Each chapter concludes with a summary of some of the key information you should take from the chapter, a large number of questions, a list of useful Web sites, and laboratory activities for you to try. Each chapter has two sets of questions. The first set of questions tests your general comprehension of the material in the chapter. The second set of questions mimics the style of the CompTIA A+ Certification exams. The questions asked here are on topics that the exams commonly probe.

Hands-on experience is the only way to become proficient in PC repair, so be sure to attempt the activities at the end of each chapter. If you can complete the activities in this text and in the accompanying laboratory manual, you should have no problem passing the A+ Certification exams. Each chapter concludes with a complete Lab Activity. Be sure to work through each of these activities. Suggested Laboratory Activities are also included. These activities are loosely structured proceedings that you can attempt on your own or if you have free time in class.

Never forget, the world of PCs changes rapidly. Consequently, PC repair and the CompTIA A+ Certification exams must change with it. Each chapter includes a list of Web sites where you can find the latest information on the topics covered. Be sure to check the CompTIA Web site (www.comptia.org) frequently for the latest information on what subjects are being added to the exams and what subjects are being dropped. Also, check the author's Web site (www.RMRoberts.com) for text updates, interesting links, and bonus laboratory material.

Acknowledgments

I would like to thank the following people who helped make this textbook possible by supplying information, details, photographs, artwork, and software.

Adam Forbes, Crucial Technology
Al Platt, US Postal Service
Beverly A. Summers, Fluke Corporation
Brian Burke, NVIDIA Corporation
Chris Keller, PC-Doctor, Inc.
David Goss, American Microsystems LTD
David Leong, Kingston Technology Company, Inc.
Erkki Lepre, F-Secure Corporation
Gabriel Rouchon, Swiftech Inc.
George Alfs, Intel Corporation
Heather Jardim, Kingston Technology Company, Inc.
Howard Burnside, Electronics Instructor, Retired
Jacqueline Romulo, Belkin International, Inc.
Jason Cambria, NeoWorx, Inc.
Jeremy VanWagnen, TechSmith Corporation
Jim Spare, Canesta, Inc.

Joanna Moore, IBM Corporation
John Stott, Citicorp
Kevin Franks, Winternals Software LP
Les Goldberg, D-Link Systems
Melody Chalaban, Belkin Corporation
Michelle Flippen, Tiny Software, Inc.
Ray Gorman, IBM Corporation
Sonel V. Friedman, GTCO CalComp, Inc.
Stu Sjouwerman, Sunbelt Software
Tom Way, IBM Corporation
Walter Ernie, Computer and Electronics Instructor
William Kautter, GTCO CalComp, Inc.
and special thanks to Carl Marchand

Trademarks

DirectX, Microsoft, MS-DOS, Outlook, Visual Basic, Windows, Windows NT, Windows Server, Windows Vista, and Windows XP are all trademarks of Microsoft Corporation.

Zip is a trademark of Iomega Corporation.

Apple, FireWire, Leopard, Mac, Macintosh, Mac OS, QuickTime, and TrueType are registered trademarks of Apple Inc.

Celeron, Celeron D, Celeron M, Enhanced Intel SpeedStep, Intel Core. Intel Core 2 Duo, Intel Core 2 Solo, Intel Core Duo, Intel Core Extreme Solo, Intel Core Quad, Intel Core Solo, Intel Xeon, Intel386, Intel486, IntelDX2, IntelDX4, Itanium, Itanium 2, MMX, OverDrive, Pentium, Pentium 4, Pentium D, Pentium II Xeon, Pentium III Xeon, and Pentium M are registered trademarks of Intel Corporation.

AMD, AMD Athlon, AMD Duron, AMD-K6, AMD OverDrive, Athlon 64, Athlon MP, Athlon Opteron, Athlon XP, ATI, and Cool 'n' Quiet are trademarks of Advanced Micro Devices, Inc.

PostScript is a trademark of Adobe Systems, Inc.

Rambus and RDRAM are trademarks of Rambus, Inc.

Other trademarks are registered by their respective owners.

CompTIA Authorized Quality Curriculum

The logo of the CompTIA Authorized Quality Curriculum (CAQC) program and the status of this or other training material as "Authorized" under the CompTIA Authorized Quality Curriculum program signifies that, in CompTIA's opinion, such training material covers the content of the CompTIA's related certification exam. CompTIA has not reviewed or approved the accuracy of the contents of this training material and specifically disclaims any warranties of merchantability or fitness for a particular purpose. CompTIA makes no guarantee concerning the success of persons using any such "Authorized" or other training material in order to prepare for any CompTIA certification exam. The contents of this training material were created for the CompTIA A+ exams covering CompTIA certification exam objectives that were current as of 2006.

How to Become CompTIA Certified

This training material can help you prepare for and pass a related CompTIA certification exam or exams. To achieve CompTIA certification, you must do the following:

1. Select a certification exam provider. For more information, please visit http://certification.comptia.org/resources/registration.aspx.
2. Register for and schedule a time to take the CompTIA certification exam(s) at a convenient location.
3. Read and sign the Candidate Agreement, which will be presented at the time of the exam(s). The text of the Candidate Agreement can be found at http://certification.comptia.org/resources/canidate_agreement.aspx.
4. Take and pass the CompTIA certification exam(s).

For more information about CompTIA's certifications, such as their industry acceptance, benefits, or program news, please visit http://certification.comptia.org.

CompTIA is a nonprofit information technology (IT) trade association. CompTIA's certifications are designed by subject matter experts from across the IT industry. Each CompTIA certification is vendor-neutral, covers multiple technologies, and requires demonstration of skills and knowledge widely sought after by the IT industry.

To contact CompTIA with any questions or comments:
Please call (630) 687-8300
or e-mail CompTIA at questions@comptia.org.

CompTIA A+ Correlation Charts

Complete mappings (correlation charts) of the CompTIA A+ 2006 objectives to the content of the *Computer Service and Repair* textbook and *Lab Manual* are located on the G-W Web site (www. g-w.com) for this textbook. On this Web site, you will find one correlation chart per CompTIA A+ exam:

- CompTIA A+ Essentials.
- CompTIA A+ 220-602.
- CompTIA A+ 220-603.
- CompTIA A+ 220-604.

Each correlation chart lists the exam objectives and the corresponding textbook pages and lab activities of where to find the related content.

Chapter Listing

Table of Contents

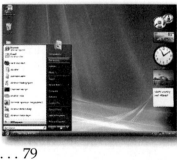

Chapter 3
Motherboards

Chapter 4
CPU

Chapter 5
Power Supplies

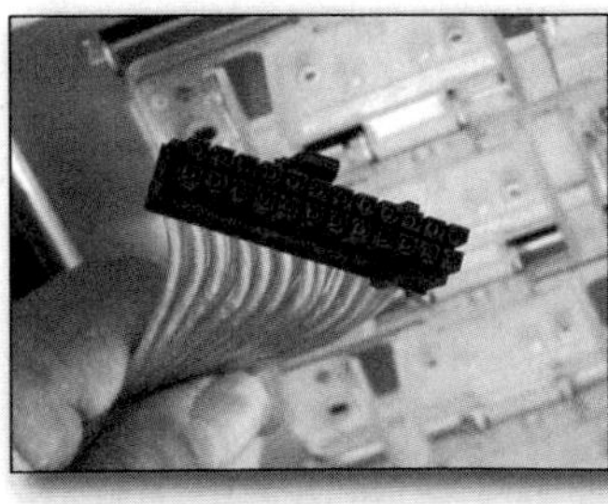

Chapter 8
Video Display and Audio Systems

Chapter 9
Magnetic Storage Devices

Chapter 10
CD Technology

Chapter 11
Printers

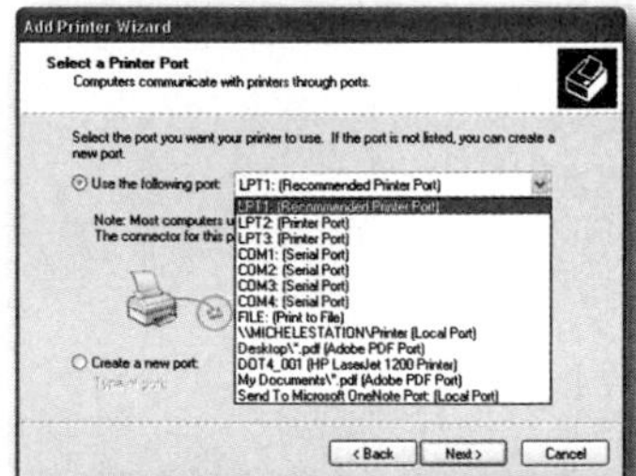

Chapter 12
Portable PCs

Chapter 13
Modems and Transceivers

Chapter 14
Viruses

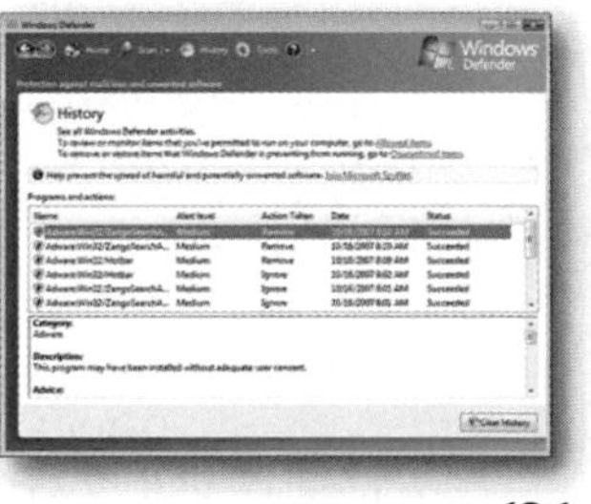

Chapter 15
PC Troubleshooting

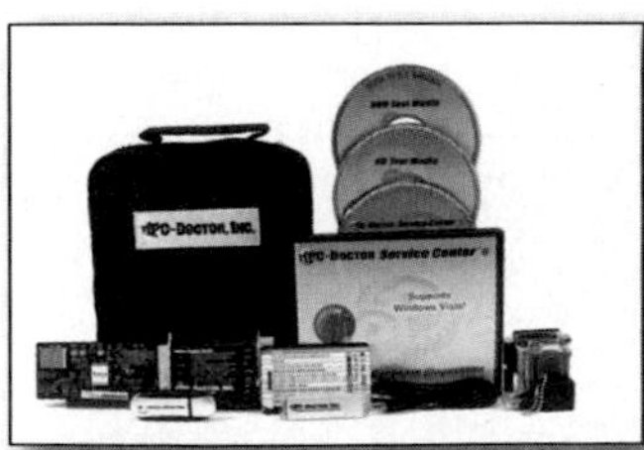

Chapter 16
Introduction to Networking

Chapter 17
Network Administration

Chapter 18
WAN

Chapter 19
Small-Office/Home-Office (SOHO) Networking

Chapter 20
Customer Support, Communication, and Professionalism

Chapter 21
CompTIA A+ Certification Exams Preparation

Chapter 22
Employment and Advanced Education

Introduction to a Typical PC

After studying this chapter, you will be able to:

- ✔ Explain the role of computers.
- ✔ Explain what a computer is.
- ✔ Describe computer data.
- ✔ Identify the major components of a typical PC.
- ✔ Describe the power-on sequence of a typical PC.
- ✔ Explain how the major components interact with each other.
- ✔ Interpret the common prefixes associated with the computer's size and speed.
- ✔ Define electrostatic discharge.
- ✔ Identify common tools used to service a PC.

A+ Exam—Key Points

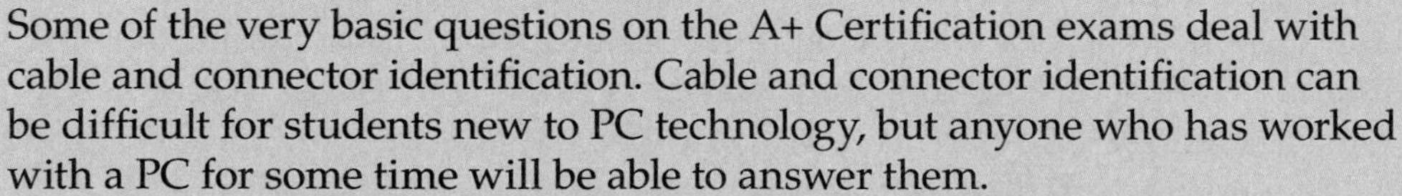

Some of the very basic questions on the A+ Certification exams deal with cable and connector identification. Cable and connector identification can be difficult for students new to PC technology, but anyone who has worked with a PC for some time will be able to answer them.

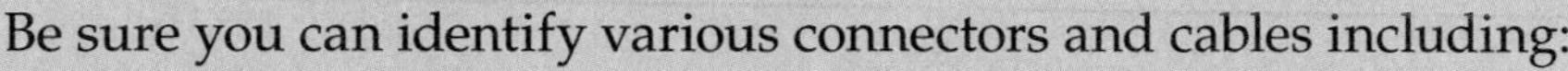

Be sure you can identify various connectors and cables including:

- ✔ DB-9
- ✔ DB-25
- ✔ RJ-11
- ✔ PS/2 or mni-DIN
- ✔ IEEE-1394
- ✔ USB

Be able to differentiate between serial and parallel data transmission. Examine and memorize all typical computer cable end connectors. For example, look at the end of the monitor cable. Does it use pins or a socket? The same goes for the PC unit. Always check the CompTIA Web page for the latest test objectives. A complete listing of hardware identification and installation requirements is listed there.

Key Words and Terms

The following words and terms will become important pieces of your computer vocabulary. Be sure you can define them.

A+ Certification
American Standard Code for Information Interchange (ASCII)
analog
anti-static wrist strap
basic input/output system (BIOS)
battery
binary number system
bit
byte
central processing unit (CPU)
complementary metal oxide semiconductor(CMOS)
CompTIA
computer
cooling fan
data
device bay
digital
electrostatic discharge (ESD)
expansion card slots
expansion cards
hard drive
hexadecimal number system
hot swap
integrated circuit (IC)
motherboard
parallel
peripherals
random access memory (RAM)
serial
word

This chapter introduces you to the basic concepts you need to know to understand computer hardware and software. It briefly covers many topics. These topics are expanded into complete chapters later in the textbook. This text presents the personal computer based on the IBM-compatible computer architecture, better known as the PC, and prepares you for CompTIA's A+ Certification exams.

CompTIA
a not-for-profit vendor-neutral organization that certifies the competency level of computer service technicians.

A+ Certification
certification awarded on successful completion of the CompTIA A+ exams.

The ***CompTIA*** organization is a not-for-profit, vendor-neutral organization that certifies the competency level of technicians through examinations written to test specific areas. The CompTIA organization has prepared the examinations to test individuals with 500 hours of PC repair, installation, and support experiences. The certification awarded on successful completion of the exams is called ***A+ Certification.*** It is recognized throughout the industry as a certification of basic PC repair and support skills. The combination of this textbook and its accompanying Laboratory Manual and Study Guide prepare you for the certification exams. There is more information in Chapter 20—A+ Certification Exam Preparation. You can also visit the CompTIA Web site at www.comptia.org for the latest information.

The Role of Computers

Computers are found in every aspect of our lives. There is not an industry that operates without a computer. Computers can be found in banks, Wall Street businesses, military aircraft, automobiles, televisions, communication systems, home appliances, satellites, submarines, and police stations. Computers can vary in size from the small, simple microprocessor that you might find in a coffeepot or a clock radio to huge mainframe systems that are used in research and government systems. **Figure 1-1** shows a microchip along with a large computer system and a typical home or business PC.

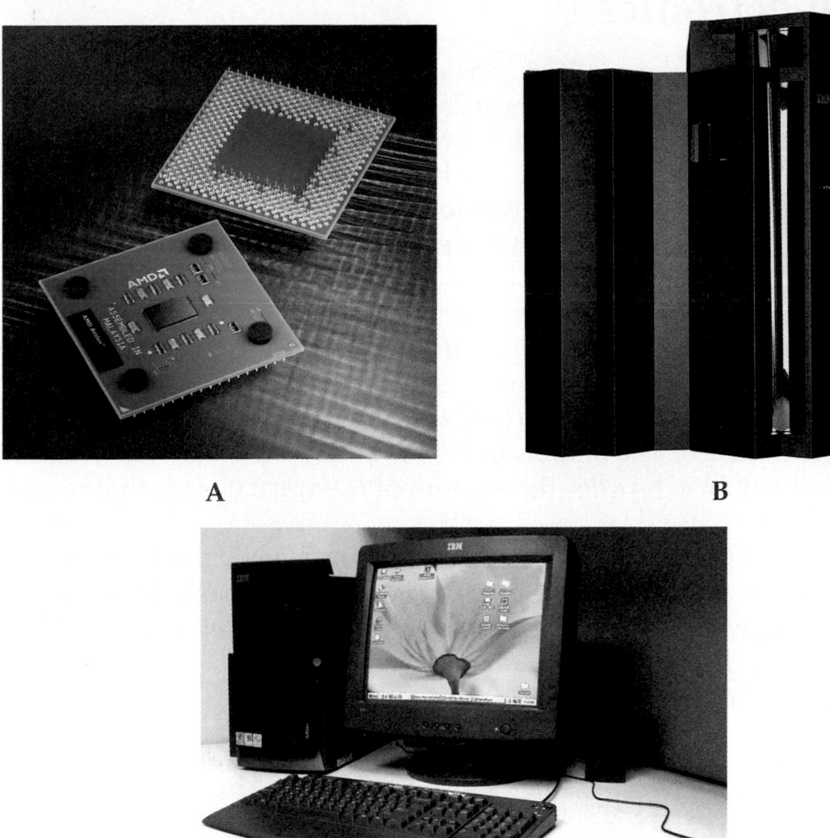

Figure 1-1. A microchip (AMD Athlon™ XP processor) alongside a large computer system for a research center, and, of course, a typical home PC. (Advanced Microprocessor Devices, Inc. and International Business Systems Corporation)

At first, the makeup of a computer can seem intimidating. However, as you progress through this text, you will see that the mechanics of a computer are quite simple. The difficulty is overcome by understanding the interaction of hardware and software, grasping different operating systems, and recognizing upgrade and compatibility issues.

If you know which part is defective, it is a relatively easy task to replace the part. The challenge is determining which part is defective or determining if the problem is hardware related or software related.

The aim of this textbook is to systematically teach you the necessary skills to be successful in the world of computer technology. In this chapter, we will take a quick look at the major components of a typical PC and introduce basic computer concepts such as computer data and software. As your studies progress through the text, each part and concept will be covered in great depth, but for now it is best to have an overall view of the PC system. No component can be fully understood without realizing how it interacts with the other components in the system. This chapter covers introductory level knowledge of the computer system before going into depth at a technician level.

Digital Electronics

digital
a system that uses discrete values.

analog
a system using a continuous, infinite range of values.

All electronic components fall into one of two categories: analog or digital. Digital electronics is a system that is best represented by a simple switch. There can only be two conditions in the switch circuit. The switch is either on or off. No other state exists. Look at **Figure 1-2,** which shows a typical switch wired to a lamp. The switch controls all the power to the lamp. The lamp can be turned on or off. No other electrical condition can exist for this simple circuit. ***Digital*** electronics in computers use on and off conditions. There is either full voltage or no voltage applied to the circuit.

Analog electronics use and produce varying voltage levels. Analog electrical circuits can be represented with a dimmer switch. **Figure 1-3** shows a dimmer switch connected to a lamp. In this circuit, the intensity of the lamp varies as the dimmer switch is turned. The light from the lamp can have different intensities because the dimmer switch varies the amount of electrical energy that reaches the lamp.

A computer is constructed of some very complex digital circuits. These digital circuits are combined into modules such as circuit board cards. As a PC technician, you will usually only be responsible for replacing the module, not repairing the digital circuits. You do not need an extensive electronics background to repair the PC.

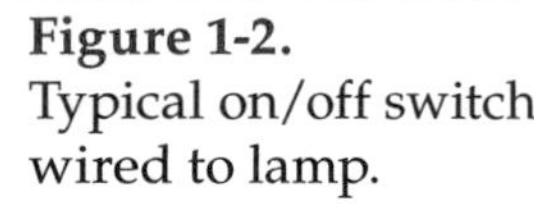

Figure 1-2.
Typical on/off switch wired to lamp.

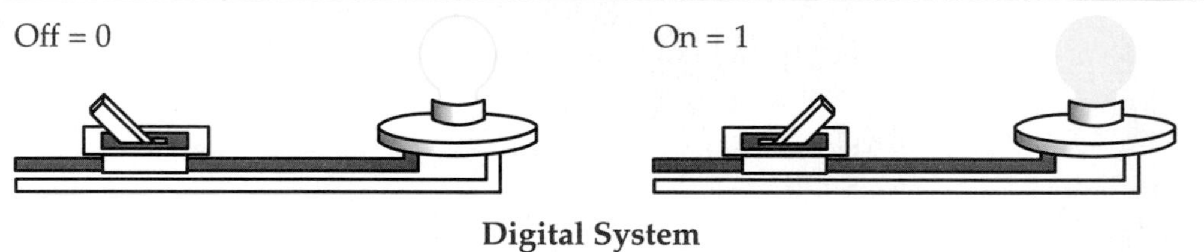

Figure 1-3.
A typical dimmer switch.

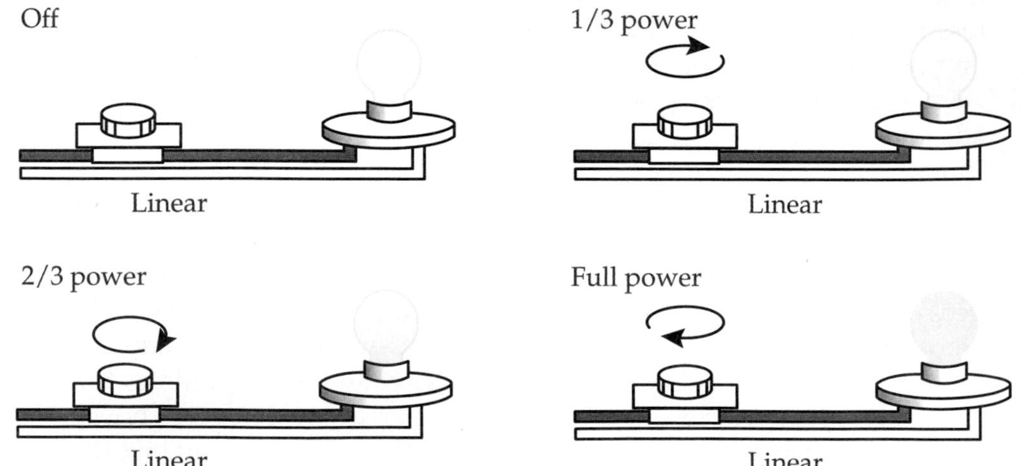

What Is a Computer?

The PC is a fantastic piece of engineering technology. A ***computer*** is an assembly of electronic modules that interact with computer programs known as *software* to create, modify, transmit, store, and display data. The computer has rapidly evolved from a simple electronic device into a highly sophisticated piece of electronic technology.

computer
an assemblage of electronic modules that interact with software to create, modify, transmit, store, and display data.

Science fiction writers have attributed human qualities to computers such as Father in *Alien: Resurrection.* The computer can appear to be intelligent, but in reality it only processes and stores data. Processing data is limited to such things as sorting items, comparing, and locating previously stored data. In addition, computers perform mathematical calculations at amazing speeds. However, the computer cannot think. The computer can only be programmed.

This leads to another basic question: What is data? ***Data*** is information. This information comes in many forms. Data can be text (such as *ABC* or *123*), graphics (pictures), and sounds (like music or voices). **Figure 1-4** is an illustration presenting text, sound, and a picture, followed by digital electrical voltage symbols.

data
information, which can be presented in alpha/numeric form (such as ABC or 123), visual form (pictures), and audible form (like music or voices).

Data inside the computer is represented electronically as high and low voltages. The voltages are pulsed through the system. These pulses of high and low voltages create what is called a *digital signal.* Many things can be done with these pulses of electrical energy. Data can be displayed on a computer monitor or can be stored in memory chips, on a hard drive, a floppy disk, or a compact disc (CD). When written to a hard drive or to floppy disks, the electrical pulses are converted to magnetic patterns on the surface of the disk.

Picture

..ctronic components
one of two categories, dig..
analog type devices. Digital
electronics has two states of
conditions, on and off. And
e expressed at many differe..
..vels between on and of..

Text

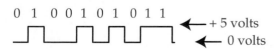

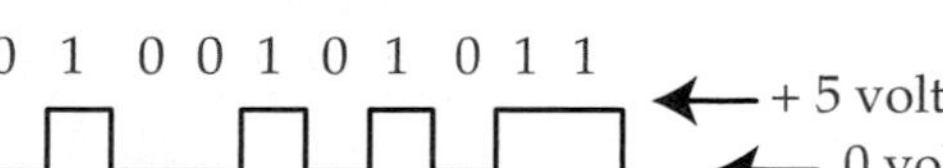

Figure 1-4. Sound, pictures, and text are all forms of data. Each can be represented by a code comprised of ones and zeros, the binary number system. (Union Tools, Inc.)

Data in a computer system is represented as ones and zeros. The pattern of ones and zeros is known as the *binary system.* You will be introduced to the binary system later in this chapter. Some of the digital patterns represent words, pictures, and sounds. Other digital patterns represent commands such as load file, find file, save file, or activate the diskette drive. Remember, the computer does not contain any intelligence. It simply manipulates, stores, and displays data.

Computer Data Codes

Data can be almost anything. It can be numbers, text, pictures, and sounds. Computer data and functions are expressed in a variety of ways. They can be expressed as voltage levels, numeric systems such as binary and hexadecimal, and symbolic codes such as ASCII. Although computer data and commands can be expressed in many different forms and still have the same meaning, the form selected should be the one that is easiest to grasp for the given material. For example, it is much easier to express memory locations as hexadecimal values rather than binary values although the memory location could be expressed in either value. The computer technician must be very familiar with each of these forms of data expression.

Binary Number Code

binary number system
a system in which all numbers are expresses as combinations of 0 and 1. Also known as the base 2 number system.

The ***binary number system*** consists of entirely ones and zeros. It is the perfect numbering system to represent digital electronic systems. Just as a digital device has only two states (on and off), the binary system uses only two numbers: *0* and *1.* Look at **Figure 1-5** to see how the binary number system is used to express different values from zero to fifteen.

Binary can be compared to a switch. If the switch is closed, the lamp will be on. This state is represented by a *1.* When the switch is in the off position, the lamp is dark. This state is represented by a *0.*

This may seem like a system too simple to represent data in a computer, but let's compare it to the Morse code system. The Morse code system consists of only two tones: a short beep and a long beep. These sounds are referred to as a dot and a dash respectively. See **Figure 1-6.** This code resembles a binary system. It has two conditions. The dots and dashes can be combined in sequences that represent the alphabet and the numerals *0–9.* The Morse code system has been used to transmit information all over the world.

Graphics are transmitted in a similar fashion using a facsimile (fax) machine. The light and dark areas are represented by the presence or absence of a transmitted voltage. Again, this is a form similar to digital electronics. See **Figure 1-7,** which depicts two rotating drums. One drum is a transmitter and the other is a receiver. As you can see, the two-state condition of digital electronics can be much more powerful than it first appears.

The ones and zeros of the binary system are used to represent the high and low voltage signals that travel throughout the computer system. They also represent data stored on disks or in memory chips.

Binary	Decimal
0000	0
0001	1
0010	2
0011	3
0100	4
0101	5
0110	6
0111	7
1000	8
1001	9
1010	10
1011	11
1100	12
1101	13
1110	14
1111	15

Figure 1-5.
The binary number system can be used to represent any integer in the decimal system. This chart shows binary numbers counting up to 15.

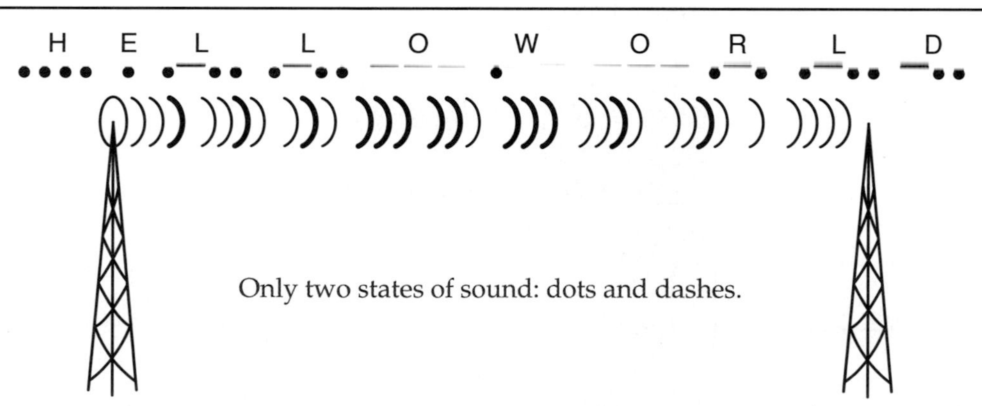
H E L L O W O R L D
Only two states of sound: dots and dashes.

Figure 1-6.
Morse code transfers letters between two antennas using combinations of two states: dots and dashes.

Hexadecimal Number Code

The hexadecimal code is based on the number base 16, similar to how the binary code is based on the number base 2. The ***hexadecimal number system*** uses 16 characters. See **Figure 1-8.**

hexadecimal number system
a system in which all numbers are expressed in combinations of 16 alphanumeric characters *(0–F)*. Also know as the base 16 system.

The hexadecimal system uses numerals *0–9* from the decimal number system and six additional characters from the alphabet, *A–F*. This combination of number and letter characters forms the hexadecimal number system. Binary numbers are too long and awkward to be used to express computer values such as memory locations. Thus, hexadecimal numbers are used instead. The hexadecimal code uses less space.

The hexadecimal system best matches the hardware system of most computers. As you will learn, data lines in a computer are eight, sixteen, thirty-two, or sixty-four lines wide. They use increments of eight and sixteen, which work beautifully with a hexadecimal system.

Figure 1-7.
Voltage highs and lows can be used to send pictures across phone lines.

Original news photograph.

The original photo is mounted on the rotating drum. A light transmitter and receiver convert the light and dark areas of the image into matching voltage levels.

A transducer moves along the drum while it spins, converting the image into electrical signals.
Rotating drum.

Copy converted from electrical signal back to photograph.

Data is converted into electrical signals. The signals are carried across telephone lines to the destination telephoto machine where the image is recreated.

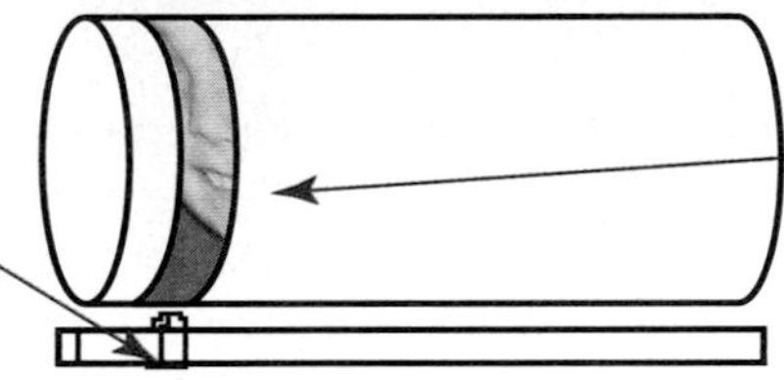
A writing stylus converts the electrical signals into an image.
Electronic voltage levels converted to drawing.

The first facsimile or "telephography" machine was put into commercial use in 1924. A transparency of a photograph was placed on a spinning drum. The image was converted into electrical signals representing the light and dark areas in the photograph. The electrical signals were converted back into a photographic image at the destination.

In addition, the number values you will encounter that are used to express memory sizes (such as 256, 512, and 1024) are increments of 16. As you can see, a number system based on 16 is used to best match the digital electronic system of computers.

Both binary and the hexadecimal numbering system will be used to express values and illustrate computer operation many times throughout the study of computer systems.

Hexadecimal	Decimal
0	0
1	1
2	2
3	3
4	4
5	5
6	6
7	7
8	8
9	9
A	10
B	11
C	12
D	13
E	14
F	15

Figure 1-8. Hexadecimal numbers include the digits *0–9* and the letters *A–F.*

ASCII Code

ASCII (pronounced *as-key*) stands for ***American Standard Code for Information Interchange.*** It was the first attempt to standardize computer character codes among the varieties of hardware and software. When a key on a computer keyboard is pressed, say the letter *M,* all computer systems display the letter *M* on the monitor screen. When the letter *M* is sent to the printer, the letter *M* is printed as expected. **Figure 1-9** is a listing of character codes and their ASCII code representatives.

American Standard Code for Information Interchange (ASCII) the first attempt to standardize computer character codes among the varieties of hardware and software.

The ASCII system was a great attempt to standardize the computer coding system, but it had limitations. The extended character set is unique to certain systems, such as IBM or equivalent machines. The extended character set must be used with a compatible software system; otherwise, unexpected characters will be generated. In addition, the standard form of ASCII does not allow for such common requirements of word-processing packages such as **bold,** *italic,* underline, or variations in fonts. ASCII was meant for symbol compatibility used for basic data files. ASCII is still used today, especially when data needs to be transferred between two different software programs.

Figure 1-9.
ASCII code.

Table of Standard ASCII Characters		
0	NUL	Null
1	SOH	Start of header
2	STX	Start of text
3	ETX	End of text
4	EOT	End of transmission
5	ENQ	Enquiry
6	ACK	Acknowledgment
7	BEL	Bell
8	BS	Backspace
9	HT	Horizontal tab
10	LF	Line feed
11	VT	Vertical tab
12	FF	Form feed
13	CR	Carriage return
14	SO	Shift out
15	SI	Shift in
16	DLE	Data link escape
17	DC1	Device control 1
18	DC2	Device control 2
19	DC3	Device control 3
20	DC4	Device control 4
21	NAK	Negative acknowledgment
22	SYN	Synchronous idle
23	ETB	End of transmit block
24	CAN	Cancel
25	EM	End of medium
26	SUB	Substitute
27	ESC	Escape
28	FS	File separator
29	GS	Group separator
30	RS	Record separator
31	US	Unit separator
32	SP	Space
33	!	
34	"	
35	#	
36	$	
37	%	
38	&	
39	'	
40	(	
41	)	
42	*	
43	+	
44	,	
45	-	
46	.	
47	/	
48	0	
49	1	
50	2	
51	3	
52	4	
53	5	
54	6	
55	7	
56	8	
57	9	
58	:	
59	;	
60	<	
61	=	
62	>	
63	?	

<table>
<tr><th colspan="2">(Continued)</th></tr>
<tr><td>64</td><td>@</td></tr>
<tr><td>65</td><td>A</td></tr>
<tr><td>66</td><td>B</td></tr>
<tr><td>67</td><td>C</td></tr>
<tr><td>68</td><td>D</td></tr>
<tr><td>69</td><td>E</td></tr>
<tr><td>70</td><td>F</td></tr>
<tr><td>71</td><td>G</td></tr>
<tr><td>72</td><td>H</td></tr>
<tr><td>73</td><td>I</td></tr>
<tr><td>74</td><td>J</td></tr>
<tr><td>75</td><td>K</td></tr>
<tr><td>76</td><td>L</td></tr>
<tr><td>77</td><td>M</td></tr>
<tr><td>78</td><td>N</td></tr>
<tr><td>79</td><td>O</td></tr>
<tr><td>80</td><td>P</td></tr>
<tr><td>81</td><td>Q</td></tr>
<tr><td>82</td><td>R</td></tr>
<tr><td>83</td><td>S</td></tr>
<tr><td>84</td><td>T</td></tr>
<tr><td>85</td><td>U</td></tr>
<tr><td>86</td><td>V</td></tr>
<tr><td>87</td><td>W</td></tr>
<tr><td>88</td><td>X</td></tr>
<tr><td>89</td><td>Y</td></tr>
<tr><td>90</td><td>Z</td></tr>
<tr><td>91</td><td>[</td></tr>
<tr><td>92</td><td>\</td></tr>
<tr><td>93</td><td>]</td></tr>
<tr><td>94</td><td>^</td></tr>
<tr><td>95</td><td>_</td></tr>
<tr><td>96</td><td>`</td></tr>
<tr><td>97</td><td>a</td></tr>
<tr><td>98</td><td>b</td></tr>
<tr><td>99</td><td>c</td></tr>
<tr><td>100</td><td>d</td></tr>
<tr><td>101</td><td>e</td></tr>
<tr><td>102</td><td>f</td></tr>
<tr><td>103</td><td>g</td></tr>
<tr><td>104</td><td>h</td></tr>
<tr><td>105</td><td>i</td></tr>
<tr><td>106</td><td>j</td></tr>
<tr><td>107</td><td>k</td></tr>
<tr><td>108</td><td>l</td></tr>
<tr><td>109</td><td>m</td></tr>
<tr><td>110</td><td>n</td></tr>
<tr><td>111</td><td>o</td></tr>
<tr><td>112</td><td>p</td></tr>
<tr><td>113</td><td>q</td></tr>
<tr><td>114</td><td>r</td></tr>
<tr><td>115</td><td>s</td></tr>
<tr><td>116</td><td>t</td></tr>
<tr><td>117</td><td>u</td></tr>
<tr><td>118</td><td>v</td></tr>
<tr><td>119</td><td>w</td></tr>
<tr><td>120</td><td>x</td></tr>
<tr><td>121</td><td>y</td></tr>
<tr><td>122</td><td>z</td></tr>
<tr><td>123</td><td>{</td></tr>
<tr><td>124</td><td>|</td></tr>
<tr><td>125</td><td>}</td></tr>
<tr><td>126</td><td>~</td></tr>
<tr><td>127</td><td>DEL</td></tr>
</table>

Bits, Bytes, and Words

Bit, byte, and word are basic computer units of data based on the binary number system. The term ***bit*** is short for *b*inary dig*it*. A bit is a single binary unit of one or zero. A ***byte*** is equal to eight bits. Early computers processed data in patterns of these eight-bit bytes.

A ***word*** is the total amount of bytes a computer can process at one time. Consequently, the length of a word can vary from computer to computer. For example, many computer systems process either 32 or 64 bits at one time. Hence, a word in those machines would consist of 32 bits (4 bytes) or 64 bits (8 bytes) respectively. Computers are often compared by the size of the word they can process.

Bit	=	0 or 1	1
Byte	=	eight bits	01011110
Word	=	1 to 8 bytes	10010010 11110000 00110011 10101010

bit
short for binary digit. A bit is a single binary unit of one or zero.

byte
equal to eight bits.

word
the total amount of bytes a computer can process at one time.

Serial and Parallel Data Transfer

Data is transferred in one of two modes in a computer system: series or parallel. Ports on a computer are similarly classified as serial or parallel ports. In a ***serial*** transfer, data is sent through a port one bit at a time in successive order. Modems are used to communicate with other computers over telephone lines. Because of the limited capacity in a telephone line, data is transferred through modems in a serial fashion. Other examples of serial data transfer are the keyboard and mouse.

In ***parallel*** transfer, more than one bit is sent side by side. In parallel port transfer, data is sent eight bits at a time. In general, data is transferred at a much higher rate through a parallel port than a serial port. Data is transferred in parallel on the computer bus system between devices such as the hard drive, RAM, and the CPU. **Figure 1-10** shows a comparison between serial and parallel data transfer.

serial
occurring one at a time. In serial transfer, data is transmitted one bit at a time.

parallel
side-by-side. In parallel transfer, more than one bit of data is transferred at a time.

Computer Numerical Values

Metric prefixes are commonly used to express the speed and size of computer systems and hardware. Prefixes are usually used in combination with the word bit (b) or byte (B). For example, *speed* is usually expressed in *bits*. *Storage space* is usually expressed as *bytes*. See **Figure 1-11** for a listing of commonly used metric prefixes.

There is some confusion when using metric prefixes for expressing computer sizes. There can be two possible values for a large expression such as a megabyte. The nominal value for megabyte using the base 10 number system is equal to 1,000,000. In computer systems, a 1-megabyte item such as memory is 1,048,576 (2^{20}) bytes (the power of 2 raised to the 20th). The large values expressed for computer systems are based on the binary number system. **Figure 1-12** compares the values of the base 10 number system and the base 2 number system.

Figure 1-10.
Serial and parallel data transfer. Serial transfers one bit at a time. Parallel transfers multiple bits, usually multiples of 8 (1 byte), at a time.

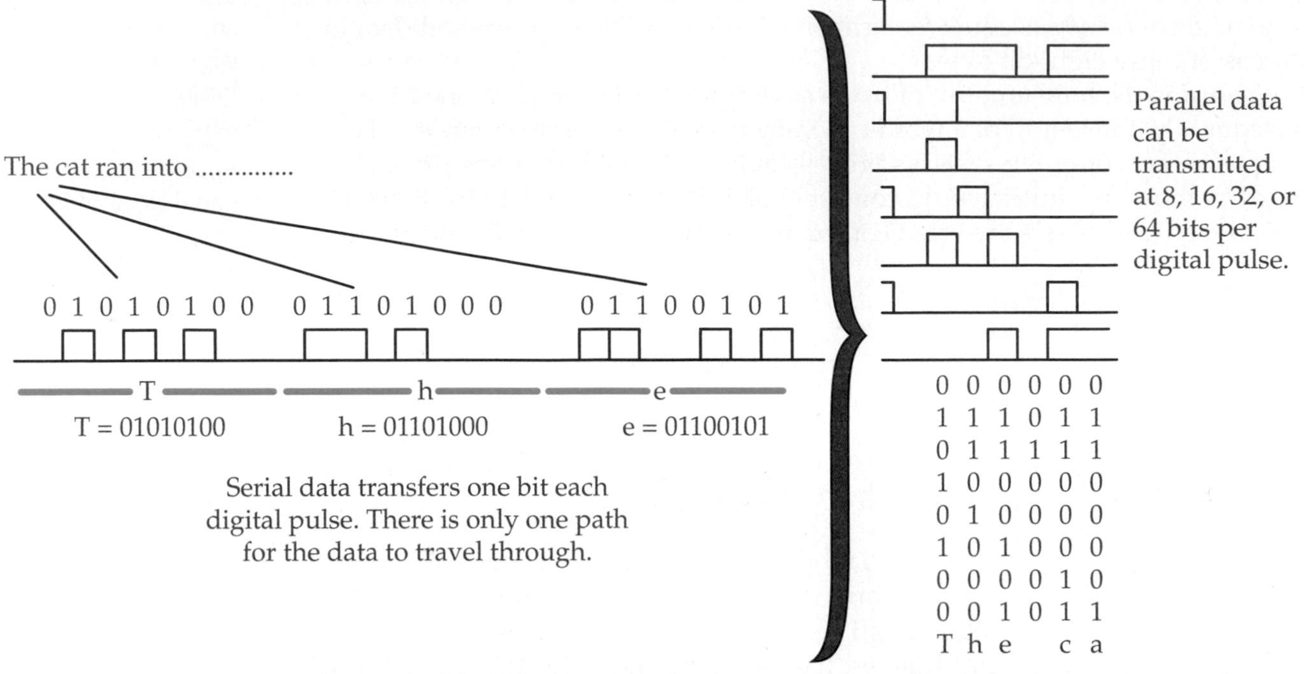

Figure 1-11.
Metric prefix chart.

Metric name	Symbol	Number base 10	Number base 2	Common name	Numeric equivalent for the base 10 number system
Pico	p	10^{-12}	2^{-40}	trillionth	0.000 000 000 001
Nano	n	10^{-9}	2^{-30}	billionth	0.000 000 001
Micro	µ	10^{-6}	2^{-20}	millionth	0.000 001
Milli	m	10^{-3}	2^{-10}	thousandth	0.001
Base unit		1			1
Kilo	k	10^{3}	2^{10}	thousand	1,000
Mega	M	10^{6}	2^{20}	million	1,000,000
Giga	G	10^{9}	2^{30}	billion	1,000,000,000
Terra	T	10^{12}	2^{40}	trillion	1,000,000,000,000
Peta	P	10^{15}	2^{50}	quadrillion	1,000,000,000,000,000
Exa	E	10^{18}	2^{60}	quintillion	1,000,000,000,000,000,000

Figure 1-12.
Base 10 and base 2 comparisons. You get more for your meg when you are using base 2 terminology.

Prefix	Base 2 number system	Base 10 number system
Kilobyte	1,024	1,000
Megabyte	1,048,576	1,000,000
Gigabyte	1,073,741,824	1,000,000,000
Terabyte	1,099,511,627,776	1,000,000,000,000
Petabyte	1,125,899,906,842,624	1,000,000,000,000,000
Exabyte	1,152,921,504,606,846,976	1,000,000,000,000,000,000

Take a Tour outside the Computer Case

Look at **Figure 1-13.** A minimal workstation consists of a computer and input and output devices. The computer is a case that houses the motherboard, CPU, memory, hard disk drive, and other associated electronics parts and modules that make up the computer system. The typical input devices found at a workstation are a keyboard and mouse, but there are many other different devices that can be used as input devices. These input devices are covered later in the textbook.

The typical output devices found at the workstation are the computer monitor, printer, and speakers. The monitor, printer, and speakers are classified as peripherals. ***Peripherals*** are optional equipment used to display data or to input data. The monitor displays data in the form of words and pictures. The printer displays data in a printed form on paper. The speakers convert data into sound such as music and spoken language.

peripherals optional equipment used to input or output data.

There are many different case styles that are used to contain and protect the electronic parts of the computer system. Some of the most common case styles are referred to as desktop, tower, mini tower, micro tower, laptop, and notebook. Case selection is usually based on individual taste. The outside of the computer system allows access to the electronic parts inside. Data can be entered into the computer system through the disk drive, CD drive, keyboard, mouse, or one of the ports in the back. See **Figure 1-14.**

Exterior Connections

The exterior connections to a computer are well worth a closer look. The following connectors are some of the more common connectors that you will find on a PC. More information is given on these connectors in the sections detailing the components with which they work.

Figure 1-13. Front view of a typical PC.

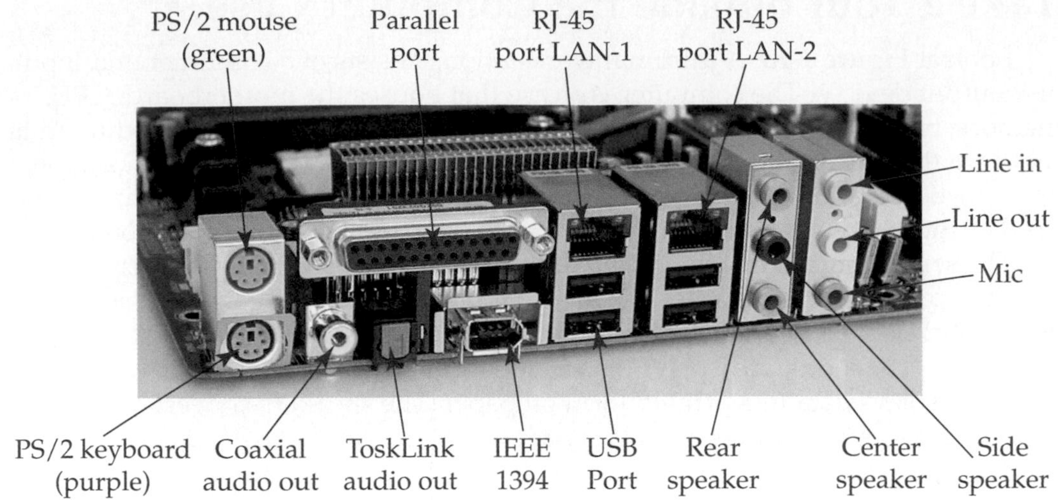

Figure 1-14. Ports accessible at the back of a typical computer.

There are a variety of exterior connectors used with computer equipment. Many times the type of connector can help reveal the identity of the card it is attached to or what type of equipment most likely connects to it. For example, the mouse and the keyboard may use the exact same style of connector, such as the mini-DIN type. However, they may not be interchangeable. The mouse must connect to the mini-DIN connector identified for the mouse cable, and the keyboard must connect to the mini-DIN connector identified for the keyboard cable. **Figure 1-15** shows the design of the DIN and mini-DIN connectors.

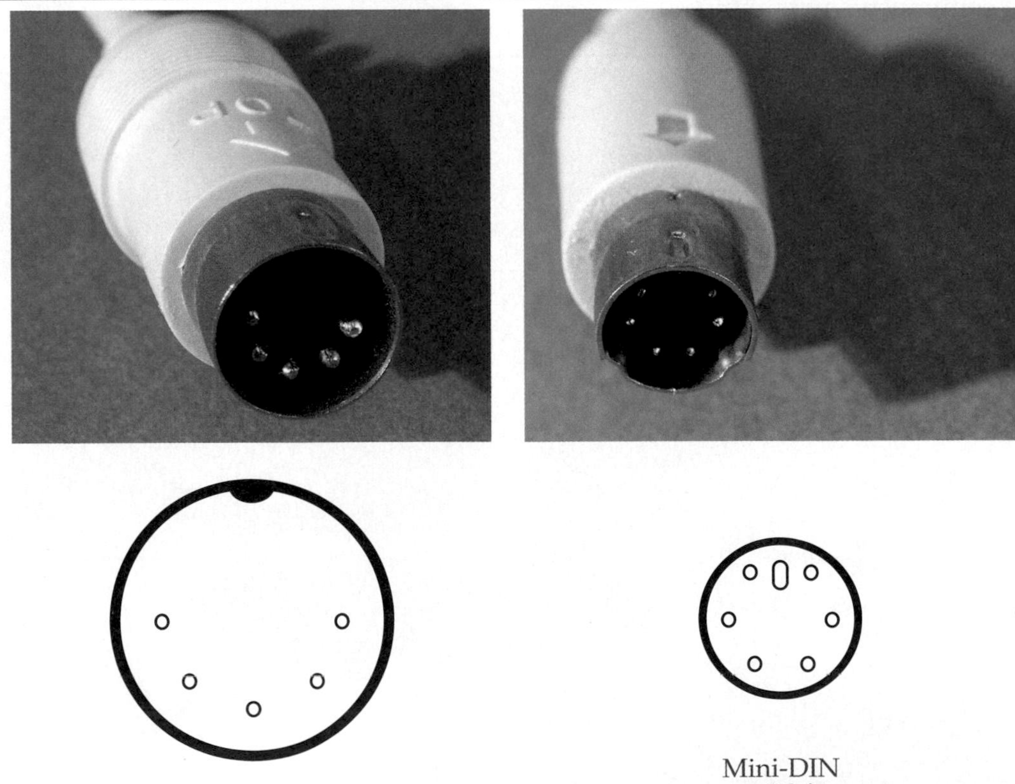

Figure 1-15. DIN and mini-DIN connectors.

The DB connector looks similar in shape to the letter *D*, see **Figure 1-16.** The DB connector typically is classified as a 9-, 15-, or 25-pin connector. The DB connector is commonly used to connect items such as a joystick, monitor, or printer. The DB connector at the back of a sound card is sometimes referred to as a game port. When a 15-pin D shell connector is arranged with three rows of five connections, it can be referred to as a HD-15. The HD represents high density and is usually used for monitor connections.

There are two types of RJ connectors commonly used with a PC: RJ-11 and RJ-45. The RJ-11 is used for modem telephone connections. The RJ-45 is used for network connections. The RJ-11 uses four conductors and four pins, while the RJ-45 uses eight conductors and eight pins, see **Figure 1-17.**

Figure 1-18 shows a picture of a network card. Network cards can come with different kinds of connectors. They may use an RJ-45, a DB-15, or a BNC connector. Some network cards come with multiple connectors to allow them to be used with any standard type of network wiring. Each type of wiring requires a different type of connector.

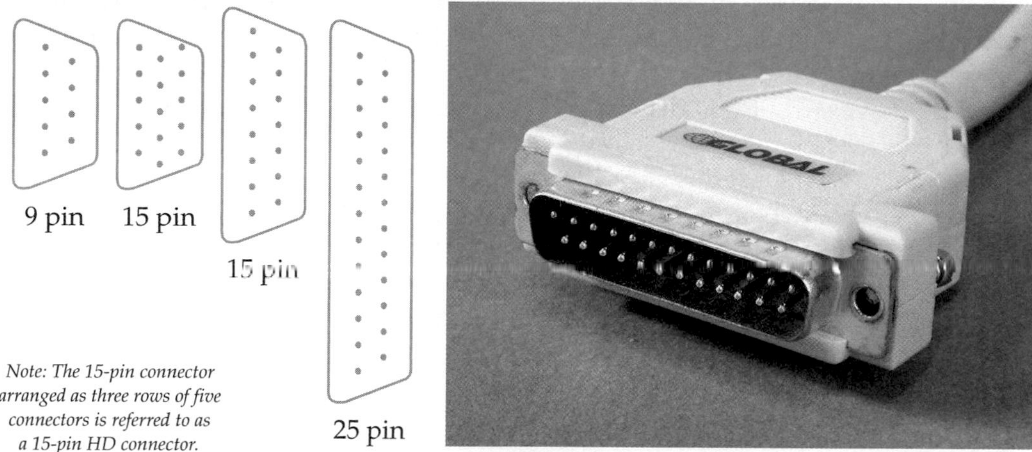

Various DB Connectors

Figure 1-16. Selection of sizes of DB connectors and a typical DB connector. DB connectors are used for both serial and parallel ports.

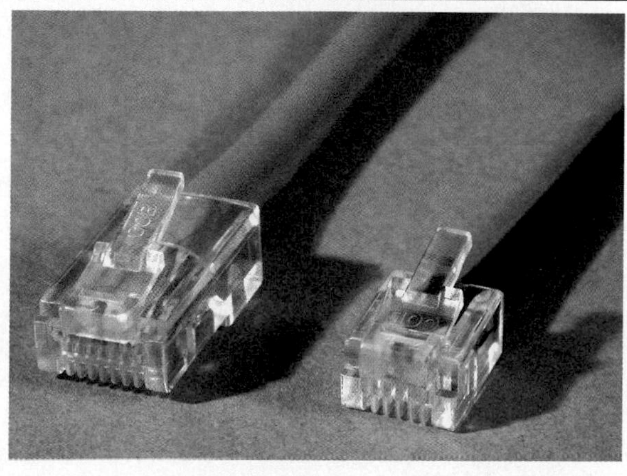

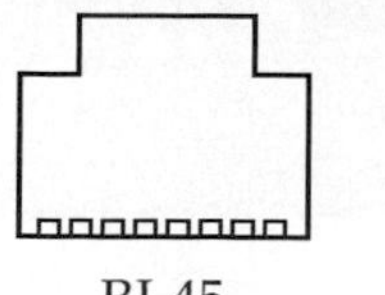

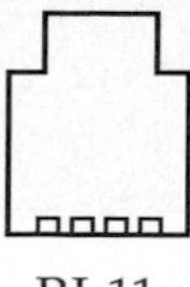

Figure 1-17. RJ-45 and RJ-11 connectors.

Figure 1-18. Typical PCMCIA network adapter for a laptop. This network adapter comes with a USB connector. Devices that convert the USB connection to other types of connections are readily available.

hot swap
to plug in or unplug a device while the PC is running.

The FireWire connector, also known as the IEEE 1394 connector, can connect up to 63 devices that can be hot swapped. The term ***hot swap*** means the devices can be plugged in or unplugged while the PC is running. FireWire was designed for Apple computers by Lucent Technologies and is proprietary. FireWire is seen more often on Apple equipment than on PC equipment. It is designed for very high-speed data transfers such as those required for video equipment. The high-speed data transfer rates make it an excellent choice to upload video images from a camera to a PC. FireWire is also used for other equipment connections such as hard disk drives, CD-ROM drives, DVD drives, and printers. **Figure 1-19** shows a pair of FireWire connectors.

The Universal Serial Bus (USB) is another type of connection used on PCs, **Figure 1-20.** The USB is a multipurpose connector that allows many different devices to connect to the PC in a daisy-chain fashion or by the use of a hub. The USB design allows for connections to peripheral devices that formerly may have required opening the PC case and inserting an adapter card. With the USB port, the need to open the case to connect many of the different devices has been eliminated.

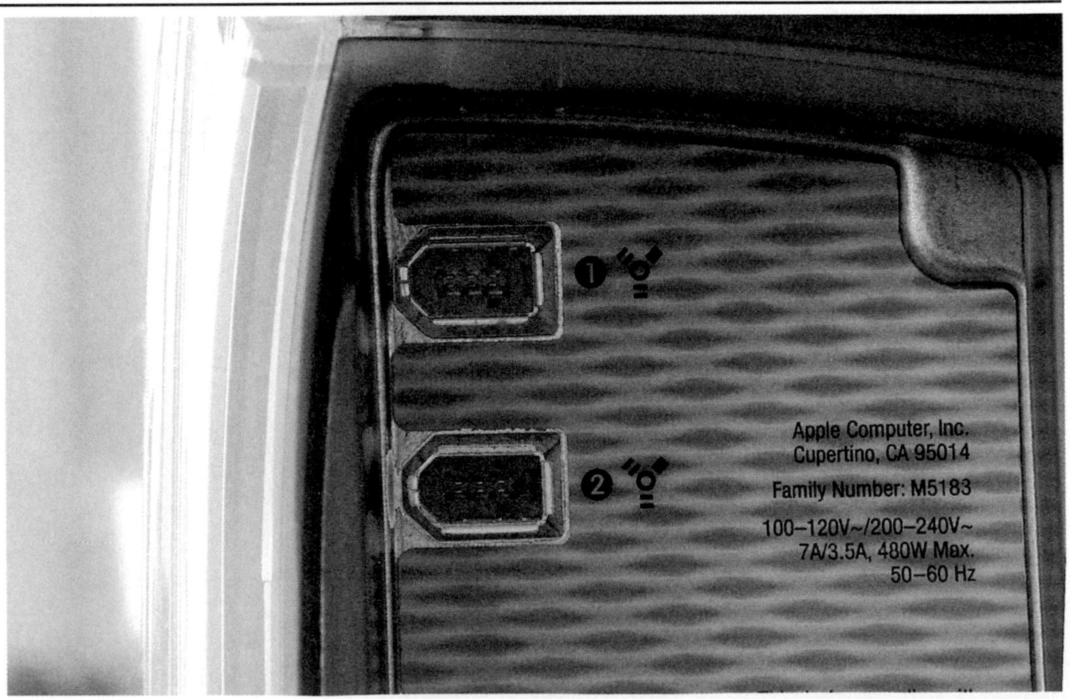

Figure 1-19. FireWire ports are high-speed connections.

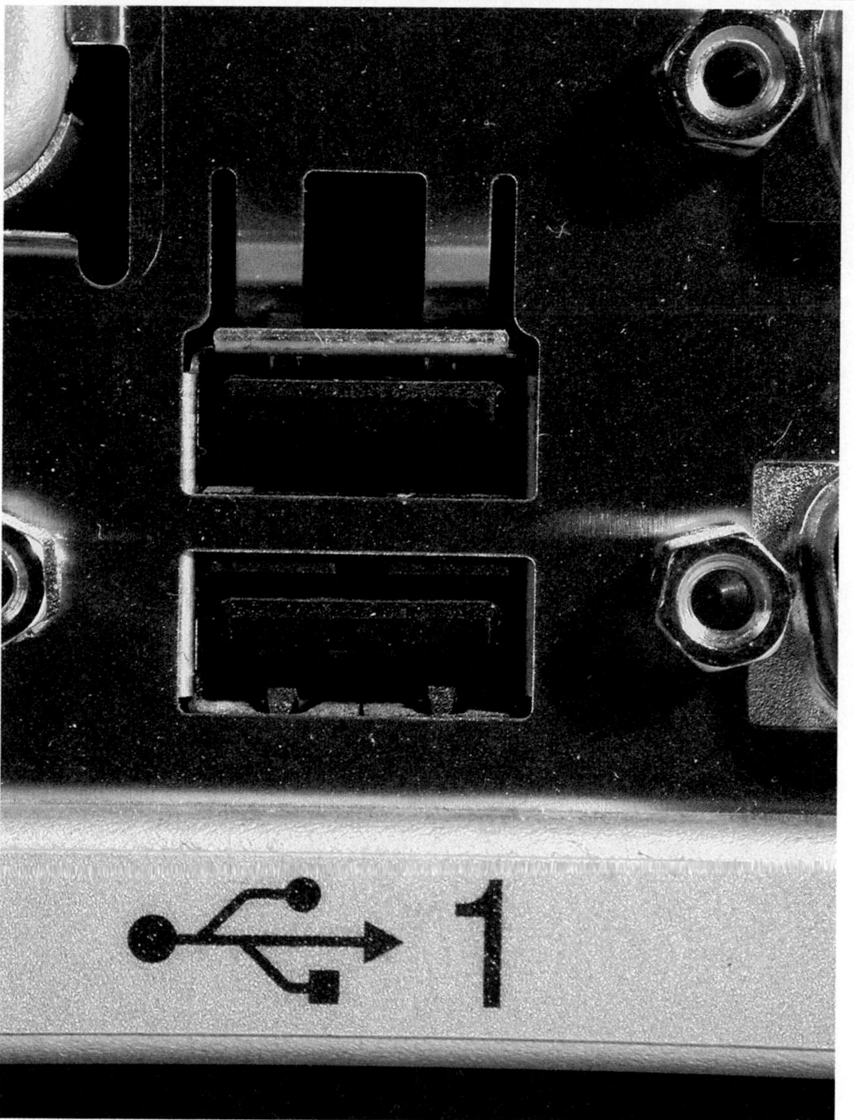

Figure 1-20.
USB ports.

Another very desirable advantage of USB is that you can connect up to 127 devices through the USB port in a daisy-chain fashion, **Figure 1-21.** Before USB, it was quite possible to run out of a sufficient number of ports to support the numerous types of equipment that might be needed for a special workstation. For example, a workstation used by a graphics designer might require connections to a scanner, digital camera, microphone, laser printer, color inkjet printer, poster-size plotter printer, and a digital graphics tablet for freehand drawings. The USB and FireWire ports are capable of supporting numerous devices required by a single workstation. Legacy workstations could only be used to support a limited number of devices.

The ***device bay*** is designed to accommodate the easy hot swap of devices such as hard drives, tape drives, CD-RW drives, and DVD drives. The device bay is prewired for either USB or FireWire and allows devices to easily slide into or out of the PC case. A device installed into the device bay looks as though it was installed internally. By installing the device into the device bay, the problem of long cords running across and around valuable desk space can be eliminated.

device bay
a drive bay designed to accommodate the easy hot swap of devices such as hard disk drives, tape drives, CD-RW drives, and DVD drives.

Take a Tour inside the Computer Case

The inside of a PC is filled with a number of standard components and expansion slots that allow each machine to be customized with a tremendous variety of interesting tools, **Figure 1-22.** The equipment that follows details only the common computer components. These are devices you will find in almost every system.

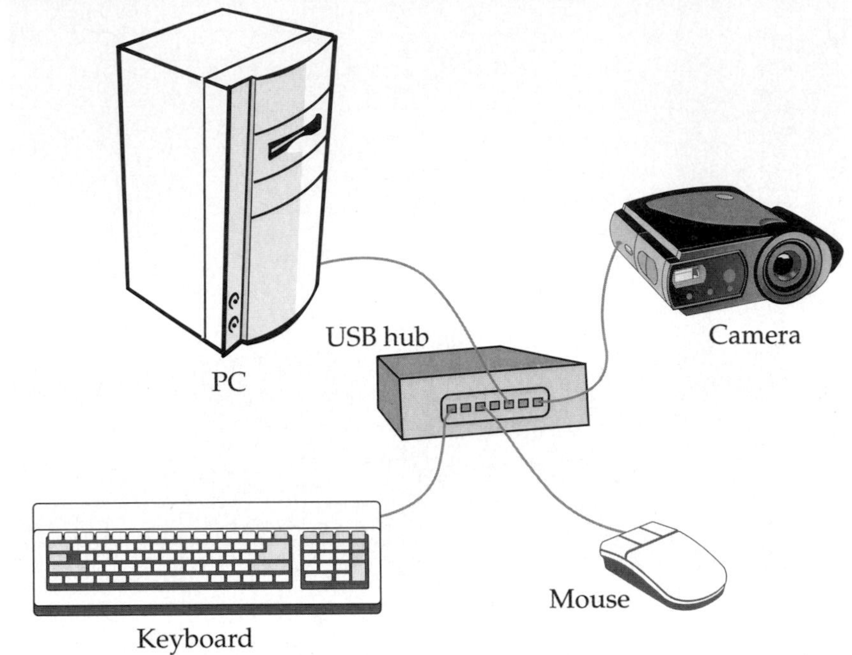

Figure 1-21. A USB hub can be used to connect multiple USB devices to a PC.

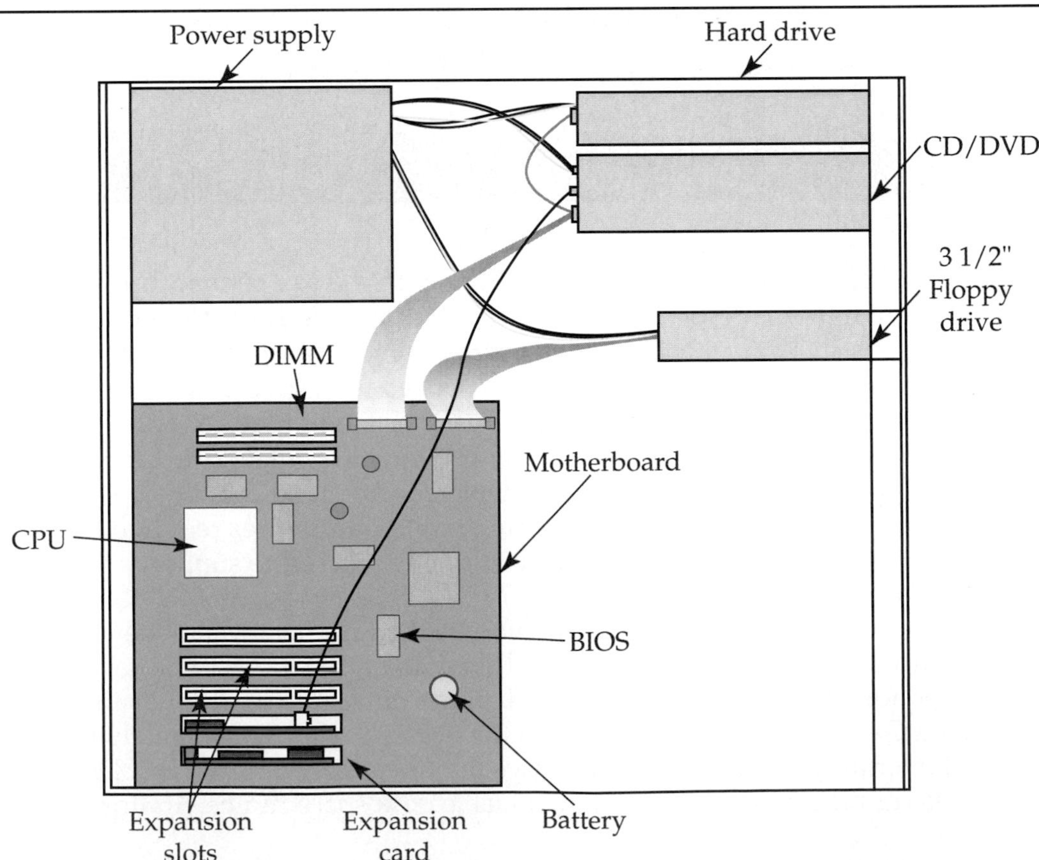

Figure 1-22. These components are common to the PC. Depending on the style of the unit (tower, desktop, or laptop), the arrangement of the parts will vary. This sketch shows a tower PC.

CPU

In the simplest of terms, the ***central processing unit (CPU)*** is the brain of the computer, **Figure 1-23.** The terms Intel® Core™ 2 Quad, AMD Turion™ 64, and others are the names given to identify various models of CPUs. The CPU consists of millions of microscopic electronic components called *transistors*. The transistors are electrically connected together in such a way they are able to interact with computer programs and process data.

central processing unit (CPU)
the brain of the computer. Most of the computer's calculating takes place in the central processing unit. In PCs, the central processing functions are carried out by a single chip, which is called a *microprocessor*.

All the other computer components depend on the actions of the CPU. The CPU controls the data in the computer. Commands are issued to the CPU via software. The CPU translates the commands into actions, such as save the data on the screen to memory, open a new file, and locate a file called MyHomeWork.

As discussed earlier, the CPU does not think or possess any human intelligence as some movies may depict. A CPU simply carries out the program codes written in the software program.

Power Supply

The power supply converts the typical 120-volt ac power from the wall outlet to dc voltage levels used by the various computer components, **Figure 1-24.** Once the 120 volts of ac power is converted to a lower dc voltage, usually 3.3, 5, or 12 volts, cables carry the electrical energy to the motherboard, disk drives, and other major components.

Hard Drive

The ***hard drive*** (also called the *internal drive* or *hard disk*) is where computer programs and data are stored, **Figure 1-25.** A hard drive is made up of several disks in a stack inside a sealed box. Computer programs and data are stored on the hard drive as magnetic impulses. Data is transmitted to and from the

hard drive
a magnetic storage media consisting of a set of magnetic disks and read/write heads housed inside a hard case.

A

B

C

Figure 1-23.
The CPU is the brain of the computer. A—An empty CPU socket on a motherboard. B—A CPU is inserted into the socket. C—A heat sink is mounted on the CPU to keep it cool.

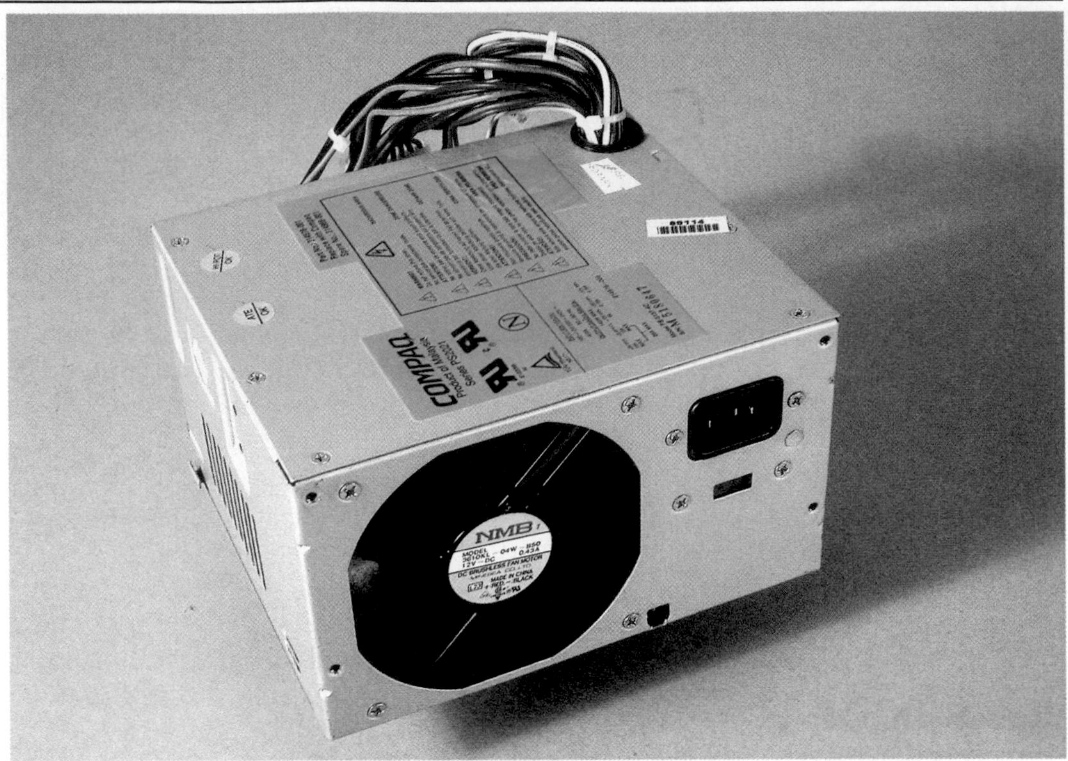

Figure 1-24. The power supply converts 120 Vac input to a much lower dc output required by the computer components.

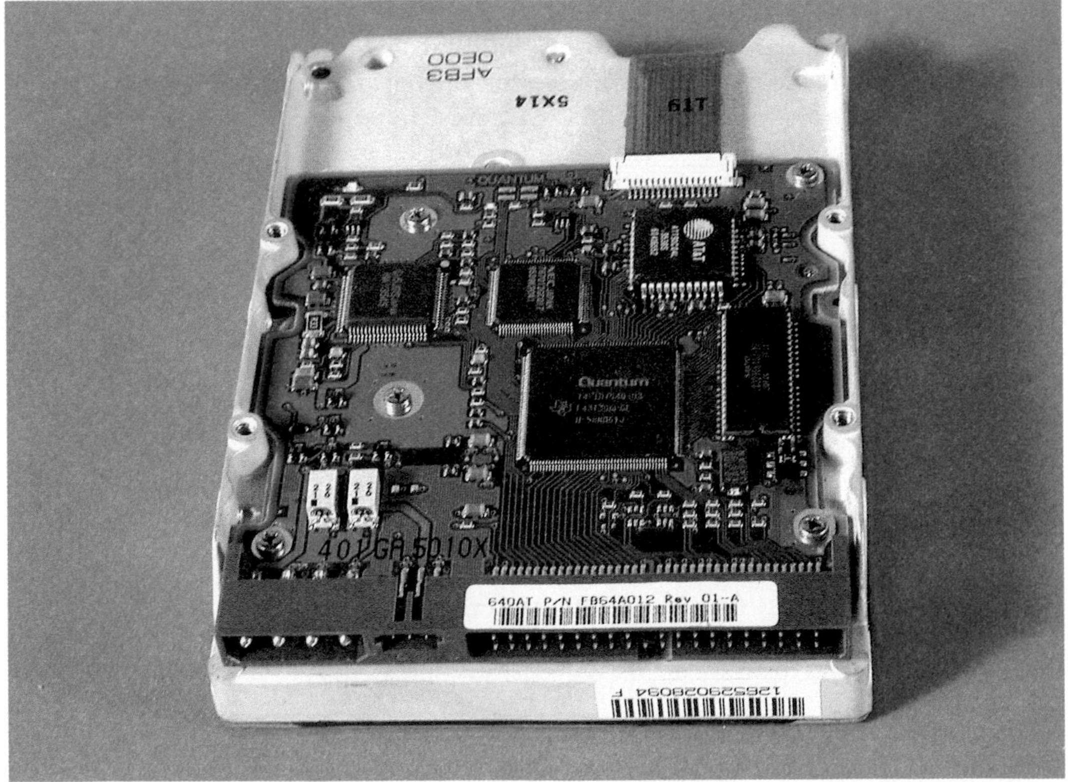

Figure 1-25. Hard drives are the most common storage device used with a PC.

hard drive through a data cable attached to the hard drive on one end and to the motherboard on the opposite end. The hard drive is connected to the power supply by several brightly colored wires that supply the electrical energy needed to run the hard drive system.

Motherboard

The motherboard is usually a rectangular piece of circuit board covered with many conductors that provide electrical energy paths to the computer components and expansion slots, **Figure 1-26.** The ***motherboard*** provides a way to distribute the digital signals carrying data, control instructions, and distribute small amounts of electrical power to the many different components mounted on the board. The electrical system of pathways is referred to as the computer bus.

motherboard
a circuit board covered by a maze of conductors which provide electrical current to the computer components and expansion slots. Also used to refer to the main circuit board and all of its electronic components (chipset).

RAM

Random access memory (RAM) is the location where computer programs are loaded to from the hard drive, **Figure 1-27.** RAM is classified as a volatile memory system. Volatile simply means that the data and programs loaded in RAM are lost when power is turned off. Increasing a computer's RAM is one of the most common computer upgrades performed. RAM is usually mounted into several parallel slots on the motherboard. The amount of RAM in a typical home PC could be 256 MB, 512 MB, 1 GB or more. Depending on the type of applications to be run, the amount of RAM required will vary.

RAM is a place where data is temporarily stored. When a computer is turned off, the RAM is emptied. When a computer is started, new information is loaded into RAM. When you draw a picture, the data that represents the picture is in RAM and is transferred to the screen. Look at **Figure 1-28.** The text on the screen is really a reflection of the data in RAM.

random access memory (RAM)
a volatile memory system into which programs are loaded. When the computer's power is shut off, all data stored in RAM is lost.

Figure 1-26. Almost all computer data runs through the motherboard.

Figure 1-27.
RAM modules are easy additions to the PC.

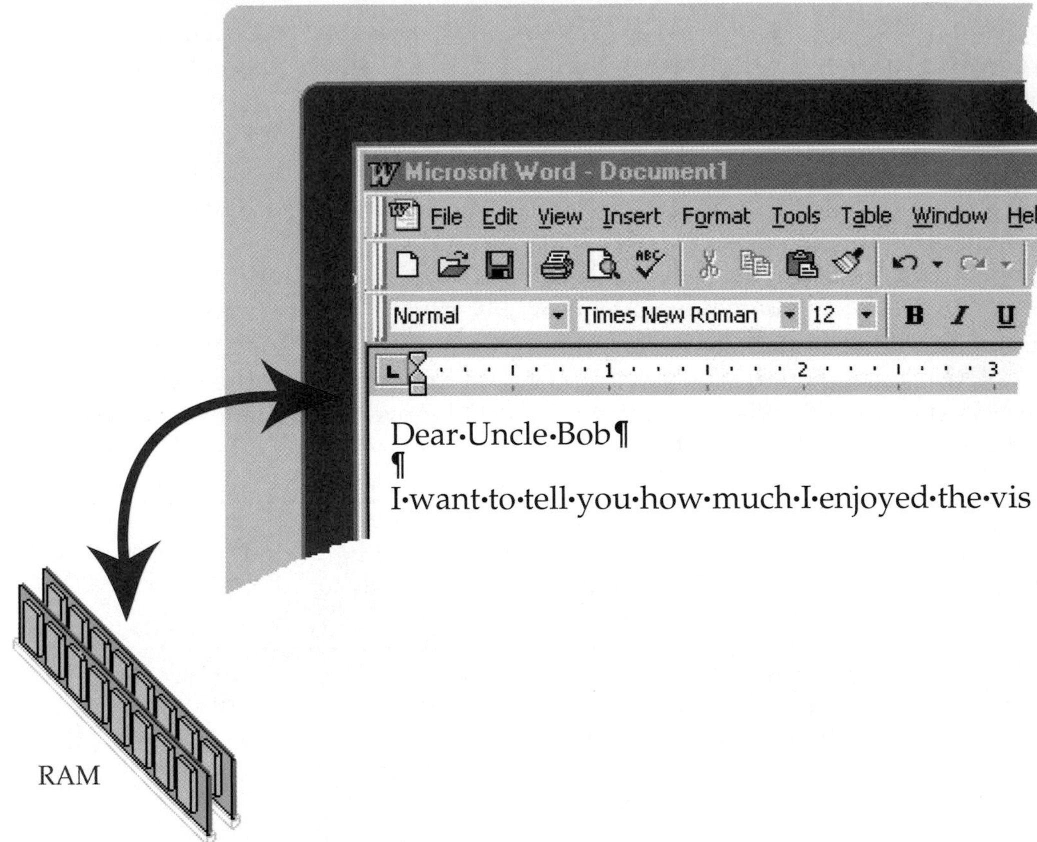

Figure 1-28.
As you type data into a word-processing program, the information is stored in RAM.

BIOS and CMOS Chips

basic input/output system (BIOS) special firmware that permits the compatibility between the CPU ad devices such as the hard drive, CD-ROM drive, and monitor.

The term ***BIOS*** is an acronym for ***basic input/output system.*** The terms BIOS and CMOS are often interchanged, but they are really two distinct concepts. The BIOS is stored in a special type of memory chip and consists of software programs that support the compatibility between the CPU and devices such as the hard drive, CD-ROM drive, and monitor. The BIOS includes the BIOS Setup program, which is responsible for setting and storing the date and time and information about the computer hardware. CMOS is a type of integrated circuit chip that stores the data required by the BIOS Setup program.

Originally, the BIOS was permanently etched into a ROM (read only memory) chip. ROM BIOS was permanent and could only be changed by replacing the ROM chip. Today, BIOS software is stored on an EEPROM (electrically erasable programmable read only memory) chip. An EEPROM is reprogrammable and is often referred to as flash ROM. Flash ROM can be erased electrically and reprogrammed with an updated version of a software program. Flash ROM retains its data when the power supply to the computer is disconnected or turned off.

The CMOS chip is a hardware component. ***CMOS*** stands for ***complementary metal oxide semiconductor,*** which describes the electronic technology used to construct the chip. The CMOS chip is where the BIOS Setup program stores information about the computer's hardware.

complementary metal oxide semiconductor (CMOS)
the chip that stores the BIOS Setup program data.

Battery

The ***battery*** supplies voltage to the CMOS chip, which contains the BIOS Setup data, **Figure 1-29.** Without the battery, the computer would lose the date, time, and all the important information about the hardware components stored in the CMOS chip when the computer power switch is turned off.

battery
the component that supplies voltage to the CMOS chip. Without the battery, the information stored in the CMOS chip would be lost every time the computer was shut off.

Expansion Cards

Expansion cards are sometimes called *interface cards* or *host adapters.* ***Expansion cards*** allow the computer to be custom-designed to meet the needs of different consumers, **Figure 1-30.** A certain computer may have video circuitry integrated into the motherboard that only allows for minimal video performance, or it may have a separate video card. The performance of this video system would be adequate for accounting or word-processing functions. However, it would be substandard for computer-aided drafting or game applications. To remedy this, a new expansion video card can be added to the computer system.

Other typical expansion cards are network interface cards, modems, and digital cameras. There are many more computer items that can be added with expansion cards.

expansion cards
a board that can be easily installed in a computer to enhance or expand its capabilities.

Figure 1-29.
Batteries allow information such as the date and time to be saved while a PC is powered down.

A

B

Figure 1-30. Expansion cards allow computers to do many different things. This is a PCIe video card.

Expansion Card Slots

expansion card slots receptacles for expansion cards which allow them to connect to the motherboard's circuitry.

cooling fan a fan that supplies a constant stream of air across the computer components.

Expansion cards fit snugly into ***expansion card slots,*** **Figure 1-31.** The expansion card slots allow the expansion card to connect directly to the electronic circuitry in the motherboard. This allows the expansion card to communicate directly or indirectly with other components on the motherboard or with the CPU. There are a number of types of expansion slots. They come with names such as ISA, EISA, and PCI. These types of expansion slots will be discussed in detail in Chapter 3—Motherboards.

Cooling Fans

The ***cooling fan*** supplies a constant stream of air across the computer components. The typical CPU comes equipped with a fan mounted directly to the CPU to assist in the cooling process, as shown in Figure 1-23C. Electronic components are damaged by excessive heat.

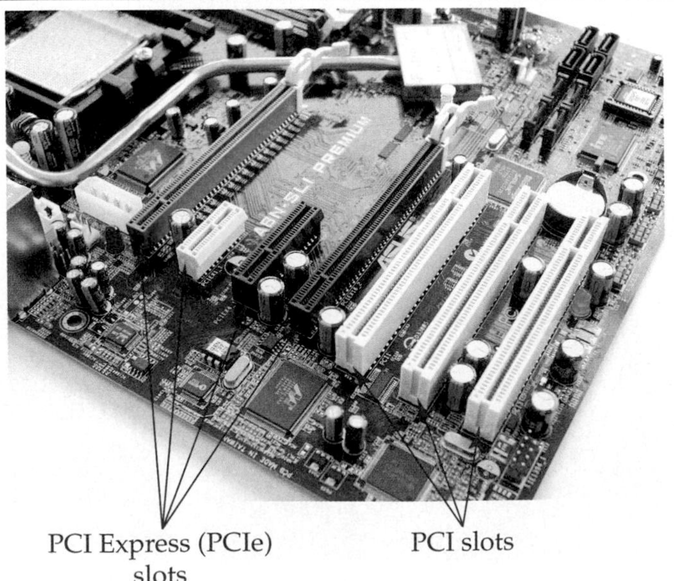

Figure 1-31. A variety of expansion slots are built into most motherboards. This motherboard has PCI and PCI Express (PCIe) expansion slots.

Cables

There are several different types of cables commonly used inside the PC case. These cables connect the motherboard to devices such as the hard drive, floppy drive, and CD-RW drive.

Figure 1-32 shows a typical flat ribbon cable used to connect a hard drive to the motherboard. The cable consists of many parallel conductors. Some of the conductors are used to transfer data and others are used to transmit control signals between the motherboard and the device.

Electrical power for the devices can also be transmitted through the flat ribbon cable, but many devices consume more electrical power than the flat ribbon cable and motherboard are designed to safely carry. When a large volume of electrical power is required for a device, a separate power cable that runs directly from the power supply is used.

Figure 1-33 shows the flat ribbon cable for a 3 1/2″ floppy drive. Note the twist in the cable used for the floppy drive. The twist is required when more than one floppy drive is connected to the motherboard. The PC control system uses the twist to separately identify the two drives.

The Flash drive has made floppy drives obsolete.

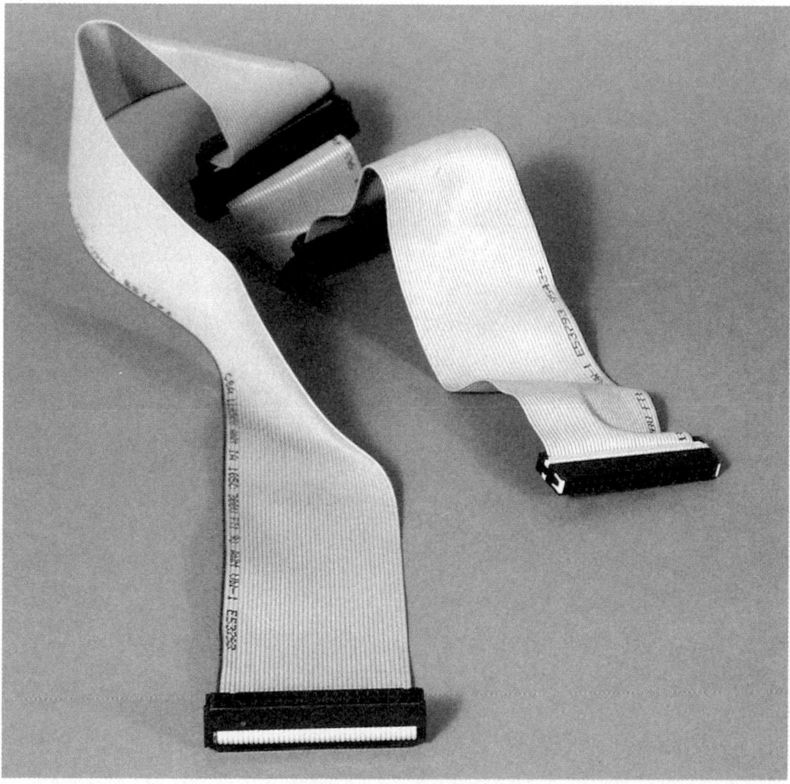

Figure 1-32. Flat ribbon cable used to connect devices such as a hard drive or CD drive to the motherboard.

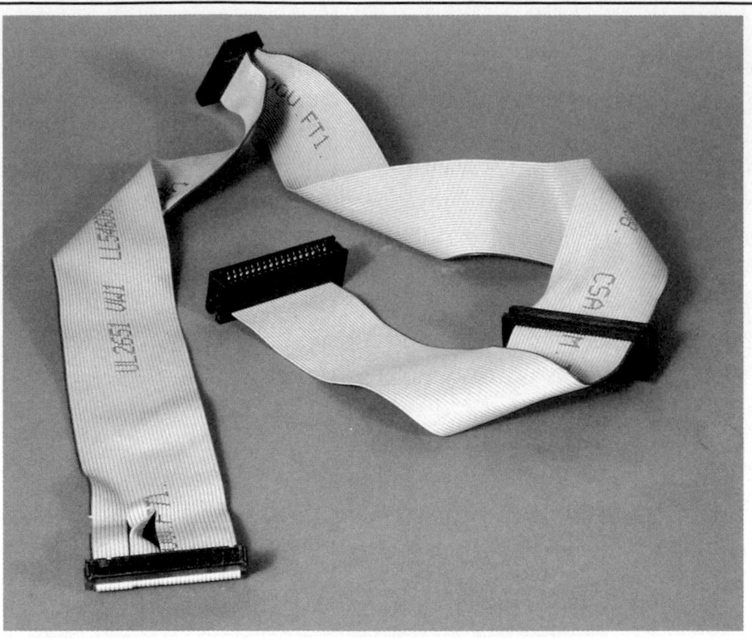

Figure 1-33.
Flat ribbon cable for connecting a floppy drive to the motherboard. Take special note of the twist in the section of cable near the connector on the left. The end with the twist connects to the floppy drive.

How the Major Parts Work Together

The following scenario traces how a sequence of events occurs in a typical PC system. In this example, a user moves from turning on the computer through saving text data. Please note that there are many different PCs. They all have unique start-up features and program interactions.

1. When the power switch is turned to the *on* position, electrical power from the wall outlet moves through the power supply where it is converted to a much lower dc voltage (or voltages). This stepped-down power is used to run the major components of the computer system including the motherboard, disk drives, and expansion cards. The fan starts up, providing a rush of cool air across the components.
2. Next, the BIOS system is activated and performs a POST. The POST (power-on self-test) checks the components in the computer system such as RAM, ROM, hard drive, and keyboard to ensure they are in proper working order. Information, such as the type and model number of the BIOS system and the amount of memory, will flash across the computer's monitor, providing information.
3. After the BIOS program checks the system, the operating system takes control. There are many different types of operating systems, but for our example, Windows software will be used.
4. The CPU now waits for activity to be generated by the mouse, keyboard, modem, or other input device. The CPU constantly checks if a key is pressed or the mouse is moved or clicked. The CPU checks these items thousands of times per second.
5. The mouse pointer is moved to an icon, and the mouse is clicked to activate a desired program—a word-processing program in this example. The software represented by the icon is activated. It now shares control of the computer with the CPU.

6. Some typing is done, and then the save command is issued by clicking a save-the-data icon in the word-processing program. The program now attempts to save to a disk. When the word-processing program saves, the operating system takes over in conjunction with the BIOS program. The operating system interprets the command issued from the word-processing program and translates it to a set of instructions that the BIOS can interpret.
7. The BIOS system, in turn, translates the instructions to the disk system. It activates the disk motor and actuator arm, moving it to the next available sector on the disk. Information about available disk space is kept in a table. The operating system and BIOS system work together until all data is transferred and recorded on disk.
8. Control is then returned to the word-processing program, so long as an error has not occurred. Possible errors are disk full or unable to read disk.

The cooperation between the word-processing program, operating system, and BIOS system goes unnoticed by the user.

Integrated Circuits

The term *chip* is often used in the computer industry. A chip is actually the final product of the manufacturing of an integrated circuit. An ***integrated circuit (IC)*** is a collection of transistors, resistors, and other electronic components reduced to an unbelievable small size. In fact, over six million transistors manufactured as an integrated circuit can fit into an area the size of a dime. Chips are commonly found on circuit boards. They are the black, square and rectangular devices.

integrated circuit (IC) a collection of transistors, resistors, and other electronic components reduced to an unbelievable small size.

Manufacturing an Integrated Circuit

The manufacturing process that creates an IC consists of many hundreds of steps in a process covering a period of several months. The first step in the manufacture of a chip is the design of the circuit. The circuit is drawn on a very large scale. When the design is completed and all drawings are finished, the manufacturing process is ready to begin. First, the drawings are photographed. The negative of the drawing's photograph is used as a template in the manufacturing process. See **Figure 1-34.**

An ingot of pure silicon is made and then sliced into thin wafers to serve as the base of the IC. Silicon is the same as most common beach sand, but it is extremely pure. The material cannot contain any impurities that might cause adverse effects in the manufacturing of the IC. A series of layers are produced over the surface of the silicon wafer using a process called *photolithography.*

Photolithography is described in the following sequence of events. First, a heat process vaporizes silicon dioxide. Then various other chemicals are used to form many extremely thin layers over the surface of the wafer. After each layer is formed, a coating of a chemical called *photoresist* is laid over the entire surface of the wafer. The photoresist reacts when exposed to ultraviolet light.

The negative from the photograph made of the circuit is used as a stencil. The negative is called the *photomask.* When ultraviolet light shines through the mask, it causes the photoresist to leave a pattern of soft and hard surfaces in

Figure 1-34.
A—A circuit drawing uses a template to form circuits on silicon wafers. B—Fine layers are created in the silicon. The layers are controlled in such a way to create the millions of transistors and other electronic components used in the integrated circuit. (International Business Systems Corporation)

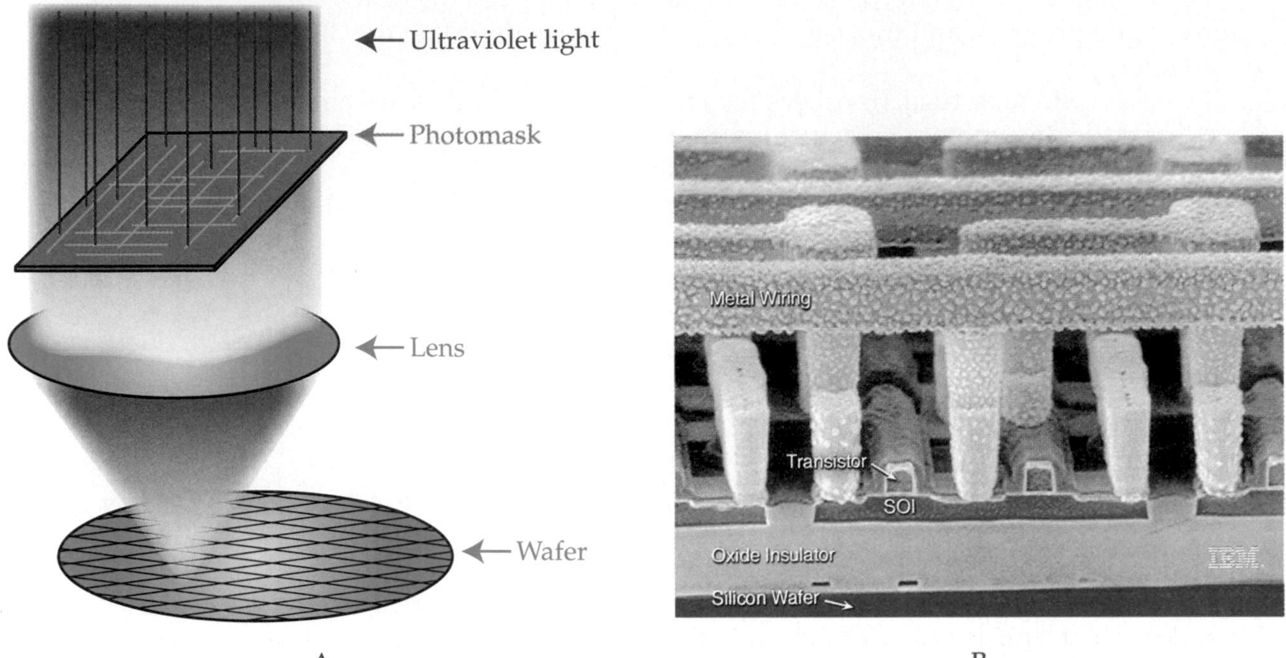

the exact pattern of the designed circuit. The soft photoresist is then washed away leaving an etched pattern of valleys and ridges on the surface of the wafer. These valleys are filled with conductive materials. The process of filling in these valleys is called *doping* or *implantation*. This process is repeated many more times until twenty or more layers are developed over the surface of the entire wafer. A single wafer consists of many integrated circuits. The wafer is cut into individual integrated circuits and then packaged.

One of the most difficult parts of packaging the integrated circuit is connecting the very fine wires between the actual wafer circuits and the much larger pins on the outside of the package. The entire wafer and thin connection wires are encapsulated in a hard insulating material resembling black plastic.

Modern computer technology would not be possible without the techniques used in building integrated circuits. The ICs used in computers have many specialized purposes. For example, the CPU is a very large and complex IC that controls all the PC activities. The computer modem, used to communicate across telephone lines, has a specialized chip that changes computer data into a stream of various voltage levels that represent the data. It also converts the stream back into digital data at the receiving end. There are various other chips scattered across the motherboard that have special purposes. Some assist the CPU with data flow across the motherboard. Others control devices such as the hard drive and floppy drive. The RAM used in computers is nothing more than a group of ICs mounted on an insulated circuit board.

Electrostatic Discharge

Electrostatic discharge, or ***ESD,*** is best defined in the world of computer maintenance as the transfer of static electrical energy from one object to another, such as a computer chip. ESD can destroy the miniature circuits inside a computer chip. Static charges are usually created by friction. When two dissimilar materials are rubbed together, an electric charge is produced.

A common example of static electricity buildup and discharge is when you walk across a surface such as a rug and then reach out and touch a doorknob. You feel a sharp snap as the electrical charge of your body discharges to the doorknob. This is ESD.

You have learned about how ICs are manufactured and can appreciate the small scale of the circuit. An electrostatic discharge will damage the tiny circuits inside the chip. To avoid ESD, technicians wear a ground strap when handling static sensitive devices, **Figure 1-35.** The ***anti-static wrist strap*** bleeds off any static charge buildup on a technician's body and allows safe handling of an integrated circuit device.

electrostatic discharge (ESD) a release of energy (electrical current), created when an object with an electrostatic charge makes contact with a conductor.

anti-static wrist strap a strap, typically worn around the wrist, that connects the technician to ground and bleeds off any electrostatic charge.

Static buildup is always greatest when the air is dry and cool.

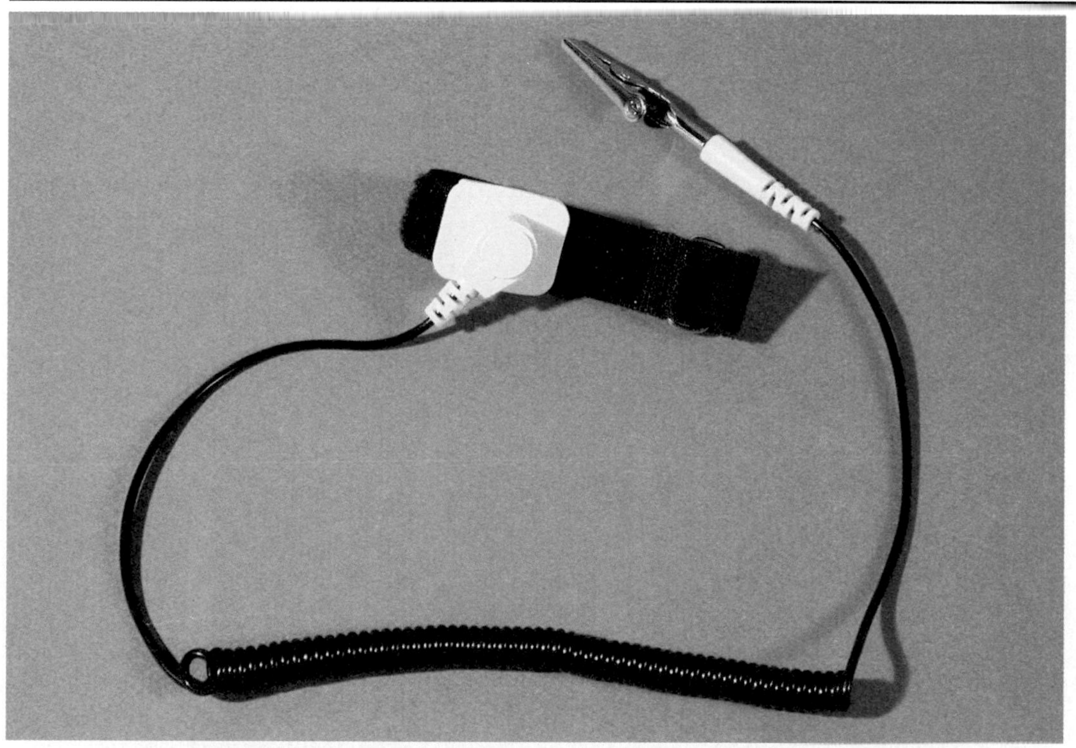

Figure 1-35. Ground strap.

Tool Kit

Computer repair requires a minimum number of tools, **Figure 1-36.** A standard tool kit can vary from a small pouch to a more elaborate tool case.

A variety of flat tip, Phillips, and star drivers are needed. Canned compressed air, a chip puller, anti-static wrist strap, multimeter, extra screws, and a Torx driver set are also helpful tools. Additionally, some type of extraction tool for retrieving dropped screws and other parts is definitely needed.

Do not use magnetic extraction devices when working on computers. In fact, you should *not* keep any magnetic devices in your tool kit, including magnetic screwdrivers. As you will learn in Chapter 9—Magnetic Storage Devices, data is often stored on magnetic computer disks and tapes. Magnetic devices such as magnetic screwdrivers or extraction tools can destroy the data. Accidents can and will happen, but many can be prevented by not having any materials around your work location that can cause such destruction.

Software Tool Kit

You will find that a software tool kit is just as important as a hardware tool kit. You will probably depend more on your skills using software than hardware to troubleshoot, diagnose, and repair PCs. As you progress through the textbook, there will be many suggestions about software to add to your tool kit. There will also be many references to third-party suppliers and shareware available for your use.

Many software tools can be found as shareware. Shareware is software programming that is freely distributed, usually by downloading from the Internet. Shareware is not always free for your unlimited use. It is usually intended for use on a trial basis only. The distributor expects the subscriber to purchase the software at a later date.

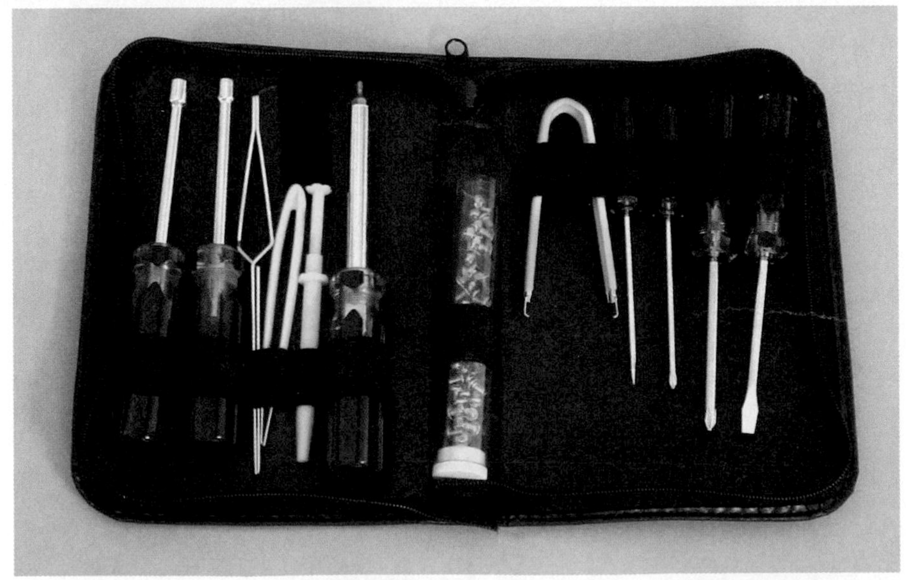

Figure 1-36. Standard small tool kit. This kit contains the basics. More elaborate kits are available.

Summary

- ✔ There are two major classifications of electronic components: analog and digital.
- ✔ An analog system consists of many various voltage levels.
- ✔ A digital system usually contains only two voltage levels.
- ✔ The three common codes associated with PCs are binary, hexadecimal, and ASCII.
- ✔ The binary system consists of only two numbers: zero and one.
- ✔ The binary number system is used to represent the digital circuits of a computer.
- ✔ The hexadecimal numbering system has sixteen characters, and it uses the digits *0–9* and the letters *A–F*.
- ✔ ASCII code is a standardized system of codes used to represent computer characters and symbols.
- ✔ A bit consists of a single *0* or *1* and is represented by the lowercase *b*.
- ✔ A byte consists of eight bits and is represented by the uppercase *B*.
- ✔ A peripheral is an optional piece of equipment used for input or output.
- ✔ A central processing unit (CPU) controls all the actions and processes data through the computer system.
- ✔ An integrated circuit (IC) is a collection of transistors, resistors, and other electronic components reduced to an extremely small size.
- ✔ Electrostatic discharge (ESD) is a static charge of electricity that can damage integrated circuits.
- ✔ *Never* use any type of magnetic tool around a PC.

Review Questions

Answer the following questions on a separate sheet of paper. Please do not write in this book.

1. Explain or compare the typical PC vs. human characteristics.
2. What components are found in a typical computer workstation?
3. Describe the difference between a digital and an analog electronic device.
4. Which of the following items acts like an analog system, and which is most like a digital system?
   a. Automobile gas pedal
   b. Streetlight
   c. Drawbridge
   d. Car horn
   e. Wind speed
   f. Slide trombone
   g. Drum
   h. Flashlight
5. Complete the following statement about the basic computer units of data. There are eight _____ in one _____.

6. Data can be _____.
   a. text
   b. sound
   c. picture
   d. All the answers are correct.
7. The binary number system consists of the decimal numbers _____ and _____.
8. List the characters for the hexadecimal number system from zero to fifteen.

   0 = ___ 1 = ___ 2 = ___ 3 = ___ 4 = ___ 5 = ___ 6 = ___ 7 = ___ 8 = ___
   9 = ___ 10 = ___ 11 = ___ 12 = ___ 13 = ___ 14 = ___ 15 = ___
9. RAM provides (temporary, permanent) _____ storage of data.
10. What is the purpose of the battery mounted on the motherboard?
11. Explain the difference between the CMOS chip and BIOS.
12. What happens during the POST?
13. Define a *bit*.
14. Define a *byte*.
15. Define a *word*.
16. What letter symbol represents bit?
17. What letter symbol represents byte?
18. How many bytes are in a 32-bit word?
19. What are the two numeric values for 1 megabit?
    a. Base 10 _____ = 1M
    b. Base 2 or binary _____ = 1M
20. Why are expansion slots provided on a computer motherboard?
21. What is the function of BIOS?
22. What is another name commonly used for an integrated circuit?
23. Why should you not have a magnetic screwdriver in your tool kit?
24. What is the purpose of an anti-static wrist strap?
25. Give an example of a serial input device.
26. Convert the following acronyms to complete words and capitalize the letter of the word used to construct the acronym. Example: CPU = Central Processing Unit.
    a. BIOS =
    b. RAM =
    c. ROM =
    d. ASCII =
    e. POST =
    f. ESD =
    g. CMOS =
    h. IC =

Sample A+ Exam Questions

Answer the following questions on a separate sheet of paper. Please do not write in this book.

1. A display monitor typically uses which type of cable connector?
   a. DB-9
   b. DB-15
   c. 9-pin serial
   d. 25-pin parallel
2. A typical hard drive uses which type of cable connector?
   a. flat ribbon cable
   b. DB-15
   c. RJ-45
   d. PS/2
3. A modem typically uses which type of connector to connect to the telephone line?
   a. RJ-45
   b. DB-9
   c. RJ-11
   d. PS/2
4. The maximum number of devices that can be connected to an IEEE 1394 connector is _____.
   a. 7
   b. 24
   c. 63
   d. 127
5. The maximum number of devices that can be connected using a USB connector is _____.
   a. 7
   b. 24
   c. 63
   d. 127
6. Firmware is associated with which of the following items?
   a. RAM
   b. BIOS
   c. DVD
   d. Speaker amplifier system
7. Which of the following is *not* a standard expansion card architecture?
   a. ISA
   b. PCI
   c. EISA
   d. ICP
8. The acronym CMOS represents which of the following answers?
   a. Complementary mechanical operating system
   b. Complementary metal oxide semiconductor
   c. Complementary media operating system
   d. Complementary metallic opposition semiconductor

9. Which is the accepted method for a technician to deal with ESD?
   a. Always use insulated hand tools.
   b. Place the PC on a rubber mat before disassembly.
   c. Disconnect the ground before servicing a PC.
   d. Always wear an anti-static wrist strap before touching PC components.
10. Which type of tool should never be used for PC repair?
   a. Stainless steel
   b. Plastic handled
   c. Magnetic tipped
   d. Wooden handled

Suggested Laboratory Activities

Do not attempt any suggested laboratory activities without your instructor's permission. Certain activities can render the PC operating system inoperable.

1. Remove the case from three different PCs and compare the hardware. The PCs may differ by age or manufacture. Take note of similarities as well as differences. Identify all the major components.
2. Select a major brand of PC and use the Internet to access the Web site of the manufacturer. Look for technical reference material to help you identify the component locations on the motherboard and on the outside of the case.

Interesting Web Sites for More Information

www.cbi.umn.edu
www.computerhistory.org
www.intel.com
www.karbosguide.com
www.pcguide.com

Chapter 1
Laboratory Activity
Part Identification

After completing this laboratory activity, you will be able to:

✔ Identify major motherboard components.

✔ Identify common motherboard ports.

Introduction

In this lab activity, you will learn to identify the major components inside a typical PC. You will be asked questions throughout the lab activity that will later be reviewed in your classroom as an instructor-lead activity. Answer all questions to the best of your ability. Short answers are acceptable. Do *not* remove any of the major components or disconnect any of the wiring connections during this activity. This is strictly a visual identification exercise. You may use your textbook to help you identify the components.

Equipment and Materials

✔ Anti-static wrist strap.

✔ Pen or pencil and notebook paper.

✔ Basic PC tool kit.

Procedure

1.______ Report to your assigned PC for this activity.

2.______ On a separate sheet of paper, answer the following question:
Is the assigned PC a desktop model or a tower?

3.______ On a separate sheet of paper, note if each of the following components are in your computer.

- Floppy disk drive.
- CD drive.
- DVD drive.

4. _______ Look at the back of the case and identify the types of port access for the computer. You may use the following figure to help you identify common ports.

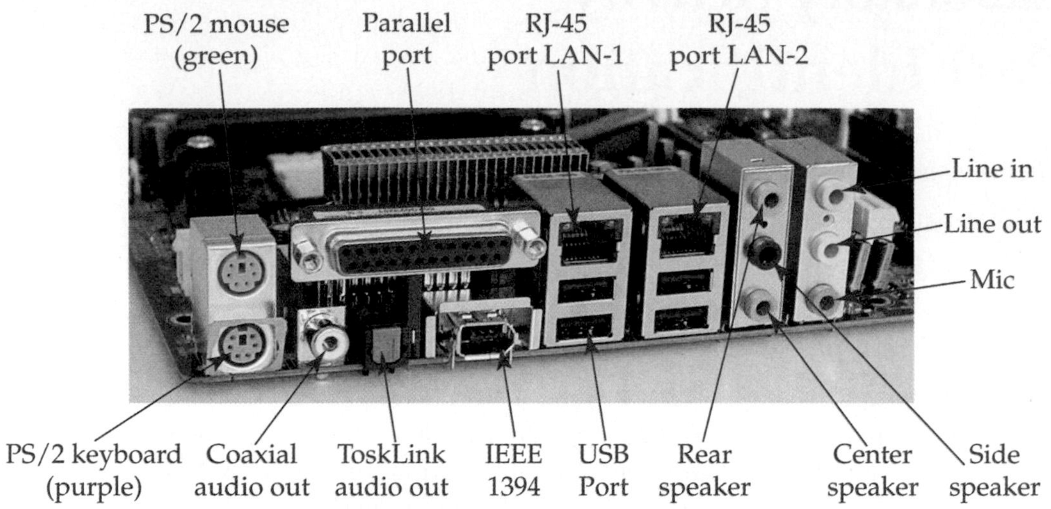

5. _______ On a separate sheet of paper, sketch and identify each of the following ports:
   - VGA, DVI, or S-Video connection port to the monitor.
   - RJ-11 telephone modem connection.
   - RJ-45 network connection.
   - PS/2 mouse.
   - PS/2 keyboard.
   - Parallel port.
   - Serial port.
   - Audio ports.
   - Game port.
   - Others.

6. _______ Observe your instructor closely as to the proper procedure for removing the computer case enclosure. There are many different variations of case styles, and it can be very difficult to properly remove a computer case enclosure. You may inadvertently damage the case if you apply force or remove an enclosure improperly.

7. _______ After removing the case enclosure, identify the power supply location. The power supply is very obvious. Look at the exterior power cord connection coming from the 120-volt wall outlet. It will connect directly to the power supply unit. You will also see a bundle of various colored wires and power connectors leading to various components inside the computer case. On a separate sheet of paper, answer the following questions:

   Does the power supply have a cooling fan?

   If yes, where is it located?

   Approximately how many connectors are associated with the power supply unit?

8. ______ Look at the power supply for information such as the voltage and wattage of the unit. On a separate sheet of paper, record the wattage rating of the power supply unit.

9. ______ Identify the CPU unit. It should be mounted directly on the motherboard with a heat sink and a fan assembly mounted on top.

10. ______ Look for the RAM modules and their location in the corresponding slots. For example, if there are four RAM slots and only two are filled, which two are filled?

11. ______ Identify the main motherboard and the type of expansion slots located on the board. Many times the expansion slot is identified by placing its name or acronym at the slot location like that shown in the following illustration.

Look closely and you will see PCI1 and PCI2 printed on the motherboard beside the corresponding PCI slots. Note that not all motherboards identify the type of slot.

12. ______ If a floppy drive is not installed, skip to the next step. If a floppy disk drive is installed, look at the back of the drive and identify the data cable. Identify the location on the motherboard where it connects. See if you can locate pin 1 or if there is a colored stripe running down one side of the cable. If yes, record the color of the stripe and its orientation to the motherboard connector. Identify the power cable connection on the floppy disk drive. How many wires does it use?

13. ______ Identify the hard disk drive. Determine if it is connected to an IDE-type of connector on the motherboard or a SATA-type connection. Again, these types of connectors usually have an ID printed on the motherboard beside the connection. Look for the letters SATA and IDE. On a separate sheet of paper, answer the following questions:

Does the hard disk drive use a flat ribbon type of data cable?

If so, does the cable have a red or blue stripe along one edge?

Do you see a power cable from the power supply to the hard disk drive?

How many wires are used for the power cable?

14. _______ Look at the various chips mounted on the motherboard. Are they soldered in place, or are they inserted into sockets?

15. _______ Locate the CMOS battery. Look for a circular silver disk approximately 1″ in diameter. The battery normally has the voltage labeled on it or a positive plus sign like that shown in the following illustration. Look at the BAT1 printed on the motherboard below the battery location.

17._______ Lastly, it is often necessary to make a sketch of the PC components' layout. The sketch is used as a guide for reassembly after certain PC components have been disassembled. For example, if you must replace the motherboard, every wire connection point should be identified. Make a sketch of the PC layout. It should look similar to that in the following figure. The one in the example is very small, and the labeling is very limited. Make yours larger on a separate piece of paper. Be sure to identify the fan, LED, and switch connections. Draw the sketch with as much detail as reasonably possible, as it will help during reassembly. Pay particular attention to how the flat ribbon cable connects to devices. Be sure to draw the orientation of the colored stripe along the cable in respect to the connection points.

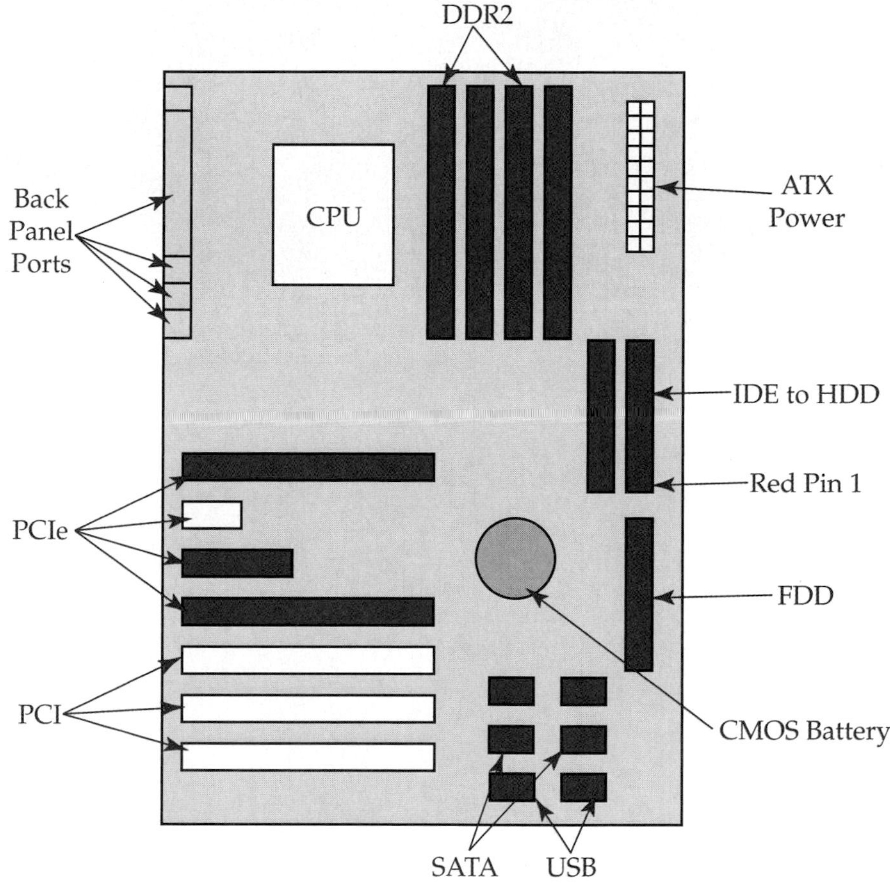

Internet Assignment

1. Locate the motherboard layout for the PC you are using in this lab activity. Go to the manufacturer's Web site and see if you can locate the motherboard schematic showing the location of all major components. Also, see if you can locate the manual that comes with the motherboard. This should provide detailed information about such items as how to access the BIOS Setup program, what type of memory can be installed on the motherboard, and which CPU can be used with this motherboard.

A cable tester is often used to test for continuity in a network cabling system.

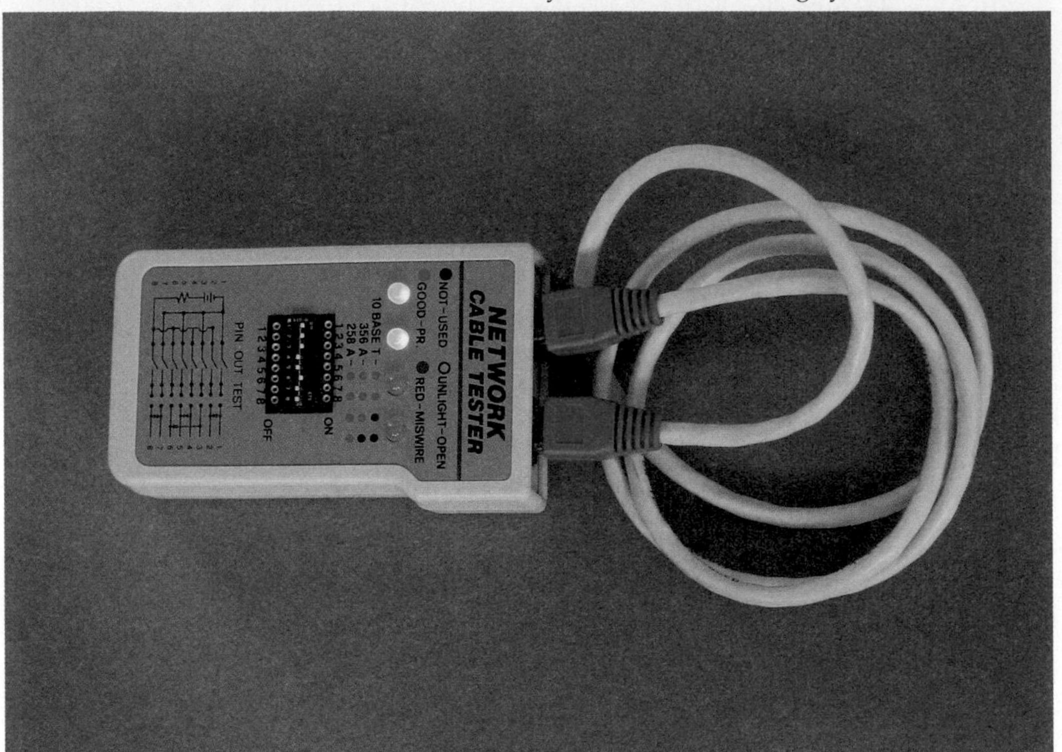

Operating Systems

After studying this chapter, you will be able to:

- ✔ Identify various computer operating systems.
- ✔ Explain minimum requirements of an operating system.
- ✔ Describe the three core DOS files.
- ✔ Identify DOS limitations.
- ✔ Explain the differences between the various versions of the Windows operating system.
- ✔ Describe the boot process.
- ✔ Describe the relationship of application software, operating systems, BIOS, and system hardware components.
- ✔ Describe the common characteristics of different operating systems.

A+ Exam—Key Points

You must know the basic text line commands such as **cmd**, **dir**, **attrib**, **mem**, **defrag**, **edit**, **copy**, **xcopy**, and **format**. These commands are required knowledge for the CompTIA A+ 602 and 603 exams. Note that many of these commands will be covered in more detail in later chapters of the textbook. Even with an excellent knowledge of the Windows operating system, the lack of sufficient knowledge of text line commands can result in failure on the CompTIA A+ Certification exams.

In addition, be sure you can define multitasking, both preemptive and cooperative.

You should also know how to navigate a directory structure from Windows Explorer and the command line and how to create and manage files and directories.

Key Words and Terms

The following words and terms will become important pieces of your computer vocabulary. Be sure you can define them.

application software
boot sequence
bootstrap program
bugs
cabinet (cab) files
cold boot
configuration file
cooperative multitasking
directories
disk operating system (DOS)
DOS system boot disk
drivers
dual-boot system
extension
external commands
file
file allocation table (FAT)
graphical user interface (GUI)
internal commands
kernel
multiple-boot system
multitasking
operating system (OS)
pathname
Plug and Play (PnP)
preemptive multitasking
registry
root directory
source code
subdirectories
text line command
virtual machine
warm boot

This chapter introduces you to various common operating systems. Understanding the operating system is essential for troubleshooting a PC system. The operating systems introduced in this chapter include MS-DOS, PC-DOS, Linux, and the Windows families (Windows 3.x, Windows 95, Windows 98, Windows Me, Windows NT Workstation, Windows 2000, Windows XP, and Windows Vista). Although, some of these operating systems are no longer in use, learning about them will give you special insight into how the Windows operating systems progressed to achieve their current features and functions.

To gain in-depth knowledge of an operating system, the operating system and its various options must be put to use. It is imperative that you supplement textbook studies with actual hands-on practice with current operating systems (Windows 2000, XP, and Vista). The Laboratory Manual for this text is designed to give you the necessary skills and first-hand knowledge required to pass the A+ Certification exams and to become a proficient PC technician.

What Is an Operating System?

Before operating systems were commonplace, users had to write code for all of the common tasks. If you wanted to save data, you had to write the code that told your computer to do so.

An ***operating system (OS)*** provides a computer user with a file system structure and with a means of communicating with the computer hardware. The operating system communicates with disk storage units, monitors, printers, memory, and other computer components. It is also the job of the operating system to make sure programs running on the computer do not interfere with each other.

operating system (OS) software that provides a computer user with a file system structure and with a means of communicating with the computer hardware.

Operating system software has evolved over the years. Think of the evolution of computer software and hardware as a group of inventors constantly building a better mousetrap. What is a leading edge operating system one day may not be the next day. In fact, it will likely become obsolete only a few years later. It is the constant evolution of the computer that makes it so confusing. Each operating system has its individual strengths and weaknesses.

The core of any operating system is referred to as the ***kernel.*** Just as plants bud and grow from a single seed or kernel, so does the operating system software. The core program is enhanced by other software applications that refine the computer system. Associated with the core can be programs that provide for user interface style, security, and specialized file systems.

kernel
the core of the operating system.

Operating systems allow application software to communicate with the BIOS, which in turn translates the request of the application software into instructions that the hardware can understand. Examine **Figure 2-1.**

An operating system provides a user with the ability to interact with the computer hardware and peripherals. As you can see, users give instructions to the computer system via application software such as word-processing, graphics, and gaming software. The operating system provides a communication system between the software application and the BIOS. In some cases, the operating system can communicate directly with the hardware components.

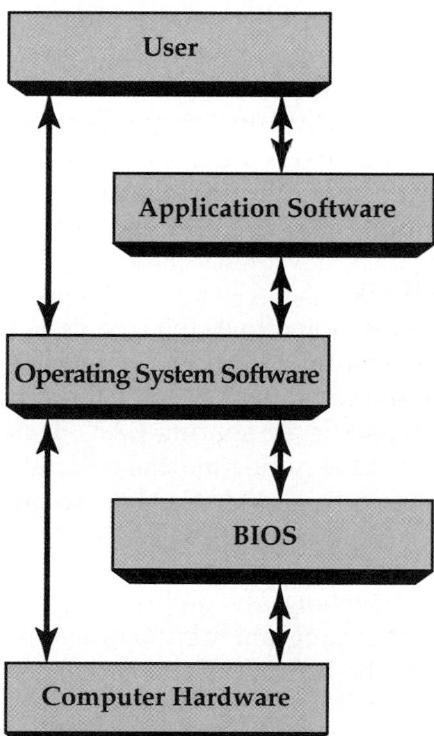

Figure 2-1.
Typical relationship of computer hardware and software components.

Operating System Characteristics

The way an operating system handles activities, such as storing data, interfacing with the user, and presenting information on the screen, can be referred to as operating system characteristics. Most operating systems appear similar when judged by their screen display. However, there are many differences in the way they handle activities, especially data storage.

Multitasking

multitasking
the ability of an operating system to support two or more programs running at the same time.

Multitasking is the ability of an operating system to support two or more programs running at the same time. With multitasking, it seems to the user that both programs are running simultaneously. However, in reality, they are not. The computer simply switches control between the programs giving the illusion they are running at the same time.

An example of multitasking is using the printer while, at the same time, using e-mail, surfing the Internet, or running another computer application such as a game. The computer runs the software in between sending packets of data to the printer.

Note that you may also hear the term *thread* or *threads* used. These terms refer to a form of multitasking when more than one CPU is installed on a motherboard. Data and parts of a program can be shared between two or more CPUs. This is called *threading* instead of multitasking.

Not all operating systems support multitasking. In addition, those that support multitasking do not all support it in the same way. DOS, for example, does not support multitasking. Only one program can be run at a time. If a second program is loaded, the first is unloaded from RAM. If the printer is printing, another program cannot run until the printer has finished. The two major classifications of multitasking are preemptive and cooperative.

Preemptive multitasking

preemptive multitasking
multiple programs sharing control of the operating system. It is sometimes referred to as *time slicing.*

Preemptive multitasking, sometimes referred to as *time slicing,* allows multiple programs to share control of the operating system. No single program can totally take charge of the computer system. All programs running in the preemptive mode of multitasking are sharing RAM. If two programs attempt to use the same area of RAM at the same time, the computer will lock up. Windows 95, Me, XP, Vista, NT, 2000, OS/2, and MAC OS X use preemptive multitasking.

Cooperative multitasking

cooperative multitasking
one program dominating the operating system but allowing another program to run while it is idle.

With ***cooperative multitasking,*** one program dominates the operating system but will allow another program to run while it is idle. This type of multitasking is common to the MAC OS 9 and earlier and Windows 3.x.

User Interface

There are two dominant user interfaces used to issue commands on a computer system: text line command and graphical user interface. Graphical user interface is usually referred to as GUI (pronounced gooey).

Text line command

text line command
commands issued by typing in text at a command prompt.

A ***text line command*** interface means that commands for the computer are issued by typing in text at a command prompt. MS-DOS, PC-DOS, Linux, and UNIX are typical text line command systems. See **Figure 2-2.**

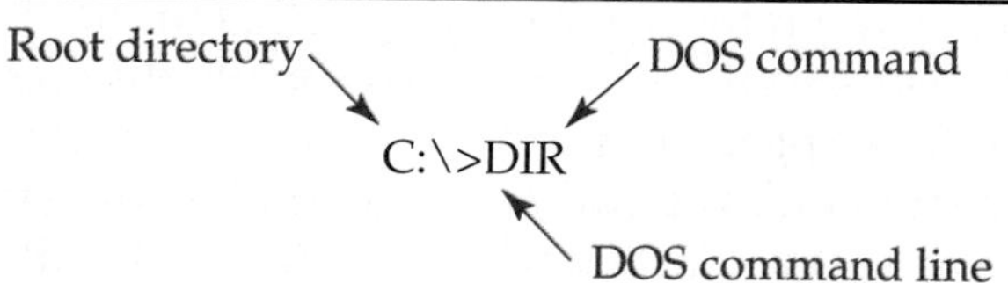

Figure 2-2.
This is a typical DOS command line.

Some common DOS commands are **dir**, **copy**, and **mem**. These commands call up a directory, copy a file or disk, and list your memory resources, respectively. See **Figure 2-3** for a chart of some common DOS commands. There are many more commands than the few listed, but these are some of the most commonly used.

Figure 2-3.
Chart of commonly used DOS commands.

Command	Example	Definition
mem	**C:\> mem**	Displays information about the type and amount of system memory.
cd	**C:\>cd\games**	Changes the command line from the current directory to another directory. In the example, a command is issued to the computer changing the current command line from the root directory of drive C to a directory on drive C called games.
copy	**C:\>copy a:memo1 c:**	Copies data from one location to another. In the example, a file named memo1 is being copied from drive A to drive C.
dir	**C:\>dir**	Displays the current directory. All the files and directories directly connected to the root directory will be displayed.
exit	**C:\>exit**	When DOS is accessed from Windows, and the command **exit** is issued at the DOS command line, DOS is closed and control returns to the Windows desktop.
md	**C:\>md c:\games**	Creates or makes a directory. In the example, a directory called games is created.
rd	**C:\>rd c:\games**	Deletes or removes a directory. In the example, the directory called games is being removed from the root directory of drive C.
chkdsk	**C:\>chkdsk a:**	Checks a disk for errors and displays the findings on the monitor.
format	**C:\>format a:**	Prepares a disk for first time usage. Today most disks are already formatted or prepared to store data and programs. You must be careful issuing the command **format** because it can erase all data on the disk being formatted. In the example, the command **format** is being issued at the DOS prompt to prepare a disk in drive A before storing data on it.

DOS was the major operating system used by PCs in the 1980s. However, DOS was difficult to use. Users had to memorize many different commands to become proficient with the operating system.

Today, text line commands are still used, especially when troubleshooting. Text line commands are particularly important when a PC fails to complete its startup process and take the user to the GUI. Troubleshooting tools such as Recovery Console, used in Windows 2000 and Windows XP, can only be run using text line commands. It is important that the technician be able to use the text line command prompt.

Windows 2000, Me, and XP do not use DOS but rather a DOS emulator. The DOS emulator has the look and feel of a real DOS prompt and functions similarly. Many of the restrictions or limitations of DOS are not found in the emulator program. For example, many of the restricted characters not allowed in DOS file names can be used.

Windows XP also uses DOS-like commands in the Recovery Console utility. The Recovery Console utility allows a computer technician to communicate with the Windows XP operating system after a system GUI failure. When a computer system fails during the startup process, there is no GUI. The only means of communicating with the computer system is by using a non-graphical user interface such as the Recovery Console. Many of the text line commands used in Recovery Console look and work exactly like the old DOS commands and DOS emulator commands. **Figure 2-4** lists the most commonly used Recovery Console

Figure 2-4. Windows XP Recovery Console commands.

Recovery Console Command	Function
attrib	View or set the attributes of a file or directory.
cd	View or change the current directory.
chkdsk	Check and display the status of a hard drive.
copy	Copy a file.
del	Delete a file.
dir	Display the files and subdirectories of the current working directory.
disable	Disable a service or a driver.
diskpart	Partition a hard disk drive.
enable	Enable a service or a driver.
exit	Exit Recovery Console.
fixmbr	Repair the master boot record.
format	Format a hard drive or floppy disk.
help	Display a list of Recovery Console commands.
md	Create a directory.
ren	Rename a file.
rd	Delete a directory.

commands. The commands are designed to look and feel like the older DOS commands so that technicians can easily understand them.

Windows Vista replaced the Recovery Console with a new utility called the Recovery Environment. The Windows Vista Recovery Environment contains access to a text-based command prompt.

There are also newer text line commands that complement today's more sophisticated operating systems. So when you hear someone say, *"DOS is dead,"* or, *"DOS is no longer used,"* you can reply, *"Yes, you are correct, but text-based commands are an essential part of troubleshooting."* There will be much more about command line support in Chapter 15—PC Troubleshooting and in the Laboratory Manual.

A+ Note:

Text line commands are still very much a part of the A+ Certification exams. To pass the exams, you must acquire a basic understanding of text line commands.

Graphical user interface

Although DOS and DOS-like systems controlled over 80% of the market during the 1980s, the user-friendly ***graphical user interface (GUI)*** system of Macintosh gained popularity. Creating GUIs for the PC in the form of Windows 3.1 and Windows NT helped Microsoft retain control of the operating system market. In most operating systems that are used today, the GUI displays the file system consisting of folders, icons, and names. One great advantage of using the GUI is that the entire file structure is easily displayed and interpreted. Examine **Figure 2-5** and **Figure 2-6.** Shown is a typical GUI display of a file system organization.

graphical user interface (GUI) an operating system interface that allows the user to perform functions by selecting on-screen icons rather than by issuing text line commands.

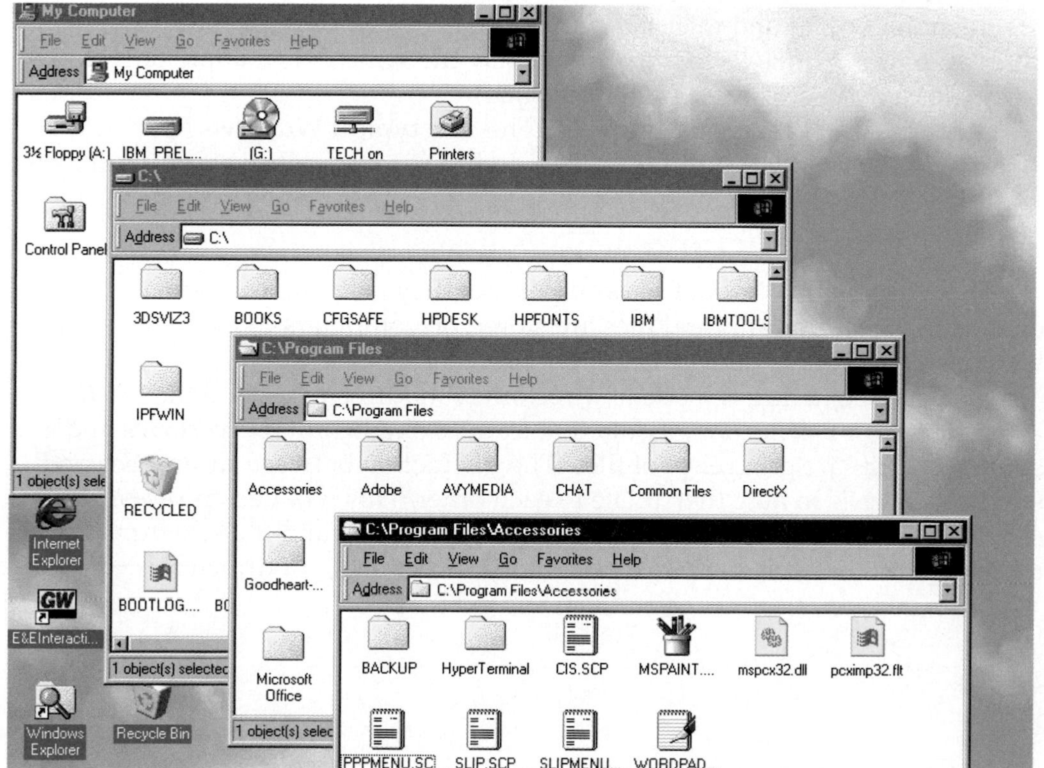

Figure 2-5. File structure is shown here through cascading windows.

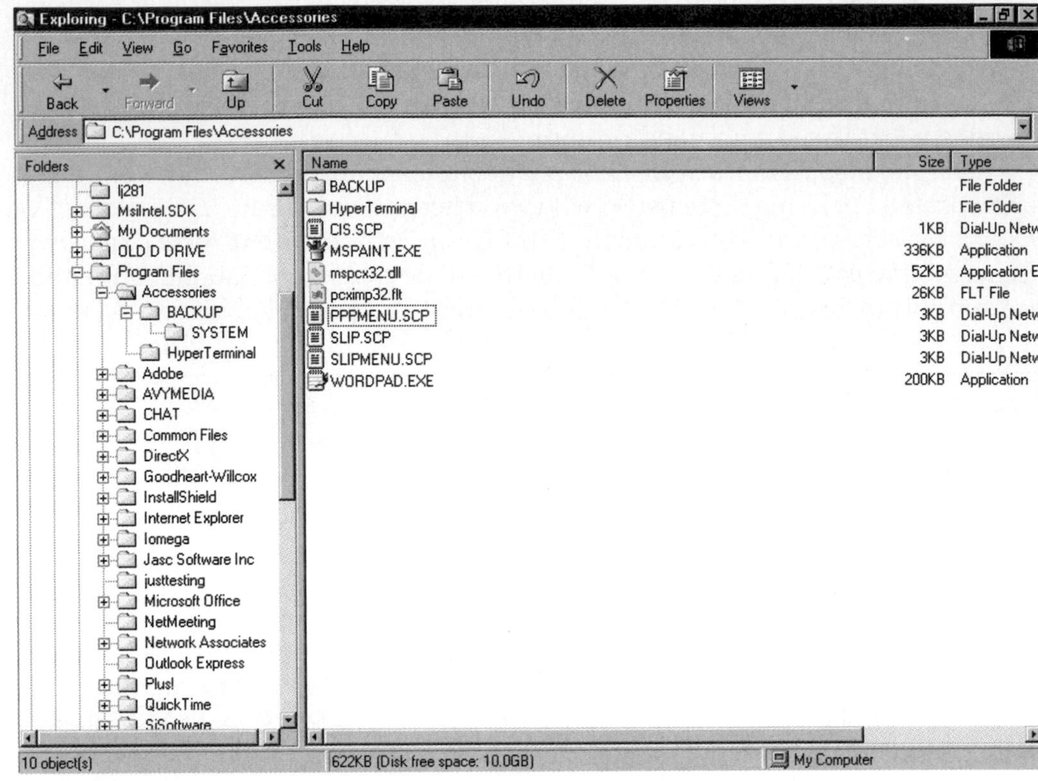

Figure 2-6. File structure can also be seen using Windows file managing software Windows Explorer.

file
a program or collection of data that forms a single unit.

directories
a file used to group other files together in a hierarchical file structure. It is analogous to a file folder in a paper filing system. Directories are referred to as *folders* in many operating systems.

subdirectories
a file that subdivides the contents of a directory. A subdirectory is analogous to a folder within a folder in a paper filing system. Subdirectories are referred to as *subfolders* in many operating systems.

The relative relationship between files and folders is simple to interpret. Two window styles appear. One is based on the program Windows Explorer, and the other uses a more traditional folder display. Each window style displays the same file structures. The two styles differ only in their presentation. Figure 2-5 uses a series of cascading windows to display information about the software's organization of files and their location in the file system on the hard drive. Figure 2-6 uses Windows Explorer to display the same information, only it resembles a more advanced DOS file structure.

A typical GUI is seen in **Figure 2-7.** This is a typical Windows XP desktop. All Windows GUIs are very similar. On the desktop are a number of program icons.

File System Structure

There are many different file systems, but they do have common characteristics. Programs and files are stored on computers in much the same way regardless of the operating system used.

The basic structure is made of directories, subdirectories, and files. A ***file*** is a program or a collection of data that forms a single unit. ***Directories*** and ***subdirectories*** are groupings of files. The distinction between directories and subdirectories is in how they relate to each other. This will become apparent shortly. Examine **Figure 2-8.** This is a typical directory and file structure. It shows the relationship of the root directory, directories, subdirectories, and files.

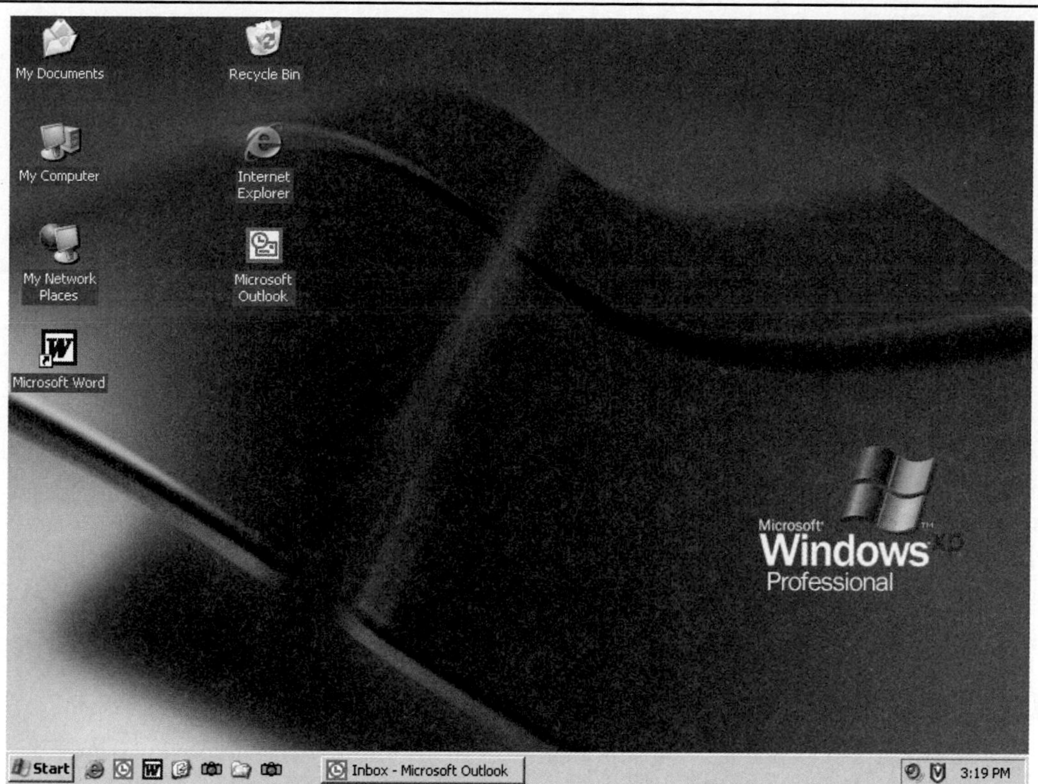

Figure 2-7. Typical opening GUI for Windows. While the mechanics behind the interface can be very different between the various versions of Windows, the appearance of the GUI has remained fairly constant.

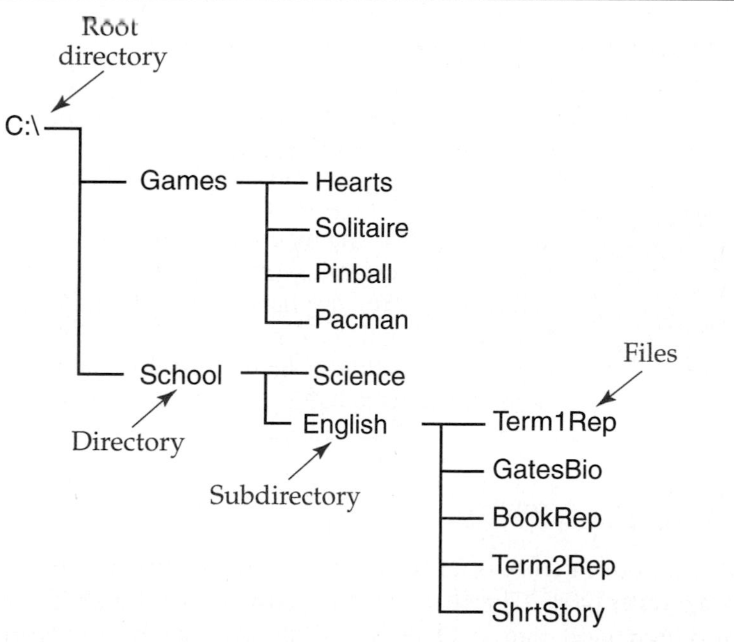

Figure 2-8. Typical directory and file structure.

root directory the top of the directory structure. A root directory is analogous to a file cabinet drawer in a conventional, paper filing system. A root directory is also referred to as the *root*.

The ***root directory*** is at the top of the directory structure. In this case, C:\ appears at the top. Thus, the root directory is C: (the hard drive). Next, there are two directories stemming from the root directory: Games and School. Directory and subdirectory are relative terms. Looking at the example again, you will see that English is a subdirectory to School. Both English and School are directories, but the placement in the structure determines which is a subdirectory in relation to the other. Directories can contain files. Under the directory Games, you can see several game files such as Hearts and Solitaire.

Pathname

pathname
a string of characters used to identify a file's location in the directory structure.

A ***pathname*** is used to identify the location of a specific file. Look again at Figure 2-6. The pathname for the file is displayed near the top of the window's dialog box. The display is C:\Program Files\Accessories. C:\ is the root directory of the file, Program Files is the first directory folder, and Accessories is the subdirectory of Program Files. The entire string of characters is referred to as the pathname.

A Closer Look at DOS

disk operating system (DOS)
an operating system typically requiring the user to issue text line commands to perform operations.

The ***disk operating system (DOS)*** is the operating system that was first widely accepted and used throughout the world. It is still used today but to a limited degree. It has been overshadowed by many more powerful operating systems. It is important to have a basic understanding of DOS because it set the standards for the other operating systems used today. In fact, DOS 7 is actually integrated into the Windows 98 operating system to ensure downward compatibility with some older programs that were designed to run under DOS.

DOS Core Files

The core files associated with DOS are io.sys, msdos.sys, and command.com. These three files are the minimum set of files required to operate a DOS-compatible computer system. The IBM system has its own version of DOS called PC-DOS. In the IBM system, the io.sys and msdos.sys files are called ibmio.com and ibmdos.sys. The command.com file is still referred to as command.com.

These are important files. If erased, the computer would fail to complete its starting routine. Command.com is a program that interprets commands, such as **copy** and **erase**, which are issued at the DOS prompt.

Note that io.sys and msdos.sys are hidden files. To prevent users from accidentally erasing them, the operating system "hides" them. You still have access to these files, but in the default operating system settings, they will not show up in your file structure. When using Windows Explorer, the option for viewing hidden files must be activated.

DOS System Boot Disk

DOS system boot disk
a floppy disk that contains the files necessary to run a computer with DOS.

A ***DOS system boot disk*** is a floppy disk that contains the files necessary to run a computer with DOS. The three files necessary are the DOS core files: io.sys, msdos.sys, and command.com. A DOS boot disk is a very handy troubleshooting tool because a computer can have one of several different problems related to the boot sequence and hard drive.

To create a DOS boot disk, you simply place a floppy disk into the drive and enter the command **format a: /s** at the DOS command prompt. DOS will then copy the necessary files to the floppy disk in **drive A:**. To test the disk, insert it into the standard 3 1/2" floppy drive while the computer is off. Then power the computer on. The computer will automatically start using the system files of the operating system located on the boot disk. A DOS prompt will appear on the screen similar to that in **Figure 2-9.**

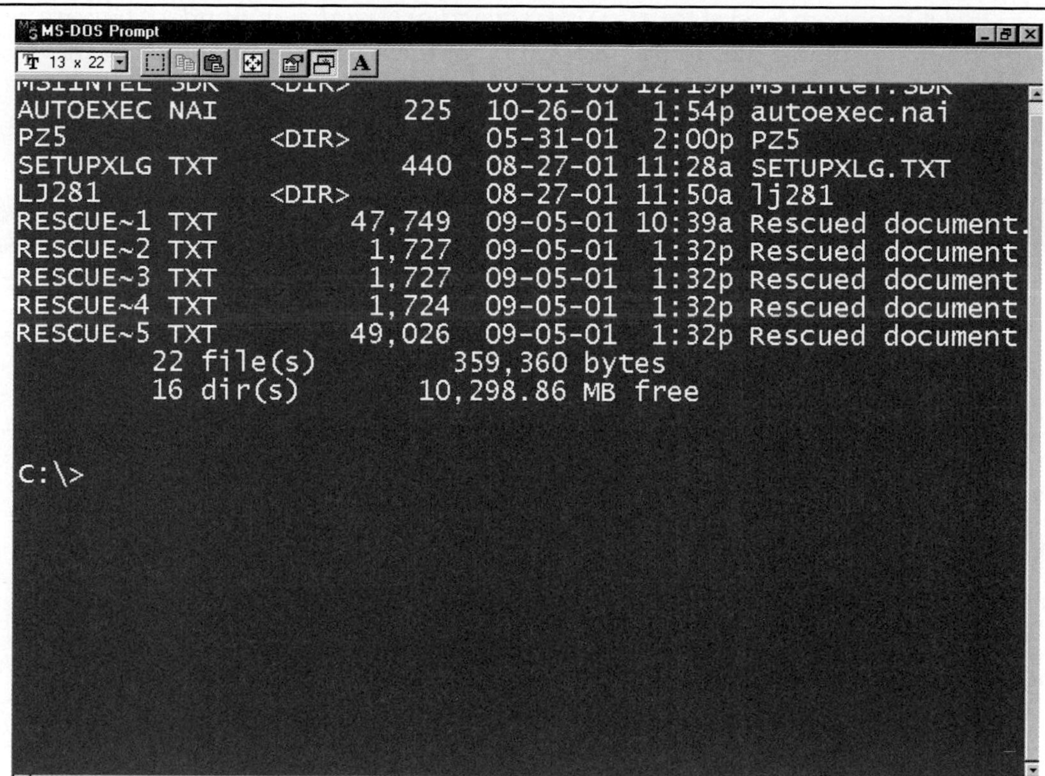

Figure 2-9. A typical command line prompt.

It is possible to create an MS-DOS boot disk in Windows Vista. If a floppy drive exists as part of the system or if you install a floppy drive through the USB port, the floppy disk can be formatted as a DOS boot disk. Simply right-click the floppy disk drive when it appears in Windows Vista Explorer. An option to format the disk will appear. When the option to format is selected, it will be followed by another option to allow you to create an MS-DOS startup disk with the minimal files required to boot the computer. This is an example of how Windows maintains backward compatibility with legacy systems.

Command.com

Command.com is a compact program that allows the user to interact with the computer using standard DOS commands. Another name for the command.com program is the *command interpreter*. The command interpreter contains a set of programs that are activated by text entered at the command prompt. These commands are known as ***internal commands*** because the required software to run these commands resides inside the command.com program file. Following are examples of several common internal commands.

internal commands a set of programs that are wholly contained within the command processor program (command.com or cmd.exe).

Command	System Response
ver	Displays the software version running on the computer.
dir	Displays a list of files, directories, and subdirectories.
time	Displays the time.
date	Displays the date.
copy	Copies a file or group of files from one location to another location.
del	Deletes a file.
rename	Changes the name of a file.

external commands individual, executable files that extend DOS's functionality beyond the limits of its internal commands.

The DOS operating system also uses several ***external commands.*** They are individual, executable files found in addition to the internal commands of the command.com file. The external commands can be viewed in the DOS directory structure. The external commands typically have an .exe file extension. Following are several examples of common external DOS commands.

Command	System Response
edit	Starts a text editor program similar to a word processor.
format	Prepares a disk for storing data.
chkdsk	Checks the condition of a disk and displays a report.
print	Prints a text file to a printer.

Windows NT-based operating systems and Windows Vista include a new command interpreter called cmd.exe. This command interpreter contains many of the same DOS internal and external commands, plus additional commands. Command.com can still be run in Windows Vista when required for legacy programs.

Msdos.sys

Msdos.sys is the kernel of the DOS operating system. This program contains many smaller programs that process all the common commands needed to communicate between the user and the hardware, such as the processor. For IBM systems with PC-DOS, the program is called ibmdos.sys.

Io.sys

The io.sys file contains generic drivers necessary for communicating with hardware devices such as the monitor, floppy drive, hard drive, and keyboard. The io.sys file works in conjunction with the msdos.sys file to boot the computer. For IBM systems with PC-DOS, it is called ibmbio.com.

Naming DOS Files

DOS has a definitive system for naming files usually referred to as the eight point three (or 8.3) naming convention. A DOS file name is divided into two parts by a period. The first part of the name consists of one to eight characters, and the second part, called the ***extension,*** consists of three characters.

extension the second part of a filename. An extension is typically three characters long and indicates the function of the file.

In most cases when you are naming a file, the second part is optional and is completed automatically by the software application. For example, a word processing application may automatically save the file with the .txt extension. **Figure 2-10** lists some common file extensions.

.bmp	A bitmap graphics file.
.com	An executable command file.
.dll	A dynamic link library—collection of data or functions that can be used by Windows applications.
.doc	A document file.
.exe	An executable file—one that is a program and will run if the name is typed at the DOS prompt.
.ini	A file containing configuration information for Windows.
.log	A file that lists actions that have occurred.
.pif	A program information file—holds information about how Windows should run non-Windows applications.
.txt	A text file.

Figure 2-10. Common file extensions.

Not all characters are available for use in a DOS name. Acceptable characters consist of the following:

A through Z
0 through 9
Underscore _
Caret ^
Dollar sign $
Tilde ~
Exclamation point !
Number sign #
Percent sign %
Ampersand &
Hyphen -
Braces { }
Parentheses ( )
At sign @
Apostrophe '
backtick `

Certain characters are *not* used as part of the file name because they have special meanings in DOS. Common characters that are not allowed include back slashes, commas, and spaces. Periods can only be used for the separation of the name and extension. Other characters that cannot be used consist of the following:

| + = * > < ? : [ ]

Many different operating systems as well as application programs restrict the use of special characters in a file name.

A Closer Look at Microsoft Windows

The most widely used operating system today is Microsoft Windows. Windows XP and Windows Vista are found on most computers. However, in this section, references to all Windows operating systems are discussed when appropriate.

A+ Note:

The A+ Certification requires knowledge of Windows 2000 and Windows XP.

Desktop

Windows 95 and later versions, including Windows NT and Windows 2000, are very similar. In fact, you might say they set the standard for today. Even the newest Linux desktop looks remarkably like a Windows desktop. The desktop allows the user easy access to many of the most common software programs used. Look again at Figure 2-7.

At the bottom left of the screen is the **Start** button. This button is used to launch and access existing programs. When the mouse arrow is clicked on the **Start** button, a menu similar to **Figure 2-11** will pop up. Many options are made available through this menu. These options include **Help**, **Find**, **Settings**, **Documents**, **Programs**, and **Shut Down**.

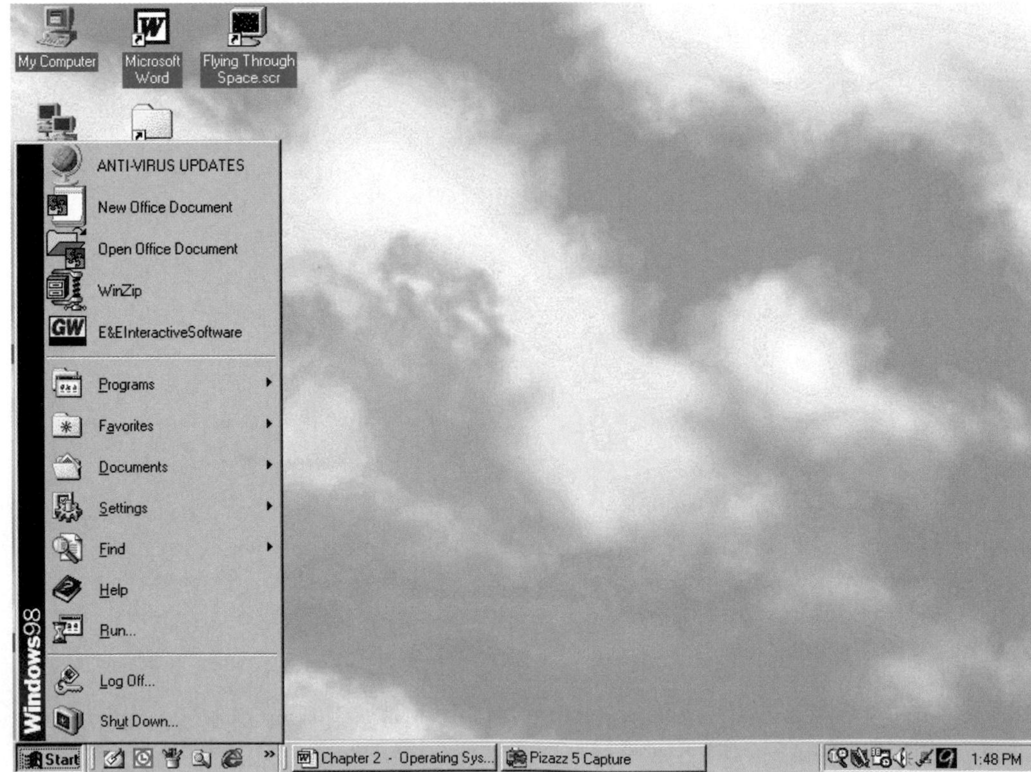

Figure 2-11. Windows desktop showing the **Start** menu.

Long File Names

Beginning with Windows 95 and Windows NT, Windows operating systems were designed to overcome the DOS file name restriction of a maximum of eight characters (the 8.3 naming convention). The long file name structure allows file names of up to 255 characters to be used.

This long file name feature allows for the content of the file to be described in some detail. This provides relief from brief, cryptic, eight-character file names. For example, using the long file name standard, a file could be saved as Term1 Science Paper The Factors Affecting Ocean Tides.

There are still certain characters or symbols that cannot be used in the file name. The characters that are still not allowed in the long file name system consist of the following:

| * > < ? : \ / "

These characters have a special meaning to the operating system and will produce errors or unwanted results when used. These symbols cannot be used even today to name files or folders in Windows XP or Windows Vista.

Windows Startup Disk

Early operating systems such as Windows 95 and 98 used a startup disk, or boot disk, for recovering from a failed or corrupt operating system. The startup disk contained only the essential system files required for a system boot operation. You could use the disk to make repairs to the operating system files and to verify or troubleshoot some of the hardware components.

A system disk is not recommended as a way to recover a failed Windows Vista operating system. It is recommended that you use the Windows Vista installation DVD to start the recovery process of the Windows Vista operating system.

Operating System Boot Sequences

A ***boot sequence*** is the step-by-step process of bringing a computer to an operational state. This involves a combination of hardware and software control to initialize hardware and load operating system files. This section serves as an introduction to the boot sequences of Windows 95, 98, Me, XP, 2000, and Vista. An in-depth understanding of boot sequences is essential to troubleshooting startup problems. Therefore, a more detailed description is presented in Chapter 15—PC Troubleshooting.

boot sequence the process of starting the computer and loading the operating system.

A+ Note:

The A+ Certification exams usually stress knowledge of the boot sequence. Exercises in the accompanying Laboratory Manual will assist you in better understanding the boot process.

Warm and Cold Booting

A computer cannot begin the boot sequence if it is not initiated. When the boot sequence is initiated, it is called *booting the computer.* There are two styles of booting a computer: a cold (or hard boot) and a warm (or soft boot). A ***cold boot*** means that the electrical power switch is used to turn on the computer. A ***warm boot*** is used to restart a computer that is already running. A warm boot can be initiated by a software program as part of a typical installation such as installing a game. Another common style of initiating a warm boot is by pressing the [Ctrl], [Alt], and [Delete] keys simultaneously.

cold boot
when the electrical power switch is used to turn on the computer.

warm boot
using the reset button or key combination [Ctrl], [Alt], and [Delete] to restart a computer that is already running. A warm boot can also be initiated by a software program as part of a typical installation such as installing a game.

bootstrap program
a short program that runs the POST, searches for the Master Boot Record (MBR), loads into memory some basic files, and then turns the boot operation over to the operating system.

POST

As you can see in **Figure 2-12,** all operating systems start out with a power-on self-test (POST). The POST is common to all operating systems, even to MAC OS X and all versions of Linux. The POST does a quick system check to determine if all major hardware components, such as the keyboard, mouse, video system, RAM, and storage devices, are in working order.

The POST is initiated by the BIOS bootstrap program. You should recall from Chapter 1—Introduction to a Typical PC that the BIOS is a special type of memory chip, called an EEPROM. It consists of software programs such as the POST, BIOS Setup program, and bootstrap program. The ***bootstrap program*** is a short program that runs the POST; searches for the Master Boot Record (MBR), which is typically located on the first section of the hard disk drive; loads into memory some basic files; and then turns the boot operation over to the operating system. The name *bootstrap* comes from the expression "to pull oneself up by one's bootstraps."

EFI

The Extensible Firmware Interface (EFI) is a modern approach to the BIOS system and an enhancement to the boot process. EFI was developed by Intel, but now a large group of computer hardware manufacturers are involved with creating a set of standards of design for EFI. The group organization is the United EFI (UEFI).

Figure 2-12. Comparison of Windows operating system boot sequences.

Windows 95, 98, and Me	Windows 2000 and XP	Windows Vista
POST	POST	POST
io.sys	Initial startup phase	Initial startup phase
msdos.sys	Boot loader phase	Windows Boot Manager phase
config.sys	Detect and configure hardware phase	Windows Boot Loader phase
command.com	Kernel loading phase	Kernel loading phase
autoexec.bat	Logon phase	Logon phase

EFI can be installed to work directly with the BIOS or as an eventual replacement for the BIOS. EFI is required on computers that wish to use a new file system directory structure referred to as GUID. In the future, EFI is expected to replace the BIOS as it exists today. There will be more about EFI and GUID later in this textbook when you have a better understanding of data storage and system files.

Windows 95, 98 and Me Boot Sequence

Windows 95, 98 and Me operating systems evolved from DOS and retained many of the features associated with it. While these operating systems are dated, a brief familiarity of their boot process and files will help you understand some of the files you might encounter while exploring Windows NT-based and Windows Vista operating systems.

Look again at the boot comparison table in Figure 2-12. The first column lists the files that are loaded in sequence when starting a computer with Windows 95, 98, or Me. Notice that after the POST, the io.sys file is loaded and executed. After io.sys is loaded, any file with an extension of .sys, .com, .bat, or .exe can be executed. Each file is loaded one after another until the GUI appears on the computer display. The user can then start running application software. The following details the Windows 95, 98, and Me boot sequence.

1. BIOS performs the POST.
2. BIOS locates the MBR and loads it into memory.
3. BIOS loads the io.sys file into memory.
4. The io.sys file loads the file allocation table into memory and then processes the msdos.sys file.
5. The io.sys file processes the config.sys, command.com, autoexec.bat, and win.com files.
6. Win.com loads the Windows kernel, the graphic device interface (GDI), the explorer shell program, various files, and network support.

The only files actually required for DOS and Windows 95, 98, and Me operating systems are io.sys, msdos.sys, and command.com. The autoexec.bat and config.sys files are not actually required, except for compatibility with earlier software applications. For example, these legacy files are in Windows Vista as you can see in **Figure 2-13.** However, they are not required for the Windows Vista operating system, but for compatibility with some earlier versions of software.

Config.sys

In early versions of Windows, it was used to customize, disable, or enable certain operating system features such as the maximum number of files that can be opened at the same time. The config.sys file also was responsible for loading device drivers that control hardware devices such as advanced video adapter boards. The config.sys file is still found in the boot process of newer operating systems, but it is included only to support legacy software applications. The registry now does the tasks formerly performed by config.sys. The registry is discussed later in this chapter.

The config.sys file is a simple ASCII text file that can be easily altered by any text editor such as Notepad. You should *never* attempt to alter or edit the config.sys file with an *advanced* form of text editor. Advanced features such as bold, italics, and special fonts can be saved into the config.sys file. This can cause the computer to crash or produce unpredictable results. Before attempting to make changes to or experimenting with your config.sys file, you should always make a backup copy. Making backup copies of files and using specific commands is covered in the Laboratory Manual for this text.

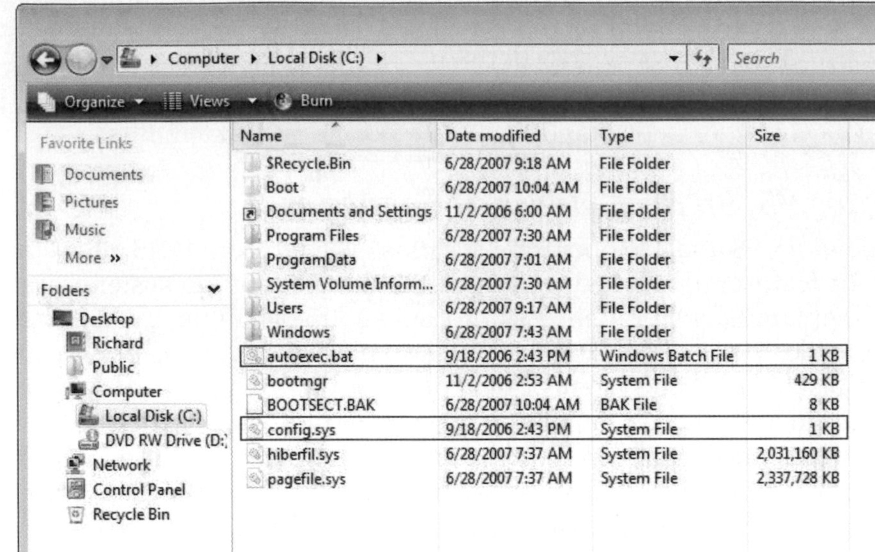

Figure 2-13. The autoexec.bat and config.sys files can be found in the root directory of Windows Vista even though they are not required. They are only used for compatibility with earlier software applications.

Figure 2-14 shows some common commands used in a config.sys file. These are only a few of the config.sys commands that can be found in a typical config.sys file.

Autoexec.bat

Autoexec.bat is a file used to load and run programs at startup. The autoexec.bat is an optional file for Windows 95 version OSR2 (Operating System Revision 2) and later. It is not required for modern operating systems. The autoexec.bat is required to run older, legacy programs usually associated with DOS. **Figure 2-15** shows some typical commands used in the autoexec.bat file. **Figure 2-16** shows an example of an autoexec.bat file taken from a Windows 95 system.

Figure 2-14. Commands that can be found in a config.sys file.

Commands	Functions
files	Used to specify how many files can be opened at one time.
devicehigh	Loads a device driver into upper memory.
buffers	Specifies how much memory is allocated for transferring files to and from disks.
lastdrive	Sets the maximum number of available drives that can be set up on a computer.
rem	Used to place text in a file as notes. Anything following the command **rem** will not be executed.
set	Sets the value for the environment such as the DOS prompt appearance.
stacks	Used to specify how much memory is reserved for hardware interrupts.

Commands	Functions
echo	Hides or displays messages on the display, using the switches on and off.
path	Sets up a search path to locate executable files.
prompt	Determines the appearance of the DOS prompt.
rem	Used to place remarks in the file that will not be executed.
set	Sets up, displays, or removes DOS variables.
shell	Used to specify the location of the command interpreter to be used.
pause	Suspends the program until any key is pressed.

Figure 2-15. Commands that can be found in an autoexec.bat file.

```
@ECHO OFF
SET BLASTER=A220 I5 D1 H5 P330 T6
SET CTCM=C:\WINDOWS
rem - By Windows Setup - C:\WINDOWS\COMMAND\MSCDEX.EXE
rem - /D:MSCD001
PATH C:\BITWARE\
```

Figure 2-16. Typical autoexec.bat file.

Windows NT-Based Boot Sequence

Windows NT was the first Microsoft operating system to be fully developed so that it is independent of the restrictions of DOS. It is a completely redesigned operating system with a new kernel. Windows 2000 and Windows XP are typically identified as Windows NT-based operating systems because they are built on the Windows NT kernel.

The Windows NT boot sequence is described as a series of phases rather than a series of files executed one after another. These phases are listed in the second column of the table in Figure 2-12. Some files are loaded into memory during the boot process and are used to provide information to the file that is presently in control of the boot operation. You might say that the boot operation is no longer a series of files taking over one by one, but rather several files working together to complete the boot operation. **Figure 2-17** provides a description of the Windows NT-based boot process files. The following details the Windows NT boot sequence.

1. BIOS performs the POST.
2. BIOS locates the MBR and loads it into memory.
3. The MBR loads the operating system loader, ntldr.
4. Ntldr reads the boot.ini file.
5. If the boot.ini file contains a reference to a SCSII disk drive system, the ntbootdd.sys file is loaded.
6. Ntldr calls the ntdetect.com program.
7. The ntdetect.com program detects system hardware information and passes the information to ntldr.

Figure 2-17.
Windows NT-based boot sequence and configuration files.

Windows NT-Based Boot Sequence File	Description
boot.ini	File used to identify the default operating system and other operating systems if more than one is present. The boot.ini file has been replaced by the Boot Configuration Data (BCD) file in Windows Vista.
bootcfg.exe	Used in dual-boot and multiple-boot systems to allow the user to select which operating system to boot.
hal.dll	Provides information and supports communication between software applications and hardware devices. Software applications are not allowed to directly communicate with hardware. Loads at the same stage as the kernel, and then works directly with the kernel.
ntbootdd.sys	The driver used to communicate with hardware devices that do not communicate directly with BIOS, such as SCSI drives and some ATA drives.
ntdetect.com	File responsible for identifying hardware information for ntldr. Ntdetect.com has been merged into the Windows Vista kernel.
ntldr	File responsible for loading the operating system. Ntldr has been replaced by the Windows Boot Manager in Windows Vista.
ntoskrnl.exe	The core of the operating system, referred to as the kernel.
winlogon.exe	The file that controls the system logon by the user.

8. Ntldr passes the hardware information and control over to ntoskrnl.exe.
9. The ntoskrnl.exe program loads the device drivers and hal.dll, and then initializes the computer settings using the values stored in the system registry.
10. Winlogon.exe loads, allowing the user to begin the logon process.
11. The user successfully logons on to the computer.

Windows Vista Boot Sequence

Windows Vista has made several changes to the boot sequence of previous Windows systems. First, Windows Vista can boot from the BIOS or an EFI system-equipped motherboard. This section focuses only on the BIOS-based boot sequence.

Look again at the table in Figure 2-12. The third column lists the major phases of the Windows Vista boot sequence. Notice that after the POST, Windows Vista progresses through the initial startup phase in similar fashion as the Windows NT-based operating systems. However, the next phase for Windows Vista is the Windows Boot Manager phase.

In this phase, the Windows Boot Manager (bootmgr) reads a registry-type file called the Boot Configuration Data (BCD) file. This file stores boot configuration information, such as the names of the operating systems to list in a boot menu, the amount of time the boot menu should be displayed while waiting for user input, and the default operating system to load if no user input is entered.

The Windows Boot Manager (bootmgr) replaces bootcfg.exe used by Windows NT-based operating systems. The Windows Boot Manager will not display a selection of operating systems if there is only one operating system on the computer. If there are two or more operating systems, the Windows Boot Manager appears for approximately 30 seconds to allow the user to select which operating system to start. If no selection is made, the default system, Windows Vista, is started.

When the Windows Boot Manager phase completes, the Windows Boot Loader (winload.exe) phase begins. First, the Windows Vista kernel (ntoskrnl.exe) is loaded into memory but not executed. The hal.dll file and registry data are also loaded into memory. The Windows Boot Loader phase ends by executing the kernel. The Kernel Loading phase begins.

In this phase, the kernel starts the Session Manager (smss.exe), which creates the system environment. Up until now, the operating system has been in a text-based mode; however, with smss.exe loaded, the operating system switches to graphics mode by loading the GUI. It is at this point that the familiar progress bar appears at the bottom of the screen.

The Windows kernel interacts with hal.dll and the registry information in memory to load hardware drivers and other files necessary to complete the boot operation. The last phase in the Windows Vista boot sequence is the logon phase, which is initiated by the loading of the Logon Manager (winlogon.exe). After a successful user logon, the desktop appears, and the user can start using the various software applications.

Certain files are automatically loaded into RAM after a successful user logon. These files are generally referred to as "startup programs," and will start quickly after they are selected from the **Start** menu or from a shortcut icon because they are already loaded into RAM. If a program is not a startup program, it will need to be loaded to RAM before it starts, thus causing a short delay in program response when selected. **Figure 2-18** provides a description of the Windows Vista-based boot process files. The following details the Windows Vista boot sequence:

1. BIOS performs the POST.
2. BIOS locates the MBR and loads it into memory.
3. BIOS locates and loads the Windows Boot Manager (bootmgr).
4. Windows Boot Manager reads the BCD file and displays the boot menu.
5. Windows Boot Manager starts the Windows Boot Loader (winload.exe) when Windows Vista is selected or if started automatically.
6. The Windows Boot Manager loads ntoskrnl.exe and hal.dll into memory and scans the registry for devices drivers to load. It then passes control to the kernel.
7. The kernel loads the device drivers and hal.dll and initializes the computer settings using the values stored in the system registry.
8. The kernel starts the Session Manager (smss.exe), which creates the system environment.
9. The operating system switches to graphics mode and the winlogon.exe file is loaded, thus starting the Logon Manager (winlogon.exe).
10. The Logon Manager allows the user to begin the logon process.

Figure 2-18. Windows Vista boot sequence and configuration files.

Windows Vista Boot Sequence File	Description
BCD	The Boot Configuration Data file, which is a registry file containing information such as the names of the operating systems to list in a boot menu.
BCDEdit.exe	Used to edit the Boot Configuration Data file. Replaces bootcfg.exe in Windows NT-based operating systems.
bootload.exe	The Windows Boot Manager file, which loads ntoskrnl.exe and hal.dll into memory and scans the registry for devices drivers to load. It then passes control to the ntoskrnl.exe.
bootmgr	The Windows Boot Manager file, which reads the BCD file and displays the boot menu.
hal.dll	Provides information and supports communication between software applications and hardware devices. Software applications are not allowed to directly communicate with hardware. Loads at the same stage as the kernel and then works directly with the kernel.
ntoskrnl.exe	The core of the operating system referred to as the kernel.
smss.exe	The Session Manager file, which creates the user session environment and the graphical user interface.
winlogon.exe	The Logon Manager file, which controls system logon by the user.

A+ Note:

When answering questions related to the Windows Vista boot sequence, remember that Windows Vista uses the winload.exe boot loader file, not ntldr.

Dual-Boot and Multiple-Boot Systems

dual-boot system a computer with two operating systems installed.

multiple-boot system a computer with more than two operating systems installed.

When two operating systems are installed on a single computer, it is referred to as a ***dual-boot system***. For example, Windows XP and Windows Vista can both be installed on the same computer, resulting in a dual-boot configuration. The Windows Vista Windows Boot Manager allows the user to select which operating system to start. If no selection is made, the Windows Vista operating system will start by default.

You could also configure a ***multiple-boot system***, which contains more than two operating systems. For example, you could have Windows 2000, Windows XP, and Windows Vista installed on the same computer. You could also add a non-Microsoft operating system, such as Linux.

Virtual Machines

When a computer is configured as a dual-boot or multiple-boot system, you can only run one operating system at a time. However, a ***virtual machine*** can be created using special software application that will allow more than one operating system to be executed at the same time. A computer that runs two operating systems at the same time is referred to as a *virtual machine* or *Virtual PC*. The Microsoft application for creating a virtual machine is called Virtual PC. There is also a third-party vender that markets VMware.

virtual machine
a computer on which more than one operating system can be executed at the same time.

When two operating systems are running at the same time, they must share the CPU and the RAM. Sharing the CPU and RAM negatively impacts computer performance when compared to a dual-boot or multiple-boot system.

The History of the Windows Family

In 1983, Windows was introduced as the first Microsoft graphic user interface for the PC operating system. It was built on top of DOS. It was not a new operating system. It simply displayed the file structure on the screen differently than the text-only screen. With the introduction of the Windows 95 came a new operating system that was not completely dependent on DOS. Many other iterations have followed. The current CompTIA A+ Certification exams no longer cover Windows 3.x or Windows 95, but it is worth taking a quick look at all versions of Windows.

Windows 3.x

The Windows 3.x programs consist of Windows 3.0, 3.1, and 3.11. These programs are known as graphical user interface (GUI) systems. These GUI systems were not truly new operating systems, but rather an additional layer placed above MS-DOS. Windows 3.x provided a graphic display in which to issue commands as opposed to entering commands from the DOS prompt.

Windows version 3.0 was not well received by all computer users. Because of the additional layer on top of the MS-DOS operating system, the computer ran slower, especially when operating gaming programs. However, the Windows system was well received by new users or people who were not adept in DOS commands and utilities.

A+ Note:

Windows 3.0, 3.1, 3.11, and Windows 95 operating systems are no longer on the A+ Certification exams. You should be familiar with them simply as a reference when compared to current systems.

Windows 95

The release of Windows 95 produced many changes in the Microsoft operating system. Some of the significant changes consisted of the following:

- ✔ Plug and Play (PnP).
- ✔ Right mouse click.
- ✔ 32-bit operating system.
- ✔ Enhanced CD player.

Plug and Play (PnP) a BIOS function that enables the automatic detection and configuration of new hardware components. Also, the automatic assignment of system resources such as DMA channels, interrupts, memory, and port assignments.

Plug and Play (PnP) allows hardware devices to be configured (installed) automatically. For example, when an adapter card is installed into a slot and the computer is turned on, the new card is automatically detected by the computer as a new piece of hardware. The computer then configures all the resources that previously required manual entry—settings such as the interrupts and memory allocation. To use the PnP capability, the device to be installed must be a PnP device. Otherwise, the computer cannot set it up automatically.

The right mouse click was new with Windows 95. The right mouse click displays a shortcut menu with access to features such as **Open**, **Explore**, **Find**, **Create Shortcut**, **Rename**, and **Properties**. See **Figure 2-19.** These features are examined in-depth in your Laboratory Manual.

Windows could now handle 32 bits of data as well as 16 bits. This meant that programs written for 32-bit systems would run much faster than on the Windows 3.x predecessor. Windows 95 maintained its downward compatibility by still including DOS as part of the operating system.

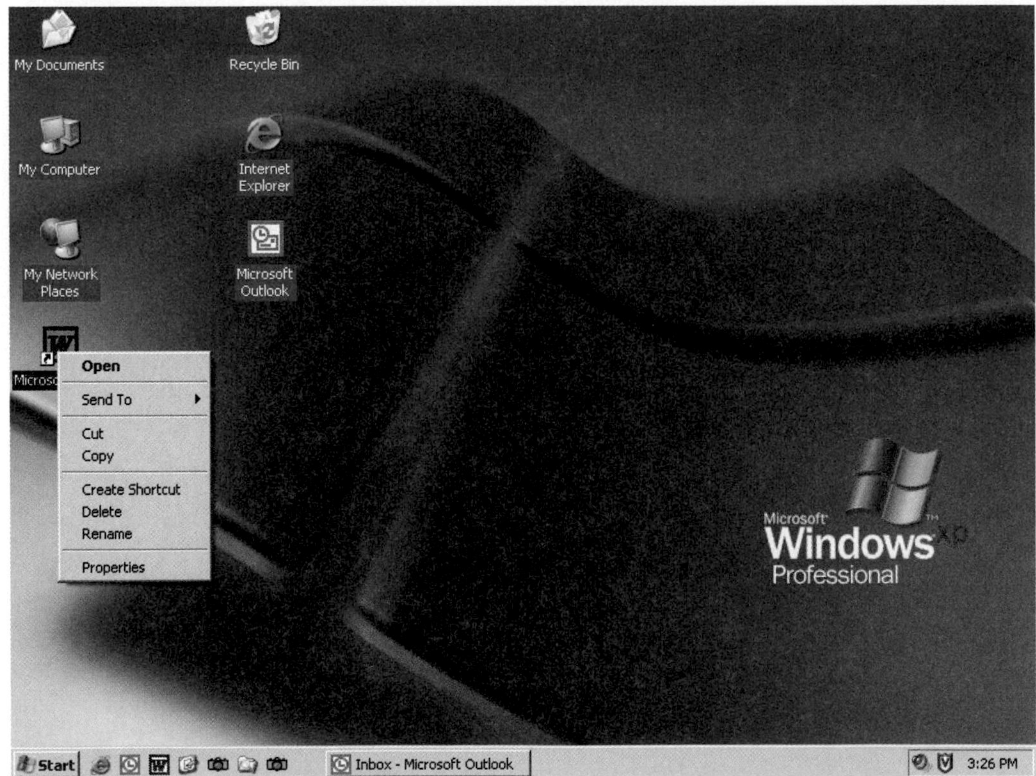

Figure 2-19.
Shortcut menu.

Windows 98

The release of the Windows 98 operating system was delayed several times. It was originally a project code-named Memphis and later called Windows 97. It offered support for new technologies such as DVD, MMX, AGP, and FAT32. Windows 98 also introduced integration of a Web browser as part of the operating system. The integration of the Web browser caused a lot of controversy and helped involve Microsoft in an antitrust suit that made its way to the United States Supreme Court. Windows 98 is downward compatible with earlier versions of Windows and DOS.

Windows NT

Windows NT (New Technology) was actually developed by Microsoft to replace the MS-DOS system but became too large and powerful for the typical PC at that time. That is why Windows NT is similar in appearance to any other windows operating system. NT is designed in two versions. One version is to be used as a PC operating system and the other as a file server operating system.

A file server is a powerful PC connected to many PCs via a network. File servers are covered in more depth in Chapter 16—Introduction to Networking. Windows NT is a 32-bit system. It supports preemptive multitasking.

Security is enhanced in Windows NT. It provides a means of limiting access to users. In fact, even if only one person is using an NT system, that single user must set up their own individual security system to be able to access the computer files and operating system.

Windows Me

Windows Me (Millennium Edition) followed the graphical user interface style that is so common with the Windows operating system. Windows Me was more stable than its Windows 98 and 95 predecessors. While the basic operating system remained the same, there were several changes in the Windows Me operating systems that were needed because of the evolution of home computing and equipment. The following are some of the changes.

At the time Windows Me was released, it was common to have more than one PC in a household. With more than one PC in the home, there needed to be a means of sharing items such as Internet connections, printers, files, and software. The home user needed to start setting up a small network system. The Windows Me system introduced an advanced network wizard designed especially for the home or small office user. It made it much easier for a novice to properly set up a network for sharing equipment, software, and Internet connections.

As the digital media world expanded and improved, the operating system needed to provide more support and more drivers for digital music and video cameras. Windows Me also included more sophisticated data compression techniques for video files.

A system restore tool was added to the system. The tool was designed to automatically capture changes in the entire PC system every ten hours or once a day. The data could be saved and used to restore the PC back to the way it was when it last worked correctly. A system file protection tool was also added to the design. It prevented a poorly written program from overwriting or replacing critical system files while installing software.

An important note about Windows Me is its technologies are written over the original Windows 95 kernel. This was the last in the series of operating systems that were written over the Windows 95 kernel. Newer systems have been written over the Windows NT kernel.

Windows 2000

Windows 2000 continues to improve the many features of the Windows operating system. One of the major changes in the operating system is the new hard drive file system known as dynamic file system (also called NFTS5.0). In Windows 2000, the standard file allocation table (FAT) file system as well as NTFS4.0 are referred to as basic file systems. The dynamic file system is a major improvement to the NTFS file system for storing and retrieving files from the hard drive. File allocation tables are discussed later in this chapter and in detail in Chapter 9—Magnetic Storage Devices. The new system improves security and allows multiple hard drives to be handled as one large volume. To the user, the multiple drives appear as one.

Microsoft named the new file system technology "dynamic disk." Technicians and writers immediately began referring to the new file system as NTFS5.0 to differentiate it from the existing NTFS4.0 file system.

Windows XP

In October of 2001, the first versions of Windows XP (eXPerience) were released. Windows XP was the first major change in the Microsoft operating system for the home user since Windows 95 came on the market. Windows Me is the last operating system technology written on the Windows 95 and Windows 98 kernel.

Windows XP is written using a modified NT kernel. The NT kernel is a much more stable operating system when compared to that in Windows 95, 98, and Me. Two Windows XP operating systems were created: one for home use, called Windows XP Home Edition, and the other for business use, called Windows XP Professional Edition.

Introduction to Windows Vista

Windows Vista is the latest Microsoft desktop operating system. It was released to the public in January 2007. Windows Vista offers many new features and is not based on the NT kernel. Since it is the latest operating system, this section will spend time introducing it. You may not clearly understand some of the features discussed in this section until you have more experience in the course of study. You should, therefore, review this section again after completing most of the textbook and related Lab Manual activities.

Significant Changes

In general, the two most significant changes made to Windows Vista when compared to other Windows operating systems are enhanced security and an enhanced user interface. The enhanced security has made many previous versions of software applications incompatible with Microsoft Vista. For example, software applications cannot directly access restricted data storage areas, such as hard disk drives, without going through the Microsoft hardware access program. Software applications cannot automatically download and install updates without following Microsoft's strict guidelines. These restrictions on software applications are intended to prevent hackers from directly accessing critical operating system files and areas of storage. This causes many software applications not to run properly or prevents them from being properly installed and configured on the computer. To overcome these problems, the software application companies must rewrite part of their software applications to meet Microsoft's security features.

The second most significant change is the enhanced appearance of the user interface called Windows Aero. This new user interface incorporates transparent and shadowy 3-D screen images for navigation. See **Figure 2-20.** These features require a faster processor, more RAM, and better graphics capabilities than previous versions of Windows. Many existing computers cannot meet the minimum hardware requirements needed to run these visual effects and, therefore, need to be upgraded or replaced.

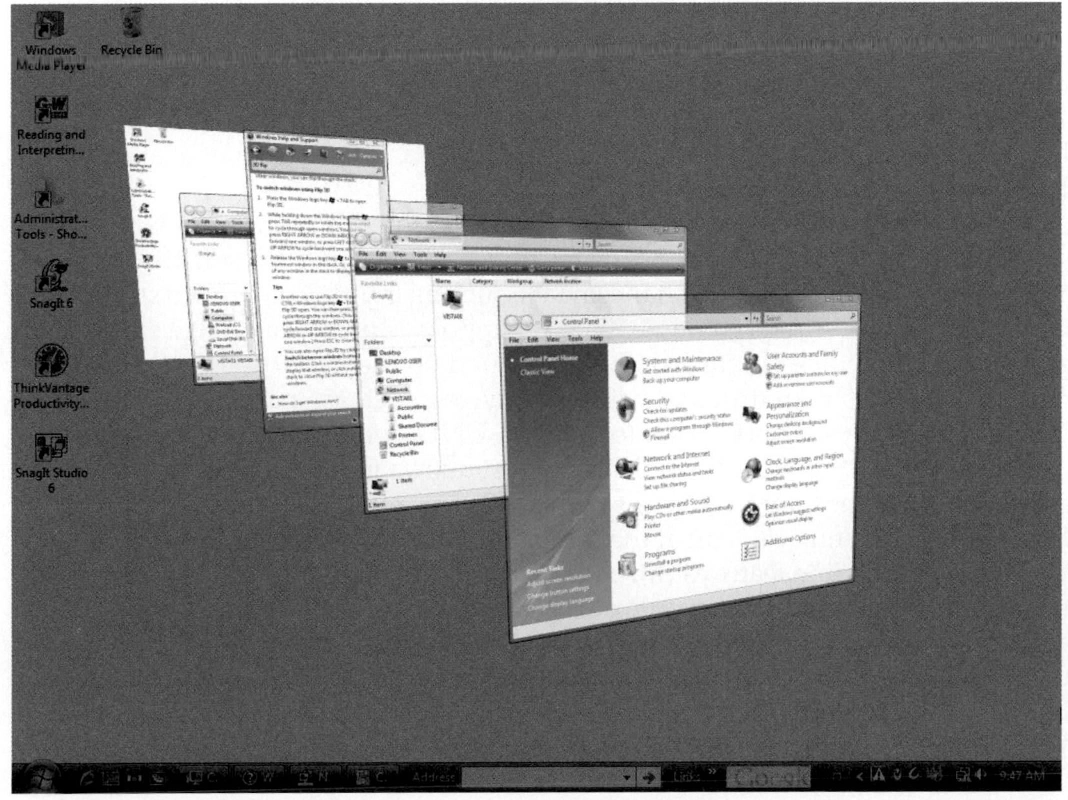

Figure 2-20.
The Windows Vista 3D flip feature, which allows the user to roll through all open programs by pressing and holding the Windows logo key and then pressing the [Tab] key. This feature requires a video card with 3D graphics support.

Microsoft has a software utility called Windows Vista Upgrade Advisor. This utility does a complete scan of the existing hardware and software on a PC to determine if it can be successfully upgraded to Windows Vista. It also determines which edition of Windows Vista would be the most appropriate for the current hardware.

Windows Vista Editions

There are six editions of Windows Vista. The following four editions are commonly available for off-the-shelf purchase:

- ✔ Windows Vista Home Basic.
- ✔ Windows Vista Home Premium.
- ✔ Windows Vista Business.
- ✔ Windows Vista Ultimate.

The versions that are not available for off-the-shelf purchase are Windows Vista Starter and Windows Vista Enterprise. The various additions can be broken down into two broad classifications: home editions and business editions. Home editions, as you might guess by the name, are mainly intended for home users, and business editions are intended for businesses.

Within each of these two broad classifications is a hierarchy based on the number of enhancements desired. Look at the Windows Vista feature comparison chart in **Figure 2-21.** This is only a partial listing of the many new or improved features of the operating system.

The very basic version, called Windows Vista Starter Edition, is designed for third-world countries that may have older, less powerful computers. Windows Vista Starter is a very limited operating system similar to Windows Vista Home Edition with built-in tutorials for first-time PC users. It is not available or advertised in the United States.

Windows Vista Enterprise Edition is designed for global and very large organizations. It contains all the features found in Windows Vista Ultimate, plus several global business enhancements, such as multiple language support, UNIX application support, and virtual PC support. Multiple language support allows more than one language to be configured on the desktop. This is ideal for multiple users with different native languages, such as Spanish and English. UNIX application support allows for a direct UNIX connection and the running of native UNIX programs. Virtual PC support allows more than one operating system to run concurrently on the same PC. For example, Windows Vista Enterprise and Linux can run at the same time on the same PC.

While these same features can be configured on other operating systems, the other operating systems would require additional software applications and additional configuration. Windows Vista Enterprise incorporates all three features. This edition must be purchased directly from Microsoft or from one of their authorized partners. You cannot purchase a boxed version of Windows Vista Enterprise through a typical software outlet, such as a chain store.

The remainder of this introduction focuses on the four commonly encountered versions: Windows Vista Home Basic, Windows Vista Home Premium, Windows Vista Business, and Windows Vista Ultimate.

Features and Capabilities	Home Basic	Home Premium	Business	Ultimate
64-bit processor support	X	X	X	X
Aero user interface		X	X	X
BitLocker Drive Encryption				X
Encrypting File System			X	X
Join a domain option			X	X
Max. RAM 32-bit	4 GB	4 GB	4 GB	4 GB
Max. RAM 64-bit	8 GB	16 GB	128 GB	128 GB
Parental controls	X	X		X
Peer-to-peer network connections	5	10	10	10
Previous Versions			X	X
Remote Desktop			X	X
Schedule backups		X	X	X
Windows Defender	X	X	X	X
Windows DVD Maker		X		X
Windows Media Center		X		X
Windows Meeting Space		X	X	X
Windows Mobility Center		X	X	X
Windows Movie Maker HD		X		X
Windows ReadyBoost	X	X	X	X

Figure 2-21. Comparison chart of common Windows Vista features.

Windows Vista Features

The Windows Vista operating system has many new features. Only a few of the most important features are introduced here. Not all of the new features are available to all versions of Windows Vista. You can use the chart in Figure 2-21 to identify which version of Windows Vista has the new feature integrated into the operating system. For a more detailed list of features, check the Microsoft Windows Vista home page at www.microsoft.com/windows/products/windowsvista or do an Internet search using the keywords "Microsoft Vista."

Windows Aero

Windows Aero is an enhanced user interface. It is much more sophisticated than the user interfaces of previous operating systems and is designed to have a glass-like appearance with various degrees of transparency, **Figure 2-22.** The Windows Aero feature is one of the main reasons a greater amount of RAM and a quality 3D graphics card or motherboard is required for this feature. Windows Aero is also one of the main reasons for the slow performance of Windows Vista when compared to Windows XP loaded on a similar PC.

Gadgets

Microsoft Vista desktop has added a new feature called *gadgets*. This feature resides by default on the right side of the desktop, **Figure 2-23.** Gadgets are mini software programs that provide services, such as an online dictionary, a notepad, a clock, a calendar, a weather report, and a CPU monitor. Third-party software vendors are continuously creating new gadgets for the gadgets toolbar.

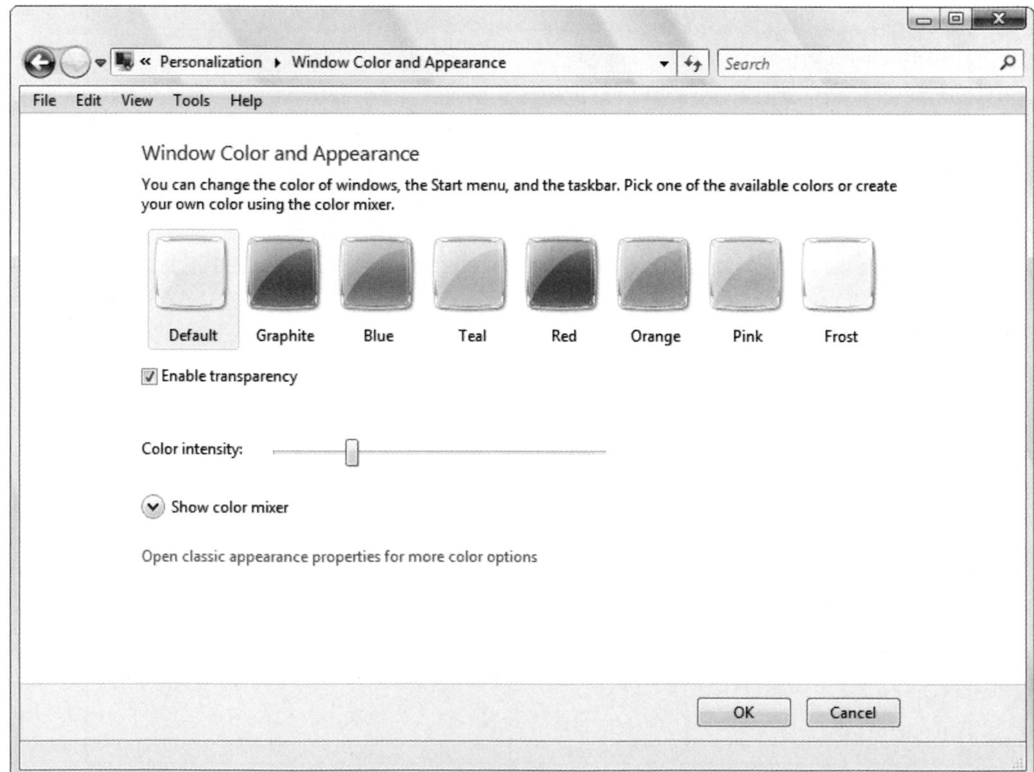

Figure 2-22. The Windows Vista Aero feature provides an adjustable transparency for Windows dialog boxes.

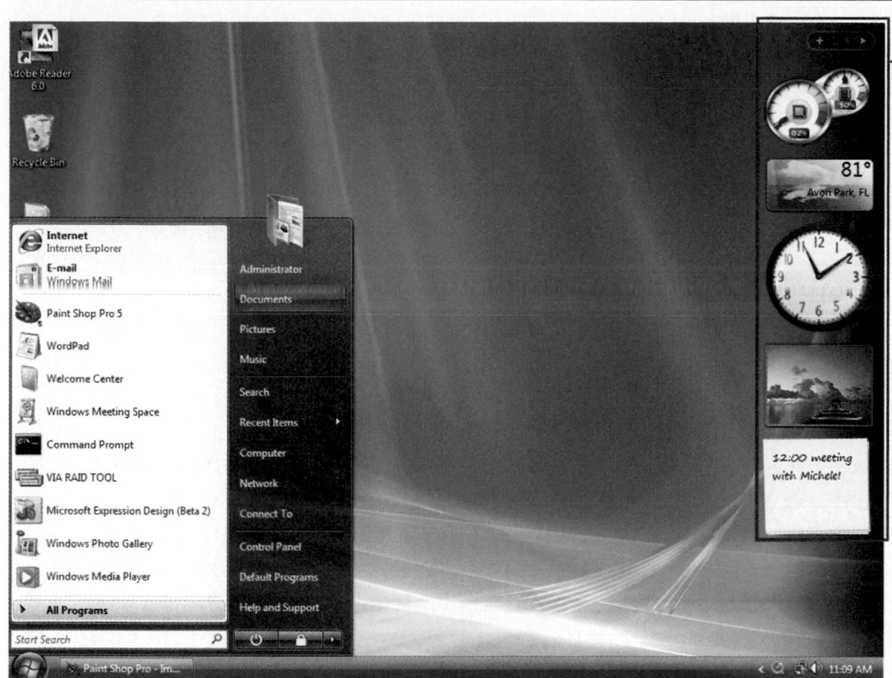

Figure 2-23. Windows Vista Business Edition desktop. Note the gadgets on the right side of the desktop.

Windows Media Center

Windows Media Center is a collection of media manipulation utilities or tools. With Windows Media Center, you can edit digital movies; modify or adjust digital photos; and record, copy, and create DVDs. If your PC has a television tuner card installed, you can also watch live television. As you can see in the feature chart, Windows Media Center is only available in Windows Vista Home Premium and Windows Vista Ultimate.

Windows Mobility Center

Windows Mobility Center provides a central location for accessing the most commonly used features for laptops, such as presentation configurations like Microsoft PowerPoint through a projector and energy conservation configurations to save battery life. It also automatically configures common network connections, such as the home connection and the office or work location connection.

The Windows Hot Start feature allows a laptop to instantly start a selected program with the touch of a single button. There is no need to wait long periods of time while the program is located, opened, and loaded into memory.

Since data theft has become a problem for laptop users, enhanced security features are incorporated into the Windows Vista operating system. These security features are covered in more depth later in this textbook.

Windows Meeting Space

Windows Meeting Space is designed for collaborating over a network. The meeting can vary from two to nine persons using their personal computers connected by cables or wireless devices. The users can share documents, PowerPoint presentations, audio, video images, and anything else that they might share in a typical meeting session.

Network Discovery

With Windows Vista, setting up a network is easier than ever before. Windows Vista automatically detects and configures a network, in most cases, and automatically sets up a share and Internet connection. It also allows files to be shared much easier in a peer-to-peer network, while still providing security from the Internet. The main exception arises if there is a router or gateway being used that is not compatible with the new Windows Vista automatic networking features.

Figure 2-24 shows the Network and Sharing Center. Notice the **Network discovery** option in the **Sharing and Discovery** section of the dialog box. This option lets you enable and disable the Network Discovery feature.

Windows Shadow Copy and Previous Versions

One of the newest features that will prove to be invaluable is the Windows Shadow Copy feature. Windows Shadow Copy automatically makes a copy of files that have changed and have been saved. This feature allows a user to go back and open an earlier version of a file using the Previous Versions feature.

To restore a file using the Previous Versions feature, open the **Properties** dialog box of the folder that held that file or of the current version of that file. Then click the **Previous Versions** tab. Previous versions of the file will be listed in the **Folder Versions** list box. Select the desired file and then click **Restore**. Notice that in **Figure 2-25** under the **Previous Versions** tab, there are two earlier versions of the document titled Chapter 5 Stormy night that can be restored.

Shadow Copy was first introduced in Windows Server 2003 and now has been incorporated into Windows Vista Business, Enterprise, and Ultimate. It is not available in the Home Basic and Home Premium editions.

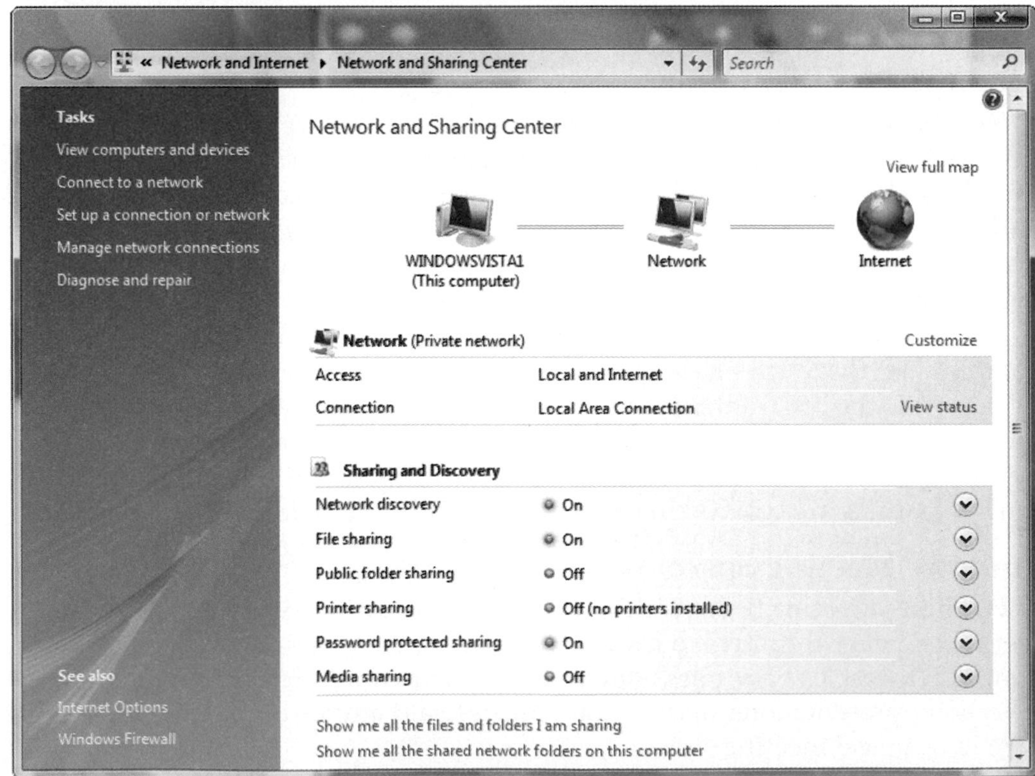

Figure 2-24. When the Network discovery option is enabled, Windows Vista can automatically detect and configure a network.

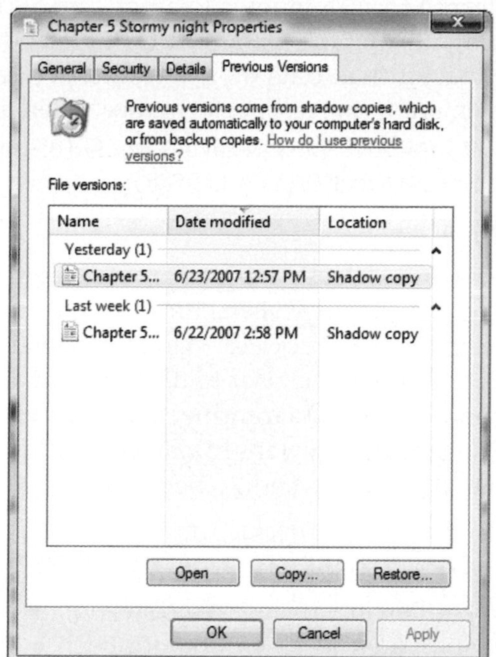

Figure 2-25. The Windows Vista Previous Versions feature allows a user to go back and open an earlier version of a file, called *shadow copies.*

Windows BitLocker

BitLocker is an encryption feature. It differs from earlier versions of NTFS encryption in that it encrypts the entire volume, including the system files required for startup and logon, rather than just data files. BitLocker ensures that data remains encrypted even when the operating system is not running. For example, if someone removes a hard disk drive and then attempts to access the data from another computer using a different operating system or software utility, BitLocker prevents the data from being accessed because the data remains encrypted.

BitLocker is transparent to the user after it is activated. BitLocker is designed to be used with a computer that has a Trusted Platform Module (TPM) or a BIOS that can read a USB Flash drive. The TPM is a microchip designed to work with the BitLocker software. The TPM ensures that encryption is intact throughout the boot sequence of the computer. If the TPM is missing or has changed, the user is required to supply a password to access the encrypted data. If BitLocker is configured on a system that does not have a TPM, a startup key is required when it is first configured.

Windows Ready Boost

Many software programs require a great deal of RAM to operate efficiently. Otherwise, the program responds slowly or may not work at all, or the system will seem to freeze up. Operating systems typically use the hard disk drive to temporarily store limited amounts of program information when the RAM is full. For example, a computer with 1 GB of RAM may use 500 kB of memory, referred to as a *page file*, to temporarily store information. This keeps the program working reasonably well when the RAM is full. However, compared to RAM, the hard disk drive is notoriously slow when accessing and manipulating data.

The technology referred to as Windows Ready Boost allows a USB Flash drive to temporarily store this information. Data on a USB Flash drive can be accessed and manipulated much faster than data on a hard disk drive. Windows Ready Boost is a great improvement to overall performance when a computer system is overworked. It is also an excellent feature for laptop computers, which typically have much less memory than desktop computers.

Windows Defender

Windows Defender works directly with Internet Explorer 7 or later to protect the computer from spyware. It scans files as they are downloaded to the computer through the Internet browser. Windows Defender identifies what appears to be spyware, but allows the user to decide what action to take. The possible actions are Ignore, Allow, Quarantine, and Always Allow. Quarantine isolates and stores the suspected spyware file, allowing the user the opportunity to install it at a later date if it is found not to be spyware.

Windows Vista Clean Install or Upgrade

An *upgrade* means that you can install Windows Vista on an existing operating system and retain files, settings, and applications. A *clean install* means that the previous operating system is completely replaced and you will lose all files, settings, and applications installed on the system. Before performing a clean install, you can save your settings and files by using Windows Easy Transfer. You can then reload your applications after the clean install.

Some previous versions of the Windows operating system require a clean install, **Figure 2-26.** Be aware that hardware used for the previous operating systems will most likely not support Windows Vista, especially its advanced features. So, before performing an upgrade or clean install, run the Windows Vista Upgrade Advisor to ensure compatibility with hardware devices.

The requirements in **Figure 2-27** will give you a good idea of the hardware needed for Windows Vista. Windows Vista Premium hardware requirements are used to describe a PC that supports advanced Vista features, such as the Windows Aero translucent windows and transition effects. A Windows Vista Capable PC will run Windows Vista, but without the special Aero effects. Some software capabilities will be limited also.

Figure 2-26. Use this table to determine if an upgrade or install should be performed based on the current version of Windows and the version of Windows Vista you wish to install.

	Home Basic	Home Premium	Business	Ultimate
XP Pro	Clean install	Clean install	Upgrade	Upgrade
XP Home	Upgrade	Upgrade	Upgrade	Upgrade
XP Media	Clean install	Upgrade	Clean install	Upgrade
XP Tablet	Clean install	Clean install	Upgrade	Upgrade
XP Pro 64X	Clean install	Clean install	Clean install	Clean install
Win 2000	Clean install	Clean install	Clean install	Clean install

Hardware Device	Windows Vista Capable	Windows Vista Premium
Processor	800 MHz	1 GHz
Memory	512 MB RAM	1 GB RAM
HDD size	20 GB	40 GB
HDD free space	15 GB	15 GB
Installation media	CD-ROM or DVD-ROM	DVD-ROM
Graphics card	DirectX 9, SVGA 800 × 600	DirectX 9, 128 MB RAM
Optical drive	CD-ROM	DVD-ROM

Figure 2-27. Windows Vista hardware requirements.

The terms used to describe Windows Vista operating system computers such as "premium" and "capable" are another way of saying "recommended" and "minimum" hardware. Capable is the minimum requirement for hardware, while premium is the recommended hardware requirement.

A+ Note:

For the A+ Certification exams, be sure you know the difference between the minimal and the recommended hardware requirements. Look for the following keyword in the question: *minimal* or *recommended.*

It is recommended that in most cases, you do a clean install after partitioning and reformatting the hard disk drive. This will eliminate any file fragments and most registry corruption from the previous operating system version. Before you perform a clean install, be sure you have all hardware device drivers available and a copy of all previously installed applications. Backup all files and be sure to turn off any antivirus programs.

Additional Non-Windows Operating Systems

The following operating systems are not covered on the A+ Certification exams. However, it can prove useful to know something of these systems as you may encounter them in the field.

Linux

Linux is a derivative of UNIX. UNIX is a mainframe computer operating system originally developed in the 1970s. Linux can run on Intel as well as Motorola processors. In other words, Linux can be installed on a Macintosh and on IBM-PC clones as well. Since it can be downloaded very inexpensively (or free), it is becoming very popular. There are several common varieties of Linux on the market such as Red Hat, SuSE, Caldera, and Debian.

source code the programming code used to make the operating system.

Linux is a powerful operating system that can be installed on a PC or file server like Windows NT. The source code can be readily downloaded. ***Source code*** is the actual programming code used to make the operating system. No other major operating system does this. Most source codes are closely guarded company secrets. Having the source code for an operating system allows you to modify it for your own needs.

A+ Note:

Linux is not covered in the A+ Certification exams. However, Linux has its own certification offered by CompTIA, called Linux+.

OS/2

OS/2 was discontinued on December 30th, 2006 and is no longer marketed or supported by IBM. The OS/2 operating system was developed by Microsoft for IBM computers. It is very similar to the Windows operating systems. At the time it was released, it was very impressive, with features that had only been found in the Macintosh operating system, such as the ability to use long file names. OS/2 is compatible with Windows and DOS as well. However, programs written specifically for OS/2 will not run on Windows or DOS. OS/2 is still used today for some industrial and consumer electronic product applications but has been replaced mainly by versions of Linux.

OS 9

OS 9 was developed jointly by Microware Systems and Motorola. Motorola manufactures the CPU found in the Macintosh computer system. OS 9 was developed in the early 1980s but is still in use today. It is the operating system behind many industrial technologies as well as WebTV boxes.

OS X

OS X is the replacement operating system for Apple computers. The last version is OS X 10.5 Leopard and was released at the end of July 2007. Originally, Apple operating systems were designed to run on the Motorola processor. Motorola no longer manufacturers processors to meet the Apple specification, and Apple was forced to change their hardware design to one based on the Intel processor. The Intel processor is the design Microsoft Windows has been using for years. The Apple OS X will run on an Intel processor just like the Windows operating systems. OS X is based on the Linux operating system, not the Microsoft operating system. The only real similarity between OS X and Windows is the fact that they can now use the same hardware.

Common Operating System Terminology

There are several technical terms that must be introduced early for your studies to be successful. The following terminology is presented at an introductory level. Throughout the following chapters, they will be introduced in more detail.

File Allocation Tables

No introduction to operating systems would be complete without mentioning file allocation tables. A ***file allocation table (FAT)*** is used by the operating system to keep track of all files on the disk. It maintains a table of all areas on the disk, and it tracks which areas are used and which are not. File allocation tables are covered in much greater depth in Chapter 9—Magnetic Storage Devices.

file allocation table (FAT)
a table used by the operating system to record and recall the locations of files on the disk.

There are several different file allocation tables with which you should be familiar. These tables are FAT12, FAT16, FAT32, VFAT, HPFS, and NTFS. The default file system used by Windows operating systems since Windows XP is NTFS. The FAT16 and FAT32 file systems are still available for use in formatting partitions under the control of Windows XP and Windows Vista. As you study operating systems more in-depth, you will see the need for other types of file allocation systems.

A+ Note:

You need to be familiar with all available file systems in preparation for the A+ certification exams.

Configuration Files

When a computer system is configured, the type of hardware and software the system planned for use is recorded in a ***configuration file.*** Configuration files contain information such as the amount of memory and the type of floppy drive, modem, and video adapter present in the system. Configuration information is stored in the config.sys file of DOS systems. Early Windows systems stored configuration information in the win.ini and system.ini files. Starting with Windows 95, configuration information is stored in the registry. The config.sys file is still in newer operating systems, but it is included only to support legacy software applications.

configuration file
a file that contains information about the system hardware and software.

Registry

The registry is found in Windows 95, 98, Me, NT, 2000, XP, and Vista. The ***registry*** is essentially a database that stores configuration information. The major sections of the registry are listed as follows.

registry
a database that stores configuration information.

- ✔ HKEY_CLASSES_ROOT: Object linking and embedding (OLE) information and how files are associated with each other.
- ✔ HKEY_CURRENT_USERS: Information for the current user of this workstation.
- ✔ HKEY_LOCAL_MACHINE: Information specific to the local computer.

- ✔ HKEY_USERS: Information for each user of this workstation.
- ✔ HKEY_CURRENT_CONFIG: Display and printer settings.

The registry is accessed by entering **regedit** in the **Run** dialog box found in the **Start** menu. **Figure 2-28** shows the Windows XP Registry Editor.

Changes in the registry can completely disable your computer operating system. Do not experiment with your registry settings unless under supervision of your instructor.

There are two main registry files: system.dat and user.dat. The system.dat files contain information about the computer settings. The user.dat file contains information about individuals who use this particular computer station. Registry files can be copied to disk, installed on another computer, backed up, and modified. The registry is repaired through the System Restore utility. Rarely does a technician need to access the registry files directly. When a technician does access the registry files, it is usually as part of repair steps outlined by Microsoft on their TechNet Web site. Direct modification of the registry is a last resort effort.

Another set of configuration files are files ending with an .ini extension. These configuration files are replaced by the Windows registry settings for the Windows 95 and later operating systems. Many computer systems still contain .ini files to maintain a downward compatibility with some software programs.

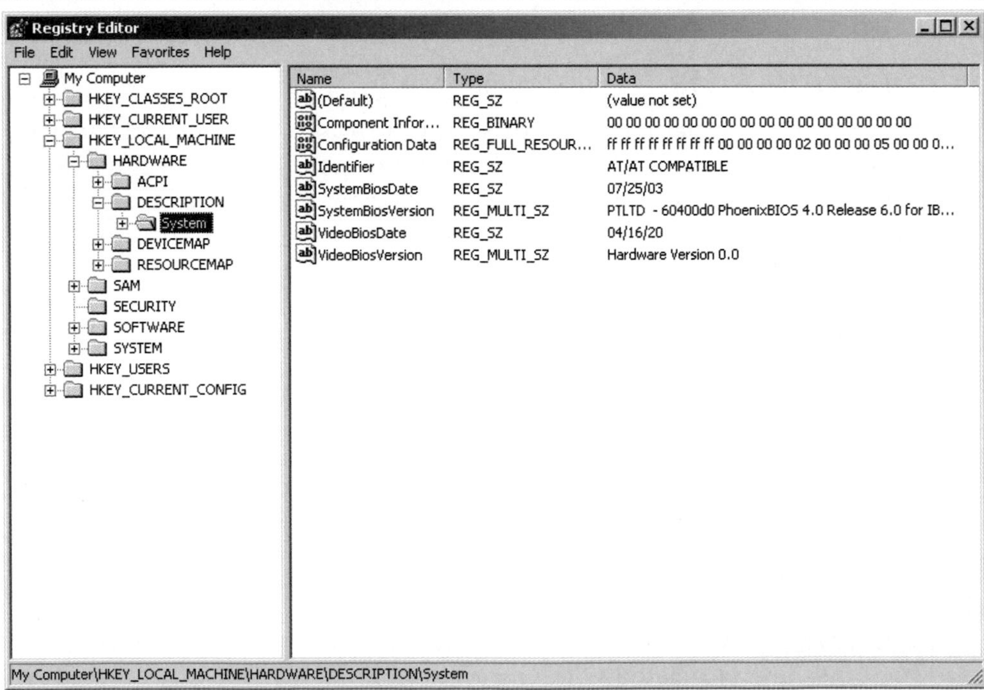

Figure 2-28. Windows XP Registry Editor.

Application Software

Application software, also referred to as end-user software, is designed for a specific purpose such as creating databases or spreadsheets, word processing, producing graphics, or just for entertainment. It is not an operating system.

The typical application software relies on the operating system to communicate with PC hardware such as the hard drive or CD-ROM drive. When a word-processing program issues a save command, the command is interpreted by the operating system, which in turn passes it through the CPU and on to the hardware.

application software software designed for a specific purpose, such as creating databases or spreadsheets, word processing, producing graphics, or just for entertainment.

Software Drivers

Software ***drivers*** are small packages of programs that need to be installed on a computer to allow proper communication between the computer and the peripheral device. Common devices that require drivers are printers, modems, monitors, and storage devices. Drivers act as translators, converting common commands issued from the CPU to the device in use.

drivers software that enables proper communication between the computer and peripheral devices.

PC and software systems are constantly evolving, but not necessarily in the same time frame. For example, you may install a printer that is much newer than the technology of the software installed on a computer. The computer may not have the software programs necessary to communicate correctly with the printer. A typical scenario is when a new printer is installed on a PC and the self-test runs perfectly. However, when a file you have created on the PC is sent to the printer, it prints out a garbled set of meaningless symbols or an endless stream of blank pages. This is a classic case of incorrect driver software.

Drivers for an MS-DOS system usually have a .sys file extension, while Windows systems usually use a .drv extension. Many driver files are stored in the Windows directory and are known as ***cabinet*** (or ***cab***) ***files.*** Cab files are compressed files that contain the software necessary to communicate with the operating system. When hardware, such as a printer, is upgraded or changed, the driver file necessary to communicate with the operating system is usually found in the .cab files.

cabinet (cab) files compressed files that contain the operating system software.

Software Patches

Software patches are fixes for operating systems and application software that have already been released. They also contain system updates when the system has been compromised. Although software systems go through countless hours of testing, many have errors in programming. These errors are referred to as ***bugs.*** Patches for software programs can assist in correcting bugs and are readily available for download off the Internet. Periodically a large collection of patches are released at once and referred to as a *service pack.*

bugs errors in programming.

Summary

- ✔ Operating systems provide a computer user with a file system structure and with a means of communicating with the computer hardware.
- ✔ The core program of an operating system is referred to as the *kernel*.
- ✔ Multitasking is the appearance to the user that two or more applications are running at the same time.
- ✔ Two types of multitasking are cooperative and preemptive.
- ✔ Computer commands can be issued through a graphical user interface or through text line commands.
- ✔ A computer system file structure is a hierarchical organization of directories, subdirectories, and files.
- ✔ The three DOS core files are io.sys, msdos.sys, and command.com.
- ✔ Command.com is the interpreter for DOS internal commands.
- ✔ Msdos.sys is the kernel of the operating system.
- ✔ Io.sys contains the generic drivers that are necessary to communicate with the BIOS and the computer hardware.
- ✔ DOS uses the 8.3 naming convention.
- ✔ Windows 95 and later use the long file naming convention allowing up to 255 characters in a file name.
- ✔ The power-on self-test (POST) is a BIOS program that does a simple check of major components when power is applied to the PC.
- ✔ Extensible Firmware Interface (EFI) can supplement the BIOS.
- ✔ The config.sys file is a text file that enables, disables, and customizes system features; it has been replaced by the registry in newer operating systems.
- ✔ Windows Vista incorporates the function of ntdetect.com directly into the kernel.
- ✔ Windows Vista replaced the boot.ini file with a Boot Configuration Data (BCD) registry file.
- ✔ A dual-boot system has two operating systems, but only one can be selected and booted.
- ✔ A virtual machine contains two operating systems and can run both at the same time, sharing the CPU and RAM.
- ✔ Plug and Play is a technology that allows many different devices to be installed automatically in a PC with minimal user intervention.
- ✔ The graphic user interface in Windows Vista is called Windows Aero.
- ✔ The file allocation table (FAT) is used to keep track of file locations on storage media such as disks.
- ✔ Files that end with .ini are configuration files.
- ✔ The registry is a database that contains information about the computer hardware and software system.
- ✔ The registry can be accessed by the Registry Editor (regedit.exe) program but should not be altered by inexperienced users.
- ✔ Software drivers are programs required to allow the CPU to communicate with hardware devices properly.
- ✔ Cabinet files are compressed files containing drivers.
- ✔ Software patches are fixes for operating systems after the original release of the program.
- ✔ A collection of operating software patches is called a *service pack*.

Review Questions

Answer the following questions on a separate sheet of paper. Please do not write in this book.

1. An operating system does what? Select all that apply.
   a. Manages file storage.
   b. Provides communication between the user and the computer system.
   c. Provides software to communicate with the BIOS.
   d. Provides communication between the user and the hard drive.
2. What is a kernel?
3. What three files are found on a MS-DOS boot disk?
4. List five symbols that are *not* allowed in Windows XP or Windows Vista naming convention.
5. List five special symbols that are allowed in Windows XP or Windows Vista naming convention.
6. Which file names are invalid using Windows 95 long name format? (Indicate why each is not acceptable.)
   myreport
   MYREPORT#12
   mymemo*for*jim
   MYMEMO/TO/JIM
   my+memo+to+jim
   mymemo:jim
   MEMO1999~CA$H
   memo1999?
   MEMOJune2001=
7. A warm boot may be initiated by pressing which three keys simultaneously?
8. Which part of the boot sequence is common to all operating systems?
9. What is the name of the Windows XP file that loads the kernel?
   a. ntdetect.com
   b. ntldr
   c. boot.ini
   d. ntoskrnl.exe
10. What is the name of the Windows XP file that detects system hardware components?
    a. ntdetect.com
    b. ntldr
    c. boot.ini
    d. ntoskrnl.exe
11. Which Windows Vista file is referred to as the kernel?
12. Which phase in the Windows Vista boot sequence replaced the boot loader phase of Windows XP?
13. Which phase of the Windows XP boot sequence allows a user to select the operating system to load when two operating systems are installed on the same computer?
14. When during the boot sequence does Windows Vista change from the text mode to the graphic mode?

15. What type of optical drive is required to meet Windows Vista Premium requirements?
16. What is the name of the Windows Vista technology that supplements the system RAM?
17. What is the purpose of Windows Defender?
18. What is the minimal amount of RAM and the recommended amount of RAM required for a Windows Vista installation?
19. The purpose of FAT is to ______.
    a. keep track of the number of times the PC starts
    b. record the amount of memory used
    c. record file locations on disk
    d. supply power to the screen display
20. A database that stores system configuration information is called the ______.
    a. autoexec
    b. sysconfig
    c. registry
    d. sysreg
21. A spreadsheet program is an example of a(n) ______.
    a. patch
    b. operating system
    c. application
    d. driver
22. A software program designed to support communication between a specific printer and a PC is commonly referred to as a(n) ______.
    a. patch
    b. operating system
    c. application
    d. driver
23. Errors in software are commonly referred to as ______ and are corrected by installing a software ______.

Sample A+ Exam Questions

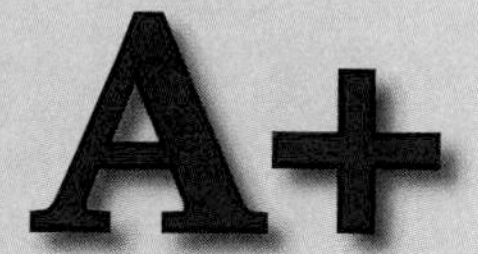

Answer the following questions on a separate sheet of paper. Please do not write in this book.

1. Which Windows XP file is responsible for loading ntoskrl.exe?
    a. hal.dll
    b. ntdetect
    c. autoexec.bat
    d. ntldr
2. The operating feature that allows two programs to appear to be running simultaneously is called ______.
    a. multiprocessing
    b. multitasking
    c. program coordination
    d. kernel sharing
3. Which operating system does *not* support multitasking?
    a. DOS
    b. Windows 98
    c. Windows 2000
    d. Windows XP
4. Which file is *not* required to boot a Windows XP operating system?
    a. command.com
    b. ntldr
    c. ntdetect.com
    d. boot.ini
5. Where is the POST program stored?
    a. Hard disk drive
    b. RAM
    c. USB flash drive
    d. CMOS
6. Which of the following are no longer required by Windows Vista? Select two.
    a. ntdetect
    b. ntoskrnl
    c. boot.ini
    d. POST
7. Which program is used to start the command prompt in Windows XP?
    a. io.sys
    b. msdos.sys
    c. cmd.com
    d. doscom.com
8. Which is executed first during the boot process?
    a. ntldr
    b. POST
    c. bootcfg
    d. ntdetect

9. Which file systems are referred to as a basic file system? Select three.
   a. FAT16
   b. FAT32
   c. NTFS 4.0
   c. NTFS 5.0
10. Which is the correct order of the typical boot process in Windows 98?
   a. command.com, autoexec.bat, io.sys, config.sys, msdos.sys
   b. command.com, io.sys, config.sys, autoexec.bat, msdos.sys
   c. io.sys, msdos.sys, config.sys, command.com, autoexec.bat
   d. autoexec.bat, io.sys, command.com, msdos.sys, config.sys

Suggested Laboratory Activities

Do not attempt any suggested lab activities without your instructor's permission. Certain lab activities could render the PC operating system inoperable.

1. Access the DOS emulator program and explore some text-based commands. To access the DOS emulator in Windows XP, type **cmd** in the **Run** dialog box located off the **Start** menu. In Windows Vista, type "cmd" into the **Search** box located on the **Start** menu. Try the following commands: **help**, **ver**, **mem**, **dir**, **dir/?**, **time**, **date**, and **cls**.

Do not attempt to use the **fdisk** or **format** commands. These commands can damage stored data.

2. Experiment with the long file naming convention. Try the special symbols and see what effect they have when attempting to save a file.
3. Do an Internet search to find more information about DOS commands.
4. Make a system startup disk and inspect the content of the disk. You can learn how to make a system startup disk by choosing **Help** from the **Start** menu. Use the search words "Startup disk" after accessing help.
5. Visit the Web site www.bootdisk.com to see the various operating system boot disks available.
6. Do an Internet search and locate information about Windows XP and Windows Vista command lines. Use the keywords "Windows XP Vista command line, cmd."

Interesting Web Sites for More Information

www.ami.com
www.dell.com
www.global.acer.com
www.ibm.com

Chapter 2
Laboratory Activity
Installing Windows Vista

After completing this laboratory activity, you will be able to:

- ✔ Install or upgrade to Windows Vista.
- ✔ Determine the minimal and recommended system Windows Vista requirements.
- ✔ Describe how to use the Windows Upgrade Advisor.
- ✔ Describe the tasks to complete before performing a Windows Vista upgrade or installation.
- ✔ Describe the tasks to complete after performing a successful Windows Vista upgrade or installation.

Introduction

There are two ways to install Windows Vista: as a clean install or a system upgrade. A system upgrade allows the computer to retain all existing user files, such as documents, images, sounds, and similar collections of information. In addition, all user configurations are retained, such as user name and password. A clean install erases all previous files created by the user. For example, all document files will no longer exist after a clean install. Do not perform a clean install unless specifically told to do so by your instructor. A clean install will destroy all previous installed software applications as well as user files on your workstation.

The Windows Vista required and recommended hardware are listed below. The difference between recommended and required hardware is that Vista will function properly using the required hardware; however, the performance will be poor. It is best to meet or exceed the Windows Vista recommended hardware specifications to have a system performance level equal or exceeding the previous operating system. For example, if you upgraded from Windows XP and met the required hardware specifications for Windows Vista, Windows Vista would perform slower than Windows XP.

Required Hardware (Minimal):

- ✔ 800 MHz CPU.
- ✔ 512 MB RAM.
- ✔ Graphics processor DirectX 9 capable.

Recommended Hardware:

- ✔ 1 GHz CPU.
- ✔ 1 GB RAM.
- ✔ Graphics processor with DirectX 9, Windows Display Driver Model (WDDM), 128 MB RAM, Pixel shader 2.0, and 32 bits-per-pixel capability.
- ✔ DVD-ROM drive.
- ✔ Audio output capability.
- ✔ Internet access capability.

Note:
Computers identified as Windows Vista Capable meet minimal system requirements, and computers identified as Windows Vista Premium meet recommended hardware requirements.

Windows Vista will run on either 32-bit or 64-bit processors. Visit the Microsoft TechNet Web site at www.microsoft.com/technet/windowsvista to find more information about Windows Vista. You can see detailed information about installing Windows Vista and common problems at the Microsoft Web site link http://support.microsoft.com/kb/918884.

There are many known issues that can cause a problem when performing an upgrade or clean install. For example, many software drivers, software applications, and hardware items will not successfully respond to a Windows Vista upgrade and may not be available for a clean install.

Microsoft provides a software program called Windows Vista Upgrade Advisor that will perform a preinstallation test to determine if the existing hardware and software are compatible for an upgrade to Windows Vista. The following shows the first screen of the Windows Vista Upgrade Advisor.

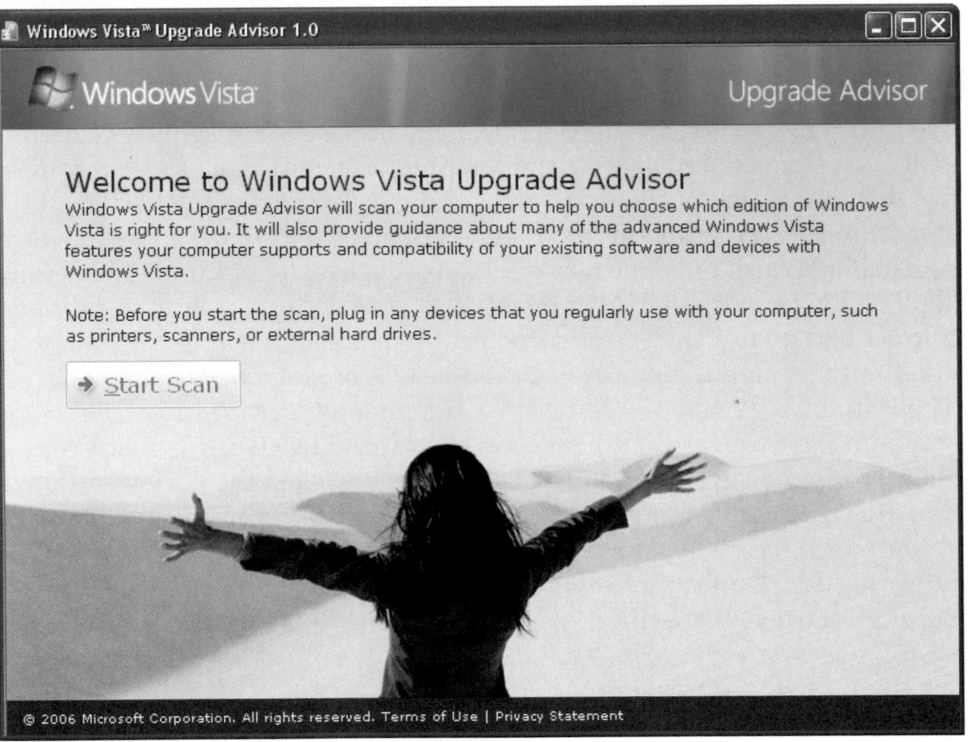

The Windows Vista Upgrade Advisor will identify known issues and display information about compatibility problems in report form. You can either download a copy of the Windows Vista Upgrade Advisor from the Microsoft Web site, or you can install and run the Windows Vista Upgrade Advisor as one of the first steps during a system upgrade.

The following shows a series of Windows Vista Upgrade Advisor screens, which provide information about Windows Vista compatibility and the computer system to be upgraded. A brief comparison of Windows Vista editions is displayed on the screen to help the user decide which version is right for them.

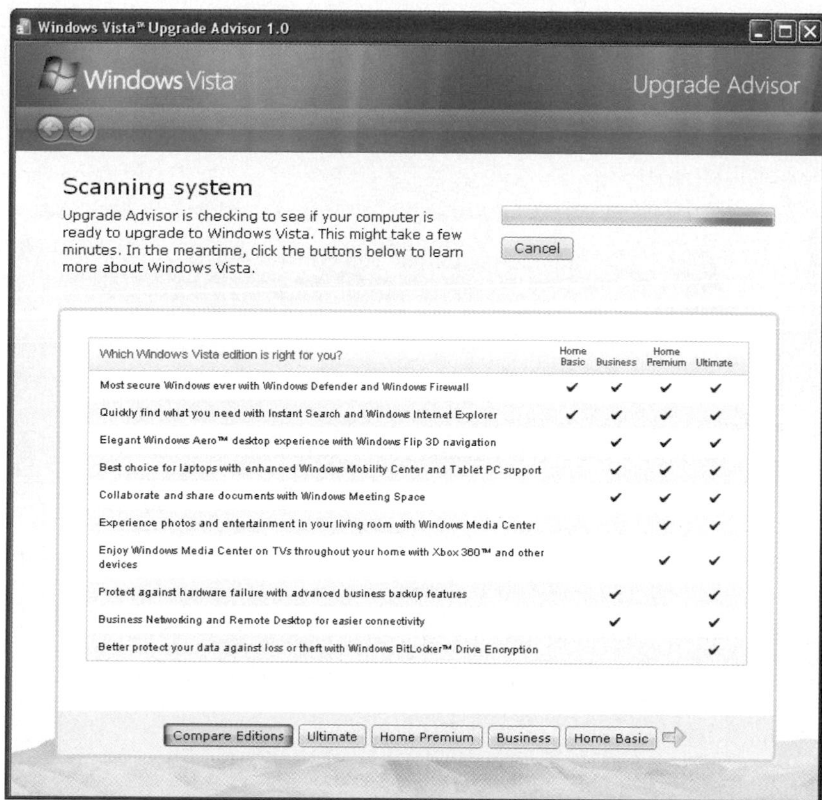

When the Windows Vista Upgrade Advisor has finished scanning the hardware and software on the computer to be upgraded, a **See Details** button will appear in the upper-right corner. You can use this button to access a detailed description of the scan.

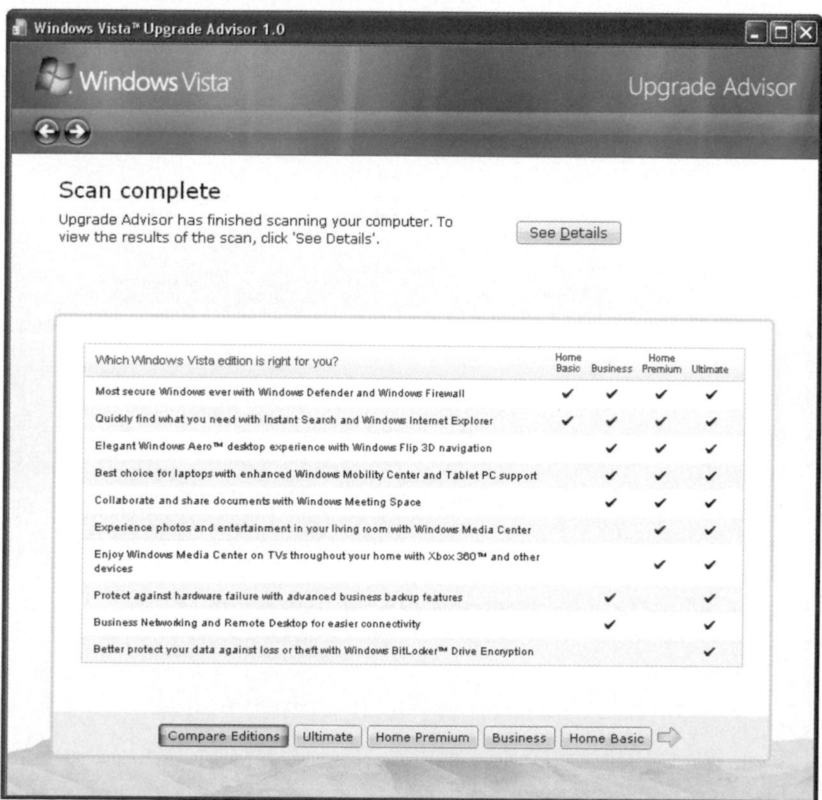

If there are no known issues, the screen capture will state that the computer can be successfully upgraded to Windows Vista.

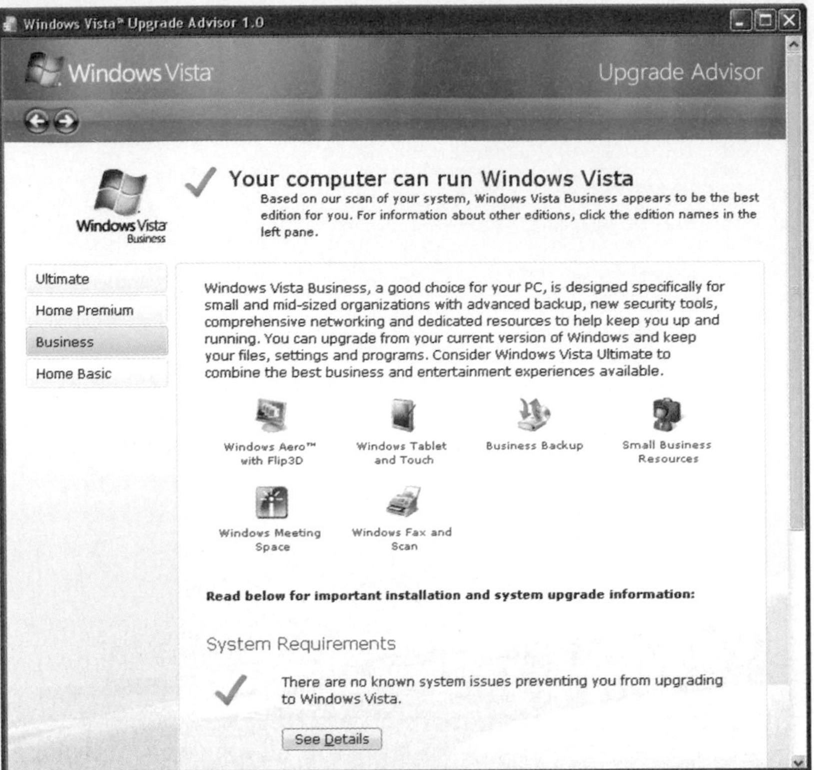

If the Windows Vista Upgrade Advisor detects known issues, it reports problems found with hardware or software and provide suggested remedies. Look at the next two screens to see how problems are identified.

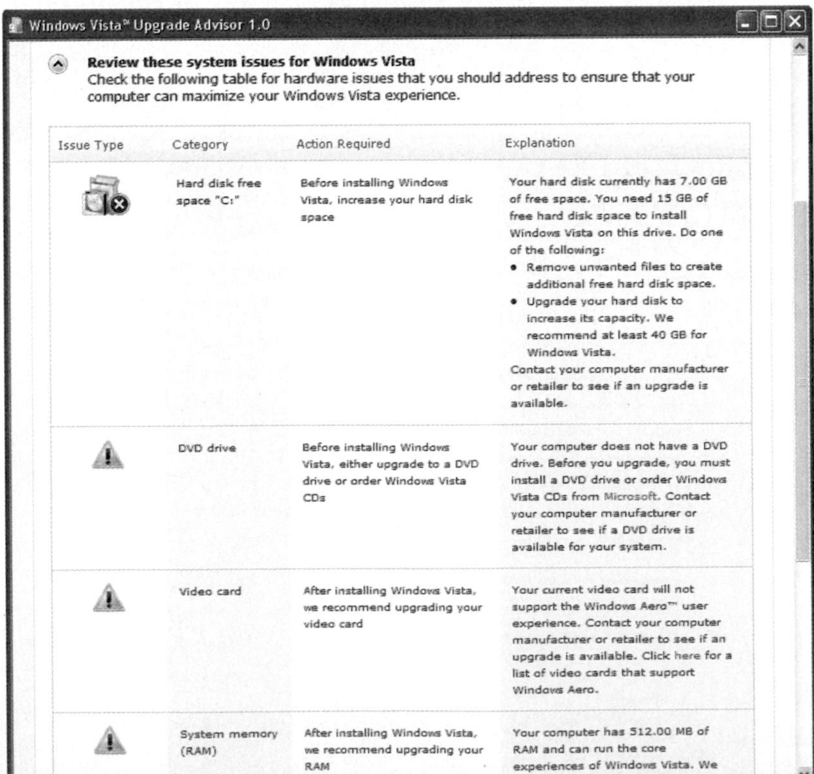

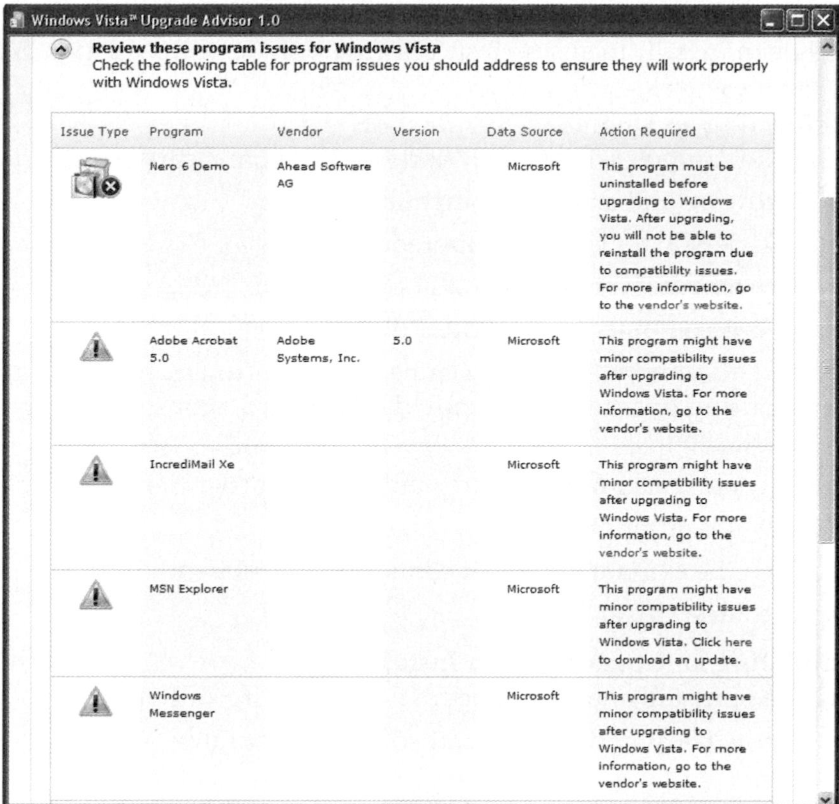

Windows Vista™ Upgrade Advisor 1.0

Review these program issues for Windows Vista
Check the following table for program issues you should address to ensure they will work properly with Windows Vista.

Issue Type	Program	Vendor	Version	Data Source	Action Required
	Nero 6 Demo	Ahead Software AG		Microsoft	This program must be uninstalled before upgrading to Windows Vista. After upgrading, you will not be able to reinstall the program due to compatibility issues. For more information, go to the vendor's website.
	Adobe Acrobat 5.0	Adobe Systems, Inc.	5.0	Microsoft	This program might have minor compatibility issues after upgrading to Windows Vista. For more information, go to the vendor's website.
	IncrediMail Xe			Microsoft	This program might have minor compatibility issues after upgrading to Windows Vista. For more information, go to the vendor's website.
	MSN Explorer			Microsoft	This program might have minor compatibility issues after upgrading to Windows Vista. Click here to download an update.
	Windows Messenger			Microsoft	This program might have minor compatibility issues after upgrading to Windows Vista. For more information, go to the vendor's website.

The Windows Vista Upgrade Advisor may perform a detailed analysis of the system prior to an upgrade operation and report that the system will upgrade without a problem. This analysis may not be true. Sometimes there will be a potential problem that has not been identified by Microsoft. For example, early releases of Windows Vista installed on an improperly installed Windows XP system may result in a failed upgrade. Windows XP had a problem identifying hard disk drives over 137 GB, SATA hard drive controllers, and some RAID systems. The Windows Vista Upgrade Advisor would indicate that there were no problems for an upgrade, but the upgrade would result in a catastrophic failure during the first reboot of the system. This is why you should always do a complete backup of all important files and possibly the entire disk before performing an upgrade.

Note:

When an upgrade installation fails, you can typically recover and revert to the original system. You simply restart the computer and watch the display carefully. An option to revert to the original operating system will appear briefly. In some cases, the option will be displayed very quickly and you must use the keyboard to quickly select the option to run the original operating system. It may take some practice before you are successful. Be aware that many times you will need a set of recovery discs to reinstall the previous operating system.

The following are lists of tasks to perform before and after a Windows Vista upgrade or clean install. To ensure a successful upgrade or installation, be sure you complete these tasks.

Before Performing an Upgrade/Clean Install:

✔ Check if the computer meets the Windows Vista hardware requirements.

✔ Check hardware and software compatibility lists.

✔ Back up all personal files for an upgrade.

✔ Create a system recovery disk for an upgrade.

✔ Check if your computer has the latest BIOS version.

✔ Disconnect all unnecessary peripherals, such as printers, scanners, and cameras, during upgrade. Leave only the keyboard, mouse, monitor, and speakers attached.

✔ Disable any antivirus, antispyware, and firewall programs for an upgrade.

✔ Find the 25-character product key.

✔ Write down the computer name if connected to a network.

✔ Collect the latest driver software.

After Completing an Upgrade/Clean Install:

✔ Reactivate or install antivirus, antispyware, and firewall programs.

✔ Check for the latest updates for your software programs.

Equipment and Materials

✔ Windows XP SP2 computer meeting at least the minimum requirements for Windows Vista.

✔ Record the following information provided by your instructor on a separate piece of paper:

Computer name: _______________

Computer workgroup/domain: _____________

User name: _________________

User password: _______________

Run the Windows Vista Upgrade Advisor during the lab activity: ______ (Yes or No)

Note:

A Windows Vista upgrade can only be installed on an existing NTFS format partition. If the partition is not NTFS, then it must be converted to NTFS before attempting to upgrade to Windows Vista. Access the following link for information about how to convert an existing FAT or FAT32 partition to NTFS: http://support.microsoft.com/kb/307881. Do not attempt a file system conversion without your instructor's permission.

Note:

Lab activity time is typically limited. For this lab activity, you will perform a simple Windows Vista Upgrade or clean install. Other options, such as checking for hardware compatibility and transferring files, are covered in other lab activities.

Procedure

1._______ Report to your assigned workstation. Boot the computer and check if it is in working order.

2._______ Run the Windows Vista Upgrade Advisor if directed by your instructor. Otherwise, proceed to the next step.

3._______ Insert the Windows Vista installation DVD. There are several versions of Windows Vista. This lab activity is based on Windows Vista Business Upgrade version. After booting the DVD, you will see a dialog box similar to the following.

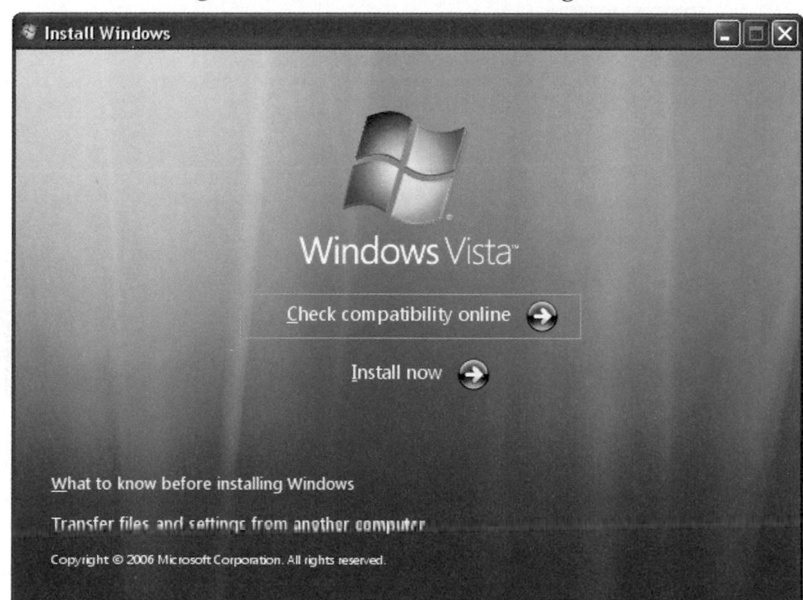

Notice that you have several possible selections: **Check compatibility online**, **Install now**, **What to know before installing Windows**, and **Transfer files and settings from another computer**.

4._______ Review the contents of **What to know before installing Windows** before proceeding. Do not spend more than a few minutes reviewing this material.

5._______ Select the **Install now** option. You do not need to run the **Check compatibility online** option at this time, unless you are directed to do so by your instructor.

The installation program will begin collecting information about the hardware and software. At the same time, a dialog box will appear asking you if you would like to go online for the latest updates. Do not select the latest updates unless you are required to do so by your instructor. You can obtain the latest updates at a later time from the Microsoft Web site.

6._______ Next, you are prompted for the 25-character product key. Enter the product key and select the **Automatically activate Windows when I'm online** option. It should be checked by default. You have 30 days to activate the copy of windows online or by telephone. Unless activated, the system will stop working in 30 days. When you select the **Automatically activate Windows when I'm online** option, the system will automatically activate Windows Vista three days after you perform your first logon.

7.______ Next, the terms of the license agreement appears on the screen. You must select the **I accept the license terms** option to proceed with the installation.

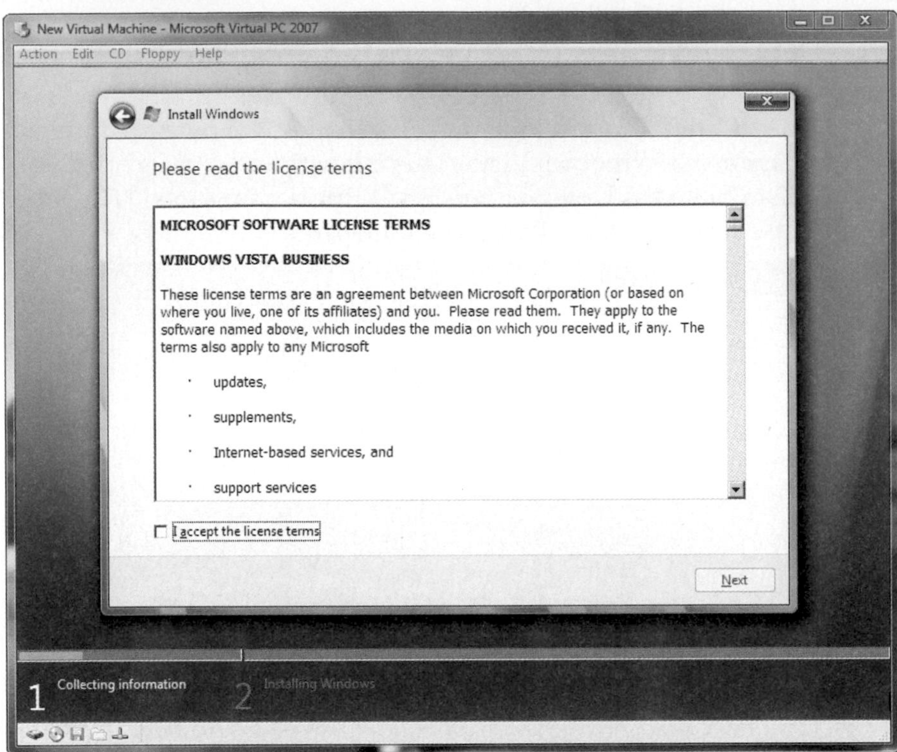

8.______ You are now presented with two installation options: **Upgrade** and **Custom**. Select the appropriate option.

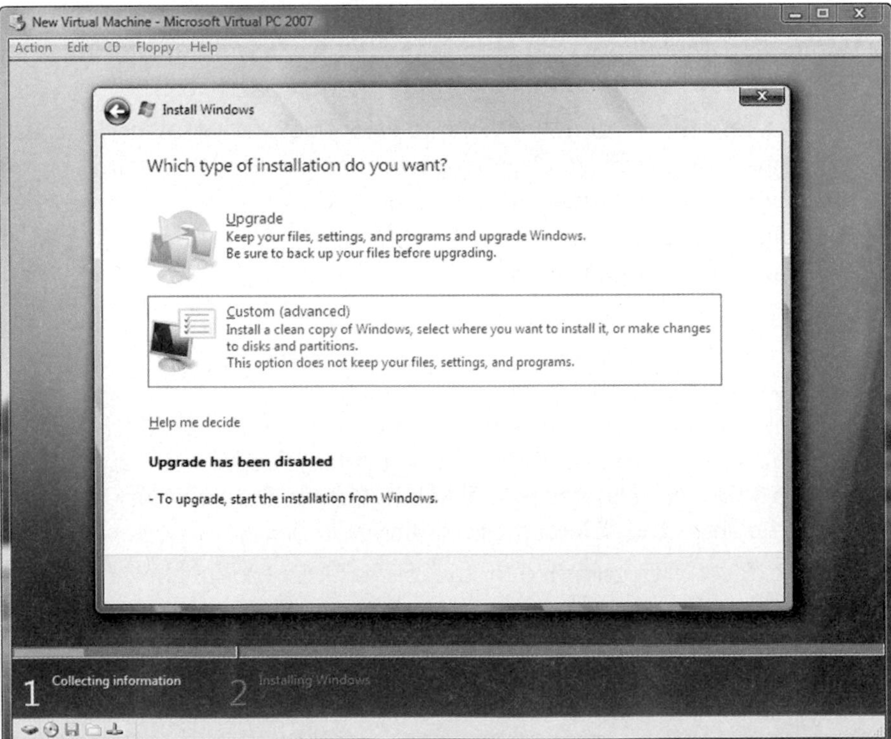

If you selected the **Upgrade** option, a compatibility report will appear if there is a known compatibility issue with the hardware or software. If the issue is not determined to be serious, you will be able to proceed with the installation.

A dialog box will appear informing you that the upgrade process has begun and that it may take several hours to complete. The actual time will depend mainly on the computer hardware. If you are installing on a computer that exceeds the hardware specifications, the actual time will be much shorter. The following screen capture lists the five major steps in the upgrade process.

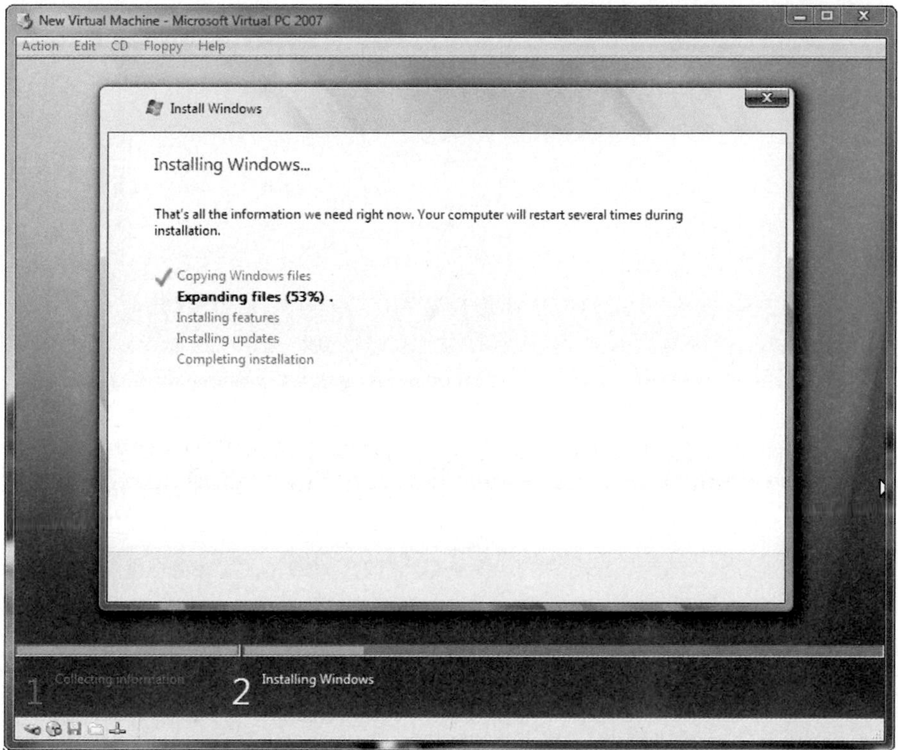

The percentage of the installation completed will appear on the screen during the upgrade process. Be aware that the computer may restart several times during this process. You should see a screen message "Please wait a moment while Windows prepares to run for the first time." After a short period or several minutes, the screen will display the "Completing upgrade" stage.

If you are performing an upgrade, proceed to step 9.

If you are performing a clean install, proceed to step 13.

9. _______ After a successful upgrade, you should see the **Help protect Windows automatically** dialog box. Select the **Ask me later** option.

10. _______ When the dialog box for setting the date and time appears, make adjustments if necessary. Also, if you live in an appropriate area that observes daylight saving time such as Arizona and parts of Ohio, select the **Automatically adjust clock for Daylight Saving Time** option.

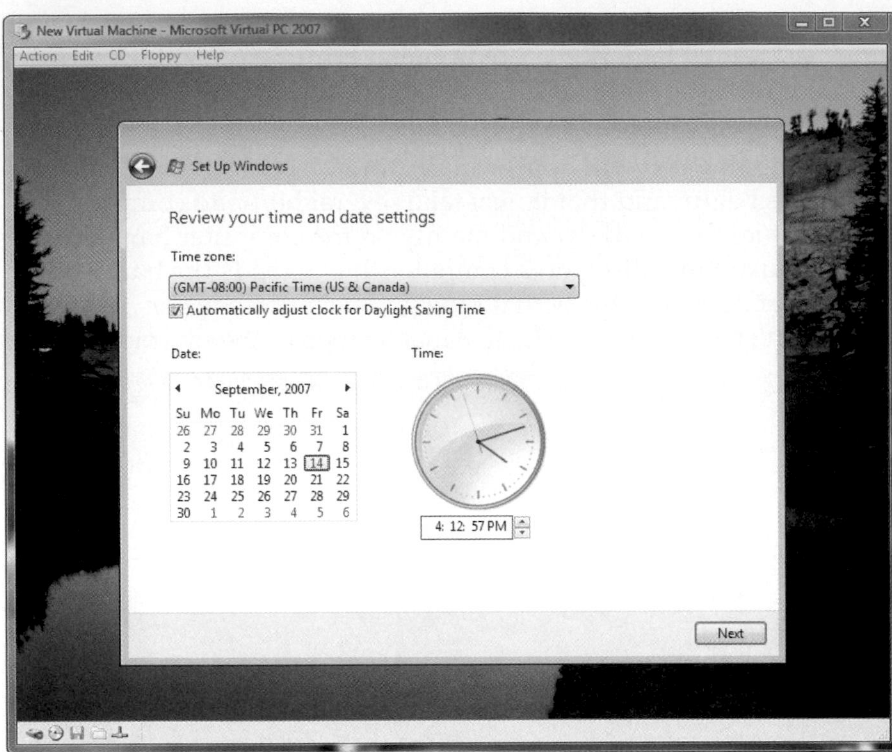

11. _______ Next, you are prompted to select your present location. The choices are **Home**, **Work**, and **Public location**. Select **Work** for this lab activity.

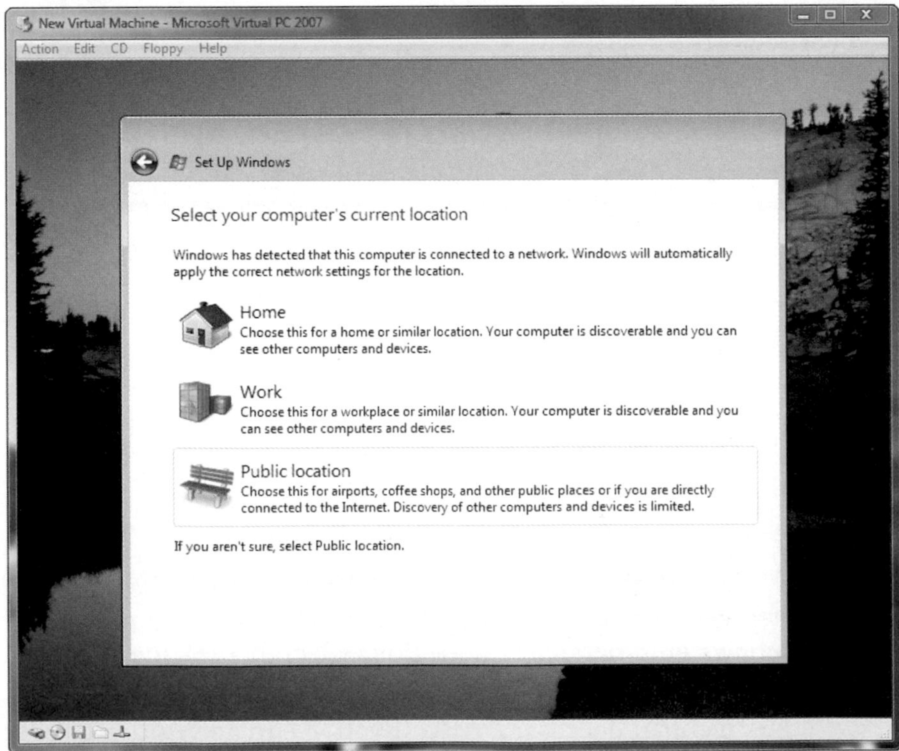

12._______ The **Set Up Windows** dialog box will display and look similar to that in the following screen capture.

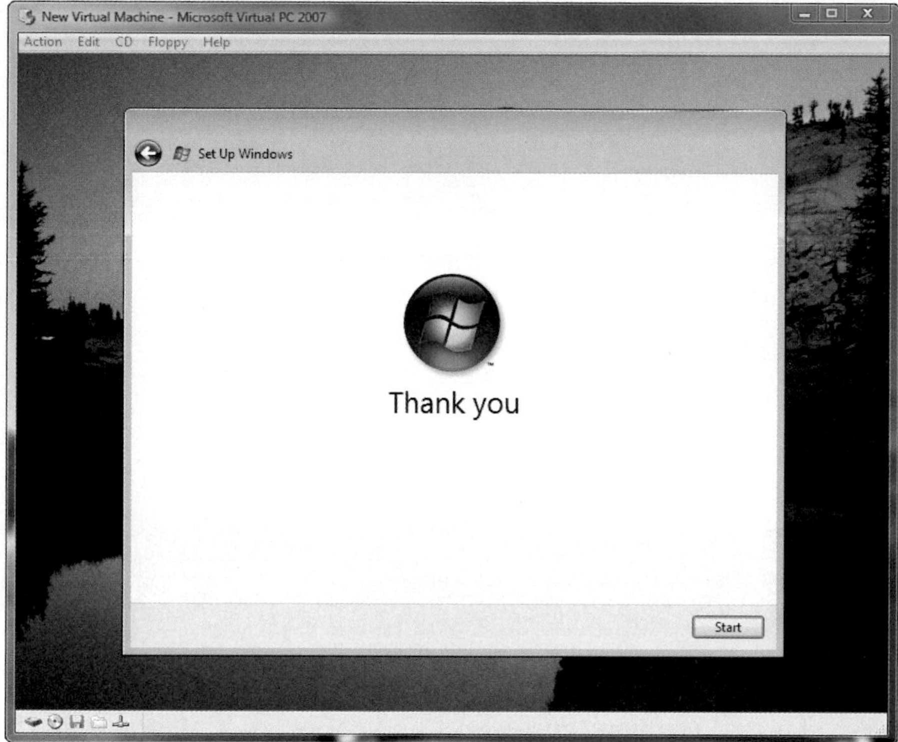

Click the **Start** button. The system will automatically check the system performance, which will take a few minutes. After it finishes, it will prepare the desktop.

You have now completed the Windows Vista upgrade or installation. Call your instructor for inspection of the lab activity and then go on to answer the review questions. Return all materials to their proper storage area.

* * * *

13._______ If you selected the **Custom** option, a dialog box like that in the following screen capture will display asking where you would like to install Window Vista.

You can install it to an existing partition or to unallocated space. You can use all of the unallocated space, or a part of it after partitioning it into one or more partitions. You can also delete an existing partition and create a new partition. After you chose a location, Windows Vista will begin installing. When Windows Vista is finished installing, the computer will reboot.

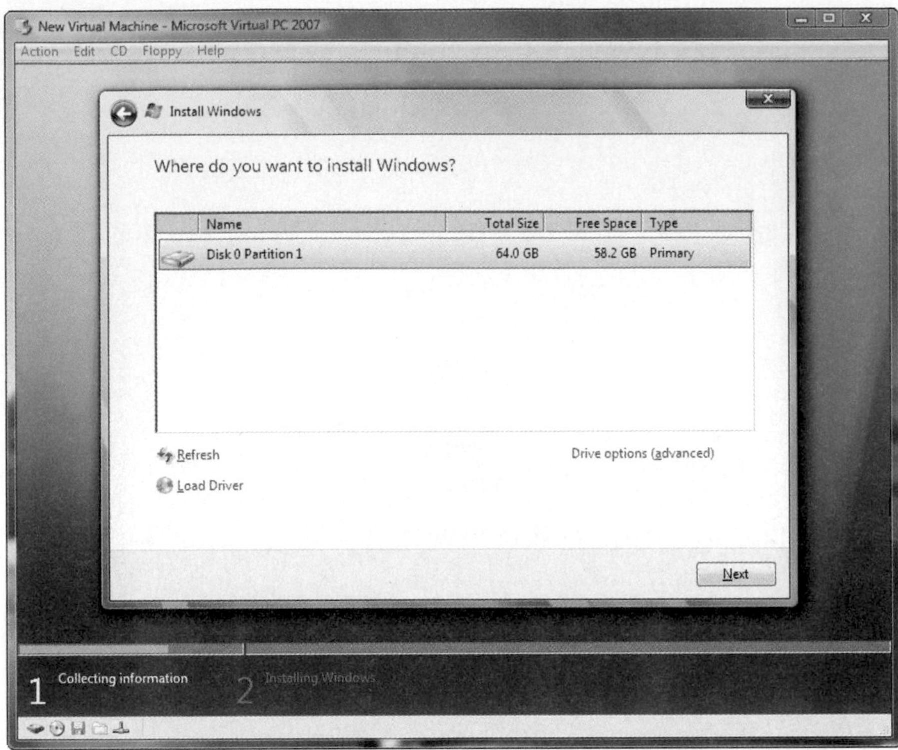

14. ________ Enter a user name, password, and password hint. While it is not necessary to have a user name and password, it is always recommended. Only configure a user name and password if your instructor has provided them.

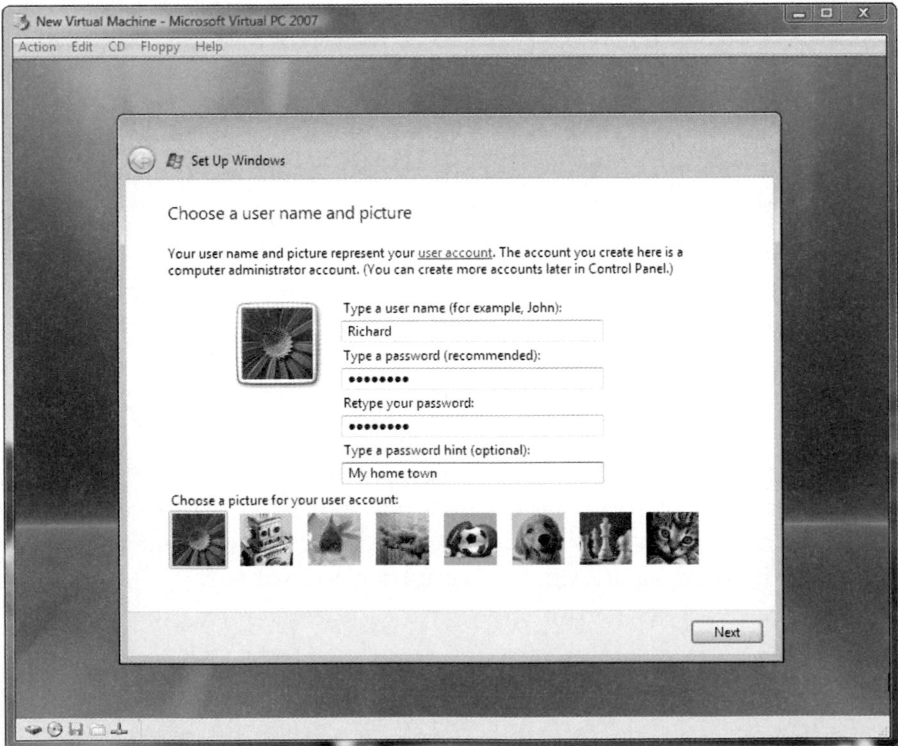

15.________ Select an icon, such as a fish or a flower.

16.________ Next, the default computer name appears. It is a combination of the user name and PC, for example, Richard-PC. Change the computer name if directed to do so by your instructor.

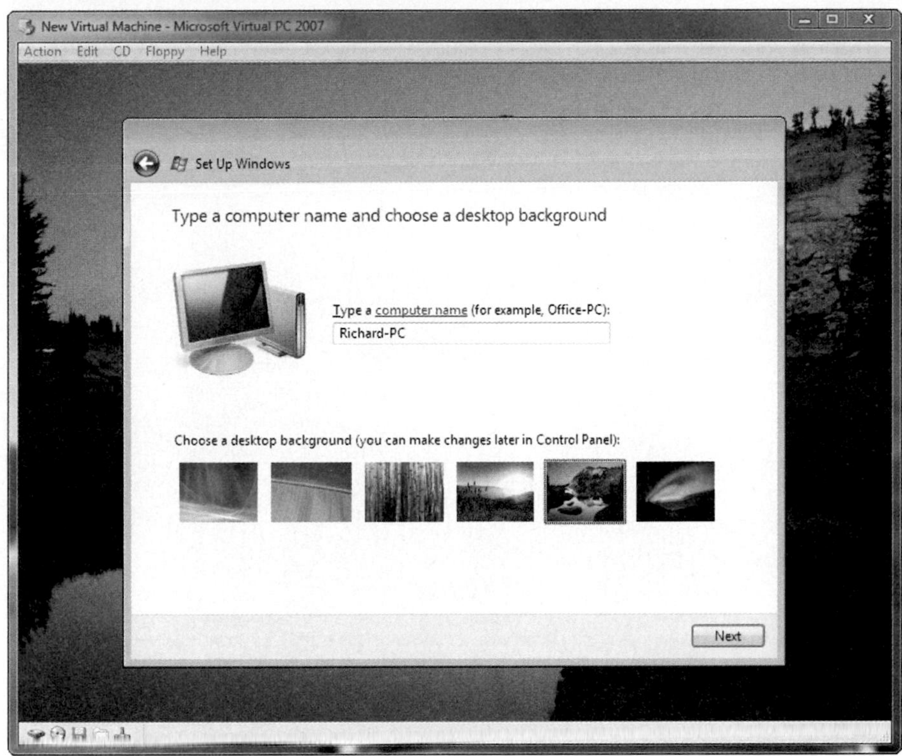

17.________ Select a desktop picture when prompted.

18.________ When prompted to set up Windows protection, choose one of the following options: **Use recommended settings**, **Install updates only**, or **Ask me later**. The **Install updates only** option is selected by default.

19.________ Set the time zone, date, and time.

20.________ Next, you are prompted to select your present location. The choices are **Home**, **Work**, and **Public location**. Select **Work** for this lab activity. The **Set Up Windows** dialog box will display.

21.________ Click the **Start** button. The system will automatically check the system performance, which will take a few minutes. Your name and icon will display, and you will be prompted for your password.

20.______ Enter your password.

21.______ The default desktop appears on the display. If an antivirus program has not been installed for the previous operating system version, you will be prompted to install one now. Microsoft will direct you to their Web site through an existing Internet connection if one exist. You may ignore this dialog box and move on to the next step

22. _______ The **Welcome Center** displays. Take a few moments to inspect the various items at this time.

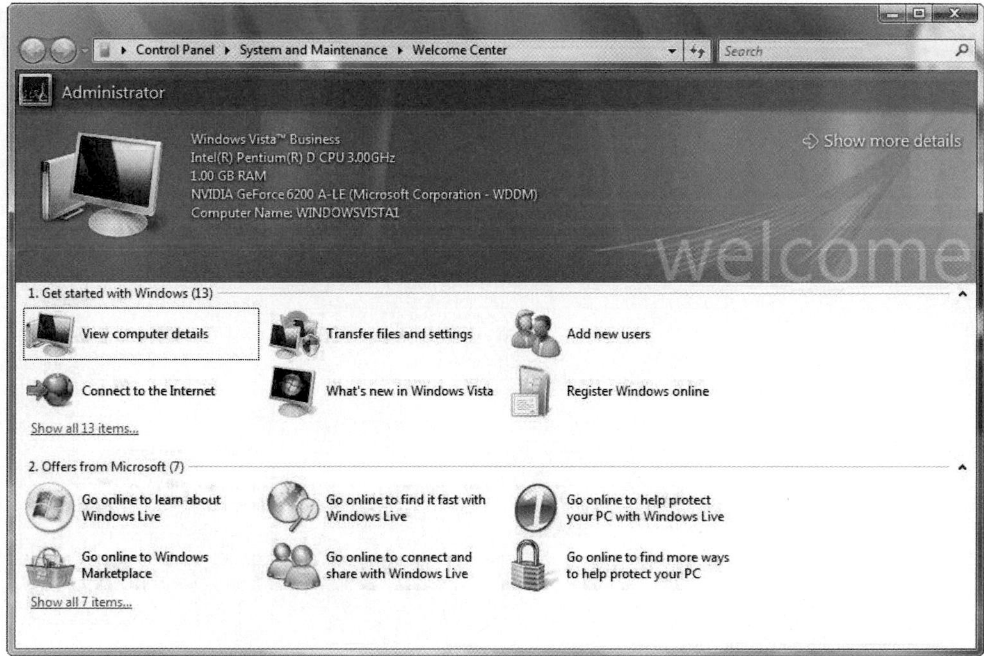

23. _______ Call your instructor to inspect your installation.

24. _______ Shut down the computer, and then reboot it once more to see the default desktop.

25. _______ Shut down the workstation and then answer the review questions. Return all materials to their proper storage area.

Review Questions

Answer the following questions on a separate sheet of paper. Please do not write in this book.

1. What is the recommended CPU speed for Windows Vista?
2. What is the minimum required CPU speed for Windows Vista?
3. What should you do before upgrading to Windows Vista?
4. What are the five major steps in the Windows Vista upgrade process?
5. What file system must Windows Vista be installed on?
6. What is the difference between a clean install and a system upgrade?

PC technicians must continuously learn about new software and hardware to meet their employer's changing demands and keep abreast of new technology.

Motherboards

After studying this chapter, you will be able to:

- ✔ Identify major parts of a motherboard.
- ✔ Identify common motherboard form factors.
- ✔ Explain motherboard bus architecture.
- ✔ Identify expansion slot architectures.
- ✔ Identify the important system resources and explain what they are used for.
- ✔ Identify and explain IRQs.
- ✔ Explain the role of a chipset.
- ✔ Explain the purpose of the CMOS Setup program.
- ✔ Explain the procedure for upgrading a Flash BIOS.

A+ Exam—Key Points

This unit will cover many of the objectives on the CompTIA A+ Essentials exam. Be sure you can access the BIOS setup program for several different computer systems and understand the terminology associated with BIOS setup. Motherboard technical manuals are available on the Internet and provide detailed BIOS setup information. Be sure to look at several thoroughly.

Since Plug and Play and USB devices have evolved and older port connection types have become obsolete, CompTIA no longer emphasizes IRQ and I/O settings for COM1, COM2, COM3, COM4, LPT1 and LPT2 on their exams.

There will be several questions concerning CMOS and BIOS. Typical questions will address the process of upgrading BIOS, changing CMOS settings, and changing and setting the CMOS Setup password.

Knowledge of expansion slot architecture will be required. There may also be a question to test basic knowledge of form factors.

Key Words and Terms

The following words and terms will become important pieces of your computer vocabulary. Be sure you can define them.

Accelerated Graphics Port (AGP)
address bus
backplane
bus
bus mastering
chipset
CMOS Setup (or BIOS Setup) program
control bus
data bus
direct memory access (DMA)
Enhanced Parallel Port (EPP)
expansion card slots
Extended Capabilities Port (ECP)
Extended Industry Standard Architecture (EISA)
field replacement unit (FRU)
FireWire (IEEE 1394)
Flash BIOS
form factor
I/O bus
I/O port address
Industry Standard Architecture (ISA)
internal bus
IRQ
local bus
memory address range
memory bus
Micro Channel Architecture (MCA)
north bridge
Peripheral Components Interface (PCI)
Plug and Play (PnP)
power bus
south bridge
Universal Serial Bus (USB)
Video Electronics Standards Association (VESA) local bus

The *motherboard* is considered the most important element of a computer's design. All major components connect to and transmit data across the motherboard. The motherboard is the communications center for input and output devices such as the memory, CPU, keyboard, mouse, parallel port, serial port, monitor, and network connection. The motherboard also provides the connection points required by the fans, speakers, on/off switches, LED indicator lights, and CMOS battery.

The motherboard provides a means for expanding and customizing the system by inserting expansion boards into slots provided as direct connections to the bus architecture. There are various special purpose chips that control communications between the different buses and devices mounted on the motherboard. The motherboard is also referred to as the *system board, main board,* and *planar board.*

Motherboard Construction

The motherboard provides a physical surface on which to mount electronic components such as resistors, capacitors, chips, slots, and sockets. The motherboard is a combination of insulating material and electronic circuit paths constructed of small thin conductors. See **Figure 3-1.** The motherboard is constructed mainly from electrical insulation material. Insulation material does not conduct electrical energy. The small electrical circuits that run across the surface of the motherboard are called *traces.* Traces provide the paths between all the different components mounted on the motherboard. This confines the

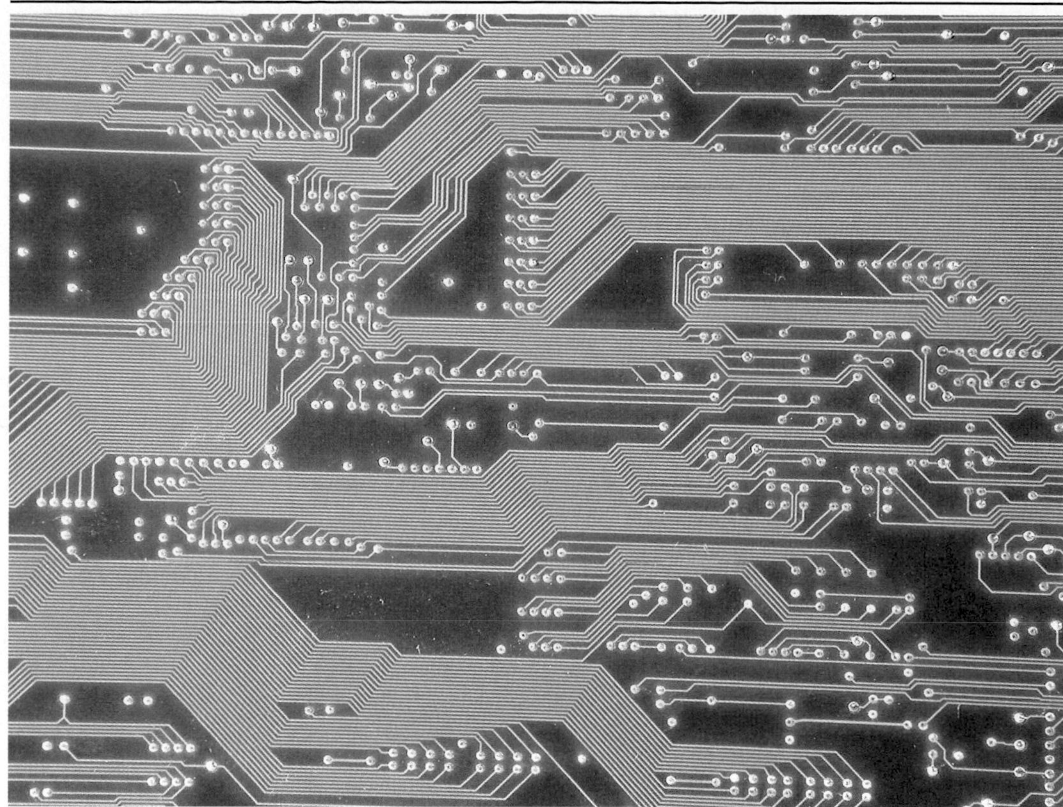

Figure 3-1. Close-up view of motherboard circuit paths.

flow of electrical energy to the path created by the traces. The electrical circuit paths provide a means of sending and receiving data between the components connected to the motherboard.

The insulated motherboard does not allow the electrical energy to come in contact with the case. An electrical short circuit would be created if electrical energy were allowed to flow to the metal PC case. A short circuit would also be created if electrical energy could flow directly between the traces on the motherboard.

The thin conductors also provide power to low-power devices. Large-power consumption devices, such as the disk drives, are provided power directly from the power supply through much larger conductors. Many of the thin conductors on the motherboard are grouped together to make up what is referred to as a bus. A ***bus*** is a collection of conductors that works together for a specific purpose.

There are many bus types, such as data bus, control bus, memory bus, internal bus, I/O bus, address bus, and power bus. The ***data bus*** is used to move data between components. The data is moved between components grouped as 8, 16, 32, or 64 bits. The amount of data that can be moved at one time is referred to as the bus width.

Signals are transmitted across the ***control bus*** to activate devices such as disk drives and modems. The ***memory bus*** connects directly to the memory, and the ***I/O bus*** (or ***expansion bus***) runs along the expansion slots. The ***internal bus*** is part of the integrated circuit inside the CPU unit. The ***local bus,*** or ***system bus,*** connects directly to the CPU and provides communications to high-speed devices mounted closely to the CPU. The ***address bus*** connects the CPU with the main memory module. It identifies memory locations where data is to

bus
a collection of conductors that connect multiple components, allowing them to work together for a specific purpose.

data bus
a bus used to move data between components.

control bus
a bus that delivers command signals from the processor to devices.

memory bus
a bus that connects the processor to the memory.

I/O bus
a bus that connects the processor to the expansion slots.

internal bus
part of the integrated circuit inside the CPU.

local bus
a bus system that connects directly to the CPU and provides communications to high-speed devices mounted closely to the CPU.

address bus
a bus system that connects the CPU with the main memory module. It identifies memory locations where data is to be stored or retrieved.

power bus
a bus system that sends electrical power to small consumption devices, such as speakers, lights, and switches.

be stored or retrieved. Lastly, the ***power bus*** is used to send electrical power to small consumption devices such as speakers, lights, and switches. Larger consumption devices such as disk drives connect directly to the power supply using larger conductors. As you can see, there are many different bus types and classifications. The name usually implies the purpose of the bus.

A bus may also be a collection of bus types. For example, the local bus consists of power, data, control, and memory bus lines. Therefore, it consists of the power bus, data bus, control bus, and memory bus. For this reason, the local bus may be referred to by other names such as the *system bus* or *memory bus.* Intel has coined the local bus as the *front side bus (FSB).* This term is used quite often when specifying motherboard bus speeds.

field replacement unit (FRU)
any major part of a computer system that could be completely replaced on site rather than repaired.

The motherboard is considered a field replacement unit. A ***field replacement unit (FRU)*** is any major part of a computer system that could be completely replaced on site. Most of the components mounted on a motherboard are chips soldered into place. Only a highly skilled electronics technician should attempt repair and replacement of motherboard chips.

Form Factors

form factor
the physical shape or outline of a motherboard and the location of the mounting holes. Also called a *footprint.*

The ***form factor*** describes the physical shape or outline of a motherboard and the location of the mounting holes. Sometimes the form factor is called the *footprint*. A motherboard form factor must be considered when upgrading a PC. The form factor determines if the motherboard will fit the PC case style you intend to use, **Figure 3-2.** Another device that conforms to a form factor is the power supply. The power supply must match the form factor of the case and motherboard. The form factors that have been developed over the years are the XT, AT, LPX, ATX, NLX, BTX, and backplane. The most common form factors in use today are microATX, ATX, and BTX.

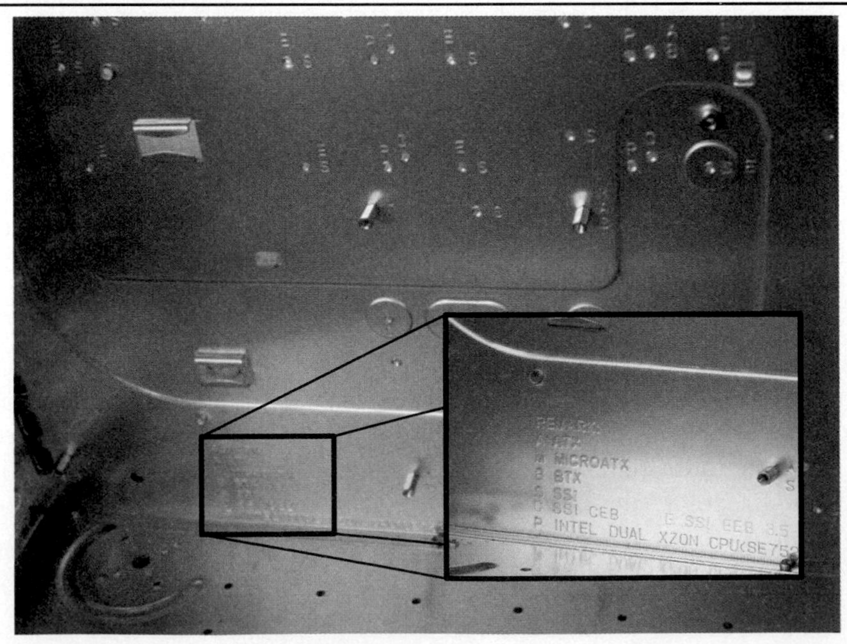

Figure 3-2.
This case can house a variety of motherboard form factors. Notice the legend at the bottom of the case (enlarged in the exploded view). The legend includes capital letters to identify the mount points for specific form factors. For example, the letter *A* represents ATX motherboard mount points, *M* represents MicroATX mount points, and *B* represents mount points BTX.

XT, AT, and Baby AT

The original PC by IBM used an XT form factor for its motherboard. This was in 1983 and was the truly first standardized form factor for motherboards. The XT used an 8-bit data bus system. The next standard size was the AT (Advanced Technology) form factor. It was slightly larger than the XT and provided a 16-bit data bus.

As chip technology advanced, it became possible to reduce the size of the motherboard back to the original size and shape of the XT. This next motherboard was called the *Baby AT.* Even though it was the same size as the XT board, there would have been a lot of confusion caused by naming it an XT. Then there would have been two different boards, one 8 bit and the other 16 bit, that were the same size. This is the reason for calling the 16-bit board the Baby AT. See **Figure 3-3.**

ATX

The Baby AT remained popular until 1996 when the ATX, a new style of motherboard, gained popularity. The ATX is incompatible with most other motherboard form factors.

ATX form factor has three common sizes: ATX, microATX, and flexATX. The flexATX is sometimes referred to as the *miniATX.* The three standard sizes are 12.0″ × 9.6″ (ATX), 9.6″ × 9.6″ (microATX), and 7.5″ × 9.6″ (flexATX), **Figure 3-4.** The overall size of the ATX motherboard is reduced by reducing the total number of adapter slots for each ATX form factor.

The ATX looks similar to a Baby AT board that has been turned 90° inside the computer case. The ATX requires a new shape of power supply so that both the motherboard and power supply will fit inside the same case. The most welcomed feature of the ATX motherboard is the new style of power supply connector mounted on the motherboard. The new power supply connector is designed to prevent the power supply from being plugged into the motherboard with the polarity reversed. This would result in a blown motherboard.

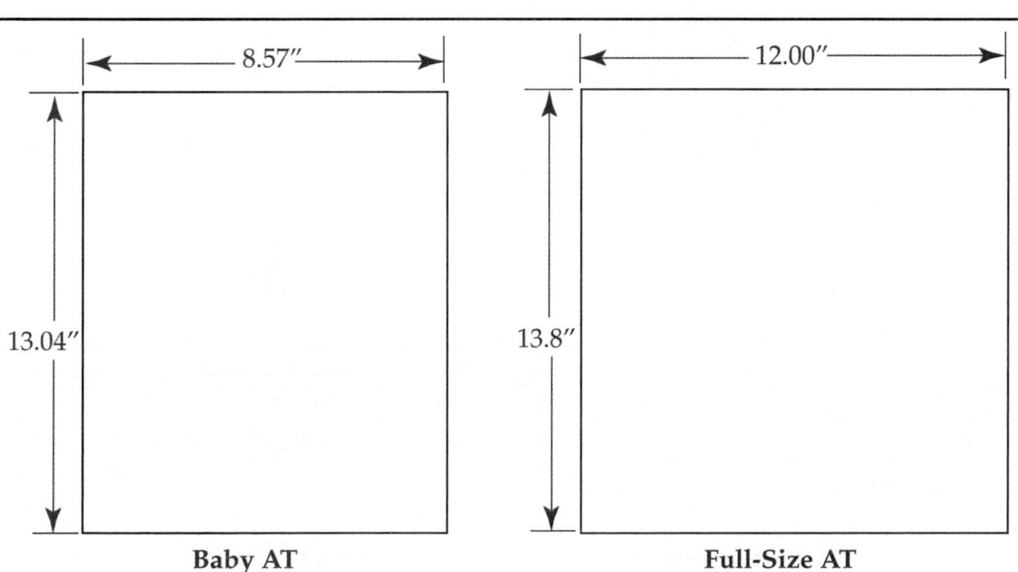

Figure 3-3. Comparison of the Baby AT and the full-size AT form factor.

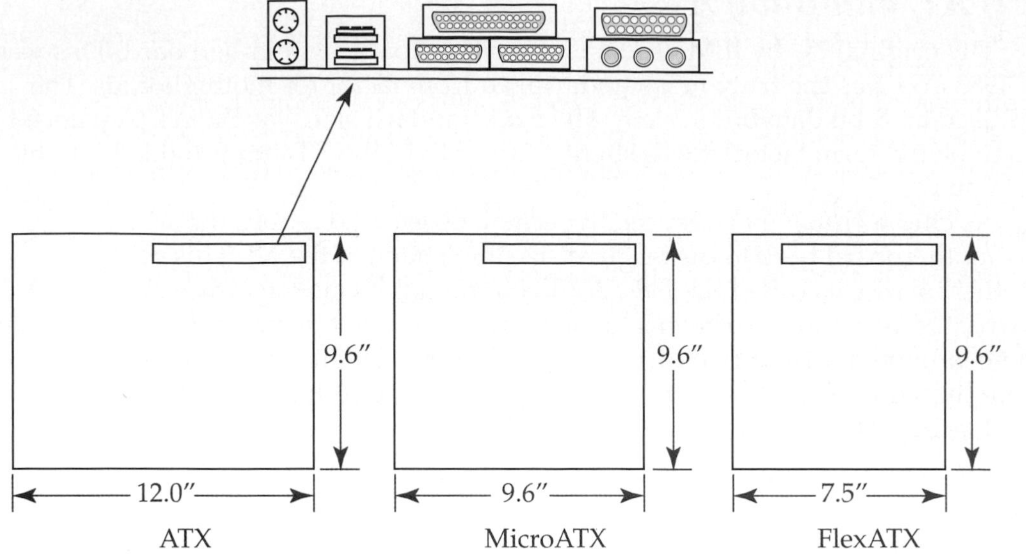

Figure 3-4.
ATX form factors and back view.

We will take a closer look at power supply connectors in Chapter 5—Power Supplies. For quick identification, an ATX form factor motherboard uses a 20-pin power supply connector, and an AT form factor motherboard uses a 12-pin connector. A newer style of the ATX form factor, called ATX12V, uses a 24-pin connector

LPX

The LPX was designed to allow for a low-profile desktop computer or a slim tower. This motherboard does not have expansion slots like a typical motherboard. Instead, it has a single expansion slot usually mounted in the middle of the motherboard. This expansion slot is used to host a bus riser card. See **Figure 3-5.**

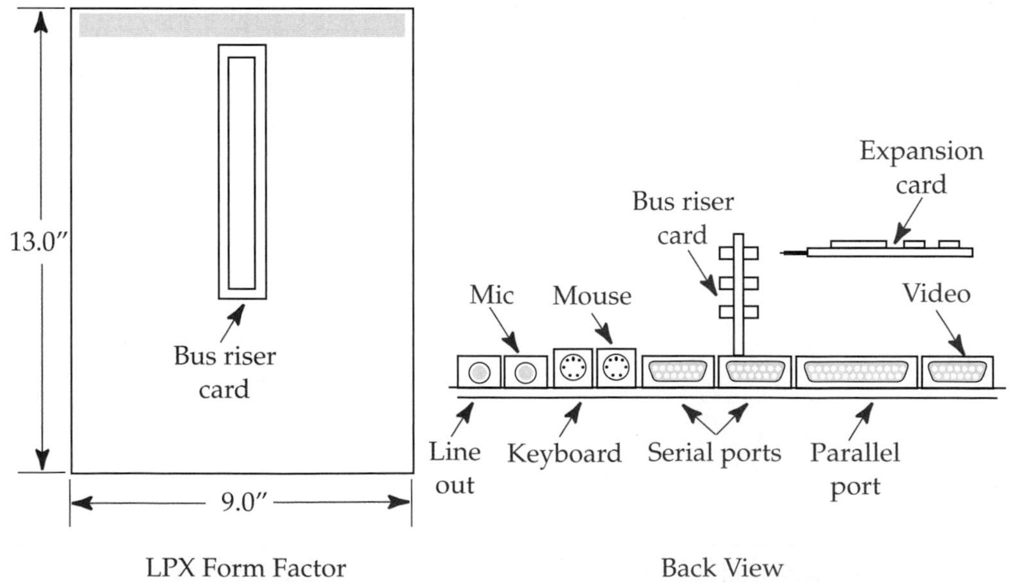

Figure 3-5.
LPX form factor and back view.

The adapter cards are plugged into the bus riser card at right angles. This style of installing expansion cards allows the cards to be inserted in parallel with the surface of the motherboard. The expansion boards installed parallel with the motherboard is what allows for the low profiles of the computer case.

The LPX is not considered a true standard that allows for upgrading. Rather, it is a proprietary style. The bus riser card is not always located in the same spot. This variation can cause a problem when changing or upgrading the motherboard. Obtaining a motherboard from the same manufacturer is usually required to get the correct layout. This style of motherboard is popular in lower-priced computer systems.

NLX

Another form factor, the NLX, uses the same principle as the bus riser card design. However, rather than placing the bus riser card in the middle of the motherboard, it is located at the end of the board. In fact, the edge of the motherboard actually plugs into the riser card.

The major advantage of the NLX board over the LPX is that the NLX is standardized in the industry. This means you can replace or upgrade any NLX board with any other NLX board in the industry. The NLX was popular among the leading PC manufacturers such as Gateway, Hewlett-Packard, IBM, NEC, and Micron. The board width is a standard 9.0″ while the length can vary from 10.0″ to 13.6″. Even though the length may vary, it is still considered a standard. See **Figure 3-6** and **Figure 3-7.**

The ATX and NLX continue to be the most popular design used by computer manufacturers. They should stay standard for some time.

BTX

Balanced Technology Extended (BTX) is the latest motherboard and PC case form factor. BTX is designed to meet the need for better system cooling and acoustics. Many PC components, such as CPUs, chipsets, and graphic cards, operate at a much higher frequency than their predecessors. Therefore, PCs require a better cooling system. The BTX form factor is designed for the best possible direct stream of air across the CPU and other heat-generating components. Another key part of the design is the ability to reduce the noise level of a PC's cooling system fans.

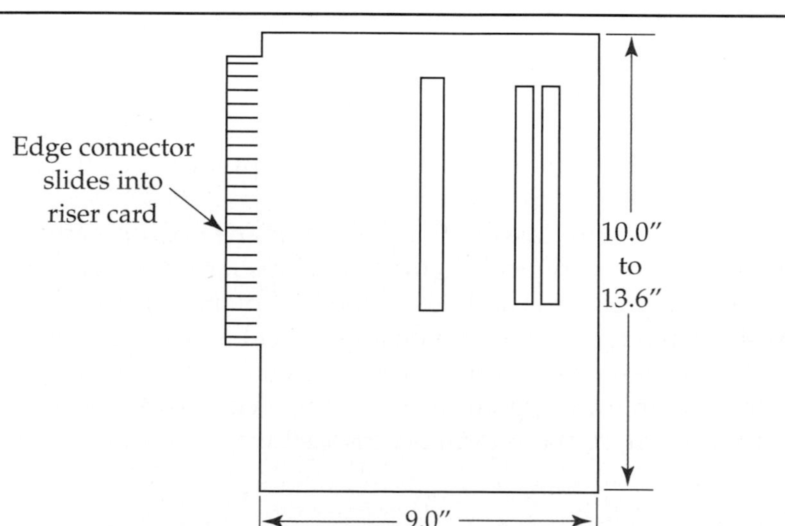

Figure 3-6. NLX form factor. Take special note of the edge connector on the left side of the motherboard. The motherboard fits into the riser expansion card.

Figure 3-7.
NLX motherboard.
(Intel Corp.)

The BTX form factor comes in three system sizes: tower, desktop, and small. The actual physical classifications are BTX, microBTX, nanoBTX, and picoBTX. The BTX design is not compatible with the ATX design, but the BTX can use a typical ATX power supply as well as any standard device that is not form factor dependent, such as DVD drives, CD-ROM drives, hard drives, CPUs, and adapter cards.

The BTX motherboard has four form factor sizes: 10.5″ × 12.8″ (BTX), 10.5″ × 10.4″ (microBTX), 10.5″ × 8.8 (nanoBTX), and 10.5″ × 8.0″ (picoBTX), **Figure 3-8.** The width of the BTX form factor is reduced by reducing the number of expansion slots. The full BTX has up to seven expansion slots, the microBTX has four expansion slots, the nanoBTX has two expansion slots, and the picoBTX has only one expansion slot.

Backplane

backplane
a circuit board with an abundance of slots along the length of the board.

A backplane is not a true form factor design, but it must be considered with a discussion on form factors and motherboards. A ***backplane*** is a circuit board with an abundance of slots along the length of the board, **Figure 3-9.** Expansion cards slide into the expansion slots. Even the CPU can insert into an expansion slot on the backplane. The main idea of the design is to ensure easy upgrades of any and all components. This style is very popular in heavy industry. The backplane is considered proprietary.

There are two main classifications of backplane boards: active and passive. In a *passive* design, all the typical circuits and chips found on the motherboard are found on the adapter cards and not on the backplane. An *active* backplane design contains the usual circuitry found on any typical motherboard with the exception of the main processor itself. The processor is usually installed into an expansion slot to allow for an easy upgrade as more advanced processors come on the market. To learn more about form factors visit www.formfactors.org.

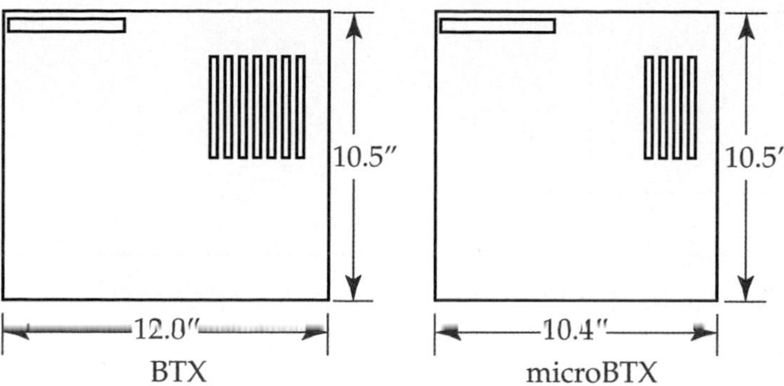

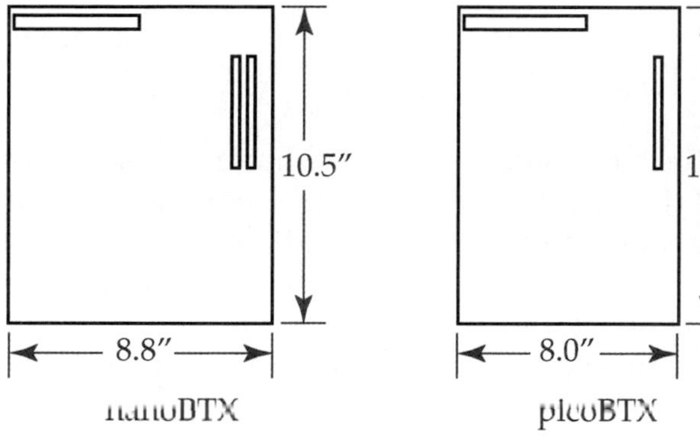

Figure 3-8.
BTX form factors. Notice that the length is retained and the width is reduced by reducing the number of available expansion slots.

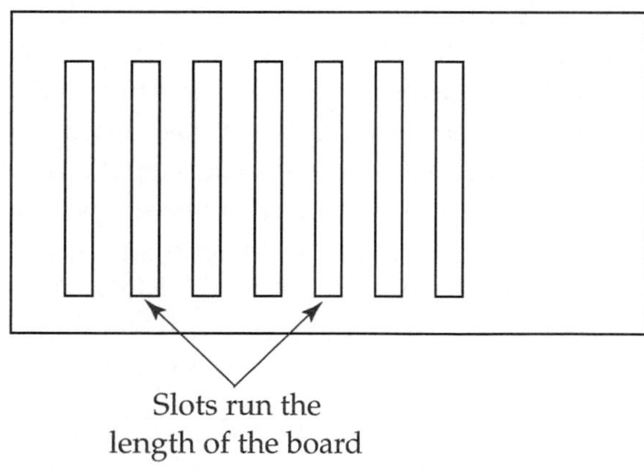

Figure 3-9.
Typical backplane design is simply a series of slots spanning across the motherboard.

Motherboard Bus System Architecture

The original PC had a simple bus architecture. One bus connected all major components to the RAM and CPU. The CPU transmitted data to and from components on the motherboard at the same speed. See **Figure 3-10.** The original bus architecture consisted of one bus. The speed of the bus matched the processor speed.

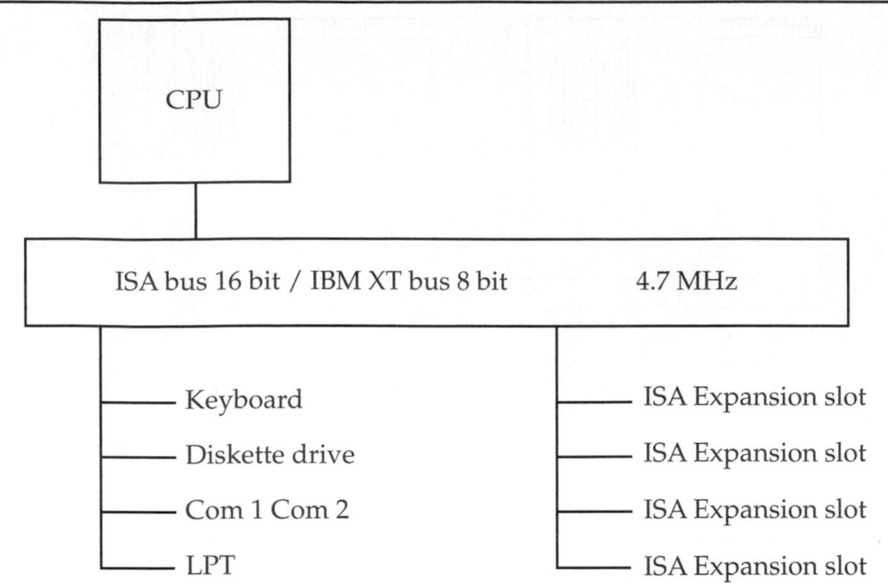

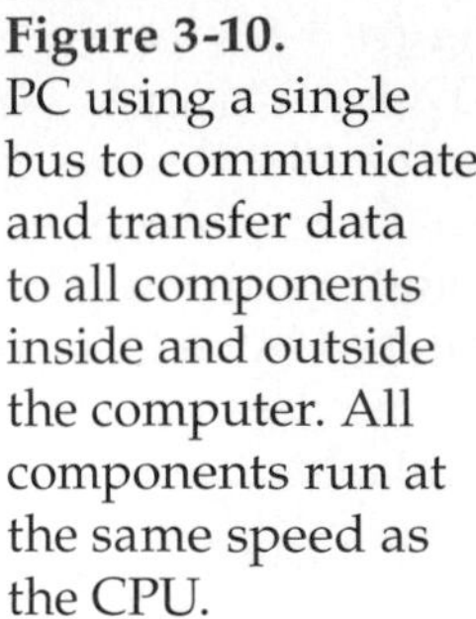
Figure 3-10. PC using a single bus to communicate and transfer data to all components inside and outside the computer. All components run at the same speed as the CPU.

As the PC evolved, the CPU processing speed increased and soon surpassed the speed capabilities of the bus structure. At high frequencies, a bus system can transmit electromagnetic energy just like a radio transmitter. The bus inside the CPU is very short. In fact, it is microscopic. This allows data to move at high speeds without generating electromagnetic interference. The bus outside the CPU is a great deal longer, and interference is a significant problem. This is the main reason for limited speed of data transmission on a bus system.

The electrical occurrence of *inductive reactance* limits the speed of electrical energy flow through a conductor. Inductive reactance has a choking effect on the flow of electrical energy. The amount of choking effect is directly related to the speed of data transmission (frequency) and the length of the conductor (bus wire length). The choking effect increases in direct proportion with the speed of data transmission and the length of the data path. Consequently, CPU transfer speeds in excess of 600 MHz are too fast for any expansion card currently on the market.

A PC is designed with several different bus speeds and chipsets that control data flow through the bus system. A current local bus is designed as a 64-bit bus. Common speeds for the local bus are 100 MHz, 133 MHz, 200 MHz, 400 MHz, 533 MHz, and 800 MHz. These speeds are too high to communicate to input/output (I/O) devices through the expansion card slots. Thus, the I/O bus, or expansion bus, became the second type of bus designed as part of the motherboard.

The two bus systems, local and I/O, are separated by computer chips that act as buffers for passing data at two or more different speeds. The chips allow the bus from the CPU and RAM to communicate with the slower I/O bus. Also, the data transmitted across the 64-bit width of the local bus is converted to the 16-bit width of a much smaller I/O bus used for an ISA adapter card. See **Figure 3-11** and **Figure 3-12** for two views of this bus system.

In Figure 3-11, note the relationship of the CPU, RAM, chip bridges, typical ports, external devices and the ISA, PCI, and USB bus architecture. Also, note that the CPU does not communicate directly with I/O devices. The CPU communicates with RAM, which in turn transmits the communication through

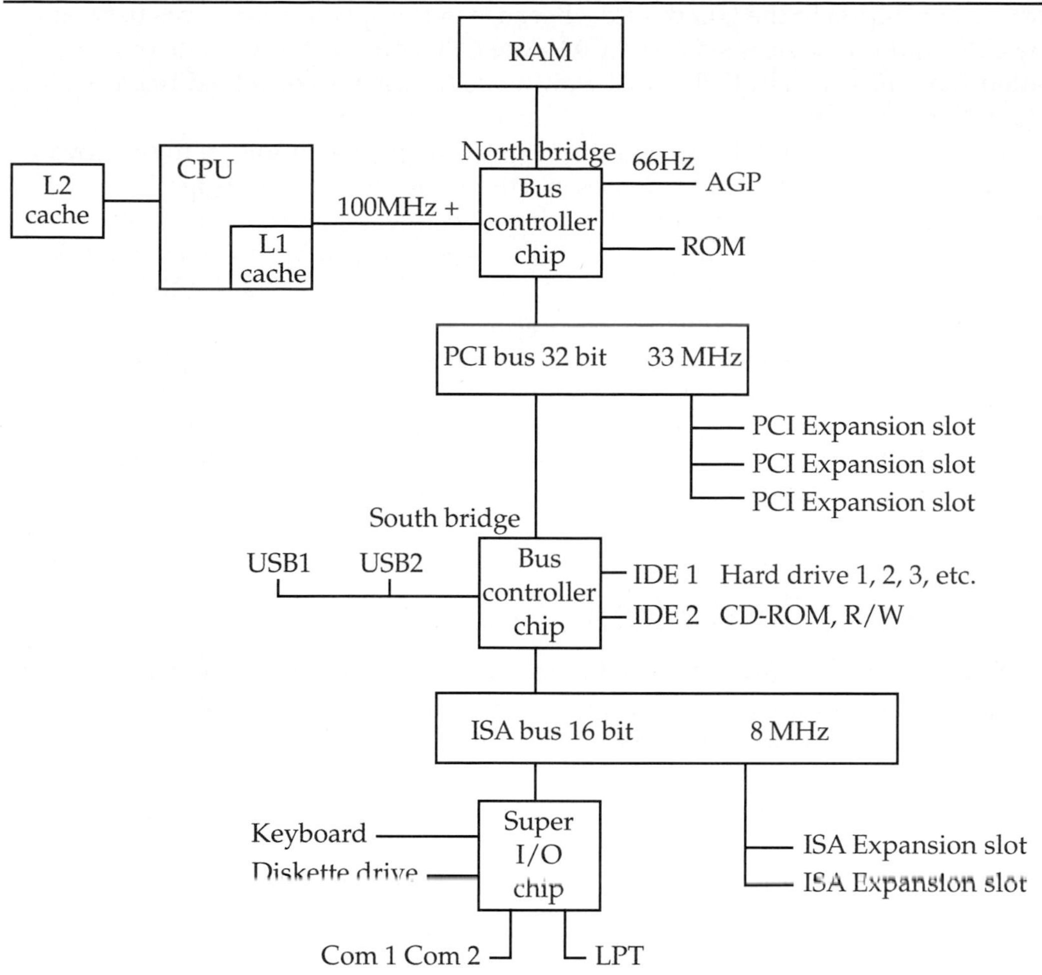

Figure 3-11.
Bus architecture with chipsets that provide communication between buses of different speeds.

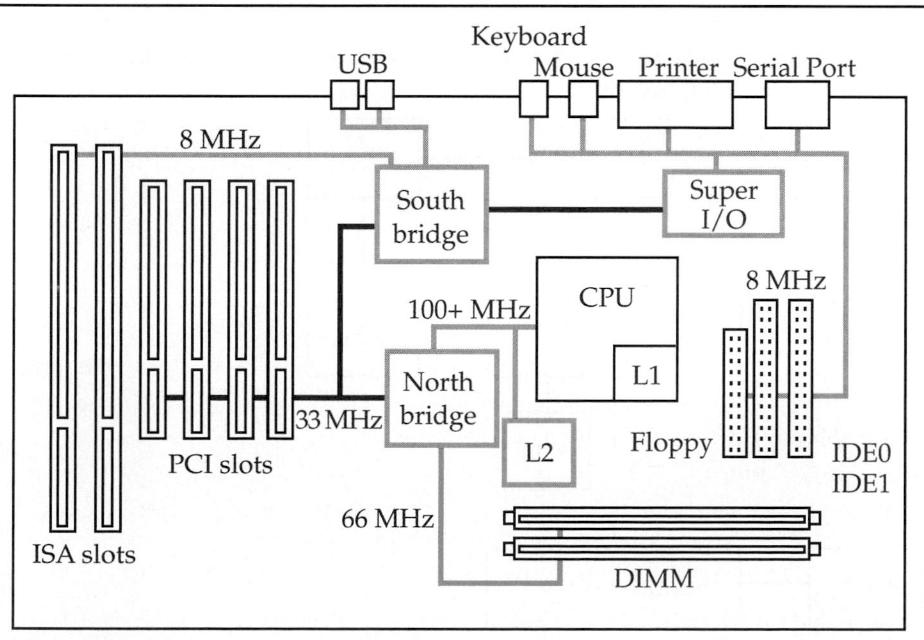

Figure 3-12.
The motherboard bus structure can be classified into two general types: local bus and I/O bus. The local bus is also referred to as the *system bus* or the *front side bus* and is the fastest bus on the motherboard. The I/O bus is slower than the local bus and is used to serve the ports and slots located on the motherboard. Notice how the chipset controls the speed of data from the CPU.

the bridge chip(s) to the I/O devices. Because of the speed differences between the CPU and the devices such as COM1, the CPU must go into a state of rest called the *wait state*. The CPU must wait while the data is converted from 16 bit to 64 bit and vice versa.

AMD invented and developed the HyperTransport technology to improve the performance of the front side bus, north bridge, and south bridge. The HyperTransport technology allows devices to connect directly to each other using bidirectional communications and to negotiate data transfer speed. It does not use a north bridge chip or an FSB. It connects directly to the south bridge, additional CPUs, or other devices. See **Figure 3-13.**

HyperTransport technology only works with processors that support the technology. For example, AMD processors work with HyperTransport bus system, but Intel processors do not. Intel is developing the Common System Interface (CSI) which is due to be released sometime in 2008. At the time of this writing, information about the CSI technology is very limited.

Expansion Card Slots

expansion card slots connectors that allow devices to be quickly and easily plugged into the bus system.

Expansion card slots provide a quick and easy method of connecting devices directly into the motherboard bus system. This allows the computer system to be modified or customized. There are several styles of expansion slots that have evolved with the computer motherboards. These expansion slots include ISA, EISA, MCA, VESA, PCI, AGP, AMR, CNR, USB, and IEEE 1394. *(USB and IEEE 1394 are not physically designed as a traditional slot. However, they are a type of hardware expansion architecture.)*

Figure 3-13.
The drawing is an example of the HyperTransport technology. Be aware that the exact design will vary by manufacturer. Notice how the memory and the CPU have a direct connection provided by the HyperTransport bus. The memory does not share a bus with other devices. The HyperTransport bus connects to a HyperTransport bridge, which replaced the traditional north bridge. The HyperTransport bridge is also referred to by many other names, even as *chipset*. The exact name used depends on the manufacturer.

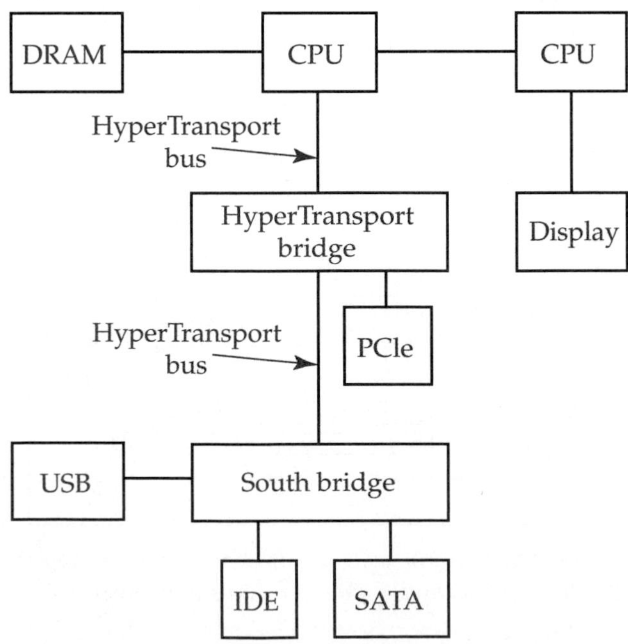

Expansion slots are designed to hold inserted cards called *adapters, expansion cards, interface cards,* and *daughter boards.* This allows the technician to modify the existing computer system for such features as network cards, which allow communications with a network. Television and radio adapter cards are available to allow tuning a favorite radio station or watching television programs on the PC.

ISA

The ***Industry Standard Architecture (ISA)*** is the oldest bus system found on PC motherboards, **Figure 3-14.** The ISA data bus is 16 bits wide, which means it communicates 16 bits of data simultaneously at a bus speed of 8.33 MHz. The original ISA bus structure of the IBM in 1981 was only 8 bits with a bus speed of 4.77 MHz.

Industry Standard Architecture (ISA) an I/O (expansion) bus system featuring a 16-bit data bus.

In addition to the 16 data lines, there are address lines on the bus that designate the location for sending the data. There are clock lines, which control the timing on the bus and voltage lines, which distribute positive, negative, and ground-level voltages for cards on the bus.

Today, the newest motherboards are equipped with PCI and PCIe slots; however, ISA is used for internal ports such as keyboard, mouse, diskette drive, and parallel ports. The ISA is the only bus system left on PC motherboards to assure backward compatibility.

MCA

Micro Channel Architecture (MCA) an I/O (expansion) bus system featuring a 32-bit data bus. MCA and ISA cards and slots are not physically compatible.

The first major revolution in bus design came with the development of ***Micro Channel Architecture (MCA)*** by IBM. MCA has a 32-bit data width and a higher data transfer speed than ISA. See **Figure 3-15.**

The MCA bus was also considered an intelligent bus system because it could automatically assign interrupt requests (IRQs) without human intervention. This was a remarkable feat at the time because most adapter devices required the

Figure 3-14.
Typical 8-bit and 16-bit ISA adapter card edges.

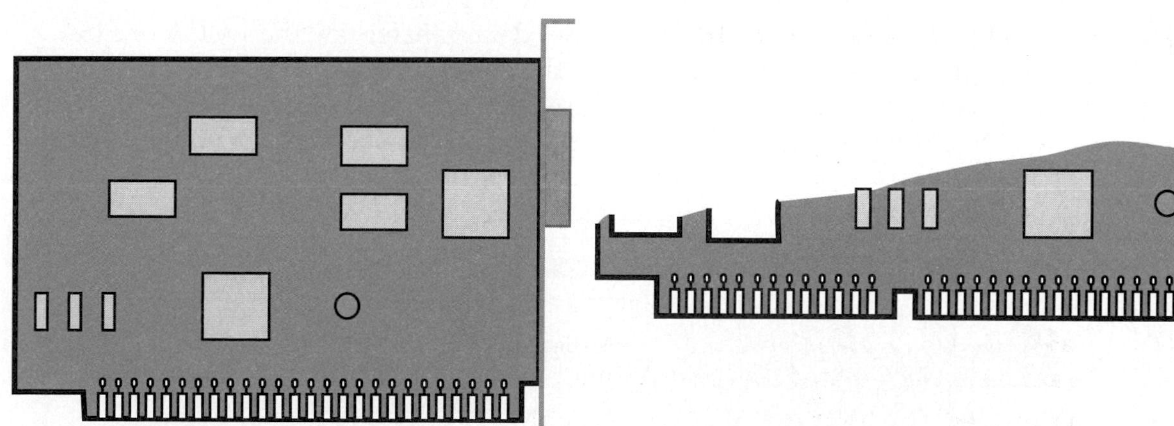

Typical 8-bit ISA Expansion Card
This card uses only 8 parallel lines for transmitting data. Note that 8-bit ISA boards can fit into slots designed for 16-bit ISA cards.
Typical 16-bit ISA Expansion Card
It has 18 more connectors than the ISA card. It transmits data over 16 data lines providing twice the data lines as 8-bit ISA.

Figure 3-15.
The MCA expansion card features Plug and Play capabilities.

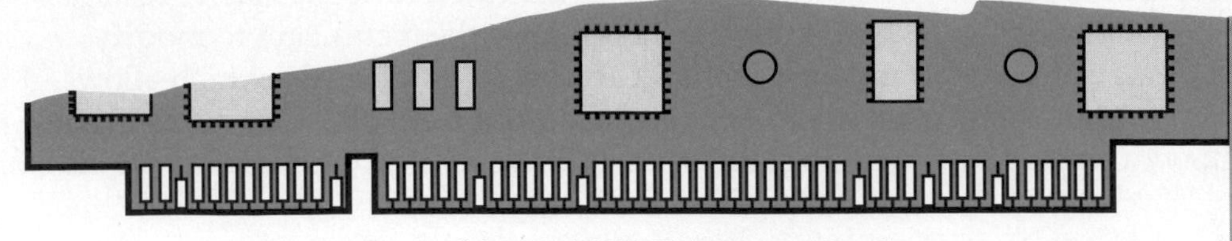

setting of switches or jumpers to identify the IRQ. One of the most significant features of the MCA bus was that it was patented by IBM and could be used by other PC manufacturers only if they paid royalties. In response to the proprietary MCA bus system came EISA.

Extended Industry Standard Architecture (EISA) an I/O (expansion) bus with a 32-bit data bus. Designed in response to IBM's MCA bus system. EISA buses are backward compatible with ISA cards. This means that an ISA card can fit and function in an EISA expansion slot.

EISA

Extended Industry Standard Architecture (EISA) was developed jointly by Compaq, AST Research, Epson, Hewlett-Packard, NEC, Olivetti, Tandy, Wyse, and Zenith Data Systems in response to the development of IBM's MCA bus system. These companies are often referred to as the "gang of nine" in the history of PC development. In contrast to MCA, EISA was developed to be royalty-free. The EISA bus is 32 bits wide with a bus speed of 20 MHz, **Figure 3-16.**

ISA and MCA are not physically compatible. However, ISA and EISA are considered physically compatible. An ISA adapter card can fit into an EISA bus slot. MCA bus slots require an adapter card physically designed according to the MCA standard.

Video Electronics Standards Association (VESA) local bus a bus system that could handle a higher data transfer rate than MCA or EISA. The VL-Bus was developed by a consortium of video adapter and monitor manufacturers.

VESA Local Bus

The ***Video Electronics Standards Association (VESA) local bus*** (often called the *VL-Bus*) was developed by a consortium of video adapter and monitor manufacturers. A consortium is an association of competitors that combine their efforts to organize something they could not do individually. In this case, the group developed a standard video system for PCs.

The VESA bus could handle a higher data transfer rate than MCA or EISA. It was placed close to the processor on the motherboard, and it transferred data at the same rate as the CPU. As CPU speeds soon increased, the VESA bus soon became obsolete. The VESA design could not keep pace with the higher CPU speeds and was soon replaced by PCI. See **Figure 3-17.**

Figure 3-16.
The EISA uses 97 connectors designed in two levels. It can transmit 32 bits of data and supports Plug and Play like the MCA card.

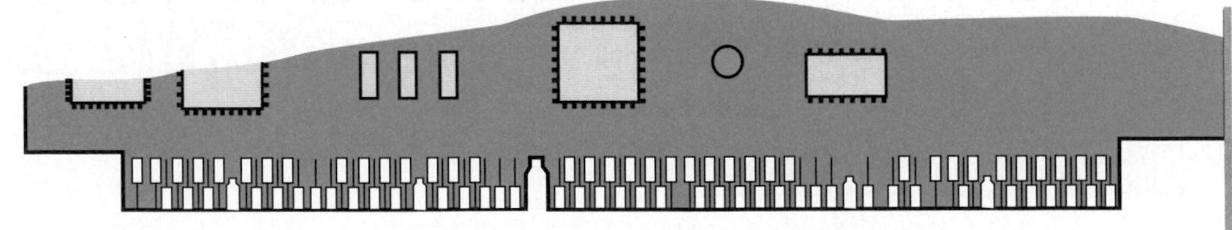

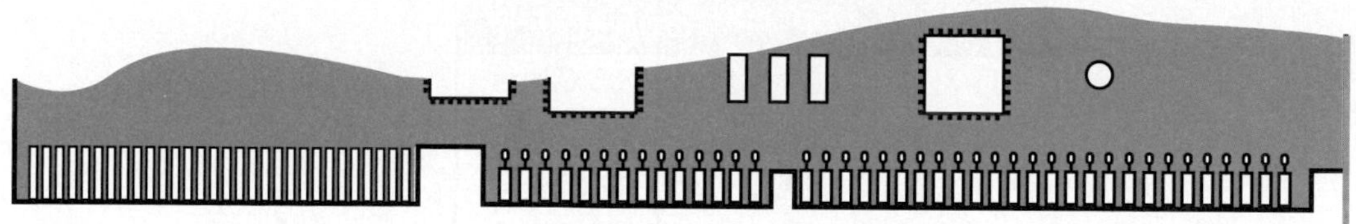

Typical 32-bit VESA Expansion Card

Figure 3-17. The VESA expansion card was designed for video adapters. It was based on the ISA standard, and the slot is compatible to ISA cards. The additional portion of the card consists of 36 more pairs of contacts to carry local bus data.

PCI

Peripheral Components Interface (PCI) was first introduced in the early 1990s and was the best choice for general purpose expansion adapters, **Figure 3-18.** PCI has a 32-bit data width that transfers data at a rate of 132 MBps. The original PCI adapter had a frequency of 33 MHz which was later increased to 66 MHz with the PCI 2.0 standard. Even this was a vast improvement over 8.33 MHz ISA.

One of the main improvements of PCI over earlier ISA technology is that PCI is flexible and can communicate with bus designs with lower frequencies, such as ISA, through the use of chipsets mounted on the motherboard. (There will be more about chipsets later in this chapter.)

PCI incorporates a chipset with a buffer, which can be used as a temporary data storage area. The buffer makes it possible to communicate with the motherboard bus of slower technology by providing a place to temporarily store data as data is transferred to the slower bus.

Network servers were the first to use PCI. PCI has dominated the motherboard adapter design for over ten years. However, demands for even greater data transfer rates spurred faster versions of PCI, such as PCI-X and PCIe.

Peripheral Components Interface (PCI) a bus system featuring a 32-bit data bus that provides a high-speed bus structure needed for faster CPUs.

PCI-X

PCI Extended (PCI-X) was designed as a replacement for PCI. It has a 64-bit data width and is capable of operating at a higher frequency (speed) than PCI. It is fully downward compatible with PCI. You can install a PCI or PCI-X in the same expansion slot. They use the same pin assignments and same voltages. The only real difference is the higher frequency capability of PCI-X, which causes high data transfer rates. For example, the standard frequency of PCI-X 1.0 is 133 MHz. PCI-X 2.0 introduced the double data rate (DDR), which operates at 266 MHz, and quad data rate (QDR) technologies, which operates at 533 MHz. These speeds are high enough to support data transfers to gigabit Ethernet network cards as the following table shows.

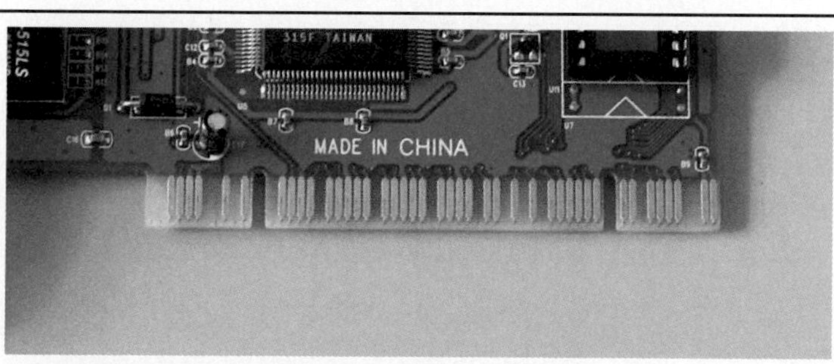

Typical PCI Expansion Card

Figure 3-18. The edge connector of a 32-bit PCI expansion card. PCI cards are not compatible with other types of expansion slots.

Bus Type	Speed	Capacity
PCI-X 1.0	133 MHz	8.5 Gbps
PCI-X 2.0	266 MHz	17 Gbps
PCI-X 2.0	533 MHz	34 Gbps

PCI-X was not widely accepted in desktop models of computers. Rather, it was limited to network servers or very high-end desktop models. PCI-X was quickly replaced by the PCI Express standard.

PCI Express

PCI Express has two common acronyms: PCIe and PCI-E. It is often confused with PCI-X. PCI Express was introduced in 2004 as an expansion adapter technology designed to replace earlier versions of adapters such as PCI, PCI-X, and AGP. See **Figure 3-19.**

While the original PCI adapter is based on parallel data transfer, PCIe uses serial data transfer. Common sense tells a person that data transferred in parallel would move much more data than a serial connection. But, when it comes to electronics, you must understand electronic principles to see the advantage of serial data transfer over parallel.

At lower frequencies, parallel data transfer is better than serial, but at high speeds, serial data transfer is better than parallel. As the speed of computers have increased over the years, serial has become the preferred method of data transfer. This is because at high frequencies there are electrical limitations imposed by the parallel data bus design. Basically, there are two main circuit construction principles that must be followed to achieve high data rates:

✔ All circuit conductors need to be the same length.

✔ All conductors need to be bundled together, or in close proximity, to reduce the effects of inductive reactance.

The simple PCIe design meets both design principles and results in higher data rates. As you will see in the following sections, all PCIe conductors are the same length and are in close proximity.

Conductor length

When conductors have the same length, data transferred across the bus system arrive at their destination at the same time. Parallel bus design involves right angle turns, which cause the length of the outside conductor to be many

Typical PCIe Expansion Card

Figure 3-19. Edge connector of a PCIe expansion card. PCIe uses serial data transfer and is designed to replace earlier versions of adapters such as PCI, PCI-X, and AGP.

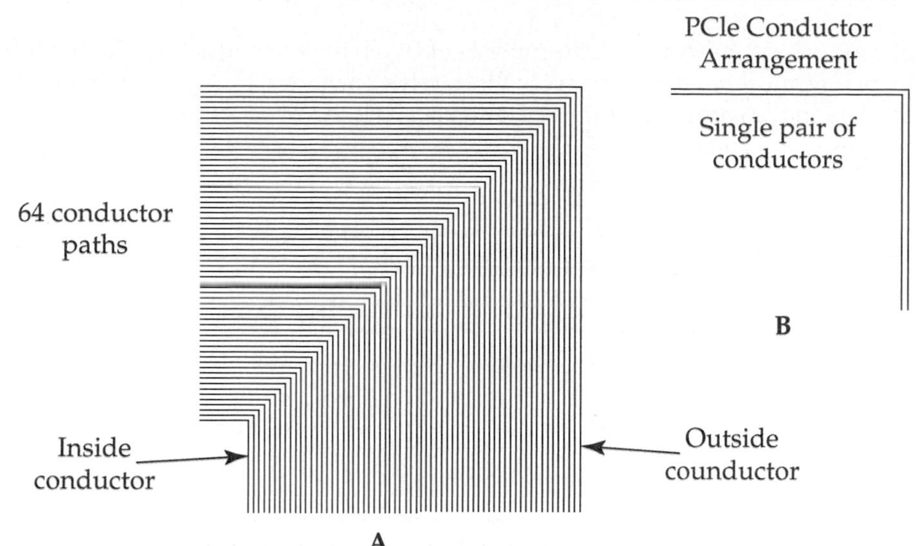

Figure 3-20.
PCIe conductor pairs in comparison to a 32-conductor path and a 64-conductor path. Notice the difference in total length of the outside conductors compared to the inside conductors. The PCIe conductor pairs closely match conductor lengths and are thus able to achieve a higher data rate.

times longer than the inside conductor, **Figure 3-20.** Notice how the outside conductor length in Figure 13-20A is drastically longer in comparison to the inside conductor. This means that if data were sent in parallel over the conductors, the data would arrive at the ends of the conductors at different times. However, when conductors are run in pairs, like in Figure 3-20B, the overall length is more closely matched and a higher data rate can be achieved.

Conductor proximity

The term *inductive reactance* is an electronics term that basically describes a resistance to electron flow through a conductor. All conductors have a degree of inductive reactance when functioning as an electrical path. Inductive reactance reduces the ability of the conductor to achieve high data rates. When the conductors are bundled together, inductive reactance is reduced to a minimum or nearly canceled, thus allowing for higher data rates than a flat ribbon data cable.

Since PCIe uses a pair of conductors in close proximity to each other, most of the effect of inductive reactance is canceled, thus allowing for high data rates. This same principle of conductor pairs is used for FireWire, USB, and SATA cables. FireWire, USB, and SATA cables have all but replaced original flat ribbon data cable designs. **Figure 3-21** compares the design of PCIe ×1 conductors to traditional parallel conductors.

PCIe is designed from serial links referred to as *lanes*. The simplest PCIe identified as PCIe ×1 consists of a single lane. A single lane consists of two pairs of conductors, or four conductors total. One conductor of each pair is used to send data, and the other conductor of each pair is used to receive data. PCIe is bi-directional, which means it can send and receive data at the same time.

The number of lanes used for PCIe is represented by the symbol "×" followed by a number. The symbol "×" represents the word *by*. For example, PCIe ×16 means "PCIe by 16" and represents a PCIe adapter with 16 lanes, or pairs of conductors. There is a PCIe ×32 specification, but it has not been applied to desktop motherboard designs at the time of this writing.

Figure 3-21.
Comparison of PCIe and parallel conductors. A—A PCIe lane consists of two pairs of conductors. Each pair forms a single communication pair. The pairs cancel most of the effect of inductive reactance, thus allowing a high data rate. B—Parallel conductors carry data in the same direction and do not cancel the effect of inductive reactance. This results in lower overall data rates when compared to PCIe.

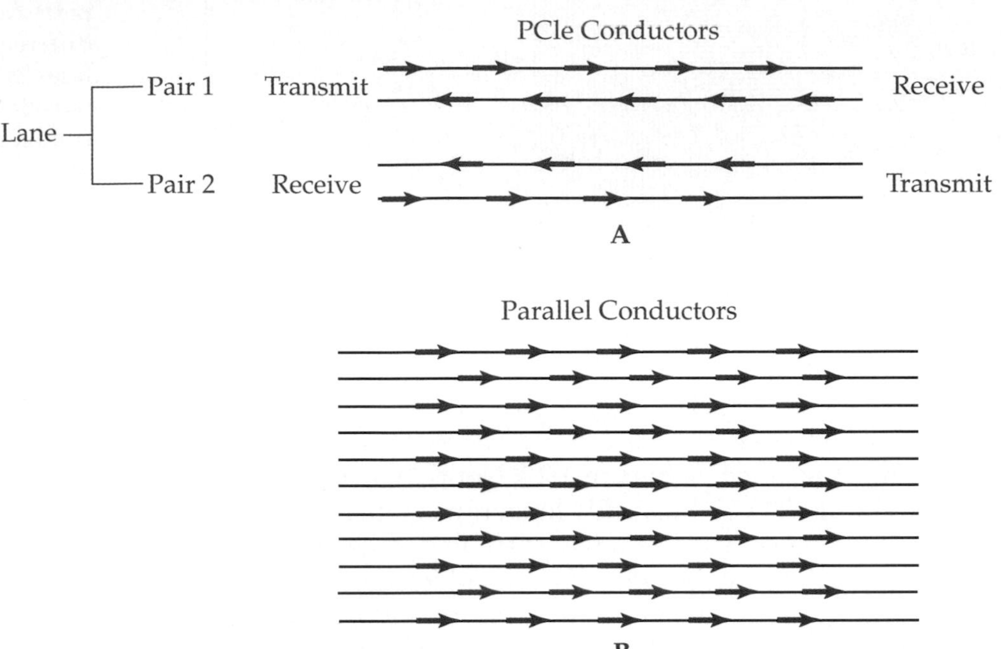

PCIe specifications

The original PCIe specification, PCIe 1.1, typically runs at 2.5 GHz and transfers data at a rate of 250 Mbps per lane. In January of 2007, the PCI Express 2.0 specification was released with an increase that doubled the throughput of data. The PCIe 2.0 specification raised the bandwidth from 2.5 GHz to 5.0 GHz and raised the data rate from 250 Mbps to 500 Mbps. PCIe is expected to reach data rates of 10 GHz in the near future.

A variety of PCIe and PCI expansion slots on a motherboard are shown in **Figure 3-22.** PCIe provides better video performance than AGP and can be used for more devices than video cards. AGP is used only for video cards.

PCIe can achieve data throughput of 80 Gbps or 6.4 GBps. Parallel circuits are most often expressed in bytes (B) and serial is expressed in bits (b). This can add to the confusion when comparing the various bus technologies. Also, consider the bus data width. Early PCI and PCI-X used 32-bit and 64-bit data bus widths. The bus width for PCIe is two, based on two pairs of conductors per lane. The chart in **Figure 3-23** compares the data speed of PCI, PCI–X, and PCIe standards. Notice that there is a tremendous performance difference between PCIe and earlier adapter technologies such as PCI.

Figure 3-22.
This motherboard has a variety of PCIe expansion slots. Notice how they compare with one another and with the standard PCI expansion slots.

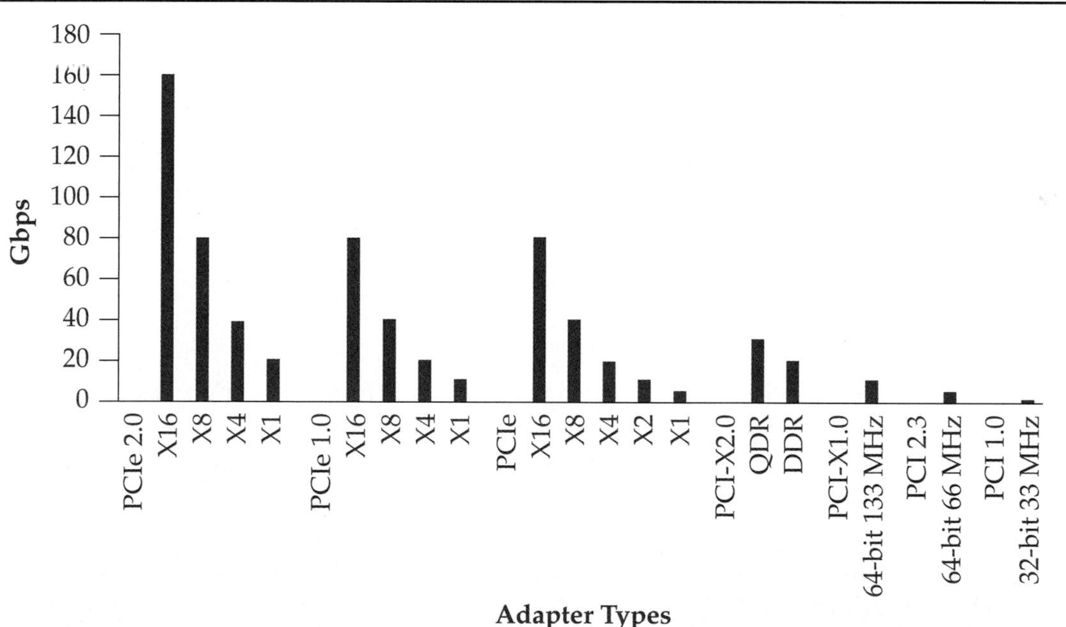

Figure 3-23.
PCI, PCIe, and PCI-X data rate comparison.

A+ Note:

The CompTIA A+ certification exams may contain several questions based on adapter speeds. You should memorize the maximum values of PCIe 1.1 and 2.0, as well as PCI-X 1.0 and 2.0.

PCIe cards are somewhat compatible. For example, a PCIe ×1 can be inserted into a PCIe ×4 slot and will perform without a problem. You cannot however insert a PCIe ×4 into a PCIe ×1 slot because it is physically impossible. To learn the latest up-to-date information about PCIe, visit the PCI SIG (Special Interest Group) Web site at www.pcisig.com/home.

Parallel Ports

Parallel port technology has changed quite a bit since it was first introduced as a high-speed data transfer port. It was considered high speed as compared to the existing serial port of that time. The parallel port was capable of transferring data through several lines at the same time, thus transferring data in bytes. Transferring data in bytes was eight times faster than serial data transfers.

Enhanced Parallel Port (EPP) a parallel port standard that allows a throughput as high as 2 Mbps. The EPP is also referred to as the IEEE-1284 standard.

Extended Capabilities Port (ECP) a parallel port standard that provides for bidirectional communication and has extended capabilities to support multiple devices.

The original parallel port standard was for a unidirectional port. The port was designed to send data to the printer. The port was used for output only. Later, the bi-directional port was designed, which allowed the parallel port not only to be used for output but also to be used for input into the computer system.

The original parallel port data transfer rate was 50 kbps, which was sufficient for dot matrix printers. The dot matrix was designed for alphanumeric character printing and low-resolution graphics. When laser printers came on the market, a standard with a higher data throughput was required. The laser printer introduced a higher quality printed image for both alphanumeric characters and graphic images. The ***Enhanced Parallel Port (EPP)*** standard met the requirements. The EPP could produce a throughput as high as 2 Mbps. The EPP was also referred to as the IEEE-1284 standard.

The next parallel printer port was the ***Extended Capabilities Port (ECP).*** The throughput was still limited to 2 Mbps, but the port's capabilities were extended, as the name implies. The capabilities were extended to support multiple devices. Common parallel port devices are printers, scanners, and faxes. The throughput of each parallel port device ranges from approximately 500 kbps to 2 Mbps. The transfer of data is bidirectional and automatically adjusts throughput to match the slowest device while exchanging data.

Universal Serial Bus (USB) a bus system deigned to replace the function of expansion slots with a data transfer rate as high as 480 Mbps. The USB is accessed by plugging a USB device into the bus at a port opening in the case. Additional devices (up to 127) can be connected to the bus in a daisy-chain configuration.

USB

Universal Serial Bus (USB) is designed to replace the existing variety of ports and expansion slots. The USB 2.0 can achieve a data transfer rate as high as 480 Mbps. USB technology conserves the use of IRQ assignments because it only requires the use of one IRQ. For example, when two or more devices are connected to a USB port, they automatically share the same IRQ address without creating a conflict. Each device takes turns communicating through the USB port. For USB to work properly, an operating system and a recently developed chipset, such as Intel's 440LX, must be used.

The USB is designed as a port rather than a traditional slot. It is accessed by plugging a USB device into the bus at a port opening in the case. See **Figure 3-24.** Devices are simply daisy chained when using USB cables and connectors. There is no need to open the computer case. Look at **Figure 3-25.** In the picture, you see two variations of the USB connector. The one on the left is a USB type A connector, and the one on the right is a USB type B connector.

Figure 3-24.
USB devices can be plugged into ports in a PC's case.

Figure 3-25.
Two variations of the USB connector: type A and type B.

The original USB (USB 1.1) supports 1.5 Mbps and 12 Mbps, and USB 2.0 supports 480 Mbps. The USB port connects to many different types of input and output peripherals and is capable of supporting up to 127 devices. The cable consists of four wires or conductors—two data lines (D+ and D–), a voltage bus (Vbus), and a ground (GND). See **Figure 3-26.**

The combination of the Vbus and GND carry power to each device connected to the USB port. Since the actual amount of electrical power carried on the electrical power lines is low, devices requiring additional power use their own electrical power supply.

Figure 3-26.
USB cable design.

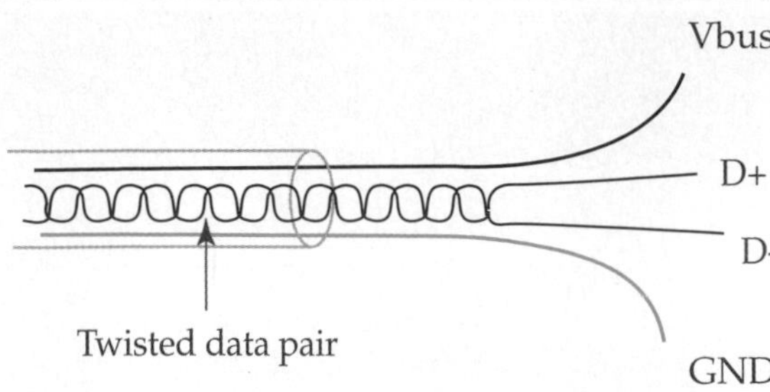

The USB carries commands and data on the two twisted data lines. The twist in the data pair is designed to support high-speed data transfers. The twist is engineered for maximum throughput. Placing a twist in cable pairs reduces the amount of inductive reactance and helps achieve the high data rates. This technique is also incorporated in some other computer high data-rate cables like newer hard disk drive cables.

The USB is designed for Plug and Play support. Devices connected to the port are automatically detected, and communication between the computer system and the device begins. The various equipment that connect to the USB port are assigned an address for identification purposes. Data is moved along the data lines as packets of information. This is similar to the way networks communicate. The topic of data packets is covered in detail in Chapter 16—Introduction to Networking.

FireWire (IEEE 1394) a bus system that provides a high rate of data transfer (speeds of 400 Mbps). A single IEEE 1394 port can serve up to 63 external devices in daisy-chain fashion.

IEEE 1394 (FireWire)

Specification ***IEEE 1394*** was first introduced by Apple computer systems and called by the trade name ***FireWire,*** **Figure 3-27.** Other manufacturers call their similar systems names such as I-link and Lynx. FireWire technology provides a high rate of data transfer (400 Mbps) needed for devices such as video cameras. A single IEEE 1394 port can serve up to 63 external devices in daisy-chain fashion.

Figure 3-27.
IEEE 1394 (FireWire) ports.

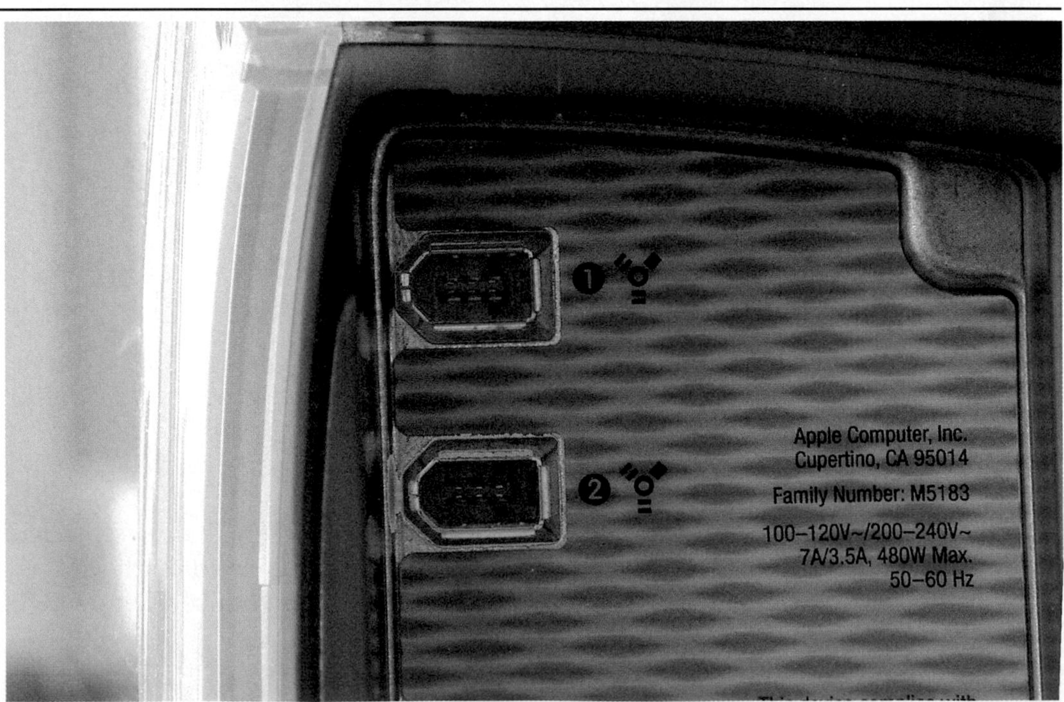

With the introduction of USB and 1394, manufacturers have been reducing the number of slots available on the motherboard. The use of USB and FireWire can eliminate the need for expansion slots as well as parallel and serial ports. USB and FireWire can be used to connect any device that presently uses motherboard adapter slot technology.

AGP

The ***Accelerated Graphics Port (AGP),*** **Figure 3-28,** was designed exclusively for the video card, especially 3-D graphic support. There is usually only one slot of this type on any motherboard. The slot is designed to fit as close as possible to the CPU and RAM to allow for high data transfer rates. The bandwidth for transferring data to and from the AGP can be significantly faster than PCI. AGP supports 32-bit data transfers at speeds of 254.3 MBps, 508.6 MBps, 1.017 GBps, and 2.034 GBps, while PCI 2.1 supports 64-bit transfers with a maximum throughput of 508.6 MBps. The actual rates vary according to PC hardware and chipsets. Chipsets are covered later in this chapter.

Accelerated Graphics Port (AGP) a bus designed exclusively for the video card. It supports data transfer of 32 bits at 254.3 MBps, 508.6 MBps, 1.017 GBps, and 2.034 GBps.

AGP offered excellent support for graphics programs until the introduction of PCIe. The most powerful feature of AGP is DIME (direct memory execution). DIME is the direct access to main memory used strictly to support the video. This means the video card can use large portions of RAM rather than only the memory modules located on the video card.

AMR, ACR, and CNR

There are many devices that are commonly used in a standard desktop computer system. By combining the functions of several separate technologies into a single unit, a more economical device can be produced. Manufacturers can combine the functions of Audio, USB, modem, DSL, Network connection (Ethernet), wireless access technologies, and more. Three special motherboard slot specifications that meet this need are Audio Modem Riser (AMR), Advanced Communications Riser (ACR), and Communications Network Riser (CNR). The combined technologies are incorporated into one riser board, which is inserted into a slot on the motherboard. See **Figure 3-29.**

CNR is a royalty free standard developed by Intel Corporation. ACR is an organization that developed the ACR standard and is supported by 3COM, AMD, Lucent Technologies, VIA Technologies, Motorola, Texas Instruments, ACER, PCTEL, and others.

The AMR technology was released first and was closely followed by CNR. CNR is the more popular choice by computer hardware manufactures because it is royalty free and uses the same space as the PCI slot. With CNR sharing a PCI slot on the motherboard, the manufacturer does not need to make a major design change in the motherboard structure and circuitry the way they would for an AMR slot. AMR was later replaced by ACR. ACR is backward compatible with AMR.

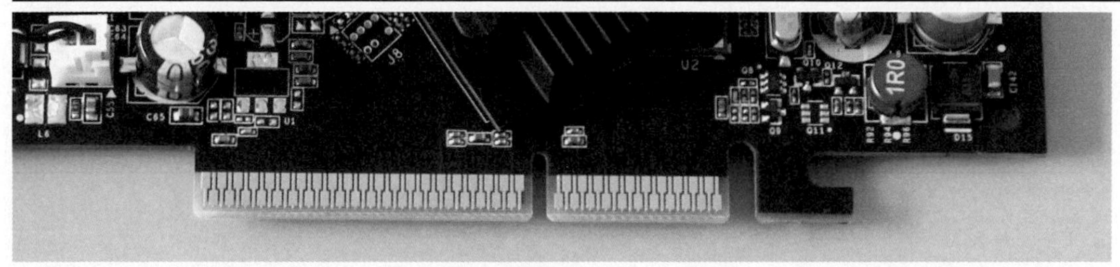

Figure 3-28. The edge connector of a 32-bit AGP expansion card.

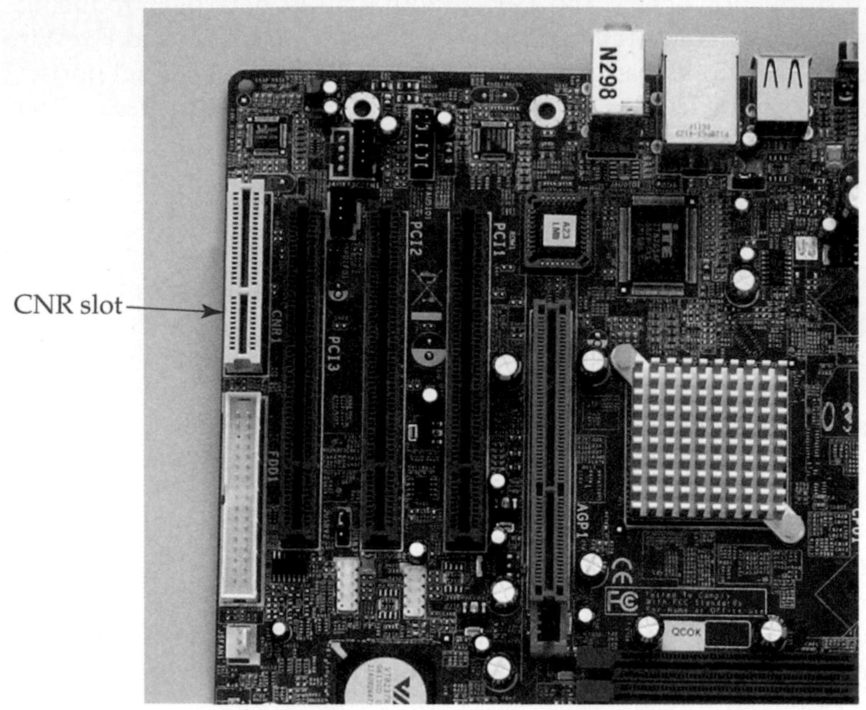

Figure 3-29. Notice that the CNR slot is located at the edge of the motherboard.

The Intel CNR board can support on a single card up to four different devices out of a possible seven types of devices. The slot location is typically located at the edge of the motherboard, far away from components that could produce interference. The riser cards incorporate audio devices whose data can be corrupted by stray electromagnetic interference generated by other high-speed components.

Riser board technology is favorable for development of low cost motherboard manufacturing, but there are two problems. First, if one or more of the devices incorporated into the riser board goes bad, the entire board will need to be replaced at a higher cost than if replacing a single item such as a modem card. Second, the cost of a replacement board is higher because you need to go through the original manufacturer.

System Resources

System resources are resources that must be assigned and made available for devices such as printers, modems, disk drives, a mouse, or a sound card. The major system resources to consider are the I/O port address, memory addresses, IRQ, and DMA settings. System resource assignments can be viewed under Device Manager in Windows.

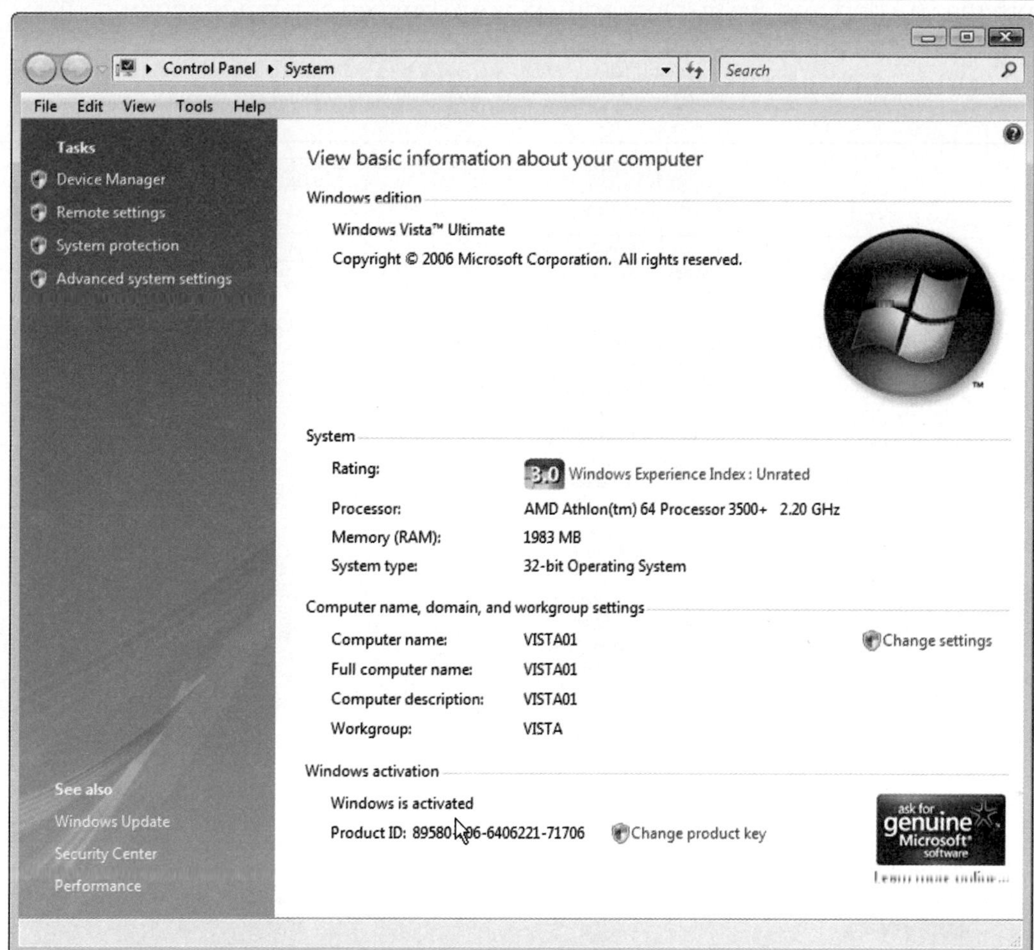

Figure 3-30.
The **System** dialog box.

To see the system resources assigned to a Windows Vista computer, right-click the **Computer** icon on the desktop. The right-click brings up a shortcut menu. Select the **Properties** option. The **System** dialog box will display, **Figure 3-30.** Choose the **Device Manager** option. You should see a screen similar to the one in **Figure 3-31.**

On a Windows XP computer, right-click the **My Computer** icon on the desktop. The right-click brings up a shortcut menu. Select the **Properties** option. The **System Properties** dialog box will display. Choose the **Hardware** tab, and then click the **Device Manager** button.

The **Device Manager** dialog box allows you to view properties of all hardware devices connected to the motherboard. In addition, the **Device Manager** dialog box allows you to change the system resource assignments.

memory address range
an assigned section of memory used as a temporary storage area for data before it is transferred.

I/O port address
a memory address expressed in hexadecimal notation, which is used to identify a computer device such as a video card.

I/O Port and Memory Address Range

Each device has a unique memory address range. Components such as DVD drives, hard drives, and monitors require part of the computer system's memory to be used for temporary data storage.

A ***memory address range*** is an assigned section of memory used as a temporary storage area for data before it is transferred. An ***I/O port address*** is assigned to a device for identification. A device must be identified for communication purposes.

Both the I/O port and the memory address are expressed as a range and in hexadecimal notation such as 03B0–03BB. Some devices have an I/O port address and a name as well, such as COM1 or LPT1, **Figure 3-32.**

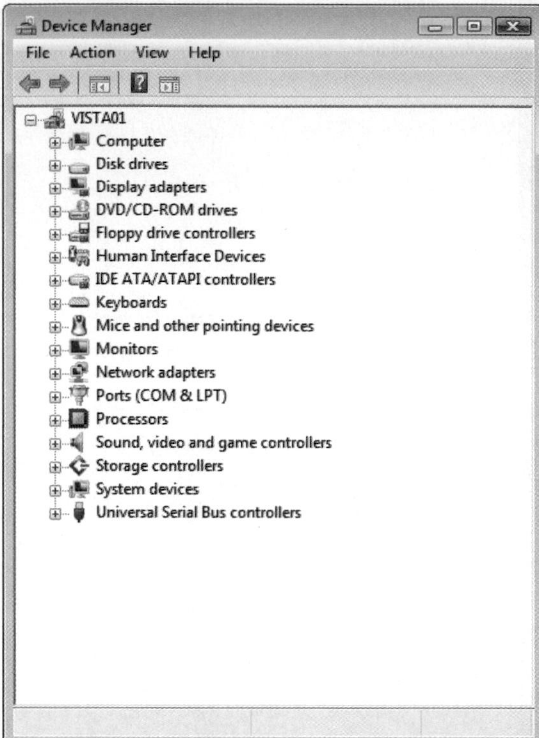

Figure 3-31. Device Manager shows a list of the devices connected to the PC.

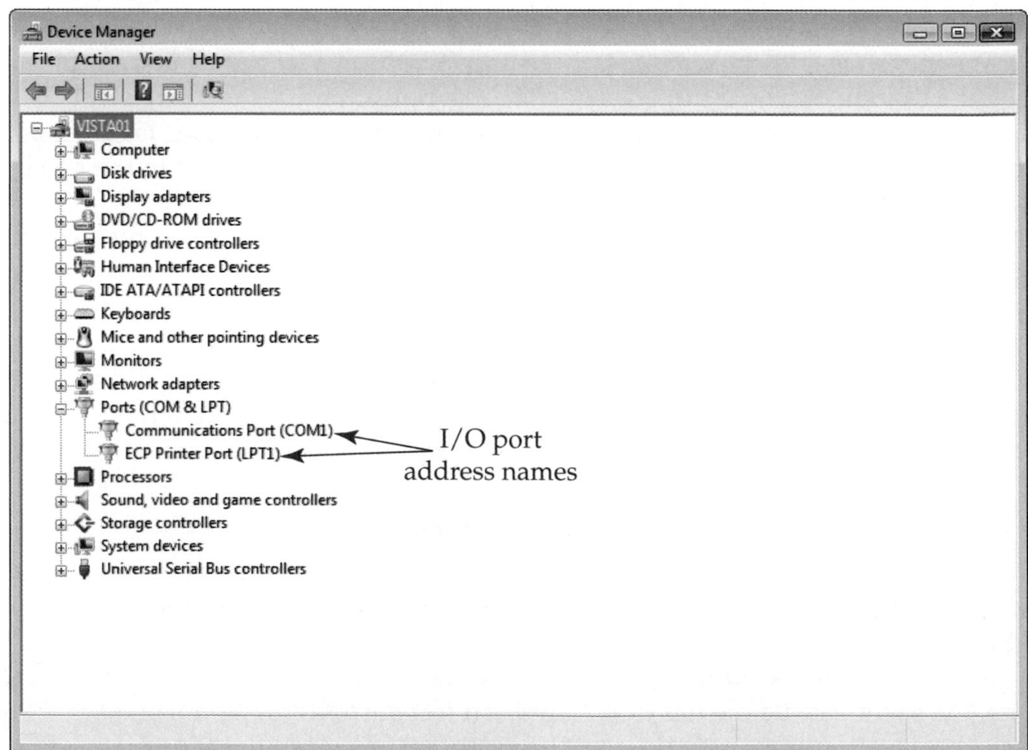

Figure 3-32. I/O port addresses expressed as a name.

A memory address is often mistaken for an I/O port address because a memory address also uses hexadecimal numbers for their assignments. Look at the resources assigned to a video graphics card in **Figure 3-33.** The memory address range is the area used to store large amounts of video information, and the I/O port is used to control communications between the video card and the CPU. For example, if a command is issued on the bus for I/O port address number 03B0, then the device that is assigned port number 03B0 accepts the command. If a large amount of video information is sent to the video card, the information is temporarily stored in the memory location range of 000B0000–000BFFFF.

Not all hardware devices have an assigned memory range, but most do have an assigned I/O port address range.

IRQ Settings

Devices connected to a computer motherboard need the attention of the CPU. The only way to share the attention of the CPU with the individual devices is through an orderly system of IRQ settings. ***IRQ*** is an acronym for interrupt request. An IRQ literally interrupts the processes taking place in the CPU to give attention to some device such as a keyboard. There are also software interrupts in addition to hardware interrupts. Software interrupts are programmed into the software and call for the CPU's attention. Hardware interrupts are physically wired to the computer bus.

IRQ
an acronym for "interrupt request." An IRQ is a signal that interrupts the processes taking place in the CPU and requests that the processor pay attention to a specific device.

The table listed in **Figure 3-34** shows a listing of typical hardware IRQ assignments. Early PC designs used only eight IRQs numbered 0 through 7. Today 16 IRQ settings are the standard, numbered 0 through 15. A number of IRQ settings, such as the system timer, keyboard, COM1, LPT, primary IDE, and secondary IDE, are standard.

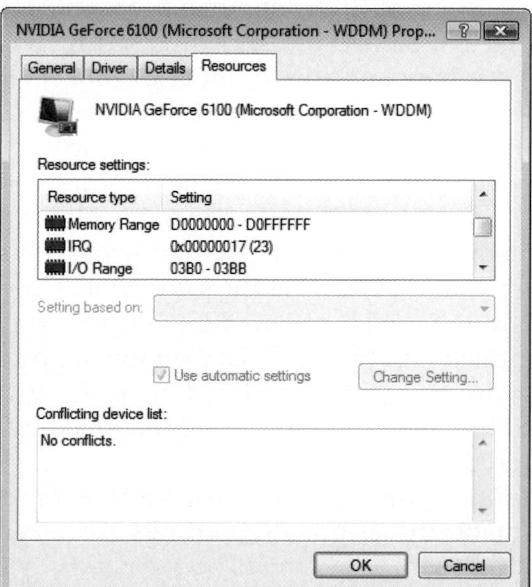

Figure 3-33. Resources assigned to a video graphics card.

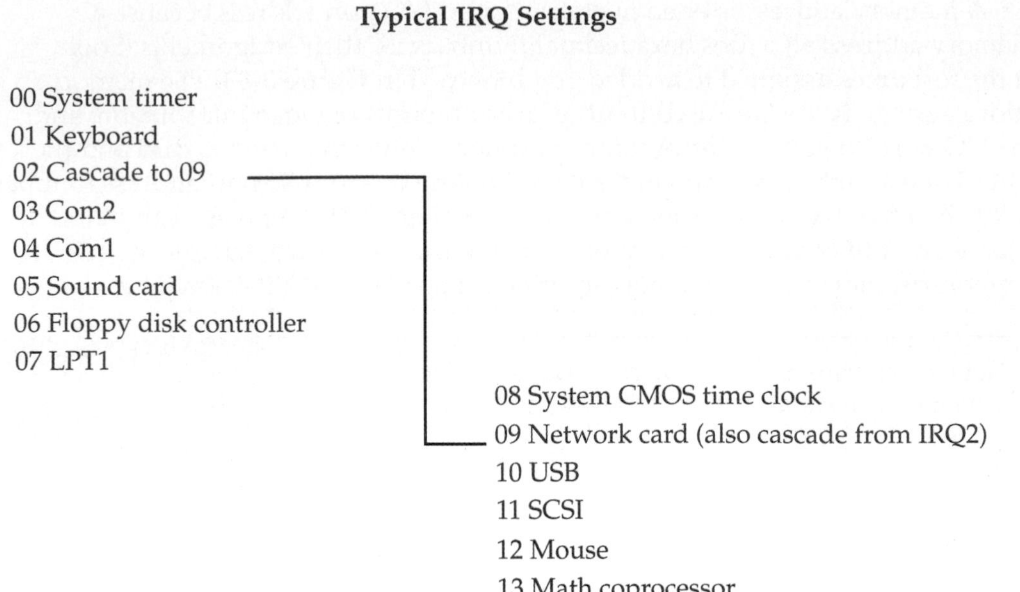

Typical IRQ Settings
00 System timer
01 Keyboard
02 Cascade to 09
03 Com2
04 Com1
05 Sound card
06 Floppy disk controller
07 LPT1
08 System CMOS time clock
09 Network card (also cascade from IRQ2)
10 USB
11 SCSI
12 Mouse
13 Math coprocessor
14 Primary IDE
15 Secondary IDE

Figure 3-34. Table of IRQ settings cascading from IRQ 2 to IRQ 9. Note that this is a typical set of IRQ assignments. They will not match all computers. Many IRQs will have more than one device assigned to them, especially controller chips.

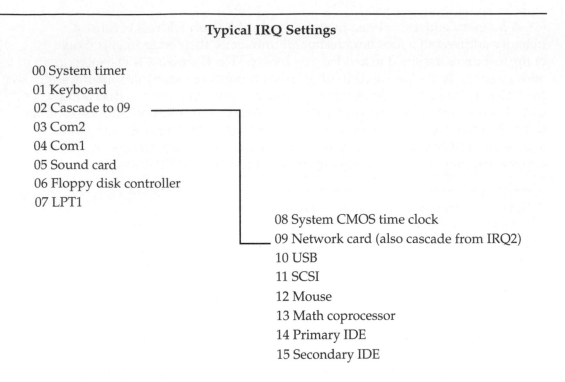

When the IRQ design evolved from 8 to 16 IRQs, it was created by cascading IRQ 2 to IRQ 9. This means that IRQ 2 should never be assigned to any device. The assignment for IRQ 2 is communicating with IRQ 9.

IRQs are also assigned priorities. A lower number for an IRQ means a higher priority. Look at the system timer on the chart. It is assigned to IRQ 0. This gives it the highest priority, as it should be. The system timer is responsible for the timing of all devices including the CPU.

Another important aspect of IRQ assignments are IRQ conflicts that arise when two or more devices assigned the same IRQ setting try to access the CPU at the same time. When this happens, the conflicting request for attention can cause some strange occurrences. Usually only one of the two devices will have access to the CPU, leaving the other the appearance of being dead.

Two IRQ assignments *can* be shared if the devices are not going to be used at the same time. An example of two such devices would be a scanner and a camera. A digital camera can share an IRQ assignment with a scanner because it is highly unlikely both would be used at the same time. However, if the mouse and a floppy drive were assigned the same IRQ setting, a problem would arise. If the mouse was identified first by the CPU, then the floppy drive would appear disabled. If the floppy drive was identified first by the CPU, the mouse would appear to be disabled. Today many chipsets are identified by IRQs and are shared with other chipsets and devices.

Plug and Play (PnP) remedies most of the assignment problems. Plug and Play technology automatically assigns IRQ settings as well as other system resources. For Plug and Play to work, the BIOS, operating system software, and hardware must all be Plug and Play compliant. Before Plug and Play technology, system resources had to be assigned manually. This was very difficult at times. With Plug and Play, the user is usually unaware of the process of system resources being assigned when devices are added. The hardware device is usually automatically detected when the system starts up. The needed resources are assigned without user intervention. There are some occasions when Plug and Play technology does not work, and system resources have to be assigned manually. This happens most often when very new hardware and legacy hardware coexist in the same system.

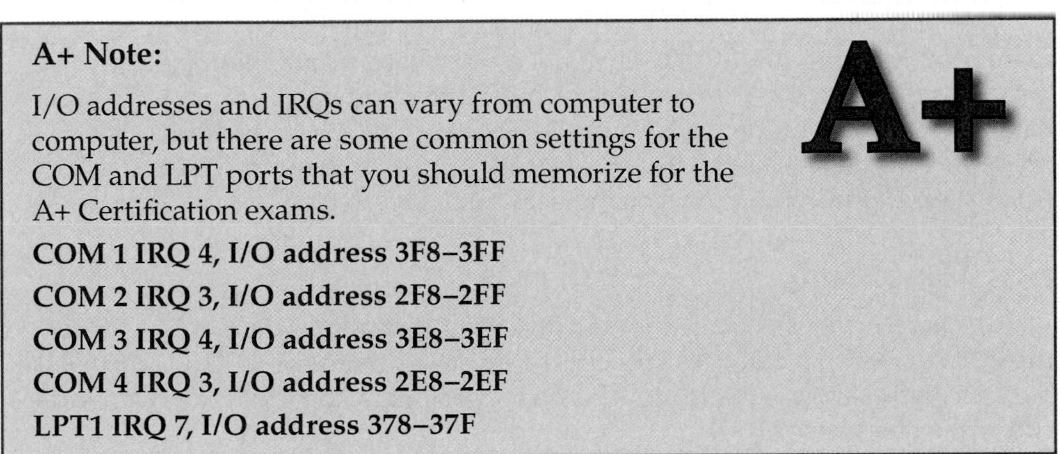

A+ Note:

I/O addresses and IRQs can vary from computer to computer, but there are some common settings for the COM and LPT ports that you should memorize for the A+ Certification exams.

COM 1 IRQ 4, I/O address 3F8–3FF

COM 2 IRQ 3, I/O address 2F8–2FF

COM 3 IRQ 4, I/O address 3E8–3EF

COM 4 IRQ 3, I/O address 2E8–2EF

LPT1 IRQ 7, I/O address 378–37F

Examine **Figure 3-35.** Here you see an interrupt request assignment viewed through the **Properties** dialog box for a system device. This window is often used to verify or change IRQ settings. To view these settings for a device, in Device Manager, double-click the device you are interested in. You can also right-click the device and choose **Properties**.

DMA Channels

In the early days of computers, the CPU was designed to control all devices and their functions. For example, when data was moved from the hard disk drive to the RAM memory, each bit would have to be transferred to the CPU, and then

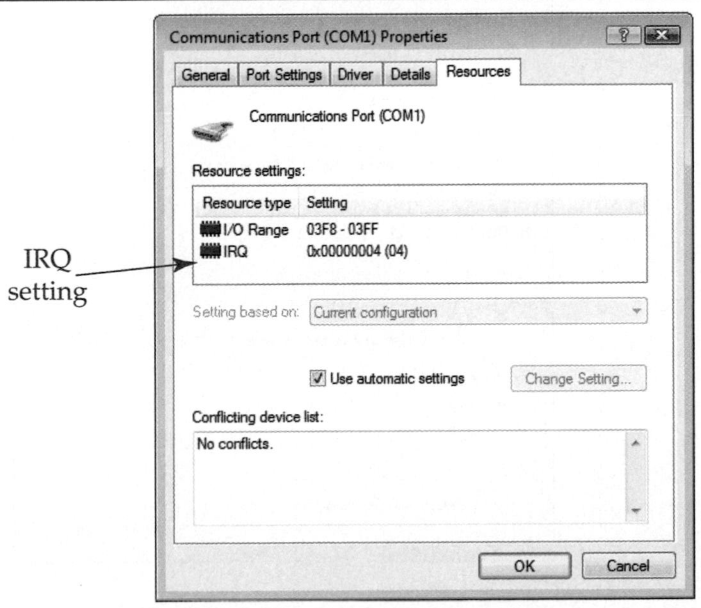

Figure 3-35. Through the **Properties** dialog box of a system device, you can view specific device properties. This can show you the IRQ being used by the device.

the CPU would transfer the bit to the memory location. DMA allows the hard disk drive to transfer all the data directly to memory without the involvement of the CPU.

direct memory access (DMA) a combination of software and hardware that allows certain system devices direct access to the RAM.

Direct memory access (DMA) is a combination of software and hardware that allows certain system devices direct access to the memory. Without DMA, all data must be transferred to memory under the control of the CPU. Waiting for the CPU to take action can cause a bottleneck for the transfer of data in the computer system. If the data does not need the CPU's special attention, a device that has DMA can transfer the data directly into memory via the DMA controller.

The DMA controller is a chip that connects certain devices directly to memory, bypassing the CPU. Each DMA controller has four channels. There is one device connected per channel. The typical motherboard has a total of eight channels available for devices. **Figure 3-36** shows the DMA assignment for LPT1 on a PC. DMA settings, like IRQs and I/O settings, can be viewed through the **Properties** dialog box for a system device.

Bus Mastering

bus mastering a feature of some buses that allows data to be transferred directly between two devices without the intervention of the CPU.

Bus mastering is another method of control that allows data to be transferred directly between two devices without the intervention of the CPU. Control of the bus is usually taken while the CPU is busy with a task that does not require the use of the bus system.

Even though bus mastering and DMA sound similar, they are different. The main difference between bus mastering and DMA is the intent of the device. Bus mastering takes control of the bus system to which it is attached, while DMA is used to access the memory system. DMA is designed to allow devices to communicate directly to and from the memory (RAM) without the intervention of the CPU. Bus mastering technology allows devices to carry out specific tasks such as communicating with each other without direct intervention of the CPU. It allows devices to carry out their individual tasks without using the CPU for each and every bit transfer. While the CPU is busy with other tasks such as calculations, the bus master controller controls the communication between two devices on the bus system.

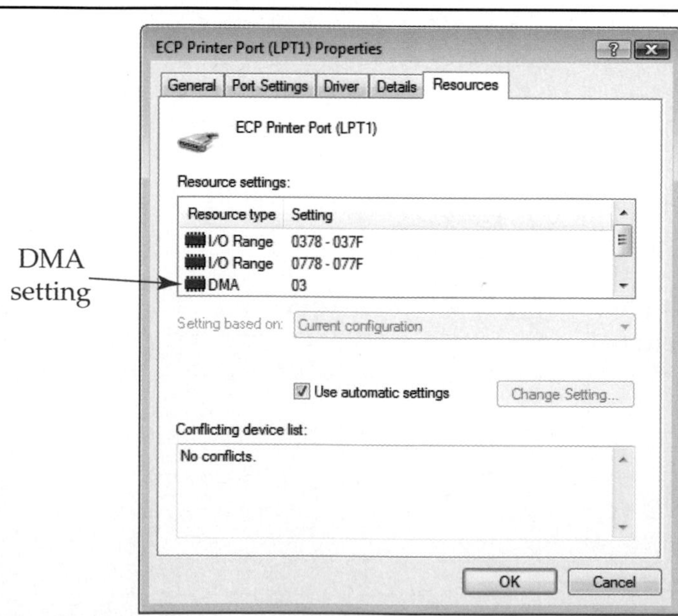

Figure 3-36. The **Properties** dialog box for a system device will also show you DMA assignments for devices.

Both DMA and bus mastering are designed to speed up the common operations involving data flow. To use either technology, the device as well as the BIOS, the operating system software, and the motherboard chipset must be designed to support the technology.

Chipsets

A ***chipset*** is designed to handle data manipulation that would otherwise need to be performed by the CPU. Chipsets handle such things as connecting motherboard buses together that run at different frequencies and connecting ports of various speeds, such as USB, FireWire, and PS/2, to the motherboard buses.

Two major chipsets are the north bridge and the south bridge. They are used to support data flow between the slower motherboard buses and the faster motherboard buses. The ***north bridge*** controls higher data speed systems such as RAM, DVD, and graphics. The ***south bridge*** supports slower devices such as the keyboard and mouse.

There are chipsets designed to handle additional functions such as enabling motherboard expansion slots to work with RAM and other computer components with minimal CPU intervention.

Without chipsets, the CPU would be required to handle all computer data operations through its own core. This would greatly reduce the efficiency of the CPU. For example, if every byte of data representing a picture transferred from the hard disk drive to the RAM had to pass through the CPU, the computer would run slowly. Some major chipset manufacturers are Intel, SIS, and VIA. Their Web sites are listed at the end of this chapter.

chipset
handles data manipulation that would otherwise need to be performed by the CPU. Chipsets also handle such things as connecting motherboard buses together that run at different frequencies and connecting ports of various speeds, such as USB, FireWire, and PS/2, to the motherboard buses.

north bridge
the portion of the chipset that controls higher data speed systems such as graphics and DVD hardware.

south bridge
the portion of the chipset that controls the slower devices associated with the PCI and ISA buses.

Plug and Play (PnP)
the automatic assignment of system resources such as DMA channels, interrupts, memory, and port assignments.

Plug and Play

Plug and Play (PnP) is the automatic assignment of system resources such as DMA channels, interrupts, memory, and port assignments. As the name implies, with Plug and Play you simply plug in a device (such as a network card) and the system software automatically assigns the system resources. There is no need to manually configure the system resources. For Plug and Play to work, the BIOS, the hardware being installed, and the operating system must all support Plug and Play technology.

Before Plug and Play, expansion cards required the installer to set jumpers or dip switches into specific configurations to identify such things as the card's IRQ setting and port address.

Plug and Play works well most of the time, but not for every case. There are times when you must intervene. Not all operating systems support Plug and Play. Windows 95 and later as well as the Windows NT series support Plug and Play to different degrees depending on the version and device drivers available.

Examine **Figure 3-37.** Jumpers are used to select certain options associated with the device they are mounted near. For example, jumper settings can determine data transmission speed or operating voltage. Jumpers are placed onto sets of pins called *headers*. Motherboards contain many headers. Some are used to configure settings, such as operating voltage, and others are used to connect devices to the motherboard, such as front panel USB ports, lights, and switches. See **Figure 3-38.**

Figure 3-37.
Set of jumpers found on a motherboard. Moving or removing jumper connections can change a variety of PC settings.

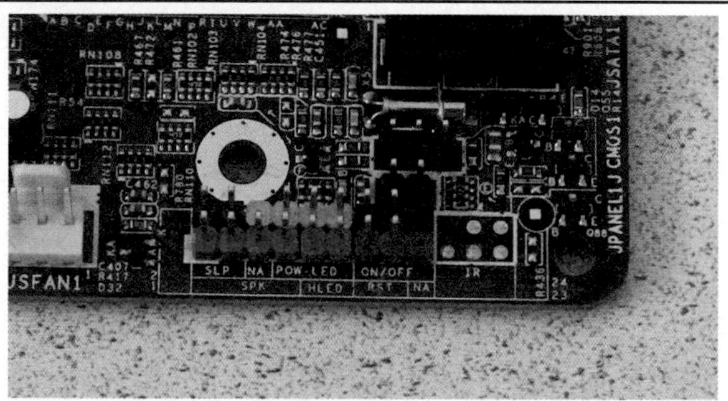

A

B

Figure 3-38.
Front panel headers and cable connectors. A—Headers for the sleep switch (SLP), speaker (SPK), power LED (POW-LED), hard drive activity LED (HLED), power switch (ON/OFF), and reset switch (RST). B—Front panel connectors are labeled. These labels do not always use the same abbreviations as those for the front panel headers.

BIOS and CMOS

Many technicians use the terms *BIOS* and *CMOS* interchangeably, but in reality they are two different distinct terms. The BIOS is a read only memory (ROM) chip that contains a group of software programs written in machine language. Machine language is a language that uses hexadecimal codes to write a program. It is the language that your computer understands. It is many times faster than other programming languages, but it is much more difficult to write.

The BIOS program is designed to initiate activities such as the power-on self-test (POST), the CMOS Setup program (also called the *BIOS Setup program*), and communications between the system hardware and operating system. The BIOS also controls the sequence of boot devices. This feature allows you to determine which device is looked at first when locating the bootstrap program. When the bootstrap program is located, it is loaded and started.

The usual setting of boot device sequence is the floppy drive, the hard drive, and last (if bootable) the CD-ROM/DVD drive. Sometimes computers are set to boot from the hard drive first as a time-saving measure or for security reasons.

Another interesting feature of the BIOS is password protection for the CMOS Setup program. By password protecting the CMOS Setup program, unauthorized personnel cannot change the settings either intentionally or accidentally. Curious PC users often inadvertently change BIOS settings.

Sometimes people forget their password. If this happens, the CMOS will have to be erased. This will allow a new password to be programmed into CMOS. Some motherboards are equipped with a jumper for erasing the data in CMOS. Moving the jumper to the "clear CMOS" position will erase all CMOS data, even the password. Moving the jumper back to its original location will allow the settings to be reentered.

The exact process and terminology of clearing the CMOS data can vary between motherboard manufacturers.

Upgrading the BIOS

Upgrading the BIOS is fairly common when upgrading hardware systems on older computers. In addition, upgrading the BIOS is not just for hardware concerns. Certain software programs can require an upgraded version of the BIOS. For example, when Plug and Play was introduced to consumers, problems arose when trying to use the new Plug and Play technology. The appropriate software operating system may have been available and a Plug and Play device installed, however, the system could not detect or support the device until the BIOS was upgraded.

To upgrade the BIOS program on early computer motherboards, the BIOS chip had to be replaced or an ultraviolet light had to be used to erase the program stored on the BIOS chip in order to reprogram it. The first programs were electrically etched into the microscopic circuitry inside the BIOS chip. The style of chip was referred to as programmable read-only memory (PROM). These were programmed once by the manufacturer and could not be reprogrammed. They simply had to be replaced.

Another variation of the BIOS chip called the erasable programmable read-only memory (EPROM) was developed. This chip had a transparent window usually covered by a foil patch. The foil patch was a sticker with the BIOS manufacturer name and part identification on it. When the label was removed, a window exposing the circuitry inside the chip was revealed. If an ultraviolet light was shined through the exposed window, the program in the chip would be erased. This process allowed the chip to be reprogrammed. These past techniques are no longer used.

Flash BIOS
BIOS that is stored on a reprogrammable chip, allowing for easy upgrades.

Modern PCs use flash BIOS. ***Flash BIOS*** is an electrically erasable programmable read only memory (EEPROM) module, which can be erased electrically and then reprogrammed. Flash BIOS is easily reprogrammed using software available through the motherboard manufacturer's Web site and an updated BIOS program file.

Upgrading the BIOS can render the PC inoperable. Visit the manufacturer's Web site first and read all information pertaining to upgrading the BIOS. Follow the manufacturer's instructions for upgrading your particular BIOS.

The following are general instructions for upgrading a flash BIOS. *Always* follow the manufacturer's instructions for upgrading a specific BIOS.

1. Download the BIOS upgrade program and the updated BIOS program file from the motherboard manufacturer's Web site.
2. Copy the BIOS upgrade program and the updated BIOS program file onto a bootable floppy disk.
3. Boot the PC with the bootable floppy disk.
4. Run the BIOS upgrade program.
5. When the BIOS upgrade program asks for the name of the BIOS program file, enter the exact name of the BIOS program file.
6. If the BIOS upgrade program asks you if you want to back up the contents of the BIOS, answer "yes." Having a backup of the BIOS is vital if you need to return the BIOS to its original state. The BIOS upgrade program will then back up the original contents of the BIOS, erase the contents from the BIOS, and write the new BIOS program file to the BIOS.
7. When the procedure has successfully completed, reboot your PC and enter the CMOS Setup program. Do not be alarmed if you do not see the new BIOS date and information in the CMOS Setup screen.
8. Enter the CMOS Setup program and set it to its default settings.
9. Save the changes and reboot the computer.
10. When the computer is rebooting, enter the CMOS Setup program again. You will now see the date of the new BIOS program.
11. Enter the correct settings for your system.
12. Save the changes and reboot the computer.

Details vary somewhat for different motherboards and BIOS upgrade procedures. For detailed steps on upgrading a particular BIOS, consult the manufacturer's Web site.

The most modern motherboard BIOS can be automatically upgraded through the Windows operating system. For example, Intel Express BIOS can be downloaded via the Internet and the BIOS upgrade will be saved as an executable file (.exe) in the default folder. To start the upgrade process, you simply double-click the BIOS upgrade file. You will see several dialog boxes similar to those in Microsoft Wizard programs. The familiar Install Shield Wizard followed by the typical license agreement will display. When you click **Finish**, the computer will automatically reboot and start the upgrade process. The status of the upgrade process will appear on the display in text format. The computer will restart once again when the BIOS upgrade process is complete. This latest procedure is by far the simplest to date.

CMOS Setup Program

The term *CMOS* (pronounced c-moss) stands for complementary metal oxide semiconductor. CMOS is a type of low-power consuming semiconductor chip technology. In the electronics field, there are many different types of devices designed from CMOS technology. In the computer field, it is understood to refer to the location where the BIOS settings or data are stored.

To store the BIOS setting in the CMOS, the ***CMOS Setup (or BIOS Setup) program*** is used. The BIOS runs a setup routine that identifies the major components and certain features for the computer. The CMOS Setup allows you to identify the type of hard drive and other storage systems. The CMOS Setup program also allows you to set up a password for accessing the machine and the BIOS settings. It also allows you to select certain power management features. The BIOS allows you to select the boot options for selecting in what order the hard drive, floppy drive, and CD-ROM drive are sequenced. It also allows you to identify the type of chipset installed.

CMOS Setup (or BIOS Setup) program
a program that allows you to identify the type of hard drive and other storage systems in the PC, set up a password for accessing the PC and the CMOS Setup program, select certain power management features, and select the boot order of bootable devices.

The CMOS Setup program is activated by a special set of keyboard strokes during the boot up period. The instructions for accessing the CMOS Setup program are often displayed on the screen. When they are not displayed, accessing a computer's CMOS Setup can be difficult. There are many different ways to access the CMOS Setup. Examine **Figure 3-39.** These key combinations could prove helpful for the troublesome machine. Keep in mind that what works for a particular brand one day may not work in the future. Another way to find the right key combination is to check the company's Web site. You may have to open the computer's case and look at the brand and model number on the BIOS chip.

BIOS Manufacturer	Key(s) to Press
AMI	[Del] or [Esc] key during POST
Award, Phoenix	[Ctrl] + [Alt] + [Esc] or [Ctrl] + [Alt] + [S] or [F2] during POST
Computer Manufacturer	
Dell	[Ctrl] + [Alt] + [Enter]
Compact	[F2] or [F10] or [Ctrl] + [Alt] + [F2]
DTK	[Esc]
IBM PS/2	[Ctrl] + [Alt] + [Del] followed by [Ctrl] + [Alt] + [Ins]
Gateway 2000	[F1]
Sony PC	[F3] while booting followed by [F1] at Sony logo
NEC	[F1] when cursor flashes on screen

Figure 3-39. Possible key combinations for accessing the CMOS Setup program.

Figure 3-40.
Screen displays for CMOS Setup program and exit.

System Time:	[14:45:47]
System Date	[06/09/2000]
Language	English
Diskette A:	[1.44 MB, 31/2]
Diskette B:	[Not Installed]
>IDE Adapter 0 Master	[C:2.2 GB]
>IDE Adapter 0 Slave	[None]
>IDE Adapter 1 Master	[None]
>IDE Adapter 1 Slave	[None]
Video Systems	[EGA/VGA]
>Memory and Cache	
>Boot Options	
>Keyboard Features	

Above is a typical first screen display of CMOS setup program.

Save Changes & Exit
Discard Changes & Exit
Get Default Values
Load Previous Values
Save Changes

Typical exit screen leaving the CMOS setup routine

Figure 3-40 shows a typical CMOS Setup routine screen. Not all CMOS Setup screens look the same, but they are similar in appearance and in function.

POST

The POST (power-on self-test) is a simple diagnostic program that is initiated when electrical power is applied to the computer system. The POST verifies that the major computer components are installed and in working order.

The devices checked may vary slightly from computer to computer depending on the BIOS. The POST checks hardware such as the CPU, ROM, RAM, keyboard, monitor, mouse, and hard drive. The test it performs is not as sophisticated as diagnostic software, but it will check for major problems. When the POST is finished, it usually makes one "beep" sound to let you know that the POST is complete and everything is in working order. If an error is detected during the POST, an error code is usually displayed on the screen and a series of beeps are heard that match the code. The codes and beep pattern vary according to the different BIOS chip manufacturers. A list of error codes and beep codes can be obtained from the Web site of the manufacturer.

Motherboard Component Identification

There are many different motherboard manufacturers. The process of identifying many of the jumper and connection locations as well as chips and other major components can be very confusing. **Figure 3-41** shows a typical component layout drawing for a motherboard.

Figure 3-41.
ATX motherboard layout.

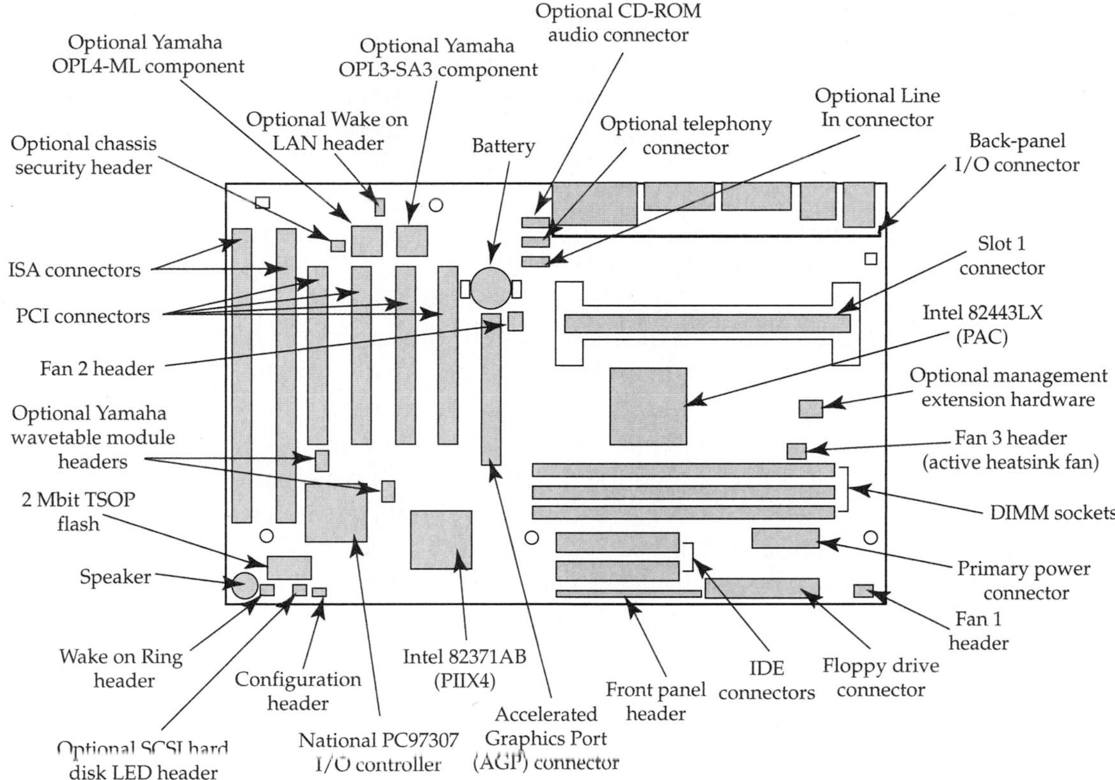

Components are identified by their relative position and outline on each motherboard. All major components can be easily identified. Component layouts are usually readily available at the manufacturer's Web site. Once the Web page for the manufacturer is located, the technician should proceed to one of the following links: site map, specifications, publications, manuals, or support. Most manufacturers have information available through downloads.

Troubleshooting Motherboards

The motherboard is one of the most expensive parts to replace, and problems with it are some of the most difficult to diagnose. Understanding all the peripheral devices that are associated with the PC is required to effectively diagnose a defective motherboard. Many times, the process of diagnosing a problem requires third-party diagnostic software or hardware.

The difficulty in diagnosing a motherboard fault is that all major components use the motherboard circuitry. For example, a technician is troubleshooting a modem problem. The technician first examines the modem and all of its connections. After all methods of diagnosing the modem have been exhausted, the motherboard chipset or circuitry could be at fault. The motherboard must be changed in order to be absolutely sure.

Substitution can be expensive when trying to determine if the CPU or motherboard is at fault. Both are expensive parts. Before replacing the motherboard, always start with a simple inspection of some common failure points. Many times electronic equipment failures are nothing more than loose connections. All the jumpers and connections on and to the motherboard should be checked. A detailed drawing of the component layout (from the manufacturer's Web site) will help locate all possible connections and jumpers. Many times, the simple act of reconnecting jumpers and connections will remedy the problem.

Sometimes a computer can be repaired simply by removing and reinstalling the CPU. The connection pins can become oxidized and stop the flow of electrical energy. Removing and reinserting often clears a sufficient amount of the thin coating of oxidation to clear the fault.

Obvious signs of lightning or high voltage surge damage should be sought. A small burnt area on the motherboard bus at the connection to a component is a sure sign. The back side of the motherboard should also be inspected for damage.

At times, a fault disappears when the cover is removed from the PC. This is often a sign of a pinched cable or a loose connection. Wires and cables can become trapped between the case and metal framework during assembly. The cable may not be completely damaged at the time it becomes caught, but, over time, the framework pinches through the cable.

As you progress through your studies, your knowledge base will grow and so will your troubleshooting skills.

Summary

- ✔ Motherboard form factor describes the shape and size of the motherboard.
- ✔ There are several types of motherboard slots available such as ISA, EISA, MCA, AGP, PCI and PCIe.
- ✔ The latest motherboard designs no longer include ISA, MCA, and EISA slots.
- ✔ The development of USB and FireWire has reduced the number of PCI slots required for system expansion.
- ✔ USB 1.1 supports data transfer rates of 1.5 Mbps and 12 Mbps, and USB 2.0 supports transfer rates as high as 480 Mbps.
- ✔ System resources are I/O port address, memory address range, interrupt request (IRQ), and direct memory access (DMA).
- ✔ Direct memory access (DMA) allows devices to communicate directly with the memory system without constant intervention by the CPU.
- ✔ Bus mastering allows devices to communicate directly with each other without constant intervention by the CPU.
- ✔ Chipsets combine many individual electronic systems into one or two chips.
- ✔ The north bridge controls communication between high-speed modules while the south bridge controls slower communications.
- ✔ Plug and Play (PnP) automatically detects new hardware and assigns system resources.
- ✔ The BIOS performs the POST, CMOS Setup, and communication between the operating system and hardware.
- ✔ The CMOS chip stores information such as time, date, and type of hard drive installed.
- ✔ The power-on self-test (POST) tests the major components (video, keyboard, mouse, memory, etc.) to see if they are working.

Review Questions

Answer the following questions on a separate sheet of paper. Please do not write in this book.

1. What are three alternate names used for motherboard?
2. What is a field replacement unit?
3. Define the following bus types.
   Memory
   Address
   Data
   Power
   Local
   Expansion
   Internal
   Control
4. A bus can consist of two or more other types of bus. True or False?
5. Form factor describes the _____ of the motherboard.
   a. bus type
   b. shape
   c. voltage level
   d. chipset
6. What is the major difference between an NLX and an LPX form factor?
7. What form factor was specifically designed for air flow across heat-generating components?
8. What does the acronym BTX represent?
9. Which is the fastest bus system?
   a. ISA
   b. EISA
   c. MCA
   d. PCI
10. An ISA adapter card will fit into a(n) _____ slot.
    a. EISA
    b. MCA
    c. PCI
    d. any standard
11. Will a Baby AT fit into the same case as an XT?
12. How many conductors are in a single PCIe lane?
13. What does the acronym PCIe represent?
14. What does the acronym PCI-X represent?
15. What is the data width of PCI?
16. What is the data width of PCI-X?
17. What is the data width of PCIe X-1?
18. What are the advantages to incorporating the CNR or ACR riser system into a motherboard design?
19. What are the four major system resources used by computer devices?
20. List how to access **Device Manager** dialog box for a Windows Vista PC. Start with *Right-click* the **Computer** icon.

21. What IRQ setting is used for COM2?
22. What IRQ setting is used for COM1?
23. What three things are necessary for Plug and Play to work?
24. Which IRQ has the highest priority?
    a. 3
    b. 5
    c. 2
    d. 15
25. What do the acronyms EPP and ECP represent?
26. What is the maximum throughput of USB 2.0?
27. What is the maximum throughput of USB 1.1?
28. Which has the highest data transfer rate: USB or IEEE 1394?
29. What is the maximum number of devices that can be attached to an IEEE 1394 port?
30. What is the total number of hardware IRQs?
31. Explain how IRQ assignments can be shared.
32. What can be done to protect the CMOS Setup program from accidental changes?
33. How many channels does a DMA controller have?
34. How many devices can be connected to each channel of a DMA controller?

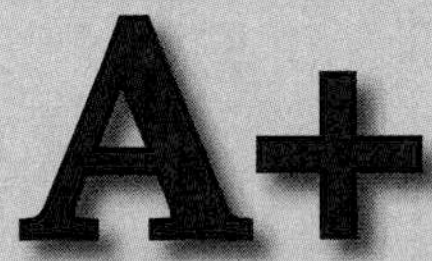

Sample A+ Exam Questions

Answer the following questions on a separate sheet of paper. Please do not write in this book.

1. Which form factor uses a bus riser card?
    a. AT
    b. ATX
    c. NLX
    d. XT
2. Which architecture supports the fastest transfer speeds?
    a. PCI
    b. USB 2.0
    c. PCIe
    d. PCIX
3. Which slot design is exclusively used for video cards?
    a. PCI
    b. AGP
    c. USB
    d. IEEE 1394
4. IRQ settings can be accessed in Windows XP through the _____.
    a. Device Manager
    b. System Resource icon in Control Panel
    c. IRQ icon in Control Panel
    d. System Resources dialog box

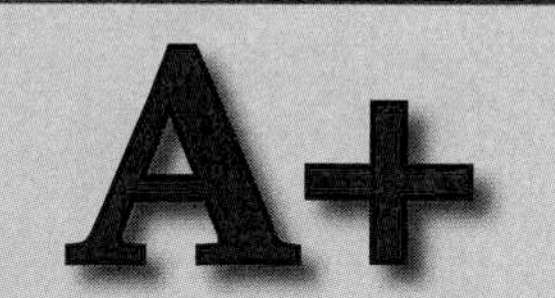

5. Which IRQ setting is associated with COM1?
   a. 3
   b. 4
   c. 5
   d. 6
6. Which I/O port address is usually assigned to COM1?
   a. 03F8
   b. 02F8
   c. 03A0
   d. 02A0
7. Where does the computer store information about the type of hard drive installed?
   a. At sector 2 of the hard drive.
   b. In the CMOS.
   c. In the system ROM chip.
   d. In the system RAM chip.
8. What is required for Plug and Play technology to work correctly? Select all that apply.
   a. Plug and Play BIOS.
   b. An operating system that supports Plug and Play.
   c. Device Manager must support Plug and Play.
   d. The hardware device being installed must be equipped to support Plug and Play.
9. Which of the following technologies is used to control data flow on the system bus?
   a. Bus mastering
   b. Bus routing
   c. Bus directory
   d. Active bus
10. Which of the following items controls the speed of data flow across different bus architectures on a motherboard?
    a. BIOS
    b. Motherboard chipsets
    c. DMA channels
    d. IEEE 1394

Suggested Laboratory Activities

Do not attempt any suggested laboratory activities without your instructor's permission. Certain activities can render the PC operating system inoperable.

1. Completely remove a motherboard. Make a drawing and label all connections to the motherboard to assist you during reinstallation.
2. Access the Web site of the motherboard's manufacturer. Look for a drawing on the site that identifies all of the major parts of the motherboard. Identify the type of chipset and BIOS that it uses. List the various features associated with the motherboard chipset.
3. Access the CMOS Setup program on your assigned PC. Write down all the settings you find in the CMOS Setup program, such as the hard drive, floppy disk drive, and CD-ROM drive configurations. Look for a **Help** option. It will usually be displayed on the screen as you move the cursor into each setting's input field. Locate the security password system in the BIOS.
4. Access **Device Manager** and study the way the system resources are displayed and assigned. Identify the IRQ, memory, and DMA assignments for various devices. Record your findings and use them as a study guide.
5. Execute **msinfo32.exe** from the **Run** program in the **Start** menu. (In Windows Vista, enter **msinfo32** into the **Search** text box.) Examine the information displayed, such as memory, DMA, and I/O assignments. Look at the various information that can be displayed and explore the options available in the **Tools** menu.
6. Access the Web site of the BIOS manufacturer American Mega Trends (www.ami.com). Locate and read the procedure for upgrading a system BIOS. Download the utility for identifying motherboards that are equipped with AMI BIOS chips. Download and print a copy of the common AMI beep and POST codes. Download and print a copy of the AMI glossary of terms.
7. Access the Phoenix Web site (www.phoenix.com) and locate the beep codes associated with the BIOS. Look for downloads and manuals.

Interesting Web Sites for More Information

www.amd.com
www.asus.com
www.formfactors.org
www.giga-byte.com
www.intel.com
www.micron.com
www.motherboards.org
www.sis.com
www.soyo.com
www.via.com

Chapter 3
Laboratory Activity
Identifying PC BIOS and Operating Systems

After completing this laboratory activity, you will be able to:

- ✔ Identify the BIOS manufacturer and version.
- ✔ Identify the Windows operating system.
- ✔ Access and modify the BIOS CMOS settings.
- ✔ Check the browser setup and version.

Introduction

In this activity, you will learn to identify the manufacturer and version of the BIOS, Windows operating system, and browser information.

The BIOS (Basic Input/Output Operating System) translates commands given by the operating system program into actions carried out by the PC system hardware. The type of hardware that makes up the PC system must be identified before the BIOS program can carry out commands that affect the system hardware. When the hardware is identified, the BIOS program stores the data in a CMOS (Complimentary Metal-Oxide Semiconductor). The CMOS must use a small battery to retain the settings after power to the computer is turned off.

The PC's hardware is usually identified automatically through Plug and Play technology. The Plug and Play technology automatically detects the hardware and assigns settings to the CMOS data collection. For the Plug and Play technology to work properly, three things must be Plug and Play compliant: the hardware being installed, the BIOS, and the operating system. For example, you may attach a Plug and Play device to a PC that is using a Plug and Play operating system, such as Windows 98. However, if the BIOS is not Plug and Play, the device will need to be installed manually. You may also upgrade the BIOS to a Plug and Play BIOS.

Typically, when the PC first boots, BIOS information is flashed across the screen. For example, a message similar to the one below may appear in the upper-left quadrant of the screen.

AMIBIOS 1992 C American Megatrends, Inc.

BIOS Version 1.00.07

0032 KB memory

Press F1 to enter setup

The above information displays the BIOS manufacturer and version. The amount of RAM is displayed, and then instructions are given for accessing the CMOS Setup program. The exact method of accessing the CMOS Setup program is not standard and is not always displayed on the screen. You may need to consult the PC or BIOS manufacturer through its Web site to identify the exact steps necessary to access the CMOS Setup program.

Equipment and Materials

✔ Typical PC with Windows 95, or later, operating system.

Procedure

1. _______ Turn on the PC and closely watch for instructions for accessing the CMOS Setup program. If the information is not displayed, you may need to ask the instructor. On a separate sheet of paper, write down the instructions for accessing the CMOS Setup program.
2. _______ After accessing the CMOS Setup program, find and record on a separate sheet of paper the answers to the questions in the following list. You will not be familiar with much of the information recorded. This is normal. The information displayed in the BIOS settings will become clear to you as you progress through the course. What is important for you to understand is the type of information contained in the BIOS settings and what can be changed. There are many different BIOS-settings programs available and not all will exactly match the information being requested below. Answer all questions to the best of your ability.

   Is the system date and time displayed?

   Can the system time and date be changed?

   Is the BIOS version displayed?

   Is the amount of extended memory displayed and if so, how much memory does the PC have?

   What information can be viewed about the floppy drives?

   What information about the hard drive is present?

   Are there any security features present and if so, describe them.

   What information about the monitor is displayed?

   What are the "Boot Options?"

   What information is provided about the serial ports?

   Is there any information about the CPU?
3. _______ Now that you have found the listed information, make special note of how the BIOS settings program is exited. You usually must exit by choosing an option such as: **Use default settings, Save changes**, or **Do not retain changes to settings**. It is important to realize that changes are not automatically retained by the CMOS.
4. _______ If time permits and you have instructor approval, change the system time indicated in the CMOS Setup program as well as the date. Again, make sure you have instructor approval first.
5. _______ Return the system time and date settings to the correct settings and then shut down the PC.

Review Questions

Answer the following questions on a separate sheet of paper. Please do not write in this book.

1. How did you access the CMOS Setup program?
2. Why aren't the CMOS settings lost after the power is turned off to the PC?
3. Where is the manufacturer of the BIOS and the version displayed?
4. If instructions for accessing the CMOS Setup program are not displayed on the screen, how could you find the information needed to determine the proper keystroke sequence for accessing the CMOS Setup program?

An Intel technician holds a wafer of microprocessor chips. Each small square on the wafer is a microprocessor. (Source: Intel Corporation)

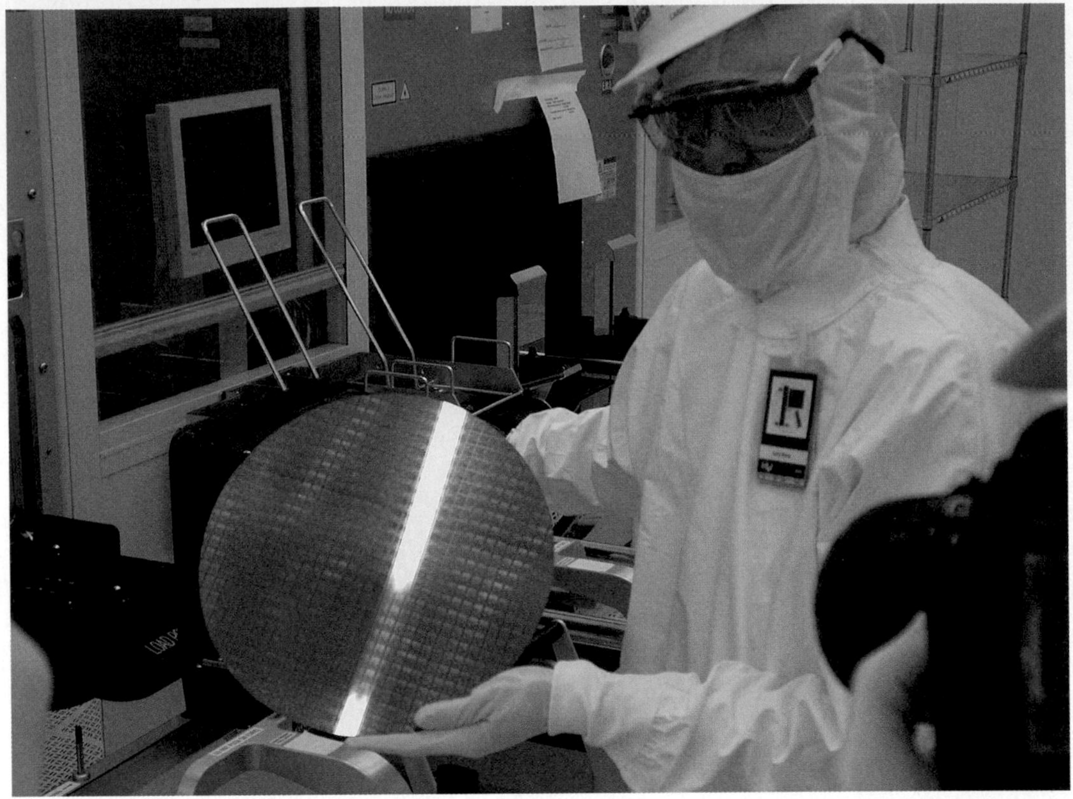

CPU

After studying this chapter, you will be able to:

- ✔ Identify the operation, function, and purpose of the CPU.
- ✔ Differentiate between the internal and external bus system.
- ✔ Identify and explain the major portions of a CPU.
- ✔ Briefly review the evolution of the CPU.
- ✔ Identify sockets and SEC connections associated with the CPU.
- ✔ Identify and explain the purpose of a voltage regulator.
- ✔ Explain real and protected modes of operation.
- ✔ Define the terms multiple branch prediction, superscalar technology, processor affinity, processor throttling, and MMX technology as it applies to the CPU.

A+ Exam—Key Points

The CompTIA A+ exams will ask basic questions about the CPU and CPU terminology. Be prepared to answer questions such as the following:

- ✔ How is CPU performance measured?
- ✔ Which CPU fits which socket?
- ✔ What effect does overclocking have on a CPU?
- ✔ What is the difference between 32-bit and 64-bit processing?
- ✔ What is the purpose of thermal compound?
- ✔ What purpose does processor throttling serve?

Key Words and Terms

The following words and terms will become important pieces of your computer vocabulary. Be sure you can define them.

arithmetic logic unit (ALU)
assembly language
bus unit
cache
clock doubling
compiler
complex instruction set computer (CISC)
control unit
decode unit
Dual Independent Bus (DIB)
dynamic execution
front side bus (FSB)
instruction set
instructions
L1 cache
L2 cache
L3 cache
math coprocessor
MMX processor
multiple branch prediction
overclocking
pin grid array (PGA)
processor affinity
processor throttling
protected mode
real mode
reduced instruction set computer (RISC)
register unit
registers
simultaneous threading
Single Edge Contact (SEC)
superscalar
System Management Mode (SMM)
thread
virtual mode
zero insertion force (ZIF) socket

CPU stands for *c*entral *p*rocessing *u*nit, and it does exactly what its name implies. It is *central* in that all other components are dependent on the CPU. See **Figure 4-1.** It is a *processor* in that it processes data. It is a *unit* in that it is very much a self-contained device that is modular in design. The CPU is replaced as an entire unit.

Instructions and Data

The CPU has been given the status of the computer's brain. It has evolved over the years from a simple chip composed of only 27,000 transistors in early 1978 to a highly sophisticated integrated chip composed of over 9 million transistors. The

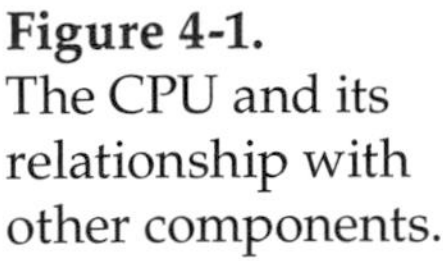
Figure 4-1. The CPU and its relationship with other components.

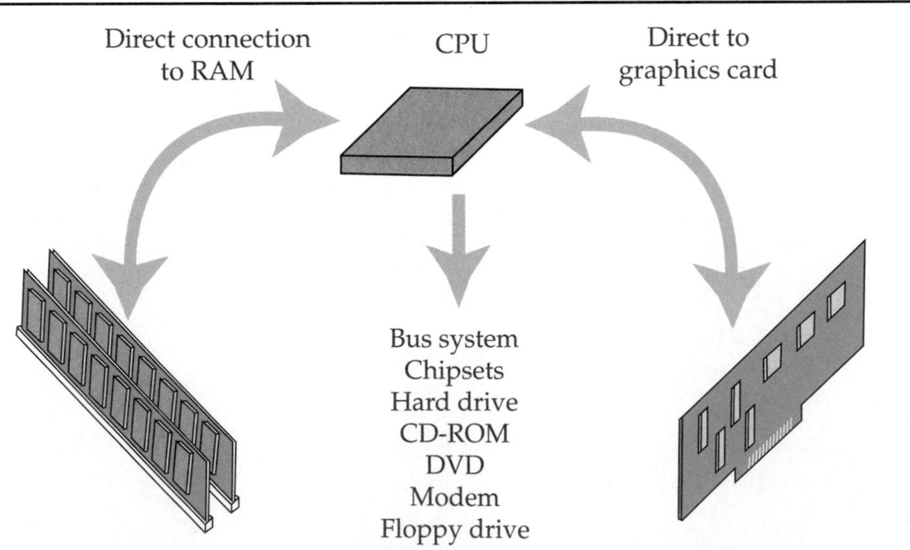

CPU follows commands called ***instructions*** and then processes data. The data is normally stored in RAM or introduced into the system by some device such as a keyboard, mouse, microphone, hard disk drive, or CD-ROM drive.

Every processor runs from a set of commands called the ***instruction set.*** The instruction set is the lowest language level used to program a computer. The instruction set is written in a language called ***assembly language.*** Assembly is one step above machine language. When code is written in a high-level language such as BASIC or C++, it must be compiled before it can run the computer as a stand-alone program or executive program. A ***compiler*** is a special program that translates the higher-level language into machine language based on the CPU's instruction set. The instruction set contains commands such as add, subtract, compare, add one to, subtract one from, get the next one, two, or four bytes from, and put the next one, two, or four bytes at.

The CPU has several registers. ***Registers*** are small pockets of memory used to temporarily store data that is being processed by the CPU. For example, when adding two numbers together, one number is stored in register A and the other number is stored in register B. The add command adds the contents of register A to the contents of register B and places the result in register C. Next, the contents can be moved from register C to a RAM address.

Assembly language programs are translated into machine language code. The program is written as a series of commands and bytes of data to be acted on byte by byte. Writing code in assembly language is painstakingly difficult. It takes an extremely long time to write even a simple program. However, it produces the fastest execution possible. Assembly translated into machine language is used when speed or compact size is a necessity. The kernel code of operating systems and BIOS programs are usually written to some degree in assembly code. Most other common programs are written for computers using a higher-level language that is then translated from the higher-level language to machine-like code. However, using a higher-level language and then compiling the code results in a larger, slower program.

The machine level programs are lengthy but appear transparent to the user because of the sheer speed at which the instructions are carried out by the computer. Programming in machine language is an entire science, but only needs to be briefly explained to give you the necessary insight on how a CPU functions with data.

instructions
commands given to the processor.

instruction set
a set of basic commands that control the processor.

assembly language
a low-level language in which a CPU's instruction set is written.

compiler
a special program that translates the higher-level language into machine language based on the CPU's instruction set.

registers
small pockets of memory within the processor that are used to temporarily store data being processed by the CPU.

CPU Operation

A CPU is in a state of constant operation. When not processing commands to process data, the CPU is:

- ✔ Refreshing memory.
- ✔ Check ing for communication from other devices through the system of hardwired IRQs and software IRQs.
- ✔ Monitoring system power.
- ✔ Performing any other programmed duties.

Look at **Figure 4-2** to see how a CPU performs the simple operation of addition. This series demonstrates how the registers are used to manipulate data. To add the numerical value of two numbers, three registers are used. The value 3 is placed in register A. The value 4 is placed in register B. Then the contents of

Figure 4-2.
Illustrated in this series are the steps that a CPU takes to add two numbers together.

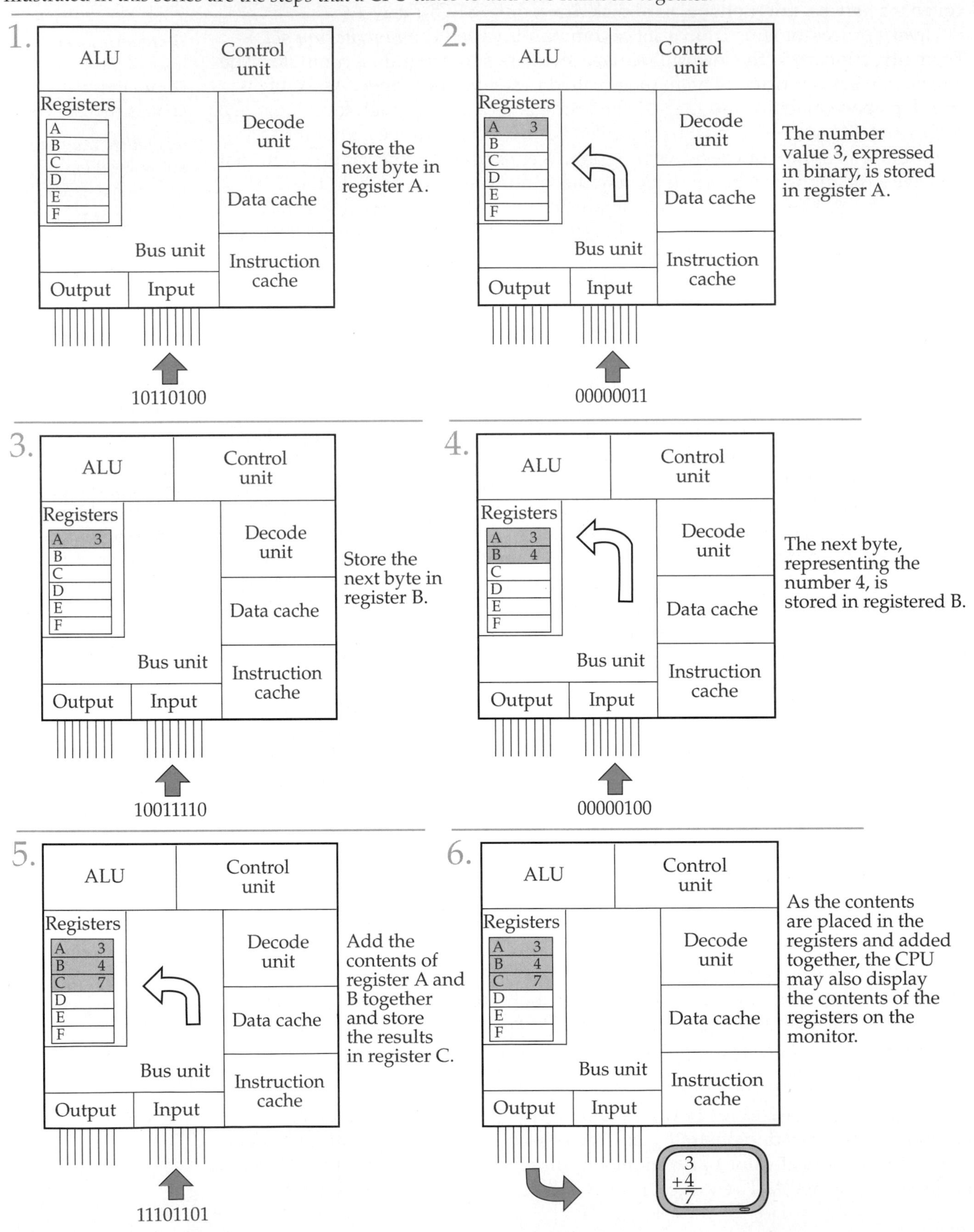

the two registers are added together and stored in register C. While this action seems simple, there are many other activities going on at the same time that are controlled by the CPU. For example, the CPU is refreshing the RAM, checking IRQ status (checking for keyboard input, mouse input, and other such input), and displaying the contents of the registers on the monitor.

CPU Parts

The following is a simplified discussion of CPU operation, but it should give you some idea of how the major parts work together to perform operations on data. The ***bus unit*** connects all the other major components together, accepts data, and sends data through the input and output bus sections. There is an instruction cache and a data cache. The term ***cache*** (pronounced cash) means a small temporary memory storage area. Cache is used to separate and store incoming data and instructions.

A ***decode unit*** does what the name implies. It decodes instructions sent to the CPU. Under the direction of a control unit, it not only decodes the series of instructions and data but also sends the data on to other areas in an understandable format.

The ***control unit*** controls the overall operation of the CPU. It takes instructions from the decode unit and directs command instructions to the arithmetic logic unit and data to be manipulated to the register area. The ***arithmetic logic unit (ALU)*** performs mathematical functions on data stored in the register area. It also performs data manipulations such as comparing two pieces of data stored in the registry unit. It can do comparisons such as "equal to," "greater than," and "less than."

The ***register unit*** is composed of many separate, smaller storage units. Each register has a unique identity. In our model, each is labeled with a letter of the alphabet. The main difference between register storage and cache is that registers contain a single data element. A single data element is a number or a letter. The data and instruction cache can hold multiple pieces of data and commands. The ALU performs manipulations on the data stored in registers, such as adding or subtracting the contents of register A to or from the contents of register B. The ALU can also do comparisons on the contents of A or B, such as determining which is larger.

Manipulating a list of words in alphabetical order is an example of a comparison of the contents of two or more registers. Each letter is given a numeric value, processed through the CPU in pairs, and then stored in either cache or RAM in the appropriate order. The series of comparisons can consist of over a thousand repetitions. The CPU operates at such a high speed that the process appears very brief. This is the great value of the computer. A computer can perform repetitive tasks such as sorting the addresses of 2,000,000 names for a phone book in a few minutes. Performed manually, the same operation would take weeks or even months to perform. Animation on the screen of the display unit has also been made possible because of the great speed of the control unit, the ALU, and the registers. See **Figure 4-3.**

bus unit
the network of circuitry that connects all the other major components together, accepts data, and sends data through the input and output bus sections.

cache
a small temporary memory area that is used to separate and store incoming data and instructions.

decode unit
a CPU component that decodes instructions and data and transmits the data to other areas in an understandable format.

control unit
a CPU component that controls the overall operation of the CPU.

arithmetic logic unit (ALU)
a CPU component that performs mathematical functions on data stored in the register area.

register unit
a CPU component containing many separate, smaller storage units known as registers.

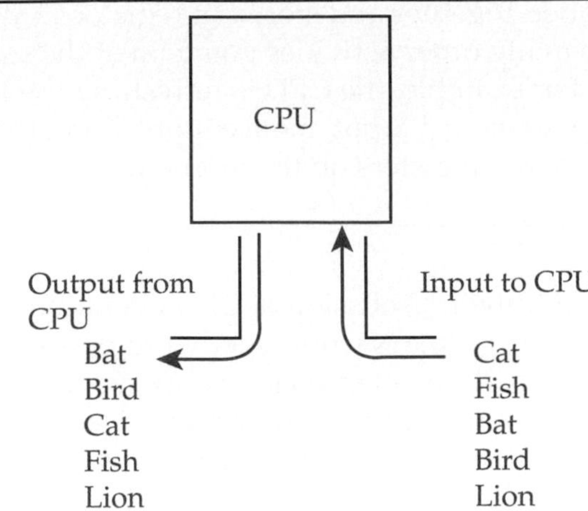

Figure 4-3. A list of words are entered into the CPU and stored in cache. The control unit sends pairs of words to the registry broken down by letter and then compares each pair until all possible combinations are exhausted.

CPU Power

Not all business conducted with a PC requires the use of a powerful CPU. A simple word processing package will work with most any CPU. However, extreme software gaming, CAD/CAM (computer-aided drafting/computer-aided manufacturing), scientific simulations and research, and large corporate financial record calculations require powerful CPUs. CPU power can be taken even further. Many of the very sophisticated operations, such as weather predictions and medical research, have requirements well beyond a PC and must turn to the use of a mainframe or a super computer.

Imagine a CAD drawing of a shopping center or mall that can be manipulated on the display unit. A person can walk through the *virtual mall* and look at the simulation as though they were actually in the mall itself. They can see the entire layout through a shopper's perspective. Or, imagine many popular game scenarios as you navigate through a maze of hallways. Animation, especially those involving three-dimensional images, is CPU intensive.

One form of animation technology requires the redrawing of every line in the image for each display change. See **Figure 4-4.** Before redrawing each line, a calculation has to be made based on the X, Y, and Z coordinates of each end of the line. The distance and angle of the new location is used as part of the algorithm. An algorithm is similar to a recipe. You simply insert the X, Y, and Z coordinates of the existing position of each line end and then input the new X, Y, and Z coordinates.

Rather than inputting the exact coordinates manually, they can be *implied* by the use of a mouse, keyboard, or game control device. To give a realistic feeling, an illustration containing hundreds or even thousands of lines must be computed in a fraction of a second and then displayed on the screen. This type of operation requires a high-speed CPU with many advanced data processing techniques.

Remember that the CPU receives a constant stream of alternating commands and data. Early CPUs required all data to be transferred through the CPU. For example, if a memo was being typed, the CPU would act on each letter in the memo. Now, modern systems allow for bus mastering and direct memory access. These additions allow repetitive actions that do not require manipulation of data to simply be passed on to memory, the screen, the printer, or data storage areas such as the hard drive.

Figure 4-4. These three illustrations show the concept behind animation technology using X, Y, and Z coordinates.

1.

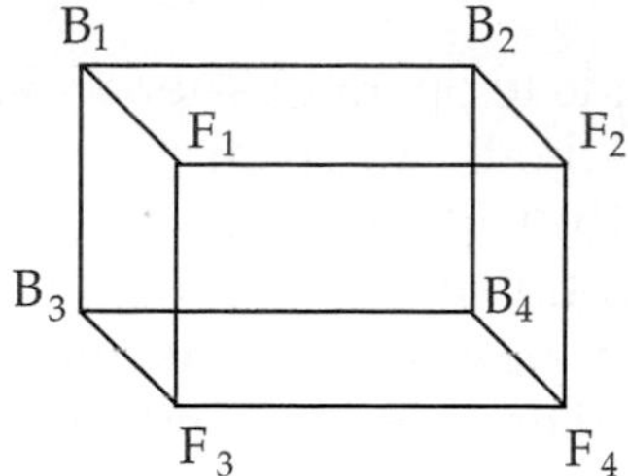

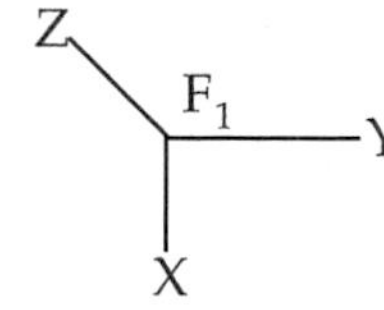

Using point F_1 as a reference, each corner of the object is calculated with trigonometric functions and the distances from F_1 based on the length of the X, Y, and Z axis.

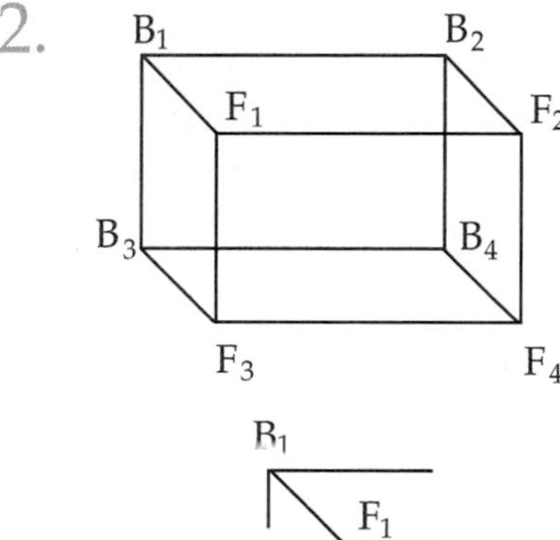

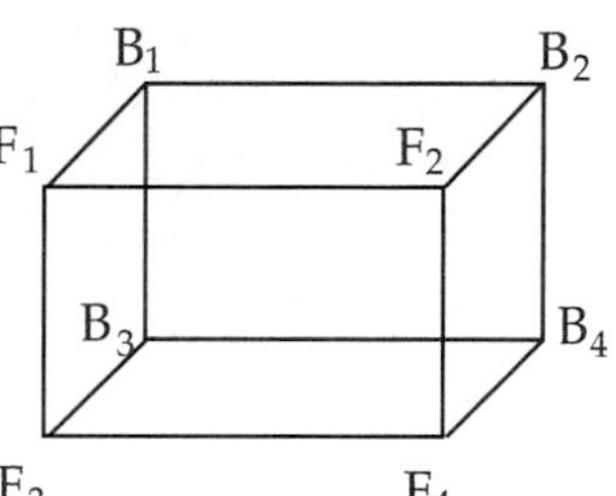

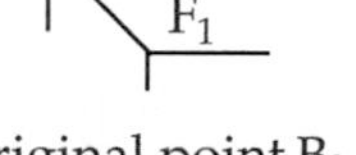

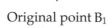

Original point B_1

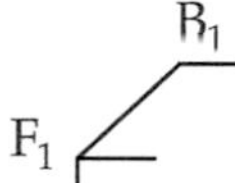

New location of point B_1

Each individual point location must be calculated and then plotted.

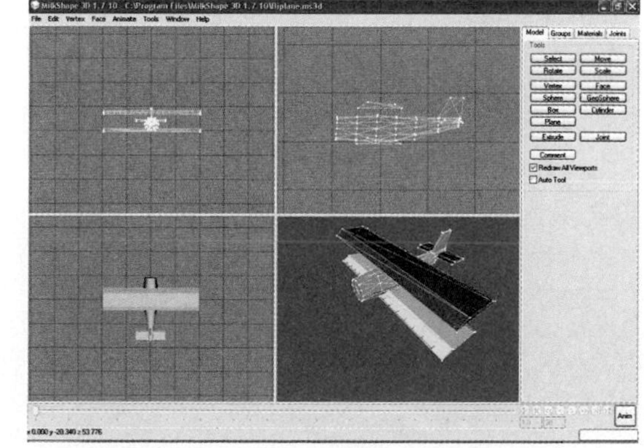

This takes a tremendous amount of computing power, especially when it is a complex drawing.

Each step of the processor requires a clock beat. The clock sends a repetitive signal to all parts of the computer system to keep all data transmissions in step with the other parts. The transmission of data throughout the PC is a combination of series and parallel transmissions and many different devices operating at different speeds. For example, the keyboard is a serial device. Keyboard data must be converted to parallel data and then be transmitted in step with the other parts of the computer.

Processor Speed

The CPU has been progressively made to operate faster and more efficiently. The modifications to data processing methods are given special names to describe their actions. Modifications to the CPU include RISC, superscalar technology, dynamic execution, and additional cache. In this next section, we will take a closer look at processor speed and these special modifications to the CPU.

Comparison of CPUs is usually based on speed and bus width. The speed is how fast the CPU can process data and commands. The bus width is how many bits can be passed simultaneously on parallel circuits, for example 8, 16, 32, and 64 bits simultaneously.

The CPU moves data and carries out commands as a series of binary numbers. The CPU or processor speed is measured in hertz (Hz), or cycles per second. With CPUs, this means the number of digital pulses in one second. A digital signal is a fluctuation of electrical energy. In digital electronics, a complete cycle is one complete sequence of the digital signal shape. Look at **Figure 4-5** to see a complete cycle of the digital signal illustrated.

The term *frequency* is used to express the number of cycles in one second. Thus, if there are 25 complete digital cycles in one second, the frequency is 25 hertz (25 Hz). A CPU that runs at 1 MHz carries out instructions and data movement at one million digital pulses per second. Bus width and speed combine to express amount of data transfer. See **Figure 4-6** for a drawing explaining the speed of a CPU.

As computer systems shifted from text-based command operating systems to Graphical User Interface (GUI), speed became an extremely important factor. For example, the intense graphics of Windows requires a faster computer system. Graphics functions demand a lot of processor attention.

Keep in mind that the speed of processing data is not entirely dependent on the speed of the electronics. The instruction set used to process data as well as special methods such as pipeline burst, RISC, and cache technique also influence the speed of processing data.

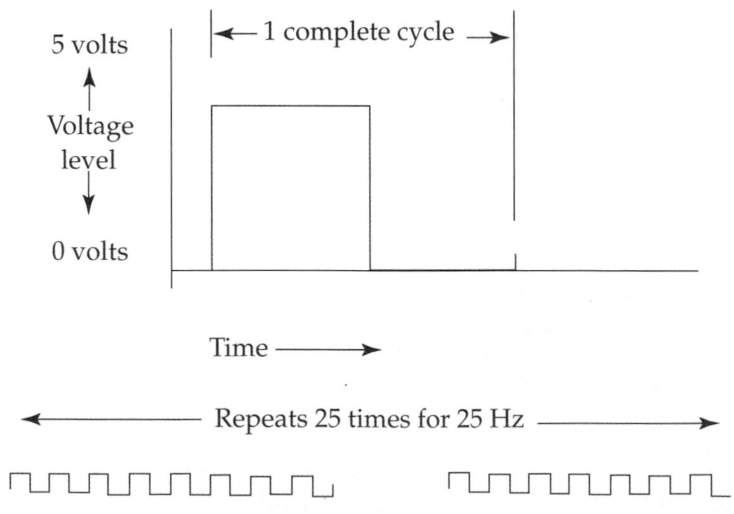

Figure 4-5. Complete cycle of a digital signal. A 5-volt digital signal rises and falls to a 5-volt level. The number of times it repeats the pattern in one second is the frequency of the signal. A 25-Hz signal repeats 25 times in one second.

10110100101101001011010010110100
11011011110110111101101111011011
00001110000011100000111000001110
00101000001010000010100000101000
11101101111011011110110111101101
00010001000100010001000100010001
11101010111010101110101011101010
10101010101010101010101010101010
11100010111000101110001011100010
11000101110001011100010111000101
10101001101010011010100110101001
11111010111110101111101011111010
00001010000010100000101000001010
11100010111000101110001011100010
01010010010100100101001001010010
11011001110110011101100111011001

Frequency of data flow is 5 MHz.

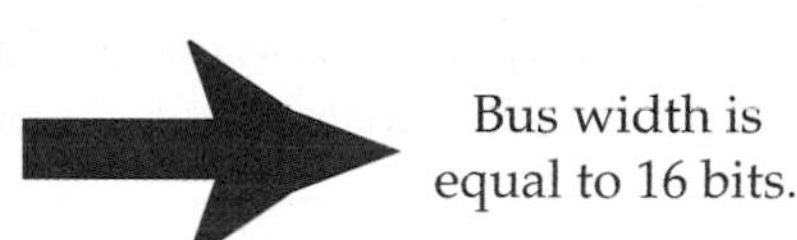

Bus width is equal to 16 bits.

Total data is equal to the bus width multiplied by the speed of the data.

16 bits x 5 MHz = 80 Mbps

Mbps (Megabits per second)

Figure 4-6.
The rate of data transfer is based on the width and speed of the bus system.

Enhancing CPU Operation

Processors are continually getting faster and more powerful. Each new generation of CPU can operate on shorter clock cycles. However, a CPU's abilities can be enhanced in a number of ways in addition to simply producing chips that operate at a faster rate. These improvements include changes to the local bus, the addition of cache, and the addition of a math coprocessor.

Local Bus

The local bus is connected directly to the CPU. It is always the highest speed bus in the entire computer system. The local bus is the bus system connecting certain components directly to the CPU. RAM and video card slots are examples of components connected directly to the CPU to better enhance performance. The local bus is also referred to as the *system bus* or the *front side bus*. A lot of the terminology used is dependent on the manufacture of the product or even the generation of the technology. The latest series of Intel Pentium processors use the term ***front side bus (FSB)*** when referencing what has been known as the local bus.

front side bus (FSB) another term for local bus.

The shorter the distance between the two devices, the higher the data transfer rate can be. It is not the length the data has to travel, but rather the effect of inductive reactance that causes a choking effect on the electrical impulses. As the length of the data path increases, so does the choking effect. The only practical way to decrease this choking effect as the length of the path increases is to lower the data flow rate. Thus, the inductive reactance slows down the speed that a processor can run.

L1, L2, and L3 Cache

The processor bus speed is the highest data transfer speed in the entire computer system. To enhance the speed of data processing, a special block of RAM was developed and manufactured as an integral part of the processor. This feature began with the 486 processor. This special memory unit is called *cache*.

L1 cache
a cache contained within the processor that is designed to run at the processor's speed.

The cache in the CPU is called the ***L1 cache.*** L1 cache is designed to run at the same speed as the CPU. It is the most costly memory to produce when compared on a per byte basis. As design engineers must create a CPU and computer system that will work at a high speed while staying within a reasonable cost that the customer can afford, L1 cache is smaller on less expensive processors.

L1 cache produces faster CPU processing of data. Data can be stored temporarily in the L1 cache rather than in a RAM module. The bus speed to L1 cache is many times faster than the bus speed from the CPU to the RAM. By storing data in L1 cache, the movement of data being manipulated by the CPU is greatly increased.

L2 cache
a cache mounted outside of the processor. (Note: The Pentium III incorporates the L2 cache in the processor.)

L2 cache is separate from the processor but mounted as close as possible to the processor to keep the transfer rates high. The ***L2 cache*** is used to increase the speed of transmitting data to and from the processor to other parts of the motherboard.

L1 and L2 cache also differ in one other significant way. L1 cache is made from static RAM technology. L2 cache uses dynamic RAM technology, which is slower than the L1 cache. The terms static and dynamic memory type will become clearer when you complete Chapter 6—Memory. **Figure 4-7** shows the layout of a modern cache system.

The Pentium III incorporates both L1 and L2 cache into the CPU die. The L1 cache is divided into a data cache and an instruction cache. The L2 cache performs at a much higher rate of data transfer than previous L2 caches since it is built in to the processing unit. Earlier models simply installed the L2 cache in close proximity to the CPU. When L1 and L2 caches are incorporated into the CPU chip, the cache on the motherboard becomes ***L3 cache.***

L3 cache
the cache mounted on the motherboard when L1 and L2 caches are incorporated into the CPU.

math coprocessor
a component of the CPU that improves the processor's ability to perform advanced mathematical calculations.

Math Coprocessor

Early processors were limited to whole number mathematical calculations. For more advanced calculations, a second chip called the ***math coprocessor*** had to be installed on the motherboard. Math coprocessors are also called floating-point units (FPU).

Beginning with the 486 CPU, the math coprocessor was integrated into the processor chip, thus eliminating the need for a separate math coprocessor chip. Math coprocessor ability was a requirement for sophisticated graphics programs such as AutoCAD. *AutoCAD* is a computer-aided drafting software program that depends on complicated math routines such as sizing drawings, changing scales, and even changing views of the object being drawn.

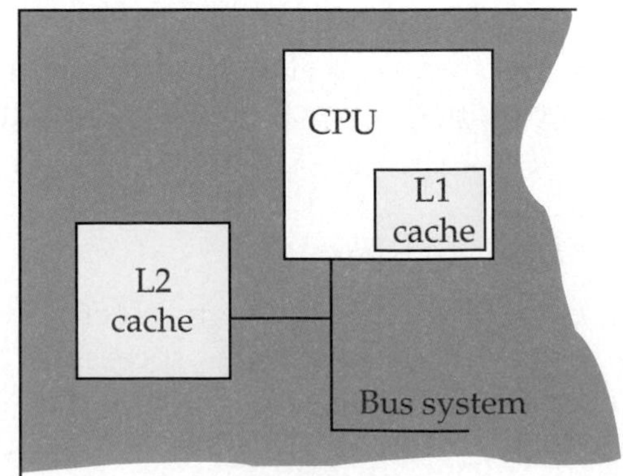

Figure 4-7.
Starting with the 486 processor, the L1 cache was incorporated into the CPU and the L2 cache was mounted on the motherboard in close proximity to the CPU.

Math coprocessor identification numbers are always one higher than the processor series they are designed to match. For example, a 386 processor would use a 387-math coprocessor.

Processor Descriptive Features

Processor descriptive features are a collection of terms used to explain, identify, and compare processing units.

System Management Mode

System Management Mode (SMM) was first developed for laptop computers to save electrical energy when using a battery. SMM was introduced in the 486SL processor and became a standard for all Pentium processors and later.

System Management Mode (SMM) a standby mode developed for laptop computers to save electrical energy when using a battery.

The power management is controlled by software usually set up by the CMOS setup program. Power management will put the CPU and the computer system into a state of rest or sleep and can actually shut down the complete PC system.

Clock Doubling

Earlier computer systems were designed with the processor in step or in synchronization with the other electronic components mounted on the motherboard. To accomplish higher processing speeds for the CPU while maintaining a common synchronization with other components on the board, CPU clock-doubling technology was developed.

The internal speed of the processor is referred to as the clock rate. Clock rate as well as bus speed is measured in hertz (Hz). As the speed of the processor has increased, the bus on the motherboard has failed to keep up with the processor speed. ***Clock doubling*** is simply the multiplying of the speed of the motherboard bus to run the CPU. Originally, the speed was multiplied by two, but multiples of three, four, and more quickly followed.

clock doubling running the CPU at a multiple of the bus frequency.

A crystal oscillator circuit produces the digital beat of the computer system. Simply put, a crystal is sliced very thin and electrical energy is connected to it. With the proper additional circuitry, a steady repetitive digital pulse is produced. This beat is the external bus speed of the motherboard.

Using microscopic digital circuitry at the clock input of the CPU, the steady beat can be doubled, tripled, quadrupled, or more. The technique is referred to as "clock doubling" even though now it more than doubles the frequency of the internal CPU digital pulse. Look at the chart in **Figure 4-8** to see how clock doubling affects the speed of the CPU while maintaining a lower motherboard bus speed that is in sync with the CPU.

Today, modern processors and motherboards use more sophisticated chipsets, which allow the processor and system bus to run at different clock rates and still remain compatible. Clock doubling is no longer a valid method used to increase computer performance. However, processors can be overclocked.

Figure 4-8.
A chart comparing the CPU internal clock rate to the motherboard bus speed and some common clock doubling speeds.

CPU	CPU speed	Clock doubling multiplier	Motherboard system bus speed
386	25 MHz	None	25 MHz
486DX	66 MHz	2	33 MHz
586	133 MHz	4	33 MHz
Pentium	100 MHz	1.5	66 MHz
Pentium	133 MHz	2	66 MHz
Pentium	200 MHz	3	66 MHz

Overclocking

Certain styles of CPU can operate at various frequencies. Sometimes CPU manufacturers substitute higher-speed processors than the computer system manufacturers order. While higher-speed processors are more expensive than lower-speed processors, the CPU manufacturers feel it is more important to be able to supply a CPU to the manufacturer when needed rather than wait until more of the requested lower-speed processors can be produced.

overclocking
forcing a processor to operate faster than its approved speed.

When computer-savvy people discovered the practice of substituting higher-speed processors in place of lower-speed processors, ***overclocking*** (sometimes called *speed margining*) was born.

Overclocking is *not* the same as clock doubling, but it is derived from the same techniques. Some motherboards are equipped with jumper settings that allow you to change the input frequency to the CPU. Consumers began to raise the input speed to the CPU to see if it would run at the higher speed. Many CPUs did, in fact, perform well.

The practice of overclocking is not supported by the manufacturing industry and voids the warranty status of the processor. When a processor runs at a higher speed than it is designed for, excessive heat develops that may damage the chip. The CPU may freeze up and come to a complete stop with or without a fatal error message. Remember that fatal error messages are issued by normally working processors that have a software or hardware problem.

A user might attempt to overclock their CPU and cause the system to fail or lock up during post. You can usually correct this problem by resetting the BIOS to its default settings. To reset the BIOS, consult the manufacturer's motherboard manual. Resetting the BIOS is typically performed by using the jumper located near the CMOS battery.

reduced instruction set computer (RISC)
a type of CPU architecture that is designed with a fewer number of transistors and commands.

RISC

Reduced instruction set computer (RISC) is a type of CPU architecture that is designed with a fewer number of transistors and commands. This architecture produces a CPU that is both inexpensive and fast. The trade-off is that the system software has to carry modifications to allow for fewer CPU instructions. This puts greater responsibility on the software written for them.

CISC

Complex instruction set computer (CISC) is, as the name implies, a CPU with a complex instruction set. The CPU die is designed to accept many machine language commands that manipulate or process complex mathematical formulas.

There is an increase in the number of transistors required to produce a CISC-based CPU. The added complexity causes an increase in clock cycles to produce the desired results. This type of system is best utilized by complex programming techniques. CISC is designed as the opposite of RISC systems.

complex instruction set computer (CISC)
a CPU with a complex instruction set.

MMX

In 1997, the ***MMX processor*** was introduced. The MMX processor was based on a standard processor with the addition of 57 commands that enhanced its abilities to support graphics technology. Many of the commands replaced functions normally carried out by the sound and video card. This allowed for faster processing of video and sound data. The L1 cache was made larger to assist in speeding the animation of frames.

The meaning behind letters *MMX* is debatable. Some claim it stands for Multi-Media eXtensions. Others claim it stands for Matrix Math eXtensions. Intel, the company that developed MMX technology, claims that MMX was not meant to be an acronym at all.

MMX processor
a processor with an additional 56 commands that enhance its abilities to support multimedia technology.

Multiple Branch Prediction

Multiple branch prediction is a technique that guesses what data element will be needed next rather than waiting for the next command to be issued. It is especially accurate in repetitive tasks and can significantly speed up CPU operations. Multiple branch prediction has proven to be over 90% accurate.

multiple branch prediction
a technique that predicts what data element will be needed next, rather than waiting for the next command to be issued.

Superscalar Technology

The 486 and all processors before it could only process one instruction at a time. Beginning with the Pentium, processing multiple instructions at the same time was possible. The act of processing more than one instruction at the same time is called ***superscalar*** execution.

superscalar
processing multiple instructions simultaneously.

CPUs are designed with two pipelines. Pipelines are parallel paths on which data travels to the CPU sections. This parallel path concept is what makes the CPU capable of performing two data manipulation functions at the same time. Two data words can be processed during the same clock tick. Again, the speed of the processor is now improved far beyond the limits of the clock. Superscalar technology is dependent not only on a new physical design of the processor, but also on an additional set of instructional commands to operate the twin pipelines while still maintaining backward compatibility with previous processors. All modern processors use superscalar technology.

Dynamic Execution

The term ***dynamic execution*** was coined by Intel to describe the enhanced superscalar and multiple branches predict features associated with the Pentium II processor. Dynamic execution is a combination of new physical features and additional instruction set commands manufactured into the processor chip. It is a technique that looks ahead at instructions coming to the processor. If an instruction can be carried out faster than the instruction preceding it, it is moved ahead of its current position and then executed.

dynamic execution
a term coined by Intel to describe the enhanced, the superscalar, and the multiple branch prediction features associated with the Pentium II processor.

Dual Independent Bus

Dual Independent Bus (DIB) is a bus architecture introduced with the Pentium Pro and Pentium II. As the name implies, there are two separate or independent bus systems incorporated into the processor chip. One bus connects to the main memory and the other connects with the L2 cache. Both buses can be used simultaneously rather than singly to increase program execution speed.

Dual Independent Bus (DIB)
a bus system architecture in which one bus connects to the main memory and the other connects with the L2 cache.

Real, Protected, and Virtual Modes

Real mode is supported by the 286 processor and later. It is used to operate within the first 1 MB of memory. In real mode, multitasking is not supported. The 286 processor acts like an 8088 or 8086 processor with the legacy limitations. In ***protected mode,*** the processor supports multitasking and accesses more than 1 MB of memory. In ***virtual mode,*** the processor can operate several real mode programs at once and access memory higher than the first 1 MB.

The various stages or modes are used in the Windows operating systems as a diagnostic tool. The operating system runs the processor as a simple device such as the early 8088 and 8086 processor. While in protected mode, each program is given its own section of memory and cannot access the other memory locations. This prevents one program from using another program's section of memory, causing a conflict that crashes the CPU.

real mode
an operating mode in which only the first 1 MB of a system's RAM can be accessed. Also an operating mode in which the 286 or later processor emulates an 8088 or 8086 processor.

protected mode
an operating mode which supports multitasking and allows access to memory beyond the first 1 MB.

virtual mode
an operational mode in which the processor can operate several real mode programs at once and access memory higher than the first 1 MB.

Simultaneous Threading

In software programming, a ***thread*** is part of a software program that can be executed independently of the entire program. When two or more threads are executed at the same time, it is called ***simultaneous threading.*** Intel coined the term *HyperThreading* to describe the simultaneous threading technology in their advertisements. Hardware and software companies often coin new terminology to describe computer technology in their advertisement campaigns. Sometimes the technology is brand new, but often only the marketing term is new.

thread
part of a software program that can be executed independently of the entire program.

simultaneous threading
executing two or more threads at the same time.

Processor Affinity

Processor affinity is the ability to select the number of CPU cores to apply to a software application. To take advantage of multi-core processors, the operating system and the software application must be designed to operate in the multi-core environment. If a software program or application is not designed to work with a multi-core processor, the software could lock up. It may be necessary to disable the multiple cores so that the software application can run properly. To disable one of the cores, you simply open the Task Manager, right-click the software program, and select **Set Affinity** from the shortcut menu. See **Figure 4-9.**

In the **Processor Affinity** dialog box, **Figure 4-10,** you can select the processor you wish to use with the software application. Simply deselect CPU 0 or CPU 1 to run the software application on a single processor.

processor affinity
the ability to select the number of CPU cores to apply to a software application.

Cool 'n' Quiet™

The Cool 'n' Quiet™ feature from AMD adjusts the processor speed and power consumption automatically based on the temperature and processing demands of a running program. Fan speed is also automatically adjusted. Intel has a similar technology called "Intel® Precision Cooling technology."

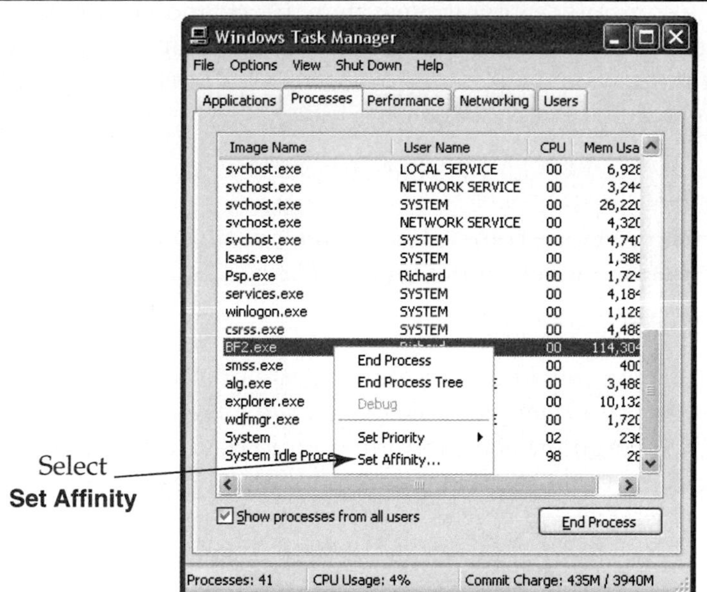

Figure 4-9.
To disable the use of multiple CPUs for a program that is not designed to work with multiple CPUs, access Task Manager and right-click the program. Select **Set Affinity** from the shortcut menu. The **Processor Affinity** dialog box will display.

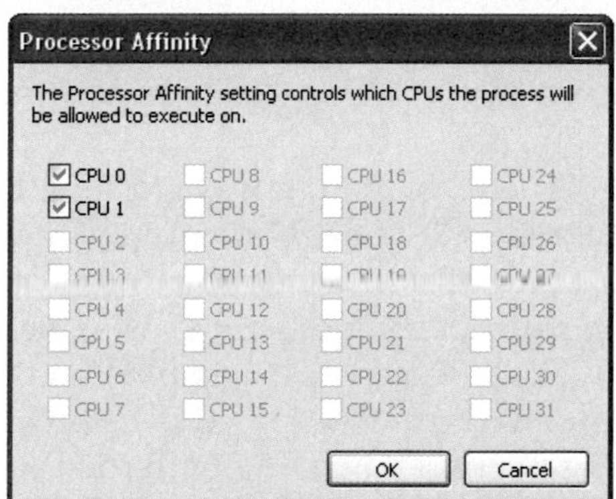

Figure 4-10.
Processor Affinity dialog box.

Controlling processor frequency is referred to as ***processor throttling.*** Processor throttling is used to conserve portable computer battery life. The frequency of the CPU is directly proportional to the demand of the software application(s) running on the system. If no software application is running, the frequency of the processor is automatically lowered to conserve battery life and produce less heat as well. There will be more about this feature in Chapter 12—Portable PCs.

processor throttling
controlling processor frequency to conserve battery life and produce less heat.

Enhanced Intel SpeedStep® Technology

Intel originally developed Enhanced Intel SpeedStep® technology for its line of portable computers. This technology is designed to change the applied system voltage and CPU frequency under certain conditions. For example, when a laptop is connected to an AC source, the CPU frequency is 2.6 GHz and the applied system voltage is 1.3 volts. The overall power consumed is 30 watts. When the same laptop is run on battery power, the CPU frequency is reduced to 1.2 GHz and the applied system voltage is reduced to 1.2 volts. The overall power consumed is 20.8 watts, a reduction of almost 10 watts. To take advantage of this technology, the computer's operating system, BIOS, and chipset must support it. Enhanced Intel SpeedStep® technology is already incorporated into Windows XP and later operating systems. It can be accessed on a portable computer under the **Power Options** icon in Control Panel.

Moore's Law

In 1965 Gordon Moore, cofounder of Intel, predicted that computers would double in calculating power approximately every 12 months. So far, he has been pretty close to correct. The amount of time has slightly lengthened to about 18 months.

Computers have evolved technically at a rate unsurpassed by any other technology in history. Other technologies have evolved at a snail's pace when compared to the computer. The continuing rapid development of the computer is difficult to predict, but most experts agree that this present rate will continue for some time.

CPU Voltages

CPU operating voltage has decreased over the years. The reason for decreasing the operating voltage levels is to reduce the amount of heat generated by the CPU when processing data.

Motherboards are designed in different ways to achieve different CPU voltage levels. Some boards are equipped with a set of jumpers located beside the CPU. Various voltage levels can be achieved by moving the jumper position. This is a very common method on third-party motherboards. Another method is the use of a voltage regulator. A voltage regulator is installed on the motherboard beside the CPU. The voltage regulator is easy to spot. It is usually equipped with its own small heat sink for cooling purposes. Starting with the Pentium, applied voltage from the motherboard was reduced from 5 volts to 3.5 volts.

Always read the motherboard documentation to ensure the correct jumper setting corresponds to the correct voltage level of the CPU. An incorrect jumper setting can easily damage the CPU.

Cooling the CPU

As the CPU evolved to higher data speeds, the heat generated by the processor circuits also increased. Electrical circuits generate heat in proportion to the speed of data flow. Electronic integrated circuits start to break down at approximately 160°F (71°C). To counteract the effect of heat generated by the processor, heat sinks and internal fan units became standard equipment for the CPU. See **Figure 4-11.**

Figure 4-11. CPUs and some chips require cooling fans to assist in removing excessive damaging heat. High heat will damage a CPU as well as other chips. The large fan in the photograph is mounted on a Pentium 4 processor. Directly behind the large fan is a smaller fan mounted on the north bridge.

A heat sink is designed to remove and dissipate heat from the CPU. Heat sinks are attached to the CPU by heat conductive paste, also called *thermal compound*. The paste ensures a good fit between the surface of the processor and heat sink. Without the paste, the heat sink could warp slightly, resulting in poor physical contact between the surfaces, and the CPU could heat up to a dangerous level.

Heat sinks come in various shapes and sizes. The heat sink is designed with a series of fins for increased surface area. The larger the surface area, the better its ability to cool. Top end, high performance computers may incorporate a cooling system similar to the one in **Figure 4-12.** This is a liquid cooling system complete with a pump, lines, a radiator heat exchange unit, and a CPU heat exchange unit. Liquid cooling provides a superior cooling effect compared to the air exchange systems. Liquid cooling is often installed on overclocked systems. When overclocked, the CPU generates higher than normal heat levels. Fan and heat sink combination units will not normally remove the additional heat generated by an overclocked CPU.

An internal fan may be attached directly to the CPU or used in conjunction with a heat sink. Never operate a CPU without a fan. Certain motherboards are designed with a heat detection device located near or under the CPU unit. The detection device reports high temperatures experienced by the CPU due to fan or heat sink failure. The motherboard's circuitry is designed to shut down the system if excessive heat is detected. The speed and temperature monitoring features are not supported by all motherboards or BIOS systems.

Figure 4-12.
Liquid cooling system. (Swiftech Inc.)

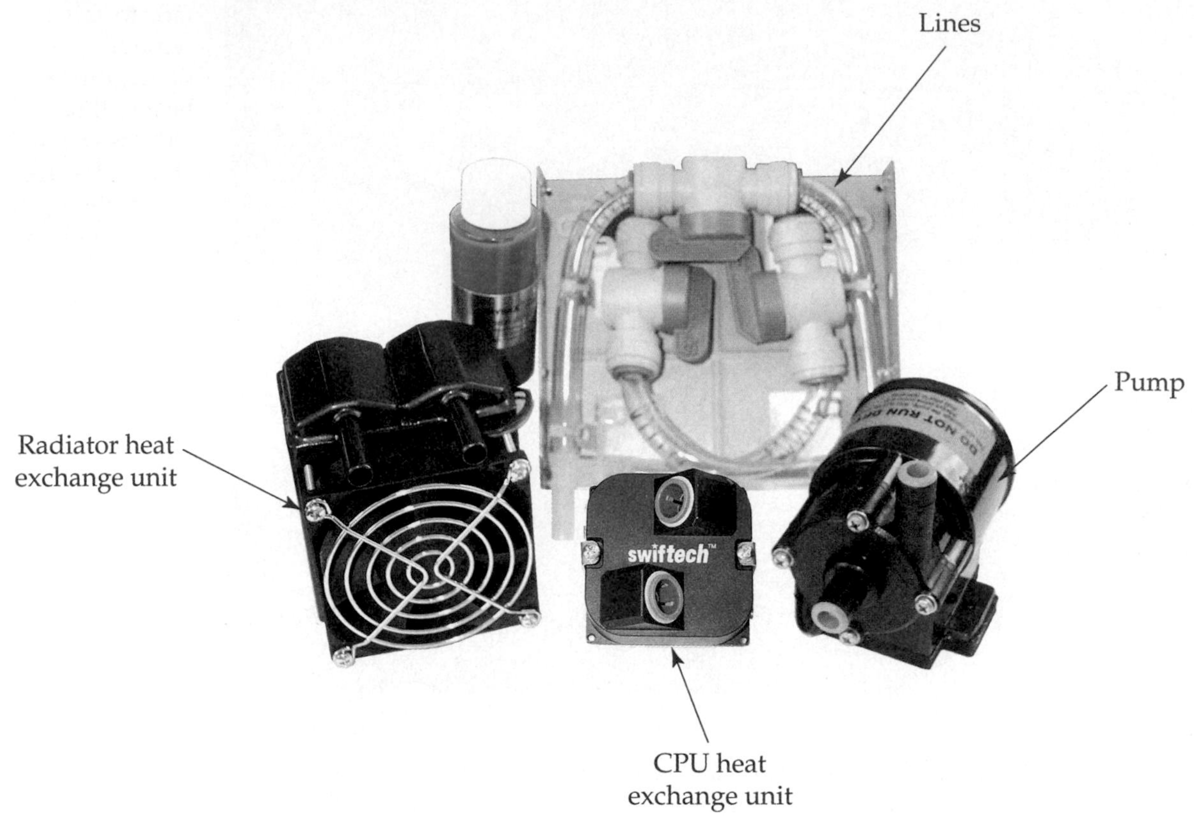

Processor Manufacturers

While there are a large number of past and present CPUs to choose from, three companies have produced most of these chips. These three competitors are Intel, AMD, and Cyrix.

Intel

Intel is the dominant force in the manufacturing of CPUs for PCs. Intel has been at the top in sales since introducing the 8086 processor to the market in the 1970s. Sales of Intel's 8088 chip were great enough to propel Intel into the Fortune 500.

Intel has continued to dominate the computer processor manufacturing market through the years. Today, Intel controls the vast majority of computer chip manufacturing. Intel not only manufactures CPUs but also chipsets, motherboards, wireless devices, and networking devices.

AMD

Advanced Micro Devices (AMD) has long been Intel's biggest competitor. Originally AMD manufactured math coprocessors, but when the math coprocessor began to be integrated into the CPU chip, AMD began manufacturing its own CPU. AMD began its series with the 486 and designed its processor to be compatible with the Intel series. Both Intel and AMD manufacture excellent CPUs.

You must be careful when upgrading a PC. For example, the AMD Slot A is physically compatible with the Intel Slot 1 design. However, the two processors do not have compatible electrical connections. The data lines and the control lines are not in the same position. You must also check if the BIOS and the motherboard chipset support the processor. Most of the information needed to determine the processor upgrade can be obtained from the motherboard manufacturer's Web site. Always check before attempting to perform an upgrade.

VIA Cyrix

Cyrix is a CPU manufacturer that was acquired by VIA Technologies. While the Cyrix CPU does not command a large portion of the desktop industry, it is a quality product at a reasonable price, especially for low-cost models.

Processor Evolution

Familiarity with the CPU evolution will assist you on the A+ Certification exams as well as give you some insight into the future development of the processor. There may be several questions on an exam asking you to identify which processor first implemented a specific feature. The following brief outline should help prepare you for such questions.

In the past, numbers such as 286, 386, 486 always identified CPUs. It was easy to identify the latest technology (and to predict the name of the next processor). Intel tried to protect their processor by trying to trademark the processor number. The courts ruled against them saying that a company cannot trademark a number. Consequently, Intel changed their practice by naming their processor line with a nonnumerical nomenclature. Thus started the Pentium, Pentium Pro, Celeron, and so on. This change in practice has made it much more difficult to identify where any particular processor belongs in the evolution of processors.

Intel 8086

The first PC introduced by IBM contained an Intel 8086 processor. The processor ran at 4.77 MHz and contained a 16-bit internal bus and was capable of a 16-bit external bus. Standard small computer systems used an 8-bit bus structure for the motherboards. At the time, making a 16-bit motherboard for the 8086 seemed like an expensive waste. This is an important point to note about the development of the PC. Simply making a more advanced processor doesn't necessarily mean the rest of the computer industry will follow suit. Developing a more sophisticated CPU also requires more sophisticated software and support hardware. A CPU that can transmit data using a 16-, 32-, or 64-bit bus width cannot be effective without other hardware and software capable of handling that same improved bus width. The 8086 was reengineered to accommodate the 8-bit external bus and was rereleased in 1979.

Intel 8088

Next in the line of development was the 8088, which was released in 1979. It was a 16-bit internal CPU that had an 8-bit external bus. The speed of the CPU was 5 MHz and 8 MHz. The 8088 is famous because it was the chip used in the original IBM PC.

Intel 80286

The 80286 (or 286) was released in 1982. It also had a 16-bit internal bus width, but the speed of the processor was significantly increased to 12 MHz. The 80286 introduced a significant advancement in computer industry known as protected mode. Protected mode, as mentioned earlier in this chapter, is the capability to assign specific areas of the computer memory to specific software programs. Each program is provided protection from interference from the other program. Look at **Figure 4-13.**

In real mode, only one computer software program could be loaded into memory at one time. To load a second program, the first had to be unloaded from memory. An interesting point to note with the 80286 is that it could change from real mode to protected mode but not return to real mode. To return to real mode from protected mode, the computer had to be rebooted. The 80286 could address up to 16 MB of memory.

Intel 80386DX

The 80386DX processor was given the DX suffix to separate it from other 386 models such as the SX and SL. The 80386 was released in 1985. It made vast improvements over the 80286. The 80386 could address up to 4 GB of memory, had a 32-bit bus width, and could boast a processor speed up to 33 MHz. The processor could also support multitasking.

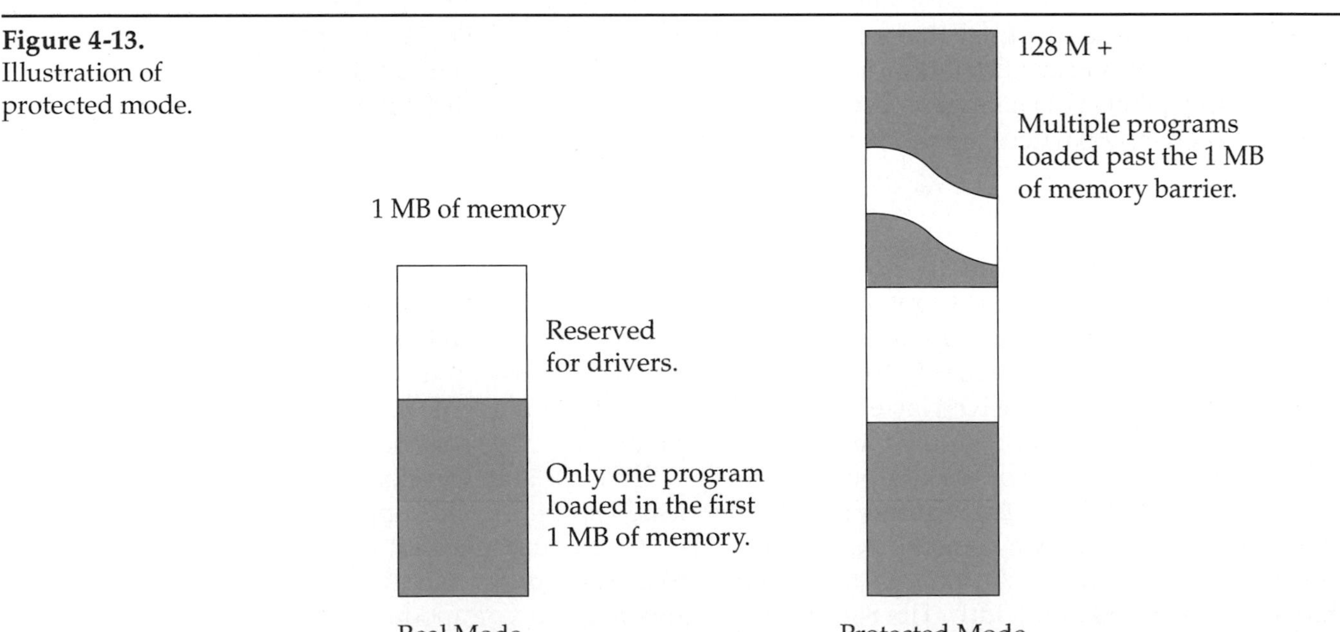

Figure 4-13. Illustration of protected mode.

Names of processors are often reduced to their last three digits. For example, an 80386 is usually referred to as simply a 386 processor.

Intel 80386SX

The 386SX model was introduced in 1988 with features similar to the 80386DX. The SX model of the 386 was designed as a less expensive version of CPU for lower-end use. It could only address a 16-bit external bus, a step back from the DX model, which could address a 32-bit external bus.

Intel 80386SL

The 386SL was introduced in 1990. It was developed with power management in mind to be used for the laptop industry. It is important to remember that portable (laptop and notebook) computers have such a restricted space to mount components in that they usually have problems performing adequate cooling. For this reason, they are usually less optimized than their full desktop or tower counterparts.

Intel 80486DX

The 486DX was introduced in 1989 and runs at speeds of 25 MHz, 33 MHz, and 50 MHz. It utilizes a built-in L1 memory cache and incorporates the math coprocessor into the CPU. This model also uses pipeline techniques.

Intel 80486SX

The 486SX model was introduced in 1991 as an inexpensive 486 model. It lacks the built-in math coprocessor and has a maximum speed of 33 MHz.

Intel 80486SL

The 486SL was introduced in 1992 with power management features.

Intel 80486DX2

The 486DX2 was also introduced in 1992. Its major feature was a clock doubler to increase the internal speed of the CPU.

Intel 80486DX4

The 486DX4 was introduced in 1994. Its major feature was the internal clock rate tripled in the CPU. The typical processor clock rates are 75 MHz and 100 MHz.

Intel Pentium

Introduced in 1993, the Pentium ran with a maximum clock rate of 200 MHz. The bus width was raised to 64 bit. It was classified as CISC architecture, and it is designed with many RISC features such as pipelining and superscaling.

Intel Pentium Overdrive

The Pentium Overdrive was introduced in 1995 with a maximum clock rate of 100 MHz. It was designed as an upgrade for the 486-based computer and was equipped with an overdrive socket mounted on the motherboard.

Intel Pentium Pro

The Pentium Pro was introduced in 1995 with a maximum clock rate of 200 MHz.

Intel Pentium with MMX

Introduced in 1997, the Pentium with MMX operates with a maximum clock rate of 233 MHz. The chip was designed for multimedia applications.

Intel MMX OverDrive

The MMX OverDrive was introduced in 1997 and operates at a maximum clock rate of 200 MHz. It was designed as an upgrade for the Pentium processor.

Intel Pentium II

Introduced in 1997, the Pentium II operates with a maximum clock rate of 450 MHz. It was the first design with the Single Edge Contact (SEC) processor package.

Intel Pentium Xeon

The Pentium Xeon processor was introduced in 1998. It was designed for high-end applications such as network servers and for communication between multiple CPUs installed on the same server. The processor has an FSB that operates at 533 MHz and a speed that ranges from 1.8 GHz to 3 GHz. The Pentium Xeon uses a socket 603 and has an L3 cache. It also has an L1 cache that ranges from 8 kB to 12 kB, and an L2 cache that ranges from 512 kB to 2 MB.

Intel Celeron

The Intel Celeron, introduced in 1999, is a budget-minded processor designed for general purpose applications. The Celeron comes in two distinct core designs: single core and dual core. Not all Celerons support 64-bit processing. There are some that only support 32-bit processing. The 32-bit Celeron design uses the 478 socket. The 64-bit Celeron design uses the 775 socket. The Celeron has excellent speed as compared to other processor models, but this can be misleading about the overall performance of the processor. The limited size of the Celeron L1 and L2 cache counters the high speed of the processor, resulting in less overall performance when compared to other Intel processor models.

Intel Pentium III

The Pentium III was introduced in 1999 and continued to be reintroduced in variations through 2000. There are 70 new instructions added to its machine language command set to increase its ability to manipulate graphics, video, audio, and speech recognition abilities. Its maximum processing speed is approximately 1 GHz. It has over 28 million transistors and can address 64 GB of memory. The CPU core voltage is 1.5 volts.

AMD Athlon

The AMD Athlon processor, introduced in 1999, is available in a wide range of speeds from 900 MHz to 1.4 GHz and has FSB speeds of 200 MHz and 266 MHz. The Athlon is designed for advanced multimedia applications. It parallels the Pentium 4 class of processors.

AMD Duron

The AMD Duron was introduced in 2000. It was designed as a low-end desktop processor to compete with the low cost Intel Celeron. The L2 cache is only a modest 64 kb. The reduced size of the L2 cache lowers the overall throughput and reduces the costs of the processor. The FSB is available in the 100 MHz and 200 MHz range, which also reduces the overall cost of the CPU. The AMD Duron installs into a Socket 462, or a Socket A. It parallels the Pentium III classes of processors.

Intel Pentium 4

The Pentium 4 was originally introduced in November of 2000. There have been many versions of the original Pentium and Pentium 4 processors. The original processor was 32 bit and was later redesigned as a 64-bit processor. The FSB increased over the years from the original 400 MHz to 633 MHz and 800 MHz.

You cannot upgrade an existing 32-bit Pentium 4 processor with a 64-bit Pentium 4. You must have a motherboard with a chipset and BIOS that supports 64-bit technology. Also note that only specific Pentium 4 models have Enhanced Intel SpeedStep® technology incorporated into the CPU.

VIA Cyrix III

The VIA Cyrix III, introduced in 2000, is built from a 0.18 micron manufacturing technology and is installed in a typical Socket 370 motherboard interface. The CPU is designed for 500 MHz to 700 MHz speeds. It has a 128 kB L1 cache and a 100/133 MHz FSB. It is completely compatible with any X86 technology. (X86 technology refers to general PC technology based on the sequence of development such as the 8086, 80286, and 80386.)

Intel Xeon MP

The Xeon MP is designed for server applications and was introduced in 2001. It has a core frequency range from 1.4 GHz to 2.8 GHz and supports an FSB of 400 MHz. The Xeon MP mounts into a socket 603. The processor contains an L1 cache of 20 kB, an L3 cache of 256 kB, and an additional L3 cache of 1 MB located on the motherboard. The three-cache system produces a very high data throughput, outperforming any processor with similar core frequency.

AMD Athlon MP

The Athlon MP processor, introduced in 2001, is designed primarily for server applications and mounts to the motherboard via a socket A. Its CPU internal clock speed range is 1.8 GHz to 2.2 GHz. The L1 cache is 128 kB, and the L2 cache is 512 kB. It supports a 266 MHz FSB. Do not confuse the AMD Athlon MP with the Intel Xeon MP.

AMD Athlon XP

The Athlon XP, introduced in 2001, can be found in servers, high-end workstations, and normal desktop computer systems. Athlon XP has 128 kB L1 and 512 kB L2 cache integrated into the CPU. An additional cache on the motherboard is referred to as L3 and ranges in size according to the motherboard manufacturer. The CPU operates at 1700 GHz to 3200 GHz with an FSB speed of 333 MHz to 400 MHz. The XP installs into a Socket 462 or a Socket A.

Intel Itanium

In 2001, Intel introduced two Itanium processors: Itanium 1 and Itanium 2. The Intel Itanium 2 processor is a high-end CPU designed for large enterprise servers and technical applications requiring a high degree of processing power.

The Itanium incorporates three levels of cache: L1, L2, and L3. The L3 motherboard cache size ranges from 3 MB to 6 MB. The L2 is 256 kB, and the on-chip L1 cache is 32 kB. It uses a 400 MHz bus.

Intel designed a plastic rail to help support the Itanium processor when mounted on the 478 socket. The 478 socket was first introduced with the Pentium 4. The plastic mounting rail surrounds the socket and is designed to ensure that the cooling mechanism makes perfect contact with the processor surface. The processor surface must be in proper alignment with and fit snugly to the heat dissipation mechanism. Without proper alignment with the processor surface, the processor would fail to transfer excessive heat to the cooling assembly. The CPU would heat in a short period of time, causing a system failure.

AMD Athlon 64

The AMD Athlon 64, introduced in 2002, is an extremely powerful desktop CPU. As the name implies, it uses 32-bit and 64-bit processing technology. L1 and L2 cache are integrated into the CPU, and an L3 cache is mounted on the motherboard. The Athlon 64 is designed to mount in a 940-pin socket. Normally the increased number of pins would increase the overall dimensions of the CPU socket. The Athlon 64 CPU, however, uses the Socket 940 micro PGA. The micro PGA reduces the socket pin grid array area, reducing the overall size of the CPU socket even with an increase in the number of pins.

Portable computer systems, such as laptops and tablet PCs, do not provide as much air flow and cooling space as desktop or tower models. In addition, portable PCs do not have sufficient room to accommodate large heat sinks. Because of CPU cooling restrictions, portable PCs do not provide the same high performance as a desktop or tower model using a similar processor.

AMD Opteron

The AMD Opteron, introduced in 2003, is a high-end processor designed and developed for network servers. The Opteron eliminated the 4 GB memory address barrier associated with earlier processors. The 4 GB memory access limitation is a trait of the 32-bit design, but the Opteron uses a 64-bit memory address design, allowing for greater memory capacity. Total possible accessible memory is 256 TB, but that number is impractical for now. The typical core processor speeds range from 800 GHz to 2600 GHz, but the processor can produce a throughput of 19 GB or more by using multiple paths to process data. The 64 kB L1 cache and the 1024 kB (1 MB) L2 cache are both integrated into the CPU chip. The Opteron mounts into a Socket 940 micro PGA.

AMD Sempron

AMD Sempron, introduced in 2004, is the successor to the AMD Duron processor and is designed for use in low-cost computer systems. The Sempron requires a socket 754 on the motherboard. The interesting thing about the Sempron is that it comes in two very different styles—HyperTransport and front side bus (FSB) with a north bridge chipset. You must be sure of which Sempron you are going to install or replace.

For CPUs that use HyperTransport, speed is represented by megatransfers per second (MT/s), not frequency (Hz). AMD claims 2000 MT/s is equal to 4 GBps in each direction of the bus. The transfer speed can also be measured as gigatransfers (GT/s), but AMD has chosen to represent the transfer speed in MT/s. To a casual reader with no real computer expertise, 2000 MT/s looks much more impressive than 2 GT/s.

AMD Athlon 64 X2

The AMD Athlon 64 X2, introduced in 2005, is a dual core processor that incorporates a new technique of accessing frequently used data. The Athlon 64 X2 cores are capable of higher data throughput than the single core Athlon 64. The Athlon 64 X2 is intended to be used in all computer systems except high-end or high-performance models.

AMD Athlon 64 FX

In 2006, AMD introduced the Athlon 64 FX and a new socket design called *AM2*. Although, the Athlon 64 FX processor is physically and electrically compatible with the socket 939 and socket 940. This means that the Athlon 64 FX can be used to upgrade an older computer that uses the previous version CPU mounted in a socket 939 or socket 940. The AM2 socket, however, is not compatible with previous version of AMD processors that fit into the socket 939 and socket 940. The Athlon 64 FX is comparable to the Intel Core 2 Extreme. Both are intended for use in high-end or high-performance computer systems, which require intense processing performance.

Intel Core Solo

The first Intel Core processor, referred to as Intel Core Solo, was introduced in the summer of 2006. The Intel Core Solo is a single core processor designed for laptop and other portable computer systems. Intel changed the physical and electrical design of its processor to meet the demands for less power consumption and high data throughput. The lower power consumption was a desirable feature for marketing laptop and portable devices. The higher data throughput is the most common design characteristic of CPU evolution and is expected in all new models. The Core Solo is also the core design utilized by the Intel dual core and quad core CPUs.

Intel Core Duo

The Intel Core Duo was also introduced in the summer of 2006. It was the first dual core processor designed by Intel and at first, was intended for the laptop market. At this point in computer development, laptops were becoming more popular than desktops. To take advantage of this growth market, Intel revised the CPU design to better capture a large market share of the laptop computer sales. This was done by developing the Intel Core Duo processor. The duo core design provided greater processing power with reduced electrical power to decrease heat.

Intel Core 2 Duo

The Intel Core Duo, introduced in 2006, is two processor cores mounted inside one CPU chip. The Core Duo differs from the AMD dual core in two main design issues. First, the Intel Core 2 Duo uses an FSB, which connects the CPU to the RAM and north bridge chipset through one common bus. The AMD dual core uses the HyperTransport bus system. Second, the Intel Core 2 Duo varies the amount of L2 cache used by each core based on program demand. The AMD design does not share the L2 cache.

Intel Core 2 Extreme

The Core 2 Extreme, introduced in 2007, is comparable to the AMD 64 FX processor. The Core 2 Extreme is also referred to as Core 2 X, where the "X" represents extreme. The Core 2 Extreme has the highest dual core processor throughput and the largest L2 cache (8 MB at the time of this writing.) The Core 2 Extreme is designed for use in intense processing computer systems such as gaming, computer-aided drafting, three-dimensional rendering, and scientific formula processing.

Intel Core 2 Extreme Quad

The Core 2 Extreme Quad, introduced in 2007, is also referred to as Core 2 Quad and Core 2 Q. The Core 2 Extreme Quad is the first quad core processor design. The Core 2 Extreme Quad houses four independent processor cores on the same CPU. It uses the same core as the Core 2 Extreme processor. The main idea is to double the capabilities of the Core 2 Extreme processor by doubling the core on one single chip. To take advantage of the quad core processing, the software application must be designed to take advantage of the four cores. Otherwise, there will not be a significant increase in software application performance.

The tables in **Figure 4-14** show a selection of characteristics for some common Intel and AMD processors. To see more information about various CPUs, visit www.geek.com/procspec/procspec.htm. This Web site has an in-depth amount of information on Intel, AMD, Sun, Alpha, VIA, and HP CPUs.

Multi-Core Processors

A multi-core processor is two or more processor cores constructed on the same die. Increased data throughput is achieved mainly by using a dual core. Both Intel and AMD manufacture multi-core processors.

Figure 4-14.
These tables list of characteristics for some common processors. A—Intel processors. B—AMD processors.

Name	Bits	Clock Speed (in GHz)	Bus Speed (in MHz)	Socket	L1 Cache	L2 Cache	Cores
Celeron D	32*	2.53–3.33	533	478	8 kB 12 kB	256 kB	1
Celeron D	32/64	3.2–3.33	533 800	775	8 kB 32 kB	512 kB	2
Pentium 4	32/64	3.0–3.8	533 800	775 478 423	8 kB 20 kB	256 kB 512 kB	1
Pentium Extreme	32/64	3.2–3.73	800 1066	775	8 kB 16 kB	2 × 1 MB 2 × 2 MB	2
Pentium D	32/64	2.66–3.6	533 800	775	2 × (16 kB + 12 kB)	2 × 1 MB 2 × 2 MB	2
Core Solo	32/64	1.06–1.83	533 667	479M	32 kB	2 MB	1
Core 2 Duo	32/64	1.86–2.66	800 1333 1066	775	2 × (32 kB + 32 kB)	2 MB 4MB	2
Core 2 Extreme	32/64	2.93–3.0	800 1333 1066	775	2 × (32 kB + 32 kB)	2 MB 4 MB 8 MB	2
Core 2 Extreme Quad	32/64	2.40–2.66	1066	775	2 × (32 kB + 32 kB)	8 MB	4

Note: The plus (+) sign indicates two L1 caches are present: the data cache and instruction cache.
*Early Celerons were 32 bit, later 64 bit.

A

(Continued)

Figure 4-15 shows the internal architecture of an AMD Athlon 64 processor and an AMD Athlon 64 FX processor. The AMD Athlon 64 processor in Figure 4-15A contains a single core and two L1 caches. One L1 cache is used to temporarily store processing instructions and commands, and the other L1 cache is used to temporary store data being processed. The two L1 caches make the processing of data twice as fast as processors that contain a single L1 cache. L1 cache is typically smaller and faster than L2 cache. The AMD Athlon 64 uses an L1 cache of 64 kB while L2 cache is typically 1 MB or more.

The DDR memory controller connects directly with RAM. The HyperTransport Link connects to other devices and buses across the motherboard. The HyperTransport technology was presented in the previous chapter.

Figure 4-14.
(Continued)

Name	Bits	Clock Speed (in GHz)	Bus Speed (in MHz)	Socket	L1 Cache	L2 Cache	Cores
Athlon 64	32/64	1.8–2.6	1600 MT/s	754	64 kB + 64 kB	512 kB 1 MB	1
Athlon 64 X2	32/64	1.9–2.1	2000 MT/s	939	2 × (64 kB + 64 kB)	2 × 512 kB 2 × 1 MB	2
Athlon 64 FX	32/64	2.6–3.0	2000 MT/s	AM2	2 × (64 kB + 64 kB)	2 × 512 kB 2 × 1 MB	2
Athlon 64 FX	32/64	2.2–3.0	2000 MT/s	939 940	64 kB + 64 kB	1 MB	1
Athlon Sempron	32/64	1.6–2.2	1600 MT/s	754	64 kB + 64 kB	256 kB 512 kB	1
Athlon Sempron	32/64	1.5–1.75	333 MHz*	A	64 kB + 64 kB	256 kB	1

Note: The plus (+) sign indicates two L1 caches are present: the data cache and instruction cache.
*At the time of this writing, there is an AMD Sempron that uses an FSB that runs at 333 MHz.

B

As you can see in Figure 4-15B, the AMD Athlon 64 FX processor consists of two complete AMD Athlon 64 processors on the same die. Each processor has its own set of L1 caches, and each has its own L2 cache. The two processors share the DDR memory controller and the HyperTransport Link.

The Intel Core Duo has two L1 caches per core, just like the AMD Athlon 64 FX processor. The big difference between the AMD and Intel multi-core processors is the L2 cache design. The AMD Athlon 64 FX processor has an L2 cache for each core; the Intel Core Duo has one L2 cache, which is shared by each core. See **Figure 4-16.** The reason Intel decided to share the L2 cache is so that the amount of L2 cache being used by each core is directly proportional to the processing demand of each core. For example, if only one core is being used, then that one core will use the entire L2 cache. If one core is running at 25% and the other at 75%, the L2 cache will also be split in a 25% and 75% ratio. This means that the entire L2 cache is used at all times. In the AMD design, the L2 cache can only be used by the corresponding processor core.

Another significant difference is the fact that the AMD multi-core design makes use of HyperTransport technology and does not use a north bridge chip. The data throughput using the HyperTransport technology is used to connect directly to the south bridge, additional CPUs, or other devices. The AMD multi-core processor also connects directly to the RAM and does not have an FSB as the Intel multi-core design does. The FSB design of Intel multi-core system requires that the RAM share the FSB with the north bridge. See **Figure 4-17.**

Figure 4-15.
The internal architecture of a single core and dual core AMD Athlon processor. A—AMD Athlon 64 (single-core) processor. B—AMD Athlon 64 FX (dual-core) processor.

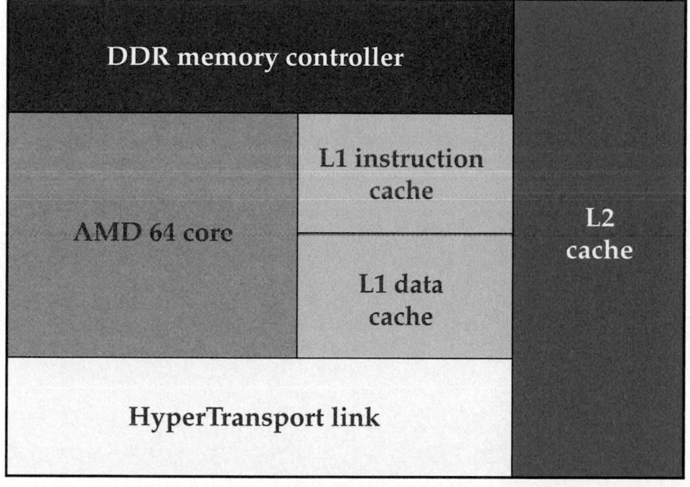

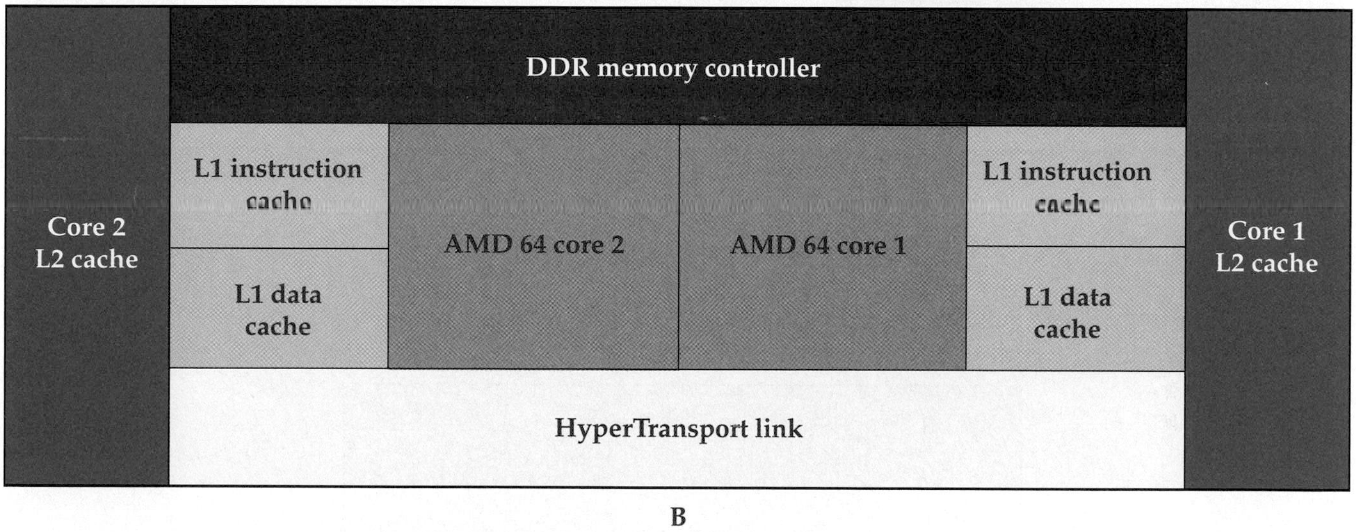

DDR memory controller
L1 instruction cache
AMD 64 core
L2 cache
L1 data cache
HyperTransport link
A

DDR memory controller
Core 2 L2 cache
L1 instruction cache
L1 data cache
AMD 64 core 2
AMD 64 core 1
L1 instruction cache
L1 data cache
Core 1 L2 cache
HyperTransport link
B

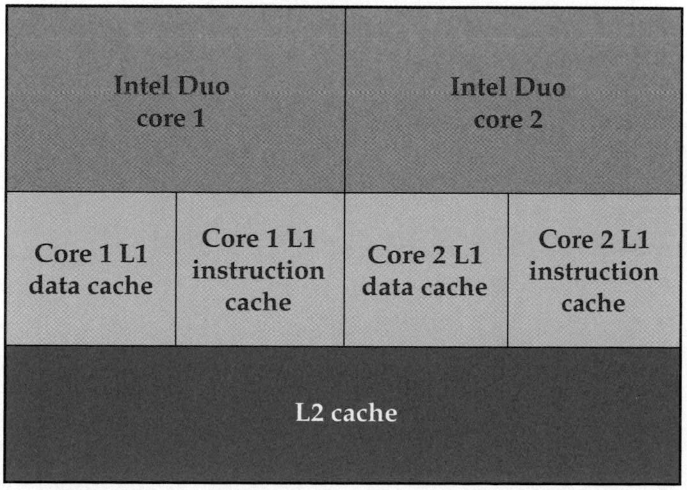

Intel Duo core 1
Intel Duo core 2
Core 1 L1 data cache
Core 1 L1 instruction cache
Core 2 L1 data cache
Core 2 L1 instruction cache
L2 cache

Figure 4-16.
Internal architecture of the Intel Core Duo. Notice it has one L2 cache, which is shared by each core.

Figure 4-17.
An AMD multi-core processor and an Intel multi-core processor interface differently with motherboard devices, chipsets, and other CPUs. A—An AMD multi-core processor connects directly to the south bridge chip, RAM, and other devices. B—The Intel Core Duo connects directly to the front side bus (FSB).

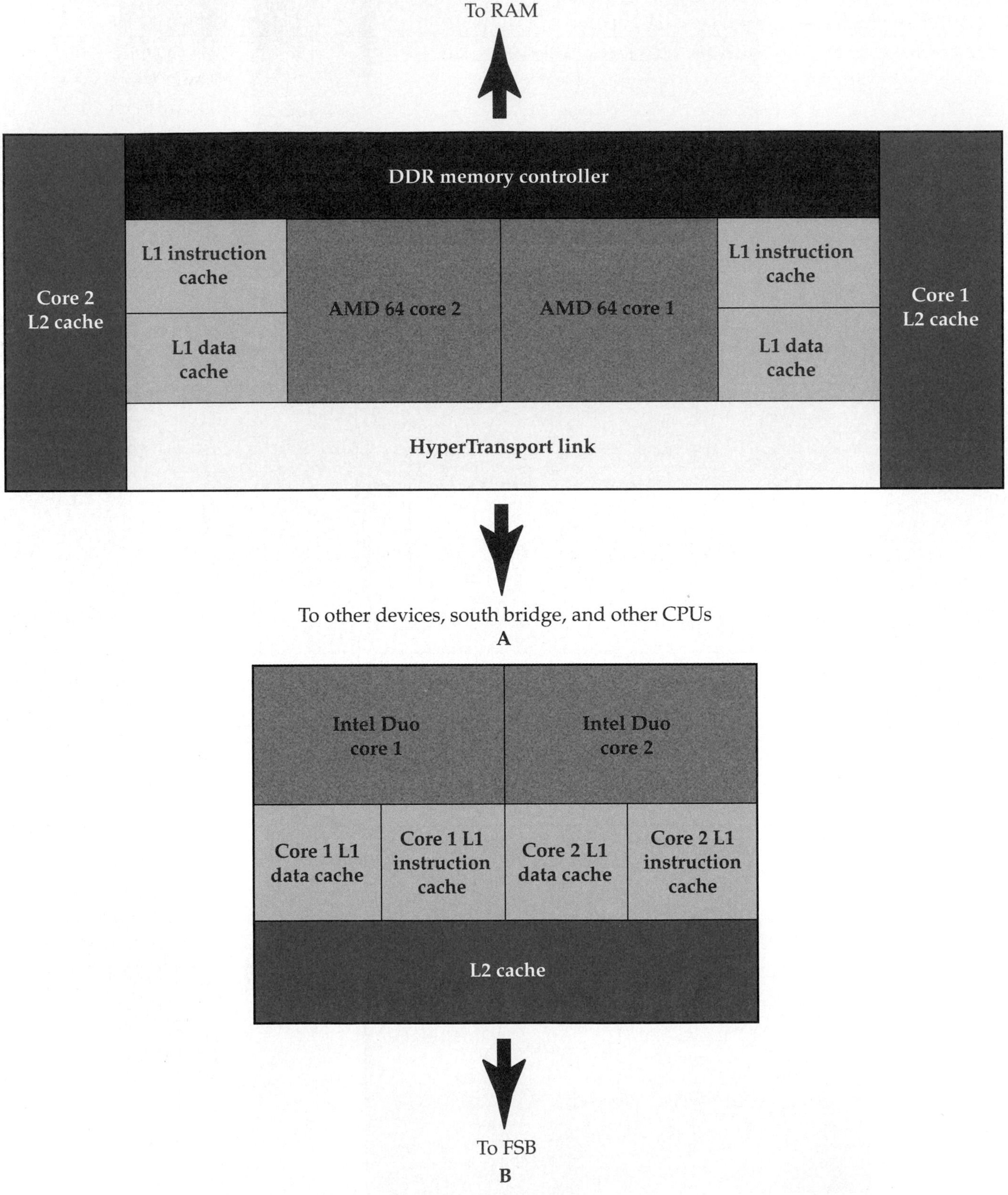

Processor Performance

Because the Intel and AMD physical designs are so different, they cannot be evaluated by the specific features. Both companies claim superior performance based on their CPU designs. The only way to fairly evaluate the CPU performance is by comparing them as they perform running software applications. There are numerous sources of performance comparisons such as www.CNET.com, www.technewsworld.com, www.PCworld.com, www.PCmag.com, and www.extremetech.com.

The true performance of a CPU can only be measured by evaluating the performance of two different computer systems using similar hardware. However, it is nearly impossible to exactly match the two systems because of the motherboard chipset and bus system. Rather than try to evaluate a specific CPU, you are better off evaluating a complete computer system and how the exact same software application performs on each computer system. There is a great interactive benchmark CPU performance chart located at www23.tomshardware.com/cpu.html.

A free CPU analyzer, called CPU-Z, is available from www.cpuid.com/cpuz.php. It will identify the CPU, size of the L1 and L2 cache, socket type, core speed, bus speed, and more. Look at **Figure 4-18.** Notice that the CPU-Z utility has identified two cores for the processor and additional related information. This is an excellent tool for identifying processor specifications as well as motherboard and memory specifications without opening the computer case and looking for part numbers.

Sixty-Four and Thirty-Two Bit Technology

CPUs and other computer devices as well as software are often referred to as 32 bit and 64 bit. What is being described by the terms *32 bit* and *64 bit* is the amount of data that can be processed in parallel during one cycle or clock beat. This is also referred to as the data width. The 64-bit technology provides

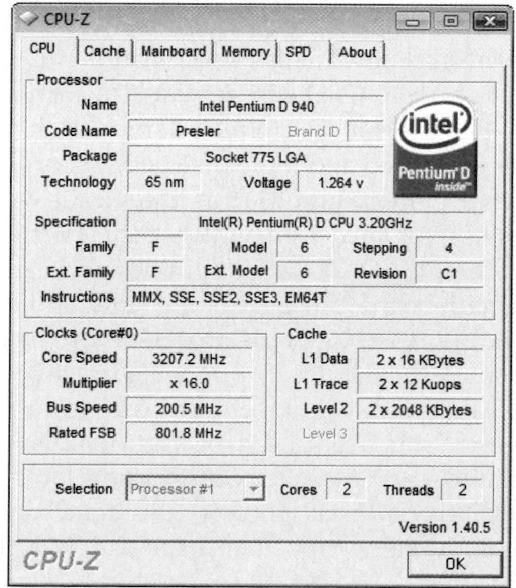

Figure 4-18. The CPU-Z utility, available from www.cpuid.com/cpuz.php, can be used to identify the CPU, size of L1 and L2 cache, socket type, core speed, bus speed, and more.

data paths twice as wide as 32-bit technology. This means that large volumes of data can be transferred much quicker with a 64-bit processor than with a 32-bit processor. The 64-bit technology is also superior to 32-bit technology when large amounts of program storage are required.

The 64-bit technology was first introduced in Windows Server 2003 and Windows XP Professional 64-bit Edition. The 64-bit technology provides access to vast amounts of memory and virtual memory for programs that require it, such as CAD/CAM, digital image creation and manipulation, in-depth financial analysis, computer games with rich graphic content, or any application requiring a great deal of memory and processor throughput.

For a computer system to take full advantage of 64-bit technology, four things are required in addition to a 64-bit processor:

- ✔ BIOS that supports a 64-bit processor.
- ✔ 64-bit operating system.
- ✔ 64-bit device drivers.
- ✔ Software applications written for 64-bit.

Take note that for data to transfer using 64-bit technology, the 64-bit operating system also requires 64-bit software device drivers, otherwise data will still be transferred as 32 bit. Also, keep in mind that a software program designed as a 32-bit system will not show any significant increase in performance when running on a 64-bit CPU using a 64-bit operating system.

Socket and Slot Styles

The CPU is physically packaged in two main styles: a socket design and a Single Edged Contact (SEC) cartridge. **Figure 4-19** and **Figure 4-20** show various socket designs and the SEC cartridge. The type and size of CPU sockets have evolved over the years. The pattern of pins is referred to as the ***pin grid array (PGA).***

pin grid array (PGA) the pattern of pins on a CPU.

zero insertion force (ZIF) socket a processor socket equipped with a lever to assist in the installation of the CPU.

Single Edge Contact (SEC) a processor configuration in which the CPU is mounted on a circuit board and the edge of the circuit board inserts into the motherboard socket.

A ***zero insertion force (ZIF) socket*** is designed with a lever to assist in the installation of the CPU. The original socket design required many pounds of force to insert the CPU pins into the CPU socket. Many times this resulted in damage to the pins and even damage to the motherboard. To alleviate the use of severe force, the ZIF socket was designed. It requires practically no force at all to insert the CPU into the socket while the lever arm is raised. Once the CPU is inserted into the socket, the lever is lowered, which in turn causes each pin to fit tightly into the socket. The ZIF socket literally clamps each pin into place.

As the system bus is expanded and more instructional code features are added, more connections to the CPU are required. Thus, the socket system has also evolved, increasing the number of pins. One design, which started with the Pentium II, was the ***Single Edge Contact (SEC).*** It is similar in design to an adapter card. The CPU is mounted on a circuit board. The edge of the circuit board inserts into the motherboard socket. The SEC cartridge-type processor also incorporates a heat sink and fan as part of the complete assembly. Examine Figure 4-20.

Both Intel and AMD have SEC cartridge-type possessors. Intel's SEC cartridge-type processors are inserted into a Slot 1 socket, and AMD's SEC cartridge-type processors are inserted into a Slot A socket. Both sockets look similar; however, they are electrically different. *Never* insert a processor designed for a Slot A socket into a Slot 1 socket or a processor designed for a Slot 1 socket into a Slot A socket.

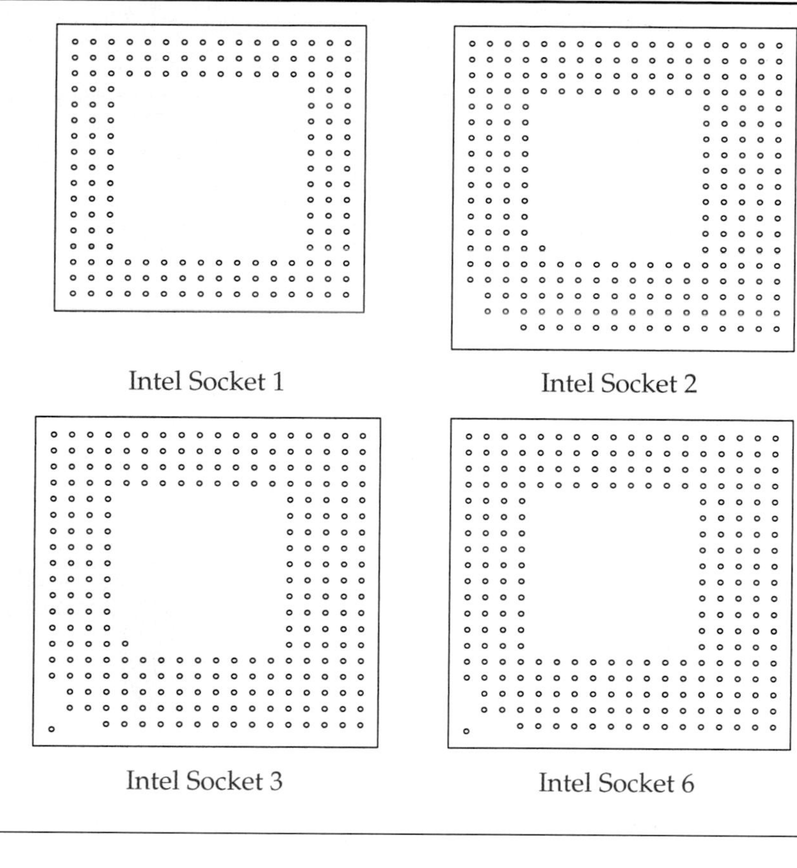

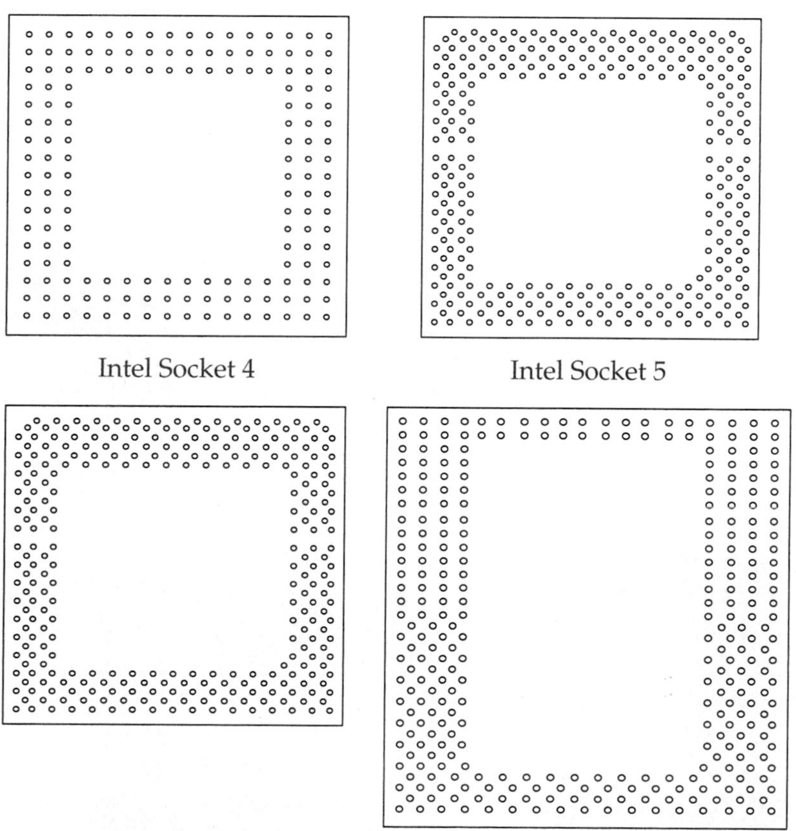

Figure 4-19. Illustration of various socket designs. A—Socket designs used for 486 processors. B—Socket designs used for the Pentium and Pentium Pro processors. C—Socket designs used for the PIII, P4, Xeon, Itanium, and Core processors. D—Socket designs used for the Athlon, Duron, and Opteron processors.

(continued)

Figure 4-19.
(Continued)

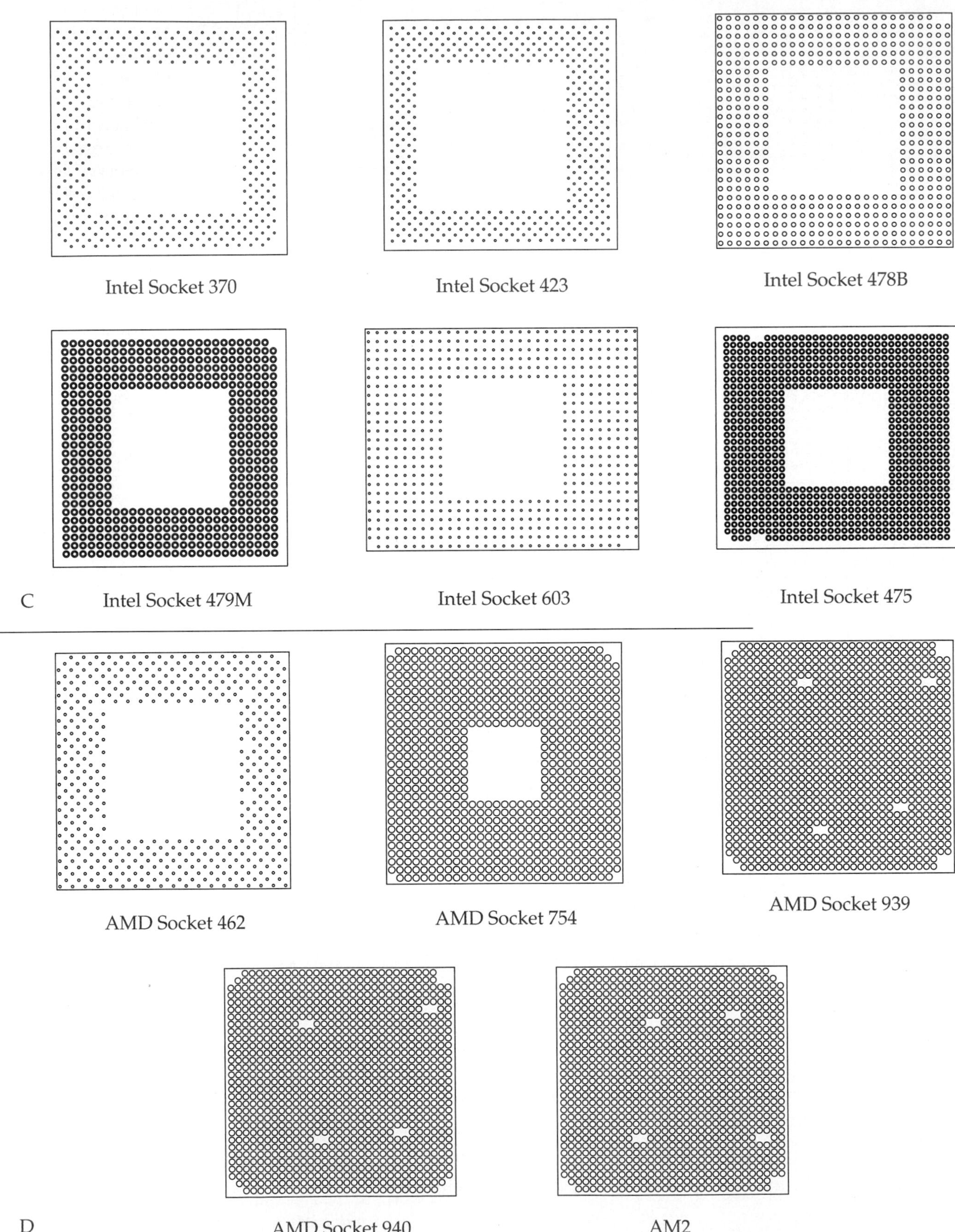

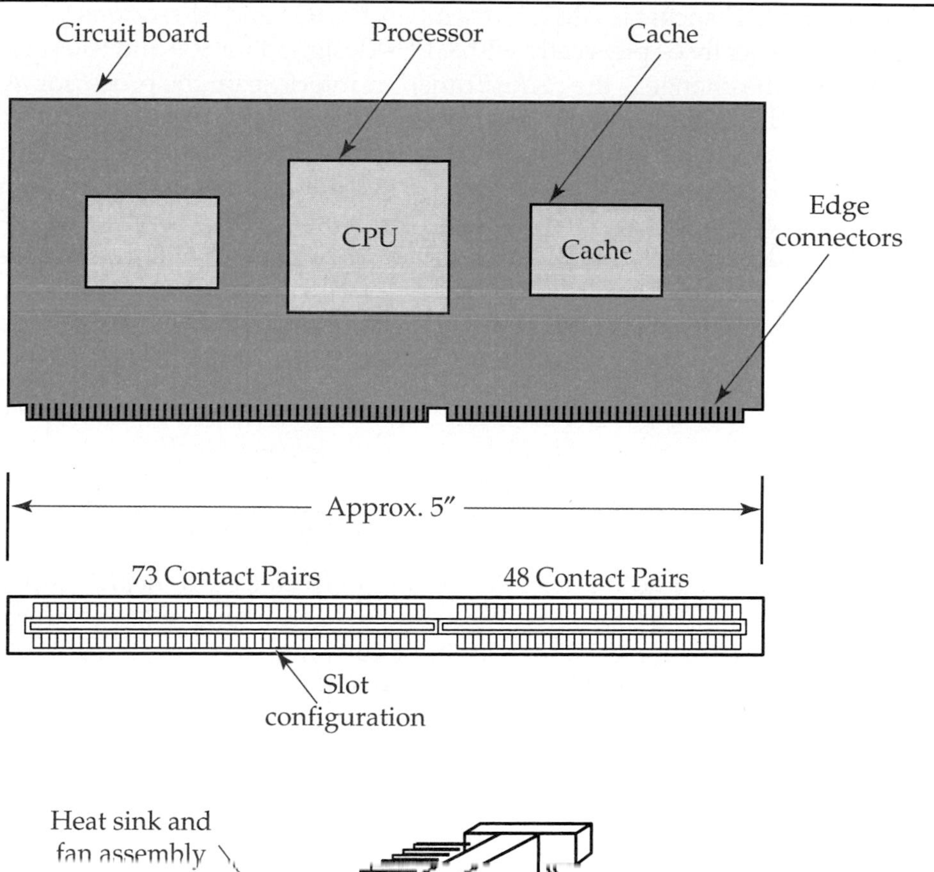

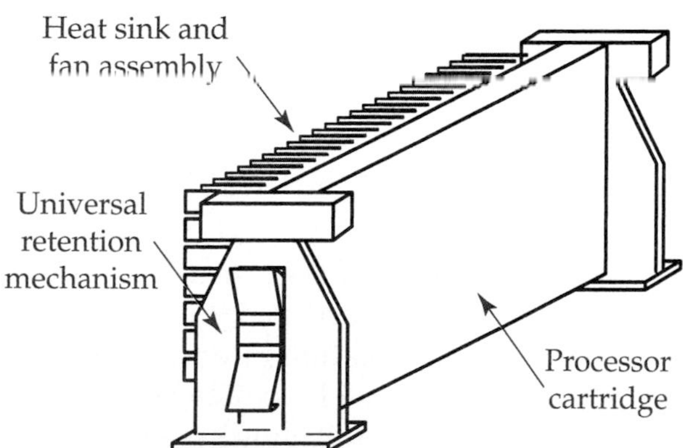

Figure 4-20. Detailed assembly of Pentium II or III SEC cartridge-type processors. The processor is mounted on a circuit board and then enclosed in a cartridge package. A fan and heat sink assembly is added for cooling. The cartridge and heat sink assembly is attached to a universal retention mechanism for weight support.

AMD features two sockets: the socket 939 and socket 940. They appear almost identical except for the one pin difference. The one pin difference is very significant. The socket 939 does not require registered RAM and socket 940 does. Registered RAM is typically used for servers and mission critical computers. Most desktop PCs do not require registered type RAM. Therefore, you will find that most AMD desktop PCs use socket 939, not 940. There will be a detailed explanation of registered RAM in Chapter 6—Memory.

Remember that Slot A is used for AMD processors, and Slot 1 is used for Intel processors. A good memory aid is to associate the uppercase “A” in Slot A with the “A” in AMD. Since the “1” in Slot 1 looks similar to an uppercase “I”, you can associate the number “1” with the letter “I” in Intel.

The latest AMD socket is AM2. It resembles the 939 and 940 sockets, but it is not compatible electrically or physically with CPUs designed for 939 and 940 sockets. The reason for the change is the HyperTransport interface on the processor. AMD CPUs that use the HyperTransport technology are no longer compatible with motherboards which use a north bridge chip in the chipset. The AMD Athlon 64 FX will physically fit into a 939, 940, and AM2 socket, but it can only take advantage of the larger L2 cache design when installed in an AM2 socket.

The AM2 socket also supports direct data transfers to DDR2 RAM. The 939 and 940 sockets do not. DDR2 RAM is a high-performance RAM that is covered in detail in Chapter 6—Memory. The original name of the AM2 socket was simply M2 but later was changed because it was confused with the M2 socket design introduced by Cyrix.

Questions to Ask before Upgrading a CPU

The process of upgrading the CPU can range from easy to nearly impossible. An important point is to be aware of the physical arrangement of the processor case before upgrading the CPU. The motherboard must be compatible with the physical style of the CPU package. The degree of likelihood for a logical upgrade is based on several computer system conditions. Questions you should first answer include:

- ✔ What are you trying to achieve by upgrading the CPU?
- ✔ Is the upgrade processor compatible physically with the motherboard socket or slot?
- ✔ Will the chipset and BIOS support the upgraded processor?
- ✔ Does the motherboard bus speed, rather than the CPU speed, limit the increase in speed you desire?

Transferring data to and from the hard drive or a scanner is mostly an issue involving the motherboard bus speed and port speeds and not the speed of the CPU. If an increase in the speed of downloading information from the Internet is the challenge, a new processor is not likely to increase the download speed. Download speed is more dependent on the cabling system between the downloading site and the computer and the modem speed. If typing is the main function performed at the computer, upgrading the CPU will have little to no effect on the user's typing speed.

As you can see, upgrading a processor may not meet your desires. If you crunch a lot of data or play games that contain intensive graphics and sound, you may very well improve the performance of the computer system by upgrading the CPU. Often, it is more practical to replace the CPU and the motherboard to achieve the desired results. The table in **Figure 4-21** can help you select a processor to meet a user's intended application and desired computer performance level.

Performance Levels and Application	Intel	AMD
High-end performance, such as intense graphics, audio, and video processing.	Core 2 Extreme	Athlon 64 FX
Average performance, such as multimedia editing and processing by the average user.	Core 2 Duo Pentium D Pentium 4	Athlon 64 X2 Athlon 64
Low performance, such as in an introductory-level PC not designed for graphics and multimedia processing.	Celeron	Sempron 64

Figure 4-21. Desired performance levels and recommended processors.

Summary

- ✔ The CPU is constantly evolving with manufacturers' attempts to improve processing power.
- ✔ Both L1 and L2 cache are small areas of memory close to the processor. L1 is usually incorporated into the integrated circuit of the processor.
- ✔ When L1 and L2 cache are incorporated into the CPU, the cache off the CPU chip is referred to as L3 cache.
- ✔ Math coprocessors became integrated into the CPU beginning with the 486.
- ✔ Clock doubling is an old technique that enabled the internal parts of the CPU to keep in step with the motherboard bus system while allowing the CPU to operate at a higher speed.
- ✔ Overclocking is running a CPU faster than the speed it is rated for.
- ✔ RISC is used to produce an inexpensive CPU.
- ✔ MMX technology was developed mainly for multimedia applications.
- ✔ The speed of the processor is increased not only by clock speed but also by data processing techniques such as superscalar technology, multiple branch prediction, and MMX.
- ✔ Superscalar technology is the ability of the CPU to carry out more than one instruction during a single clock beat.
- ✔ Real mode is when a CPU is running under the standard DOS restrictions such as only 1 MB of memory and no multitasking.
- ✔ Protected mode is running the CPU with multitasking capabilities.
- ✔ Moore's law states that the calculating power of the CPU doubles every 12 months. In reality, it is actually approximately every 18 months.
- ✔ Processor throttling is a method of controlling the running frequency of a processor in order to conserve battery life and produce less heat.
- ✔ To combat the heating problem associated with the higher CPU speeds, heat sinks and internal fans became part of the CPU assembly.
- ✔ The voltage required to operate the CPU has also been reduced from 5 volts to 3.5 volts or lower.
- ✔ A multi-core processor has two or more processors built into the same die.
- ✔ Virtual memory is located on the hard drive and is used to supplement RAM.

Review Questions

Answer the following questions on a separate sheet of paper. Please do not write in this book.

1. What three methods or devices are used to cool the CPU?
2. What is cache?
3. Which processor first introduced L1 cache?
4. Which processor was specifically designed for improved video animation?
5. What three methods are used to combat the CPU heat problem?
6. What does the term *superscalar* mean?
7. When did superscalar begin?
8. What is System Management Mode?
9. What does the arithmetic logic unit do?
10. What is a math coprocessor?
11. What is a ZIF socket?
12. Where is L3 cache located?
13. What does the term *clock doubling* mean?
14. What does overclocking mean?
15. What is a dual independent bus, and when was it introduced?
16. Which processor first integrated the math coprocessor into the CPU chip?
17. State Moore's law.
18. What is protected mode?
19. What is real mode?
20. How many more instructional commands were added to the instruction set of a CPU with MMX technology?
21. What is Intel's term used for simultaneous threading?
22. What does MT/s represent?
23. What is Enhanced Intel SpeedStep® technology?
24. What is processor affinity?
25. Which AMD desktop processor is comparable to the Intel Core 2 Extreme?
26. Which AMD desktop processor is comparable to the Intel Celeron D?
27. Does the AMD Sempron use an FSB or a HyperTransport bus system?
28. What socket is used for an AMD Athlon 64 processor?
29. Which socket is used for an Athlon processor: Slot A or Slot 1?
30. Which AMD processor is most similar to the Intel Celeron?
31. Which Athlon processor contains the largest L2 cache?
32. What type of socket is used for the Pentium 4?
33. What is the main difference between the AMD 940 and 939 sockets?
34. What four things are required of a computer system to take full advantage of 64-bit processing?

Sample A+ Exam Questions

Answer the following questions on a separate sheet of paper. Please do not write in this book.

1. Which of the following are true statements concerning the L1 cache? Choose all that apply.
   a. It is generally incorporated into the CPU.
   b. It generally transfers data faster than external cache.
   c. It is usually much larger in storage size than motherboard RAM.
   d. It is a form of temporary memory storage.
2. A CPU register is best described as what?
   a. A cache memory used to store hardware information
   b. A temporary memory storage unit
   c. The CPU clock signal generator
   d. The trademark associated with the brand of CPU
3. Which statement best describes the location of the FSB?
   a. The FSB connects directly to the USB port.
   b. The FSB connects directly to the CPU.
   c. The FSB connects directly to the back side bus.
   d. The FSB connects directly to the HDD interface connector.
4. Which is the best definition of the term *superscalar*?
   a. A CPU die that is unusually physically large in cross-sectional area
   b. A CPU specially designed with a set of instructions to scale AutoCAD drawings
   c. A CPU design that supports the processing of more than one instruction at the same time
   d. A CPU design that automatically overclocks the processor speed
5. Which mode allows the CPU to access more than 1 MB of RAM?
   a. Real mode
   b. Protected mode
   c. RISC mode
   d. Safe mode
6. When upgrading a CPU, which three items below should be given consideration?
   a. BIOS version
   b. CPU socket/slot type
   c. Size of the RAM
   d. Motherboard chipset
7. The acronym SEC represents what?
   a. System energy control
   b. Secret encryption code
   c. Single edge contact
   d. Solid edge connector
8. Which technology was developed for multimedia applications?
   a. RISC
   b. PGA
   c. MMX
   d. SMM
9. Which factors directly affect the speed of data manipulation by the CPU? Choose two.
   a. Clock frequency
   b. Bus width
   c. Voltage level
   d. System temperature

10. When replacing or upgrading the CPU, you should always do what?
    a. Leave the fan assembly off and run the system for awhile to be sure the new CPU is operating correctly.
    b. Move the jumpers on the motherboard to test for the highest overclocking speed that the CPU can safely handle.
    c. Check the manufacturer's Web site for the latest upgrade or replacement information.
    d. Replace the BIOS as a matter of routine practice.

Suggested Laboratory Activities

Do not attempt any suggested laboratory activities without your instructor's permission. Certain activities can render the PC operating system inoperable.

1. Go to the AMD Web site and access the instructions for installing and replacing an AMD processor.
2. Go to the Intel Web site and access the instructions for installing/replacing Intel Core 2 Extreme and Intel Core 2 Quad.
3. Select a PC in the lab, visit the manufacturer's Web site, and locate step-by-step procedures for replacing the CPU.
4. Go on the Internet and download a shareware utility to measure CPU performance.
5. Visit the Intel Web site and AMD Web site and research the latest CPU technologies.
6. Go to www.cpuid.com and download and install a copy of the free CPU analyzer.
7. Open the Task Manager and view the **Processor Affinity** dialog box for a multi-core processor.
8. Go to the AMD Web site and locate the AMD Builders Guide or use the "AMD Builders Guide" for a keyword search on Google. Survey the material, including how to install the various types of AMD processors.

Interesting Web Sites for More Information

http://support.intel.com/support/processors/pentium4/inuse.htm
www.amd.com
www.amd.com/us-en/assets/content_type/white_papers_and_tech_docs/31684.pdf
www.amdcompare.com/us-en/desktop/
www.ibm.com
www.idt.com
www.intel.com
www.intel.com/design/quality/celeron/parts.htm
www.intel.com/design/quality/celeron/ppga/integration.htm
www.mips.com
www.motorola.com
www.nec.com
www.sun.com
www.ti.com

Chapter 4
Laboratory Activity
Installing a Pentium 4 Processor

After completing this laboratory activity, you will be able to:

- ✔ Identify the required socket used for an Intel Pentium 4 processor.
- ✔ Explain the key steps to installing an Intel Pentium 4 processor.
- ✔ Explain the importance of properly applying the thermal compound.

Introduction

In this lab activity, you will install a Pentium 4 processor and fan and heat sink assembly. The Pentium 4 is designed by Intel, and installs into a 478-pin micro pin grid array (µPGA). The symbol for micro (µ) is often used in the acronym. The micro PGA uses less space on the motherboard for the socket because the pins are placed closer together than in any other previous socket design.

The installation of the Pentium 4 processor can be quite complex compared to earlier processor installations. One of the most critical aspects of installing the processor is the installation of the fan and heat sink assembly. The fan and heat sink assembly requires electrical power to operate properly. Electrical power is provided by a three-pin connection located on the motherboard in close proximity to the processor.

Note:
You may need additional instructional sheets if the fan and heat sink assembly does not match the one in this lab activity.

Heat exchange between the cooling unit and the processor is also critical. Simply mounting the fan and heat sink assembly on the processor is not sufficient. A thermal compound must be installed between the processor and fan and heat sink assembly to ensure heat will dissipate in the most efficient manner. Without the thermal compound, the heat conduction between the processor and the fan and heat sink assembly is significantly reduced and can cause the processor to overheat. Excessive heat can damage the processor.

The thermal compound looks like a cream-colored, grease-type material. The thermal compound may come in a separate container or be already spread on the processor and protected by a clear plastic cover. If it is already spread on the processor, the protective plastic cover must be removed before installing the fan and heat sink assembly.

Sometimes thermal compound is supplied in a tube. When in a tube, simply open the tube and squeeze the compound onto the base of the heat sink or onto the surface of the processor. Rather than using your finger, you may use a small piece of plastic that comes with the packaging to smear the thermal compound evenly across the surface area.

Note:
When replacing a defective processor, some of the thermal compound may be removed and should be replaced.

Some key points to remember while installing a processor include the following:

- ✔ Always wear a ground strap when handling static-sensitive devices such as a processor.
- ✔ Always place the static-sensitive materials (processor and motherboard) on an anti-static mat or inside the original plastic package. Never lay them on a workbench unless the workbench has been designed to handle static-sensitive devices.
- ✔ The fan and heat sink assembly must be designed specifically for the Pentium 4 processor model you are installing.
- ✔ Thermal compound must be installed between the processor and the fan and heat sink assembly.
- ✔ If the thermal compound is already spread on the fan and heat sink assembly and protected by a clear plastic cover, the protective plastic cover must be removed before installation.
- ✔ A Pentium 4 processor requires a special motherboard with a 478-pin micro pin grid array (μPGA) and a power supply with a rating sufficient to support the processor. The power supply should indicate that it is designed for a Pentium 4 processor.

For more information on Pentium 4 installation procedures, visit Intel's support Web site at www.support.intel.com/support.

Equipment and Materials

- ✔ Pentium 4 processor (model determined by instructor) and fan and heat sink assembly.
- ✔ Motherboard with a 478-pin mPGA socket and retention frame.
- ✔ Anti-static mat or packaging for processor and motherboard.
- ✔ Additional instruction sheets may be required for this lab activity, especially if the fan and heat sink assembly do not match the one in this activity.

Procedure

1. _______ Gather all materials required for this lab activity and report to your assigned lab location.

Note:

When handling the motherboard or the Pentium 4 processor, be sure to take the proper electrostatic discharge (ESD) precautions.

2. _______ If available, read the motherboard manual prior to installing the processor. Read the section specific to processor installation.
3. _______ If the retention frame is not already installed on the motherboard, remove the four white pushpins from the black fasteners in each corner of the frame. The four black fasteners should remain fully seated in the retention frame.

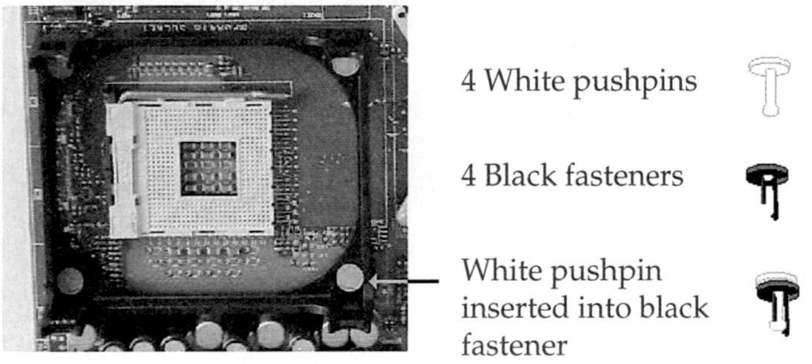

4 White pushpins

4 Black fasteners

White pushpin inserted into black fastener

4. _______ If the retention frame is already installed, skip to step 8.
5. _______ Place the retention frame on the motherboard, aligning it with the four corner holes that surround the processor socket.
6. _______ Secure the retention frame to the motherboard by gently pressing on the black fasteners until they snap into place.
7. _______ Insert the four white pushpins into the black fasteners, one at each corner of the retention frame.
8. _______ Carefully remove the processor from its box. Do *not* handle or touch the processor pin area.

9.______ Place the socket ZIF lever in the fully released position. The fully released position is when the lever is in the upright position.

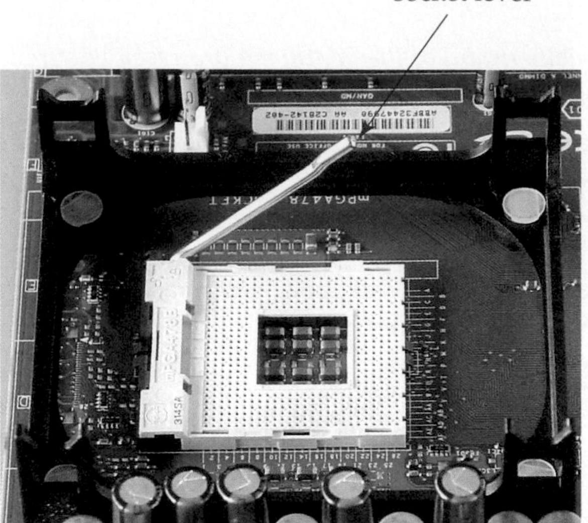

10.______ Look closely at the processor pin grid pattern to ensure the pin pattern on the processor matches the pin pattern of the socket. The socket has one corner pin hole missing near the hinge area of the ZIF socket lever. This is where pin 1 is located. Align pin 1 on the processor with pin 1 on the socket and insert the processor. There is a dot on the back of the processor, which indicates pin 1. No force is required to insert the processor pins into the socket.

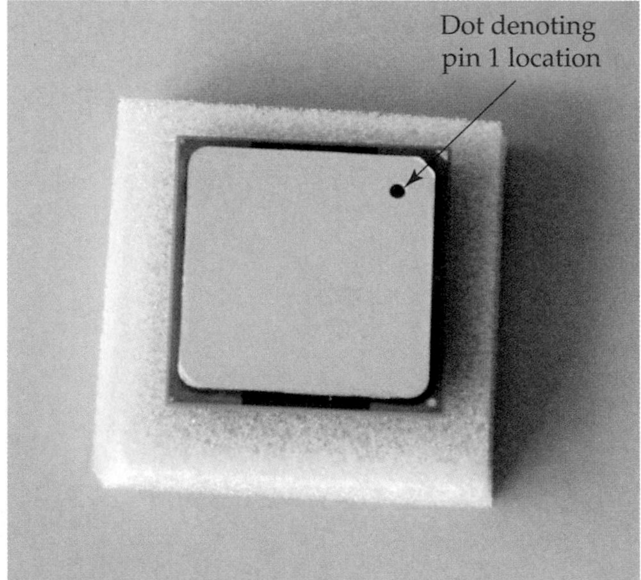

11.______ After the processor has been inserted into the socket, close the ZIF socket lever by pushing the lever down to its lowest position.

12._______ If the processor fan and heat sink assembly already have thermal compound applied, remove the plastic cover. Do *not* touch the white patch containing the thermal compound.

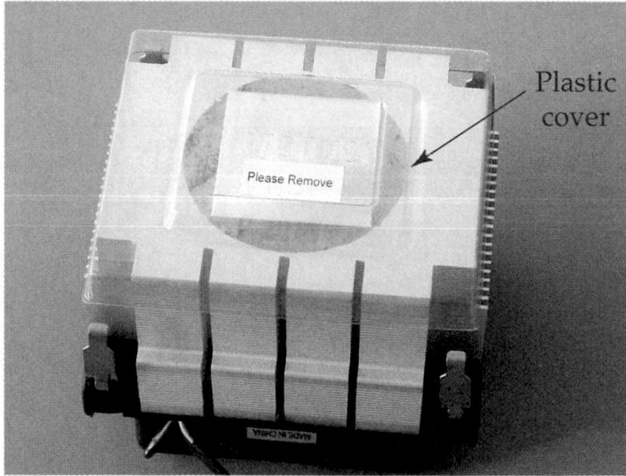

13._______ If the thermal compound is included in an applicator with the processor, apply the entire thermal compound material to the center of the processor's surface.

14._______ Make sure the lever of the fan and heat sink assembly is in the unlocked position. (See the following illustration.)

15._______ Align the fan and heat sink assembly with the retention frame (the fan and heat sink assembly is symmetrical with the retention frame) and place it on the processor. The retaining clips on the fan and heat sink assembly should align with the holes in the retention frame. Make sure the fan and heat sink assembly cable is not trapped between the assembly and retention frame. Allow the heat sink base to compress (without rotating or twisting) the thermal compound material.

16.________ Move the lever of the fan and heat sink assembly to the locked position. The lever action will insert all four retaining clips into the holes of the retention frame. It is important to *not* allow the heat sink assembly to rotate or twist on the processor's surface. Securing the fan and heat sink assembly while closing the lever ensures the thermal interface material is not damaged and the processor will operate correctly.

17.________ Once the lever is locked, verify that the fan and heat sink assembly is securely retained and that the retaining clips are properly engaged with the retention frame.

18.________ Connect the fan and heat sink assembly fan cable to the motherboard fan power header. Consult the motherboard manual to determine the correct fan header to use.

19.________ Call your instructor to have your project inspected. Do *not* energize your project until the instructor has inspected and approved it.

Review Questions

Answer the following questions on a separate sheet of paper. Please do not write in this book.

1. Why should a ground strap be worn during installation or removal of a processor?
2. How do you properly install the Pentium 4 processor?
3. What does the acronym μPGA represent?
4. How many socket pins are used with a Pentium 4 processor?
5. What is the purpose of the thermal compound?
6. Where would you look to find more specific information about the Pentium 4 processor?
7. Any power supply can be used with Pentium 4 processor. True or False?

Power Supplies

After studying this chapter, you will be able to:

- ✔ Define electrical energy.
- ✔ Describe the terms *ampere, volt,* and *ohm* in relation to electrical energy.
- ✔ Explain the wattage rating of a power supply unit.
- ✔ Determine power supply requirements for a PC.
- ✔ Identify possible commercial power problems.
- ✔ Use a digital multimeter to troubleshoot a power supply.
- ✔ Apply wattage values when selecting the proper power supply and computer devices.
- ✔ Identify various power supply form factors.
- ✔ Explain the use of UPS and power protection devices.

A+ Exam—Key Points

There will be some basic questions about meters and reading resistance of wires and fuses. There will also likely be a basic question about wattage.

Key Words and Terms

The following words and terms will become important pieces of your computer vocabulary. Be sure you can define them.

- Advanced Configuration and Power Interface (ACPI)
- Advanced Power Management (APM)
- alternating current (ac)
- amperes (A)
- backfeed
- continuity
- current
- cycle
- dedicated circuit
- direct current (dc)
- fuse
- metal oxide varistor (MOV)
- mini connector
- Molex connector
- power
- power good signal
- rails
- resistance
- soft power
- standby power connection
- uninterruptible power supply (UPS)
- voltage
- volt-amperes (VA)
- volts (V)
- watts (W)

This unit introduces you to the basic concepts of electrical energy. This chapter is not intended to turn you into an electronics technician. Rather, this chapter will familiarize you with the terminology and basic electrical concepts needed to ensure success as a computer technician and success on the A+ Certification exams.

You will learn how to use a multimeter to test voltage and resistance and to test the standard features of computer power supplies. The basis of this chapter is the discussion and illustration of the PC power supply unit. The power supply is easy to understand and simple to replace, but making a mistake connecting a power supply can damage the motherboard. This would be a very expensive mistake.

What Is Electrical Energy?

Electrical energy is best defined as the flow of electrons. Most people only know that electricity can be supplied from a wall outlet or from a battery. This is fine for what you need to achieve in this unit. In fact, these will likely be the only two areas of concern you will have when working with PCs.

The flow of electrons is described by terms that express electrical values such as voltage, current, resistance, and power. Each term will be explained on an individual basis and in relation to each other. The terminology may seem confusing at first, but it is fairly simple. Familiarity with these terms is essential for A+ certification.

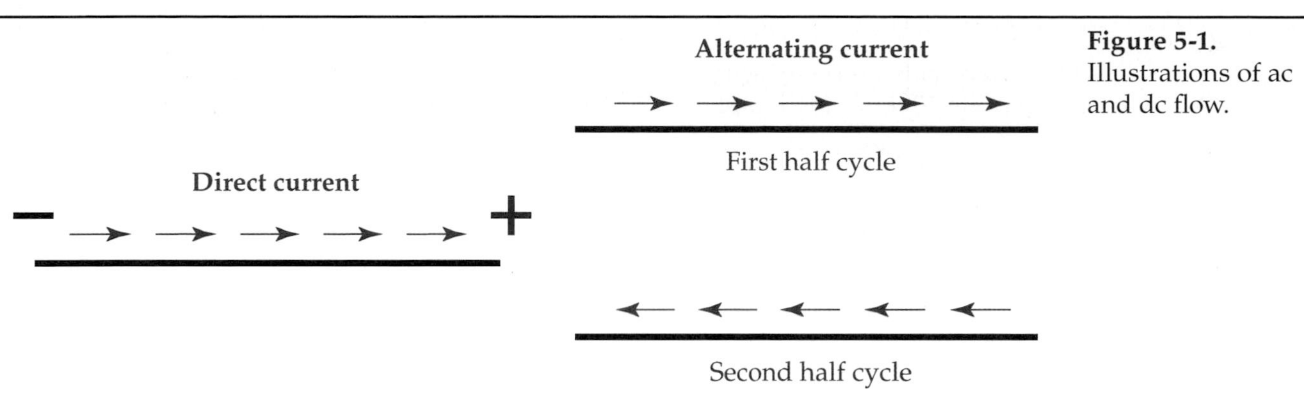

Figure 5-1. Illustrations of ac and dc flow.

AC and DC

Direct current (dc) electrical energy flows from negative to positive. A dc power source has two terminals: one positive and the other negative. The positive terminal is indicated by the color red and a plus (+) sign. The negative terminal is indicated by the color black and a minus (–) sign. DC electrical energy flows in a steady motion from negative to positive. Look at the left side of **Figure 5-1.**

direct current (dc) electrical current that flows in one direction.

Alternating current (ac) has no negative or positive markings because an alternating current system is in a state of constant change or alternating polarities. The current in an ac circuit flows in one direction and then in the opposite direction. Examine the right side of Figure 5-1. The completed sequence of flow, first in one direction and then in the other is called a ***cycle.*** Current flows in one direction during the first half cycle and then in the opposite direction the next half cycle. See **Figure 5-2** for an illustration of one ac cycle.

alternating current (ac) electrical current that reverses direction cyclically.

cycle the completed sequence of flow, first in one direction and then in the other.

This pattern is repeated as long as power is applied to the circuit. The frequency of how often the cycle is repeated is expressed in hertz (Hz) and is based on a time period of one second. Standard household electrical energy is 60 Hz. This means that the direction of the current changes at a rate of 60 times per second, or 60 Hz. See **Figure 5-3.**

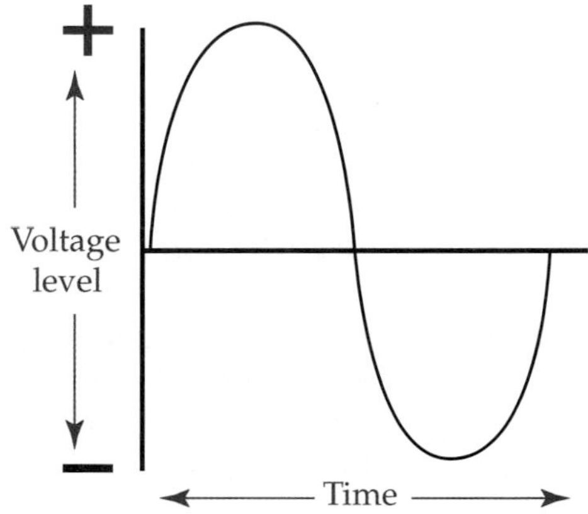

Figure 5-2. An ac voltage is commonly plotted as a graph with the voltage level plotted along the vertical axis and the time plotted along the horizontal axis.

Figure 5-3.
A complete ac cycle is illustrated with a series of ac cycles. The cycle pattern represents the rise and fall of a voltage level. This pattern repeats 60 times in one second (60 Hz) for standard household electrical energy.

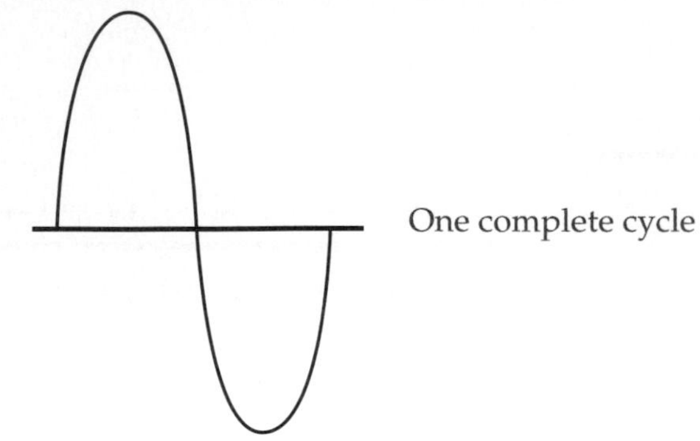

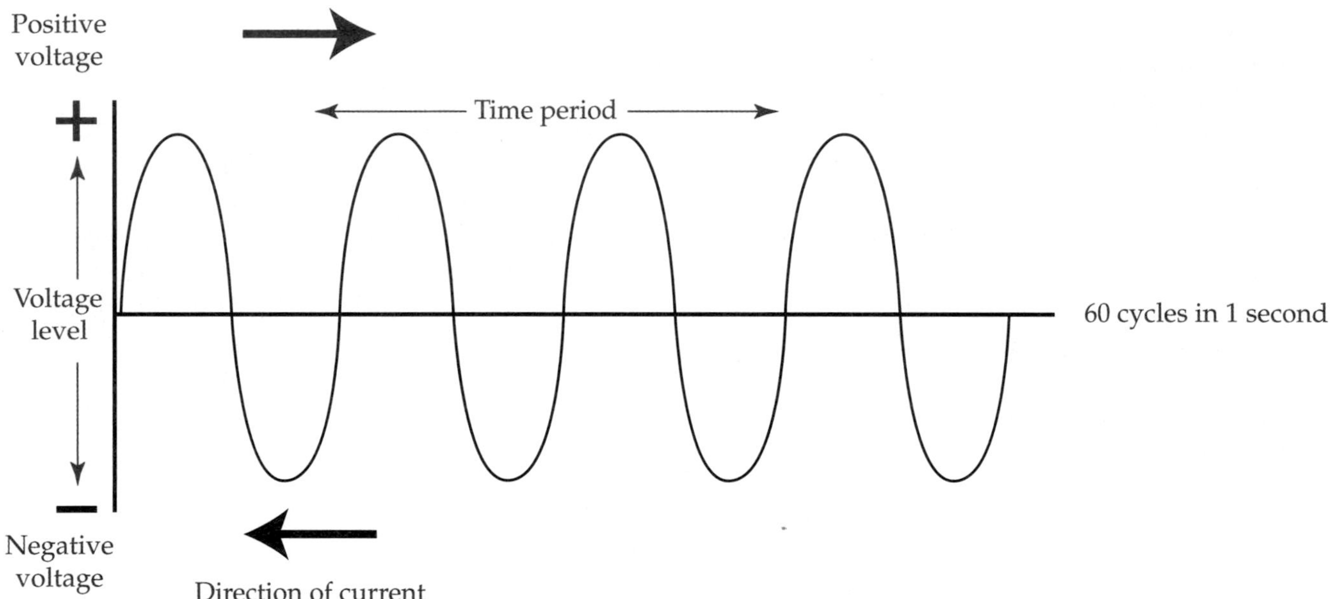

voltage
the amount of electrical pressure present in a circuit or power source.

volts (V)
a scale used in measuring electrical pressure (electromotive force).

current
the electron flow in a circuit.

amperes (A)
a scale used in measuring the volume of electron flow in a circuit.

Voltage and Current

Voltage and current are two measures of electrical power that are tested by technicians in the diagnosis of problems related to the PC. Measurements are usually taken with a universal multimeter. The multimeter and its operation are covered later in this chapter.

Voltage and current are directly related to each other when measuring electrical quantities. ***Voltage,*** measured in ***volts (V),*** is the amount of electrical pressure present in a circuit or power source. ***Current,*** measured in ***amperes (A),*** is the amount of electron flow. Do not mistake the ampere measurement of electrical energy as speed. It is the measure of volume of electrical energy flowing through the system.

Electrical energy can be compared to water in a pipe. Water flow is measured in gallons per minute (GPM) as well as pounds per square inch (PSI). GPM is the rate of flow or volume of water while PSI is the amount of pressure used to produce the flow. Electrical energy is similar. The voltage of the electrical source produces the force for moving the amount of electrical energy, or current, flowing through the wires and devices. The letter *V* represents voltage and the letter *A* or the abbreviation *amp* usually represents amperes.

Resistance

Resistance is the opposition to the flow of electrical energy. The unit of resistance is the ohm and is expressed with the letter symbol *R* or the symbol omega (Ω).

resistance
the opposition to the flow of electrical energy.

Electrical components that manipulate the voltage and current levels in a circuit have measurable resistance values that can be expressed in ohms. Computer technicians very seldom, if ever, are required to take accurate resistance readings. The resistance readings taken by PC technicians are usually to check for electrical continuity. ***Continuity*** is the ability of a device or component to allow an unobstructed flow of electrical energy. Examine **Figure 5-4.**

continuity
a state of connectedness. In electronics, an unbroken circuit is said to have continuity.

In the illustration, there are two electrical wires. These wires are referred to as *conductors* when using electrical terminology. A complete conductor, one that has no breaks, will have a resistance reading of zero. There is no significant resistance to be measured. When a conductor has a break in its path, referred to as an *open*, there is an immeasurable amount of resistance. This extreme condition of high resistance is referred to as *infinity.* As the term *infinity* implies, the reading is so high it is beyond the capability of the multimeter to read it. It is imperative that you learn these two readings, what they mean, and the conditions that cause them. This is the key to using the ohmmeter function to troubleshoot certain PC items.

Now let's look at a switch and a fuse. A ***fuse*** is constructed of two metallic end pieces with a thin strand of wire stretched between them. The wire is engineered to burn open at a predetermined ampere value. The fuse is covered in either a tube of clear glass or opaque ceramic material.

fuse
an inexpensive, passive component that is engineered to burn open at a predetermined amperage, protecting the rest of the circuit from overload.

To check a fuse with a multimeter, the meter function should be set to measure resistance. Place the meter probes across the fuse, one probe on each end of the fuse. The reading should be zero for a good fuse and infinity for a bad fuse. A bad fuse is when the small wire inside the fuse is burnt to an open condition. The path for the electricity no longer exists, **Figure 5-5.**

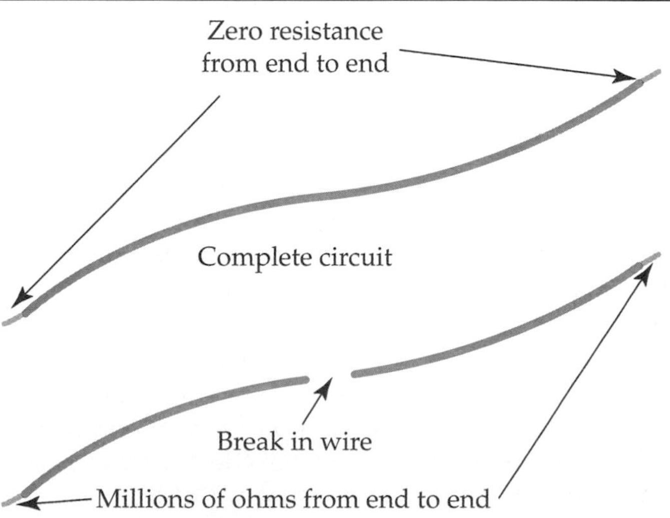

Figure 5-4.
Drawing of two wires, one complete and the other open. A complete circuit has (almost) no resistance. An open circuit (like a broken wire) has a very high or infinite resistance.

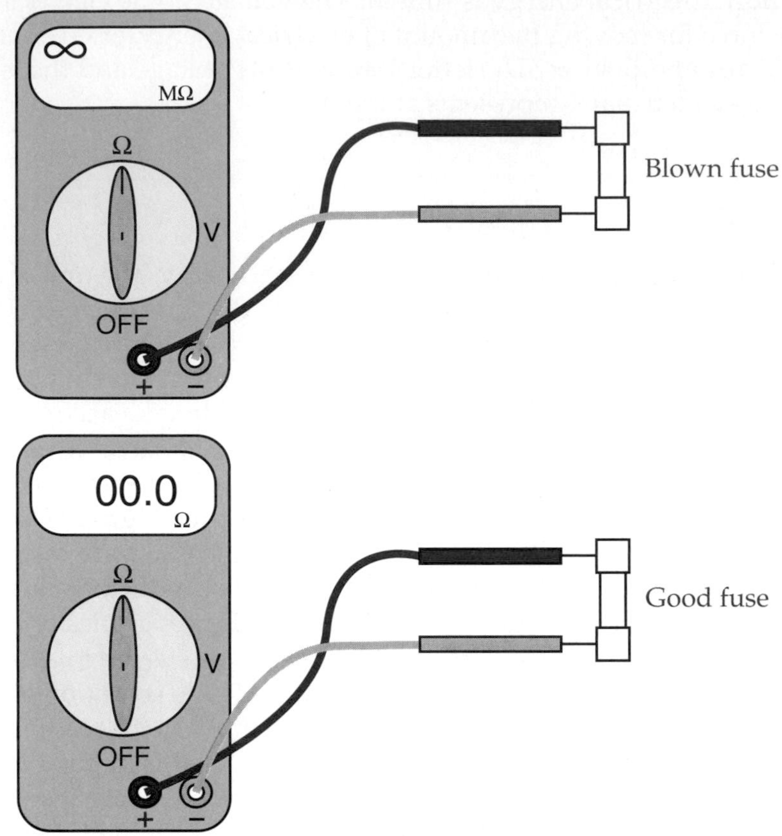

Figure 5-5. A blown fuse will have a resistance reading too high to be displayed, even in the megaohm range. A good fuse will display zero resistance.

Be sure the electrical power supplying the fuse is turned off.

Testing switches is very similar to testing fuses. An open switch will show an infinite resistance. A closed switch should show zero ohms of resistance, **Figure 5-6.** As with testing a fuse, *make sure the electrical power to the switch is disconnected.*

Backfeed

Resistance values can fool an untrained electronics technician. There is a situation when a resistance reading taken on a circuit component such as a switch will give false information. An open switch can, in fact, have what appears as a resistance value other than infinity. The meter may be reading through the electronic components mounted in the system and indicate a value anywhere between zero and infinity.

backfeed
a type of ohmmeter reading in which the resistance is measured through the circuit components even though the circuit is open.

Look at the drawing in **Figure 5-7.** In the illustration, the ohmmeter is reading through the circuit components even after the switch is opened. This is referred to as ***backfeed*** and is a very common condition. To avoid backfeed situations, the component to be read should be removed from the circuit whenever possible. This is not always practical. At times, it is more appropriate to take voltage readings to indicate the condition of fuses, breakers, and switches.

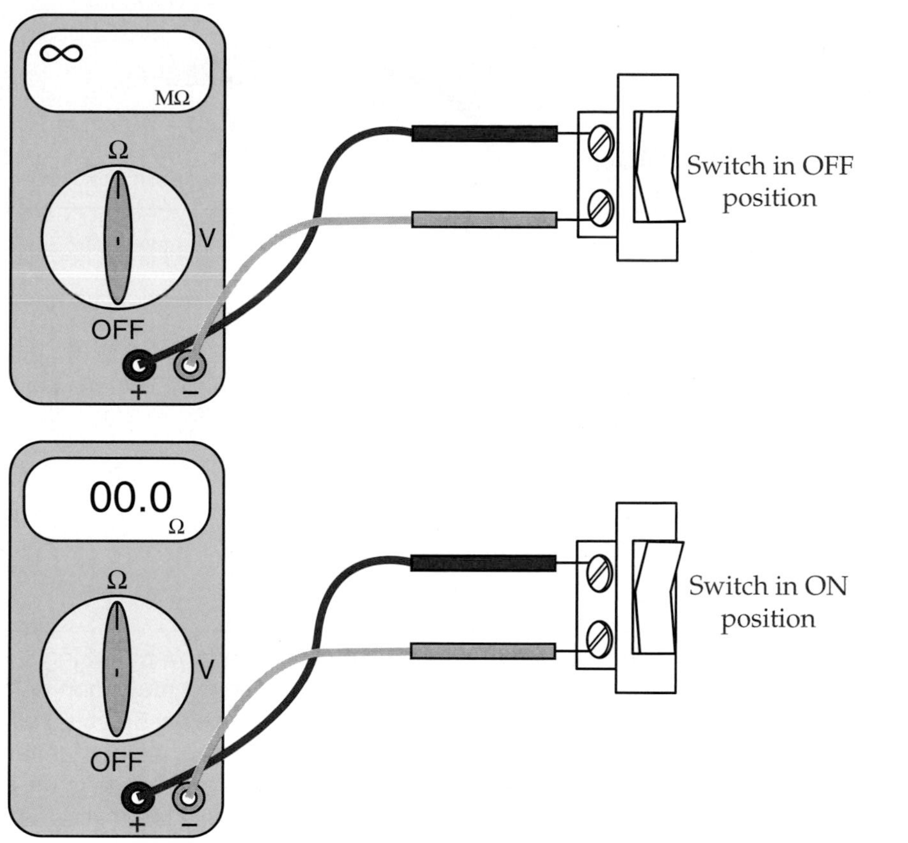

Figure 5-6.
A closed switch has zero resistance while an open switch shows infinite resistance.

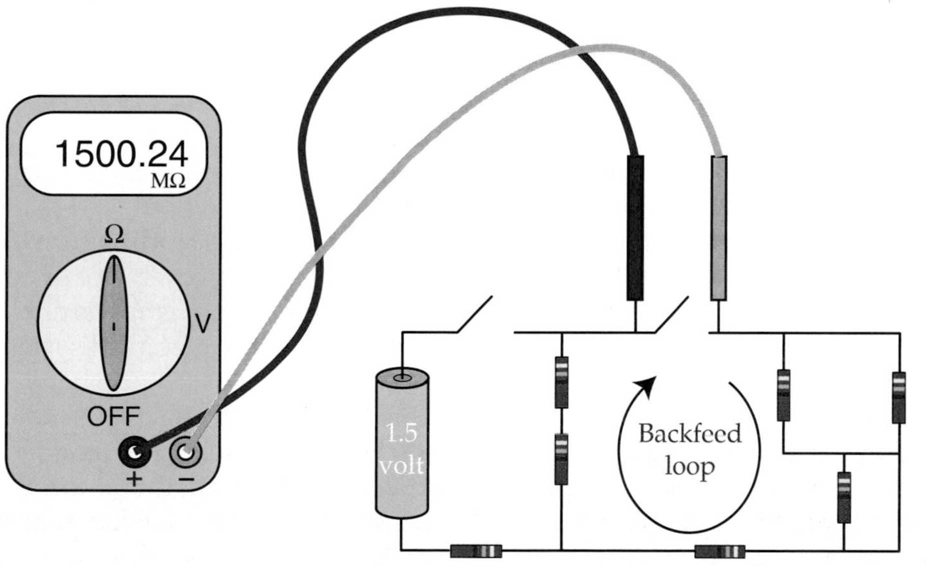

Figure 5-7.
Reading resistance across an open switch can give you a false resistance reading. The ohmmeter reads the resistance through the rest of the circuit instead of the resistance across the open switch.

Checking Power Outlets

Checking a power outlet is a very common task. See **Figure 5-8.** The meter probes are simply inserted into a wall outlet to check for electrical power. There is no polarity when reading ac voltage sources, so the polarity markings on the meter need not be observed.

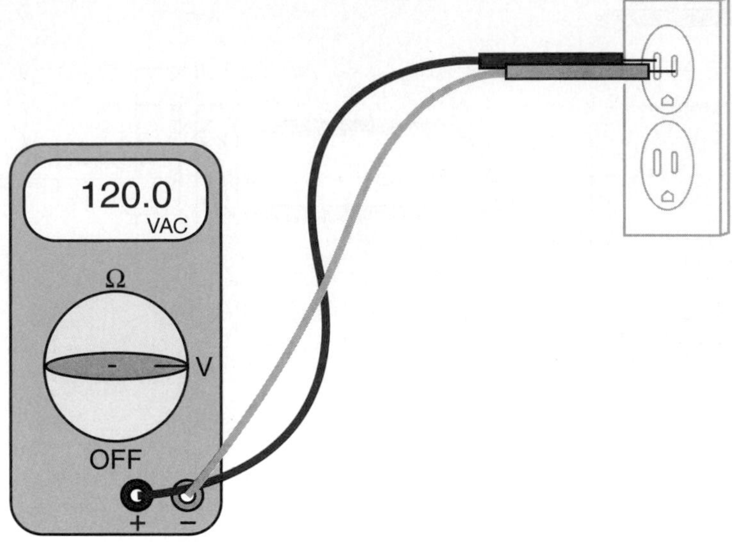

Figure 5-8. Meter connected to a wall outlet. Polarity need not be observed. Be careful when making this test. Keep your fingers away from the exposed probe tips.

Never touch the tips of the meter leads when taking readings. Once you start this practice, it may soon develop into a very bad habit. Low voltages (below 50 volts) will not normally harm you, and you normally do not feel any electrical sensation. Touching a 120-volt ac line is an entirely different story. You will definitely feel the sensation of electrical energy. It is possible to incur a permanent injury or even death. Safety is a habit. Develop safe habits when reading low voltages and you will automatically use the same habits when reading a much higher voltage.

A good voltage reading is considered to be plus or minus 10% of the 120-volt rating. In actuality, the voltage can drop or rise considerably more before affecting a PC.

Two other important considerations when taking voltage readings are the weather and the time of day. Low voltage is common on extremely hot or cold days when electrical heat or air conditioning control building temperature. Heating and air conditioning call for a large demand on the electrical system inside a building. The highest demand for electrical power is usually between the hours of 4:00 PM and 6:00 PM. During this time period, most households are actively using power because of those coming home from school or work. The demand for heat or cooling increases and often combines with the power needed for the preparation of the evening meal. During the same time period, many businesses are still operating. This is the time period that most brownouts occur.

When checking for low voltage, it is best to have the air conditioning or heating system operating at maximum so that you can see the system under maximum strain. This is especially important when checking an intermittent problem and a low voltage condition is suspect.

Clean Electrical Power

Clean power is a term that means the commercial electrical supply is steady, at the correct voltage level, and does not contain voltage spikes. Clean power can be difficult to obtain without additional equipment being added to the supply system. High voltage power line switching, lightning, cars hitting electric poles, or routine line maintenance can cause voltage spikes. When a spike occurs, an abnormally high level of voltage is sent through the electrical system. See **Figure 5-9** for an illustration of line spike in relation to normal ac voltage pattern.

Line voltage spikes can be reduced or eliminated by the use of line conditioning equipment. A common method of ensuring a constant clean power supply is the use of uninterruptible power supplies (UPS). The UPS system will be discussed later in this chapter.

Power

The amount of electrical energy provided or used by equipment is ***power,*** and it is measured in ***watts (W).*** Wattage is the product of voltage and current. In other words, to determine the amount of power expressed in watts that a dc circuit is using, the electrical pressure measured in volts is multiplied by the electrical current measured in amps.

Watts = Volts × Amps

A computer drawing 3 amps when connected to a 120-volt source would consume *approximately* 360 watts of electrical energy. Notice that the term *approximately* is used here. When calculating wattage values associated with ac power, there are other electrical factors, such as induction, to be taken into account. The power value of an ac circuit is expressed as ***volt-amperes (VA).***

A power supply's output capacity is rated in watts and in VA. Watts and VA are not the same expression. Wattage is considered the "true" power rating of a device. It is measured with a very expensive wattmeter or calculated with a more exact formula. VA is considered the "apparent" power. It is called the apparent power because the voltage and ampere values derived from a multimeter are not true values. These values are distorted from electrical factors in the circuit, such as induction. Look at **Figure 5-10.** Total load is calculated from a group

power
the amount of electrical energy provided or used by equipment.

watts (W)
a scale used in measuring electrical power.

volt-amperes (VA)
an alternative scale for measuring electrical power.

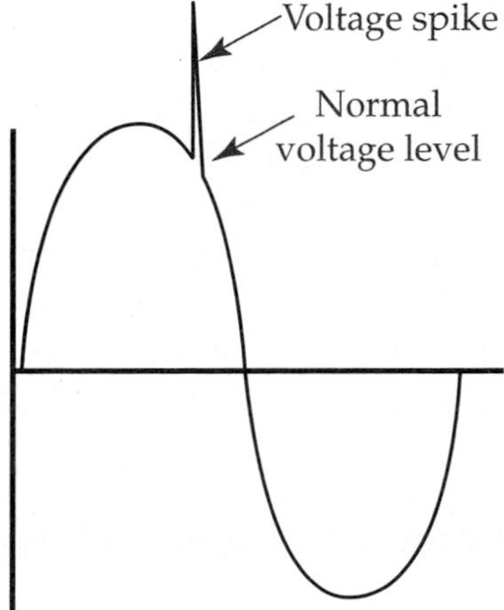

Figure 5-9.
A voltage line spike can be caused by many things (motors, switches, lightning). The increased voltage in the spike damages electronic components by exceeding the voltage limitation of the component.

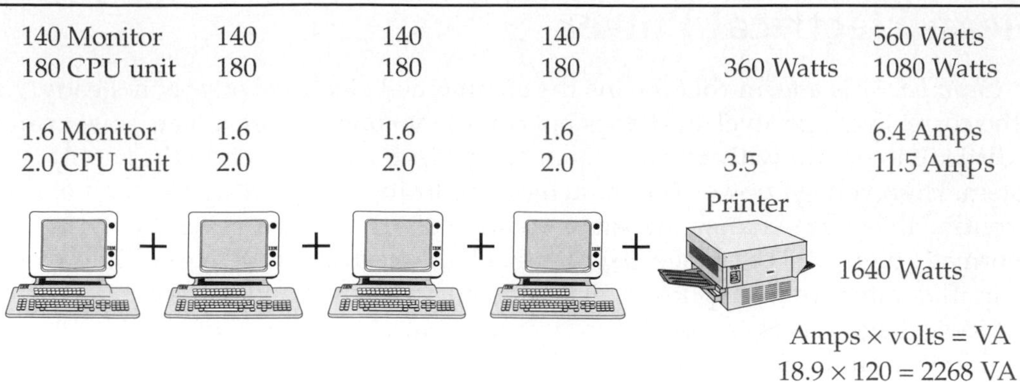

Figure 5-10. The total wattage rating can be quite a bit different than the calculated wattage rating based on the formula of volts × amps. It is not unusual for the calculated wattage using volts and amps to be larger than the wattage totals.

of computers and a printer, which are rated by current, amperes, and wattage. Notice that the calculated power rating derived from the formula V × A is higher than the total power rating derived from adding the individual watt values. The power rating derived from adding the individual watt values is the true power rating. This is a very brief explanation of a very complicated topic. The electronic theory involved for a complete understanding of electronic system loads is beyond the scope of this text. If you have a real desire to know more about electronics, an introductory level course in basic dc and ac circuits is recommended.

When sizing the load capacity of a computer configuration, there are two choices. All the watt values can be added together to arrive at the total load in watts, or all the ampere loads can be added together and then compared to the amperage rating of the power supply.

Wattage measurements are used in two primary ways: power consumption and power supplied. The amount of power consumed by devices such as monitors or hard drives is expressed in watts. When wattage is written on a device that uses or consumes electrical power, the watts label is used to express the amount of power used or consumed by that device. When watts is used as a label on a device that supplies electrical energy such as a generator or power supply, it represents the amount of power that can be provided safely from that unit. Power supplies and generators can actually supply more power than they are rated for. However, when excess amounts of power are taken from a power supply, excessive heating occurs. This can permanently damage the power supply.

When changing power supplies, a power supply with equal or greater wattage marked on the label must be used. A power supply with less wattage capability may work for a while, but it will surely burn up after a period of time.

To determine how much equipment can be connected to a power strip, the wattage ratings of each piece of equipment should be added together. A typical power strip should not connect to a total of over 1600 watts of equipment. Also, *never* daisy chain (string in series) power strips, **Figure 5-11.** When daisy chained together, the first strip carries the total load of both strips.

Another consideration when using extension cords is wire size. A cord with less than number 16-gauge wire should not be used. Wire smaller than 16 gauge can pose a fire hazard. Wire gauge is used to indicate the size of wire and also how much current it can safely handle without excessive heat. Remember, the larger the number, the smaller the wire. **Figure 5-12** shows a wire size chart with current ratings.

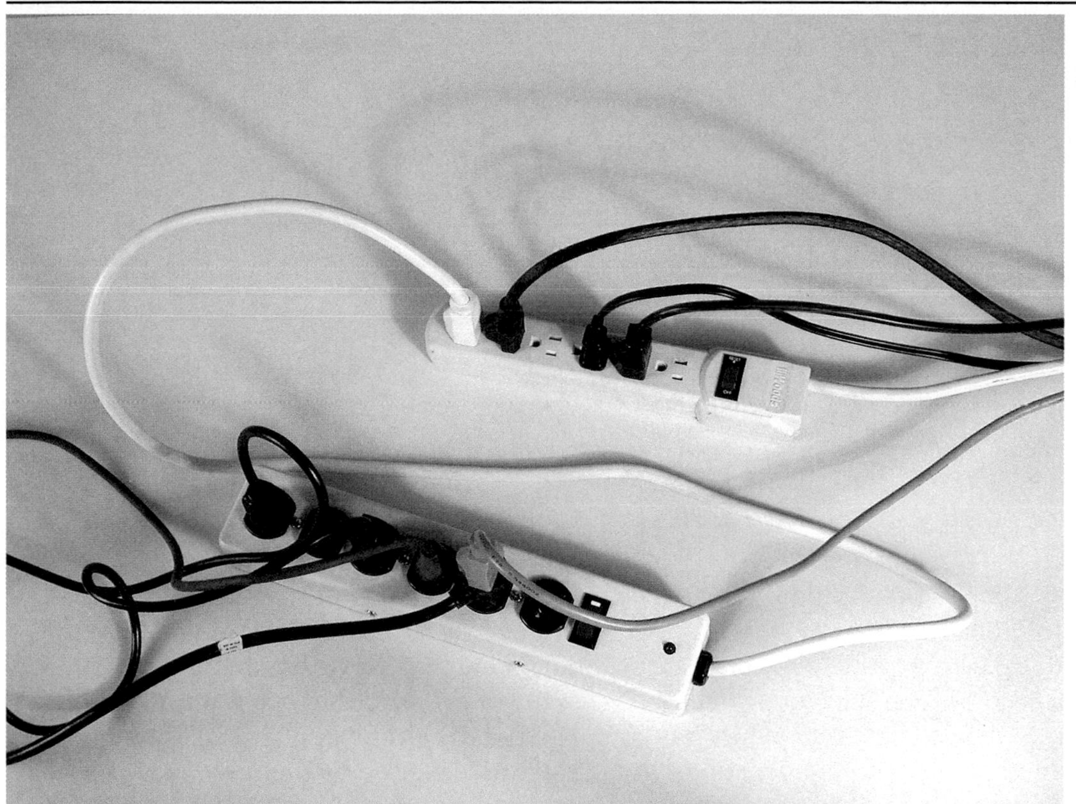

Figure 5-11.
Daisy chaining power strips is very unwise.

Wire Size	Ampere Rating
12	20
14	15
16	7
18	5

Figure 5-12.
Wire size chart with current ratings. Note that this chart reflects current carrying capacities of typical conductors. It does not take into consideration the type of insulation or the application, which can change the current rating for the listed conductors.

Parts of a Digital Multimeter

A digital multimeter is used to measure current, resistance, and voltage values. As the name implies, the meter is constructed from digital circuits, and it is used in place of multiple meters. The multimeter replaces the use of individual volt, ohm, and amp meters. It is an all-in-one type of meter. Look at **Figure 5-13.** Shown is a typical digital multimeter with major parts labeled.

The display area displays a numeric value of the electrical quality being measured such as voltage, current, or resistance. The numeric display expresses the value with a decimal point when appropriate. The numeric value displayed in the meter window is coordinated with the range dial setting and with the location of where the meter leads are plugged.

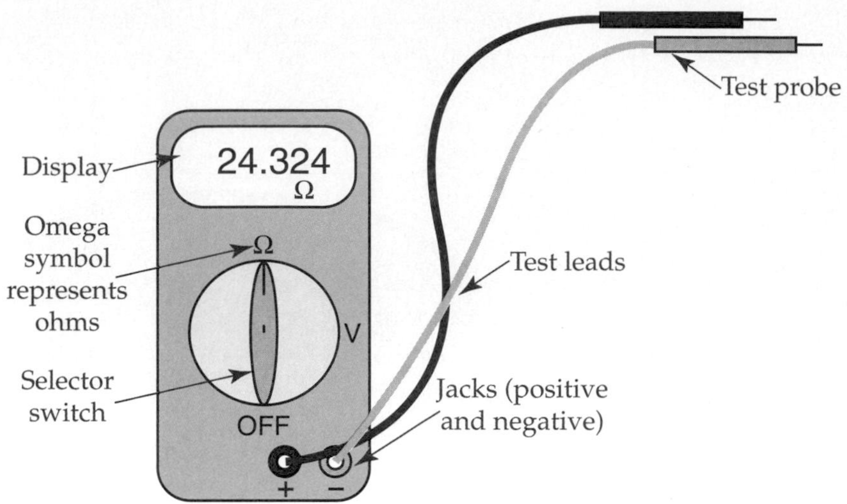

Figure 5-13. A typical auto-range meter is very simple in design. You simply select the function you wish (volts or resistance), and then touch the parts with the probe tips.

The range should be set to a level higher than the expected value to be read. In other words, a meter with voltage ranges of 5, 50, and 500 should be set to 50 to take an expected 12-volt reading. Some meters come with automatic range selection. The selector switch dial is set to voltage, and the meter automatically sets the correct range when it is connected to the circuit being measured.

There are several locations where the test leads can be plugged. Examine **Figure 5-14.** Notice the plug-in points (or jacks) on the meter. One is black with a negative (–) symbol beside it and the other is red with a plus (+) sign beside it. These identify the appropriate polarity position of the electrical input. The

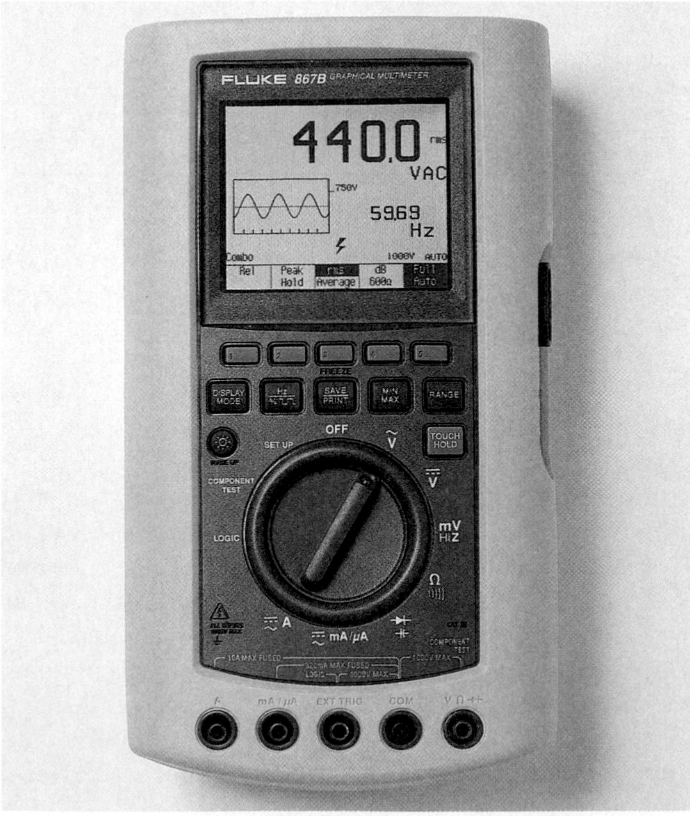

Figure 5-14. Meters come with multiple jacks for the test probes. Be sure to place the test probes in the proper jacks. (Fluke Corp. Reproduced with permission.)

test leads correspond in the colors red and black, which represent positive and negative power respectively. Also, take special note of the ac marking on some of the meter jacks. Be sure the test leads are plugged into the appropriate jacks when taking current readings.

Probes

The meter is equipped with two test leads with probes at the end of each. The probes are for touching test points. One test lead is black and the other is red. This color combination is universal. The black lead is for the negative side of a reading. It plugs into the meter at the jack that is marked in black, has a negative sign, or both. The red lead plugs into the jack with the red marking or the plus sign for voltage and resistance readings. For current readings, there is usually a different position in which to be plugged. As a PC technician, you typically never need to take a current reading. Current readings are much more complicated and require knowledge of electronic components to correctly connect the meter. Voltage readings and occasionally resistance readings are required.

Never touch the probes with your fingertips when taking readings even when the voltage is low. Make electrical safety a habit. Forming safe habits is essential. If you touch the bare tip of the probe during routine checks of low voltage where there is not sufficient voltage to harm you, you may create a bad habit. This can lead to touching the tips when reading dangerously high voltages.

Display Area

The display area is where the measured value is displayed. For example, when reading voltage, the display will give a numeric value of the voltage and possibly indicate if it is an ac or dc voltage value. It may also indicate if you are out of the correct range selection value.

Range Selection

The range selector is used to choose the appropriate value to be read: voltage, current, or resistance. The dial indicator should be placed in the lowest range that is greater than the value to be read. If it is placed higher than the next highest value, an accurate reading will not be obtained. The reading will be a rounded-off value, rather than an accurate reading. If you go below the desired level, you will probably not get a reading at all. In fact, a warning will appear in the display area of most good meters.

Some meters are equipped with an auto-range feature. It will automatically select the correct range for the reading you are taking. I highly recommend this type of meter for anyone not familiar with basic electronics.

Procedures for Reading Voltage

Before taking any readings, you should have some idea of the level of voltage you expect to read. For example, a common wall outlet is 120 volts ac. A power supply unit might be 12, 5, or 3.3 volts dc depending on the exact power supply connection.

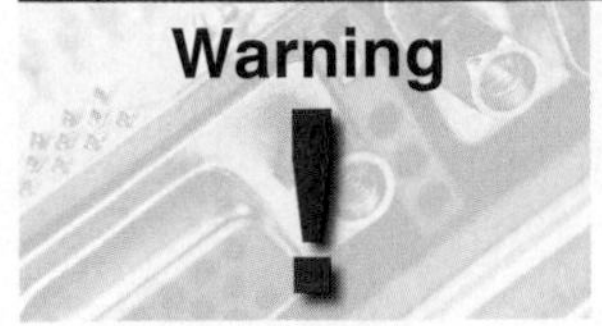

Never wear an anti-static or ground strap while taking meter readings. The ground strap makes you an excellent conductor of electricity, which is a dangerous situation when taking meter readings.

To read ac or dc voltages:

1. Insert the meter leads into the appropriate jacks on the face of the meter. The red lead is inserted into the jack marked with the letter "V" or a "+" symbol. (Generally, you will never use the jacks marked with an "A" or a "mA" as they are used for current readings.)
2. Insert the black lead into the jack marked "COM" or with the "–" symbol. The common is usually black and the input voltage jack is usually red.
3. Turn the selector switch to voltage AC. On some meters this can require the use of two separate switches. One switch selects ac or dc voltage and the other switch selects the voltage range. If you do not have an auto-range meter, set the range selector to the next highest voltage level over what you expect to read. (This is where an auto-range meter is handy.)
4. Touch the test locations with the probes. Keep your fingers away from the tips of the probes.
5. Read the display and record the voltage. It should be within 10% of the expected voltage level.

Procedures for Reading Resistance

To read resistance:

1. Insert the meter leads into the appropriate jacks on the face of the meter. The red lead is inserted into the jack marked with the letter "V" or a "+" symbol.
2. Insert the black lead into the jack marked with "COM" or with a "–" symbol. The common is usually black.
3. Be absolutely sure the power is OFF before attempting to read resistance.

Electrical voltage can damage a meter if the meter is set up to read resistance.

4. Set the selector switch to the *highest* value of resistance.
5. Touch the test probes together to see if the meter is working properly. The reading should be zero. If not, the battery inside the unit could be weak. The ohmmeter portion of a multimeter depends on battery power to take a resistance reading.
6. Touch the probes to the part (fuse or cable) to be tested.
7. When doing a resistance check on a fuse or a cable, you should read either zero resistance or infinity. A good fuse will cause a reading of zero resistance as will a good cable. A bad fuse will cause a reading of infinity as will a cable that is not complete from end to end.

Checking Fuses, Cables, and Switches

When checking fuses, cables, and switches there are only two resistance values that are typically displayed on a digital meter display: zero ohms and infinity. A typical low ampere value fuse found in electronic equipment is simple in construction. The fuse is a cylinder shape of glass or ceramic with a metal cap on each end. Inside the cylinder is the fuse link. The fuse link is a thin metal wire that burns and splits into two parts at a predetermined ampere value.

The easiest way to tell if the fuse is good (or not) is to remove it from the fuse holder and take a resistance reading across the fuse. Since the fuse is made of a small metal wire, it will have very low resistance. When tested with the ohmmeter, the meter will indicate zero resistance. If the fuse is burned open, it will have a resistance value too high to read. You would be trying to read through the air or space inside the tube. This reading is known as infinity. This means the resistance reading is beyond the capabilities of the meter range.

The same principle applies to a cable and switches. Before reading a switch or cable with an ohmmeter, they must be removed from the PC. A cable should read zero resistance from one end to the other. A cable with a broken wire will read infinity. See **Figure 5-15** for an illustration of a cable with a meter attached, illustrating both a good reading and a bad cable reading.

A switch can be difficult to remove from the circuit and the type of switch present must be identified. Some switches used today are capacitor-type switches. These switches cannot be adequately diagnosed with an ohmmeter. Capacitor switches are usually very small in comparison to the physical size of mechanical

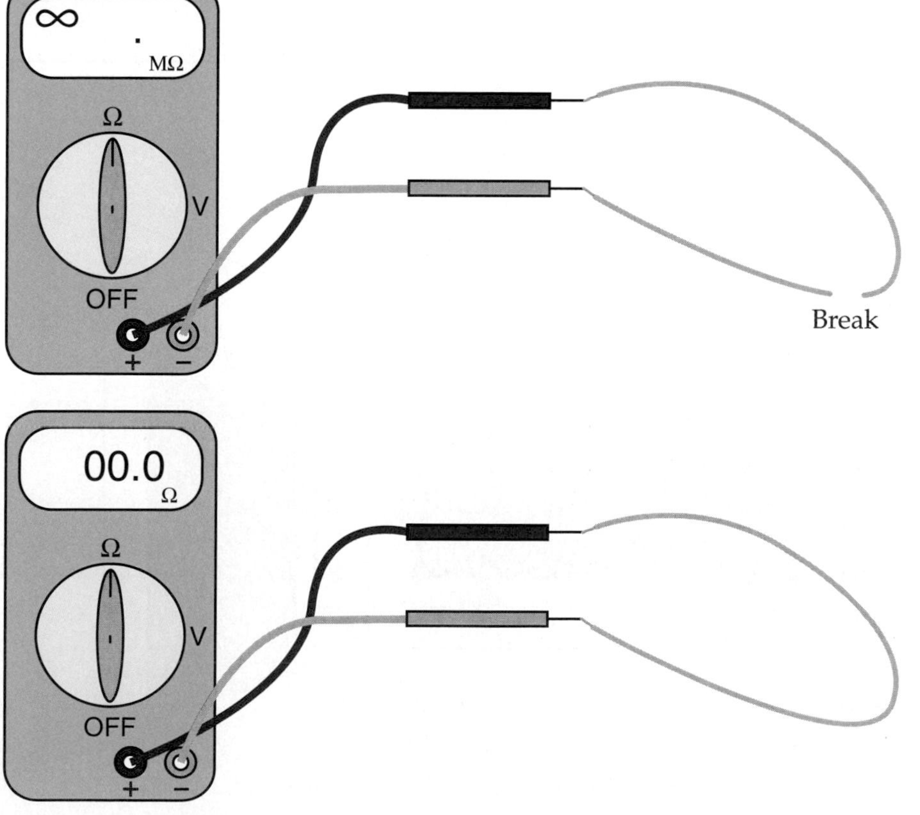

Figure 5-15. A good conductor will read zero resistance. A conductor with a break (or open) will read infinity, the highest possible resistance reading.

switches. If a switch is suspected as the problem, it may be best to simply replace the switch with a known good switch rather than attempting to diagnose it with a meter.

Branch Circuits

Many computer problems can be generated by the electrical system inside the residential home or small business. A typical electrical panel distributes electricity to electrical circuits throughout a home. The electrical power in home settings and some businesses all tie back to the same electrical panel. Electrical equipment running anywhere in that environment can cause a power problem for the computer system.

For example, the operation of a vacuum cleaner or a power tool can generate voltage spikes that can disrupt the computer process. The computer can be damaged, develop a glitch, or simply lock up. It is imperative that a surge protector of some sort be installed at the computer location. See **Figure 5-16** for a drawing of a typical home distribution system.

A branch circuit is the technical name for the wiring from an electrical panel to the final outlet on that circuit. A typical commercial installation uses two electrical distribution panels: one panel for lighting and the other panel for distributing power to equipment. **Figure 5-17** is an illustration showing side-by-side panels. One panel is for lighting and the other is for power.

Computers are located in every type of business location from small travel agency offices to heavy manufacturing operations. It is important to know the type of equipment that a company operates from the same electrical distribution panel that serves the computer station.

Figure 5-16.
Typical home distribution.

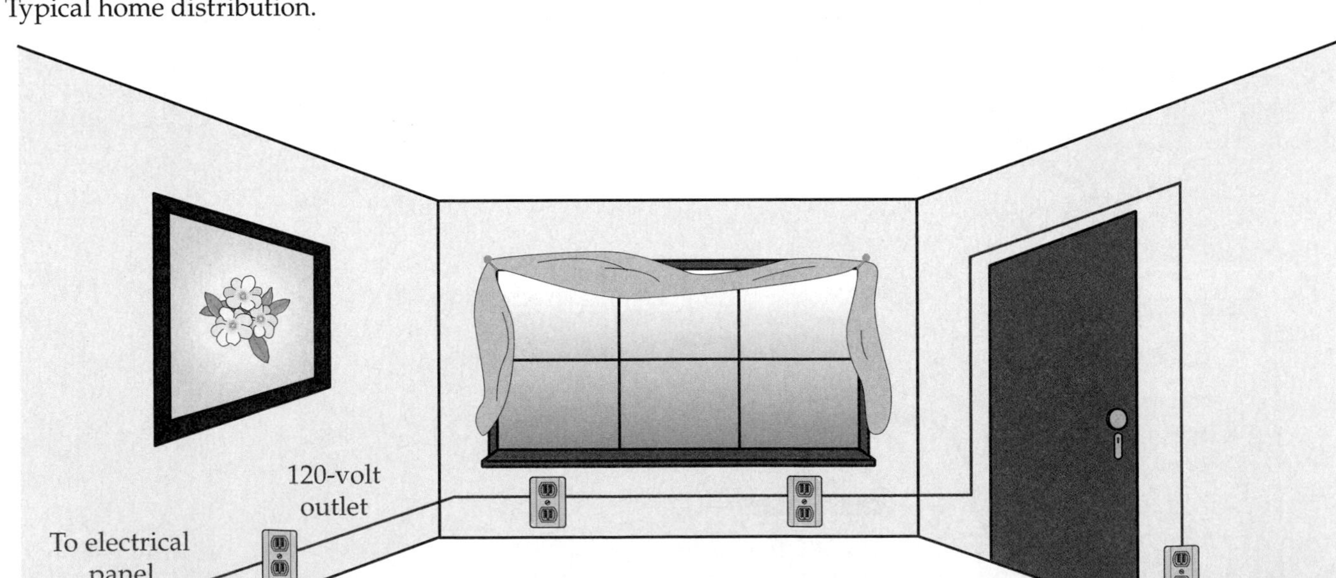

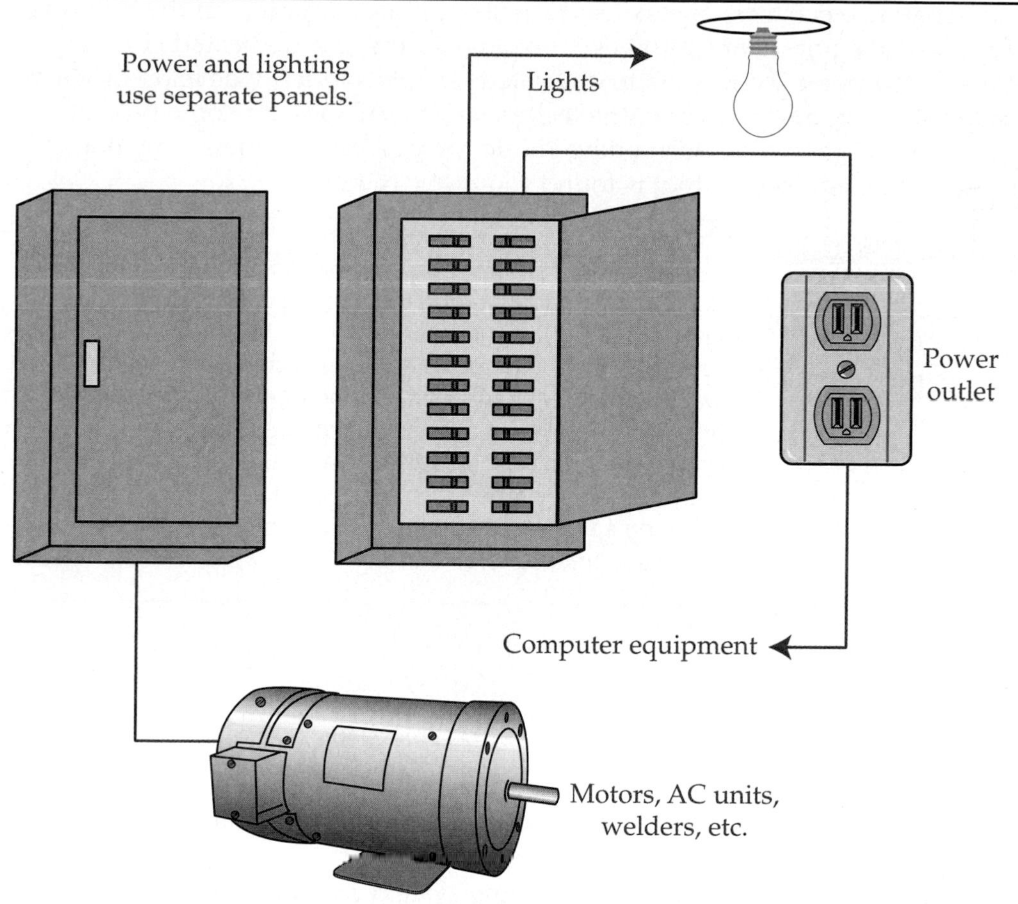

Figure 5-17. Heavy machinery should have its own electrical panel. It should not be on the same panel as computer equipment.

The type of electrical distribution and the equipment connected to that electrical system is of major concern to reliable computer operation. An office location in the form of a large industrial building can be misleading to a technician. While the immediate environment may look like a typical office setting, the same electrical circuits in the office environment can be serving heavy printing press equipment directly behind the office wall. A surge protector power strip may not be adequate in this type of location. A more reliable approach to ensure dependable operation of this computer system would be the installation of a quality uninterruptible power source (UPS) system. UPS systems are covered later in this chapter.

Dedicated Circuit

A ***dedicated circuit*** is one that is installed in an electrical power distribution system that is designed to serve *only* computer equipment. A dedicated circuit is wired separately from other electrical circuits. A typical installation uses an isolation transformer to separate the computer electrical power from other power circuits. An isolation transformer converts electrical energy to magnetic energy and then back to electrical energy again. The transformer helps to buffer the circuit against voltage spikes generated outside the building as well as from inside the building.

dedicated circuit
a circuit installed in an electrical power distribution system that is designed to serve only computer equipment.

A separate electrical panel is used strictly for the computers in the building. No additional equipment should ever be plugged into the dedicated circuit outlets. If computers connected to dedicated circuits suddenly develop problems that appear to be power related, the technician should look for some type of equipment that may have been plugged into the dedicated outlets. Any non-computer type equipment that is found should be removed.

An interesting, and all too common, occurrence happens to network equipment and office computer systems that are left constantly in the "on" position. When office workers return to work in the morning, they find their computers locked up or crashed. After rebooting, everything appears fine again. However, a few days later, or even the next day, the computer system is down again. This problem is usually solved when it is discovered that the overnight cleaning service is using the dedicated circuits to power their vacuum cleaners.

Grounding

Improper grounding conditions can cause serious problems to computer equipment. After all other attempts to solve a power problem have been exhausted, the technician should investigate the grounding system. An improperly installed or damaged grounding system can cause problems that appear as voltage problems.

To check out the grounding system, a certified electrician or power company technician should make the inspection. There is specialized equipment used to perform grounding tests. It is expensive and special training is needed to use it. This is one time when the computer tech must call on another specialist.

The PC Power Supply

The power supply is responsible for converting standard 120-volt ac power from the wall outlet to dc voltage levels appropriate for the electronics systems of the computer. Typical dc voltage levels are +12, +5, +3.3, –12, and –5. These voltages are provided to the motherboard, which, in turn, distributes these voltage levels to motherboard components and expansion slots. The expansion slots provide the voltage levels required by adapter card electronic parts. Voltages are also distributed to peripherals inside the computer, such as the hard drive and DVD drive.

Power supplies have form factors just as motherboards do. The power supply must fit into the case and also allow room for the motherboard. Some of the standard form factors are named after the motherboard form factors such as AT, Baby AT, LPX, ATX, ATX12V and NLX. In addition, they can be broken down further to tower or desktop models. You should be aware of a variety of nonstandard power supplies that are proprietary. The color coding on the wiring for these types of power supplies are not truly standard. You must be careful. As a matter of fact, any implied standardization should not be taken for granted. Always check with the manufacturer's specifications for definitive information about color and voltages.

Main Power Connectors

To assist in making the proper voltage level connections, power plugs have a special shape that matches the voltage level required by the motherboard or peripheral. **Figure 5-18** illustrates two styles of motherboard main power connection. Figure 5-18A shows the ATX and Figure 5-18B shows the newer style of ATX power connection, the ATX12V. Notice that both connectors in Figures 5-18 have a PWR_OK connection. This refers to the power good signal. This signal is transmitted from the power supply to the motherboard and on to the CPU. The ***power good signal*** is used to verify the power supply is working properly during POST.

The +5VSB (standby) connection provides voltage even when the power switch is set to off. The computer is said to "wake up" on an event. The exception is when the AC plug is physically unplugged from the wall outlet or the power supply. ***Standby power connection,*** also called ***soft power,*** provides power to the keyboard when the computer system is in sleep mode. Power is reduced to the entire system, but some power must remain on to reactivate or wake up the system. This is the purpose of the standby power connection. The power on and

power good signal a signal sent from the power supply to the motherboard that verifies the power supply is working properly.

standby power connection provides power to reactivate or wake up a system in standby mode.

soft power another term for the features provided by a standby power connection.

Figure 5-18.
ATX and ATX12V main power connections.

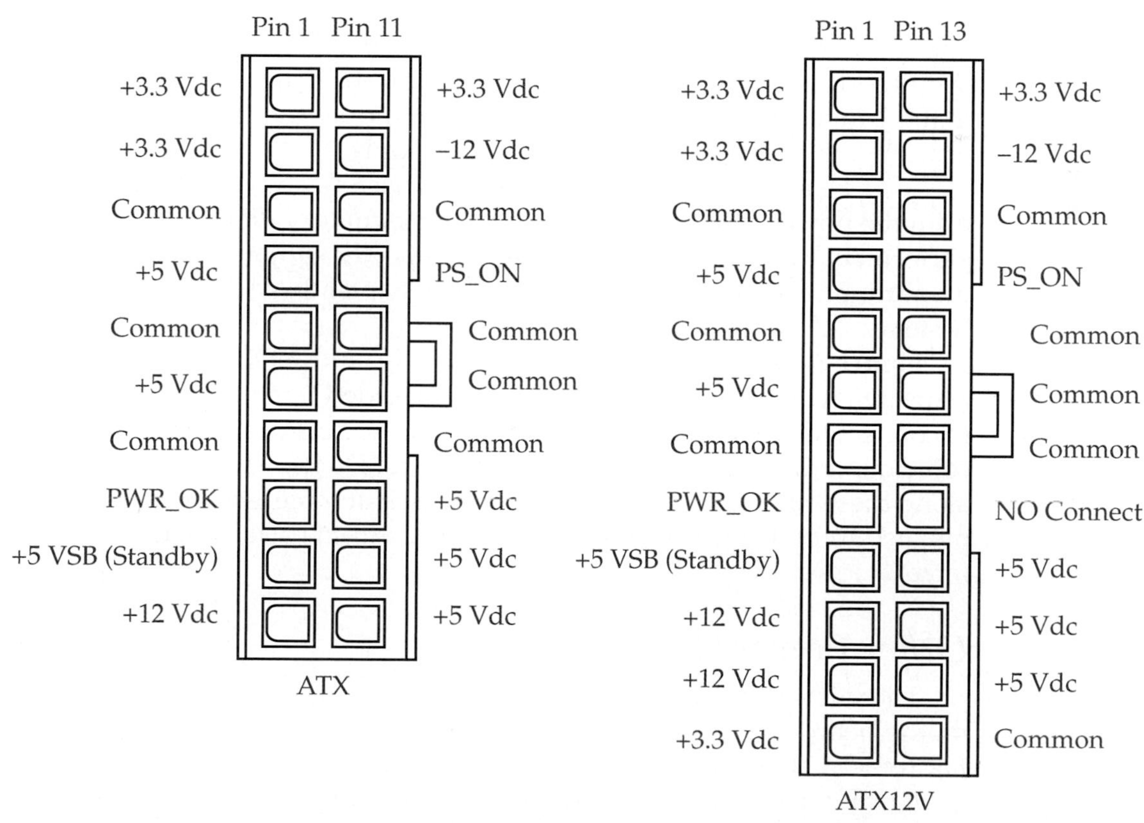

the standby power connections are also used jointly by Windows 9x software to turn the computer off using software commands rather than a physical switch. For example, the +5VSB connection can provide electrical power to a network card so that the computer can be activated when a network event occurs. The BIOS Setup program is used to configure the computer to "wakeup on LAN," which means network activity can wake up or start up the computer system. This is a common feature of all modern computer systems.

The ATX and ATX12V form factors also have 3.3-volt power connectors. The addition of 3.3 volts at the power connection has eliminated the need for a voltage regulator located at the CPU. The regulator was used to convert the 5 volts from the power supply to the lower voltage required by the new CPU units. ATX is one of the most popular power supply form factors on the market.

The ATX12V power supply is a redesign of the ATX power supply. Changes in the design were made to accommodate new power requirements such as that for PCIe devices and power-hungry video cards. The ATX motherboard main power connection has 20 pins. The newer ATX12V motherboard main power connection has 24 pins. Look closely at Figure 5-18 and you can see the main difference between the 20-pin and 24-pin connection is the bottom four pins. These four additional pins on the ATX12V are used to supply additional electrical power required by the more modern motherboards.

Most ATX motherboard designs will accept the new 24-pin ATX12V. The standard is intended to ensure a backward compatibility with older motherboards when purchasing the newer power supply to replace a defective ATX type power supply. Conversion kits are available to change a 20-pin connector into a 24-pin connector and also the opposite, change a 24-pin to a 20-pin connector. Many motherboards have no problem with a pin conversion kit. The conversion kit is simply two connections, one 24-pin and one 20-pin joined by wires. If you study the pin assignments carefully in Figure 5-18, you will see that the first set of 20 pins of an ATX power supply connector closely match the first 20-pins or the 24-pin ATX12V power supply.

Also, be aware that there are power connectors designed to connect directly from the power supply to a PCIe card. For example, video cards with high-performance processors require a separate power supply connected directly to the card. There will be more about this in Chapter 8—Video Display and Audio Systems.

Figure 5-19 and **Figure 5-20** show the ATX and ATX12V power connectors respectively. The plastic of these plugs are molded to permit the connector to connect to the motherboard in only one way. This prevents an improper connection that will destroy the motherboard. Do keep in mind that nothing along these lines is truly impossible. If sufficient force is applied, it can be plugged in backward. The connector should attach easily. If it does not, do not force it.

Other Power Connectors

There is a wide assortment of power connectors besides the main motherboard power connectors that can be used with a computer power system. **Figure 5-21** shows four of the more common you will encounter. The +12-volt power connector, Figure 5-21A, is also referred to as a 2 × 2, 12-volt connector. The designation 2 × 2 represents the pin configuration as two pins in two rows. The 2 × 2 designation is a way to differentiate the 4-pin power connector from the

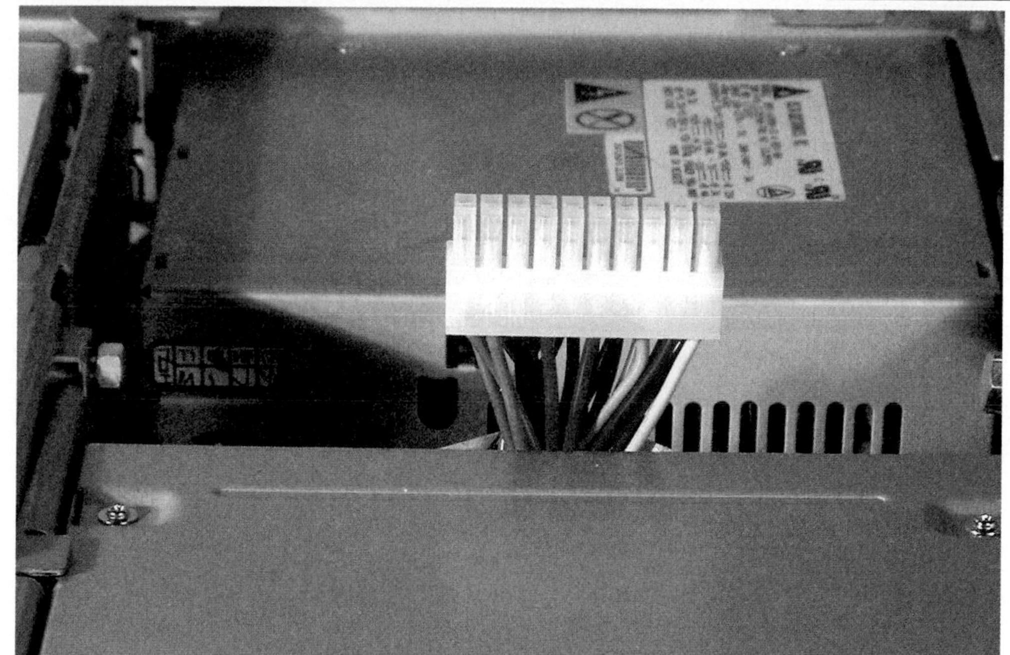

Figure 5-19. ATX motherboard power connector.

Figure 5-20. ATX12V main motherboard power connector. Most motherboards designed to work with a 20-pin ATX power supply will work with a 24-pin ATX12V power supply.

4-pin peripheral power connector. The 4-pin peripheral power connector would be designated as 1 × 4. There are also 2 × 3, 12-volt power connectors, **Figure 5-22**, and 2 × 4, 12-volt power connectors on many power supplies. You will often see power supply main motherboard connectors referred to in the same fashion. For example, a 20-pin ATX connector is referred to as a 2 × 10 connector, while the 24-pin ATX12V connector is referred to as a 2 × 12 connector.

Figure 5-21. Assorted power connectors.

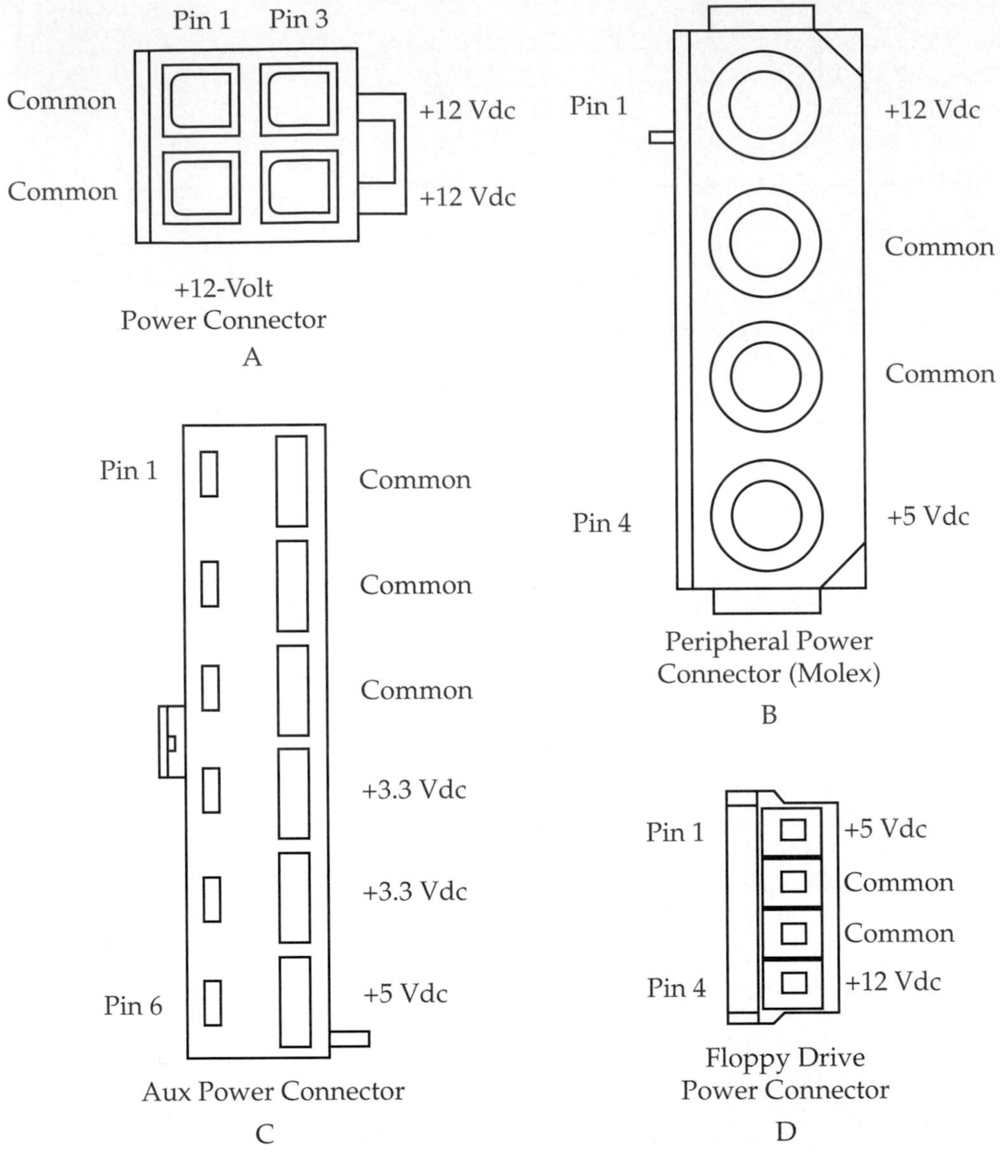

Pin 1 Pin 3
Common
Common
+12 Vdc
+12 Vdc
+12-Volt
Power Connector
A

Pin 1
+12 Vdc
Common
Common
Pin 4
+5 Vdc
Peripheral Power
Connector (Molex)
B

Pin 1
Common
Common
Common
+3.3 Vdc
+3.3 Vdc
Pin 6
+5 Vdc
Aux Power Connector
C

Pin 1
+5 Vdc
Common
Common
Pin 4
+12 Vdc
Floppy Drive
Power Connector
D

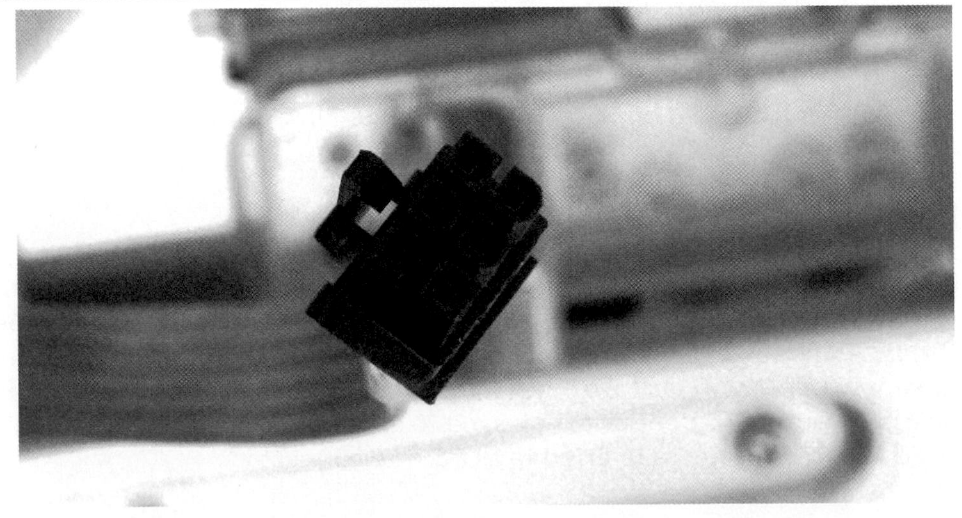

Figure 5-22. Two by six (2 × 3) 12-volt power connector.

The 4-pin peripheral power connector, Figure 5-21B, is also called a ***Molex connector.*** It is used to connect to ATA hard drives, CD-ROM drives, and DVD drives. These devices typically use the +12 volt level from the connector. The floppy drive power connector, Figure 5-21D, is also called a ***mini connector.*** This connector is used for 3½″ floppy drives. **Figure 5-23** shows a picture of the Molex connector, and **Figure 5-24** shows the mini connector.

Molex connector a four-wire, D-shaped connector that delivers +12-volt and +5-volt signals from the power supply.

mini connector a two-pin connector that delivers a +5 volt signal from the power supply. A variation of this connector has four wires and delivers both +12-volt and +5-volt signals.

The term *Molex* is commonly used and universally accepted to identify the large four-connector peripheral power connection. This is incorrect. Molex is the name of the company who designed and markets this type of connection.

An auxiliary power connection, Figure 5-21A, is used to supply 12 volts to newer high-performance CPUs. The voltage applied to the processor was raised from 5 Vdc to 12 Vdc. Therefore, the ATX12V power supply uses a 4-pin or more power connector attached directly to the motherboard near the processor rather than through the main motherboard power connector. **Figure 5-25** shows an auxiliary power connector.

The ATX style could only carry voltage and higher current to the CPU through the very thin conductors on the motherboard referred to as traces. Traces are very limited in the amount of current that they can carry. Power connections made directly to location on the motherboard as well as directly to devices overcome the current limitations of motherboard traces. The power connection near the CPU is critical on motherboards with high-performance processors. Without the direct connection, the computer will not boot.

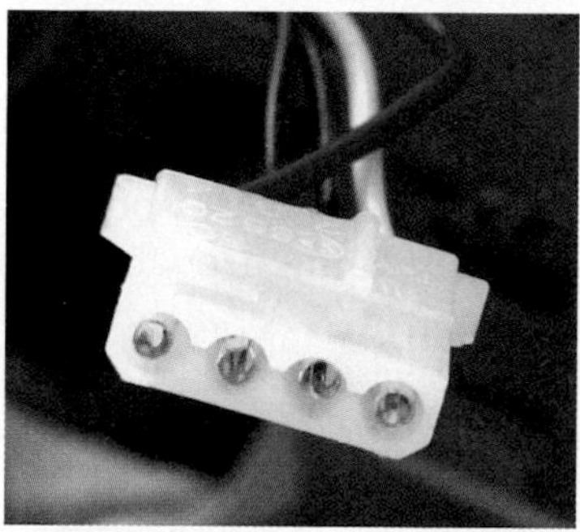

Figure 5-23. Peripheral power connector. This connector is typically used to power ATA hard drives, CD-ROM drives, and DVD drives.

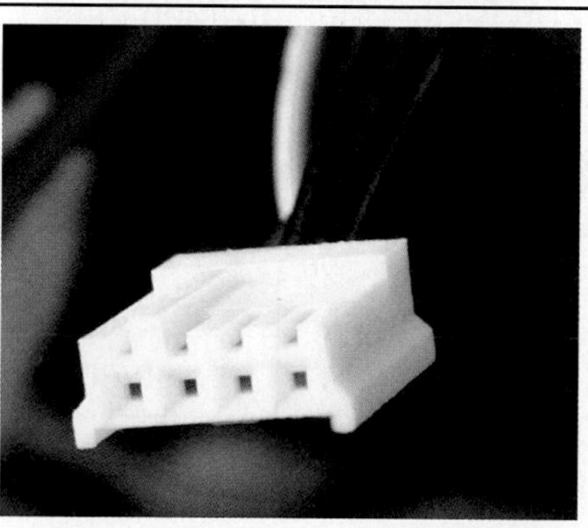

Figure 5-24. Mini connector. This connector is used to power 3½² floppy drives.

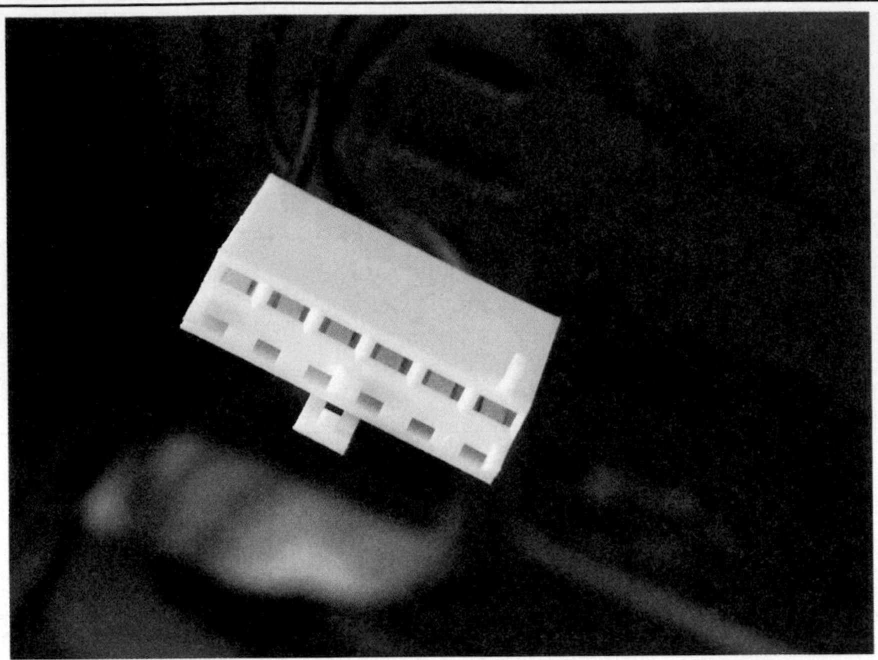

Figure 5-25. Auxiliary power connector.

Always check your motherboard manual or support documentation to determine the location of and type of power connections to use.

The four-pin connector is also used to provide power directly to many high performance video cards. There will be more about video card power requirements later in the textbook.

Serial ATA (SATA) hard drives use a SATA power connector, **Figure 5-26,** which has 14 pins at three different voltage levels. There are adapter wiring kits available so that you can connect an SATA hard disk drive to a power supply that does not have a SATA power connector.

Input and Output Voltage Levels

Input voltage levels specified by Form Factors Organization located at www.formfactors.org. Form Factors Organization makes a set of recommended nonbinding specifications that are used as a guideline for power supply manufacturers, as shown in the following table.

Input	Minimum VAC	Nominal VAC	Maximum VAC
115 Vac	90	115	135
230 Vac	180	230	265
Frequency (Hz)	47	50/60	63

Figure 5-26.
SATA power connector and pin outs.

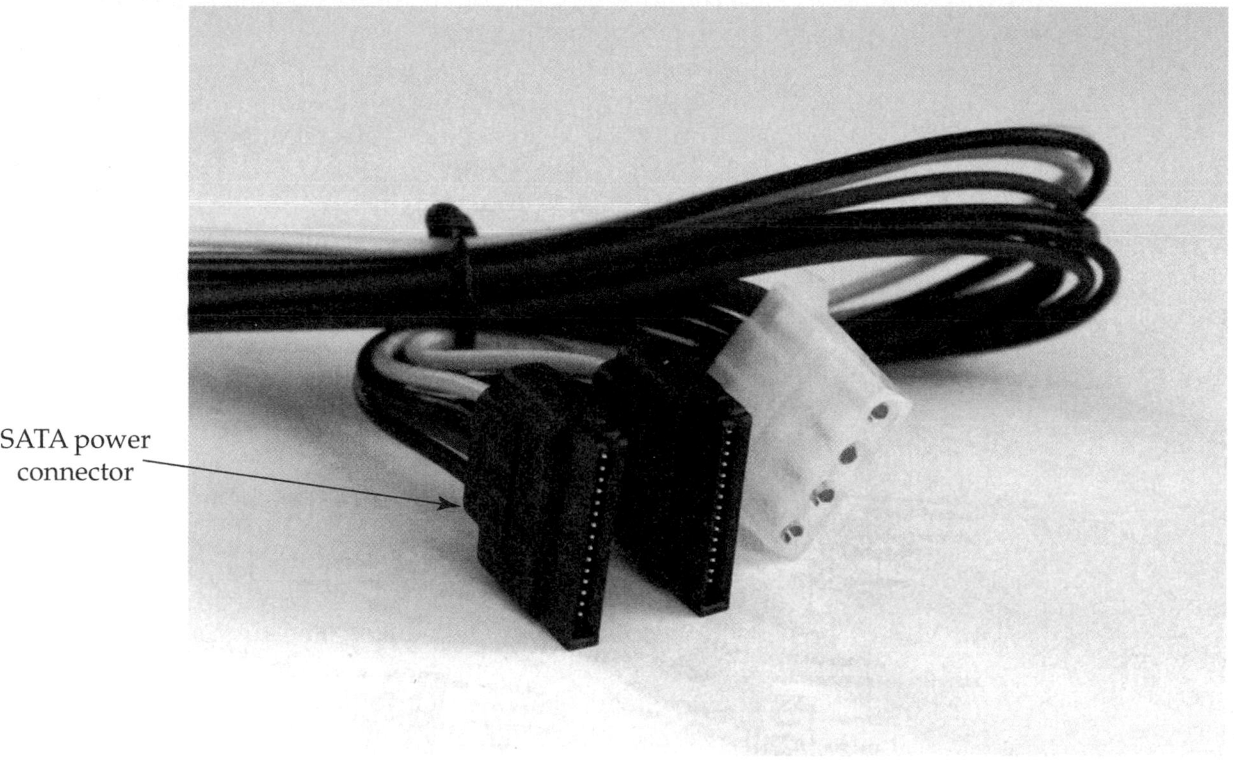

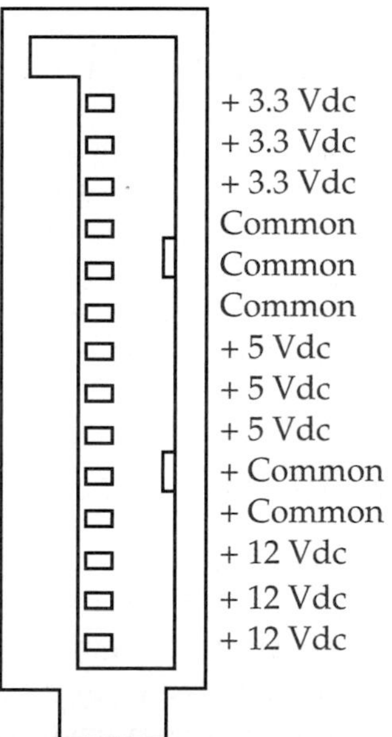

Computers are used worldwide, and as a result, they are typically designed with two voltage levels available either through use of a switch or by automatic electrical sensing and switching circuitry. Most countries in the world use 50-Hz electrical power rated at 230 volts. Some use 115 volts at 50 Hz. The USA is one of the few countries that use a 115/230-volt 60-Hz electrical system. While a computer will run on 230 volts at 50 Hz, the 120-volt 60 Hz standard USA electrical plug will not fit physically into the 230-volt 50-Hz wall outlet. A special adapter must be used to make the computer power supply physically compatible. Always check the foreign country the client or customer is going to so you can best advise them as to the electrical requirements.

To learn more about specific countries throughout the world visit the following Web site: www.kropla.com/electric2.htm. The Kropla Web site has a comprehensive list of countries and their standard electrical power systems, voltage, and frequency.

The DC output levels of an ATX12V power supply are +12, –12, +5, and +3.3. The following table lists the tolerance levels for these voltages. Thus, a connection that is designated to output +12 volts may actually output +11.40 volts to +12.60 volts.

Output Vdc	Range	Minimum	Maximum
+12	± 5%	+11.40	+12.60
+5	± 5%	+ 4.75	+ 5.25
+3.3	± 5%	+ 3.14	+ 3.47
-12	± 10%	–10.80	–13.20

rails
the conductor paths inside the metal power supply case of an ATX12V power supply. There is one rail for each voltage level. Each rail then supplies the electrical voltage level to all connectors that require that specific voltage.

The ATX12V power supply specification introduced a new term called ***rails.*** All power supplies use a transformer that converts the voltage levels identified in the following table. These voltage levels are distributed by rails, which is the electrical term used to describe the conductor paths inside the metal power supply case. There is one rail for each voltage level. Each rail then supplies the electrical voltage level to all connectors that require that specific voltage. In other words, every connector that requires +5 volts will connect to the same 5+ rail inside the power supply.

Some power supplies use a dual rail for a specific voltage. For example, a power supply designed to provide large amounts of wattage will have dual +12-volt rails, each supplying 18 to 20 amperes. When you look at a set of manufacture specifications for a specific power supply, the voltages available will be stated by rail.

Power Management Standards

Advanced Configuration and Power Interface (ACPI)
an open industry power management standard for desktops, laptops, and servers. ACPI allows the operating system to control the power management features.

Power management is a critical issue when it comes to power consumption of desktops, laptops, and servers. Controlling power consumption on laptops is critical for battery life before charging is required. Controlling power consumption for desktops and servers can result in significant electrical energy costs, especially in an environment of several hundred or even thousands of computers. Turning off computer displays and putting the computer into hibernation can save thousands of dollars in energy costs. The savings are not just directly related to electrical energy consumed by the computer system, but also to electrical energy consumed by air conditioning. Computers and displays generate a lot of heat, especially CRT displays.

Advanced Configuration and Power Interface (ACPI) is an open industry power management standard for desktops, laptops, and servers. ACPI allows the operating system to control the power management features. The original implementation of computer power management was ***Advanced Power Management (APM).*** APM was designed for the BIOS to control power management features of the computer system, **Figure 5-27.** APM was configured in the BIOS setup and determined the amount of time before the display screen and hard disk drive would be turned off. It was later replaced by Advanced Configuration and Power Interface (ACPI).

ACPI is enabled by the BIOS but not controlled or configured by the BIOS Setup program. ACPI is configured through the operating system and determines when to implement the energy saving features. Look at the Windows XP power options in **Figure 5-28** and the Windows Vista power options in **Figure 5-29.**

Windows Vista provides three general options for power savings: **Balanced**, **Power saver**, and **High performance**. To the right of each option, you can see the relationship of energy savings to computer performance. For example, the **Power saver** option would be the best choice for the maximum life of a laptop

Advanced Power Management (APM) power management standard that allows the BIOS to control power management features of the computer system. APM is configured in the BIOS Setup program and determines the amount of time before the display and hard disk drive are turned off.

Full On	The system is at full power.
APM Enabled	The APM power system is on and unused devices are powered down.
APM Standby	The system appears asleep. Most devices are shut down but can be powered back up almost instantly.
APM Suspend	The system is not operating and is in a state of suspended animation. Operation parameters have been saved to disk. The system can be brought back to the APM enabled state but with some delay.
Off	The power supply is off. The system is completely shut down.

Figure 5-27. Chart of the five conditions possible with APM technology.

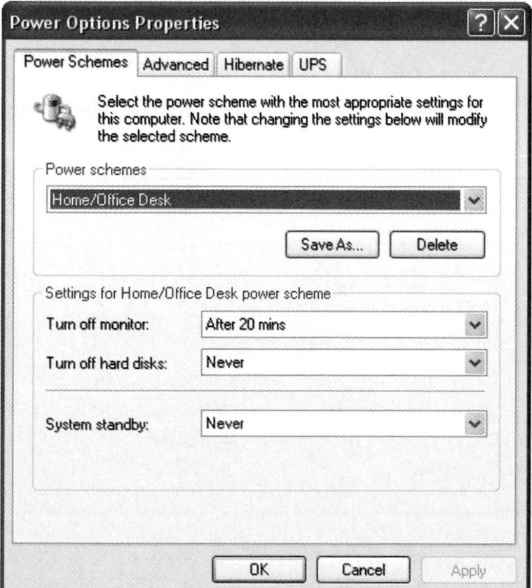

Figure 5-28. Windows XP power options.

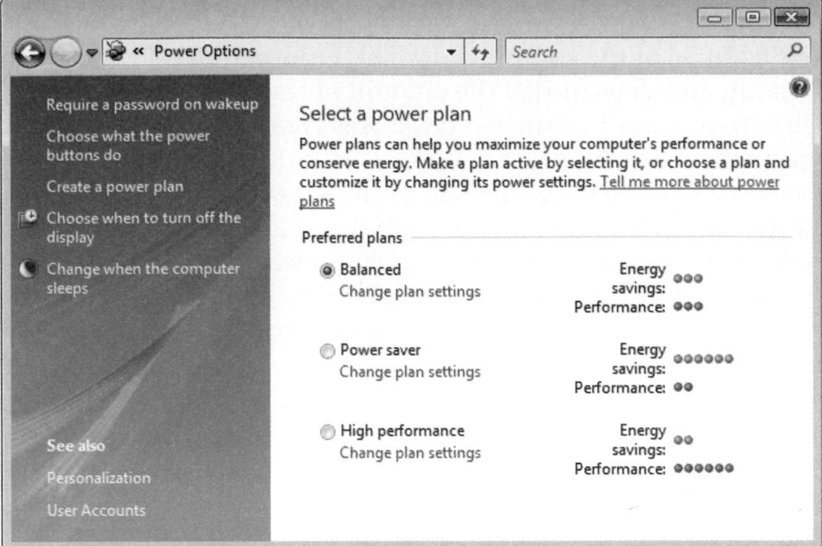

Figure 5-29. Windows Vista power options.

battery charge. There will be much more about power saving and laptops later in Chapter 12—Portable PCs. The **Power Options** dialog box accessed through **Control Panel | Performance and Maintenance** in Windows XP, and **Control Panel | System and Maintenance** in Windows Vista. If your folders are set up to use the classic view, the **Power Options** dialog box is accessed through **Control Panel | Power Options** in both Windows XP and Windows Vista.

Windows uses dynamic processor throttling to control the processor when in certain processor management modes. The Windows operating system can automatically throttle CPU performance to conserve electrical energy. The following table lists the various modes.

Mode	Description
None	Run at highest performance possible.
Constant	Always run at lowest possible performance to conserve maximum energy.
Adaptive	Performance based on demand.
Degrade	Always run at lowest performance state. Used mainly for laptops to conserve maximum amount of energy.

A+ Note:

On the A+ Certification exams, you will most likely see a question concerning power options for desktop and laptop computers. Be sure you can identify which power options are available for all current Windows operating systems.

Troubleshooting the Power Supply

See **Figure 5-30** for a picture of the inside of a power supply. A power supply is usually sealed to make it difficult to open. In general, there are no serviceable parts inside the power supply. It is considered a field replacement unit. Although it is possible to repair a power supply, it is not cost effective. The cost of most power supplies does not come near the cost of having an electronic technician repair the unit.

The bulleted list that follows contains signs that a power supply might be bad. Although some of the indicators can be caused by other system components, it is most likely that the power supply has caused the occurrence. Power supply failure is quite frequent when compared to the failure of other computer components.

These common signs of a defective power supply include the following:

- ✔ **Inoperable cooling fans:** Cooling fans that are not running are a fairly consistent sign that the power supply has failed. (Cooling fans receive their power directly from the power supply.)
- ✔ **Smoke:** Smoke coming from the power supply is an indicator of electronic component or circuit board damage. Electronic components usually burn up from an overload condition. This almost always results in excessive heat, which generates the smoke.

  The distinctive smell of burnt electrical device in proximity of a failed computer is also a very common indication that the power supply is defective. The smell can linger for hours after a system failure.
- ✔ **Circuit breaker tripping:** If a circuit breaker is tripped, it is most likely caused by the power supply unit in the computer. With the exception of the monitor, no other component will generate a condition to trip the breaker. To verify that the problem is with the power supply, unplug the monitor to isolate the computer power supply.

Figure 5-30.
Inside a power supply. Power supplies are field replacement units.

- ✔ **Automatic rebooting:** If the computer reboots itself while on standby or during normal operation, it is a good indication of a bad power supply. The power level dropping and rising is a common occurrence as the power supply breaks down. This fluctuating voltage level causes the computer system to reboot for no apparent reason.
- ✔ **Electric shock:** Any electric shock received from the computer case is a sign of a bad power supply or one that is breaking down. *Always use extreme caution when troubleshooting a suspected power supply unit. Remember that 120-volt ac power can be deadly.*
- ✔ **Excessive heat:** This troubleshooting diagnosis is made through experience. Even a normally functioning power supply will produce a certain amount of heat. Heat is a normal by-product of electrical equipment. However, excessive heat is a sure sign that complete failure of an electronic component is imminent. The excessive heat in combination with the other signs can leave little doubt that the power supply is failing. If the power supply is too hot to touch, it has excessive heat. Electronic components usually start to break down at 160°F (71°C).

Electronic technicians can repair power supplies, but it is usually not cost effective. The time taken to diagnose the power supply, locate the component, and replace the defective component is simply cost prohibitive. It's much quicker and more economical to replace rather than repair. Power supplies are very low cost components. The cost of labor and availability of replacement parts are the major factors that determine when a unit is repaired or replaced.

Figure 5-31 shows a typical ATX power checker with the cover removed to better expose the LED indicators. The LEDs light up to indicate the presence of +12, –5, +5, –12, and +3.3 voltage levels corresponding to the ATX main motherboard connection. This is the preferred method of checking power. Also, notice that the two large white rectangular areas at the top corners of the device are resistors. The resistors are used to simulate an actual electrical load. To measure a true voltage output level, some electrical load must be used. Many

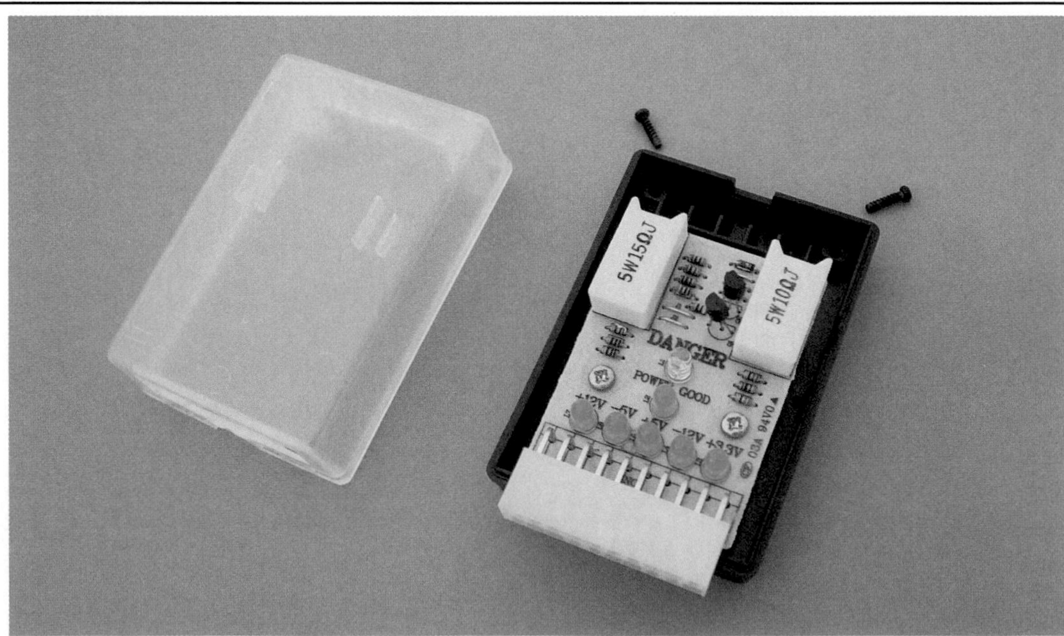

Figure 5-31. A typical power supply check device.

times a false good reading is indicated on a voltage power supply output when there is no electrical load. This is one of the short comings of using a digital voltmeter to check the power supply output voltage.

Replacing a Power Supply

Replacing a power supply is an easy task. You must make sure the replacement is an acceptable form factor to match the case and motherboard. You must also make sure there is an adequate watt capacity provided by the replacement unit. *The watts capacity should either match or exceed the unit being replaced.*

Steps for power supply replacement:

1. Be absolutely sure the power is off. (Do not use an anti-static wrist strap for this operation.)
2. Sketch of all the connections between the old power supply unit and the other computer components. (This will save you a great deal of time later.)
3. Remove the power connections carefully. Try not to disturb other cable connections on the motherboard or other devices. Also, remove the power cord attached to the power supply.
4. Remove retaining/mounting screws from the case that secure the power supply in place.
5. Place the new power supply into the case and secure the retaining/mounting screws.
6. Reconnect the power connections to the motherboard and devices using your sketch as a map.
7. Place any extra connections from the power supply in a neat bundle. Keep the loose connectors away from the motherboard. A loose connector could easily slip over a motherboard bare jumper causing destruction during power on or can catch in the fan blades thus stopping the fan and causing the CPU to overheat.
8. Take one last look around at the connections. Verify that they are all secure, and then power on the computer before replacing the case cover. The cover should be left off until you are satisfied the PC is working properly. Any error messages at this time could be generated by a loose or improper connection during installation.
9. If everything is fine, replace the case cover and power on the PC once more. When replacing the case cover, be careful not to pinch any of the cables between the case frame and cover.

Surge Protection Devices

An electrical surge, brownout, or blackout can happen at any time. A surge is when a higher voltage than desired is present in the electrical system. A brownout is when low voltage is present. In a blackout condition, there is no voltage present. A momentary blackout can happen at any time and go completely unnoticed by the human eye. All that is required is the absence of one electrical cycle of power, or less, to cause a computer crash or lockup. **Figure 5-32** shows a series of cycles with one flatlined. Below it is a series of digital signals with a large group of flat digital pulses in relation to the one cycle.

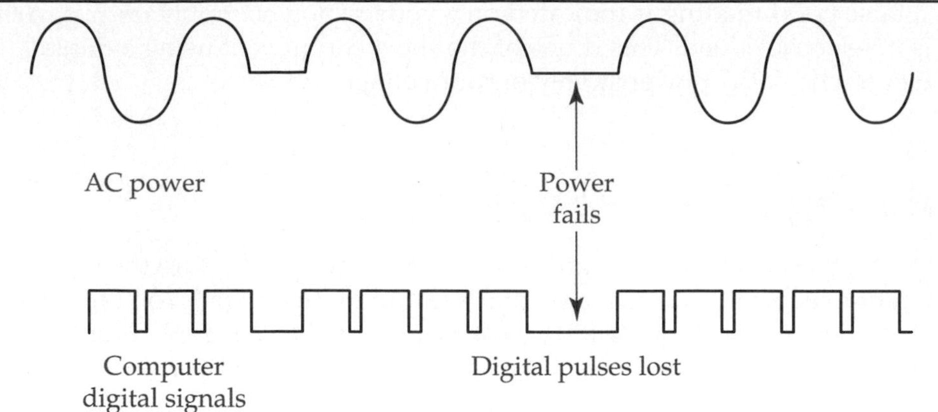

Figure 5-32. Series of cycles with a few cycles flatlined. Below it is a series of digital signals with a large group of flat digital pulses. A few lost cycles can eliminate many digital pulses.

Surge protection devices are designed to protect computer and other electronic devices against harmful surges of electrical energy. Two of the most common methods of providing protection are the use of power strips and UPS systems. UPS systems also protect against brownouts and blackouts.

UPS System

uninterruptible power supply (UPS) a power supply that ensures a constant supply of quality electrical power to the computer system.

An ***uninterruptible power supply (UPS)*** is designed to ensure a constant supply of quality electrical power to the computer system. Quality power means a power supply that eliminates surges and low voltage as well as complete power outage conditions. **Figure 5-33** illustrates a typical UPS system showing outlets, surge protection, batteries, and charger. **Figure 5-34** shows two typical UPS systems.

A UPS system monitors the power input to the computer while maintaining a fully charged battery. The AC/DC inverter is used to convert some of the 120 Vac from the outlet to 12 Vdc used to keep the batteries fully charged. When commercial power fails, the inverter changes the 12 Vdc from the battery back into 120 Vac. The 120 Vac is then used to maintain power to the computer until the PC can be properly shut down, preventing the loss of data. Without the UPS system, the PC would crash when the power failed, and all data in RAM would be lost.

Low voltage situations and brownouts are common occurrences in electrical distribution systems. Some low voltage occurrences last only a few milliseconds and go completely unnoticed by the users. Even low voltage levels of a few milliseconds can cause a computer crash. Remember that the digital traffic in a computer is traveling at megahertz values. Many commands can be issued in a few milliseconds or thousands of bits of data can be sent. All of it could be lost during the momentary voltage loss. Many computer system lockups are caused by momentary low voltage conditions. This condition can be prevented by using a UPS. A power strip does not provide protection against blackout or brownout conditions.

metal oxide varistor (MOV) a gate in a surge suppressor that becomes conductive at a given voltage, causing current to bypass the equipment plugged into the suppressor.

Power Strips

Not all power strips provide protection against power surges. Some are designed as a strip of convenient outlets to plug equipment into. Power strips that are designed for power surge protection have a ***metal oxide varistor (MOV)*** connected across the internal electrical line.

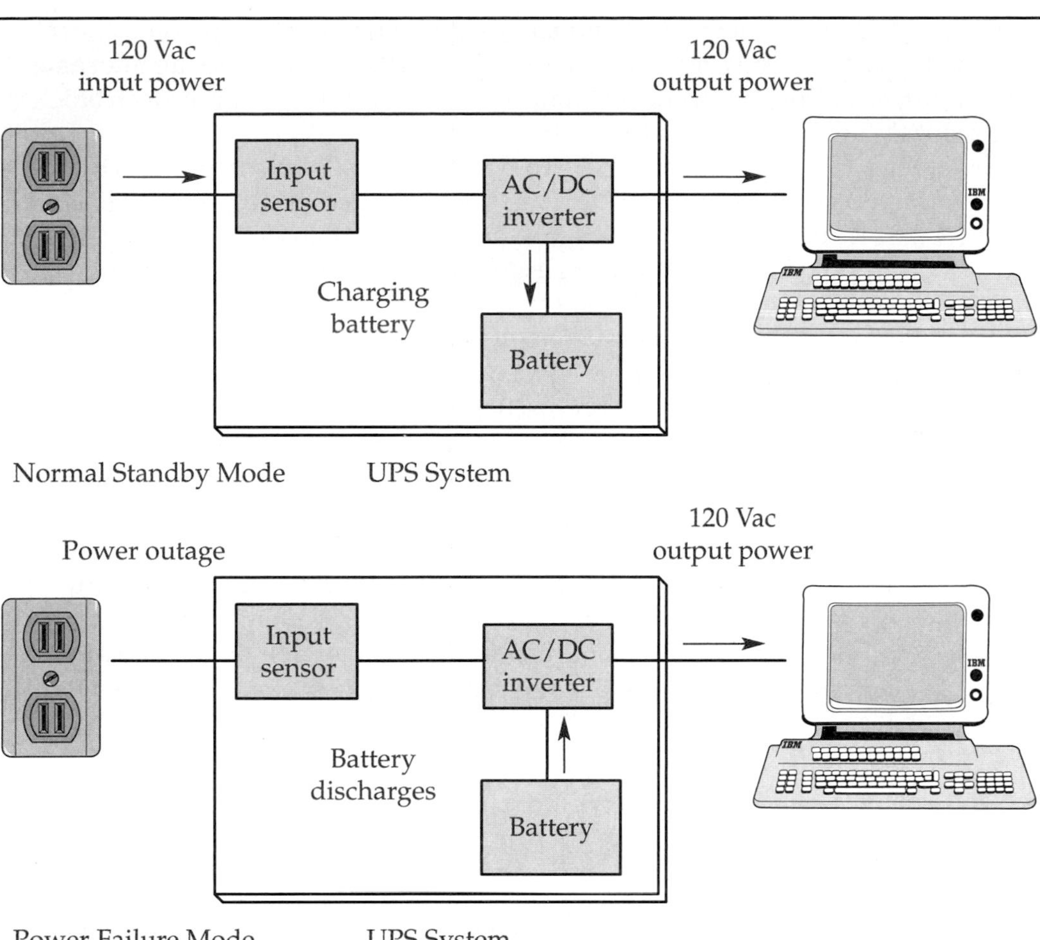

Figure 5-33.
A typical UPS monitors the 120 Vac input. When power is normal, the battery is kept fully charged and ac power is supplied to the computer. When the 120 Vac input fails, the battery discharges through the inverter to create 120 Vac for the computer.

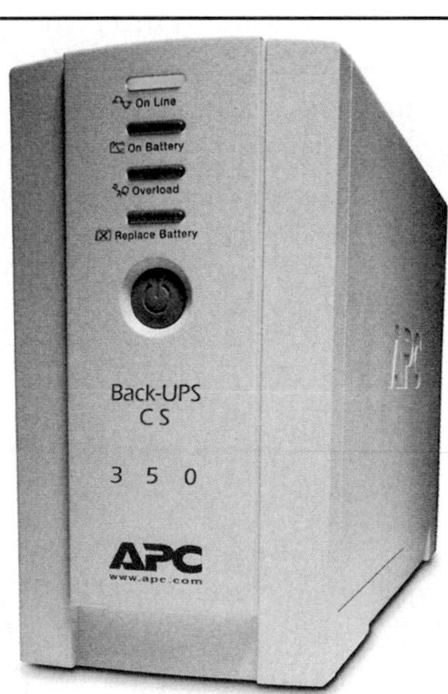

Figure 5-34.
Uninterruptible power supply systems protect PCs and servers from power loss and power surges. All critical PC systems should be protected by a UPS. (APC)

The MOV does not normally conduct electricity until a certain voltage level is reached. Then the MOV acts much like a direct short. It provides an alternate path for current. This diverts the current from the path through the electronic equipment that is plugged into the strip.

Power strips offer some degree of protection against power surges. While there is no true protection against extreme power surges, such as those generated by a direct hit from a bolt of lightning, the surge protector does protect against lower forms of power surge. A power surge can occur naturally many times a day in high-voltage power distribution systems. Most of them go unnoticed, but there are some that are quite severe. Surges are produced in the normal course of events such as in the opening and closing of electrical switch gear. Electrical distribution systems are normally rerouted while performing routine or emergency maintenance.

Other sources of voltage surges are caused by running brush-type motors such as those found in vacuum cleaners, drills, saws, and most any type of power tool or appliance. These types of surges show up as line spikes. See **Figure 5-35.**

These surges can produce very large spikes in the electrical system many times greater than the normal voltage. These spikes can damage sensitive electronic equipment. Many electronic components have maximum operating voltages. When a voltage surge exceeds this value, the component is damaged.

Batteries

Computers keep a variety of information stored in their CMOS. In this way, when your computer is turned on, it knows the settings describing the hard drive and floppy drive as well as items like the time and date. BIOS setup information cannot be stored in ROM and must match the hardware installed in that exact computer. BIOS setup information is saved to the CMOS chip and maintained by a battery so that the setup information remains intact even when the computer power is disconnected or turned off. Thus, a battery is used to power the CMOS chip when the main power supply to the computer is shut down. Look at **Figure 5-36.**

Batteries are constructed in a simple manner. When two dissimilar metals are placed in contact with a chemical solution, called an electrolyte, a voltage is produced. See **Figure 5-37** for an illustration of the principles behind a battery. It shows two metal plates and an electrolyte with a lightbulb as the load.

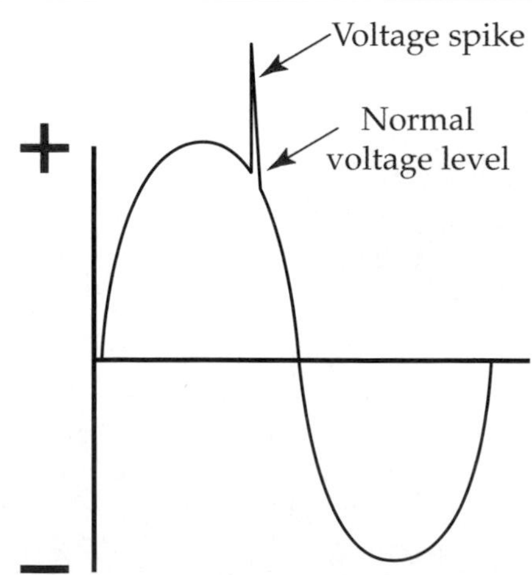

Figure 5-35. Voltage spikes can be caused by many things. The increased voltage in the spike damages electronic components by exceeding the voltage limitation of the component.

Figure 5-36. Typical motherboard battery.

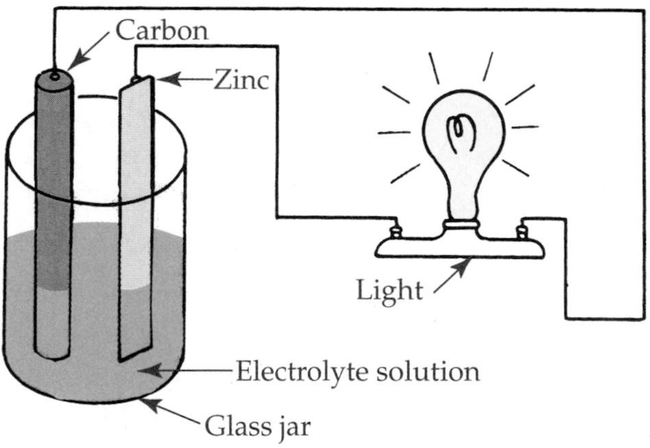

Figure 5-37. Illustration of the battery principles. Two metal plates in an electrolyte solution producing energy to power a light.

The most common types of batteries used for motherboards are alkaline, nickel metal hydride, nickel cadmium (also called NiCad), and lithium. All are rechargeable batteries. The charge on a lithium battery lasts longer than the other three types of battery. This is why lithium is also the preferred choice for laptop computers.

A sure sign of failure of the CMOS battery is the PC's failure to correctly keep the date and time. Battery failure can also cause the system to fail to recognize the hard drive and other devices that store information about themselves in the CMOS settings. A typical PC battery should last five to seven years, but they have been known to fail sooner. You can usually reset the CMOS settings and use the computer as normal until the battery is replaced.

The batteries used for a UPS system are usually lead-acid or a jell-type. These batteries can provide power for a substantial period of time. The biggest advantage of jell-type is the lack of regular maintenance required as compared to lead-acid. Newer lead-acid batteries should also be maintenance free. Both types should be periodically inspected for corrosion on the battery terminals.

Battery Disposal

Batteries must be disposed of in the manner outlined by the Environmental Protection Agency (EPA). Most manufacturers will readily accept the old battery in return when purchasing a new one. They have the proper means of disposal at hand that the typical technician does not. You simply do not throw an old battery into the trash, especially large UPS batteries.

More information on battery recycling can be found on the EPA's Web site. The site is located at www.epa.gov.

Summary

- ✔ Electrical voltage provides the pressure needed to push electrons through a circuit.
- ✔ Amperes or current is used to express the amount or volume of electrical energy flowing through the circuit.
- ✔ Electrical current is expressed in amperes.
- ✔ Resistance is the opposition to current and is measured in ohms.
- ✔ Electrical power is expressed in watts.
- ✔ Power is calculated by multiplying voltage times amperes. If the circuit is a dc circuit, this value is expressed in watts (W). If it is an ac circuit, this value is expressed in volt-amperes (VA). Watts is not the same as VA.
- ✔ The highest possible resistance reading is called infinity.
- ✔ A good fuse or cable has a zero resistance reading.
- ✔ Clean electrical power does not have any undesirable electrical characteristics such as spikes or low voltage slumps.
- ✔ An auto-range meter selects the proper range automatically.
- ✔ A dedicated circuit is used only for computer equipment.
- ✔ Computer systems must be properly grounded.
- ✔ PC power supplies have form factors to match cases and motherboards.
- ✔ The ATX power supply uses a 20-pin connector while the ATX12V uses a 24-pin connector.
- ✔ The ATX12V power supply is compatible with a motherboard designed for an ATX 20-pin connector.
- ✔ Power management standards are designed to conserve electrical energy consumed by desktop, laptop and server computer systems.
- ✔ Windows operating systems use dynamic processor throttling to control the performance of the CPU to conserve electrical energy.

- ✔ Advanced Configuration and Power Interface (ACPI) is controlled by the operating system, and Advanced Power Management (APM) is controlled by the BIOS Setup program.
- ✔ A UPS system provides protection against power surges and temporary power outages.
- ✔ A surge protector power strip provides protection against power surges.
- ✔ An MOV is used to stop voltage surges in electrical power strips and UPS systems.

Review Questions

Answer the following questions on a separate sheet of paper. Please do not write in this book.

1. Define electrical energy.
2. Water pressure, expressed in PSI, is similar to what value in electronics?
3. What value in electrical energy is similar to gallons per minute in water?
4. Opposition to electron flow is expressed in _____.
5. Wattage and VA are exactly the same. True or False?
6. The wattage rating on a power supply unit is an indication of how much _____.
    a. electrical energy can be safely supplied to the PC's devices
    b. electrical energy the power supply will consume
    c. current the power supply unit will draw from the PC's devices
    d. voltage the power supply unit needs to operate the PC
7. What resistance value will a good fuse indicate on a digital multimeter?
8. A blown fuse should indicate how much resistance on an ohmmeter?
9. A good cable should read how much resistance from one end to the other end?
10. What is a dedicated circuit?
11. What are the typical dc voltage levels from a PC power supply unit?
12. What is the difference between an ATX and an ATX12V motherboard main power connection?
13. What is the typical electrical voltage supply in European countries?
14. What should you warn a computer customer about when they plan a trip to Europe and they want to take their laptop along with them?
15. What is the minimum input voltage level of a standard ATX12V power supply used in the United States?
16. What is the name of the connector that is used to supply power to a hard drive unit?
17. What is the difference between APM and APCI?
18. What are the three main power conservation settings available in Windows Vista systems?
19. What is a metal oxide varistor used for?
20. What is the difference between an electrical surge and a brownout?

21. A UPS unit delivers a constant level of power to a PC during _____. Select all that apply.
    a. electrical surges
    b. low voltage
    c. power outage conditions
    d. brownouts
22. All power strips provide surge protection. True or False?

Sample A+ Exam Questions

Answer the following questions on a separate sheet of paper. Please do not write in this book.

1. Select the best definition of a PC power supply.
    a. A power supply converts 120 Vac power into 3.3, 5, and 12 Vdc levels that are used by the motherboard and various components.
    b. A power supply converts 120 Vdc power into 3.3, 5, and 12 Vdc levels that are used by the motherboard and various components.
    c. A power supply converts 120 Vac power into 5, 12, and 18 Vdc levels that is used by the motherboard and various components.
    d. A power supply converts 120 Vdc power into 5, 12, and 18 Vdc levels that is used by the motherboard and various components.
2. Which unit below is used to express electrical pressure?
    a. Ampere
    b. Volt
    c. Watt
    d. Ohm
3. Which electrical characteristics does a digital multimeter measure? Select all that apply.
    a. Voltage
    b. Resistance
    c. Amperes
    d. Wire size
4. Which item listed below ensures a steady and clean supply of electrical energy during power outages?
    a. VOM
    b. DMM
    c. UPS
    d. APC
5. Electrical power is usually expressed by which letter?
    a. V
    b. A
    c. W
    d. R

A+

6. What is the maximum electrical load that may be connected to a typical 120 Vac power strip supplying computer equipment?
   a. 1000 W
   b. 1600 W
   c. 2000 W
   d. 2400 W
7. Which of the following is the closest to the resistance reading of a blown fuse?
   a. 0 Ω
   b. 120 volts
   c. 10 MΩ
   d. Infinity
8. Which is a typical procedure when a power supply is suspected to be bad?
   a. Open the power supply unit and replace the fuse.
   b. Check the output voltage levels of the wall outlet.
   c. Run **msinfo32** from **Run** in the **Start** menu to diagnose the power output.
   d. Put on an anti-static wrist strap and then open the power supply box to replace the fuse.
9. Which system is controlled by the operating system to conserve electrical energy?
   a. ACPI
   b. APM
   c. DDR
   d. DMA
10. Which DC voltage levels are associated with a typical ATX power supply?
    a. 3.3, 5, 12
    b. 5, 12, 18
    c. 3.3, 5, 12, 18
    d. 12, 18, 24

Suggested Laboratory Activities

Do not attempt any suggested laboratory activities without your instructor's permission. Certain activities can render the PC operating system inoperable.

1. Remove a power supply from a typical PC and then reinstall it.
2. Practice taking ohm readings of various conductors.
3. Gather several small batteries of different voltages. Practice taking dc voltage readings.
4. Take voltage readings of the 120 Vac outlets in your classroom. See what the actual voltage levels are. Take readings throughout the day to see if the voltage levels change.
5. Take voltage readings from the output of a typical PC power supply. Take notes of the voltage type (whether ac or dc) and the voltage levels.
6. Take resistance readings of a fuse known to be good and then a fuse known to be blown. Compare the results.
7. Go to a multimeter manufacturer's Web site, such as www.fluke.com, and download a user's manual for one of their digital multimeters.

Interesting Web Sites for More Information

www.acpi.info
www.apcc.com
www.bestpower.com
www.duracell.com

Chapter 5
Laboratory Activity
Exploring and Replacing the Power Supply

After completing this laboratory activity, you will be able to:

- ✔ Replace a PC power supply unit.
- ✔ Determine if a power supply is defective.
- ✔ Check the voltage input and output of a power supply unit.

Introduction

One of the most common PC problems encountered is a defective power supply. The power supply is considered a field replacement unit. A field replacement unit is any module in a PC system that is commonly changed in the field and does not need to be brought back to the repair shop to be replaced or upgraded. The power supply is used to convert 120-volt ac input into 12-, 5-, and 3.3-volt dc outputs. It supplies the correct dc voltage to the PC's modules and devices, such as the motherboard, hard disk drive, and CD-ROM drive. Some of the dc voltages are positive while others are negative. Some of the connections will have no voltage indicated at all. These usually indicate a ground used by system components. Power supplies come in a variety of styles and arrangements. Their physical appearance depends on the motherboard and case style.

Power supplies are classified by their wattage ratings. The wattage rating is an indication of how much electrical energy can be safely supplied to the PC's devices. In general, a higher wattage rating means that more devices can be connected to the power supply. In a typical repair scenario, you would replace a power supply with one that has the same wattage rating. However, if additional devices have been added to the machine, then the power supply may need to be upgraded to a higher wattage rating.

In this lab activity, you will remove the existing power supply and then reinstall it in the same PC. After reinstalling the same power supply, you will record the voltage output of the connectors.

Equipment and Materials

- ✔ Typical PC with an Intel Pentium 4 or later processor.
- ✔ Digital multimeter to take voltage readings.

Procedure

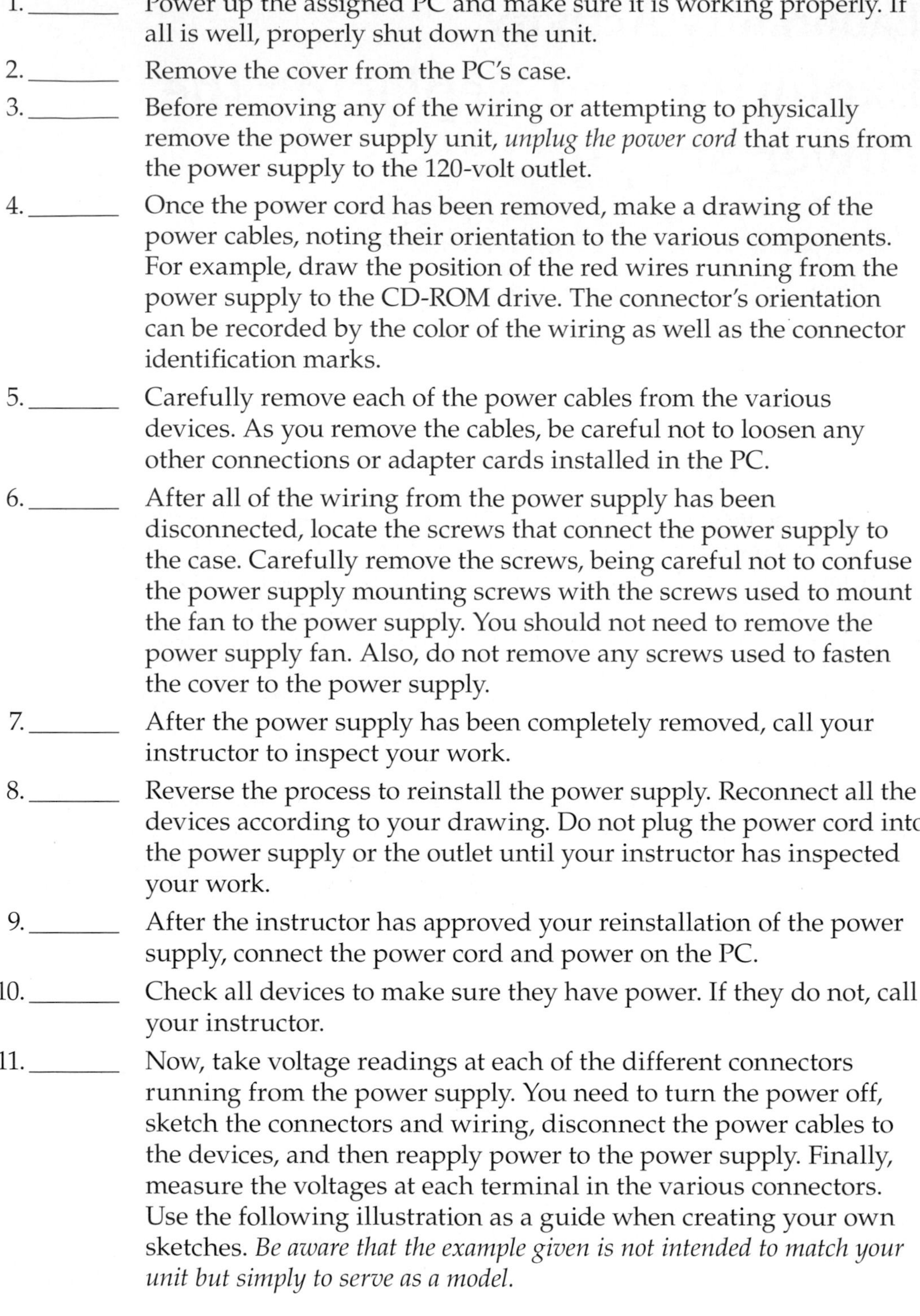

1. _______ Power up the assigned PC and make sure it is working properly. If all is well, properly shut down the unit.
2. _______ Remove the cover from the PC's case.
3. _______ Before removing any of the wiring or attempting to physically remove the power supply unit, *unplug the power cord* that runs from the power supply to the 120-volt outlet.
4. _______ Once the power cord has been removed, make a drawing of the power cables, noting their orientation to the various components. For example, draw the position of the red wires running from the power supply to the CD-ROM drive. The connector's orientation can be recorded by the color of the wiring as well as the connector identification marks.
5. _______ Carefully remove each of the power cables from the various devices. As you remove the cables, be careful not to loosen any other connections or adapter cards installed in the PC.
6. _______ After all of the wiring from the power supply has been disconnected, locate the screws that connect the power supply to the case. Carefully remove the screws, being careful not to confuse the power supply mounting screws with the screws used to mount the fan to the power supply. You should not need to remove the power supply fan. Also, do not remove any screws used to fasten the cover to the power supply.
7. _______ After the power supply has been completely removed, call your instructor to inspect your work.
8. _______ Reverse the process to reinstall the power supply. Reconnect all the devices according to your drawing. Do not plug the power cord into the power supply or the outlet until your instructor has inspected your work.
9. _______ After the instructor has approved your reinstallation of the power supply, connect the power cord and power on the PC.
10. _______ Check all devices to make sure they have power. If they do not, call your instructor.
11. _______ Now, take voltage readings at each of the different connectors running from the power supply. You need to turn the power off, sketch the connectors and wiring, disconnect the power cables to the devices, and then reapply power to the power supply. Finally, measure the voltages at each terminal in the various connectors. Use the following illustration as a guide when creating your own sketches. *Be aware that the example given is not intended to match your unit but simply to serve as a model.*

3.3 V+	3.3 V+
12 V-	3.3 V+
0	0
0	5 V+
0	0
0	5 V+
0	0
5 V-	0
5 V+	5 V+
5 V+	12 V+

Disconnecting a power connector from any device while the device is energized could result in permanent damage to the device. This is especially true for the motherboard.

12._______ After recording all voltages at each power connection, return the PC to its original condition.

Review Questions

Answer the following questions on a separate sheet of paper. Please do not write in this book.

1. What other components of the PC affect the power supply's appearance?
2. Do all power supplies supply the same voltages?
3. What is the power supply function in the PC?
4. What is the wattage rating of the power supply in your test unit?
5. What is the rated input voltage and frequency? (Look on the power supply.)

As a PC technician, you must be able to recognize the many different types of power connectors and to be aware of the power levels at each of their connection points.

Memory

After studying this chapter, you will be able to:

- ✔ Identify major issues concerning memory upgrades and replacement.
- ✔ Describe how to properly upgrade RAM.
- ✔ Identify and classify the various types of memory available.
- ✔ Identify memory map areas and functions.
- ✔ Identify typical memory problems.
- ✔ Upgrade system memory.

A+ Exam—Key Points

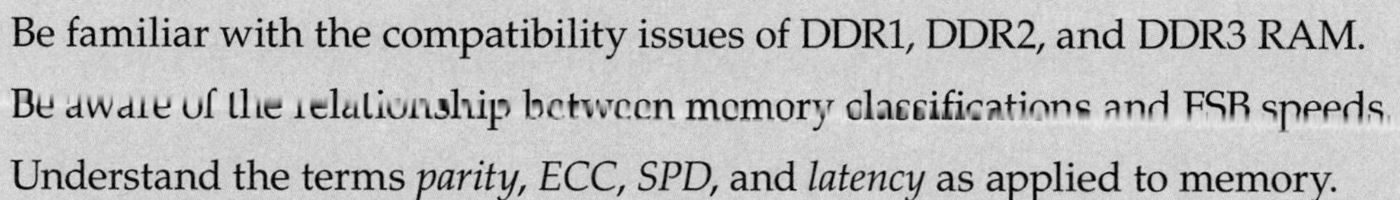

Be familiar with the compatibility issues of DDR1, DDR2, and DDR3 RAM.

Be aware of the relationship between memory classifications and FSB speeds.

Understand the terms *parity*, *ECC*, *SPD*, and *latency* as applied to memory.

Key Words and Terms

The following words and terms will become important pieces of your computer vocabulary. Be sure you can define them.

buffer
Column Address Select (CAS)
conventional memory
dual in-line memory module (DIMM)
dual in-line package (DIP)
dynamic RAM
electrically erasable programmable read only memory (EEPROM)
erasable programmable read only memory (EPROM)
error code correction (ECC)
even parity checking
expanded memory standard (EMS)
extended memory system (XMS)
fake parity
Flash memory
Flash ROM
heap
high memory area (HMA)
hot swap
nanosecond (ns)
odd parity checking
page file
parity
programmable read only memory (PROM)
random access memory (RAM)
read only memory (ROM)
registered memory
reserved memory
Row Address Selection (RAS)
safe mode
serial presence detect (SPD)
single in-line memory module (SIMM)
single in-line package (SIP)
Solid State Disk (SSD)
static RAM
upper memory
virtual memory

The memory in a computer is one of the most difficult parts of the computer to explain and understand. It is imperative that you carefully examine the illustrations provided in this chapter while studying the concept of memory. You may also need your instructor's help to completely grasp this difficult concept. While memory is, without question, one of the easiest upgrades that can be made to a PC, understanding system memory and its evolution is very complex and confusing.

The original disk operating system (DOS) could only access 1 MB of memory for program use. This restriction existed for many years to ensure compatibility with legacy software systems. Consequently, this restriction is still part of memory terminology and structure. With the introduction of Windows 95 and Windows NT, memory could be handled as one large unit, referred to as the *heap*. However, the memory restrictions were in effect in Windows if the PC was using legacy programs (programs designed to run under DOS).

This chapter covers memory types, memory terminology, memory diagnostics, and memory management used by the various Microsoft operating systems. It will also help you understand the complexity of PC memory and develop troubleshooting strategies. A large part of the A+ Certification exams is dedicated to questions regarding memory systems and terminology. The terminology associated with memory can be very confusing, but with a little concentration and effort, you will master the subject of PC memory.

Questions to Ask before Upgrading Memory

Before you begin your study of memory types, let's look at the issues you must consider when upgrading memory. There are a number of items of which you must be aware. Novices simply plug memory modules into motherboards and expect the amount of memory and performance to increase. This will not always be the result. Improperly identified memory modules and improper installation can decrease PC performance and possibly permanently damage the motherboard.

The questions that need to be answered before upgrading memory involve the following:

- ✔ **Compatibility:** Are you upgrading or replacing DDR1, DDR2, or DDR3?
- ✔ **Quantity:** What is the total amount of RAM desired? Are you adding to existing RAM or replacing it?
- ✔ **Parity or Non-parity:** Does the existing memory have parity checking? Does the existing system support parity checking?
- ✔ **Speed:** Will the existing chipset support the speed (frequency) of the memory module?
- ✔ **Memory Specifics:** Must the memory be installed in pairs? Must the size and latency match when installed in pairs? Are there any other specifics that must be adhered to?

These questions should all be answered before attempting a memory upgrade on a PC. Deciding on these issues will save time and money. The rest of this chapter assists with answering these questions. It also covers important concepts that will aid in your understanding of technical manuals and memory issues.

Physical Memory Packages

PC memory chips are packaged in several different physical styles. Some of these are SIP, DIP, SIMM, and DIMM. Physical size of the memory package is very important when the technician is assessing an upgrade or a replacement.

SIP

A ***single in-line package (SIP),*** as the name implies, is a single row of connections that run along the length of a chip, **Figure 6-1.** SIPs are sometimes referred to as SIPPs, single in-line pin packages, because the row of connections along the modules are pins. This type of module is not often used today because it has a high physical profile and the pins are easily bent.

single in-line package (SIP)
a memory chip containing a single row of connections, which run along the length of the chip.

DIP

A ***dual in-line package (DIP)*** is a chip that has two rows of connections, one row per side of the chip, **Figure 6-2.** This style is commonly used for cache memory or for memory that must be mounted permanently on a circuit board. You can see memory of this type on older model motherboards. It is mounted in rows near the CPU.

dual in-line package (DIP)
a memory chip that has two rows of connections, one row per side of the chip.

Figure 6-1.
Early PC memory modules were SIPs.

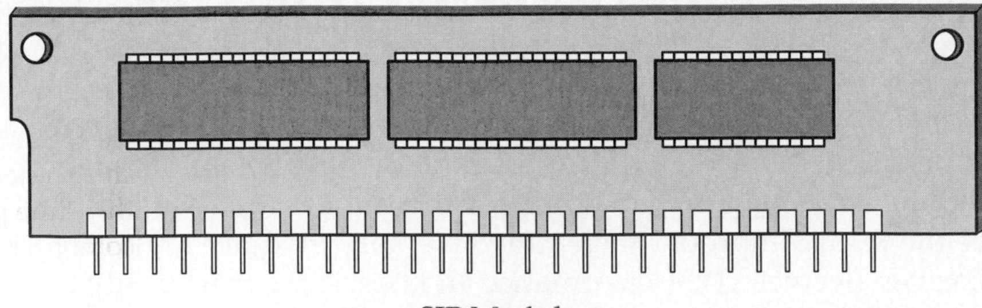

Figure 6-2.
Another early form of PC memory was the DIP.

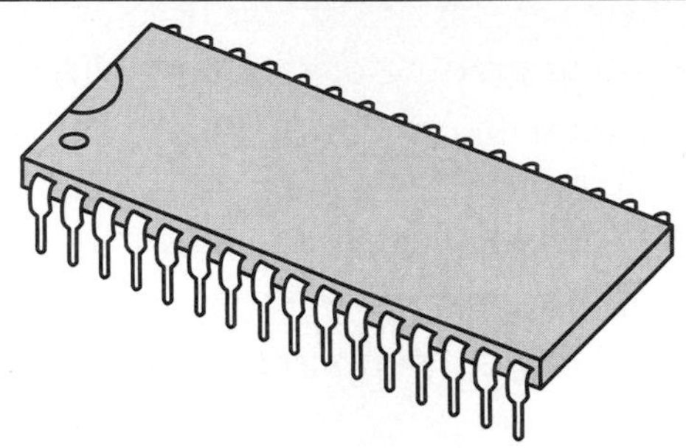

SIMM

single in-line memory module (SIMM)
a memory module containing a row of DIP memory chips mounted on a circuit board.

A ***single in-line memory module (SIMM)*** is a row of DIP memory chips mounted on a circuit board. The circuit board has flat contacts that run along both sides of the bottom edge. This type of connection is called an edge connector. The circuit board is then inserted into a SIMM memory slot on the motherboard. The SIMM is designed so that, when plugged into the memory socket, each side of the edge connector is the same circuit. This eliminates easily damaged pins. SIMMs come in 30-pin and 72-pin packages.

Flat edge contacts are also referred to as pins.

DIMM

dual in-line memory module (DIMM)
a memory module in which the edge connectors are located directly across the circuit board from each other and do not connect electrically.

A ***dual in-line memory module (DIMM)*** is constructed much like a SIMM. The major difference is that the edge connectors located directly across the circuit board from each other do not connect electrically. They are not the same electrical connection as they are on the SIMM board. The DIMM design allows for more electrical connections per inch than the SIMM design, **Figure 6-3.** DIMMs come in 168-pin, 184-pin, and 240-pin packages.

SO-DIMM and SO-RIMM

Small outline DIMM (SO-DIMM) and small outline RIMM (SO-RIMM) are a small outline package of regular DIMM and RIMM modules made especially for laptop applications where space is compact. The small outline package is designed to fit easily into the small confines of the interior of the laptop.

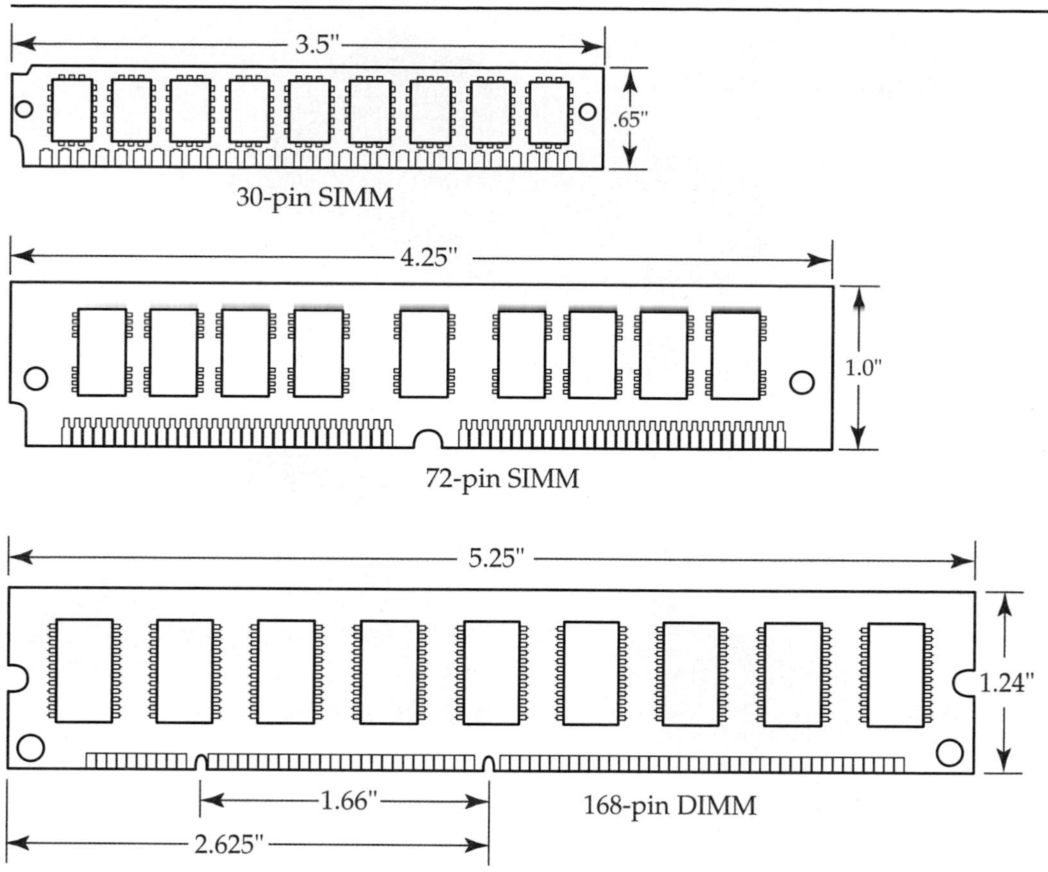

Figure 6-3. The various packages of memory can be easily identified by size. Shown are two SIMMs and a 168-pin DIMM.

Micro-DIMM

Micro-DIMM is a more compact version of the standard SO-DIMM package. Kingmax Semiconductor coined the term "Micro-DIMM" to distinguish it from the already existing SO-DIMM package and to emphasize its smaller size. Other memory manufacturers such as Kingston use SO-DIMM as the name of the smaller module. Either way, the module is quickly identified because of the overall smaller dimensions and pin count. The Micro-DIMM has a 172-pin count while the standard SO-DIMM module has a 200-pin count, **Figure 6-4.** The Micro-DIMM memory module is used in many notebook and laptop computers, not in desktops.

ROM and RAM Memory

Computer systems contain both ***read only memory (ROM)*** and ***random access memory (RAM)*** memory. ROM is designed to store the program information in a permanent fashion, while RAM is designed to be loaded with data or programs, which can then be erased and reloaded again and again. All programming and data in RAM is lost when power is removed from the chip. ROM retains any data and programs after power is removed.

To help you understand the difference between RAM and ROM, think of a typical "white board" found in classrooms or in corporate boardrooms. The white board requires the use of a nonpermanent marker. If information is written

read only memory (ROM)
memory that stores information permanently.

random access memory (RAM)
memory type that can store information, be erased, and have new information written to it.

Figure 6-4. Micro-DIMM is a compact version of the standard SO-DIMM. Some manufacturers also call the Micro-DIMM a SO-DIMM. (Kingston Technology)

on a white board using a permanent marker, the information will remain on the board forever, similar to the information written in a ROM memory chip. If an erasable marker is used on the white board, the information can be wiped clean from the board, allowing new and different information to be written on the white board. This is similar to RAM.

The terms *volatile* and *nonvolatile* are often used to describe computer memory. RAM is considered volatile memory. Like RAM, a volatile memory chip loses its data when power is removed from the computer. ROM chips are nonvolatile. Nonvolatile memory chips retain their information when the power is removed from the computer.

Types of ROM

There has been a good deal of innovation involving ROM memory. Not all ROM chips have programs that are permanently embedded. Many variations of ROM chips can actually be reprogrammed with different data or programs. They are still classified as ROM chips because, in normal applications, they retain their information even after power is removed from the computer.

PROM

The original ROM chips were manufactured with a program etched into the chip. The technically correct term for this type of ROM chip is *mask ROM.* The manufacturer uses a mask to create the circuitry. This circuitry represents the program when the chip is manufactured. Recall the discussion from Chapter 1—Introduction to a Typical PC about the chip manufacturing process. The programs in these chips cannot be altered.

Programmable read only memory (PROM) is similar to mask ROM. It is used extensively in computer program development. Blank ROM chips are purchased and then programmed using a device called a *PROM burner.* A PROM burner is connected to a PC. A program or data is written on the PC and then transferred to the burner where it permanently electrically burns the program into the blank PROM chip. The PROM chip then retains the program indefinitely, but it cannot be reprogrammed.

programmable read only memory (PROM)
read only memory that can be written to only once.

EPROM

Erasable programmable read only memory (EPROM) was an advancement of the PROM. These chips can be programmed, erased, and then reprogrammed. The EPROM has a small clear window that exposes the miniature circuitry inside the chip. The chip is erased by shining an ultraviolet light through the window. This returns the EPROM back to its original blank state.

erasable programmable read only memory (EPROM)
read only memory that can be erased with an ultraviolet light and written to more than once.

EEPROM

Electrically erasable programmable read only memory (EEPROM) eliminated the need for using an ultraviolet light to erase the memory chip. The EEPROM uses a higher electrical charge to erase the chip than the original charge used to program it. EEPROM was designed to be erased one bit at a time. In this way, part of a program could be erased rather then the entire program at one time.

electrically erasable programmable read only memory (EEPROM)
read only memory that can be erased electrically and written to more than once.

Flash ROM

Flash ROM behaves in a similar manner to RAM. It is possible to replace the memory contents of Flash ROM. It is similar to EEPROM, but it uses a much higher voltage to erase the chip and also erases the entire block of memory at one time.

It is important to note that EEPROM and Flash ROM can only be reprogrammed a limited number of times. At some point, the chip will become damaged by the application of the higher than normal voltage used in the erase operation.

Flash ROM
ROM that can be erased in blocks using a high voltage.

Types of RAM

Random access memory is a matrix of individual storage areas where information can be stored as bits. The name *random access* means that the CPU can access any bit anywhere in the memory. The CPU does not have to go through the memory in sequential fashion. The early computer systems did not have the advantage of RAM chips or disk drive systems. They used ROM chips and stored data on magnetic tape. The data on the tape was stored sequentially, bit by bit, along the entire length of tape. To access any information on the tape, the tape would have to play back bit-by-bit until the desired information could be retrieved.

Dynamic RAM vs. static RAM

There are two basic forms of RAM. One type, dynamic RAM, uses capacitors to store the information. The second type, static RAM, uses devices called flip-flops.

dynamic RAM
a type of integrated circuit that utilizes capacitors to assist in storing data in the transistors.

static RAM
an integrated circuit using digital flip-flop components.

Dynamic RAM (referred to as DRAM, pronounced *dee-ram*) is a type of integrated circuit that uses capacitors to assist in storing data in the transistors. Capacitors are capable of storing electrical charges. The presence or absence of the electrical charge in the capacitor represents the binary data being stored. Because of their microscopic size, the capacitors in the integrated circuit lose their charge over a short period of time. To retain the charge, the capacitors must be constantly refreshed (recharged) with electrical energy. Dynamic RAM is used in the CPU because it is very small and is low cost when compared to static RAM.

Static RAM (referred to as SRAM and pronounced *es-ram*) is an integrated circuit technology based on digital flip-flop components. The flip-flop does not use a capacitor to hold the data condition as the dynamic RAM does. It transmits data faster than dynamic RAM because it does not have to be constantly refreshed. To take advantage of the faster data transfer speed, most PC cache systems use static RAM as opposed to dynamic RAM. However, SRAM is approximately four times larger than DRAM, and it is considerably more expensive. Consequently, a computer's RAM will be some variant of DRAM.

DRAM

The basic *dynamic RAM (DRAM)* is the typical memory chip installed in older PCs, **Figure 6-5.** When someone says a computer has 2 GB of RAM, they are generally saying that the computer has DRAM. DRAM memory chips must be refreshed periodically to retain the information stored on them.

EDO DRAM

Extended Data Output DRAM (EDO DRAM) is faster than conventional DRAM. Conventional DRAM accesses only one block of memory at a time and then passes the data completely on to the next component before it transfers in new data. EDO DRAM is designed to access and start transferring in new data before the previous data stored on the chip is finished being transferred out. This technique greatly improves the transfer rate of memory.

BEDO DRAM

Burst Extended Data Output DRAM (BEDO DRAM) is an improved version of EDO DRAM. BEDO DRAM can transfer data in groups or bursts of four memory addresses at one time. EDO DRAM cannot keep up with a motherboard bus that runs faster than 66 MHz. Consequently, there are few current applications for this type of memory.

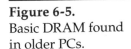

Figure 6-5.
Basic DRAM found in older PCs.

SDRAM

Synchronous dynamic RAM (SDRAM) is much faster than conventional DRAM, **Figure 6-6.** SDRAM can transfer data at speeds exceeding 100 MHz. The SDRAM synchronizes the transfer of data with the CPU chip. Synchronizing data transfer timing increases data transfer rates. This is because the chip does not have to wait for the next tick of the CPU clock system to begin transferring data. SDRAM can be found on video cards because of its high-speed transfer rate.

DDR1

Double Data Rate-SDRAM or simply *DDR1* was designed to replace SDRAM. DDR1 was originally referred to as DDR-SDRAM or simply DDR. When DDR2 was introduced, DDR became referred to as DDR1. Names of components constantly change as newer technologies are introduced, especially when the newer technology is based on a previous one.

The principle applied in DDR is exactly as the name indicates. DDR doubles the rate at which data is transferred by using both the rising and falling edges of a typical digital pulse. Earlier memory technology, such as SDRAM, transferred data after one complete digital pulse. DDR transfers data twice as fast by transferring data on both the rising and falling edges of the digital pulse. Look at **Figure 6-7.** As you can see, DDR can transfer twice the data as SDRAM.

DDR2

DDR2 is the next generation of memory developed after DDR. DDR2 increased the data transfer rate, referred to as bandwidth, by increasing the operational frequency to match the high FSB frequencies of the motherboard and by doubling the prefetch buffer data rate. There will be more about the memory prefetch buffer data rate later in this section.

DDR2 is a 240-pin DIMM design that operates at 1.8 volts. The lower voltage counters the heat effect of the higher frequency data transfer. DDR1 operates at 2.5 volts and is a 184-pin DIMM design. DDR2 uses a different motherboard socket than DDR1 and is not compatible with motherboards designed for DDR1. The DDR2 DIMM key will not align with DDR DIMM key. Forcing a DDR2 into the DDR1 socket will damage the socket, and the memory will be exposed to a high voltage level.

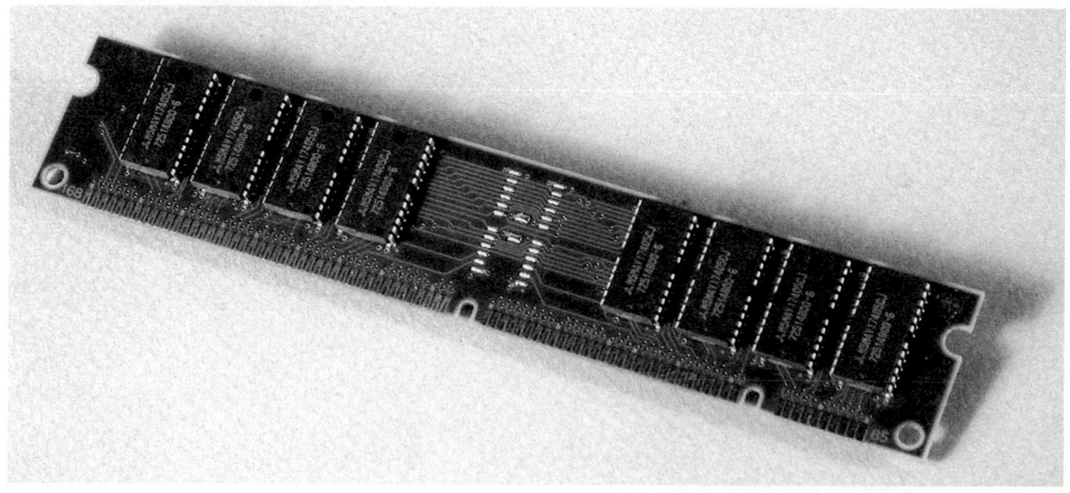

Figure 6-6. SDRAM found in many desktop PCs.

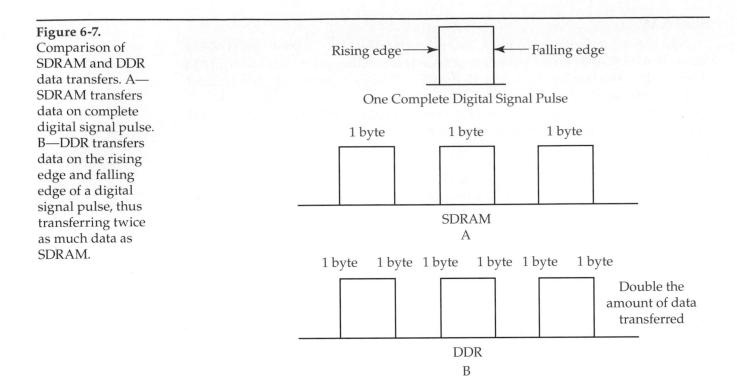

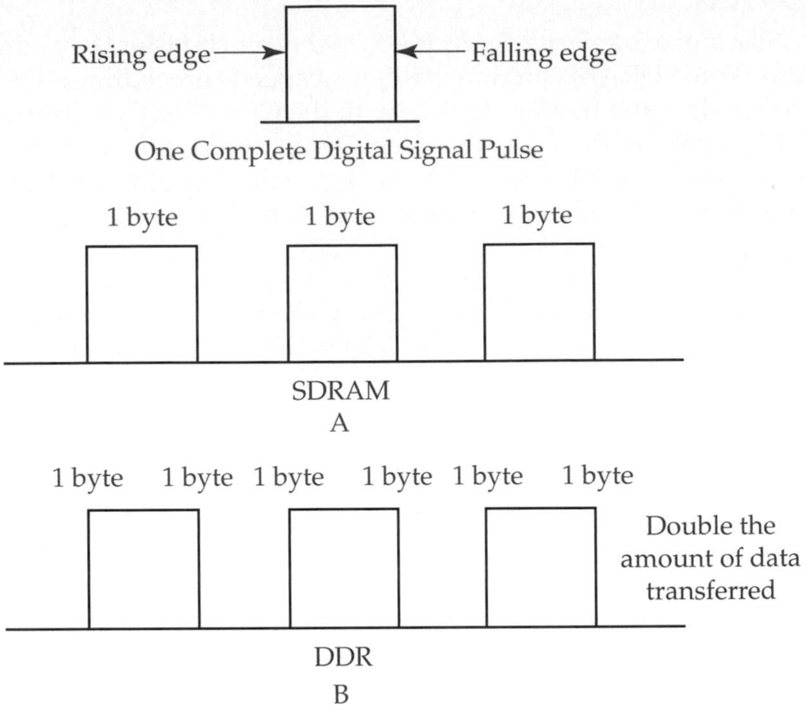

Rising edge → ← Falling edge

One Complete Digital Signal Pulse

1 byte 1 byte 1 byte

SDRAM
A

1 byte 1 byte 1 byte 1 byte 1 byte 1 byte

Double the amount of data transferred

DDR
B

Figure 6-7. Comparison of SDRAM and DDR data transfers. A—SDRAM transfers data on complete digital signal pulse. B—DDR transfers data on the rising edge and falling edge of a digital signal pulse, thus transferring twice as much data as SDRAM.

DDR3

DDR3 was introduced in the summer of 2007 and is the natural successor to DDR2, **Figure 6-8.** DDR3 increased the prefetch buffer size to 8 bits and increased the operating frequency, resulting in higher data transfer rates than DDR2. In addition, the voltage level was lowered to 1.5 V to counter the heating effects of the high frequency. By now, you can see the trend of memory is to increase the prefetch buffer size and chip operating frequency and lower the operational voltage level to counter heat.

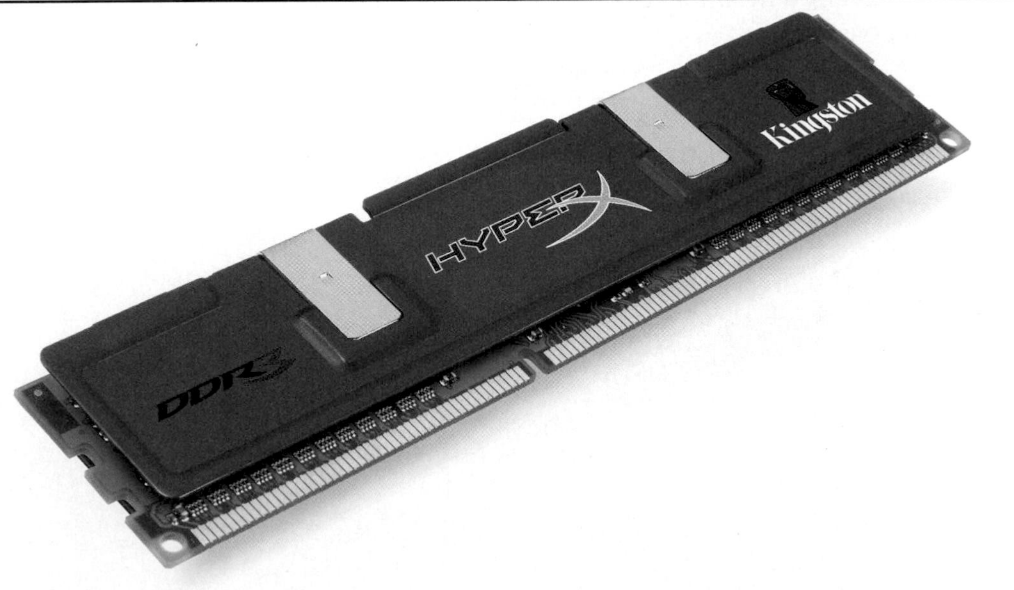

Figure 6-8. Kingston DDR3 DIMM. (Kingston Technology)

The DDR3 is also designed with 240 pins like the DDR2, but the notched key is in a different position to prevent the insertion into a DDR2 socket. DDR3 is both electrically and physically incompatible with previous versions of RAM. Look at the various memory module designs in **Figure 6-9.** Pay particular attention to DDR1, DDR2, and DDR3. Look close at the location of the notch placed along the bottom edge of the memory module. The notch is used to match the proper memory module to the proper socket. Insertion of the wrong memory module into the wrong socket will damage the RAM socket.

You cannot upgrade DDR1 to DDR2 or DDR2 to DDR3. They are not compatible physically or electrically. DDR is 2.5 Volts, DDR2 is 1.8, and DDR3 is 1.5 Volt. Be aware that some manufacturers may use a slightly different voltage level for their memory module.

In addition to high frequency and lower applied voltage level, the DDR3 has a memory reset option. The memory reset allows the memory to be cleared by a software reset action. Other memory types do not have this feature, and thus their memory state is uncertain after a system reboot. The memory reset feature ensures that the memory will be clean or empty after a system reboot. This feature causes a more stable memory system.

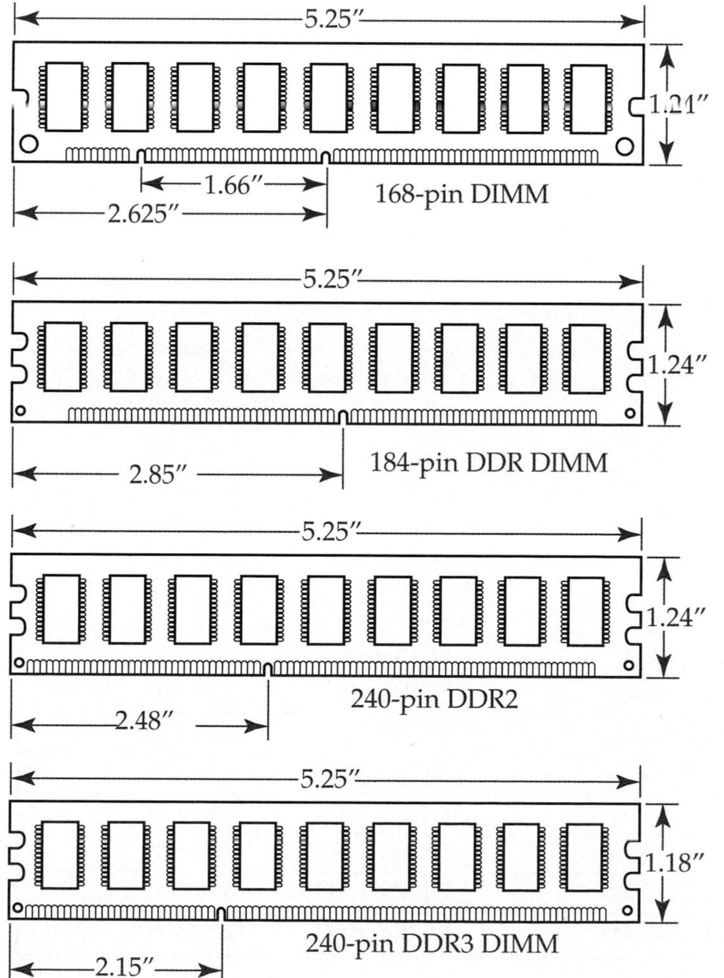

Figure 6-9. Various memory module designs.

Figure 6-10 lists the memory module PC classification, memory chip classification, and memory module bandwidth of various SDRAM and DDR memory modules. The memory chip classification correlates to the memory chip frequency design. For example, a DDR2-400 is designed to operate at 400 MHz. The memory module PC classification correlates to the memory module frequency times 8. For example, a DDR2-400 would be identified as a PC2-3200. The 3200 is equal to 8 times the 400 MHz.

The memory module bandwidth is the theoretical amount of data that can be transferred, even though it is expressed as an exact value such as 12.8 GB. The table is based on theoretical throughputs and does not take into account the memory controller, BIOS, or chipset. For a motherboard designed with dual-channel architecture, the memory module bandwidth is theoretically doubled. The theoretical speed is just a value used to compare the various RAM types and classifications.

You will see many video cards with a specification of GDDR3 as the main memory type mounted on the video card. Do not confuse this with DDR3. GDDR3 is only designed for video cards.

Dual-channel DDR memory

Dual-Channel DDR memory takes advantage of dual-channel technology developed by Intel in 2003. The RAM bus system, also known as the front side bus (FSB), consisted of a single bus system. The Intel Corporation redesigned the motherboard to provide two memory busses between the RAM and the north bridge chipset, **Figure 6-11.** The north bridge chipset contains the memory controller, which controls the flow of data between the RAM and CPU. Dual-

Figure 6-10. Memory chip and memory module classifications. The memory chip classification correlates to the memory chip frequency design. The memory module PC classification correlates to the memory module frequency times 8.

Memory Module PC Classification	Memory Chip Classification	Memory Module Bandwidth
PC100	SDRAM	800 MB
PC133	SDRAM	1.10 GB
PC1600	DDR	1.60 GB
PC2100	DDR	2.10 GB
PC2700	DDR	2.70 GB
PC2-3200	DDR2-400	3.20 GB
PC2-4200	DDR2-533	4.20 GB
PC2-5300	DDR2-667	5.30 GB
PC2-6400	DDR2-800	6.40 GB
PC2-8500	DDR2-1066	8.50 GB
PC3-6400	DDR3-800	6.40 GB
PC3-8500	DDR3-1066	8.53 GB
PC3-10600	DDR3-1333	10.67 GB
PC3-12800	DDR3-1600	12.80 GB

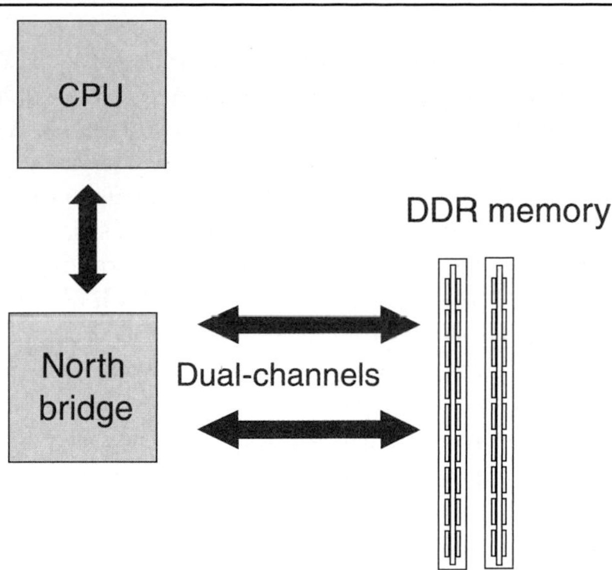

Figure 6-11. The Intel dual-channel DDR memory motherboard architecture significantly increases the data throughput from the RAM to the north bridge.

channel technology doubles the data flow between the chipset and the RAM but does not actually double the data rate to the CPU. There is still at the time of this writing only a single bus between the CPU and chipset. While data rates are significantly higher, they have not reached double the rate when tested in the field.

To implement dual channel, you must install DRAM as a pair. The pair does not necessarily need to match, but it is highly recommended that they match for best performance. When the pair does not match, the memory module with the least amount of memory will be matched by the other memory module. For example, a 512 MB memory module and a 1 GB memory module paired in a dual-channel arrangement will result in the same effect as two 512 MB not 1 GB pair. Also, be aware that the worst latency will apply to both modules as a pair.

When installing pairs of memory in dual channel architecture, the size, speed, and latency should be matched; otherwise, unexpected and intermitted problems could occur. Latency is covered later in this chapter.

VRAM

Video RAM (VRAM), also called *Video DRAM (VDRAM),* is a type of RAM used to enhance data transfer rates between the video card and the display unit. It is designed with two paths, one to the CPU and one to the display unit. This design allows for a much higher transfer rate.

WRAM

Windows RAM (WRAM) is specially designed memory used in video adapter cards to enhance Windows multimedia applications. It is much faster than traditional video RAM found in PCs.

SGRAM

Synchronous Graphics RAM (SGRAM) is used to enhance the video qualities of video cards. SGRAM is designed to work with advanced video card systems that contain their own controller. The design moves video RAM as large blocks of data rather than a stream. Moving the video data in large blocks makes for a more efficient system. SGRAM is found in many high performance 3D video card systems.

RDRAM

Rambus DRAM (RDRAM) was developed by Rambus, Inc. RDRAM is a proprietary memory system, **Figure 6-12.** The RDRAM uses a DDR (double data rate) technique to double the speed of the data transfer. Data transfer rates as high as 800 MHz can be accomplished using RDRAM and a motherboard and CPU that supports a 400 MHz front side bus. Intel originally incorporated Rambus RDRAM into their line of motherboards but has since discontinued it.

RIMM is the trade name for Direct Rambus memory module. It is longer than a 168-pin DIMM, and it reaches speeds of 800 MHz. It also uses a package capable of dissipating the heat generated by the high-speed data transfer rate. The package is an aluminum sheath, called a *heat spreader,* which covers the chips and acts as a heat sink.

RIMM must be installed in pairs to function. However, one RIMM module may contain more than enough memory for a user. In that case, to achieve the effect of two RIMM modules when using only one RIMM module, a continuity RIMM (C-RIMM) must be installed in the second slot, **Figure 6-13.** The C-RIMM does not contain any memory chips; it simply acts as an electrical connection allowing data to pass through as if there were an additional RIMM installed.

Figure 6-12. RDRAM has data transfer rates of up to 800 MHz.

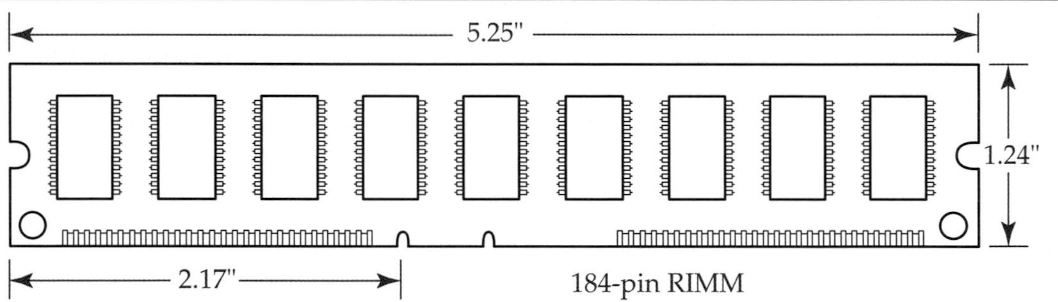

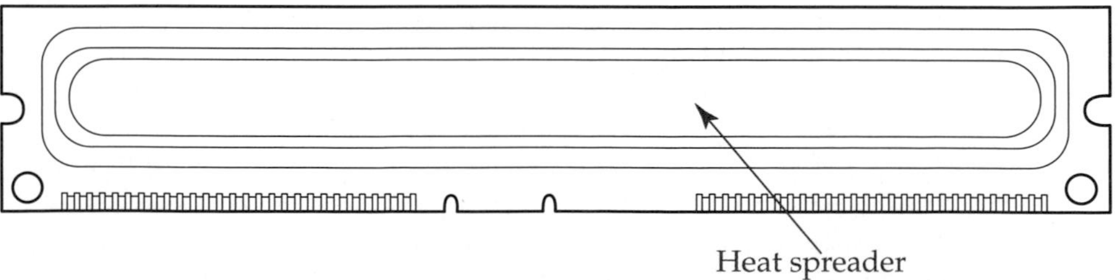

Figure 6-13. Sketch of RIMM and C-RIMM. In the diagram, the RIMM is shown with the heat spreader removed, exposing the individual memory chips.

When C-RIMM is used in conjunction with a RIMM, the exact slot sequence should be checked against the manufacturer's specifications.

FPM RAM

Fast page mode RAM (FPM RAM), or page mode memory, is a DRAM that allows for faster transfer rates. It was developed mainly for video systems in which large chunks of sequential data are needed for graphic displays. The RAM uses a technique that divides memory into 512-byte pages, or smaller, and then accesses the pages sequentially. With this technique, only half the normally required address is used.

Memory can be thought of as a matrix of memory cells. Column and row addresses are used to identify the memory cells, **Figure 6-14.** When FPM RAM is applied, the start of the addresses is equated to a certain column and row. After the initial column and row is supplied, only the column is needed for the next series of consecutive addresses. This technique eliminates the need of row identification, thus allowing for faster transfer time.

Memory chip technology is rapidly changing. There has been at least one new memory type developed every year for the last five years.

DDR Prefetch Memory Buffer

Memory chips can operate at extremely high frequencies inside the memory chip structure. The frequencies of the logic transistors inside the chip operate at a much higher frequency than the outside connections, such as the FSB or the HyperTransport bus. The transferring data is positioned into a buffer located on the chip and then awaits the proper time to transfer the data to the bus on the motherboard. The entire operation is referred to as the memory prefetch.

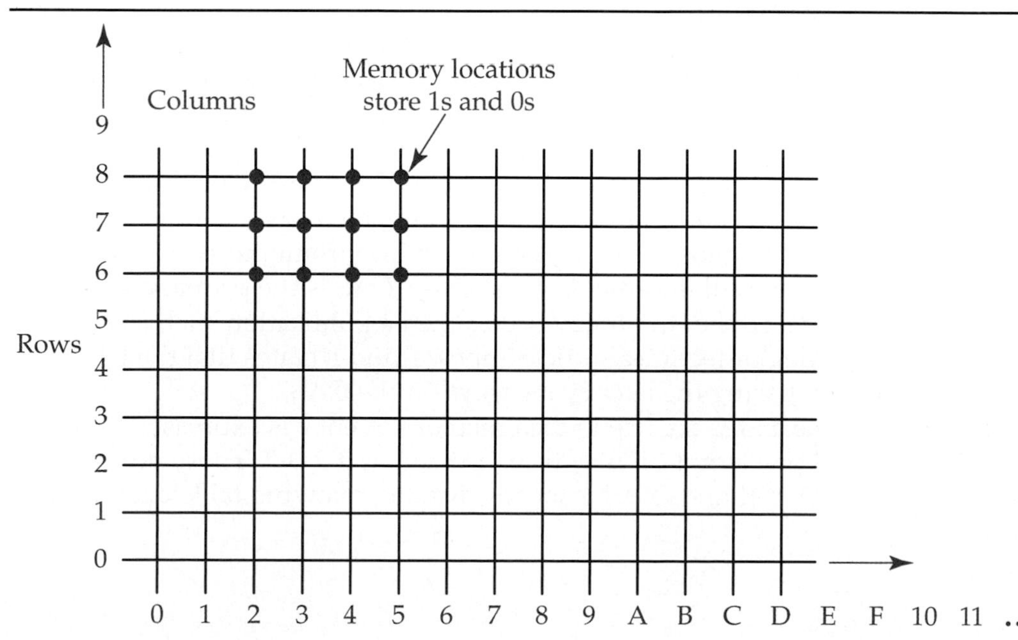

Figure 6-14. Each memory location in the matrix is described by a column and a row hexadecimal number such as 08A2h 3B5Fh.

The term *prefetch* is followed by the lower case letter *n* and a number that represents the number of data bits. For example, DDR1 has a prefetch 2n, which means it can store 2 bits of data in each prefetch buffer. DDR2 uses a prefetch 4n, or 4-bit buffer, thus doubling the amount of data transferred from the buffer as compared to DDR1. DDR3 uses a prefect 8n, which doubles the size of the prefetch used in DDR2. Look at the following table and compare the prefetch buffer, voltage level, and FSB data rates of DDR1, DDR2, and DDR3.

	DDR1	DDR2	DDR3
Prefetch Buffer	2-bits	4-bits	8-bits
Voltage Level	2.5 V	1.8 V	1.5 V
FSB Data Rates (in MHz)	200, 266, 333, 400	400, 533, 677, 800	800, 1066, 1330, 1600

Increasing the size of the prefetch buffer and the memory bus operational frequency allows each generation of DDR to increase the overall throughput.

Latency

To understand latency, you must first understand how computers locate and transfer data stored in memory locations. The RAM can be thought of as a matrix of storage bins, each bin containing a bit of information in a binary format. Each location corresponds to a specific column and row identification. Look again at Figure 6-14.

Reading or writing to a memory location takes time. The time required to complete a memory read or write operation is measured in clock signals. A clock signal is when the voltage level switches between high and low. There are two main measurements and several minor measurements of read-write access: RAS and CAS.

Row Address Selection (RAS) describes the time it takes to start a memory read or write to the row location in the memory matrix. RAS is the first step of a memory access operation.

Column Address Select (CAS) describes the time it takes to access the exact column location in the memory matrix after RAS.

Row Address Selection (RAS) is a term that describes the time it takes to start a memory read or write the row location in the memory matrix. RAS is the first step of a memory access operation. This is followed by CAS.

Column Address Select (CAS) is a term used to describe the time it takes to access the exact column location in the memory matrix after RAS. There is a minimum amount of time the CAS must remain active to complete the read operation. For example, a CAS 3 means that there will be three clock signals required before the CAS can complete the read of the memory location.

CAS is considered by most experts as the most important number when expressing latency. You will find that in most cases, CAS is the primary way latency measure is described. In other words, when a publication such as a computer parts catalog or technical article appears, and it states that the latency is 5, they are generally basing the latency measure on the CAS.

Other latency measures are used when memory latency is expressed as a series of numbers. For example, it may be expressed as 3-3-3-5. These numbers represent tCL, tRCD, tRP, and tRAS respectively. The following table describes each term.

Term	Description
tCL	This is equal to CAS or Column Access Strobe.
tRCD	The amount of delay between the RAS and CAS.
tRP	How long it takes to precharge the RAS.
tRAS	The delay to precharge the RAS.

Now you can see why most articles simply use the CAS value. These other latency terms require a more in-depth understanding of digital electronics; otherwise, they are very cryptic to the average reader.

In general, the lower the number used to describe the latency, the better the performance. There is an exception to this general rule. You must compare latency between similar DDR technologies for a fair comparison. As frequencies rise, memory latency rises. For example, DDR has latencies in the range of 1.5 to 3. DDR2 has latency range from 2 to 5, and DDR3 has latency from 7 to 11. While DDR3 has the largest latency number compared to DDR1 or DDR2, it provides much better system performance. If you double the memory frequency, you will of course double the latency.

Be aware that most computers will develop memory errors if the latency of the memory modules paired do not have matching latency. This is an important consideration for memory upgrades or replacements.

SSD

Solid State Disk (SSD) is a storage system designed with no moving parts and that consists entirely of DRAM chips. The SSD is also referred to as a RAM drive. The SSD is very advantageous to laptop designs because it requires less electrical power, is much lighter than mechanical drives, boots faster, and does not generate noise the way mechanical drives do. It is also not damaged as easily as mechanical drives when dropped or experience mechanical shock.

SSDs are designed mainly for laptops and other forms of portable equipment. As the cost to produce SSD drives drop, they will become common on desktop models of computers. There will be more about SSD in Chapter 12—Portable PCs.

Solid State Disk (SSD)
a storage system designed with no moving parts and consists entirely of DRAM chips. The SSD is also referred to as a RAM drive.

Cache

Cache can be found throughout the computer system. *Cache* is a small amount of high-speed memory designed to speed up the transfer of data between components and peripherals. The term *small* is relative, of course. The cache is small when compared to total system RAM.

An example of a common use of cache is transferring data from system RAM to a hard drive. Transferring and writing data to a hard drive can be very time-consuming compared to the speed of transferring and writing data to RAM. By incorporating a cache on the hard drive circuit board, data transfer can be accelerated, thus releasing the system to perform other tasks. The memory chips used for cache store data at least ten times faster than storing data directly to the hard disk system.

Another important reason for using cache is the data remaining in cache can be accessed faster than accessing the hard disk drive. Anywhere data transfer is taking place, you can be sure there is a cache system designed in the circuit board. Discussion of L1, L2 and L3 cache can be found in Chapter 4—CPU.

SPD

serial presence detect (SPD) a technology used to identify the type of RAM installed on a computer. It involves the presence of an extra chip on the memory module that contains technical information about the RAM module.

Serial presence detect (SPD) is a technology used to identify the type of RAM installed on a computer. It involves the presence of an extra chip on the memory module that contains technical information about the RAM module. The information provided by SPD is used by the BIOS to automatically configure the BIOS RAM settings to match the installed RAM. You can still change the RAM settings manually in the BIOS, but this is not advised.

Increasing the RAM access clock speed is commonly performed by PC enthusiasts who wish to increase the performance of their computer. This group of enthusiasts is referred to as "overclockers." They not only overclock the RAM performance, but also the CPU. When you manually override the automatic SPD detection and configuration in BIOS, you run the risk of overheating the memory chips and causing a system failure or lockup. After failing to tweak the speed of the RAM, the computer BIOS must be reset, thus allowing the SPD to automatically reconfigure the BIOS RAM configuration correctly.

Installing RAM Modules

Adding memory is one of the easiest upgrades you can make to a computer. You simply insert the module and the computer's BIOS recognizes the new memory when you start your computer. However, the memory and the slots on the motherboard can be damaged if you are not careful, so there are a few important facts to keep in mind when installing memory.

Do not force the memory module into the socket. Doing so may damage the memory module or socket. The memory module should fit snuggly but experience only a little physical resistance. You can check the motherboard documentation for the correct memory type that is compatible with the motherboard and motherboard chipset.

Memory modules are extremely sensitive to static discharge. Always wear a standard static or grounding wrist strap when handling memory chips. You must also properly identify the orientation of the SIMM or DIMM before inserting it into the memory slot. Both the SIMM and DIMM packages are physically designed to prevent backward insertion into the slot. If too much force is applied when inserting the memory modules into the slots, permanent damage may result to both the memory module and the slot.

The SIMM is inserted at a 30° angle, **Figure 6-15.** It is then rotated up to a final position perpendicular to the motherboard. The notch in one end of the SIMM is used for proper insertion into the slot. If the notch does not line up with the locking clip, the SIMM is being inserted backward. Take special note of the

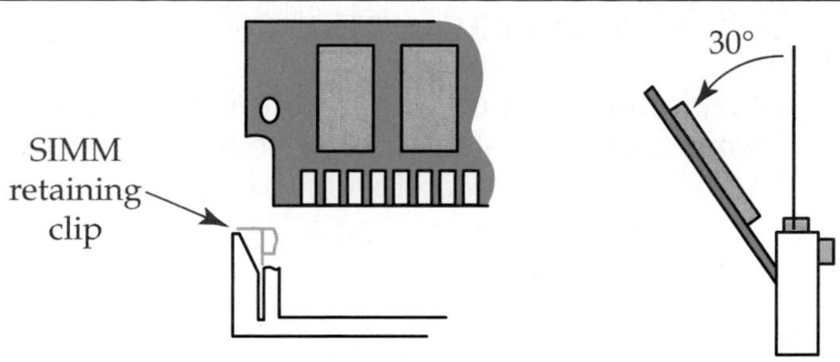

Figure 6-15.
With the retaining clips open, a SIMM is inserted at approximately a 30° angle. It is then tilted to the perpendicular. The retaining clips are then closed to lock it in place. The procedure is reversed for removal.

notch or notches on the edge connector. The notch or notches are used to identify the proper voltage and the type of memory compatible with the PC system.

DIMM memory is inserted straight into the DIMM slot. You do *not* use the 30° angle used with SIMMs. DIMM modules also use special ejector tabs to assist in the removal and installation of memory, **Figure 6-16.**

In most instances, SIMM memory modules must be installed in pairs. A few motherboards were produced that allowed single SIMMs to be installed. The reason most SIMM memory modules have to be installed in pairs is because of the way information is transmitted to and from most SIMM modules. Memory access speed is increased when data is stored in a pattern that alternates between the two SIMM modules rather than just one. DIMM modules do not have to be installed in pairs. The DIMM module circuitry is designed to simulate two separate memory modules. Only one DIMM needs to be installed to increase memory.

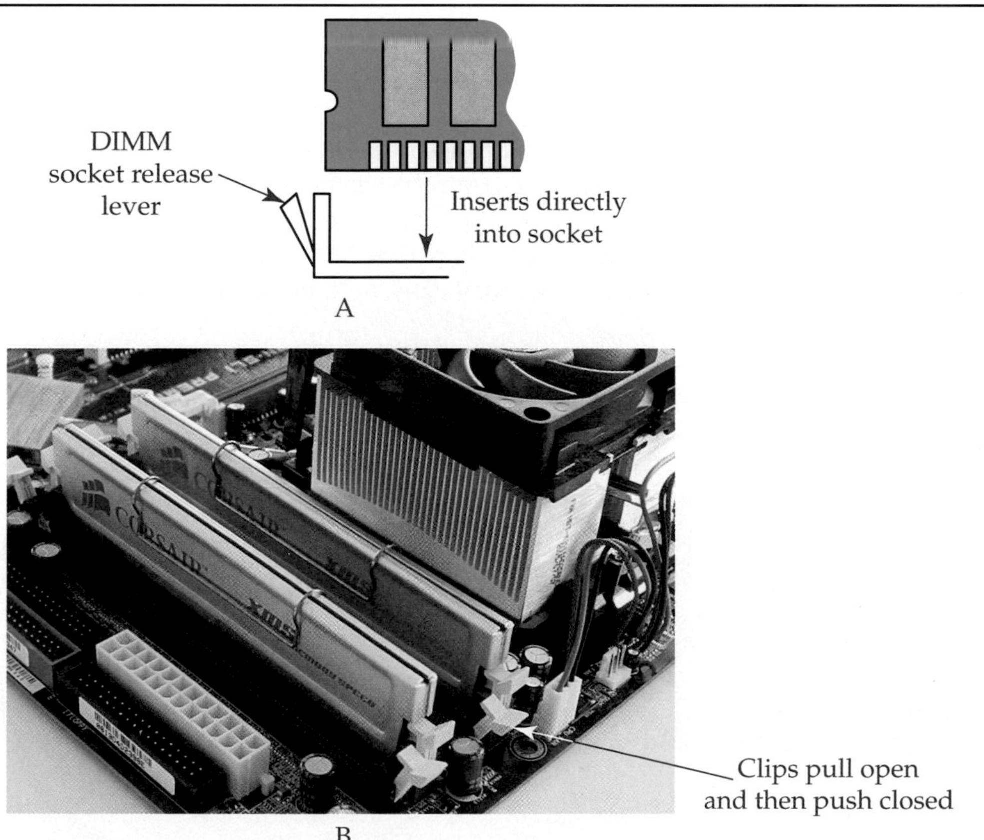

Figure 6-16.
A DIMM is inserted directly into the socket. There is no need to tilt the DIMM. Simply move the DIMM socket release lever outward. A—DIMM socket with release lever that snaps back into position. B—Corsair DDR memory modules. Notice that the clips for DDR DIMM sockets must be opened and then closed manually. (Corsair)

Matching RAM Characteristics

When adding or replacing RAM modules, it is important that certain characteristics of the modules are matched. The two most important characteristics of RAM chips are the speed and the integrity of the chips. These two characteristics need to be studied.

Memory Chip Speed

nanosecond (ns) equal to one billionth of a second.

The speed of the CPU is measured in megahertz (MHz) or gigahertz (GHz). Memory chip speed is measured in nanoseconds. A ***nanosecond (ns)*** is equal to one billionth of a second.

When adding more memory to a PC, it is best to match the speed of the existing memory chips. If faster memory chips are added to an existing slower memory chip bank, the newer faster chips will run at the same speed as the existing chips. The chips will run, so if you have them, they can be used successfully. However, as they will run at a slower speed, they are not cost effective.

Another consideration is the maximum speed that the motherboard system bus can support as well as the chipsets. You must check the PC, chipset, and BIOS documentation before attempting to upgrade RAM. This is especially true if the PC you are attempting to upgrade is several years old.

While faster RAM will slow down to run on a computer with a slower bus speed, RAM modules with a speed slower than that of the motherboard bus will *not* run. For example, a 133 MHz SDRAM module can run on a motherboard with a 100 MHz bus, but will operate at 100 MHz. However, a 100 MHz SDRAM module will not work on a motherboard with a 133 MHz bus, **Figure 6-17.**

Memory Data Integrity

Data can become corrupted while waiting in memory. Some causes of data corruption are electrical voltage leaking from the memory module, electrical interference, power surges, and electrostatic discharges. Even cosmic rays can corrupt data. Think for a moment about a 16 MB SIMM memory module. That module is composed of 128 million memory cells, so there is always a possibility

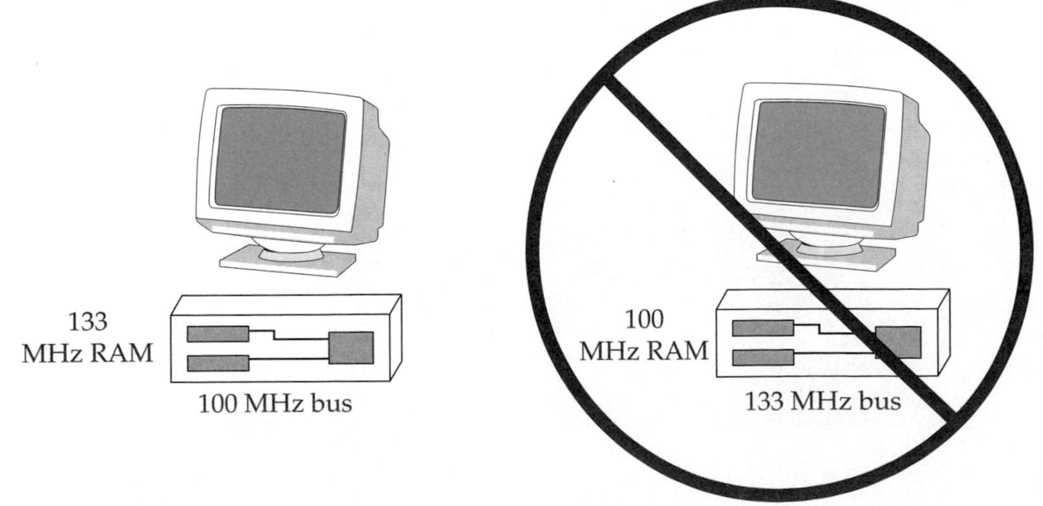

Figure 6-17. RAM must be as fast or faster than the system bus it is installed in.

of corrupted data being transmitted. Corrupt data that is processed through the RAM can result in mathematical computation errors as well as program run errors that can cause a computer system to lock up. There are two common methods for checking the integrity of data transferred in and out of memory: parity and error correction code.

Parity

As you have learned, all data transmitted through a PC system is comprised of ones and zeros together in groups of eight. These groups of eight are known as bytes. ***Parity*** is simply the counting of either odd or even bits of the bytes being transmitted.

parity
the counting of either odd or even bits being transmitted.

To understand the role of parity, we must first look at how memory is constructed. A memory chip consists of millions of tiny cells that store data. Each cell can contain either a zero or one. The ones and zeros represent the state of electrical charge in the cell. Typically, a 5-volt electrical charge represents a one and no electrical charge represents a zero. The cells are grouped together in sets of eight cells (one byte).

When memory chips and data transfer techniques were first developed, they were not as reliable as they are today. Out of the millions of cells designed in the memory module, a few of the individual cells might be flawed. These flawed cells tend to lose their electrical charge. Cells that lose their charge are said to *leak.* If a single cell changes its charge state from 5 volts to 0 volts while it is stored, then the data it represents also changes. For example, the stored binary number 00001010 represents the decimal number *10.* If one cell loses its charge, the binary format of the data could look like 00000010. It now represents the decimal number 2. The data stored as a byte has changed its value from the decimal *10* to the decimal 2. Data stored in a changing byte is not limited to data that represents numbers. The stored byte could represent letters, sound, part of an illustration, or even a program command.

Data can also change while being transferred from one module to another. Remember that data is processed through a PC. It could be loaded from a disk to the memory (RAM) and then moved to the CPU to be manipulated and then routed simultaneously to the screen and to RAM. While the data is being transferred around the PC system, any of the bits that form a complete byte could be changed by outside electrical interference or by a slightly defective part such as a circuit board trace that is starting to fail.

odd parity checking
a data integrity checking method in which every time the number of bits counted is odd, an extra bit of data is transmitted as a one to indicate odd.

To check that data received by RAM and transferred to other parts is still valid, parity was developed. Instead of just the usual eight bits being stored to represent one byte, an additional bit was added to make a total of nine bits. The ninth bit is referred to as the *parity bit.* The parity bit reflects the number of ones and zeros contained in the data byte.

For example, assume the number of ones being transmitted to or from the memory is counted. Every time the number of bits counted is *odd,* a parity bit of one is sent to indicate the number of bits is odd. This is an example of ***odd parity checking.*** The system could also be designed to do ***even parity checking*** by transmitting an extra bit each time there was an even number of bits in the byte of data being transmitted. See **Figure 6-18.** Parity checking is not simply limited to memory; it is also used for transmitting data across telephone and network lines.

even parity checking
a data integrity checking method in which every time the number of bits counted is even, an extra bit of data is transmitted as a one to indicate even.

The only problem with a parity check using this method is it assumes that only one bit will change. If two bits change, the parity will not change and the error will go undetected.

Figure 6-18.
A table showing streams of bytes representing odd and even totals followed by a parity bit. In this example, the parity bit is generated as a one each time the total number of bits that equal one is odd. A zero is generated if it is even.

Data byte bit location	0 1 2 3 4 5 6 7	Parity bit	Result
Data bit value	1 0 0 0 1 0 1 0	1	ODD
Data bit value	1 0 1 0 1 1 1 1	0	EVEN

fake parity
when the parity bit is always set to one regardless of the true number of ones contained in the byte.

Today, memory chips and circuit board designs are very dependable. Relatively few errors are generated by individual memory cells or motherboard parts. Many PCs use memory modules that do not check parity, or they use what is described as fake parity. With ***fake parity,*** the parity bit is set to a constant value, say, for instance, a one. This is done by electronic circuit design. Since the parity bit is always set to one regardless of the true number of ones contained in the byte, parity will always match when data is transferred. In other words, a true parity check is never performed. The fake parity bit always confirms the data as good. Some PC systems *require* parity checking memory modules. On systems that require parity checks to be made, fake parity memory modules can be used.

The term *fake parity* can also refer to the manufacture of memory chips that are advertised as containing parity but in reality are fake. Memory designed with actual parity checking costs more than memory that is not designed with actual parity checking. Using fake parity in place of true parity checking memory brings additional profit.

SIMM modules usually contain eight chips used for stored memory and a ninth chip to check parity. The only way to be certain if a memory module uses fake parity checking or not is to check the part number. All information needed about the chip is usually listed on the company Web site.

Error code correction

error code correction (ECC)
an alternative form of data-integrity checking.

Another form of checking the integrity of data is error code correction. ***Error code correction (ECC)*** not only checks for errors but also corrects most errors. Parity checking simply generates an error code, which is displayed on the screen and then stops the program. Error code correction requires an additional chip designed especially for this type of error checking and correcting. ECC cannot correct all errors, only the usual corrupt single bit. If multiple bits are corrupt, the ECC chip cannot correct the data.

ECC is not often found in desktop PCs. It is usually only found in high-end machines such as servers.

Buffered Chips

buffer
an area to temporarily store data before transferring it to a device.

The term ***buffer,*** in relationship to a PC, can be likened to a temporary waiting or holding area. Data can be temporarily stored for a few microseconds before continuing its journey. Remember that there are several different bus systems on the computer motherboard, and all of them are running at different speeds. In addition, many of the devices attached to the computer have speeds much slower than memory chips. For this reason, fast memory requires buffering when exchanging data with other components in the PC.

Figure 6-19.
Buffering and voltage can be identified by the position of the notch at the bottom of the DIMM. This is how manufacturers ensure the correct type of DIMM is installed on the motherboard when replacing or upgrading memory modules. The variances in the notch locations on DIMMs are slight but sufficient. Forcing an incorrect DIMM into the slot will result in damage to the DIMM or to the slot. Memory modules should be inserted into the slot with minimum effort.

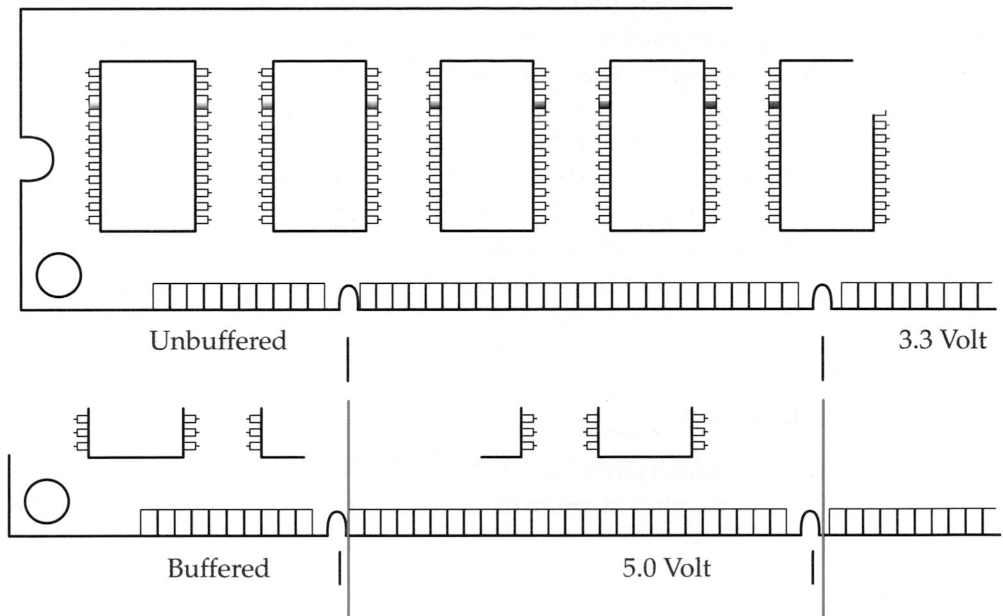

The buffer area can be provided in the motherboard chipset or as an additional chip on the memory module. DIMM memory modules have definitive notch patterns that match the memory module slots on the motherboard. This design prevents improper installation of a buffered DIMM into a motherboard that already contains memory buffer chips. See **Figure 6-19** to view a drawing of notch locations on a DIMM and how they vary.

Registered Memory

registered memory a memory module that incorporates driver and synchronizing electronics as part of the unit.

Registered memory is a memory module that incorporates a registry chip to drive and synchronize itself without depending on the motherboard. Typical motherboards incorporate a chipset with functions to drive and synchronize the memory unit with the motherboard bus system. Registered memory is sometimes referred to as buffered memory because it works in a similar fashion as buffered memory. Some computer systems incorporate a memory register or buffer on the motherboard. The important thing to remember is that registered and nonregistered memory modules cannot be mixed. Registered memory is not typically found on standard PCs. It is found more commonly on high-end PCs and network servers.

Flash Memory Devices

Flash memory
memory type that stores data but does not require a power source to retain the data.

Flash memory is a solid-state, reusable data storage device that can retain data even when the electrical power is disconnected. It is derived from EEPROM technology and takes advantage of the EEPROM's ability to be programmed and reprogrammed. However, unlike the original EEPROM, Flash memory only stores data, not computer programs. Like the EEPROM, Flash memory does not require a power source to retain data. Since it does not require a power source, the size and weight is reduced significantly.

Flash memory devices are often referred to as "Hot Swappable" devices. The term ***hot swap*** means that the device can be plugged into or unplugged from a computer system while the computer is running.

hot swap
a technology that allows a computer device to be plugged into or unplugged from a computer while the computer is running.

Some typical devices that use Flash memory technology are miniature data drives, personal digital assistants (PDAs), global positioning systems (GPS), digital cameras, cellular phones, pagers, electronic instruments, MP3 players, and personal computer systems. A few of the many devices commonly found are presented in the following sections.

USB Flash Drives

A typical Flash drive is constructed from EEPROM chips. Data is "flashed" to the EEPROM chip similar to the way BIOS chips are flashed. There are many different names used for the EEPROM memory devices such as pen drives, jump drives, micro drives, thumb drives, micro vaults, stick drives, and more. In this textbook, the term *USB Flash drive* will be used. USB Flash drives are reusable storage systems that connect to the computer system via a USB port, **Figure 6-20.** The electrical power for energizing the USB Flash drive is also delivered by the USB port. There is no need for an external power supply. After data is transferred to the USB Flash drive, the drive can be removed from the system and will retain the data for a long period of time. The data on the USB Flash drive can be transferred to another computer or to a similar device. The USB Flash drive can have additional data added to it or it can be completely erased similar to most other storage media.

At the time of this writing, USB Flash drives range from a modest 128 MB to 16 GB. A 21 GB USB Flash drive has the same storage capacity as approximately 10,200 floppy drives or 24 standard 650 CD-RW discs or approximately 4-4.7 GB DVDs. This is an incredible amount of data for such a compact device. USB Flash drives will compete with traditional hard disk drives soon and most likely will replace the use of common floppy disks and possibly compact discs. The main advantage of the USB Flash drive is it has no moving parts to wear out or misalign. The entire system is designed from integrated chip technology.

Figure 6-20.
USB Flash drive.

When connected to a computer system through the USB port, the device is recognized as a removable hard drive. Look at **Figure 6-21.** The USB Flash drive is listed beneath **Devices with Removable Storage** and is identified as **drive F:**.

A USB Flash drive is automatically detected and configured when inserted into the computer system's USB port. As a precaution, the USB Flash drive should be deactivated before removing it from the USB port. This is especially true while data is being transferred to or from the USB Flash drive. **Figure 6-22** shows a Windows XP **Safely Remove Hardware** dialog box.

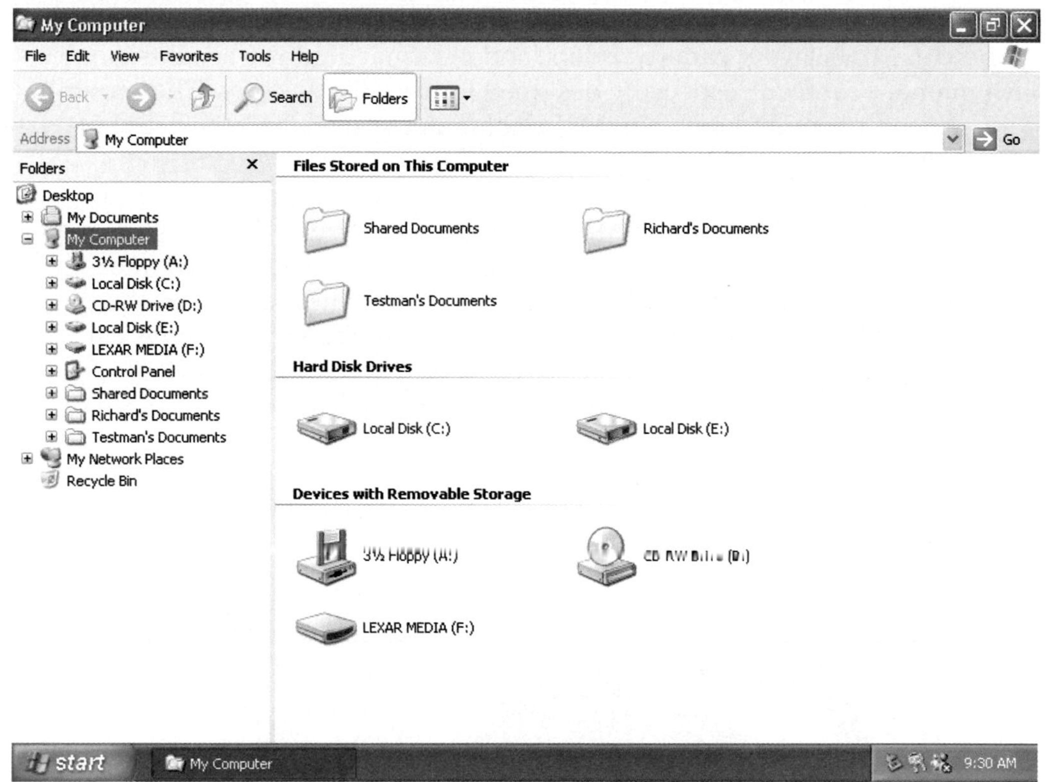

Figure 6-21. Removable storage devices such as the USB Flash drive are automatically detected on boot and are listed in **My Computer** beneath **Devices with Removable Storage**.

Figure 6-22. The USB Flash drive, as with any other removable computer device, should first be stopped with the Safely Remove Hardware program.

The **Safely Remove Hardware** dialog box identifies the USB Flash drive as a **USB Mass Storage Device**. The user simply clicks the **Stop** button and then proceeds to unplug the USB Flash drive from the USB port. Many users simply unplug the USB Flash drive, unaware of the possible damage that could occur to the drive.

Flash Memory Cards

Flash memory cards hold text data, image data, and sound data. Flash memory technology has been incorporated into many digital systems, such as cameras, music players, notebook computers, cell phones, electronic test equipment, MP3 players, cam recorders, and personal digital assistants. Some Flash memory cards are especially designed for security systems. They contain user passwords required to log on to the computer system, and they support data encryption.

Flash memory cards go by many different names such as SmartMedia, CompactFlash, MultiMediaCard, Memory Stick, and Secure Digital. The names vary because of the individual competing companies who developed and marketed the Flash memory cards. Although they are all designed on the same principles of Flash memory technology, they differ in their overall physical design, electrical characteristics, and software system requirements for reading and writing to the media. Because they have different attributes, you have to either match the card type to a particular reader or use one of the readers that support multiple card formats.

One such card reader is the Belkin 8-in-1 Media Reader/Writer, **Figure 6-23,** which reads and writes to eight different types of Flash memory cards. The reader connects to any standard PC through the USB port.

Figure 6-23.
The Belkin 8-in-1 Media Reader/Writer reads a variety of Flash memory card types. (Courtesy of Belkin Corporation)

Memory Map Structure and Development

Memory map structure is a description of the way memory is allocated in the PC. Because of the issue of backward compatibility in the PC industry, the development of the memory structure has become complex and confusing. The desire for the latest computer system to be compatible with ancient 8-bit system technology has created the evolution of a difficult memory structure. There have been many different software attempts to overcome these structural limitations.

The terminology of memory structure dates back to the original PC and the oldest DOS operating system. The early PC could only access 1 MB of memory (1,024,000 bytes). The restrictions of 1 MB of memory are DOS and Windows 3.x restrictions. They do not apply to Windows 95 or later operating systems. Windows 95 and later follow the DOS memory pattern *only* when dealing with legacy cards or 16-bit software programs. Windows NT, Windows 2000, Windows XP, and Windows Vista are not affected at all by DOS memory structure. NT, 2000, XP, and Vista operating systems handle individual memory areas as one big block, referred to as the ***heap.*** The memory is then portioned out as needed. Let's look at how the memory system structure was designed and labeled.

heap
how Windows refers to the entire memory.

Conventional Memory

The memory structure is illustrated in **Figure 6-24.** This illustration shows the layout of conventional, upper, high, and extended memory.

The original PC was limited to 1 MB (1024 kB) of random access memory. This first memory was originally divided in half (512 kB each). After the original PC was on the market for a short time, the memory system was redesigned into parts that were no longer equal. The bottom part was given 640 kB and was called ***conventional memory.*** The top part was given 384 kB and was called ***upper memory*** or ***reserved memory.*** This division of the first 1 MB of memory into two unequal parts, conventional (640 kB) and reserved (384 kB), became the industry standard.

conventional memory
the first 640 kB of a PC's RAM.

upper memory
term for a PC's memory range between 640 kB and 1 MB.

reserved memory
another term for upper memory.

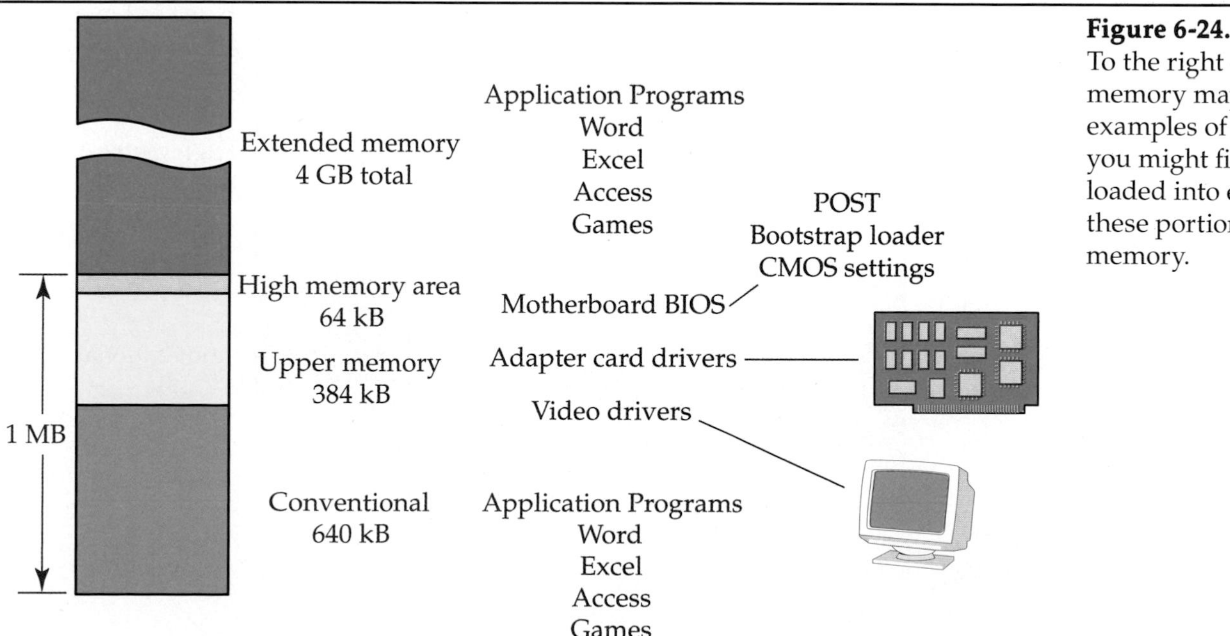

Figure 6-24.
To the right of the memory map are examples of what you might find loaded into each of these portions of memory.

Conventional memory is where application programs are loaded. The reserve memory was reserved for use by the video system, expansion cards, and the BIOS. The reserve memory is dedicated (or reserved) for hardware drivers and cannot be used by application programs. For many years, conventional memory (640 kB) was referred to as the *memory barrier*. Early computer programmers were required to write programs that could fit into the 640 kB space of conventional memory.

The term *conventional memory* is still in use. However, the 32-bit operating systems of newer models easily work around the 640 kB barrier. Programs, as well as drivers, can be loaded into memory well beyond the first 1 MB.

Read through **Figure 6-25.** This illustration diagrams the relation of the various areas in RAM and how they developed.

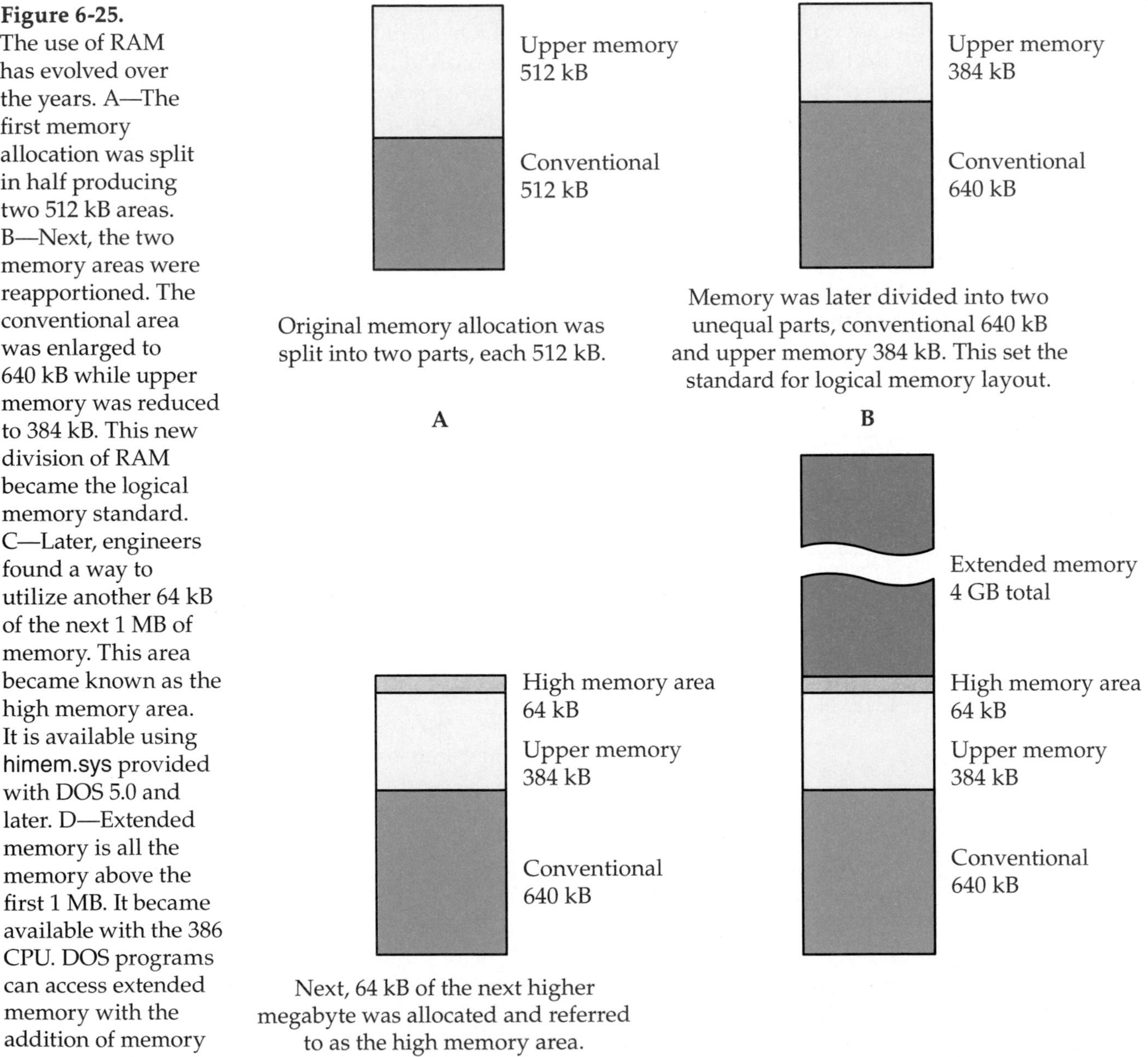
Upper memory
512 kB
Conventional
512 kB
Original memory allocation was split into two parts, each 512 kB.
A
Upper memory
384 kB
Conventional
640 kB
Memory was later divided into two unequal parts, conventional 640 kB and upper memory 384 kB. This set the standard for logical memory layout.
B
High memory area
64 kB
Upper memory
384 kB
Conventional
640 kB
Next, 64 kB of the next higher megabyte was allocated and referred to as the high memory area.
C
Extended memory
4 GB total
High memory area
64 kB
Upper memory
384 kB
Conventional
640 kB
D

Figure 6-25. The use of RAM has evolved over the years. A—The first memory allocation was split in half producing two 512 kB areas. B—Next, the two memory areas were reapportioned. The conventional area was enlarged to 640 kB while upper memory was reduced to 384 kB. This new division of RAM became the logical memory standard. C—Later, engineers found a way to utilize another 64 kB of the next 1 MB of memory. This area became known as the high memory area. It is available using himem.sys provided with DOS 5.0 and later. D—Extended memory is all the memory above the first 1 MB. It became available with the 386 CPU. DOS programs can access extended memory with the addition of memory management programs.

Upper Memory Area (Reserved Memory)

The upper memory area (UMA), or reserved memory, is the 384 kB of memory remaining after the first 640 kB of conventional memory. The term *reserved* means that only the PC system software drivers used to run and interface with the system hardware components can be loaded into this area. The reserved memory cannot be used for application software such as word processor programs, gaming, or other software.

The upper memory is divided into sections that are determined by their function. The first part of the UMA (128 kB) is used for the video system. The information about the computer monitor is stored in this area. The next part of the UMA (128 kB) is used for adapter boards mounted in slots on the motherboard. Examples of these adapter boards are boards for the modem or network cards. VGA adapter cards sometimes utilize the first 32 kB of this area of memory. The last part of the UMA (128 kB) is used for the motherboard BIOS, CMOS settings, POST program, and bootstrap program.

Many types of device drivers are also loaded into the UMA. A section of UMA can also be occupied by a memory manager program, which permits certain programs to use memory beyond the 1 MB barrier. Again, modern operating systems have no problem accessing RAM beyond the first 1 MB. This was a restriction of earlier operating systems.

High Memory Area

It is easy to confuse a high memory area with upper memory. The ***high memory area (HMA)*** is the first 64 kB of the extended memory area. (Actually it is 16 bytes short of a full 64 kB.)

high memory area (HMA)
the first 64 kB of the extended memory area.

This area was first discovered as a design flaw in the memory access data lines, but it soon became the standard method to gain more conventional memory space. Conventional memory not only holds application programs but also basic DOS files, such as the kernel, needed to operate the PC. The DOS kernel file is approximately 45 kB in size. Transferring a DOS kernel to the high memory area releases 45 kB of conventional memory space for use by application programs. To use the HMA, the line **DOS=HIGH** is added to the config.sys file.

In DOS 5.0 and later versions, the **DOS=HIGH** command loads the DOS program kernel into the high memory area. The high memory area can also be used to store a software driver instead of the DOS kernel, but note that only one program can be stored in the high memory area.

Expanded Memory

Expanded memory was an early method to move past the 1 MB memory barrier. ***Expanded memory standard (EMS)*** was designed to increase the amount of memory available for applications. An expanded memory adapter board loaded with memory chips was inserted into a motherboard expansion slot. Unlike RAM, the expanded memory adapter board is not accessed directly by the CPU, but rather by a software-driver program, which is loaded into reserved memory. The software-driver program transfers data to and from the memory adapter board to the 64 kB EMS window established in upper memory. See **Figure 6-26** for a memory map illustrating the 64 kB EMS window and expanded memory available on the expanded memory adapter board.

expanded memory standard (EMS)
an early method to move past the 1 MB memory barrier.

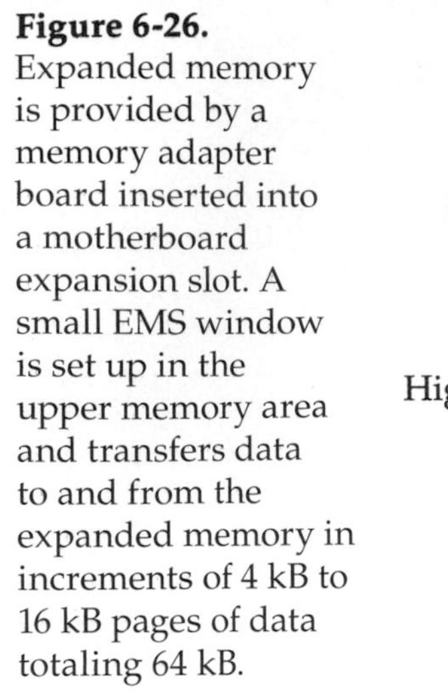

Figure 6-26.
Expanded memory is provided by a memory adapter board inserted into a motherboard expansion slot. A small EMS window is set up in the upper memory area and transfers data to and from the expanded memory in increments of 4 kB to 16 kB pages of data totaling 64 kB.

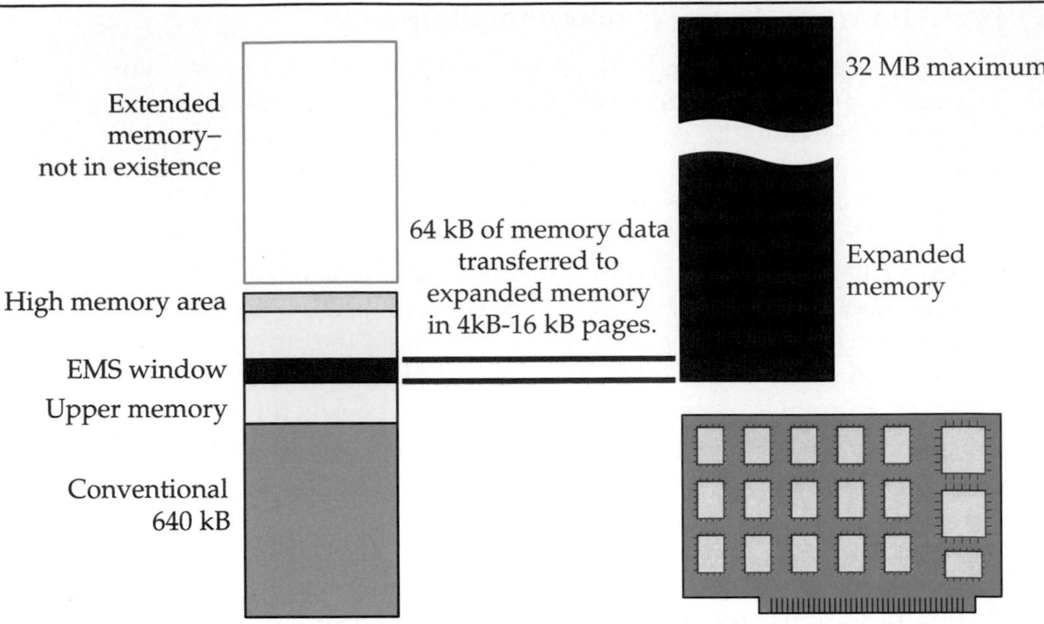

The memory adapter board could contain a maximum data content of 32 MB. Data was transferred through the EMS window in 16 kB segments, or pages, to and from the memory on the adapter board.

EMS is obsolete, and the memory boards are no longer manufactured. The transfer rate of data with EMS is extremely slow because it is limited to the speed of the motherboard bus slot. EMS was designed for the ISA bus slot, which is very slow when compared to the data transfer rates of SIMM or DIMM. SIMM and DIMM connect via the system bus, directly to the CPU. The concept of EMS was readily accepted when memory space was needed and the 1 MB barrier was a problem.

Extended Memory

extended memory system (XMS) all of the PC's memory beyond the first 1 MB when the CPU is running in real mode.

The ***extended memory system (XMS)*** includes all of the PC's memory beyond the first 1 MB when the CPU is running in real mode. As operating systems evolved over time, the CPU was designed to access more memory than the early predecessors. Today, a 32-bit operating system can access 4 GB of RAM. A 64-bit operating system can access theoretically 16 TB (terabytes) of RAM. The 64-bit upper memory access limit is not realistic at this time. No computer system hardware is designed to allow for 16 TB of memory. A more realistic maximum RAM value of 8 GB to 128 GB can be expected for desktops.

Real Mode, Protected Mode, and Safe Mode

Real mode is designed on the DOS system of memory access. When operating in real mode, only the first 1 MB of RAM can be accessed. *Protected mode* includes all of real mode plus extended memory. Multitasking can only occur in protected mode.

Safe mode is accessed by pressing the [F8] key during the startup or boot operation for all versions of Windows operating system. Computers systems boot very fast now and it is almost impossible to press the [F8] key at the exact time between the finish of the POST and the loading of the operating system. The best way to enter safe mode is to repeatedly press [F8] during the boot operation, starting during the post and continuing until the menu options or Advanced Boot Options menu (in Windows Vista) appears.

safe mode
mode that boots the computer with minimum required drivers and programs to allow for troubleshooting.

Starting Windows in safe mode is a very common troubleshooting technique. Safe mode will only load minimal drivers and limit the memory access to the first 1 MB of RAM, thus eliminating any problems caused by 32-bit drivers and software applications. If the computer starts in safe mode, then it is a good indication that the problem is software related rather than a hardware problem. Many troubleshooting features are available while in safe mode. This feature will be covered in-depth in the Chapter 15—PC Troubleshooting.

Windows 98, Windows Me, and Windows XP allow you to directly access safe mode by pressing the [Ctrl] key during the boot operation. This feature is not available in Windows Vista.

Virtual Memory

Virtual memory is memory that supplements physical memory known as RAM. Virtual memory is located on the hard disk drive and is referred to as a ***page file*** or *swap file*. The virtual memory is divided into units called *pages*. RAM is used to hold data content as well as the software application. If data or sections of an application program are not accessed for a period of time, then the data or application section is transferred to virtual memory as a page of information. The transfer to the page file is called *paging* or *swapping*. When needed, the data is transferred back to RAM from the hard disk drive page file.

virtual memory
a section of the hard disk drive reserved to supplement RAM.

page file
a file that is located on a special section of the hard disk drive used to supplement RAM.

Figure 6-27 shows the virtual memory configuration page in Windows Vista. It is accessed through **Control Panel | System | Advanced System Properties**. The **Advanced** tab of the **System Properties** dialog box will display. Click **Settings** under the Performance section. A similar configuration feature is available in all Windows operating systems.

One sign that the computer is running out of RAM and using the page file is when there is a lot of hard disk drive activity. The use of virtual memory causes an overall drop in software performance. You need to install more RAM if virtual memory is being used.

A new feature in Windows Vista used for virtual memory is ReadyBoost. ReadyBoost allows removable storage devices, such as USB Flash drives, to supplement the memory installed on the computer system.

ReadyBoost will not work with all types of USB Flash drives. You should only use USB 2.0 or later. However, the device may still fail to work properly. When the removable storage device is attached to the PC, the operating system will automatically detect it and display a menu option for ReadyBoost like that shown in **Figure 6-28.** The option **Speed up my system using Windows ReadyBoost** is located at the bottom dialog box.

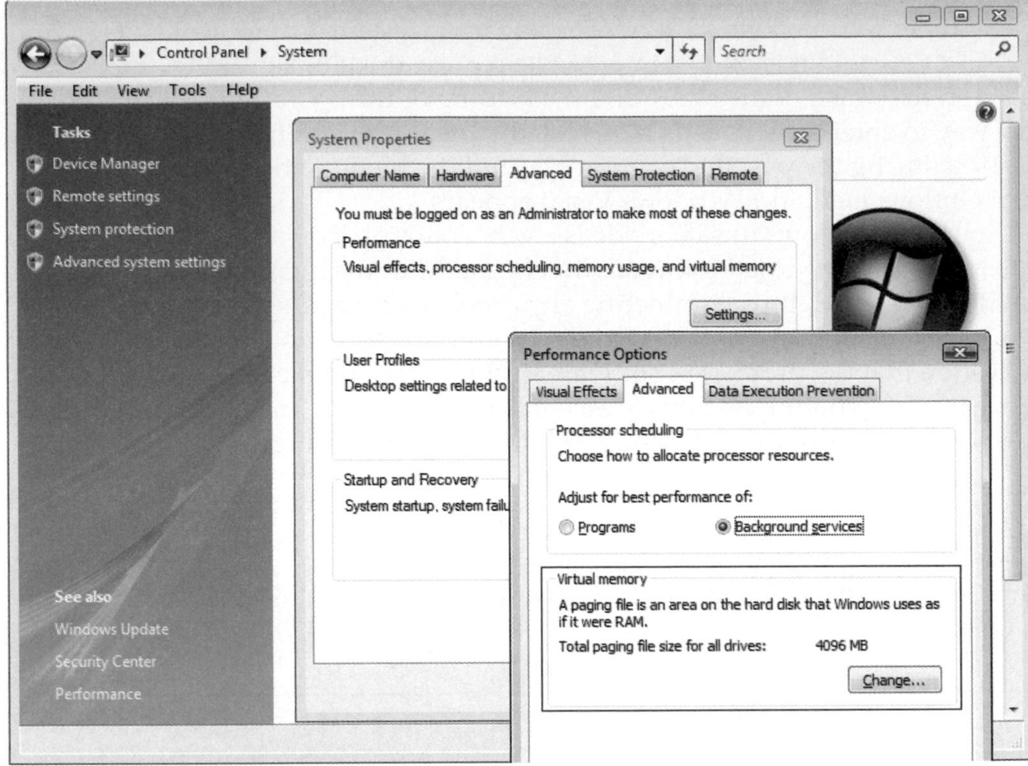

Figure 6-27. Virtual memory setting can be configured in Windows Vista in the **Performance Option** dialog box under the **Advanced** tab.

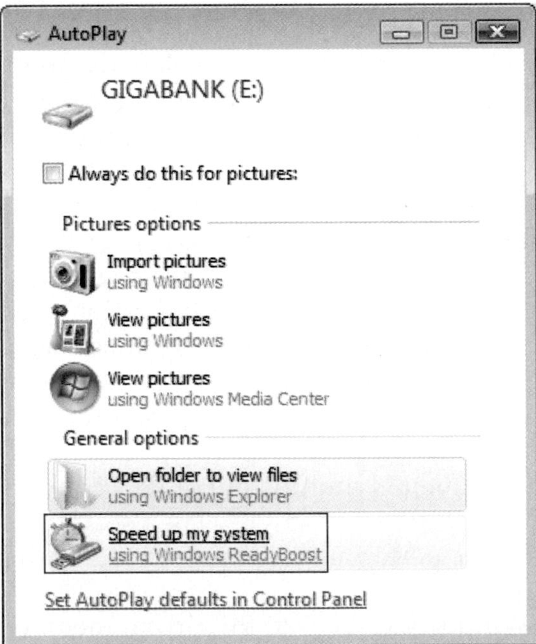

Figure 6-28. The **Speed up my system using Windows ReadyBoost** option appears in the **AutoPlay** dialog box when a removable storage device is attached to the PC.

If the removable drive is compatible with the ReadyBoost feature, a dialog box like that in **Figure 6-29** will appear after choosing the **Speed up my system using Windows ReadyBoost** option. You can select to use or not use the removable device. The device in the example is limited to only 350 MB, so it would not provide sufficient space to supplement the 2 GB of RAM already installed on the PC. You could delete files from the removable device to free up space, which would allow more space to be usable by ReadyBoost.

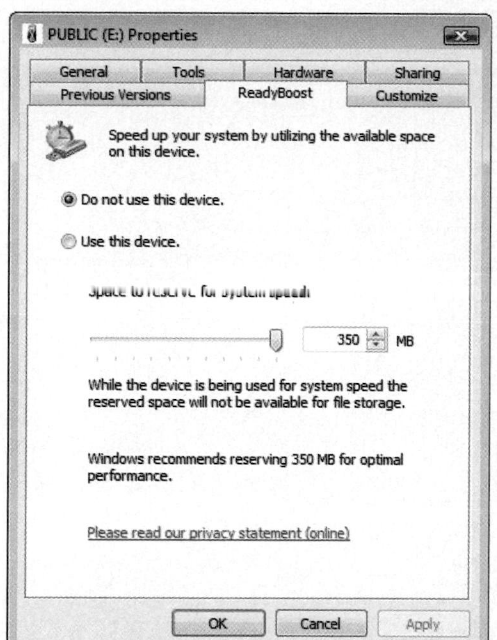

Figure 6-29.
In the **ReadyBoost** dialog box, you can select to use or not use the removable device.

Microsoft recommends the space on the removable drive be one to three times the amount of installed physical RAM. For example, if the system has 512 MB of RAM, the recommended maximum amount of USB Flash memory is 1.5 GB. ReadyBoost will perform faster than the page file system that uses space on the hard disk drive. The USB Flash drive has a faster read and write rate than the hard disk drive.

Windows Memory Diagnostics Tool

A new memory diagnostic utility introduced in Windows Vista is the Windows Memory Diagnostics Tool. You start the tool from the command prompt. You must be the system administrator or equal to run this tool. Enter **mdsched** in the **Search** box on the **Start** menu or at the command prompt. You will be prompted to have Windows automatically restart the computer to begin the memory diagnostics or to start the diagnostics the next time the computer reboots. When the Memory Diagnostics Tool does run, it will look similar to that in **Figure 6-30.**

For a quick check to see how much memory is installed in a Windows XP PC, right-click **My Computer** and then select **Properties** from the shortcut menu. You will see a dialog box similar to that in **Figure 6-31.** This is similar to the **System Properties** dialog box available in Windows Vista. You access the Windows Vista **System Properties** dialog box the same way.

You might use the command prompt to display what appears as the total amount of memory for the computer system, but the result would be inaccurate. **Figure 6-32** shows a screen capture of Windows Vista after the **mem** command has been issued at the command prompt. Look at the amount of conventional memory, largest executive program size, total contiguous extended memory, and total extended memory available. Notice that only 1 MB of memory is indicated.

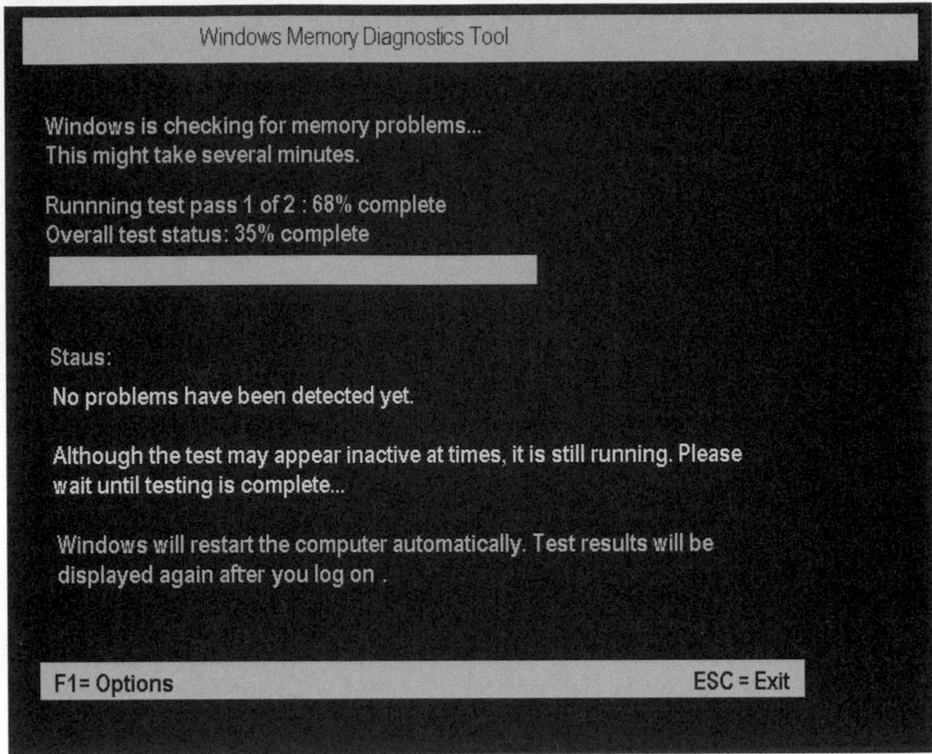

Figure 6-30. Windows Memory Diagnostics Tool.

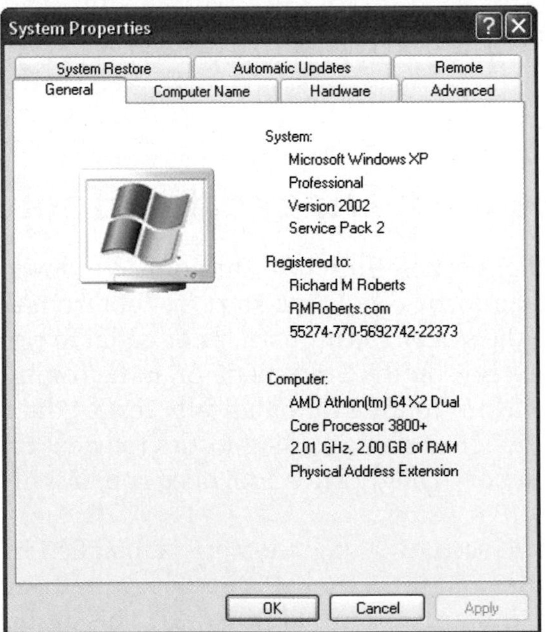

Figure 6-31. You can quickly check how much memory is installed in a PC through System Properties.

This is incorrect for this particular computer. The **mem** command is a DOS-based memory command and cannot detect memory above 1 MB. The command failed to identify the total amount of physical memory installed in this computer. The total physical memory for this system is 2 GB. Using the **mem** command is not recommended for determining the amount of memory installed.

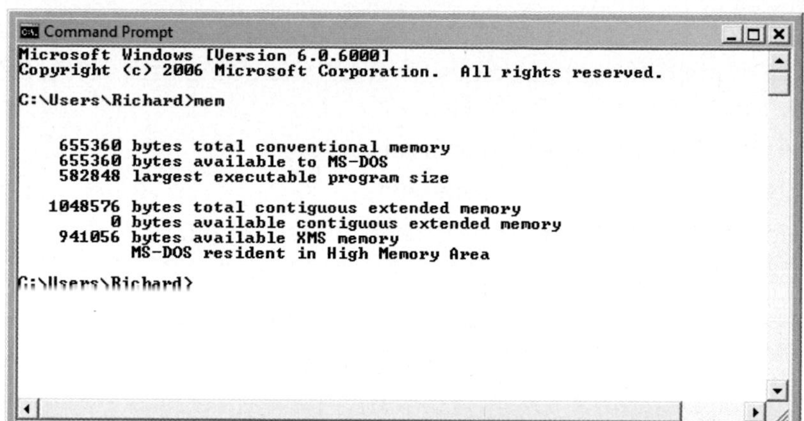
Microsoft Windows [Version 6.0.6000]
Copyright (c) 2006 Microsoft Corporation. All rights reserved.

C:\Users\Richard>mem

655360 bytes total conventional memory
655360 bytes available to MS-DOS
582848 largest executable program size

1048576 bytes total contiguous extended memory
0 bytes available contiguous extended memory
941056 bytes available XMS memory
MS-DOS resident in High Memory Area

C:\Users\Richard>

Figure 6-32. The **mem** command only gives memory information for the first 1 MB of memory.

Microsoft has made Windows Memory Diagnostics Tool available for download. It is located at http://oca.microsoft.com/en/windiag.asp#top and can be used with a bootable CD or floppy disk.

Gold Vs. Tin Edge Connectors

There are two types of edge connector finishes used on memory modules, gold and tin. The memory module (SIMM or DIMM) edge connector should match the connector finish inside the expansion slot. When two different types of metal are in contact with each other, a condition occurs that causes increased oxidation. When first installed, the memory will not show any signs of a problem. It should work perfectly. But as time goes by, oxidation develops. The PC starts to generate error codes, such as parity errors, more frequently. The amount of use and the conditions of the environment determines how long the oxidation process will take. Once it reaches a point that the electrical connection between the memory edge connector and the slot connector has totally degenerated, errors will constantly occur.

Some oxidation can be removed by simply removing and reinserting the memory module. This action alone may correct the error. However, the condition can also be so bad as to render the motherboard slot useless. Always match the type of metals used.

Memory and Heat

Heat will destroy a chip or cause temporary chaos in a computer. A common symptom of excessive heat causing memory problems is when a PC works fine for a short period of time (20 minutes) and then locks up. At the time the PC locks up, a sufficient level of heat has been generated to cause a circuit problem inside one of the memory chips. This causes the PC to fail. Fans should be checked, filters cleaned, and dirt and dust removed to prevent heat buildup.

Summary

- ✔ There are many different packages for RAM including SIPs, DIPs, SIMMs, and DIMMs.
- ✔ ROM retains data after the power is removed.
- ✔ RAM loses data after power is removed.
- ✔ Dynamic RAM (DRAM) must be constantly refreshed.
- ✔ Static RAM (SRAM) does not need to be refreshed.
- ✔ Flash memory is derived from EEPROM technology and takes advantage of the EEPROM's ability to be programmed and reprogrammed and to retain data without depending on a power source.
- ✔ DDR1 has 184 pins and DDR2 and DDR3 have 240 pins.
- ✔ SPD represents serial presence detect and is used to identify the RAM installed on the computer.
- ✔ Registered memory modules can only be used on systems designed for registered memory.
- ✔ Hot swap technology allows a computer device to be plugged into or removed from a digital system without requiring the system power to be turned off.
- ✔ Windows can utilize RAM as one large block of memory if there are no legacy programs or hardware in the system.
- ✔ The four logical areas of RAM are conventional, upper, high memory, and extended memory.
- ✔ Conventional memory is the first 640 kB of RAM.
- ✔ Upper memory is the next 384 kB after conventional memory.
- ✔ High memory area is 64 kB after upper memory or the first 64 kB (minus 16 bytes) of the second megabyte of RAM.
- ✔ Extended memory is all the memory above the first 1 MB of RAM and is used by Windows in protected mode.
- ✔ The maximum amount of RAM accessible when using a 32-bit operating system is 4 GB.
- ✔ The maximum amount of RAM accessible when using a 64-bit operating system is 16 TB.
- ✔ Real mode means addressing only the first 1 MB of memory.
- ✔ Protected mode is an operating mode that supports multitasking and allows access to the extended memory area.
- ✔ Safe mode is accessed by pressing [F8] during the boot operation.
- ✔ Virtual memory is located on the hard disk drive and is used to supplement the available RAM.
- ✔ Virtual memory is accessed in sections referred to as pages.
- ✔ The **System Properties** dialog box displays the amount of RAM installed in a Windows computer.
- ✔ The Windows Vista ReadyBoost feature allows a USB Flash drive to supplement the amount of RAM installed in a computer.
- ✔ ReadyBoost should be configured at one to three times the amount of existing physical RAM.

✔ The Memory Diagnostics Tool (mdsched.exe) is new in Windows Vista and can be run from the command prompt to perform a memory diagnostic routine.

✔ You should not use the **mem** command to determine the amount of memory installed in a computer.

Review Questions

Answer the following questions on a separate sheet of paper. Please do not write in this book.

1. Compare an ink pen and a pencil with an eraser to RAM and ROM memory.
2. What is the difference between SO-DIMM and MicroDIMM?
3. What is the maximum data rate for a PC3200 memory module used in a motherboard with a FSB of 200 Mbps?
4. What is the PC2 classification of a DDR2-800 memory module?
5. What is the bandwidth of a PC2-6400 memory module?
6. What will happen to latency when you double a memory module frequency?
7. Why can you not replace a DDR2-800 with a DDR3-1600 memory module to achieve better overall PC performance?
8. Briefly describe dual-channel DDR memory technology.
9. What is the purpose of memory SPD?
10. RAM chip speed is measured in _____.
11. How much memory can DOS access?
12. What is the difference between expanded and extended memory?
13. What is the maximum amount of RAM that the original PC's processor could access?
14. What are the four logical areas of RAM?
15. Draw the logical memory layout of RAM for DOS and label each part and indicate the size in kB.
16. What is another name used for upper memory?
17. Application programs run from _____ memory.
18. Video drivers are loaded into the _____ memory area of RAM.
19. System BIOS is transferred into the _____ memory area of RAM.
20. System video BIOS is usually stored in the _____ area of RAM.
21. What is the maximum amount of memory accessible by a 32-bit operating system?
22. What is the maximum theoretical limit for RAM access when using a 64-bit operating system?
23. What is virtual memory?

Sample A+ Exam Questions

Answer the following questions on a separate sheet of paper. Please do not write in this book.

1. During the system boot, the following error message is displayed onscreen: "Parity check failure!" What particular system component would the message be referring to?
   a. RAM
   b. ROM
   c. HDD
   d. USB
2. In the Windows XP operating system, how would you display the amount of RAM installed on a PC?
   a. Select the **Start** menu, right-click **My Computer**, and select **Properties** from the shortcut menu.
   b. Select the **Start** menu, right-click **My Computer**, and then select **System Status** from the short cut menu.
   c. Open **Control Panel** and double-click the **RAM** icon.
   d. Open **Control Panel** and double-click the **System Memory** icon.
3. Which command will evoke a memory diagnostic routine for Windows Vista?
   a. **mdsched**
   b. **sysconfig**
   c. **msinfo32**
   d. **memprob**
4. Which processor mode will only allow access to the first 1 MB of memory?
   a. Real mode
   b. Protected mode
   c. Limited mode
   d. Extended mode
5. Which type of memory must constantly be refreshed to retain the stored data?
   a. SRAM
   b. PROM
   c. DRAM
   d. CRIMM
6. A memory location at 2 MB would be considered part of which memory area?
   a. Upper memory
   b. Conventional memory
   c. Expanded memory
   d. Extended memory
7. How can you access safe mode when using Windows XP operating system?
   a. Hold down [F1] during the POST.
   b. Press [F8] immediately after the POST.
   c. Press [Ctrl] [Alt] [Delete] at the same time.
   d. You cannot access Safe mode when using a Windows XP operating system.
8. A memory chip's speed is measured in which standard unit?
   a. Megahertz
   b. Gigahertz
   c. Nanoseconds
   d. Cycles per second

9. Which memory module is designed with DDR2 memory chips?
   a. PC2100
   b. PC2700
   c. PC2-6400
   d. PC3-12800
10. Which items listed below should be practiced to ensure correct installation of additional memory? Select all that apply.
   a. Use an ESD wrist strap.
   b. Put the PC into real mode to prevent accessing the upper memory area until after the installation is complete.
   c. Turn off all electrical power to the system.
   d. Disconnect all peripheral components until after complete memory installation has been verified by system setup.

Suggested Laboratory Activities

Do not attempt any suggested laboratory activities without your instructor's permission. Certain activities can render the PC operating system inoperable.

1. Run **msinfo32** and reveal the properties of the memory.
2. Remove the RAM chips from a lab PC and observe the boot operation. Observe all proper ESD precautions. Does the system boot? If it does, what part of the system startup sequence does not rely on RAM? Also, observe any error messages that are displayed.
3. Add additional memory to a lab PC.
4. Identify any markings on the lab PC (such as the manufacturer, serial number, and model number) and then try to obtain a definitive identification from the Internet Web sites.
5. Go to www.kingston.com and download their memory manual. It contains pages of information about system memory.
6. Visit the Intel Web site and look up the specifications of several Intel motherboards. Find out what is the maximum RAM support by the motherboard. Be sure to include servers for motherboards as well as desktop models.
7. Run the **mem** command from the command prompt and view the information concerning conventional, XMS, extended, and HMA memory.
8. Start the computer and use the [F8] key to access the startup menu. View the options available, such as safe mode.

Interesting Web Sites for More Information

http://oca.microsoft.com/en/windiag.asp#top

www.fujitsu.com

www.hitachi.com

www.intel.com

www.kingston.com

www.kingston.com/products/pdf_files/FlashMemGuide.pdf

www.kingston.com/ukroot/press/primages/flash.asp

www.memorysuppliers.com/memoryguide.html

www.micron.com

www.mitsubishielectric.com

www.mosys.com

www.nec.com

www.oki.com

www.samsung.com

www.toshiba.com

Chapter 6
Laboratory Activity
Viewing RAM and Virtual Memory Information

After completing this laboratory activity, you will be able to:

- ✔ Identify the amount of RAM installed in the PC.
- ✔ Identify the amount of virtual memory.
- ✔ Access the Resource Monitor utility.

There are several different ways to identify the amount of memory installed in a typical PC. The amount of memory is revealed to the user during the power-on-self-test (POST). The RAM is tested and the results are displayed on the screen during the POST. On many computers, the POST is hidden from view because a splash screen is displayed during the POST. To see the POST, you may need to access the BIOS Setup program and select the BIOS option that will allow the POST to be viewed.

In Windows XP, you can view the amount of RAM installed by accessing **Control Panel | System**. The **System Properties** dialog box will display and reveal the amount of physical RAM installed as well as the type of processor.

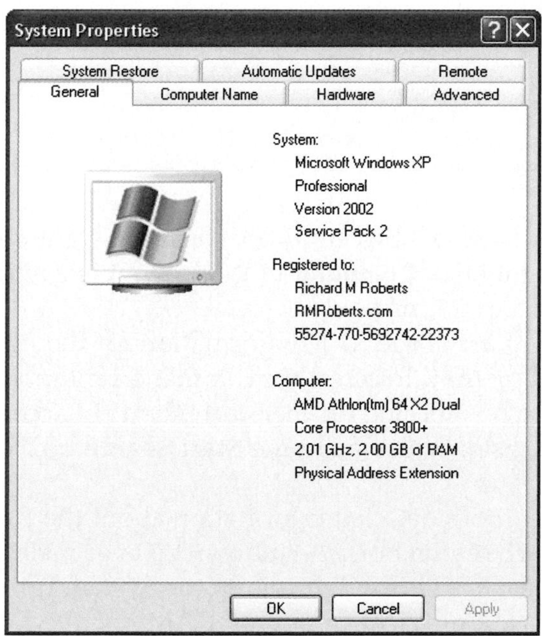

In Windows Vista, you can view the amount of RAM installed by accessing **Control Panel | System**. The Windows Vista **System Properties** dialog box reveals similar information as Windows XP.

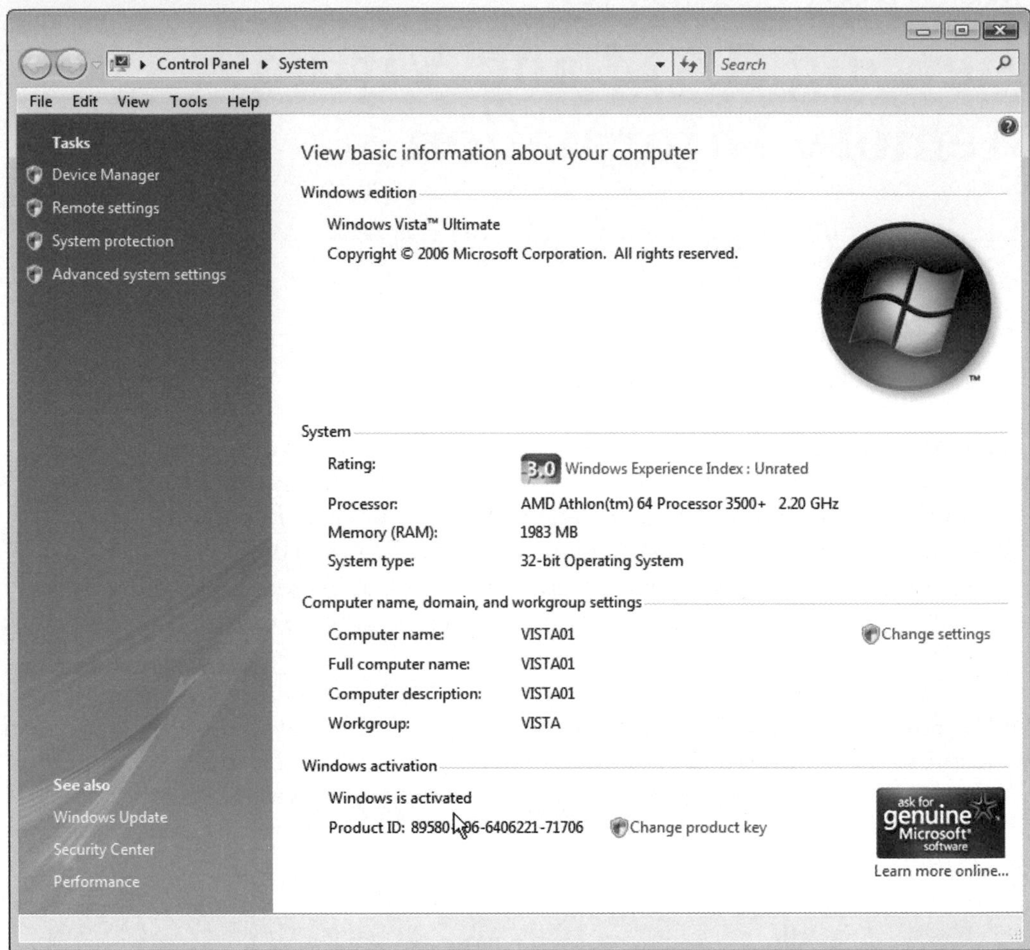

The quickest way to access System Properties is to right-click on **My Computer** in Windows XP or right-click **Computer** in Windows Vista and then select **Properties** from the shortcut menu.

You can also view part of the RAM information for the first 1 MB by entering **mem** at the command prompt. To access the command prompt in Windows XP, type **cmd** in the **Run** dialog box located off the **Start** menu. To access the command prompt in Windows Vista, type **cmd** in the **Start Search** box located off the **Start** menu.

You can also view more detailed information about the RAM by typing **msinfo32** into the **Start Search** box in Windows Vista or **msinfo32** in the **Run** dialog box in Windows XP. This will bring up the System Information program. This program reveals the physical amount of RAM installed in the system, the total amount of virtual memory, the amount of virtual memory available, and the size of the page file.

Virtual memory is actually a portion of the hard disk drive that is assigned to function as RAM when the entire available RAM has been committed to software programs. Some programs are memory intense, which means they require a lot of memory to perform. Some examples of memory-intense software programs are programs designed to edit pictures, images, music, and videos. These types of data collections require large blocks of memory.

Virtual memory can fill these requirements when all available RAM has been used. Virtual RAM is not as fast as physical RAM, but it will allow you to run software programs that would not be available to you if the entire RAM was used. Check the Help and Support files located on the Windows operating system to learn more about virtual memory.

If you are using Windows Vista for this lab activity, you will also access the Resource Monitor to view information about system memory.

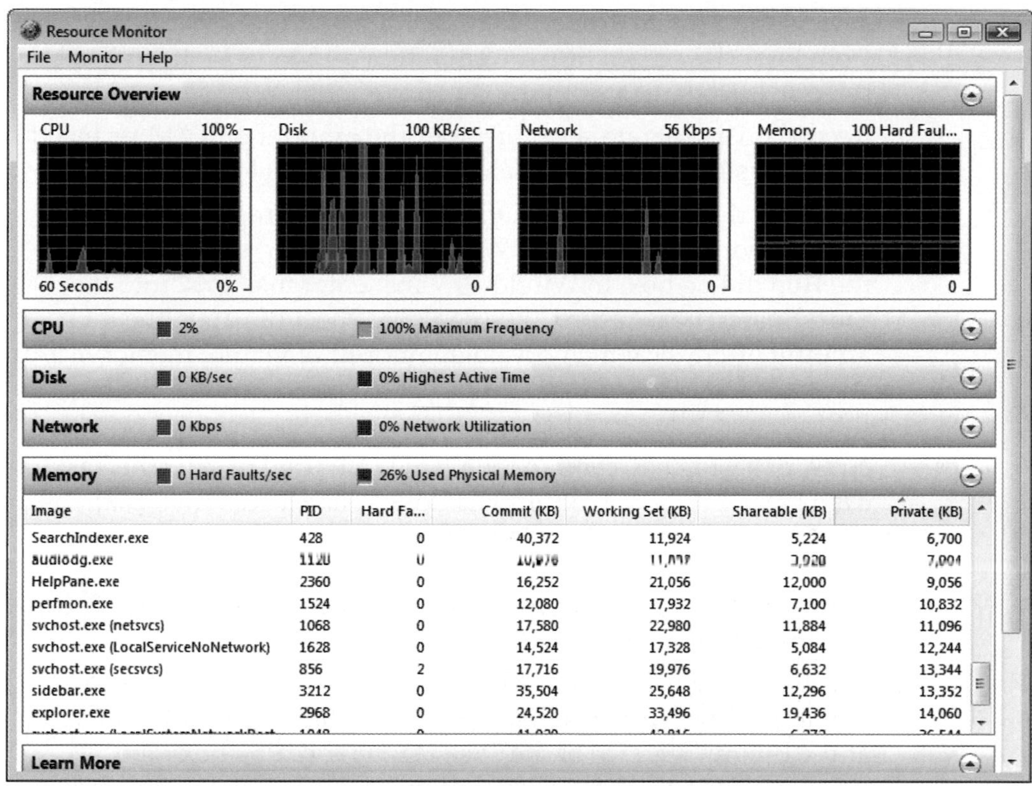

Resource Monitor contains very detailed and extensive information concerning the system memory, CPU, disk drives, and network system. There will be more about the Resource Monitor program in later lab activities.

Equipment and Materials

✔ Typical PC with 500 MB RAM and Windows XP or Windows Vista.

Procedure

1. _______ Report to your assigned workstation.
2. _______ Boot the PC and watch the display closely for the RAM information displayed during the POST. If a splash screen is used to hide the POST results, you may change the BIOS configuration if you have your instructor's permission to do so. Once the BIOS is changed to reveal the POST results, start the computer once more and observe the RAM information.
3. _______ Access the **System Properties** dialog box by right-clicking **My Computer** (Windows XP) or **Computer** (Windows Vista) and then selecting **Properties** from the shortcut menu.
4. _______ Record on a separate sheet of paper the amount of RAM revealed by the **System Properties** dialog box and then close the dialog box.
5. _______ Now use the System Information (**msinfo32**) program to view information about RAM. In Windows XP, enter **msinfo32** into the **Run** dialog box. In Windows Vista, enter **msinfo32** into the **Start Search** box. Record, on a separate sheet of paper, the total amount of physical memory, total amount of virtual memory, available virtual memory, and page file space. After recording the information, close the dialog box.
6. _______ Now, press the key combination [Ctrl] [Alt] [Del] to start the Task Manager in Windows XP. In Windows Vista, press [Ctrl] [Alt] [Del] and then select **Start Task Manager**. After Task Manager appears, select the **Performance** tab to see information about the performance of the computer. On a separate sheet of paper, record the amount of memory available.
7. _______ If you are using Windows XP for this lab activity, skip this step. If you are using Windows Vista, select the **Resource Button** located at the bottom left side of the **Task Manager** dialog box. The System Resource Monitor dialog box will display. This dialog box provides detailed information about the system memory.
8. _______ Close all programs and return the PC to its original condition. Then, answer the review questions. You may leave the PC running so that you can access the Windows Help and Support files to assist you with answering some of the review questions.

Review Questions

Answer the following questions on a separate sheet of paper. Please do not write in this book.

1. Where is virtual memory located?
2. What is the purpose of virtual memory?
3. Approximately how much memory is revealed when you run **mem** at the command prompt?
4. Explain how to use the **msinfo32** command to view system information in Windows XP and in Windows Vista.
5. How do you access Task Manager in Windows XP and Windows Vista?

Input Devices

After studying this chapter, you will be able to:

- ✔ Explain how a keyboard scan code is generated.
- ✔ Modify input device properties of a keyboard or mouse using Control Panel.
- ✔ Explain how devices such as the keyboard, mouse, joystick, scanner, and digital camera operate.
- ✔ Explain how to access input device information using Device Manager.

A+ Exam—Key Points

Basic input devices are always a source of questions on the A+ Certification exams. Be sure to be familiar with wireless input device technologies, OCR, Wi-Fi, and scanner operation.

Key Words and Terms

The following words and terms will become important pieces of your computer vocabulary. Be sure you can define them.

bar code reader
Bluetooth standard
carpal tunnel syndrome
digital camera
digitizer pad
input devices
light pens
mouse
optical character recognition (OCR)
scan code
scanner
synchronous
touch screen displays
track ball
Ultra-Wideband (UWB)
universal peripheral interface (UPI)
Wi-Fi
Wireless USB (WUSB)

input devices equipment that provides the computer with data.

Input devices include a wide variety of items that are used to communicate with the PC system. The standard keyboard is a common serial input device. It changes keystrokes into computer data. See **Figure 7-1.**

The keyboard is one of the most common and useful input devices, but there is a broad spectrum of input devices for computers. Some devices, such as the mouse, find widespread use in a variety of different computer applications. Other input devices, like bar code scanners, have more specific uses.

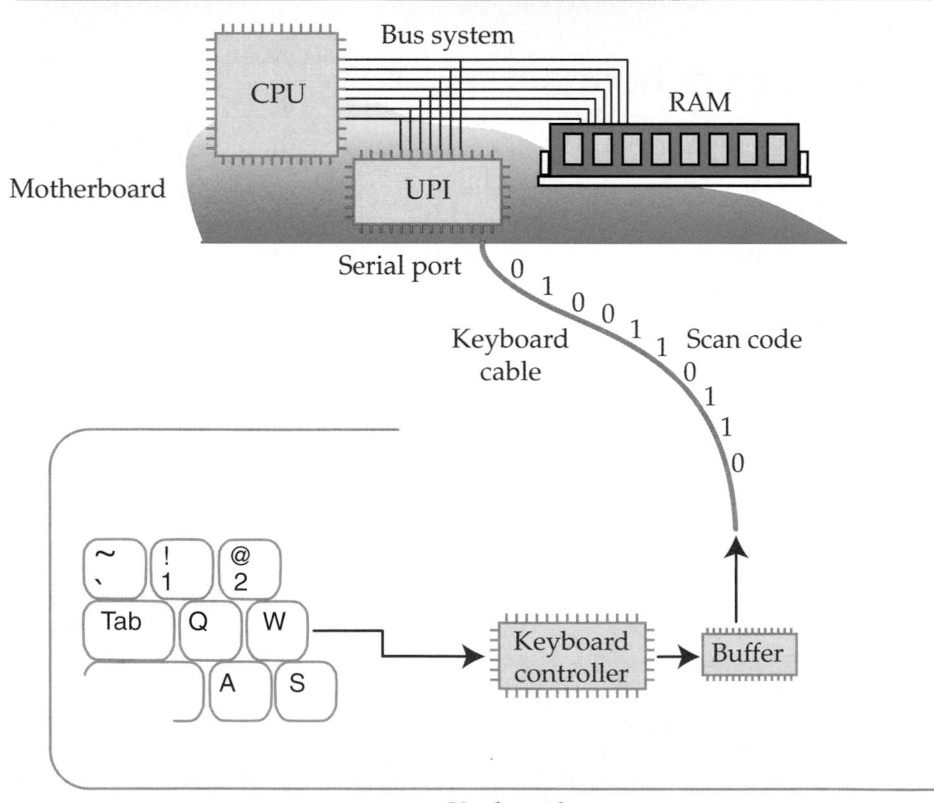

Figure 7-1. A typical keyboard and how it works.

While specific plugs and jacks are common to certain input devices, you may encounter a keyboard, mouse, or other input device that installs in some unique way. Some devices have standard connections on the back of the motherboard. The keyboard and mouse usually attach this way. Other devices require a card to be inserted into a motherboard expansion slot. In addition, almost all new input devices are offered in the universal serial bus (USB) format.

Keyboard

The typical keyboard has a small microprocessor such as the Intel 8048, Intel 8049, or Motorola 6805 processor installed as a keyboard controller. The keyboard controller is not as powerful as the processor inside a PC. Rather, it is a limited processor used for small device applications such as telephones, automobiles, and appliances. The keyboard also contains a buffer, which is a temporary memory storage device similar to RAM.

When a key or a combination of keys is pressed, an electrical circuit is completed to the keyboard controller. The keyboard controller turns the electrical signal into a ***scan code.*** Look again at the drawing in Figure 7-1. Each key or combination has its own unique scan code. The scan code is sent to the keyboard buffer. The buffer temporarily stores the scan codes.

From the buffer, the scan code is sent to the ***universal peripheral interface (UPI)*** mounted on the motherboard. The UPI is a microcontroller device. You can think of a microcontroller as a mini computer that is programmed to do a specific set of tasks. The UPI is manufactured with a small 8-bit CPU and a small amount of ROM and RAM. It will typically accept up to 90 programming instructions. A UPI can be designed to support any peripheral device associated with a computer.

The keyboard UPI chip then sends an interrupt signal (IRQ1) to the CPU, letting it know that the keyboard is attempting to transmit data. The CPU receives the data and determines if it is simply text, a command for the application software, or a command for the CPU such as "save." If it is simply text, the code is temporarily stored in RAM. The code can also be a command for the software application that is loaded in RAM. If so, it will also be transmitted to RAM where the application software is stored.

scan code
a data signal created from electrical signals sent by an input device.

universal peripheral interface (UPI)
a chip on the motherboard that directs communications between the CPU and the input device.

Key Construction

Several types of switches are used under the keys in keyboards. See **Figure 7-2.** The most common types include the following:

- ✔ Mechanical.
- ✔ Membrane.
- ✔ Rubber dome.
- ✔ Capacitor.

The mechanical switch, Figure 7-2A, is constructed from a set of typical electrical contacts that are normally open (separated). When the key is pressed, the contacts snap closed.

Figure 7-2.
The mechanics of the four most common types of keyboard switches.

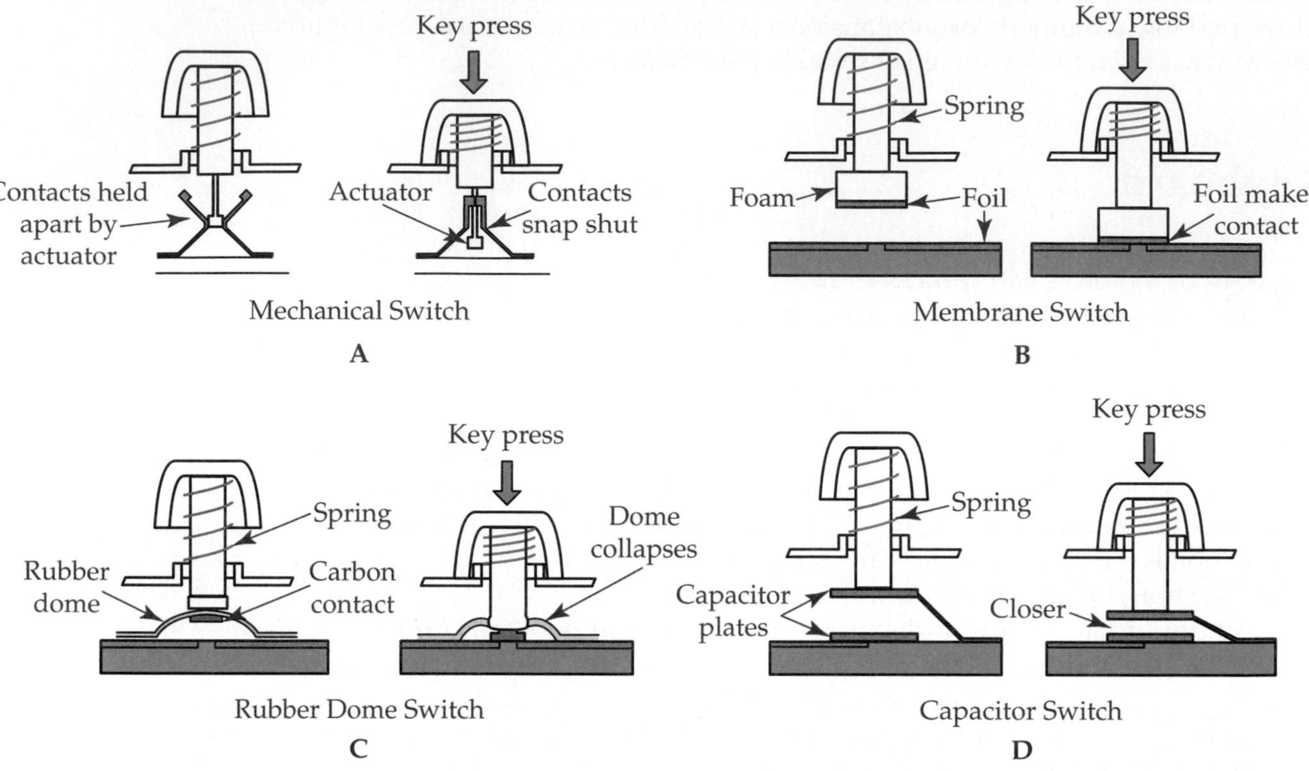

A membrane switch, Figure 7-2B, is constructed differently than the typical contact switch. A piece of foam with foil on one side is attached to the switch actuator. A circuit board is used as the base of the switch. The circuit board has a pair of contact points on the surface of the board. When the key is pressed, a conductive piece of foil located on the foam completes the circuit across the circuit board contact points.

Another type of keyboard switch is the rubber dome, Figure 7-2C. The rubber dome is constructed as the name implies, with a small rubber dome under the actuator. When the key is pressed, the rubber dome folds down. This causes a small carbon contact to complete the circuit on the circuit board. The rubber dome switch is less likely to allow dirt particles to accumulate between the carbon contact and the circuit board contact area. This keeps the switch working reliably.

The last type of switch is the capacitor switch, Figure 7-2D. The capacitor switch derives its name from the fact that it operates on the principle of an electronic capacitor. A capacitor is simply two plates of metallic material in close proximity to each other. The distance between the two capacitor plates directly affects the strength and electrical characteristics of the capacitor. When the key is pressed on the capacitor switch, the plates move closer together, but they never touch. The capacitor switch is the most reliable type of keyboard switch available. Dirt particles or corrosion will not affect the switch. The other three types of switches are susceptible to corrosion, which causes an open circuit and a failure to complete the electrical circuit.

When comparing types of switches, the first obvious difference is the tactile feel of the switch. While the difference in the "feel" of the various switches may not be important to a PC technician, it may be the most important characteristic to a professional typist. Most PC users have a keyboard preference even if they do not realize the reason for the difference. Because of this, you may be required to install an older keyboard when replacing an old PC with a newer one.

Keyboard Scan Codes

The keyboard is a matrix of electrical connections. Each junction in the matrix is a key location. Each position on the matrix has an assigned number. When a key is pressed, the electrical signal (digital binary) is sent to the keyboard controller as a scan code. The scan code is interpreted by the system BIOS and the application software and is turned into an ASCII character. The scan code represents the position of the key being pressed. Another scan code is generated when the same key is released.

The scan code is not the ASCII code nor is it the printed letter, number, or symbol on the physical key. The scan code is used to identify the exact symbol to be displayed on the screen or to be printed on the printer. Keyboards can have multiple sets of scan codes. Programmers use the scan codes to convert the action of a certain key being pressed into an action by the computer. Usually, the action is converting the code to an ASCII character, but not always. The scan codes are what allow multiple languages to be assigned to a particular computer. The scan code from the key is converted into the letter symbol of the language for which the system has been set up.

Look at **Figure 7-3** for a listing of scan codes for several keys. Note that the key press and release codes are expressed in hexadecimal values.

Keyboard Connectors

There are two traditional types of keyboard connectors: 5-pin DIN (XT/AT style) and 6-pin mini-DIN (PS/2). The 6-pin mini-DIN, **Figure 7-4,** is currently the most common style. However, USB wireless keyboards are becoming more common.

The difference in the two connectors is their physical shape, not their electrical qualities. Even though the 6-pin mini-DIN has an extra pin connector, the extra pin is a no connects (NC). The NC means that there is no electrical connection made by that particular pin. Each style transmits the same

Key	Key Press Code	Key Release Code
A	1E	9E
B	30	B0
Esc	01	81
F2	3C	BC
Home	E047	E0C7
Delete	E053	E0D3
Page Down	E051	E0D1
Space bar	39	B9
4 $	05	85

Figure 7-3. Hexadecimal scan codes for the pressing and releasing of selected keys.

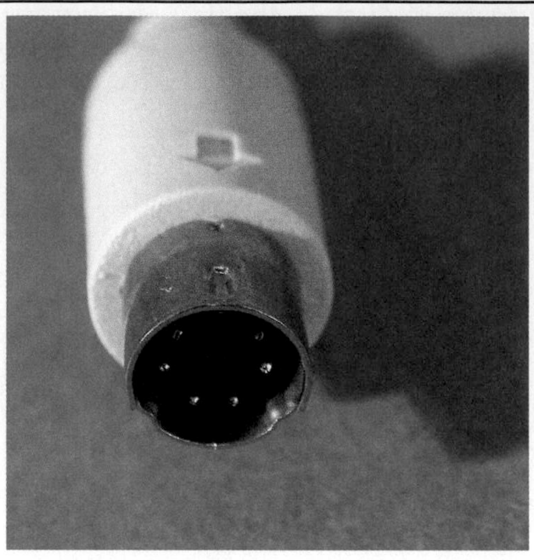

Figure 7-4. A six-pin mini-DIN and diagram. The six-pin mini-DIN is commonly used to connect wired keyboard and wired mice to a computer motherboard.

Key

6-pin DIN (PS/2)

1. Clock
2. Data
3. NC
4. Ground
5. +3.0, +3.3, +5.0 Vdc
6. NC

information to the motherboard. There are adapters made that change the physical connection of either plug to make them compatible with the motherboard.

Data is sent through only one of the five connectors. The keyboard is a serial device. The data sent to the motherboard is sequential. After the data reaches the motherboard, it is converted into parallel form, usually two bytes. There is also a clock signal transmitted through the keyboard connector wiring. The keyboard data transfer is ***synchronous.*** This means that the data is transferred based on that clock signal.

synchronous data transferred on the same timing as the computer.

Ergonomic Keyboards

Ergonomic keyboards are keyboards shaped for comfort and to help prevent injury. Many people suffer from carpal tunnel syndrome. ***Carpal tunnel syndrome*** is an inflammation of the tendons in the hands and especially the wrist. Carpal tunnel syndrome is caused by repeating the same movement over and over again

carpal tunnel syndrome an inflammation of the tendons in the hands and especially the wrist.

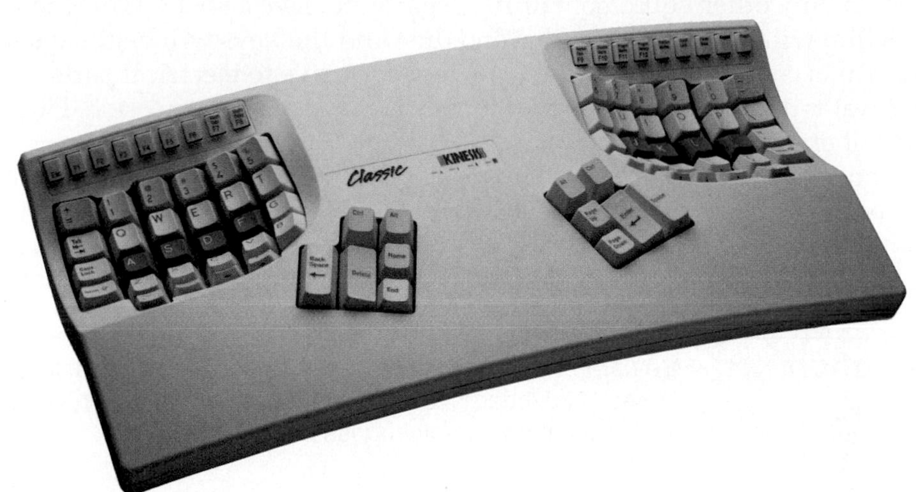

Figure 7-5. Ergonomic keyboards are designed to relieve stress on the hands and wrists caused by typing with hands in an uncomfortable position.

without proper rest or support. An example of this type of repetitive movement, and a common cause of carpal tunnel syndrome, is inputting data at a keyboard day after day.

It is believed that by shaping a keyboard so the hands and fingers contact the keyboard in a more natural alignment, carpal tunnel syndrome can be prevented. A variety of different designs for keyboards have been developed. See **Figure 7-5.**

Troubleshooting Keyboards

In general, it is not cost effective to repair damaged keyboards. It is usually less expensive to simply replace the keyboard. However, preventive maintenance can be used to extend the life of a keyboard.

Preventive Maintenance

Most of the problems with keyboards are associated with dirt in and around the keys. As you have seen, the keyboard keys can easily be disabled by dirt or corrosion. A keyboard should be cleaned on a regular basis. A small vacuum cleaner or a can of dry compressed air can be used to clean the keyboard.

When using vacuum cleaners, remember that they generate a lot of electrical noise and static. Electrical noise consists of high voltage spikes. If the vacuum is plugged into the same outlet as the computer being cleaned, be sure the computer is off. Do not equate a computer being off as a computer in a suspended state. When in doubt, unplug the computer. Also, remember that computers other than the one being cleaned might be connected to the same circuit. A battery-operated vacuum is the safest, but be sure it contains sufficient power. Be careful of static electricity. Static electricity is a common and hazardous by-product produced by the plastic parts on a vacuum cleaner. Be sure to follow all anti-static procedures to prevent damage to equipment.

Most computer users understand the hazards of keeping liquids (coffee or soda) near the computer equipment. If a liquid is spilled on the keyboard, the keyboard should be flushed with distilled water as soon as possible. Residue from soda or any other liquid containing sugar will leave a sticky film when dry. This film will quickly collect dirt and dust and the keys will begin to stick. Certain drinks contain materials that are very corrosive to electrical parts. Distilled water does not contain any minerals that will cause corrosion. Flush the keyboard liberally with distilled water.

Keys on the keyboard can be easily removed using a chip puller. A paper clip can also be bent to hook under the individual keys. Care should be used when attempting to remove the space bar. The typical space bar can be very difficult to reconnect to the keyboard after removal.

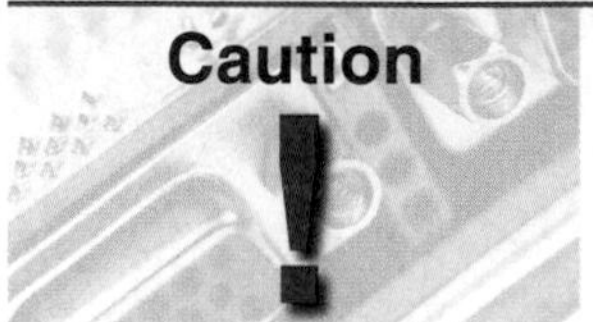

Be careful when entirely disassembling a keyboard. Many styles of keyboards are assembled at the factory in ways that make them nearly impossible to reassemble.

Adjusting Keyboard Properties

Certain keyboard properties can be adjusted for preference in the **Keyboard Properties** dialog box. The **Keyboard Properties** dialog box for Windows XP is located at **Control Panel | Printers and Other Hardware | Keyboard**. For Windows Vista, the **Keyboard Properties** dialog box is located at **Control Panel | Hardware and Sound | Keyboard**.

A+ Note:

Many times a question will appear on a, A+ certification exam asking for the correct path to an option such as the **Keyboard Properties**. Be sure to learn the paths for both Windows XP and Windows Vista.

Windows XP and Windows Vista use a very similar **Keyboard Properties** dialog box. You can easily change the repeat delay and the repeat rate as well as the cursor blink rate, **Figure 7-6.** Under the **Speed** tab, you will find the **Repeat delay** and **Repeat rate** adjustments, which control the actions of a pressed key. These adjustments control the length of a pause after pressing a key and the time required to hold a key in place before it repeats a character. A typical application of this timing method is when a user holds the space bar down to continuously move the cursor across the screen. The number of times per second a character can be typed is usually expressed as characters per second (CPS). The **Cursor blink rate** is simply how fast the cursor blinks on and off. It does not affect your typing in any way.

The computer can also be configured to allow a different language to be displayed on the screen. The computer is an international electronic device marketed worldwide, not just in the United States. This window allows you to add and change the language entered by the keyboard. There are keyboards for all major languages in the world. Language is configured in the **Regional and Language Options** dialog box, **Figure 7-7.**

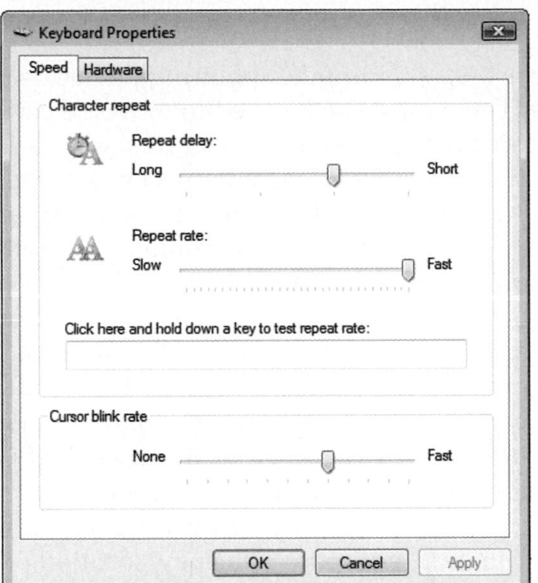

Figure 7-6. Windows Vista **Keyboard Properties** dialog box. This box is accessible through **Control Panel**.

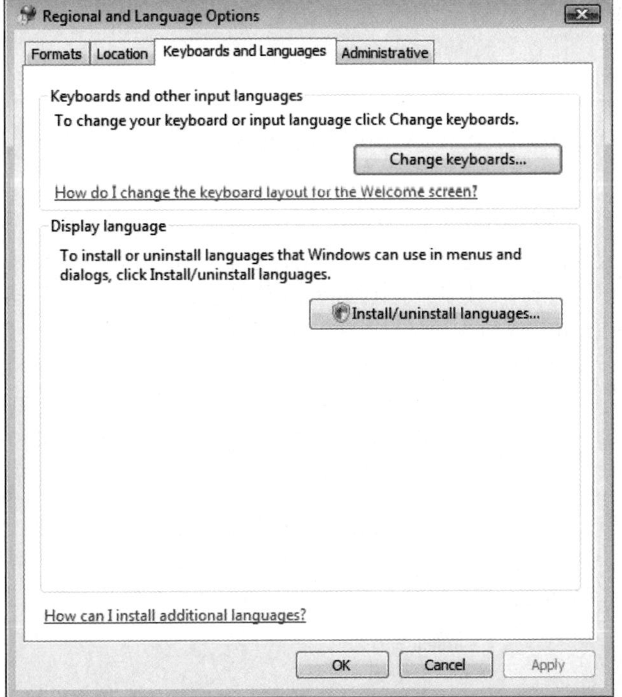

Figure 7-7. Keyboards and languages are changed through the **Regional and Language Options** dialog box. In Windows Vista, it is located in **Control Panel | Clock, Language, and Region | Regional and Language Options**.

In Windows Vista, you can access the **Regional and Language Options** dialog box through **Control Panel | Clock, Language, and Region | Regional and Language Options**. In Windows XP, you can access the language options by **Control Panel | Date, Time, Language, and Regional Options | Regional and Language Options**. Changing the physical keyboard layout in Windows XP to match the language is not as easy as it is in Windows Vista and requires several additional steps.

Mouse

mouse
a computer pointing device used to manipulate an onscreen pointer.

The ***mouse,*** **Figure 7-8,** is a computer pointing device used to manipulate an on-screen pointer. The mouse can be used to move, select, or change items on your computer screen. There are a variety of mouse styles. They can come with two or three buttons, and many come with a center wheel or lever that is designed for ease in scrolling through documents or Web pages.

The typical mouse is a very interesting combination of electrical and mechanical applications. See **Figure 7-9.** Take a good look at the major parts of the assembly: the light receiver, light transmitter, shutter disk, and the y-axis and x-axis contact points with the ball. As the ball inside the mouse rolls across the surface of a mouse pad, the movement causes either shutter disk (or both) to rotate. An infrared beam is emitted from an LED (light-emitting diode) across from the shutter. As the shutter disk revolves, it causes the light beam to be chopped. The number of chops is directly proportional to the distance the ball rolls. The combined effect of the x- and y-axis is transmitted to the motherboard as a digital signal. The digital signal plots the new location of the mouse cursor on the screen. The buttons on a mouse close very small microswitches. There is one switch under each button.

track ball
a pointing device similar to a mouse that is operated upside down.

The typical ***track ball*** is simply a mouse that is configured upside down. The same principles of the mouse apply to the track ball.

Mouse Interface

The mouse is available in two interface styles:

- ✔ Motherboard PS/2.
- ✔ USB.

Most keyboards and mice connect to the computer system directly through the motherboard PS/2 port. Even wireless mice and keyboards connect through the PS/2 port. The motherboard provides two mini-DIN connections referred to as PS/2 ports. However, they are not interchangeable. The two connections are easy to swap by mistake. There should be some indication on the back of the computer showing whether the connection is for the mouse or for the keyboard. If not, refer to your motherboard manual.

Figure 7-8.
Selection of mice.

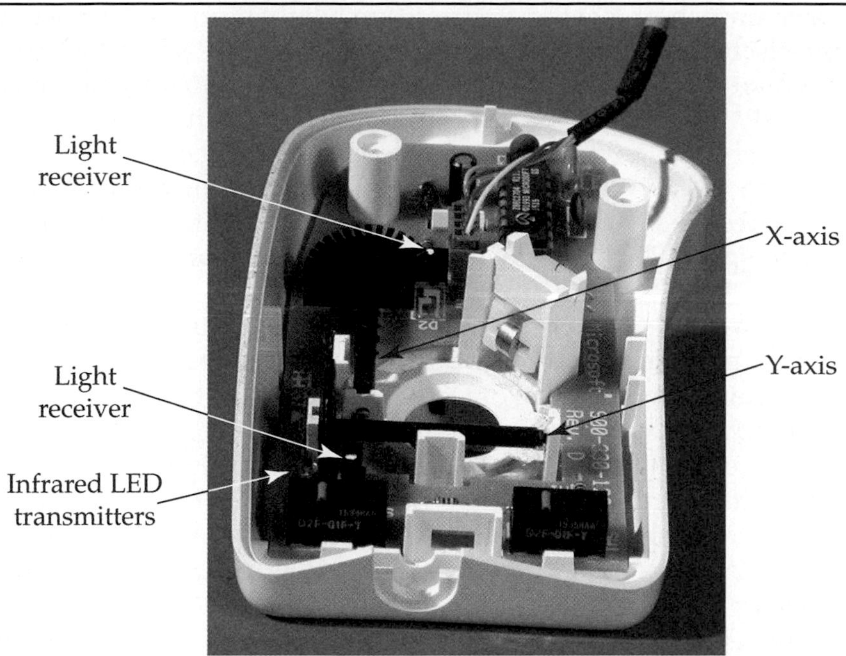

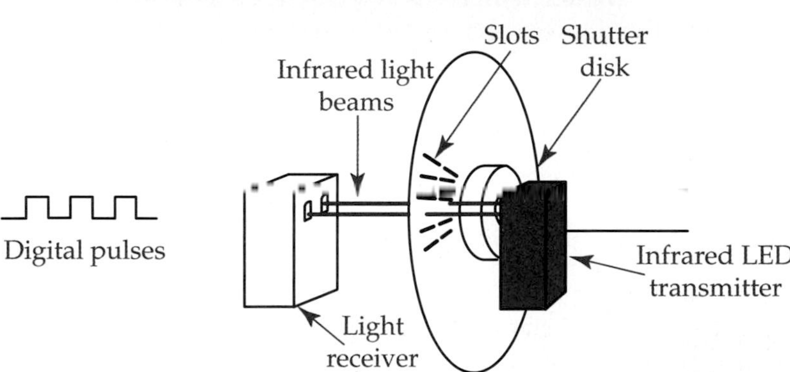

Figure 7-9.
Shown are the insides of a typical mouse. The mouse ball moves two wheels that determine the x- and y-axis movement of a mouse pointer on screen.

The mouse connector built into the motherboard is the most common means of connection. The IRQ setting for a motherboard interface mouse connection is typically IRQ12.

The other method of connecting a mouse or keyboard is by using a USB port. This is most common on laptop computers. When the mouse or keyboard is connected to the laptop via the USB port, the keyboard or mouse is automatically configured and can be immediately used.

The USB is not physically compatible with the other connector styles, so it is impossible to plug into the wrong socket. While the mouse may not require the speed that USB can provide, the USB is a standard socket that all new PCs have. This makes the USB connection a safe choice for mouse manufacturers.

Optical Mouse

One problem with the traditional mouse is a buildup of dirt in the inner workings of the device. The mouse ball picks up the dirt and transfers it to other parts. The latest input technology for a mouse eliminates the need for the ball, preventing dirt buildup problems. All of the moving parts from a traditional mouse are replaced with a CMOS digital camera.

Optical mice trace movement by transmitting a light beam to a surface. The light beam is reflected back from the surface to a built-in receiver in the mouse. The receiver contains the CMOS digital camera, which captures a small image of the surface directly under the mouse. The images are taken in rapid succession and compared to one another to determine the direction of motion. The optical mouse may take thousands of images in a single second. A microprocessor inside the mouse compares the images and translates the images into relative direction of movement and speed. There are no mechanical moving parts as found in a ball mouse.

Optical mice have far superior performance when compared to roller ball type mice. Optical mice do not need to be cleaned near as often as ball mice. There are no mechanical parts to fail or to be clogged by dust and lint as often occurs with ball mice and roller mice.

Two light sources commonly used with optical mice are LED and laser. A laser can produce much more precise movement increments than LED mice. LED light depends on a light-shaping optical lens mounted in the mouse to produce a fine beam of light. A laser has a natural fine line of light and requires no special light-shaping lens.

Mouse quality is measured and compared by frames per second (FPS) and dots per inch (DPI). The term *frames per second* as related to an optical mouse means how often the mouse sensor reads the surface and transmits the data collected. DPI is the degree of accuracy that a mouse can produce when sliding across a surface. The higher the number represented by DPI and FPS, the better the quality of the mouse system.

It is not unusual for a laser light mouse to produce increments of 1600 DPI and transfer 6000 FPS or more. This is quite an improvement over earlier versions of ball-type mouse movement of less than 100 DPI and 100 FPS.

Some modern office furniture designs incorporate a clear plastic or glass writing surface. You should avoid using an optical mouse on a transparent surface or material.

Troubleshooting the Mouse

As with keyboards, it is not cost-effective to spend any large amount of time fixing a malfunctioning mouse. However, proper maintenance and adjustments can make them last longer and work more efficiently.

Mouse Maintenance

Maintenance for a mouse or track ball is very easy. Most failures are caused by a buildup of lint or dirt on the roller that contacts the ball. This buildup is usually caused by a dirty mouse pad or from using the mouse without a pad on dirty furniture surfaces or on pads of paper. Paper tablets contain a great deal of paper lint particles. Using a mouse directly on a paper tablet will cause the mouse to fail after a relatively short period of time.

Another large cause of problems is hand lotion. People who use hand lotion on a regular basis will inadvertently contaminate the mouse ball with a film from the lotion. This film rapidly picks up dust and lint.

The best way to maintain a mouse is to keep the mouse or track ball and socket very clean. The ball under the mouse is easily removed, **Figure 7-10.** A small plate usually twists off and the ball drops out. The rollers inside the mouse can be sprayed with compressed air. The mouse ball can be rinsed with water.

Adjusting Mouse Properties

As with keyboards, certain properties of the mouse can be adjusted for preference. There is a **Mouse Properties** dialog box for making adjustments to the mouse. See **Figure 7-11.** This dialog box can be accessed in Windows XP through **Control Panel | Printers and Other Hardware | Mouse**. In Windows Vista, it is accessed through **Control Panel | Hardware and Sound | Mouse**.

Once the properties window for the mouse is open, adjustments to functionality, such as speed of pointer travel across the screen and the speed used to double-click can be adjusted. The type of mouse being used can be selected. One special change allows you to reverse the features (such as dragging) associated with the right and left buttons. Adjustments for purely aesthetic reasons can be performed here as well. For example, the length of the trailing mouse tail can be adjusted. The style, color, and size of the pointer can also be changed, **Figure 7-12.**

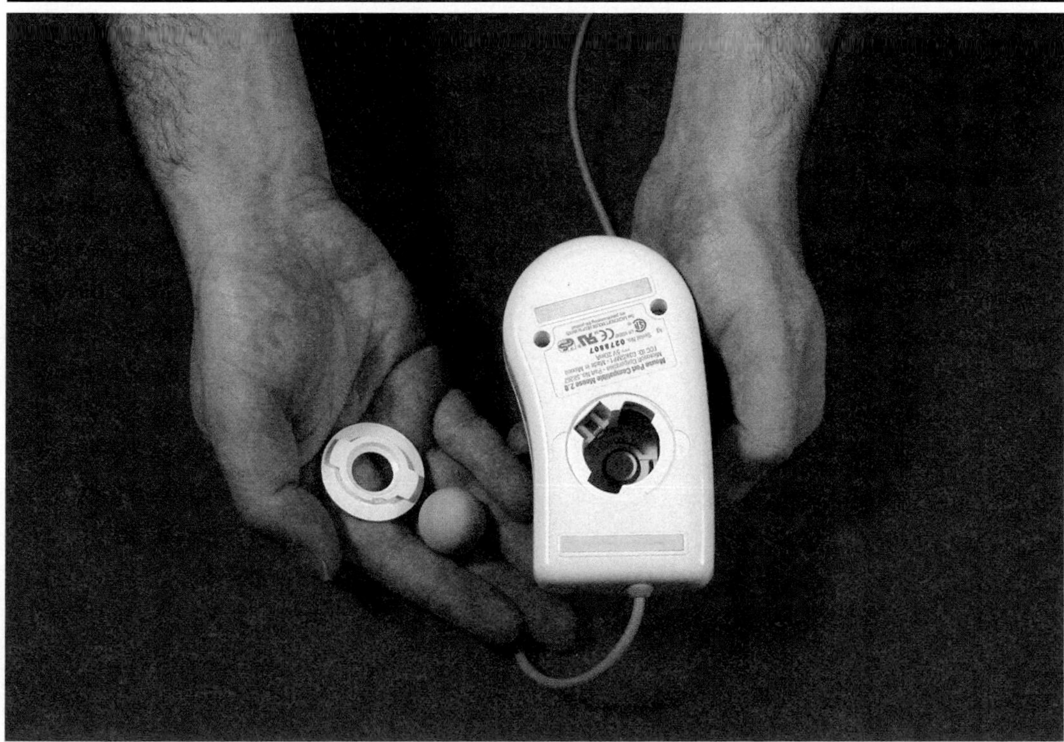

Figure 7-10.
Opening a mouse for cleaning is a simple task.

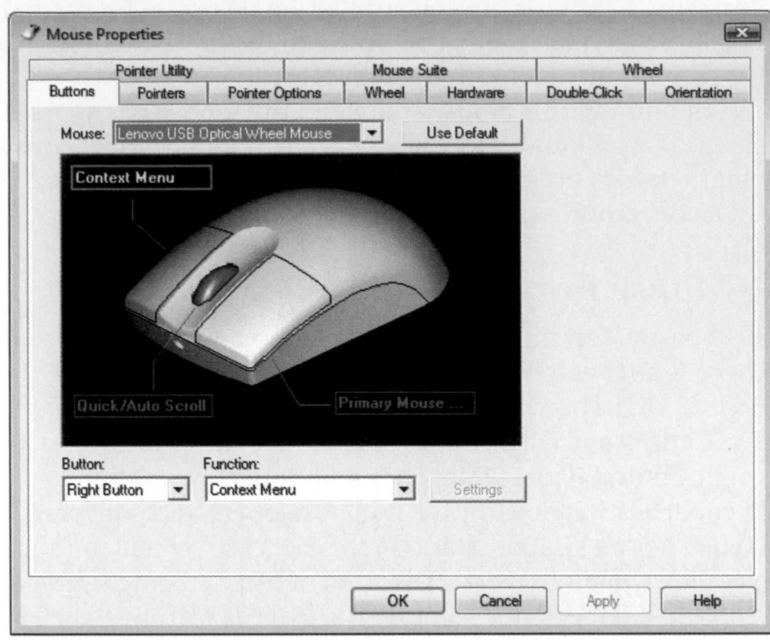

Figure 7-11. The **Mouse Properties** dialog box in Windows Vista. The appearance of this box will vary depending on the mouse installed.

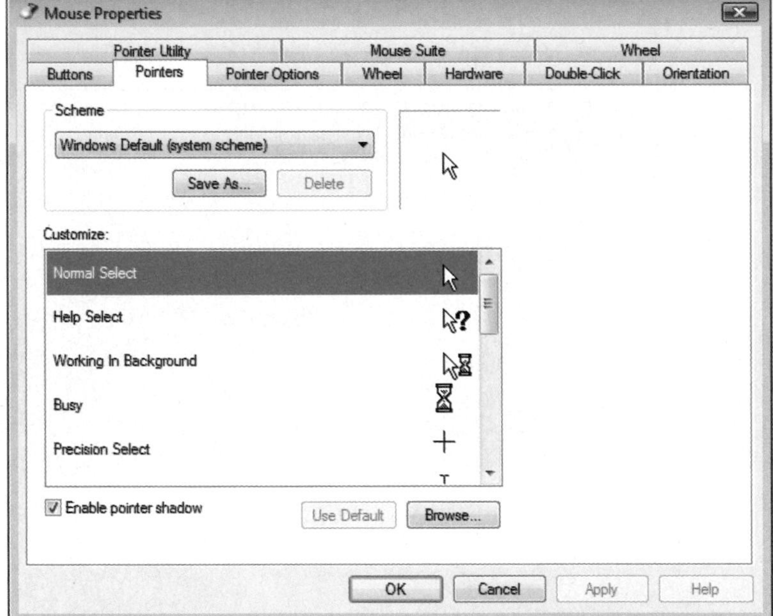

Figure 7-12. The **Mouse Properties** dialog box allows you to adjust the mouse for purely aesthetic reasons in addition to functional reasons.

Game Controllers

The earliest game controller, other than the keyboard or mouse, was the joystick. The first joysticks were of a simple box construction with a lever (the stick) extending from the top, **Figure 7-13.** Often, it had one or two push buttons. When the lever was moved, its position was converted into x- and y-screen coordinates. The buttons operated microswitches concealed inside the box. The buttons were typically fire control buttons for games that used weapons. Today, the simple joystick has evolved into a more complicated game controller. It has the same functions as the original joystick design and more, **Figure 7-14.**

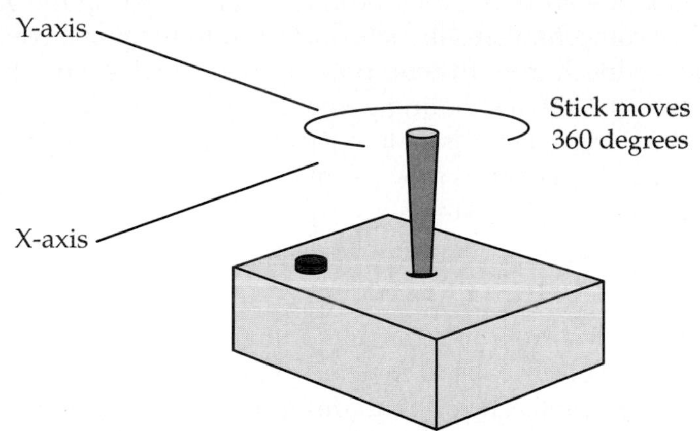

Figure 7-13.
Very early (and basic) joystick.

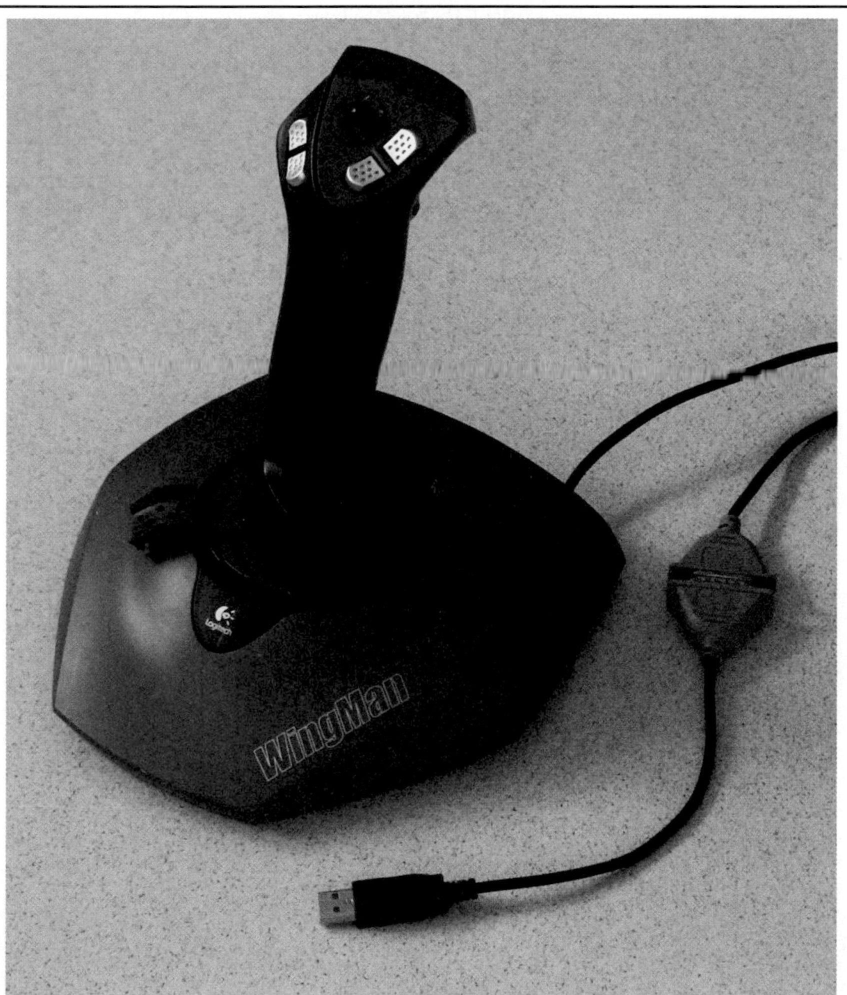

Figure 7-14.
Modern joysticks still resemble their predecessors, but they offer many more options. They have more buttons and controls, and some offer force feedback from the games they play.

The additional features on most controllers are top hat control and force feedback. The top hat control located at the top of the stick is used as an additional control. It can plot x- and y-coordinates, or it can be used as an additional switch.

The force feedback feature is a method that creates "feel" at the game stick control. A set of servomechanisms is incorporated into the game controller. These operate on feedback from the computer. When a wall is struck in a driving game or a weapon is fired in a shooting game, the game software package generates an electrical signal that is sent to the game stick. The signal activates a servomechanism, which generates movement or vibration in the game controller that simulates the action in the game.

Game Controller Construction

A game controller is similar in construction to the mouse except that there are many variations on the electrical and mechanical mechanism that generates the electronic positioning signal. The original designs were based on two variable resistors called *potentiometers*. A potentiometer is a resistor device that is capable of varying its resistance to current. The styles of potentiometer used for gaming devices usually ranges from 0 to 100 kilohms of resistance. One potentiometer is used for the x-axis and the other for the y-axis. The range of resistance values is directly proportional to the x- and y-coordinates on the display screen. See **Figure 7-15** for an illustration of a screen and its coordinates.

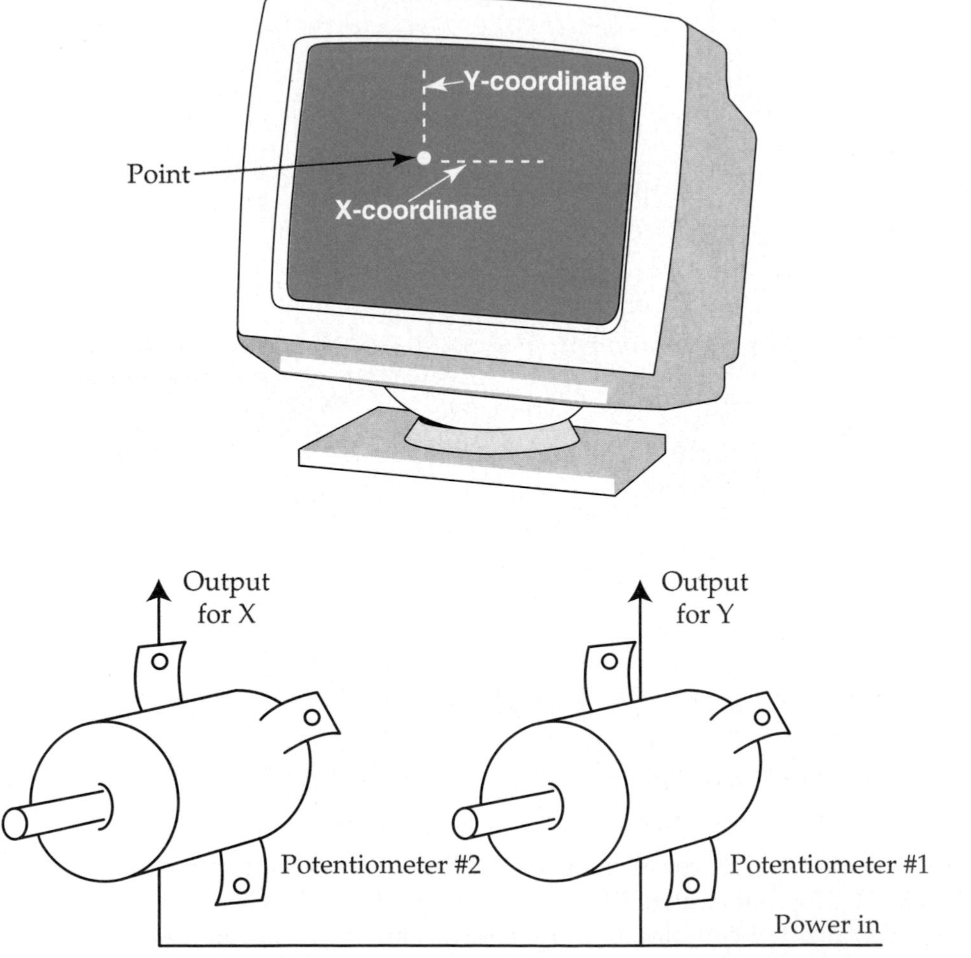

Figure 7-15. Two potentiometers and the screen coordinates they produce.

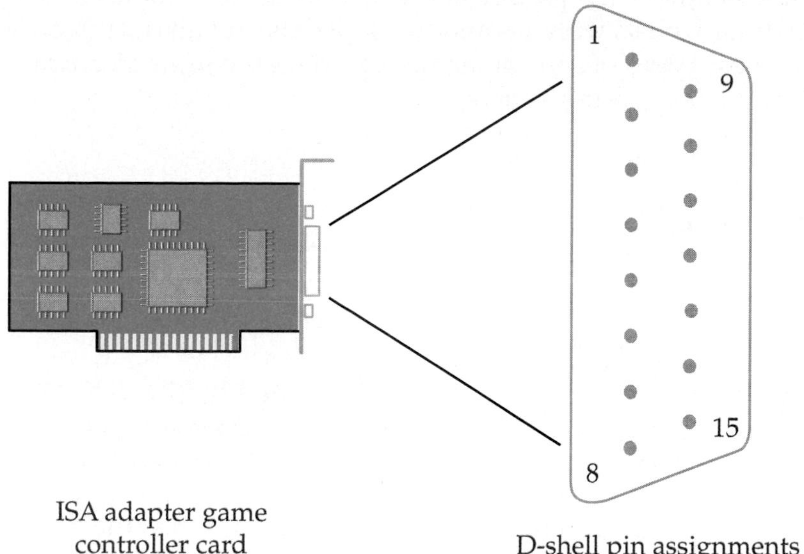

Figure 7-16.
Game controller card with a 15-pin D-shell connector. Most game peripherals are USB or wireless devices.

Game Controller Port

The game port is usually a 15-pin, two-row D-shell connector, **Figure 7-16.** The game controller connects to the motherboard through fifteen conductors. All new game adapters today are either USB, wireless, or a combination of both. These take advantage of the speed and abundance of USB ports.

The chart in **Figure 7-17** identifies the function of each of the fifteen conductors involved in a typical application. Note that this chart represents a typical application, not a typical game controller. The actual use of pins can vary or be modified for a particular brand of game controller. Also note that this chart reflects conditions for using two game controllers (one called A, and the other B), since many games are set up for two players.

Pin #	Function Description
1	Provide +5 volts to game controller A.
2	Provide input from switch located on game controller A.
3	Provide input about position along x-coordinate of game controller A.
4	Used as ground.
5	Used as ground.
6	Provide input about position along y-coordinate of game controller A.
7	Provide input from second switch on game controller A.
8	Provide +5 volts to game controller A.
9	Provide +5 volts to game controller B.
10	Provide input from switch located on game controller B.
11	Provide input about position along x-coordinate of game controller B.
12	Used as ground.
13	Provide input about position along y-coordinate of game controller B.
14	Provide input from second switch located on game controller B.
15	Provide +5 volt input to game controller B.

Figure 7-17.
Chart of pin use in a typical application of a game controller. Pin use can be modified by the game controller.

Some game adapters are quite elaborate in appearance. Some are designed to imitate steering wheels with gas and break pedals and aircraft steering yokes with pedals. These types of controls are all based on the same electrical and mechanical principles discussed here.

Digitizer Pad

digitizer pad a pointing device consisting of a tablet and a puck or pen-like stylus.

A *digitizer pad* came into use long before graphical user interfaces, **Figure 7-18.** The pad served the same purpose as the GUI does today. This results in very few current applications for digitizer pads.

The digitizer pad is connected to the computer motherboard, usually through a serial port. The pad is constructed with a matrix under the symbols displayed on the pad. A mouse-like device called a puck is moved across the pad and centered above the desired command. Commands such as circle, line, and square are typical for computer-aided drafting systems. When the pointer button is pressed, the coordinates under the pointer device transmit the coordinates from the digitizer pad to the computer. The software system responds to the appropriate request.

Bar Code Readers

bar code reader a device that converts bar code images into data.

A ***bar code reader*** simply converts bar code images into data. The operation of a bar code scanner is simple, **Figure 7-19.** It is designed with a light source transmitter and a light source receiver. The light source transmitter projects a light beam across the bar code. The bar code is made up of dark lines of varying width and spacing. The widths of the dark lines combine with the white spaces to form a code that represents ASCII letters and numbers. Look at **Figure 7-20,** which shows a typical bar code.

The light from the source is reflected by the white spaces and absorbed by the dark lines. The receiver converts the reflected light into electrical pulses representing the data contained in the bar code. The electrical pulses are then

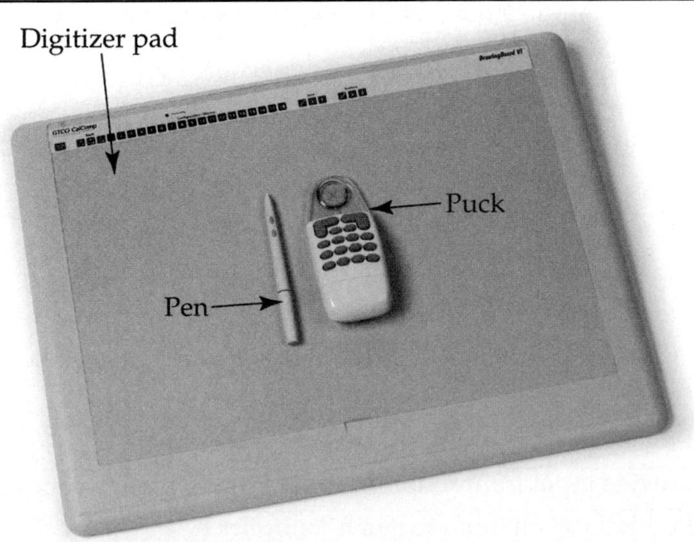

Figure 7-18. Digitizer pad, puck, and pen. (CalComp)

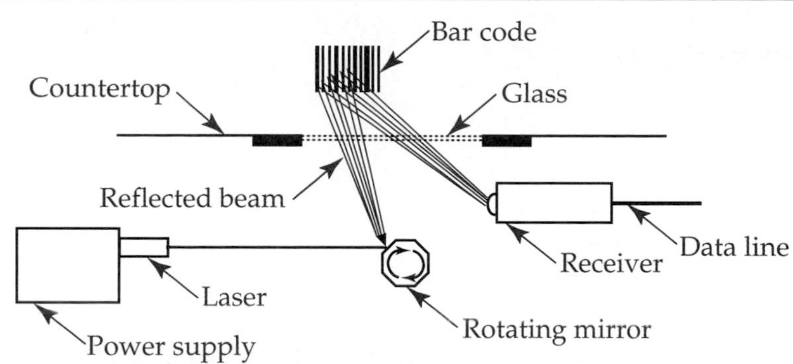

Figure 7-19. Shown are the workings of a bar code reader that can be found at the checkout counter of many stores. Using these fixed readers, objects have their bar codes dragged across the glass for reading.

Figure 7-20. A typical bar code. Note the variation in the thickness of the black lines of the code.

passed along as ASCII data to the PC through either a wireless or a wired connection. The PC has software driver programs that use the ASCII data for application programs that manage inventory or drive a cash register program.

scanner
a device that digitizes printed images and text.

optical character recognition (OCR)
a type of software that is able to distinguish between the various letters, numbers, and symbols in a scanned image.

digital camera
a type of camera that captures and stores images as digital data instead of on photographic film.

Scanners and Digital Cameras

A ***scanner*** is a tool that takes in an optical image and digitizes it, **Figure 7-21.** Scanners can be used to read text into a computer or to create a digital version of a photo. To read text into a format that can be used with word-processing software, a scanner uses optical character recognition software. This ***optical character recognition (OCR)*** software determines which letters, numbers, and symbols match with images taken by the scanner. The output is a fairly accurate text version of a printed document. A ***digital camera*** takes pictures like a regular camera, but it captures and stores images as digital data instead of on photographic film. See **Figure 7-22.**

The secret to scanner and digital camera operations is the charged-coupled device (CCD). Think of a CCD as a series of light-activated transistors contained in a single chip. These transistors convert light into electrical energy. When light strikes the CCD, a voltage is produced in direct proportion to the intensity of the light.

Figure 7-21.
A scanner changes reflected light into digital signals.

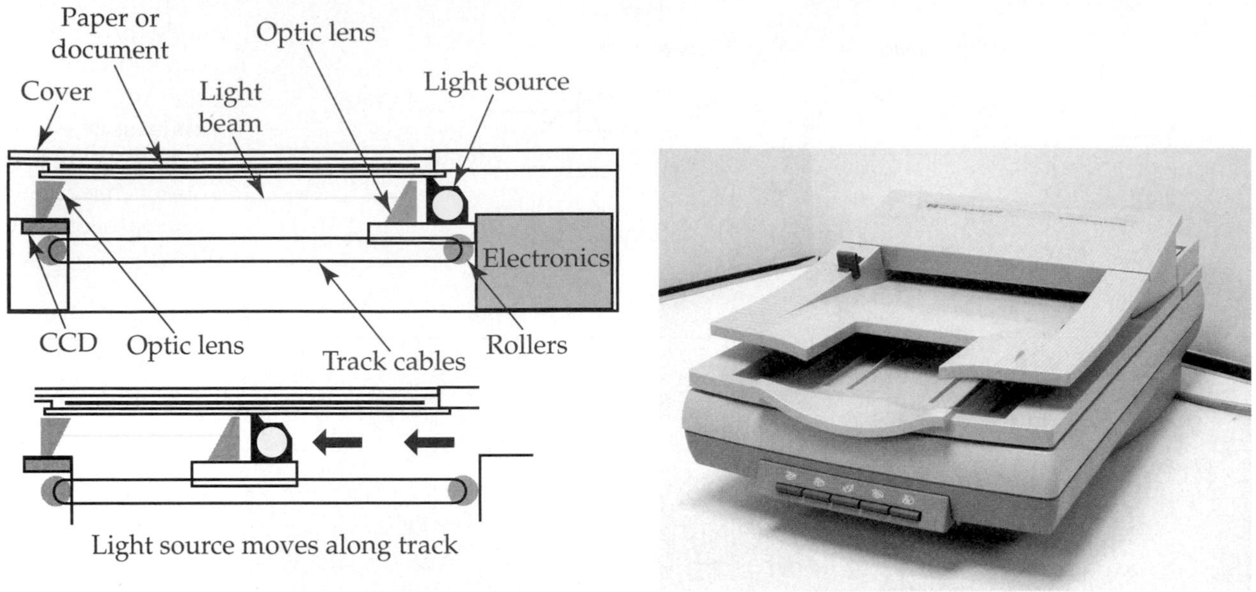

Figure 7-22.
Digital cameras are similar to scanners in that they both use charge-coupled devices to produce their images.

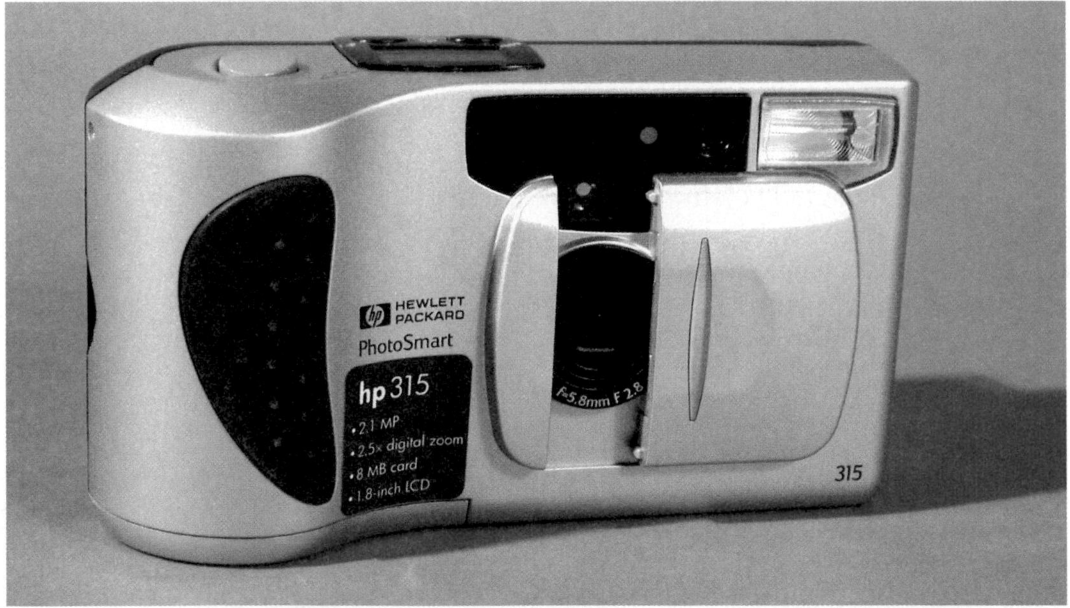

The voltage produced is analog, which means the voltage level is a continuously variable signal. To be utilized by a computer system, the voltage must be converted to a digital signal, a sequence of discrete voltages. A special chip called an *analog-to-digital converter (ADC)* receives the analog electrical charge from the CCD and converts it to a series of digital signals that represent the light intensity of the image. The digital pulses are stored in memory to be accessed by graphical software programs. See **Figure 7-23.**

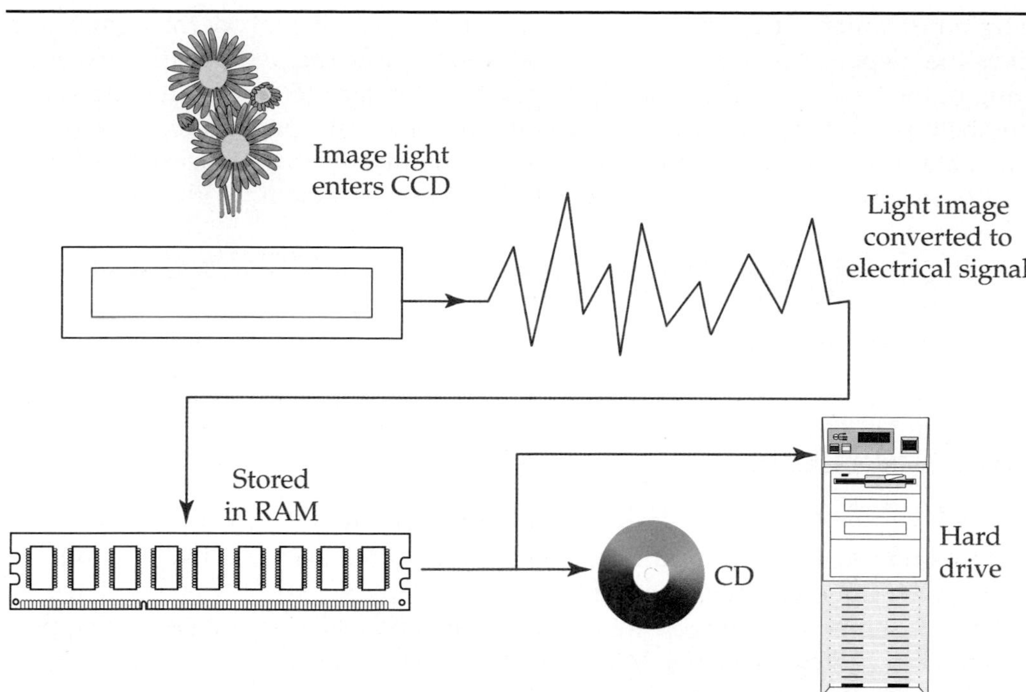

Figure 7-23. Illustration of a graphic stored as impulses.

The flat bed scanner uses a cable to move the light beam along the image placed on the bed of the scanner. The scanner captures the image one line at a time. After a line of the image is captured, the CCD is moved down the image a fraction to capture the next line. This process continues until the entire image has been captured.

The CCD device in a camera consists of an array of tiny windows. The entire image is captured at once rather than line by line as in the scanner application. Color filter lenses are used for color images. Each color is captured separately by incorporating a set of color filters into the lens units.

Light Pen

light pens input devices that interact with the light beam that creates the image on the monitor.

Light pens interact with a light beam that strikes the monitor screen. The raster or movement of the light across the screen is explained in detail in Chapter 8—Video Displays and Audio Systems. For now, imagine the computer screen image as being generated by a light beam sweeping across the screen thousands of times a second. The beam moves from left to right. After each pass of the beam from left to right, it moves down the screen just a fraction. This process continues until the beam has covered the entire screen. The process is repeated approximately sixty times a second. The light intensity of the beam changes as it crosses the screen to produce an image. The travel of the beam is a product of precise timing of horizontal and vertical electronic controls.

The light pen is plugged into an adapter card that is inserted into one of the expansion slots in the motherboard. Light pens are also available as a USB device. The end of the light pen is light sensitive. The light pen can detect the beam from the monitor as it sweeps across the computer display screen. The screen area has a graphical user interface displayed. It can be a menu or a list of products. When the light pen touches the screen area where an image is displayed, the light beam strikes the display screen and actuates the input area of the pen. It is this exact timing of the beam that allows the light pen adapter card to convert the location of the pen into screen coordinates. The software program converts the screen coordinates into user information such as "one hamburger with cheese," or "open bay door number 2." The command can be anything associated with the image on the screen.

Light pen technology requires light generated from a CRT-type of display. Because the CRT is rapidly becoming obsolete, touch screen technology will soon replace light pen technology.

Touch Screens

touch screen displays computer display that is modified to accept input by touch.

Touch screen displays are computer displays modified to accommodate input information by touch. The input area on the touch screen is activated by a touch, as the name implies, or by using a stylus.

A touch screen system requires a touch screen panel assembly, controller, port connector, and software driver. The controller can be a separate unit attached by cable to the touch screen or incorporated into the edge of the touch screen frame. The typical connection to the computer system is made through a USB port, **Figure 7-24.** Special PCI cards may be used in place of a USB port. The PCI card can serve as a port connection to the computer and incorporate the necessary electronics to act as the system controller.

A software driver program must be installed in the computer system during the installation of the touch screen. The software driver provides the necessary support for interpreting the digital signal sent by the controller. Installing the necessary driver is similar to installing a driver for any other computer input device.

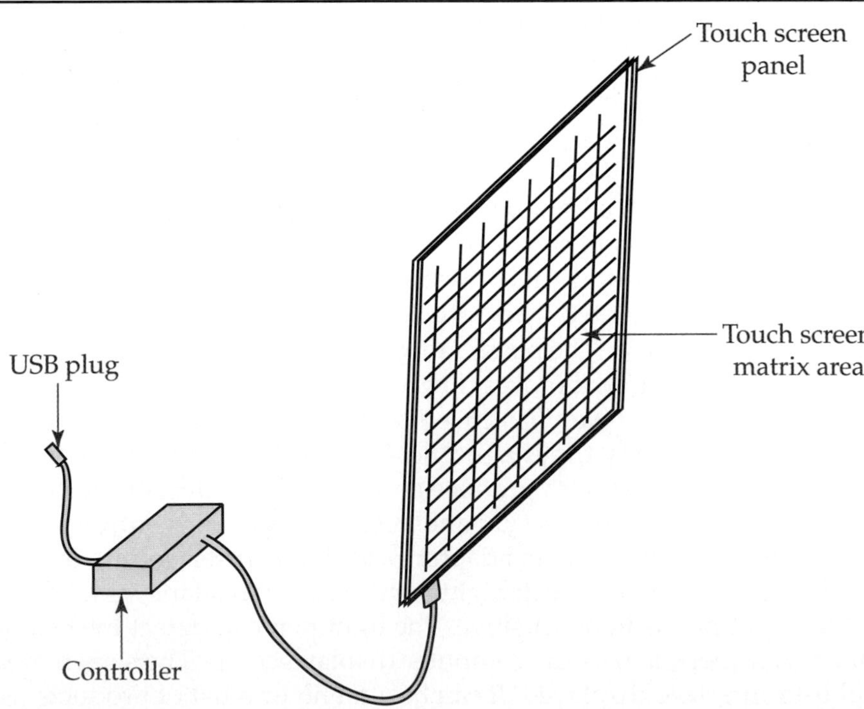

Figure 7-24. This touch screen connects to the USB port of a PC. The controller is a separate unit attached to the cable.

Touch screens are often incorporated into a computer system when a mouse or keyboard would not be a practical input device or as a convenience for users. Touch screen applications have been applied to interactive computer communications such as those in hotel lobby information panels, manufacturing assembly line controls, hospital surgical rooms, and the food service industry.

Touch screen technology falls into five major sensor categories: resistance, capacitance, near field effect, infrared, and acoustical wave. All touch screen technologies operate in a very similar manner. The main difference is the touch screen surface construction and the type of electronic transmitters and receivers or sensors used.

Resistance

Touch screens that utilize the electronic principle of resistance are one of the most common and inexpensive to design. The touch screen consists of two layers of conductors separated by very tiny spacers. The first layer is a series of vertical translucent electrical conductors, and the second layer is a series of horizontal translucent electrical conductors. The two layers combine to form a matrix pattern. The two layers are assembled into a flexible transparent cover, which fits neatly over the monitor display.

The monitor typically displays command buttons or similar graphics, which represent menu commands such as open, save, view files, and exit. When the screen is touched, a connection is made at that point in the matrix, **Figure 7-25.** Each area on the resistance touch screen produces a unique electrical resistance value. The electrical resistance value is interpreted by the screen controller and then passed to the computer operating system as a screen location. The digital signal is sent into the computer system through a USB port or through a PCI card designed for this purpose. Resistance touch screens work well in dusty or humid environments.

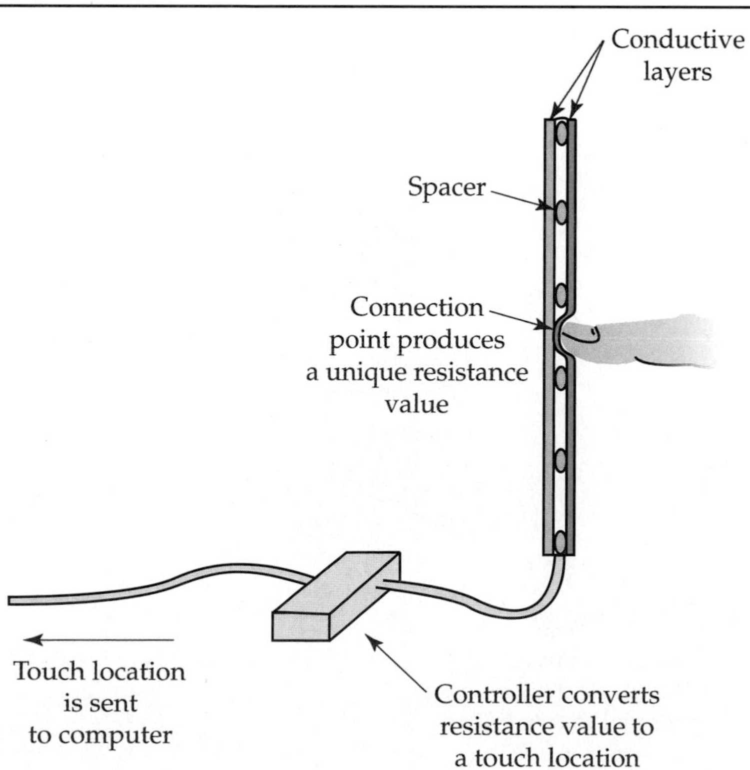

Figure 7-25. Basic operation of a resistance touch screen.

Capacitance

Capacitance touch screens operate on the principle of capacitance. See **Figure 7-26.** The touch screen is coated with a transparent metal oxide. A slight electrical charge is applied to the metal oxide, which creates an equally distributed electrical field across the inside of the touch screen. When the screen is touched, the electrically charged field is disturbed. A drop in the electrical potential at that point in the screen is transmitted to the touch screen controller. Capacitance touch screens do not work well in a humid environment.

Near Field

Near field touch screens also operate on the principle of capacitance. However, the near field touch screen is constructed from two laminates of glass, each with a pattern of a transparent metal oxide coating. The main difference between the two technologies is that you need not touch the screen, but rather place your finger near the screen area. A finger or any other pointing device near the screen area is sufficient to disturb the electrical field between the two screen plates. Near field touch screen works well in an industrial or medical application where the user may have gloved hands.

Infrared

The infrared touch screen forms a matrix created by a row of infrared transmitters and receivers along the edges of the screen, **Figure 7-27.** The infrared transmitters are specially designed LEDs that transmit infrared light to the receivers. The receivers are light activated transistors, which act like a switch that is turned on and off by the presence or absence of the infrared light beam.

Figure 7-26.
Basic operation of a capacitance touch screen.

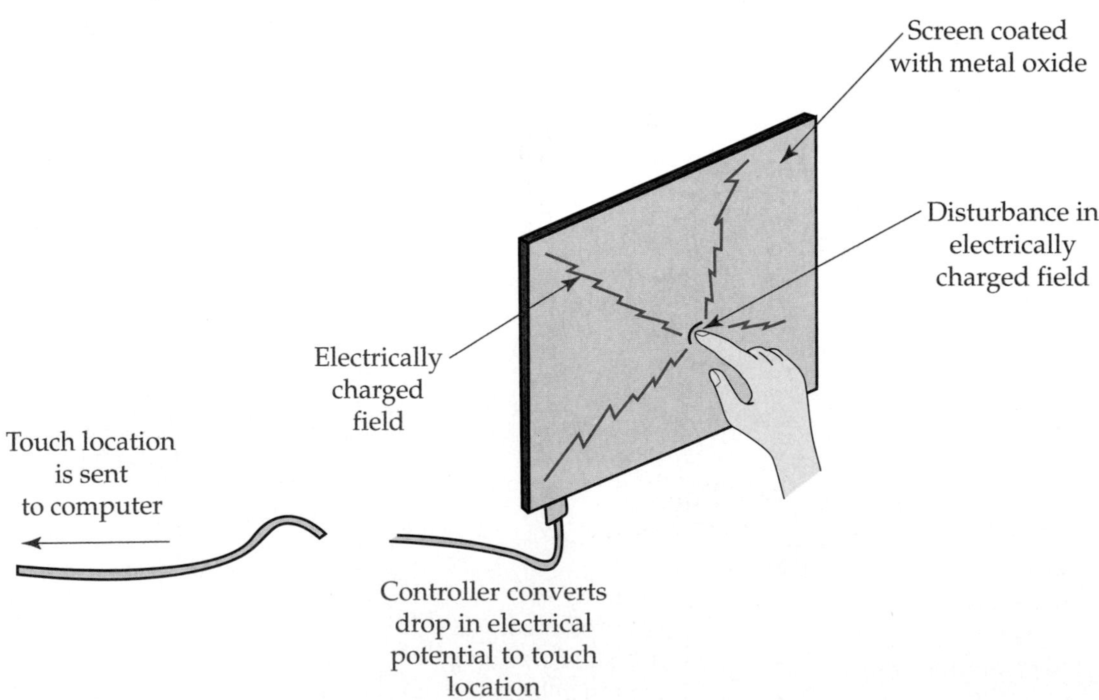

Figure 7-27.
Basic operation of an infrared touch screen.

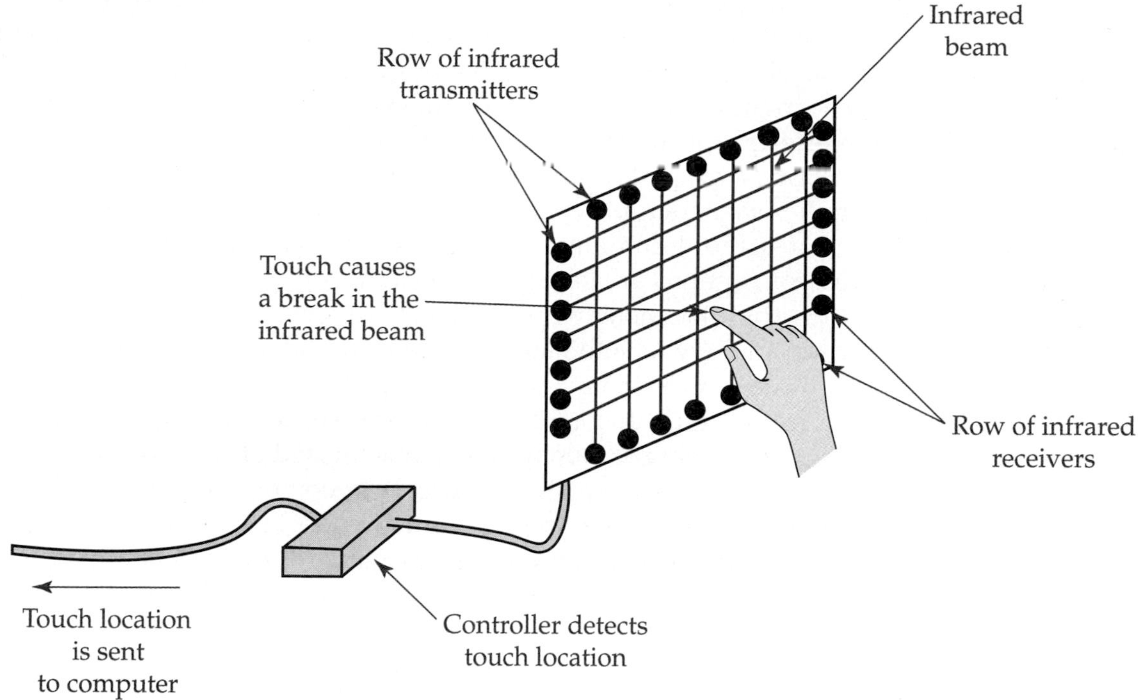

When a touch interrupts the infrared beam, the receivers in that matrix area send a signal to the controller. The controller determines the touch location and sends this location to the computer.

Acoustical Wave

The acoustical wave touch screen is similar in design to the infrared screen. The acoustical touch screen, however, uses a matrix of sound waves. The edges of the panel are lined with acoustical sound wave transmitters and receivers. When an object such as a finger interrupts the sound wave, the location of the interruption is transmitted to the screen controller. The infrared and acoustical do not work well in a dusty environment.

Wireless Input Devices

Wireless input devices use either radio signal (RF) or infrared (IR) light to transfer information between an input device and a computer system. Typical wireless input devices commonly encountered are mice, keyboards, microphones, game input devices, Web cams, and digitizer pads. There are four major classifications of radio frequency used for input devices for computers: 27 MHz, 2.4 GHz, Bluetooth, and Wi-Fi. The information in this section will be limited to how wireless input device technology correlates to common PC wireless input devices. Other wireless technologies will be introduced in later chapters.

Infrared Devices

Infrared communications for computer specifications have been established by the Infrared Data Association (IrDA). Infrared devices use light to establish the connection between the input device and the computer. These devices work in similar fashion as a television remote control. The one main problem with infrared controls is that they require line of site between the transmitter and receiver. The main advantage of infrared devices is that they are not susceptible to radio interference as many other wireless devices are. Infrared device communication is typically limited to only two devices. Wireless technology based on radio waves is typically used for two or more devices and does not require line of site for a communications link between the devices.

Infrared connections are usually established automatically when devices are brought within one meter of each other. Microsoft operating systems use ActiveSync technology to automatically establish and synchronize a connection between infrared devices such as a PC and a personal digital assistant. You can access the infrared setup and configuration wizard in Windows Vista by typing "irda" in **Microsoft Help and Support**, which is located off the **Start** menu.

You can only establish one infrared link between two devices, but the two devices can provide support for more than one software application at the same time. For example, you can transfer the contents of a calendar program, a business card program, and e-mail program in one session using one common infrared link.

There is several data transfer speeds associated with infrared technology. Serial IrDA (SIR) is 115.2 kbps, Fast IrDA (FIR) is 4 Mbps, and Very Fast IrDA (VFIR) is equal to 16 Mbps. Ultra Fast IrDA (UFIR) is currently under development and should be released with a data transfer rate of 100 Mbps. Each generation of IrDA is backward compatible with the previous version. For example, a VFIR device can communicate with a SIR device at the SIR data rate of 115.2 kbps.

IR Technology	Data Rate
SIR	115.2 kbps
FIR	4 Mbps
VFIR	16 Mbps
UFIR	100 Mbps

Infrared devices are configured in Control Panel or Device Manager of Windows operating systems. However, if the infrared device does not exist, you will not see an option to configure the device.

RF Devices

Radio Frequency (RF) devices use radio waves to communicate between the remote device and the receiver. The early radio remote control devices used the 27 MHz frequency for their wireless devices. This is the same frequency used by model remote control planes, cars, and other toys such as robots. The use of specific radio frequencies for devices is controlled by the Federal Communications Commission (FCC). It is their responsibility to assign radio frequencies and enforce rules regulating the devices using radio waves.

The radio frequency can transmit through solid material and does not need to be in line of sight like infrared. RF can transmit through solid objects but within limits. RF can easily pass through wood, sheet rock, glass, concrete block, and other common building materials. However, if the material is very dense, the RF may not pass through. For example, a thick concrete wall containing steel reinforcement may totally block the RF signal. Do not expect RF to pass through metal, such as metal walls or a wall covered with metal file cabinets. The metal will most likely block the RF signals.

Many RF devices are designed as proprietary devices. This means that the technology was designed by a specific company and may not be used by other manufacturers without the original manufacturers' permission. One of the drawbacks to a proprietary design is that it may not be compatible with other devices that perform a similar function. For example, a mouse designed by Logitech that uses a 27 MHz radio frequency may not be compatible with another brand of mouse receiver. This means when you replace a 27 MHz Logitech mouse, you must use another 27 MHz Logitech mouse. You cannot use a Microsoft or a Bluetooth mouse.

Wireless Technology Standards

As you study the characteristics of wireless devices, be aware that there are many overlapping RF standards which can create a lot of confusion. For example, Logitech Fast RF is not a radio frequency standard but rather a Logitech proprietary standard developed for their brand of input devices. Fast RF is not intended to be compatible with devices manufactured by other manufacturers.

The IEEE organization developed and released a set of wireless standards for networking, which is referred to as the EEE 802.11 wireless standard. The IEEE 802.11 standard specifies how 2.4 GHz and 5 GHz RF is used for networking devices.

ZigBee is a wireless standard used for home entertainment systems. Wireless USB is a standard developed by the USB organization to replace wired USB devices with wireless USB devices. Wireless WiMedia is an International Standards Organization (ISO) radio standard which has been adopted by several other organizations that are responsible for their own individual set of radio standards.

As technology evolves, some standards are absorbed into other original standards which add to the confusion. For example, the Bluetooth wireless standard is slow compared to some other wireless technologies. To stay competitive, Bluetooth is now evolving into the UWB standard, which will allow Bluetooth to exchange data between devices at a competitive rate. The Bluetooth organization will retain the "Bluetooth" name to identify Bluetooth standard devices even after they conform to UWB.

A+ Note:

You will most likely be asked questions about wireless technology frequencies and speeds. Keep in mind that standards for computer and electronic devices constantly change. You should always check the manufacturer Web site for the very latest information about assigned RF and bandwidth.

Bluetooth

Bluetooth standard a standard that connects low-powered devices over a short distance using the assigned 2.4 GHz frequency.

The ***Bluetooth standard*** was developed by a special interest group of electronics manufacturers who wanted to produce a standard way to connect low-powered devices over a short distance using the assigned 2.4 GHz frequency. Anyone can use the 2.4 GHz frequency for a wide assortment of devices. The Bluetooth organization was interested in developing a standard to be followed by manufacturers to share communication with each other's devices. For example, a cell phone that could automatically transfer information between the cell phone and a computer. Bluetooth was originally designed for only very low-power devices that would transmit data over the 2.4 GHz frequency. As the demand for wireless devices expanded, so did the Bluetooth list of products. Wireless keyboards and mice conform to the Bluetooth standard.

Bluetooth is often confused with other 2.4 GHz RF devices. The main difference is Bluetooth is a design standard of how the device should operate using the 2.4 GHz radio band. When manufacturers apply the Bluetooth standard to their devices, their devices can communicate with any other Bluetooth standard devices no matter who manufactured the device. For example, a PC that uses the Bluetooth standard can communicate with any cell phone that uses the Bluetooth standard.

The Bluetooth standard specifies that all Bluetooth devices should use the same "protocol" when communicating between devices. The formal definition of a protocol as defined for use with computer and network communications is as follows: a protocol is a set of rules used to govern communication between two devices. The set of rules outline information about how the data is organized that is to be exchanged between the two devices. A protocol sets the standards for such items as the following.

- ✔ How the devices are to be identified (by numbers or letters) and the exact number of characters.
- ✔ The maximum amount of data that can be transmitted at one time.
- ✔ The speed at which each of the electronic devices should operate.
- ✔ If information should be encrypted, and if so, by what method.

There are over 1200 pages in the current Bluetooth standard that manufacturers must follow to ensure compatibility with other Bluetooth devices. The Bluetooth specification as well as many other wireless specifications must adhere to regulations set by the Federal Communications Commission (FCC). There are three general wireless power classifications described by the FCC, as shown in the following table.

Class	Power in Milliwatts (mW)	Maximum Range in Meters (m)
Class 1	100	100
Class 2	10	10
Class 3	1	1

The classes are Class 1, Class 2, and Class 3. The amount of power of each classification is directly related to the maximum distance an RF device can transmit. The power output of radio devices is measured in milliwatts (mW). A milliwatt is very little energy as compared to other electronic type devices.

Most common short range RF input devices are rated as a Class 3 device with a maximum range of 1 meter. There are some instances of Class 2 input devices. In general, the maximum distances indicated in the table are for ideal conditions. If there is a significant amount of radio interference, the maximum distance will be reduced. If the radio interference is excessive, the wireless device will fail to operate entirely.

Wireless devices will operate either in the 27 MHz range or the 2.4 GHz Bluetooth range. There are 2.4 GHz devices that are not Bluetooth. Bluetooth is a standard, not a specific frequency; although, it is assigned to use a specific frequency. When Bluetooth is used to connect to the computer receiver, the typically maximum range is approximately 6′. When using the 27 MHz frequency, the range can be significantly farther. Both the 27 MHz and the 2.4 GHz radio frequencies can be interfered with by other devices, such as cordless phones, microwave ovens, garage door openers, and baby monitors.

The wireless receiver connects to the computer either through a USB port or through a PS/2 port. Keyboards and mice often connect through a wireless receiver that in turn connects to the PS/2 port intended for wired keyboard and mouse connection. Other wireless input devices use USB port connection for their receivers.

Wi-Fi

Wi-Fi is another wireless standard designed by a special interest group in much the same way Bluetooth was developed. Wi-Fi alliance was originally organized to produce a specification for interfacing with 2.4 GHz networking devices and network applications. It closely follows the IEEE 802.11 standard. Since the original Wi-Fi standard was released, it has expanded to include cameras, Web cams, laptops, phones, printers, game consoles, and many other devices that were once dominated by Bluetooth. Interestingly, Microsoft and Logitech have chosen not to include Wi-Fi as a choice for their mice and keyboard communications. Wi-Fi has similar power limitations as Bluetooth mainly because all radio equipment used in the USA must meet the FCC regulations.

Wi-Fi
the registered trademark of the Wi-Fi Alliance organization and that applies to any IEEE 802.11 wireless device that conforms to the Wi-Fi Alliance standard.

Be aware of the fact that both Bluetooth and Wi-Fi devices operate at the same RF frequency of 2.4 GHz and can cause interference for each other if they are in close proximity. In addition, Wi-Fi has devices that also operate at 5 GHz, but these devices are not typical short-range input devices.

Wireless USB

One of the latest specifications is the ***Wireless USB (WUSB)*** radio specification, which was developed by the USB organization. Essentially, WUSB is their implementation of wireless devices that use the radio frequencies between 3.1 GHz to 10.6 GHz. Wireless USB is designed to configure wireless communications between the PC and many common PC devices such as cameras, projectors, printers, scanners, and MP3 players. In general, USB wireless devices transfer more data per second than Bluetooth and Wi-Fi products. The USB wireless data rate at the time of this writing is 480 Mbps at 3 meters and 110 Mbps at 10 meters. As the distance between the wireless devices increases, data throughput decreases.

Wireless USB (WUSB)
the specification for USB wireless devices that uses the radio frequencies between 3.1 GHz to 10.6 GHz.

1394 Wireless FireWire

The 1394 FireWire cable system followed the same wireless path that USB followed, thus providing a wireless connection to 1394 FireWire devices in similar fashion as USB. 1394 wireless is based on the IEEE 802.15 standard. The IEEE 802.15 standard was developed for small personal wireless networks such as networks found in homes or offices. IEEE 802.15 data rates are between 11 Mbps and 55 Mbps and limited to 200 wireless devices. Future data rates are predicted at 110 Mbps and 480 Mbps.

Ultra-Wideband

Ultra-Wideband (UWB)
a short distance (10 meter) radio communication standard developed by the WiMedia Alliance.

Ultra-Wideband (UWB) is a short distance (10-meter) radio communication standard developed by the WiMedia Alliance. The WiMedia Alliance is a group of industry professionals who share a common interest in developing a high-bandwidth short-range wireless medium specification. UWB standard specifications use the 3.1 GHz to 10.6 GHz radio frequencies in contrast to other technologies that use the 27 MHz, 2.4 GHz, and 5 GHz radio frequencies. The USB and FireWire cable technologies actually base their wireless media on the UWB specifications. Even Bluetooth is in the process of developing a Bluetooth technology that will run on top of the higher-bandwidth UWB standard. This will allow Bluetooth to achieve data rates as high as 480 Mbps. At the time of this writing, the Bluetooth version 3.0 has not yet been released.

There will be more about wireless technologies presented in other chapters throughout the textbook when subjects such as laptop computers and networking are presented.

Synchronizing the Wireless Device

A typical wireless mouse and keyboard, **Figure 7-28,** is ready to use after installing or charging the batteries. The products are usually synchronized at the factory before shipping them to retailers. Synchronizing is the operation of matching a pair of devices to each other so that they recognize each other and not other wireless devices in the same general area of use.

After a few months of use, the device batteries may fail, or radio interference from another device other than the matched keyboard and mouse may interfere with the operation of the wireless device. In this case, the device must be synchronized with the receiving unit. Synchronization typically requires that a button on each device be pressed so that they can identify each other and then connect using the same frequency and an assigned channel. **Figure 7-29** shows the instructions printed on the back of the keyboard.

The diagram shows to first press the button on the receiver unit and then to press the button on the bottom of the mouse. The two wireless devices will establish a link as long as they are in range. The diagram indicates to wait 20 seconds for the synchronization to occur and then to repeat the process for the wireless keyboard. **Figure 7-30** shows a close-up of a synchronization button located on the bottom of a keyboard. As you can see, the button is labeled "CONNECT."

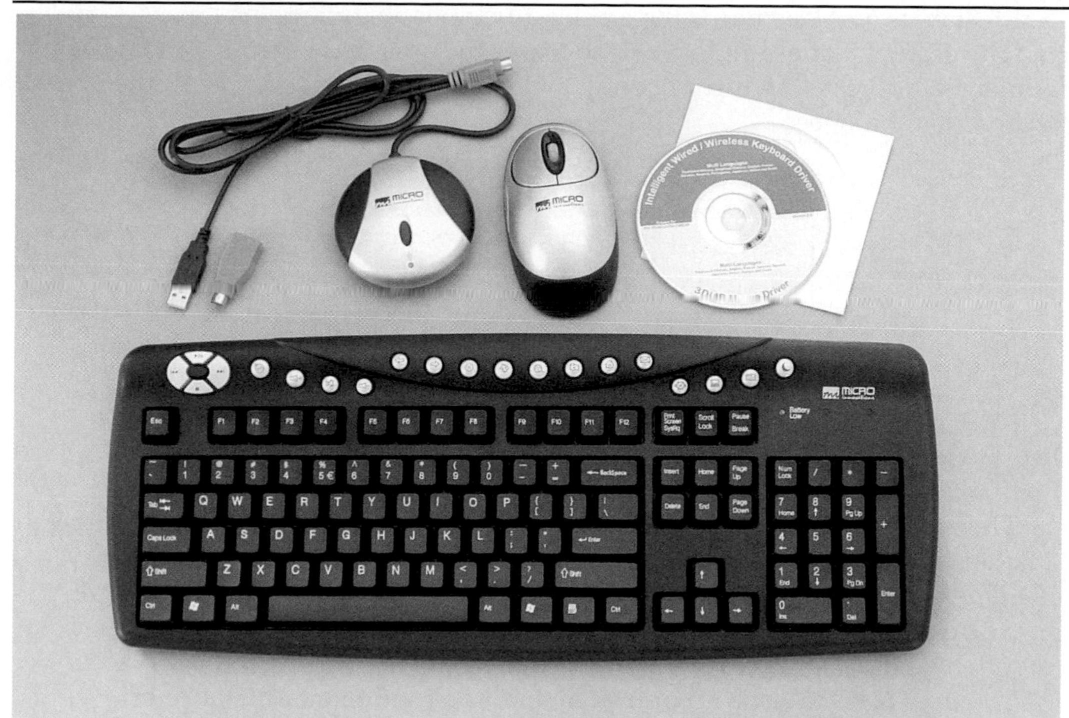

Figure 7-28.
Wireless keyboard and mouse with installation software.

Figure 7-29.
The back of this Logitech keyboard displays instructions for synchronizing the receiving unit with the mouse and keyboard.

Figure 7-30.
Close-up of the CONNECT button which is pressed when synchronizing the keyboard with the receiving unit.

Most mice and keyboards have at least two possible channels for communication. For example, Microsoft uses the assigned channels and frequencies indicated in the following table to match the receiver with the keyboard and mouse.

Device	Channel 1	Channel 2
Keyboard	27.095 MHz	27.195 MHz
Mouse	27.045 MHz	27.145 MHz

Wireless Device Failure

The most common reason for wireless input device failure is battery failure. A battery will last six months on average. You can expect more or less battery life depending on how much the device is used each day. Also, some batteries provide energy longer than others. Rechargeable batteries last much longer. They can often be used for up to five years or more before requiring to be replaced.

You may need to clean an optical mouse as a routine maintenance or troubleshooting problem. First, clean the optical lens area using a dry lint-free cloth or use dry compressed air designed for this purpose. If this fails to clean the unit, check the manufacturer's Web site or product literature to see what chemical cleaners, if any, are safe to use on the unit.

Another common reason for failure is radio interference. Many other electronic devices use the same radio frequency that is assigned to wireless devices. For example, baby monitors, garage door openers, microwave ovens, wireless phones, and more.

Many times you can counter the effects of radio interference by using a different assigned channel. Some wireless devices have several different channels to choose from when configuring the device. If radio interference is suspected as a cause for wireless connection failure or very low data rates, you may want to change the assigned channel. You can locate the exact method to change an assigned channel by checking the device documentation or the manufacturer's Web site. There will be much more about wireless technology in later chapters.

Virtual Keyboard

Canesta has developed a virtual keyboard designed to work with PCs, personal digital assistants (PDAs), smart phones, and any application where an input device might be required. The Canesta system consists of three main components: the sensor module, the infrared light source, and the pattern projector, **Figure 7-31.**

The infrared light source and pattern projector work together to create an image of a keyboard. The keyboard image can be projected onto any surface. The light of the keyboard image is reflected off the surface to a set of light sensors. The user simply types on the image just as though it was a real keyboard. The user's finger motions interrupt the light pattern representing the keyboard. The light sensors detect interruptions in the reflected light. The light sensor module converts the interruptions into digital signals that represent the keys touched by the user. See **Figure 7-32.**

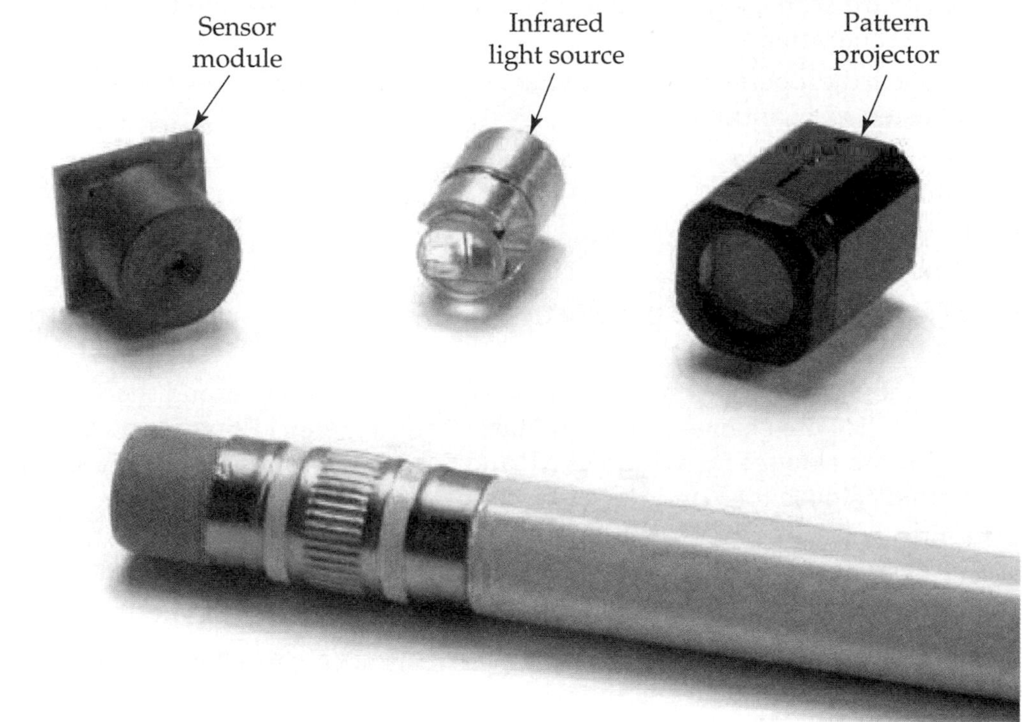

Figure 7-31.
The virtual keyboard by Canesta is constructed from three main devices: the sensor module, the infrared light source, and the pattern projector. (Canesta, Inc.)

Figure 7-32.
The user's finger movements interrupt the light pattern representing the keyboard. The light sensor module detects the interruptions and converts them into digital signals that represent the keys touched by the user. (Canesta, Inc.)

Summary

- ✔ There are four standard types of keyboard input switch designs: mechanical, membrane, rubber dome, and capacitor.
- ✔ Keyboard scan codes are interpreted by the BIOS and sent to the CPU as an ASCII character.
- ✔ Keyboard properties such as characters per second and repeat delay can be adjusted via Control Panel.
- ✔ The common styles of keyboard and mouse connectors are the 6-pin mini-DIN and USB.
- ✔ Ergonomic keyboards are shaped for comfort and help prevent carpal tunnel syndrome.
- ✔ If a mouse is connected directly to the motherboard, it is usually assigned IRQ12.
- ✔ The mouse properties such as size and style of the pointer and the speed of the click are changed through **Start | Control Panel | Printers and Other Hardware | Mouse** for Windows XP and **Start | Control Panel | Hardware and Sound | Mouse** for Windows Vista.
- ✔ Optical mouse movement is rated in DPI and FPS.
- ✔ The game port usually can be a 15-pin, two-row D-shell connector or a USB connector.
- ✔ The major touch screen technologies are resistance, capacitance, near field effect, infrared, and acoustical wave.
- ✔ Wireless input devices operate using infrared light or radio transmission.
- ✔ Infrared is a line of sight medium which means the transmitter and receiver must have a direct, unobstructed view between them.
- ✔ RF signals can pass through most building materials, but the thickness and type of material may reduce or completely block the signal.
- ✔ Bluetooth, Wi-Fi, and the IEEE 802.11 standard all use the 2.4 GHz radio frequency.
- ✔ Wi-Fi and 802.11 also use the 5 GHz radio frequency.
- ✔ Ultra-Wideband (UWB) is a radio communication standard developed by the WiMedia Alliance that utilizes the 3.1 GHz to 10.6 GHz radio frequencies.
- ✔ The most common reason for wireless device failure is batteries.

Review Questions

Answer the following questions on a separate sheet of paper. Please do not write in this book.

1. Scan codes are always equal to ASCII codes. True or False?
2. What are the four types of keyboard switches?
3. What are the two main keyboard connector styles called?
4. Is the keyboard a parallel or a serial device?
5. What is carpal tunnel syndrome?
6. How do you clean a keyboard that has a sugary drink spilled on it?
7. What is the path to the **Keyboard Properties** dialog box in Windows XP?
8. List two advantages of an optical mouse.
9. What is the commonly used IRQ setting for a mouse with a direct motherboard interface?
10. What is a CCD?
11. What measurements are used to compare optical mice?
12. Identify five touch screen technologies that are incorporated into the touch screen matrix.
13. What type of touch screen would you use in a dusty environment?
14. What type of touch screen would you choose for a medical surgical room where the staff commonly wears rubber or latex gloves?
15. What are the four major wireless radio input device classifications?
16. What common radio frequency does Bluetooth and Wi-Fi use?
17. What standard is associated with wireless keyboard and mouse devices?
18. What is the main advantage of RF over infrared technology?
19. List four devices that can interfere with a wireless RF device.
20. What frequencies are supported by the UWB specifications?
21. What three main parts comprise the Canesta virtual light keyboard?

Sample A+ Exam Questions

Answer the following questions on a separate sheet of paper. Please do not write in this book.

1. Which two connection ports are most commonly associated with keyboards? Select two.
   a. 15-pin D shell
   b. PS/2
   c. USB
   d. LPT1
2. What is a keyboard buffer?
   a. A mechanical device designed to keep the individual keys from striking the keyboard backing too severely.
   b. A special IC designed to suppress electrical surges directed from the keyboard.
   c. An IC designed as a small memory unit to temporarily store keyboard-generated signals.
   d. A mechanical device designed to remove debris and shine keyboard keys.
3. A ball mouse is behaving erratically. When moved in certain directions, it seems to work fine. However, when moving in different directions, it skips or stalls. What would most likely remedy the condition?
   a. Reinstall the mouse driver software.
   b. Check the connection for a bent pin.
   c. Clean the mouse ball and rollers.
   d. Open the **Mouse** dialog box in **Control Panel** and adjust the movement speed of the mouse pointer.
4. Which best defines a keyboard scan code?
   a. A keyboard scan code is a signal generated when a key is struck on the keyboard. It determines what symbol is displayed on the monitor.
   b. A keyboard scan code is a signal generated by the keyboard scan generator. It checks what key is being pressed and then generates the corresponding ASCII symbol.
   c. A keyboard scan code is a binary code that records the duration that a key is held down.
   d. A keyboard scan code is generated by the CPU and then sent to the keyboard to identify which key is being pressed.
5. The physical design of a keyboard is referred to as what?
   a. Ergonomics
   b. Ecology
   c. Carpelmatics
   d. Physiology
6. Which of the following items is best for cleaning a keyboard?
   a. Windex
   b. A solution of 50% alcohol and 50% water
   c. Distilled water
   d. Any vacuum cleaner

7. Which technology does an optical mouse use?
    a. It is a wireless radio communication model.
    b. It uses a rotating wheel that breaks up a light signal into digital pulses.
    c. It uses CCD CMOS technology similar to digital camera technology.
    d. It uses an optical rubber ball that lights the surface of the material it passes over.
8. Which frequency is typically associated with Bluetooth and Wi-Fi devices?
    a. 2.4 GHz
    b. 24 MHz
    c. 5 GHz
    d. 5 MHz
9. Which is the correct path to access the mouse configuration speed setting on a Windows XP computer?
    a. **Start | Mouse | Settings**
    b. **Start | Control Panel | Printers and Other Devices | Mouse**
    c. **Start | Control Panel | Pointing Device**
    d. **Start | Control Panel | Device Manager**
10. What similar light-sensitive device do scanners and digital cameras use to acquire an image?
    a. OCR
    b. CMOS
    c. ADC
    d. CCD

Suggested Laboratory Activities

Do not attempt any suggested laboratory activities without your instructor's permission. Certain activities can render the PC operating system inoperable.

1. Change the keyboard properties, such as the **Repeat rate** and **Repeat delay** settings, to see the effects on the keyboard. For Windows XP, access the **Keyboard** icon through **Control Panel | Printers and Other Hardware**. For Windows Vista, the **Keyboard** icon is accessed through **Control Panel | Hardware and Sound.**
2. Try installing a second language for the keyboard in Windows Vista. This is done through **Control Panel | Clock, Language, and Region | Change display options**. You will most likely need the operating system installation CD.
3. Unplug the keyboard and restart the system. Observe any error codes that may appear. Also, listen for any beep sounds indicating a problem. Repeat the experiment by unplugging the mouse.
4. Open the **Mouse Properties** dialog box and change the appearance of the tail, the click speed, and the type of icon used for the mouse pointer. Access **Mouse Properties** in Windows XP through **Control Panel | Printers and Other Hardware | Mouse**. In Windows Vista, the path is **Control Panel | Hardware and Sound | Mouse**.

Interesting Web Sites for More Information

www.americanmicrosystems.com

www.blackbox.com/Tech_Support/Technical-documents/connector-guide.aspx

www.irda.org

www.logitech.com

www.microsoft.com

www.mobileinfo.com/Bluetooth/FAQ.htm

www.palowireless.com/infotooth/tutorial.asp

www.usb.org

www.wi-fi.org/knowledge_center_overview.php

Chapter 7
Laboratory Activity
Windows Vista Keyboard Properties

After completing this laboratory activity, you will be able to:

✔ Adjust typing characteristics of a typical keyboard.
✔ Explain the purpose of the **Roll Back Driver** option.
✔ Explain the purpose of the **Update Driver** option.
✔ Explain the purpose of a digital signature as related to hardware drivers.

Introduction

As a PC technician, you may be called to make certain adjustments to the keyboard. Many people, especially professional secretaries, are sensitive to keyboard characteristics such as the repeat rate of a pressed key. In this lab activity, you will make adjustments to the keyboard typing rate characteristics. You will also select a set of language characters, other than English, to be output by the keyboard.

You will also see where the software driver options are located. You will be able to install a new version of a driver. You will also see the location of where to reverse the installation of a software driver.

This lab activity will also introduce you to some of the software driver options available to you in both Windows XP and Windows Vista. The following is a screen capture of one of the **Keyboard Properties** dialog boxes of Windows Vista. It is also very similar in Windows XP.

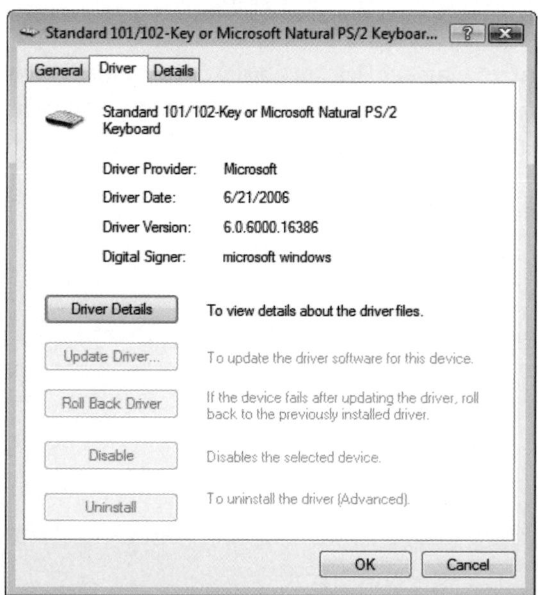

There are several driver option buttons you need to be aware of. These choices are available for all hardware devices.

- ✔ **Driver Details:** Used to display details about the software drivers such as the manufacturer, version, copyright, and if the file is digitally signed. A digitally signed driver ensures that this driver is the real software driver from the stated manufacturer and not malware.
- ✔ **Update Driver:** Allows you to install a newer version of the software driver.
- ✔ **Roll Back Driver:** Removes the latest software driver version installed and replaces it with the previously installed driver.
- ✔ **Disable driver:** Disables the device.
- ✔ **Uninstall Driver:** Removes the installed driver.

These buttons may be shaded and not available as an option if no previous version of the driver exists. These options are available for all types of hardware devices. This is also the preferred method of removing a driver. Never attempt to delete the driver file manually or use some other method to replace or remove the driver. There will be more about driver replacement in other lab activities.

Note:
When some software driver features are not available through the keyboard properties dialog box, they may be available through ***Device Manager****. The* ***Device Manager*** *is intended for technicians, while the simple* ***Keyboard Properties*** *dialog box is typically used by common users.*

Equipment and Materials

- ✔ Typical PC running Windows XP or Windows Vista.

Procedure

1. _______ Report to your assigned workstation and boot the computer. Wait for the desktop to be displayed.
2. _______ Access the **Keyboard Properties** dialog box. For Windows XP, use **Control Panel | Printers and Other Hardware | Keyboard.** For Windows Vista, use **Control Panel | Hardware and Sound | Keyboard**. You should see a dialog box similar to the following.

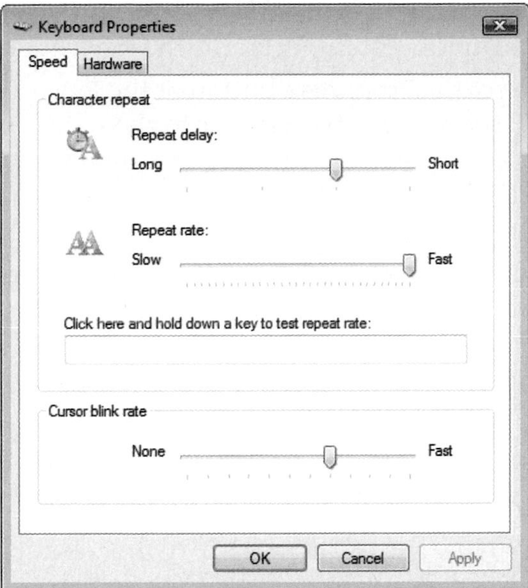

The *repeat delay* is the adjustment for the amount of delay before the first keyboard character will appear after the key is pressed.

The *repeat rate* is the delay between each character appearance on the display or how rapidly the characters appear.

3. ________ Before making any adjustments, test the repeat rate and repeat delay by typing in the text box provided.

4 ________ Adjust both the repeat delay and the repeat rate, and then test the new rates by typing into the test text box. Experiment to see the effects of each.

5. ________ Adjust the cursor blink rate. The rate should change immediately after changing the position of the **Cursor blink rate** slider.

6. ________ Select the **Hardware** tab located at the top of the dialog box. You will see a dialog box similar to the following.

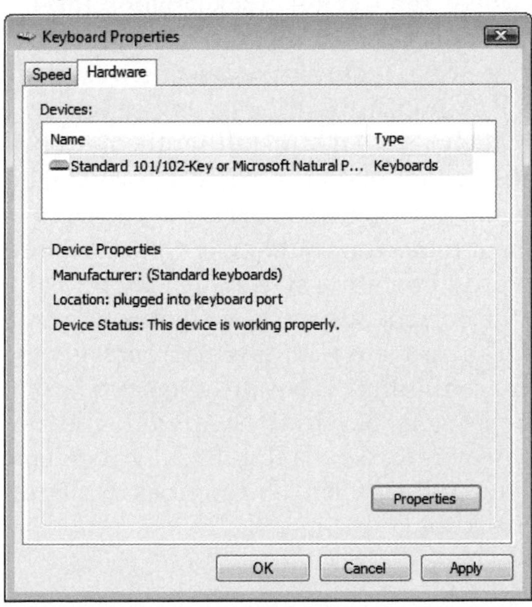

The **Hardware** tab reveals information such as the manufacturer, port used, and most importantly, the device status.

7. _______ Now, select the **Properties** button at the lower right-hand corner. You will see a dialog box similar to the following.

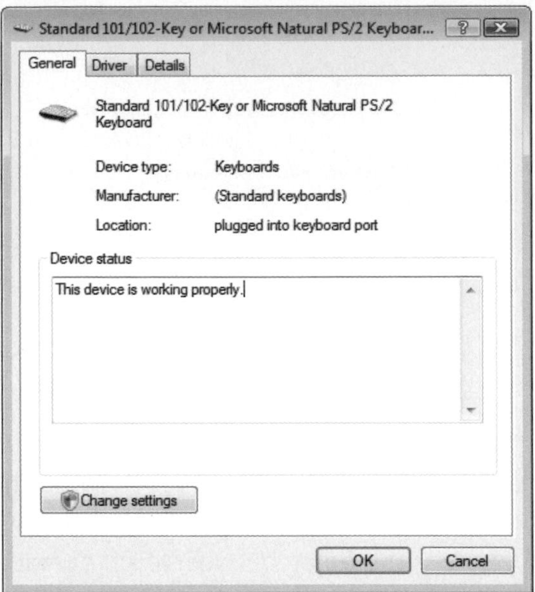

The **Device status** textbox provides a general condition of the hardware device. In the screen capture, you see that the device is working properly. When the device is not working properly, a possible explanation and related information will be presented in the textbox. The same detailed information is revealed under the **Details** tab.

8. _______ Select the **Driver** tab. You will see information about the software drivers installed for the keyboard. Pay particular attention to the **Update Driver** and the **Roll Back Driver** buttons. The **Roll Back Driver** option is very handy and is the preferred method to undo a software driver that was incorrectly installed. For example, a hardware manufacturer offers a newer version of a software driver for your keyboard. After installing the newer driver, the keyboard does not function properly. There are several options to repair this situation. You could install a complete system backup, which would take a lot of time. You could do a system restore. A system restore is a Microsoft operating system feature that allows the system to replace the current operating system configuration with an earlier version. The problem with this approach is that it may change other hardware configuration besides the keyboard. It will also convert to earlier software applications as well. The most sensible and effective way is to use the Roll Back Driver feature. Later in this course, you will perform lab activities explaining this feature and system backups.

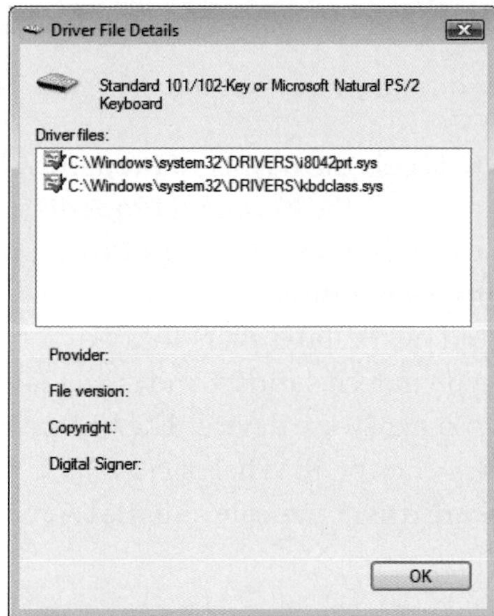

The **Driver Details** option reveals information about the provider, file version, copyright, and digital signature. If the **Driver Details** option does not appear, try selecting one of the files listed in the text box by clicking it with the mouse. No detail information will appear unless a file is selected.

Also, be aware that the exact location or path of the driver file is indicated in the text box. In the example, the kbdclass.sys file is located in the Windows\system32\drivers directory. This is where all the 32-bit software drivers are generally located for Windows XP and Windows Vista.

Try using Windows Explorer to locate the file. You must have administrative rights to access system files.

9. _______ Under the **Driver** tab of **Keyboard Properties**, notice the **Disable Driver** option. This option is available for all hardware devices. It allows you to temporarily disable a hardware device while troubleshooting or for some other reason. For example, suppose you are using a laptop that has a built-in keyboard and you wish to use a USB full-size keyboard instead. Most of the time, the operating system will identify the USB keyboard and make it the default, but there are times when the two might conflict with each other. You could temporarily disable the default keyboard by clicking the **Disable Driver** button after opening the corresponding properties dialog box.

10. _______ Take a few minutes to practice accessing the **Keyboard Properties** dialog box starting from the **Start** menu.

11. _______ Go on to answer the review questions. Then, return all materials and leave the workstation in the condition you found it.

Review Questions

Answer the following questions on a separate sheet of paper. Please do not write in this book.

1. What is the path to access the **Keyboard Properties** in Windows XP?
2. What is the path to access the **Keyboard Properties** in Windows Vista?
3. Why would you use the system **Roll Back Driver** option rather than a system backup or system restore?
4. Where are the Windows 32-bit drivers located?
5. A customer calls you in tech support and says that they cannot roll back the driver for a hardware device. The button is there, but nothing happens when they click on it. What is *most likely* the reason?
6. Why does a software driver indicate a digital signature?

Video Display and Audio Systems

After studying this chapter, you will be able to:

- ✔ Describe the basic operation of the CRT.
- ✔ Describe the basic operation of an LCD panel.
- ✔ Explain screen resolution.
- ✔ Define screen pitch.
- ✔ Explain the major steps for installing a video adapter card.
- ✔ Explain the major steps of installing a sound card.
- ✔ Define different display systems.
- ✔ Explain how data compression works.
- ✔ Explain how MIDI produces sound.
- ✔ Compare WAV file and MIDI file types.
- ✔ Explain how sampling rate and number of bits determine the quality of analog-to-digital conversion.

A+ Exam—Key Points

Be very familiar with screen resolutions associated with different displays, especially VGA and XGA. A scenario question concerning the assignments of system resources may be asked about a sound or video card.

Key Words and Terms

The following words and terms will become important pieces of your computer vocabulary. Be sure you can define them.

active-matrix display
alternating-frame rendering
aspect ratio
bitmap (.bmp)
buffering
cathode ray tube (CRT)
codec
color palette
color/graphics adapter (CGA)
contrast ratio
deflection yoke
digital-to-analog converter (DAC)
dot pitch
electron guns
enhanced graphics adapter (EGA)
extended graphics array (XGA)
field
gas-plasma displays
liquid crystal display (LCD)
monochrome
Motion Picture Experts Group (MPEG)
multicolor/graphics array (MCGA)
multimedia
musical instrument digital interface (MIDI)
native resolution
passive-matrix display
persistence
pixel
pixel pitch
polarized light
raster
refresh rate
resolution
response time
run-length encoding (RLE)
sampling
shadow mask
split-frame rendering
Super VGA (SVGA)
thin film transistor liquid crystal display (TFT-LCD)
vector graphics
video graphics array (VGA)
viewing angle

The display system of a computer consists of two main components: the display and the adapter. The video adapter is often called a *video card*, or *graphics card*. There are some references made to legacy video systems in this chapter. Many of these legacy systems are no longer manufactured. This brief information, however, will help you understand the development of the computer video system as well as help you identify obsolete systems when you encounter them. There are still a number of these old technologies in existence. Being unable to identify them can be extremely frustrating and embarrassing to any technician.

A computer video display can be very dangerous. The inside of a computer monitor has voltages present in excess of 20,000 volts. In addition, the monitor can store high voltages for a long period of time after the power has been disconnected.

A monitor should only be opened by a trained and qualified electronics technician. The scope of this textbook is not to train you as a monitor repair person but rather to give you the necessary skills to install, calibrate, and diagnose common monitor problems. Do *not* open a computer monitor case for any reason.

Display Aspects

There are a number of features common to all monitors. These features, such as dot pitch and size, greatly affect the quality of the picture produced as well as the price you will pay for the unit.

Monitor Size

Sizes of monitors are similar to television sets. The length of a diagonal drawn from one corner to the opposite corner determines the size of a monitor. See **Figure 8-1.**

Standard monitor sizes are 14″, 15″, 17″, 19″, and 21.″ The actual viewing area is approximately 10% less than the diagonal measurement, though it varies from monitor to monitor.

A+ Note:

Most PC systems use a three-row 15-pin D-shell connector for the monitor. The game port is usually a two-row 15-pin D-shell connector. The A+ Certification exams may ask a question about identifying one of these two ports on the PC.

dot pitch
the distance between two color dots on the screen, measured in millimeters.

Dot Pitch

The ***dot pitch*** is the distance measured in millimeters between two color dots on the screen. The dot pitch is a measurement that reflects the quality of the image displayed. Generally, if the monitor has a smaller dot pitch, it produces a higher quality (sharper) image. An acceptable standard dot pitch is from 0.28 mm to 0.25 mm. The dot pitch cannot be adjusted. It is manufactured into the screen.

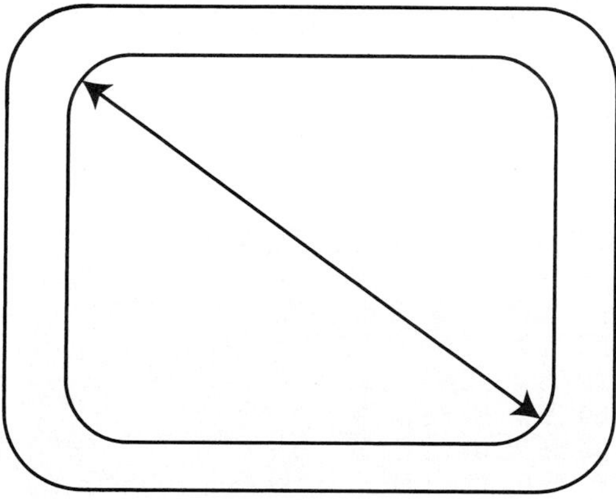

Figure 8-1. Computer display screen sizes are measured on the diagonal.

Color Display Values

The color display quality is determined by the number of bits used to represent the individual colors of red, green, and blue. The number of bits used to represent each color can determine the possible number of color shades. A byte contains 8 bits. This means that there are a total of 256 possible combinations of 1s and 0s in a byte. This means that an 8-bit color pattern can reproduce 256 intensities of a specific color. By mixing the intensities of red, blue, and green, other colors can be produced.

Figure 8-2 is a listing of common standard color display values, expressed in bits. As the number of bits increases, so does the number of possible colors produced.

The color mix guide in **Figure 8-3** shows the application of 256,000 color intensities and the total spectrum of color produced by the monitor. This illustration is a screen capture taken from the **Edit Colors** command from Microsoft's Paint program. Paint can be found in the **Accessories** section of Windows. Using the **Edit Colors** dialog box, you can create your own pallet of colors beyond the standard colors. By moving your mouse across the sample of colors in the display, the amount of red, blue, and green that make up the custom color is varied. In the bottom-right corner are three numeric text boxes. Each box contains the value of the color used to make the color indicated under the cursor. The values correspond to the 8-bit range (0 to 255). This is an example of a 24-bit color system.

Display Resolution

resolution
the amount of detail a monitor is capable of displaying.

The term ***resolution*** refers to the amount of detail a monitor is capable of displaying. This term is also used to describe the detail produced by printers, digital cameras, and any similar type of graphic equipment. High resolution equals finer, better detail than low resolution. Look at **Figure 8-4** for a comparison of resolution patterns.

Figure 8-2.
Common standard color display values.

Color Display Value	Number of Colors
8-bit	256
16-bit (True color)	65,536
24-bit (True color)	16,000,000
32-bit (True color)	4,000,000,000

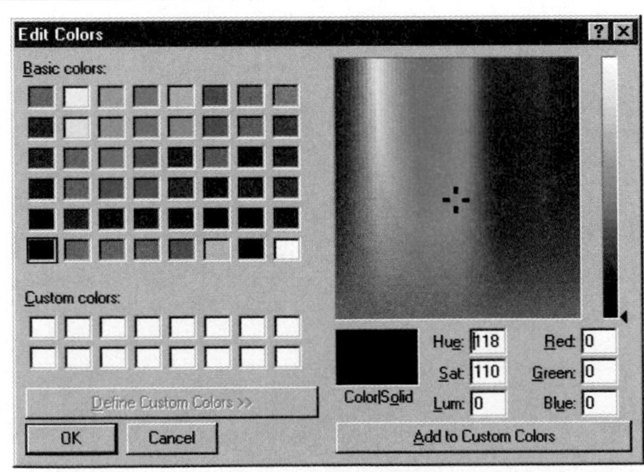

Figure 8-3.
With this color mix guide, you can display 256,000 color intensities and the total spectrum of color produced by the monitor.

Figure 8-4.
A comparison of resolution patterns. The image of the PC setup is shown on the left at high resolution (300 dpi). On the right, the same image is shown at a low resolution (72 dpi).

Resolution is measured in pixels (*pic*ture *el*ement). A ***pixel*** is the smallest unit of color in a screen display. Think of it as a small dot. A typical VGA system has a resolution of 640 × 480. This means a VGA has a screen layout of 640 pixels by 480 pixels or a total of 307,200 pixels. The most common resolutions are listed in **Figure 8-5.**

When PCs first came to the marketplace, most displays were monochrome display adapters (MDA). ***Monochrome*** technology uses only one color. Usually the color was amber or green. The adapters were designed to display text only, not graphics. Graphics required a good deal of memory, and at that time large amounts of memory were too expensive for most users. Early computers were used for business and research, not for entertainment. The screen resolution was 720 × 350, which presented a very sharp, clear image for text only.

In 1981, IBM introduced the ***color/graphics adapter (CGA).*** It offered two resolutions: 320 × 200 in four colors (from a choice of sixteen colors) and a higher resolution of 640 × 200 in two colors. Another company offered the Hercules adapter card. It met the requirements of graphics programs (such as AutoCAD) that the IBM adapter could not fulfill. The Hercules adapter card resolution was 720 × 348.

In 1987, IBM introduced the ***enhanced graphics adapter (EGA).*** The EGA system could display 16 colors in 640 × 200 or 320 × 200 resolution on a standard IBM color monitor. In monochrome, it could display a 640 × 350 resolution. When the EGA was attached to an enhanced color monitor, it could display 16 colors (from a choice of 64) in a resolution of 640 × 350.

pixel
the smallest unit of color in a screen display.

monochrome
a monitor type that displays only a single color, usually amber or green.

color/graphics adapter (CGA)
a video standard that featured two resolutions: 320 × 200 in four colors and a higher resolution of 640 × 200 in two colors.

enhanced graphics adapter (EGA)
a video standard that improved on the resolutions and color capabilities of the CGA standard.

Resolution	Acronym	Designation
640 × 480	VGA	Video Graphics Array
800 × 600	SVGA	Super VGA
1024 × 768	XGA	Extended Graphics Array
1280 × 1024	UVGA	Ultra VGA
1400 × 1050	SXGA	Super XGA
1600 × 1200	UXGA	Ultra XGA
1920 × 1200	WUXGA	Wide Ultra XGA

Figure 8-5.
Chart of common resolutions.

video graphics array (VGA)
the minimum standard for video adapters, that displays at a resolution of 640 × 480 with 16 colors or 320 × 200 with 256 colors.

color palette
a collection of possible different colors that may be displayed on a monitor.

The ***video graphics array (VGA)*** is the baseline for video adapters today. The VGA standard was first introduced in 1987 with the IBM PS/2. VGA is the true minimum standard for video monitors at a resolution of 640 × 480 and 16 colors. Up to 256 colors can be displayed, but the resolution is reduced to 320 × 200.

The VGA palette contains 262,144 (256K) different colors. A ***color palette*** is a collection of possible different colors usually in degrees or shades, which can be displayed on a monitor. The palette contains a large variety of possible colors, but the total number of colors in the palette cannot be displayed at the same time on a monitor. For example, a video system such as VGA that can display up to 256 colors in the 320 × 200 mode can only use 256 colors from the total 262,144 colors possible in the palette.

Think of the color palette as the total number of tubes of color an artist has available to purchase from a supplier. While there may be 262,144 colors in the store, the artist can only afford to buy 256 tubes. Thus, the actual number of colors used for the painting is limited to the 256 colors. In the same way, while there are 262,144 colors that can be displayed in VGA, the video adapter can only support 256 of the total number at one time.

When a computer system detects a malfunction, it will start in safe mode, which only supports the minimum video standard of VGA. The VGA mode driver is located in the first 1 MB of memory while more sophisticated drivers require memory above the first 1 MB.

Also in 1987, the PS/2 display adapter 8514 was also introduced. It had better resolution than VGA and offered more colors. It supported a resolution of 1024 × 768 pixels with 256 colors. There were some disadvantages to the system, however. First, the system plugged into IBM micro-channel architecture. Second, to take full advantage of its capabilities, an 8514 color display monitor had to be used. This PS/2 display adapter was replaced by the IBM XGA standard.

It is interesting to note that EGA, VGA, and the PS/2 adapter 8514 came out at about the same time. However, only VGA survived the consumer marketplace.

multicolor/graphics array (MCGA)
a video standard that supported CGA and also provided up to 64 shades of gray.

super VGA (SVGA)
a video standard that supports 16 million colors and various resolutions up to 1600 × 1200.

Another standard of the time was ***multicolor/graphics array (MCGA)***. The MCGA adapter could support CGA, and also provided up to 64 shades of gray when more color variations than the standard CGA were required to be displayed.

Super VGA (SVGA) supports 16 million possible colors and various resolutions such as 800 × 600, 1024 × 768, 1280 × 1024, and 1600 × 1200. The exact number of colors that can be displayed at the same time on an SVGA monitor is determined by the amount of memory. The higher the memory, the higher the number of colors produced.

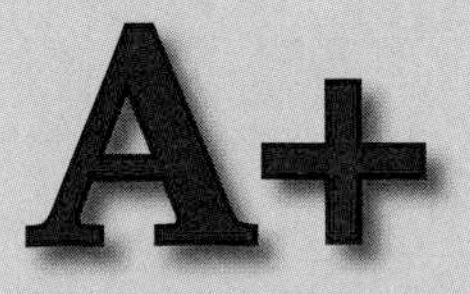

A+ Note:

All the previously mentioned types of display adapters with the exception of VGA have been discontinued. The reason that they are mentioned in this text is to keep you on alert for difficult questions on the A+ Certification exams. For example, if given EGA and XGA as answers for a multiple-choice question about video properties, confusion could result in an incorrect response.

In 1990, IBM introduced the ***extended graphics array (XGA).*** It is capable of a resolution of 640 × 480 while supporting 65,536 colors and 1024 × 768 with 256 colors. It also supports all of IBM's older graphic standards.

extended graphics array (XGA)
a video standard that supports a resolution of 640 × 480 with 65,536 colors, or 1024 × 768 with 256 colors.

You will see the label Ultra VGA used in advertising. Ultra VGA is not a true standard but rather a marking terminology that is used by manufacturers to describe their video adapters and monitors in an enhanced description.

The UVGA, SXGA, UXGA, and WUXGA screen resolution naturally evolved from the original VGA and XGA screen resolutions and are the most commonly encountered today. They are all capable of producing over 16 million colors and are capable of supporting the new HDTV standard of resolution. When you see a display that is very wide, it will be usually UXGA or WUXGA. These resolutions are normally used to match the very wide display units.

When the Windows Vista operating system starts in safe mode, the screen resolution changes to 640 × 480, the original VGA standard. Compare the 640 × 480 resolution, **Figure 8-6,** to the standard 1024 × 768 XGA resolution, **Figure 8-7.** Notice how much larger the desktop icons appear when in the VGA screen resolution of safe mode. There will be more about safe mode in Chapter 15—PC Troubleshooting.

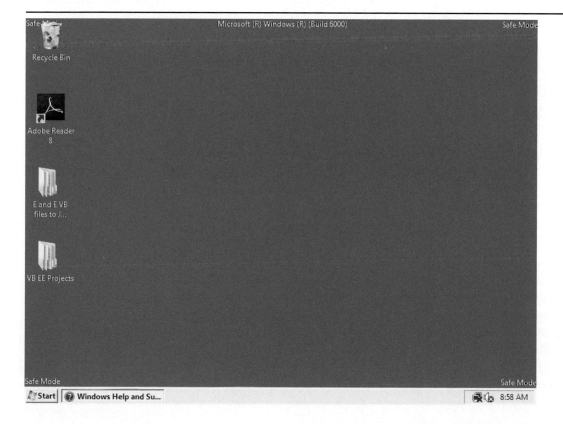

Figure 8-6. Windows Vista in safe mode. The resolution is 640 × 480, which is the resolution of the original VGA standard.

Figure 8-7. Windows Vista desktop in 1024 × 768 XGA resolution.

A+ Note:

The A+ Certification exams will often contain a question referring to the VGA resolution. This is because VGA is the default resolution during the safe mode startup process.

Types of Video Displays

There are a number of different types of display systems for computers. The two most common types are the *cathode ray tube (CRT)* and the *liquid crystal display (LCD)*. See **Figure 8-8** and **Figure 8-9.** As the television industry merges computer and television technology into a single display unit, it will no longer be possible to distinguish a computer monitor from a television. Because of this, the gas plasma display will also be discussed in this section. This section covers the basic operation and principles of all three display technologies and the terminology with which they are commonly associated.

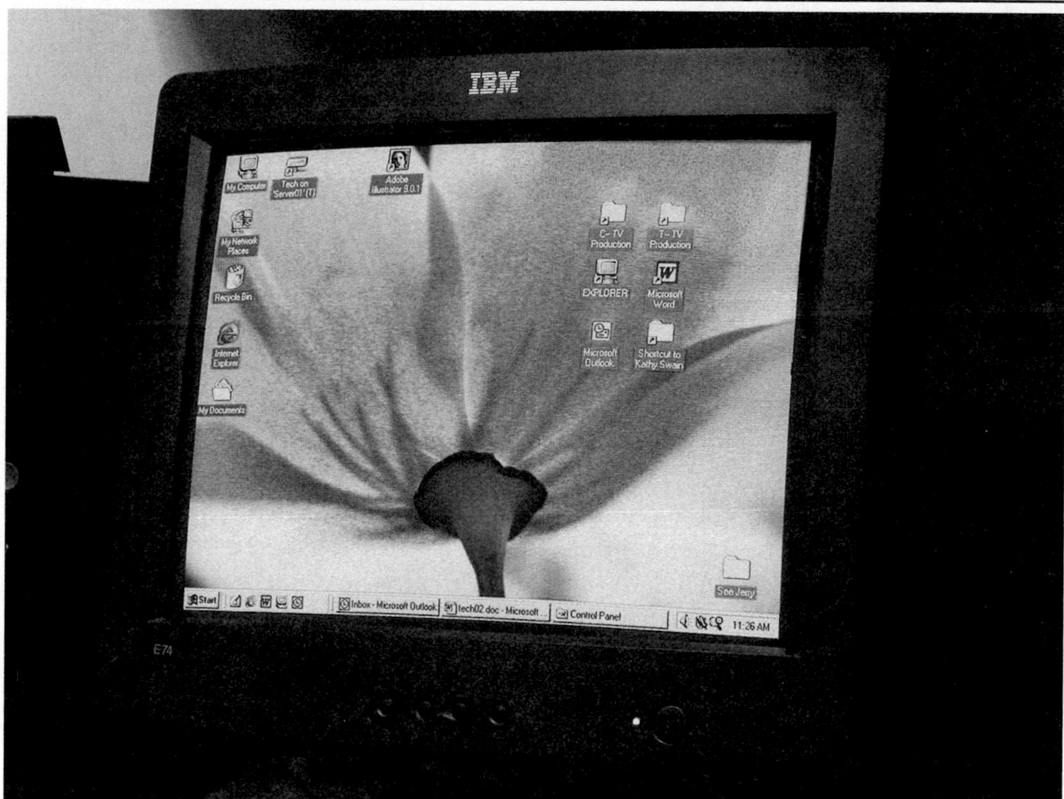

Figure 8-8.
CRT display used with a desktop computer.

Figure 8-9.
The LCD monitor, because of its thin profile, takes up less desktop space than the CRT.

Cathode Ray Tube Displays

cathode ray tube (CRT)
a picture tube in which a beam of electrons sweeps across the glass tube, exciting phosphorous dots in the screen.

A ***cathode ray tube (CRT)*** is a glass tube in which electrons are used to produce a picture. To understand how a CRT monitor works, you must first understand some basic electricity concepts. A brief discussion of electron theory will help you understand how the flow of electrons can create an image on a screen.

When electrons flow through a wire, similar to a filament in a lightbulb, heat and light are produced. The filament is placed inside a glass-enclosed vacuum. A vacuum contains no oxygen. Oxygen is needed for supporting fire, thus the vacuum prevents the destruction of the filament by burning. The vacuum prevents the wire from burning while producing the heat and light.

This is the most you usually need to know about a lightbulb. But, in addition to the heat and light, a cloud of electrons forms around the filament. The greater the electron flow through the filament, the larger the cloud of electrons. The movement and direction of the cloud of electrons can be controlled by a magnetic field. By shaping a magnetic field into a ring, the electron cloud can be shaped into a beam of electrons. The beam direction can also be deflected by magnetic fields. The formation of an electron beam and the action of deflecting the direction of the beam are the underlying principles behind producing an image on a computer monitor as well as on a television screen. See **Figure 8-10.**

Figure 8-10.
Televisions and CRT computer monitors use the same electronic principles to produce images. (Sylvania-GTE)

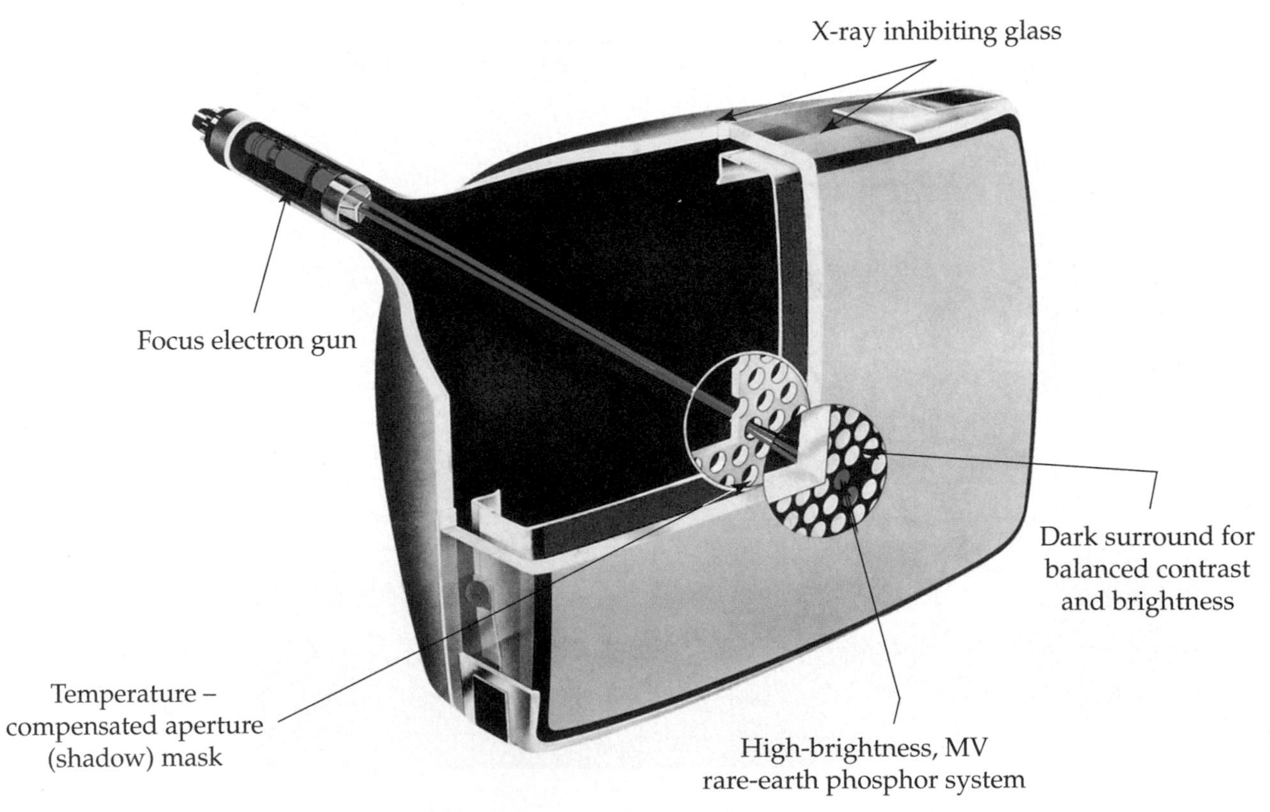

A second important safety concern is implosion. A CRT is under a vacuum condition. When broken, the pieces of glass will at first be sucked into the glass envelope and will then burst out into the surrounding area. Severe damage to personnel can occur from a monitor tube bursting.

Three ***electron guns*** are located at the back of the CRT. The guns produce the electron beam, which sweeps across the inside of the monitor screen. The CRT ***deflection yoke*** area contains electromagnets. The intensity of the magnets can be changed to deflect the electron beam horizontally and vertically. The deflection yoke controls the location where each of the three electronic beams strikes the screen area.

The beam then passes through a metal mesh called a ***shadow mask.*** The shadow mask is designed as a pattern of triangular or rectangular holes. The shadow mask pattern of holes limits the area of the screen the electron beam can strike. The design of the shadow mask holes produces a much sharper image than would be produced without the shadow mask. The shadow mask determines the dot pitch of the monitor. The beam passes through the shadow mask and strikes the inside of the display screen. The screen area is coated with phosphorus material. The phosphor material is spread across the screen of the monitor in a pattern of red, blue, and green. When the electron beam strikes the color areas, they glow red, blue, and green accordingly. The intensity of the electron beam is directly related to the intensity of color produced in the area struck by the beam. The phosphor areas continue to glow after the electron beam ceases to strike the area. The continuation of the glow after the beam leaves the area is called ***persistence.*** The persistence of the color glow must last long enough so that it does not disappear before the electron beam strikes the phosphor again. By mixing the intensities of the three colors, a complete spectrum of colors can be produced. Look at **Figure 8-11.**

electron guns
the components that produce the electron beam, which sweeps across the inside of the screen.

deflection yoke
the electromagnets used to deflect the electron beam in a CRT.

shadow mask
a metal mesh with triangular holes that a CRT's electron beam passes through, creating a crisper image.

persistence
the continuation of the glow after the electron beam ceases to strike the phosphor areas.

Figure 8-11.
Red, green, and blue are the basic colors used in a CRT.

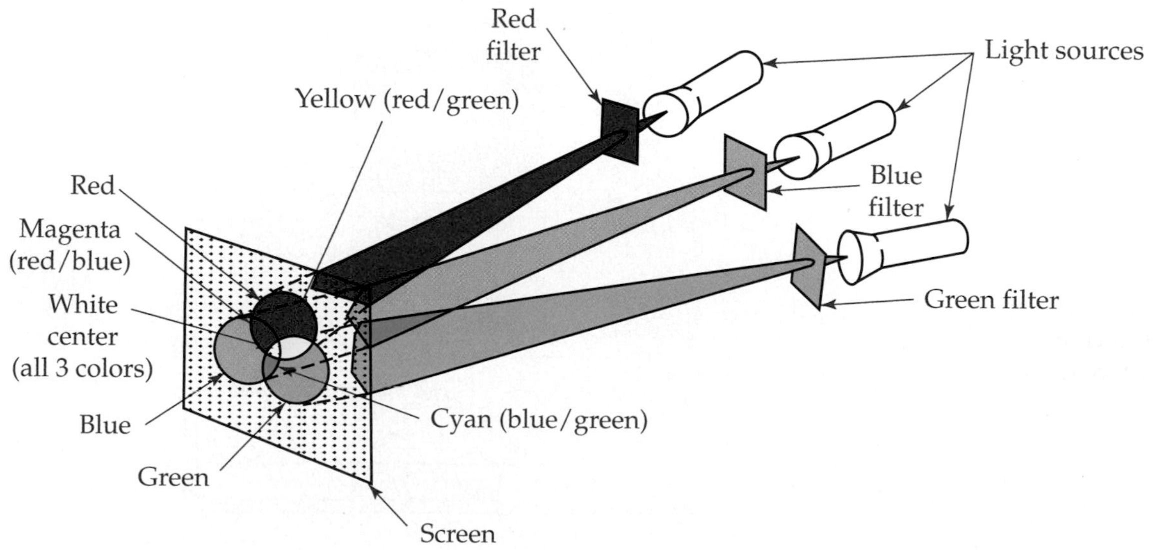

As you can see in the illustration, the color white is produced when each of the three colors is at equal intensity. The color black is produced when there is complete absence of intensity. Varying the degree of intensity of the three-color combinations produces other color hues.

Refresh rate

refresh rate
the rate at which the electron beam sweeps across the screen.

The rate at which the beam sweeps across the screen is called the ***refresh rate.*** The refresh rate of most computer monitors can be adjusted in **Control Panel** using the **Display Properties** dialog box. Often screen flicker can be corrected by increasing the refresh rate. A high refresh rate is good for someone who must spend long hours in front of a computer display because it reduces eyestrain. The downside of a high refresh rate is that it takes away from CPU time that could otherwise be used for processing information. Most current systems will choose their own optimal settings, **Figure 8-12.**

Raster display

raster
the sweep of the electron beam.

field
a complete sweep of the entire video display area orientation.

The electronic beam sweeps across the screen horizontally from left to right. The sweep of the beam is called a ***raster.*** The sweep from left to right is repeated, each time lower on the screen, until the bottom of the screen is reached. This method of producing a picture on a monitor is called *raster display.* A complete sweep of the entire screen area is called a ***field.*** The entire field is completed sixty times each second.

Not all monitors make one continuous sweep vertically down the screen. Some complete the process in two steps. First, all of the odd number lines are swept, and then all of the even lines are swept. This method of producing a complete frame is called *interlacing.* Some display units, especially LCD panels, use a technique known as progressive scan. *Progressive scan* displays the image on the monitor line by line in sequence from top to bottom.

The time it takes to complete the entire screen sweep is referred to as the monitor's *refresh rate.* The refresh rate of the monitor can be controlled with software in **Control Panel**. The refresh rate can be adjusted higher or lower.

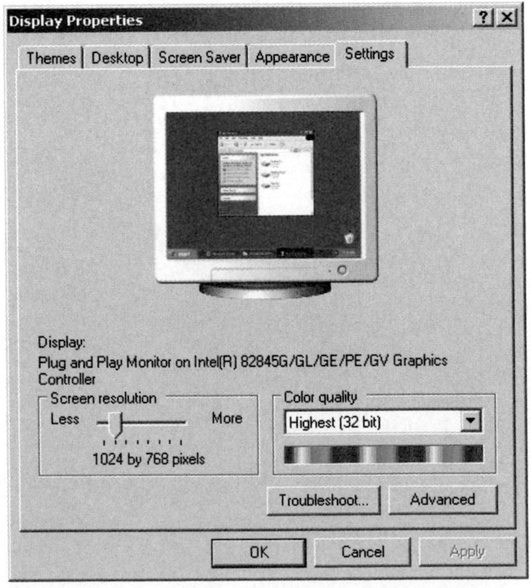

Figure 8-12. Most monitors are by default set to the "Optimal" refresh rate setting. You can find your adjustments for this setting in the **Display Properties** dialog box in **Control Panel**. Click the **Settings** tab. Choose **Advanced**, and then choose the **Monitor** tab.

The typical PC technician should never disassemble a monitor. If for some reason it is required, *never* wear an anti-static wrist strap when working on a monitor. You must avoid grounding yourself. Remember that a CRT can contain voltage in excess of 20,000 volts even when unplugged! The CRT tube can retain a high voltage charge for some time, similar to a capacitor.

Liquid Crystal Displays

The most common flat-panel display is the ***liquid crystal display (LCD).*** The liquid crystal display operates on two principles. The first is polarized light. The second is the effect of an electrical voltage applied to a crystal structure.

liquid crystal display (LCD)
a type of monitor that uses polarized light passing through liquid crystal to create an image on screen.

A typical light beam is composed of numerous waves of light. The waves of light travel in parallel but at different wave angles. When a thin slot is cut in a material such as metal, only light waves with an angle matching the slot can travel through the slot. The light that travels through the slot is polarized light. ***Polarized light*** is light energy composed of light beams with a matching wave angle.

polarized light
light energy composed of light beams with a matching wave angle.

The second principle is based on the effect of electrical voltage applied to a crystal structure. When an electrical voltage is applied to a crystal, the crystal changes shape slightly or twists. The degree of twist is directly related to the amount of voltage applied to the crystal. Light normally passes through the crystal in a straight line. When a light is shined through a crystal and voltage is then applied to the same crystal, the angle of the light wave changes as it passes through the crystal. These two principles, polarized light and voltage effect on crystals, is the basis of how all LCD displays work.

How liquid crystal displays work

To fully understand how the typical liquid crystal display works, follow along while referring to **Figure 8-13.** The LCD panel is constructed of several thin layers of material. A thin fluorescent backlight is used as the source of light energy for the display. When the backlight strikes through the first layer, only

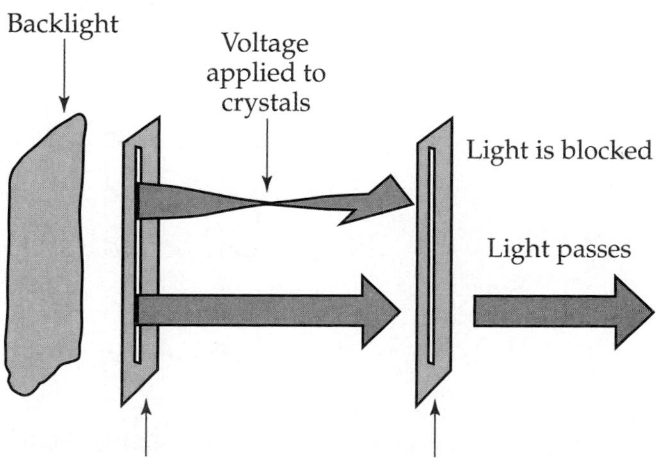

Figure 8-13.
The liquid crystal is used to twist the light wave.

light waves with an angle matching the slot can pass through the filter. The light waves that pass through the slot are polarized light because they all have a matching wave angle.

The polarized light passes through the array of crystals. Each crystal has a transistor connected to it. The transistor acts similar to a dimmer light switch, which can be turned on in varying degrees. The amount of voltage applied to each crystal by the individual transistors determines the amount of twist in each crystal. Any crystal that has voltage applied to it causes the angle of the light beam to change as it passes through the crystal. The amount of change in the light wave angle is determined by the amount of voltage applied to each crystal.

The second filter is used to screen out light waves that are no longer polarized. The amount of change in each light wave determines how much of the polarized light can pass through the second filter. For example, a light beam passing through a crystal with a maximum voltage applied will have its angle changed to the extent that none of the light energy will pass through the second filter. This creates a dark pixel image on the display. A light beam passing through a crystal with no voltage applied will not have its angle changed and will therefore pass through the second filter. This creates a full brightness pixel image. The amount of light and dark pixels directly relates to the applied voltage at each crystal.

passive-matrix display
an LCD display in which a grid of semitransparent conductors is run to each of the crystals that make up the individual pixels.

Passive-matrix display

There are two types of electrical circuitry used to energize the crystal area: passive and active, **Figure 8-14.** In a ***passive-matrix display,*** a grid of semitransparent conductors run to each crystal, which is used as part of the individual pixel area. The grid is divided into two major circuits: columns and rows. Transistors running along the top and the side of the display unit head the columns and rows. A ground applied to a row and a charge applied to a column

Figure 8-14.
In an active-matrix display, each individual cell in the grid has its own individual transistor. The active-matrix provides a better image than does the passive.

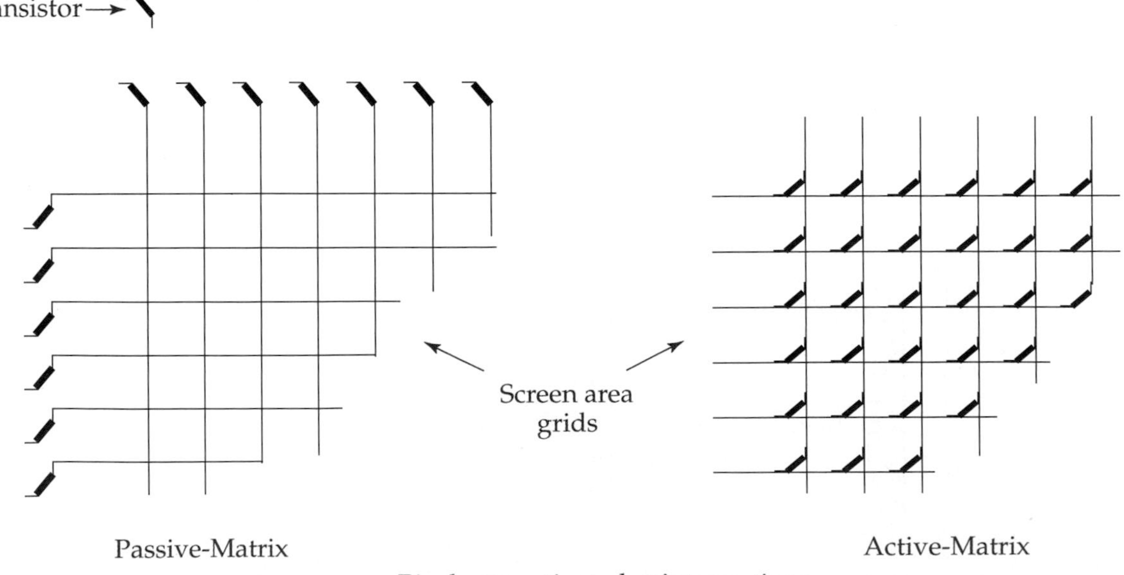

activates a pixel area. The voltage is applied briefly and must rely on screen persistence and a fast refresh rate. Because current must travel along the row and column until it arrives at the designated pixel, response time is slow.

Active-matrix display

In an ***active-matrix display,*** each pixel in the grid has its own transistor. The active-matrix provides a better image than the passive-matrix. The active-matrix image is brighter because each cell can have a constant supply of voltage.

The most common active-matrix display is the ***thin film transistor liquid crystal display (TFT-LCD).*** Often, this type of display is referred to simply as a TFT display. The TFT display consists of a matrix of thin film transistors spread across the entire screen. Each transistor controls a single pixel on the display. There are over one million transistors in a display, three transistors at each pixel area, one transistor for each color pixel, **Figure 8-15.** The liquid crystals in the TFT display are energized in a pattern representing the data to be displayed.

The conventional television has used the CRT to display images because the original LCD design had limitations that could not compete with larger display units. As the size of the display unit grew to over 18", problems developed with the brightness of the display and in converting the analog television signal to a digital signal and to a wide-angle viewing area without image distortions. These problems were solved with the introduction of thin film transistor LCD technology.

active-matrix display an LCD display in which each individual cell in the grid has its own individual transistor.

thin film transistor liquid crystal display (TFT-LCD) a display that consists of a matrix of thin film transistors, in which each transistor controls a single pixel.

Advantages of LCD over CRT displays:

- ✔ LCDs can be constructed much smaller and are lighter in weight than CRT displays.
- ✔ LCDs are more economical to run because they require less power.
- ✔ LCDs generate less heat.
- ✔ LCDs create more detailed images.
- ✔ LCDs produce less electromagnetic interference (EMI).

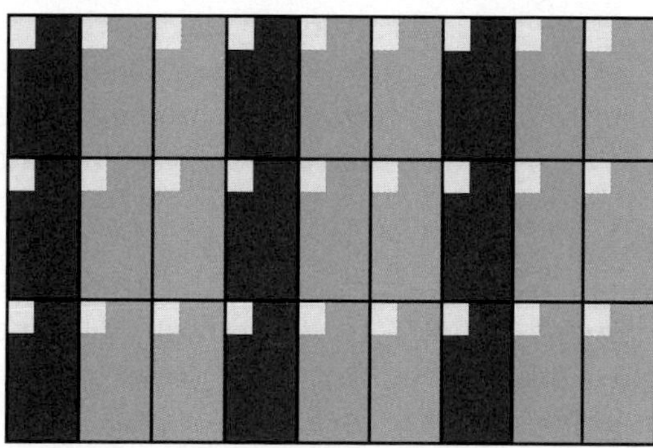

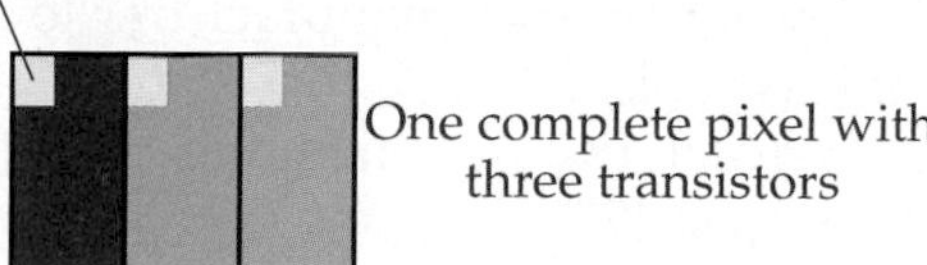

Figure 8-15. Each pixel area on the TFT display consists of three transistor-controlled color fields. The three, color fields—red, green, and blue—are combined to form various shades and hues of color.

Disadvantages of LCD as compared to CRT displays:

- ✔ Lack of an industry-wide standard.
- ✔ Complexity of scaling images without distortion.

Contrast ratio

contrast ratio
a numeric expression in the form of a ratio that describes the amount of contrast between the darkest and lightest pixel in the image.

Contrast ratio is a numeric expression in the form of a ratio that describes the amount of contrast between the darkest and lightest pixel in the image. The higher the ratio, the better the colors will be represented on the display unit. This is a very important display characteristic that correlates closely to the overall quality of the display. For example, a display with a high contrast ratio will be able to do a better job of displaying finer details of an image. Contrast ratios typically range from 500:1 to 1000:1. A contrast ratio of over 800:1 is considered a high-quality display.

Brightness

Brightness in an LCD is produced by the fluorescent backlight. The maximum amount of brightness produced in the display is determined by this light source. Brightness levels typically range from 200 cd/m^2 (candela per square meter) to 250 cd/m^2. A candela is a light measurement based on candle illumination. Many people confuse light measurement with watts or wattage. Wattage is a measurement of electrical energy, not light energy. While electrical energy often directly relates to the amount of light produced, there is not a direct correlation between electrical energy and light when comparing different light technologies such as the case of incandescent and fluorescent light. For example, a fluorescent light and an incandescent light use two different electrical technologies for generating light. The amount of power consumed measured in watts does not accurately represent the amount of light provided when comparing different technologies. The same is true for computer displays. To accurately compare brightness levels between a CRT display and an LCD, you must use candela per square meter. For a general comparison, a typical CRT screen displays approximately 120 cd/m^2. An LCD screen would need to display at least 120 cd/m^2 to produce the same amount of brightness as a typical CRT display.

Brightness is also a main factor for determining if the monitor will adequately display an image in a bright environment such as an outdoor area.

Viewing angle

viewing angle
a measurement of the angle at which a person can adequately see an image on a display without it looking excessively distorted.

The ***viewing angle*** is a measurement of the angle at which a person can adequately see an image on a display without it looking excessively distorted. As a person's angle to the screen increases, the image displayed becomes increasingly washed out until the image disappears. See **Figure 8-16.**

The viewing angle of early models of LCD panels was quite limited and could not compete with CRT screens. Today, the viewing angle is of less concern because almost all LCD panels have a very acceptable viewing angle. The actual viewing angle of a display varies from manufacturer to manufacturer, but the minimum viewing angle is typically 150°. Top of the line displays have a viewing angle of 170° or more. To match the viewing angle of a CRT, the viewing angle of the LCD panel must be at least 170°.

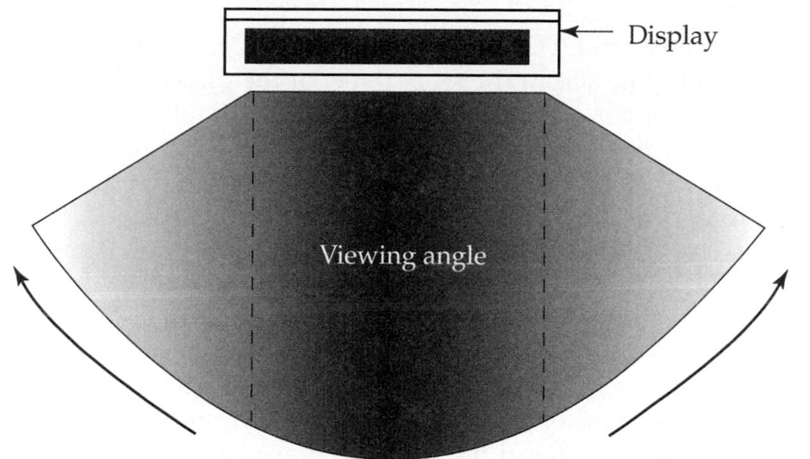

Figure 8-16. The viewing angle defines the locations where the screen can be viewed comfortably without distortion. As the angle of view increases, the image appears increasingly washed out until the image disappears.

Pixel pitch

Pixel pitch is similar to CRT dot pitch. Pixel pitch is the distance between two same color pixels on the display area. In other words, pixel pitch is the distance between two red pixels or two green pixels. Each color pixel is composed of three pels, one pel for each of the three colors that compose a pixel. Pixel pitch is expressed in millimeters (mm) per inch.

pixel pitch the distance between two same color pixels on the display area.

Native resolution

An LCD is capable of displaying a number of different resolutions. The ***native resolution*** is the resolution that matches the pixel design of the display. For example, if a display has a native resolution of 1280 × 1024 then it will display images best at 1280 × 1024. If a resolution other than the native resolution is chosen, an image will appear slightly blurred in some areas. Earlier in this chapter, bitmap distortion was explained for bitmap images that change scale. The LCD is manufactured with a set number of pixels. Because a set number of actual pixels are used to generate an image, the display will operate as a bitmap device, its image blurring when the scale is changed. When a screen resolution other than native is selected, the display controller must either add or remove pixels from the image before it is displayed on the screen. The process of adding or removing pixels causes the image to appear slightly blurred. This is especially true when displaying a much higher or much lower resolution image.

native resolution the resolution that matches the pixel design of the display.

Response time

The ***response time*** is the amount of time it takes a TFT pixel to display after a signal is sent to the transistor controlling that pixel. Response time is measured in milliseconds (ms). A typical response time ranges from 15 ms to 40 ms. The lower the response time, the better the quality of the display unit. A quick response time is required for quality animation. A high response time can result in a slight flicker or in breaks in the animation presented on the screen. It is interesting to note that at this time, the CRT is better at displaying animation or full motion video then the LCD. The CRT has an almost instantaneous response time, which produces a better full motion video display.

response time the amount of time it takes a TFT pixel to display after a signal is sent to the transistor controlling that pixel.

Monitor size

The monitor size of an LCD is measured in a similar fashion to a CRT screen, in a diagonal line across the front panel of the display. The big difference between the LCD monitor and the CRT monitor is no display size is lost to the area around the perimeter of the screen. As you recall from earlier in the chapter, a CRT monitor has an actual image display smaller than the screen's measured size. An LCD screen size is the same as the image to be displayed. There is no display size loss. A 16″ LCD monitor can and will display a 16″ image, while a 16″ CRT monitor will display less than the measured size.

Aspect ratio

aspect ratio ratio of a display area's height and width.

Aspect ratio refers to the ratio of the display area's height and width. A typical CRT screen is based on the television standard ratio of 4:3. The width is represented by the number 4 and the height is represented by the number 3. A newer wide-aspect ratio became a standard with the introduction of HDTV. The wide-aspect ratio found on most new LCD panels is 16:10. See **Figure 8-17** for a comparison of the two aspect ratios.

The wide-aspect ratio width allows more information to be displayed on the monitor and matches the new HDTV standard for display systems. The development of the wide-aspect ratio has created a need for newer video resolution standard identification, which allows a user to select a resolution that more closely matches the design of the monitor. The newer resolution standards designed for wide-aspect ratio use the prefix "W" to describe the modified standard resolution. For example, an XGA resolution based on the traditional 4:3 ratio would be identified as WXGA when based on the 16:10 ratio.

Gas-Plasma Displays

gas-plasma displays a display that operates on the principle of electroluminescence.

Gas-plasma displays are flat panel displays that operate on the principle of electroluminescence. Electro-luminescence is the display of light created when a high frequency passes through a gas to a layer of phosphor, resulting in the release of photons. The electrical energy from releasing photons is better known as producing light.

Figure 8-17.
The aspect ratio is an expression of the relationship of height to width of the screen area. The aspect ratio for HDTV screens is wider than traditional screens.

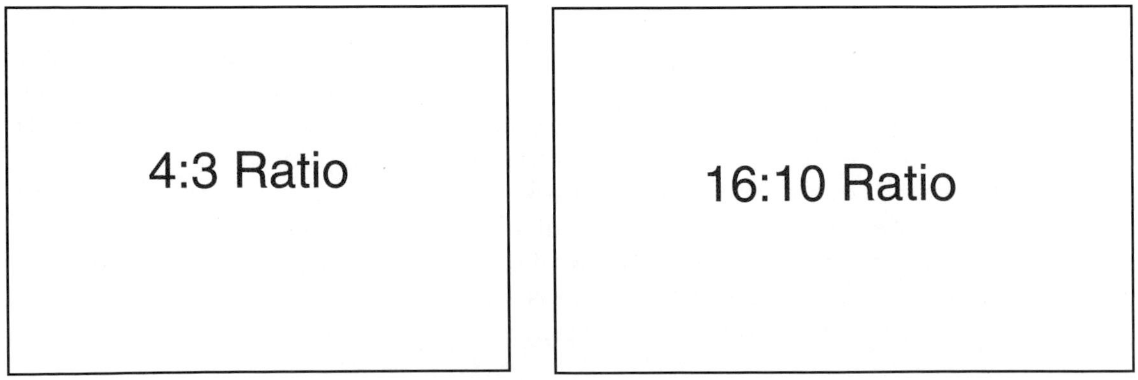

4:3 Ratio

16:10 Ratio

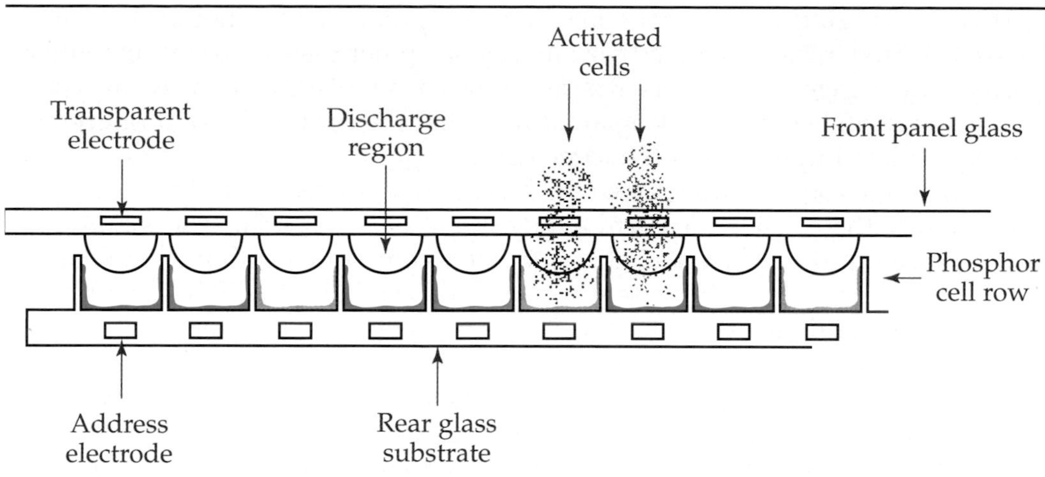

Figure 8-18. Gas-plasma technology.

A gas-plasma display consists of millions of tiny cells sandwiched between two glass plates. See **Figure 8-18.** Each cell contains an inert gas and is coated with a phosphorous material of red, blue, or green. Transparent electrodes run horizontally behind the front panel on top of the cells. Address electrodes run vertically along the rear glass panel beneath the cells. When the address electrodes and its corresponding transparent electrode are energized, the gas, in an exited, plasma state, releases an ultraviolet light. The ultraviolet light strikes the phosphorus coating inside the cell causing the cell to release a light corresponding to its color. By varying the pulses of current, the entire light spectrum can be duplicated such as orange, yellow, and brown.

The top electrode is called the *row electrode* and the bottom electrode is called the *column electrode*. A column and row electrode forms a junction point. Each junction point conforms to a memory address. The microprocessor sends information to the memory address and to the monitor. The junction points become energized in a pattern reflective of the computer memory pattern.

The biggest difference between an LCD and a gas-plasma display is the plasma display does not require a backlight. Each cell in a gas-plasma display generates its own light. For this reason, a gas-plasma display can be manufactured much thinner than an LCD.

Troubleshooting Video Displays

Troubleshooting displays is quite simple since there are no serviceable parts inside CRT or LCD monitors. You simply replace a suspected monitor with another. Before changing the monitor, you should do the following:

✔ Check if the monitor is turned on.

✔ Check if power cord is plugged in.

✔ Check if the wall outlet has voltage.

✔ Check the video cable between the computer and the display unit.

✔ Replace the display with a known good display.

✔ Reseat the video card.

✔ Reinstall video card drivers.

✔ Replace the video card.

If after changing the monitor you still have a problem, you should check the video card. First, reseat the video card in its slot. Sometimes an oxidation builds up on the card edge connections. Reseating the card will remove the oxidation, and the card will begin to work again. If reseating the card does not produce the desired results, simply replace the video card.

Many motherboards incorporate the video chipset directly on the motherboard; there is no video card in any slot. When this is the case, simply install a video card into any available slot that is compatible with the video card. This will not always work because when the video chipset is built in as part of the motherboard and it is defective, it may prevent another video card from working. It will mainly depend on the type of electronics failure in the chipset. Also, be aware that other items such as a telephone modem or network card could prevent a computer system from completing the POST and thus make it appear as a video problem. There will be more about this type of scenario in Chapter 15—PC Troubleshooting.

Before replacing the video card, you should reinstall or update the video card drivers. Drivers often become corrupt and many times replacing the drivers or updating the drivers corrects the problem.

A+ Note:

On the A+ Certification exams there is always at least one question on how to troubleshoot a display unit. The tips in this section should provide sufficient information to answer most questions concerning the display unit.

Cleaning Video Displays

There is always much debate and conflicting methods for cleaning displays. Always consult the manufacturer documentation. The following information contains the generally-accepted guidelines for properly cleaning displays.

- ✔ Never clean a display while it is energized. Always unplug the electrical supply before cleaning the display.
- ✔ Clean the display area using a lightly dampened lint-free soft cloth. Never use detergent to clean the plastic display case surface. Detergents will often leave a white residue on the surface after drying. CRT monitors have a glass covering while LCD do not. LCD uses a plastic cover and can be easily damage by chemical solutions, except ones designed specifically for cleaning LCD displays.
- ✔ Never use a paper towel to clean an LCD monitor. Paper towels are often made with course fibers which can scratch a plastic LCD screen. Use only soft lint-free cloth.
- ✔ Never spray liquid directly on the display. Too much spray causes the liquid to run down the display and enter the display through the seam along the edge of the screen. When the liquid enters inside the display, it can short out the electronic components.
- ✔ Never use the following chemicals to clean a monitor: acetone, ethyl alcohol, ammonia, products containing chlorine or chloride products.

A+ Note:

The A+ Certification exams always have a question about proper cleaning of display units.

Never locate a display unit in direct sunlight such as when placed in front of a window. Direct sunlight will cause excessive heat buildup inside the display. This may damage the electronics. Also, direct sunlight can damage plastic cases, resulting in yellowing or fading of colors. The direct sunlight can also cause the plastic case to become brittle, which may cause the case to crack.

Place the display unit in an area of relative low humidity. High humidity in the range of 80% to 100% can damage electronic components. Avoid moving devices in and out of drastic temperature changes with high humidity present. This is often the case with laptop computers. When moving laptops, try to keep the laptop inside a carrying case designed for the laptop. This will provide some temperature and humidity control.

Video Adapter Cards

Monitors can attach to a computer in one of two ways. The monitor can plug into a video adapter card, which is inserted into a PCI or an AGP slot on the motherboard. They can also attach directly to the motherboard, which incorporates the same electronic components found on a video adapter card.

The heart of the video adapter card is a specialized chip known as a digital-to-analog converter. The ***digital-to-analog converter (DAC)*** converts the digital signal from the computer to an analog signal that is displayed on the computer's monitor. The DAC can consist of one single chip or three chips, one chip for each color. The card also contains RAM, ROM, a video processor, and BIOS. The entire video adapter card is similar to a complete computer that has been specialized for video display.

digital-to-analog converter (DAC) a chip that converts the digital signal from the computer to an analog signal that is displayed on the computer's monitor.

A VGA monitor uses a 15-pin D-shell connector to connect to the video display adapter card or to the video port on the motherboard. **Figure 8-19** shows a diagram of a standard VGA 15-pin D-shell connector. The chart next to the diagram lists the function of each pin on the connector.

Video adapter cards are installed in PCI, PCI-X, PCIe, or AGP slots on the motherboard. As you can see in **Figure 8-20,** the PCIe design produces the highest throughput of the two technologies. Although, note that PCIe, because it transfers information in a serial fashion, is expressed as bits per second (bps), not bytes per second (Bps).

Video performance also depends on the amount of available memory that can be used to create and process images. When the graphics controller is incorporated into the motherboard, the controller uses the RAM that is installed on the motherboard for video images. This means that the motherboard RAM must be used for all software functions that require RAM as well as for video performance. When a video adapter card is used, the performance is greatly increased. The total effect on video performance is determined by how much RAM is incorporated into the video adapter card. As a general rule, the more

Figure 8-19.
Standard VGA 15-pin connector diagram. In this arrangement, pin 5 is used for testing the monitor. Some manufacturers use pins 4, 11, 12, or 15 to identify or detect the type of monitor connected to the motherboard. Pin 9 is usually missing by design; other pins may be missing as well if not used by that particular manufacturer.

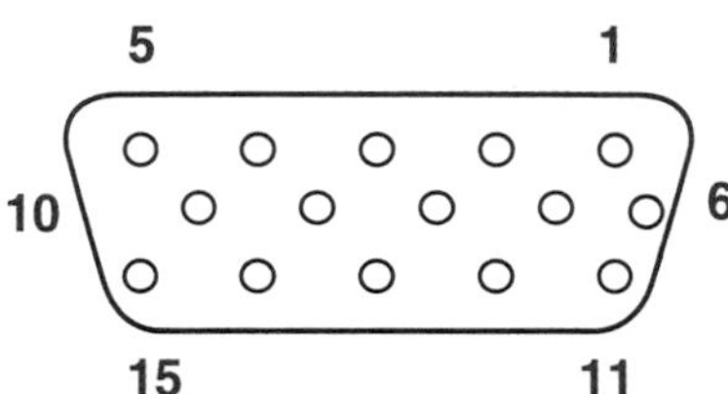

Pin Number	Function
1	Red video
2	Green video
3	Blue video
4	Monitor ID 2
5	TTL ground test pin
6	Red analog ground
7	Green analog ground
8	Blue analog ground
9	Plugged hole
10	Sync ground
11	Monitor ID 0
12	Monitor ID 1
13	Horizontal sync
14	Vertical sync
15	Monitor ID 3

Figure 8-20.
Comparison of video adapter card bus types.

Bus Type	Throughput MBps	Speed in MHz	Width in Bits
PCI	127.2	33	32
PCI 2.1	508.6	66	64
AGP	254.3	66	32
AGP ×2	508.6	66 × 2	32
AGP ×4	1017.3	66 × 4	32
AGP ×8	2034.4	66 × 8	32
PCI–X	1060.0	133	64
PCI–X	2150.0	255	64
PCIe	***2000.0	NA	NA
+++PCIe 2.0	***4000.0	NA	NA

*** PCIe is not measured in MBps but rather in Mbps. MBps is a parallel bus measurement while Mbps is a serial bus measurement. The speed of PCIe expressed in the chart is noted incorrectly as MBps so that it can be compared to other parallel bus types.

+++ PCI 2.0 has not been released at the time of this writing but is expected to be released in late 2009 or early 2010.

video RAM incorporated into the video adapter card, the better the overall video performance. Other factors that influence video performance are the version of operating system, the motherboard chipset, and the video adapter card BIOS.

AGP

The accelerated graphics port (AGP) is a slot used strictly for AGP adapter cards. It is designed with graphics as a priority, using a computer's memory to work more effectively with graphics. It also operates at a faster bus speed than standard PCI slots.

Typically, there is only one AGP slot on a motherboard. The AGP slot looks similar in design to the PCI slot, only in reverse. It is slightly shorter than a PCI slot, and it is usually a different color. To readily identify the AGP slot, look for the slot closest to the CPU and offset from the alignment of the PCI slots.

PCI-X

PCI Extended (PCI-X) was designed as the successor to the PCI bus. You can see the increase in throughput in Figure 8-20. These are theoretical speeds for PCI-X and can be much slower when the bus is shared with other types of devices. PCI-X is not used by many video card systems today but may still be encountered occasionally in older systems. You may wish to review the information concerning PCI-X and PCIe bus types in Chapter 3—Motherboards.

PCI Express

PCIe ×16 is the preferred bus type for video cards at this time of writing. PCIe ×16 provides approximately twice the graphics data throughput as AGP ×8. PCIe 2.0 is expected to be released in late 2009 or early 2010. The PCIe 2.0 specification will be designed to produce twice the throughput as the original PCIe ×16. This will be equal to four times the throughput of AGP ×8.

Using Multiple Video Cards

Computers can be configured with two or more video cards to increase overall video performance. This is most desirable for graphic-intensive applications such as games, computer aided drafting, video editing, and graphic arts 3D design programs. The increase in performance is due to the parallel processing power of joining the two video cards together. The two or more video cards share the workload by using either slip-frame rendering or alternate-frame rendering.

When using ***split-frame rendering,*** each card is responsible for half of the frame image. If four cards are used, each card is responsible for one-fourth of each image.

The second method is ***alternating-frame rendering.*** This method is as the name implies. Each card is responsible for rendering every other frame. If four cards are used, then each card is responsible for the fourth frame image. Some cards are capable of both split-frame rendering and alternate-frame rendering.

split-frame rendering
a method of sharing the video workload in which each card is responsible for an equal part of the frame image. For example, if four cards are used, each card is responsible for one-fourth of each image.

alternating-frame rendering
a method of sharing the video workload in which each card is responsible for rendering every other frame. For example, if four cards are used, then each card is responsible for the fourth frame image.

SLI

Scalable Link Interface (SLI) is a proprietary video card system owned by the NVIDIA Corporation. The original SLI system required that both cards be identical. This meant that each video card was to have a matching Graphics Processing Unit (GPU) and the same amount of RAM and bus speed. Today, SLI no longer requires identical video cards. However, when the video cards do not match, the best performance is based on the slower of the two cards.

Figure 8-21. Two GeForce 8800 video cards installed in an SLI configuration (NVIDIA Corporation).

Figure 8-21 shows two NVIDIA® GeForce® 8800 video cards installed in an SLI configuration. Notice the SLI bridge connector at the top of the cards.

Originally the acronym SLI was introduced as Scan-Line Interleave by the 3DFX company. When 3DFX sold the technology to NVIDIA, NVIDIA renamed the acronym to Scalable Link Interface

ATI CrossFire

ATI CrossFire™ is the multiple card technology introduced by ATI Technologies Inc. Two or more cards are configured for the computer. The two cards do not need to match but must be compatible. One card is referred to as the master and the second card is referred to as the slave. Both SLI and CrossFire must be installed in matching PCIe types of slots. For example, you cannot use one card in a PCIe slot and the other in an AGP slot. You must use two PCIe ×16 slots.

In theory, using two video cards would produce an overall video rate of double, but in reality, an overall 170% to 180% increase is typically achieved at best. There is some software overhead that must be implemented that reduces the theoretical doubling speed and the speed of other processes running in the background.

To see how to install an SLI video card, visit the NVIDIA Web site at www.slizone.com/object/slizone_howto_install.html. To see how to install a CrossFire system, visit the ATI AMD Web site at http://ati.amd.com/technology/crossfire/howitworksdemo.html. If either of these links expire, simply conduct a search using the keywords, "SLI install how to" or "CrossFire install how to."

Installing a Video Adapter Card

Installing a video adapter card is easy. The steps that follow are generic in nature, but there should not be much variation in installation between different cards.

Before beginning any installation of hardware, always back up critical computer files. It is very easy to accidentally destroy data on a computer. Sometimes drivers do not work the way they should resulting in a total lockup of the computer system. In the course of recovering the system, most anything can happen. The worst-case scenario is losing hard drive data. Always back up the hard drive or critical data before working on a PC.

Steps for installing an adapter card:

1. Back up all computer files.
2. Power off the computer and unplug the power cord from the wall outlet.
3. Read the installation procedures and specification sheet that came with the adapter card. Verify that your new card is compatible with the type of display unit being used.
4. Take normal static precautions.
5. Before attempting to insert the video adapter card into the expansion slot, check for debris in the slot.
6. Insert the card by applying even force to the top of the card. Do not rock the card into the slot.
7. Connect the monitor to the new card and turn on the PC. The card should auto detect if it is Plug and Play and you are using a modern Windows operating system.
8. If Windows cannot find its own driver when the system attempts to detect the card, it will ask you to supply a new driver. The driver should have been packaged with the expansion board either as a floppy disk or a CD-ROM. It is also a good idea to check the card manufacturer's Web site for any patches or upgrades needed for the driver. Prepackaged drivers will often be dated. The most up-to-date drivers can be downloaded from their Web sites.
9. As the drivers are loading, follow the screen prompts to complete the installation.
10. A message box will display on the screen when the installation is complete. If a problem occurs, a message will appear saying that the installation is not complete. Reread the installation procedures. Also, check for bent pins on the video adapter. A pin can easily bend when assembling the system. Another area to check is your computer's BIOS. In particular with older machines, you may need to upgrade the BIOS on the motherboard to use your new card. If problems still persist, check both the card manufacturer's and the motherboard manufacturer's Web site. Some motherboards have a video adapter integrated into the circuit board. If this is the case, you may have to disable the integrated system before the new adapter board will work. It is *always* a good idea to consult the Web site of the motherboard manufacturer for the latest updates before you begin.
11. If all has gone well, you should be able to close the case and reboot the system.

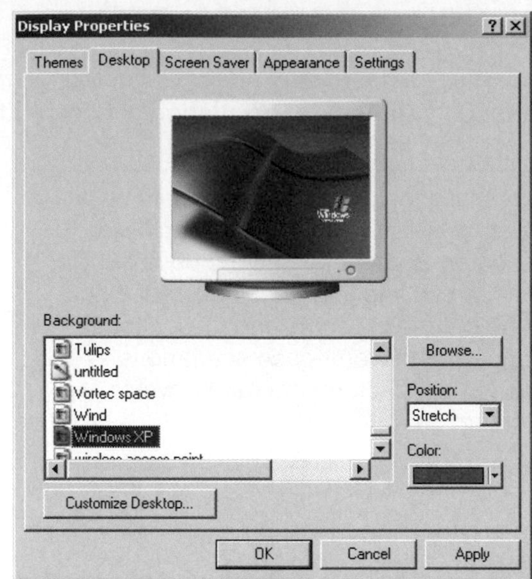

Figure 8-22. The Windows XP **Display Properties** dialog box.

Changing Display Properties

In the Windows operating system, many adjustments can be made to the display. In Windows XP, these adjustments are made in the **Display Properties** dialog box, **Figure 8-22.** The **Display Properties** dialog box can be accessed through **Control Panel | Appearance and Themes | Display**. There are a number of options in the properties of the video display. This dialog box allows you to change "look and feel items" like the desktop theme, screen saver, or computer wallpaper. It also allows you to adjust hardware issues such as the monitor's refresh rate or the type of display used (e.g. CRT or flat panel).

In Windows Vista, the various display adjustments are made through several dialog boxes accessed through **Control Panel | Appearance and Personalization | Personalization**. For example, the refresh rate is adjusted in the **Display Settings** dialog box and the appearance is adjusted in the **Windows Color and Appearance** dialog box.

Television and Computers

Computer and television technology has rapidly merged since the development of HDTV and the availability of flat panel display technology such as TFT and gas-plasma. It is not unusual for a display unit to be designed to serve as both a television display and a computer display, **Figure 8-23.** The merger of the two technologies has produced many conflicting standards within the television and computer industry. This conflict in standards has resulted in a variety of connector designs used to connect various displays to computers and television receivers. **Figure 8-24** shows some of the connection designs associated with computer and television systems.

All of the connection designs carry the acronym DVI, which stands for Digital Visual Interface. The DVI-I is a combination-type connector designed for both digital and analog connections. The DVI-D is designed for a digital

Figure 8-23.
This flat-panel, gas-plasma TV is capable of both television and computer applications. (ViewSonic Corp.)

Figure 8-24.
Various connection designs and a DVD-D connector.

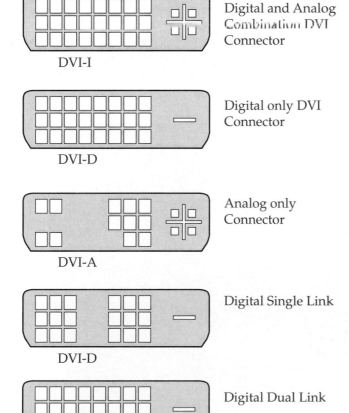

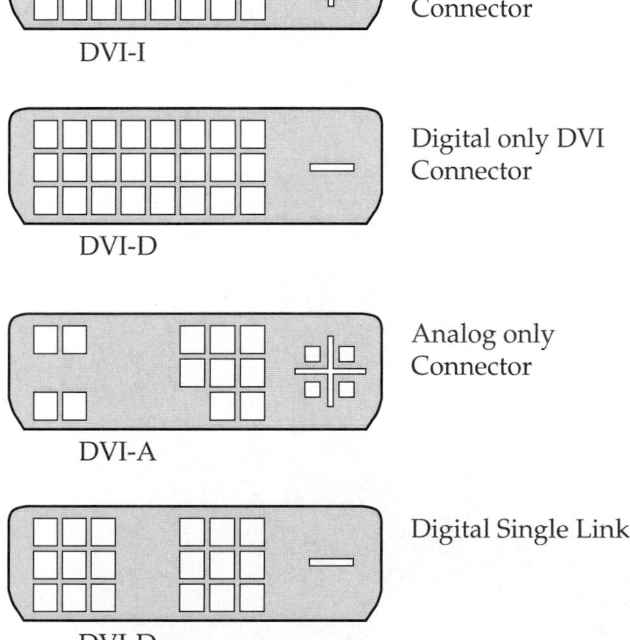

DVI-D Connector

only connection. It can be used to connect devices that support compatible digital resolutions. The DVI-A is used with digital-to-analog conversion. It is not commonly used today because of rapid advances in digital video and the fading out of analog systems.

The references to DVI-D single link and DVI-D dual link relate to the amount of bandwidth that can be transmitted by each connection design. The single link can carry a bandwidth equal to 165 MHz, which is the matching bandwidth for HDTV. It is capable of producing a maximum resolution of 1920 × 1080 at 60 Hz. The dual link can carry twice the bandwidth of the single link and can produce a resolution as high as 2048 × 1536.

Some video adapter cards provide several connection types to choose from. **Figure 8-25** shows a video adapter card with a variety of video display ports: a DVI port, a TV port (S-Video), and a DB-15 VGA monitor port.

Some video adapter cards are manufactured to support two monitors at the same time. Web page designers often require more than one display unit while designing Web pages. By having more than one display connected to the computer station, they can view the Web page they designed at different resolutions.

High-Definition Television Resolution

High-Definition Television (HDTV) displays have become the center of home entertainment systems and have created a demand for computer displays that are compatible with the same resolution and aspect ratio as HDTV. The display resolutions and overall physical shape of the viewing area are designed to support HDTV as well as other media center options, such as watching movies and editing video and digital photography.

Original analog television resolution is approximately equal to 720 × 480. The two most common HDTV formats are HD 720 and HD 1080. HD 720 is nothing more than an enhanced original analog television resolution of 720 × 480. True HDTV resolution requires a display resolution of at least 1080 × 720.

Figure 8-25. This video card is equipped with a variety of video display ports.

The two most commonly encountered television connectors associated with HDTV are S-Video and Component Video. These connectors are discussed in a later section.

Windows Media Center

Today more computers are being set up as a media center in the home. Windows XP first introduced a Media Center version of its operating system that emphasized audio and video media. By adding a television tuner either as an expansion card or as a USB device, the computer is able to receive analog and digital television signals.

Windows Media Center is incorporated into Windows Vista Home Premium and Windows Vista Ultimate editions. As more and more homeowners incorporate Windows Media Center into their home entertainment center, PC technicians will need to become very familiar with the cable connections and equipment used in a media center system.

Home Entertainment Center Connection Types

A home theater or entertainment center can consist of many different electronic devices connected together. The system may consist of a high-definition LCD or plasma television, cable TV, antenna or satellite source of signal, speakers, DVR, and a computer. The equipment that comprises a complete home entertainment center may involve a wide variety of cable connections. You need to be able to identify each type and understand its capabilities.

The signal that is supplied by the local cable television company or through a satellite dish system typically connects to the initial receiver in the home from a single coaxial cable. Original media systems consisted of a single coaxial cable that connected to a cable box and then another single coaxial cable to the television. Today, the single coaxial cable that supplies the cable television signal or satellite disk signal is separated into multiple audio and video signals which are processed by much more sophisticated equipment. The overall product is enhanced audio and video that requires a variety of connections and cables.

You need to be aware that audio cables, such as the cable used for speakers, is low frequency—less than 20 kHz. It does not require shielding from interference or cause interference the way video signals do. The speaker wiring does not use a carrier wave. It simply transmits the sound pattern as an analog signal.

Video signals are typically either UHF or VHF, each of which are high frequency in the hundreds of megahertz range. Hence, video cables must be shielded to protect the video signal from interference and to prevent the video cable from broadcasting radio wave interference to surrounding devices. Coaxial type cable is used for video signals while nonshielded cable is used for speakers. The speaker wires will have a much larger core conductor diameter when compared to RG-6 cable, which is a type of coaxial cable. The large diameter ensures less signal loss as the audio signal travels the length of the cable.

Component Video

The Component Video connection consists of three RCA-type connectors typically identified as Y, P_b (C_b), P_r (C_r). See **Figure 8-26.** Component Video, Figure 8-26C, is found on high-performance devices and produces a better quality picture than an S-Video, Figure 8-26B, or Composite Video, Figure 8-26A,

Figure 8-26.
Various home entertainment center connections and cables. A—Composite Video. B—S-Video. C—Component Video. D—Audio. E—Home entertainment center connections.

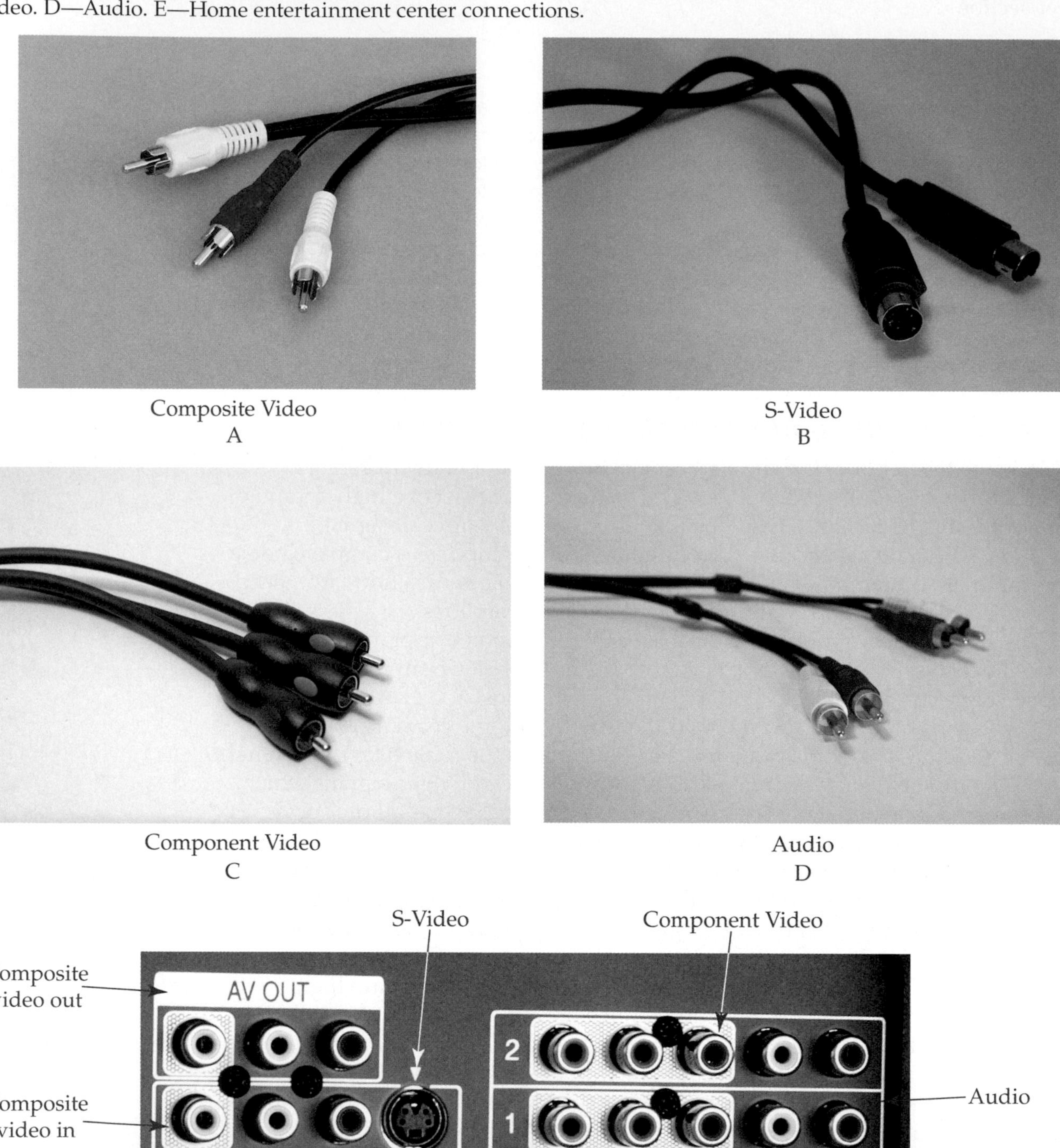

connection. The cables used are constructed from flexible coaxial cable. Each individual cable consists of a single conductor surrounded by a dielectric and a shield to protect it from receiving or generating interference. Component Video does not carry the audio signal. Audio signals are typically supplied through two separate ports using cable, Figure 8-26D, similar to the Component Video and Composite Video cables.

Composite Video

Composite Video, Figure 8-26A, resembles component video connections and cables. Notice that Composite Video uses an RCA-type connector similar to Component Video; however, it uses only one cable for the video signal and two more for stereo sound. The Composite Video cable uses a larger diameter cable (the one with the yellow connector) for video. The larger diameter cable is an RG-59 coaxial cable. The other two cables are used for audio and do not use coaxial shielding. Composite Video provides a better signal than F-type or RF cable connections but does not provide a signal as good as S-Video or Component Video.

S-Video

S-Video, Figure 8-26B, is a four-pin round connector that delivers separate signals for video signal chrominance (color) and luminance (brightness). It is a very simple way to connect components together because there is no way to misconnect the audio and video cables. S-Video supports better signal quality than Composite Video, but not as well as Component Video.

A nine-pin version of S-Video is used for video in and video out (ViVO) configurations, **Figure 8-27.** The nine-pin connector allows for video to be streamed in both directions. A four-pin connector is used for applications that only require video in one direction. Many video computer cards have the nine-pin S-Video connector, which is used commonly for video editing. The video is copied to the computer from the source, edited on the computer, and then sent back to the source.

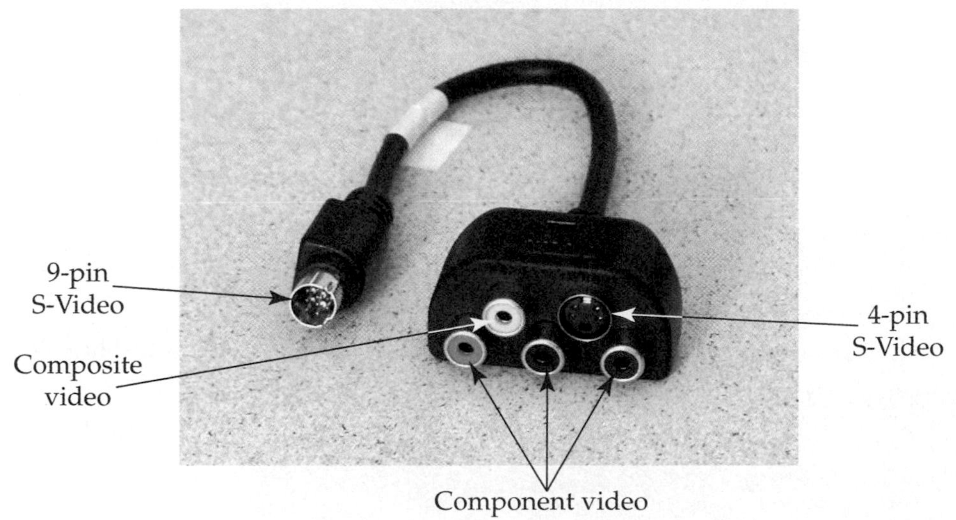

Figure 8-27. An S-Video adapter with a nine-pin S-Video connector on one end and a combination 4-pin S-Video, Component Video, and Composite Video connection on the other end.

HDMI

The High Definition Multimedia Interface (HDMI) connector is used to supply video and audio in an uncompressed, all digital signal format. See **Figure 8-28.** Only one cable assembly is needed between devices such as satellite receivers and the HDTV. HDMI supports an enhanced HDTV format and Dolby 5.1 using a single shielded cable. HDMI, Figure 8-28A, can support a digital audio signal as high as 192 kHz, a digital video signal as high as 350 MHz, and a data signal as high as 10.2 Gbps.

Figure 8-28.
HDMI and ToskLink connectors and connections. A—The HDMI connector closely resembles the standard USB connector found on PCs. B—The ToskLink connector is protected from damage by plastic end pieces. The connectors are susceptible to damage from scratches or even dust collected on the ends. C—HDMI, ToskLink (optical), and RS-232 connections on the back of an HDTV system. The RS-232 connection connects to a diagnostic device that is used to troubleshoot the high-definition television.

A

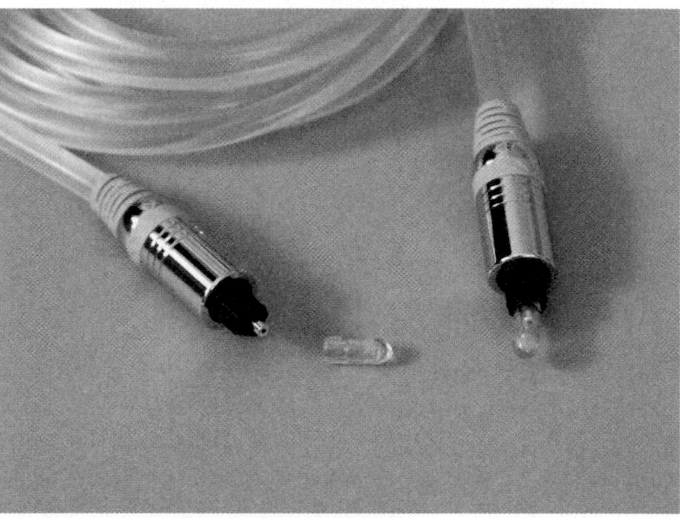

B

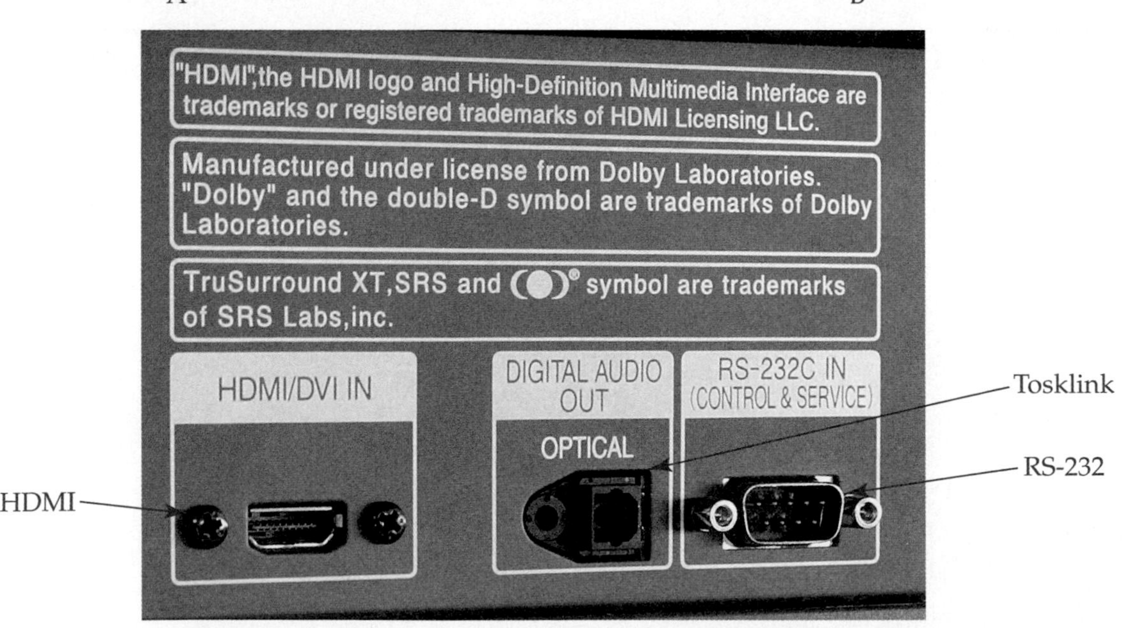

C

At the time of this writing, HDMI provides the best picture and sound quality available. The HDMI uses the new xvYCC standard, which is an enhanced color standard that exceeds the HDTV standard. The xvYCC is short for Extended YCC Colorimetric for Video Applications. The term *colorimetric* means identification of colors using three sets of numbers representing red, green, and blue. This new standard was designed to enhance the viewing experience and can support 1.8 times as many colors as existing HDTV signals. The new standard is also designed to support Blu-ray technologies for Digital Video Disc (DVD) and newest video game technology. The HDMI connector is commonly found on many high-end computer video cards.

ToskLink

The ToskLink optical connector, Figure 8-28B, is a proprietary connection developed jointly by Sony and Phillips. The ToskLink cable is limited to audio at this time and supports audio signals between home theater equipment. The ToskLink cable is fiber-optic with a glass or plastic core. Fiber-optic cable ensures a high-quality transfer of audio signals because it is immune to radio and magnetic interference. The fiber-optic cable light signal is not susceptible to interference emitted from other cables and radio signal sources. More and more manufacturers are incorporating ToskLink ports into their motherboards in addition to traditional audio ports.

RF and F-type

RF and F-type connections in general provide the poorest quality video images when used between home entertainment center devices. They are generally used only with old technologies to support connections between devices. The RF and F-type cables are a standard coaxial cable consisting of a solid or stranded copper core conductor, **Figure 8-29.** The core conductor is surrounded by a thick insulator material. The insulator material is covered by a conductive mesh or foil referred to as the shield. The shield protects the core conductor from outside electromagnetic interference.

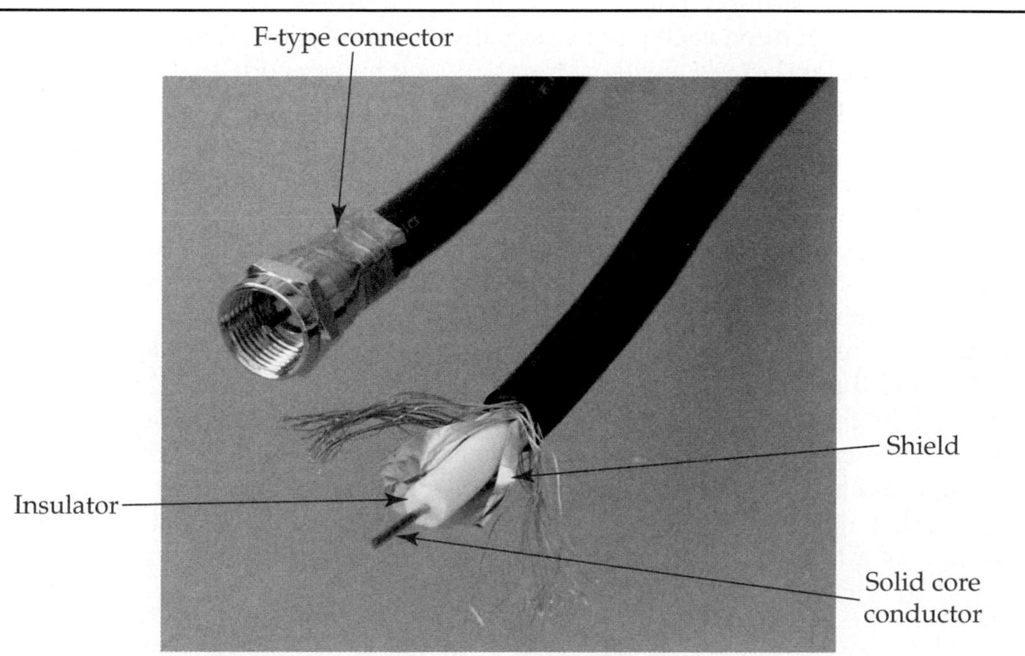

Figure 8-29. Coaxial cable with F-type connector.

RF and F-type cables provide the poorest signal quality transfer between home entertainment devices. Other cabling technologies, such as Component Video, S-Video, and HDMI, provide better signal support. Do not confuse the use of transferring a signal between devices with bringing in the raw signal that comes directly from a satellite or Broadband cable television. The other types of cabling other than coaxial are not typically used to bring a raw signal into a complete system. The exception is fiber-optic cable, which is now being introduced in many areas to bring the raw signal into a final destination.

The following is a comparison of video connection technologies.

Video Connection Type	Comparison
HDMI	Best
Component Video	Excellent
S-Video	Good
Composite Video	Poor
RF	Poor

ToskLink has been excluded from the table because it is limited to audio at this time. If ToskLink was included, it would be ranked equally with HDMI.

Bitmapped Graphics

bitmap (.bmp) a graphics standard for uncompressed encoding of images.

There are many different methods used to code the data of an image. One of the standards is the ***bitmap (.bmp),*** also referred to as a ***raster image.*** A display screen or printed image is made from thousands or millions of pixels. As discussed earlier, a pixel is the smallest screen element. The number of bits used to encode the pixel determines the color and shades of that color.

For example, an 8-bit code is capable of 256 different binary number patterns. Each of the binary number patterns can represent a different color or shade of gray. On a color monitor, each pixel is actually a combination of three different colors: red, blue, and green. Each color has an 8-bit binary code that can represent 256 shades of the color. The three individual 8-bit colors combine to form a 24-bit code that represents the actual color of the pixel image. See **Figure 8-30.** The 24-bit color code is referred to as *true color* and can produce over 24 million colors when mixed together.

Figure 8-30 is a screen capture of the Edit Colors tool in Microsoft's Paint program. Take note of the color reference window. All the different possible colors in the window are created from mixing various shades of red, blue, and green. At the bottom right are the three colors listed with a box beside each. Displayed in the boxes is a numeric value that can be varied from 0–255. Notice that these are the same total number of values that an 8-bit binary code can represent. By varying the numeric value displayed in the boxes, the three colors (red, blue, and green) can be mixed to form new colors in addition to the basic 28 colors that are given in the Paint program for drawing bitmap pictures. This technique of mixing colors is standard for most drawing programs.

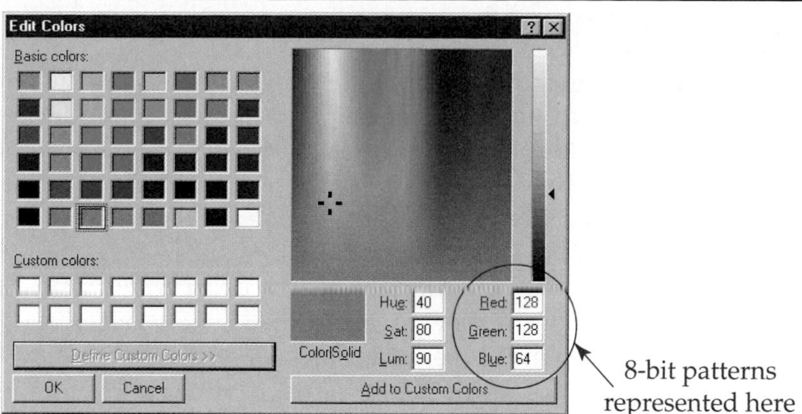

Figure 8-30.
In Microsoft's Paint program, you can see three 8-bit patterns forming a 24-bit pattern to represent the final color. The three patterns are represented by three 8-bit numbers, which describe the amount of red, green, and blue used.

Vector Graphics

vector graphics a graphic standard based on a series of mathematical formulas that can be converted into geometric shapes representing the image to be displayed.

Vector graphics is based on a series of mathematical formulas that can be converted into geometric shapes representing the image to be displayed. Vector graphics are typically produced by drawing programs, not by photographic images. One main advantage of vector images is they can be resized or scaled without losing the quality of the image. When a bitmap image is enlarged or reduced in size, the number of pixels must be increased or decreased accordingly. This means adding or removing pixels, which distorts the original image. The software program performing the bitmap conversion must decide what color to add as the image is increased. It chooses the pixel color closest to the original pixel. When the image is reduced, the software erases an existing pixel.

Since vector graphic images use mathematical formulas to represent the lines in the figures, the picture retains its original picture quality no matter which size it is changed to. The lines that compose the image are simply multiplied or divided by the applied scale factor. For example, all the line segments and circle diameters are multiplied by 2 for a drawing that is to be increased in scale by 200%.

A vector drawing could scale an infinite number of times and never lose its quality. In comparison, a bitmap image that was resized only a few times would become completely distorted.

Software programs that produce bitmap images are often referred to as *paint programs*. Software programs that produce vector images are often referred to as *draw programs*.

Vector image technology is used in critical drawing applications such as Computer Aided Drafting (CAD) programs and in many different animation software programs. Bitmap is mostly associated with photographic images. It is important to note that you can convert a vector image to a bitmap image, but you cannot convert a bitmap image to a vector image.

Graphic Compression

Graphics applications require a lot of memory space for storage. Even a small graphic can require several million bytes of memory depending on the resolution and the number of colors used to create the graphic. To decrease the amount of memory space needed, drawing data can be compressed. There are many different compression methods. However, they all use similar techniques to accomplish the compression.

A close inspection of a typical graphic reveals the color pixels repeated many times sequentially in an area of the picture. **Figure 8-31** shows a series of apple images. Each successive photo in this series looks progressively closer at the apple to expose the pixel pattern of colors. In the first image, you see what appears as very subtle variations of shades of green and red. As the picture is enlarged, you can see that many of the pixels are the same color. These repeating pixels of the same color are the secret to file compression. Instead of describing every pixel, a compressed file can describe a series of similar pixels with a short piece of code.

For a file compression technique to be effective, it must convert the same information stored in the image but use less memory space. This image was saved as a Windows true color image, meaning that the image pixels are each

Figure 8-31.
What appears to be finely detailed can be broken down into a series of pixels, some of which repeat.

composed of three 8-bit bytes. Consequently, each picture element shown uses 24 bits to represent the pixel. Look at the magnified images of the apple. Notice several continuous rows of pixels. If a row has 20 pixels, it would require 60 bytes of information.

One compression method worth looking at is run-length encoding. ***Run-length encoding (RLE)*** replaces a series of repeated pixels with a single pixel and the length of the series (run). The longer the runs and the greater number of runs there are, the greater the compression that will be achieved.

run-length encoding (RLE)
a graphics compression format that reduces image file size by recording strings of identical pixels.

Figure 8-32 shows a comparison of labeled binary codes. The first set of binary codes represents the color white for 20 pixels. The second set of binary codes shows a condensed version of the same information.

In the compressed file, the first byte gives the location of the first pixel. The next three bytes represent the color white, which is equal to decimal 255 (or binary code 11111111). The color white is composed of equal parts of red, blue, and green. Thus, the color is coded as three bytes, all consisting of eight 1s. The last byte of information contains the number of times necessary to repeat the pattern of white pixels. In the example, the last byte represents the decimal number 20. As you can see, the size of the compressed file, containing only 6 bytes, is very small in comparison to the original file that required 60 bytes of data.

Looking again at Figure 8-31, you can see many different colors that form a repeating pattern in the image. Each of these areas can be encoded the same way. This is the basic concept of compression. There are many different programs available to compress files. While they all do not work exactly as demonstrated, they do work in a similar fashion. File compression techniques are used not only for graphics but also for other forms of data such as sound files. Some compression techniques can achieve a compression ratio as high as 12:1.

The color white is equal to equal color parts of red, green, and blue.

Red	Blue	Green			
11111111	11111111	11111111	11111111	11111111	11111111
11111111	11111111	11111111	11111111	11111111	11111111
11111111	11111111	11111111	11111111	11111111	11111111
11111111	11111111	11111111	11111111	11111111	11111111
11111111	11111111	11111111	11111111	11111111	11111111
11111111	11111111	11111111	11111111	11111111	11111111
11111111	11111111	11111111	11111111	11111111	11111111
11111111	11111111	11111111	11111111	11111111	11111111
11111111	11111111	11111111	11111111	11111111	11111111
11111111	11111111	11111111	11111111	11111111	11111111

Original file information needed for the row of white pixel images.

10010011 11100111	11111111 11111111 11111111	00010100
Location of first pixel	The three colors	Repeat (length of run)

Compressed file information for same section.

Figure 8-32. Compression techniques can tremendously reduce the amount of code used to store an image or text. Here repeated data is reduced from 60 bytes to 6 bytes.

Audio

Audio is the second half of the multimedia experience. All PCs come with a small internal speaker, but that is not enough for most users. Fancy sound cards, subwoofers, and microphones have become standard equipment on many systems. The first step in learning audio systems is to understand sound itself and how it is created. The next step is to see how audio devices interface with the PC.

What Is Sound?

Sound is comprised of vibrations that are put into motion through a medium such as air or water. We are most familiar with air as the medium. The air itself actually carries a vibrating wave action. If you place a piece of tissue paper in front of a speaker, you can see it move from the sound vibration. If you are anywhere near some cars that have megawatt speakers turned up very loudly, you are familiar with the "feel" of sound.

If all air is removed and only a vacuum exists, there would be no sound. A vacuum is completely empty. There is no medium to carry the vibrations produced that we call sound. This concept can be demonstrated by placing an alarm clock inside a sealed, glass container. In this experiment, air is removed from the container. When the alarm goes off, it cannot be heard. There is no medium present to transport the pattern of vibrations called *sound,* **Figure 8-33.**

The human ear can detect sounds from approximately 20 Hz to 20 kHz. This is known as the frequency response range of the human ear. Vibrations above or below this range go undetected by human ears.

Sampling

sampling measuring an analog signal at regular intervals.

Measuring an analog signal at regular intervals is called ***sampling.*** Sampling is required before converting an analog signal into a digital signal. The quality of any type of analog-to-digital conversion is based primarily on the sampling rate and number of bits used to represent the height or voltage level of the signal. Sampling rates are incorporated into many different technologies. Weather radar units, security systems based on voice and image identification, and automatic piloting of aircraft are only a few examples.

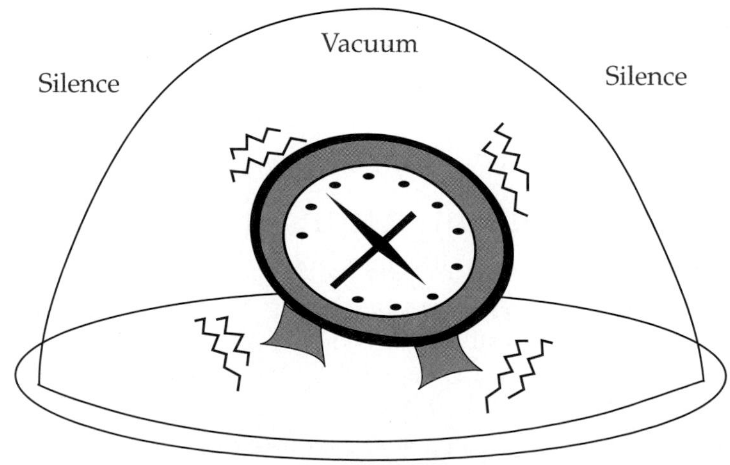

Figure 8-33. The alarm can be set off in a vacuum, but no sound will be transmitted.

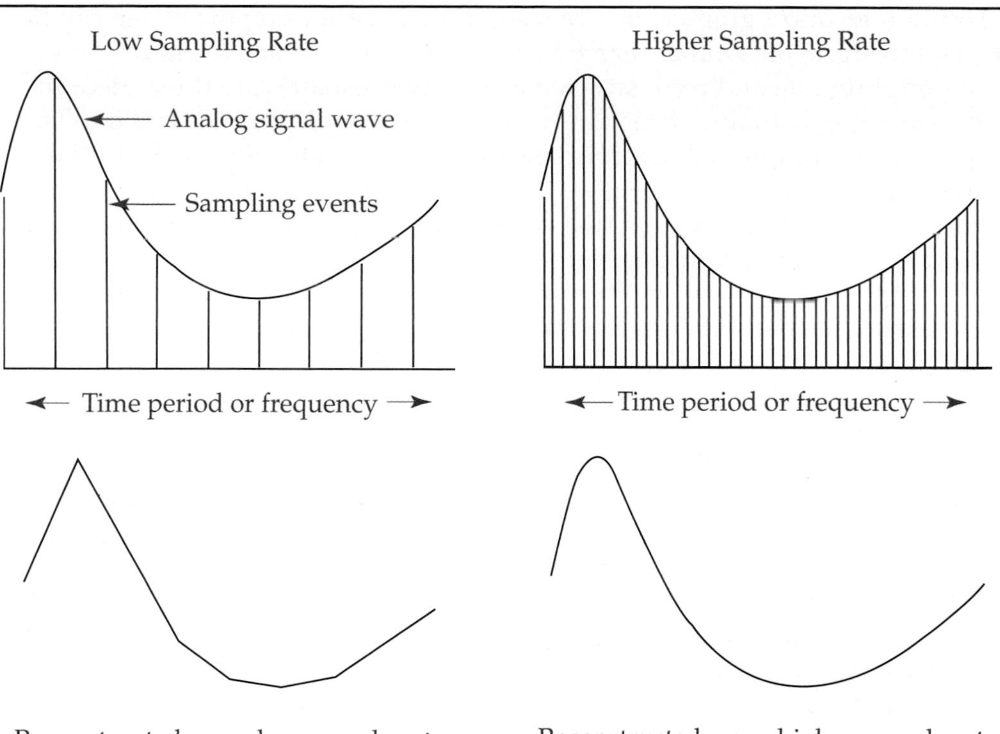

Figure 8-34. A higher sampling creates a more accurate reproduction of the original waveform.

A high frequency of sampling (frequent samples taken) results in a better quality of sound. **Figure 8-34** shows two different sampling rates taken from the same wave. See how the resultant waves differ with high and low sampling rates by comparing the reconstructed analog wave shapes.

A high sampling rate gives a better representation of an analog signal shape. In the illustration, an analog wave shape is sampled at two different rates. When the two wave shapes are reconstructed by connecting the points of sampling, you can see that the higher sampling rate gives a shape closer to the original analog wave shape. The quality of the sampling is directly affected by the sampling rate and by the number of bits used to indicate the height of the signal at the sampling points. The size of the file storing the signal data needed to reconstruct the sound wave also increases proportionately with the sampling rate.

Several factors affect the choice of sampling rates. Sampling rates vary depending on what is being recorded. Music would require a high sampling rate in comparison to a simple voice recording. The quality of sound may not be an issue when leaving a voice mail message. However, most listeners are fairly discriminating regarding the quality of their music.

Audio Resolution

The original sound card was an 8-bit card. Today, most quality sound cards are 16-bit. You can record a better image of the original sound using a 16-bit rather than an 8-bit card. A system based on 8-bit sound is limited to using 256 levels, or binary codes, to store a binary image of the sound wave sample. A 16-bit sound card can use 65,536 binary codes to store the sound wave pattern during each sampling. The 16-bit system can save a more detailed representation of the analog sound wave pattern than an 8-bit system.

Think in terms of graphic picture resolution. A better graphic image can be produced using 16 bits, rather than 8 bits, per pixel. Look back to Figure 8-34 where sampling rate and reconstructed analog wave shapes are illustrated. In the illustration of sampling rates, the height of the sample is measured in bits. A more detailed graph can be reconstructed by using more bits for the initial readings taken.

Audio resolution is based on two key factors: sampling rate and number of bits used to represent the analog sound. Sampling rate is how often a sample or snapshot of the sound is taken. The number of bits used to represent the analog sound determines the sensitivity of the analog measurement represented as a voltage level. Together these two quantities determine the quality of the sound captured and played back.

The original sound card was 8-bit which meant that there were 256 possible levels of audio sound level that could be captured during each momentary sampling period. A 16-bit card can capture 65, 536 discrete levels of sound. A 24-bit card can capture 16,777,216 discrete levels of sound. Today, most quality sound cards are 16-bit, 24-bit, and higher. The more bits used to record the audio image of the sound, the better the quality of the sound.

A typical sampling rate is 44.1 kHz or 44. This is equal to 100 times per second for 16-bit and 96 kHz for 24-bit. A 24-bit sound card with a sampling rate of 99 kHz will record 4 bytes of data 99,000 times a second. A 24-bit 96 kHz sampling rate will result in 33 MB of storage for a one minute recording. As you can see, audio recordings require a significant amount of data storage.

MIDI Files

musical instrument digital interface (MIDI) a file standard developed for music synthesizers.

Musical instrument digital interface (MIDI) is a file standard developed for music synthesizers. Synthesized music is electronically simulated music sounds rather than recorded sounds. A chip, or set of chips, can produce the sounds of many instruments, **Figure 8-35.** To play music, input through the chips is made from a database containing information such as the type of instrument to play, the actual note to play, the length of sound, and any special effects such as an echo chamber effect. The music is actually a sequence of coded instructions sent to the chips that make the sounds. An advantage of MIDI is that it is a universal file format. A disadvantage is that many MIDI audio systems sound like artificial music to the ear. After all, they are artificial sounds produced by chips rather than real instrument recordings.

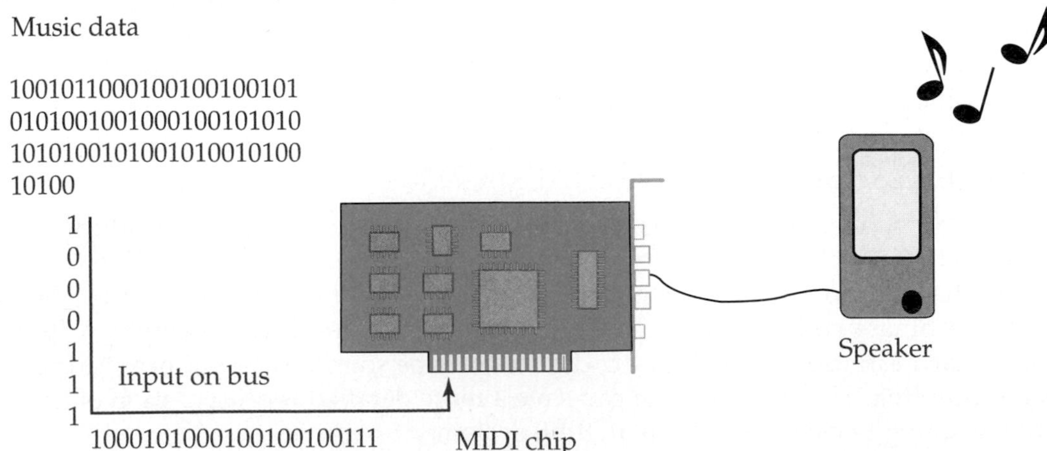

Figure 8-35. A MIDI chip is capable of reproducing sound from a selection of instruments that are stored in its memory.

Figure 8-36.
A typical keyboard (left) with its MIDI interface (right).

MIDI can be created electronically by connecting a PC to a sound synthesizer or keyboard, **Figure 8-36.** The keyboard has selector switches from which the user can select dozens of different instruments. A song can be recorded in MIDI data format to be saved and played back on the PC. Once the sound track is saved, it can be manipulated to add special effects. A single musician can create music similar to a complete orchestra of instruments.

Audio Devices

There are numerous audio devices for the PC. They include both input devices, such as the microphone, and output devices, such as the speaker. Most of these devices are tied into the PC through the sound card.

Microphones

A microphone is a simple electronic device used to convert sound waves into electrical energy. The microphone converts the air vibration that strikes it into voltage levels that are in direct proportion to the strength and frequency of the vibrations. The electrical energy is analog in nature. **Figure 8-37** shows sound waves striking a microphone and their conversion to digital data.

When the signal reaches the sound card, the analog electrical signal is converted to a digital signal, which allows it to be stored in RAM, on a hard drive, or on a CD. When the sound is stored as a digital code, it is often referred to as a "wave" file because it usually has a .wav file extension. A one-minute .wav file can vary in size from 500 kB to over 20 MB depending on variables. Some of these variables are the speed of the sampling frequency, whether monaural or stereo sound is being recorded, whether 8-bit or 16-bit sampling is used, and what compression technique is being used (if any).

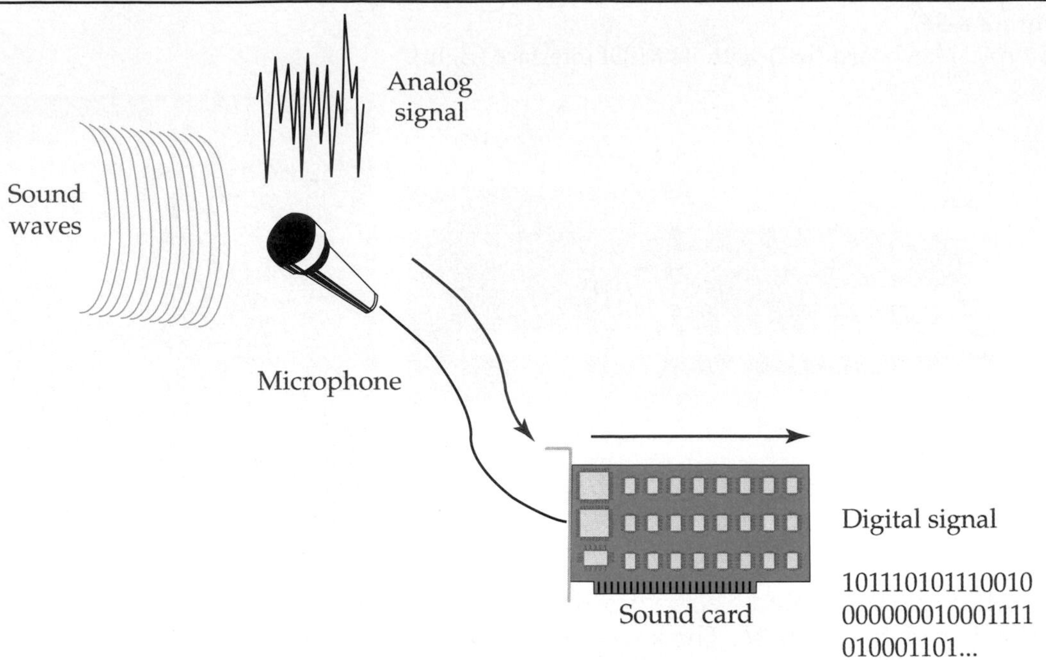

Figure 8-37.
An analog sound signal is turned into an analog electrical signal by a microphone and then into a digital electrical signal by a sound card.

Speakers

A speaker converts electrical energy back to sound energy. Look at **Figure 8-38** to see a digital sound passing through a sound card and out through a speaker.

To listen to stored digital code, the code is sent back through the sound card and is then converted back to an analog electrical signal. As the electrical energy varies in strength, the speaker cone is vibrated at a rate proportional to the analog electrical signal.

Take note of the 120-volt converter unit. The 120-volt converter unit is used to power the amplifier inside the speaker. The speaker amplifier takes the small analog signal it receives from the sound card and powerfully reproduces it. A typical sound card cannot provide ample power to drive a speaker. Most sound cards only produce approximately 2 watts of energy. This is sufficient to drive only a headphone set, not a desktop speaker. When a speaker has its own built-in amplifier, it is called an *active speaker.* A speaker without amplification is called a *passive speaker.*

Sound Cards

Most sound cards purchased today are PCI adapter cards. This means they are Plug and Play technology. All system resources (IRQ, DMA, I/O port addresses, memory addresses) are automatically detected and assigned. Older 8-bit ISA adapter type cards will most likely require system resources to be manually assigned through software or physically assigned by setting jumpers or dip switches.

System conflicts are quite common for older ISA type cards. Always check the system resource assignments when problems arise, especially after newer hardware has been installed to an existing system. Software diagnostic programs included in most operating systems can diagnose conflicts. Windows 98 and higher versions have diagnostic software to assist you with conflicts with system

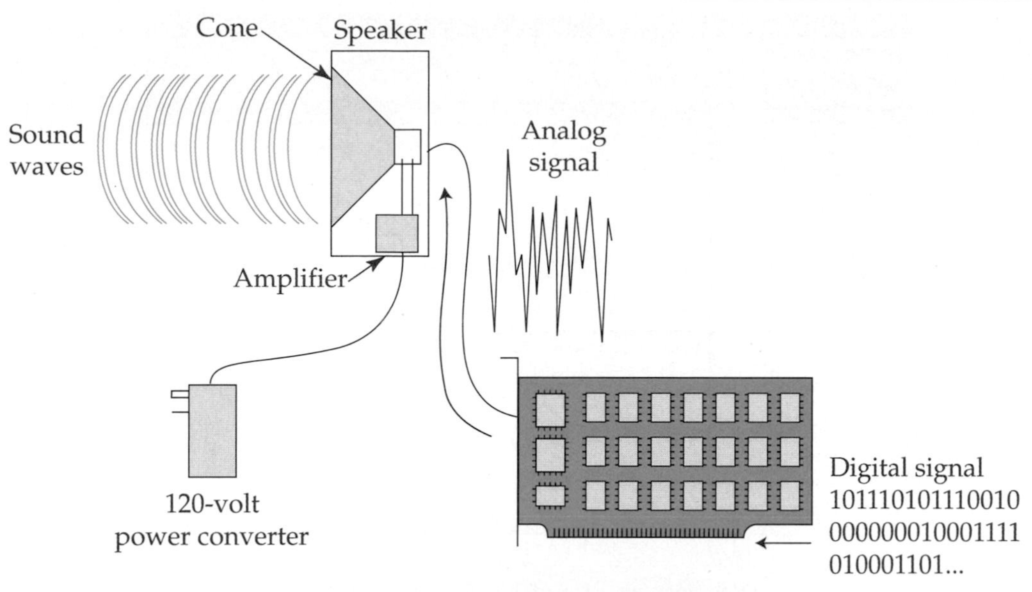

Figure 8-38.
The sound card changes a digital signal back into an analog electrical signal. This electrical signal is used to produce sound by the speaker.

resources. These tools can be accessed through **Start | All Programs | Accessories | System Tools | System Information**. **Figure 8-39** shows the **Microsoft System Information** dialog box. It can assist you when solving system resource conflicts. You can use this window to analyze conflicts arising from system resource assignments.

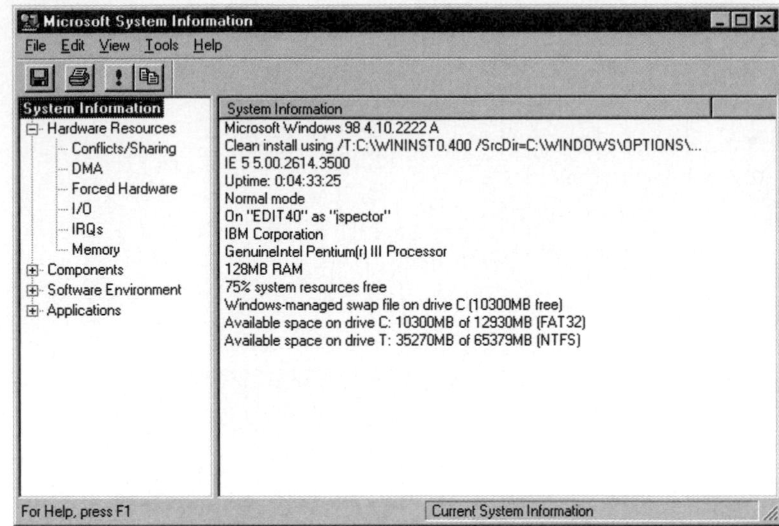

Figure 8-39. The **Microsoft System Information** dialog box can be used to help troubleshoot conflicts. It shows the IRQs, DMAs, and I/O port addresses a computer's components are using.

Installing a Sound Card

Installing a sound card before Plug and Play could be very frustrating. The source of frustration came from system resource assignments. There was almost a guarantee of a system resource conflict appearing with legacy sound cards. Multimedia type cards use all areas of system resources. Before installing any legacy sound card, review the IRQs, DMA, memory addresses, and I/O port address topics covered earlier in the textbook.

Although Plug and Play should eliminate most conflicts, there can still be problems, especially when upgrades are performed. As new technologies evolve, there will be the need to upgrade current technologies. In other words, Plug and Play operates well now, but a new technology will appear in the future that will also require Plug and Play to be upgraded or redesigned. The following steps are used for the installation of a typical sound card:

1. Power off the computer and unplug the power cord from the wall outlet.
2. Read the card procedure and specification sheet.
3. Take normal static precautions.
4. Check for debris in the expansion slot.
5. Insert the card into the slot by applying even force to the top of the card. Do *not* rock the card into the slot.
6. Check if there are any cables that might interfere with the sound card. Voltages can be induced by wires in close proximity to the sound card. This can cause distortion of the sound quality. Keep cables away from sound cards.
7. Connect the speakers to the computer and connect the speaker's power supply to the speakers. Turn the speakers on before powering on the computer.
8. Power on the computer.

The card should be auto detected if it is Plug and Play. You may have to supply the driver for the new adapter card when the system detects the card. The Windows system may not have the correct driver for the card. The driver should have been packaged with the sound card as a CD-ROM. Also check the manufacturer's Web site for the latest patch or upgrade for the driver. Follow the screen prompts to complete the installation. If all has gone well, you should be able to turn off the power, install the cover, and then reboot the system. If the installation failed, reread the installation procedure. Check for simple things first. For example, is the power supply module for the speakers plugged in? Or, is there a bent pin at one of the connection points? Check if the volume is turned up. You may also need to upgrade the BIOS on the motherboard. Check the Web site of the motherboard manufacturer and the sound card manufacturer for the latest updates.

Multimedia

Interaction with audio and video is referred to as ***multimedia.*** Attempts to create and play multimedia files more quickly and clearly has been one of the major driving factors in the computer industry. The computing power needed to render three-dimensional images and the storage needed to store or even play movies have caused the processing speeds of CPUs and the RAM considered "minimum requirements" on PCs to increase over the last few years. The greatest recent changes in PC operating systems are changes to how they handle multimedia.

multimedia
incorporating sound or video.

MPEG Formats

The ***Motion Picture Experts Group (MPEG),*** (pronounced empeg), is an organization made up of professionals from all areas of the motion picture industry. The goal of the organization was to develop a standard format for recording motion picture video and sound. Together they developed data compression standards and file formats for storing both audio and video data. The two main formats are MPEG-1 and MPEG-2. MPEG-1 is similar to videotape quality. MPEG-2 is a higher quality compression used for PC CD video, Digital Versatile Disc (DVD) (also called *Digital Video Disc*), and HDTV.

The MP3 standard (short for *MPEG* layer 3) is used for music. It is a derivative of the MPEG-2 standard. (To avoid confusion, MP3 is also a well-known Web site, but the site takes its name from the format.) MPEG-4 came out in 1999, and there are several more MPEG standards under development. Check the Web page provided by the Motion Picture Experts Group for the latest updates.

Motion Picture Experts Group (MPEG)
a standard format for recording motion picture video and sound.

Codecs

A term frequently used in compression is ***codec.*** The term *codec* is a contraction of the two words compression and decompression. A codec is any hardware, software, or combination hardware and software that can compress and decompress data. The term is used most often in the video industry and telecommunications. MPEG is only one form of codec. There are others such as Indeo, Cinepak, QuickTime, and DVsoft. When setting up properties for audio and video equipment using Windows, the many compression techniques will be referred to as choosing a method of codec.

codec
any hardware, software, or combination hardware and software that can compress and decompress data.

Buffering

buffering a technique used to play a downloaded file without skips or quiet spots during playback.

Buffering is a technique used to play a downloaded file without skips or quiet spots during playback. When downloading music from a site, it must travel hundreds or even thousands of miles from the source to your PC. Unless you have a high-bandwidth connection such as a T1 or cable, you will have difficulty maintaining a steady stream of data from the other site. In Chapter 13—Modems and Transceivers, more detailed information about various connection mediums, such as T1 lines, is presented.

Data is sent across phone lines to your PC in packets that average 1500 bytes each. As noted earlier, data for sound is quite large. A music sample may be constructed from thousands of the 1500-byte packets. The data does not arrive as a consistent series of packets. Many data packets will even arrive out of their original order. The reason the data packets can arrive out of order is that the data route to and from the site is constantly being updated. The Internet is composed of millions of miles of lines. Many of the lines become congested with data traffic. At times, data packets are rerouted to achieve a faster transmission rate. If a quicker route is discovered by the transmission system while data is transferred, the balance of the data will be transmitted through the new route, **Figure 8-40.** If another route is discovered or the present one becomes very busy, an alternate route is chosen. As the routes continue to change, some of the packets arrive out of the original order.

In addition, the steady stream of packets can be momentarily stopped due to congestion on the lines. In the last few years, the dramatic increase in video and audio data packets has created a lot of traffic on the data lines resulting in an apparent slow down of the entire system. A good example of these seemingly slow systems can be seen on many college campuses where scores of students are downloading music and video files from the Internet at one time.

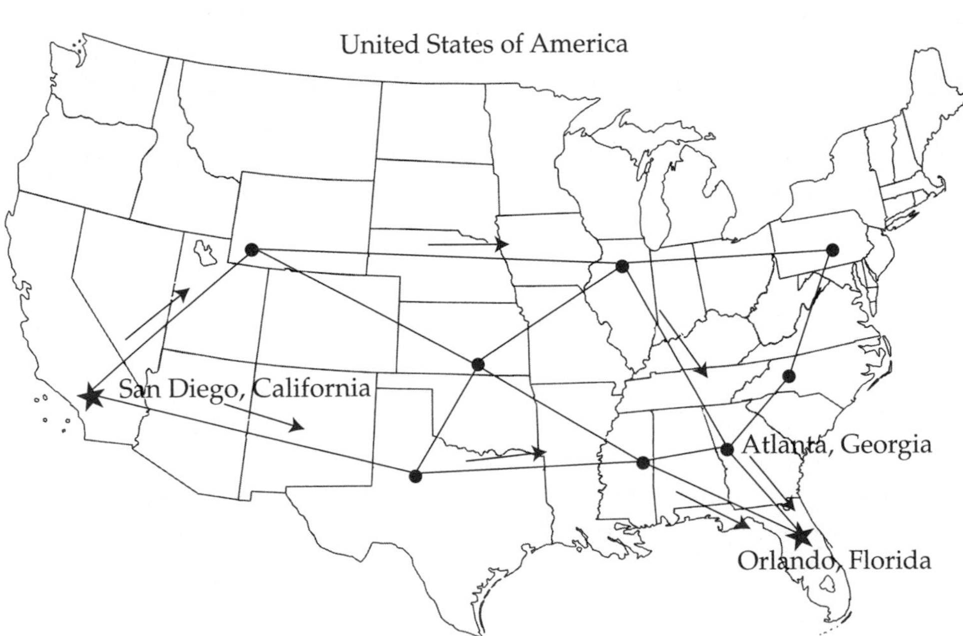

Figure 8-40. Different routes for data flow. The shortest route is not always the quickest.

The packets must be reassembled at their destination. Buffering collects all the downloaded data and reassembles it in its original order. It then provides a steady stream of data. In the case of downloading a song, the act of buffering means the song data is downloaded into RAM. It is then assembled and transferred to the player. The player plays the song from a steady stream of data located in RAM rather than from the site. With buffering, there are no interruptions in the continuous stream of music.

Audio and Video Players

To access sound and video tracks recorded on the PC or taken from the Internet, you need a player which is often called a *plug-in*. A player is used to decode compressed multimedia files converting them to audio and video. Players can convert more than one type of compression, but when a new or enhanced compression format is developed, you will need to download an updated version of the player. See **Figure 8-41.**

A large variety of media players are available through the Internet at no charge. Some of the players are only designed to allow you to play through the Internet browser. They will not actually record.

Figure 8-41. Microsoft includes Windows Media Player with its operating system.

The quality of the multimedia presentation is directly related to the quality and capacities of the computer system you use. However, upgrading a single component on an existing system may not show any real improvement. Too often, novices assume that upgrading the CPU or adding more RAM will greatly improve the performance. A system needs to be studied as a whole before a decision is made about enhancing multimedia performance. For example, upgrading the CPU and adding more memory will do little to improve the quality of the multimedia performance if the system uses an 8-bit sound card inserted into an ISA slot. A major improvement may have resulted by simply replacing the sound card with a 16-bit PCI sound card.

Summary

- ✔ There is a danger from high voltage levels inside a CRT computer monitor. Never open a computer monitor.
- ✔ There is a danger from implosion when handling CRT computer monitors.
- ✔ Pitch is the distance between pixels on a video screen.
- ✔ All colors produced on a display monitor are derived from red, blue, and green.
- ✔ Screen resolution expresses the amount of detail that can be displayed on a screen or in an image. Resolution is usually measured in pixels.
- ✔ An image is formed on a CRT monitor by a stream of electrons striking the phosphorous coating inside the CRT.
- ✔ A shadow mask ensures a sharp image on a CRT-type display.
- ✔ Liquid crystal material twists when energized.
- ✔ The two main types of LCD panels are active and passive.
- ✔ Contrast ratio is a measurement of contrast between the darkest and lightest pixel that can be displayed.
- ✔ Native resolution is the resolution that is based on the number of actual pixels designed in the monitor.
- ✔ Aspect ratio expresses the relationship of height to width of a display.
- ✔ Gas-plasma displays do not require a backlight.
- ✔ Analog-to-digital conversion takes a periodic sample of the voltage levels in an analog signal and stores them in digital format.
- ✔ Digital-to-analog conversion converts the stored digital information patterns back into analog wave shapes.
- ✔ AGP was developed strictly for use by video cards.
- ✔ PCIe ×16 is the preferred bus type for video cards.
- ✔ Most sound card problems are generated by system resource conflicts.
- ✔ A bitmap image distorts when changed to a different scale; a vector image does not.
- ✔ A vector image is stored as a series of mathematical formulas that represent the image.
- ✔ Compressing a file is a technique that summarizes redundant information contained in a file.
- ✔ Codec is any technology that compresses and decompresses a file.
- ✔ Buffering is a technique that downloads a stream of data packets and reassembles them in correct order before using the data in an application.

Review Questions

Answer the following questions on a separate sheet of paper. Please do not write in this book.

1. What two dangers should you be concerned with when working around CRTs?
2. How is monitor size determined?
3. The distance between two color pixels is called _____.
4. Dot pitch is measured in _____.
5. The smaller the dot pitch the (better, worse) the screen resolution.
6. What is a pixel?
7. Which type of standard display has the highest resolution?
   a. VGA
   b. XGA
   c. SVGA
   d. WUVGA
8. Which type of standard display has the lowest resolution?
   a. VGA
   b. XGA
   c. SVGA
   d. WUVGA
9. What is the screen resolution for XGA?
10. What is the screen resolution for WUXGA?
11. What screen resolution is used when Windows XP or Windows Vista is in safe mode?
12. What three colors are produced by the electron guns inside a color CRT?
13. What is raster?
14. Describe the difference between progressive scan and interlacing.
15. What is the difference between passive and active matrix?
16. What two factors determine the quality of converting an analog signal into a digital signal?
17. Define the term *contrast ratio* when describing LCD displays?
18. What is the unit of measure for a LCD display?
19. What is native resolution?
20. What affect does a high response time have on animation?
21. Why does a gas-plasma display not require a backlight?
22. What should you use to clean an LCD display?
23. Which motherboard slot type will produce the fastest graphics?
24. What does the acronym SLI represent?
25. What ATI technology is similar to NVIDIA SLI?
26. What does the acronym DVI represent?
27. What type of image retains its quality after resizing?
28. Explain how a picture image is compressed.
29. What is codec?

Sample A+ Exam Questions

Answer the following questions on a separate sheet of paper. Please do not write in this book.

1. When a PC boots in safe mode, which video mode is used by the system?
   a. VGA
   b. SVGA
   c. XGA
   d. CGA
2. Which of the following is the best definition of dot pitch?
   a. The distance between two color dots measured in pixels
   b. The distance between two color dots measured in inch fractions
   c. The distance between two color dots measured in millimeters
   d. The distance between the diagonal of the screen corners measured in millimeters
3. Which screen resolution provides the greatest image detail?
   a. VGA
   b. XGA
   c. SVGA
   d. UVGA
4. Which is a standard VGA resolution?
   a. 640 × 480
   b. 860 × 1280
   c. 320 × 480
   d. 1280 × 960
5. A typical VGA monitor connects directly into which type of adapter card connector?
   a. 9-pin D-shell
   b. 15-pin D-shell
   c. 25-pin D-shell
   d. Any of the above may be used.
6. A customer complains of eyestrain when using a CRT computer monitor. Which action would *most likely* remedy the problem?
   a. Increase the monitor's refresh rate.
   b. Lower the screen intensity and resolution.
   c. Increase the screen contrast and resolution.
   d. Lower the monitor's refresh rate.
7. Which example would provide the best quality for a sound recording?
   a. An 8-bit, high frequency sampling rate
   b. A 16-bit, high frequency sampling rate
   c. An 8-bit, low frequency sampling rate
   d. A 16-bit, low frequency sampling rate
8. The term *codec* best relates to which of the following answers?
   a. Sound quality measurement
   b. Picture quality measurement
   c. A compression and decompression technique
   d. A sound transmission media type

A+

9. A music file is being downloaded and played at the same time. The music constantly starts, stops, and skips repeatedly. What is *most likely* the reason?
   a. Insufficient amount of RAM. The amount of memory should be increased.
   b. The modem speed needs to be increased to 112 baud.
   c. This is a normal effect caused by low download speeds.
   d. The DMA channels are blocked by too much bus traffic.
10. The smallest picture element on a monitor display is called what?
    a. Raster element
    b. Pixel
    c. Byte mark
    d. Color element

Suggested Laboratory Activities

Do not attempt any suggested laboratory activities without your instructor's permission. Certain activities can render the PC operating system inoperable.

1. Make sound recordings and experiment with changing the sampling rates.
2. Use Control Panel to install and modify the properties of a digital camera input system.
3. Create a new set of sounds for closing, opening, and maximizing windows. To do this in Windows XP, access **Control Panel | Sounds, Speech, and Audio Devices | Sounds and Audio** and select the **Sounds** tab. In Windows Vista, access **Control Panel | Hardware and Sound | Sound**.
4. Adjust the refresh rate of the monitor and observe the effects. In Windows XP, this is usually accomplished by clicking the **Advanced** button in the **Settings** tab of the **Display Properties** dialog box. Next, the **Monitor** tab should be selected from the video adapter **Properties** dialog box. A list of available refresh rates can be found in the drop-down list box, but be aware that not all video cards and monitors allow adjustments to the refresh rate. After you have experimented with changing the refresh rate, return the refresh rate back to its default setting. To adjust the refresh rate in Windows Vista, access **Control Panel | Appearance and Personalization | Personalize | Display Settings**. Click the **Advanced Settings** button, and then the **Monitor** tab.

Some video cards and monitors cannot support higher than normal refresh rates.

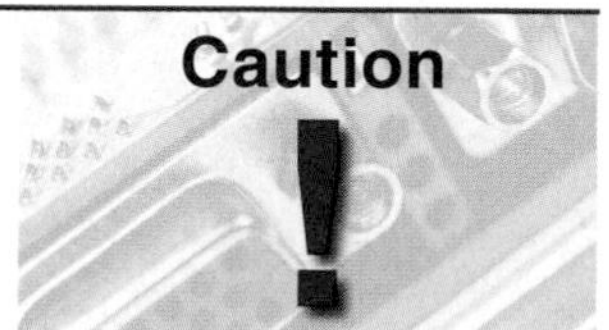

5. Locate and identify the driver for the monitor. This information should be provided in the video adapter's **Properties** dialog box. Detailed instruction for accessing this dialog box is given in the previous activity.

6. Download new audio clips from the Web. Use one of the audio clips to greet PC users after they boot the system. Remember that new system sounds are assigned in Windows XP by accessing **Control Panel | Sounds, Speech, and Audio Devices | Sounds and Audio** and select the **Sounds** tab. In Windows Vista, it is accessed through **Control Panel | Hardware and Sound | Sound**.
7. Experiment with various wallpapers in the **Background** tab of the **Display Properties** dialog box in Windows XP and in the **Desktop Background** dialog box in Windows Vista. Change the screen saver by selecting the **Screen Saver** tab of the **Display Properties** dialog box in Windows XP or by accessing the **Screen Saver** dialog box in Windows Vista.
8. Create a unique desktop wallpaper using the Windows Paint program.
9. Download a Paint Shop Pro or SnagIt trial program and create a unique animated screen saver.
10. Use a digital camera to create a unique desktop wallpaper for your assigned PC. Make it a computer "techie" theme.
11. Install a new multimedia system, including a newer sound card, video card, and CD-ROM drive, in an older PC. Before starting, make sure the PC is upgradeable. Check the PC and multimedia manufacturers' Web sites for hardware concerns, such as BIOS support.

Interesting Web Sites for More Information

http://apple.com/quicktime

www.alesis.com

www.ATI.AMDcom

www.bell.com

www.ddwg.org

www.echoaudio.com

www.korg.com

www.lucent.com

www.microsoft.com

www.midiman.com

www.mp3.com

www.nVidia.com

www.roland.com

www.sony.com

www.soundblaster.com

www.vesa.org

www.yamaha.com

Chapter 8
Laboratory Activity
Display Properties

After completing this laboratory activity, you will be able to:

- ✔ Modify the appearance of the desktop area.
- ✔ Change the screen saver.
- ✔ Adjust the screen resolution.
- ✔ Change the monitor's refresh rate.

Introduction

This laboratory activity will familiarize you with the many setting options available for a standard display. You will change many of the display settings, and then restore the original settings. Throughout the laboratory activity, you will be prompted to write down the settings before you change or experiment with them. This will assist you when attempting to restore the system to its original configuration.

In Windows XP, the **Display Properties** dialog box can be used to change the appearance of the desktop, screen saver, windows, and dialog boxes. The more advanced settings in the **Display Properties** dialog box affect the technical performance of the monitor, such as refresh rate and energy management. The variety and effect of display-setting options depends on the display manufacturer's hardware and drivers. For example, not all monitors allow you to change the refresh rate. For some monitors, refresh rate is determined entirely by the hardware and the driver software.

In Windows Vista, the various display adjustments are made through several dialog boxes accessed through **Control Panel | Appearance and Personalization | Personalization**. The following screen capture shows the locations for changing the color and appearance of the windows and dialog boxes, desktop background, screen saver, and refresh rate and resolution.

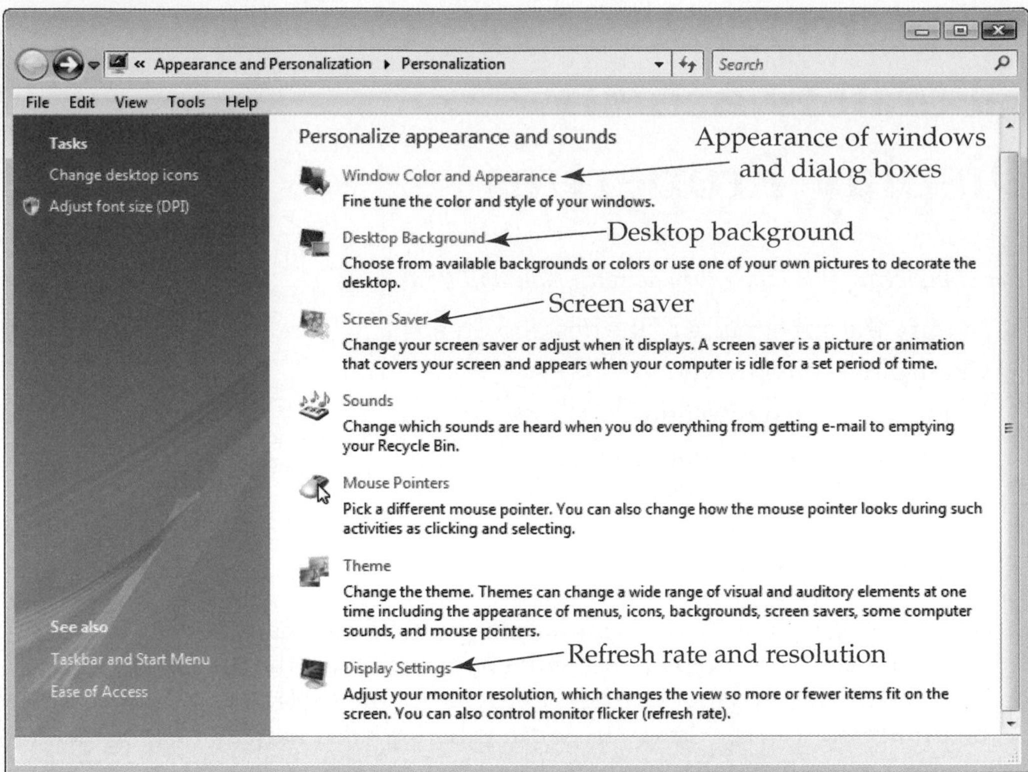

Some of the settings will be viewed but not used in this lab activity. Do not make any permanent changes to the desktop area. If you follow the information in the lab activity, you will not permanently change any of the settings. The settings you change will only be temporary.

Equipment and Materials

✔ Typical PC with a SVGA monitor and Windows XP or Windows Vista installed. (A VGA monitor may be substituted.)

Note:

This lab activity is divided into two parts. The first part provides procedures for adjusting the display setting in Windows XP and the second part provides procedures for adjusting properties in Windows Vista. If you have access to both operating systems and ample lab time, perform both parts of the lab activity. This will give you the opportunity to compare the display settings of both operating systems.

Part I (Windows XP)

Procedure

1. ______ Boot the PC and wait for the desktop display.
2. ______ Access the **Display Properties** dialog box through **Control Panel | Appearance and Themes | Display**. You can also access **Display Properties** by right-clicking the desktop and selecting **Properties** from the shortcut menu. The **Display Properties** dialog box should appear similar to the one that follows.

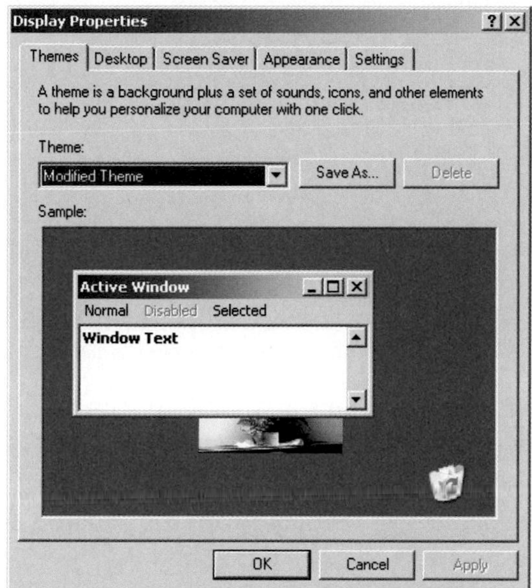

3. ______ On a separate sheet of paper, list the tabs found in the **Display Properties** dialog box. For example, the first tab is **Themes**.
4. ______ Select the **Settings** tab. A dialog box similar to the following will display.

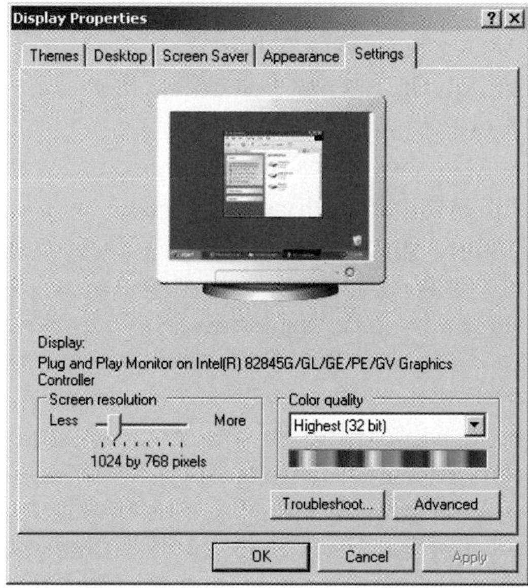

5. _______ Next, click the **Advanced** button. This opens a dialog box that incorporates your video card name in its title bar. On a separate sheet of paper, list the names of the tabs available in this dialog box.

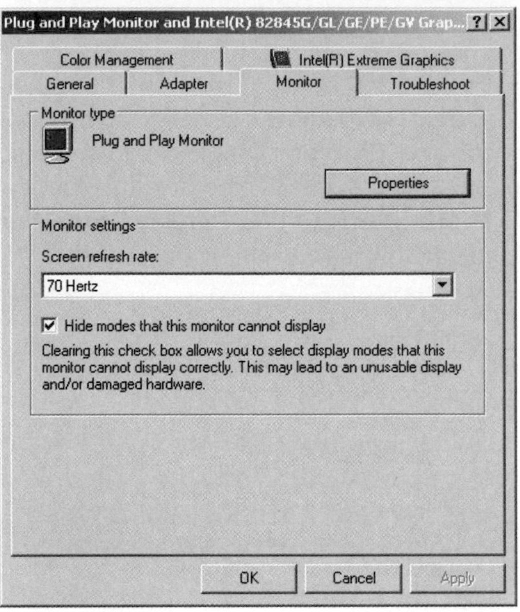

6. _______ Compare the sets of tabs available in this dialog box and the **Display Properties** dialog box. Can you tell which set is used for cosmetic purposes and which set is used for the display's technical settings?

7. _______ Now go back to the **Display Properties** dialog box by clicking the **Cancel** button in the new dialog box.

8. _______ Select the tab marked **Desktop**. This is where the screen's background can be changed. Another name for background is *wallpaper.* A list box beneath the word **Background** lists all of the files in the selected directory that can be used as wallpaper. The currently selected wallpaper is highlighted in the list. On a separate sheet of paper, record the name of the current wallpaper so that you can restore it when you are finished.

9. _______ Scroll through the list and select Ripple. Notice that the image of the monitor in this dialog box previews your selection.

10. _______ Select several other types of wallpaper and watch their effect.

11. _______ Restore the original wallpaper selection.

12. _______ Next, select the **Screen Saver** tab at the top of the **Display Properties** dialog box. This screen is where different screen savers can be selected and installed. Write down the name of the screen saver that is displayed in the **Screen Saver** list box so you can restore it after your experiment.

13. _______ Try selecting some different screen savers, and then clicking the **Preview** button to see their effect on the display.

14. _______ Next, select the **Appearance** tab at the top of the **Display Properties** dialog box. Look at the list box labeled **Color Scheme**. This is the title of the screen appearance now selected. Record it on a separate sheet of paper.

15. _______ Experiment by selecting different schemes.

16. _______ Next, restore the original scheme color.

17. _______ Select the **Settings** tab. This tab allows you to change the technical properties of the display, such as refresh rate. Click the button labeled **Advanced** to open a video card properties dialog box. This dialog box is where you can select or identify your video card (also referred to as video adapter) and your monitor. From this dialog box you can also change your refresh rate and accelerate the graphic display.

Note:

The refresh rate can be changed to a higher setting to help relieve eyestrain. The optimal setting is usually fine, but at times it may need to be faster to relieve eyestrain. The eye can perceive the raster moving across the screen even though the brain allows us to see only the image presented. Nevertheless, the action of the raster can cause eyestrain and headaches after a long period. A screen that has an apparent flicker usually needs a higher refresh rate.

18. _______ Take the rest of the time allocated for this lab activity to experiment with the settings available in the **Display Properties** dialog box. If you intend to do the second part of this lab activity, spend only a few minutes and then go on to part two.

    Before changing any settings, write down the current setting. After you have experimented with a new setting, immediately restore the original setting before changing the next. Change only one setting at a time. Changing several settings at the same time can lead to confusion when trying to return the display to its original state. For your first experiment, change the **Screen resolution** setting, which is listed under the **Settings** tab. See how this affects the screen display area.

19. _______ You may leave the PC on and the **Display Properties** dialog box open while answering the review questions. After you have answered all the questions, return all display properties to their original settings and properly shut down the PC.

Review Questions (Windows XP)

Answer the following questions on a separate sheet of paper. Please do not write in this book.

1. Name two ways of accessing the **Display Properties** dialog box in Windows XP.
2. What tab would you select in the **Display Properties** dialog box to change the desktop background?
3. What other name does Microsoft use for desktop background?
4. What tab in the **Display Properties** dialog box would you select to change the color scheme of Windows dialog boxes and screens?
5. What tab in the **Display Properties** dialog box would you select to adjust the resolution of the screen display?
6. What happens to the size of the screen icons when you select a higher resolution on the **Screen resolution** slider?
7. Where would you change the monitor's refresh rate?

Part II (Windows Vista)

Procedure

1. _______ Boot the PC and wait for the desktop display.
2. _______ Access the **Personalization** window through **Control Panel | Appearance and Personalization**. You can also access **Personalization** by right-clicking the desktop and selecting **Properties** from the shortcut menu. On a separate sheet of paper, list the options found in the **Personalization** window. For example, the first option is **Window Color and Appearance**.
3. _______ Select the **Display Settings** option and then click the **Advanced Settings** button. This opens a dialog box that incorporates your video card name in its title bar. On a separate sheet of paper, list the names of the tabs available in this dialog box.
4. _______ Compare the sets of tabs available in this dialog box and the options listed in the **Personalization** window. Can you tell which set is used for cosmetic purposes and which set is used for the display's technical settings?
5. _______ Now go back to the **Personalization** window by clicking the **Cancel** button in the opened dialog boxes.
6. _______ Select the **Desktop Background** option. A dialog box similar to the following will display. This is where the screen's background can be changed. A list box next to the word **Picture Location** lists all of the types of backgrounds that can be used. The pictures for the background types are listed as a thumbnail in the center window. The currently selected background (thumbnail) is highlighted. On a separate sheet of paper, note the current background so that you can restore it if you need to.

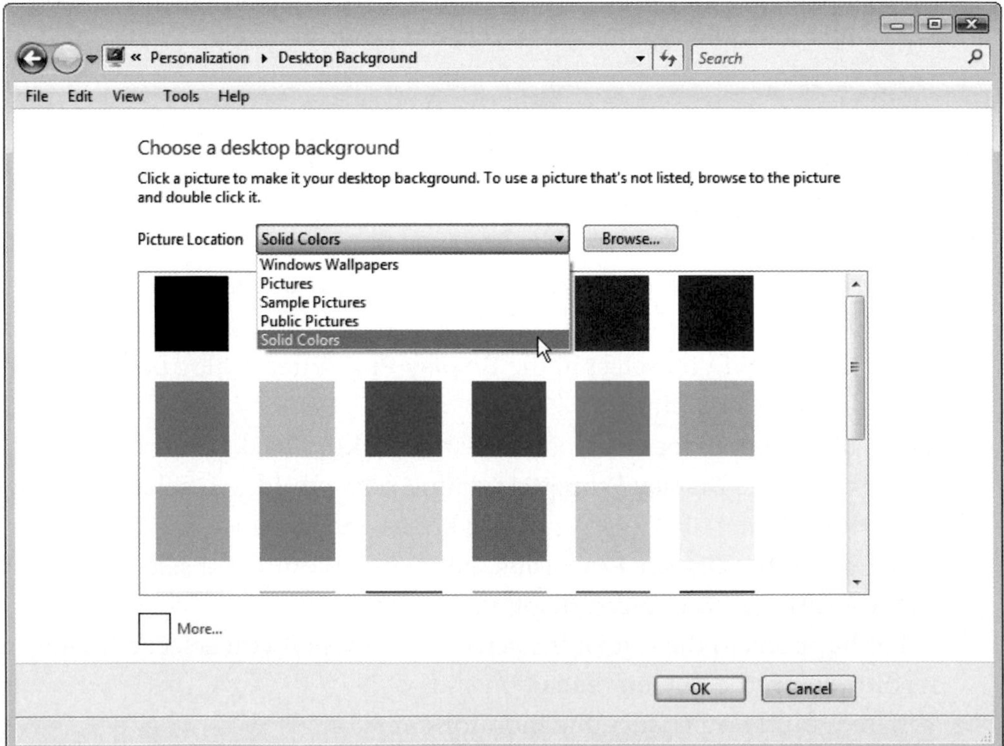

7. _______ Select the different types of backgrounds and look at the available backgrounds for each type.
8. _______ Click **Cancel** to return to the **Personalization** window.
9. _______ Next, select the **Screen Saver** option. This screen is where different screen savers can be selected and installed. Write down the name of the screen saver that is displayed in the **Screen Saver** list box so you can restore it after your experiment.
10. _______ Try selecting some different screen savers. Watch the effect on the monitor image in the dialog box. To see the effect on your display, click **Preview**.
11. _______ Click **Cancel** to return to the **Personalization** window.
12. _______ Select the **Color and Appearance** option. Look at the list box labeled **Color Scheme**. The title of the current screen appearance is highlighted. Record it on a separate sheet of paper.
13. _______ Experiment by selecting different color schemes.

Note:

To take advantage of Windows Aero features, a computer must meet the recommended requirements or be Premium Ready.

14. _______ Next, restore the original color scheme and then return to the **Personalization** window.
15. _______ Select the **Display Settings** option. This option allows you to change the technical properties of the display, such as refresh rate. Click the button labeled **Advanced Settings** to open a video card properties dialog box. This dialog box is where you can select or identify your video card (also referred to as video adapter) and your monitor. From this dialog box you can also change your refresh rate and accelerate the graphic display.
16. _______ Take the rest of the time allocated for this lab activity to experiment with the settings available in the **Personalization** windows. Before changing any settings, write down the current setting. After you have experimented with a new setting, immediately restore the original setting before changing the next. Change only one setting at a time. Changing several settings at the same time can lead to confusion when trying to return the display to its original state. For your first experiment, change the **Resolution** setting, which is listed under the **Display Settings** option. See how this affects the screen display area.
17. _______ You may leave the PC on and the **Personalization** window open while answering the review questions. After you have answered all the questions, return all display properties to their original settings and properly shut down the PC.

Review Questions (Windows Vista)

Answer the following questions on a separate sheet of paper. Please do not write in this book.

1. Name two ways of accessing the **Personalization** window in Windows Vista.
2. What option would you select in the **Personalization** window to change the desktop background?
3. What option would you select in the **Personalization** window to change the color scheme of Windows dialog boxes and screens?
4. What option would you select in the **Personalization** window to adjust the resolution of the screen display?
5. Where would you change the monitor's refresh rate?

Magnetic Storage Devices

After studying this chapter, you will be able to:

- ✔ Explain how magnetic principles are used for data storage.
- ✔ Understand disk geometry.
- ✔ Explain how disk fragmentation occurs.
- ✔ Explain the purpose of using ScanDisk and Chkdsk.
- ✔ Identify major parts of common disk storage units.
- ✔ Select the appropriate file storage system.
- ✔ Explain how to install a second hard drive.

A+ Exam—Key Points

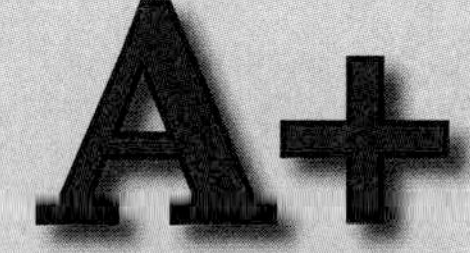

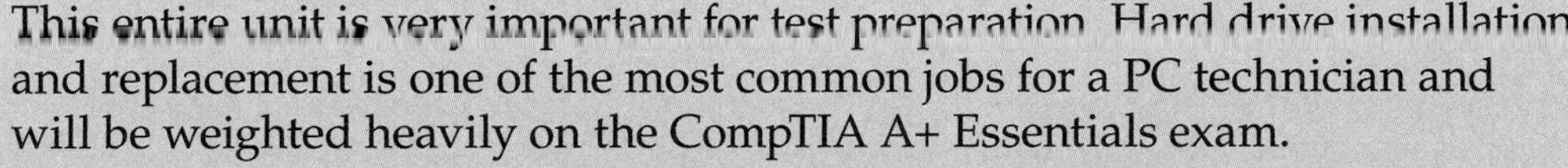
This entire unit is very important for test preparation. Hard drive installation and replacement is one of the most common jobs for a PC technician and will be weighted heavily on the CompTIA A+ Essentials exam.

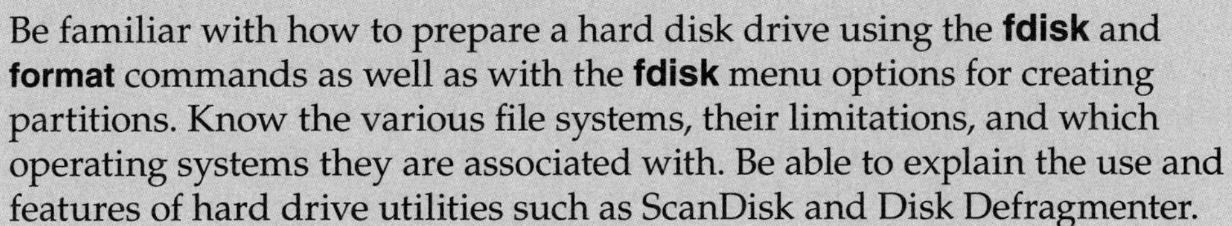
Be familiar with how to prepare a hard disk drive using the **fdisk** and **format** commands as well as with the **fdisk** menu options for creating partitions. Know the various file systems, their limitations, and which operating systems they are associated with. Be able to explain the use and features of hard drive utilities such as ScanDisk and Disk Defragmenter.

In addition, thoroughly familiarize yourself with the hard drive terminology listed in the Key Words and Terms section.

Key Words and Terms

The following words and terms will become important pieces of your computer vocabulary. Be sure you can define them.

active partition
actuator arm
AT Attachment (ATA)
basic disk
benchmark tests
cluster
cylinder
defragment
dual boot system
dynamic disk
encrypted file system (EFS)
Enhanced Integrated Drive Electronics (EIDE)
FAT16
FAT32
floppy disks
floppy drive
formatting
fragmented
High Performance File System (HPFS)
high-level format
Integrated Drive Electronics (IDE)
interleave factor
logical drives
logical unit numbers (LUN)
low-level format
LS-120 drive
master
Master Boot Record (MBR)
multiple zone recording (MZR)
New Technology File System (NTFS)
partitions
read/write head
ScanDisk
SCSI ID number
Serial Attached SCSI (SAS)
sectors
slave
Small Computer System Interface (SCSI)
Solid State Drive (SSD)
tracks
virtual file allocation table (VFAT)
volume mount points
Zip disk

This chapter will prove to be one of the most important units covered in the entire textbook. It will give you incredible insight as to how an operating system organizes, stores, and retrieves data. This information can prove invaluable when troubleshooting system failures. Magnetism has been used to record data for many years. Magnetic storage devices have been the mainstays of the PC industry. This chapter thoroughly covers magnetic storage systems such as hard drives, floppy disks, and tape systems. First, electromagnetic principles are explained to provide the proper foundation for understanding how magnetic storage devices work.

Electromagnetic Principles

To understand complex devices like hard drives and other disk drives, you first need some background in electromagnetic principles. These principles allow hard drives and floppy disks to store volumes of data. However, these principles also place restrictions on their use and construction.

Converting Data to Magnetic Patterns

Electrical energy can produce magnetism, and magnetism can produce electrical energy. This principle is the basis of magnetic storage device operation. A fine layer of iron oxide covers the data storage area of a typical storage device such as tape or a disk platter. Iron oxide is easily magnetized when it is exposed to an energized conductor. A conductor is any material that allows for the easy flow of electricity. Any energized conductor is surrounded by a rotating magnetic field. The direction of the rotation determines the north and south characteristics of the magnetic field. The direction of rotation around the conductor is determined by the direction of current in the conductor.

Look closely at **Figure 9-1.** It shows the relationship of current direction and the magnetic field surrounding a conductor. The conductor is wound around the top of the magnetic ***read/write head*** to increase the amount of magnetic energy created by the electrical current. At the bottom of the magnetic head, there is a gap. This gap is used to transfer the magnetic energy to the oxidized surface of a floppy disk, hard disk, or magnetic tape. All magnetic recording devices use this same principle.

read/write head the mechanism that records information to and reads information from a magnetic medium.

A digital signal is composed of rising and falling voltage levels. These rising and falling voltage levels produce a changing current direction. As the current (digital signal) changes direction through the conductor wound around the read/write head, the magnetic field at the gap changes. As the digital signal flows through the read/write head, a magnetic pattern is impressed on the iron oxide. The magnetic pattern represents the digital pattern sent to the read/write head. This is how data is stored on a magnetic disk or tape.

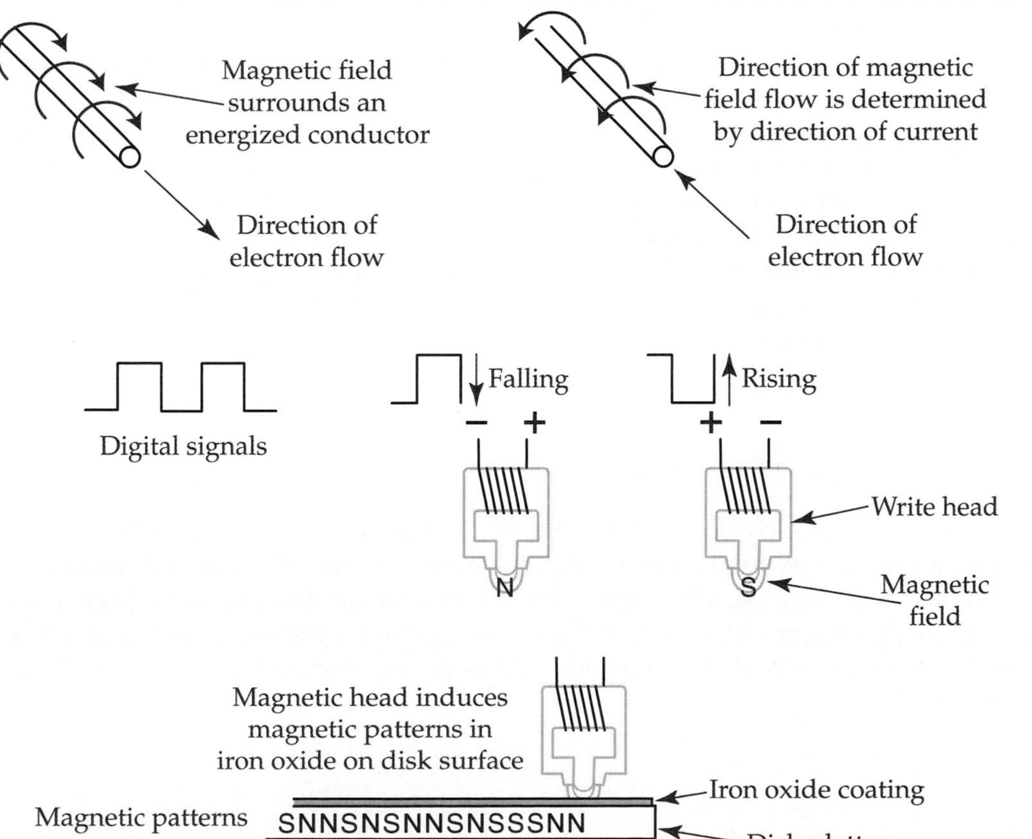

Figure 9-1. At the top, current flowing through a conductor produces a magnetic field. This field is concentrated in a magnetic write head (middle). The write head is then used to create patterns on a disk or tape surface (bottom).

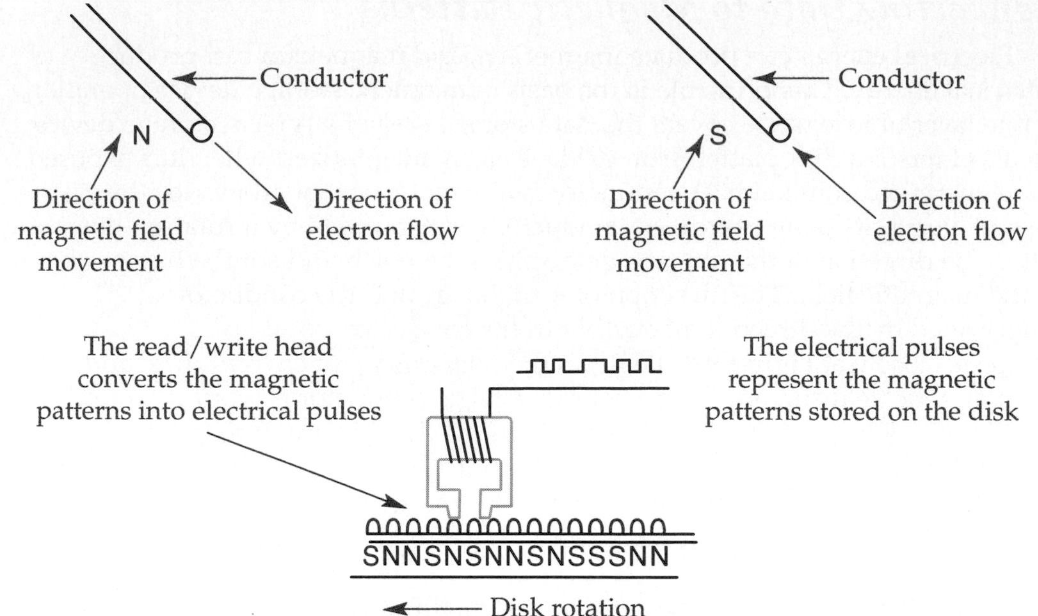

Figure 9-2. The magnetic patterns stored on a disk platter are converted back to electrical pulses representing the data stored on a disk. As the platters spin rapidly under the read/write head, the magnetism creates electrical energy in the read/write head.

Converting Magnetic Patterns into Computer Data

To read the data back from a disk or tape, an electrical signal is generated from the magnetic patterns. Electrical energy can be produced by the motion of a magnetic field near a conductor. Look at **Figure 9-2.** The direction of the current produced in the conductor is directly related to the north and south property of the magnetic field.

As you now know, a magnetic disk has a magnetic pattern along its surface. As the magnetic pattern on the surface of the disk passes rapidly under the read/write head, electrical energy is produced in pulses. The electrical pulses that are generated match the pattern on the magnetic code stored on the disk. The pulses of electrical energy are very small, so an amplifier circuit is needed. The amplifier magnifies the electrical energy produced from the magnetic patterns stored on the media to a level high enough to be used by the computer circuitry and components. The amplifier is integrated into the electronic circuitry on the media drive's circuit board.

Hard Disk Structure

A typical hard drive consists of several platters in a stack. The platters can be made from glass, an aluminum alloy, or even ceramic. The top and bottom of the platter are coated with a thin film of metal oxide. The metal oxide records the magnetic patterns introduced to the disk platter by the read/write head. The read/write head is located at the end of an ***actuator arm,*** which moves the head over the disk.

actuator arm
the device that moves the read/write head over the disk.

At one time, the head was constructed of very small wire coils. Read/write head technology has now evolved to such microscopic size that the same technology used to manufacture chips is also used to create the read/write head. The read/write head can produce extremely compact magnetic patterns exceeding 10,000 bits per inch.

The hard disk drive is simple in design but very impressive when you consider the tolerances within which it operates. See **Figure 9-3.** The read/write head does not actually touch the platter. Instead, it rides over the platter on a cushion of air. The distance from the surface of the disk platter is only a few microns. Since the head travels so closely to the platter, the platter must be absolutely flat and free of defects. Any defect on the surface of the platter would destroy the read/write head on contact.

Hard drives have filters to catch any microscopic particles that might be produced during normal read/write operations. Remember that the actuator mechanism is mechanical and will produce some particles through friction between the moving parts.

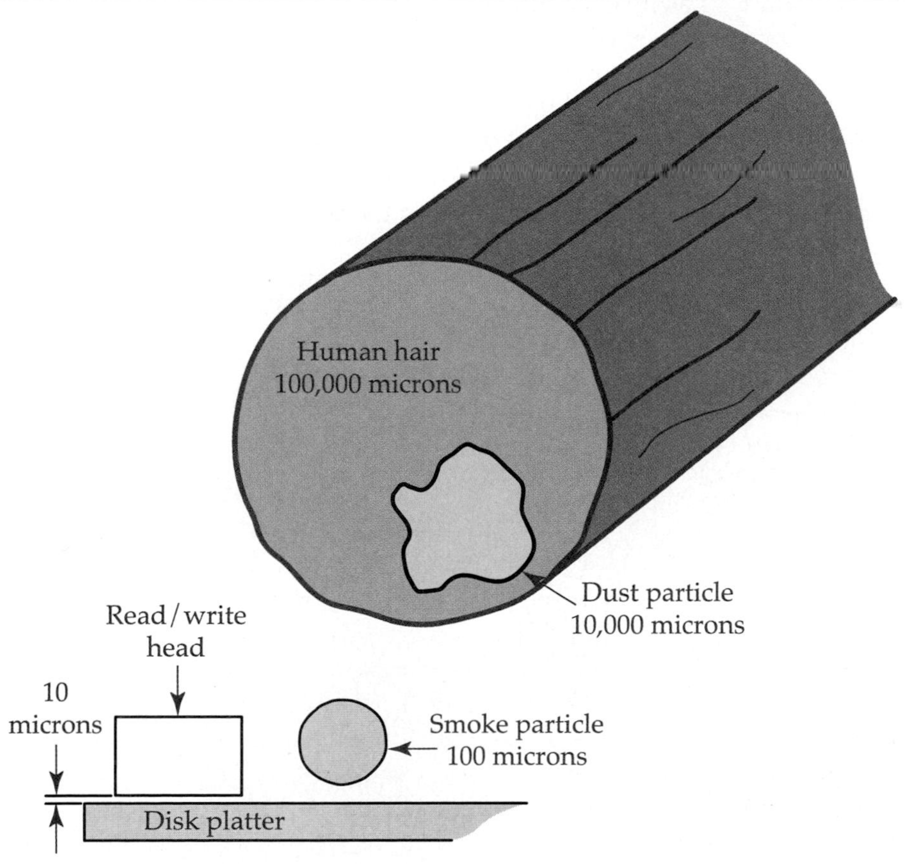

Figure 9-3.
The read/write head floats just above the spinning disk of a hard drive.

Disk Geometry

formatting
preparing a disk to receive data in a systematic, organized manner.

tracks
the concentric circles of data storage areas on a disk.

sectors
subdivisions of tracks, usually about 512 bytes in size.

cluster
composed of one or more sectors and are the smallest unit that a file will be stored in. Also referred to as allocation units.

cylinder
a vertical collection of one set of tracks.

Before a floppy or hard disk can be used to store data, it must be formatted. ***Formatting*** a disk prepares it to receive data in a systematic, organized manner. The surface of the disk is divided into sections that are used as storage areas for the data. The layout of the sections on the disk surface must be recognized by the computer operating systems. The sections used to record data on a disk drive are described in terms such as *sectors, clusters, tracks,* and *cylinders,* **Figure 9-4.**

A set of concentric circles represents the ***tracks*** where data is stored. The tracks are subdivided into physical sections called ***sectors.*** The term ***cluster,*** or ***allocation units,*** is used as a description of file storage space and usually consists of one or more sectors. The smallest sector or cluster size is 512 bytes.

A sector is a "*physical*" description of a portion of a track. A cluster is a "*logical*" file storage unit, which may span several sectors.

While a floppy disk is a single layer, a hard disk drive consists of a stack of platters. Each platter has its own tracks, clusters, and sectors. A ***cylinder*** is a vertical collection of one set of tracks. There is one cylinder for every stack of tracks. The read/write heads move across the platters in unison. All tracks are written to simultaneously. Thus, data files are stored in cylinders for fast access.

When writing to a disk, each head writes data to the disk sequentially. Head 1 writes data on the first available sector on the top surface of platter one. When another sector is needed, head 2 writes data on the bottom of the top platter. Head 3

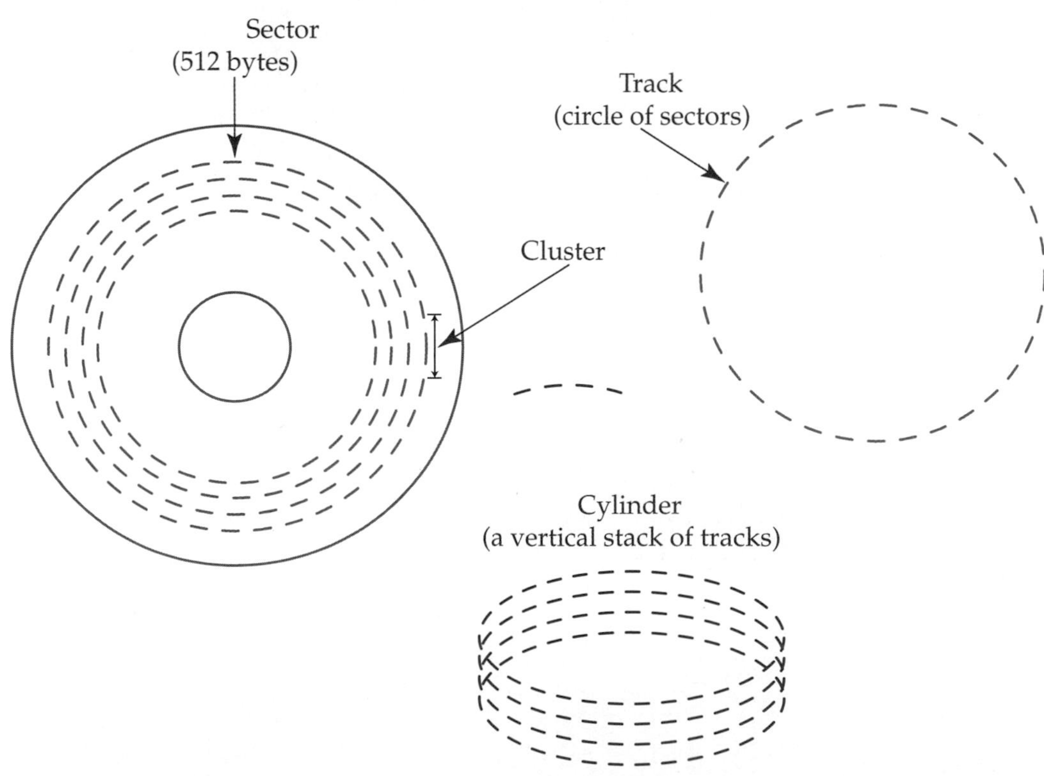

Figure 9-4. Typical disk geometry. Disks can be subdivided into sectors, tracks, and cylinders.

writes data on the top of the second platter and so on. This scheme of data recording is continued using the read/write heads in sequence until all the data has been recorded. Thus, the data of a single file can be spread over several disk platters.

A typical cluster size range is from 4 kB to 32 kB each. It is important to note that the size of the cluster is directly related to the size of the hard disk drive when using certain file systems such as FAT12, FAT16, FAT32, and NTFS. These file systems are discussed in detail later in this chapter.

File systems often derive their names from the amount of available space used to identify the clusters in binary form and to store the value in the file allocation table. The file allocation table binary code space is as follows:

FAT12 = 2^{12} entries

FAT16 = 2^{16} entries

FAT32 = 2^{28} entries

FAT32 only uses 2^{28} of the available 2^{32} possible entries. It saves the rest as spares for future development.

Data or a typical program stored on disk will span many clusters. There needs to be an organized way to keep track of all the clusters of data on a disk. Clusters open for storage space and those filled with data must be identified. The computer needs to know where clusters of a particular data group begin and end. The computer must also know which clusters on a disk are already being used for storage and which clusters are available for storage. Special areas on a disk are used to organize and keep track of all of this information. The Master Boot Record contains partition information and a small amount of executable code that starts the computer operating system.

In a FAT16 or FAT32 formatted system, the file allocation table (FAT) contains information about where each file starts on the disk. In a system formatted as NTFS, a master file table (MFT) contains similar information for the NTFS system. See **Figure 9-5.**

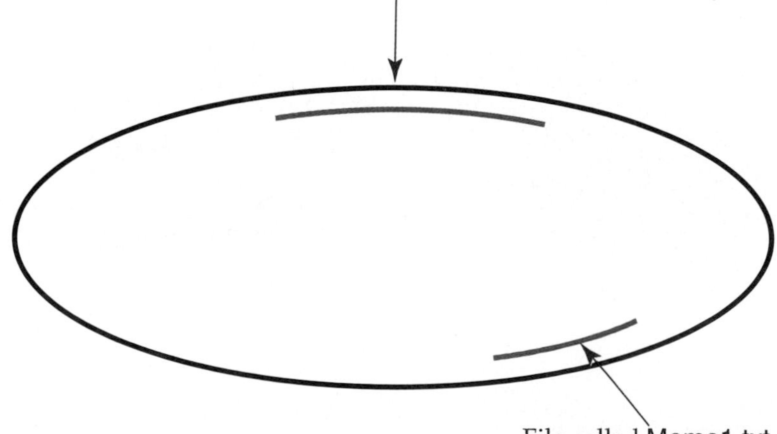

Figure 9-5. Three pieces of information are necessary to locate a file on a disk: the drive letter (to locate the drive the data is stored on), the name of the file or directory, and the cluster locations of the file.

Two DOS commands are used to prepare a disk for storage: **fdisk** and **format**. These commands are covered in detail later in this chapter. The disk geometry is created by the command **format**. When the **format** command is issued, the disk is prepared to store data by organizing the surface of the magnetic media into tracks containing sectors and clusters. To keep track of how the clusters are organized on a disk, a boot record is installed when the disk is formatted.

Multiple Zone Recording

multiple zone recording (MZR) a method of sectoring tracks so there are twice as many sectors in the outermost tracks as there are in the innermost tracks.

Early disk drive geometry provided an equal number of sectors on the innermost and outermost tracks. To improve storage capacity of the platters, a new method of sectoring the tracks was developed. Because there is wasted space in the outer tracks on the platter, multiple zone recording was developed. ***Multiple zone recording (MZR),*** also called *zone bit recording*, provides twice as many sectors in the outermost tracks as compared to the innermost tracks. See **Figure 9-6.**

Master Boot Record

Master Boot Record (MBR) an area of the hard disk that contains information about the physical characteristics of the drive, the disk partitions, and the boot procedure. Also referred to as the boot sector.

The most important area on a hard disk is the Master Boot Record. The ***Master Boot Record (MBR)*** contains information about the disk partition areas such as the number of bytes per sector, number of sectors per cluster, number of clusters per track, number of tracks, total number of clusters, number of read/write heads, and the type of storage media (floppy disk or hard drive). It also contains the boot software program used to access or transfer control of the computer system to the operating system.

The MBR is created when a disk is partitioned. It is located at sector one, cylinder zero, head zero. **Figure 9-7** shows the critical files pattern on a hard disk. This pattern is standard for FAT16 file systems. Other compatible systems have also followed this design to maintain downward compatibility.

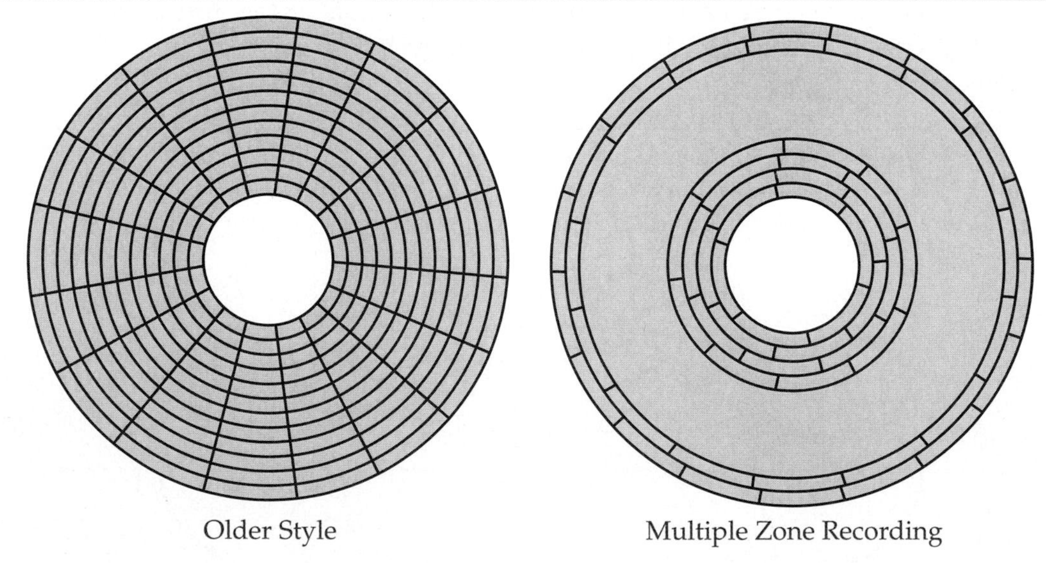

Figure 9-6. Multiple zone recording allows for more sectors on the outer tracks of a disk. The disk on the left reflects the older style for setting up sectors on a hard drive. Inner and outer tracks contain the same number of sectors. The disk on the right shows multiple zone recording. There are more sectors on outer tracks than inner tracks with multiple zone recording.

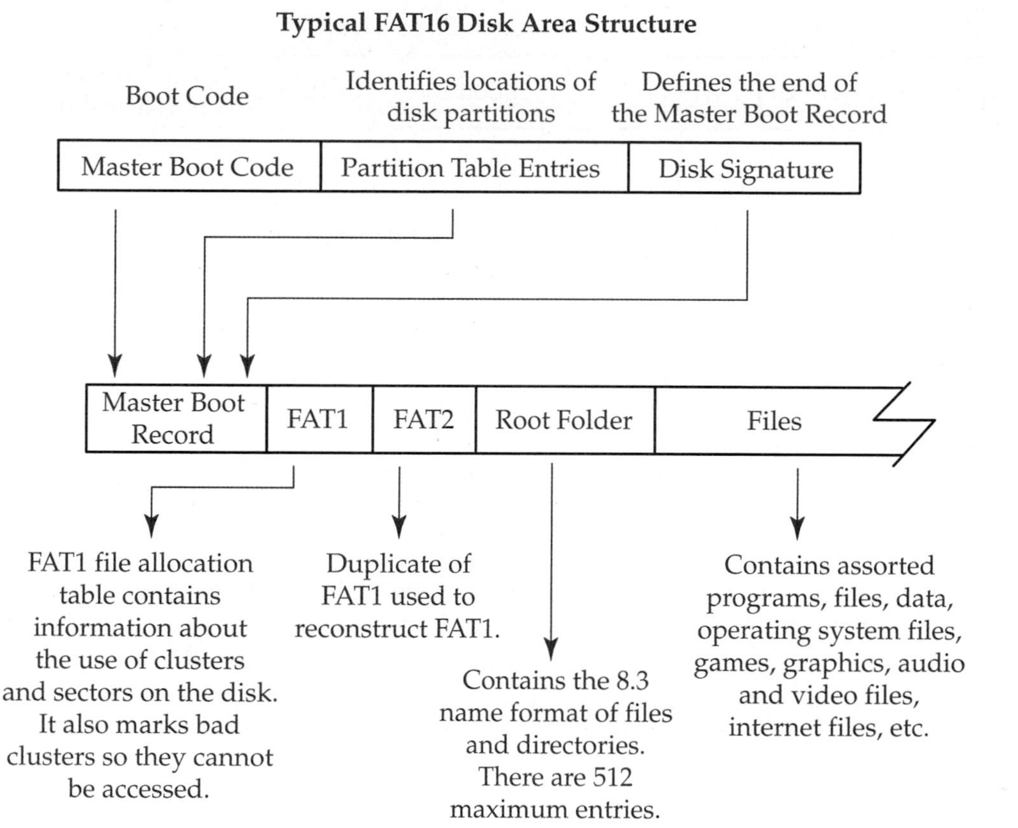
Typical FAT16 Disk Area Structure
Boot Code
Identifies locations of disk partitions
Defines the end of the Master Boot Record
Master Boot Code
Partition Table Entries
Disk Signature
Master Boot Record
FAT1
FAT2
Root Folder
Files
FAT1 file allocation table contains information about the use of clusters and sectors on the disk. It also marks bad clusters so they cannot be accessed.
Duplicate of FAT1 used to reconstruct FAT1.
Contains the 8.3 name format of files and directories. There are 512 maximum entries.
Contains assorted programs, files, data, operating system files, games, graphics, audio and video files, internet files, etc.

Figure 9-7. Layout of a typical FAT16 system.

A bad sector or cluster anywhere on a disk simply causes a loss of that particular file. Often, parts of a file can be recovered using a third-party utility program, such as Norton Utilities. When the MBR is corrupted or infected by a virus, access to the entire disk is lost. The MBR may be recoverable if precautions have been taken. One method of recovery is to have a copy of the MBR saved on floppy disk so that it can be reinstalled to replace the corrupted sector that contains the MBR.

A hard drive can be divided into two or more logical drives called ***partitions.*** Having one hard drive with multiple partitions simulates having multiple hard drives. Each partition has its own boot record, but one partition must contain the master boot record. The master boot record is located on the partition that is used to boot the operating system. See **Figure 9-8.**

partitions areas on a hard drive that simulate separate drives. Also referred to as logical drives.

Tech Tip: There can be a lot of confusion concerning proper terminology of the Master Boot Record. Often, the MBR is referred to as the boot record, boot sector, master boot sector, and boot program. This text uses terminology as defined by Microsoft in the *Microsoft Resource Kit.*

Root Directory

The root directory identifies the files and directories by name. It also identifies files that are associated with various directories and their location on the disk. It stores information such as the file extension, file attribute, time, date, and location of the first cluster.

Figure 9-8. A disk drive can be divided into many sections called partitions. Each partition is identified with a drive letter such as C, D, E, up to the drive letter Z.

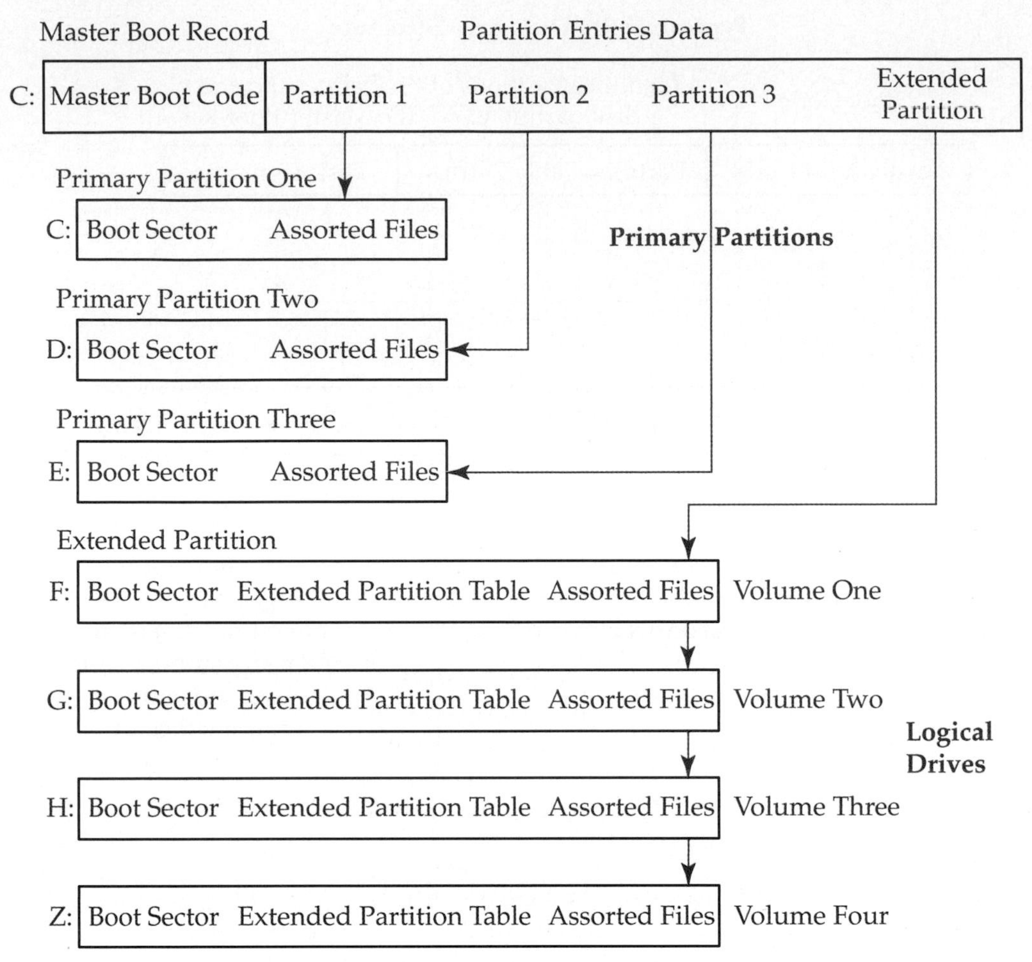

FAT16 has a limit to the number of files (512) that can be contained in the root directory. This does not imply that a hard disk storage unit can only contain 512 files. It means that there can be only 512 unique names of files and directories in the root directory of a FAT16 file system. There can be more files on the hard disk by the use of directories and subdirectories. A directory in the root directory appears as a single file, but it can have an unlimited number of files contained under it as files and subdirectories.

Disk Partitions and Fdisk

Hard drives are partitioned for several reasons. The user may wish to have more than one operating system on a computer. When two logical drives are created from one hard drive, one partition of the drive could be used for Windows XP and the other for Linux. A multiple operating system installation is usually referred to as a ***dual boot system.*** When the computer boots, the user is prompted to choose which operating system is to be used. If no selection is made, the default system is booted after a given length of time.

dual boot system a system in which multiple operating systems are stored. The user chooses the operating system when the computer boots.

Hard drives can also be divided into several partitions to separate different types of files such as business files and games. This important aspect of partitioning makes it easy for the user to make backups of critical files. If the original is destroyed or lost, a backup still exists on another partition.

It is normal to partition a disk that is larger than 2 GB when using DOS. One of the limitations of DOS is that it can only directly access a maximum of 2 GB of space. For example, a drive with 8 GB of storage space may be partitioned into four 2 GB areas. All areas can be used for storage of programs and data. Each of the partitioned areas of the drive will have a unique drive letter (C, D, E, and F).

When a disk is partitioned, it is divided into separate storage areas. The separate storage areas are often referred to as ***logical drives.*** Logical drives are not physically separate drives even though they appear to the user as a separate drive. See **Figure 9-9.** In this screen capture, a 10 GB hard drive has been partitioned into several areas. Notice how many hard drives are displayed. You can see five hard drives indicated by the letters C, D, E, F, and G. These are five logical hard drives created from one large physical hard drive.

logical drives separate storage areas on a single drive that simulate separate drives. Also referred to as partitions.

Another reason for partitions is security. In Figure 9-9, drive C is set up on a network as a share. The hand under the drive is the symbol for a shared drive. The term *shared* means that the drive can be used or shared by other computers on the network. The other drives on this computer are not shared and cannot be accessed by other users on the network.

The **fdisk** command is used to partition a hard drive. When multiple partitions are created on a hard drive, only one of the partitions is designated as the active partition. The ***active partition*** is where the operating system will boot. It is the designated boot disk for the system. The master boot record can be reconstructed using the command **fdisk/mbr**. It is a commonly used method of restoring the hard disk once the disk failure has been analyzed and determined to have a bad or corrupt MBR.

active partition the designated boot disk for the system.

The use of the fdisk command destroys any existing data on the hard drive. In addition, you do not necessarily have to issue the command fdisk to obtain the same disastrous results. It is common for the computer to ask if you want to partition or repartition a hard drive while installing an operating system.

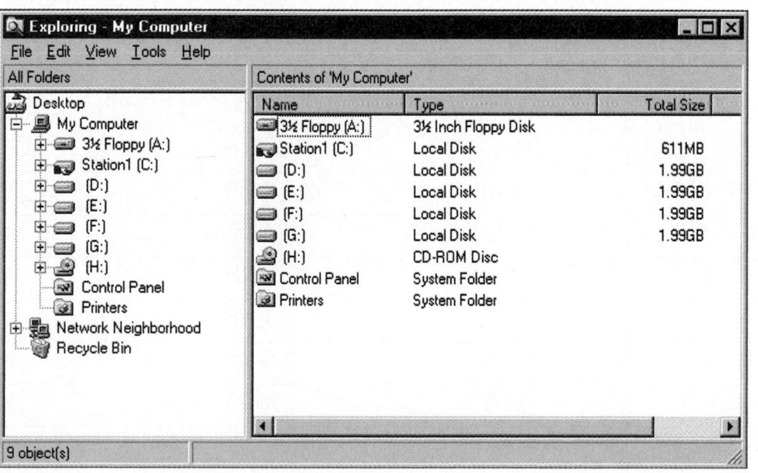

Figure 9-9. Windows Explorer showing a 10 GB hard drive partitioned into drives C through G.

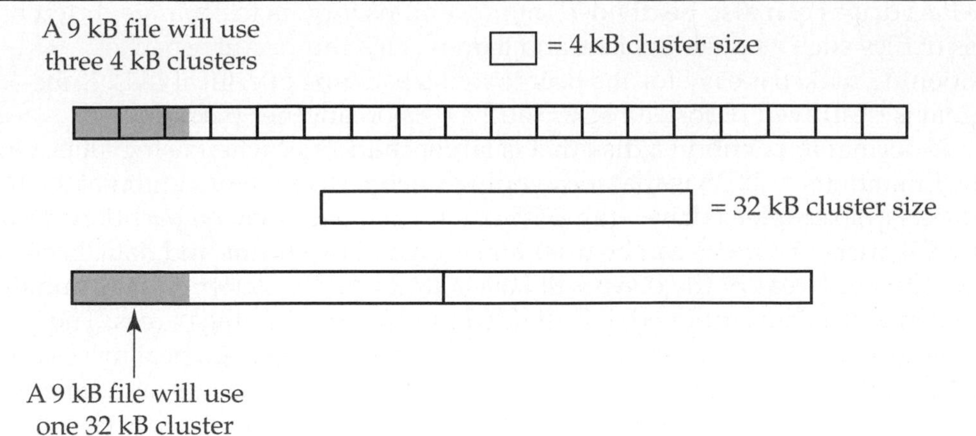

Figure 9-10. Comparison of cluster utilization of disk storage area for a 9 kB file. The 4 kB cluster format wastes only 2 kB of storage space when storing the file. The 32 kB cluster format wastes 23 kB of space.

The minimum amount of space a file can occupy is a cluster. The size of clusters on a hard drive is directly related to the size of the hard drive. Larger hard drives have larger clusters. The hard drive can have clusters as large as 64 kB. With 64 kB clusters, even if a file size were only a few hundred bytes total, the entire 64 kB cluster would be required for storing the small file. Examine **Figure 9-10.**

By partitioning a hard drive, smaller cluster sizes can be used. Since the cluster size is directly related to partition size, you can have more efficient use of disk space by using more than one partition. For example, a 20 GB hard drive formatted with FAT32 as one partition will contain 16 kB clusters. The same 20 GB hard drive formatted with FAT32 but divided into two equal partitions will contain 8 kB clusters. Partitioning improves the efficiency of disk storage space.

The size of the cluster is also dependent on the FAT system used. The chart in **Figure 9-11** details cluster size in relation to hard drive size and the FAT system used. Note the NTFS cluster sizes compared to FAT16 and FAT32. The NTFS system uses much smaller cluster sizes than FAT16 and FAT32. This results in better use of hard disk space.

Figure 9-11. Comparison of cluster size for FAT16, FAT32, and NTFS. NTFS allows the smallest cluster for larger partitions. This data is based on the Windows 2000 Resource Book.

Volume or Partition Size	FAT16 Cluster Size	FAT32 Cluster Size	NTFS Cluster Size
7 MB–16 MB	2 kB	NA	512 bytes
17 MB–32 MB	512 bytes	NA	512 bytes
33 MB–64 MB	1 kB	512 bytes	512 bytes
65 MB–128 MB	2 kB	1 kB	512 bytes
129 MB–256 MB	4 kB	2 kB	512 bytes
257 MB–512 MB	8 kB	4 kB	512 bytes
513 MB–1024 MB	16 kB	4 kB	1 kB
1025 MB–2 GB	32 kB	4 kB	2 kB
2 GB–4 GB	64 kB	4 kB	4 kB
4 GB–8 GB	NA	4 kB	4 kB
8 GB–16 GB	NA	8 kB	4 kB
16 GB–32 GB	NA	16 kB	4 kB
32 GB–2 TB	NA	NA	4 kB

File Allocation Tables

The file allocation area is referred to as the file allocation table (FAT). The FAT contains information about how the clusters on the disk are being used and which ones are associated with each other. For example, a file may span four clusters of storage on the disk. The FAT retains a record of which clusters are used to store a particular file, such as clusters 127, 128, 129, and 130. It is important to note that there are two file allocation tables on a disk. One is the primary FAT and the other is a duplicate of the first. The second FAT is used to reconstruct the first in case of corruption.

FAT16 and FAT32

There are several forms of FAT. The original DOS and the original release of Windows 95 used ***FAT16.*** The 16 represents the number of bits used to identify stored data. The maximum storage area for a FAT16 system is limited to 2 GB.

FAT16
a file system in which file storage information is recorded with 16 bits of data.

As demand for greater storage capability evolved, the ***FAT32*** system was designed. Starting with Windows 95 OSR 2, this new FAT was available. Windows 95 OSR 2 and later Windows 9x operating systems can use either FAT16 or FAT 32. FAT32 uses 32 bits to identify stored data, and its upper limit for storage is theoretically 2 TB (terabytes). However, Windows 2000 limits the size to 32 GB. A number of different operating systems and the file systems that they support are listed in the table of **Figure 9-12.** Note that Windows Vista must be installed on an NTFS partition. However, additional partitions can be created with the Windows Vista operating system and formatted with FAT32. Also, Windows Vista can save data to a FAT16 or FAT32 partition or networked drive.

FAT32
a file system in which file storage information is recorded with 32 bits of data.

VFAT

Virtual file allocation table (VFAT) is not a truly independent file allocation table system but rather a method of programming related to the existing FAT16 root directory. This programming allows the FAT16 to appear to have long file name capabilities similar to FAT32. The long file names span over several normal 8.3 file name spaces on the FAT16 file allocation table, thus allowing the system to reflect long file names. This system is used for operating systems prior to Windows 95 OSR 2.

virtual file allocation table (VFAT)
a method of programming the FAT16 file system to allow long file capabilities similar to FAT32.

Operating System	File System(s) Supported
DOS	FAT16
Windows 95/98/Me	FAT16, VFAT, FAT32
Windows NT4.0	FAT16, NTFS
Windows 2000/XP/Vista	FAT16, FAT32, NTFS4.0, NTFS5.0
OS/2	FAT16, HPFS
LINUX	FAT16, FAT32, NTFS

*Windows Vista must be installed on an NTFS partition; however, it is backward compatible with FAT16 and FAT32.

Figure 9-12.
File systems. Note that each of the file systems maintains downward compatibility with the original DOS FAT16 system.

The VFAT system of storing file names in its root directory significantly reduces the total number of root directory files it can handle. NTFS and the Windows 2000 dynamic disk system has long file name capabilities without limiting the number of files that can be listed in the root directory.

NTFS

New Technology File System (NTFS) a file system found in Windows NT and Windows 2000. NTFS features improve security and storage capacity and are compatible with FAT16.

The ***New Technology File System (NTFS)*** was designed specifically to operate with the Windows NT operating system. Microsoft Corporation realized the limitations of FAT that included a 2 GB size limit for a volume on a hard drive and large cluster sizes. These factors resulted in wasted disk space. The NTFS was designed to ensure that much larger hard drives could be accommodated. The maximum hard drive volume that can be used with NTFS is 16 EB (exabytes). NTFS also limits the size of clusters, which results in less wasted space on the hard drive.

NTFS supports long file names for user convenience and security access features that are not available in FAT systems. NTFS is compatible with FAT16 but not with FAT32. Windows 2000 further developed the NTFS with additional features and called its file system *dynamic disk.* NTFS was originally more commonly found on a file server or an NT workstation than on a typical PC. However, with the introduction of Windows XP, Microsoft moved the home user to an NTFS-based file system.

Since the introduction of the dynamic disk file system, the name has been changed to NTFS5.0. The original NTFS is now called NTFS4.0. This can lead to a lot of confusion. Technical literature written during and before the year 2000 uses the terms *NTFS* and *dynamic disk,* while literature produced post 2000 uses *NTFS4.0* and *NTFS5.0.* Microsoft still uses the term *dynamic disk* in their own literature when describing the new file system, but publications that originate outside of Microsoft use NTFS5.0. In addition, Microsoft refers to FAT16, FAT32, and the original NTFS as *basic disk systems.*

Encrypted file system

encrypted file system (EFS) an NTFS native encryption system that uses a file encryption key (FEK) to encrypt and decrypt the file contents.

The ***encrypted file system (EFS)*** is the native encryption system used with NTFS. NTFS uses a file encryption key (FEK) to encrypt and decrypt the file contents. A single file, folder, or a complete data drive may be encrypted. A common way to use EFS is to create a folder in a directory and then set the properties of the folder to encrypt. After the folder is set for encryption, any file that is dropped into the folder will be encrypted. The encryption and decryption process is transparent to the authorized user of the file. EFS is an ideal security measure that can prevent confidential data from being accessed by unauthorized users.

The compression and encryption features in Windows XP can be accessed by right-clicking the item to be encrypted (file, folder, or data drive), selecting **Properties**, and then **Advanced. Figure 9-13** shows the **Advanced Attributes** dialog box.

EFS is not available in Windows XP Home Edition because the Home Edition does not support NTFS. Also, you cannot encrypt a file that is compressed.

NTFS compression

NTFS supports its own file compression system. The NTFS file compression allows you to compress a single file, a folder, or an entire volume. Like file encryption, file compression is transparent to the user. A compressed file opens and closes in a fashion typical to an uncompressed file. The only time

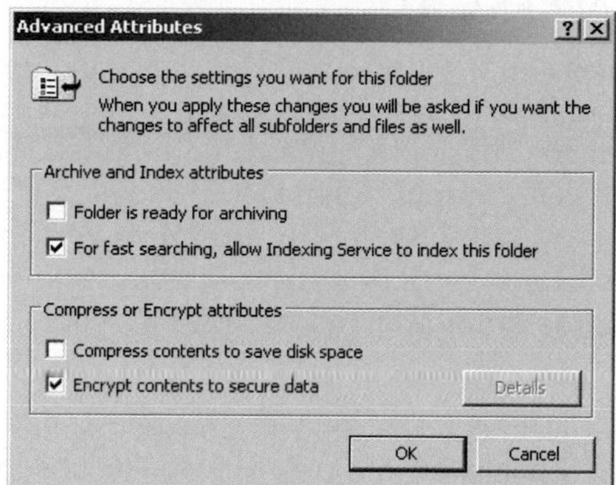

Figure 9-13. The **Advanced Attributes** dialog box can be used to encrypt or compress a file in an NTFS directory system.

file compression is obvious to the user is during the initial compression of a large folder or volume. An entire volume could take hours to compress. After it is compressed, the time it takes to open and close is comparable to an uncompressed volume.

Compression does not always achieve the desired effect. For example, if a user is trying to create more disk space by compressing graphic files, they may notice very little difference in file size after compression. Most graphic file systems, such as JPEG and GIF, already use a file compression technique. Additional compression has little or no effect on the file size. Also be aware that files that are compressed may be difficult or impossible to recover after a complete system failure.

HPFS

High Performance File System (HPFS) was developed jointly by Microsoft and IBM for the IBM series of computers. HPFS was first introduced as part of the OS/2 operating system, which is also unique to IBM. This file system was written to overcome the limitations of DOS and is similar to NTFS. It provides security and multiple naming conventions. Although HPFS is not compatible with NTFS4.0, HPFS is compatible with the DOS version of Windows 3.0. HPFS was designed to meet the needs of a larger computer system, such as those encountered on a network, but it can be used on a desktop.

High Performance File System (HPFS) file system developed for IBM PCs to overcome the limitations of DOS.

A+ Note:

There are many more file systems in existence than the ones listed here. The others are very limited or proprietary in nature. The A+ Certification exams are based on the Microsoft family of file systems at this time. For the current exams, you may need to know that HPFS is an IBM file system and is not compatible with NTFS4.0

Dynamic Disk (NTFS5.0)

basic disk
the traditional FAT16, FAT32, and NTFS file storage systems.

dynamic disk
an improved version of the NTFS file system.

Windows 2000 Professional, Windows XP Professional, Windows Vista Business, Windows Vista Enterprise, and Windows Vista Ultimate handle two types of disk configurations: basic disk and dynamic disk. ***Basic disk*** refers to the traditional FAT16, FAT32, and NTFS file storage system. ***Dynamic disk*** is based on NTFS technology, but with significant improvements. It has improved disk security as well as lifted restrictions normally associated with NTFS. As discussed, dynamic disk is often referred to as ***NTFS5.0.***

Note that NTFS5.0 also supports the FAT32 file system. Earlier versions of NTFS would not support FAT32 until service pack 4.

While Microsoft recommends you use dynamic disk, you can set your system to use basic disk. You might wish to use a basic disk file system because of compatibility features. Some software may not run on the NTFS5.0 system.

Microsoft Active Directory can only be installed on a drive that is formatted as dynamic disk (NTFS5.0).

You can install a basic disk file system on your computer and upgrade at any time without losing data, but you probably will not be able to reverse the operation without losing data. Microsoft recommends against reversing the process, though there are some third-party utilities that claim they can do the job. Use them at your own risk.

There are a number of important changes for NTFS5.0. Disk quotas can be set using NTFS5.0. That means when a hard disk drive is shared by several users, each user can be allocated a portion of the disk for storage and cannot use more space than they have been allocated. This prevents one user from using up all the disk space for photos and such.

volume mount points
allow a volume or additional hard drive be attached to a directory structure. Volume mount points can be used to integrate a dissimilar file system into a logical file system.

In addition, the traditional method of allocating additional space on a large disk system by using partitions and additional logical drives is no longer needed. Dynamic disk treats the entire disk as one large volume of data. It appears seamless to the user. The usual long list of additional drive letters such as R, P, S, and Z is no longer required to appear on the screen to the user. Instead, a system of volume mount points can be established. This gives the user an illusion of one long continuous file structure.

Volume mount points allow a volume or additional hard disk drive to be attached to a directory structure. Traditionally, adding a new hard disk drive required a new partition and new directory assigned such as E: or F:. With the volume mount point feature, a new volume or disk can be attached to an existing directory. See **Figure 9-14.**

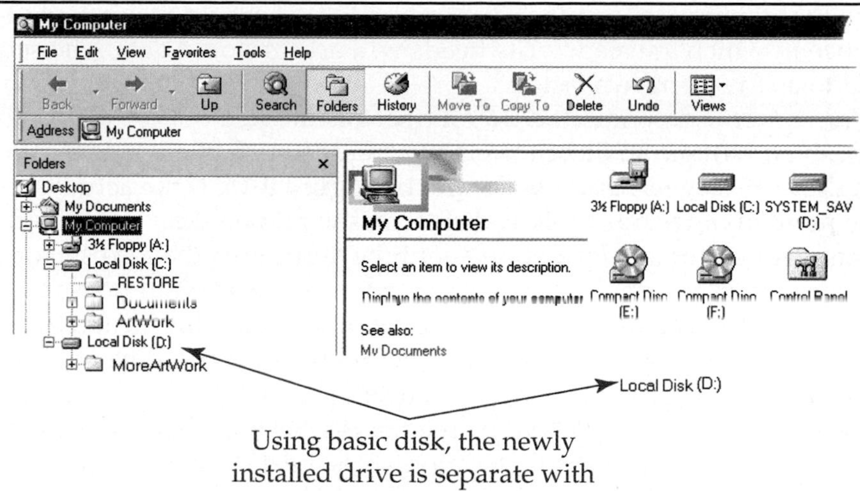

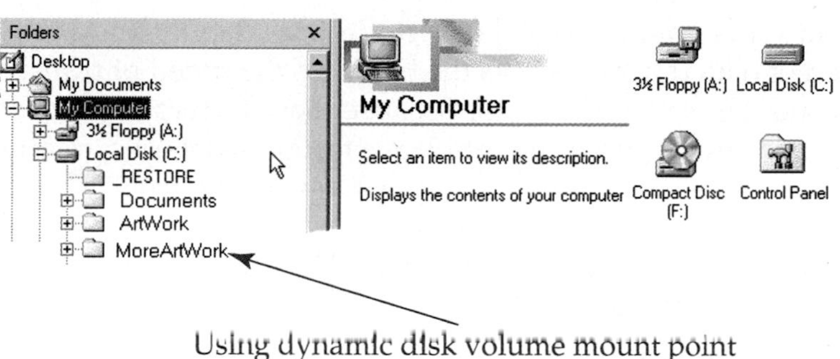

Figure 9-14. The volume mount points, new in NTFS5.0, allow additional volumes or disk drives to appear as a folder in the existing directory rather than as a separate drive letter.

When the new disk is installed, it can be spliced into an existing file structure rather than appear as a separate drive with an individual drive letter. Basic file systems are limited in the number of drives that can be installed and in the maximum number of partitions that can be created. The maximum number of partitions is equal to the letters of the entire alphabet minus the letters used for assignment to floppy drives, CD-ROM drives, and other disk drives. Since the volume mount point technology does not require a separate drive letter, there is no practical limitation to the number of drives assigned to a system. This is especially important on network systems.

Format

The **format** command is used to prepare the disk for data storage. The command creates a new root directory and a file allocation table. The **format** command also checks for bad areas on the disk surface. When a bad area is found, it is identified in the file allocation table so that it will not be used to store data.

There are two classifications of formatting for hard drives: low-level format and high-level format. Generally, a hard drive comes with low-level formatting already performed at the manufacturer. The ***low-level format*** performs

low-level format a process that determines the type of encoding to be done on the disk platter and the sequence in which the read/write heads will access stored data.

operations that determine the type of encoding to be done on the disk platter and the sequence in which the read/write heads will access stored data. The sequence is referred to as the interleave factor.

interleave factor describes how the sectors are laid out on a disk surface to optimize a hard drive's data access rate.

Interleave factor describes the way the sectors are laid out on a disk surface. Many times you will see an illustration showing sectors laid out side by side. In reality, they are staggered across the tracks, **Figure 9-15.** If the actual sectors were in sequential order side by side, disk access would be slow. At the end of each cluster or sector is information about the location of the next sector or cluster. If the sectors were side by side, the read/write head would pass the next sector before the location information could be processed. This means the disk would need to make a complete revolution before the data could be read from the next sector. By staggering the sectors across the disk track area, a hard drive's data access rate is optimized. When the read/write head passes over the end of the sector, all information about the location of the next storage sector can be processed before the read/write head reaches it. This means the disk read/write head does not need to wait for a complete disk revolution to read the stored data in the next data storage sector.

The interleave factor is unique to each disk design. It takes into account disk rpm, the speed of data transfer across the bus, and the speed of transfer through the chips and the read/write head. Because these factors differ greatly from manufacturer to manufacturer, the interleave factor also varies greatly. The interleave factor is only important for performing a low-level format. The low-level format arranges the locations of the sectors on the disks. High-level formats performed by the **format** command simply identify the sector locations and construct the file allocation tables.

high-level format a process that prepares the disk for file storage.

High-level format prepares the disk for file storage. It determines the file allocation table, checks the physical condition of all sectors, marks bad sectors so that they cannot be used to store data, and identifies the operating system being used. A low-level format actually destroys all data on a disk. While a high-level format is said to destroy all data, in actuality, the sectors/clusters still contain the original data. A high-level format erases only the contents of the file allocation table so that no file name is associated with the data clusters.

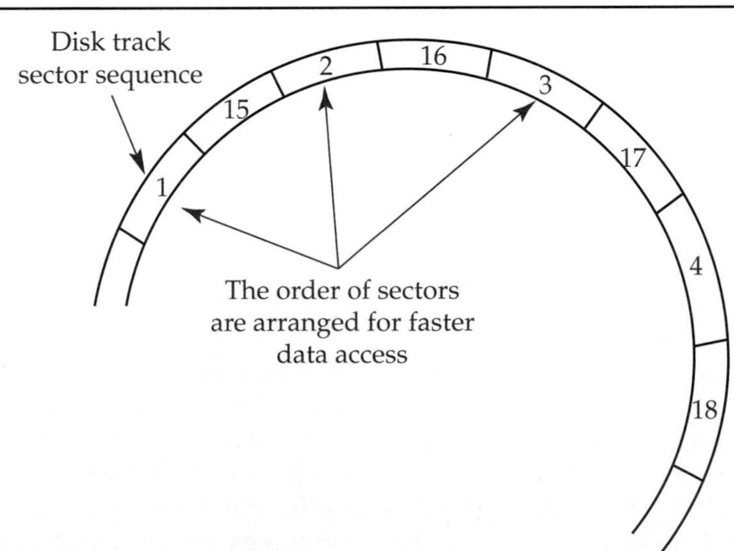

Figure 9-15. The interleave factor describes the pattern in which sectors are laid out on a disk. Sequential sectors are not side by side.

Data can be recovered after a high-level format takes place. The collection of clusters that contain the file data can be identified and given a file name using third-party tools. Also, certain third-party disk editor utilities can display the ASCII contents of a file after the disk has been formatted or the file deleted.

Windows offers two high-level format methods: full format and quick format. Quick format is used on a disk that has already been formatted once. Rather than prepare the entire disk surface for storage, only the FAT table and the root directory are changed. This is much quicker than the full formatting process, which prepares the entire disk. The full formatting process typically would be used for an unformatted disk. This process was useful when floppy disks were sold unformatted. Since disks are now formatted during manufacture, this process is not needed as often.

File Fragmentation

File fragmentation is a common occurrence on disks. Files are assigned to disks by clusters. A file is ***fragmented*** when the clusters used for storage of the data are not consecutive. File fragmentation occurs through normal disk activities such as saving new files, erasing older files, opening files, and adding additional data to files.

fragmented stored in nonconsecutive clusters on the disk.

Figure 9-16 illustrates a possible sequence of events leading to fragmented files on the hard drive. The first three files saved (A, B, and C) show no file fragmentation. Each file is stored in a consecutive series of clusters. When file B is erased, it creates an opening in the sequence of clusters, which can now be used

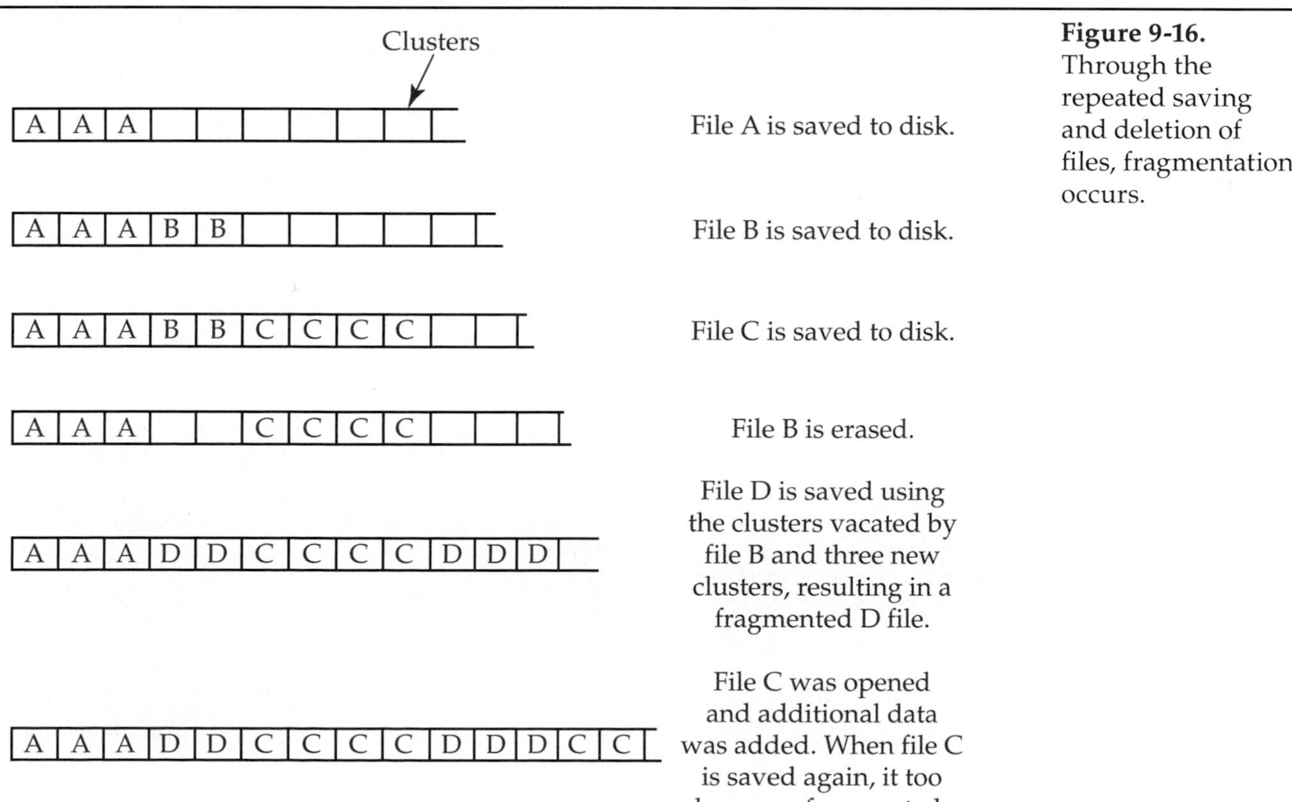

Clusters
A A A
File A is saved to disk.
A A A B B
File B is saved to disk.
A A A B B C C C C
File C is saved to disk.
A A A C C C C
File B is erased.
A A A D D C C C C D D D
File D is saved using the clusters vacated by file B and three new clusters, resulting in a fragmented D file.
A A A D D C C C C D D D C C
File C was opened and additional data was added. When file C is saved again, it too becomes fragmented.

Figure 9-16. Through the repeated saving and deletion of files, fragmentation occurs.

for the storage of new data. When file D is saved, it uses the two clusters left open by the deletion of file B as well as three additional clusters. File D is a fragmented file because the clusters used to store the data are not sequential. Next, file C is opened and used by the computer. As file C is used, it grows in size. When file C is saved back to the disk, it uses the four original clusters and two additional clusters at the end of the file system. File C is now fragmented also.

The more often files are opened, modified, closed, or erased from a disk, the more fragmented the system becomes. The more fragmented a file becomes, the longer it takes to load and use the file. It is more difficult for a data recovery utility to identify the cluster sequences of fragmented files. As part of routine file maintenance, a hard disk should be defragmented (defragged) on a regular basis. When you ***defragment*** your hard drive, the computer moves the clusters around so that all files have their clusters organized sequentially. The Windows Disk Defragmenter utility program is located at **Start | All Programs | Accessories | System Tools | Disk Defragmenter**.

defragment rearranging clusters on the disk so each file is stored in consecutive clusters.

Figure 9-17 shows what the Disk Defragmenter program looks like while it is in operation. Each small square represents a cluster on the disk. The progress of the program is displayed in graphic form on the screen. A color code is used to indicate items such as damaged areas on the disk, data that is currently being read, and free disk space.

Windows 2000 automatically prevents fragmentation of files by only storing files in sequential clusters. This operation is accomplished by skipping over small clusters of available storage space that are not large enough to contain the file being saved.

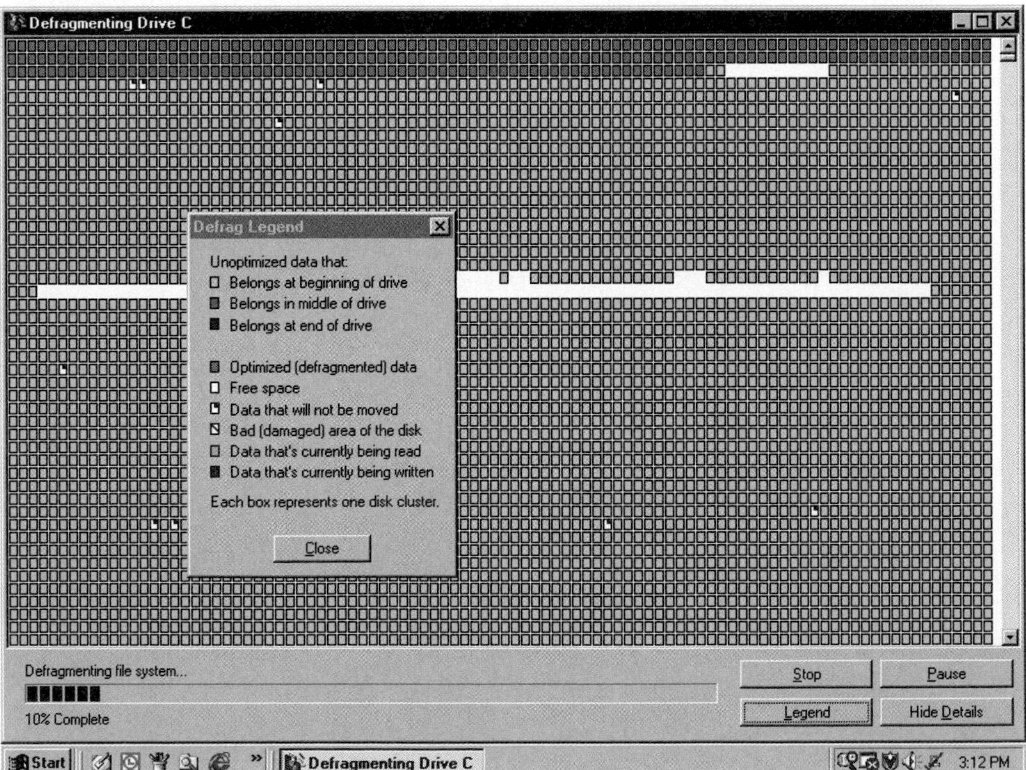

Figure 9-17. Disk defragmentation in process. This tool reorganizes your files to optimize hard disk access times.

Defragmenting can take a long time to complete, especially on large hard drive systems. Performing routine disk defragmentation can save time. The more operations performed between defragmentation, the longer the time required.

ScanDisk

The ***ScanDisk*** program is used to inspect the surface of a disk and identify bad and lost clusters, **Figure 9-18.** Many times the program will repair lost clusters.

After ScanDisk has inspected disk surface integrity, a report can be viewed, similar to the one in Figure 9-18. The report summarizes the findings by identifying bad sectors, reporting the number of files, and reporting the available disk space. The ScanDisk program can be accessed through **Start | Programs | Accessories | System Tools | ScanDisk**. ScanDisk is useful when troubleshooting a possible data storage problem.

ScanDisk is not included in Windows operating systems starting with Windows XP. Chkdsk, a similar utility, is still available and performs all the same functions as ScanDisk.

ScanDisk
a program included in Windows operating systems that is used to inspect the surface of a disk and identify bad and lost clusters.

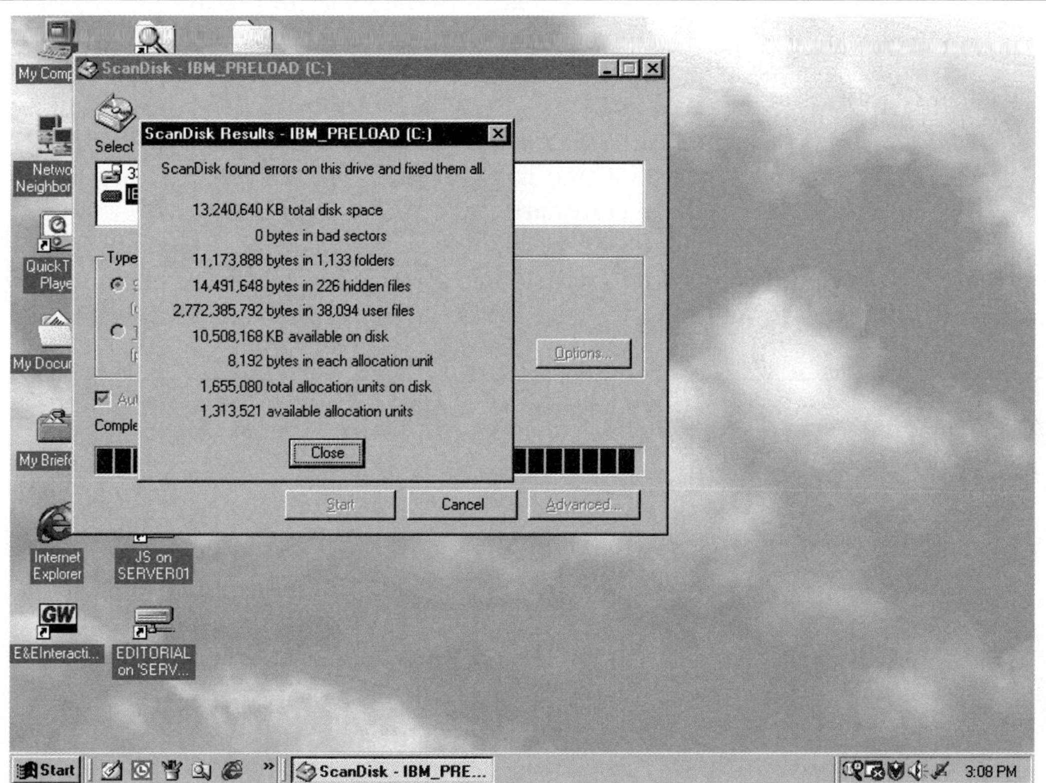

Figure 9-18.
ScanDisk program in operation.

ScanDisk is a DOS utility program. There are two versions of ScanDisk available. The oldest version from Windows 95 OSR1 supports only 8.3 file names. Versions from Windows 95 OSR2 and later support long file names. If you use the older version on a file system that contains long file names, the long names will be converted to an 8.3 file name. Always label the versions of repair disks that you create.

Chkdsk

Chkdsk is a command line tool used to check and repair the integrity of the file system on a hard disk drive. Disk problems such as bad sectors, lost clusters, cross-linked files, and directory structure errors can be detected and repaired automatically. Chkdsk can be run from the command prompt or from the GUI. **Figure 9-19** shows the results of the **chkdsk** command run on a Windows XP computer from the command prompt.

When the Chkdsk utility is run from the command prompt, it will identify but not repair problems found. To automatically repair problems found, the **chkdsk** command must be run with the **/r** switch.

To run the Chkdsk utility as part of a GUI, simply access the Windows Explorer view of the desired drive or partition you wish to test. Then, right-click the partition or drive and select **Properties** from the shortcut menu. You will see the drive's **Properties** dialog box similar to that in **Figure 9-20.**

Under the **Tools** tab, click the **Check Now** button to check the partition or drive. The Chkdsk utility will run as a GUI. When completed, the results will be displayed in GUI format similar to the Windows Vista screen capture in **Figure 9-21.** Notice the reference to "Chkdsk" listed in the results. The results are very similar to when Chkdsk is run from the command prompt.

Chkdsk must have exclusive control of the volume it is checking. This is a problem when attempting to run Chkdsk on the default boot partition when it contains the complete operating system. A message will appear indicating that

Figure 9-19. The results of the **chkdsk** command run on a Windows XP computer.

```
Command Prompt
C:\Documents and Settings\Richard>chkdsk
The type of the file system is NTFS.

WARNING!  F parameter not specified.
Running CHKDSK in read-only mode.

CHKDSK is verifying files (stage 1 of 3)...
File verification completed.
CHKDSK is verifying indexes (stage 2 of 3)...
Index verification completed.
CHKDSK is verifying security descriptors (stage 3 of 3)...
Security descriptor verification completed.
CHKDSK is verifying Usn Journal...
Usn Journal verification completed.
CHKDSK discovered free space marked as allocated in the volume bitmap.
Windows found problems with the file system.
Run CHKDSK with the /F (fix) option to correct these.

 122881153 KB total disk space.
 104546912 KB in 197039 files.
     72612 KB in 17838 indexes.
         0 KB in bad sectors.
    325797 KB in use by the system.
     65536 KB occupied by the log file.
  17935832 KB available on disk.

      4096 bytes in each allocation unit.
  30720288 total allocation units on disk.
   4483958 allocation units available on disk.
```

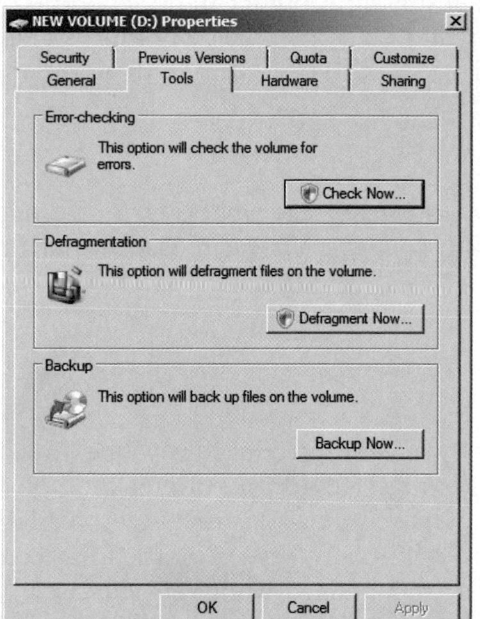

Figure 9-20. Chkdsk can be run from the GUI by right-clicking the drive, selecting **Properties** from the shortcut menu, selecting the **Tools** tab, and clicking **Check Now.**

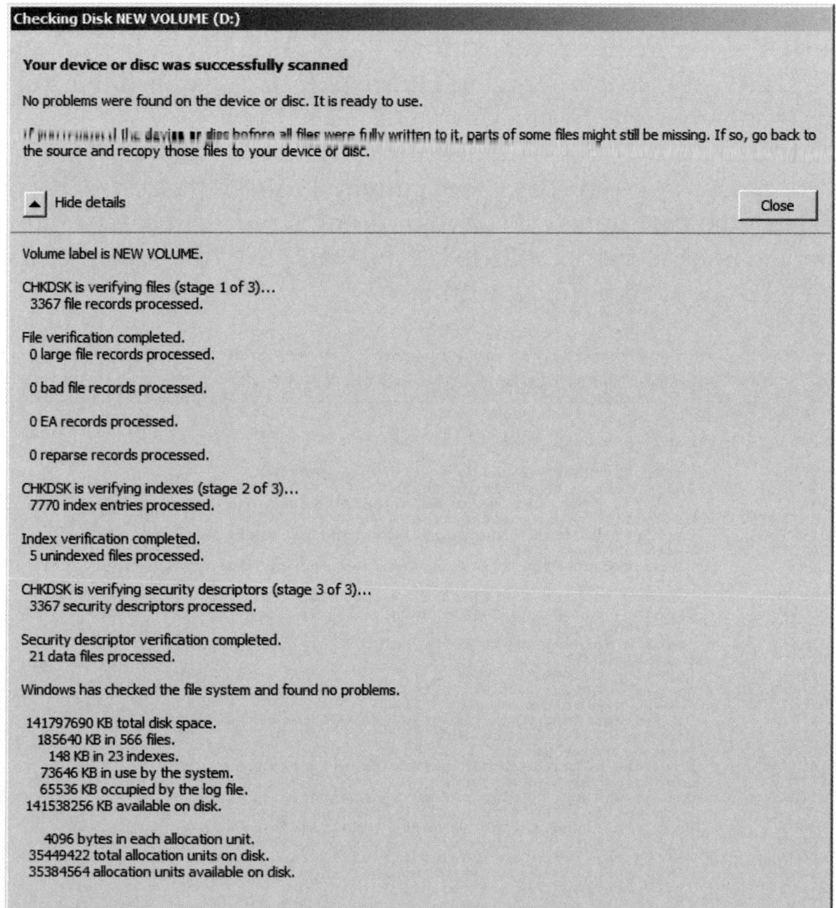

Figure 9-21. GUI results of the Chkdsk command.

Chkdsk cannot be run at this time, but it can be scheduled to run automatically when the computer is restarted. When the computer is restarted or shut down and started at a later time, the Chkdsk utility will automatically start up and run on the boot partition.

Note:

While Chkdsk is often run as a routine attempt to repair a volume, Microsoft recommends backing up your data before running Chkdsk with the automatic repair option.

DiskPart

The DiskPart utility was first introduced in Windows 2000 Server and Windows XP. It is used to manage disk partitions and volumes from the command prompt. The **fdisk** command is no longer available in Windows Vista. DiskPart has replaced the functions served by the **fdisk** command. Today, disks, partitions, and volumes are managed using the Microsoft Management Console (MMC) or Computer Management, but there will be times when you will need to use the DiskPart utility, especially when you cannot access the MMC or Computer Management, for example, during some troubleshooting operations while trying to recover a failed operating system.

See the list of commands revealed from the command interpreter after issuing the DiskPart **help** command in **Figure 9-22.** Only a partial list of commands is shown in the figure.

The DiskPart utility is much more complex than the Fdisk utility. Commands typically use two or more words in the command line syntax. Also, be aware that you must select the partition, disk, or volume before you can carry out many of the commands. Look at **Figure 9-23** to see an example of the sequence used to view the details about a selected partition.

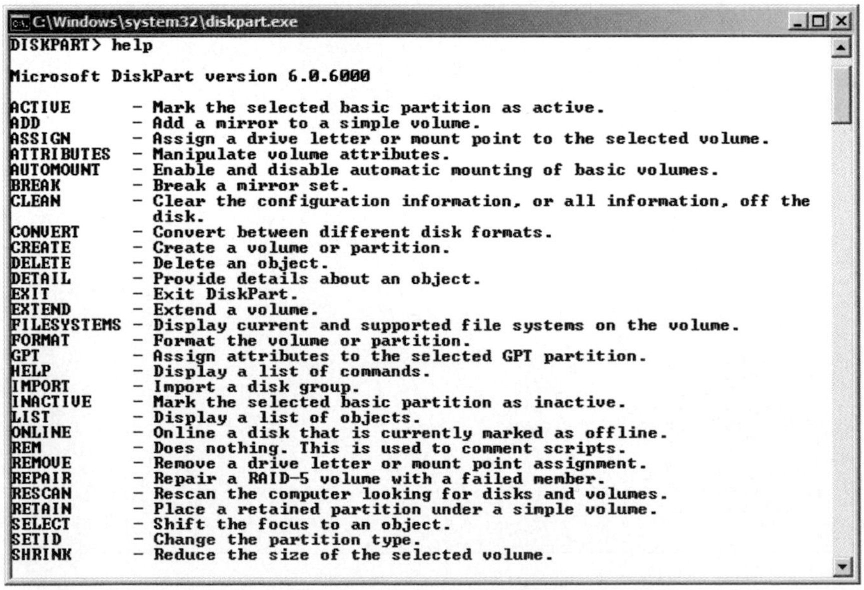

Figure 9-22. Issuing the **Help** command in the DiskPart utility displays a list of DiskPart commands.

```
C:\Windows\system32\diskpart.exe
DISKPART> help

Microsoft DiskPart version 6.0.6000

ACTIVE      - Mark the selected basic partition as active.
ADD         - Add a mirror to a simple volume.
ASSIGN      - Assign a drive letter or mount point to the selected volume.
ATTRIBUTES  - Manipulate volume attributes.
AUTOMOUNT   - Enable and disable automatic mounting of basic volumes.
BREAK       - Break a mirror set.
CLEAN       - Clear the configuration information, or all information, off the
              disk.
CONVERT     - Convert between different disk formats.
CREATE      - Create a volume or partition.
DELETE      - Delete an object.
DETAIL      - Provide details about an object.
EXIT        - Exit DiskPart.
EXTEND      - Extend a volume.
FILESYSTEMS - Display current and supported file systems on the volume.
FORMAT      - Format the volume or partition.
GPT         - Assign attributes to the selected GPT partition.
HELP        - Display a list of commands.
IMPORT      - Import a disk group.
INACTIVE    - Mark the selected basic partition as inactive.
LIST        - Display a list of objects.
ONLINE      - Online a disk that is currently marked as offline.
REM         - Does nothing. This is used to comment scripts.
REMOVE      - Remove a drive letter or mount point assignment.
REPAIR      - Repair a RAID-5 volume with a failed member.
RESCAN      - Rescan the computer looking for disks and volumes.
RETAIN      - Place a retained partition under a simple volume.
SELECT      - Shift the focus to an object.
SETID       - Change the partition type.
SHRINK      - Reduce the size of the selected volume.
```

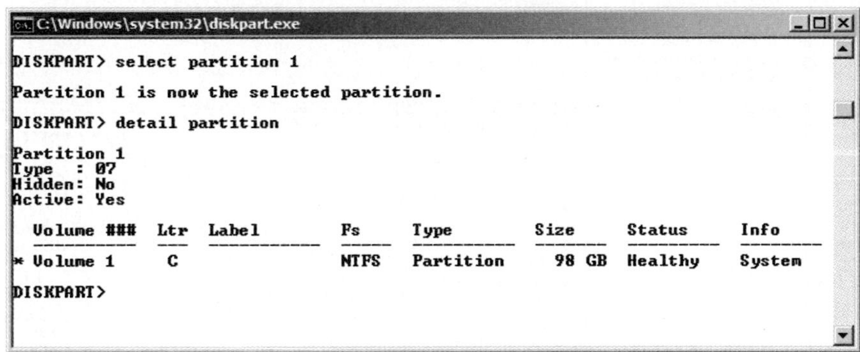

Figure 9-23.
The DiskPart utility can be used to display information about hard drives and their partitions. Notice that the object (such as hard drive, partition, and volume) to be viewed must first be selected with the **select** command (**select partition 1**). The **detail** command (**detail partition**) can then be used to display information about the object.

First, the command **select partition 1** is entered at the command prompt. The DiskPart utility responds with a text message saying, "Partition 1 is now the selected partition." After the partition has been selected, the command **detail partition** is entered to reveal the details about partition 1. If you issue the **detail partition** command without first selecting the partition, an error message will be generated. DiskPart command information is available at the Microsoft Web site at http://support.microsoft.com/kb/300415. If the link has changed, conduct a search using the key words "Microsoft DiskPart."

Computer Management Console

The preferred, easy-to-use disk management tool is located in the Computer Management console. This console has a default collection of commonly used tools for managing the computer system. One such tool is Disk Management. The Disk Management tool provides easy access to all installed disk drives and allows information to easily be displayed about each drive and its partition(s). You can view the drive type, the file system used, and the status of each drive. Look at **Figure 9-24** to see an example of the Windows Vista Computer Management console with the **Disk Management** option selected. Also, note the shortcut menu items listed for the partition when you right-click the mouse on the selected partition.

The Windows Vista Computer Management console is very similar to the Windows XP version. In addition to displaying information about the disk system, there are tools that allow you to extend or shrink the size of a partition, add additional drives and partitions, format the partitions, change the drive letters, allocate amount of space each user can use (disk quota), convert a basic disk to dynamic disk, and run Chkdsk and Disk Defragmenter.

Accessing the Computer Management console is accomplished by right-clicking **Computer** (Windows Vista) or **My Computer** (Windows XP) located off the **Start** menu and then selecting the **Manage** option from the shortcut menu.

A customized console can be created with the Microsoft Management Console (MMC). Typing **MMC** or **MMC.exe** into the **Run** dialog box of Windows XP or

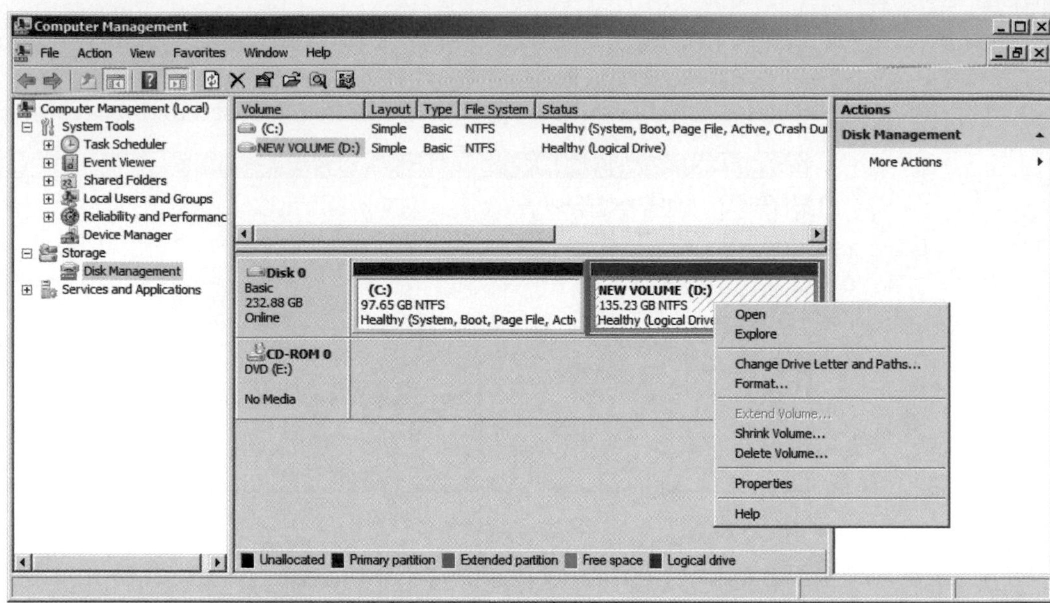

Figure 9-24. The **Disk Management** option in the Computer Management console can be used to display information about the disk system and to perform maintenance-related task such as extend or shrink the size of a partition, add additional drives and partitions, and format the partitions.

the **Start Search** dialog of Windows Vista will generate a blank MMC that can be customized to include the tools you want. The MMC will be explored more in the related lab activities. There is also a lot of information about the MMC located in **Help and Support** located off the **Start** menu. You can also do a Web search using the key terms "Microsoft MMC."

Performance Measures

benchmark tests performance tests used to compare different hardware and software.

Benchmark tests are performance tests that are conducted to compare different hardware and software. Industry journals and third-party organizations often do comparisons to rate the quality of hardware and software. Many times these same performance tests are conducted by the manufacturer and then used in advertisement campaigns. Always check who conducted the performance test. Based on this information, the results of the test should be viewed with caution.

Hard drive performance is judged on such items as *access time, latency,* or *seek time.* Access time, latency, and seek time mean the same thing when it comes to performance. These terms refer to the amount of time taken to position the read/write head over the proper sector. This is usually measured in microseconds (ms).

Another standard of measure is data transfer rate. This rate refers to the speed of transfer of data to and from the disk. The actual time it takes must include the fact that cache memory is used to give the appearance of higher transfer rates. Disk data transfer rates are usually measured in megabytes per second (MBps).

The fastest and easiest way to compare disk drive systems is to load the two drives that are to be compared with a Windows operating system. Place one or two typical software applications in the system's Startup folder so that they launch when Windows opens. The two systems should then be booted. Compare the length of time it takes to boot and load the software systems. Any technician can perform this simple test. When comparing two devices, all other hardware must be equal. The only variation can be the actual piece of hardware or software being compared in the test.

ATA (IDE and EIDE) Hard Disk Interface

IBM introduced the first hard drive in 1957. It was constructed of fifty 24-inch platters with a total storage capacity of 5 MB. IBM would not sell the hard disk, but, at that time, it could be leased for approximately $35,000 per year. The entire disk drive system was physically enormous by today's standards. It was as big as a refrigerator box. Today's hard disk has a thousand times more storage space at a fraction of the size and cost.

Early PC hard drive controller circuitry was mounted on an adapter card and installed into an ISA slot. A cable ran from the adapter card to the hard disk drive. A second hard disk drive standard was introduced by IBM and was used with the MCA slot. It was used to interface with the MCA bus system. It is now obsolete.

As the hard disk drive became more popular, the card was integrated into the hard drive device so that the adapter card and physical hard disk drive became one unit. This was the beginning of a third standard called the ***AT Attachment (ATA),*** developed for the 80286 model. The original ATA was a 16-bit data transfer system using a 40-pin cable connector that attached to the motherboard and to the circuit board mounted on the hard disk drive.

The ATA design is in use today and is referred to as IDE or EIDE. The term ***Integrated Drive Electronics (IDE)*** came from the adapter card being integrated into the hard drive device. ***Enhanced Integrated Drive Electronics (EIDE)*** was a term introduced by Western Digital Corporation, a major hard drive manufacturer. EIDE hard drives originally used a new ATA standard known as ATA-2, Fast ATA, or Fast ATA-2.

AT Attachment (ATA)
a standard for disk drive interface that integrates the controller into the disk drive. Often referred to as IDE or EIDE.

Integrated Drive Electronics (IDE)
an early standard for a disk drive interface that integrated the controller into the disk drive. The term is still commonly used when referring to the AT Attachment.

Enhanced Integrated Drive Electronics (EIDE)
an enhanced version of the IDE disk drive controller standard. The term is commonly used when referring to the AT Attachment.

Since the development and release of the SATA standard, the traditional acronym ATA is now often referred to as PATA, representing parallel ATA.

Programmed Input Output (PIO) was introduced in 1995. The PIO standard was used in relation to early ATA and ATA-2 systems to classify data transfer rates, **Figure 9-25.** The PIO ATA system used the CPU to process the data transfer before DMA became standard. PIO is only mentioned because it has ocurred in the CompTIA A+ exam objectives in recent years.

All the different terminology around the ATA/IDE drive connection can prove very confusing. Some manufacturers didn't wait for new standards to be implemented and came out with similar sounding names. Other manufacturers have changed the requirements for their standard. The requirements for EIDE have changed many times. Refer to **Figure 9-26** for ATA standards.

Some ATA designs use an adapter board inserted into the PCI slot to take advantage of higher data transfer speeds. When using the expansion slot to upgrade to a higher ATA standard, check if the motherboard chipset will support the higher ATA standard. Otherwise, the desired higher transfer speed of the newer ATA design may not be reached.

After all these advancements, many people still refer to the ATA design as IDE or EIDE, so when you are in the field talking to other technicians, remember that they are talking about the connection to the mass storage devices other than SCSI.

Figure 9-25.
ATA PIO data rates.

ATA Version	PIO	MBps
ATA	0	3.3
ATA	1	5.2
ATA	2	8.3
ATA-2	3	11.1
ATA-2	4	16.6

Figure 9-26.
ATA standards.

Drive Specification	Features
ATA-1	The original ATA design released in 1988 used a 40-pin ribbon cable connector and featured a master, slave, and cable select option. It also used a programming technique to automatically identify itself to the BIOS system during setup.
ATA-2	Released in 1996, it allowed other storage devices to be connected to the bus system not just hard disk drives. It allowed disks up to 8.4 GB to be accessed easily. It was also called Fast ATA because it featured faster DMA data transfer speeds than ATA-1.
ATA-3	A revised ATA-2 that allowed password protection for hard disk drive security and a few other minor changes.
ATA-4	A 1998 revision that allowed data transfer rates as high as 33 MBps. It is also referred to as UDMA/33 and Ultra ATA/33. ATA-4 also introduced an optional 80-conductor ribbon cable for the standard 40-pin connector. This modification reduced electrical effects that limited data transfer rates. The ATA-4 specification also integrated the ATAPI standard, which allows for the attachment of CD-ROM, tape drives, and other forms of mass storage devices that required an ATAPI interface.
ATA-5	Introduced in 1999 with a standard 80-conductor ribbon cable. The 80-conductor ribbon cable allowed for transfer rates as high as 66 MBps as long as the motherboard is designed to take advantage of the ATA-5 design. If not, the transfer rate is only 33 MBps. The ATA-5 is also referred to as UDMA/66.
ATA-6	ATA-6, released in 2000, offers transfer rates as high as 100 MBps. An 80-conductor ribbon cable is again used with this design. If the motherboard is not designed for the ATA-6 specification, then the highest transfer speed will probably be 33 MBps.
ATA-7	ATA-7, also known as ATA/133, is the latest and fastest version of the ATA series. It is capable of producing a transfer data rate of 133 MBps. ATA-7 was introduced in 2005 and uses Ultra DMA 133 and an 80-pin data cable.

ATA Hard Disk Installation

Figure 9-27 illustrates two drives, one slave and one master, connected to a motherboard using an IDE interface connection point. Typical motherboards provide two sets of connections identified as IDE0 and IDE1. They provide two channels of communication to hard drives and to other devices such as CD-ROM, CD-RW, or tape drive systems. Each channel can provide an interface with the computer bus system for two hard drives, creating a total of four separate physical drives. Each channel consists of one drive designated as a master and the other designated as a slave. Moving jumper settings on the hard drive sets the designation of master and slave. See **Figure 9-28.**

When two or more drives are installed on the same PC system, one drive must be designated the ***slave*** and the other the ***master.*** The jumper settings are required because the two drives share the same communication cable. Failure to configure one device as master and the other as slave can result in hard drive

slave
a secondary drive on an IDE channel.

master
the primary drive on an IDE channel.

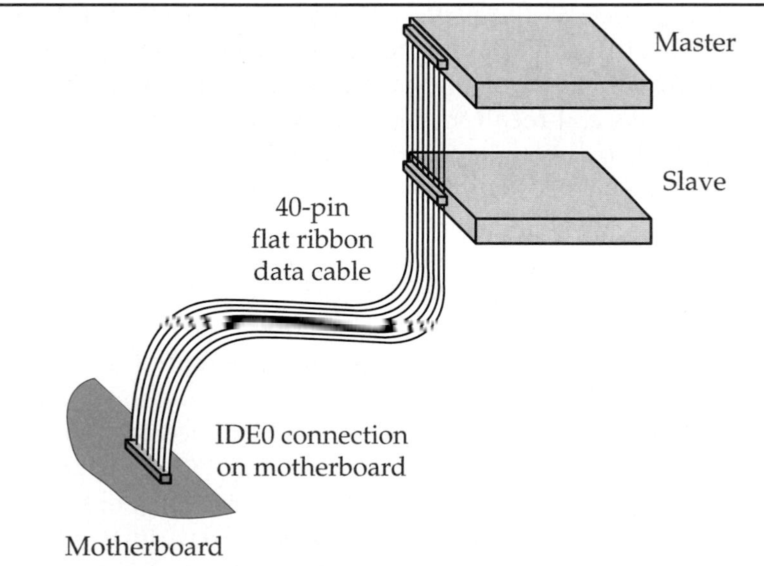

Figure 9-27.
Illustration of two IDE hard drives connected to a motherboard. Two hard drives are connected as shown. One hard drive is the master and the other is the slave.

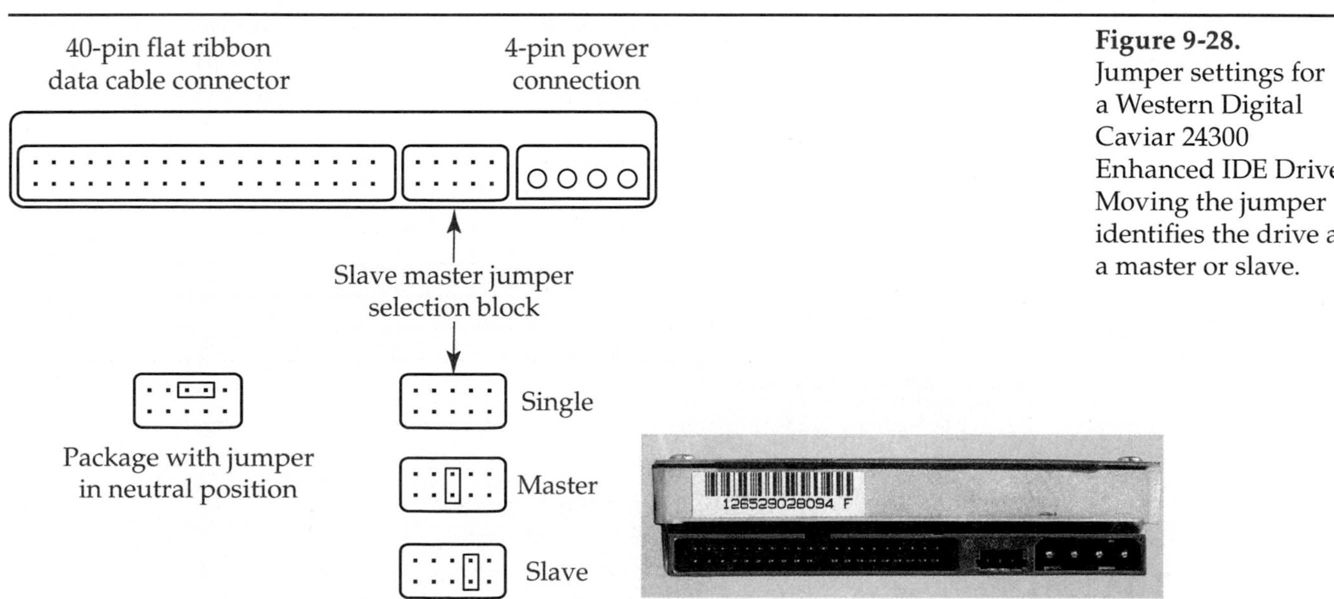

Figure 9-28.
Jumper settings for a Western Digital Caviar 24300 Enhanced IDE Drive. Moving the jumper identifies the drive as a master or slave.

failure. Think about the partitions in the hard disk drive system. When the PC is booted, it must be able to differentiate between the two or more drives. How can the BIOS system search out the active boot partition if it cannot tell the difference between the two hard disk drives installed on the same PC? By making one the master and the other the slave, one drive becomes the extension of the other. The BIOS system can now differentiate between the two drives and try each one out as it searches for the master boot partition.

Serial ATA

Serial ATA (SATA) was developed to overcome the limitations of the ATA drive. The SATA 1.0 maximum transfer rate is 150 MBps. The transfer rate is expected to reach as high as 600 MBps as other versions of SATA are developed and released. SATA has a higher performance than ATA because it moves data to the motherboard in a series of packets in a similar fashion to USB and FireWire. The ATA transfer rate is slower because it is limited to the clock frequency of the motherboard and to the effect of induction caused by the design of the flat ribbon cable. The SATA design can achieve a higher data rate because it generates its own frequency for the data transfer, and its cable is designed to reduce the effects of electrical induction. As you recall from earlier chapters, induction can limit the frequency of data traveling through a conductor, reducing data transfer speeds.

The SATA drive uses a thin, flat or round cable with 7 conductors and a 7-pin cable connector. This is quite a reduction in cable width compared to the width of the 40-pin and 80-pin ATA cables. Because of the width reduction, the SATA cable is much easier to route inside the computer chassis.

Look at **Figure 9-29.** Three of the seven conductors in the illustration are identified with the letter *G*, which represents ground. The pair of conductors used to transmit data are marked DT– and DT+. The pair of conductors used to receive data are marked DR– and DR+. The pairs of cables and the grounds are twisted together to reduce the negative effect of electrical induction on the data transfer rate.

The SATA cable connectors are keyed to prevent a user from incorrectly connecting the cable to the motherboard or to the hard drive. The SATA cable is connected to the motherboard at locations identified as SATA 0 and SATA 1, **Figure 9-30.**

The SATA drive is designed with only two sets of connectors: power and data. See **Figure 9-31.** There are no master/slave jumper pin connections to worry about. Each device is automatically set as master. There is no slave in the SATA design.

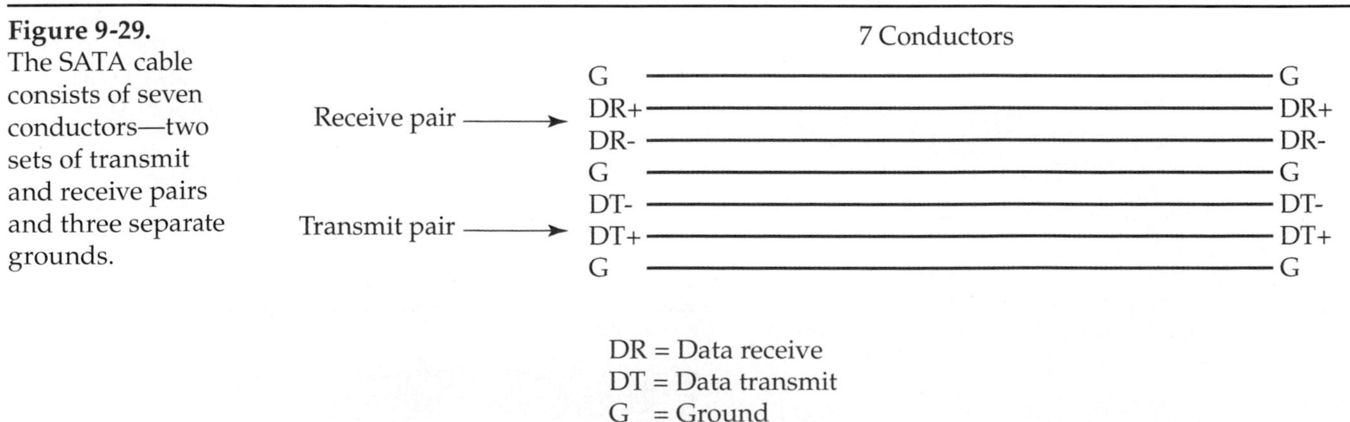

Figure 9-29. The SATA cable consists of seven conductors—two sets of transmit and receive pairs and three separate grounds.

Figure 9-30.
SATA connections on a motherboard.

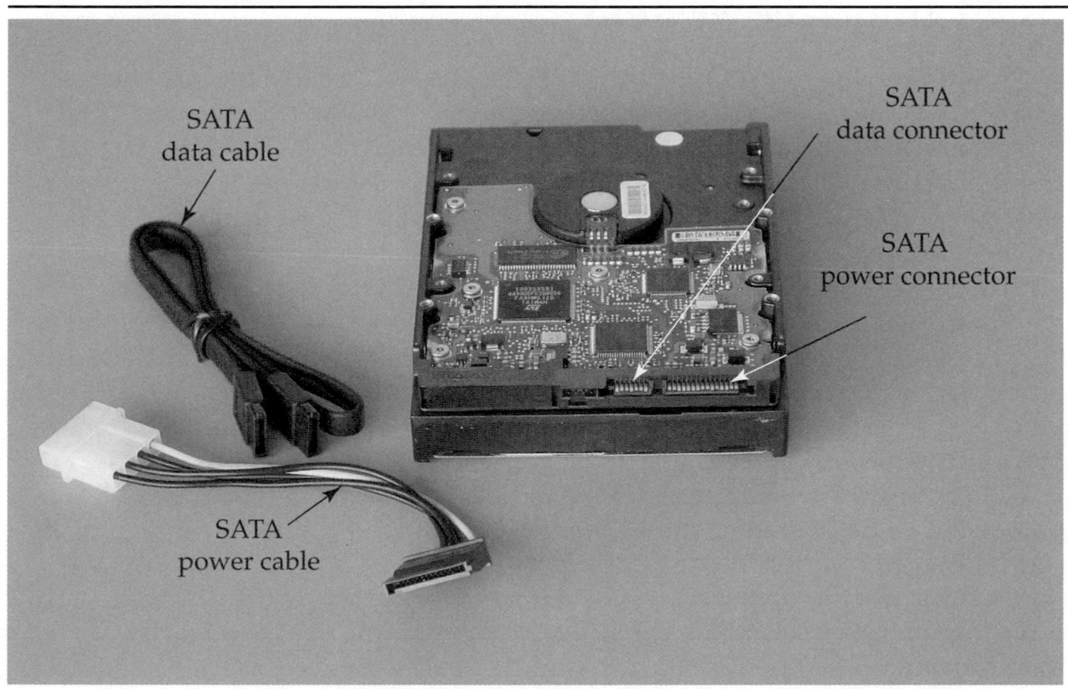

Figure 9-31.
SATA drive and cables. A SATA drive has only two connectors: a data connector and a power connector.

An existing computer system may be upgraded to SATA by using a SATA host adapter card. The host adapter card is installed in an available PCI slot. The SATA drive is then connected to the host adapter card using a SATA cable. When using a host adapter card, you must check that the BIOS and motherboard will support the SATA technology. Even if SATA is supported, the motherboard BIOS may report the SATA drive as a SCSI drive. The SATA system should perform normally even if it is identified as a SCSI drive. Also note that only one SATA drive can be connected on a SATA cable. This means that there can only be a total of two SATA drives connected to motherboard or to the host adapter card.

During the early implementation of SATA, regular ATA drives were fitted with a bridge adapter and a SATA conversion chip at the manufacturers and then marketed as SATA drives.

SATA II

Technically speaking, SATA II is the name of the organization that designed the specification for the second generation of SATA. The SATA II organization changed its name to Serial ATA International Organization (SATA IO) to help alleviate the confusion. The term *SATA II* has become synonymous with the second generation SATA 3 Gbps data rate. You will see SATA second generation hard disk drives listed as either SATA II or as SATA 3 Gb/s drives and also as SATA 2.0. The third generation of SATA should be available in 2008 and will most likely be identified as SATA 6.0 Gb/s. Only time will tell.

SCSI Interface System

Small Computer System Interface (SCSI) the standard that allows up to 7 or 15 devices to be connected to a SCSI adapter board.

Small Computer System Interface (SCSI), pronounced *skuzzy,* uses an adapter board and connects up to seven devices on one flat ribbon cable. This is the standard system used by Macintosh/Apple and many UNIX mainframe systems to connect peripherals. Because it was fairly expensive, SCSI technology was slow coming to the PC market. It was first used in the IBM market for file servers that required a lot of disk storage. File servers are like super PCs that control network systems. They are covered in more detail in later chapters.

The SCSI standard was developed, in part, to remedy compatibility problems between PCs and aftermarket hardware. Original market concerns created proprietary systems in early PCs. PC upgrading and expansion was a challenging task because of the compatibility issues. SCSI was designed to eliminate some of these issues by creating a standard that was available to all manufacturers.

The SCSI system was also designed to free the CPU from the burden of processing all data transactions. SCSI interfaces with a PC through an intelligent controller card inserted into the expansion bus. A SCSI bus cable connects the SCSI card to a series of devices. These devices, as directed by the controller card, can communicate freely along the bus cable, eliminating the need for the CPU's involvement.

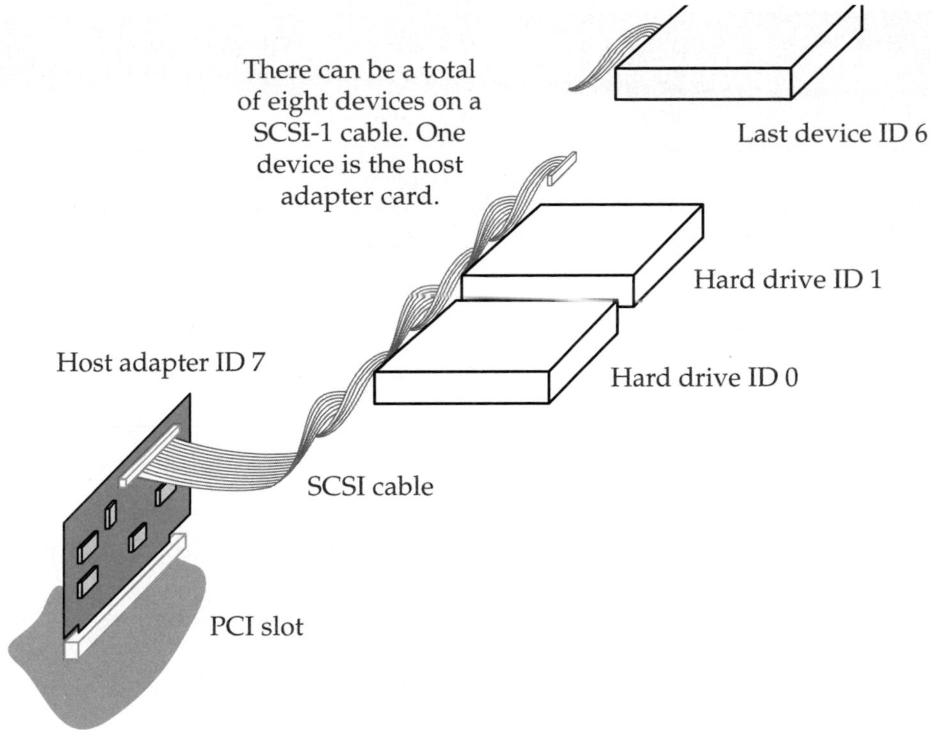

Figure 9-32.
Typical SCSI setup. There can be a total of eight devices including the adapter card.

Figure 9-32 shows a typical SCSI-1 installation. The SCSI-1 standard allows for eight devices at maximum to be connected to a SCSI-1 cable. One of these is the host adapter card. The ID numbers assigned range from 0 to 7 (eight numbers total). SCSI-2 allows for 16 devices (host adapter included) to be assigned.

A+ Note:

The quantity of SCSI devices allowed can make for a tricky question on the A+ Certification exams. When asked how many devices can be connected to a SCSI-1 cable, the correct answer is eight. However, eight may not be one of the multiple-choice answers. In that case, the answer is seven. Examine how the question is worded. Eight devices can be connected to the cable. Seven devices can be connected to a host adapter card. In various reference materials, you will see it written that seven devices can be connected to a SCSI-1 cable. This is written because the host adapter card is understood to be a necessary part of the installation. Read and answer the question carefully.

There are many styles of SCSI that have developed over the years. The main three classifications are SCSI-1, SCSI-2, and SCSI-3, **Figure 9-33.** There are variations of these three SCSI styles that can easily be confusing. Some of the names are Wide SCSI, Fast SCSI, Fast Wide SCSI, Ultra SCSI, Ultra2 SCSI, and Wide Ultra2 SCSI. When selecting SCSI hardware to install or replace, you must

Figure 9-33
SCSI standards.

Controller	Maximum Number of Devices	Typical Devices	General Information
SCSI-1	8–the host adapter plus seven devices	Hard drive, CD-ROM, scanner	Low transfer rate 5 MBps
SCSI-2	8 to 16–the host adapter plus 7 or 15	Hard drive, CD-ROM, CD-RW, DVD, tape drive, scanner	Fast SCSI is 10 MBps Fast Wide is 20 MBps
SCSI-3	16–the host adapter plus 15	Hard drive, CD-ROM, CD-RW, DVD, tape drive, scanner	Various speeds from 20 MBps to 160 MBps

exercise caution. Though SCSI was originally created to help solve compatibility problems, many of the SCSI systems are still not compatible with each other. The problem lies in the many proprietary variations.

You must be careful to match the device to the proper SCSI technology. *SCSI-1* uses an 8-bit system and supports data transfer rates as high as 5 MBps. It was the first SCSI technology. It uses a 25-pin flat ribbon cable. *SCSI-2* is similar to SCSI-1, but it uses a wider, 50-pin connector and supports up to 7 devices on one cable. *Wide SCSI* uses a wider cable with 68-pins, hence the name "Wide SCSI." Wide SCSI can transfer 16-bits of data at one time. *Fast SCSI* uses an 8-bit bus similar to SCSI-1, but has a much higher transfer rate of 10 MBps. There are also Fast-20, Fast-40, and Fast-80 SCSI systems. The last two digits of the name reflect the speed of data transfer in megabytes per second (MBps). The speed of each can be doubled by the use of a Fast/Wide device. Hence, a Fast/Wide-20 will produce a data transfer speed of 40 MBps.

Be careful when checking the speed of a device. When abbreviated, megabits per second is Mbps while megabytes per second is MBps. The small change in the case of the "b" means a very large change in the speed of the device.

Serial Attached SCSI (SAS)
A SCSI device that transfers data in serial fashion rather than in parallel. The SAS design allows 128 devices to be attached directly and can be expanded to as many as 4,032 storage devices.

Serial Attached SCSI (SAS) is the latest development for SCSI technology. Serial attached SCSI is similar in design to SATA. The SCSI device transfers data in serial fashion rather than in parallel. The SAS design allows 128 devices to be attached directly and can be expanded to as many as 4,032 storage devices. The SAS can be expanded to 4,032 devices total through the use of edge expander devices.

SAS has achieved data transfer rates as high as 3 Gbps. Note that a SAS is expressed in gigabits per second (Gbps) not gigabytes per second (GBps). Gbps is used as a measurement for serial data transfers. Since SAS transfers data in a serial fashion, Gbps is technically correct. For comparison to other SCSI standards, 3 Gbps is equal to 375 MBps. This is more than twice as fast as the 160 MBps transfer rate associated with the SCSI-3 standard.

Advanced SCSI programming interface (ASPI) is a programming language developed by Adaptec, Inc. It was developed for issuing commands between SCSI devices. It is the standard for programmers developing SCSI utility programs.

Advantages of SCSI

One advantage of SCSI is that SCSI devices can be connected inside or outside the computer case, leaving some flexibility for the user. IDE and EIDE are designed to install hardware inside the case. SCSI also has very high data transfer rates. Older SCSI hard drives were much faster than IDE hard drives. (New EIDE drives have closed that gap.) Most SCSI devices are also fully compatible with the Windows Plug and Play specification making installation simple. Some older SCSI systems may not be Plug and Play compatible.

A big advantage of SCSI in a multitasking environment is its ability to disconnect the communication between devices when the device is not needed, thus conserving resources. For example, when a tape is rewinding, it does not need to maintain its connection to another device. SCSI can disconnect the communication to and from the tape for a period of time and then go back and check if it is ready for additional communication.

In the SCSI technology system, equipment can be easily exchanged. At the most, the driver may need to be upgraded. To a SCSI host adapter, all hard drives look the same, as do other SCSI devices such as printers and optical drives. Of course the total capacity of the drives may differ. There is no need for slave and master arrangements as there is with IDE/EIDE. Each device is given its own unique ID number.

SCSI ID

SCSI devices must have a unique ***SCSI ID number.*** The ID range for the typical SCSI-1 is from 0 to 7 (eight ID numbers). When two devices attempt to control the SCSI bus at the same time, the device with the highest number takes control.

SCSI ID number
a unique number assigned to a device on a SCSI chain and used to identify that device.

While any device connected on the SCSI cable can have any ID number assigned, there are some common assignments. The host adapter is usually assigned the number 7, and hard drives are usually assigned 0 and 1. The host adapter is usually given the highest priority number. These are normal SCSI assignments, but they are not mandatory nor a recognized standard. It is simply a general practice.

The original SCSI limit of eight devices was first expanded by the use of SCSI bus extenders. The bus extenders were integrated circuit cards that connected as SCSI devices. They allowed an additional seven devices to be connected within a SCSI system. See **Figure 9-34.** As the SCSI-1 system was expanded, an additional system of identification was needed. The additional devices connected to the SCSI extender are identified using ***logical unit numbers (LUN)*** from 0 to 7.

logical unit numbers (LUN)
an identifier used with SCSI extenders to distinguish between (up to) eight devices on the same SCSI ID number.

Expanders can also be found in some SCSI-2 systems. They may be referred to as expanders, repeaters, and regenerators. The use of LUN ID is not limited to only SCSI storage drives. LUN ID is often used to identify nonstorage devices connected on a common SCSI cable, such as SCSI compatible CD-ROM, DVD, and tape drives.

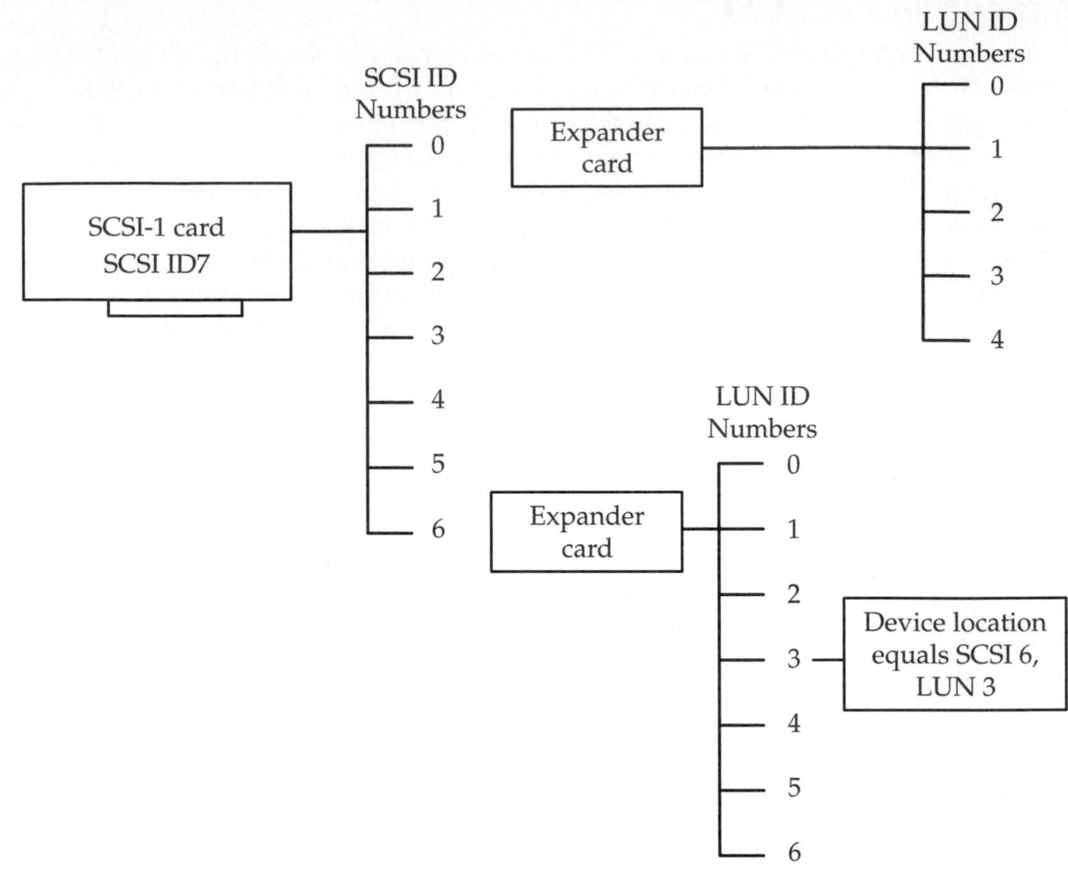

Figure 9-34. The SCSI limit of seven devices can be expanded by using expander cards. Each expander card allows an additional seven devices to be connected to the SCSI system. A LUN number is assigned so the system software and BIOS can identify each of the additional units.

SCSI ID Jumpers

Older SCSI systems used jumpers to identify devices. Look at **Figure 9-35.** The picture illustrates how a set of pins and jumpers might look on a SCSI device. The pins are actual electrical connections and the jumpers are used to make an electrical connection across the pairs of pins. The jumpers are set in the binary pattern that represents the SCSI ID number. If you have trouble interpreting the jumper patterns, you may wish to review the first chapter in the textbook, which illustrates and discusses binary numbers.

LVD and HVD

SCSI systems communicate using two different voltage levels identified as High Voltage Differential (HDV) and Low Voltage Differential (LVD). HVD uses 5 volts for a high and 0 volts for a low. LVD uses 3.3 volts for a high and 0 volts for a low. The high and low voltage levels are represented by a binary one or zero respectively. The advantage of HVD is that data can be transmitted on longer cables than on LVD. HVD can transmit data on cables up to 25 meters long while LVD is limited to cables 5 meters long.

The SCSI trade organization has excellent reference material, such as detailed charts of SCSI connectors, at their Web site www.scsita.org. Also, Adaptec and other hard drive manufacturers listed at the end of this chapter contain SCSI information.

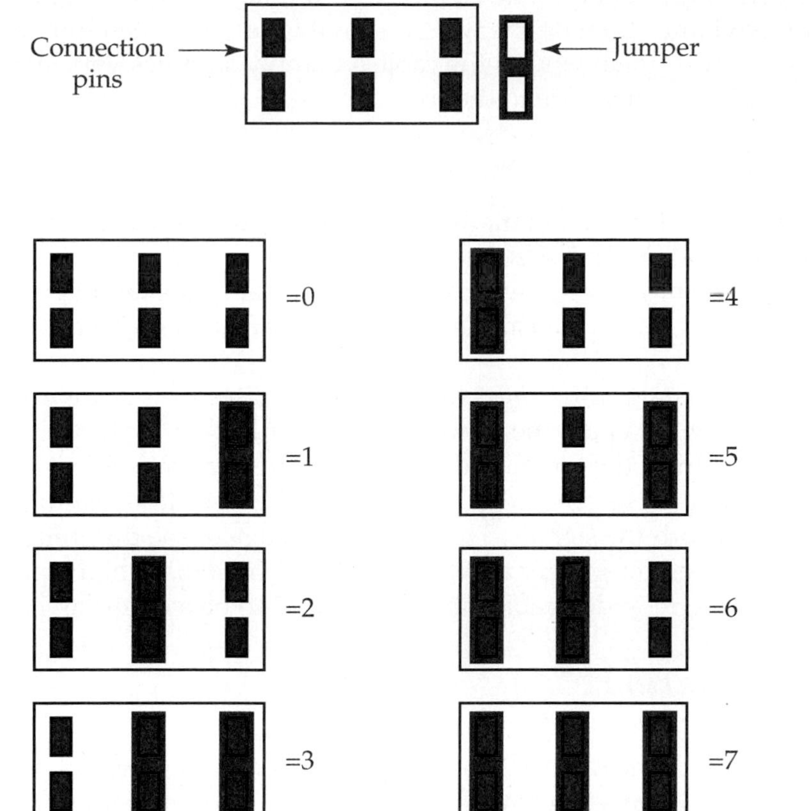

Figure 9-35.
SCSI binary patterns.

SCSI Commands and Terminology

In the SCSI system, there are two classifications of hardware that relate to communication between SCSI devices. They are targets and initiators. The SCSI host adapter card is usually the initiator, while the devices connected to the SCSI bus (printers, hard drives, tape drives, and other SCSI devices) are usually the targets.

SCSI has its own set of commands, which are used to control the flow of data and the communications between devices, targets, and initiators. There are also nine special control signals used in a SCSI system. They are as follows:

1. **C/D (Control/Data):** This control signal allows the target to signal if it will return a command or data to the initiator. The initiator will wait for the data or command.
2. **I/O (Input/Output):** This indicates whether the target will be sending or receiving on the data bus.
3. **MSG (Message):** The target uses this control signal to send error messages or status conditions back to the initiator.
4. **REQ (Request):** This control signal allows the target to obtain data from the bus.
5. **ACK (Acknowledge):** This is a reply signal sent back after the REQ signal. It acknowledges the REQ signal and takes control of the bus.
6. **BSY (Busy):** This control signal lets other devices know that a device is busy.
7. **SEL (Select):** This control signal is used to select a target device.
8. **ATN (Attention):** This control signal informs the target that a message is coming.
9. **RST (Reset):** This control signal resets all devices on the bus system.

These signals are sent on wires inside the complete cable assembly. By placing a high- or low-voltage level on the wire, a signal is sent between initiator and target devices. Additional wire in the cable assembly supplies data and power. These commands are invisible to the user.

SCSI Cable

SCSI cables are designed in many variations, **Figure 9-36.** The cable is either single-ended or differential. A single-ended cable simply carries the signal from the initiator to the target. Each wire carries the signal to the target and to a common ground. There is a terminating resistor located at each end of the cable to absorb stray signals.

In the other design, called *differential*, a pair of wires is used for each signal transmitted. By using a pair, the signal travels simultaneously from the initiator to the target and from the target to the initiator. This transmission cancels the effects of electrical noise generation. The system still uses terminating resistors at each end to absorb the signals. The main advantage of the differential design is that it can be used for greater distances, up to 25 meters. In high-speed data transmissions, single-ended cable may be required to be as short as 1.5 meters.

SCSI Termination

Each end of the SCSI cable must be terminated immediately after the last device on the end of the cable. Without the terminators, data would be garbled. The high-speed transmission of data through the cable would produce an effect similar to radio broadcast waves. These waves would echo and return to the ends of the cable causing the data to be garbled.

Cable termination is classified as either active or passive. Passive termination uses resistors to terminate the cable on each end. Passive termination is powered through the cable itself and is good for short runs of up to one meter. Passive termination works well for cables limited to the inside of the PC case. Active termination requires the use of an external power supply. It uses a voltage regulator and resistors to control the amount of voltage transmitted inside the

Figure 9-36.
Typical SCSI device and cabling. The back of this SCSI CD-RW drive has two SCSI cable connectors. The photo on the right shows the ends of a cable connector. Compare the cable connector on the left (SCSI) to the cable connector on the right (parallel).

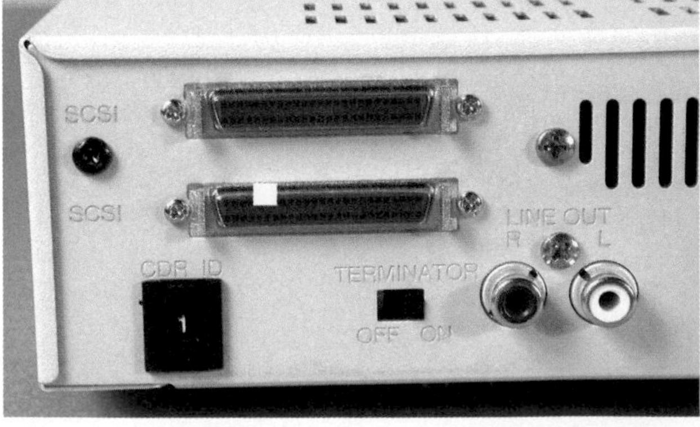

cable and to absorb the signals at the end of the cable. The active terminator allows greater lengths of SCSI cable to be used. It is typically used for cable runs outside the computer case to connect devices such as flat bed scanners.

SCSI Bus Operation

The first part of communication on the SCSI bus is the control of the bus. The control of the bus can only be attempted while there is no active BSY or SEL signal on the bus. Both BSY and SEL must be idle. Only one device can communicate on the bus at a time, so the device must gain exclusive control of the bus. The device that has control is the initiator. When a device is attempting to take control of the bus, it is called the *arbitration phase*. Once a device (the initiator) has taken control of the bus, it identifies the target device. Identification of the target device is called the *selection phase*.

The individual devices negotiate the control of the SCSI bus. When two devices attempt to take control of the bus at the same time, the device with the highest assigned ID number wins control. This is the reason that the host adapter is usually assigned the highest number. In a SCSI-2 system, the host adapter is usually assigned the number 7.

The initiator sends a BSY signal a SEL signal. After the initiator has transmitted data or a command, it then releases the BSY signal. The target then receives the data and issues a BSY signal until a reply with data or a command such as ACK is transmitted. The following steps are an example of how a typical communication might take place between two devices:

1. The system checks that the bus is idle with no BSY or SEL signal.
2. Arbitration takes place until the device chosen as the initiator takes control.
3. Selection of the target takes place.
4. The target device acknowledges the communication link.
5. The target notifies the initiator that it is ready to receive data.
6. The data is transferred to the target device.
7. Status of the data transfer is maintained. For example, are there any errors?
8. A message indicating all the data has been transferred is sent.
9. The bus is released to all devices.

When putting a SCSI system together with multiple devices, one device at a time should be installed after the host adapter card is installed. Using this method, it is easy to isolate a problem with an individual device if it arises during assembly. Also, note that all devices on your SCSI chain must support (or not support) parity. Some SCSI devices use parity and others do not.

Solid State Drives

Solid State Drive (SSD)
a storage device that uses Flash memory chips.

A ***Solid State Drive (SSD)*** uses Flash memory chips in place of disks and discs for storage. The advantage of SSD over disk and disc storage devices is SSD transfers data quicker, uses less power, is silent, and does not have any moving parts which can wear out in time. SSD does not have latency issues when accessing a data location as do storage devices that use disks or discs. Also, computers that use an SSD from which to boot the operating system, boot faster than disk systems.

The cost of SSD storage at the time of this writing is more expensive than disk drives, but as time goes by, the cost will greatly drop due to demand. The most commonly found place for SSDs is in the portable computer or laptop models. However, soon they will be found on desktop models. SSDs weigh less than and are much smaller in physical size than traditional laptop storage drives. This helps to make the laptop and portable device lighter and thinner. The SSD uses both ATA-6 and SATA data interfaces.

Tape Drive

Magnetic tape storage was the earliest removable storage media used with computer systems. Tapes can hold a tremendous amount of data and have long been used for backing up large amounts of data. Tape drives were also the preferred method of sending data from one location to another before the full development of the Internet, **Figure 9-37.**

Figure 9-37.
Typical tape drive.

A storage tape is created by covering a plastic tape with a thin flexible coating of metal oxide, similar to the coating on floppy disks and hard disk platters. A read/write head transfers data to and from the tape. The data is stored on the tape as a long series of magnetic pulses. The principles used to store and retrieve data on a hard drive also apply to the magnetic tape system, **Figure 9-38.**

The tape uses a format similar to disks. A file allocation table is used to keep track of sectors on the tape. A tape must also be formatted before it can be used. Formatting a tape is similar to formatting a disk except that it takes a great deal of time because of the tape's large capacity. Tapes are generally preformatted when they are purchased, saving hours of valuable time. Some of the top-of-the-line tape systems can format a tape as they are being used.

The one main disadvantage of using tape is that the data must be read sequentially. That is to say you must start at the beginning of the tape and search through the data sequentially until you find what you need. Hard drives, floppies, and CD-ROMs allow you to access data anywhere on the disk without having to pass through all of the data saved previously. Still, for inexpensive, dependable backups of large data systems, the tape has been the preferred media. However, with the development of CD-RW and DVD disc systems, tape drives have diminished in popularity. CD-RW and DVD give the advantages of both large storage capabilities and random access. Tape systems will continue in industry as conversion from tape to disc continues, but they will soon be obsolete.

The importance of system backups cannot be overemphasized. Once total loss of data or programs has been experienced, the need to back up becomes obvious. Most cases of a total loss of data revolve around the failure of a hard drive that contained all original data. While operating system software can be reinstalled, original data can be lost forever. Data recovery techniques are discussed later. However, data recovery techniques are not always successful, and they are certainly more time-consuming than replacing files with copies from a backup disc or tape.

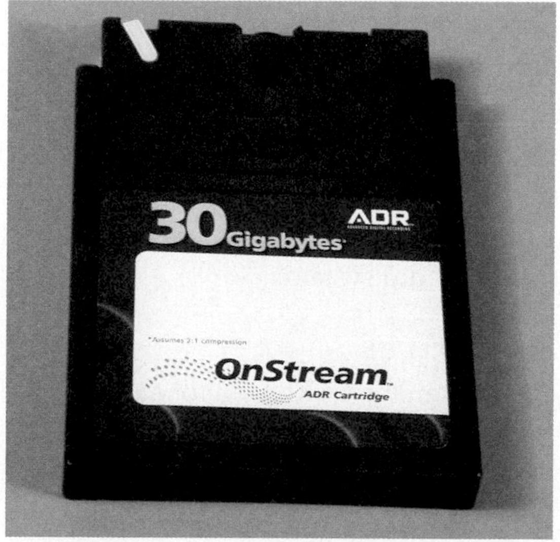

Figure 9-38.
Large storage tapes are often used to back up systems. This tape can hold 30 GB of data.

Tape Formats

Early tape drive systems were not standardized. If data was saved on any particular manufacturer's tape drive system, it most likely could not be read by a different tape drive system. Manufacturers used different recording schemes and, at times, even the physical sizes of the tapes were not compatible. Due to the demand for standardization, the Quarter-Inch Cartridge (QIC) was developed by a group of manufacturers. Tapes are identified by a combination of letters and numbers such as QIC-40 or QIC-80. The numbers are strictly identification numbers. They do not correlate to the length of tape or the amount of data.

In 1983, the first tapes were based on the 4″ × 6″ × 5/8″ original size of recording tapes. Later, the 3 1/4″ × 2 1/2″ × 3/5″ cartridge was developed. The larger cartridge would not install in a typical PC bay, hence the need for the smaller physical size standard. The larger cartridge was referred to as a data cartridge (DC), and the smaller tape cartridge was called a minicartridge (MC). Minicartridges can contain over 13 GB of data on a single tape. By using compression techniques, some tape standards such as digital linear tape can reach capacities of over 70 GB.

Minicartridges are not all compatible. The compatibility issue is caused by mechanical differences between tape drives, especially in the read/write mechanism. Never assume that a mini tape recorded on one system can be read by a different tape drive. If the tape is to be used exclusively by one tape drive, there should be no problem.

There are other common tape systems. While QIC is the most common tape media, there are quite a few others that have been developed. Digital audio tape (DAT) uses a system to record data similar to the music industry. Exabyte Corporation has an 8 mm tape similar to the video industry. Digital Linear Tape (DLT) is a technology with very high storage capacities and long lasting tapes. It is an expensive system, but it has rapidly gained favor for backing up network systems. The 3M Company created the Travan cartridge tape as a patented proprietary system. Its different styles are identified as T-1 through T-4 type tapes.

Choosing a Tape Drive

When choosing a tape backup system, there are some things that should be considered. These factors include the following:

- ✔ The amount of data that needs to be backed up.
- ✔ The capacity for future growth of the system.
- ✔ The compatibility with other tape systems in the same or affiliate companies.
- ✔ The overall cost of the system as compared to other data backup systems.
- ✔ The speed of data recording and retrieval.

A balance between all factors should be made. Not all scenarios will require the same equipment for a backup system.

floppy disks
soft magnetic disks used for storing small amounts of information.

floppy drive
a device that reads and writes to floppy disks.

Floppy Disks and Drives

Floppy disks are soft magnetic disks used for storing small to moderate amounts of information, **Figure 9-39.** It is similar in design to the hard drive except that the media disk is readily accessible. The ***floppy drive*** reads and writes to floppy disks, and it has been a standard device on PCs for quite some time. There have been many predictions about the end of the floppy drive, but they are still hanging in there, **Figure 9-40.**

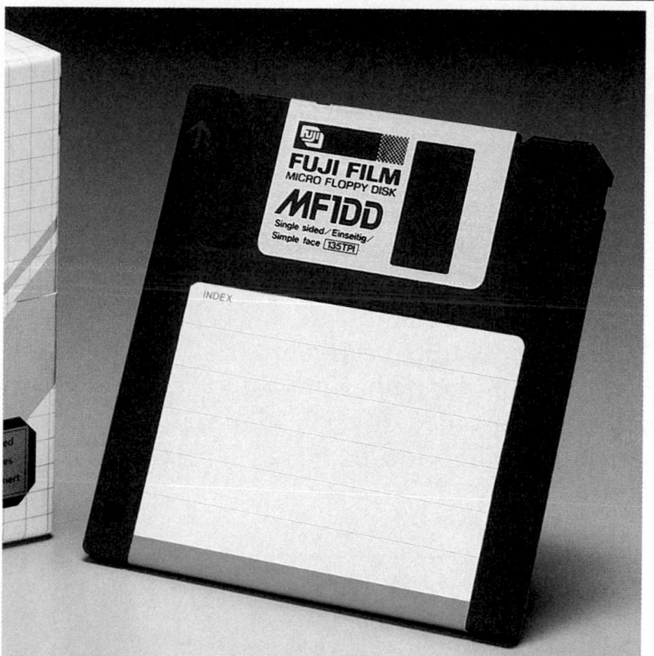

Figure 9-39.
Early floppy disks were very flexible, earning them the name "floppy." Today's disks have hard shells that have little flexibility.

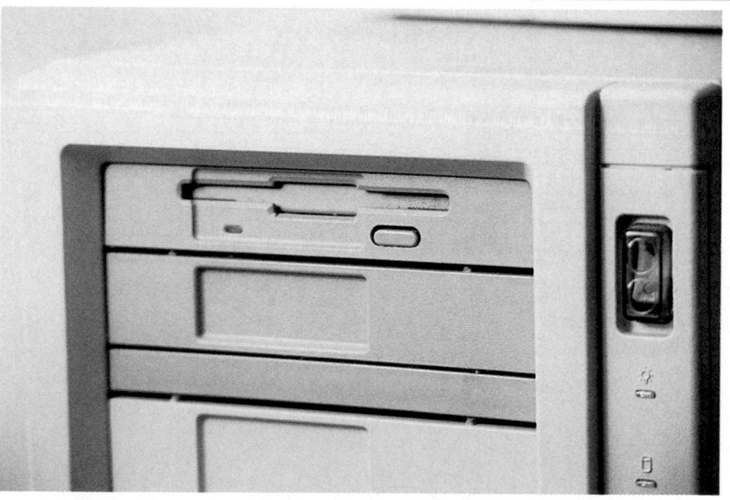

Figure 9-40.
Typical floppy disk drive.

Think of a floppy drive as an unsealed hard drive package. In the hard drive system, the data is stored on platters. In the floppy drive system, the data is stored on removable diskettes.

The original disk media was a thin, Mylar (plastic) disk covered with metal oxide. It was stored inside a paper jacket when not in use. This media was easily exposed to the environment, and data was often lost due to improper handling. Users were taught not to touch the disk media with bare hands and to avoid laying the disk down without the protective jacket. These early disks were easily damaged. The 3 1/2" diskette was designed with a durable plastic case surrounding the entire disk media. The protective jacket and the data media were supplied as a single unit rather than as two separate pieces. This provided much more security for the disk. The data on the media was well protected when not inserted in the floppy drive. The added rigidity of the plastic case of the

3 1/2″ diskette gave even more protection. The original floppy disks could easily be bent or warped resulting in failure of the disk inside the disk drive. Data on the newer plastic diskettes is protected from dust and lint particles. The older style floppy was exposed to contaminants even when properly stored.

The floppy drive, as we know it, has evolved from a large 8″ disk, to a 5 1/4″ disk, and to the standard 3 1/2″ disk with which we are all familiar, **Figure 9-41.** The early 8″ and 5 1/4″ diskettes were packaged in a hard paper or thin layer of cardboard or plastic. Today's diskettes are packaged in a thicker, durable plastic. However, the diskette inside the package is still "floppy," giving the medium its name. With the improvement of manufacturing capabilities, the physical size of diskettes steadily decreased while the amount of storage available on a diskette greatly increased. The 3 1/2″ floppy has proven to be one of the most dependable and popular devices ever installed on a PC. **Figure 9-42** shows a table listing the three common storage capacities for the 3 1/2″ floppy. The 1.44 MB format is the widely accepted format.

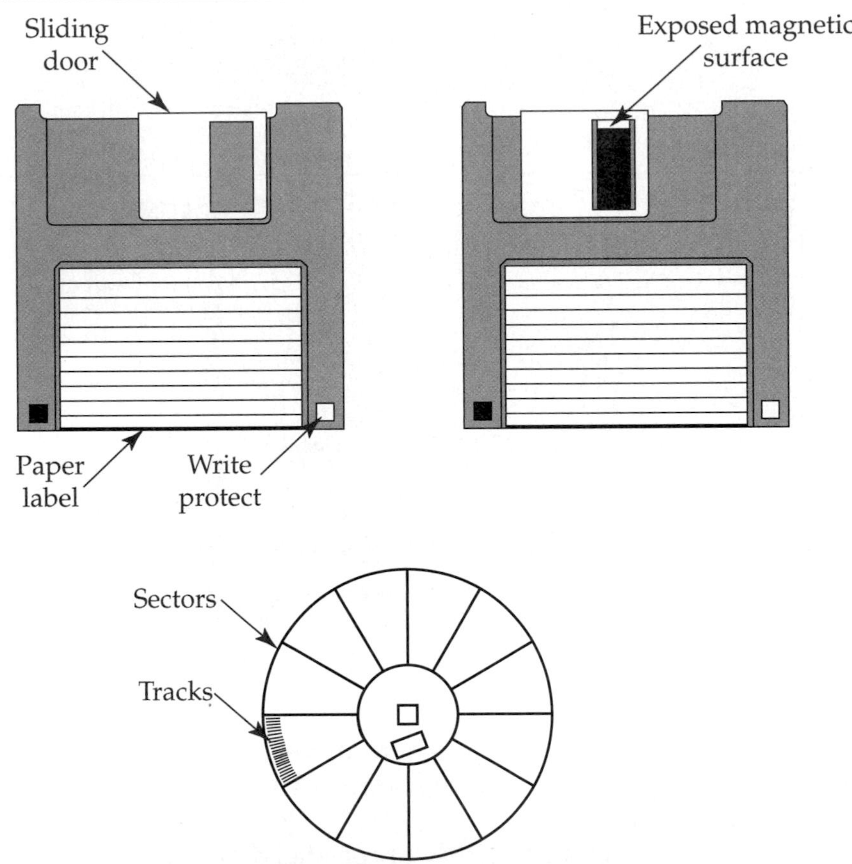

Figure 9-41. The features of a typical floppy disk.

Figure 9-42. Floppy disk capacities.

Physical Size	Type	Capacity
3.5	Double density	720 kB
3.5	High density	1.44 MB
3.5	Extra-high density	2.88 MB

Figure 9-43 diagrams a typical floppy drive. The operation of a floppy drive is simple. The disk spins inside the drive at 300 revolutions per second. A read/write head, similar to the one discussed with hard drives, moves across the disk's surface through an opening in the disk cover called the *head window.* The read/write head moves into position over one of the concentric tracks to read or write as necessary.

Figure 9-44 shows power and cable connections for a floppy drive. The data cables for floppy drives have a twist near one of the connectors. The connector near the twist is attached to the drive unit.

The file system on a floppy disk is similar to that on a hard disk with the exception of partitions. A floppy disk cannot be partitioned. As with hard drives and tapes, floppy disks must be formatted before they can be used to store data. Most disks are preformatted when purchased.

The Windows operating system gives the user two options for formatting a diskette: quick or full. See **Figure 9-45.** The quick format simply erases the FAT. The full format erases information across the entire disk and checks for bad sectors.

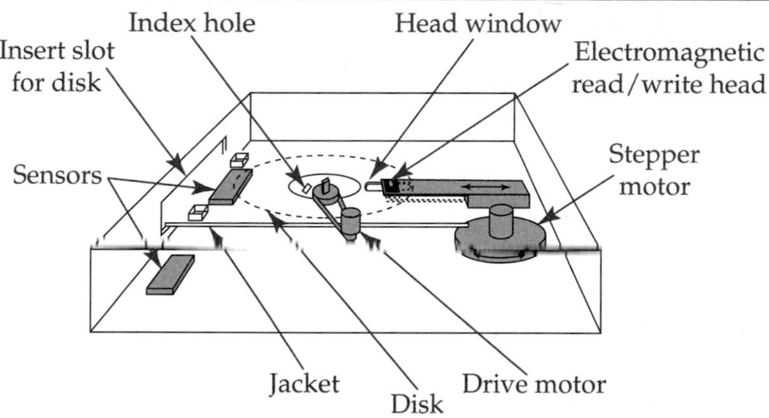

Figure 9-43. Parts of a floppy disk drive.

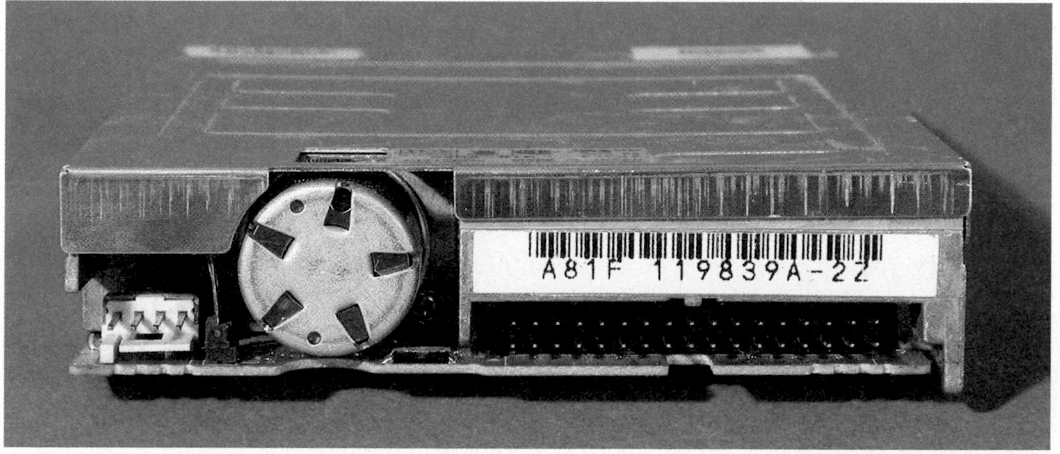

Figure 9-44. Cable and power connections for a floppy drive. The data cabling is the same for all floppy drives. However, many drives come with a two-jack mini power connector.

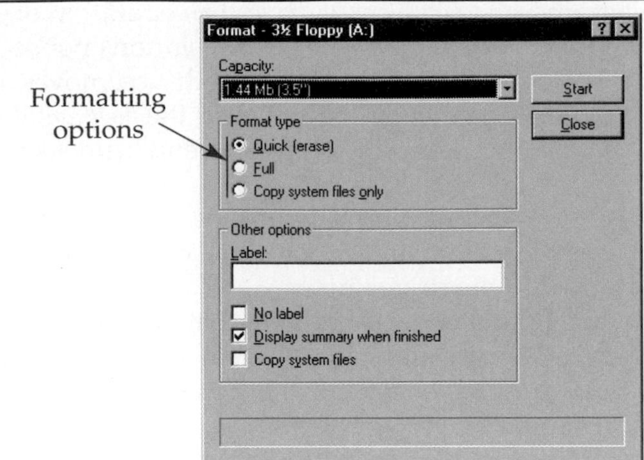

Figure 9-45. When formatting a floppy disk, there are two formatting options, quick and full. Quick can only be used on a floppy that has been previously used or formatted. Most floppy disks are now formatted by the manufacturer.

Floppy Disk Drive Repairs

Repairing a floppy drive is practically obsolete. The replacement of a 3 1/2″ drive is so inexpensive that labor costs for a typical disk repair far exceed replacement.

Cleaning

Floppy drive repair is usually limited to cleaning the read/write head. A commercial head cleaner kit can be used and is recommended over cleaning the head manually with alcohol and a foam swab. Cleaning the head manually involves removing the floppy drive from its mount. A commercial kit involves inserting a special cleaning floppy disk.

Disk Drive Alignment

Disk alignment is important. A misaligned disk drive will probably go unnoticed… until you attempt to use a floppy disk created on another computer. A misaligned disk drive will not read a disk from a properly aligned disk drive, or the material it does read will seem to be plagued with data errors. A misaligned disk drive will also find errors when attempting to read a floppy disk from an original software package.

Disk alignment is a questionable repair. The easiest and quickest solution is to replace the drive. Attempting to realign the read/write head is typically a waste of valuable time. Correcting a misaligned head involves purchasing software to assist in the realignment, as well as mechanically adjusting the head alignment.

Before replacing a misaligned disk drive, remember to copy all floppy material to the hard drive or to some other backup media. Once the drive has been replaced, all of the old floppy disks will become unreadable. Just as a misaligned floppy drive cannot read data from an aligned floppy drive, an aligned floppy drive will not be able to read the disks created on the old misaligned floppy drive.

If there is a large amount of data stored on floppies created by the old drive, there is one other solution. You can install an additional 3 1/2″ drive in an available bay space on the PC. With this option, the original misaligned floppy drive allows you to access any disk recorded with the old drive. As each old disk is discovered, the data can be transferred from the bad drive to the new 3 1/2″ drive.

LS-120 Drive

The ***LS-120 drive,*** also called a ***floptical,*** is a very high capacity disk drive that is able to store 120 MB of data, **Figure 9-46.** This is quite an increase when compared to the 1.44 MB capacity of an ordinary floppy disk. The *optical* part of fl*optical* infers that an optical system is part of this drive. However, the optical system is not used to record data. Data is recorded in a manner similar to any typical floppy drive or hard drive. The difference between the floptical and regular floppy drive is in the size and number of tracks per disk. The LS-120 uses many more tracks in thinner lines. It can also simultaneously write to 20 tracks, creating a much higher data transfer rate than the typical disk drive.

LS-120 drive
a very high capacity disk drive that is able to store 120 MB of data on a single disk.

This technology requires a much more precise alignment than the typical alignment found on a 3 1/2″ drive. An optical system guides the read/write head into proper alignment each time the disk is run. An alignment track is permanently etched into the recording disk. A laser beam is reflected from the alignment etch and this keeps the read/write heads in perfect alignment each time data is transferred to or from the disk. The laser alignment is used in place of the typical mechanical alignment of a read/write head. By using the laser for tracking the alignment, the disk can store over 80 times the data of a typical floppy disk of the same size. An additional advantage of the LS-120 is that it can also read/write to regular floppy disks.

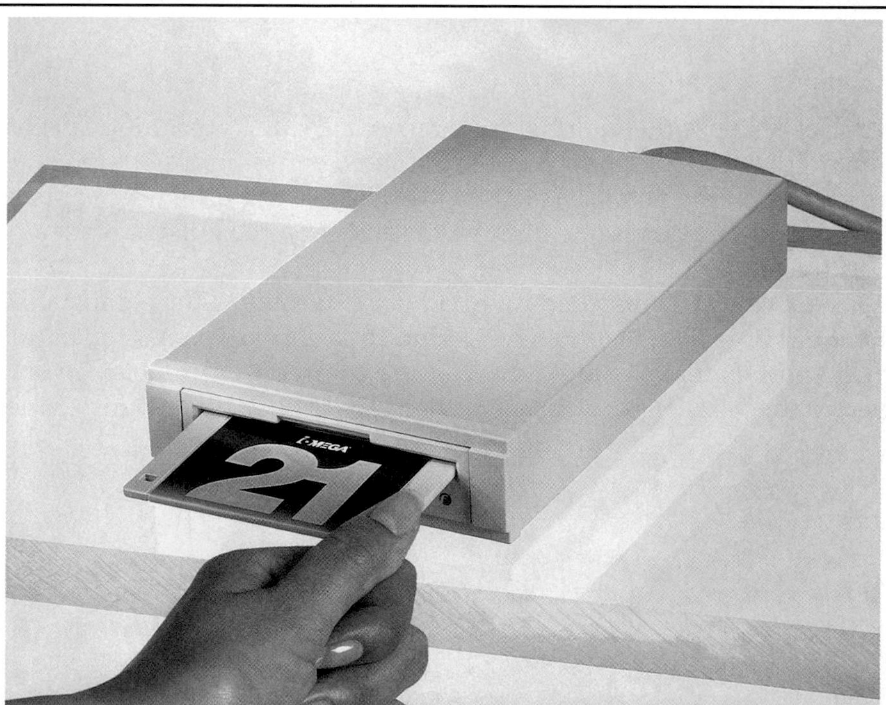

Figure 9-46.
Floptical drives, like the one shown here, can read and write to regular floppy disks as well as to their own high storage disks.

Zip Drives

Zip disk
a form of removable computer data storage that can contain over 200 MB of data.

A ***Zip disk,*** **Figure 9-47,** is another form of removable computer data storage. The Zip disk is similar to a floppy disk in physical size. Like the floppy disk, a Zip disk contains a flexible metal oxide covered disk surrounded by a hard plastic shell. The typical Zip disk, however, can contain over 100 MB of data.

The Zip drive, **Figure 9-48,** differs from conventional floppy disks in the head design. The head used for reading and writing in a Zip drive is approximately one-tenth the size of that used for a floppy drive. This allows the Zip drive to write data using 2118 tracks as compared to 135 tracks on a floppy.

Figure 9-47.
A Zip disk is slightly larger than a floppy disk.

Zip drives also use the multiple zone recording (MZR) technique used on modern hard drives. This technique, as discussed earlier in this chapter, allows for more sectors on the outer portions of the disk leaving little wasted space. A typical floppy disk has the same number of sectors on the outside track as on the innermost track.

The Zip drive can be installed internally or externally. Internal installations use either SCSI or (E)IDE technology. Externally, a Zip drive uses the parallel port or USB port. Before CD-ROM drives were common, a portable Zip drive connected to the parallel port was a popular way to back up or transfer files.

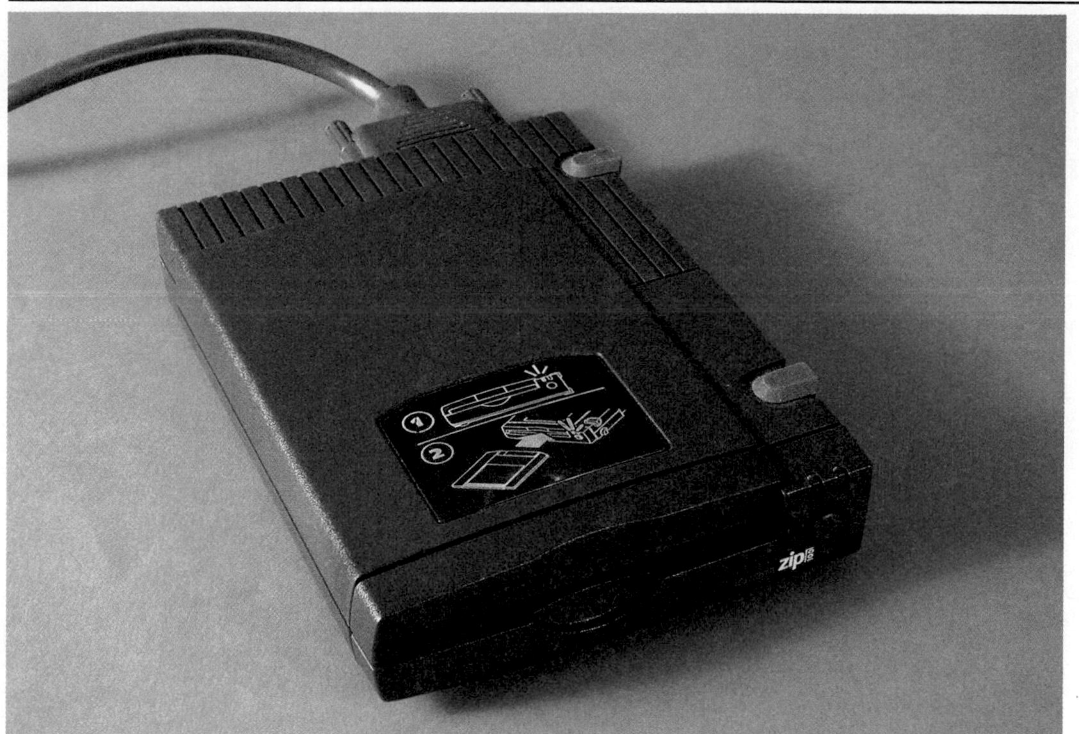

Figure 9-48. Standard external Zip drive.

Summary

- ✔ The hard drive is divided into sectors, cylinders, and tracks.
- ✔ A sector spans 512 bytes of storage space.
- ✔ The smallest unit of storage on a disk is a cluster.
- ✔ A cluster is composed of one or more sectors.
- ✔ Another name for cluster is *allocation unit*.
- ✔ Tracks are concentric circles of data storage areas on a disk.
- ✔ A cylinder is a vertical collection of tracks spanning two or more platters.
- ✔ Hard drives can be divided into multiple partitions to simulate additional drives.
- ✔ **Fdisk** and **format** are commands used to partition and format disks.
- ✔ The file allocation table contains information about how the clusters on a disk are being used and which clusters are associated with others.
- ✔ FAT16, FAT32, and NTFS are common file storage technologies.
- ✔ Encrypted file system (EFS) is the native encryption system used with the NTFS file system.
- ✔ Files become fragmented under normal disk operations.
- ✔ FAT16 is compatible with most operating systems.
- ✔ The ScanDisk program checks the disk surface integrity.
- ✔ Chkdsk is a command line tool used to check and repair the integrity of the file system on a hard disk drive.
- ✔ The DiskPart utility must be used in Windows Vista to partition a hard drive because Fdisk is not available.

- ✔ The manufacturer of the hard disk drive performs low-level formats. Technicians or users generally perform high-level formatting.
- ✔ SCSI is a bus system that typically connects up to seven devices on a high-speed connection to a PC. There are many different styles of SCSI.
- ✔ SCSI devices connect to the PC through an adapter board, and each device is configured to have its own ID number.
- ✔ SCSI must be terminated at each end of the cable. There are two types of SCSI terminator used: active and passive.
- ✔ Tape drives can be used to back up large amounts of data.
- ✔ An LS-120 drive, also called a *floptical*, can store 120 MB of data, and it can read/write to a standard 3 1/2" 1.44 MB floppy disk.
- ✔ Zip drives are like large floppies that can be used to store over 100 MB of data.

Review Questions

Answer the following questions on a separate sheet of paper. Please do not write in this book.

1. The magnetic polarity produced by a conductor is directly related to the direction of _____ through the wire.
2. The magnetic patterns left on a disk represent _____ numbers.
3. What is another term used for allocation units?
4. What DOS command is used to partition a hard disk?
5. What is multiple zone recording?
6. When is the MBR created?
7. Each primary partition or volume must contain a(n) _____.
8. What is the maximum size hard drive that can be formatted using a FAT16 file system without more than one partition?
9. What information is contained in the file allocation table?
10. What are the three major interface technologies used for hard disk systems?
11. On which file system can EFS be used?
12. What is the purpose of Chkdsk utility?
13. Does Windows XP support the ScanDisk utility?
14. Does Windows XP support the Chkdsk utility?
15. Does Windows Vista support the Chkdsk utility?
16. Does Windows Vista support the ScanDisk utility?
17. What switch must be used with the **chkdsk** command that will enable it to automatically make repairs to the disk?
18. Which operating system no longer recognizes the **fdisk** command?
19. What command line utility has replaced the functions of Fdisk utility?
20. How do you access Computer Management in Windows XP?

21. What is the maximum number of physical hard drives that can be installed on a typical PC with two IDE channels?
22. How many drives are designated as master on a PC with two channels and four physical hard drives?
23. How many logical drives can a typical FAT file system contain?
24. What is the maximum data transfer rate of SATA 1.0?
25. How many SATA drives can be connected to a SATA cable?
26. How many hard drives can be installed on a type SCSI-1 interface?
27. How many devices can be attached to a SCSI-1 cable?
28. How many devices can be attached to a SCSI-2 cable?
29. What is the expected high-voltage level of SCSI HDV and LDV?
30. How is so much more data stored on a Zip drive diskette as compared to a conventional 3 1/2″ high-density floppy?

Sample A+ Exam Questions

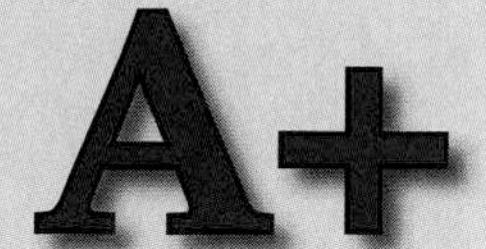

Answer the following questions on a separate sheet of paper. Please do not write in this book.

1. You install a new second hard drive to increase the total storage capacity of a PC. Both hard drives are installed on the same data cable. When you boot the system, the computer displays the BIOS information and the RAM test on the screen. After the RAM test is completed and passed, the PC hangs up. What is *most likely* the problem?
   a. The BIOS needs to be upgraded to match the new hard drive.
   b. A virus has been introduced into the system from the new hard drive.
   c. The jumper settings identifying master and slave are incorrect.
   d. The two drives' positions are reversed on the data cable.
2. Where in a FAT16 file system is the MBR located?
   a. In the first disk sector
   b. In the last disk sector
   c. The exact location varies according to the number of cylinders.
   d. An MBR is only on a hard disk system formatted for NT4.0.
3. Which command is used to partition a hard drive?
   a. **format**
   b. **format /s**
   c. **fdisk**
   d. **fdisk /part**
4. On which of the following file systems must Windows Vista be installed?
   a. FAT16
   b. FAT32
   c. VFAT
   d. NTFS

5. When preparing a new disk, the **format** command performs which of the following functions? (Select all that apply.)
   a. Creates a root directory
   b. Sets the first partition to active
   c. Checks for bad sectors on the disk surface
   d. Creates a master boot record
6. A certain file consists of 12 sectors. The sectors are not contiguous but rather they are divided into two separate areas of the disk. Which of the following technical terms is used to describe this condition of file storage?
   a. Cross-linked sectors
   b. File fragmentation
   c. Multiple zone recording
   d. Multiple sector storage
7. Which of the following technologies is not used for disk storage?
   a. ATA
   b. IDE
   c. SCSI
   d. DDS
8. What is the size, in bytes, of the smallest typical disk sector?
   a. 256
   b. 512
   c. 1024
   d. 2048
9. What is the maximum number of hard drives that can be installed on a SCSI-2 configuration?
   a. 5
   b. 9
   c. 15
   d. 24
10. Where on a Windows Vista operating system is the ScanDisk utility located?
    a. **Control Panel | Utilities**
    b. **Start | Programs | Accessories | System Tools | ScanDisk**
    c. **Start | Programs | ScanDisk**
    d. Windows Vista does not support ScanDisk.

Suggested Laboratory Activities

Do not attempt any suggested laboratory activities without your instructor's permission. Certain activities can render the PC operating system inoperable.

1. Using a lab PC identified by your instructor, experiment with the **fdisk** command. Try to set up multiple partitions on one physical drive. Also, try to create FAT32 and FAT16 file systems. Boot the system before formatting any of the partitions to observe the error generated. Format the same hard drive and reboot the system to observe the error generated. Now format the partition using the **/s** switch, which installs system files to the partition. Boot the system once more to see if any errors are generated. Remember, the **fdisk** command is not available in Windows Vista.
2. Install a second disk drive sharing the same data cable as the original drive.
3. Use the **fdisk/status** command issued from the DOS prompt to reveal information about the hard drive's partition tables. If using Windows Vista, use the DiskPart utility.
4. Access Seagate or Western Digital's Web site. Download any hard drive utilities that are available. There are usually hard drive utilities that will identify the type of hard drive installed, perform diagnostics, or allow access to hard drives too large for DOS and older BIOS systems.
5. Check a floppy disk and a hard drive with ScanDisk. Choose to perform a thorough scan.
6. Access the BIOS setup utility and find information about the hard drive configuration. See if it is auto detected or assigned a number. See if there is information about the number of heads, cylinders, and sectors. See if you can find controls to change the boot order (which boots first: floppy, hard drive, or CD-ROM drive). Do not make any changes to the BIOS setup without your instructor's approval.

Interesting Web Sites for More Information

www.adaptec.com
www.ibm.com
www.maxtor.com
www.quantum.com
www.scsita.org
www.seagate.com
www.westerndigital.com

Chapter 9
Laboratory Activity
Typical ATA (EIDE) Hard Drive Installation

After completing this laboratory activity, you will be able to:

- ✔ Replace a hard drive on a typical PC.
- ✔ Add a second hard drive to a PC.

Introduction

The replacement of a hard disk drive is a common PC repair. Fortunately, the mechanics of the replacement are very simple. Back up any important data before beginning this activity. When replacing a hard drive or adding an additional hard drive to a PC, *always* back up important files. The original hard drive can be inadvertently damaged during the installation process. For example, confusion or distraction could result in executing commands such as **fdisk** or **format** to the wrong drive.

This laboratory activity, with slight alterations, can be used to add an additional hard drive to a computer. If your instructor has you add an additional hard drive, skip the removal portion of the activity (steps 2 through 7).

Equipment and Materials

- ✔ Typical PC with Windows XP operating system or later.
- ✔ Additional hard drive.

Procedure

1. _______ Back up your data!
2. _______ Be sure the power is off to the PC. Remove the cover of the PC unit. Follow all anti-static procedures.
3. _______ Inspect the position of the hard drive and cables. Make a drawing of all cable positions if necessary.
4. _______ Remove the cables (power and data) from the existing hard drive. Do *not* forcibly pull on the cables. Make sure you remove the cables by pulling on the connector and not the cable itself. Some cable assemblies are poorly made, and the cable can be pulled apart from the connector.

5. _______ Hard drives mount in various ways. Inspect the mounting carefully before removing any of the screws. Unscrew the hard drive mounting screws. Place the screws in a safe location so they will not be lost. A paper cup or small container will prove very handy.

6. _______ Slide the drive out of the mounting. *The drive should remove easily.* If there is a lot of resistance when trying to remove the drive, check for an additional screw.

7. _______ If there is more than one hard drive on the computer you are working with, check the jumper positions on the hard drive you have removed for slave or master identification.

8. _______ Check the jumper settings on the hard drive you are about to add. Make sure the master/slave jumper on the new drive is set to match the drive removed. If there will be only one hard drive in the computer, the jumper should be set to master or single (no setting).

   If you are installing an additional hard drive, the jumper setting will be determined by where you install the drive and what is already installed in your computer. If you are adding the drive to an empty cable, the drive can be set as master or single. If you are adding the device to a cable that already has an EIDE device attached, the settings of the preinstalled and new device must be checked. One device must be set as a master and one device must be set as a slave. (Note that the hard drive you will be booting from must be set as a master.)

9. _______ Insert the new drive. Mount it into position using the mounting screws.

10. _______ Attach the power and data cables. When attaching the flat ribbon data cable, be sure to align pin 1 on the hard drive to the colored stripe on the cable assembly. Pin 1 on the hard should be identified by a number stamped on the drive. It is usually the pin closest to the power connection. The stripe on the cable is most often red, though it can be blue. Some cables will have the number *1* printed on the proper conductor. See the illustration.

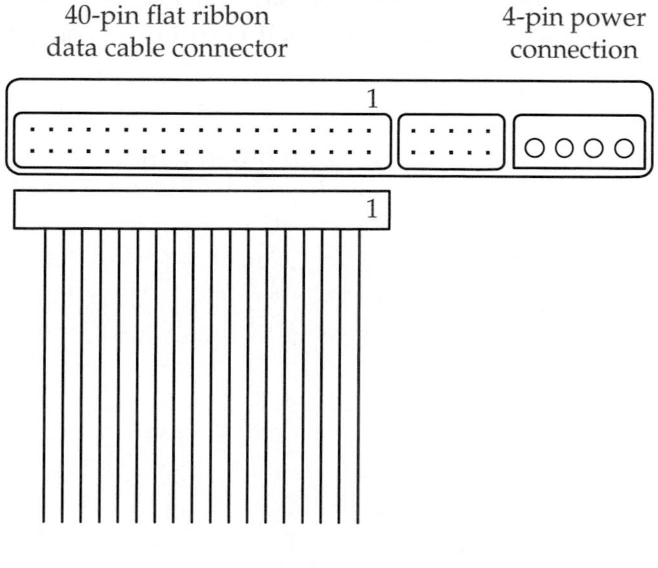

11.________ Before closing the PC cover, power on the PC and boot the system.

12.________ The new drive should be automatically detected by the Windows operating system. If the drive is not detected, you may have to adjust the CMOS settings. Some drive manufacturers supply a disk with software for their hard drives should a problem arise.

13.________ When everything is normal, power down the system and attach the PC case.

14.________ After the new hard drive has been installed, you need to use the **fdisk** command or DiskPart to set up partitions on the new drive, even if it will only have one partition. After you partition the drive, proceed to format each partition.

If the computer will not boot up, check that all cables are connected properly. Cables can come loose when installing a new component inside the PC. Also, check if the BIOS supports the drive you are installing. You may need to upgrade the BIOS. Check the Web site of the drive manufacturer for the latest information. Many manufacturers provide free downloads of diagnostic software for their drives.

In the field, before you replace a suspected bad hard drive, you will want to verify that the hard drive is actually bad. Try installing the suspect drive in another PC to verify it is indeed bad. There are many items, such as the data cable, the EIDE on the motherboard, or a boot sector virus, that would make the hard drive appear to be defective.

Review Questions

Answer the following questions on a separate sheet of paper. Please do not write in this book.

1. What is the first thing you should do before you install a new hard drive? Why?
2. What are the possible jumper settings if your PC has only one hard drive? What are your jumper options with two hard drives?
3. How is proper data cable alignment assured to prevent connecting the cable backward to the hard drive or motherboard?

CD Technology

After studying this chapter, you will be able to:

- ✔ Explain how data is stored and retrieved using optical storage devices.
- ✔ Describe how CD and DVD discs are constructed.
- ✔ Explain different CD formats such as CD-ROM, CD-R, CD-RW, and DVD-RW.
- ✔ Describe major parts of a CD and DVD storage device.
- ✔ Define Sierra format.
- ✔ Explain the steps for installing an optical drive.
- ✔ Discuss the compatibility of different CD and DVD formats.
- ✔ Explain the CD file systems ISO 9660 and UDF.
- ✔ Distinguish between CD, DVD, HD-DVD, and Blu-ray Disc storage technologies.

A+ Exam—Key Points

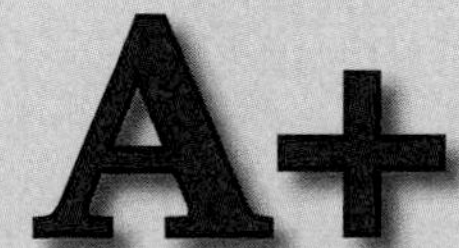

- ✔ Know the differences between CD types and DVD types of discs.
- ✔ Be familiar with the different storage capacities of disc types.
- ✔ Be familiar with disc compatibility.
- ✔ Know the various ways that disc drives can be added to an existing computer system, such as SCSI, EIDE, SATA, USB, and FireWire.
- ✔ Be familiar with the disc standard (colored) books. Know which colors describe which specifications.

Key Words and Terms

The following words and terms will become important pieces of your computer vocabulary. Be sure you can define them.

- access time
- Advanced SCSI Programming Interface (ASPI)
- AT Attachment Packet Interface (ATAPI)
- CD-ROM File System (CDFS)
- colored books
- Compact Disc Read Only Memory (CD-ROM)
- Compact Disc-Recordable (CD-R)
- Compact Disc-ReWritable (CD-RW)
- constant angular velocity (CAV)
- constant linear velocity (CLV)
- data transfer rate
- Digital Versatile Disc (DVD)
- High Sierra format
- ISO 9660
- ISO image
- lands
- magneto-optical (MO) drives
- Numerical aperture (NA)
- packet writing
- photocell
- pits
- Universal Disk Format (UDF)

Optical data storage began with the CD-ROM. It revolutionized the methodology for storing and retrieving data. Great amounts of data could be stored in much smaller physical areas. The CD-ROM paved the way for economical computer storage of music, graphics, and video. This chapter discusses and explains CD and DVD technology associated with the PC.

CD-ROM

Compact Disc Read Only Memory (CD-ROM) an optical disc able to store very large amounts of data.

In 1978, Philips and Sony Corporations developed the ***Compact Disc Read Only Memory (CD-ROM),*** an optical disc able to store large amounts of data. CD technology was originally developed to replace plastic records and tapes used in the music industry and not directly for computer storage, **Figure 10-1.**

Figure 10-1. Typical CDs. CDs can hold 650 MB to 700 MB of information.

Note that spelling *disc* with a *c* is a common practice to indicate optical disc or CD. Spelling *disk* with a *k* is used when discussing floppy and hard disks.

The first CD-ROM devices were large 12″ platters. By 1982, the 4.72″ platter became the standard.

To see the layers built into a CD-ROM, look at **Figure 10-2.** A typical CD-ROM is composed of a polycarbonate (plastic) wafer approximately 1.2 mm thick. The base of the wafer is coated with an aluminum alloy. This is where the actual data is encoded. A final layer of plastic polycarbonate is used to seal the aluminum alloy layer. A label is then placed on the top of the CD. The data is read from the bottom of the CD, not the label side. Data is recorded on the aluminum disc as a series of pits and lands.

The ***pits*** are holes etched into the disc and ***lands*** are the flat areas. The lands reflect the light of the laser beam. The pits disperse the light rather than reflect it back. Digital data is recorded to the CD track as a series of pit and land sequences. The pits and lands convey the binary values of 1 and 0. Changes from lands to pits and pits to lands create 1s. Lack of change for defined periods of time creates 0s.

pits
the holes etched into a compact disc in order to record data.

lands
the flat areas between the pits in a compact disc.

Most CD-ROMs are mass-produced using a laser to etch the surface of a disc known as the *master*. The master is then used to stamp out copies of the original data pattern onto many more plastic discs. The mass-produced discs are copies of the original. The plastic disc is then coated with a thin film of aluminum reflective material. The aluminum material follows the pits and lands etched into the plastic. An additional layer of plastic seals the aluminum material, and the outside is given a smooth finish to allow the laser light to pass freely through the surface.

A CD-ROM drive uses a laser diode to read the disc, **Figure 10-3.** The laser diode produces a laser light when energized. The laser produces a low-energy infrared beam. A servomotor in the drive follows commands issued by software to position the beam on the track on the disc. The pits defuse the light, while the lands reflect the light. The reflected light strikes a photocell, which is sometimes referred to as a photo detector. A ***photocell*** is an electronic component that changes light energy into electrical energy.

photocell
an electronic component that changes light energy into electrical energy.

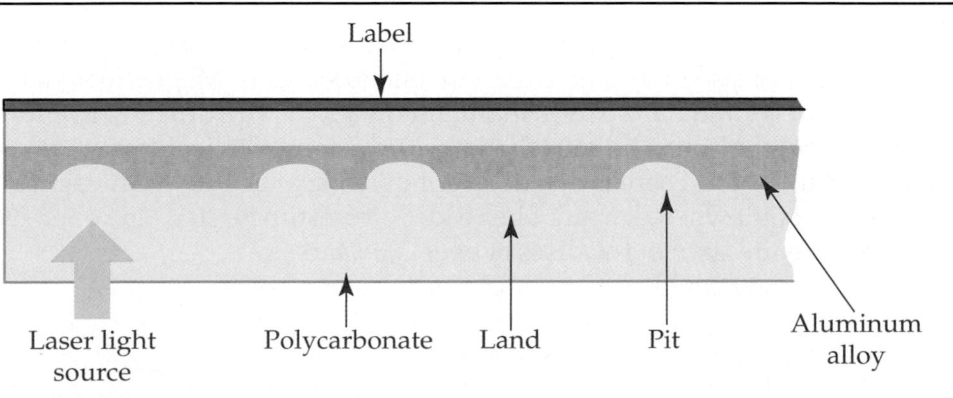

Figure 10-2. Cutaway view of a typical CD.

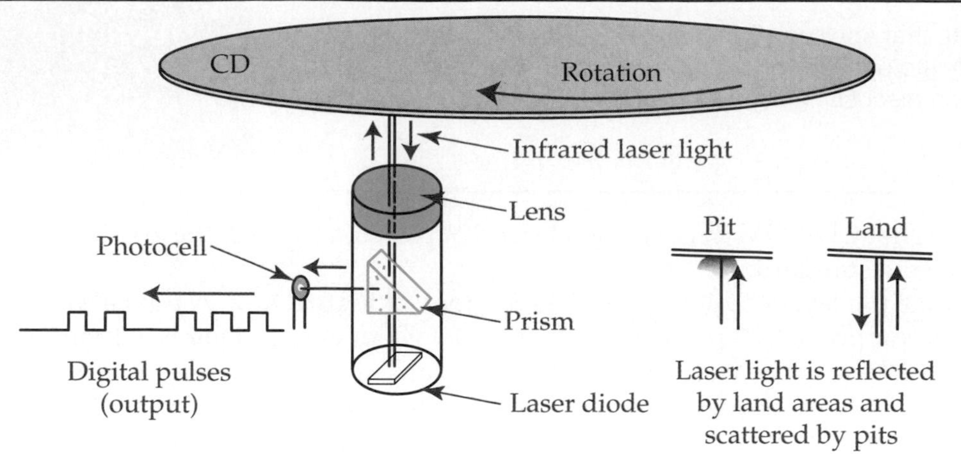

Figure 10-3. A laser diode sends a beam of light through a prism and onto the CD. If the light hits a land, the light is reflected. Pits disperse the light. The reflected light travels back through the prism, which sends some of the light to a photocell. The photocell turns the light into digital electrical pulses.

The light reflected off the CD produces a pattern that replicates the data stored on the disc. The light is reflected to the photocell where it generates electrical pulses. These electrical pulses are reproduced as a digital signal (on or off), and they represent the binary codes used to encode the data on the CD. Once the information stored on the CD is converted to digital signals, it can be utilized by the computer system. A typical CD-ROM contains between 650 MB and 700 MB of information.

Permanent damage can result to the retina of the eye when working with any laser source. There are specially designed safety glasses for working on lasers. As a computer technician, you should *never* work directly on the parts inside a CD device. The CD device is considered a field replacement unit.

The CD data is organized somewhat differently than on a hard drive platter. The CD uses a spiral technique to record data rather than dividing the platter into sectors, **Figure 10-4.** By using a spiral technique, it is possible to increase storage capacity. There is no wasted space as is found on the conventional hard disk platter.

Two major advantages of optical storage over magnetic storage are capacity and stability of data storage. Using the same physical amount of storage area, much more data can be stored using optical systems than magnetic systems. Optical systems are also more stable than magnetic systems. Magnetic systems such as floppy disks and hard drives maintain data for approximately five to eight years before they must be refreshed (written again). Optical storage does not have this limitation. There is debate over how long a CD-ROM can last before it degrades to a point where it cannot be read. Some estimate 10 to 25 years. Other estimates put the life span of the discs at over 100 years.

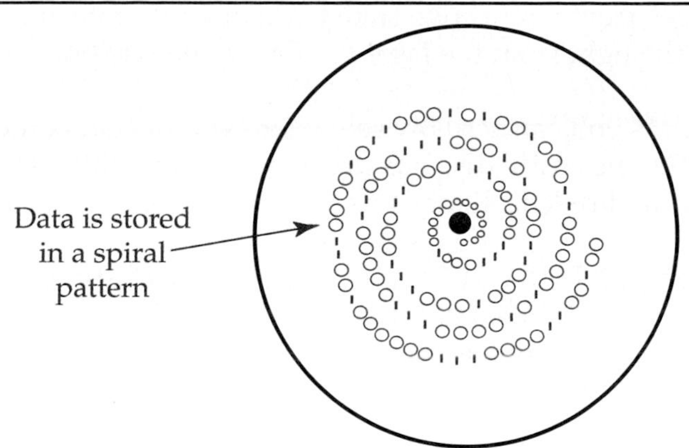

Figure 10-4.
CDs store data differently than hard drives. CDs do not use sectors.

CD-R

With ***Compact Disc-Recordable (CD-R)*** technology, you have a CD on which you can write data. This type of disc was first called CD-WORM (Write Once Read Many). With CD-R, data *can be* erased and the disc *can be* written to again. However, it cannot be written to a previously recorded sector. A previously recorded area *cannot* be recorded on again. When an area on the CD is said to be *erased,* the data is actually still present. It simply can no longer be accessed. Consequently, every time a file is updated on a CD-R, the existing file is made inaccessible and a new section of the CD-R is used to store the newest version of the file. **Figure 10-5** shows a typical CD-R disc.

Compact Disc-Recordable (CD-R) an optical storage media that uses photosensitive reflective dye to simulate the pits and lands of a standard CD.

A CD-R is designed with a photosensitive transparent organic dye layer placed against an aluminum alloy layer inside the CD. The photosensitive layer reflects light in its natural state. Thus, in its natural state, it appears as one long land to the CD reader. When exposed to the recording laser light, the

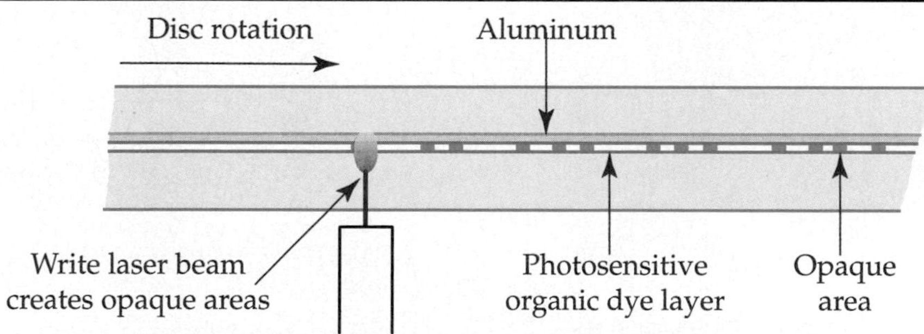

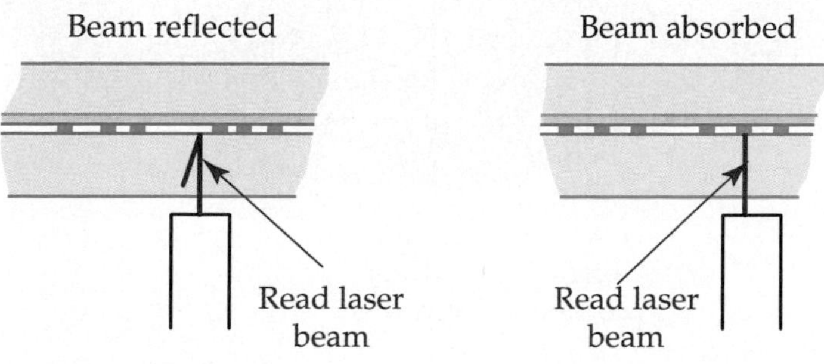

Figure 10-5.
One laser writes to the CD-R while a second laser is used for reading.

photosensitive layer changes from a reflective state to an opaque state. Instead of reflecting light, it absorbs the light from the laser similar to the pits used in the standard CD.

Note that with these discs you can actually see where you have recorded your data. With the stamped CDs, the entire disc has universal shine. With CD-R discs, the area that has been recorded reflects light differently than the unrecorded area, **Figure 10-6.**

CD-R has been replaced by CD-RW (discussed next). You will still encounter the CD-R in existing PCs for some time, but virtually all new PCs come with combination CD-RW and DVD recordable systems.

CD-RW

Compact Disc-ReWritable (CD-RW) an improvement over the CD-R technology, featuring special discs that can be erased and rerecorded.

The ***Compact Disc-ReWritable (CD-RW)*** is an improvement over the CD-R. The CD-RW read and write technology allows the same sections of a CD to be written to many times instead of only once. A special polycrystalline structure is sandwiched inside the plastic platter, **Figure 10-7.** The polycrystalline is a composite silver-indium-antimony-tellurium layer.

This technology uses a laser beam that has two states of heat intensity: low and high. When the polycrystalline structure is exposed to the high heat 932°F–1292°F (500°C–700°C), it loses its reflective quality. When the low power beam of the laser 392°F (200°C) is applied, it changes the surface back to a reflective quality. By applying the high and low beam heat effects on the polycrystalline structure, the reflective quality of the disc can be arranged (and rearranged) into

Figure 10-6. Notice the change in the appearance of the CD-R disc. Data has been recorded on the inner circle.

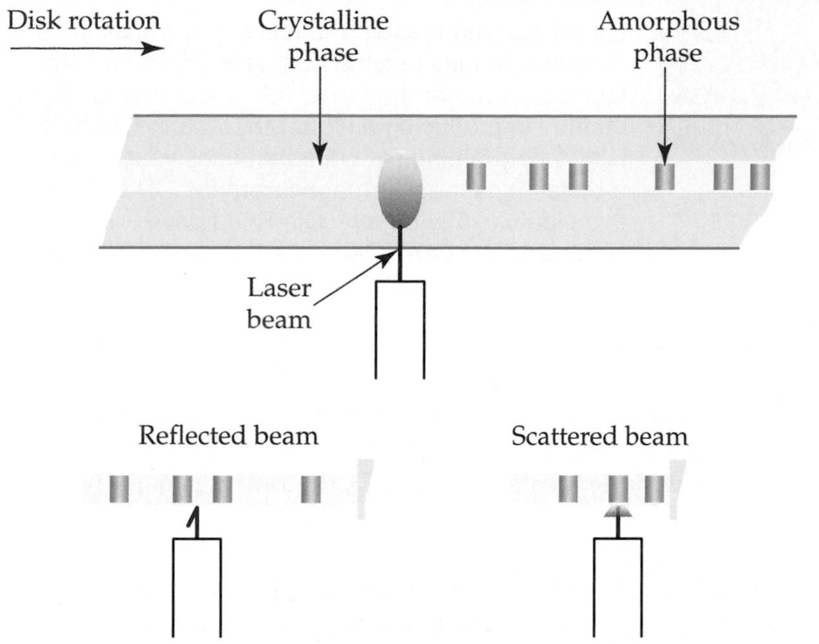

Figure 10-7. With the CD-RW process, firing a laser at its high intensity causes the disc to lose its reflective quality. The firing of a low intensity beam returns the reflective quality to the material.

a state similar to the land and pit technique. This means that previously recorded areas of the disc can be rewritten to, allowing for a data-recording media similar to a hard drive or floppy disk. The CD-RW has become a cost-effective media for low-volume data backups.

Compatibility issues have, at times, plagued the CD industry. Older CD players will often not be able to play new CDs, in particular CD-RWs. This lack of recognition is related to the intensity of the light used to represent the lands and pits on newer discs. The original CD standards required that the CD reflect at least 70% of the light striking the land. With the pits, no more than 28% of the light could be reflected. On the modern CD-RW, the land areas reflect no more than 15% to 25% of the light striking the surface of the land. This is well below the early standard of 70%.

Today's modern CD and CD-RW systems can read older technologies and make adjustments for the various light reflective intensities. However, the older technologies cannot make these adjustments. Consequently, a CD-RW made on a PC today, may not be readable by a CD system that is not CD-RW capable. Typically, only a CD-RW can exchange data with another CD-RW.

CD Specifications

Two of the most common CD specifications are data transfer rate and access time. The ***data transfer rate*** is a measurement of how much data can be transferred from the CD to the PC random access memory in a set period of time. This standard is usually given in kBps or MBps. If a manufacturer claims a transfer rate of 1 MBps, they are claiming that the CD can transfer a steady stream of data at 1 megabyte per second. Data transfer rate is more important if you transfer a lot of data from a CD on a continual basis. Playing games off of a CD is one use where you would like a high data transfer rate.

data transfer rate a measurement of how much data can be transferred from a CD to RAM in a set period of time.

Be careful when reading manufacturers' claims. Sometimes, they use the numbers based on compression techniques rather than true data transfer time. Another method of producing a higher-than-normal transfer figure is by incorporating software that uses your hard drive as a buffer to cache information from the CD system. With this type of software, any CD-ROM drive will appear to be faster and any CD-ROM system can be used this way.

access time
the amount of time that passes between the issue of the read command and when the first data bit is read from the CD.

The access time for a CD is measured in much the same way as it is for a hard disk. The ***access time*** is the amount of time that passes between the issue of the read command and the point in time when the actual first data bit is read after it has been located on disc. Because the amount of time delay varies according to where the data is physically located on the CD, the rating is usually an average. If you run applications where you periodically access a CD, access time becomes a more important time factor.

When upgrading a CD-ROM drive, be sure of what you are trying to achieve. Consider why you are upgrading. A better access time and transfer rate will not deliver a significant difference in performance to the average user. However, if the drive is being used as part of a tower in a network system, it can make an important difference in the performance. **Figure 10-8** shows a comparison of CD-ROM drive access and data transfer rates.

Figure 10-8.
Table showing the access times and the data transfer rates of a selection of speeds of CD-ROM drives.

Speed	Access Time	Data Transfer Rate
1X or Single-speed	600 ms	150 kBps
2X	320 ms	300 kBps
3X	250 ms	450 kBps
4X	135–180 ms	600 kBps
6X	135–180 ms	900 kBps
8X	135–180 ms	1.2 MBps
10X	100–150 ms	1.6 MBps
12X	100–150 ms	1.8 MBps
16X	100–150 ms	2.4 MBps
24X	100–150 ms	3.6 MBps
32X	100–150 ms	4.8 MBps
40X	50–100 ms	6.0 MBps
48X	50–100 ms	7.2 MBps
52X	50–100 ms	7.8 MBps
60X	50–100 ms	9 MBps
72X	50–100 ms	10.8 MBps

The X represents the base speed of the original music CD. For example, a 24X CD spins 24 times faster than a 1X CD.

The access time and data transfer rates indicated in the chart are intended as a guide for comparison. Actual drive access times and data rates will vary widely by manufacturer.

Note that CD-ROM drives are commonly advertised as 8X, 24X, or 40X. This naming convention is relative to the speed at which the disc is spinning, with 1X set by the speed at which the early CD-ROM drives turned.

There are two methods of reading data from a CD: constant linear velocity and constant angular velocity. ***Constant linear velocity (CLV)*** was used on earlier CD drives. It varied the speed at which the CD was spinning to keep points on the inside and outside of the disc spinning at a constant linear velocity. To better understand this concept, we must look at the relationship of data location on the disc and the speed of disc rotation. **Figure 10-9** shows the relationship between the speed of rotation on the surface of a disc and the distance from the center of the disc.

constant linear velocity (CLV) a method of reading data from a CD where the speed of the CD drive adjusts so that points on the inside and outside of the disc are read at a constant linear velocity.

All points on the surface of a disc that is spinning at a constant speed rotate at the same rpm. However, the farther any point is from the center, the faster that point will move. The point farther from the center has a longer distance to travel to complete its revolution, yet it has the same amount of time in which to complete it. Thus, data patterns at the outer edge of a CD move more quickly than data patterns in the center of the disc. CLV technology maintains the same speed of data transfer by varying the speed of the disc. When reading data from the outer areas of the disc surface, the rpm is reduced. When reading data from the inside areas, rpm is increased. By varying the speed of the spinning disc, a steady stream of data flow is maintained.

Modern drives use constant angular velocity technology. ***Constant angular velocity (CAV)*** maintains the same rpm regardless of the data location. These drives permit the data flow rate to change. With CAV technology, there is no more lost time while the CD-ROM drive adjusts its speed. Thousands of revolutions could be wasted with the CLV method while the drive sped up or slowed down to the proper speed.

constant angular velocity (CAV) a method of reading data from a CD where the drive maintains the same RPM regardless of the data location.

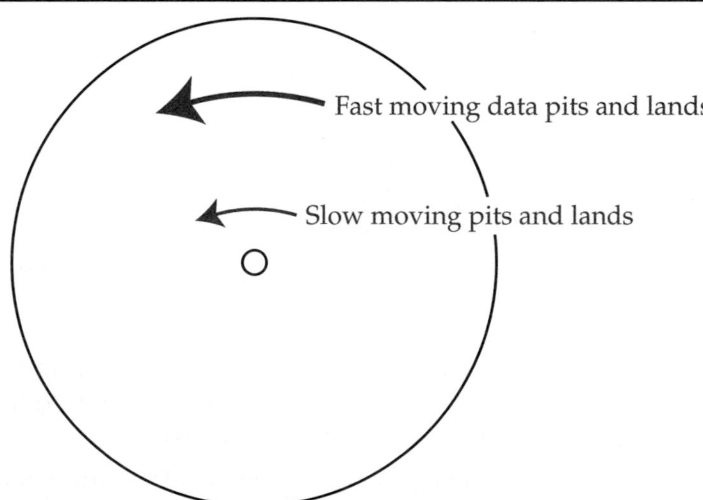

Figure 10-9. Although the rpm of a CD remains constant, the speed of the CD varies from point to point. A point farther out on the disc has a longer distance to travel per revolution. Consequently, the point moves at a faster speed.

CD-ROM Formatting

Without some standard method for coding CDs, a CD generated on one CD device would be unreadable to a CD device made by a different manufacturer. Producers of CD technology foresaw these problems and met to set some standards for the industry. The first set of standards became what is known as the High Sierra format. This format was later modified into ISO 9660. This format is the worldwide standard for CD-ROMs. An additional format, UDF, was developed for ***packet writing*** of information. This format was developed primarily for the CD-RW and DVD systems.

packet writing records data in small blocks similar to the way hard drives store data.

High Sierra format a standard for compact discs that was created so that CDs could be read on any CD device.

High Sierra Format

The ***High Sierra format*** is a standard for compact discs that was created so that CDs could be read on any CD device. The format got its name from the meeting place at the High Sierra Hotel near Lake Tahoe. CD-ROM industry representatives were interested in combining their efforts to achieve a common format they could all share. All members would benefit if they could use their CDs on any type of CD device.

The following explains the standard in simple terms. The first track on the CD identifies the CD itself as the media. It also synchronizes the CD with the drive mechanism. The disc also identifies the directories of data on the volume. The CD contains a Volume Table Of Contents (VTOC). This tells the CD drive how the data is laid out on the disc, similar to the FAT on a hard drive.

The spiral path of data on the CD does have sectors and clusters, but there is no need of tracks since the disc consists of one long spiral. The CD also contains a directory. The directory is used for organizing the data stored on the CD, but in contrast to the DOS system that relies on the directory structure to access information, a CD system can directly access files and information without going through the directory.

ISO 9660

ISO 9660 the file system standard that CD-ROMs use, which is an update on the High Sierra format.

CD-ROM File System (CDFS) another name used for ISO 9660.

In 1988, the High Sierra format was transformed into ***ISO 9660.*** The two standards are identical in content. However, the exact formatting is different. The ISO 9660 format is the CD-ROM format used today. An interesting note to the ISO acronym is that it is also a Greek word "iso," which translates to mean "equal." The ISO 9660 is also called ***CD-ROM File System (CDFS).***

The ISO 9660 is a file system structure very similar to FAT16 but with many improvements. There is no limit to the size of the root directory, and it can contain up to eight levels of files and directories. Look at the example that follows:

F:\LEV1\LEV2\LEV3\LEV4\LEV5\LEV6\LEV7\LASTFILE

The root directory is F:\ and then there are seven levels of subdirectories ending with the file LASTFILE.

ISO 9660 supports long file names. However, if you intend to use it with an operating system like DOS, you must use the eight by three naming convention. The ISO standard for CD-ROMs allows only uppercase letters, digits, and the underscore when naming a file or directory. Remember DOS allows the use of many special symbols in the name. The CD-ROM files are stored by sectors, usually 2048 bytes long, but they can be made larger or smaller. The sectors are numbered consecutively starting with sector zero.

An ***ISO image*** makes an exact copy of the contents by copying all sectors containing data and ignores the file system being used. For example, if you need an exact copy of an operating system, creating an ISO disk will copy all disk sectors containing data and will ignore the file system being used.

ISO image
an image that is the exact copy of data. It is made by copying all sectors containing data and ignoring the file system used.

Only Windows Vista Business edition and Ultimate edition are capable of creating an ISO image disk. All other Microsoft operating systems cannot create an exact ISO image of a disk without the use of a third-party software package, such as Nero 8 Ultra Edition or Roxio Easy Media Creator 10 Suite. ISO disc images are a common way of distributing software operating systems and an excellent way to back up a computer system.

UDF

The Optical Storage Technology Association (OSTA) was formed by manufacturers to create a file system structure that could be used for CD-RW, magneto-optical disc, and DVD technology. The file structure called ***Universal Disk Format (UDF)*** defines the new file system structure. It is the successor to the ISO 9660 file structure.

Universal Disk Format (UDF)
the file system standard accepted for CD-RW, magneto-optical disc, and DVD technology.

One of the greatest improvements of the UDF file system structure is that it allows for a bootable disc. One of the reasons CD-RW discs cannot be read by CD-ROM technology is the way the UDF file structure is organized.

Disc System Standards

Disc system standards are outlined in a series of specifications referred to as the ***colored books***. Each set of specifications is classified by book color. The *red book* describes the physical properties of compact disc audio and graphics. The *yellow book* was written to describe the requirements of using CD technology for computer data storage systems. The *green book* describes the specifications of interactive CD technology (CD-i). The *orange book* standard describes recordable CD media. The *white book* is used for video standards. The *blue book* is an expanded version of music standards referred to as *CD Plus* or *Enhanced Music CD* discs.

colored books
the set of books that outline disc system specifications.

The CD standards contain information about the physical description of tracks and overall physical dimensions as well as data formats, data encoding, disc compression, light reflection intensities, and error correction techniques. The standards are designed to allow for compatibility between different manufacturers in the industry.

Magneto-Optical Drives

Magneto-optical (MO) drives combine magnetic and optical principles to store and retrieve data on a CD-like disk. The MO disk is constructed of a magnetically sensitive metal crystal that is sandwiched between two plastic disks.

magneto-optical (MO) drives
disk drives that combine magnetic and optical principles to store and retrieve data.

When writing to the MO disk, a laser heats the plastic surrounding the metallic crystal. This allows the crystal to change its orientation on the disk when exposed to the magnetic field of the write head. When the plastic cools, the metallic crystal is aligned along the disk track representing the binary information, **Figure 10-10.**

To read the data from the disk, the CD is spun while the laser is focused on the track. This time the laser uses much less power and simply provides light to be reflected back to the photodiode. The reflected light is slightly polarized by

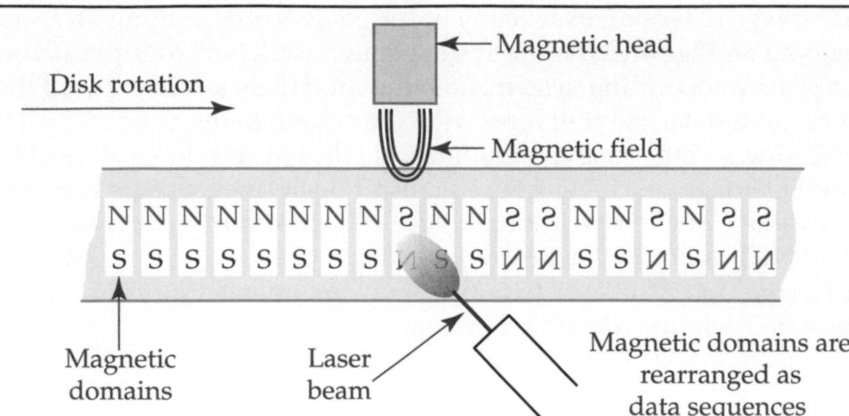

Figure 10-10. The crystals on a magneto-optical disk are fixed until the plastic around them is heated with a laser. During this heating process, the crystals are susceptible to having their orientation changed to store data.

the magnetic domain. The direction of the polarization represents the bit pattern stored on the disks. For example, a north pole orientation may represent a binary one, while a south pole orientation may represent a binary zero.

DVD

Digital Versatile Disc (DVD) the highest storage capacity of all laser-based CD storage types. Also called *digital video disc.*

Digital Versatile Disc (DVD) offers the highest storage capacity of all laser-based CD types thus far. The very same technology is also referred to as *digital video disc*. DVD is a standard that was pushed by the motion picture industry so that they could release films on CD rather than traditional tape systems. DVD obtains its higher storage capacity by using a shorter wavelength of light, **Figure 10-11,** to

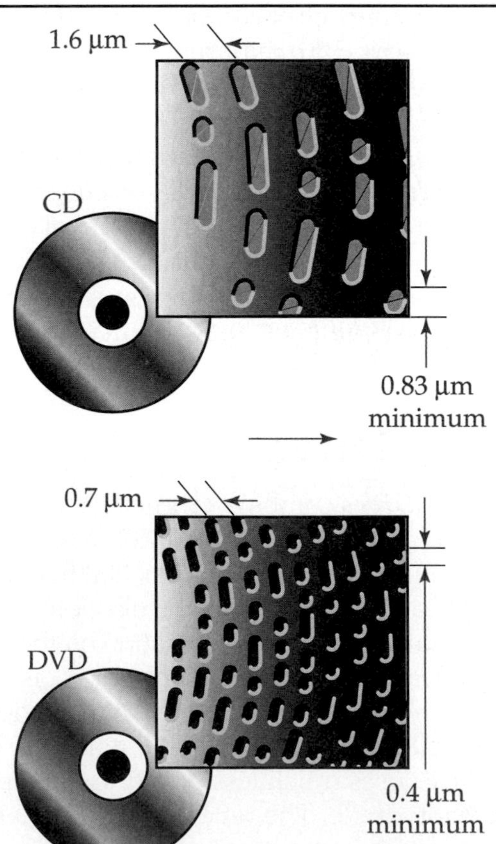

Figure 10-11. DVD players use a laser with a shorter wavelength than the infrared of traditional CD players. This allows data to be more tightly packed.

record and play back data. DVD uses a shorter wavelength red light as opposed to the infrared used by CDs. DVDs with an even shorter wavelength, blue laser are starting to appear. DVDs also use a smaller track technology, smaller pit and land length, and advanced data compression techniques such as MPEG-2. **10-12** lists the various DVD speeds and their data transfer rates.

The DVD Forum developed DVD-RW standards, which are not compatible with DVD-RAM developed by manufacturers that did not wait for a standard to be developed. DVD-Read Only Memory (DVD-ROM) was developed mainly to focus on multimedia in order to store video and sound on the same disc space. DVD-ROM is a playback only media and cannot be used to record. DVD-RAM is made to be written to and played back many times and also features random access of data. The directory does not have to be accessed first to locate a particular file, photo, or special sequence of data.

DVD Disc Structures

The DVD disc comes in several structure styles to increase data storage capacity. See **Figure 10-13** for a drawing of DVD disc structures.

The 4.7 GB single-sided, single-layer DVD disc structure consists of a single layer of reflective film that contains the pit and land areas that represent stored data. It is similar in construction to the typical CD-ROM. However, the 4.7 GB DVD storage capacity far surpasses the CD-ROM's 650 MB capacity, **Figure 10-14.**

The 8.5 GB dual-layer, single-sided structure contains two reflective film layers, a gold layer and a silver layer. For this technology to operate, the laser beam is run at two different intensities. The first layer is gold. When the laser is run at high intensity, this layer is partially transparent to the laser beam. This allows the data on the second layer, the deepest silver reflective film, to be read. When intensity is lowered, it cannot penetrate through the gold reflective layer. The gold layer data is read when the beam is in low intensity mode.

The 9.4 GB single-layer, double-sided disc structure is accessed from both sides. Think of the 9.4 single-layer, double-sided disc as two 4.7 GB back-to-back. The double-sided disc works with a DVD drive that has two lasers, one to read the top and another to read the bottom of the disc. If the DVD drive has only one laser, the disc must be turned over to read the other side.

DVD Speed	Data Transfer Rate
1 X	1.32 MBps
2 X	2.64 MBps
3 X	2.64 MBps
4 X	5.28 MBps
5 X	6.6 MBps
6 X	7.93 MBps
8 X	10.57 MBps
10 X	13.2 MBps
12 X	15.85 MBps
16 X	21.13 MBps

Note: This chart is for comparison purposes. DVD 1X is approximately equal to the CD 9X data rate.

Figure 10-12. Comparison of DVD speeds and data transfer rates.

Figure 10-13.
Different DVD structures allow for a variety of storage capacities. DVDs can store up to 17 GB of data.

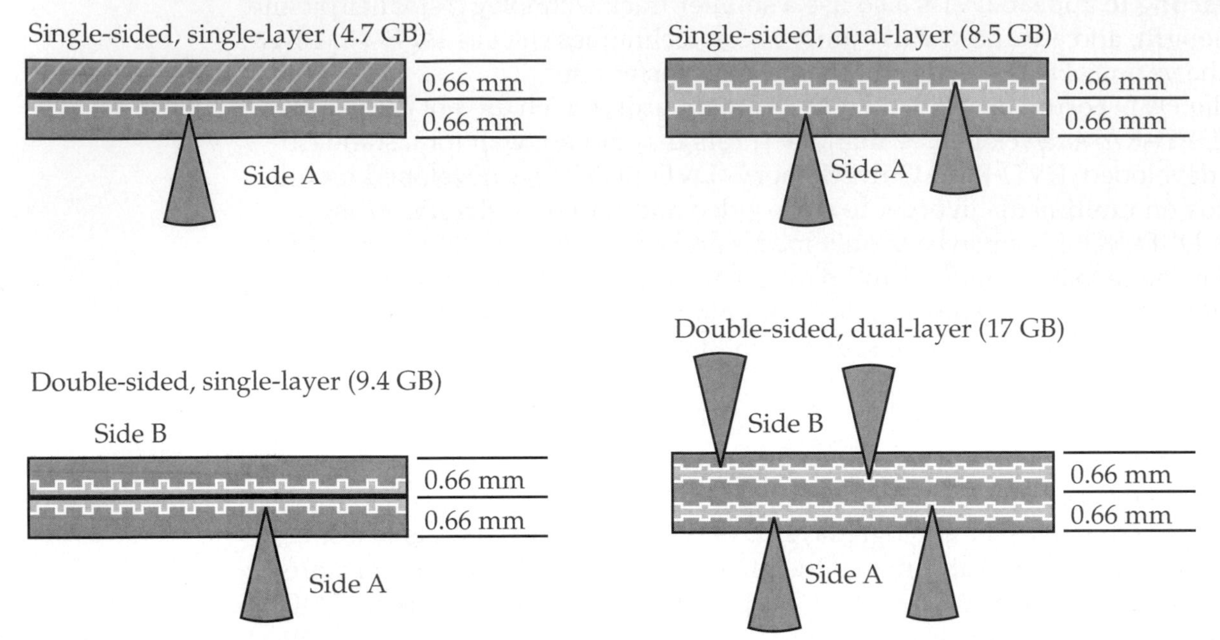

Figure 10-14.
The storage capacity of a DVD is a significant increase above the CD, and a tremendous increase above the old storage king, the Zip disk.

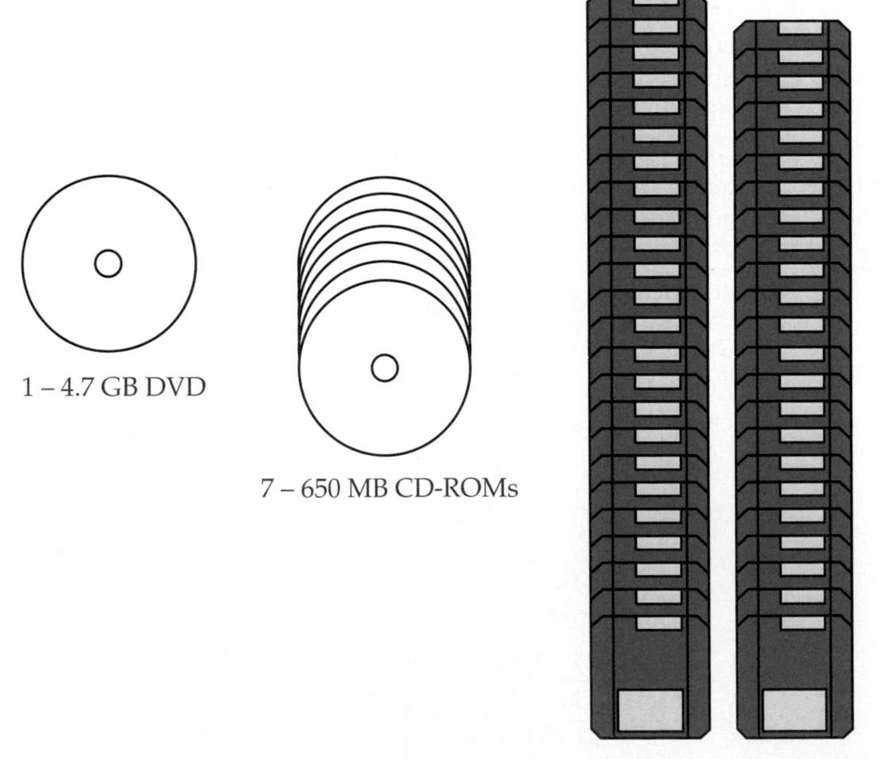

The 17 GB is dual-layer and double-sided. It is similar to two 8.5 GB dual-layer, single-sided discs joined back-to-back. The same technology of a gold/transparent layer is applied to this disc structure. Again, as with the 9.4 GB double-sided disc, there must be two lasers or the disc must be turned over to access data on both sides of the disc.

In a race to have the first dual-layer, double-sided discs available to the public, some compatibility problems developed. The manufacturers did not wait for a standard to be fully developed and implemented. Usually, if the disc is referred to as 17 GB DVD-Random Access Memory (DVD-RAM), it is not compatible with 17 GB DVD-RW.

Advantages of DVD

In addition to the obvious advantage of tremendous storage capacity, there are several other advantages to DVDs and DVD drives. One of the best advantages of purchasing a DVD drive is its downward compatibility with CD technology. A DVD drive will read most older CD technologies in addition to the new DVDs. DVD players have no trouble reading CD-ROMs; however, some players may have difficulty with CD-Rs and CD-RWs. The newer DVD players should be able to handle all the older CD technologies. Unfortunately, older CD technology drives will not read DVD discs because the laser intensities are different.

Another advantage of DVD is that video cards can incorporate MPEG standards of decompression directly onto the adapter card. This eliminates the use of the processor to decompress the files. This means faster overall performance.

DVD Compatibility Issues

Manufacturers raced to release DVD technology to dominate the market, and the consumer was therefore left with enormous compatibility issues. Consequently, there are several DVD standards that are not compatible with each other. This is a common cause of customer complaints about making a DVD on one DVD recorder and not being able to access it on another. Presently, there are two formal organizations dictating standards: the DVD-RW Alliance and the DVD Forum. Interestingly, there are some manufacturers like Sony and Ricoh that are members of both organizations. The following section covers DVD format standards for both groups.

DVD-R

DVD-R is a write once DVD recordable format introduced by the DVD Forum. The DVD-R format is compatible with most DVD players. DVD-R comes in two types: general use and authoring. The authoring type is a higher quality than the general type. The DVD-R type must match the recorder being used for the initial writing, but it can be read back on either type.

DVD-RW

DVD-RW is a ReWritable format introduced by the DVD Forum. DVD-RW can be reused over 1000 times. Most DVD players will read DVD-RW, but not all. It is not as compatible as the DVD-R format.

DVD+R

DVD+R was introduced by the DVD+RW Alliance and functions similar to DVD-R. There are some minor differences that are sufficient to prevent compatibility with the DVD-R format. It is also interesting to note that DVD+R is not compatible with all DVD+RW players. Most DVD players support both DVD+R and DVD+RW formats.

DVD+RW

DVD+RW is again similar to DVD-RW except for minor differences in the format structure. One of the main differences is that DVD-RW was designed to allow drag-and-drop file exchange, which earlier formats did not support. The drag-and-drop capability is often referred to as the Mount Rainier drag-and-drop support. The Mount Rainier version is also referred to as +MRW.

Early DVD players will have the most problem reading the variety of formats available. Today, it is common to purchase a DVD player that cannot only read, but can also write in any of the mentioned formats.

DVD-RAM

DVD-RAM is used primarily as a video format but originally was designed as a data storage format. One problem with DVD-RAM is it will not work in a standard DVD-ROM player.

HD-DVD and Blu-Ray Disc

The demand generated by HD television and movie industries for better video recording media has lead to the two latest disc formats: HD-DVD and Blu-ray Disc (BD). Blu-ray Disc (BD) is a new high-definition video and data format developed jointly by the Blu-ray Disc Association, which was started by Sony. HD-DVD and Blu-ray Disc are not just for recording multimedia. They are also used for data storage. Sony released the first laptop computer with a Blu-ray Disc device in the summer of 2006.

The DVD Forum approach is to preserve as much previous DVD design technology to ensure downward compatibility while increasing storage capacity. The Blu-ray Disc Association is more concerned with achieving the greatest possible storage capacity while not necessarily ensuring downward compatibility with previous CD and DVD designs. The Blu-ray Disc Association does encourage downward compatibility, but does not require it in its specifications for the design of Blu-ray devices.

A standard CD can store approximately 650 MB of data, and a DVD disc can store 4.7 GB of data, which is far less than what is required to record movies and television programs in HD format. However, single-layer HD-DVD has a capacity of 15 GB, and single-layer Blue-ray Disc has a capacity of 25 GB. The storage capacity doubles for dual-layer disc formats. For example, dual-layer HD-DVD can store 30 GB, and dual-layer Blu-ray Disc can store 50 GB. Future storage capacities are expected to exceed 100 GB or more as the technology is refined. See **Figure 10-15** for a comparison of the various disc technologies.

Notice that HD-DVD and Blu-ray Disc use the same laser wavelength of 405 nm; however, they are incompatible. The main difference between HD-DVD and Blu-ray Disc technology is the laser lens numerical aperture (NA) setting.

	CD	DVD	HD-DVD	Blu-Ray Disc
Storage Capacity	0.65 GB	4.7 GB	20 GB	25 GB
Approx. Data (1X) Transfer Rate	0.15 MBps	1.32 MBps	4.36 MBps*	4.29 MBps*
Video Resolution	Varies	720 × 480	1920 × 1080	1920 × 1080
Wavelength	750 nm (infrared)	650 nm (red)	405 nm (blue-violet)	405 nm (blue-violet)

*HD-DVD and Blu-ray Disc data transfer rates are typically specified in bits per second (bps), but are presented here in bytes per second to simplify their comparison to CD and DVD data transfer rates. The bits per second data transfer rate is 36.5 Mbps for HD-DVD and 36 Mbps for Blu-ray Disc.

Figure 10-15. Disc technology comparison.

The ***numerical aperture (NA)*** is a numerical expression for the way the light is gathered and focused into a single point. The Blu-ray Disc NA setting is 0.85. HD-DVD is 0.65. As a result, the tracks written on a Blue-ray disc can be spaced closer than those on an HD-DVD. Also, the Blu-ray laser does not penetrate the disc structure as far as an HD-DVD laser. This also allows for more tracks per disc surface. See **Figure 10-16.**

numerical aperture (NA) a numerical expression for the way the light is gathered and focused into a single point.

The Blu-ray Disc surface is sealed using a much more scratch-resistant material than CD and DVD discs. The harder disc surface is required because scratches would more easily prevent the reading of data from the smaller and closer disc tracks used in Blu-ray.

As with DVD, there are several different formats of HD-DVD and Blu-ray Disc. These are listed and described in **Figure 10-17.**

Since the release of HD-DVD, the original DVD is now often referred to as SD-DVD.

CD and DVD Interface

There are several ways to interface CD or DVD technology with existing PC technology. They include SCSI/ASPI, IDE/ATAPI, and SATA. Exterior connections can also be made easily using USB or FireWire ports.

The ***Advanced SCSI Programming Interface (ASPI)*** was developed by Adaptec to allow CD devices to communicate with the SCSI system components. ASPI became the de facto standard for SCSI CD devices. Remember that SCSI was used in PCs before the CD became standard equipment. Beginning with SCSI-2, the CD device could be installed as part of the internal or external system.

Advanced SCSI Programming Interface (ASPI) an interface that allows CD devices to communicate with SCSI system components.

Figure 10-16.
The numerical aperture (NA) and the depth of laser penetration of Blu-ray allows for more disc tracks than HD-DVD. Notice the difference in track pitch between HD-DVD and Blue-ray Disc and the depth of penetration of each laser.

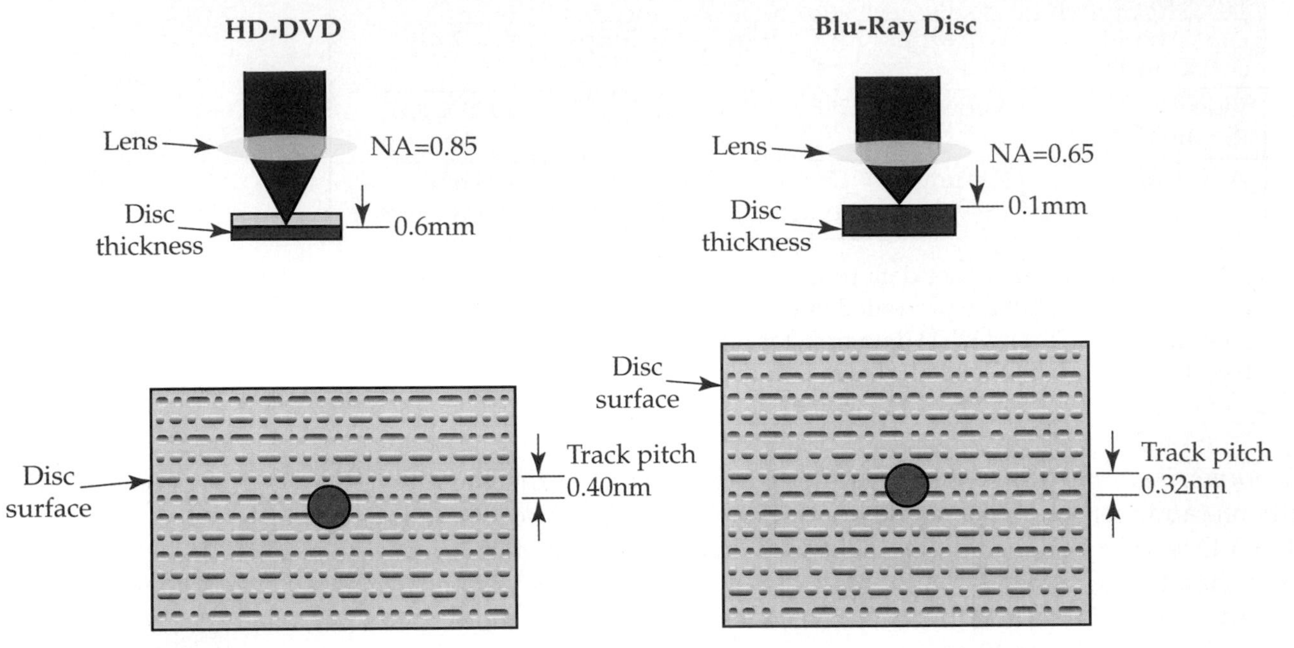

Figure 10-17.
HD DVD and Blue-ray Disc formats.

Formats	Storage Capacity	Description
HD DVD-R	15 GB single-layer 30 GB dual-layer	The disc can only record once.
HD DVD-RW	*	The disc can be used to record, erase, and rerecord.
BD-R	25 GB single-layer 50 GB dual-layer	The disc can only record once.
BD-RE	25 GB single-layer 50 GB dual-layer	The disc can be used to record, erase, and rerecord.
BD-ROM	25 GB single-layer 50 GB dual-layer	Used for prerecorded media such as movies.

*The standards for HD DVD-RW have not been released at the time of this writing.

De facto standards are standards that have not been defined by an organization. They are standards that have become so widely used, that they are accepted as the standard by industry.

The IDE port was designed as a hard drive interface. As CD technology became popular, the IDE system was modified to accept a CD upgrade, hence the development of ***AT Attachment Packet Interface (ATAPI).*** ATAPI is the interface used for standard IBM PC AT and compatible systems for accessing CD devices. ATAPI drives are also referred to as Enhanced IDE drives.

AT Attachment Packet Interface (ATAPI)
the interface used for standard IBM PC AT and compatible systems for accessing CD devices.

When upgrading a PC with a CD or DVD drive attached to the IDE port on the motherboard, it is advisable *not* to connect the CD or DVD drive to the same IDE port that connects the hard drive. Depending on the software that is running and the purpose of the CD or DVD drive, the IDE channel can have problems sharing the channel. For example, when recording music on a CD-RW, it is desirable to avoid interruptions in the data transfer process. Having the CD-RW share the same IDE channel with a hard drive can create problems arising from use of the hard drive. SCSI is a preferred way of connecting a CD or DVD device because of the much higher data transfer rates of which it is capable. Also, the CD or DVD device can completely take control of the SCSI bus, allowing for fewer problems caused by interruption of the data transfer process.

The easiest way to add a new CD or DVD drive to a PC is through the use of the parallel port, FireWire port, or USB port. The PC does not have to be opened, and the drive can be used for more than one PC. Before purchasing a new drive for a business, look at the corporate environment. It may not be necessary to install a CD-RW on every PC in the corporation. A portable CD-RW can be used to upgrade software systems and for installing large programs. A CD tower can be shared over a networked system.

Physical Connections

The connection points on a CD or DVD drive are similar to a hard disk drive with the addition of an audio and digital output connection. See **Figure 10-18.** This figure shows the back and front view of a typical CD device. The power and data connection cables are similar to the ones found on a hard disk drive.

The difference between the hard drive and the CD or DVD drive is the audio and the digital output connections. The CD or DVD audio connection connects to the sound card. This connection provides sound from the disc drive to the sound card. The digital output connection can be connected to an audiotape or other recording device for direct data transfer to the device. Installation of CD and DVD technologies can be made using EIDE as well as SCSI and SATA. SCSI was the preferred method for high data transfer rates, but SATA is most common and works well for most consumer PCs.

Note that master/slave selection jumpers must also be installed if the CD or DVD drive is to share a channel with another EIDE device such as a hard drive. It is recommended that hard drive channels not be shared with a CD or DVD device if possible. Sharing the same channel with the CD or DVD device can cause some unusual problems.

Figure 10-18. Connections for a typical CD or DVD drive.

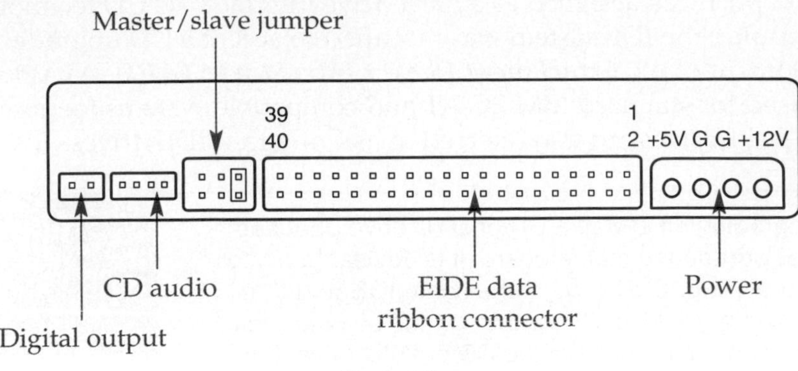

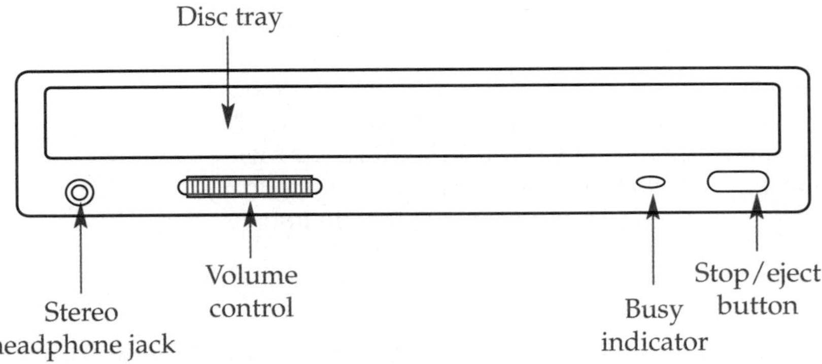

The DVD SATA drive is often not detected or automatically configured by the Windows operating system. This is because the motherboard BIOS software (firmware) may need to be upgraded. Often a motherboard can be two or more years old even in a newly purchased computer system. When a new technology is developed, the system BIOS often has a problem detecting the new technology and requires a firmware upgrade.

Summary

- ✔ CD and DVD technology use laser light reflected from the CD disc to generate electrical pulses that represent the data stored on the disc.
- ✔ Patterns known as land and pit areas represent data stored on a CD-ROM.
- ✔ A typical CD-R uses a chemical that changes from a transparent to an opaque color when exposed to laser light.
- ✔ A typical CD-RW uses a special crystalline structure that changes its reflective quality after exposure to heat generated by laser light.
- ✔ Most CD-ROM drives cannot read CD-RW discs.
- ✔ Magneto-optical drives use a combination of laser and magnetic properties to store data. The magnetic properties are used to polarize reflected light from the magneto-optical storage disc.
- ✔ DVD offers the same flexibility that a CD has, only at much higher storage density.
- ✔ Higher storage for DVD was accomplished by using a shorter wavelength of laser light, smaller pit and land areas, and closer track spacing.
- ✔ While DVD can read CDs, CD drives cannot read DVD discs.
- ✔ HD-DVD and Blu-ray Disc was developed to meet the needs of high storage capacity directly related to HDTV.

Review Questions

Answer the following questions on a separate sheet of paper. Please do not write in this book.

1. When was the CD-ROM introduced?
2. How do pit and land areas affect the laser light?
3. What does a photocell do?
4. What is the typical storage capacity of a CD-ROM?
5. What precaution should be taken when working around lasers?
6. How does the track on a CD differ from the track arrangement on a hard drive?
7. Why must a CD-R use a new section of the CD to store a file after the file is modified?
8. What other CD acronym could be used in place of CD-WORM?
9. How does a typical CD-RW have the ability to reuse the same areas for storage of data?
10. What is the difference between a CD-ROM and a CD-R?
11. What is the difference between a CD-R and a CD-RW?
12. Why is a drive designed as a CD-ROM player *not* able to read a CD-RW disk?
13. What does data transfer rate mean when used in specifications?
14. What does access time mean when used in specifications?
15. What does the "X" represent on a CD drive when printed as 24X?
16. What is High Sierra format?

17. What four factors give DVD a higher storage capacity than CD-ROM?
18. What is the typical storage capacity of the smallest capacity DVD disc?
19. What are the four ways in which DVD discs are constructed? List them starting with single-sided, single-layer.
20. What is the wave length of Blu-ray?
21. What is the wave length of HD-DVD?
22. Which stores more information, HD-DVD or Blu-ray Disc?
23. What is a numerical aperture?
24. Which disc technology provides the most storage capacity?
25. After installing a CD-RW to an EIDE, it fails to work. What might be some of the reasons for failure?

Sample A+ Exam Questions

Answer the following questions on a separate sheet of paper. Please do not write in this book.

1. Which is the most appropriate and advisable scenario for the installation of a CD drive?
   a. Install the new CD drive on the same IDE interface and data cable as the existing hard drive. This allows the remaining IDE interface to be used for future expansion.
   b. Install the new CD drive and format it using FAT16 to ensure compatibility with the existing hard drive.
   c. Do not install the new CD drive on the same IDE interface as the existing hard drive to avoid possible conflicts.
   d. Install the new CD drive on either IDE interface, but format the new CD drive using the same file system as the hard drive.
2. Which is true about MO disk technology?
   a. The read/write head uses intense magnetic fields to change the arrangement of the magnetic particles embedded in the disk drive.
   b. The read/write process uses laser technology to heat the plastic surrounding the magnetic storage particles being written to.
   c. The laser head is used to melt the reflective material embedded in the plastic disk leaving a bit pattern matching the data.
   d. The read/write head cuts small notches, which represent binary data, into the surface of the plastic disk. The individual notches reflect laser light back, which is then interpreted as data by the BIOS system.
3. Which are the standards for CD file storage? Select two.
   a. UDF
   b. CDUF
   c. CDRW
   d. CDFS
4. The amount of storage on a typical CD-ROM is equal to _____.
   a. 2.88 MB
   b. 650 MB
   c. 1.6 GB
   d. 1.44 GB

5. Which interface can be used for a CD drive installation? Select all that apply.
   a. EIDE
   b. ATA
   c. USB
   d. IEEE1394
6. Which of the following technologies offer the greatest storage capacity?
   a. DVD
   b. Dual-layer HD-DVD
   c. CD-ROM
   d. Single-layer Blu-ray Disc.
7. Which book describes the standards for audio and graphics compact discs?
   a. Red book
   b. Yellow book
   c. Brown book
   d. Cyan book
8. How does CD-RW technology work?
   a. A typical CD-RW uses a special crystalline structure that changes its reflective quality after exposure to heat generated by laser light.
   b. A typical CD-RW uses metallic particles suspended in plastic, which are heated by a laser and moved magnetically into patterns representing the data.
   c. The CD-RW technology is based on polarized light formation caused by a polarizing magnetic light read/write head crossing the plastic surface.
   d. A typical CD-RW is exactly the same as a CD-ROM only using a much more powerful laser.
9. A couple brings in their laptop computer and complains that when they make a video disc using their HD-DVD player/recorder on the laptop, they cannot play the video on their older desktop PC that has a DVD player. What is *most likely* the cause of the problem?
   a. The HD-DVD is copy protected and cannot be played back on another player.
   b. The newer HD-DVD player has a much more powerful laser and has burned the disc severely preventing playback on the older player.
   c. The BIOS on the desktop must be upgraded to match the laptop HD-DVD player/recorder.
   d. The density of the HD-DVD disc is too high to be read by the older DVD player.
10. What is the purpose of the VTOC on a CD-ROM?
    a. Its function is similar to a FAT. It describes how the data is laid out on the disc.
    b. It controls the volume level on the disc so that it will not blow the speaker system during playback.
    c. It controls the speed of the compact disc to make it compatible with other systems such as DVD.
    d. It is a special identification data tag to protect against copyright infringements.

Suggested Laboratory Activities

Do not attempt any suggested laboratory activities without your instructor's permission. Certain activities can render the PC operating system inoperable.

1. Format and then copy a file to a CD-RW disc. You can go to the CD-RW manufacturer's Web site and access information about the steps necessary to record data.
2. Install a CD-RW into a PC. After installation, test the CD-RW by accessing data from an existing CD.
3. Install a CD-ROM, CD-RW, or a DVD in combination with a sound card.
4. Check the Microsoft hardware compatibility list at Microsoft's Web site (http://www.microsoft.com/whdc/hcl/default.mspx) to see if all CD drive and DVD drive systems are compatible with Windows 98, Windows 2000, Windows Me, Windows XP, and Windows Vista operating systems.
5. Open **Device Manager** and see what the system resource assignments are for an existing CD drive.
6. Download a driver for a CD drive from a manufacturer's Web site.

Interesting Web Sites to Visit

www.hp.com
www.iomega.com
www.philips.com
www.sony.com
www.verbatim.com

Chapter 10
Laboratory Activity
CD/DVD Drive Installation

After completing this laboratory activity, you will be able to:

- ✔ Install any type of IDE CD or DVD drive.
- ✔ Identify common problems associated with CD or DVD drive installation.
- ✔ Identify the major parts required for CD or DVD drive installation.

Introduction

In this laboratory activity, you will either be installing a new drive in a PC that didn't previously have one, or you will be replacing or upgrading an existing CD or DVD drive. The exact type of procedure will be assigned by your instructor. The installation process is similar for both types of installation.

Installing a CD or DVD drive system is a simple task. The installation can be more complicated when a sound card is used in combination with the CD or DVD drive. When a sound card is incorporated with the CD or DVD drive for enhanced audio, some problems may develop. Usually the sound card and CD or DVD drive will share the same IRQ assignment.

The original Plug and Play technology often failed to correctly identify a new CD or DVD drive. This is rarely a problem today, but it still does occur occasionally. When Plug and Play fails to correctly identify the new drive, you will need to use the installation CD that accompanies it. Follow the instructions in the drive's installation manual. When an installation manual is not available, you can usually obtain the information from the manufacturer's Web site as well as the required software drivers or the latest updated driver.

Loading the proper driver can be another problem when installing a CD drive. When the new drive is installed and the computer is booted, the operating system should automatically detect the CD or DVD drive and load the appropriate driver. For example, in Windows XP, Plug and Play identifies the new device and then automatically extracts the driver files from the cab files and installs them. Cab files are located on the hard drive as part of the Windows XP installation. They are compressed files supplied by the manufacturer and are included in the Windows XP installation disc.

However, new drives are placed on the market daily. The operating system you are using may not contain the very latest drivers needed for the installation. In this case, you will need to find the latest driver and install it manually. A driver is usually included when the CD drive is purchased, but it may not be the latest. It is, therefore, a good idea to check the manufacturer's Web site for the latest driver for the device as well as information about known problems. Checking the Web site can save many frustrating hours during an installation.

Keep in mind that Windows Vista has changed the way driver files are handled by using two distinct steps: staging and installation. During staging, the driver is added to what Microsoft refers to as the driver store. The driver store is the collection of drivers used for all the hardware installed on the computer. A driver can be added to the driver store before the physical hardware is actually installed. Microsoft has a list of "bad drivers" which Windows Vista will not allow to be installed. The bad drivers have been identified by Microsoft and can cause the operating system to lock up or fail. During the installation step, Windows Vista automatically detects the new hardware item and then automatically installs the correct driver from the driver store. The changes to Windows Vista are part of Microsoft's efforts to prevent the installation of software that can harm the operating system.

To manually install a hardware device in Windows XP or Windows Vista, you will need to open **Control Panel** and then select **Classic View** option. The **Add New Hardware** icon is no longer part of the Windows XP or Windows Vista default Control Panel listing of services. Running Windows XP or Windows Vista Control Panel in classic view will provide you with the **Add Hardware** icon, thus allowing you to perform a manual installation of a hardware device.

Proper connection of the CD drive can be another troublesome area during the installation. When installing a CD drive, avoid sharing the IDE connection with the hard drive. Sharing the same IDE connection can create compatibility problems between the CD drive and the hard drive. One problem is resolving the master/slave issue between the two devices. The other is the data transfer speed. An older hard drive will most likely have a much slower data transfer rate than the newer CD drive. This condition will cause the CD drive to transfer data at the lower rate, matching the hard disk drive and thus hurting the performance of the CD drive.

The mechanics of installing a CD drive are quite simple. The only real concern is the possibility of loosening a connection to one of the other drives while installing the CD drive cables. The following illustration of a typical CD drive shows the connection points on the end of the drive.

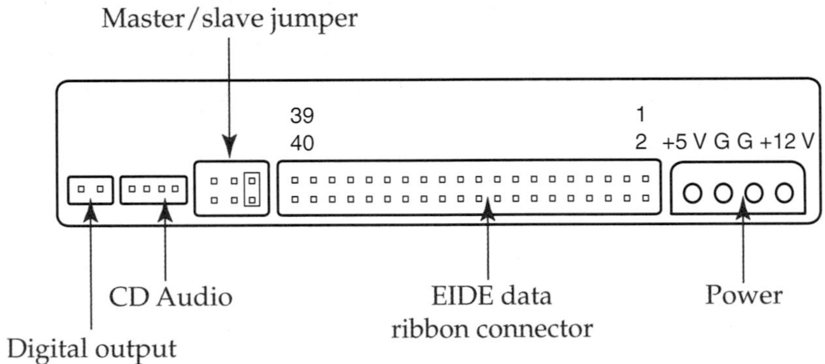

Note the master/slave jumper selection area. The master/slave jumper setup is similar to that found on hard drives. When more than one device is connected to an IDE or EIDE connection, one device must be designated the master and the other as the slave.

Equipment and Materials

- ✔ Typical PC running Windows XP or later.
- ✔ CD or DVD drive.

Procedure

1. _______ Boot the PC to be sure it is in working order before you begin the installation procedure.
2. _______ Once you have verified that the assigned PC is in working order, properly shut it down and turn off the power.
3. _______ Remove the PC cover and select the bay in which the new CD or DVD drive will be installed. If you are replacing an existing drive, sketch the drive and its cable connections. Take care to mark the proper orientation of the cables, as you will most likely have to reinstall the original drive at the end of the lab. Once you have sketched the drive setup, disconnect the cables and remove the mounting screws from the mounting rails. Slide the CD or DVD drive out of its bay. This procedure will vary based on the make and model of the drive and the case.
4. _______ If you are performing a new installation, install the mounting rails to the bay now. For a unit replacement, check the existing mounting rails for compatibility with the new drive. You may need to remove the existing mounting rails and replace them with a set of rails compatible with the new drive. Before securing the CD or DVD drive into the case, check the master/slave jumper settings. Be sure to choose the correct setting for the installation. Check the drive's documentation or look on the side of the drive for a chart of jumper settings.
5. _______ Mount the CD or DVD drive into the bay using the mounting rails. Be careful not to overtighten the mounting screws. Use only the mounting screws that were provided with the drive. Screws that did not come with the drive may be too long and may damage the CD or DVD drive during installation.
6. _______ Attach the power cable to the CD or DVD drive.
7. _______ Attach the ribbon cable between the CD or DVD drive and the IDE controller port on the motherboard.
8. _______ Next, attach the audio cable to the sound card, if the computer is equipped with one. You may need to read the sound card documentation to locate the correct connection for the audio cable. The audio cable may connect to the motherboard if the sound system is integrated into the motherboard.
9. _______ Have the instructor inspect your installation now.

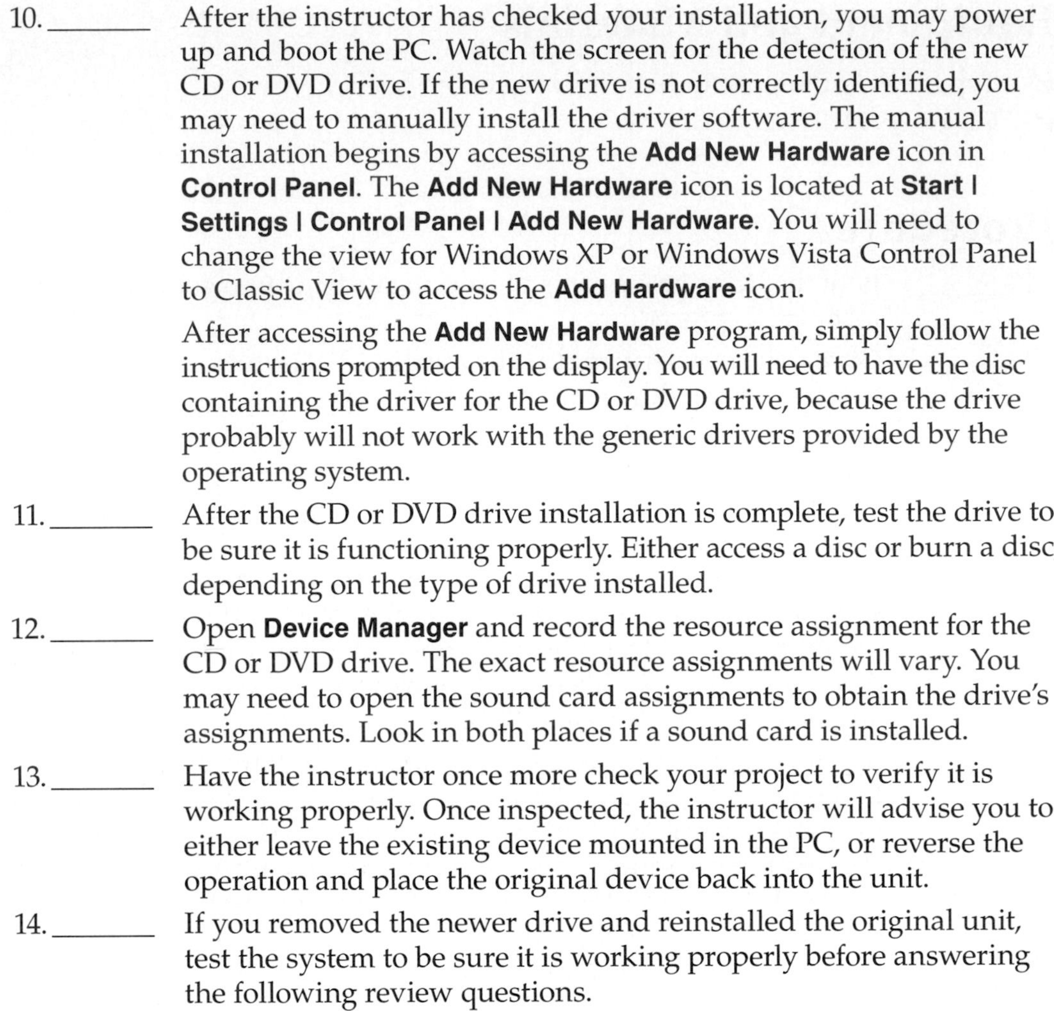

10._______ After the instructor has checked your installation, you may power up and boot the PC. Watch the screen for the detection of the new CD or DVD drive. If the new drive is not correctly identified, you may need to manually install the driver software. The manual installation begins by accessing the **Add New Hardware** icon in **Control Panel**. The **Add New Hardware** icon is located at **Start | Settings | Control Panel | Add New Hardware**. You will need to change the view for Windows XP or Windows Vista Control Panel to Classic View to access the **Add Hardware** icon.

After accessing the **Add New Hardware** program, simply follow the instructions prompted on the display. You will need to have the disc containing the driver for the CD or DVD drive, because the drive probably will not work with the generic drivers provided by the operating system.

11._______ After the CD or DVD drive installation is complete, test the drive to be sure it is functioning properly. Either access a disc or burn a disc, depending on the type of drive installed.

12._______ Open **Device Manager** and record the resource assignment for the CD or DVD drive. The exact resource assignments will vary. You may need to open the sound card assignments to obtain the drive's assignments. Look in both places if a sound card is installed.

13._______ Have the instructor once more check your project to verify it is working properly. Once inspected, the instructor will advise you to either leave the existing device mounted in the PC, or reverse the operation and place the original device back into the unit.

14._______ If you removed the newer drive and reinstalled the original unit, test the system to be sure it is working properly before answering the following review questions.

Review Questions

Answer the following questions on a separate sheet of paper. Please do not write in this book.

1. What problems might arise during a CD or DVD drive installation?
2. Why should you avoid connecting the CD or DVD drive on the same IDE controller on the motherboard?
3. What are the two stages used by Microsoft Vista for driver installation?
4. Since Windows Vista no longer has the **Add Hardware** icon available in the default view of **Control Panel**, how can you install hardware manually in Windows Vista?
5. What does the stripe running along the ribbon cable indicate?
6. Where could you locate the latest driver for the CD or DVD drive you are installing?
7. Why should you use only the screws designed for the mounting of the drive unit?

Printers

After studying this chapter, you will be able to:

- ✔ Explain the operating principles of a laser printer.
- ✔ Explain the operating principles of an inkjet printer.
- ✔ Explain the operating principles of a dot matrix printer.
- ✔ Explain how to install a printer.
- ✔ Install print driver software.
- ✔ Complete printer installation and setup.
- ✔ Identify and diagnose common laser printer faults.
- ✔ Explain how fonts are generated and installed.

A+ Exam—Key Points

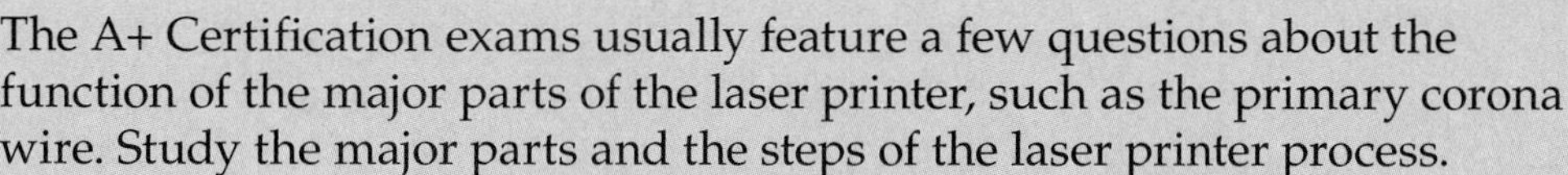

The A+ Certification exams usually feature a few questions about the function of the major parts of the laser printer, such as the primary corona wire. Study the major parts and the steps of the laser printer process.

You should also understand how printer drivers are installed and how to solve common printer problems.

Key Words and Terms

The following words and terms will become important pieces of your computer vocabulary. Be sure you can define them.

bubble jet printers
CMYK
color thermal printer
dot matrix printer
dye-sublimation printers
electrophotographic process (EP)
font
inkjet printer
local printer
paper jams
paper train
pitch
points
printer
queue
solid ink printer
spooling

printer
an electromechanical device that converts computer data into text or graphic images printed to paper or other presentation media.

A ***printer*** is an electromechanical device that converts computer data into text or graphic images printed to paper or other presentation media. PC technicians are responsible for the installation, setup, modification, and troubleshooting of printer systems. A PC technician is not usually responsible for making physical repairs to the electromechanical parts of the printing engine, but a good knowledge base of the electromechanical operation of printers can prove valuable when troubleshooting a printer system. The electromechanical repair of printers is a specialization area. In this chapter, you will learn the basic operation of the most common styles of printer.

Laser Printer Operation

electrophotographic process (EP)
a photographic process that uses a combination of static electricity, light, dry chemical compound, pressure, and heat.

Traditional printing is based on wet ink applied to paper using several different processes. Laser printing uses a process called the electrophotographic process. ***Electrophotographic process (EP)*** is a combination of static electricity, light, dry chemical compound, pressure, and heat. To better understand this process and the role that the major parts of the laser printer perform in the printing process, view the step-by-step series of illustrations shown in **Figure 11-1,** parts A through G. A black-and-white laser printer is shown here.

Step 1. Charging the Drum (Part A):

The primary corona wire is charged to approximately 6000 volts. The high voltage creates an electrical condition known as *corona*. The corona is a static charge surrounding a high-voltage conductor. The primary corona wire is in close proximity to the drum. The primary corona wire applies a large negative charge of approximately 600 volts to 1000 volts to the surface of the drum.

Figure 11-1A. Charging the drum.

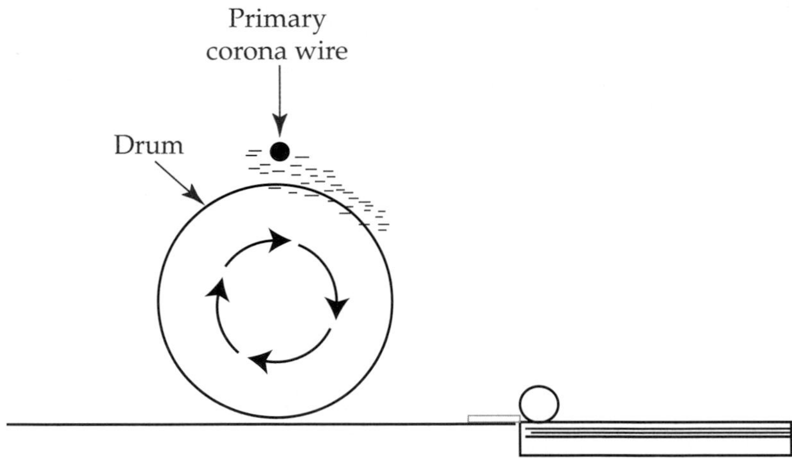

Step 1. The primary corona wire charges the surface of the drum with a negative charge of approximately 600 to 1000 volts.

A

The laser printing process uses extremely high levels of voltage. Never attempt to repair or disassemble a laser printer. Repairing a laser printer requires special training and safety precautions. PC technicians do not normally replace printer parts other than toner cartridges.

Step 2. Writing the Image (Part B):

The image is written to the drum using laser light. The laser light changes intensity according to the light and dark patterns encoded by the data describing the image. A rotating pentagon-shaped mirror reflects the laser beam horizontally across the surface of the drum.

After each horizontal trace is complete, the drum rotates by a small increment and the next trace begins. A typical laser printer makes 300 to 1200 increments of rotation per inch. The drum is coated with a light-sensitive photoconductive material. The special coating on the drum conducts electricity when struck by intense light. As the laser beam is reflected across the drum, the areas struck by the beam become conductive and lose most of their negative static charge. For example, when a typical image or business letter is to be printed, the white areas of the image are struck by the laser beam while the dark areas, such as letters and lines, are not struck by the laser light. The parts of the drum that are not exposed to the light retain the 600-volt to 1000-volt negative charge.

Step 3. Developing the Image (Part C):

As the drum turns, the image created by low and high static charges on the drum pass by the toner cartridge. The toner is attracted to the static charge on the drum. Think of toner as a form of very fine plastic dust particles.

A roller is incorporated in the toner cartridge to assist with dispersing the toner from the cartridge. The image to be printed is now formed on the drum.

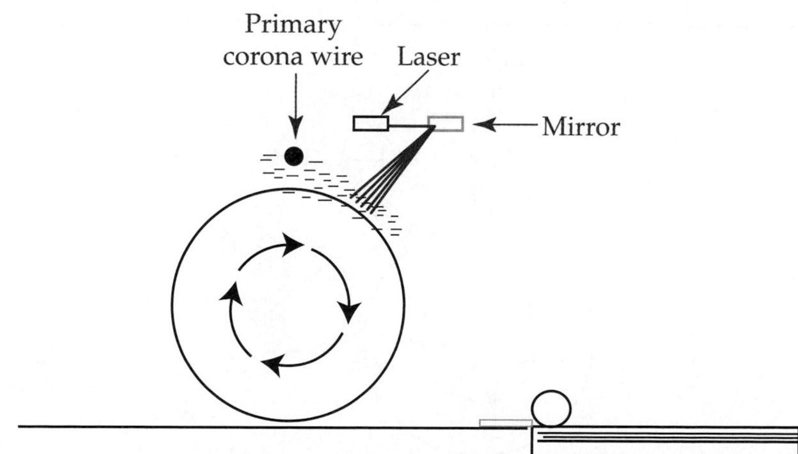

Step 2. A laser beam pulses to a spinning mirror which reflects light across the negatively charged drum. The laser light draws the outline of the image to be produced.

B

Figure 11-1B. Writing the image to the drum with a laser.

Figure 11-1C. Toner is drawn to the drum.

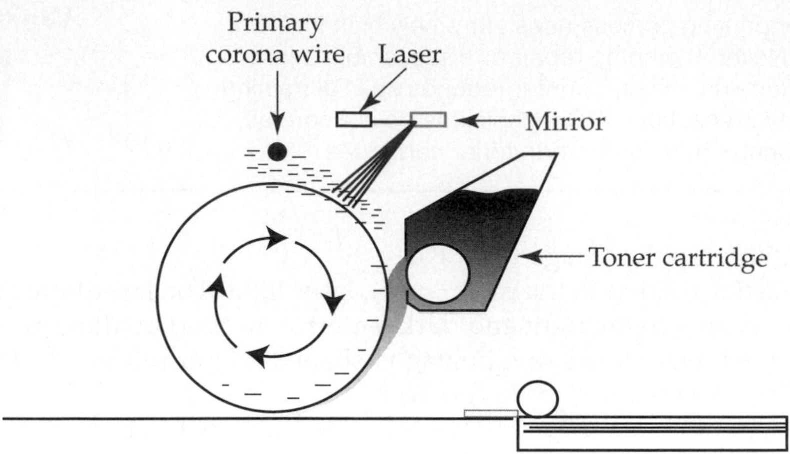

Step 3. The toner is attracted to the static charge on the drum. The static charge is in the shape of the image to be printed.

C

Step 4. Transferring the Image (Part D):

As the drum continues to rotate, the paper is fed under the drum. A set of rollers called *pickup rollers* lift one sheet of paper at a time from the paper tray. The paper is fed into position under the drum. A device known as a *separator* makes sure only one sheet of paper is sent into the drum area. The separator is located at the edge of the paper tray near the pickup rollers.

Just before the paper passes under the drum, it is given a positive charge by the transfer corona wire. The transfer corona wire works much like the primary corona, only using the opposite charge. The paper now has a positive charge of

Figure 11-1D. The paper is charged and drawn under the drum.

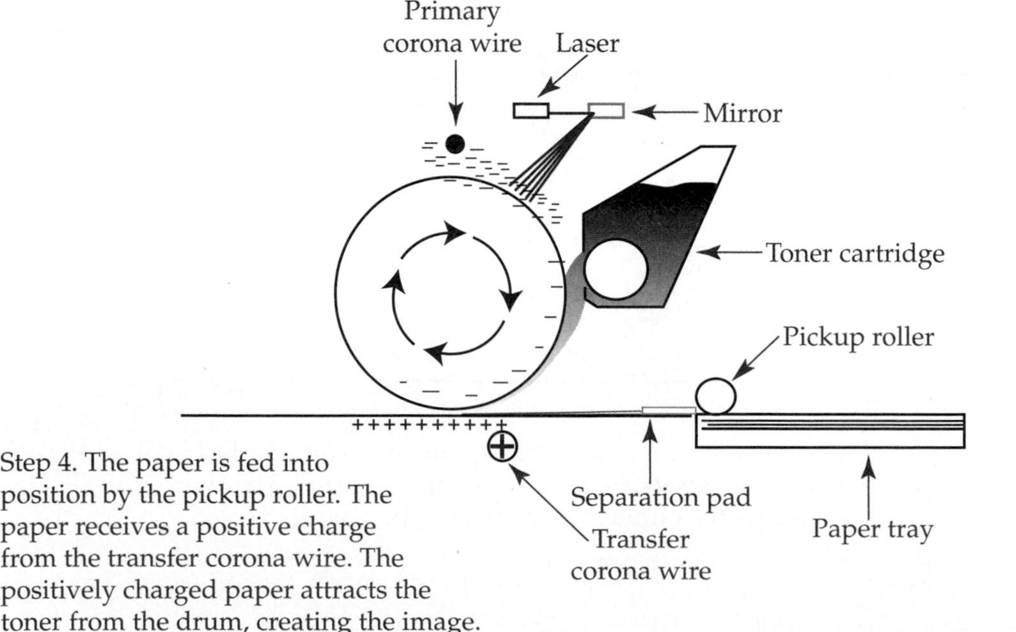

Step 4. The paper is fed into position by the pickup roller. The paper receives a positive charge from the transfer corona wire. The positively charged paper attracts the toner from the drum, creating the image.

D

static applied to its surface. As the positively-charged paper passes under the negatively-charged toner on the drum, the toner is attracted to the paper. (As you should remember from a basic physics class, opposite charges attract.)

Step 5. Fusing the Image (Part E):

There is no longer a need for the static positive charge on the paper. A static brush makes contact with the paper and drains off any charge remaining on the paper. If the charge was not removed from the paper, it would cause the paper to stick to the negatively charged drum and would also make the paper difficult to handle after leaving the printer.

Covered with a dry toner image, the paper passes through the fuser. The fuser consists of a pair of rollers, one of which is heated to a very high temperature. As the toner-covered paper passes through the fuser rollers, the heat and pressure melt the toner, fixing it to the paper's surface.

Usually, a quartz lamp is used to produce the high temperature of the fusing unit. The lamp generates a temperature of over 356°F (180°C). As a safety precaution, there is usually a temperature sensor installed near the fusing unit. This sensor will shut off power to the fusing unit if the temperature gets too high.

The area around the fusing unit in the printer can cause severe burns when touched. Never attempt to work inside a laser printer unless it has been off for at least 15 minutes.

Step 6. Cleaning the Drum (Part F):

The drum must be prepared before the next image can be printed. A cleaning unit removes any toner that might still be on the drum. The unit consists of a simple rubber scraper or blade that removes any residual toner left on the drum. The particles of toner are collected inside the cleaning unit container. The blade or scraper is specially designed not to scratch the drum surface. Any scratches on the drum would remove the photosensitive finish. This would result in poor quality printed images.

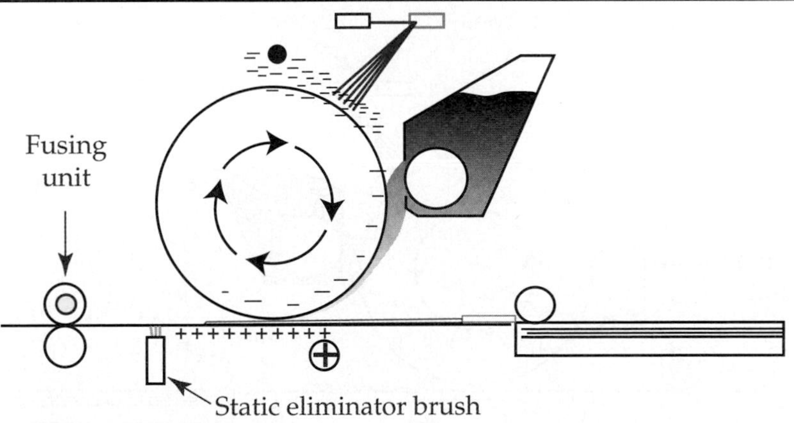

Step 5. The fusing unit rollers heat the toner and paper until the toner melts and bonds to the paper. The static eliminator brush removes the static charge from the paper.

E

Figure 11-1E. Toner is fused to the paper.

Figure 11-1F. The drum is cleaned of excess electrical charge and toner.

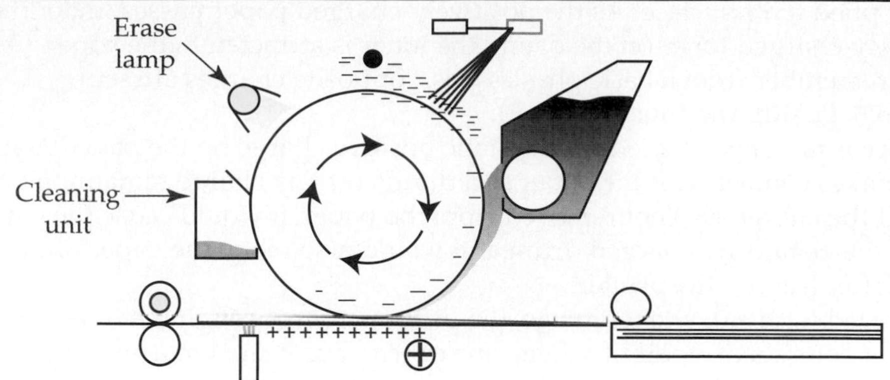

Step 6. The cleaning unit removes any residual toner that might remain on the drum. The erase lamp shines a bright light on the drum to remove any remaning charge. The drum is now ready to begin the process over again.

F

A high-intensity light is also beamed onto the drum to remove any remaining charge from the drum's surface. The drum is now ready to be charged again by the primary corona wire, and the printing process can be repeated. Figure 11-1G shows all the parts together.

Note that in the example of the laser printing process, the drum illustrated was negatively charged. The same process can occur using opposite polarities. Different manufacturers use different charging levels and polarities to create the same printing process that was shown in our example.

These principles of operation employed in the black-and-white laser printer can also be applied to a color laser printer. A color laser printer uses four separate print engines, one for each of the major colors. The major colors used in a color

Figure 11-1G. Shown are the vital parts of the laser printer in relation to each other. This illustration shows a negatively charged drum. Some printers place a positive charge on the drum and a negative charge on the paper. The process is the same with the polarities reversed.

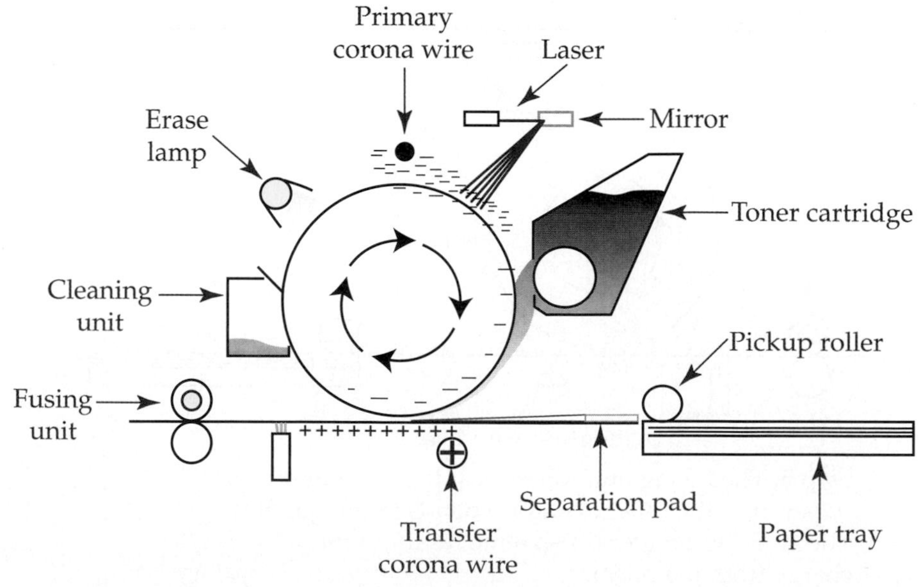

G

laser printer are blue, red, yellow, and black. Often the blue color is represented by the color cyan and the red is represented by the color magenta.

Color Inkjet Printer Operation

An ***inkjet printer*** uses specially designed cartridges that spray a fine mist of ink as it moves horizontally in front of a sheet of paper. Some inkjet printers are commonly referred to as ***bubble jet printers.***

inkjet printer printer that uses specially designed cartridges that spray a fine mist of ink as they move horizontally in front of a sheet of paper.

bubble jet printers an inkjet printer.

The inkjet printer head is the part that fires the ink onto the paper. The construction of an inkjet printer head is fairly simple, **Figure 11-2.** Ink must be forced out of the printer head. The two most common types of inkjet printers use either a *thermoresistor* or *piezocell crystal* to produce a force that fires a drop of ink through a nozzle directly onto the paper.

Figure 11-2 is an exploded view of a single nozzle and its major parts: nozzle, firing chamber, and (in this model) thermoresistor. The ink flows into the firing chamber from the ink cartridge reservoir. An electrical pulse from the computer enters the thermoresistor and the ink in the firing chamber is instantly heated to over 1112°F (600°C). The extreme heat expands the ink in the chamber, causing it to fire through the nozzle and onto the paper. As the chamber cools, a vacuum is created that draws more ink into the firing chamber from the ink cartridge reservoir. An inkjet printer can fire its chamber many times a second.

The single ink droplet is quite small. A typical low-cost inkjet printer can produce 720 × 720 dots per square inch (dpi). High-quality inkjet printers can produce a dpi of 1200 × 1200 and higher.

A piezocell could be used instead of the thermoresistor. A piezocell is a crystal that deflects or bends when energized by an electrical pulse. When a piezocell is used in place of the thermoresistor, the piezocell flexes every time an electrical pulse is sent. When the piezocell crystal flexes, the ink drop is fired through the nozzle. When the electrical pulse stops, the crystal returns to its original shape. This creates a vacuum in the firing chamber (like with the thermoresistor), which draws more ink into the chamber.

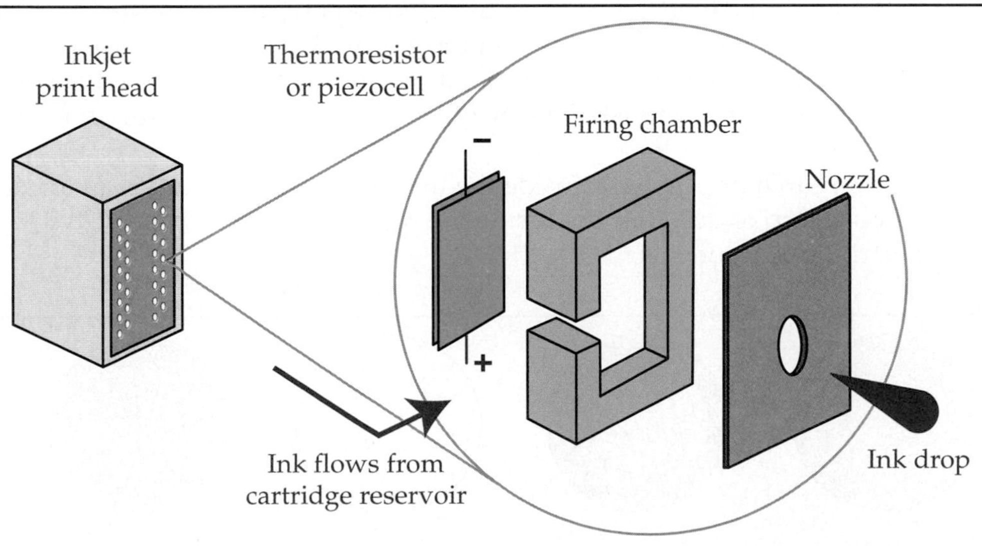

Figure 11-2. Exploded diagram of typical color inkjet printer head.

CMYK
standard combination of colors (cyan, magenta, yellow, and black) used by color inkjet printers.

A color inkjet printer uses four hues of ink: cyan, magenta, yellow, and black. This is a standard combination of colors often referred to simply as ***CMYK.*** Note that the letter *K* is used to signify black rather than *B*, which is used for blue in the RGB (red, green, blue) system. See **Figure 11-3.** These colors are standard in the printing industry. They can be mixed to make other hues such as green, orange, brown, and gray.

Inkjet Printer Cleaning Guidelines

Inkjet printers operate on the principle of controlling a fine mist of ink to print images on the paper. Because of this printing technique, the mist of ink often collects on the inside and outside of the printer case. To remove ink deposits from the outside of the printer case, you should use a soft cloth and water. If the case will not clean properly with water, you may use a mild detergent diluted in water. The water should be distilled water. Cleaning a printer with water that has severe mineral deposits can make the printer case look worse than before it was cleaned. Never clean a printer case with alcohol or any form of strong commercial cleaners. Harsh chemicals will ruin many plastics.

A+ Note:

The A+ Certification exams will most likely only list water or very mild detergent as the correct answer.

Most printer designs have been engineered to allow for some accumulation of ink inside the printer. In general, you should never attempt to clean the inside of the printer with alcohol or any commercial solvents. Alcohol, solvents, and water can damage the electrical components inside the printer. The only areas inside the printer that may require cleaning are the printer cartridges. The printer should only be turned off after the printing process has completed. When the printer has finished printing, the ink cartridge is returned to "home" position. The home position is engineered to cover the ink ports to prevent them from drying out. Inkjet ports often dry out because of long periods of nonuse.

A small, fine brush or an anti-static vacuum should be used to remove paper dust and lint. Do *not* use compressed air to remove dust. The compressed air may actually force the dust deeper inside the printing mechanism and result in more harm than good.

Never attempt to lubricate parts inside the inkjet printer. Lubricants can cause an increased buildup of dust and lint inside the printer. Lubricants can also damage electronic components.

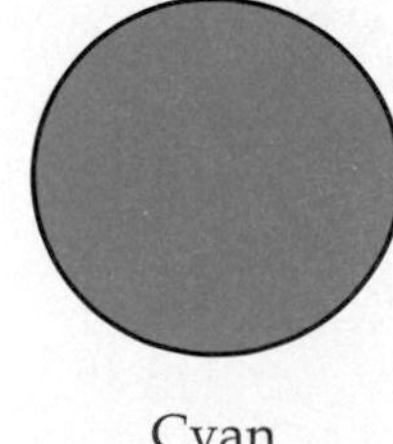

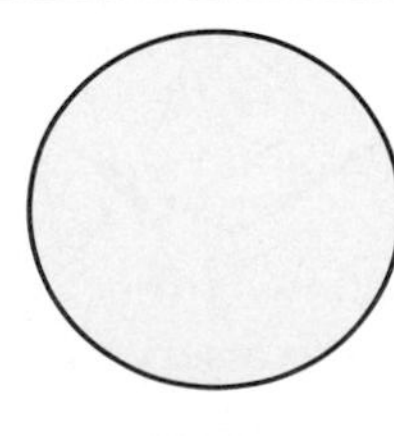

Cyan Magenta Yellow Black

Figure 11-3.
CMYK stands for cyan, magenta, yellow, black. These are the colors used for ink printing. They can be mixed to produce a broad spectrum of colors.

These are general guidelines to follow and may vary somewhat when working with specific printers. The best policy is to download a copy of maintenance and cleaning instructions for the exact printer model from the manufacturer's Web site.

Dot Matrix Printers

The ***dot matrix printer*** derives its name from the pattern, or matrix, of very small dots it prints to create text and images. Dot matrix printers were some of the earliest printers. They are now much less common and tend to be used only for special purposes.

dot matrix printer printer that uses a pattern of very small dots to create text and images.

The dot matrix print head consists of a line of small metal rods called print pins, **Figure 11-4.** In appearance, they look much like a series of small nails. An electrical coil, called a solenoid, controls each print pin. When energized, the solenoid creates a magnetic field. The print pin is constructed with a magnet at one end. When the solenoid is energized, the magnetic end of the pin is attracted to the coil and the print pin rapidly moves forward, striking an ink ribbon. Each energized solenoid causes that individual print rod to strike the ribbon, leaving a dot of ink on the paper.

To form a letter, such as the letter *A* in the illustration, a series of electrical pulses is sent to the print head. The pulses are coded in a sequence that forms the letter *A* on the paper as the entire print head moves horizontally across the paper. The two most common print head styles are 9-pin and 24-pin.

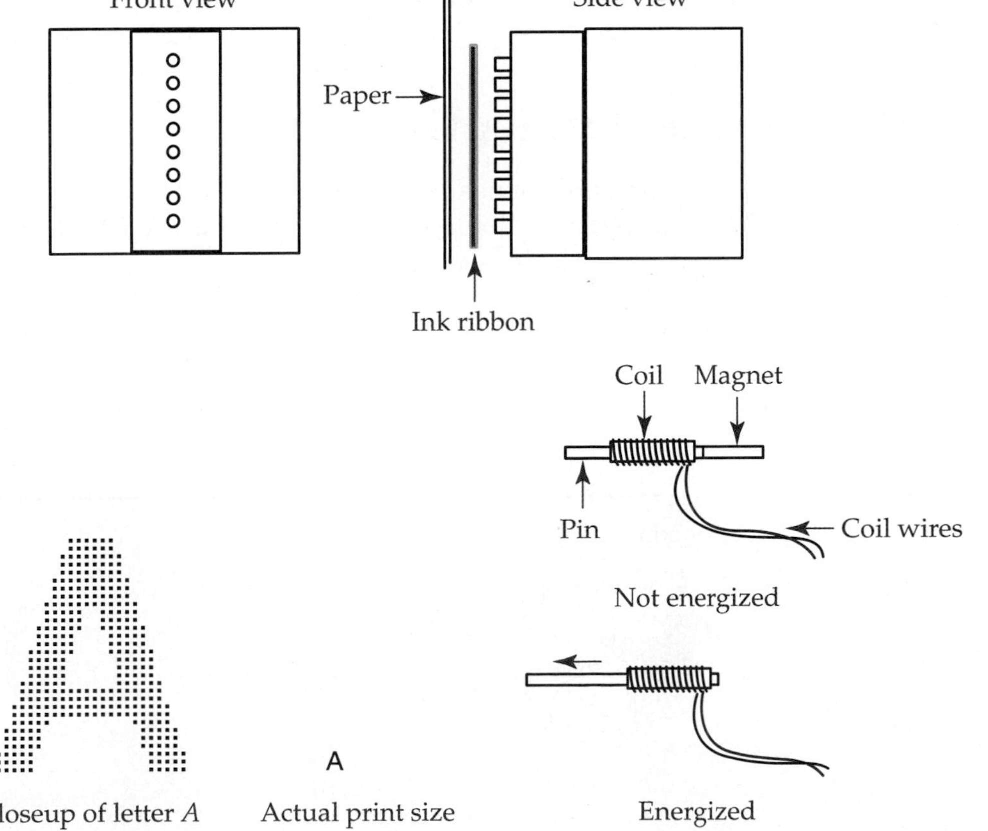

Figure 11-4. The dot matrix print head close up. Dot matrix printers generate a pattern of dots to create images.

Dot matrix printers are quite slow and noisy. To achieve finer detail, the print head may have to make multiple passes on the same line. Dot matrix printers are used primarily for spreadsheets and other text applications in businesses. When graphics with fine detail are desired, other printers such as inkjet or laser are typically used.

Color Thermal Printer Operation

color thermal printer printer that applies color by heating a special ribbon that is coated with wax-like material.

Color thermal printer operation is based on the principle of applying color by heating a special ribbon that is coated with wax-like material. Heat is used to melt the wax. The wax is then sealed to the surface of the paper by Teflon coated rollers. See **Figure 11-5.**

The heating unit consists of an array of small heaters that melt the wax in small dots. The small dots of heated wax represent the data sent from the PC to the printer. The paper must be run through the process four separate times. Each time the paper is run through, a new color is added to the paper. The colors are cyan, magenta, yellow, and black (CMYK). The process is similar to the dye-sublimation process described in the next section. The difference is that in dye sublimation the color actually penetrates the paper, while in thermal print operation the color is printed to the surface of the paper.

Color thermal printers are used for high quality presentation drawings and illustrations. Many corporations use them for special applications such as CEO reports to the board when color photos and charts are required. They are not commonly found in home use. They have high quality print but at a relatively high cost per sheet since they use special paper and expensive color wax supplies. Color thermal printers are not used for mass copies, just high quality.

Dye-Sublimation Printer Operation

dye-sublimation printers printer that produces near photo quality printed images by vaporizing inks, which then solidify on paper.

Dye-sublimation printers produce near photo quality printed images by vaporizing inks, which then solidify onto paper. *Sublimation* is a scientific term that means changing a solid material into a gas.

The major parts used in the dye-sublimation process are the drum, transfer roll, and heater, **Figure 11-6.** A special paper is mounted directly on the drum. The transfer roll is a long sheet of plastic material coated with CMYK colors. As the drum rotates, the plastic transfer sheet (roll) passes under the drum and across the heater.

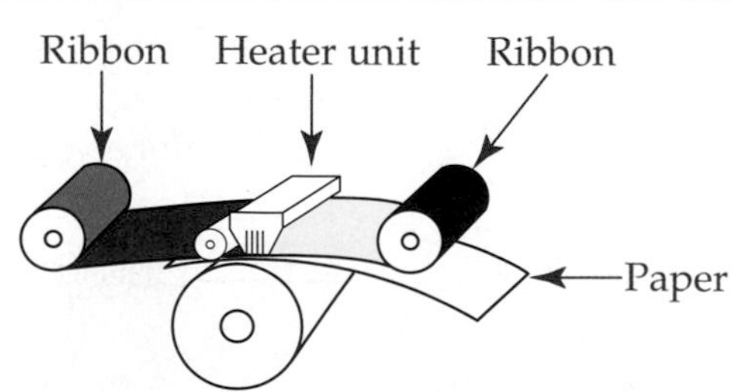

Figure 11-5. Sketch of a color thermal printer.

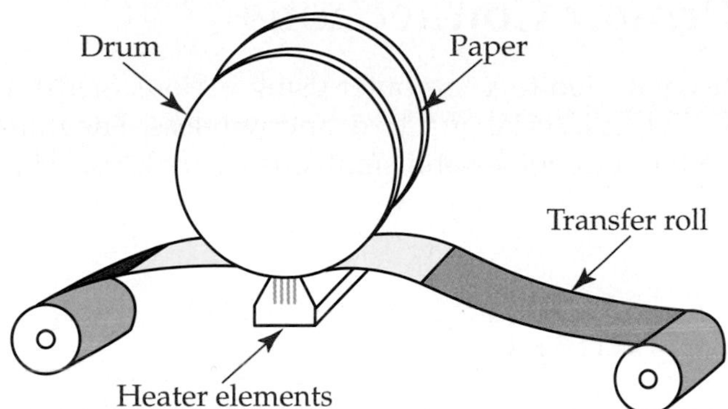

Figure 11-6.
The important parts of a dye-sublimation printer.

The heater consists of thousands of tiny heating elements arranged in a close array. These elements heat up in patterns representing the data patterns sent from the computer system. The heating elements can heat to 256 different temperature levels, which cause the dye to be transferred at 256 different levels of intensity.

The drum rotates four times. During each revolution of the drum, a different color passes from the transfer roll into the paper. The color is absorbed into the fibers as opposed to coating the top of the paper. The four colors sublimate to the paper and combine to create over 16 million colors.

Dye-sublimation printers and materials are very expensive. However, the dye-sublimation process gives much higher resolution and better color representation than the laser or inkjet processes.

Solid Ink Color Printer Operation

A ***solid ink printer*** uses solid ink cartridges similar to wax. The print head consists of four long rows of many individual nozzles. Each of the four rows produces one of the CMYK colors. The four colors are heated and flow into individual reservoirs. As the paper passes by the print heads, the nozzles are fired, releasing a fine mist of color to the paper.

solid ink printer printer that uses solid ink cartridges similar to wax.

An advantage of the solid ink color printer is that it uses ordinary paper for its process. However, printer and ink supplies are expensive when compared to laser and inkjet supplies.

All-In-One Products

In recent years, manufacturers have introduced all-in-one products, especially for home and small office use. The all-in-one units are a combination of four common office devices that rely on printing techniques to accomplish their tasks. They are a combination of printer, fax, copier, and scanner. The all-in-one devices are a cost-effective way to purchase office equipment. The downside is that when the all-in-one device fails, typically you cannot use any of the devices.

Common Printer Connections

Printers can be connected to a computer using various media such as USB, IEEE 1394, RJ-45, SCSI, serial, infrared, and wireless. The most common connections encountered in homes and small offices are USB, IEEE 1394, wireless, and RJ-45.

Local Printer Installation

local printer printer that connects directly to a specific PC.

The term ***local printer*** refers to a printer that connects directly to a PC. The printer is *local* to that particular PC. Not all printers are local printers. A printer can be connected to a PC through a network and shared by many different PCs. This type of connection is covered later.

When a printer is connected to a PC, a port address must be assigned before the PC can communicate with the printer. Common computer ports are given a name such as LTP1 or COM1 rather than a port number such as 037Fh. The usual choices for a printer are LPT1, LPT2, COM1, COM2, COM3, or COM4. Originally, the letters LPT represented *line printer terminal,* but today, it's simply *printer.* The letters COM were an abbreviation for communication.

During the DOS era, printers were a real challenge to set up. They had to be set up manually. The printers were usually equipped with several DIP switches that had to be set (flipped) into certain positions to match the type of ASCII code it was to use. Switches also controlled other printer characteristics or commands. For example, placing a carriage return after every line of text or double spacing between lines of text could be set by mechanical adjustments or by software commands. It could take many hours to set up a printer correctly.

Today, most systems are Plug and Play compliant, which usually means an easy, automatic setup. However, not all setups are simple. Sometimes, parts of the setup program must be accomplished manually. A technician must become familiar with the setup options and properties available for printer systems. Be aware that the users you serve are easily frustrated by inoperable equipment or by new computer equipment that does not perform to expectations. Knowledge can generate confidence in the user and lessen some frustrations during setup or repair.

Manual printer installation begins with opening the **Printers and Faxes** dialog box in Windows XP, and the **Printers** dialog box, **Figure 11-7,** in Windows Vista. The **Printers and Faxes** dialog box in Windows XP and the **Printers** dialog box in Windows Vista are located directly off the **Start** menu.

In Windows XP, the **Printers and Faxes** dialog box can also be accessed through **Control Panel** by selecting **Printers and Other Hardware** in the category view. In the Windows Vista, the **Printers** dialog box can be accessed through **Control Panel | Hardware and Sound | Printers**.

After accessing the **Printers and Faxes** or **Printers** dialog box, any printers for which the PC has been set up will appear in the window. Notice the **Add Printer** option shown in Figure 11-7. The **Add Printer** option is activated to add a new printer to the PC. When activated, the **Add Printer** wizard screen appears, **Figure 11-8.**

This wizard steps you through the installation procedure. You will be required to manually intervene, even when using the wizard. In one of the wizard steps, you must select the printer for which the drivers are to be installed, **Figure 11-9.**

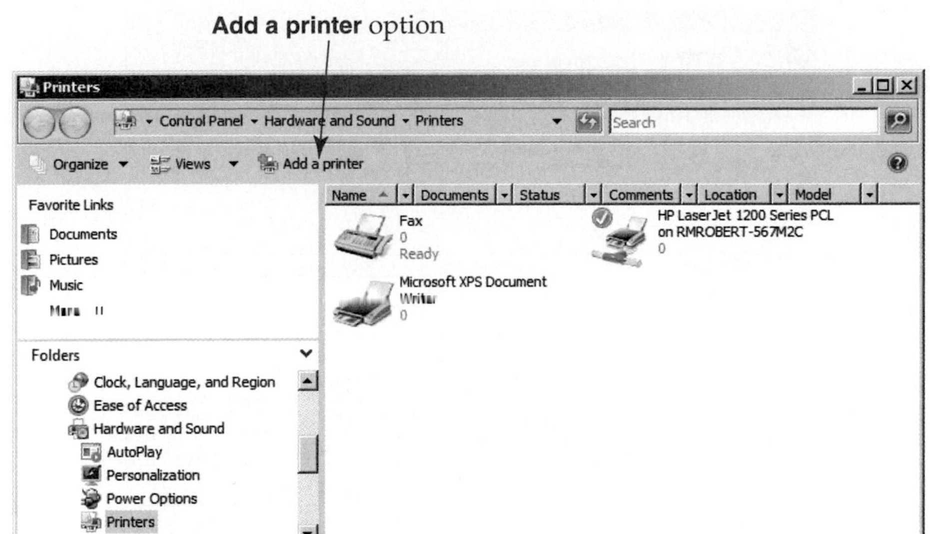

Figure 11-7.
Windows Vista **Printers** dialog box.

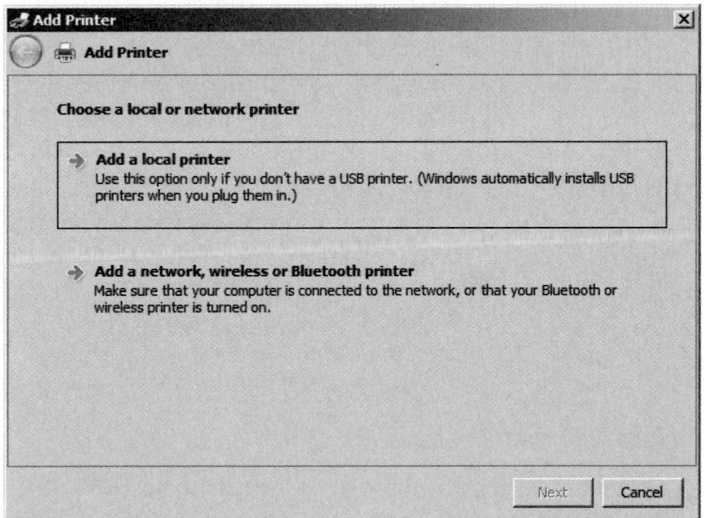

Figure 11-8.
The Windows Vista **Add Printer** wizard takes you through the installation of a new printer.

In the illustration, notice the window used to identify the printer for which the drivers must be installed. A printer driver contains the code necessary to allow the computer to communicate to the printer. Without the correct driver, the printer may operate incorrectly or may not operate at all. When you attempt to print without the correct driver, some common actions are a constant ejection or feed of paper, printing copy with no margins, and printing gibberish or unrecognizable symbols. The correct driver for the printer is essential to ensure proper printing of the desired text or image.

Look again at Figure 11-9. On the left side is a list of printer manufacturers. After a printer manufacturer is selected, the models of the printers associated with the manufacturer appear on the right. Windows has over 800 models from which to choose. Some technicians load all available printer drivers on the hard disk as part of a regular installation procedure. This way, all the printer drivers at the time of the operating system release are available on the hard drive. However, this is not always the case. If the needed driver was not loaded during

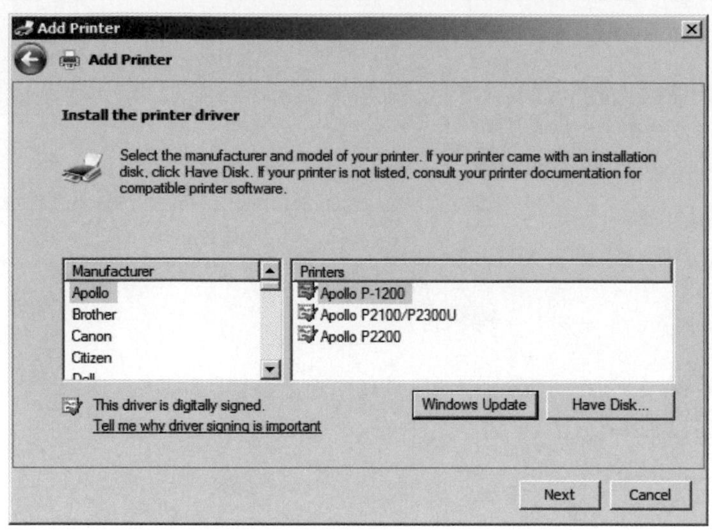

Figure 11-9. The **Add Printer** wizard offers a selection of manufacturers to choose from. First choose your manufacturer. Next, pick out the model you are installing.

installation, when you click the **Next** button after choosing your printer, the wizard will ask you to insert your Windows operating system CD and to click **OK**. The wizard will then find the correct driver on the CD.

Sometimes, the printer you are installing will not be listed. New models of printers are constantly being developed and the desired driver may not be present. When the model to be installed is not listed, click the **Have Disk** button shown in Figure 11-9. With this button, you supply the driver from a CD. A CD with drivers should come in the packaging with the printer. (Though, don't forget to check for the latest drivers at the manufacturer's Web site.) Clicking the **Have Disk** button brings up the screen shown in **Figure 11-10.** If the drivers included with the printer are on a CD, be sure to change from **A:** to **D:** or to the correct CD drive letter for your PC.

PC Printer Resources

Printers are connected to computers in several different ways. For example, they can be connected to the computer directly through the parallel port, USB port, or a wireless device. Wireless connections include Infrared, Bluetooth, and IEEE 802.11 wireless. Printers are almost never connected as a serial device.

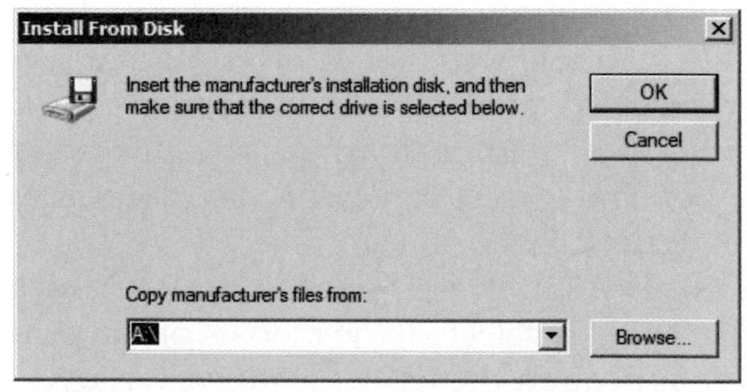

Figure 11-10. To use a driver supplied by a manufacturer, click **Have Disk** and then enter the path to the driver (floppy or CD). If you have downloaded a driver from a manufacturer's Web site, you need to point to the folder on your hard drive in which you saved the file.

The older method of using COM and LPT ports is mentioned here so that you will be familiar with the technology if you run into it on the A+ Certification exams. Also, some older printers are still in use.

The printer may use COM ports, LPT ports, or DOT4 ports for the connection between the local printer and the computer. COM ports are serial ports and are seldom used. There are usually four COM ports identified as COM1, COM2, COM3, and COM4. COM1 and COM3 share the same IRQ assignment, and COM2 and COM4 share the same IRQ assignment. Look at the table in **Figure 11-11** to see the assigned IRQ and port memory address for each COM and LPT port.

LPT is a parallel port used to connect to a printer or other device that requires a parallel connection. It too has an assigned IRQ and a port memory address. LPT ports are still in use to some extent for printers.

The preferred cable connection for printers is USB. When USB is used to connect to a printer, the port is identified as a DOT4 port, **Figure 11-12.** This port is a virtual port, not an actual physical port in the sense that COM and LPT ports are. The DOT4 port provides two-way communications between the printer and

	IRQ Assigned	Port Address	Comment
COM1	4	3F8h-3FFh	Serial port
COM2	3	2F8h-2FFh	Serial port
COM3	4	3E8h-3EFh	Serial port
COM4	3	2E8h-2EFh	Serial port
LPT1	7	378h-37Fh	Parallel port
LPT2	Any available	278h-27Fh	Parallel port

The lowercase letter h signifies a hexadecimal number.

Figure 11-11.
COM and LPT ports and their resources.

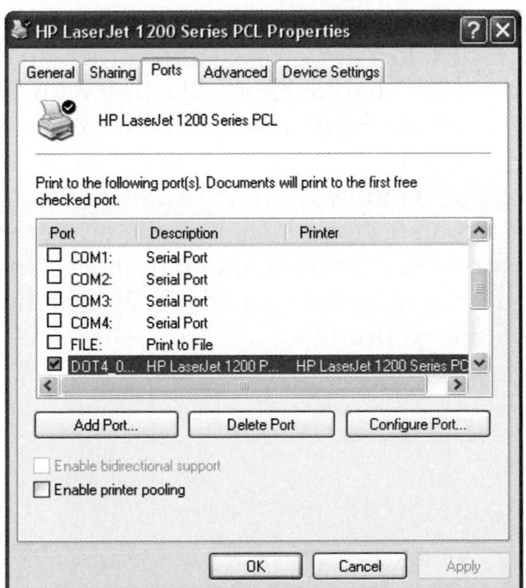

Figure 11-12.
USB ports are identified as DOT4.

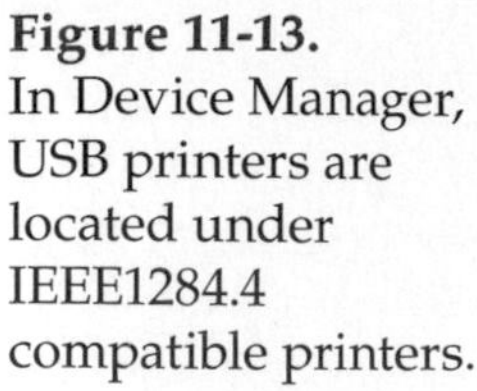

Figure 11-13.
In Device Manager, USB printers are located under IEEE1284.4 compatible printers.

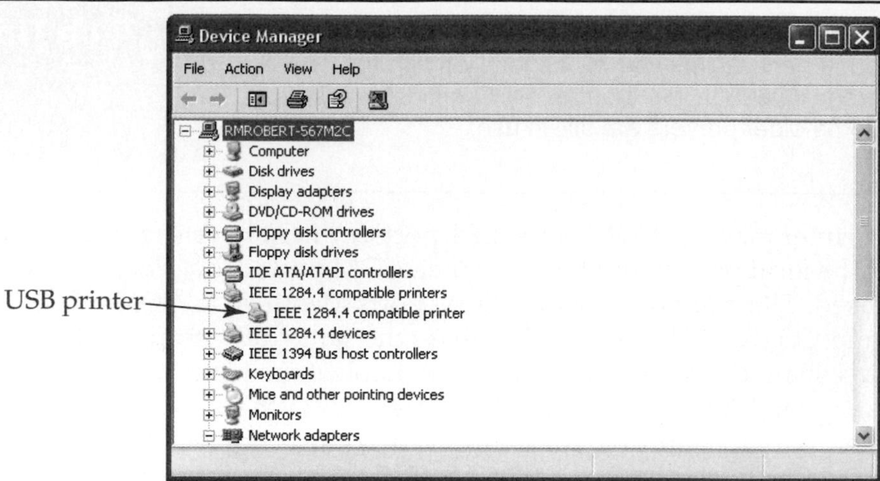

the computer. This allows the printer to send messages back to the computer indicating things such as "out of paper" or "toner/ink low."

When the printer is connected as a USB device, you can view the connection in Device Manager, but it will be listed under IEEE 1284.4 compatible printers. **Figure 11-13** shows this connection in the Windows XP Device Manager.

Sharing Printers

Printers are commonly shared over wired networks or wireless networks. Sharing by network is covered in more detail in Chapter 16—Introduction to Networking.

When a printer is connected directly to a PC, it is referred to as a local printer. When the printer is connected via a wired or wireless network connection, it is referred to as a network printer or as a Bluetooth connection. Printers can also be shared or connected to over the Internet. Mechanical switches were often used in early printer sharing scenarios, but they are seldom encountered today.

Look at **Figure 11-14** to see how a shared printer is indicated in the Windows XP **Printer and Faxes** dialog box. In Windows XP and earlier, an open hand under the printer indicates that it is a shared device. Starting with Windows Vista, the open hand is no longer used. A shared resource is simply shown as a printer icon connected to a network cable.

A wizard is available in Windows XP and earlier products. In Windows XP, the **Add Printer** wizard has an option for sharing the printer in a network. In Windows Vista, when the **Printer Sharing** option in the Network and Sharing Center is enabled, the operating system automatically searches for local printers and configures them as shared printers.

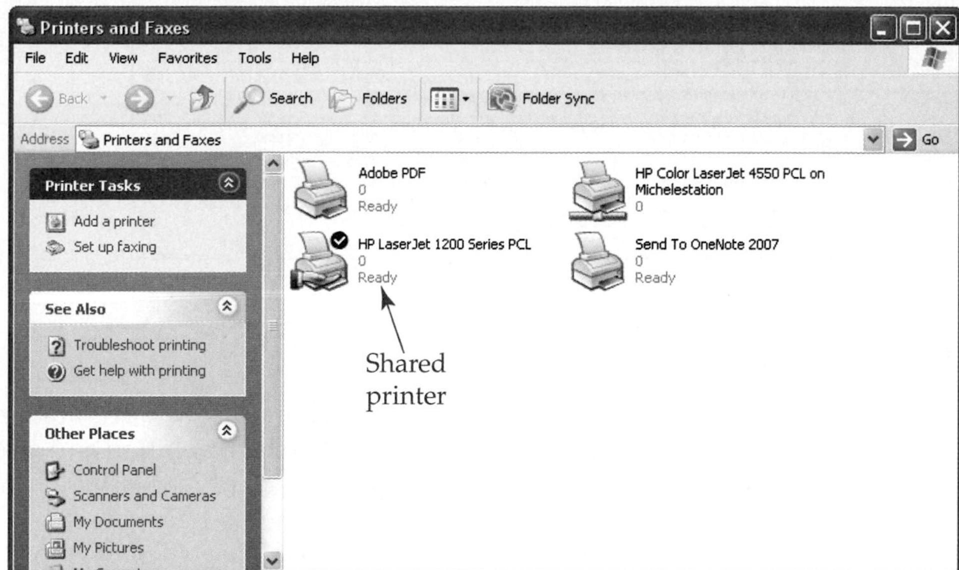

Figure 11-14.
A shared printer in Windows XP is identified by an open hand.

Printer Spooling

In early computer systems, no other operation could be accomplished until the computer finished printing. Today, when a file is sent to the printer, other activities can be performed on the PC without waiting for the printer to complete its job. This is accomplished through a technique called ***spooling.*** Many I/O devices and operations use spooling to temporarily store data, freeing up CPU resources and allowing other activities to be performed on the PC. When a printer uses spooling, it stores the data to be printed in a buffer. The printing operation can be completed in the background while the user performs other tasks on the PC.

spooling
a technique that stores in memory data to be printed so that printing operations can be completed in the background while other tasks are performed by the PC.

Many printer jobs can be sent to the printer at the same time. The computer, rather than sending multiple printer jobs directly to the printer, sends them to the spooling buffer. The buffer can be RAM or hard disk area. With the data in the buffer, the documents can be accessed by the printer one at a time as the printer completes its printing jobs. Print jobs waiting to be completed are stored in the print ***queue*** (pronounced like the letter *Q*). **Figure 11-15** shows a print queue with multiple documents in line. You can check a printer's queue at any time. It is accessed through the **Printers** folder by double-clicking the icon for the printer you wish to inspect.

queue
list of print jobs waiting to be completed and their status.

The print jobs are displayed in a Windows print queue window. Notice that the status of the current print job is shown and is indicated as "printing." Other status possibilities are "paused" and "spooling." If the printer is shared by more than one PC, the owner of the job will be displayed.

In Figure 11-15, the same print job is repeated several times. This is a very common occurrence. When a page fails to print, a novice user will attempt to print the document several times before calling for technical support. One of the first things a technician should do when responding to a print call is to purge all the duplicate print files from the queue. Sometimes a printer is locked up because of a document sent by a shared user. By purging a particular user's document, the printing problem may be cleared and the remaining documents will print as they should.

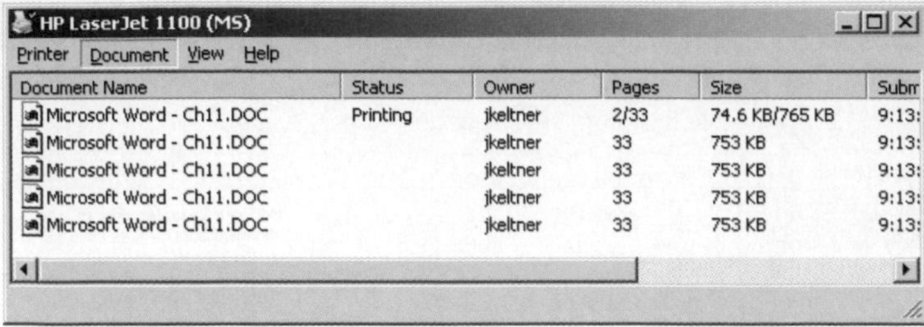

Figure 11-15. The printing queue shows the status of the current print job and the documents that are queued to follow.

Printer Memory

Printers usually have memory in the form of SIMMs or DIMMs. The amount of memory with which a printer is equipped determines the resolution and size of the subject to be printed. If a printer does not have sufficient memory to print a file, it will generate an error code. Error codes are common when printing large, memory-intensive, graphic images. The exact error code will depend on the printer manufacturer and model. When a printer prints only a portion of an image, it is a sure sign of insufficient memory.

Installing more printer memory is a relatively simple task. Once the printer documentation is consulted about the appropriate memory type to use, the memory installs just as it would to the RAM banks on a motherboard. Review the *Installing RAM Modules* section from Chapter 6—Memory. The amount of memory in the printer can usually be verified by a self-test performed at the menu on the printer.

Error Codes

Error codes produced on some printer LCD displays provide a frequent source of confusion. Some errors generated are straightforward such as "Paper Jam" or "Refill Paper Tray." Other errors are cryptic and require decoding. They simply refer to a number such as "40 ERROR" or "22 ERROR." Some of these errors can be translated by using the owner's manual. Other times, you may need to access the manufacturer's Web site.

Some of the codes are not published for the general public. The manufacturers feel these repairs involve work beyond the typical user's expertise.

Paper Jams

paper jams
when a printer pulls one or more sheets through its mechanism and the paper becomes wedged inside.

Paper jams are when a printer pulls one or more sheets through its mechanism and the paper becomes wedged inside. They are a very common problem associated with most printers. With proper care, most printer jams can be avoided. There are many causes of paper jams.

Paper quality is an important issue when it comes to paper jams. Low-quality paper produces a lot of paper lint. Paper lint accumulates in all printers. Accumulation around sensitive printer parts can cause jams.

Another issue is moisture. When paper arrives from an outside storage area that is not climate controlled, condensation (moisture) can be created due to the change in temperature. This can make the paper damp. Damp paper is almost sure to jam in a printer. Paper should be stored at the same room temperature and humidity level as the printer for approximately twenty-four hours.

Another common cause of paper jams is worn parts along the paper train. The ***paper train*** is the route that the paper follows through the printer. The train consists of several rubber rollers and a paper separator pad. The paper separator pad is designed to allow only one sheet of paper at a time to enter the paper train from the paper tray. As the paper separator pad wears, jams become increasingly more common. In this case, the only remedy is to replace the separator pad. Worn pickup rollers can also cause jams. Sometimes, cleaning the rollers or removing paper lint can solve the problem. Other times, the pickup rollers have to be replaced.

paper train
the route the paper follows through the printer.

The direction of paper can influence the number of jams created in the printer. Most paper is manufactured with a natural curve. Typically, the outside wrapper of the paper will indicate the side of the stack of paper that should be used first in any printer or copy machine. The wrapper is often marked with an arrow. However, not all paper packages are marked with an indicating arrow. If you are experiencing a definite curl to the finished printed page, check for markings on the paper wrapper for the correct positioning of the paper into the paper tray.

One way to avoid paper jams is to discard the first sheet of paper where the fold of the wrapper comes together. Many times this sheet of paper contains glue residue from the sealing process. The glue can collect inside the printer on the rollers and separator as well as on the fusing unit or drum. *Always* discard the first sheet from a new package of paper.

Toner Spills

Toner will be spilled from time to time especially when replacing toner cartridges. Toner is composed of extremely small particles usually a combination of carbon and polyester resin. Since the particles are so small and the toner is designed to permanently adhere to paper and similar products, there are some precautions that should be observed.

Small spills should be cleaned up with an approved vacuum cleaner. An approved vacuum cleaner designed for toner spills is made with a dust-tight motor. Normal household vacuum cleaners do not have dust-tight motors and can create static discharge inside the vacuum cleaner housing. A static discharge can cause an explosion of toner particles, especially since one of the main ingredients is carbon. Approved toner vacuums also have a conductive hose. The conductive hose is designed to prevent static discharge created from the moving parts inside the vacuum.

The approved vacuum typically has a High-Efficiency Particulate Air (HEPA) filter. The HEPA filter can filter out smaller particles than a normal household vacuum cleaner. Attempts to vacuum toner spills with a normal household vacuum will only result in producing a cloud of toner particles in the air that could cause harm when breathed.

Do *not* use a standard household vacuum cleaner to remove toner spills. Only an approved vacuum expressly designed to clean toner spills should be used.

Small toner spills on hard surfaces such as tile can be swept with a broom. Be sure to use a slow, sweeping action so not to create a cloud of toner dust. Never use hot water to wipe or mop a toner spill. Hot water will set the toner, causing a permanent stain. This is especially true for clothing. Try to always remove loose toner from clothing before washing. Use only cold water to wash clothing covered with toner.

Spills on a printer case can be removed with a soft dry cloth. Toner can be removed from case areas that are difficult to clean with a cloth by using a small paint brush. Again, slowly brush the areas as not to create a cloud of toner dust.

For information about any special precautions or dangers associated with toner and other chemical products, you can consult the material safety data sheet (MSDS) for that specific product. By law, all chemical products must have an MSDS available on request to answer all questions about how the product should be handled. This includes safe handling and cleanup. Printer toner is considered safe when handled in the intended manner.

Recycling Toner Cartridges

Products associated with technical equipment, such as printers, generate billions of tons of waste which can be harmful to our environment. To reduce the impact on our environment, most manufacturers such as Xerox and Hewlett Packard have recycling programs that allow a consumer to recycle toner and ink cartridges as well as other consumables. You can view the manufacturer's Web site to obtain information about their recycling program.

Diagnosing Laser Printer Problems

Laser printers are the most common printer you will encounter. Understanding the complete printing process of the typical laser printer based on the electrophotographic process will give you a quick insight to the problem. Most printers are equipped with a self-test program as part of a diagnostic routine. Running the printer self-test can eliminate many printer faults.

The following covers twelve most common problems you may encounter with a laser printer. Examine them along with their causes and solutions.

```
$$%34693%@%&&#^&bsr ]]]]]]]]]]]]]]]]]]]]]]]]]]
#^tbsss$%^^%#$#%$%^%%^%&LK$J^$%JYS}
}}}$@L#K!!K@#LL$K#$T)$U))_$          #KS)$%)LFX
)$I)$# )#$L    )$##@)#^&B%PO("R
@!@RGXR^*&*)%Y%^%&&R(T)(+{&^@$^%^%E
R^*^R<LTG*&T<A#$^E&I&R*KFEA$^%E&HEW$
#^%DB$%&%4985)(*&(()*)(Q@LJ9984jlk
094/94"3434W%$))$E)$I)@LR_%%+@<V<
%)$##########)I$#$%&*()_&E<?""})_(%#R$%*(&
:$*&L(MN?){"_W^((D%^*(*E$^JJ&*O)(PAE$^^%
*P_VHJ*%&K<M?":"?><O)*%$#&(**>&T%$#^*&
&())?><R$%E$%O*&#^%*&)(*&^%Q%*D*$B^&(
*@R****D^U^E&I^%*R*KS%$*&T(IAY$Q@$%*(*
JYR#^%E(*&(OYT$A^%(*&(HRE^%&(I^R*%*UI&
^O$%*D%&%&Y^%*IKM^%^&^)%%%%%%%
%%%%%%%%%%
```

Figure 11-16. If your printed page looks like this, there is likely a problem with your printer driver.

Printing Gibberish

If the printer is printing gibberish or unintelligible symbols, **Figure 11-16,** but prints fine during the self-test, you probably have the wrong printer driver loaded or a corrupted driver.

An incorrect printer driver can be loaded when a user attempts to use a disk from another PC with a different printer installed. Some word processing packages save the printer setup as well as the document to disk. When the document is loaded on a different PC with a different printer, it can cause the printer to print gibberish or just continually print a series of blank pages. Check the **Printers and Faxes** window (Windows XP) or **Printers** window (Windows Vista). If you see printers other than the one you are using, this is most likely the problem.

You may also have a corrupt printer driver and may need to reinstall the printer driver. A computer "hiccup" can corrupt a driver. Reinstalling the printer driver will correct this problem. Reinstalling the driver is done just like the initial installation, using the **Add Printer** wizard. The computer will install the new driver over the old, corrupt driver.

Pages Have Light Streaks

If pages are printing light images or have light streaks vertically down the page, **Figure 11-17,** the printer is low on toner. Remove the toner cartridge, shake it gently from side to side, and then reinstall it. If the quality of the printed pages improve, replace the toner cartridge.

Pages Print Solid Black

When pages print solid black or if there is a great deal of gray in the areas that should be white, the most likely problem is the toner cartridge is seated improperly, allowing toner to dump on the paper, **Figure 11-18.** It is also possible

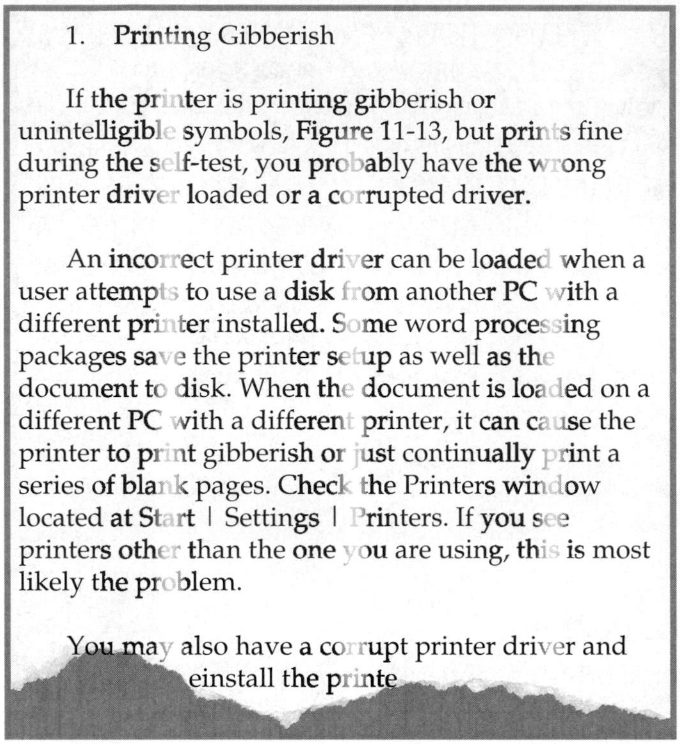

1. Printing Gibberish

If the printer is printing gibberish or unintelligible symbols, Figure 11-13, but prints fine during the self-test, you probably have the wrong printer driver loaded or a corrupted driver.

An incorrect printer driver can be loaded when a user attempts to use a disk from another PC with a different printer installed. Some word processing packages save the printer setup as well as the document to disk. When the document is loaded on a different PC with a different printer, it can cause the printer to print gibberish or just continually print a series of blank pages. Check the Printers window located at Start | Settings | Printers. If you see printers other than the one you are using, this is most likely the problem.

You may also have a corrupt printer driver and einstall the printe

Figure 11-17. When toner cartridges run low, the printed page will show insufficient toner coverage.

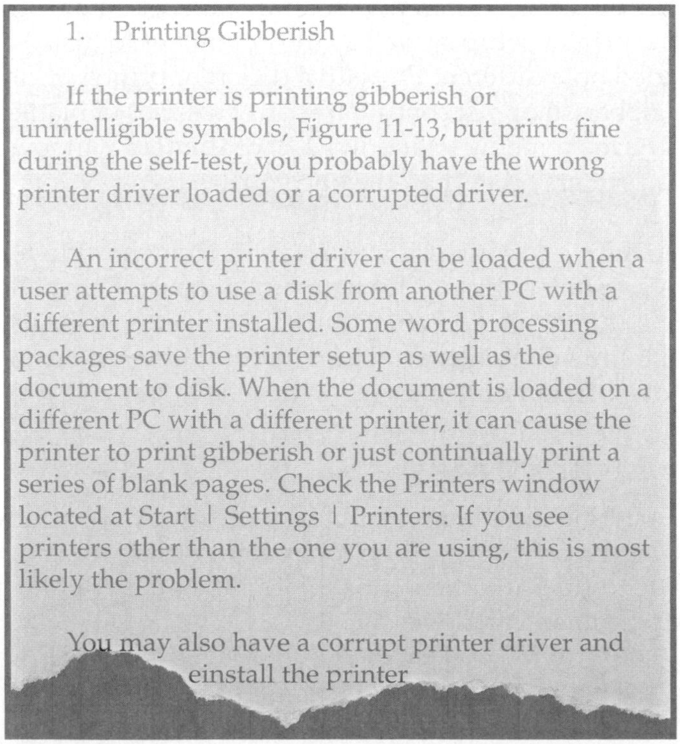

1. Printing Gibberish

If the printer is printing gibberish or unintelligible symbols, Figure 11-13, but prints fine during the self-test, you probably have the wrong printer driver loaded or a corrupted driver.

An incorrect printer driver can be loaded when a user attempts to use a disk from another PC with a different printer installed. Some word processing packages save the printer setup as well as the document to disk. When the document is loaded on a different PC with a different printer, it can cause the printer to print gibberish or just continually print a series of blank pages. Check the Printers window located at Start | Settings | Printers. If you see printers other than the one you are using, this is most likely the problem.

You may also have a corrupt printer driver and einstall the printer

Figure 11-18. If extra toner appears on a page, you should first check if the toner cartridge is seated correctly.

that the toner cartridge is defective. Fixing an improperly seated toner cartridge is as simple as removing the cartridge and replacing it correctly.

Although less likely, there is also the possibility that the laser may not be working or the mirror may be defective. The primary corona wire could also be at fault. When the primary corona wire is at fault, there is no initial charge placed on the drum. Remember that the polarities used depend on the manufacturer. The polarities used determine if the page prints totally black or totally white. You must first determine whether the laser on the printer writes the images or writes the background. If any of these parts have gone bad, a qualified technician needs to be contacted.

Pages Print Blank

Always check the easy things first. A common error that causes blank pages occurs when the toner cartridge is changed. Often users fail to remove the sealing tape that keeps the toner slot closed during shipping and transfer. If you are getting blank pages, always remove the toner cartridge first to ensure that the sealing tape has been removed.

The wrong driver or a corrupt driver can also cause blank pages. If only alternate pages or just the first page is blank, it is probably a printer setup problem. The driver is the place to look. Try reinstalling it.

If all the pages of the print job are blank, the transfer corona may be at fault. Without a charge on the paper, it cannot attract toner from the drum. A qualified technician must be called for this problem.

Printer Quality Has Suddenly Become Poor

With poor quality prints, first check that the toner cartridge is not low on toner or completely empty. Also, check if the printer is set up for economy or draft mode. The economy or draft mode is used to conserve on toner. This option usually can be accessed in the printer dialog setup window of the operating system and through the printer menu options controlled by the buttons on the printer. Usually, any settings on the printer will override settings created with the operating system interface.

Toner Smears on Paper

As stated earlier, always check the simplest thing first. With toner smears, the easiest thing to check is if the printer was loaded with the wrong type of paper. Some printers require special paper. If there are multiple types of printers at a location, there is a chance the wrong type of paper may have been placed into the paper tray.

However, when toner smears across the paper when touched, **Figure 11-19,** it is a good indication that the fusing unit is out. With the fusing unit out, the toner is never melted to the paper.

The Printer Acts Completely Dead

If a printer acts dead, check if the printer is offline. If there is no response, check the printer cables, as they may have become loose. Of course, never forget to check the power cable and to make sure there is power at the outlet. A dead printer can also be a driver problem.

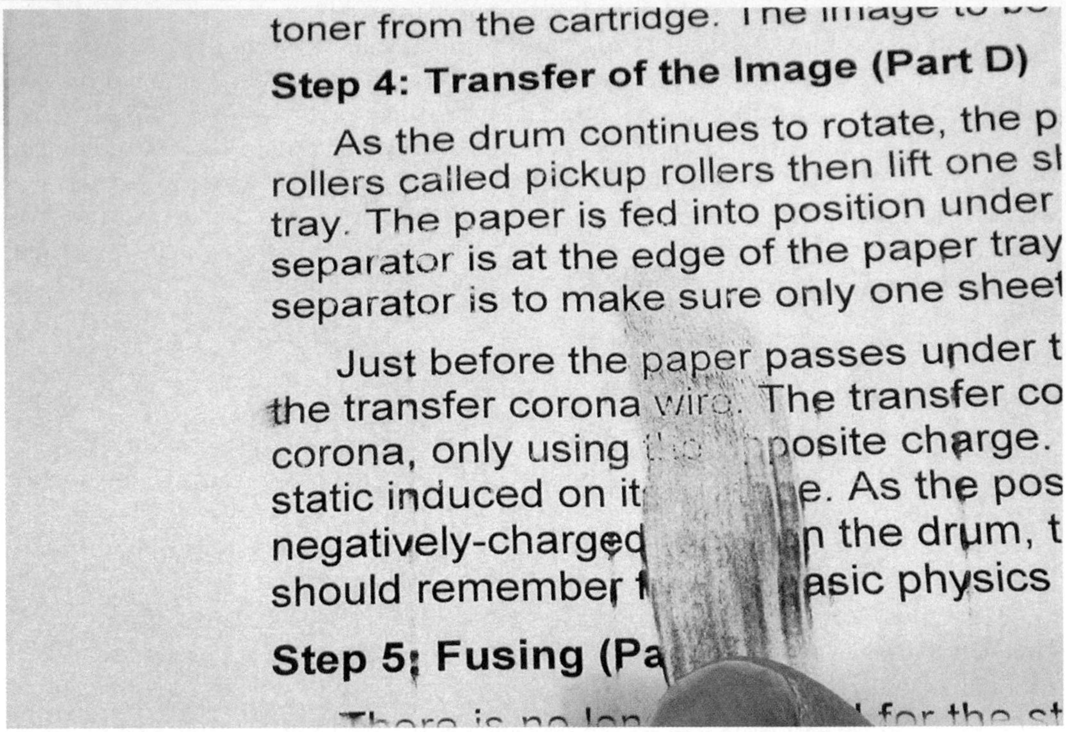

Figure 11-19.
If toner is not sealed properly to paper, it smears easily.

Printed Characters Are Fuzzy

With fuzzy printing, check the type of paper loaded into the printer. If the wrong type of paper is used, the toner may scatter outside the character outline.

Constant Dark or White Spots

If you find dark or white spots that appear in the same place on multiple printed sheets, it is likely that the drum is scratched. With a scratch on the drum, it may not be able to hold toner or it may hold toner on the spot at all times. Replacement drums can be purchased and installed fairly easily for most laser printers.

Ghost Images on the Paper

A ghost image is a second image that appears on the paper in the background of the image you are trying to print, **Figure 11-20.** A ghost image is usually a sign that the erase lamp is burnt out. When the erase lamp is out, the image of the last print run will remain on the drum.

Blank Areas Appear in Parts of the Printing Job

If blank areas are appearing on the printing job, there is a good chance the wrong paper length has been selected at setup. Check if there is a mismatch in paper length.

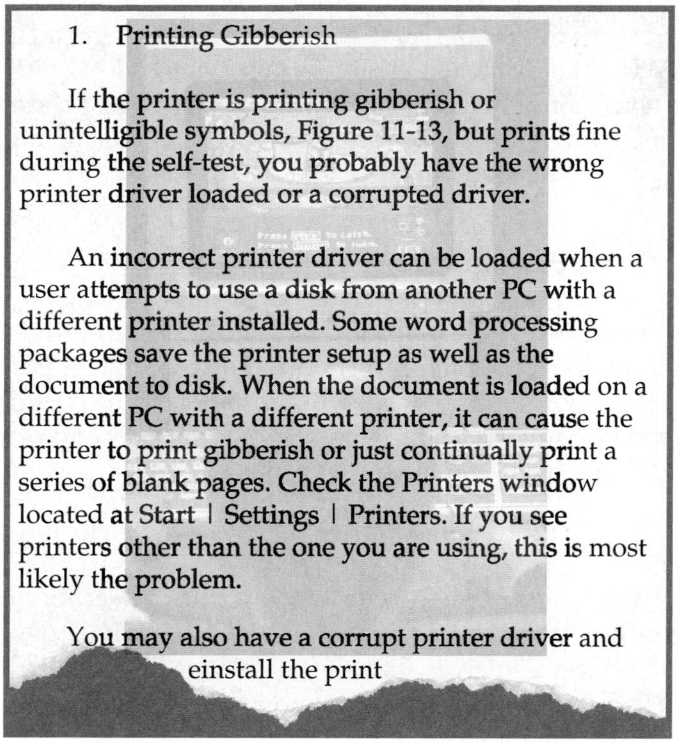

1. Printing Gibberish

If the printer is printing gibberish or unintelligible symbols, Figure 11-13, but prints fine during the self-test, you probably have the wrong printer driver loaded or a corrupted driver.

An incorrect printer driver can be loaded when a user attempts to use a disk from another PC with a different printer installed. Some word processing packages save the printer setup as well as the document to disk. When the document is loaded on a different PC with a different printer, it can cause the printer to print gibberish or just continually print a series of blank pages. Check the Printers window located at Start | Settings | Printers. If you see printers other than the one you are using, this is most likely the problem.

You may also have a corrupt printer driver and
einstall the print

Figure 11-20.
Ghost images appear when the image from a previous print is not erased from the drum.

Printer Trips the Circuit Breaker

If the circuit breaker trips when the printer is running, it is a good sign that electronic or other parts of the printer are failing. However, you must remember that a printer uses heat to fuse the toner to the paper. A printer may draw as much as 15 amps of current while processing a page. If the printer is on the same circuit as another piece of heavy-load equipment, the two running at the same time can trip a breaker. A coffeepot, copy machine, toaster oven, and microwave are good examples of equipment that may be found on the same circuit breaker as the printer. The combination of these types of equipment sharing the same breaker as the printer can cause frequent breaker trips. Check carefully. A circuit can span more than one room. The overloaded equipment may not be near the printer location.

Diagnosing USB Printer Problems

The USB connection has become the standard cable type connection for printers, thus replacing the parallel cable and earlier serial connections. While USB is easy to install and typically configures automatically, there are several problems commonly associated with this type of connection.

Insufficient or No Electrical Power

It is most important to mention that you should always check for the simplest and easiest solution first when dealing with printer problems. Check if the printer is turned on and is online. An LED generally indicates power to a printer. If the

LED is lit, the USB port selected for the printer connection may not be providing sufficient electrical power to operate the printer. While the majority of electrical power is supplied to the printer through its own electrical plug, the USB cable also provides a small amount of energy required to run the printer. This problem is easily remedied by installing a powered USB hub capable of supplying the higher electrical power needed by the printer.

Printer Is Offline

A printer can have power but be offline or on standby. A printer cannot print while in the offline mode. An offline printer may sound like too simple of a problem or too obvious, but the problem often occurs. When giving support over a telephone, the power source and whether the printer is offline should be checked first. Don't be surprised if the person on the other end of the telephone does not exactly know what you mean by "offline."

Conflicting Devices

USB devices are not supposed to conflict, but this is in theory only. Occasionally, conflicts do arise and are generally caused by either the BIOS setup program or the USB device driver. One of the devices may be programmed to take over the bandwidth of the port, causing the other devices to go into a hibernation state or simply lockup.

Microsoft furnishes basic device code to developers to use and modify for their USB devices. Microsoft will also test the software and the hardware compatibility for a small charge. If the device passes Microsoft testing, the device is added to the Microsoft Hardware Compatibility List (HCL) for the operating system version for which it was tested. However, some manufacturers develop their own driver software and only refer to the Microsoft guidelines. For whatever reason, they do not submit their code for testing or it is tested after the release of the hardware device. If a problem is found, the manufacturer will simply provide a "patch" at their Web site.

To troubleshoot a USB device, remove all other USB devices from the port that the printer is connected to. This will help eliminate the possibility of a conflict between the devices connected to the same port.

Check Device Manager for a problem with the USB port indicated by an exclamation mark or question mark. These symbols indicate that the printer is not properly recognized or configured and are most likely related to the printer driver or BIOS setup. The software drivers or BIOS, or both, may need to be upgraded. Check the printer manufacturer's Web site for more information.

Windows Help and Support

Windows provides the Printer Troubleshooter feature in its Help and Support software. The Printer Troubleshooter feature is designed to help solve printer problems, **Figure 11-21.** This feature can be accessed by entering the keywords "printing troubleshooting" in the **Search** text box of Help and Support.

The Printer Troubleshooter feature asks a series of questions about the printing problem and provides possible solutions. There are also many topics about printers in Windows Help and Support, such as adding a printer, setting up a printer on a network, and changing printer settings.

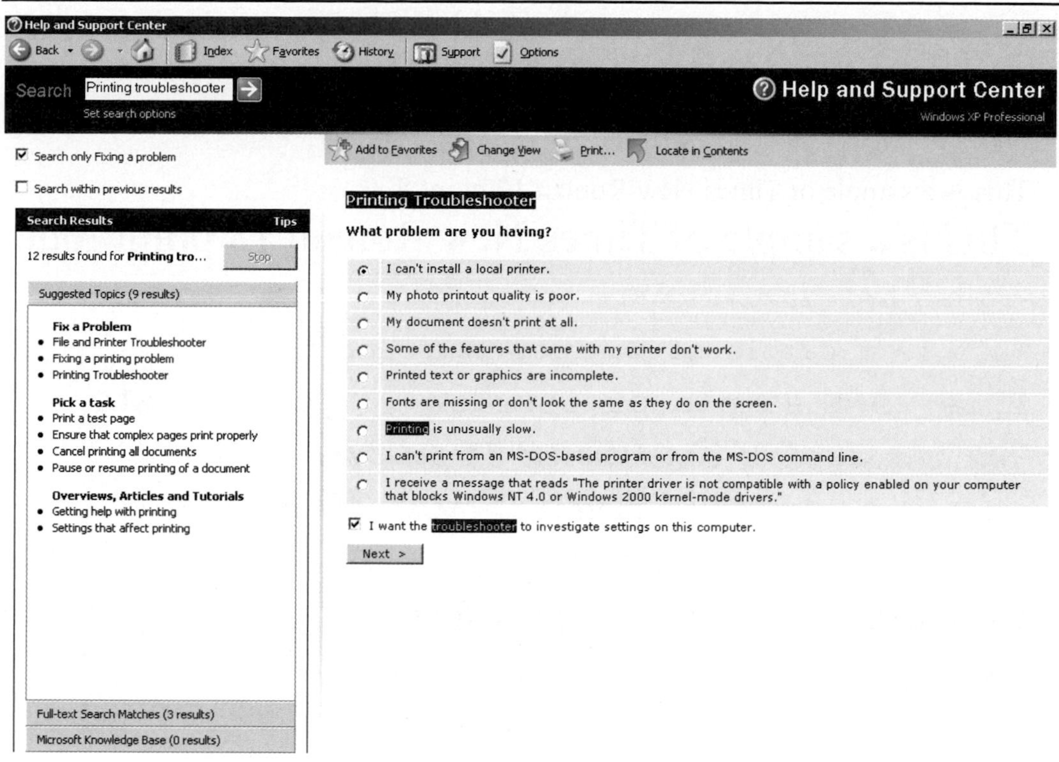

Figure 11-21. The Printing Troubleshooter is located in Windows Help and Support.

Fonts

A ***font*** is a design for a set of symbols, usually text and number characters. A font describes characteristics associated with a symbol such as the typeface, size, pitch, and spacing between symbols. Look at **Figure 11-22.**

font
a design for a set of symbols, usually text and number characters. A font describes characteristics associated with a symbol such as the typeface, size, pitch, and spacing between symbols.

The two main classifications of fonts are *bitmap* and *vector*. Bitmap fonts use a pattern of dots to represent each letter. The bitmap images of the text are stored in memory. As you type, the bitmap images are placed on the screen by a process similar to a cut-and-paste process. Each and every different font requires a different bitmap pattern. A bitmap font must also use a separate bitmap for each size of the letter.

A vector font is also referred to as an outline font. A vector font draws the outline of the letter rather than storing a separate bitmap pattern for each font. The angles, turns, and distances are calculated for each character. A vector font is easily scaled to larger or smaller sizes because the letter is based on an algorithm.

Bitmap fonts look better than vector fonts when displayed on low-resolution devices such as monitors. On high-resolution devices, such as some printers, vector fonts look better than bitmap fonts.

The physical size of a font is described in points and pitch. The height of a letter is measured in ***points.*** The width is measured in ***pitch.*** Each point is equal to 1/72 of an inch.

points
unit of measure for the height of a font. Each point is equal to 1/72 of an inch.

pitch
unit of measure for the width of a font.

Vector fonts are used with Page Description Language (PDL). Common PDLs are Adobe PostScript and Microsoft TrueType. A page description language treats everything on a page as a graphic image. The PDL translates the picture on the monitor into a set of printer codes that will exactly duplicate the image seen on the screen. This is often referred to as "what you see is what you get" (WYSIWYG).

Figure 11-22. Samples of common typefaces and point-sizes.

Sample Fonts

This is a sample of Times New Roman 8 point font.

This is a sample of Times New Roman 12 point font.

This is a sample of Times New Roman 18 point font.

This is a sample of Courier 8 point font.

This is a sample of Courier 12 point font.

This is a sample of Courier 14 point font.

This is a sample of Brush Script 16 point font.

This is a sample of Brush Script 20 point font.

This is a sample of Tahoma 10 point font.

This is a sample of Tahoma 14 point font.

This is a sample of Myriad 10 point font.

This is a sample of Myriad 16 point font.

This is a sample of Myriad 16 point italic font.

This is a sample of Myriad 16 point bold font.

Figure 11-23 shows all the ways the Word program can manipulate a font. The manipulation feature is typical in most word processing packages. Available fonts can be viewed in Windows XP by accessing **Start | Control Panel | Appearance and Themes** and then selecting **Fonts** located under **See also** in the side panel, **Figure 11-24.** In Windows Vista, available fonts are located under **Start | Control Panel | Appearance and Personalization | Fonts**. **Figure 11-25** shows the Font folder and available fonts. You can print a sample of the selected font by right-clicking the folder and selecting **Print** from the shortcut menu.

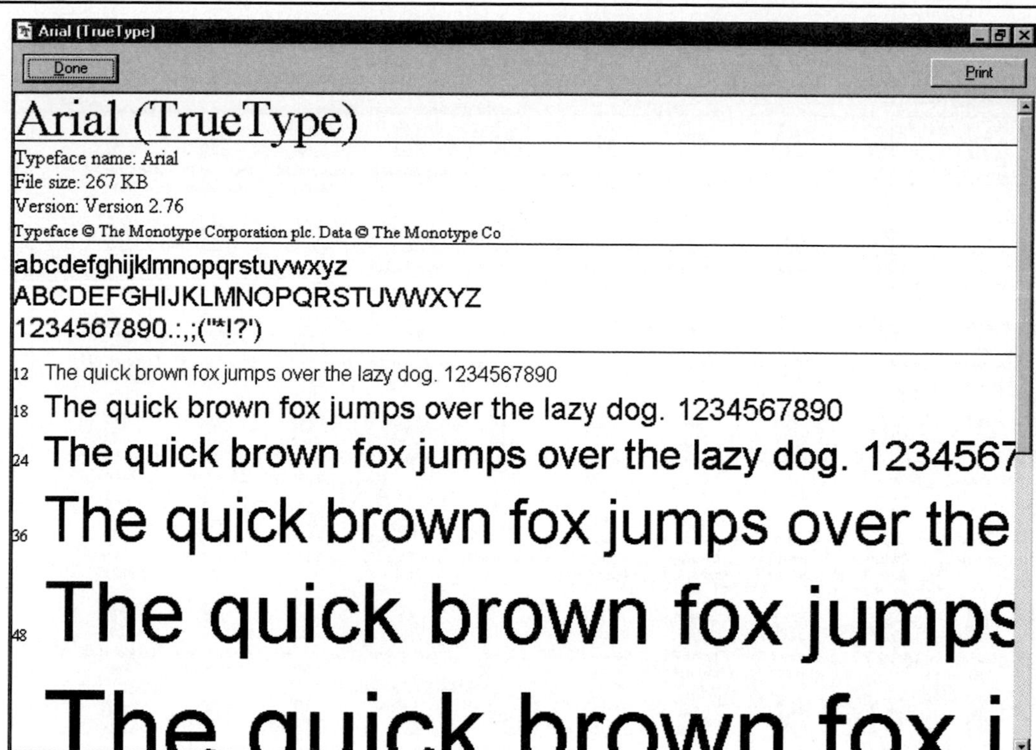

Figure 11-23.
A sample of the Arial typeface printed from the **Font** folder in **Control Panel**.

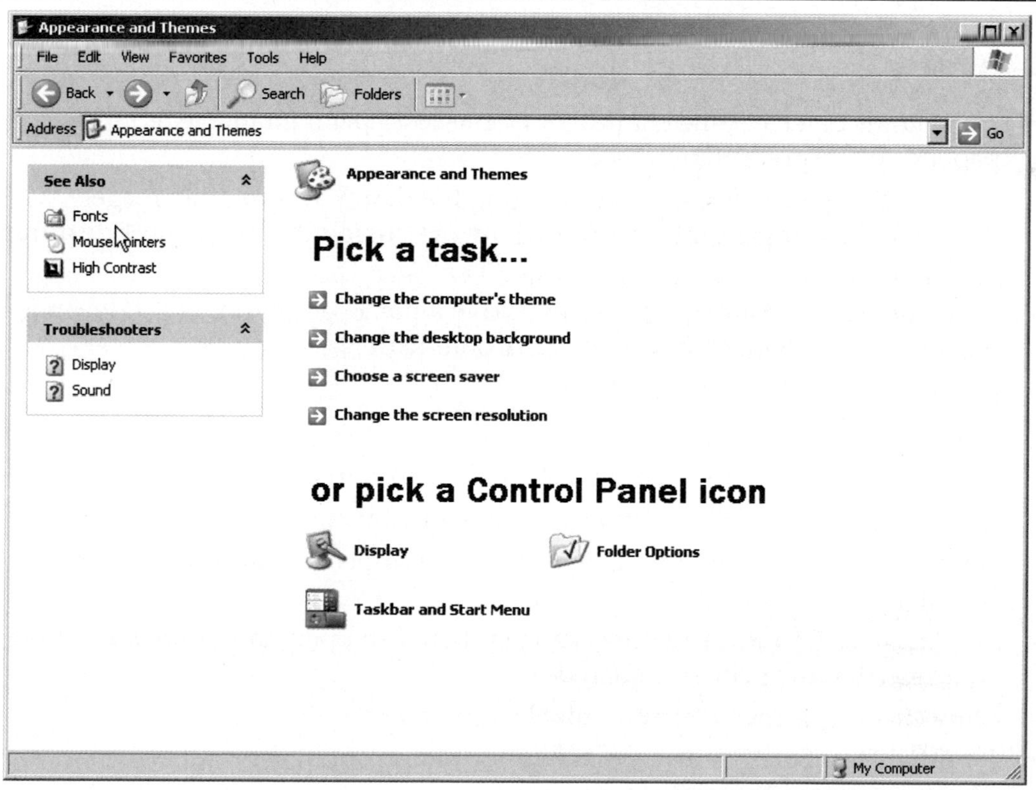

Figure 11-24.
In Windows XP, the Fonts folder is accessed through **Start | Control Panel | Appearance and Themes | Fonts**.

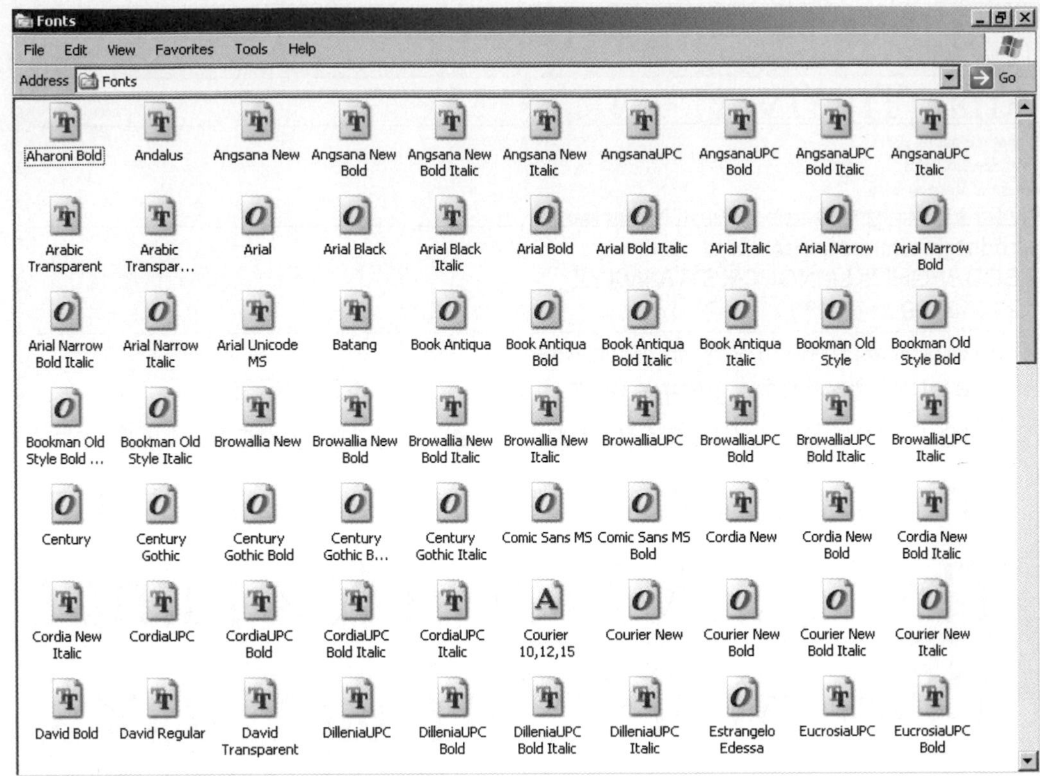

Figure 11-25. Windows Font folder showing available fonts.

Summary

- ✔ A printer is an electromechanical device used to print an image or text to paper or other presentation media.
- ✔ The six laser printing stages are charging the drum, writing the image, developing the image, transferring the image, fusing the image, and cleaning the drum.
- ✔ Inkjet printers use either a photoresistor or a piezocell crystal to produce the force needed to spray a fine mist of ink onto paper.
- ✔ COM1 and COM3 share IRQ 4.
- ✔ COM2 and COM4 share IRQ 3.
- ✔ A USB printer is identified as an IEEE 1284.4 item in Device Manager.
- ✔ USB printers use a DOT4 virtual port for a printer connection.
- ✔ A printer can be shared by either a wired or wireless network or over the Internet.
- ✔ In Windows XP and earlier operating systems, an open hand under a printer indicates that the printer is shared.
- ✔ Only use an approved vacuum for cleaning toner spills.
- ✔ Material Data Safety Sheets contain information about the safe handling of and any dangers associated with a chemical product.
- ✔ Many printer problems are simple and can be easily solved by users or technicians.
- ✔ A font is a description of the characteristics of a symbol such as letters and numbers and describes the attributes of the symbol.

Review Questions

Answer the following questions on a separate sheet of paper. Please do not write in this book.

1. After a laser printer prints a page of text, the toner smears when touched. What might be the problem?
2. A paper jam constantly occurs when using a printer. This is a recent problem. What might be the cause?
3. An error code appears on the printer panel that you are not familiar with. What should you do?
4. Place the following steps in the correct order.
   Toner is attracted to the drum.
   The static brush removes the charge from the paper.
   The laser writes the image on the drum.
   The transfer corona charges the paper.
   The fusing section melts the toner.
   The drum is erased of all charge.
   The primary corona wire places a charge on the drum.
5. How is a USB printer identified in the Device Manager?
6. How is a shared printer indicated in Windows XP?
7. Describe what print spooling does.
8. What is the print queue?
9. What is the difference between a bitmap font and a vector font?
10. How can the font folder be accessed in Windows Vista? Start with **Start |** _____ **|** _____ **|** _____.
11. The height of a font is measured in _____.
12. The width of a font is measured in _____.

Sample A+ Exam Questions

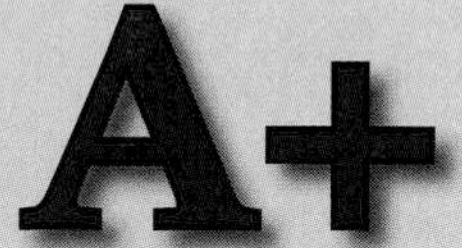

Answer the following questions on a separate sheet of paper. Please do not write in this book.

1. What type of printer uses piezoelectric technology?
   a. Laser
   b. Dot matrix
   c. Dye-sublimation
   d. Inkjet
2. What type of printer uses pins driven by a solenoid striking a ribbon to make dots conforming to letters, symbols, and pictures?
   a. Laser
   b. Dot matrix
   c. Dye-sublimation
   d. Inkjet
3. Which type of printer utilizes thermoresistors to force the ink from a reservoir?
   a. Laser
   b. Dot matrix
   c. Dye-sublimation
   d. Inkjet

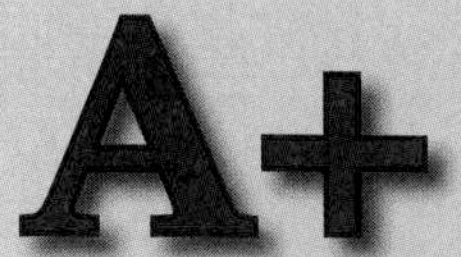

4. In the electrostatic process, the term *fusing* can best be described as which of the following answers?
   a. The protective device installed in electrostatic laser printers to prevent electrical overload of the circuits.
   b. The transfer of toner to the paper to construct the printed image.
   c. The bonding of the toner to the paper.
   d. A special module that prevents the voltage from exceeding the 600 volts positive charge.
5. Which of the following includes all the correct processes in correct order for electrostatic printing?
   a. Charging the drum, writing the image, developing the image, transferring the image, fusing the image, cleaning the drum.
   b. Charging the drum, transferring the image, writing the image, developing the image, fusing the image, cleaning the drum.
   c. Cleaning the drum, charging the drum, transferring the image, developing the image, charging again, writing the image, fusing the image.
   d. Writing the image, charging the drum, developing the image, transferring the image, fusing the image, cleaning the drum.
6. The acronym LPT represents which of the following?
   a. Local printer transferring-port
   b. Line printer terminal
   c. Local printer terminal
   d. Line port terminal
7. What does the printer term *spooling* mean?
   a. It describes the mechanical device that holds the ribbon in place on a dot matrix printer.
   b. It is a method of connecting a local printer to an area network printer group.
   c. It is the method used to store print jobs waiting to be processed in an orderly fashion.
   d. It is a method of determining the amount of rotation or "print spooling" required for blank spacing between lines of text in a document.
8. LPT1 is usually assigned to which IRQ?
   a. 5
   b. 6
   c. 7
   d. 8
9. A paper comes out of a laser printer, and its printed surface is completely black. What is *most likely* the cause?
   a. The toner cartridge is seated improperly.
   b. The charge is too low on the drum.
   c. The laser is defective.
   d. The fuser is overheating the paper.
10. A laser printer prints a page, and the document smears when touched. What is the *most likely* cause of the image smear?
   a. The primary corona is defective.
   b. The transfer corona is defective.
   c. The toner is damp.
   d. The fuser is defective.

Suggested Laboratory Activities

Do not attempt any suggested laboratory activities without your instructor's permission. Certain activities can render the PC operating system inoperable.

1. Install and set up a local printer using Windows XP.
2. Practice downloading a printer driver file.
3. Set up a printer to print to paper in landscape orientation.
4. Send the same print job to a printer three or four times. Open the **Printers and Faxes** folder (Windows XP) or **Printers** folder (Windows Vista) and look for a listing of files being printed. Stop the file printing process and purge the duplicate files.
5. Try printing to a printer while it is turned off and observe the error code.
6. Go to a major printer manufacturer's Web site and access information about how to care for the printer. What is the routine maintenance that should be performed?
7. Using a laser printer that cannot be salvaged, carefully disassemble the printer and identify all the major parts. You may try to use the manufacturer's Web site to assist you. Do not be surprised if you cannot find information about the disassembly process. Usually the manufacturer does not want persons who are not fully qualified to disassemble their printers.
8. Add memory to an existing laser printer. Go to the manufacturer's Web site for step-by-step instructions. Do not attempt to disassemble a working laser printer without instructions on how to access the memory chips. Attempting to access the memory chips without knowing how can result in damaging the printer's plastic assembly.
9. Draw out the step-by-step electrostatic printing process. When presented, this is one of the most commonly missed questions on the A+ Certification exams by PC technicians.
10. Go to the HP Web site and download a list of common error codes associated with an HP4L printer.
11. Go to a major printer manufacturer and obtain a copy of a toner MSDS. Look over the sheet to see what precautions are recommended when handling toner.

Interesting Web Sites for More Information

www.epson.com
www.hp.com
www.ricoh.com

Chapter 11
Laboratory Activity
Installing a Printer

After completing this laboratory activity, you will be able to:

- ✔ Install and set up a typical printer.
- ✔ Explain the various printer options available.

Introduction

The installation of a new printer is a common procedure. During the early years of personal computers, printer installation could be quite difficult. Now, in the era of Plug and Play and wizard programs, printer installation is much easier. In this exercise, you will install a printer driver. For the purpose of lab instruction, an HP laser printer is used, although the exact model will not be specified. You should substitute the manufacturer and model of your own printer in its place.

A printer driver is necessary for communications between the software that uses a printer and the printer hardware. The driver translates the communications between processor and printer. The processor communicates in hexadecimal or binary codes. The printer driver translates those and reissues them as commands that the printer can understand. In turn, the printer starts a new page, changes font size or style, copies an image from RAM, or prints a line.

If the correct driver is not selected, many things go wrong. An endless stream of paper may be ejected from the printer, completely blank or filled with unintelligible symbols. The printer may simply sit there and appear dead.

To install a printer in Windows XP, access the printer installation program either through Control Panel or from **Start | Printers and Faxes**. Once the **Printers and Faxes** dialog box is open, click **Add a Printer**, which is listed under **Printer Tasks**.

Equipment and Materials

- ✔ Typical PC with Windows XP installed.
- ✔ Windows XP Installation CD.
- ✔ HP laser printer or equivalent.

Note:

The lab is compatible with most printers. Simply substitute the brand and model you are using in place of references made to the HP laser printer.

Procedure

1. _______ Boot the PC and wait for the Windows desktop to appear.
2. _______ Access **Printer and Faxes** located off the **Start** menu. The **Printer and Faxes** dialog box will appear similar to the following.

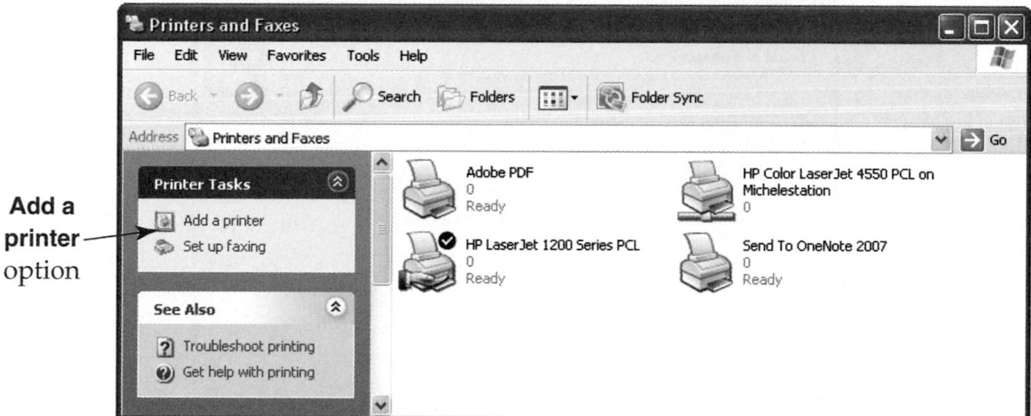

3. _______ Select the **Add a printer** option located under **Printer Tasks** on the left side of the window. The Add Printer wizard should start automatically and will look similar to the following.

4. _______ Click the **Next** button. The **Add Printer** wizard dialog box should look similar to the following. You must make a choice of printer connection by selecting either the **Local printer attached to this computer** or **A network printer, or a printer attached to another computer** option.

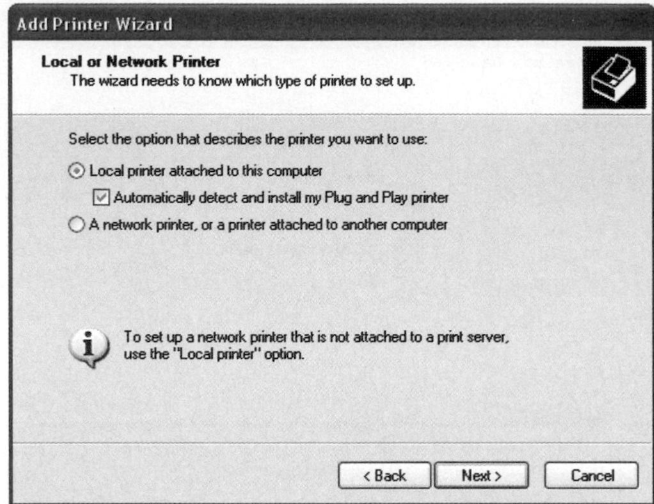

A local printer is one that is directly connected to the PC, while a network printer is one that is accessed via a network. In this lab activity, you should select **Local printer attached to this computer**.

When installing a local printer, the Windows XP operating system usually correctly detects and identifies the correct printer and will automatically configure the correct drivers. For this lab activity, unselect the check box indicating **Automatically detect and install my Plug and Play printer**. This will allow you to see the screens provided for a manual installation.

5. _______ Click **Next**. A dialog box similar to the following will appear, prompting you to select a port. Select the default LPT1 port so that you can see the options available.

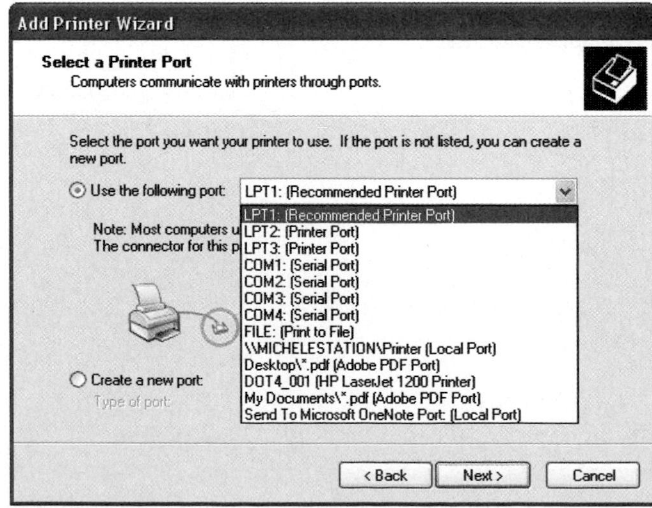

6._______ Click **Next** again. A dialog box similar to the following will appear. This dialog box allows you to manually select the printer manufacturer and printer. There is also an option to use a driver that came on a disc with the printer. This option allows you to install a printer not identified in the list.

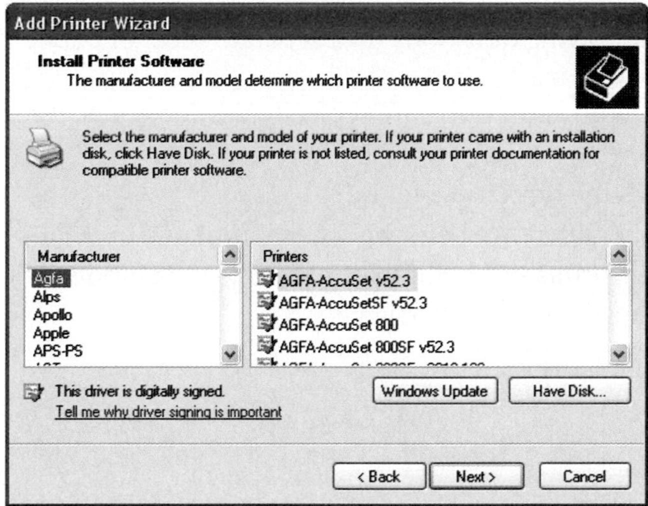

7._______ Cancel out of the manual installation by clicking **Cancel**, unless your instructor wants you to continue with a manual installation.

If you continue with the manual installation, you will be prompted to enter a printer name. The name you choose should be designed to assist you in identifying the printer at a later date. This is especially true of a network shared printer. For example, the printer name might be "LaserJet Room 114."

Before you finish the installation, a screen will appear similar to the following giving you an option to print a test page. Always test the printer configuration by printing a test page.

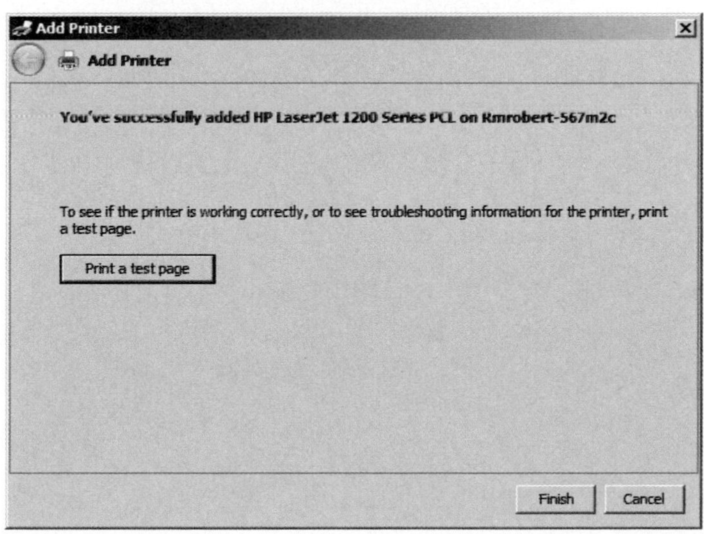

8. _______ Answer the review questions, and then return the workstation to its original configuration.

Review Questions

Answer the following questions on a separate sheet of paper. Please do not write in this book.

1. Which two physical ports are typically used to connect to an older model printer?
2. What does the printer driver do?
3. What is the difference between a COM port and an LPT port?
4. If a printer prints unintelligible characters or symbols when first installed, what is most likely the problem?

Portable PCs

After studying this chapter, you will be able to:

- ✔ Distinguish between laptops, notebooks, palmtops, and personal digital assistants.
- ✔ Identify the parts that are different in full-size PCs and portable PCs.
- ✔ Explain the difference between the types of batteries used in portable PCs.
- ✔ Identify the three standard PCMCIA cards.
- ✔ Identify the two widths of ExpressCards.
- ✔ Define what the Bluetooth standard does.
- ✔ Describe how Windows Briefcase is used.
- ✔ Describe direct cable connection communications.

A+ Exam—Key Points

You can count on at least one question about PCMCIA cards and batteries. Also, you may be asked a question about a null modem cable, its use or construction.

Key Words and Terms

The following words and terms will become important pieces of your computer vocabulary. Be sure you can define them.

ad-hoc network
alkaline battery
application service provider (ASP)
biometrics
Bluetooth
bridge
docking station
encryption
ExpressCard
infrastructure network
laptop
lithium-ion (Li-ion) battery
nickel-cadmium (NiCd) battery
nickel-metal hydride (NiMH) battery
notebook
palmtop
PCMCIA cards
personal digital assistants (PDA)
port replicator
smart card
Windows CE
wireless access point

The portable PC is a computer that is designed to go wherever the user needs it. There are a variety of portable PCs on the market. They go by names such as laptops, notebooks, palmtops, pocket PCs, and personal digital organizers. All modern portable PCs are battery-powered devices that use some type of flat-panel screen technology to keep weight and power consumption to a minimum.

Portable PCs generally have equal computing power to full-size PCs, though they are more expensive than the equivalent full-size model. However, as their numbers have increased, their price per unit has come down. When electronic devices are manufactured in limited numbers and with the latest technology, the prices are always higher. The classic electronic calculator is an excellent example. The first calculators, which provided only basic mathematical functions, cost $325 or more. Now, a small-sized calculator, which can perform nearly any desired mathematical function, preprogram math formulas, and plot graphs on an LCD screen, can be purchased for much less. This same trend is in progress with laptops, palmtops, and personal digital assistants.

laptop
a lightweight, portable computer with the monitor, motherboard, processor, disk drives, keyboard, and mouse molded into one unit.

notebook
lightweight, portable computer with the monitor, motherboard, processor, disk drives, keyboard, and mouse molded into one unit. It is slightly smaller than a laptop.

palmtop
portable computer that can rest in the palm of the hand.

Laptops, Notebooks, and Palmtops

There are several types of true portable computers including laptops, notebooks, and palmtops, **Figure 12-1.** All are lightweight, portable machines with the monitor, motherboard, processor, disk drives, keyboard, and mouse molded into one unit. Laptops are the largest of the group. Each classification is determined by the physical size of the computer. A ***laptop*** is considered slightly larger than a ***notebook,*** which is slightly smaller and thinner. However, this is a little ambiguous. When exactly does a laptop become a notebook computer? For the purpose of this textbook, the terms *laptop* and *notebook* will be used interchangeably.

With a palmtop computer, **Figure 12-2,** there is no argument. The ***palmtop*** rests in the palm of the hand. Despite its size, the palmtop is a true portable computer that provides the services that its full-size PC counterpart provides.

Even newer devices such as cellular phones are becoming more and more accessible for use as wireless computers. These devices can be even smaller than a palmtop.

Figure 12-1.
Typical portable PCs.

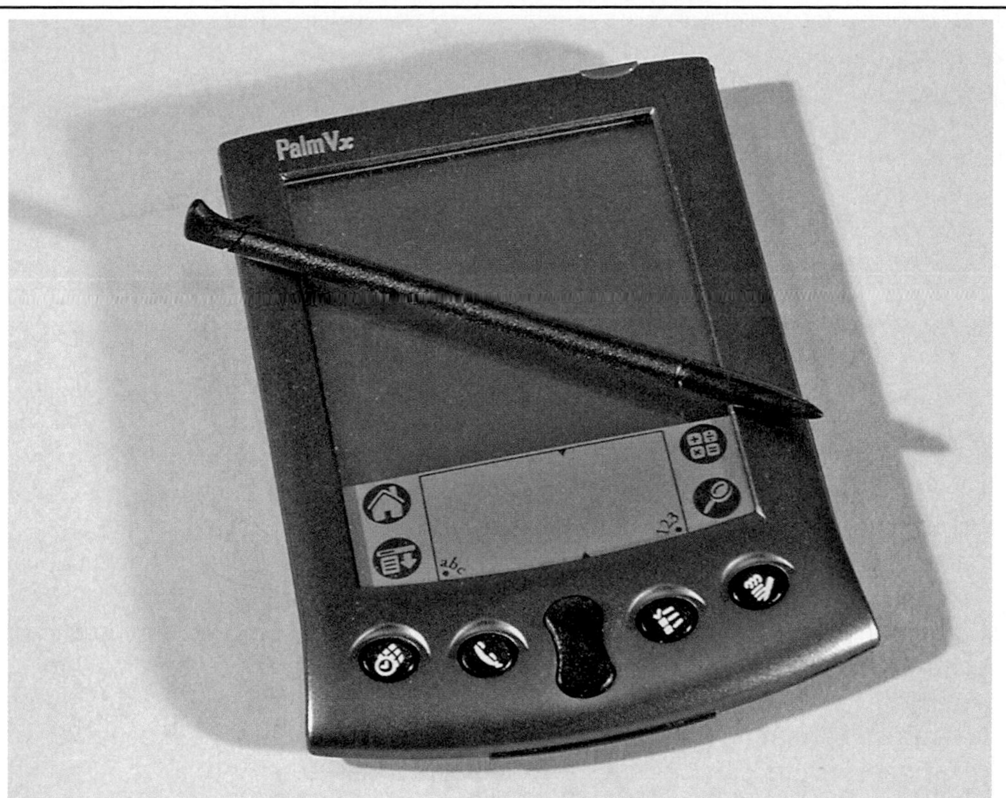

Figure 12-2.
Typical palmtop PC.

Parts of Portable PCs

A portable PC functions very similarly to a full-size PC. However, alterations have been made to the design of the portable PC to allow it to be carried easily, used anywhere, and connected quickly to other PCs and networks. To allow this functionality, laptop computers are equipped with some parts that full-size PCs don't have (large storage batteries) and have had other common PC components altered significantly (such as the mouse). In addition, to keep laptops adaptable like their full-size counterparts, PCMCIA and ExpressCards were developed. PCMCIA and ExpressCards allow new devices to be added to laptops easily.

Batteries

Batteries are a vital part of portable computing, **Figure 12-3.** There are four major types of batteries found in use for portable computers:

- ✔ Alkaline.
- ✔ Nickel-cadmium (NiCd).
- ✔ Nickel-metal hydride (NiMH).
- ✔ Lithium-ion (Li-ion).

The type of battery is extremely important when selecting a portable PC. It determines the number of hours a PC can be used independently, and it also greatly affects the weight of the PC. All four types of batteries are rechargeable.

The ***alkaline battery*** is a common battery found in small devices such as TV remote controls and some of the older palmtops. They are not used much today with computers.

alkaline battery
a common battery found in small devices such as TV remote controls and some palmtops.

Figure 12-3. This laptop battery is a lithium-ion. It is found in most modern portable PCs.

nickel-cadmium (NiCd) battery rechargeable battery used in early portable computers. Has a problem with memory effect.

The ***nickel-cadmium (NiCd) battery,*** called ***NiCad*** for short, was a standard portable computer battery for many years. It is one of the least expensive batteries. However, NiCad has some drawbacks. NiCad batteries can take up to 12 hours to fully recharge. Also, older NiCad batteries are subject to a phenomenon known as *memory effect.* When NiCad battery-powered equipment is recharged before the battery is completely drained, the battery operates for a shorter time before it appears to be completely discharged. Batteries that are not fully drained cannot be fully recharged. They show a "memory" of previous use. For example, a battery should last four hours, but the equipment is only run for one hour and then recharged. With future uses, the battery appears completely drained after one hour. This is not a problem with today's batteries.

All batteries have limits to the number of recharges. For NiCad, the average number of recharges is approximately 1000. This number of recharges can last an average user up to 2 1/2 years. Cadmium is a very toxic material, which presents a problem with disposal of spent batteries.

nickel-metal hydride (NiMH) battery second generation of rechargeable battery used for portable computers. Has no problem with memory effect and holds a charge longer than the NiCad battery.

The ***nickel-metal hydride (NiMH) battery*** is an improvement over the NiCad battery. It can store up to 50% more charge time than a NiCad battery. It does not have the memory effect problem, so it can be recharged anytime during its discharge cycle. The NiMH battery has a shorter number of total recharges then NiCad. It can usually only be recharged about 500 times.

lithium-ion (Li-ion) battery rechargeable battery found in most new portable computers. Has no problem with memory effect and holds a charge longer than NiCad and NiMH batteries.

The ***lithium-ion (Li-ion) battery*** has the highest electrical potential of all the batteries discussed here. As with NiMH batteries, they also do not suffer from a memory effect. Lithium-ion is both lightweight and compact, making it the most popular battery type used for laptop computers. Lithium-ion batteries contain no poisonous metals and are relatively safe for the environment. The only disadvantage to lithium-ion batteries is that they are more expensive than their counterparts.

Laptop battery disposal

Most rechargeable batteries are regulated because of the hazardous waste materials they contain. The exact method of disposal varies according to local government authority such as cities, counties, state, and the federal government. Almost all states have adopted their own set of guidelines that exceed the federal regulations. Following is a list of common battery types and why they can be dangerous:

- ✔ **NiCad batteries:** NiCad batteries contain the toxic metal cadmium.
- ✔ **Mercury batteries:** Mercury batteries contain the toxic metal mercury.

- ✔ **Lithium-ion batteries:** Lithium-ion batteries contain lithium, which is highly reactive with water. (Not all lithium-ion batteries are considered a waste hazard.)
- ✔ **Lead-acid and lead-gel batteries:** These batteries contain the toxic metal lead.

In most areas, there is a recycling facility that takes old batteries and either recycles them or sends them to another facility for recycling.

If a battery is rechargeable, it is usually recyclable. Do not attempt to disassemble a battery for recycling. It takes a highly skilled and trained individual and special safety equipment to disassemble a battery for recycling.

Never attempt to incinerate a battery.

Never attempt to solder wire leads to a battery.

Never short circuit (connect the positive and negative terminal with a wire or any conductive material) a battery. Batteries can explode or catch fire.

Never puncture, crush, or physically damage a battery. Some battery vapors are hazardous.

As a PC technician, you and your company will encounter more than the average number of recyclable batteries. You must adhere to all laws and regulations when disposing of batteries. The regulations vary according to the amount of batteries accumulated over a set period.

Docking Station

A ***docking station*** is like an electronic cradle for the laptop. The laptop slides into the docking station and snaps into place. Once in place, the laptop can operate from power provided by the docking station rather than from a battery or a battery charger. Some docking stations contain slots for expansion devices and bays for additional storage devices. Many times the docking station automatically connects the laptop to the company network or the Internet.

docking station an electronic cradle that provides power for a laptop, allowing users to turn the laptop into a full-size PC.

Docking stations essentially allow users to turn their laptops into full-size PCs when portability is not necessary. By connecting to the docking station, you can easily connect a full-size keyboard, mouse, or other less portable equipment to your machine.

Normally, a portable computer needs to have the desired configuration identified while docking or undocking. For example, a laptop is equipped with an LCD screen but a docking station may use a CRT screen as a display. When the laptop is connected to the docking station, the video must be configured for the CRT display. When the laptop is removed from the docking station, it must be reconfigured for the LCD screen. Windows XP, however, automatically configures the laptop video. Windows XP introduced a feature called *hot docking*. The hot docking feature allows users to dock or undock their laptop computer without the need to change hardware configurations. Windows XP automatically detects when a portable computer is placed into or removed from a docking station.

Port Replicator

port replicator
an external computer device that provides additional ports to be used by a computer system.

A ***port replicator*** is an external computer device that provides additional ports to be used by a computer system. The most common computer systems to use a port replicator are notebook computers, cell phones, and PDAs. Portable devices typically have a very limited number of ports available due to their compact design. For the same reason, it is often difficult or impossible to add additional ports by using expansion cards. Adding a PCI card to a laptop, cell phone, or PDA is not a practical solution. A port replicator solves the problem of adding additional ports.

A port replicator allows for the addition of devices such as a printer, camera, joystick, external CD or DVD drive, monitor, extra hard drive, external modem, scanner, keyboard, mouse, or any other digital device used by a full-size PC. In many ways, the port replicator serves the same function as a docking station. The use of a port replicator is not limited to just small digital devices. You can also use a port replicator to add additional ports that are not usually found on a typical computer, such as SCSI ports. It is also important to note that a USB hub designed to add additional USB ports can also be classified as a port replicator.

Portable Motherboards

Portable PC motherboards do not follow a standard form factor, **Figure 12-4.** The form factors are proprietary. To help keep the PCs small, most portable PCs incorporate the processor directly into the motherboard. The processor is often

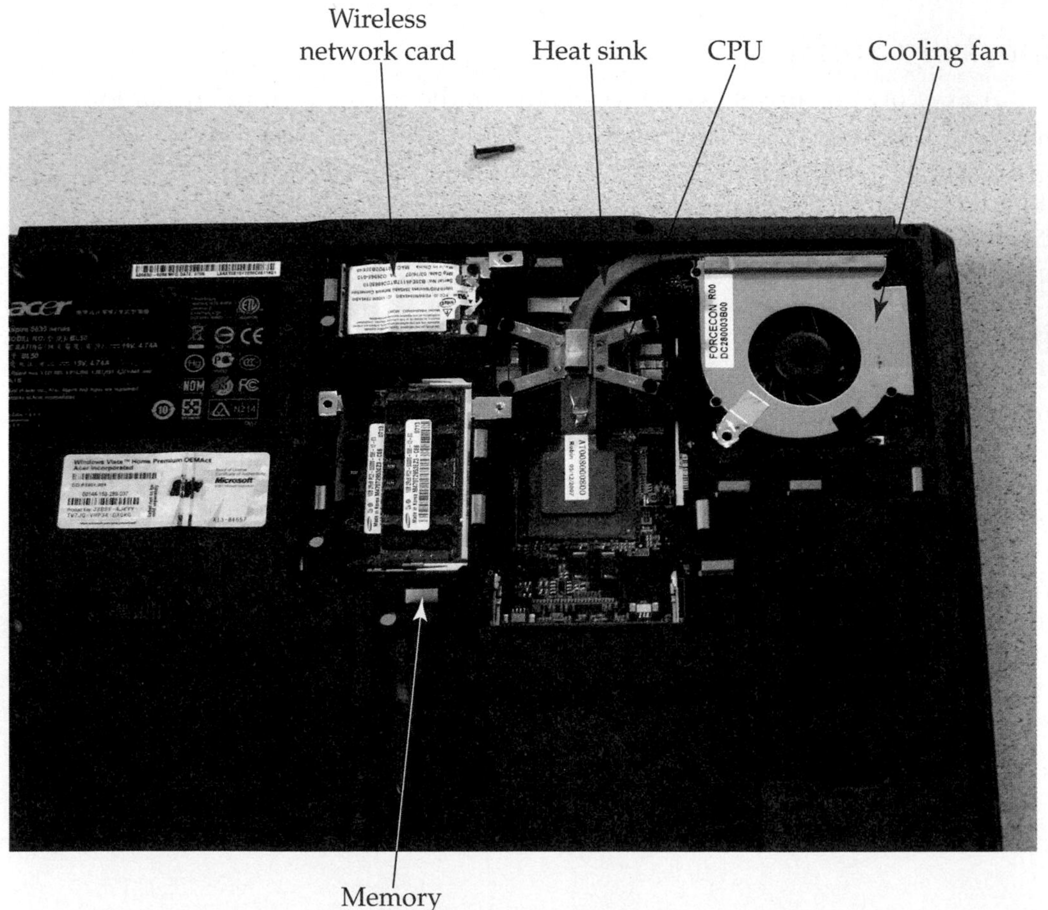

Figure 12-4. Laptop PCs, such as this unit, have the same internal components as full-size PCs. However, the layout of a laptop machine is very different to keep size and weight down.

purposely set to run at a lower speed than it is capable of if installed in a full-size PC. The reason for the slower speed is to reduce heat in the portable PC. Portable PCs leave little room for cooling because of the compact design. They incorporate large, flat heat sinks inside the case, but there is not sufficient room for a full-size cooling fan.

Mouse

To avoid having to find a flat surface to work a mouse, portable PCs incorporate a mouse or a mouse substitute into the case of the computer, **Figure 12-5.** The mouse can be incorporated into the portable PC as a simple roller ball alongside two flat switches. Some computers use an eraser-looking joystick that is located in the middle of the keyboard, Figure 12-5A. A small touch pad is standard on other models, Figure 12-5B.

If room to work is available, many people prefer to add a standard, full-size mouse to the laptop. This is easily accomplished by connecting a mouse to an available port on the laptop.

Infrared Devices

Data is often transferred between computer devices using infrared beams of light. One of the most common uses of this transfer is to move data from full-size PCs to laptops and vice versa. Almost all laptops are equipped with an infrared port for this purpose. The infrared beam of light is broadcast from an infrared transmitter located on one PC to another PC. Infrared ports can also transmit to other equipment, such as a printer.

The infrared port is sometimes referred to as an *IrDA transceiver port.* The IrDA stands for Infrared Data Association, a group responsible for a set of standards for infrared transmission of data. The term *transceiver* is used because the term implies a device that cannot only transmit a signal but can also receive a signal. Think of the term transceiver as a combination of the words *transmit* and *receive.*

Figure 12-5.
A—Some portable computers have a small joystick-like device mounted on the keyboard. This device, along with two buttons below the keyboard, takes the place of a mouse. B—Other keyboards come with a touch pad.

Printers and many other devices that are not designed with infrared ports can be modified to accept the infrared signals. An infrared port can be added to existing equipment typically through the serial COM port, a USB port, or by adding an expansion card to an expansion slot. If the Plug and Play feature does not recognize the device during startup, the device can then be set up manually through **Control Panel | Add New Hardware**.

The infrared light beam is pulsed in patterns representing the data being transferred. Transfer rates as high as 115 kbps are typical through a standard serial port. Speeds as high as 4 Mbps can be achieved going directly to and from infrared transceivers.

PCMCIA Cards

The Personal Computer Memory Card International Association (PCMCIA) designed a set of standards for adding memory and expanding a portable PC through the use of devices resembling thick credit cards. These cards are called PCMCIA cards. A ***PCMCIA card*** is installed in a PCMCIA slot on the side of the PC. These slots are used in place of expansion slots as the way to install additional devices. As with USB connections, many PCMCIA cards are hot swappable (can be swapped without powering off the computer).

***PCMCIA card** card designed by the Personal Computer Memory Card International Association (PCMCIA) to add memory or expand a portable PC. The PCMCIA card is often referred to as simply a "PCM" or "PC" card.*

All PCMCIA cards have the same rectangular (85.6 mm by 54 mm) shape, but they vary in thickness, **Figure 12-6.** Their thickness classifies the cards. There are three classifications of cards. The classifications are as follows:

- ✔ **Type I:** 3.3 mm thick. These cards are used primarily to add memory to the PC.
- ✔ **Type II:** 5.0 mm thick. These cards are usually used to add modems and network cards to the PC. The cards are equipped with either RJ-11 or RJ-45 connectors. The RJ connectors look like telephone jacks.
- ✔ **Type III:** 10.5 mm thick. These cards are designed to support hard drives or to support external CD, DVD, or tape drives.

There is a selection of slots to go with the cards. A Type I slot can hold one Type I card. Type II slots can hold one Type II card or two Type I cards. Type III slots can hold one Type III card or one Type I card and one Type II card. All of the smaller cards fit into larger slots on their own.

Type IV cards are in the works, but they have not been ratified by the PCMCIA consortium at this time. Type IV cards are expected to be 16 mm thick. They will be used for large-capacity hard drives.

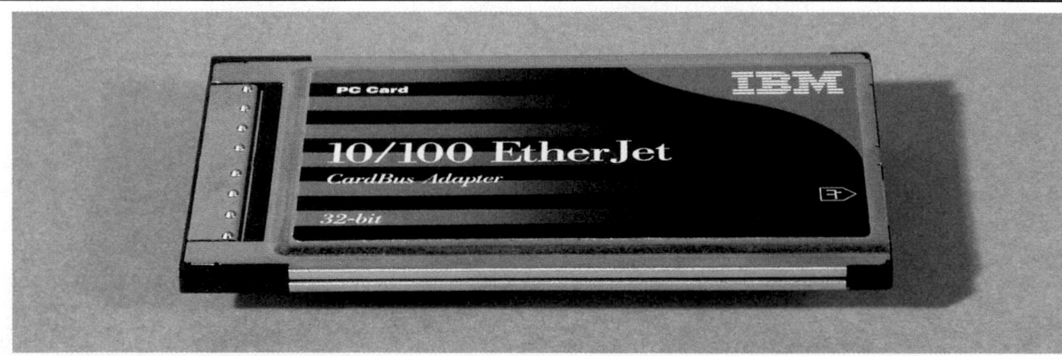

Figure 12-6. Typical Type II PCMCIA card. This card is used to connect a laptop PC to a network.

ExpressCards

The ***ExpressCard*** is rapidly replacing the PCMCIA card as the choice for laptop computers because it can achieve high data rates. Look at **Figure 12-7** to see an ExpressCard. ExpressCards can be used for modems, analog and digital television tuners, wireless network cards, exterior SATA connections, and to expand the PCIe bus to connect other devices.

ExpressCard
card that is used to add memory or expand a portable PC. It is designed to connect internally to either the USB 2.0 bus or the PCIe bus.

The card is available in two widths: 34 mm and 54 mm. Look at **Figure 12-8** to see what each width looks like. The exact choice of width is based on the type of device the card incorporates.

ExpressCards are designed to connect internally to either the USB 2.0 bus or the PCIe bus. When using the USB 2.0 bus, the data rate for the ExpressCard is 480 Mbps. When using the PCIe bus, the data rate is 2.5 Gbps. The bus type is automatically detected and configured by the software drivers. Visit the www.pcmcia.org Web site to learn more about the latest PCMCIA and ExpressCard standards.

There is also a legacy version of the ExpressCard that fits into a PCMCIA slot.

Special Function Keys

Portable PCs typically have special keyboards not found on the standard keyboard associated with desktop PCs. The keyboards are made very compact and also incorporate special function keys typically associated with laptop needs.

The special function keys typically are activated by pressing the [Fn] key in combination with other function keys identified in blue, **Figure 12-9.** You can see the [Fn] key in Figure 12-9A which is positioned on the left side of the keyboard and the function keys, Figure 12-9B, which are positioned on the right side of the keyboard. These function keys share the key space with the arrow keys. Other special function keys are located along the top or along the right side of the keyboard.

Figure 12-7.
This ExpressCard provides two FireWire ports. (Courtesy of Belkin International, Inc.)

Figure 12-8.
ExpressCards come in two widths: 34 mm and 54 mm.

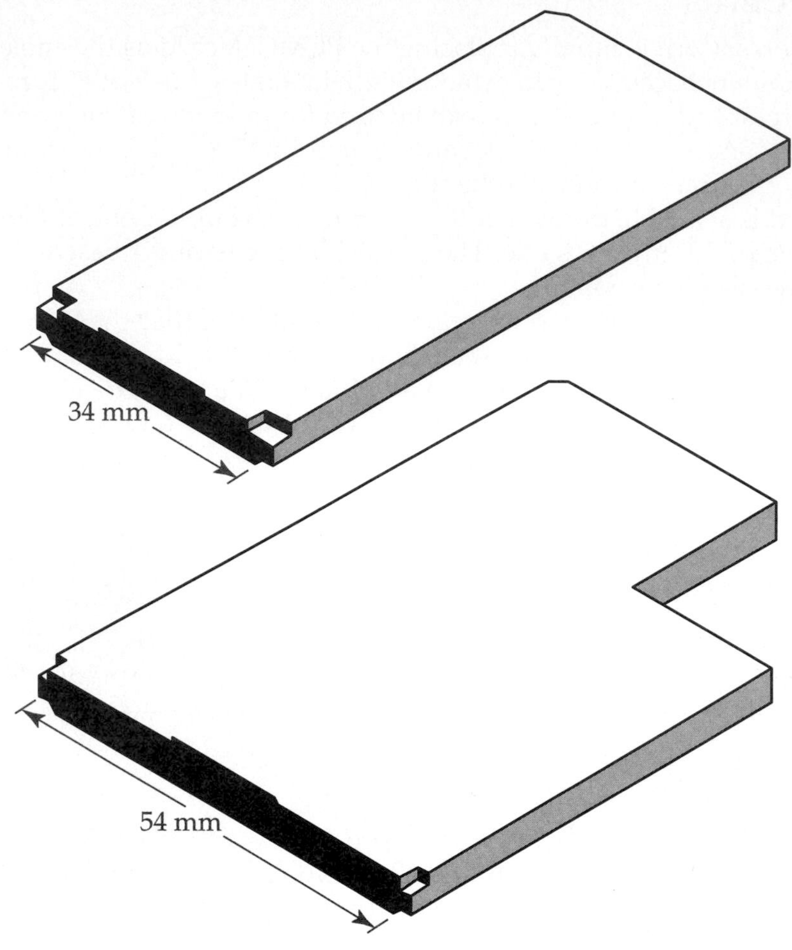

Figure 12-9.
To access special laptop functions, simultaneously press the [Fn] key and the desired function key.

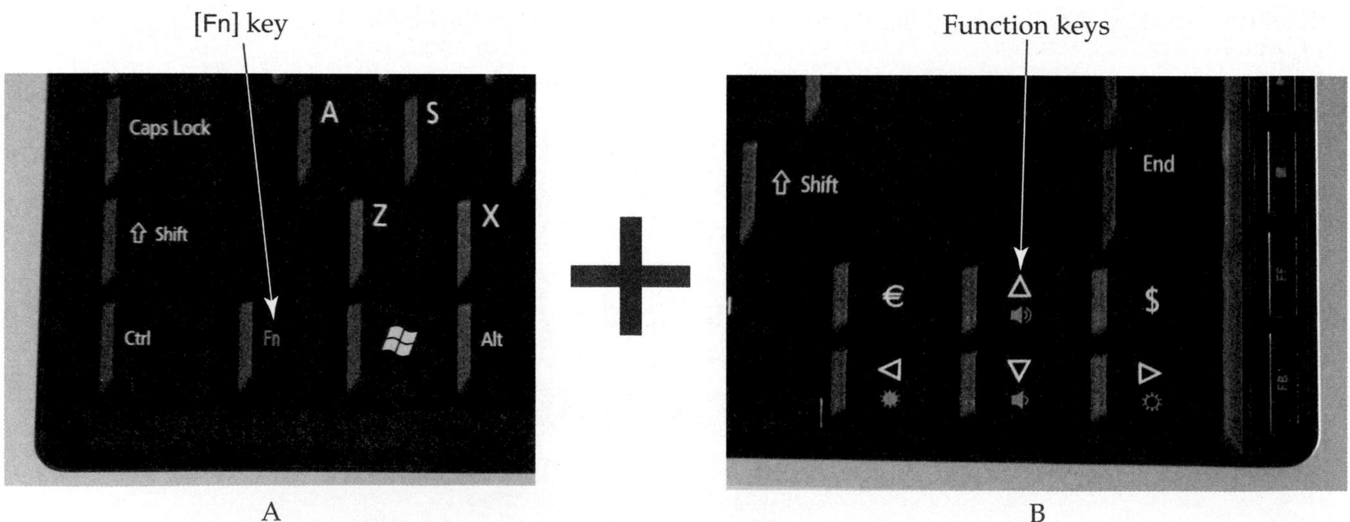

Many times a new laptop user will inadvertently hit a combination of keys which result in unexpected results while typing a word document. They may turn off the sound, put the laptop in sleep mode, change the brightness of the display, automatically connect or disconnect from the Internet, and more. The user may make the same mistake several times and cause the user to think that something is wrong with the laptop. At times, a new user will repeatedly make the same mistake and think they have a virus. They call tech support to resolve the problem, and if misdiagnosed, the laptop may be packaged and sent to a repair depot needlessly.

Power Management

Power management is a very important aspect of laptop computers. Configuring the power management incorrectly can reduce the battery power length of time considerably. The power management configuration reduces the amount of power used by the three major power consumption devices: display, CPU, and hard disk drive.

APM and ACPI

Automatic Power Management (APM) and Automatic Configuration and Power Interface (ACPI) are industry standards for automatically configuring power on portable devices. The difference is APM was first available in Windows 95 and was incorporated as a BIOS configuration option to conserve electrical power. The simple APM design simply powered down the computer after a predetermined amount of inactivity. It also included a suspend or sleep switch typically located at the front of the computer case. APM was enabled by default and could not be accessed directly by the operating system. APM is also known as *Advanced Power Management*. APM is no longer used.

ACPI replaced APM as a natural evolution in power management. It was first introduced in Windows NT and Windows 98 operating systems. APCI has many more advanced options not found in the original APM. ACPI is not limited to managing power consumed by the display and CPU. ACPI can manage the power of any hardware device added to a computer. For example, it can power down a device that is not being used after a short period of time, such as a modem, wireless card, or network card. It also includes features to awaken or bring devices automatically out of the power-down state when needed. For example, a network card in a sleep state can be wakened by network activity directed to that particular network card while ignoring all other network activity.

ACPI also provides a feature referred to as soft-off which allows the computer to be turned off by the software. Previous to this add-on feature, the computer had to be manually turned off with a switch. Some companies did design a proprietary soft-off switch before the ACPI standard. Another feature of ACPI is support for a switch that can be used to place the computer automatically in sleep mode. All the features associated with ACPI are controlled by the BIOS. The configuration is stored in CMOS. ACPI allows the operating system to directly control the power configuration features. Microsoft has incorporated energy configuration features in all their products.

Power management is not limited to portable devices. Desktop systems also have power management configuration management options to conserve electrical energy.

Windows Vista Power Management Options

Microsoft Vista power management options are based on preconfigured power plans, or power profiles. The power plans are a way to choose between long battery life and computer performance. They are located in **Start | Control Panel | Hardware and Sound | Power Options**.

Look at **Figure 12-10.** Notice that there are three power plans available in Windows Vista: Balanced, Power saver, and High performance. The *balanced power* plan equally emphasizes battery conservation and system performance. The *power saver* plan slows the performance of the CPU and lowers the backlighting of the LCD display. Both actions save considerable electrical energy. *High Performance* sacrifices battery life but allows for top computer performance. Best performance is often required for intense activities such as viewing movies, playing graphic-intense computer games, and editing photos.

Other power management features allow you to configure the power buttons and password protection. The settings for these features are located in **Start | Control Panel | Hardware and Sound | Power Options | System Settings**.

Look at **Figure 12-11.** Notice that you can select how the laptop will react when the power button or the sleep button is pressed or when the laptop lid is closed. The options for each are **Do nothing**, **Sleep**, **Hibernate**, and **Shut down**. The **Do nothing** and **Shut down** options are straightforward. They should need no further explanation, but **Sleep** and **Hibernate** do require some explanation.

The **Sleep** option saves all documents and folders that are in use at the time sleep is invoked. When the computer is awaked, the same open files automatically reappear on the desktop. Sleep mode has very little drain on laptop battery.

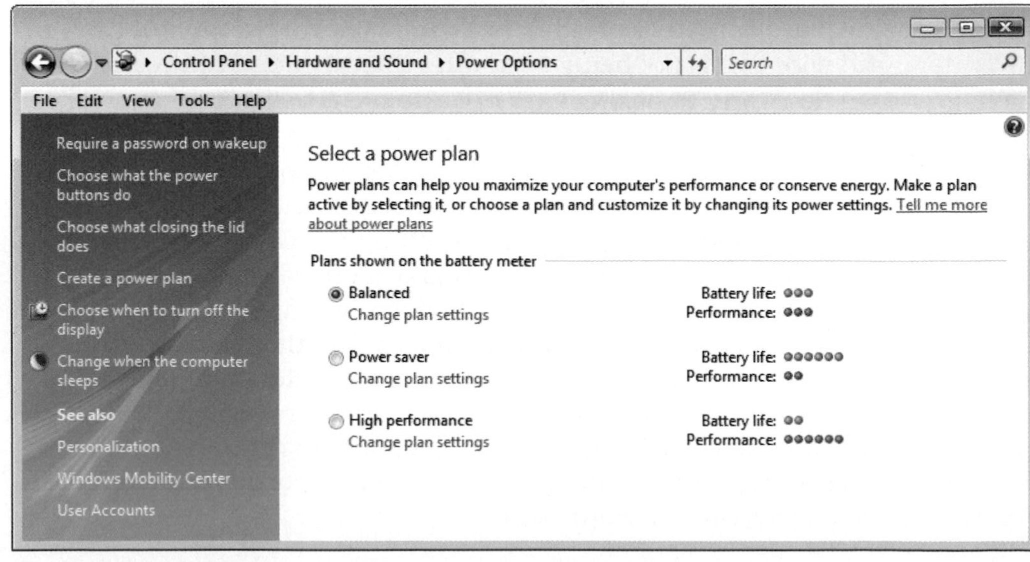

Figure 12-10. Windows Vista power plans are located in the **Power Options** dialog box.

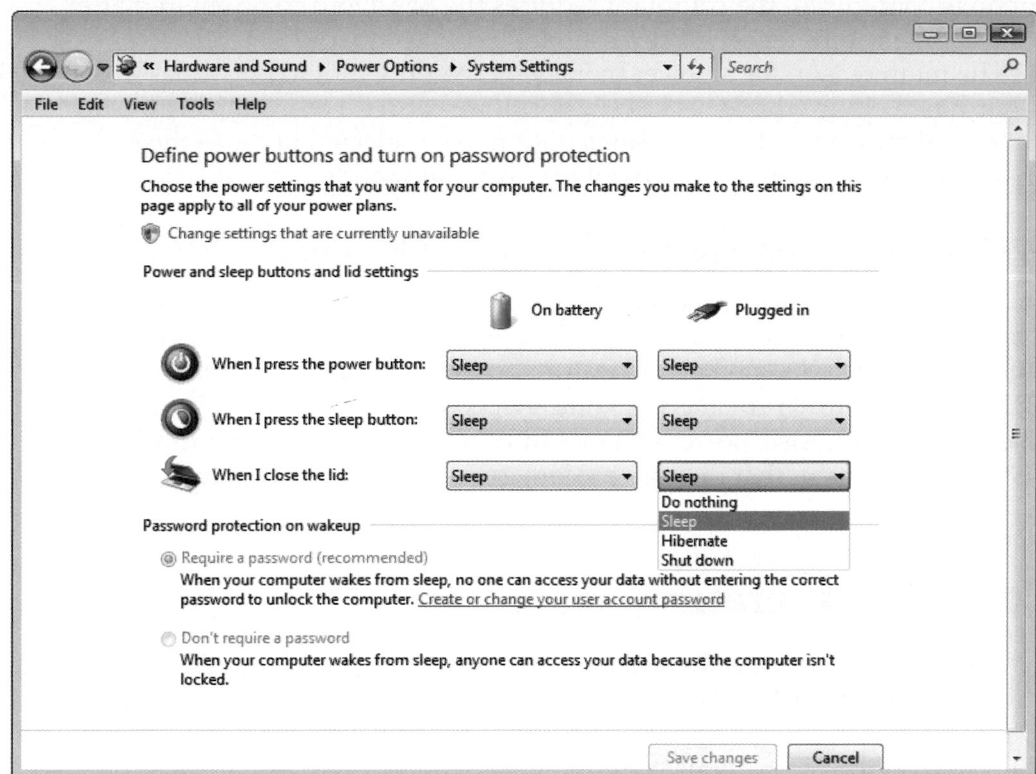

Figure 12-11. Windows Vista allows you to define your PC's power buttons and to enable password protection.

The **Hibernate** option saves your open files and current work to the hard disk drive, and when the PC is awaked, it reopens the files and current work. The hibernate mode uses less battery life than sleep mode. The main difference between sleep mode and hibernate mode is where the open files and current work are saved. Sleep saves the files and current work in RAM, and hibernate saves the files and current work to the hard disk drive. Hibernate mode takes longer to recover from than sleep mode because sleep mode stores the files in RAM. Open files and work can be lost when a laptop is placed in sleep mode and the power is disconnected, such as when removing the battery or during battery failure with no AC plugged in. In Figure 12-11, notice that each of the selections is correlated to when the laptop is supplied battery power or AC power.

Some computers have a hybrid sleep feature that saves working files to both RAM and the hard disk drive while in sleep mode. The computer still has fast recovery when awakened and also has protection against data loss due to lost power or battery failure. Hybrid sleep requires a BIOS that supports this feature.

Another Windows Vista power management feature is password protection. Password protection is provided as an option for scenarios such as when closing the lid of the laptop and leaving the area. Anyone could awaken the laptop from sleep mode by simply opening the lid of the laptop. The password option is used to ensure security against unauthorized access to the laptop. When the password option is configured, the computer requires the password to be entered after bringing the computer out of sleep mode.

The main reason for a power management option not to be available is a BIOS or hardware device that does not support that feature. For example, an older video card may now allow the **Sleep** option to be selected because the software drivers for the old video card do not support sleep mode.

Windows XP Power Management Options

Windows XP power management options are quite a different layout when compared to those in Windows Vista, **Figure 12-12.** However, notice that Windows XP includes a hibernate feature (under the **Hibernate** tab). The Windows XP hibernate feature provides the same effect on the system as the Windows Vista hibernate feature. Also, power schemes in Windows XP are similar to Windows Vista power plans in that they are preconfigured power configurations.

Portable Operating Systems

When installing older Windows operating systems, such as Windows 98 and Windows Me, the technician would make a choice between several installation options that were related to the size of the operating system being installed. The usual options were **Typical**, **Portable**, **Compact**, and **Custom**. These options were presented because the older portable devices were not nearly as powerful as desktop PCs, and in many cases, did not have sufficient hard disk drive space or sufficient RAM to run a full version of the operating system with all options installed. The **Portable** option was used for laptop computers and similar devices.

When installing operating systems such as Windows Vista and Windows XP, there are generally only two installation options—one of which is a custom installation. The custom option allows you to choose which features you want to install on the computer. For example, you could choose the Windows Mobility Center feature because it is designed specifically for use with a laptop.

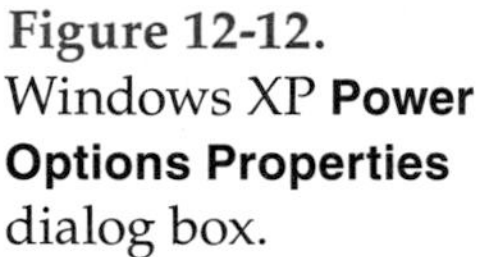

Figure 12-12.
Windows XP **Power Options Properties** dialog box.

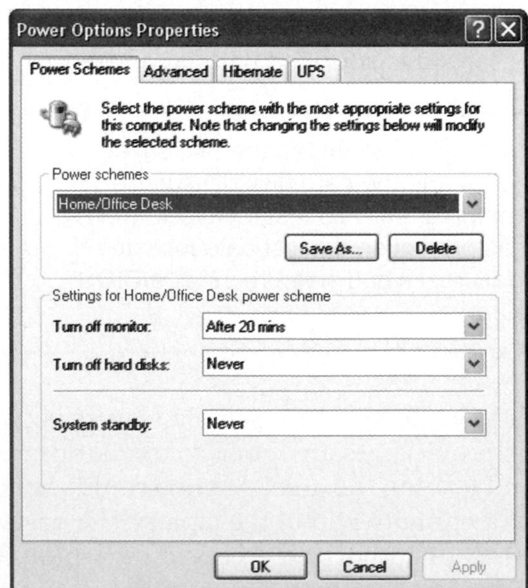

Windows Vista Mobility Center

The Windows Mobility Center was introduced with Windows Vista. This feature contains a collection of the most common utilities and configurations used by laptops. **Figure 12-13** shows a typical **Windows Vista Mobility Center** dialog box. As you can see, the most commonly used configurations are readily available, such as Volume, Battery Status, and Wireless Network. See **Figure 12-14** for a description of each feature.

The Brightness Control configuration (not shown) controls the brightness of the LCD monitor. In the screen capture of Figure 12-13, you do not see the Brightness Control. This is because the screen capture was taken on an Acer laptop that has modified the Mobility Center by eliminating the brightness control and adding Acer Sharing Service (Shared Folder) and the Acer User Guide Drivers and Utilities (Software Page). For this particular Acer laptop, a special function key is used to control the brightness from the keyboard.

Hardware manufacturers often modify Windows dialog boxes to match their own hardware needs.

Windows CE

For personal digital assistants and palmtops, Microsoft has an operating system called ***Windows CE***. The "CE" is thought to stand for Compact Edition. Space is limited on palmtops and very limited on personal digital assistants. The Windows CE operating system has been modified to meet the needs of the smaller units. The Windows CE program is similar in appearance to any of the Windows operating systems. It has a control panel and uses the registry system

Windows CE version of Windows designed for less powerful devices, such as PDAs or smart appliances.

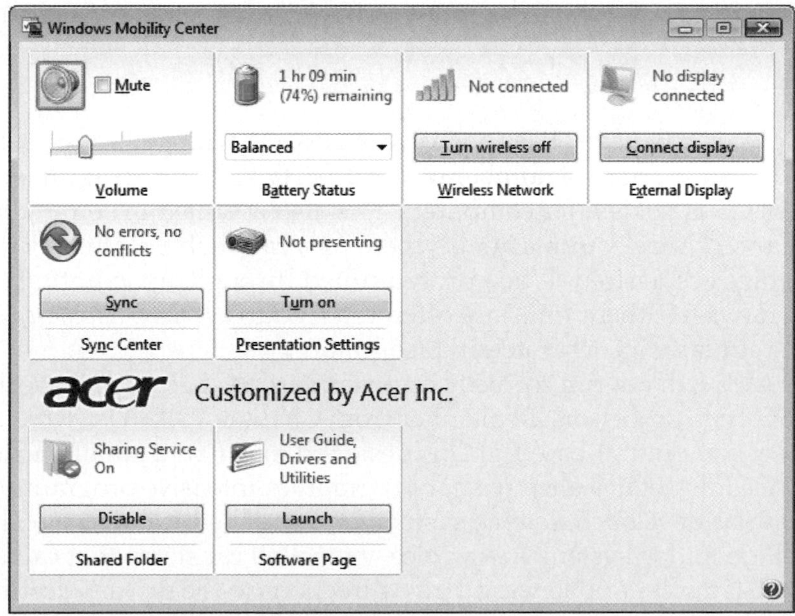

Figure 12-13. The Windows Mobility Center allows a user to access laptop-related utilities and configuration settings.

Figure 12-14. Common Windows Mobility Center features and their description.

Windows Mobility Center Feature	Description
Battery Status	Allows you to modify the battery usage by selecting a different power plan for the laptop.
Brightness	Controls the brightness of the LCD monitor.
External Display	Used to automatically set up a second or third display. An external display is often connected to a laptop PC via a cable or docking station.
Presentation Settings	Allows you to preconfigure presentation settings, such as the volume or which projector to use if more than one projector is typically connected. The projector can be automatically detected through a wizard, or you can enter the URL or a UNC address of the projector. After the presentation settings are configured, you can simply access the present configuration and start your presentation immediately without a further configuration.
Sync Center	Maintains the very latest version of a file or collection of files that are commonly transferred between the laptop and another device. This feature is only available in Windows Vista Business and Windows Vista Ultimate editions. Sync Center is short for Synchronize Center.
Volume	Allows you to adjust the portable laptop speaker volume.
Wireless Network	Displays the status of a wireless network connection. Also includes an option to enable and disable the wireless network adapter.

to control devices and users. Files and directories are arranged in the same way. Windows CE also supports a number of third-party software programs.

Windows CE is not just for computers. It is also installed in some stereos, telephones, and other electronic items where programmable features such as memory storage are desired. When programmed through an operating system such as Windows CE, these units are often referred to as *smart appliances*. These systems are regularly incorporated into common toys.

Windows CE will not run correctly on a standard PC because it is designed to work on RISC-type processors. Remember from Chapter 4—CPU, a RISC (reduced instruction set computing)-based CPU is designed to run on a smaller instruction set. Windows CE is not designed to support graphics-intensive programs.

Microsoft has developed a stereo system for cars called AutoPC, which uses the Windows CE operating system. It is a voice-controlled car stereo that can check and read e-mail, dial a cellular phone, and give directions to the driver's destination.

Personal Digital Assistants

A ***Personal digital assistant (PDA)*** is not as powerful as a laptop or palmtop computer. They are limited in memory space because of their overall physical size, but they do perform many valuable services. They can be used to retain to-do lists and store personal data such as phone numbers, addresses, and company information. They connect to the Internet to display text-only versions of Web pages. They can check and transmit e-mail.

personal digital assistant (PDA) portable computer comparable in size to a palmtop. Has a limited amount of memory and is used mostly to retain to-do lists, store personal data, connect to the Internet, and send and receive e-mail.

With the innovation of application service providers, they function more like the palmtop. An ***application service provider (ASP)*** can provide software applications such as word processing packages, spreadsheets, databases, or even games. However, the operational concept is to download the application from a provider as needed rather than to permanently load it on the machine. By using an ASP, valuable storage space is saved on the PDA or palmtop. Also, by using an ASP, the latest version of the software is always available.

application service provider (ASP) provides software applications to a personal digital assistant (PDA) or palmtop by downloading the application from a provider as needed.

One important difference between a PDA and a palmtop is that a PDA does not have a keyboard— a palmtop does. Without a keyboard, the PDA relies on a stylus for inputting data. A *stylus* is a small pen-like object used to write on a touch screen. Software like Microsoft Transcriber converts cursive or printed handwriting entered by the stylus into data recognized by the operating system. Some PDA systems use a small, onscreen keyboard for entering data.

A second big difference between the PDA and a palmtop is that a PDA does not have a hard drive. Due to the lack of a hard drive, memory modules are often used to retain data and serve to function as a PDA hard drive. All data is stored in RAM and held there by battery backup. The RAM is proportioned by software into two sections. One section is used as traditional RAM that is erased when power is removed. The other section is used for storage similar to a hard drive. This difference may disappear as hard drives are developed that have no moving parts— the entire hard drive storage consists of memory technology similar to RAM.

The last major difference between a palmtop and a PDA is the screen. Palmtops usually have a high-resolution color screen while PDAs usually have monochrome screens with fairly low resolution.

A PDA can come with many accessories, such as a docking station that has a built-in charger. A keyboard can also be purchased as an input device. An automobile charger is always a nice accessory too. A charge on a PDA can last for two weeks or more, but it is always convenient to have a charger when needed.

PDAs can upload to full-size PCs using an infrared portal, a telephone modem, a USB port, or a network connection. The PDA can also be synchronized with a CD-ROM on a desktop model enabling it to download programs and files.

Bluetooth Standard

Bluetooth royalty-free standard developed for short-range radio links between portable computers, mobile phones, and other portable devices so that major manufacturers could develop compatible equipment.

Bluetooth is the name of a standard developed for short-range radio links between portable computers, mobile phones, and other portable devices. The standard was created by many of the world's leaders in mobile computing equipment. It is a royalty-free standard enabling major manufacturers to develop compatible equipment. PCs, PDAs, and mobile phones using the Bluetooth standard are able to communicate with one another. A small transmitter and receiver are incorporated into the devices. They transmit data and commands on a 2.45 GHz radio band. Bluetooth standards support data transfer speeds as high as 1 Mbps. Actual speed, however, is 700 kbps to 800 kbps. The use of the standard allows for many innovative applications. Some examples include the following:

- ✔ **Office:** You arrive at your office or worksite and your PDA automatically downloads files from home or downloads entries that you may have made while on the road. As you inspect an industrial location, you download information about each piece of equipment as you pass by. Items such as total running hours, number of items manufactured, and next and scheduled downtimes are recorded to be later downloaded at the office.
- ✔ **Home:** When you arrive at home, you can automatically open the garage door, unlock the door, turn on outside lights, turn off the security system, and turn on the furnace, stereo, or TV. If an item operates on electricity, it can be turned on, off, or have its settings modified as long as the item is Bluetooth compliant.
- ✔ **Travel:** You arrive at an airport and automatically check in using your PDA rather than standing in a long line. Arriving at your destination, you automatically notify the car rental and have your car sent to you. If you are a tourist on vacation, you can automatically download maps or directions to your PDA. You can automatically check in or check out of a hotel. You can also monitor your billing at the hotel or resort. You can check on a restaurant, download its menu, and check on the waiting time for the next available table.

ad-hoc network
a wireless network formed between two or more wireless devices such as a full-size PC and a notebook PC.

infrastructure network
a wireless network that contains a wireless access point.

wireless access point
a device that is used to support communications between wireless devices and a hard-wired network system.

bridge
a device that is used to connect two dissimilar networks.

Wireless Data Transfer

A wireless connection is commonly used to connect a notebook PC to a full-size PC or to join a small network. A wireless connection can be made using radio waves or by using infrared light. A much more detailed description of wireless networking is covered later in this textbook. This section covers terminology related to wireless data transfer.

Ad-Hoc Network

When a wireless network is formed between two or more wireless devices such as a workstation and a notebook, it is called an ***ad-hoc network.*** You can think of an ad-hoc network connection, **Figure 12-15,** as a direct cable connection that uses radio waves as the connection media rather than cable.

Wireless Infrastructure Network

Another classification of wireless connection is called ***infrastructure network.*** An infrastructure network differs from an ad-hoc network in that it contains a wireless access point (WAP). A ***wireless access point*** is a device that supports communications between wireless devices and a hard-wired network system, **Figure 12-16.** A wireless access point is often referred to as a bridge. A ***bridge*** is a device that is used to connect two dissimilar networks. In this example, the network access point is bridging the connection between the hard-wired network and the wireless network.

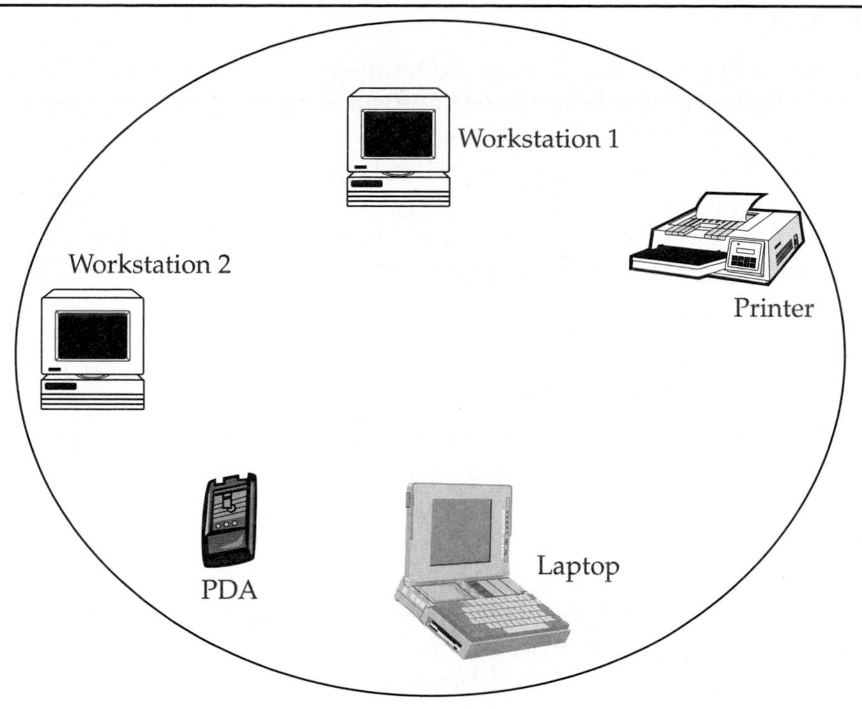

Figure 12-15.
Some devices are connected together by radio waves in an ad-hoc network. An ad-hoc network can consist of 2 to 64 wireless devices.

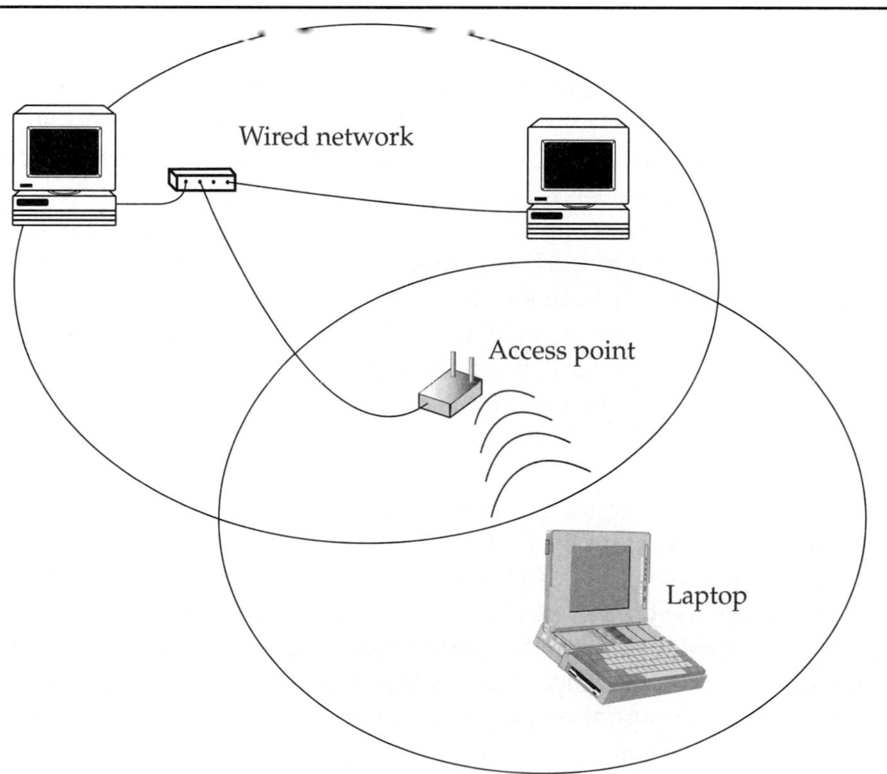

Figure 12-16.
A wireless access point acts as a bridge between the wireless device and the wired network system.

Radio Waves

Radio waves are used to deliver or exchange information all over the world. To prevent radio waves from interfering with each other, radio frequencies are regulated by the FCC. The FCC assigns specific radio frequencies to various types of equipment. For example, toy remote control cars are typically 27 MHz and 40 MHz. When you tune your car radio, you are actually selecting a radio frequency. When you select a radio station such as 104.5 FM, you are tuning the radio receiver to a transmitted carrier wave of 104.5 MHz. The carrier wave is a set frequency, which is used to carry the information from the transmitter to the receiver.

Radio Signal Interference

Radio signal interference is a radio wave transmission that corrupts a desired radio wave signal. Some common sources of wireless computer communication devices are wireless telephones, medical equipment, microwave ovens, and cell phones. While all electronic equipment generates some interference, these specific devices share the same radio wave frequencies that wireless network cards use, approximately 2.48 GHz. Other electrical devices and appliances containing electrical motors can also cause problems.

A wireless connection rated at 11 Mbps, may actually be only 5 Mbps or as low as 1 Mbps or less. Another major factor that affects wireless communication is the distance between the source and destination. As the distance between the source and destination increases, the throughput decreases. This is because the greater the distance of the transmitted radio signal, the weaker the signal becomes. As the signal becomes weaker, it is more susceptible to radio interference.

On average, the maximum advertised distance for IEEE 802.11b wireless devices is approximately 250 meters indoors and 450 meters outdoors. There is no definitive maximum distance because of the variables that affect radio waves. Realistic distances for wireless transmissions will be much shorter distances than advertised because wireless systems rarely operate in ideal environments.

Another factor that affects radio signals is physical objects in the radio wave area. Objects placed directly between the source and destination weaken the radio signal. The most common object that affects radio signals are building partitions, file cabinets, furniture, fireplaces, appliances, and similar objects. The density and material these objects are made from affect the signal. For example, a wall constructed of concrete block will weaken a signal more than a wall constructed of sheet rock. A metallic partition commonly used to create an office cubicle will block a radio signal. A wireless connection to exchange data directly between a notebook computer and a PC should not be affected by building structures. If you are using a notebook on a patio to access an Internet connection through a PC inside the home, the distance and building materials will affect the signal to a great extent. Windows XP and wireless device manufacturers have utilities that allow you to monitor the wireless network. **Figure 12-17** shows the strength of the wireless signal displayed as a bar graph. The speed of the data is also displayed as 11.0 Mbps.

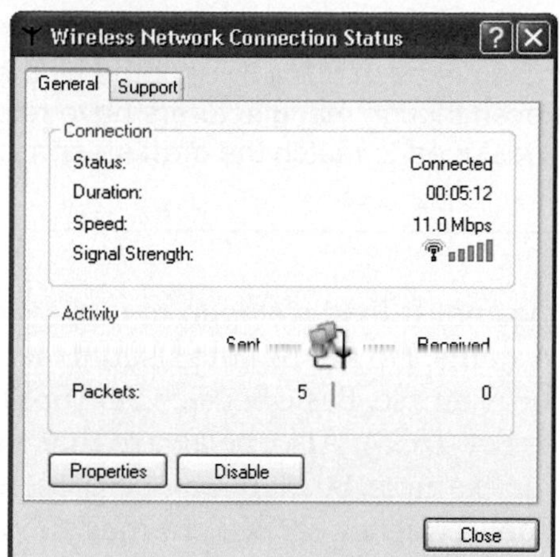

Figure 12-17. The **Wireless Network Connection Status** dialog box displays the strength of the signal and the speed of the transmission.

Wireless Standards

The IEEE organization has developed and released several standards that deal specifically with wireless communication. The standards serve as guidelines for how the equipment should function. Remember that standards are developed so that equipment developed by different manufacturers can communicate with each other. The wireless standards, 802.11, 802.11a, 802.11b, 802.11g, and 802.11n recommend characteristics and specifications for wireless networking. Some of the items specified are frequencies, maximum bandwidth, and communication procedures.

The original 802.11 standard was first developed to standardize wireless devices that would transmit data at 1 Mbps and 2 Mbps. The frequency, or radio band, assigned to 802.11 by the FCC is 2.48 GHz. It was a very short time before it had to be modified to provide for higher data rates and was soon followed by 802.11a and 802.11b. Although both standards were released at the same time, 802.11b became the de facto standard for small office and home wireless devices.

The 802.11a standard specifies a frequency of 5 GHz and a maximum bandwidth of 54 Mbps. While 802.11a has a much higher bandwidth than 802.11b, it has less range, approximately half that of 802.11b. It is not backward compatible with 802.11.

The 802.11b standard allows for data transmission rates at 1 Mbps, 2 Mbps, 5.5 Mbps, and 11 Mbps. The 11 Mbps throughput, however, is only achieved at optimal conditions. Optimal conditions are short distances with no radio interference and only two devices. As distance increases between two wireless devices, the bandwidth drops drastically. Building materials and furnishings can also interfere with radio wave transmissions. Other devices such as portable phones, microwave ovens, wireless industrial communication control devices, and wireless medical devices assigned to the same frequency, can generate radio interference. 802.11b is backward compatible with 802.11 and is assigned the same 2.48 GHz frequency.

The 802.11g standard was the next to be developed. It operates at the 2.4 GHz frequency with a maximum transmission rate of 54 Mbps. It is compatible with 802.11a and 802.11b.

The 802.11n standard is referred to as Multiple In Multiple Out (MIMO) device. As the name MIMO implies, the device is capable of multiple input and output transmissions at the same time. 802.11n is proposed to have a data transfer rate as high as 248 Mbps, approximately five times faster than 802.11g. The high data rate meets the data throughput requirements for HDTV video streaming. The 802.11n standard is backward compatible with 802.11a, 802.11b, and 802.11g.

At the time of this writing, IEEE 802.11n is in draft form and has not been officially adopted by the IEEE organization, even though manufacturers have released products designed to match the draft standard of 802.11n.

Wireless technology has not fully developed to one set of de facto terminology to describe the wireless systems. Do not be surprised to see that terms vary among manufacturers. For example, Basic Service Set (BSS) may be listed as Independent Basic Service Set (IBSS). Also, be aware that the specified frequency of a standard will vary. For example, 802.11b may be presented as 2.5 GHz, 2.4 GHz, and 2.45 GHz. The frequency for 802.11a may be presented as 5 GHz, 5.1 GHz, and 5.8 GHz. In actuality, the frequency is not one set frequency, but a range of frequencies. The following table lists the assigned frequency ranges.

Wireless Standard	Frequency Range
IEEE 802.11	2.4 GHz–2.4835 GHz
IEEE 802.11a	5.15 GHz–5.850 GHz
IEEE 802.11b	2.4 GHz–2.4835 GHz
IEEE 802.11g	2.4 GHz–2.4835 GHz
IEEE 802.11n	2.4 GHz–2.4835 GHz
	5.15 GHz–5.850 GHz

In general, wireless technologies are classified as 2.4 and 5 GHz. However, the actual ranges are almost never used in product identification.

Wireless Devices

Most laptops come with a wireless device incorporated into the motherboard or as an add-on. The exact type of wireless technology will vary. When the wireless device is not already incorporated into a laptop, a PCMCIA, an ExpressCard, or a USB device is used to provide wireless network support. **Figure 12-18** shows a PCMCIA card which is somewhat similar in design to an ExpressCard. The ExpressCard in **Figure 12-19** supports the 802.11n wireless standard.

Security

Security is a high priority at all times, especially when dealing with portable PCs. The portable PC may contain important company information such as customer lists, contract information, proposed business ventures, and other sensitive communications. Information for connecting to the company network may also be contained on the hard drive. Security is even more important for portable PCs issued to people in police departments, the FBI, or the CIA. As you can see, laptop security is a vital issue.

Figure 12-18. A PCMCIA wireless network card.

Figure 12-19. An ExpressCard wireless network card. (D-Link)

Encryption

Encryption is used as part of the security system. ***Encryption*** is a way to code data that cannot be converted back to meaningful words without an encryption key. The encryption key is not a physical device but rather a mathematical formula for substituting values in strings of data. For example, a text-based code could be developed based on the number five. The data in a file would be stored with every letter changed to one that is four places further in the alphabet. See **Figure 12-20.**

encryption
method of encoding data that must be converted back to meaningful words by using an encryption key. The encryption key is a mathematical formula for substituting values in strings of data.

The message is rewritten in code and then stored. To read the message, you would need the code. This is a simple example. A true encryption code is more complex.

Sample message:

THIS IS THE TIME FOR ALL GOOD MEN…

Change the position of all letters by four positions in the alphabet.

A B C D E F G H I J K L M N O P Q R S T U V W X Y Z
E F G H I J K L M N O P Q R S T U V W X Y Z A B C D

Coded message:

XLMW MW XLI XMQI JSV EPP KSSH QIR…

Figure 12-20. Very simple encryption code.

NTFS versus FAT

The NT kernel that comes with Windows NT, Windows 2000, and Windows XP provides many security features needed for this security. It is very difficult to hack into an NT station as compared to some other home operating systems. Security was an important design issue for the NT system.

A typical security system using FAT16 or FAT32 allows for only two types of file access when shared: full access and read only. These options are set when a file or directory is shared. NTFS4.0 and NTFS5.0 allow more choices when file and directory security are set up. There are many options to choose from when a file share is created. These options are referred to as permissions.

For example, a Windows 9x system using FAT16 or FAT32 can only set file access options to either full access, read only, or no access. With full access capabilities, another user can do anything to the file that the file originator can do. The user can delete the file completely, copy the file, or create a new file. When the NTFS system is used, access to the shared file can be controlled through more precise options. These options include read only, modify, read and execute, write, and list files. The people who have the right to modify or delete the file can be tightly controlled.

A FAT system can be set up with similar file restrictions used for NTFS when running the NT operating system. However, the file restrictions are lost when the files are transferred to another directory or operating system.

The strongest security feature for NTFS is its encryption capabilities. NTFS allows for file encryption. FAT does not. This means that a low-level disk editing utility can be used to access the contents of a hard drive formatted with FAT. NTFS system files are protected.

Figure 12-21 shows a text file that was created and saved to the hard drive of a FAT system and viewed through the Norton Disk Editor. The Norton Disk Editor program is used to inspect the disk storage system and reveal the contents of the clusters byte by byte. In Figure 12-21, you can see the contents of a file located at cluster 291,629. The Norton Disk Editor reveals the contents as ASCII code on the right side of the screen and as hexadecimal codes on the left side.

Notice the hexadecimal number 73 in the center field of hexadecimal numbers. The number 73 is equal to the ASCII character code for the letter *s*. If you count the hexadecimal position locations, you can see that the hexadecimal code 73 occurs at the fourth, seventh, and eleventh position in the line of hexadecimal characters. These three locations correspond to the location of the ASCII text for the letter *s* on the right.

With NTFS, you could not view the file system this way. NTFS has encryption capabilities built into the system. The files created by the user can be saved as encrypted files that would have no meaning to the person opening them in Norton Disk Editor.

Figure 12-21.
An unencrypted text file viewed through a disk editor. The ASCII code can be read and translated.

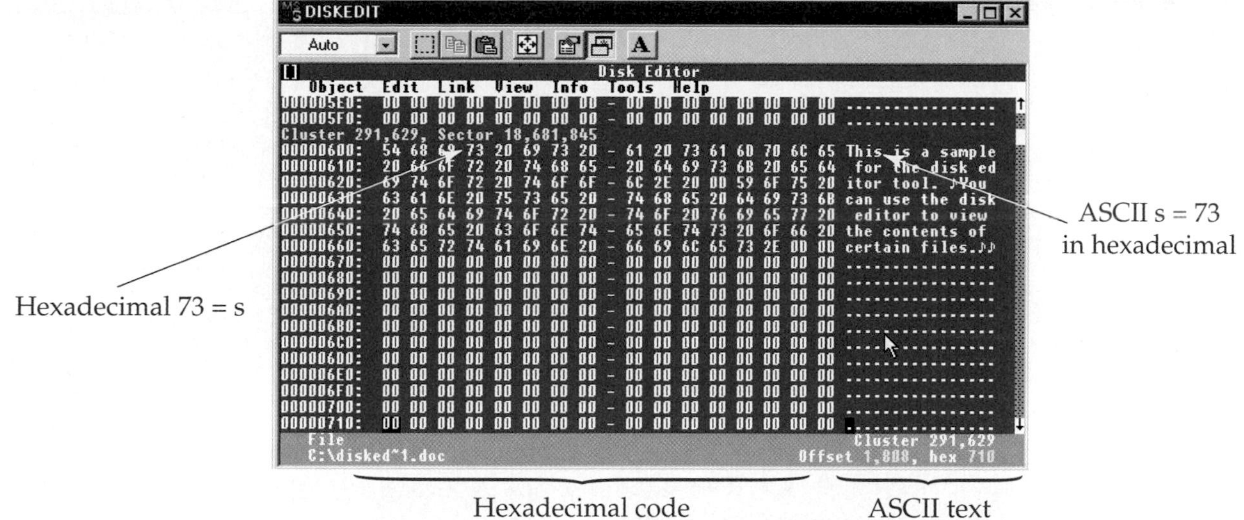

There are many third-party vendors that have encryption software for FAT systems. The best programs hide and/or encrypt files using the registry system. The ones that are not difficult to hack leave a trail in the autoexec.bat file. They are easily bypassed. The NTFS system comes with its own standard encryption software.

Another feature of NTFS that makes it more suitable than FAT for portable PCs is NTFS uses smaller cluster sizes when formatting the drive. Portable systems generally have less storage space available than full-size PCs because of their physically smaller hard drives, **Figure 12-22.** The smaller NTFS cluster sizes result in less wasted space on a hard drive system, making it the preferred storage file system for portable PCs.

Smart Cards and Biometrics

Use of a smart card is another clever way to protect your laptop. A ***smart card*** is identical in size and feel to a credit card. Smart cards store information on a chip located within the body of the card. These chips can hold a variety of information. They can be used commercially for retail or vending operation. They can be used with pay phones or for gaming. With portable computers, they work very well for security. A smart card setup can be used to allow you to access the laptop (or full-size) PC. Without the card, the computer cannot be accessed. The smart card works in conjunction with a smart card reader, which is placed in the PC. The typical smart card connects through a standard RS-232 connection or a Type II PCMCIA card slot. The smart card is supported by all the latest Microsoft operating systems and by many other operating systems.

smart card
credit card-like device with a chip embedded in the plastic. The chip allows the card to be used for a variety of purposes.

Figure 12-22.
The form factor of a laptop hard disk drive is much smaller than a desktop PC hard disk drive.

biometrics
the science of using the unique physical features of a person to confirm their identity for authentication purposes.

Biometrics is the science of using the unique physical features of a person to confirm their identity for authentication purposes. For example, a person can use their fingerprint or eye color patterns to log on to a computer system. **Figure 12-23** shows an IBM ThinkPad laptop with a built-in biometric device. The biometric device is a fingerprint reader that is used to verify the identity of the user at logon.

Figure 12-23.
This IBM ThinkPad computer has a fingerprint reader that is used to verify the identity of the user at logon. (International Business Machines Corporation)

Wireless Security

Wireless networks have an inherent security problem because the communications media they use is radio waves. All wireless devices, however, are capable of using wired equivalent privacy (WEP), which is an encryption technique used for wireless transmissions. WEP uses 64-bit and 128-bit encryption keys to encode and decode messages. Wireless devices are assigned a unique coding key that encrypts and decrypts messages. Anyone without the unique encryption key can still receive or send messages, but they will not be able to decode them.

Windows Vista increased wireless security by adding WPA and WPA2 security for wireless networks. WPA was developed jointly by the Wi-Fi Alliance and IEEE organizations. WPA is a more advanced security application than WEP. It provides a better authentication that WEP. WPA2 is the second release of WPA and provides even better security that WPA. A wireless adapter must be designed to support the later versions of WPA and WPA2; otherwise, WEP will be the only security option available when configuring the device. Most older wireless devices can only support WEP. Network security will be presented in more depth later in the textbook.

Another common practice is to encrypt the files located on the wireless devices. The Windows NTFS encrypted file system (EFS) is typically used to encrypt files located on the devices such as laptop computers.

Exchanging Data with Full-Size PCs

Laptops and other portable devices exchange data with full-size PCs for a variety of reasons. One very common reason is to exchange information between home and work computers. For example, when someone brings work home from the office or from a road trip or takes work into the office from home or from a road trip.

Direct connection between a PC and a laptop can be accomplished with a serial null modem cable, parallel null modem cable (also known as a *parallel link interlink cable*), USB link cable, crossover network cable, infrared ports, and wireless connection.

Figure 12-24 shows how a null modem cable is wired. Both serial and parallel null modem cables are difficult to find today. The most common methods used to exchange data are USB link cable, wireless, or a small network system using a hub and two network cables.

The USB link cable is a special USB cable with matching connectors on each end. The center typically contains an integrated chip which allows the two devices to exchange data. A regular USB cable extension will not allow the direct exchange of data.

Wireless is fine for exchanging small amounts of data, but for large volumes of data, a USB cable works better. Wireless often suffers from radio interference, and Bluetooth devices have a very limited data rate at this time.

The best way to exchange large volumes of data is to create a small network using a network hub or switch. Speeds in the range of 100 Mbps to 1 Gbps can be nearly achieved in a small network system. Networks systems such as this will be presented in later chapters that cover networking. Look at **Figure 12-25** for a quick comparison of direct data exchange methods.

Figure 12-24. A null modem cable is designed by switching the transmit and receive connections on one end of the cable. This allows data from the transmit connection on one computer to be sent to the receive connection on the other computer.

Pin	Pin
2	3
3	2
7	7

DB-25 connection

Pin	Pin
3	2
2	3
5	5

DB-9 connection

3-wire serial null modem cable pinout connections

Pin	Pin
2	15
15	2
3	13
13	3
4	12
12	4
5	10
10	5
6	11
11	6
25	25

11-wire parallel null modem cable pinout connections

Figure 12-25. Comparison of direct data exchange methods.

Media	Theoretical Data Rate	Comments
Infrared	115 kbps– 4 Mbps	Uses a direct line of sight but is immune to radio and magnetic interference.
Network Cable	10 Mbps–1 Gbps	Excellent for large volumes of data exchange.
Parallel null modem	500 kbps–2 MBps	Rate too low to be used today.
Serial null modem	115 kbps	Rate too low to be used today.
USB link cable	480 Mbps	Excellent for high volumes of data exchange.
Wireless (Includes Bluetooth)	700 kbps–254 Mbps	Wireless devices vary greatly because of all the various standards. They are not immune to radio interference.

Direct Connection

In Windows XP you can create a direct connection using the New Connection Wizard located at **Start | All Programs | Accessories | Communications**. Look at **Figure 12-26.** As you can see, in the New Connection Wizard, the fourth option is **Setup an advanced connection**. This option allows you to connect two computers using a serial, parallel, or infrared port. To see a detailed information guide on how to configure a direct connection using Windows XP Home Edition, use the following link: http://support.microsoft.com/kb/814981. If this link is no longer available, conduct an Internet search using the keywords "Microsoft direct cable connection."

Since almost all modern laptops have built-in wireless technology, Windows Vista no longer has a direct connection option. To configure a direct connection in Windows Vista, you need to use either an ad-hoc wireless connection or a small network connection using wireless or cable media. You can still connect two Windows Vista computers using a USB link cable because the USB link cable comes with required support software on disc.

Look at **Figure 12-27** to see the **Set up a connection or network** dialog box. This dialog box is accessed by opening the **Start** menu, right-clicking **Network** and selecting **Properties** from the shortcut menu, and then clicking **Set up a connection or network**. As you can see, there is no option for a direct cable connection as in Windows XP and earlier operating systems. Wireless and networking are the preferred methods of direct data exchange in Windows Vista.

Briefcase

Briefcase is a Microsoft program that is designed to exchange programs between laptops and full-size PCs while keeping the most recent version on both devices. For example, you want to take several files to work on while away from the office. You can simply copy the file to a removable storage device or use Briefcase. Many people have difficulty when copying files to/from floppies and PCs. They become confused as to which is the latest edition of a file. Briefcase determines which file has the latest changes, and it issues warnings about updating a file before action is taken.

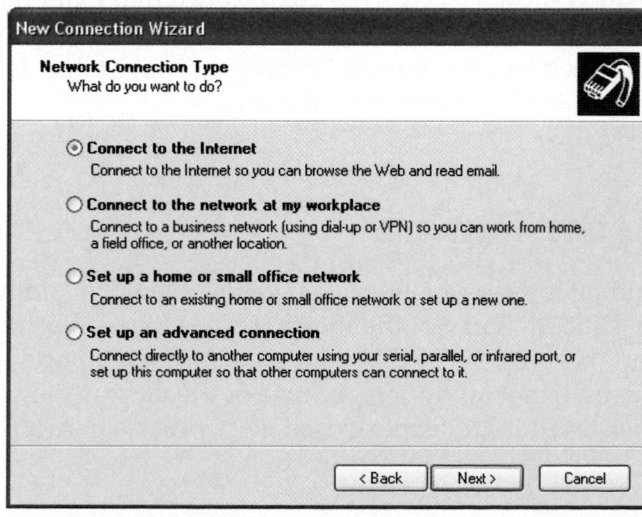

Figure 12-26. The Windows XP New Connection Wizard can be used to set up a direct connection.

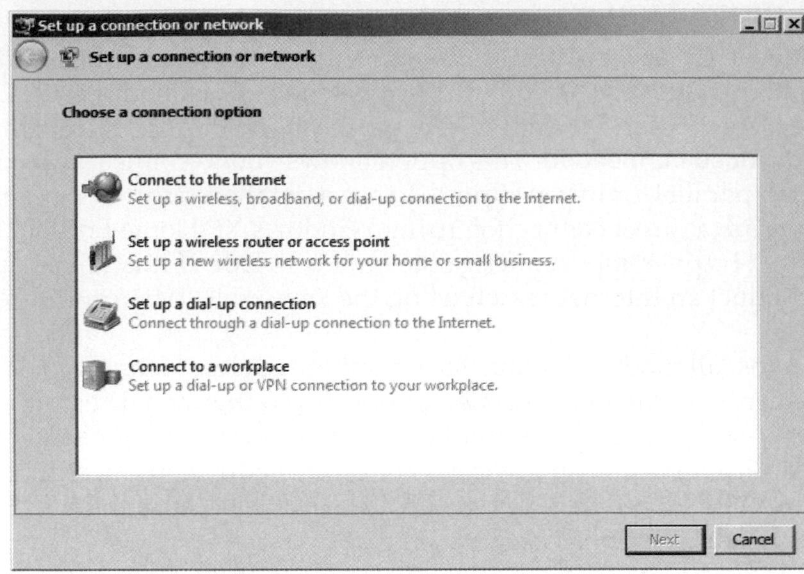

Figure 12-27. Windows Vista does not have an option to set up a direct connect. Direct connections in Windows Vista are set up through ad-hoc wireless connections or wired connections using a network hub.

Briefcase can be copied across a network or loaded to a floppy or USB Flash drive. To use Briefcase, simply copy the files you wish to work on to the **Briefcase** icon on the desktop. You can simply drag each file onto the **Briefcase** icon. Then drag the briefcase icon onto a floppy disk or USB Flash drive. Take the PC home, complete your work, and then reverse the operation.

Sync Center

Windows Vista continues to support Briefcase but has added a feature called Sync Center. The Sync Center is designed especially for mobile device data exchange to ensure that the very latest file version is available and not confused with an older file version. The Sync Center only works with files that are configured for sharing in a network environment, even a small home network containing only two devices. Once the desired folder is set up as a share, the file can be synchronized using the Sync Center. This will enable the latest version of the file to always be available for use by either device.

The Sync Center is shown in **Figure 12-28.** Notice that it allows folders and files to be accessed, viewed, and modified offline. You can synchronize the contents of a folder used by two or more computers or portable devices so that the very latest version is always available for use.

Upgrading the Laptop

Notebooks and laptops can be upgraded easily. Memory and hard drive upgrades are not difficult. Some of the internal parts for laptops are smaller and more delicate than their full-size PC versions, so handle all parts with care. The CPU upgrade is usually not an option because of the design. Upgrading a CPU is a very difficult task, even for an experienced electronics technician.

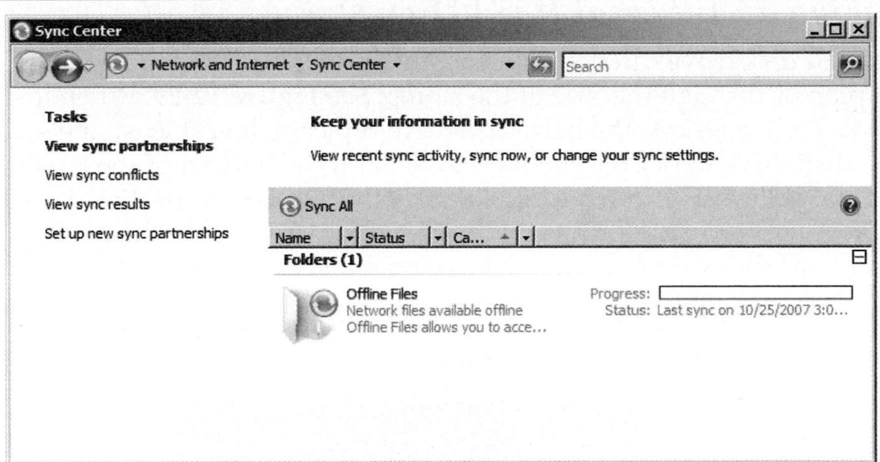

Figure 12-28. Windows Vista Sync Center.

PDAs and palmtops also have limited upgrades. You can add additional memory or any accessory through a port. Hardware repairs must usually be made at an authorized factory. Software is another matter. By now you are aware that most computer repairs are required because of software or operator error. Third-party downloads and add-ons can cause a system lockup or crash. Most repair techniques related to software or operator error that are used for a full-size PC work equally as well on portables.

Upgrading Memory

Adding or replacing memory is a very common laptop upgrade. The memory modules for laptops are accessed through panels under the laptop. Laptops use SO-DIMM. The SO represents "Small Outline." Installing SO-DIMM is not difficult, but you should consult the manufacturer's documentation before performing the memory replacement or upgrade. The following lists the general steps for replacing or upgrading SO-DIMM memory in a laptop.

1. Before performing any hardware replacement or upgrade, remove the laptop battery and unplug the power cord or adapter.
2. Remove the retaining screw(s) that hold the memory access panel in place.
3. Either gently pull the retaining clips from each end of the memory module or rotate the memory module to a 45° angle. (You should consult the manufacturer's information about this procedure before attempting to remove and replace the memory.)
4. Align the memory module key notch to ensure the correct direction and alignment of the memory module into the memory socket.
5. Gently press the memory module into the socket until it is seated evenly and snuggly.
6. Replace the memory module access panel and replace the retaining screw(s).
7. Replace the power cord and battery.
8. Power up the system and check **Properties** dialog box to see that the new RAM is properly identified by size. If not, you may need to reseat the memory module. Be sure to remove the battery and the power cord. Most of the time, a memory upgrade or replacement failure is caused by improperly seating the memory in the socket.

Replacing an Internal Hard Disk Drive

The hard disk drive can be accessed either under an access port on the bottom of the laptop or through the side of the laptop. See **Figure 12-29.** When installed in the side, Figure 12-29A, the hard disk drive typically has at least one screw to keep the disk drive in place. When it is located on the bottom of the laptop, it may have several screws, Figure 12-29B. Replacing the physical hard disk drive is an easy task. You must use a form factor designed for laptop computers. Desktop computer hard disk drives are much too large to fit inside a laptop.

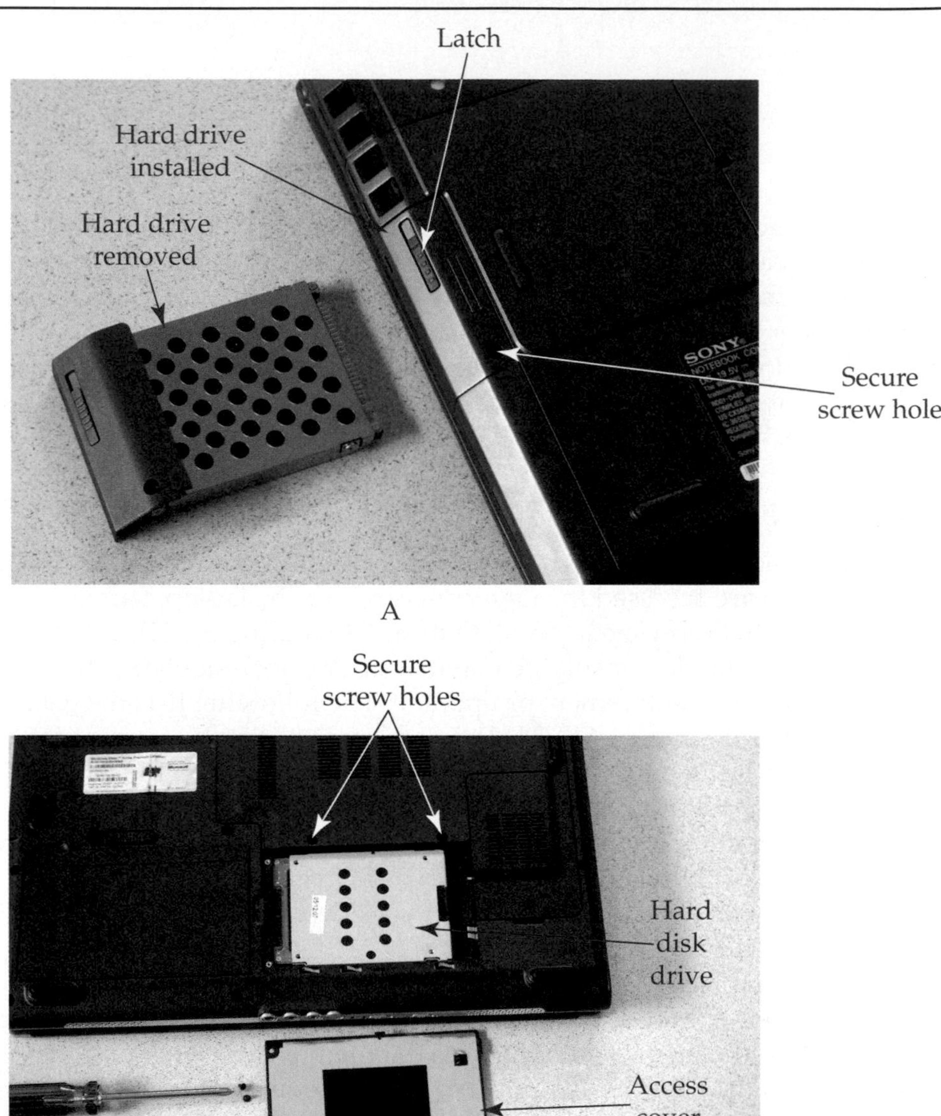

Figure 12-29. Laptop hard disk drive removal. A—The Sony laptop hard disk drive is removed from the side access panel of the laptop. B—The Acer laptop hard disk drive is removed from the bottom of the laptop.

Replacing the Battery

Before performing any repairs on a laptop computer you should first remove the battery and disconnect any AC source of power. Some areas of the motherboard are still energized by battery power or by AC through the power adapter even when the laptop is turned off. Working inside a laptop with a battery or the AC adapter still plugged into an AC source could cause a short circuit and damage the motherboard or other components because the motherboard is still partially energized.

Figure 12-30 shows two common ways batteries are mounted in a laptop configuration. In some models, the battery slides out of the side of the laptop, Figure 12-30A. In other models, the battery is removed from the bottom of the laptop, Figure 12-30B. For both configurations, a latch is used to secure the battery in place.

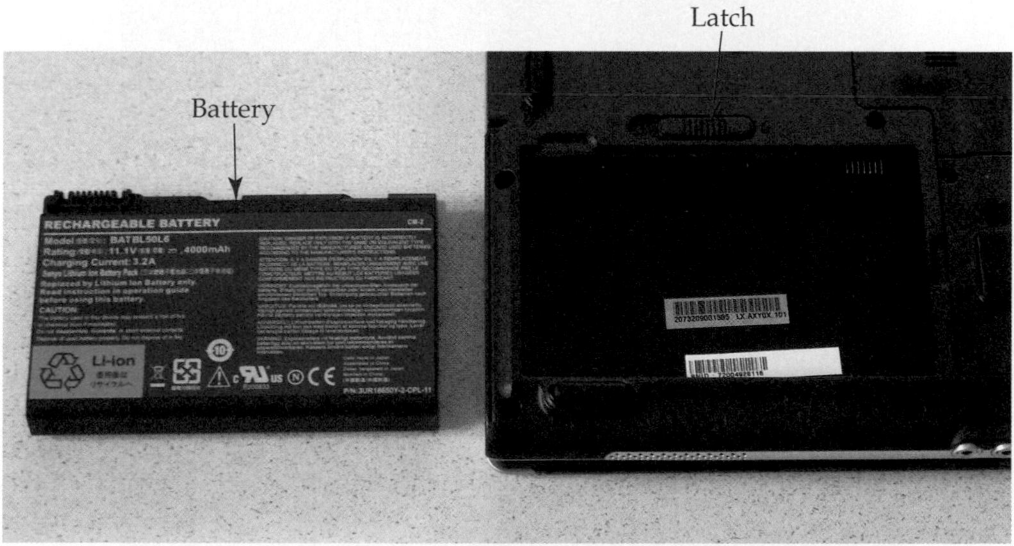

Figure 12-30. Laptop battery removal. A—The battery snuggly fits inside the back of this Acer laptop and is held in place by a spring latch. B—In this image, a spare battery is resting beside the installed battery of a Sony laptop computer. This laptop uses a latch to hold the battery in place. The battery is inserted from the bottom of the case.

Replacing a Wireless Card

Almost all laptops have a wireless card installed inside the case. Older laptops use wireless devices connected through the exterior of the case via a USB port, PCMCIA slot, or ExpressCard slot.

Figure 12-31 shows a wireless network card installed inside an Acer laptop. It is held in place by a bracket. There are also two wires, one black and one white, that run from the card through the inside of the case into the LCD display housing where the antenna is installed. A common error by new technicians is forgetting to reconnect the wires running from the card to the antenna.

Replacing the CPU

Replacement of the CPU is not an easy task. You should never attempt to replace the CPU without first studying the manufacturer's manual on that particular laptop model. The replacement of the CPU often requires a tedious disassembly of the cooling fan and heat sink and may involve the removal of other parts. Looking at **Figure 12-32,** you can see that the CPU is covered by the heat sink assembly and may also require the removal of the cooling fan before removing the heat sink.

Troubleshooting the Laptop

There are some very common laptop troubleshooting practices you need to be familiar with. This section is brief and intended only as an introduction. For more in-depth troubleshooting check Chapter 15—PC Troubleshooting.

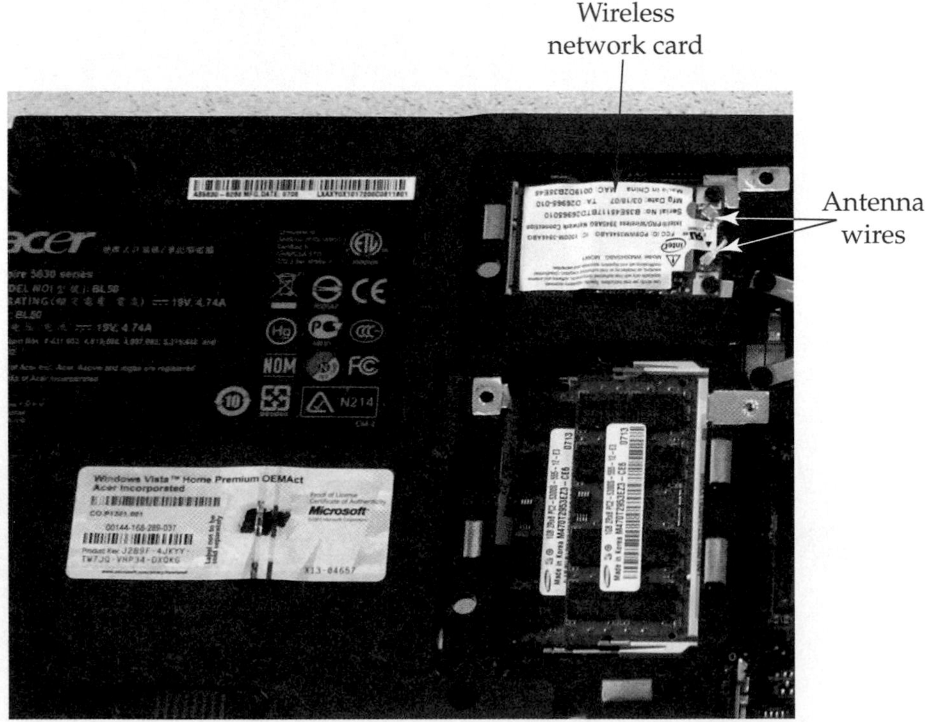

Figure 12-31. A wireless network card installed inside a laptop PC. Notice the black and white wires that connect the network card to the antenna.

Figure 12-32. To replace a laptop CPU, the heat sink and possibly the cooling fan needs to first be removed.

Be sure to remove the battery from a laptop or portable device before attempting any repairs that involve disassembly of the unit. A screwdriver tip can short circuit the motherboard, even when the laptop is turned off. This is because the battery still supplies power to parts of the motherboard.

Symptom 1:

No power LED or other LEDs are lit when the laptop is plugged into an ac power source.

Items to check:

This is an indicator that a major power problem has occurred in the laptop, most likely on the motherboard. Laptops do not have a power supply as desktops do. The power input is incorporated into the motherboard. The laptop uses dc power. You may try changing the ac adapter first. Be sure to use an adapter that matches the voltage and current output. Also, be aware that not all adapter plugs are physically the same size and shape.

If the motherboard is at fault, the laptop should be returned to the laptop manufacturer for motherboard repair issues. Most technicians do not repair laptop motherboards. If the laptop is out of warranty, the motherboard should be replaced.

Symptom 2:

The laptop seems to boot, but there is no display.

Items to check:

When the laptop boots and the display appears black, gray, very dim, or discolored, it is a symptom that the LCD back lamp is defective or the LCD inverter has failed. Active matrix LCD displays used two main parts to produce the required back lighting: a florescent lamp and an inverter. A florescent lamp, also referred to as the cold cathode florescent lamp or by the acronym CCFL, produces the light necessary for the LCD display. The inverter is a small circuit board that converts the low dc voltage to a much higher ac voltage. An inverter may produce anywhere from 500 Vac to over 1000 Vac from a 12-volt to 18-volt laptop battery.

Symptom 3:

Slow laptop, and too many popups.

Items to check:

The laptop is infected with spyware. Install and run a reputable antispyware program.

Symptom 4:

Laptop freezes up and will not respond, even to the power button.

Items to check:

Unplug the power cord and remove the battery from the laptop. Replace the battery and power cord, and the laptop should reboot and respond normally.

Symptom 5:

Laptop is booting slower and slower over time.

Items to check:

Typically, too many programs and downloads have been installed on the computer. The programs are all being loaded at startup into RAM, thus slowing the overall boot time and slowing computer performance. Remove unnecessary programs from the laptop. You can also stop many programs from loading during startup by running the System Configuration Utility (msconfig.exe) and selecting which programs to load at startup. Using the System Configuration Utility is covered in Chapter 15—PC Troubleshooting.

Symptom 6:

A blue screen appears during the boot process and an error message appears on the screen.

Items to check:

This symptom is typical of a major problem. The easiest way to remedy this problem is to completely reinstall the Windows operating system. Be aware that a complete reinstall may cause you to lose all data and files stored on the laptop. This is a major reason why you should frequently back up valuable data!

Symptom 7:

The laptop acts strangely.

Items to check:

When the laptop "acts strangely" and unpredictable results occur when certain programs or certain actions are taken, it is a good sign that the laptop has a virus or malware. The computer may randomly stop running, automatically shut down, or take you to a Web site you did not intend to launch. All these symptoms are usually a good indicator that a virus has infected the computer. Install and run an antivirus program.

Symptom 8:

Incorrect characters appear on the screen.

Items to check:

A very common client complaint is that the laptop prints characters on the screen when the number keys are pressed. Again, this is very common, especially for new users. The most likely cause is that a function key or function key combination has been pressed, setting the default state of the keys to characters rather than numbers. Also, be aware that laptop keyboards often have many more special function keys than the traditional full-size keyboard. This causes many other problems for users who are not familiar with that particular laptop keyboard or who have recently changed from a desktop system to a laptop.

A great reference site for laptop repair is Laptop Repair 101 located at www.laptoprepair101.com. Most repairs have step-by-step illustrated repair procedures. Another great Web site is www.irisvista.com, which includes information about how to disconnect a wireless network card antenna from inside the laptop.

A+ Note:

Be sure you are familiar with the disassembly of a laptop computer. Download a copy of the laptop repair manual and study the procedure for at least two different types of laptops. This will prove to be a valuable aid if you are planning to take the CompTIA 602 IT Tech certification exam.

Preventive Maintenance

Preventive maintenance of laptops and portable devices are always outlined in the user manual that comes with the device. They are very common for all such devices. The most common preventive maintenance tips are as follows:

- ✔ Never store a portable device or laptop in direct sunlight. Direct sunlight can harm the plastic case, causing it to yellow and make the plastic brittle, which can cause the case to easily break when dropped.
- ✔ Never leave a portable device in a car. Extreme heat can damage the components, such as the motherboard capacitors. Extreme cold can cause condensation problems when taking the portable device from a very cold car into a hot and humid environment, causing water to condensate inside the case. Condensation can damage motherboard components.
- ✔ Never use harsh chemicals to clean the case, especially the screen area.
- ✔ Do not spray liquids directly on the screen area as they can drip down and enter the display at the display edge. This can cause damage to the inverter or other components. When you must use a spray, spray the liquid directly on a soft cloth and then use the damp (not wet) cloth to wipe the screen.

- ✔ Clean the keyboard with compressed air or a small paintbrush. Never use liquid or sprays directly on the keyboard. The keyboard is mounted over the motherboard, and any liquid that seeps through the keyboard will wet the motherboard components and cause a short circuit.

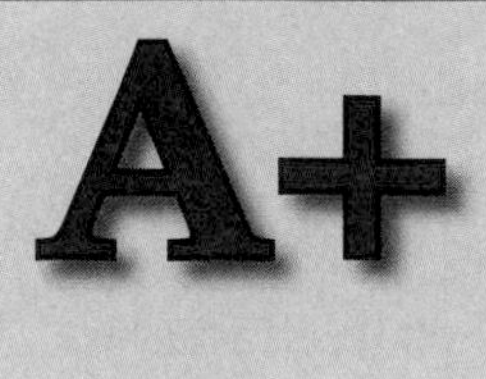

A+ Note:

To better prepare for the A+ Certification exams, download one or two laptop manuals and review the information about preventive maintenance and common repairs. Check the Gateway support Web site for a list of devices and available manuals.

Summary

- ✔ Several types of portable computers include laptops, notebooks, and palmtops.
- ✔ A palmtop computer is small enough to rest in the palm of the hand.
- ✔ The most common battery types associated with portable equipment are alkaline, nickel-cadmium (NiCd), nickel-metal hydride (NiMH), and lithium-ion (Li-ion).
- ✔ Portable PCs usually use lithium-ion type batteries because they are relatively lightweight and have a greater charge holding capability than other types of batteries.
- ✔ Portable computers can expand their capabilities through the use of PCMCIA cards and ExpressCards.
- ✔ There are three types of PCMCIA card: Type I for memory, Type II for communication devices such as modems and network connectors, and Type III for hard drives or CD drives.
- ✔ The two ExpressCard types are 34 mm and 54 mm.
- ✔ Portable computers rely on energy management software to lengthen the life of the batteries.
- ✔ A port replicator is used to provide additional ports for computer devices.
- ✔ The portable option in the Windows installation installs additional features that are used with portable computers.
- ✔ NTFS is the preferred file system for portable computers because of its encryption capabilities and its ability to use smaller clusters than those used by FAT16 and FAT32.
- ✔ IEEE 802.11a transmits at 5.8 GHz and has a maximum bandwidth of 54 Mbps.
- ✔ IEEE 802.11b transmits at 2.48 GHz and has a maximum bandwidth of 11 Mbps
- ✔ IEEE 802.11b devices transmit farther than IEEE 802.11a devices.

- ✔ IEEE 802.11g transmits at 2.48 GHz and has a maximum bandwidth of 54 Mbps.
- ✔ IEEE 802.11n transmits at 2.4 GHz–2.4835 GHz and 5.15 GHz–5.850 GHz and is backward compatible with 802.11a, 802.11b, and 802.11g.
- ✔ Other radio devices in the same assigned frequency as well as other electrical devices and appliances can interfere with wireless communications.
- ✔ As the distance between two wireless devices increases, the transmission rate decreases.
- ✔ Wired equivalent privacy (WEP) is used to encode wireless transmissions.
- ✔ Data can be exchanged between two computers using a null modem cable, a parallel cable, or infrared technology.
- ✔ Folder contents are synchronized using Briefcase in Windows XP and earlier operating systems and Sync Center in Windows Vista.

Review Questions

Answer the following questions on a separate sheet of paper. Please do not write in this book.

1. What is the difference between a PDA and a palmtop?
2. Name four types of batteries commonly associated with portable PC products.
3. Which battery is the preferred choice for portable PCs?
4. Which type of battery has memory effect?
5. What is the most lightweight and compact battery?
6. What type of PCMCIA card is used for hard drives?
7. What type of device is associated with a Type I PCMCIA card?
8. Which type of PCMCIA card is the thickest?
9. What are the two ExpressCard widths?
10. What is the data rate of an ExpressCard using a USB 2.0 bus?
11. What is the data rate of an ExpressCard using a PCIe bus?
12. What is the function of a docking station?
13. What device can be used to provide additional ports for a portable or compact digital device?
14. List five devices that can be connected through a port replicator.
15. What are the three power schemes available in Windows Vista?
16. What is the difference between sleep mode and hibernate mode?
17. What is hybrid sleep?
18. What are the three styles of wireless devices used for laptop systems when a wireless network adapter is not already incorporated into the system?
19. What is the frequency and the maximum bandwidth associated with IEEE 802.11b devices?
20. What is the frequency and bandwidth associated with IEEE 802.11a devices?

21. How does distance affect wireless device communications?
22. What items can interfere with radio wave communications?
23. Why is security so critical for a portable PC?
24. What does the acronym WEP represent?
25. What role does WEP play in wireless communications?
26. What are the three most common methods of exchanging data between a laptop and desktop today?
27. What is the name of the Windows Vista program that synchronizes the contents of a folder shared between two computers?
28. What is the name of the software program that is used to synchronize the exchange of data between two Windows XP operating systems?
29. Why is it difficult to upgrade the CPU in a portable PC?
30. What should be removed from the laptop before disassembling a laptop?
31. What two devices are used to produce the back lighting of an LCD display?
32. What is the purpose of an LCD display inverter?
33. What utility can you use to select the programs that are allowed to run at startup?

Sample A+ Exam Questions

Answer the following questions on a separate sheet of paper. Please do not write in this book.

1. A Type I PCMCIA card port is typically used for which application?
   a. It is typically used to install a PCMCIA hard drive.
   b. It is typically used to install a PCMCIA CD-ROM.
   c. It is typically used to install additional RAM.
   d. It is typically used to install a floppy drive connection.
2. Which type of memory is most commonly used for laptop computer RAM?
   a. SIMM
   b. SO-DIMM
   c. EPROM
   d. DIMM
3. When exchanging information directly from a laptop PC to a full-size PC, both with Windows XP installed, which cable would you *most likely* use?
   a. Rollover cable
   b. Straight through network cable
   c. 15-pin D shell serial connection cable
   d. Null modem cable

4. Which is the best example of battery memory effect?
   a. A battery supplies the same level of voltage when connected to various types of laptop computers because it remembers the voltage level required the last time it was used.
   b. A battery loses its charge after the amount of time lapse of its last usage, even if the battery is designed to last longer.
   c. A battery is designed to remember the total length of warranty and will cease supplying voltage after the expiration date.
   d. A battery remembers the orientation of the connection polarity after being removed from the case for reinstallation at a later date.
5. Which type of battery would you *most likely* find in a new laptop computer?
   a. Lithium-ion
   b. Alkaline
   c. NiCad
   d. Nickel-metal hydride
6. When using a Windows XP operating system, which program, located under **Accessories | Communications**, would you *most likely* use to transfer data to and from a laptop PC to a full-size PC?
   a. New Connection Wizard
   b. Network Connections
   c. Modem Connection
   d. Hyper Terminal
7. Which statement is true for proper disposal of a laptop battery?
   a. They must be disposed of by incineration to protect the environment.
   b. You must follow local, state, and federal guidelines.
   c. Any container that is lined in plastic can be used.
   d. Lithium-ion batteries do not need to be disposed of because they can be recharged indefinitely.
8. Which situation best describes an ad-hoc network?
   a. An Ethernet network with two wireless access points: one for WAN and the other for LAN service
   b. A notebook PC connected to a full-size PC transferring files by radio signal
   c. A group of computers using radio waves to communicate through a centralized access point on a 1000BaseT network
   d. A network consisting of several access points each using a different frequency
9. What is the maximum data transfer described by the IEEE 802.11b standard?
   a. 2 Mbps
   b. 5 GHz
   c. 11 Mbps
   d. 54 GHz
10. What form of security is typically implemented on an IEEE 802.11b network system to prevent compromising sensitive data?
    a. PPTP
    b. WEP
    c. PGP
    d. SLIP

Suggested Laboratory Activities

Do not attempt any suggested laboratory activities without your instructor's permission. Certain activities can render the PC operating system inoperable.

1. Set up a laptop PC to access your home or school PC. You will need a laptop with a modem port or you can install a PCMCIA modem card into the laptop.
2. Transfer a file from a laptop to a full-size PC using a direct cable connection.
3. Try installing and using the Briefcase program available through Microsoft Windows.
4. Locate and use the infrared port feature to transfer files from a laptop to a full-size PC.
5. Explore the power management settings on a typical portable PC. Be sure to record the settings before changing any.
6. Set up a portable PC for use by multiple users. Each user should have their own password and they should be able to retain their personnel desktop settings. For example, change the desktop display so each user has a different desktop.

Interesting Web Sites for More Information

www.3com.com
www.bluetooth.com
www.comdex.com
www.compaq.com
www.hp.com
www.ibm.com
www.motorola.com
www.palm.com
www.sun.com

Chapter 12
Laboratory Activity
Wireless Ad-Hoc Installation and Configuration

After completing this lab activity, you will be able to:
- ✔ Install a typical ad-hoc network.
- ✔ Identify key elements associated with an ad-hoc network.
- ✔ Identify common causes of problems with an ad-hoc network.
- ✔ Define and describe an Independent Basic Service Set (IBSS).
- ✔ Define WPAN.

Introduction

In this lab activity, you will install and configure an ad-hoc network using two computers. The ad-hoc network is mostly encountered in a small peer-to-peer network or to form a direct connection between a notebook computer and a full-size PC.

Note:
Microsoft technical information refers to an ad-hoc arrangement as an Independent Basic Service Set (IBSS), while most wireless device manufacturers use the term ad-hoc.

Two configuration modes are used for wireless computer communications: ad hoc and infrastructure. In ad-hoc mode, two or more computers communicate directly with each other. In infrastructure mode, a wireless access point is required to coordinate communications between wireless devices and devices in a LAN consisting of network cabling. The wireless access point controls communications between all wireless devices within its range. It also controls communications between any wireless device and a device on the wired LAN.

Note:
A small wireless network such as a home-office network is referred to as a Wireless Personal Area Network (WPAN).

In this lab activity, you will be using wireless devices based on the IEEE 802.11b standard. The 802.11b standard is assigned the 2.4 GHz frequency band as specified by the FCC for radio wave communications. The data rates specified in 802.11b are 1 Mbps, 2 Mbps, 5.5 Mbps, and 11 Mbps. The highest rating of 11 Mbps can only be achieved when the two devices are in close proximity. As the distance increases between two wireless devices, the data rate drops. The typical range for an 802.11b wireless ad-hoc network is 100 meters maximum. This distance may vary because of conditions and building structure materials. For example, a wireless system installed inside a building and transmitting through walls of concrete block will not achieve the 100-meter through 150-meter distance.

Note:

Some wireless card manufacturers advertise rates of 22 Mbps for their cards, but these rates are not specified by the 802.11b standard. They are compatible but are not a recognized standard data rate.

The 802.11a standard is assigned the 5 GHz frequency band and supports data rates as high as 54 Mbps. The 802.11a standard is preferred for applications such video and conferencing. While the 802.11a standard provides a higher throughput, it does not support the same distances as 802.11b. The expected range is approximately half the range of the 802.11b device.

A third standard, 802.11g, combines the 802.11a and 802.11b characteristics. The 802.11g standard uses the higher data rate, 54 Mbps, for shorter distances and the lower frequency, 2.4 GHz, for longer distances. This is a relatively new standard, and at the time of this writing, the cost of the 802.11g devices is more than the 802.11b devices.

All wireless networks require a service set identifier (SSID), which is the name used to identify the network. Both wireless modes of operation, ad hoc and infrastructure, require the use of an SSID. For devices to communicate with each other on a wireless network, all devices must be identified by the same SSID. Wireless devices usually have a default SSID already assigned by the manufacturer. For example, Dell uses "wireless" and Linksys uses "linksys."

Note:

One reason wireless networking devices from the same manufacturer seem to work automatically when first installed is that the default settings match. When devices from different manufacturers are installed on an ad-hoc network, the SSID must be changed to match the other device(s).

The 802.11b assigned frequency of 2.4 GHz shares the Industrial Science and Medical (ISM) radio frequency band. This means equipment that falls into these categories and uses radio waves for communication may interfere with a wireless 802.11b system. For example, microwave ovens and portable telephones assigned to the 2.4 GHz band will disrupt the wireless communication between the computers.

The placement of the antenna also influences the distance and quality of the radio transmission and reception. For example, the antenna on the back of a PC should be oriented in a vertical position and placed where metal filing cabinets or metal furniture, such as room partitions, will not block the path of the radio signal. A separate antenna can be connected to the wireless card by flexible coaxial cable. This will allow the antenna to be placed in a spot that will support better transmission and reception.

Although setting up a wireless network is simple, there may be times you will experience problems. The following is a list of items to check:

- ✔ Check Device Manager to be sure the wireless device is installed and the device driver is loaded.
- ✔ Check that all wireless devices are in the same mode of operation: ad hoc or infrastructure.
- ✔ Check that encryption has been enabled, and if so, that the passphrase matches on each device.
- ✔ Check for sources of radio interference from microwave ovens, portable telephones, medical devices, industrial devices, garage door openers, wireless

PA systems, portable microphones, and any other form of equipment that may transmit radio waves.

- ✔ Check that the SSID matches on all devices. Matching the SSID is mandatory in the ad-hoc mode. This is especially true for matching devices from different manufacturers. In infrastructure mode, the matching SSID can be automatically overwritten when an access point is scanned and then selected.
- ✔ Check that the same channel is assigned.

This lab activity is written specifically for Windows XP operating system. You may substitute a Windows Vista operating system computer but only as a last resort. Windows XP is much more difficult to configure than Windows Vista. If you can configure the more difficult Windows XP ad-hoc network, you will have very little problem configuring a Windows Vista system.

Many wireless device manufacturers produce wireless devices that exceed the IEEE wireless standard. For example, the IEEE 802.11g standard states that the highest data rate for the standard is 54 Mbps. Many manufacturers exceed this standard and produce IEEE 802.11g compatible devices with a maximum data rate of 108 Mbps or double the standard rate.

The very latest proposed wireless standard IEEE 802.11n promises data rates as high as 248 Mbps using the existing radio frequencies used by 802.11g. The range is expected to double that of 802.11g. It is proposed to be backward compatible with existing wireless standards and can operate at the 2.4 GHz and 5 GHz frequencies.

Note:

The 802.11n is still a proposed standard at the time of this writing. You may wish to verify that the information is accurate after the release of the official standard by checking the IEEE Web site or other respected Internet sources.

Equipment and Materials

- ✔ PC with Windows XP and an 802.11b wireless device installed. The wireless device may be a USB, PCI, or PCIe type.
- ✔ Notebook computer with Windows XP and an 802.11b PCMCIA wireless card. (You may use a laptop that is already wireless enabled in this lab activity if approved by your instructor.)
- ✔ You will also need the product guide for the 802.11b PCMCIA wireless card. If you do not have the product guide on hand, you can download the product guide from the manufacturer's Web site. Familiarize yourself with the PCMCIA card before beginning this lab activity.

Note:

While this lab activity is designed for a notebook computer and a PC, you may substitute a second PC for the notebook and achieve similar results.

Procedure

1. _______ Gather all materials and report to your assigned workstation. Boot the computers and check that they are in working order.
2. _______ Install the wireless card into the notebook computer. You may need to install the device drivers and software for the PCMCIA card before actually installing the card. While Microsoft Windows XP is designed to automatically detect and configure wireless cards, some manufacturers prefer that you use their software in place of the Windows XP software and drivers. Problems with the wireless card could result from using the Windows XP automatic detection and configuration. Check the PCMCIA wireless card's documentation and take appropriate action before moving on.
3. _______ After installing and configuring the wireless card, you may need to reboot the system for proper setup.
4. _______ If both wireless devices are configured for ad-hoc mode, they should automatically start communicating with each other, especially if they are made by the same manufacturer. When the wireless devices connect automatically, it is referred to as zero configuration. Zero configuration means that no configuration is necessary. The wireless devices automatically configure for any wireless connection they find. Not all network devices offer zero configuration.

   To check if the wireless devices are communicating, you can simply open **My Network Places** to see if the other wireless computer is listed.
5. _______ Open **Start | Control Panel | Network and Internet Connections | Network Connections** and then right-click the identified wireless connection. A shortcut menu similar to the following will display.

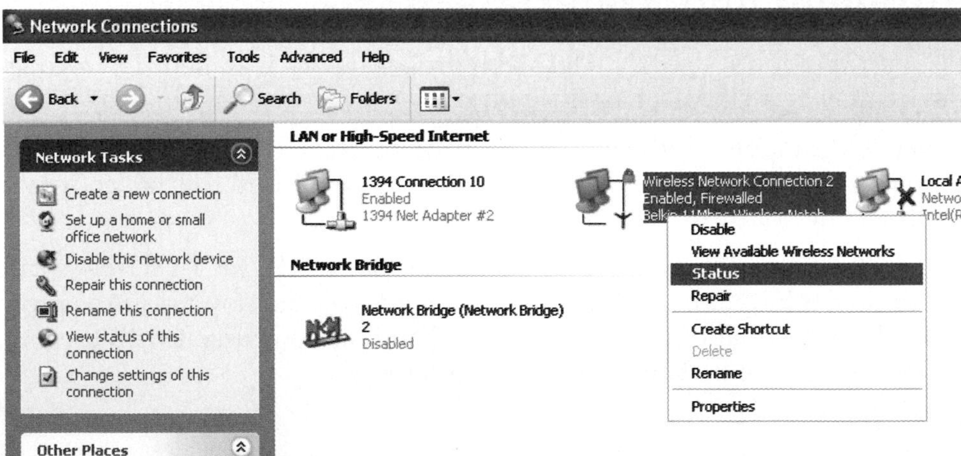

You are given a range of commands: **Disable, View Available Wireless Networks, Status, Repair, Create Shortcut, Delete, Rename,** and **Properties**.

6.______ Select **Status**. A dialog box similar to the following will display.

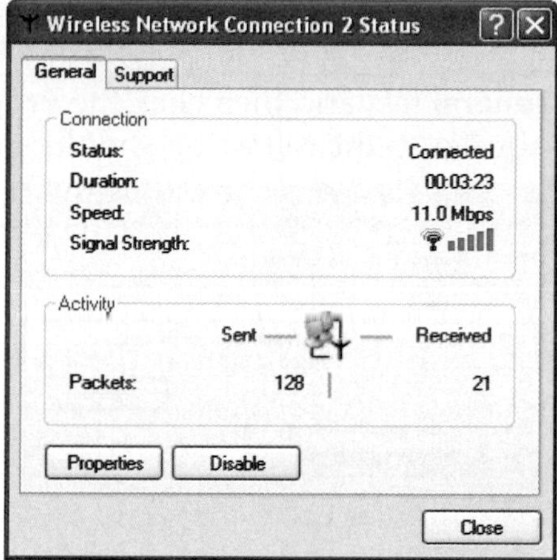

The **Wireless Network Status** dialog box displays the signal strength of the wireless device. In the screen capture, a strong signal is indicated by the bar graph showing all five bars. Also, notice that the connection speed indicated is 11 Mbps. The combination of the speed and signal strength is an indication of an excellent wireless communication condition.

Wireless devices send and receive data in the form of packets in the same way wired networks communicates data. The number of packets sent and received is indicated in the dialog box and can help diagnose a problem with the connection. For example, if there are a number of packets sent but none have been received, this would indicate that a connection has not been established.

7.______ Select the **Support** tab. You should see a dialog box similar to the following. The support tab reveals the TCP/IP properties assigned to this particular wireless card.

8. _______ Click the **Details** button. Look at the information revealed, such as the physical address (MAC address), DNS server address, and the WINS server address. After viewing the contents, click **Close**.

9. _______ Select the **General** tab, and then click the **Properties** button. A dialog box similar to the following should appear.

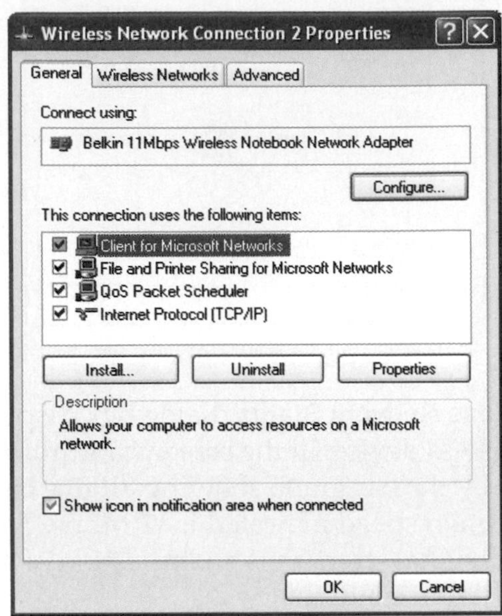

In the **Wireless Network Connection Properties** dialog box, you see the list of familiar settings associated with a typical network card. You can choose to add or remove clients, TCP/IP settings, and protocols and to set up file and print sharing.

10. _______ Select the **Wireless Networks** tab. A dialog box similar to the following should appear.

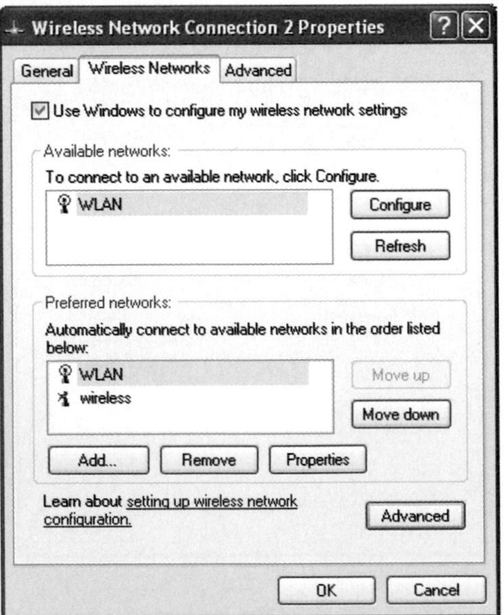

Pay particular attention to the option **Use Windows to configure my wireless network settings**. When this option is selected, Windows XP configures the network device, not the software provided by the network wireless card manufacturer. This is critical for proper operation of the wireless device.

11. _______ Select the **Use Windows to configure my wireless network settings** option. The button labeled **Advanced** becomes available.

12. _______ Click the **Advanced** button. The **Advanced** dialog box will display. This is where you configure the wireless device for use in ad-hoc or infrastructure mode. The mode of all devices must match for proper operation. Pay particular attention to the option **Automatically connect to non-preferred networks**. When this option is selected, the wireless device is capable of connecting to any wireless device within its range, even if the SSID does not match. If it is unchecked, you may be able to see the other wireless devices when surveyed by the software, but not be able to communicate with the other device because of the configuration values that are set. Be sure the **Computer-computer (ad-hoc) networks only** option is selected, and then close the dialog box. You should return to the **Wireless Network Connection Properties** dialog box.

13. _______ Now select the **Advanced** tab. A dialog box similar to the following should appear.

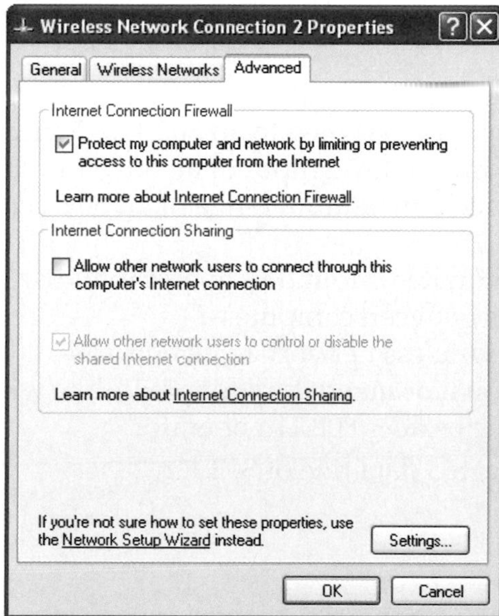

The **Advanced** tab reveals options for enabling the Internet connection firewall and also for setting up an Internet connection share. These options are used when a wireless infrastructure mode is configured. They are also used if the computer is using a direct wireless satellite connection. When using a direct satellite connection, you will want to enable the firewall to protect the computer from unauthorized intruders.

14. _______ Now, feel free to experiment with the various settings and options available in the **Wireless Network Connection Properties** dialog boxes. Try changing the mode of operation as well as the SSID to see the effects on the ad-hoc system. Set up a share on one of the two computers and attempt to copy and transfer the contents of the share. Do not experiment with the encryption settings at this time. You will experiment with the encryption in the next lab activity. Also, use Help and Support to learn more about wireless ad-hoc networks.

15. _______ Return all materials to their proper storage area and then go on to answer the review questions.

Review Questions

Answer the following questions on a separate sheet of paper. Please do not write in this book.

1. What are the two modes of wireless operation?
2. Which mode does not require an access point?
3. What does Microsoft call an ad-hoc wireless configuration?
4. An ad-hoc network is most similar to which type of network, a peer-to-peer or a client/server?
5. What are the four typical data rates for an 802.11b standard wireless device?
6. What is the assigned FCC frequency for an 802.11b wireless device?
7. What is the frequency assigned to an 802.11a device?
8. What is the maximum throughput of an 802.11a wireless device?
9. What is the expected maximum range of an 802.11b wireless ad-hoc network?
10. What two common items found in homes will disrupt wireless communications between computers?
11. What is a small wireless network referred to as?
12. Is the SSID optional or mandatory for an ad-hoc wireless network?
13. At what frequencies does 802.11n operate?
14. What is the expected data rate of 802.11n?

Modems and Transceivers

After studying this chapter, you will be able to:

- ✔ Identify basic features of telephone wiring systems.
- ✔ Explain the operation of a modem.
- ✔ Explain how modems negotiate a connection.
- ✔ Set up a standard modem.
- ✔ Use the **Phone and Modem Options** dialog box.
- ✔ Explain ISDN, DSL, Cable, and T-carrier lines.
- ✔ Identify several basic AT commands.
- ✔ Diagnose common modem problems.

A+ Exam—Key Points

Telephone applications and setup will be on the A+ Certification exams. More questions will be included on the tests as more computer telephone services develop. Be familiar with standard modem negotiation terminology and acronyms such as CD, RTS, and CTS. Also, be able to compare and contrast ISDN, DSL, cable, and telephone modem characteristics.

Key Words and Terms

The following words and terms will become important pieces of your computer vocabulary. Be sure you can define them.

bandwidth
baud rate
Cable modem
Data Over Cable Service Interface Specification (DOCSIS)
digital subscriber lines (DSL)
DSL modem
Integrated services digital network (ISDN)
Internet Service Provider (ISP)
modem
protocol
T-carrier lines
telephone jack
universal asynchronous receiver-transmitter (UART)

One of the basic functions of the modern PC is communication with other computers, usually through Internet access. In this section, you will learn about the modem, basic residential telephone system wiring, modem installation, and communications software setup. Some of the material covered here will be seen again in the chapters discussing the basics networking.

Modems allow you the freedom to surf the Internet, connect with others through e-mail, send pictures around the world, take part in conference calls, and participate in many other activities relating to communications. While the modern modem is a Plug and Play device, there is still much to learn about modems and modem-related issues. We will begin this chapter with a brief description of the public telephone system and residential telephone wiring.

Public Telephone System

To understand the complete communications model, we must first take a look at the standard telephone system. The public telephone system has been serving the general public for over 100 years. As telephone system technology evolved, it has retained its own downward compatibility to existing equipment. The original telephone system was designed to transmit voice as an analog signal across the country and world. This system only had to be able to accommodate the frequency spectrum of sound associated with voice communications. The voice frequency spectrum for the telephone industry operated between 200 Hz and 4000 Hz. This frequency spectrum is more than adequate for carrying voice. However, it is not adequate for high-speed modem connections. High-speed connections demand higher bandwidth. This is the main reason why people switch to Cable television carriers for Internet access. The cables used for Cable television can carry much higher frequencies than the simple twisted-pair telephone cable. This large bandwidth allows for much more information to be transported in shorter spans of time.

bandwidth
the range of frequencies that an electronic cable or component is designed to carry.

The ***bandwidth*** of a cable or device is the range or limit of frequency that an electronic cable or component is designed to carry. For example, a cable with a bandwidth of 4 kbps is designed to carry a maximum frequency of 4 kbps. Note that bandwidth is also used to describe a portion of the frequency spectrum. For example, television channels use a bandwidth of 6 MHz for each channel. This means that each channel has a frequency range of 6 MHz.

Telephone technology has made tremendous advances over the years, but the downward compatibility issue has made it difficult to implement all the latest technologies. The main bottleneck of the entire telephone system is the last few hundred feet of connection that serve each building, especially in private homes. Most of the public telephone network system (PTNS) is constructed of high-speed fiber-optic cables, microwave transmitters and receivers, digital equipment, and computerized telephone control units. While all of these major parts of the telephone network system are composed of cables and media that have high data transfer rates, the last few hundred feet of twisted pair from the main system to the individual connection point severely limit the speed of data transmission.

The public telephone system is often referred to as POTS, which is an acronym for *plain old telephone system.*

Residential Telephone Wiring System

The typical residential telephone wiring system is simple in design while a system for a commercial enterprise is somewhat more complicated. The simple residential system consists of two to four wires running throughout the residence and connecting to telephone jacks. See **Figure 13-1.**

RJ-11 and RJ-14 connectors look very similar. Their physical shape is similar. The difference in classification is determined by the number of electrical contacts inside the connector. Four contacts for four wires is an RJ-14, and two contacts for two wires is an RJ-11.

The telephone wiring in a residential dwelling is typically #22 copper conductor run in a daisy chain fashion throughout the residence. Older homes may have a two-wire system, but four-wire systems are most common. Two wires are the minimum number used for one telephone to communicate with another telephone. The pair of connections are referred to in telephone technician terminology as the "tip and the ring." The additional two wires from the four-wire system can be used for an additional phone or to connect to electrical power for electrical lighting or other electrical device on the phone.

Phone lighting does not use 120 volts. A transformer is used to step the voltage level down to 12 volts, which is used to light the phone dial. The voltage level at the phone jack is considered low voltage. It reaches an approximate 48 volts when the phone is ringing. This voltage can be felt by touch, but is not considered deadly. To see how a typical phone line might be run through a home, look at **Figure 13-2.** As you can see, the cable runs through the residence from room to room. This is the usual style, but each individual jack could have its own run of cable from a junction box. The daisy chain style is preferred because it uses less cable, which means it is less expensive.

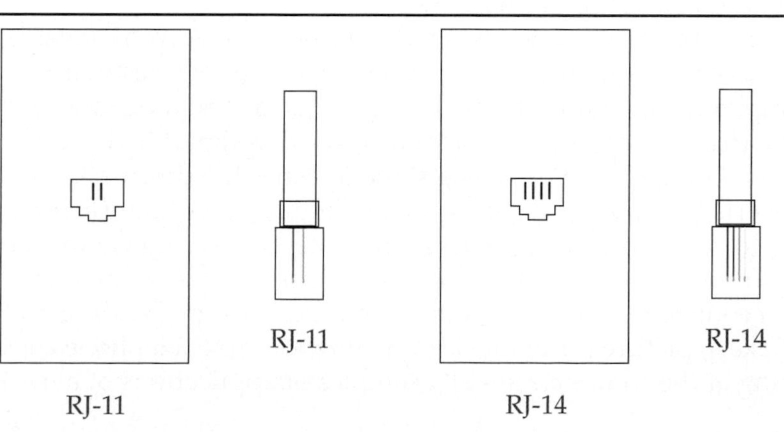

Figure 13-1. Most modern homes are wired with RJ-14 four-wire cable. Two wires are used for one telephone connection. The other two wires can be used for an additional phone line or for electrical power for phone lighting.

Figure 13-2.
The telephone jacks in a home are run using one common line.

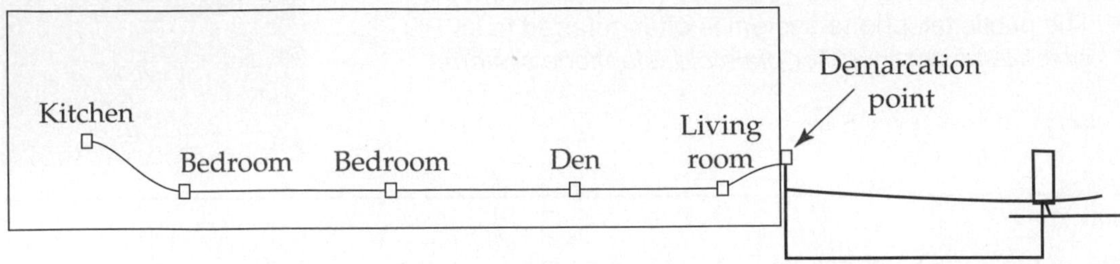

Never work on a telephone line when there is a storm in the area. Lightning strikes can travel many miles across a telephone system and exit anywhere along the system. You could be injured during a lightning storm.

telephone jack
where the telephone line connects into the cabling. This is a standard connection used to attach devices such as modems and telephones to the wiring system.

A ***telephone jack*** is where the telephone line connects to the cabling. This is a standard connection used to attach devices such as modems and telephones to the wiring system. The telephone jack is usually an RJ-11 or an RJ-14. The RJ-11 is a two-wire system, while the RJ-14 is a four-wire system. Since the deregulation of the public telephone system some years ago, the wiring inside the residence is typically the responsibility of the owner and not the local telephone company. A *point of demarcation* is where the telephone company system ends and the residence ownership begins.

Modems

modem
electronic device that is used to convert serial data from a computer to an audio signal for transmission over telephone lines and vice versa.

A ***modem*** is an electronic device that is used to convert serial data from a computer to an audio signal for transmission over telephone lines and vice versa. The term *modem* is a contraction of two words: *mo*dulator and *dem*odulator. It is derived from the field of electronics. A modem can be integrated into the motherboard, it can be installed in the form of an adapter card, or it can even be connected outside the computer case as a peripheral device. A modem must be used to transmit data across traditional telephone lines. The modem simply converts a digital signal into an analog signal, and then transmits a signal across telephone lines. Another modem on the receiving end converts the analog signal back to a digital signal. See **Figure 13-3.**

A modem is sometimes referred to as a transceiver. A transceiver is an electronic device that not only transmits data but also receives data.

Two computers can communicate using modems. The modem converts the digital signal from the computer system to an analog signal that can be carried over telephone lines. When the analog signal reaches the destination PC, the modem converts the analog signal back to a digital signal. Some common uses for modems are to gather information across the Internet, to connect to an office PC from home, to connect to a home or office PC from a laptop while on the road, and to establish a connection to a mainframe computer system. Sending and receiving facsimiles (faxes), pictures, and music or having a simple telephone conversation while working at the computer are all examples of applications of a modem.

Figure 13-3.
These two computers are connected by a modem. The signal coming from the first computer is digital until it passes through its modem. The modem coverts the digital signal to an analog signal and passes it through the phone lines. The second computer's modem receives the analog signal and converts it back to a digital signal that the computer can read.

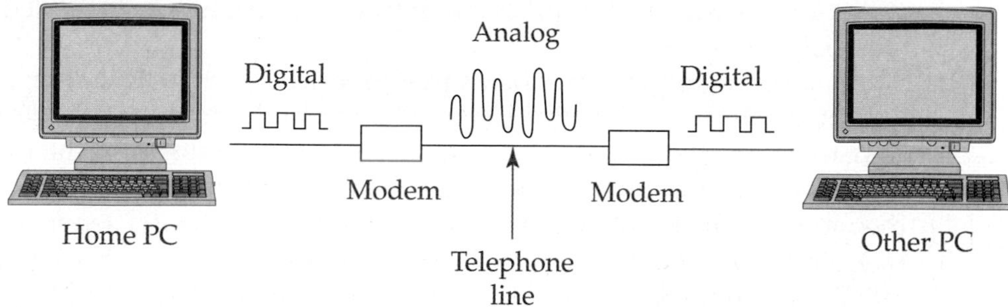

Modem Construction

The modem is simple in construction and only requires a few electronic components. See **Figure 13-4.** The main chip is the ***universal asynchronous receiver-transmitter (UART).*** The main purpose of the UART is to change parallel data to serial data and vice versa. Data moves as bytes on the computer bus system. The telephone uses a single wire to communicate in one direction. Thus, the byte, which is a parallel arrangement of data, must be converted into a series or single string of data bits.

universal asynchronous receiver-transmitter (UART)
main chip in a modem that changes parallel data to serial data and vice versa.

The modem must also change the data into a form that can be transmitted across telephone lines. Digital data from the computer system cannot travel across typical phone lines because of its high frequency and wave shape. To operate over traditional phone lines, the digital signal must be modulated. This means that the digital signal is changed into an analog signal and its frequency is slowed down. The rate of data flow inside the computer is far too high to pass through traditional phone lines.

The rate of the analog frequency that a modem transmits at is known as the ***baud rate.*** When the original modem was designed, the baud rate and data transfer rate were very close. Today, the baud rate and data rate are two distinct speeds. Baud rate reflects the actual analog signal rate. However, now there are a number of modulation techniques that can get a higher data transfer rate from the same baud rate. Some of these techniques include *frequency shift keying, quadrature amplitude modulation,* and *phase shift keying.* These systems of

baud rate
analog frequency rate of modem transmission.

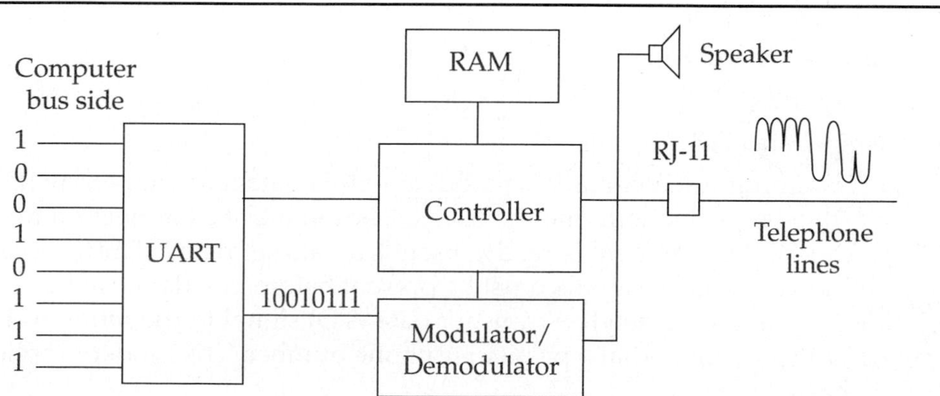

Figure 13-4.
There are only a few major components in a modern modem. The UART is the most important.

encoding are very difficult to fully understand without an adequate electronics background. For now, just know that these techniques allow data to be a multiple of a single baud rate. For example, a baud rate of 900 can be changed to a data rate of 1800 or 3600 bits per second (bps). Even bits per second is not the actual data speed. The actual data speed is increased by data compression techniques as well. Compression techniques were introduced in Chapter 8—Video Display and Audio Systems.

In addition to the components that produce signal modulation, modems need a memory chip component. The data flow from the computer bus is too fast to transmit directly through the modem. Data must be stored in the modem and transmitted more slowly. This is the job of a simple RAM chip incorporated into the modem. The RAM chip holds large chunks of data and sends it at a slower rate, a rate the modem can handle. When a modem receives data, the same action takes place in reverse. The data received is stored in RAM until the computer bus system is ready to receive it.

Modems also come with an audio device, such as a small speaker. This speaker allows you to hear the audible tones dialed by the modem when activated. This will assist you when troubleshooting. The speaker allows the user to hear the tones used in the transmission of data, usually at start up. When you connect to the Internet through your modem, you can hear the modem dial out to your Internet service provider. If you don't hear any tones when the modem is dialing out, the modem may be set up incorrectly or the modem may have failed. However, some people turn off the sound to the modem, so lack of sound does not always indicate a problem.

The job of coordinating the entire operation of the modem is left to the control chip. The control chip controls the flow of data and the interaction of all the parts of the modem. It is similar to a minicomputer and is often referred to as a microcontroller.

Modem Connection Process

There are several steps that must be performed to make and maintain a connection to another computer. The act of connecting to another computer using a modem is often referred to as *modem negotiation.* Often these steps can be observed on an exterior modem through the use of lights (LEDs). The process of making the connection is a series of signals and commands, which include the following:

- ✔ Data Terminal Ready (DTR).
- ✔ Data Set Ready (DSR).
- ✔ Carrier Detect (CD).
- ✔ Request to Send (RTS).
- ✔ Clear to Send (CTS).
- ✔ Transmit Data (TD).

A software program commands a modem with a data terminal ready (DTR) signal, which tells the modem that the user wishes to make a connection to another location. If the modem is ready, it sends a data set ready (DSR) signal back to the software. Both signals must be present before any data can be transmitted. Next, the PC sends a transmit data (TD) signal to the modem. This commands the modem to dial a particular phone number. The modem replies with a receive data (RD) signal and proceeds to open a connection on the phone line, which is referred to as "off the hook." A series of electrical pulses flows from the modem through the telephone line. This is the same as dialing a number. When the other modem receives the hailing signal, it responds back to the originating modem. The modem now uses a carrier detect (CD) signal to let the originating PC know that a carrier signal has been received from the modem. An example of this conversation is shown in **Figure 13-5.**

There are many different modem styles and software systems, so the two modems now communicate back and forth trying to establish a common ground for exchanging data. The communication includes such matters as the transmission speed, the number of stop and start bits, and the type of parity that will be used. The handling of half/full-duplex must also be resolved. Data speed or baud rate must be the same for both modems. The absolute base speed is 300 baud, but normally it will be above 1200 baud. Start/stop bits must be established.

Figure 13-5.
Modems send signals back and forth to set up a conversation.

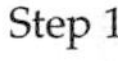

Step 1

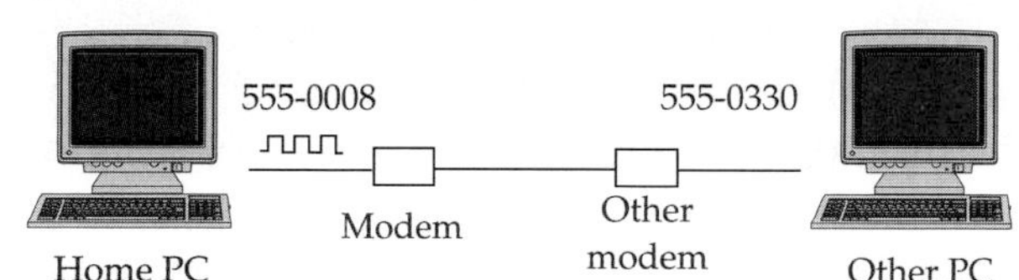

Hey modem, are you ready?

Yes, I'm ready.

Data Terminal Ready (DTR)
and Data Set Ready (DSR)

Step 2

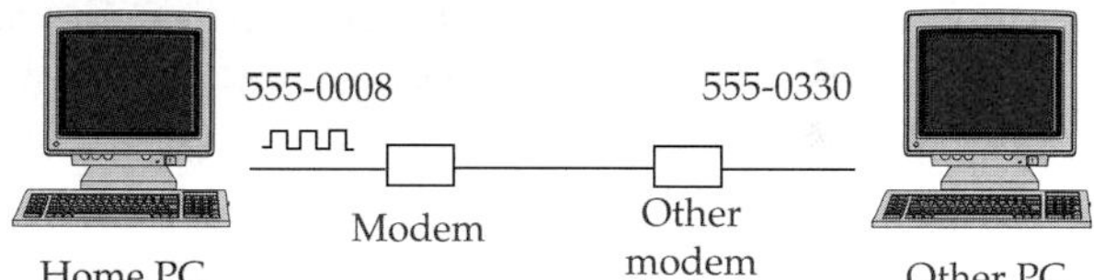

Hey modem, call this
number for me: 5550330

OK, will do.

Transmit data (TD) : call the 5550330 number.
Carrier Detect (CD): is there a phone line available?
When line is available, the 5550330 number is dialed.

Step 3

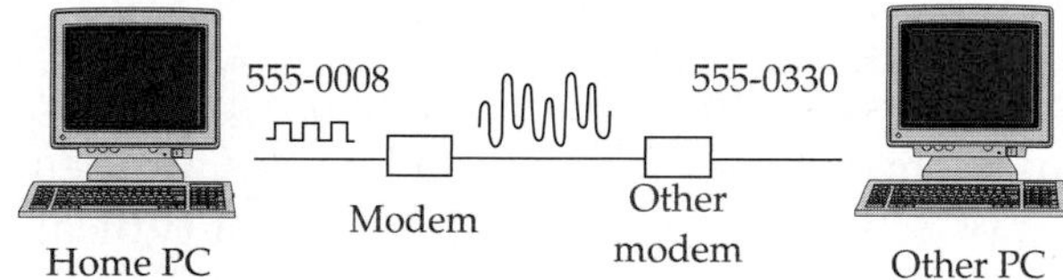

Hey 5550330. I'm calling you.

I'm here 5550008.

How fast do you run?

I run at 28,000 bps. Can you keep up?

No problem. Do you use parity?

Yes.

Odd or even?

How about odd?

That's fine. Are you going to display images on both screens or shall I?

You called, so why don't you do it.

Ok.

The rules of communication have been negotiated.

Step 4

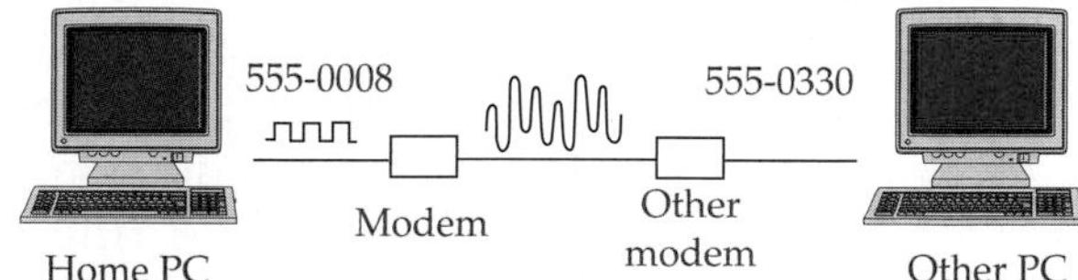

Hey 5550330, I'm going to send you a request to send (RTS) each time I send you some data, and you reply with a clear to send (CTS) if you are ready. I know that the CPU can be quite busy and your RAM could be full.

Thanks 5550008, I'll do the same for you.

The process of data exchange continues until one of the parties hangs up.

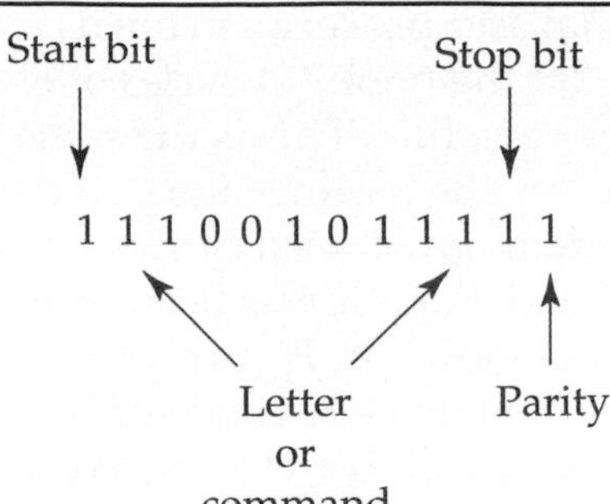

Figure 13-6.
Typical modem data packet. Surrounding the data is a start bit, stop bit, and parity bit.

Data sent across telephone lines by a modem is sent in packets. A single bit is used to mark the beginning of a packet and either one or two bits are used to mark the end of the packet. Look at **Figure 13-6.**

The type of parity must also be agreed on. There are three options: no parity, odd parity, and even parity. Parity is a way to check the accuracy of the data packet being sent. When the number of bits inside the data packet is added up, it will equal an odd or an even number. The systems agree to send an additional bit that represents either an odd number or an even number. A zero can represent odd or even parity and the same is true for a one. The receiving system adds up the bits in the data and compares that number to the parity bit to check for errors.

The last item to resolve is the half/full-duplex condition. The two communicating systems must agree which system will be responsible for half-duplex transmission and which will be responsible for full-duplex transmission. The terminal responsible for full-duplex is responsible to display data on the screen for both PCs. The other PC need not be responsible. If this condition is not agreed on, neither system will display the data on the screen, or both systems will display data on the screen. This means the data will be displayed twice on each screen.

After all the responsibilities have been negotiated between systems, messages can begin to be transmitted. The modem sends a request to send (RTS) signal asking if the other modem is ready to receive data. It replies with a clear to send (CTS) signal. The two computers can send data back and forth in continuous operation and actually both can transmit data over the line at the same time.

Many of these commands and activities can be monitored when using a modem connected outside the PC unit. The exterior type of modem has a series of lights that indicate different stages of activities. **Figure 13-7** is a list of typical light abbreviations and their definitions.

The entire operation of the modem is a combination of coordinating the operating system software, modem controller chip, and UART chip. The entire process seems complicated, but in effect it appears transparent to the typical user. The user simply clicks an icon and connects.

Modem and Dialing Properties

There are many different properties associated with a telephone modem. Plug and Play modems are easy to install. But, as easy as it is to install a Plug and Play modem, there will be times when you will need to be familiar with the various property settings associated with the telephone modem and modem connections to the Internet. During troubleshooting scenarios, you may need to reconfigure a dial-up modem or talk a customer through various changes and verifications when performing customer support.

AA (Auto Answer)	Ready to accept incoming calls automatically.
CD (Carrier Detect)	The modem has detected a carrier signal.
HS (High Speed)	The modem is operating at its highest speed.
MR (Modem Ready)	Modem is ready to operate; the power is on.
OH (Off Hook)	Same as taking the receiver off the telephone hook.
SD (Send Data)	Data is being received from the other modem.
TR (Terminal Ready)	Modem indicates it has received a (DTR) from the software package.

Figure 13-7. External modem light abbreviations and definitions.

When a new telephone connection is first set up, you will use the **New Location** dialog box, **Figure 13-8.** The **New Location** dialog box looks very similar in Windows XP and Windows Vista and requires information about several items. These items are described in **Figure 13-9.**

The **Area Code Rules** tab reveals how the area code should be entered. For example, what number(s) or prefixes are to be used and in what sequence. The **Calling Card** tab, shown in **Figure 13-10,** allows you to select the calling card company you wish to use with the dial-up connection. As you can see, you must include a calling card account number and a personal identification number (PIN).

The **New Location** dialog box is located through **Start | Control Panel | Phone and Modem Options** when in the Classic View. In the Category View, it is accessed through **Start | Control Panel | Printers and Other Hardware | Phone and Modem Options**. This dialog box is similar in Windows XP and Windows Vista.

In Windows Vista, you can access **Phone and Modem Options** through **Start | Control Panel | Hardware and Sound | Phone and Modem Options**. You may also access the **Phone and Modem Options** dialog box using the Classic View setting of **Control Panel** to reveal the **Phone and Modem Options** icon.

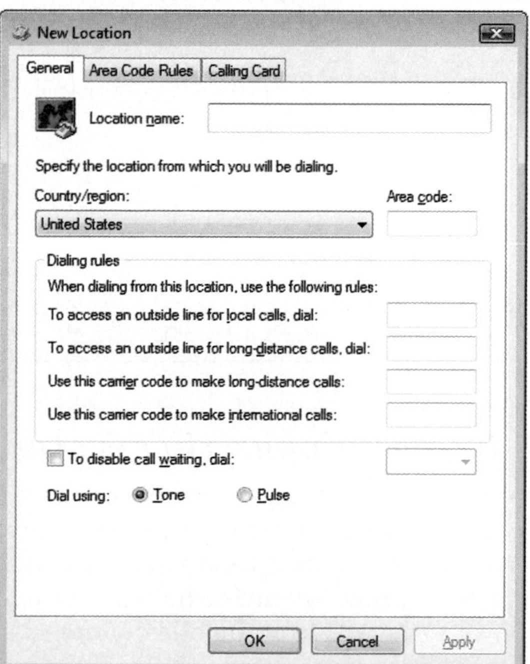

Figure 13-8. The **New Location** dialog box allows you to examine and change settings for your modem.

Figure 13-9.
New Location dialog box properties and description.

Property	Description
Location Name	A name that identifies the location to which the modem will connect. This is very important if there are more than one dial-up connection, such as one to your Internet service provider and one to your work location.
Country/Region	Country or region of the location you are calling from.
Area code	The area code of the telephone line you are calling from, not to.
Dialing Rules	Special numbers required to place an outside call. For example, a number such as *9* or *1* may need to be dialed before a connection outside the facility can be established.
Call Waiting	Used to disable call waiting. Some service providers require that you disable the call waiting feature. The local telephone provider will supply the required number(s) to disable the call waiting feature.
Dial using	Options are **Pulse** or **Tone**. Pulse phone dialing is used with the rotary dial phone. In the U.S., touch tone dialing is used almost everywhere.

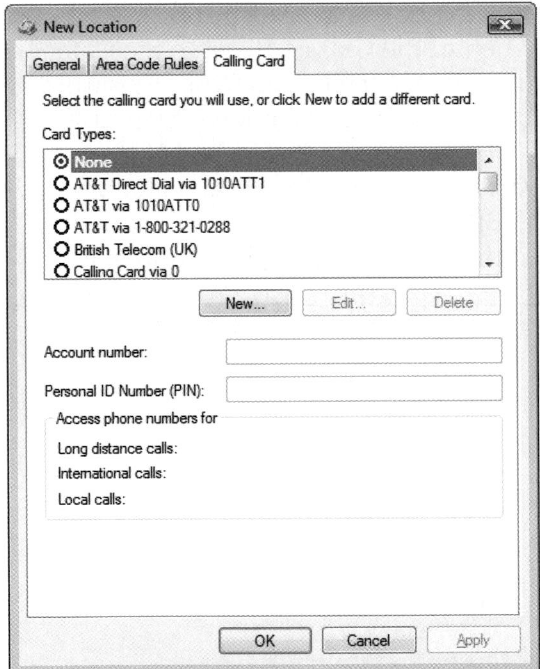

Figure 13-10.
Beneath the **Calling Card** tab is a list of many calling card companies with which to use your dial-up connection. Notice that you must also enter your account number and personal identification number (PIN).

Windows Vista Internet Connection Features

Windows Vista has drastically changed how network and Internet connections are made. The Windows Vista operating system automatically detects installed devices, such as modems and network connections and then automatically starts the appropriate wizard to help a user to configure the device. However, when Windows Vista fails to automatically detect an installed device, it modifies the dialog input boxes and wizards according to which devices are detected. For example, if a telephone modem has not been installed or configured, Windows Vista will not display an option for the device. Look at the differences between the dialog boxes shown in **Figure 13-11.** Notice the option **Show connections that this computer is not set up to use**. After selecting this option, the dialog box displays other devices that can be configured for Internet access, such as a dial-up modem or ISDN. Therefore, the option to configure a dial-up connection is displayed, thus allowing you to configure a modem, even though it was not automatically detected. The **Dial-up** option allows you to manually configure a dial-up connection if the Windows Vista operating system has failed to automatically detect the modem.

Some of the features that were standard in earlier versions of Windows operating systems have been absorbed into other setup programs. For example, a direct telephone dial-up feature is no longer available, but the same service can be provided through the Connect to a workplace wizard.

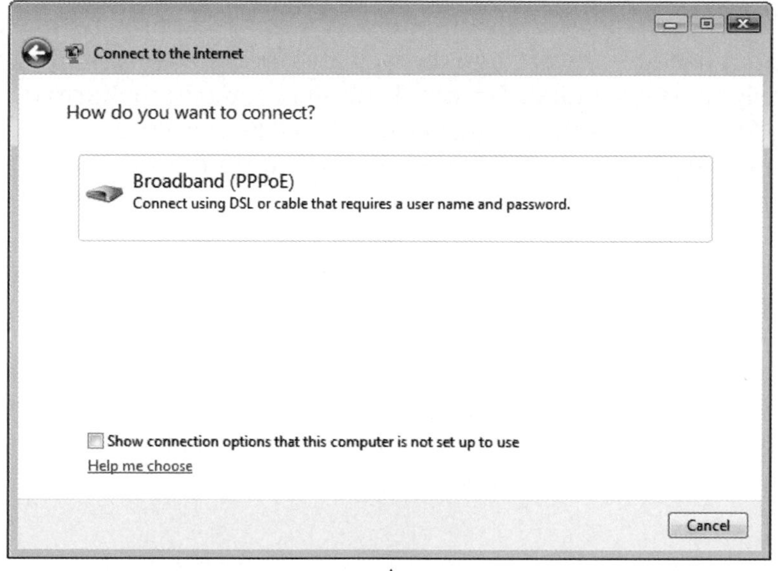

A

Connect to the Internet
How do you want to connect?
Broadband (PPPoE)
Connect using DSL or cable that requires a user name and password.
Dial-up
Connect using a dial-up modem or ISDN.
Show connection options that this computer is not set up to use
Help me choose
Cancel

B

Figure 13-11. Windows Vista modifies the dialog input boxes and wizards according to which devices were detected. A—The **Dial-up** option is hidden because the operating system did not detect the modem. B—With **Show connection options that this computer is not set up to use** selected, the **Dial-up** option is displayed.

Many times a feature not seen in Control Panel can be viewed and accessed by changing the default Control Panel view to Classic View. For example, **Phone and Modem Options** is directly available under Classic View but not in the Category View, which is the default view.

Integrated Services Digital Network

integrated services digital network (ISDN) standard that allows a completely digital connection from one PC to another.

Integrated services digital network (ISDN) is a standard that allows a completely digital connection from one PC to another. Like the regular dial-up service, ISDN uses phone lines to transfer data. Although, to use ISDN services, you must be within approximately 3 1/2 miles of the actual digital equipment of the telephone company. To use ISDN lines for communication, you must use a terminal adapter (TA) rather than a modem. A terminal adapter is like a modem, only it does not need to convert signals back and forth between analog and digital. The signal stays digital. Terminal adapters come in the form of adapter boards or exterior devices that connect directly to the serial port.

ISDN can be used to carry voice and digital information simultaneously. Traditional phone lines only allow voice or data. They cannot handle both at the same time. On a standard ISDN line there are three channels: one D channel and two B channels. The D channel is designed to carry control signals and operates in a range of 16 kbps to 64 kbps. The two B channels are used for voice and data and can carry data at speeds up to 64 kbps. The two B channels can be combined to carry data up to 128 kbps.

ISDN provides services for businesses as well as for private use. The price is much higher for digital service than for traditional phone lines. This makes its use prohibitive for many private users.

Digital Subscriber Lines

digital subscriber lines (DSL) provides high-speed Internet access over telephone lines. A DSL can provide a constant connection to the Internet and can send both voice and data over the same line.

Digital subscriber lines (DSL) provide high-speed Internet access over telephone lines and has become one of the most popular methods for connecting to the Internet. There are many different variations of DSL available, such as ADSL, HDSL, VHDSL, and SDHL. In this textbook, we will use the acronym DSL to represent the technology in general and will not address any particular type of DSL.

A DSL can provide a constant connection to the Internet and can be used to send and receive both voice and data over the same line. Regular telephone lines are designed to carry low-frequency voice communications in a range of 0 kHz to 4 kHz. DSL telephone lines are designed to carry much higher frequencies at 25 kHz to 1 MHz. The higher frequencies can be used as a high-speed Internet access. DSL is not available in all areas, and it is more expensive than regular telephone line service.

The maximum distance DSL can span is limited by the high frequencies it uses. The typical maximum distance for DSL is 1000′ to 1800′ measured from the DSL modem to the telephone central office. The exact limit depends on the type of DSL used and any special equipment, such as loading coils, or media such as fiber optic, that might exist on the telephone line.

A loading coil is used to amplify analog voice signals. It will not amplify a DSL signal. In fact, the loading coil reduces or blocks the higher frequency DSL signal. The media might also change between the subscriber location and the central office. For example, the copper conductor cabling may change to fiber-optic cabling at some point, which will prevent the application of DSL. DSL technology is applied only to copper wiring, not fiber optic.

The actual physical attributes of the copper core in the cable is another factor that determines the maximum distance DSL can be applied. The cable copper core length, diameter, and number of twists per foot in the cable pairs affect the actual distance and throughput of the DSL service. The diameter of the cable is expressed in a measure referred to as AWG, which is the acronym American Wire Gage. The three common diameters range are 22, 24, and 26 AWG. The 22 AWG is the largest diameter, and the 26 AWG is the smallest diameter. The smaller the diameter of the cable and the greater the number of twists in the cable pairs, the shorter the distance the cable can span and the lower the frequency it can carry. The most significant factor affecting DSL performance is the cable overall length.

DSL Types

There are many types of DSL systems. They vary in upstream and downstream bandwidths as shown in **Figure 13-12.** The term *downstream* is used to describe the data flow direction from the carrier or provider's site to the customer. The term *upstream* is used for the data flow direction from the customer to the carrier.

ADSL is the original DSL service and is commonly used by Internet service providers for residential services. An ***Internet Service Provider (ISP)*** provides connection to the Internet, and it usually provides many other services as well. Services such as e-mail, tools, and space to set up your own Web site, search engines, and local information are provided by most ISPs.

Internet Service Provider (ISP) provides a connection to the Internet and to other services.

ADSL2+ is an improved version of the original ADSL and has greater service distances and higher rates. VDSL is a high-speed, short-distance DSL service that is typically used for short runs from the home or office to a higher speed fiber-optic cable service. VDSL2 and VDSL2+ are the latest DSL service technologies designed to provide combined voice, video, and data to support high-definition television.

DSL Type	Upstream	Downstream	Maximum Distance
ADSL	800 kbps	1.5 Mbps–8 Mbps	12,000–18,000
ADSL2+	2 Mbps	24 Mbps	5000
HDSL	1.544 Mbps	1.544 Mbps	15,000
SDSL	1.544 Mbps	1.544 Mbps	10,000
VDSL	1.5 Mbps–2.3 Mbps	13 Mbps–52 Mbps	1000–4500
VDSL2	1 Mbps–16 Mbps	30 Mbps	4000
VDSL2+	2 Mbps	24 Mbps	5000
RADSL	1 Mbps	7 Mbps	1000–18,000
G.lite ADSL	192 kbps–2.3 Mbps	192 kbps–2.3 Mbps	14,000

Figure 13-12. DSL types and their upload and download speeds. Typical maximum distances are also listed.

SDSL and HDSL are both symmetric services, which mean that the upstream and downstream data rates match. Services that start with the letter *A* are asymmetric. This means the upstream and downstream data rates do not match. SDSL is a basic service, while HDSL is a high-speed data rate form of DSL.

RADSL stands for Rate Adaptive DSL. Rate adaptive means the connection is shared and the actual connection speed will vary depending on the number of persons using the service. When more people are using the service, the actual connection speed drops in increments. For more information on the various DSL technologies, visit www.xdsl.com.

When comparing information about xDSL from other sources, you will see that data rates and maximum distances will vary greatly. This is because some sources only reflect their company's technologies. A major factor is the electrical characteristics of the copper wire.

DSL Modem and Cables

DSL modem transceiver that allows for high-speed Internet access over existing phone lines.

A ***DSL modem*** allows for high-speed Internet access over existing phone lines. It is also referred to as a DSL transceiver. A typical DSL modem is shown in **Figure 13-13.** Also shown are a power adapter, telephone cable, and Ethernet cable. The power adapter converts the standard 120 Vac to 12 Vdc in order to power the modem. The telephone cable connects to the back of the DSL modem to the telephone wall jack using RJ-11 connectors. The Ethernet cable is a standard Cat 5 or Cat 5e cable. The Ethernet cable connects to the back of the DSL modem and then to the network adapter card installed in the PC, **Figure 13-14.** Some DSL modems use a USB cable to connect to the PC's USB port. No network adapter is required to be installed in the PC if a USB cable is used.

Figure 13-13.
DSL modem, cables, and power adapter.

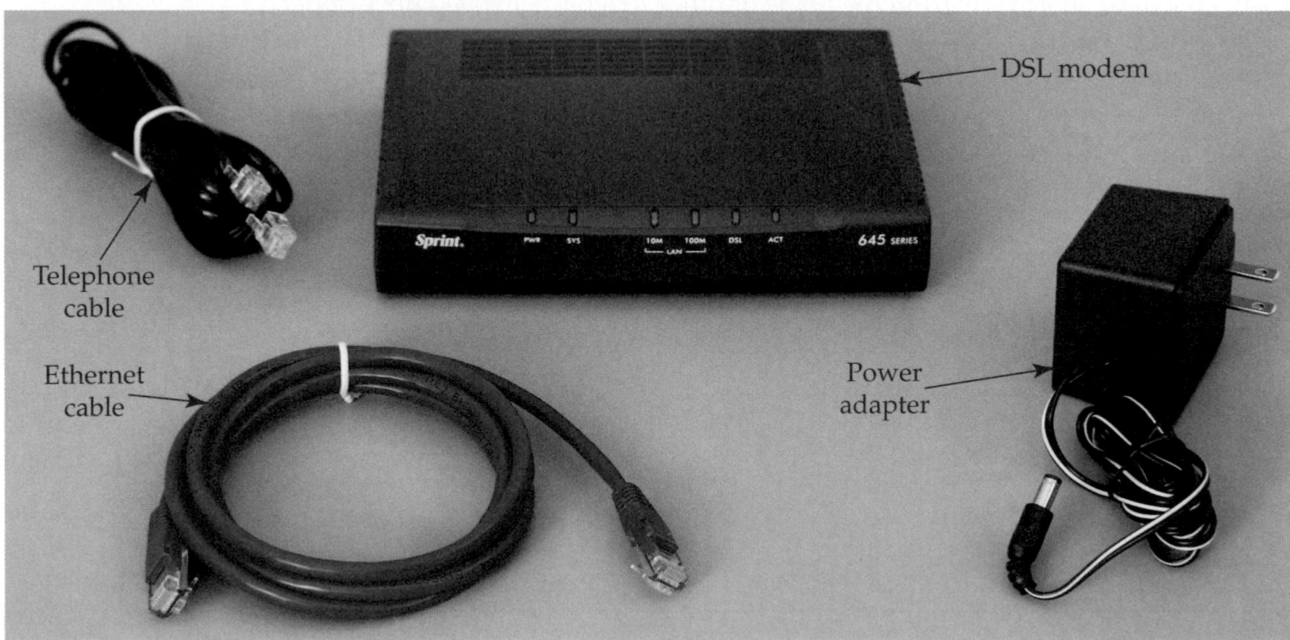

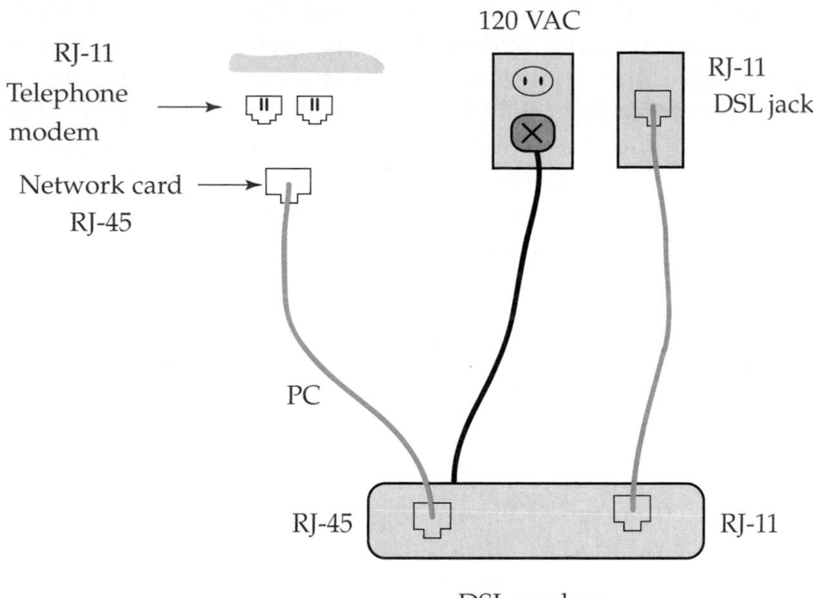

Figure 13-14.
The DSL modem is connected between the DSL telephone line and the network card on the PC.

An additional device called a *filter* may be required if there is other equipment connected to the same telephone line used for Internet access. Other equipment types are fax machines or telephones. Fax machines and telephones can be plugged into the same DSL line as the PC, but they must do so through a filter. The filter prevents lower frequency signals to and from these devices from interfering with or corrupting the higher frequency signals used for the Internet connection. A filter is never installed in the line between the DSL modem and the PC because it will block the high frequency signals used by the Internet connection.

DSL is a point-to-point connection. This means it will provide a steady bandwidth and will not fluctuate like other broadband connections. For example, Cable television access used for Internet connections are shared by other connections in the local neighborhood. Cable television bandwidth varies according to how many other people are accessing the Internet using the shared cable.

Both Cable Internet access and DSL can be used to support multiple devices such as other computers or gaming consoles. A device called a *router* or *gateway* is installed after the modem, or the modem can be a combination of router and modem. The router can distribute additional connections using cable or wireless radio signals.

Cable Internet Service

Cable Internet service provides high-speed Internet access using lines designed for Cable television. It uses a Cable modem to connect you to the Internet without having to dial in. It can provide you with a continuous connection. Your connection will not time out for lack of use like it may with a dial-up Internet service provider. ISPs set a time-out value so that they can take back the IP address and make it available to other users. With a Cable Internet service, you have your own IP address. IP addresses are discussed later in this chapter.

DSL and Cable provide much more bandwidth than a 56 k telephone modem. DSL has several different speed options running from 250 kbps to over 1.5 Gbps. A drawback of Cable is that its Internet bandwidth varies greatly depending on the number of users accessing the Internet through the shared connection. Thus, as more people access and use data-intense services, such as video and audio downloading, your data speeds will slow. You can expect 300 kbps to 500 kbps on average from each of the Internet services, despite their claims of speeds in the very high Mbps range. In some cases, you can expect speeds as high as 1.5 Mbps or slightly higher. Another drawback of Cable Internet service is there is typically only one choice of Cable service provider per neighborhood. So, if you are unhappy with your service provider, the only way to get a new one is to move.

Cable Media

There are two major types of Cable television media used for access: fiber-optic cable and coaxial cable. See **Figure 13-15.** Coaxial cable consists of a solid copper conductor surrounded by a thick insulating material. An outer conductor is made of braided copper or a foil jacket surrounding the insulating material. An insulating jacket, used to provide physical protection to the cable assembly, covers the entire assembly. Special coaxial cable connectors are crimped onto the ends. Coaxial cable is easily spliced or extended. Coaxial cable has a maximum data transfer speed of 350 MHz. The coaxial cable is used to download from the Internet, while conventional telephone lines make the connection to the Internet. The coaxial cable is not currently a two-way data transmission system.

Fiber-optic cable consists of a glass or plastic core. Each core material, glass or plastic, is quite small in cross-sectional area and is very flexible. Fiber-optic cable transmits light rather than an electrical signal through the core. Fiber-optic cable has many advantages over coaxial cable or any type of copper core cable. It is lightweight, resistive to corrosion and water, and immune to electrical interference. It also provides excellent security because it is almost impossible to tap into. One very big advantage of fiber-optic cable is that it is immune to strikes by lightning. When lightning strikes traditional metal core cable, a high current can run through the cable and damage sensitive electronic equipment, including

Figure 13-15.
A—Coaxial cable. Note the center conductor surrounded by layers of insulation. B—Fiber-optic cable. Fiber-optic cable has several outer layers. The layers protect the cable and reflect the light down the cable.

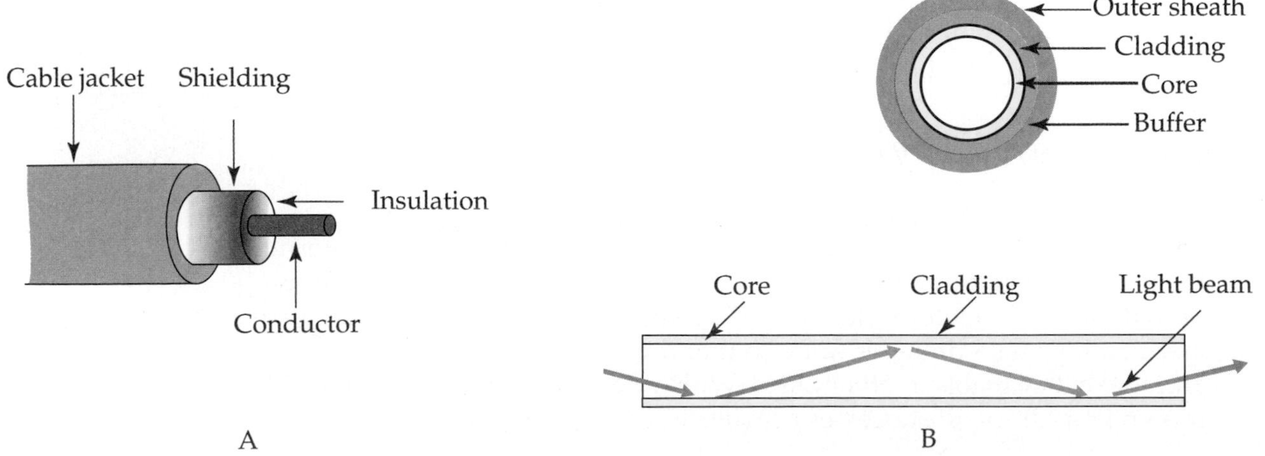

computers and monitors. Fiber-optic cable can also be run for longer lengths with less signal loss than conventional copper core cables.

The downside of fiber-optic cable is essentially price. Fiber-optic cable is expensive to install. Also, special equipment is required for splicing the cable.

Fiber-optic cable through the television company is usually divided into many different channels. Each channel uses a 6-MHz channel to transmit each separate television channel or network, such as ABC, CBS, or NBC. The same principle is used for Internet connections. Two channels, each 6 MHz, are provided to transmit data to and from the Internet. Currently, there is not a single standard for Cable modem specifications. You must check with the local ISP cable company to see what type or brand of cable modem you will need. One standard that has been established for cable modems is called ***Data Over Cable Service Interface Specification (DOCSIS).*** This standard allows any DOCSIS Cable modem to communicate with any other DOCSIS cable modem. Also, you will need to install a cable splitter. The cable splitter divides the signal between your modem and your television. Remember, the same cable provides both television and Internet access.

Data Over Cable Service Interface Specification (DOCSIS) standard for cable modems that allows any DOSIS Cable modem to communicate with any other DOCSIS cable modem.

Cable Modem

A ***Cable modem*** is a transceiver similar to a DSL modem and allows existing Cable television coaxial cable to be used for Internet access. Look at the Cable modem connection in **Figure 13-16.** The Cable modem is installed between a splitter and the PC. In this configuration, the coaxial cable can supply a television signal to the television as well as provide Internet access for the PC. The Cable television coaxial cable connects to the Cable modem from the splitter. An Ethernet cable or USB cable is used between the Cable modem and the PC. More than one PC can use the Cable Internet connection if a router or gateway is installed. The router or gateway need not be a separate device. Some cable modems are a combination modem and router.

Cable modem transceiver similar to a DSL modem that allows existing Cable television coaxial cable to be used for Internet access.

Figure 13-16.
The Cable modem is installed between a splitter and the PC. The splitter separates the Cable television signal from the Internet signal.

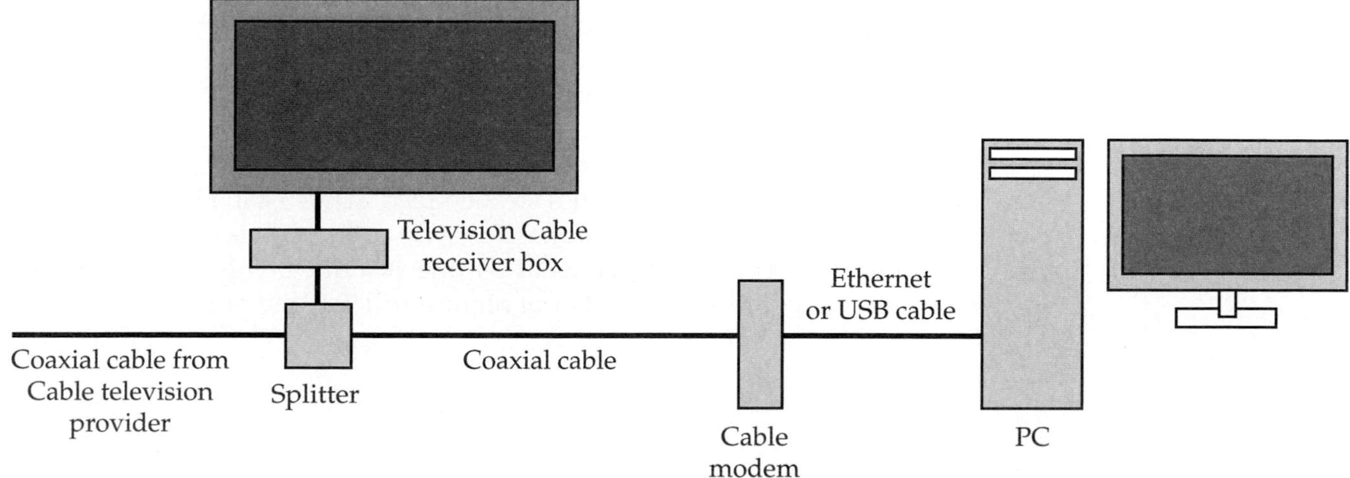

DSL and Cable modem ISPs typically include a setup CD. The setup CD automatically configures the connection to the ISP. The DSL and Cable modem require an IP address before making a connection to the Internet.

Satellite

Satellite systems can be used for Internet access and are ideal for remote locations when a home or office is located a great deal away from city services. Satellite Internet service typically costs more to set up than other residential forms of service. You typically must either buy the satellite equipment for several hundred dollars or rent it.

The data rates for satellites vary greatly. The common downstream speed varies from 512 kbps to 1.5 Mbps. The common upstream data rates vary from 128 kbps to 256 kbps. The satellite provides a constant connection to the Internet in similar fashion to xDSL and cable systems. Satellite systems are line-of-sight systems, which mean they must have an unobstructed direct view to the source. Trees and buildings can obstruct the satellite receiver from the source. The satellite system is also susceptible to weather conditions, such as heavy rain storms.

T-Carrier Lines

T-carrier lines lines designed to carry voice and data at a much higher rate than traditional phone lines.

T-carrier lines were first introduced in 1993 by AT&T. They are designed to carry voice and data. The lines have the ability to carry data at a much higher rate than traditional phone lines. An important part of the T-carrier line system is the use of a *multiplexer* and a *demultiplexer.* A multiplexer is a special electronic device that controls the flow of data and voice over a T-carrier line. Think of it as a funnel that combines lower frequency lines together to take advantage of the higher frequency transmission rates of the T-carrier. Look at **Figure 13-17** to view a multiplexer and T-carrier.

As you can see in the illustration, there are several low-speed lines tied into the multiplexer. As data is transmitted through the multiplexer, it is reorganized into smaller packages called *data packets.* The multiplexer sends the data packets through the T-carrier in an organized manner. The data packet then travels at the maximum speed of the T-carrier. At the opposite end of the T-carrier there is a demultiplexer that reverses the process. It rearranges the packets back into their original structures and releases them to lower data rate lines. Businesses, government, and educational institutions are the primary customers who lease T-carrier lines. The levels of T-carrier lines are identified in the list in **Figure 13-18.**

An additional label, called a fractional T-1, is a T-1 line that is only partially issued to a customer. Think of a fractional T-1 line as a line being shared among different parties who, individually, do not require full T-1 line capacity.

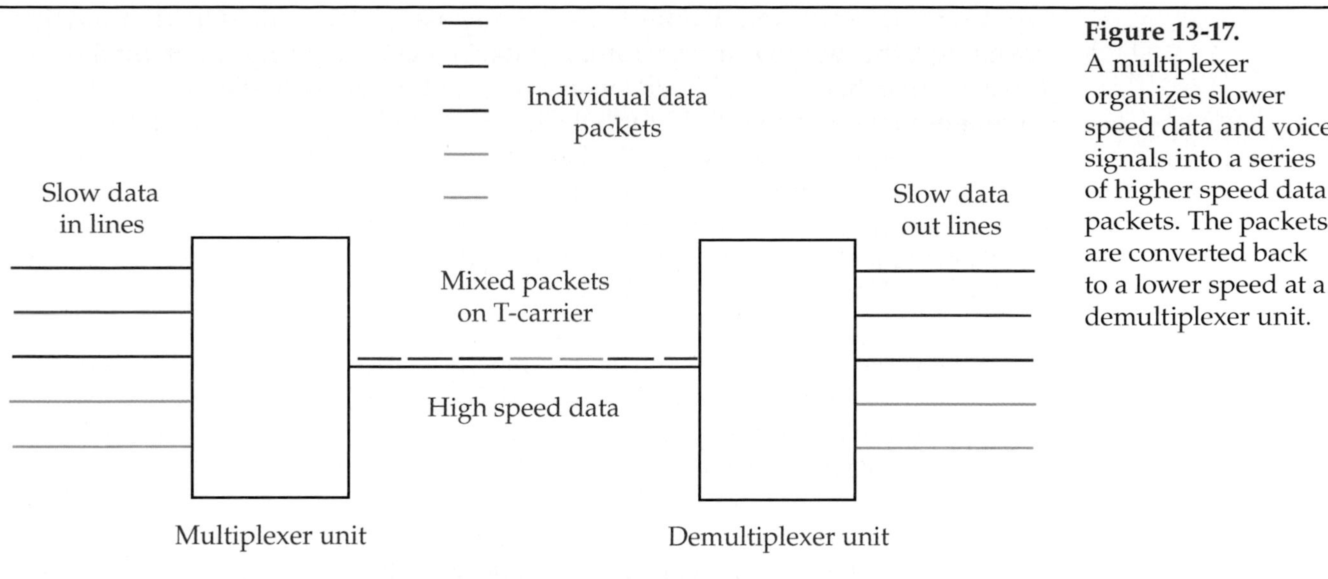

Figure 13-17. A multiplexer organizes slower speed data and voice signals into a series of higher speed data packets. The packets are converted back to a lower speed at a demultiplexer unit.

T-carrier
T-1 = 1.544 Mbps or 24 voice channels
T-2 = 6.312 Mbps or 96 voice channels
T-3 = 44.736 Mbps or 672 voice channels
T-4 = 274.176 Mbps or 4032 voice channels

Figure 13-18. T-carrier identifications.

Setting Up a Residential Internet Connection

A residential Internet connection can be easily set up. The term *residential* is used because setting up an Internet connection for a network system is different. The requirements for a large network are covered later in this textbook. Most of the residential setup is done using a setup wizard program, but even the setup wizard will need some information from you.

Most ISPs provide CD-ROMs to assist you in automatically connecting with their services. Running these discs starts a wizard that helps you set up your connection to the Internet. In addition, most PCs purchased today have setup software for several ISPs loaded onto the desktop. These ISPs can be added quickly by clicking the associated icon on the display. Usually, all this will work automatically. At times, you may be required to do some configuring manually. This is especially true in a business environment or in a PC with a security system such as a firewall.

For a typical home PC, you will need to enter the telephone number of the ISP, your user ID such as JonesB, and a password issued by the ISP. Other items that you may need to enter are the name of the e-mail server being accessed at the ISP location and type of e-mail protocol being used, such as POP3. These last two items are usually provided by the ISP. You might also need to select the type of protocol used to transmit data to the ISP over the telephone line such as PPP or SLIP. Typically, PPP is used.

When you are setting up your Internet connection, you may be required to input a choice of protocol. A ***protocol*** is a set of rules much like the rules that are used by two modems. The standard protocol used for the Internet is TCP/IP, which stands for Transmission Control Protocol/Internet Protocol.

protocol set of rules for formatting the data stream transmission between two computers or devices and for describing how to transmit data, usually across a network.

A number, called an IP address, is usually associated with TCP/IP. You will have to get this number from your ISP if it is not automatically set up by the software installation. An IP address is a series of numbers that identifies the computer you are using. The numbers are separated by periods (dots) into four groups (for example 192.168.27.132). Each group is called an *octet*. An octet is a number that is comprised of eight bits. As you know, you can form 256 numbers (0–255) using eight bits. The Internet actually communicates using these series of numbers to identify a site as opposed to using the site name (such as www.g-w.com) that you are used to seeing. Software converts the numeric ID (IP address) into the name of the site you are trying to reach.

Since you are connecting to the Internet and expect other Web sites and people to respond to you, your PC also will have an IP address. If you use a dial-up ISP, the IP address you use may not be permanent. Rather, the address is newly issued each time you access the Internet through your ISP. This allows the ISP to have a smaller number of IP addresses and distribute them to users as they need them. The phone number dialed as you access the Internet is just the phone number of the ISP used by your PC. It is not your IP address. If you have a Cable modem, you will most likely have your own dedicated IP address.

McAfee Internet Connection Speedometer

A good free utility to test the actual speed of the Internet media is the McAfee Internet Connection Speedometer, **Figure 13-19.** It is located at http://us.mcafee.com/root/speedometer/default.asp. The MacAfee Internet Connection Speedometer tests the transfer of data packets for both upstream and

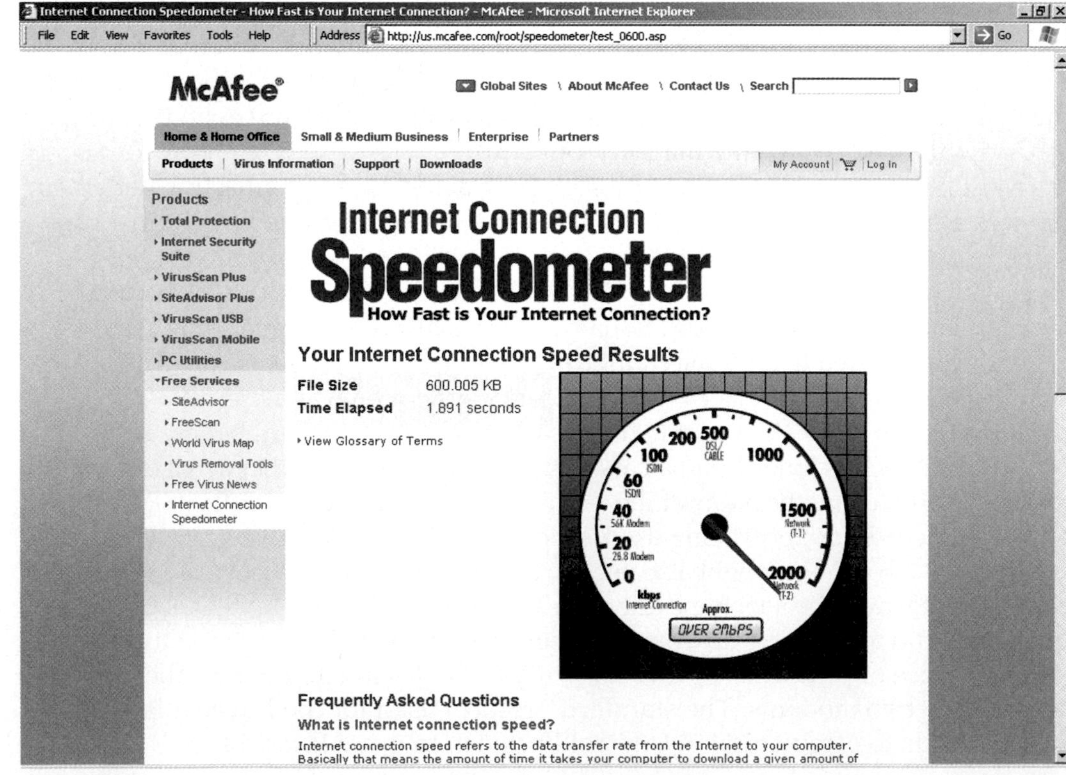

Figure 13-19. The McAfee Internet Connection Speedometer is an excellent utility to determine the speed of your Internet connection. It is located at http://us.mcafee.com/root/speedometer/default.asp.

downstream connections and then displays the result in the dial. In Figure 13-19, you can see that a 600 kB file was used to test the connection and the average speed obtained was 2000 kbps. The McAfee Internet Connection Speedometer is one the best free utilities available to test your connection speed.

Modem Signaling Standards

Data sent between two modems must use some type of communication standards after the initial process of setting up communication rules. The standards are used for data compression techniques and error correction after an error has been detected. When there were only a few telephone companies operating, this was not an issue. The Bell Telephone Company developed a set of standards known as the Bell standards. Bell 103 was the first widely accepted standard used for modems operating at 300 baud. Later, Bell 212A was the accepted standard for 1200 bps. After deregulation of the telephone companies in America, however, a number of standards were used.

A dominant standard was the *International Telecommunications Union (ITU).* This was not actually a single standard but rather a collection of standards. The standards resolved issues such as volume, minimum and maximum tone sound, and synchronous or asynchronous transmissions. As the speed of modems increased, new standards had to be developed based on the new techniques and technical parameters. Communication is now a worldwide event and involves standards from Europe also. As computer network systems evolved, another set of standards was developed called the *Microcom Networking Protocol (MNP).* This was developed in the mid-1980s. This set of standards deals mainly with the rules of communication between two computers.

In addition to the standards, a system is needed for telephone data communication between two points. A modem standard is developed so that two modems can communicate effectively. After a communications standard is established, the modem must have a way to determine data and command codes. A system is needed to show how the electrical pulses and fluctuations will be used to represent data. A modem simply transports packets as a series of electrical fluctuations. A protocol is needed to represent the data and how it is to be encoded. You can think of a protocol as the organized manner and the rules used to represent the data being transmitted. Some common communication protocols are Kermit, ASCII, Zmodem, Ymodem, and Sealink. There will be much more information about protocols later in this textbook when covering network fundamentals.

Basic AT Commands

There are sets of modem commands that are usually automatically issued by software in the GUI environment. You simply click the feature you want, and it automatically issues the command to the modem for you. However, at times, you may want to use a command directly from the keyboard, especially when using HyperTerminal or troubleshooting a modem.

HyperTerminal is an old style of communication for computers. It is still used today, but not so much for communication between computers. It is more for testing the modem and for programming remote equipment such as routers. You can transfer files between computers using HyperTerminal, but the files must be in ASCII format. Some colleges still offer downloading of files from their mainframes using HyperTerminal.

There are many AT commands, but only the basic commands will be covered here. You can download information on more commands from the Internet. You can use the basic AT commands for troubleshooting purposes. For example, you could start HyperTerminal, and then enter **AT** at the command line to verify that the modem and PC are communicating with each other. After the [Enter] key is pressed, the HyperTerminal screen should display "OK" on the screen. You can also type **AT&F** to reset the modem to its original factory settings. Examine some other basic commands in **Figure 13-20.**

There are other AT commands that can set the number of rings before a phone is answered, set the phone for a manual answer rather than automatic, save the phone profile or setup, cause the modem to briefly turn on, and more. The commands illustrated here are just to familiarize you with AT commands. They can be used when troubleshooting a standard modem.

Figure 13-20.
AT commands.

Command	Response	Description
AT&F	OK	Restore factory default settings.
ATZ	OK	Soft modem reset.
ATE1	OK	Enable the echo command. This allows commands to be viewed.
ATE0	OK	Turns the echo command off.
A/	OK	Repeat the last command issued.
+++	OK	This command gets the attention of the modem.
ATDT####	Connect ####	This command dials the phone number indicated by the #### symbols.
ATDT#, ##	None	The comma tells the modem to pause after dialing #.

Modem Troubleshooting

Use the following suggestions when troubleshooting a modem:

- ✔ Always check the modem connections first. Do not waste valuable time until you check the most obvious and the most common problem. People tend not to check cabling unless told to do so. A modem connection can be easily disturbed by vacuum cleaners, plugging in other equipment, or moving furniture. Always check the cable first.
- ✔ Start HyperTerminal and type **AT** at the command prompt to see if the modem responds. The response should be "OK." The OK response tells you that communication between the PC system and modem is working. Do not disassemble the PC.
- ✔ Try dialing a local or test telephone number. Use the computer's Phone Dialer to call the phone number of a phone on a neighboring desk. The phone should ring.
- ✔ Check the computer's IRQ and COM port settings. Look for conflicts.
- ✔ Check the call waiting function on the modem or dialer setup.
- ✔ Check if there is a time-out feature being used for the modem. Some modems cut off after a set time period of no activity.
- ✔ Check the telephone cable and telephone line. Faulty wiring along the telephone cable can be the cause. Try plugging in a standard telephone.
- ✔ Check with the phone company if any lines are out. Look for communications vehicles in the area of the company or residence with a modem problem. If you are called to a business for a modem problem and you see a communication vehicle sitting beside a ditch on your way there, it may save you a lot of frustration troubleshooting the modem if you stop and ask a few questions.
- ✔ If the modem is connecting but you are receiving or transmitting gibberish, then you probably have a software issue. Check the manufacturer's Web site for last minute upgrades and patches.
- ✔ Always assume that someone has already attempted to correct the problem before you were called. You may have to correct several problems before you detect the original one.

Summary

- ✔ An RJ-11 is a standard telephone cable connector.
- ✔ The term *modem* is a combination of the words *modulate* and *demodulate*, which describe the electronic action of the modem.
- ✔ The central electronic component of a modem is the universal asynchronous receiver transmitter (UART), which changes data from parallel to serial.
- ✔ A modem is designed to communicate by converting the digital data from the PC to an analog signal transmitted across telephone lines or other media.
- ✔ Baud rate reflects the speed of the analog frequency and not the true data transfer rate.

- ✔ Parity is used to ensure the data received is the correct bit pattern.
- ✔ Some standard communications media are telephone wiring, coaxial cable, and fiber-optic cable.
- ✔ A multiplexer is used to convert multiple individual data inputs into one series of serial data output.
- ✔ A demultiplexer is used to separate serial data input to separate parallel output data that matches the original data configurations.
- ✔ Actual data speeds will vary greatly from advertised speeds of Cable and DSL services.
- ✔ AT commands are used for modem communications.

Review Questions

Answer the following questions on a separate sheet of paper. Please do not write in this book.

1. What is the most important task of a phone modem?
2. Name several specific tasks that can be done by using a modem.
3. What is the main factor that limits the speed of data transfer over the residential telephone system?
4. What is the designed frequency spectrum for voice communication over traditional telephone lines?
5. What is RJ-11?
6. What was the original modem maximum speed?
7. Describe the difference between baud rate and data rate.
8. Describe the difference between a protocol and a standard.
9. Arrange the following commands in the expected order of implementation.
   CTS
   RTS
   DTR
   DSR
   CD
10. Why does a modem negotiate a connection with another modem?
11. What is an octet?
12. Write an example of an IP address.
13. Give five advantages that fiber-optic cable provides over coaxial cable and typical telephone wiring.
14. What does the **AT** command **ATDT5551010** do?

Sample A+ Exam Questions

Answer the following questions on a separate sheet of paper. Please do not write in this book.

1. Which statement best describes the operation of a modem?
   a. A device that converts digital signals from the PC bus system to analog signals that are transmitted across telephone lines.
   b. A device that transmits digital signals across telephone lines.
   c. A device that converts analog signals from a USB port to digital signals that are transmitted across telephone systems.
   d. A device that sends digital signals across various network systems until a digital signal reaches a predetermined PC connection.
2. Which of the following has the slowest data transfer rate?
   a. ISDN
   b. DSL
   c. Cable modem
   d. Dial-up modem
3. Which is the correct example of using an **AT** command to dial the phone number 555-6186?
   a. **AD 555-6186**
   b. **ATDT5556186**
   c. **ATD5556186**
   d. **AutoDial555-6186**
4. What does the LED marked "CD" on a modem *most likely* indicate?
   a. The call has been disconnected: CD = Call Disconnect.
   b. The phone code has been deployed: CD = Call Deployed.
   c. The carrier has been detected: CD = Carrier Detect.
   d. The carrier has been called or dialed: CD = Carrier Dialed.
5. Which of the following is an example of an IP address?
   a. 00 03 A4 34 C5 1F
   b. 123.67.103.114
   c. JohnJK12@hotmail.com
   d. JohnDoel23.456.ACME
6. Which connection type is typically found in a residential telephone jack outlet?
   a. RJ-45
   b. RJ-11
   c. BNC
   d. AT-45
7. Which connection type is typically found between a PC and a DSL modem?
   a. RJ-45
   b. RJ-11
   c. BNC
   d. AT-45

8. What would *most likely* affect the bandwidth of a Cable Internet connection?
   a. The amplitude of the signal modulation.
   b. The number of subscribers sharing the Cable line.
   c. The distance from the Cable modem to the Cable provider.
   d. Changes in media between the subscriber location and the central office.
9. What is the maximum bandwidth using an ISDN line?
   a. 56 kbps
   b. 1.54 Gbps
   c. 128 kbps
   d. 256 kbps
10. A T1 line is capable of reaching what data transfer speed?
   a. 56 kbps
   b. 1.54 kbps
   c. 1.54 Mbps
   d. 2.56 Mbps

Suggested Laboratory Activities

Do not attempt any suggested laboratory activities without your instructor's permission. Certain activities can render the PC operating system inoperable.

1. Install and set up NetMeeting to communicate with another PC.
2. Install and set up HyperTerminal to connect to a remote PC and exchange a file.
3. Inquire about what types of Internet service are available in your area. The services to inquire about are DSL, ISDN, Cable modem, and satellite. Use the Internet to inquire about availability in your area.
4. Download and read a DSL and Cable modem user manual. Pay special attention to the modem's ports, physical installation, and software configuration.

Interesting Web Sites for More Information

www.56k.com
www.cablelabs.com
www.catv.org
www.teledata-networks.com
www.usrobotics.com
www.verizon.com

Chapter 13 Lab Activity
Modem Installation

After completing this lab activity, you will be able to:

- ✔ Install and configure a typical dial-up modem.
- ✔ Explain the options available under the various modem properties tabs.
- ✔ Explain how to test a modem.

Introduction

In this lab activity, you will explore how to install and manually configure a telephone modem. It will not be necessary to physically install a modem. Most student labs do not have dial-up available for each workstation.

The term *modem* is a contraction of the two electronics terms *modulation* and *demodulation*. Modulation is the process of modifying an electrical signal or waveform by encoding data into the electrical signal. Demodulation means to extract information from the electrical signal or waveform. A telephone modem encodes the computer digital signal information into the analog signal used on plain old telephone system (POTS) designed for voice communications. In essence, the modem converts the digital signal from the computer into an analog signal and then transmits it over conventional telephone lines. At the destination modem, the analog signal is converted back to a digital signal that can be used by the computer.

The main electronic component inside a telephone modem is the universal asynchronous receiver transmitter or UART. The UART converts the parallel digital signal into a serial analog signal.

Modems can be integrated into the motherboard (onboard modem), installed as a separate unit outside the computer (external modem), or installed inside the computer as an adapter card.

The exact software installation and configuration requirements and steps are similar for Windows XP and Windows Vista. Basically, the modem you first set up as a hardware device and then configure it for a dial-up connection. A telephone modem is typically automatically detected by the operating system and requires very little technician intervention, except for the actual entering of the telephone number, area code, and other information used to identify the telephone connection. The following is a list of troubleshooting tips to help you in case you have problems with the installation.

- ✔ First, check the telephone line to and from the computer to be sure it is connected. Telephone lines often become loose or disconnected.
- ✔ Dial-up modems only work with analog telephone lines. If the phone line is DSL, you must use a DSL modem, not a dial-up modem.
- ✔ Check and verify that the telephone modem is configured for dialing an outside line when required. For example, the telephone modem may require "9" to be dialed to access an outside line.

- ✔ You can plug a working, analog-type phone into the telephone modem line and listen for a dial tone. This will verify that the line to the telephone company is intact.
- ✔ Open Device Manager and locate the telephone modem. See if a problem is indicated.
- ✔ Consult the telephone modem installation manual or manufacturer's Web site for information, especially for error code messages relating to the modem and for troubleshooting tips.
- ✔ As a last resort, call the telephone provider to verify the line is OK.

Equipment and Materials

- ✔ Typical PC with Windows XP or Windows Vista installed.
- ✔ A 56 k modem as an external device, adapter card, or integrated into the motherboard. This will be determined by your instructor. You may also need a device driver for the modem.
- ✔ Telephone number provided by the instructor of the line to be used.

Note:

You may need a number to access an outside line, especially in a school or office building setting.

Procedure

1. _______ Boot the PC and wait for the Windows desktop. This verifies the system is working properly.
2. _______ If you are simulating the installation, go on to step 3. If you are going to physically install an internal telephone modem, shut the computer down. Read the installation manual for additional information required to complete the modem installation.

   If you are installing an external modem, be sure the computer is powered down before connecting the modem cable to the PC.

3. _______ In Windows XP, access **Control Panel | Printers and Other Hardware | Phone and Modem Options**. You should see a dialog box similar to the following.

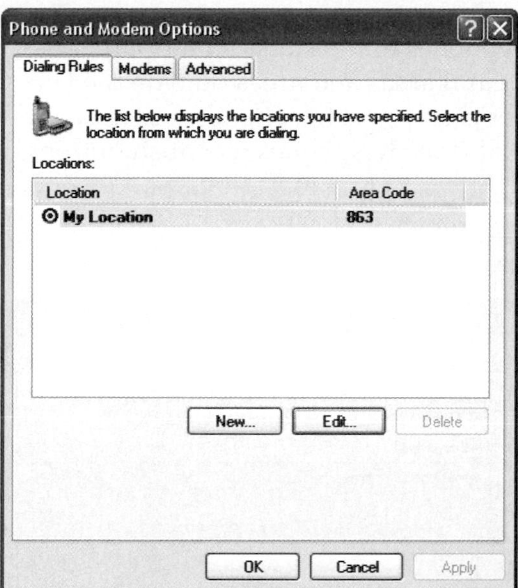

If you are using Windows Vista computer, access **Control Panel | Hardware and Sound | Phone and Modem Options**. The dialog box will be very similar to the previous Windows XP screen capture.

4. _______ Click the **New** button to set up a new phone connection. The dialog box **New Location** will display and look similar to the following for Windows XP or Windows Vista.

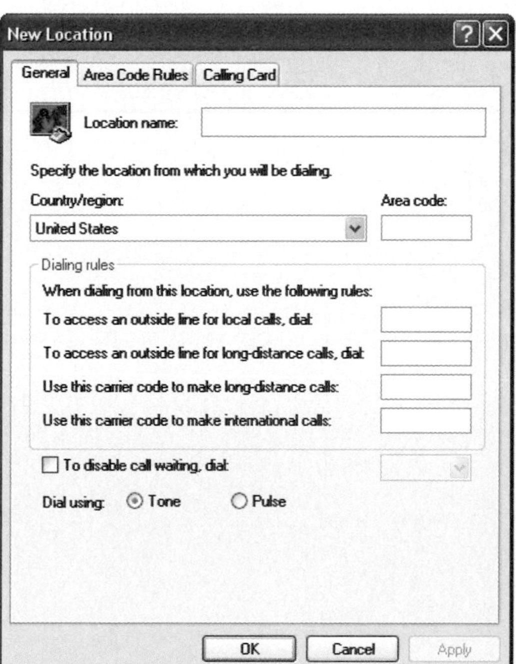

This dialog box is used to configure essential information about the telephone connection. You would put in the location name, area code, and other information required as needed. The **Dial using** option at the bottom of the dialog box has **Tone** selected by default. Most telephones in the United States are tone-type telephones. In some rural areas and areas outside the United States, you may encounter pulse-type telephones. Pulse-type telephones use a rotary dial. Tone telephones use push buttons.

5. ______ Select the **Area Code Rules** tab and look at the options in the new dialog box, which is similar to the following. There will most likely be no area code rules defined at this time.

6. _______ Click **New**. The **New Area Code Rule** dialog box will display.

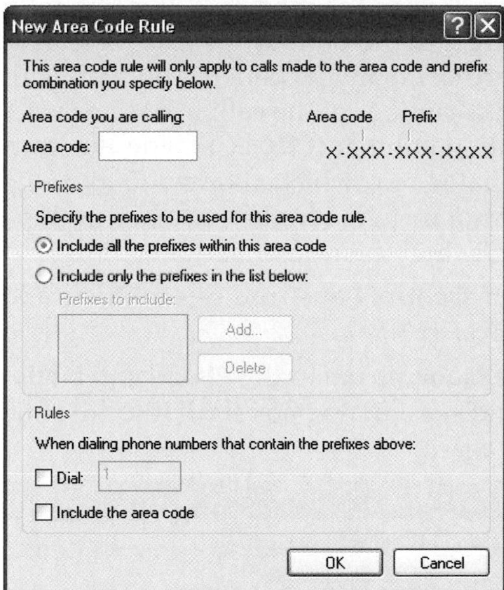

This is where you configure additional information required to dial certain area codes and prefixes. Close this dialog box by clicking **Cancel**.

7. _______ Select the **Calling Card** tab on the **New Location** dialog box. You should see a dialog box similar to the following.

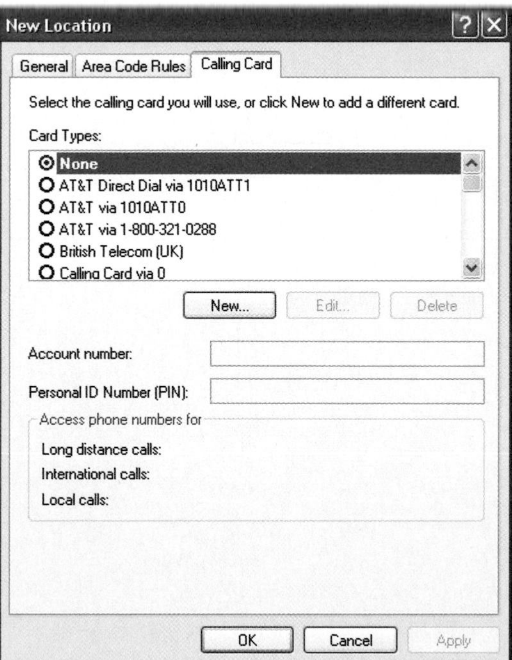

This dialog box allows you to select a calling card to be used when placing a call from the modem. All major calling card companies are identified in the **Card Types** list. You can add an additional calling card company if needed. You would also configure the account number of the calling card as well as the personal identification number (PIN). Clicking the **New** button to reveal another dialog box, which allows you to configure a calling card company not included in the list. Look at the information contained there briefly and then close all dialog boxes.

8._______ Now, open **Control Panel** and select **Phone and Modem Options** as you did in step 3.

9._______ Select the **Modems** tab in the **Phone and Modem Options** dialog box. You should see a dialog box similar to the following. If not, repeat the steps again.

10. _______ Click the **Add** button. A dialog box similar to the following will display.

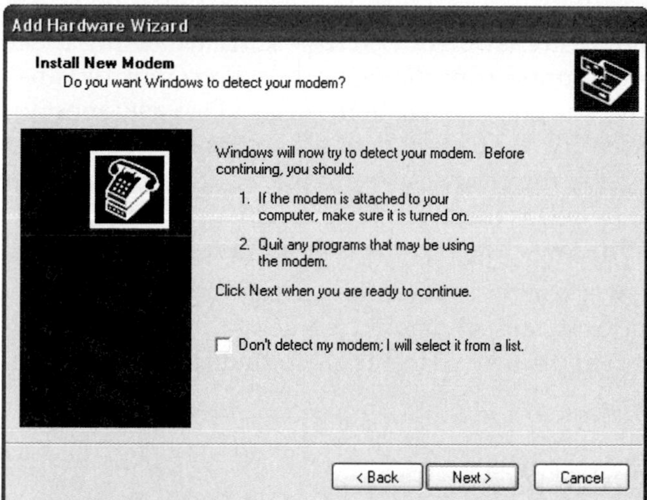

You have now started the Add Hardware Wizard. You would use this wizard to add a new physical modem to the existing computer. Select the **Don't detect my modem; I will select it from a list** option, and then click **Next**. A dialog box similar to the following will display.

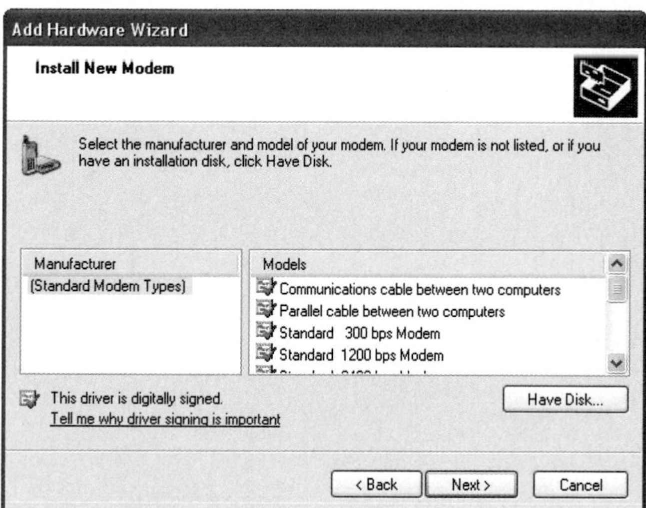

The Add Hardware Wizard will provide you with a list of modem types and corresponding models. You would now scroll through the list to select the correct model. Go ahead and scroll down the list to view the models, but do not select one at this time.

After you explore the list of models, look at the button labeled **Have Disk**. This button would be used if you have a disc supplied with the telephone modem you are installing and the modem is not identified in the list. You would insert the disc into the drive and then click **Have Disk**. The disk would be detected by the operating system and the correct drivers would be automatically installed.

11. _______ Close all dialog boxes by clicking the **Cancel** button. Take a few minutes to practice opening the telephone modem properties dialog boxes. Be sure you know how to access them after opening **Control Panel**. You may also wish to practice accessing the telephone modem properties dialog boxes when Control Panel is set to Classic View. The A+ Certification exams often ask questions requiring you to identify the correct path to the **Phone and Modem Options** dialog box, starting from either the **Start** button or from **Control Panel**. You will be responsible for both the default view (called Category View in Windows XP) and the Classic View.

12. _______ Answer the review questions. You may use Windows Help and Support to assist you with some of the questions. When you are finished, return all materials to their proper storage area.

Review Questions

Answer the following questions on a separate sheet of paper. Please do not write in this book.

1. What does the acronym UART represent?
2. Does a telephone modem convert the outgoing signal from analog to digital or digital to analog?
3. What does the acronym POTS represent?
4. What does the acronym PIN represent?

Viruses

After studying this chapter, you will be able to:

- ✔ Identify common virus characteristics.
- ✔ Explain virus detection.
- ✔ Explain how viruses are spread.
- ✔ Explain the prevention of virus infection.
- ✔ Define virus signature.
- ✔ Classify viruses by their action or description.

A+ Exam—Key Points

Data backup may be covered on the A+ Certification exams, as well as the installation of antivirus software.

Key Words and Terms

The following words and terms will become important pieces of your computer vocabulary. Be sure you can define them.

adware
back door virus
botnet
browser hijacker
computer virus
cookie
data miner
dialer
grayware
hoax
keylogger
logic bomb
macro virus
MBR virus
password virus
pharming
phishing
polymorphic virus
rootkit
spam
spyware
stealth virus
Trojan horse
virus signature
worm

This chapter covers the fundamentals of virus infection, protection, and its elimination in the computer environment. Viruses cause a tremendous amount of destruction and aggravation. Sooner or later, you will encounter a virus or worm. You must have a knowledge base to deal with these threats. This may be one of the most important chapters you read.

What Is a Computer Virus?

computer virus
a maliciously created software program that is written for the express purpose of causing damage to a computer system.

A ***computer virus*** is a maliciously created software program that is written for the express purpose of causing damage to a computer system. It is typically written to duplicate itself and, in the process, cause problems and possible permanent damage to a computer. A virus usually has three phases: infection, replication, and execution.

The infection arrives from a source such as a floppy disk, CD, e-mail, or network connection to a computer, such as the Internet. Replication is when the virus duplicates itself to other programs, files, drives, or other computers on a network. If a virus continually replicates itself, it can easily use all available disk space. Execution can take many forms. Some are harmless and just annoying. Others can be very destructive. They can erase files and lock up hardware.

virus signature
combination of characteristics that defines a particular virus, including such things as its length, file name(s) used, mode of infection or replication, and more.

Viruses are said to have *signatures*. A ***virus signature*** describes a particular virus. It is a combination of characteristics that include such things as its length, file name(s) used, mode of infection or replication, the areas of the system that are attacked, the type of software programs that are attacked, and the name or length of the file attachment. These signatures are what antivirus software use to catch viruses on your computer.

Virus Classifications

The term *computer virus* has taken on a very broad definition with the public. Most malicious programs that infect computers are referred to as viruses. However, the software companies that develop antivirus software programs have developed a variety of classifications. These classifications vary somewhat from company to company. In addition to a virus, there are other malicious programs called *worms*. Each program has its own features. Common classifications of computer infections are Trojan horse, logic bomb, macro, worm, password, back door, and hoax. While some classes will seem similar, there are sufficient variations in their style to allow a classification system to be used. Note that there are many viruses and worms that are composed of the features of multiple classifications.

Worm

worm
destructive program that contaminates files on the infected computer and spreads itself to other computers without prompting from the user.

While many viruses attach themselves to other programs to slip into your computer, worms operate on their own. Technically speaking, a ***worm*** is not a true virus, but rather it is its own destructive program. A virus replicates itself on one computer and infects files on that particular computer. A worm contaminates files on the infected computer, but it also spreads itself to other computers without prompting from the user. This method of spreading itself is what makes it different from a virus. Worms are also referred to as bacterium virus by some authorities.

It is also important to note that worms are self-replicating. Once infection takes place, the worm can replicate or transmit itself to other computers without user intervention. A classic example of its reproduction is through an e-mail application. When a worm is sent out as a file attachment, it replicates itself by using the list of contacts in the user's e-mail database. The recipients of the e-mail then inadvertently infect the people on their lists. The infection rate is exponential. See **Figure 14-1.** The infamous Melissa and I Love You viruses are both worms.

Trojan Horse

The Trojan horse classification is named after the Trojan horse from Homer's Iliad. In the legend, the Trojans leave a huge wooden horse to the city of Troy, presumed as a gift that symbolized the end of the Trojan War. The horse was taken inside the walls of the city. However, the horse was hollow inside and filled with Greek soldiers. In the secret of night, the Greek soldiers climbed out of the horse, attacked the guards, and opened the gates to the city. This allowed the Greek soldiers to enter and defeat the city of Troy. The city was captured and burned to the ground. The virus acts very much like the Trojan horse in the legend.

Trojan horse class of virus that appears as a gift, such as a free download of a game or utility program, an e-mail attachment, or some other item.

The ***Trojan horse*** class of virus appears as a gift. It may be a free download of a program such as a game or utility program, an e-mail attachment, or some other item that is attractive to a user. When opened, the virus becomes activated. Some cause immediate damage. Others wait until a later date. The Trojan horse

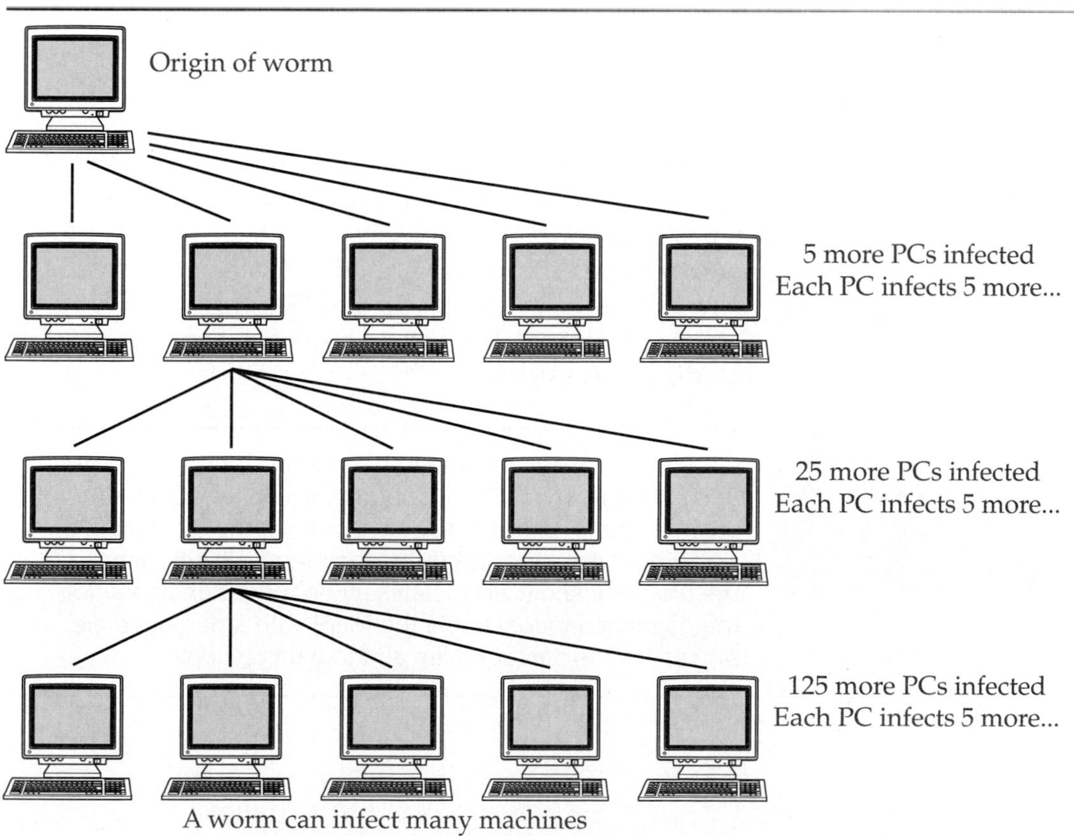
Origin of worm
5 more PCs infected
Each PC infects 5 more...
25 more PCs infected
Each PC infects 5 more...
125 more PCs infected
Each PC infects 5 more...
A worm can infect many machines
across the globe very rapidly

Figure 14-1. E-mail is the most common method of transmitting a worm. Using this method, the worm multiplies at an exponential rate.

can have a harmless outward appearance. It often advertises itself as a utility to assist with some sort of computer operation. Since the Trojan is disguised, users may not even realize that they have infected their computer. After a time, unusual operations or glitches appear in the computer. The hard drive may be erased or written over leaving no space for any other files to be saved. There are too many possible symptoms of Trojan horses to list them all, but you can expect many unusual operations on the computer and may not recognize the problem until damage has been done.

Macro Virus

macro virus
a common virus created using a macro programming language. It is attached to documents that use the language.

A ***macro virus*** is named after the macro software-programming tool. It is a virus created using a macro programming language, and it is attached to documents that use the language. A standard macro program is designed to assist a computer user by converting repetitive tasks into one simple key code or name. Macros can record a set of user keystrokes and then save the set of keystrokes under a file name. When needed, the set of keystrokes can be easily loaded any time. For example, a set of keystrokes used to create a template that will be used over and over again can easily be created using the macro feature in Microsoft's Word program. A typical letter heading including a company's name, address, phone number, and contact person is an example. When loaded, the macro automatically recreates the keystrokes, producing the desired information.

This same method is used to create some virus programs. They are often distributed as e-mail attachments. Once a computer is infected, the virus attaches itself to any new file created with the infected software application. Macro viruses are very common. In fact, macro viruses are estimated to account for 75% of all viruses.

MBR Virus

MBR virus
an extremely destructive virus that attacks the master boot record (MBR) of a hard disk, resulting in hard disk failure.

An ***MBR virus,*** a virus that attacks the master boot record (MBR) of a hard disk, is considered extremely destructive. When activated, the virus plants hexadecimal codes in the master boot record, rendering it useless. This results in hard disk failure. Damage is usually limited to only the master boot record, which can be rebuilt if backups have been made. Many antivirus programs perform MBR backups as part of their installation and require a floppy to save necessary records for rebuilding the system.

One point of particular interest is the **fdisk/mbr** command used to repair the MBR. Certain known virus programs, such as the Monkey virus, actually move the location of the MBR. Applying the **fdisk/mbr** command will not remedy the problem, and it will most likely do more damage when the command reconstructs the MBR with a damaged file and saves the damaged file as the backup copy.

Logic Bomb

A ***logic bomb*** is a destructive program that is slipped into an application and waits dormant until some event takes place. The event could be the arrival of some date or time, the entering of a certain number, word, or file name, or even the number of times the application is loaded. The idea behind the design of a logic bomb is to wait for a period of time, allowing the virus to spread to other computers before releasing its payload of destruction.

logic bomb
a destructive program that is slipped into an application and waits dormant until some event takes place, allowing the virus to spread to other computers before releasing its payload.

Back Door Virus

A ***back door virus*** is designed to go undetected and leave a back door into your system. A back door is a hole in the security system of a computer or network.

The back door virus is not designed to be directly destructive like the typical virus or worm. Rather, it is used to breach security systems. Once the back door is created, the computer file system can be accessed in spite of password and other standard security setups. Back doors are usually associated with network systems but can also be used on a single computer.

back door virus
a virus designed to go undetected and leave a back door into your system. A back door is a hole in the security system of a computer or network.

Password Virus

A ***password virus*** is not designed to destroy a system or replicate itself. Rather, like the back door virus, it is designed to breach security. These viruses steal passwords. The passwords are stolen and then redirected to another location possibly on some other system on the Internet to be accessed later. Often, the system that is housing the stolen passwords is not even aware that it is being used to hold stolen material.

A password virus is closely associated with a back door virus, and both may be used in combination. The password virus and back door virus are designed for illegally accessing networks, though either can be used to access a single computer when it is connected to the Internet.

password virus
a virus that steals passwords.

Stealth Virus

A ***stealth virus*** hides from normal detection by incorporating itself into part of a known, and usually required, program for the computer. The signature of a stealth virus is difficult to acquire unless the original computer system has an antivirus program installed when new. When the antivirus program is installed on a clean computer, the program monitors changes in all files, especially those susceptible to a stealth virus. For example, if the important files change in length, it is a sign that it has been infected with a stealth virus.

stealth virus
a virus that hides from normal detection by incorporating itself into part of a known, and usually required, program for the computer.

Polymorphic Virus

To resist detection, a ***polymorphic virus*** changes as it evolves. It can randomly change its program length, and it can also change the location or type of file it chooses to infect. By constantly changing its virus profile, it can go undetected by antivirus programs that compare the signature or profile of the known virus. The most modern and dangerous viruses use both the polymorphic and stealth characteristics to protect themselves.

polymorphic virus
a virus that changes as it evolves so that it may go undetected by antivirus programs.

Hoaxes

hoax
a false message spread about a real or unreal virus.

A ***hoax*** is not actually a virus. Instead, a hoax, as the name implies, is a false message spread about a real or unreal virus. These messages could be classified as pranks. While hoaxes do not directly damage the computer or destroy files, they are not harmless.

Hoaxes can cost money through the loss of production time. If a hoax warns of a virus such as a logic bomb that will activate at 12:00 on June 5, people who believe the hoax will stop working and use antivirus software to clean their computer before resuming work. It may take some time before they find out that the message was just a hoax and that no real virus exists. If this message spreads through a large corporation, thousands of computers could be shut down. Another trick used by hoaxes is to pick the name of a legitimate file used by a computer's operating system and claim that it is a virus. You are then warned to delete the file. Many people lost their ability to read long file names when one of these hoaxes passed through.

A hoax is considered harmful because it too can cause losses. While the damage is not usually directed to the computer or data system files, money is lost in the form of labor costs. The best way to prevent against being fooled by a hoax is to visit one of the Web sites of an antivirus software manufacturer. These sites have pages dedicated to discussing common hoaxes.

Rootkit

rootkit
a collection of software programs that an intruder installs on a computer that allows the intruder to take total control at a level equal to the system administrator.

A ***rootkit*** consists of a collection of software programs that installs on a computer that allows an intruder to take administrative control. What makes a rootkit so difficult to detect and remove is that it boots and runs before the operating system does. This allows it to take over the computer before the operating system can. It is similar to having two operating systems installed on the computer running simultaneously. Rootkits are difficult to remove and often require a step-by-step manual removal procedure. At times, the only way to eliminate a rootkit is to do a complete low-level format of the hard drive.

Botnet

botnet
a collection of infected computers that are controlled by a source computer.

grayware
a collection of malware that is not regarded as very dangerous, but rather more of a nuisance. Examples of grayware are popups, adware, joke programs, spyware, and data mining software.

One of the latest viruses is the ***botnet*** or ***robot network.*** Botnet is also referred to as a bot network. The term *bot* represents robot when used in variations of the name. A botnet is a collection of infected computers that are controlled by a source computer. The collection of robot networks can be used to simultaneously send out spam or newsletters to millions of computers connected to the Internet. This type of arrangement can also be used to create a denial of service (DOS) attack. A denial of service attack is when a network server or Web server is flooded with requests to the point that it cannot fulfill the requests. This causes the requests to time out. A Web server would appear to the requester as being out of service, and in the practical sense, it is.

Grayware

The exact definition of ***grayware*** depends on which antivirus producer Web site you visit. In general, grayware refers to a collection of malware that is not regarded as very dangerous, but rather more of a nuisance. Examples of grayware are popups, adware, joke programs, spyware, and data mining software. Examples that are not considered grayware are Trojans, MBR virus, and destructive worms. Grayware does slow computer performance because it often uses the Internet connection to send information back to the originator or collection point.

Spam

Spam is unsolicited junk e-mail or junk electronic newsletters. Spam is responsible for drastically reducing the bandwidth of the Internet. Millions of pieces of spam are circulating in the Internet at any given moment. Spam is illegal in most countries, but it is difficult to stop when coming from a country that does not have laws against spam. Also, many times spam is distributed by taking over a computer and using the computer as a source of spam e-mail. For example, a malicious software package can be downloaded and installed on an unsuspecting user's computer. The computer is under the control of a hacker and is used for other purposes, such as forwarding e-mail spam. The computer is therefore considered as a zombie.

spam
unsolicited junk e-mail or junk electronic newsletters.

Keyloggers

A ***keylogger*** is malware that after being installed on a computer keeps track of all keys pressed by the user. It records the keystrokes in a file, which can later be retrieved. The data collected from the keylogger program can be accessed remotely and then used to learn the user logon name, password, and other confidential information. Keylogger programs are often distributed through Trojans attached to e-mail.

keylogger
malware that after being installed on a computer keeps track of all keys pressed by the user. It records the keystrokes in a file, which can later be retrieved in order to learn the user logon name, password, and other confidential information.

Adware

Adware is so named because it is designed to support advertisements such as popups and may also gather information about the user. Adware is also referred to as spyware by some antivirus software programs.

Adware most commonly infects computers through free downloads such as screen savers, free trial software programs, and file sharing programs. Adware is not overtly destructive as many malware programs are. However, adware can cause computer performance to suffer. The adware program often sends data back to the originating source to keep track of the user's Internet habits. Computer performance suffers because while the user is trying to use the Internet and search the Web, the adware program may keep sending information back to the original source, thus reducing bandwidth and causing computer performance to suffer.

The right to use adware on the computer is typically stated in the end user license (EUL) agreement that most users never read. When you click on the **I agree** button while installing the software, you have agreed to let the company spy on you or gather information about you and your browsing habits. This is completely legal. Many antivirus programs do not remove adware. You should install an additional program designed specifically for removing adware and spyware. Two very common free versions are Ad-Aware by Lavasoft Corporation and Spybot—Search & Destroy by software programmer Patrick Kolla. Windows Vista now includes a copy of Windows Defender as part of the installation package. Windows Defender is designed to combat adware and spyware and is discussed later in this chapter.

adware
designed to support advertisements, such as popups, and may also gather information about the user, which it sends data back to the originating source to keep track of the user's Internet habits.

Be aware of the fact that some antiadware software companies make agreements with some software distributors not to remove their adware. Do not be surprised to find that if you run two different antiadware software packages on a computer that you obtain different results.

Spyware

spyware
designed to track a user's habits, such as their Web browsing habits.

Spyware is designed to track a user's habits such as their Web browsing habits. Spyware is often included as part of a free download software package. Many software companies include spyware as part of the trial or free software package. The main difference between spyware and adware is that spyware is considered malicious or illegal because you have not given your consent to install the program on your computer. Spyware and adware can be used to generate popups on a computer as you surf the Internet. Some forms of spyware may monitor the user's keystrokes and read cookie contents stored on the computer.

Data Miner

data miner
used to gather information about a user's Web browsing habits for marketing purposes. Data miner programs are classified as spyware by most antivirus organizations.

Data miner is another name for spyware. Data miners are used to gather information about a user's Web browsing habits for marketing purposes. Data miner programs are classified as spyware by most antivirus organizations. Data miners are also considered a form of grayware. Data miner programs are often embedded into downloaded software, especially free applications or trial versions of software. It is usually legal because when you download the software or trial version, the user agreement often states that the user will be using a data miner to gather information about their use of the product and their browsing activities. When the user selects the **I agree** button at the end of the license agreement, they have given their permission to allow the company to mine data from their computer or simply put, to spy on you.

Browser Hijackers

browser hijacker
a program that changes the Internet Explorer browser configuration, such as by replacing the default home page or browser.

A ***browser hijacker*** is a program that changes the browser configuration, such as by replacing the default home page or default browser. The new browser was not intentionally installed by the user. Some forms of browser hijackers are identified as adware by some antivirus software packages. Some browser hijacker programs simply install undesired icons or modify the toolbar. The purpose is to take the user to a Web site that they did not intend to connect to or view.

Dialers

dialer
a program that automatically disables a telephone modem that is dialing a number and automatically switches to another phone number.

A ***dialer*** is a program that automatically disables a telephone modem that is dialing a number and automatically switches to another phone number. The new phone number is typically an expensive (900) number. The user unknowingly is creating a very expensive phone bill.

Phishing

Phishing (pronounced fishing) is an e-mail used to impersonate a legitimate company or institution, thus fooling the user into believing the e-mail is from some trusted source. The phishing e-mail requests information from the user, such as the user name, password, account number, social security number, or some combination of personal information. A very common phishing scam is to send millions of e-mails that look like legitimate e-mails from E-bay requesting that the user confirm their personal information, such as the user name, password, and account number. If the user responds to the bogus e-mail, then their account is compromised by the criminal. Phishing is also considered a form of social engineering.

phishing
an e-mail used to impersonate a legitimate company or institution, thus fooling the user into believing the e-mail is from a trusted source. The phishing e-mail requests information from the user, such as the user name, password, account number, social security number, or some combination of personal information.

Pharming

Pharming is the deceptive practice based on poisoning a Domain Name Service (DNS) server with an incorrect IP address for a Web site. Pharming is also referred to as DNS cache poisoning or simply as DNS poisoning. All Web sites have a name address known as a domain name and a numerical address known as the IP address. DNS servers are located all over the Internet at different levels. For example, each Internet Service Provider (ISP) is responsible for running a DNS server at their location. When you request a Web page, such as www.rmroberts.com, your request is sent to the local ISP. When it reaches the local ISP, the IPS's DNS server matches the domain name to the domain name's IP address, such as 65.254.254.34. It is the IP address that is then used to find and connect to the requested Web site.

Pharming takes place when the domain name requested is realigned with a different IP address such as 192.122.12.16. When this happens, any requests through the DNS server is redirected to the counterfeit or bogus Web site. For example, you request to connect to a company selling computers. The bogus Web site is an exact replica of the real site. When you find the computer you want at a great price, you purchase the computer by providing your name, address, credit card information, and more. What has happened is the bogus Web site has collected all your information needed to use your credit card anywhere in the world. Pharming is a very sophisticated method of identity theft and is relatively new.

The Pharming strategy takes place on a remote computer so that traditional antivirus, antispam, and other malware protection programs cannot prevent pharming. Pharming can only be prevented at the DNS server by ensuring that the DNS server is using protection mechanisms.

pharming
the deceptive practice based on poisoning a Domain Name Service (DNS) server with an incorrect IP address for a Web site.

Cookies

A ***cookie*** is a small text file used to send information about a user to a server. The original design was to assist a user to find topics or information on a server that they should be interested in. For example, if a user browses a Web site and purchases a fishing pole, a cookie will be generated and stored on the user's computer. The next time the user visits that particular Web site, information is displayed relating to fishing poles, such as wading boots, fishing lures, and any related fishing merchandise that might be on sale. The cookie and the text information stored in it identify the special interest of the user.

cookie
a small text file used to send information about a user to a server.

Creation of Viruses

By understanding something of how a virus is created, you may better be able to detect a virus. Viruses are created in a number of different ways using many different programming tools. For example, one common way viruses are created is through macros. As discussed in the section on macro viruses, a macro is a short program written to save keystrokes. Macros are written in macro language programs, such as visual basic or similar programming tools. They were developed to help users. However, the same techniques used to save you time can also be applied for destructive purposes. Programming software such as Visual Basic, C++, and ActiveX are commonly used tools to develop viruses and worms. Even the simple macro editor that comes with Microsoft Word can be used. There are Web sites that will even sell password, back door, and worm programs. They are advertised "for educational use only."

Most virus and worm paths can be tracked. They can often be traced backward to the original source, especially when delivered by e-mail. Look at **Figure 14-2.** Notice how the e-mail properties can be revealed to expose the real e-mail address, e-mail server name, and originating IP address. Once the TCP/IP address is known, a trace can begin. The ISP can revoke access to any user who violates privacy or harasses another computer site. Remember that accessing another person's computer without their express permission and distributing a virus is a crime.

Well-Known Viruses

There are many more viruses than the viruses that follow, but these are some of the significant viruses. Each listed virus is well-known and documented. Understanding viruses from the past will help you understand how to identify and defend against new viruses as they continue to arrive.

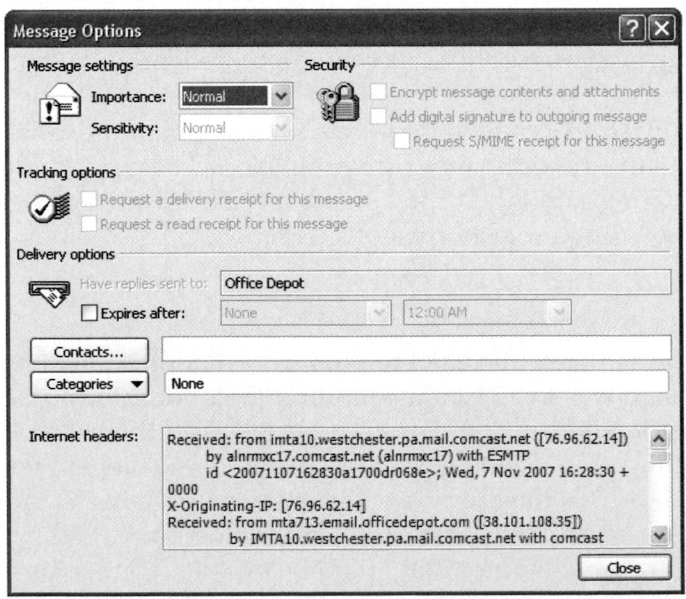

Figure 14-2. The source information of an e-mail can be revealed in Microsoft Outlook through **Message Options**. This dialog box is accessed by opening the e-mail and then clicking **View | Message Options**.

Be aware that antivirus software producers often use different names for the same virus. This is because they discover the new virus at approximately the same time and then name it. Because the naming takes place at different venders on approximately the same date, they can have more than one name in circulation used to identify the same malware. The only time a malware becomes identified with a single name is when the media (press or television) reports a story on the malware, and then the name they use becomes the default name for the virus. Look at the following table to see how the same virus is identified by various antivirus companies.

Company	Malware Name
Kaspersky Lab	Worm.P2P.Harex
McAfee	W32/Spybot.worm.gen.e
Symantec	W32.Mexer.C.Worm
Sophos	Win32/Harex-A
Grisoft	Worm/Harex.A
Trend Micro	Worm_HAREX.A

Michelangelo

On March 6, 1992, millions of computers were predicted to have their hard drives erased. The cause was the Michelangelo virus. The Michelangelo virus was named such because the trigger for this logic bomb was the birth date of the famous artist. Michelangelo was the first virus widely publicized in the media.

While certainly not harmless, Michelangelo was not as disastrous as predicted. The prediction of millions of computers crashing was not achieved, but an estimated 10 to 20 thousand computers did get hit that year. While the virus is still around, it is fairly rare. The destructive nature of this virus keeps it from spreading. By wiping out the hard drive of its host computer, the virus destroys itself as well.

Melissa

The Melissa virus first appeared in March of 1999. Melissa was a macro e-mail virus that, when activated, sent an infected message to the first fifty people on a user's Microsoft Outlook e-mail list. The message sent out from the infected computer would say, "Important message for (insert the person's name from e-mail list)." The body of the message would say, "Here is that document you asked for." The attached document is the infected document. Melissa was also able to infect additional documents on your computer. This means that almost any document could be sent, regardless of whether it was insignificant, high security, or simply embarrassing.

Melissa attracted attention because of how quickly it spread and the large number of computers it affected. The volume of e-mail generated by computers in some corporate networks forced the networks to shut down temporarily. The Melissa virus is estimated to have caused 80 million dollars in damage.

I Love You

The subject of the e-mail said "I Love You," **Figure 14-3**, and the e-mail body contained the note "Kindly check the attachment." The attached file name was Love-Letter-For-You.txt.vbs. When the attachment was opened, it not only infected the host computer, it also e-mailed itself to all the addressees in the computer's Microsoft Outlook e-mail address book.

While this worm was similar to Melissa in its method of distribution, it was considerably more destructive. The worm would attack any graphics file with a .jpeg or .jpg extension and any file with a .vbs, .vbe, .js, .jse, .css, .wsh, .hta, or .sct extension. The worm would overwrite those files with copies of its source code and then append the .vbs extension to the files. It also caused Windows Explorer to produce a blank page for the home screen. Over twenty variations of this worm were created and released. The I Love You virus spread even faster and did more damage than Melissa.

Pretty Park

The Pretty Park virus had a combination of malicious features. This program was a worm, Trojan horse, back door, and password-stealing virus. It first appeared in June 1999 and then cropped up again in March 2000. This is a particularly nasty virus. It attaches itself to e-mail and is distributed as Pretty Park.exe. It included an icon as an attachment using a character from South Park, the cartoon show.

When activated, this virus does several things. It hides itself on the user's system by changing its file attribute to hidden. It also creates a file called files32.vxd, duplicates itself, and then places itself into files32.vxd. It then alters the registry so that files32.vxd is called every time the computer attempts to run an executable (.exe) file. If the user erases files32.vxd, none of the .exe files on the computer will operate. The files32.vxd reference in the system registry must be removed first. The virus can be removed easily by changing the registry and removing files32.vxd, but it must be done in that order.

One of the characteristics of the Pretty Park virus is that it attempts to attach the infected computer to one of several chat rooms. By invading a chat room, the author can monitor the chat room and determine which computers are infected. The virus author can invade any infected computer by using the back door that the virus creates. Any files on the system can then be accessed.

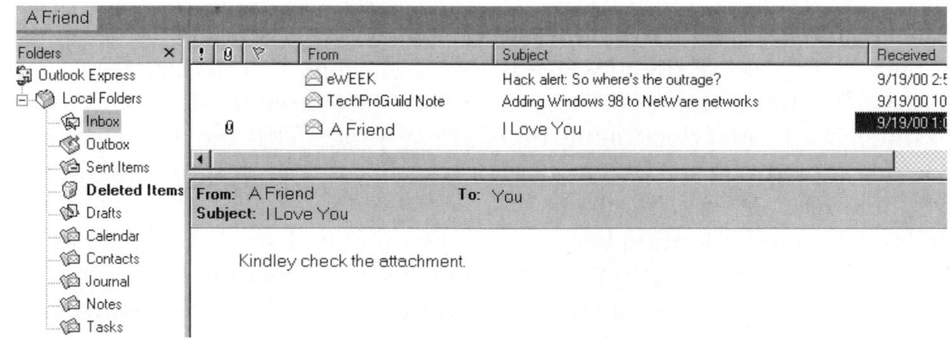

Figure 14-3.
The I Love You virus spread quickly across the globe. Unlike Melissa, this virus was destructive to the computers it struck.

Chernobyl

The Chernobyl virus was written as a logic bomb designed to go off on April 26, the anniversary date of the Chernobyl nuclear accident in Russia. Variations of the original virus were created and set to deliver its payload on the 26th of any month. One part of the payload overwrites the hard drive. A second part overwrites the Flash BIOS program, effectively killing the computer. A computer attacked by the virus may need a new BIOS chip, or if the BIOS is soldered to the motherboard, it may need a new motherboard.

Interestingly, the Chernobyl virus uses a method of infection called a *fragmented cavity attack*. It looks for unused space in the file it is infecting. Then, the virus breaks itself into smaller pieces and inserts itself into the empty space. Thus, files infected by this virus can be the same size as the original. The Chernobyl virus affects only computers running the Windows 9x line of operating systems. Windows NT and Windows 2000 are not affected.

Kakworm

Kakworm took advantage of a design flaw in Windows Internet Explorer browser and Outlook Express mail programs. This bug limited itself to these two programs and could not affect other browser or mail programs. It was a selective virus. What made this worm unique and dangerous was that you didn't need to open an attachment to become infected. You only needed to view an infected e-mail to infect your computer.

When Kakworm is activated, it plants itself in the Windows startup folder. On the first of any month after 5:00 pm, the worm displays the following message, "Kagou-Anti-Kro$oft says not today." After the message is displayed, the computer shuts itself down, **Figure 14-4.**

Laroux

Laroux is a macro virus written to attach Microsoft Excel spreadsheets. The code hides in two macros named auto_open and check_files. When activated, it looks for a file called personal and, if found, Laroux is planted inside it. If the personal file is not found, one will be created. The virus does no damage to the computer or its files. It only replicates itself.

Picture Note

Picture Note is a back door and Trojan horse combination virus. It does no direct harm to files or to the system, but it does have the potential for damage. It comes in the form of an e-mail attachment named picture.exe. When activated, it searches for any America Online user information such as the user name and password of the local computer. This information is then sent to a specific e-mail address for retrieval.

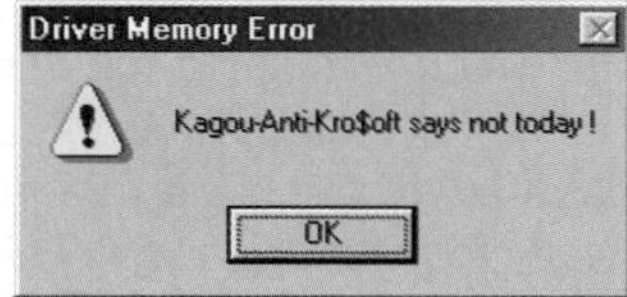

Figure 14-4. This error message indicates that your computer has been infected with Kakworm.

Sobig

One of the latest virus programs to cause havoc for Internet e-mail users is the Sobig virus. As of August. 2003, it was considered one of the most costly viruses in years. Sobig displays the characteristics of a time bomb, worm, Trojan horse, and a back door virus. When it infects a computer, it lays dormant until the following Friday. It then sends e-mail to everyone on the host computer's e-mail list and to certain Web sites. It continues to send e-mail until the virus is removed. By starting on a Friday, the virus can spread over the weekend, creating the best opportunity to infect a large majority of computers before the start of the business week on Monday morning. When business employees check their e-mail early Monday morning, the Sobig virus is activated through the infected attachments by unsuspecting users. The result is a severe slowdown on the Internet because of the heavy traffic generated by businesses opening all of the infected e-mails generated over the weekend. Business e-mail servers are flooded with bogus, infected e-mails. Certain Web sites are also inundated with excess traffic and cannot meet the requests of real users.

The e-mail attachment typically has a .pif extension and a file name such as "Thank_you," "Details," "Application," "wicked_screen," "Movie0045," and others. The subject titles used typically correspond to the file such as, "Your Details," "My Details," "Your Approved," "Your Application," "That Movie," and others. The virus is not spread until the attached file is opened. The address from the infected system is used in the e-mail "From" textbox.

The lesson to be learned here is that when an unusually large number of e-mails are on the incoming e-mail server, you probably need to suspect the worst.

Storm Botnet

The Storm botnet accounted for as much as 8% of all computer virus infections in 2007. The Storm botnet is designed to infect computers through a worm or Trojan, and it controls the infected computers, which are much like a league of zombies. The entire collection of infected computers behaves as one large super computer and is used to send out spam or whatever the originator desires. There are many variations of and names for the Storm botnet. Some other names used to identify the Storm botnet are CME-711, Downloader-BAI, Win32.Agent.bet, and Win32.Nuwar.

Virus Prevention

Keeping a computer free of viruses can be a task. Most viruses can be prevented, but with new viruses appearing all the time, it is difficult to prevent them all. Worms make use of existing program security flaws. For worms, there is no other protection than to avoid all contact on networks and the Internet. For most people, this is not an option.

A virus or worm designed to crack an e-mail list will be specific to a particular e-mail software package. Since each e-mail system has a unique program design, each e-mail software package must have a virus designed especially for that package. This means other e-mail software packages cannot be cracked by the same worm.

Most virus infections can be prevented following some simple practices. Additional practices will help keep the damage to a minimum if you are infected. The following suggestions will help keep your computers and networks safe:

- ✔ Always use a firewall to protect your computer from Internet access.
- ✔ Always install an antivirus program to combat malware.
- ✔ Never open unsolicited e-mail or e-mail attachments.
- ✔ Never reveal your password to anyone or transmit a password in an e-mail.
- ✔ Never respond to any e-mail that requests your password, account numbers, social security number, or any other information that could put you at risk.
- ✔ Don't accept file attachments on e-mails from unknown sources. It is true that you can still get a virus from a known source. This happens when the friendly source does not know that they are spreading a virus. However, your chances are lessened by accepting attachments from only known sources. Regular acceptance of file attachments from completely unknown sources will almost surely cause a problem sooner or later.
- ✔ Never load a file from a floppy disk or other media that you have not checked first with up-to-date antivirus software. The number of infections that have occurred by simply exchanging disks (especially games) is enormous.
- ✔ Before giving a file to anyone, check the storage media using an antivirus program. Many forms of media such as floppy disk and Flash drives have a write protection feature. Use it to prevent the media from being written to from an infected system.
- ✔ Encrypt your important files. Encrypted files are usually useless to another user without the encryption key. Even if you have files stolen, minimal damage is done.
- ✔ Back up your important files.
- ✔ Always perform regular daily backups of important files. Not all malware can be stopped before doing damage to a computer system. Performing regular backups are your best insurance against a malware disaster.

If you have any doubts about taking the time to protect yourself or taking the time to back up your files, ask yourself the following questions regarding your options if a virus destroys your files.

1. Do you have the discs to reload everything, from your operating system to your leisure programs?
2. How much time would it take to reconstruct everything on your computer?
3. How many of the items on your computer are one of a kind?
4. Are there important documents on your hard drive? Do you have term papers, legal papers, financial data, income tax forms, and other unique items stored on your computer?
5. Do you have any hard copies of this information?
6. What happens to you if you are responsible for a corporation?
7. How much would the corporation lose if the computer was wiped out? Could it lose a list of thousands of customers? Could it lose a 200-page catalog sitting on the hard drive or file server?

After thinking about the individual or corporate losses, it is easy to see the benefits of protecting your computer and backing up all of your important files.

Windows Defender

Windows Defender is an antispyware program that detects spyware and provides additional utilities. It was introduced with Windows Vista and installs automatically with the operating system. Windows Defender maintains a history log, **Figure 14-5.** The history log contains information about every spyware and adware program identified on the computer.

The Software Explorer identifies and displays what programs are currently running on your computer. Look at **Figure 14-6.** Notice the **Categories** box that allows you to view startup programs, currently running programs, network connected programs, and Winsock Service Providers. Winsock is a Microsoft application that is required for certain program-specific sockets that are used for a network connection. Sockets and their relation to networks are discussed in later chapters.

Lavasoft Ad-Aware

Ad-Aware by the Lavasoft Corporation is designed specifically to identify adware and spyware. Ad-Aware is a commercial utility package, but there is also a free version available for home users.

Figure 14-7 shows the results of an Ad-Aware scan. Ad-Aware will sort the various adware by classifications and inform the user as to which poses a threat to the system and to what degree. Some of the detected programs are used by Internet Explorer and other legitimate software programs to provide special functions, such as cookies to help identify the user when entering certain Web sites. Not all adware is dangerous, but some is and is usually classified as spyware.

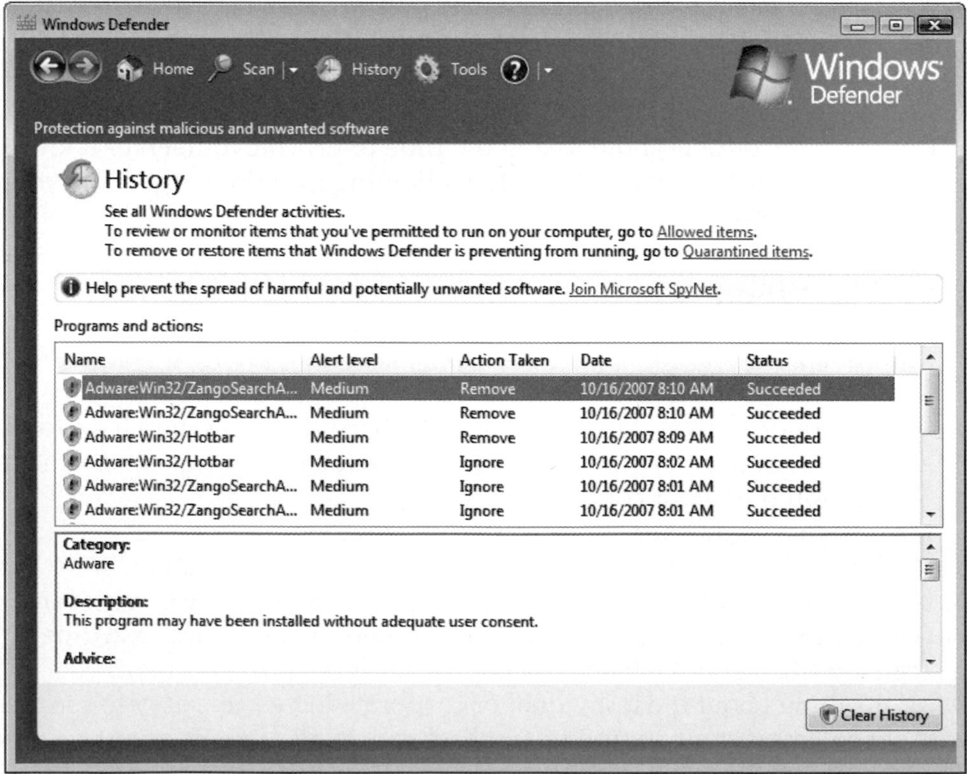

Figure 14-5. The Windows Defender history log lists all of the adware and spyware detected on a computer.

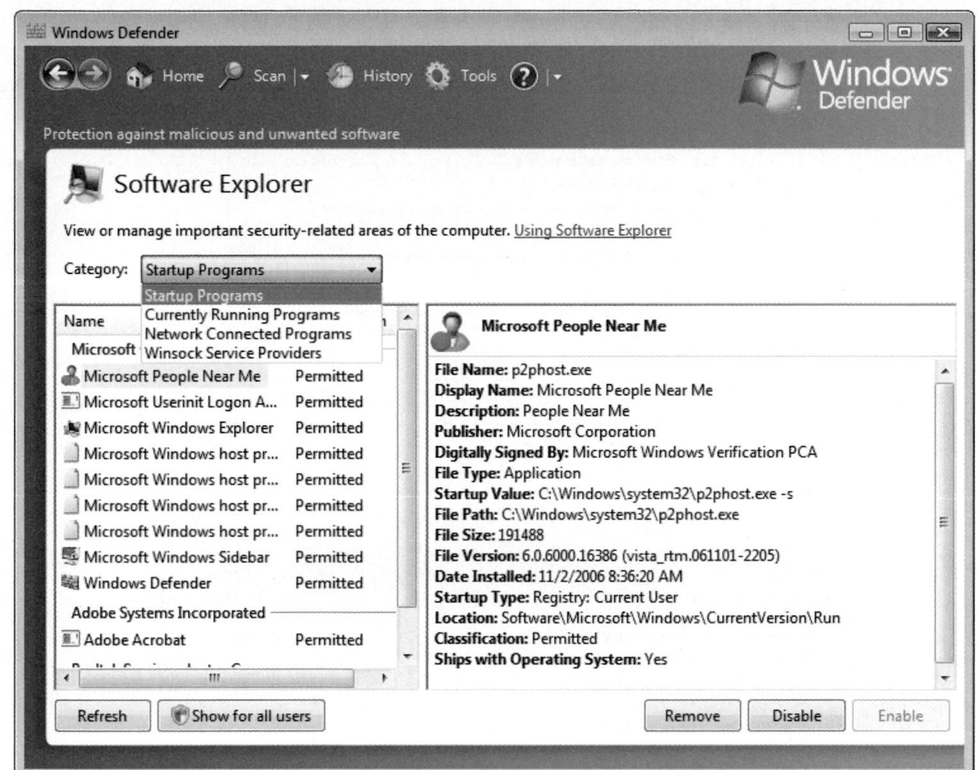

Figure 14-6. Windows Defender Software Explorer allows you to view information about the programs on your computer.

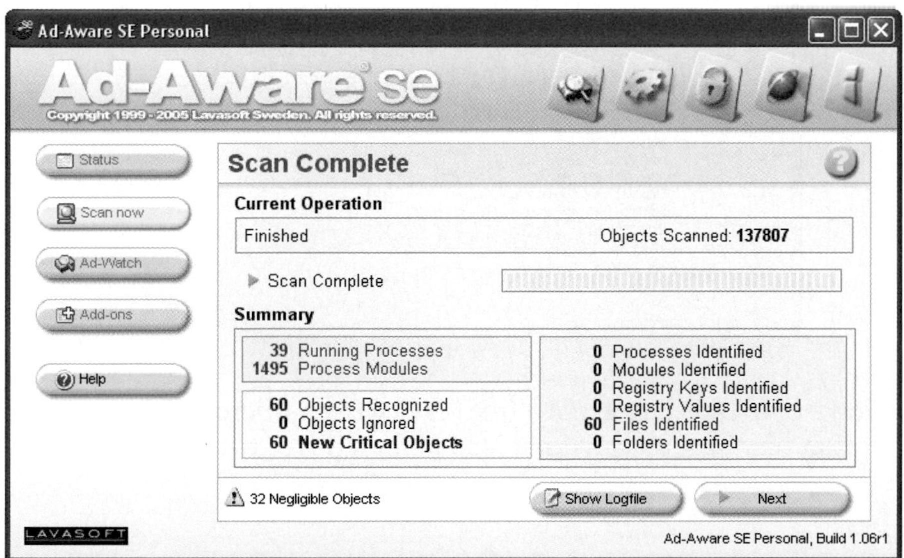

Figure 14-7. The Ad-Aware program by Lavasoft identifies all adware on the computer and indicates its threat level.

Windows Live OneCare

Windows Live OneCare is a software suite consisting of antivirus, antispyware, antiphishing, firewall, backup and restore, and performance tune-up software.

In **Figure 14-8,** you can see that Windows Live OneCare will remove unnecessary files, defragment the hard drive, check for viruses, perform file backups, and check for the latest security update from Microsoft. **Figure 14-9** shows Windows Live OneCare performing a tune-up.

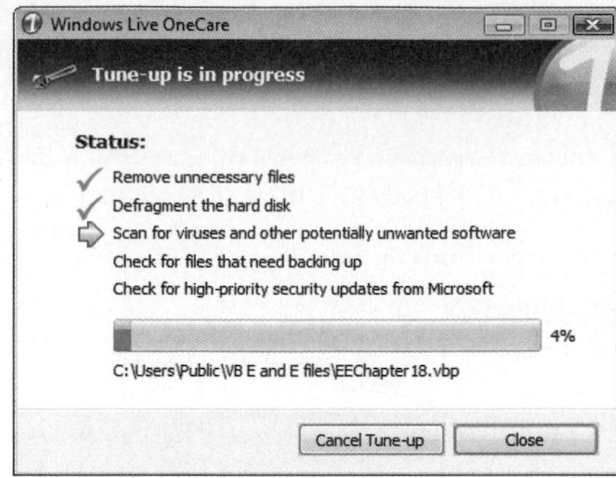

Figure 14-8. Windows Live OneCare tune-up in progress.

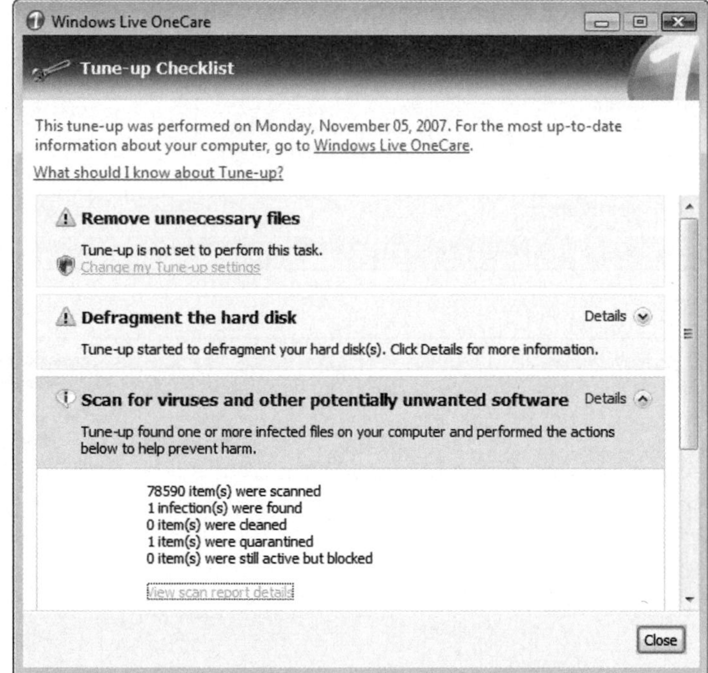

Figure 14-9. Windows Live OneCare tune-up results.

Windows Live OneCare is not a free service from Microsoft, but rather a subscription service. You can download a limited free trial version from Microsoft.

Virus Removal

While preventing the arrival of a virus or worm is ideal, there is a good chance that at some point you will encounter an infected computer. Remember that a virus or worm is simply a program designed to annoy, amuse, or destroy. You eliminate a virus that has never been run as you would any unwanted program. You delete it. Place it in the **Recycle Bin** and empty it.

However, once the virus has been activated (run on your computer), it can be a much more complicated task. The removal of some viruses and worms is as easy as locating and erasing the file containing the virus. In most cases, removal often involves removing many various files, installing a software patch, and adjusting registry settings. Most antivirus manufacturers provide a small downloadable program that does many of these tasks automatically. When a widespread virus is first discovered and publicized, your first move should be to go to the Web site of your antivirus provider and check their alert bulletins for a description and remedy.

The first step in virus removal is to identify the virus. Just because a computer is acting strangely does not mean it has contracted a virus. Any number of things can produce the same effects of known viruses. Check your antivirus software manufacturer Web site for information about the particular virus characteristics. The characteristics of a virus, or its signature, can be found there. This will give you a complete description of the virus and what it does. This includes its symptoms and size, where it is generally located, how it spreads, and what areas of the computer system are affected. Most viruses and worms have hidden, system, or read only file attributes set to help protect it.

The next step is the actual removal. Usually, antivirus manufacturers provide a removal tool, which is an executable program you download and run. The executable program does all the complicated steps for you. Behind the scenes, it removes all the infected files, and, if need be, corrects any altered registry settings. If there is no removal tool prepared, you can usually find step-by-step instructions on the Web. You will have to manually delete all infected files. If registry changes are needed, you must open the registry program and make the alterations as specified. You must be extremely careful when altering the registry. If you make a typo in your registry alteration, great trouble may ensue.

A virus may make additional copies of itself so that it can re-infect your computer if the original is erased. For example, it can attach itself automatically to any drive when files are saved to that drive. This means that while the bug has not been detected and you save a file to a floppy disk, CD-RW, or even to a network hard drive, the virus also saves a copy of itself to the same media. When the media such as the floppy is used to load a file to a hard drive or to RAM, the virus tags along, loading itself as well. This is one way many viruses spread. As part of eliminating a virus, all CDs and Flash drives must be scanned. This is the only way to ensure the complete removal of the virus.

Legal Aspects

Legal punishment for the creation and distribution of a virus is severe. In addition, individuals can be held liable for the cost of financial losses suffered by any corporation harmed by the virus. The FBI National Computer Crime Squad (NCCS) has classified computer crimes into certain categories. These categories include the following:

- ✔ Intrusions of the public phone system.
- ✔ Major computer network intrusions.
- ✔ Network integrity violations.
- ✔ Privacy violations.
- ✔ Industrial espionage.
- ✔ Pirated software.
- ✔ Other crimes committed by using a computer.

In addition to the federal crime statutes, most states have their own crime statutes that are comparable to the federal statutes. Computer crimes are not taken lightly. An example of harsh consequences can be seen in the cases of a number of young students who have used new computer systems to break these laws. The final outcome is usually simple. While the students serve no time for their mistakes, their entire computer systems have been confiscated, and they may be banned from using a computer for five years or more.

You may be wondering why there are laws dealing with intrusion into the public telephone system. The public telephone system provides a medium for a tremendous amount of Internet use. Many hackers have attempted to gain, or have successfully gained, access to telephone company records. This has allowed them to use other people's identifications when accessing the Internet for illegal purposes. Illegal access to the public telephone system carries severe penalties.

The last classification, "other crimes committed using a computer," is a catchall. If a computer crime is not specifically listed, then the act of any criminal nature committed using a computer will fall under this statute. This law is important because people who are determined to do damage or illegally use computer systems invent new crimes on a continual basis.

Mistaken Identifications (or Oops)

Many times a problem occurs on a computer and the computer software automatically assumes it to be a virus. Some technicians automatically assume that many difficult-to-solve problems are caused by a virus. However, users do make errors when using their computers and often the results can appear similar to problems caused by a virus. A classic problem is when a user accidentally hits a key combination that has devastating effects. For example, a key combination struck in error can cause an entire manuscript to disappear. When the key combination [Ctrl] [A] is struck in Microsoft Word, the entire text document is highlighted. The very next keystroke will replace all text in the document with the next letter typed. A major disaster has now occurred, and the computer user may have no idea that they actually caused the problem. It would be easy to assume that a virus has attacked their computer system.

A follow-up phenomenon is the repeat of the keystroke error. Once a mistake is made, human nature allows that person to repeat the same mistake again. Since the technician will probably never view the error in progress and will only get a verbal description of the situation, it may be difficult to diagnose the problem. A frantic description of time lost on a document does not make for easy computer diagnosis. The assumption is that it must be a virus. A few simple steps can help if the user has not tried to repair the error first. Typing [Ctrl] [Z], the shortcut combination for undo, can save the day if the user has not typed too many additional keystrokes before you arrive.

Users often assume a virus has attacked their computer as things go wrong. However, there are many different reasons that a computer can exhibit unusual actions. Possibilities include power glitches, magnets too close to the computer or monitor, network glitches, and more. A strong magnetic field can completely erase computer disks. When this happens, it will probably be reported as a virus.

Summary

- ✔ A computer virus is a software program that is written for the purpose of causing damage to a computer system.
- ✔ Virus infection is a real danger that can destroy data, slow down a computer system, fill up unused space on a hard drive, or do relatively nothing.
- ✔ A worm contaminates files on the infected computer and also spreads itself to other computers without prompting from the user.
- ✔ Viruses are spread easily by e-mail, and passing copies of floppies and CDs.
- ✔ Most virus infections can be prevented by not accepting file attachments on e-mails from unknown sources, turning off Windows scripting, and never loading a file from a floppy disk or other media that has not been checked.
- ✔ Legal punishment for the creation and distribution of a virus is severe.
- ✔ Not all puzzling computer problems are caused by viruses. Human error is one of the leading causes of computer catastrophes.

Review Questions

Answer the following questions on a separate sheet of paper. Please do not write in this book.

1. What are the three major stages of a computer virus?
2. How is a worm different than a virus?
3. How can replication harm a computer system?
4. What is a Trojan horse virus?
5. Define *macro*.
6. What is a polymorphic virus?
7. What is a hoax virus?
8. What is a botnet?
9. What is grayware?
10. What is a zombie?
11. What is a keylogger?
12. What is the difference between adware and spyware?
13. Why can't antivirus software prevent pharming?
14. What steps can you take to prevent virus attacks?
15. What are the six major categories of computer crime as identified by the FBI?

Sample A+ Exam Questions

Answer the following questions on a separate sheet of paper. Please do not write in this book.

1. Which is the *least likely* way to contract a virus?
   a. Loading a game program on a computer from a Flash drive given to you by a trusted friend.
   b. Downloading a file from a reputable Internet site.
   c. Connecting to another computer on a corporate network.
   d. Loading a new operating system from a DVD taken directly from a sealed shrink-wrapped box.
2. Which of the following is the best definition of a macro?
   a. A short program used to diagnose system resources.
   b. A short program used to detect viruses designed to infect text editors.
   c. A software program designed to take repetitive tasks and combine them into one simple set of keystrokes.
   d. A program named for the Macromaniac virus first released in 1993.
3. Worms are typically spread by which of the following methods?
   a. E-mail attachments.
   b. Exchanged Flash drive contents.
   c. The system BIOS whenever two computers connect together on the Internet.
   d. Exclusively by text editor programs.
4. How does a virus typically cause problems for a computer?
   a. It loads itself into the video ROM, which results in poor video performance.
   b. It resides on the hard disk drive and uses up valuable disk space by replicating itself.
   c. It is loaded as an e-mail attachment. Once it is activated, it spreads to other computers via the e-mail list of users on the computer.
   d. Viruses spread by installing new operating system software supplied through venders.
5. Which is the best definition of a polymorphic virus?
   a. A polymorphic virus is a combination worm and Trojan horse virus.
   b. A polymorphic virus constantly changes its virus profile to resist detection by antivirus programs.
   c. A polymorphic virus can infect multiple parts of the same computer system.
   d. A polymorphic virus lives forever by constantly re-infecting the same computer, thus preventing it from ever being removed.
6. The characteristics which describe the uniqueness of a virus are referred to as a _____.
   a. signature
   b. reputation
   c. payload
   d. morphic synopsis

7. Which of the following is generally considered a form of grayware? (Select three)
   a. Adware
   b. Pop-ups
   c. Trojan
   d. Data miner
8. Which malware type changes the DNS server address of a legitimate Web site and replaces the IP address with a bogus Web site?
   a. Phishing
   b. Zombie
   c. Trojan
   d. Pharming
9. What effect does data miner and adware programs have on a computer?
   a. They slow system performance during browsing.
   b. They increase the amount of time it takes to write to the hard disk drive.
   c. They do not adversely affect computer performance.
   d. Only data miner programs classified as malware affect computer performance.
10. Which technique or software program is based on poisoning the DNS database of a DNS server?
    a. Rootkit
    b. Phishing
    c. Pharming
    d. Data Mining

Suggested Laboratory Activities

Do not attempt any suggested laboratory activities without your instructor's permission. Certain activities can render the PC operating system inoperable.

1. Visit some antivirus manufacturer Web sites. Download and install trial versions of their antivirus program.
2. Open Microsoft's Word program. Explore how macros are made. Make a macro that will automatically type your name and address on a form when a combination of two keys is pressed.
3. Visit www.eicar.org and download their virus test program.
4. Download the latest security patch for Microsoft e-mail. While at the Microsoft Web site, look for other patches to update security for your computer.
5. Visit www.lavasoft.com and install and run the free version of Ad-Aware.
6. Visit www.onecare.live.com and download and install the limited free trial version of Windows Live OneCare.
7. Visit several different antivirus Web sites and scan their virus encyclopedias.

Interesting Web Sites for More Information

http://onecare.live.com
www.antivirus.com
www.cert.org
www.datafellows.com
www.datarescue.com
www.fedcirc.gov
www.f-secure.com
www.lavasoft.com
www.mcafee.com
www.norman.com
www.ontrack.com
www.stiller.com
www.symantec.com
www.virusbtn.com
www2.sans.org

Chapter 14
Laboratory Activity
Virus Test Software

After completing this laboratory activity, you will be able to:

- ✔ Test a typical antivirus program to ensure it is installed correctly.
- ✔ Build the EICAR virus test program.

Introduction

In this lab activity, you will access the EICAR Web site at www.eicar.org and download a copy of the EICAR utility. The utility is designed to test an installed version of any antivirus software.

EICAR (European Institute for Computer Antivirus Research) has developed a virus test program that checks if an antivirus program has been installed correctly and is working. The EICAR test file is a simple text file that contains the following symbols:

X5O!P%@AP[4\PZX54(P^)7CC)7}$EICAR-STANDARD-ANTIVIRUS-TEST-FILE!$H+H*

You can copy the line of text above using Notepad or WordPad and save it as a plain ASCII text file named EICAR with the file extension of .com, .dll, or .exe. When typing the line of text, be sure to enter the third letter symbol as the capital letter *O* and not as a zero. All the letters should be entered as uppercase letters.

The antivirus program installed on your computer should prevent you from saving the EICAR antivirus file. When the EICAR file is activated, you should see a window similar to the McAfee dialog box that follows. The look of the dialog box will vary according to the brand of antivirus software you are using.

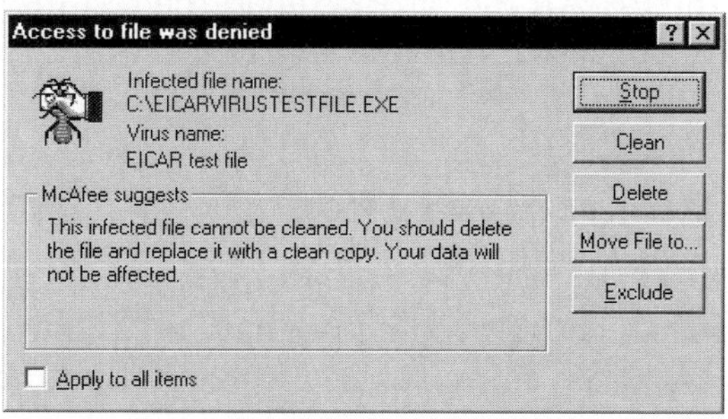

Seeing a window similar to this window means that the software is working. However, it does not ensure that all options for the antivirus utility are correctly configured. It just lets you know that the general antivirus program is installed and working. For example, it does not mean the antivirus program you are using is up-to-date and contains the latest virus definitions or that the program is scanning e-mail automatically.

The following screen captures are another sample of dialog boxes triggered by the EICAR.COM program.

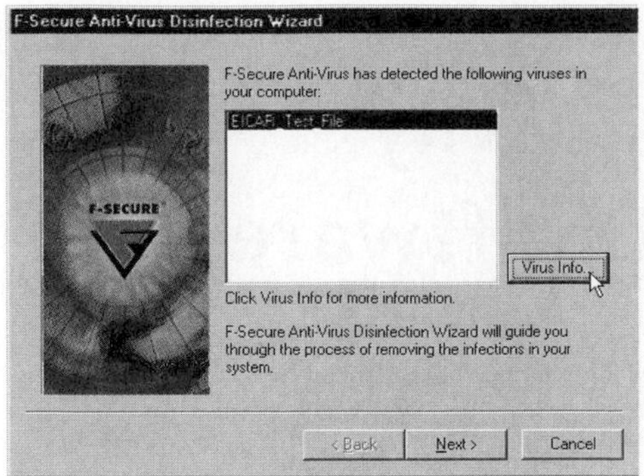

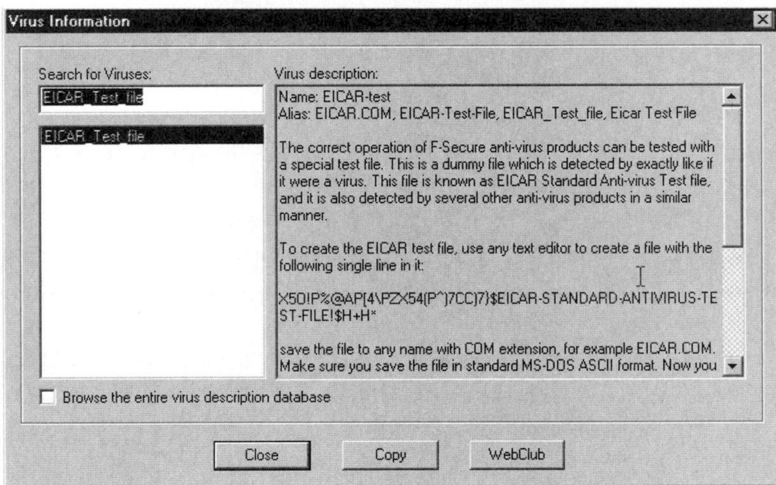

These two images are windows created by the F-Secure Anti-Virus software utility. If your computer is not equipped with an antivirus utility package, you can download an evaluation package from www.fsecure.com. After downloading the evaluation package, install the antivirus utility following the screen prompts. You can either create the EICAR file or download the test file from most antivirus Web sites. The file is free to download and use to test antivirus programs.

Equipment and Materials

- ✔ Typical PC with Windows 98 or later operating system, Internet access, and an antivirus program installed. (If you do not have an antivirus program installed, you can download a 30-day antivirus trial version from many different sites including www.symetec.com, www.mcaffee.com, and www.fsecure.com.)
- ✔ Floppy disk for saving the EICAR file.

Procedure

1. _______ Boot the computer and open Notepad (not Microsoft Word or any other high-end word processor). The file must be a plain ASCII text file.
2. _______ Type the following list of symbols exactly as they appear and save as a file called eicar.txt to the floppy disk or Flash drive. The string of characters must appear exactly like the list that follows. You may also download this file from www.eicar.org/anti_virus_test_file.htm.

   X5O!P%@AP[4\PZX54(P^)7CC)7}$EICAR-STANDARD-ANTIVIRUS-TEST-FILE!$H+H*

   If you have trouble activating the EICAR file by typing the string of symbols, try a downloaded copy. Note that the file should be saved as a .txt file not as a .com, .dll, or .exe. If you attempt to save this file as any of these three file extensions, it may trigger any antivirus program installed on your computer. When you wish to use the file for testing antivirus software, you change the file extension to .com, .dll, or .exe. You can name the file anything you wish. It does not have to be named EICAR. You can name it VirusTestProg.exe for example.
3. _______ Test the antivirus program by attempting to save the eicar.com file to the hard disk drive from the floppy drive or Flash drive. (Note that any attempt to save the EICAR file to the floppy drive or Flash drive may activate any existing antivirus software already loaded on the computer.) The exact reactions to the EICAR program vary from one antivirus utility to another.
4. _______ Experiment with the EICAR file by changing the type of file extension and by changing your antivirus software settings. You should also try changing one or two characters in the character string inside the EICAR file. Try installing the file in different directories. See what happens.
5. _______ After you are done with your laboratory experiments, remove the EICAR test program from the computer and return the comuter to its original condition.

Review Questions

Answer the following questions on a separate sheet of paper. Please do not write in this book.

1. What types of file extensions are used with the EICAR virus test program?
2. What does the acronym EICAR represent?

The SANS Institute (www.sans.org) is dedicated to combating viruses and providing security information. Check out their white papers on computer security.

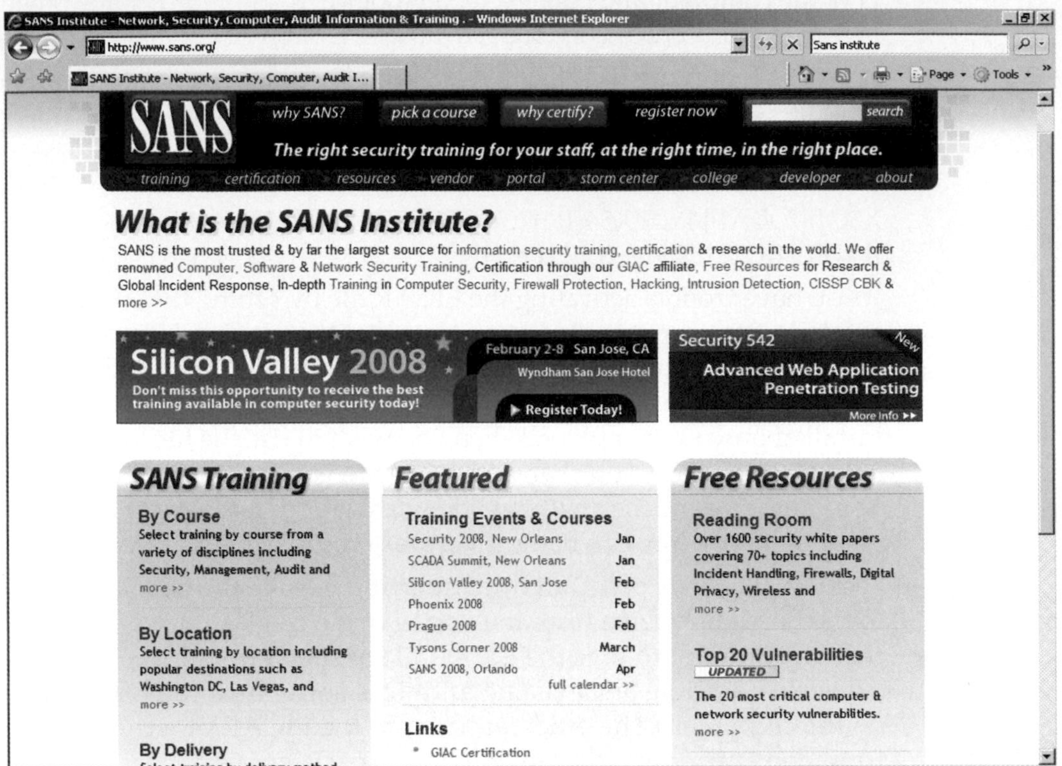

PC Troubleshooting

After studying this chapter, you will be able to:

- ✔ State commonly practiced troubleshooting steps.
- ✔ Identify the three stages of computer operation.
- ✔ Recognize common startup problems and understand their causes.
- ✔ Restart a PC in a variety of troubleshooting modes.
- ✔ Identify the appropriate diagnostics utility to use given a specific problem.
- ✔ Step through a PC's boot sequence.
- ✔ Explain basic data recovery methods.

A+ Exam—Key Points

The A+ Certification exams place a great deal of weight on knowing the basics of troubleshooting. You need to become familiar with the tools, their limitations and their purpose. The best way to become familiar with troubleshooting tools is by using them. Study the menu options, such as **Safe Mode**, and how to access them.

It is very important to study the setup readme.txt files that come with each version of Windows installation CDs. They contain a lot of information that is used on the A+ Certification exams and that is usually not found in textbook material.

Key Words and Terms

The following words and terms will become important pieces of your computer vocabulary. Be sure you can define them.

blue screen error	kernel mode
clean room	Microsoft Dynamic Link Library (DLL)
differential backup	startup problem
incremental backup	user mode

Troubleshooting a PC requires a combination of the technician's knowledge, intuition, and experience. There are many diagnostic tools that are included as standard programs for Microsoft software systems. There are also many diagnostic tools available from third-party vendors that can assist in the troubleshooting process. Third-party vendor programs range from freeware and shareware to systems costing several thousands of dollars. The more expensive programs include a diagnostic board that plug into the PC's expansion slots.

Most problems can be diagnosed without expensive system diagnostics. The value of expensive diagnostic tools is they can be used to save time and money when trying to identify problems that may be caused by two or more components. For example, it can be difficult to determine if a problem is caused by a troublesome CPU or a bad motherboard. When this situation arises, a simple solution is to substitute a known or good CPU for the suspect CPU. However, this substitution alone can be a very expensive proposition.

Common Sense Practices

Remember, when troubleshooting and repairing PCs that "time is money." When diagnosing PC failures and problems, always take the quickest and easiest path first. When troubleshooting, there are some common sense practices you should follow:

- ✔ Determine the major area at fault.
- ✔ Determine what action occurred just prior to failure or problem.
- ✔ Write down settings before you change them.
- ✔ Go slowly.
- ✔ Think, think, think!

Determining the Major Fault Area

The first step is to try to determine what major area is the most likely source of the fault. There are three major fault areas to be considered:

- ✔ Hardware failure.
- ✔ Software failure.
- ✔ User-generated problems.

The most common error or problem is the user-generated problem. Some users like to tinker with Control Panel, and others will try to solve their problems alone. Users with a little technical knowledge can be the most dangerous. They often attempt to fix a problem alone before calling the technician. When this happens, you may very well be faced with more than one problem. First, the original problem likely still exists, and then there are additional problems created by the user. Repairing computers in a school setting can be the most frustrating. Some students love to experiment on the settings on a school's computer before trying the activity on their home computer.

What Happened Last?

It is critical to determine from the computer user what the last action on the computer was prior to the problem occurring or before computer failure. Often, the last action taken by the user can lead the technician directly to the problem. Find out if the user recently installed some new software. Perhaps, there has been a recent hardware upgrade to the problem PC. Has the user recently downloaded a file from the Internet? Ask as many questions of the user as possible. This can save valuable time.

Proceed Carefully

Do not rush when diagnosing problems. Operating in a hurry will lead to sloppy work. This can create new problems or cause you to overlook something important. In contrast, do proceed in a methodical yet constant pace. Customers will not appreciate a technician who is standing around drinking coffee, talking, socializing, or any other activity that appears to be a nonproductive use of energy. Customers are typically paying a premium price for service and are losing the use of their computers while they are inoperable. Don't waste their money, or, next time there is a problem, someone else will be called.

Write Things Down

Do not rely on your memory alone while performing troubleshooting. Before you change a setting, write down the current setting. If you are going to delete a file, write down the file name. You can make the problem much harder to find if you create another problem along the way. If a problem is not cleared after changing a setting or deleting a file, you should return the system file or setting to the way you found it. Do not simply move on and try something else.

Think

Think the problem through. Don't try operations out of desperation. Desperate technicians will often run the same test twice knowing the results from the first test were valid. These are acts of desperation, and they occur when a technician is stumped.

When you run out of tests—*stop and think* about the situation. Writing things down in a list helps. Make two lists. First, make a list of what you know is not the problem. Then, make a list of possible problems that could still exist. Check the Web site of the manufacturer of the PC, the BIOS, and the operating system. There could be corrections posted for exact symptoms you are encountering. Many times, a problem is discovered that affects a particular setup or particular combination of hardware and software programs.

Don't hesitate to contact the manufacturer of the hardware or software in question by e-mail with a description of the problem. Most questions will be answered in 24 to 48 hours at no cost for the service. You can get much faster replies by calling, but that service is seldom free.

Your fellow technicians are another very important source of information. As you progress in the PC repair world, you will make many friends. It is a standard practice to share information with a colleague who may have encountered a similar problem. A peer may have a quick and easy answer to a problem that you have not encountered before. Other times, simply discussing the problem with a peer can be quite helpful. Explaining the problem forces you to summarize the situation and describe it in logical terms. Just the act of verbalizing the problem may allow you to solve it. Never be embarrassed to use this form of assistance.

Troubleshooting Overview

There is no one foolproof method to troubleshooting. There are too many variables that can cause a computer to fail, but there are recommended procedures that can be used to help you organize your approach to solving a computer problem. The causes of failure discussed are not all inclusive and should be interpreted as a guide to solving a computer-related problem or complete system failure.

When troubleshooting computer problems, the first thing you must do is isolate the problem. You must determine if it is a hardware problem, software problem, or user-generated problem. This is easier said than done. The best way to go about this is to decide when the problem is occurring. In other words, at what stage of computer operation is the problem occurring? Did the failure or problem happen during the POST, during the loading and initialization of the required operating system files, or after the logon and running the services and application software? This section discusses the common causes of failure related to the three stages of computer operation. The first stage is the POST. The second stage is loading the required operating system files and initializing the hardware system. The third stage is after the logon. It comprises loading the startup programs and running applications and services.

First Stage

If the problem occurs during POST, it is most likely a hardware failure. In this stage, no operating system software or allocation software has been loaded. The post may fail to complete if a damaged hardware device fails POST or fails its own diagnostic routine. For example, a telephone modem that has been damaged during a thunderstorm may cause the computer to lock up during the POST or immediately after.

If you just built the computer system and it fails to successfully boot the first time during POST, chances are you have improperly installed the RAM, CPU, or CPU cooling device. A high-speed CPU that has an improperly installed cooling fan and heat sink may generate excessive heat in a few seconds, causing the computer to freeze while performing the POST. Improperly seated RAM may also cause the computer to fail during POST. When memory is improperly seated, a beep code typically will be issued, indicating a problem with RAM. Go back and reinstall these devices and remove all unnecessary devices, such as adapter cards that are not required for system operation, and reboot the system.

If the problem still persists, you can either substitute parts to determine which hardware device is causing the failure during POST or use a third-party utility that uses a POST card to diagnose the POST problem. A very popular third-party utility suite used by repair centers is PC-Doctor Service Center 6. The complete PC-Doctor Service 6 kit is shown in **Figure 15-1.**

The kit includes all the software and hardware you need to perform a thorough testing of all computer hardware components. PC-Doctor is used by Circuit City firedog technicians as well as Staples to perform computer diagnostics in the service department.

The PC-Doctor POST card, **Figure 15-2,** is inserted into any PCI slot and used to diagnose errors during POST caused by hardware failure such as the CPU, RAM, or the motherboard. A POST error code is displayed on the LEDs. The technician can then match the code to the diagnostic chart in the user manual.

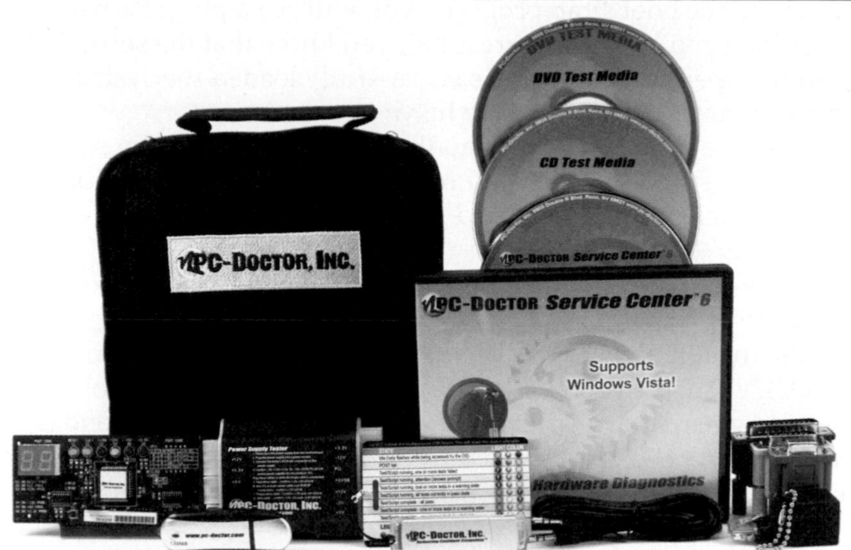

Figure 15-1.
The PC-Doctor Service Center 6 is a complete kit for diagnosing computer hardware. (PC-Doctor, Inc.)

Figure 15-2.
PC-Doctor PCI POST card. (PC-Doctor, Inc.)

Without a POST card, a technician would have to substitute the CPU, RAM, and motherboard with a known good component. Part substitution can be very time-consuming and expensive. The technician runs the risk of damaging a part during the substitution process.

For more information on problems that can occur during the POST stage, see the following chapter sections: Typical Startup Problems, Hard Drive Failures, Additional Mechanical Problems, and Boot Sequences.

Second Stage

If the problem occurs during stage two—operating system loading and initialization—the problem is most likely related to a corrupt operating system file or a driver. You can identify when stage two starts by observing the screen display. Many computer systems display the results of the POST as it occurs. You will see the RAM check verified on the screen as well as the hard disk drive identified and other devices present. Soon after the POST turns over loading the operating system to the boot strap program, you will see a progress bar appear on the screen. When you see the progress bar, you know that the second stage has begun and the operating system has successfully loaded the system kernel. The operating system then initializes the hardware devices.

Failure during the second stage is usually the result of a corrupt required operating system file such as ntldr or failure to properly detect and initialize a piece of hardware such as the sound card. It can also be the failure of a required hardware driver file.

The fastest way to repair a system failure that occurs during the loading and initialization of the operating system is by reinstalling required system files. Simply insert the installation CD/DVD and then reboot the computer. When the installation CD/DVD boots, follow the screen prompts. For more information on problems caused by hard drive failure that can occur during the second stage, see the Hard Drive Failures section. Detailed troubleshooting methods for this stage are covered in the Recovering from a System Startup Failure section.

Third Stage

System logon is the end of the second stage. Keep in mind that not all operating systems require a logon. The third stage is when the desktop first appears. During the third stage, startup programs, services, and applications are loaded. The most common problems that can occur during this time are usually due to corrupt or incompatible drivers and files.

File corruption

Files can become corrupt in various ways such as by virus attacks and hardware failures. For example, an intermittent RAM failure can corrupt files also if the file contents is being transferred or copied during the time of RAM failure. Files are also corrupted by being stored in an area of the hard drive that has a bad sector. All data saved to the bad sector is lost, thus corrupting the contents of the complete file.

Overwritten DLL file

Microsoft Dynamic Link Library (DLL) an executable file that can be called and run by Microsoft software applications or by third-party software programs.

Certain files such as DLL can cause a system failure when inappropriately applied in a software program or when they become corrupt. A ***Microsoft Dynamic Link Library (DLL)*** file is an executable file that can be called and run by Microsoft software applications or by third-party software programs. Rather than write code from scratch each time a new software application is written, a programmer can simply call a DLL from within the program they have written and run the function they need automatically. One DLL can be used by more than one software program at the same time. By reusing the same code contained in the DLL, a programmer saves time and the computer uses less memory and disk space. The term *dynamic* is used because the file can be loaded, run, and then unloaded from computer memory when no longer needed.

One of the major software problems in the past is when a user loads a software application from a disc that contains the necessary DLL files required to run their software application. All too often, the DLL file on the software disc overwrites the existing DLL already residing on the computer. If an older DLL file overwrites a newer DLL file, an error can occur when the user starts an application other than the one just loaded. A classic example is when a user loads an older version of a software game on a computer that has other games requiring the similar DLL file. While the older game runs perfectly, one or more of the other games may now run incorrectly or may not run at all.

DLL files usually have a DLL file extension such as mon.dll. Sometimes the DLL will have an .exe file extension. Look at **Figure 15-3** to see the results of a search for files with the "dll" extension. There are 11,497 files that have a "dll" extension on this particular computer. As you can see, there are thousands of possible DLL files that can be used as part of software application programs and hardware drivers.

Blue screen error

The system may also experience a blue screen error. A ***blue screen error*** is a blue screen that appears with an error code and then freezes the system. Microsoft also refers to blue screen errors as *fatal errors, stop errors,* and *stop error messages* because the system is not recoverable at the time of the error. The system must be restarted before you can attempt to remedy the problem. Some of the most common causes for blue screen errors include the following:

- ✔ Defective hardware, such as memory chips and video adapter cards.
- ✔ Corrupt files on the hard drive.
- ✔ System BIOS settings that are beyond the capabilities of the hardware.
- ✔ Third-party software containing bad code.
- ✔ Bad code in the Windows operating system.

blue screen error a blue screen that appears with an error code and then freezes the system. Also referred to by Microsoft as fatal errors, stop errors, and stop error messages.

The error codes displayed on the blue screen can be quite cryptic. You should copy the error code and use it as a reference when searching Microsoft's support Web site.

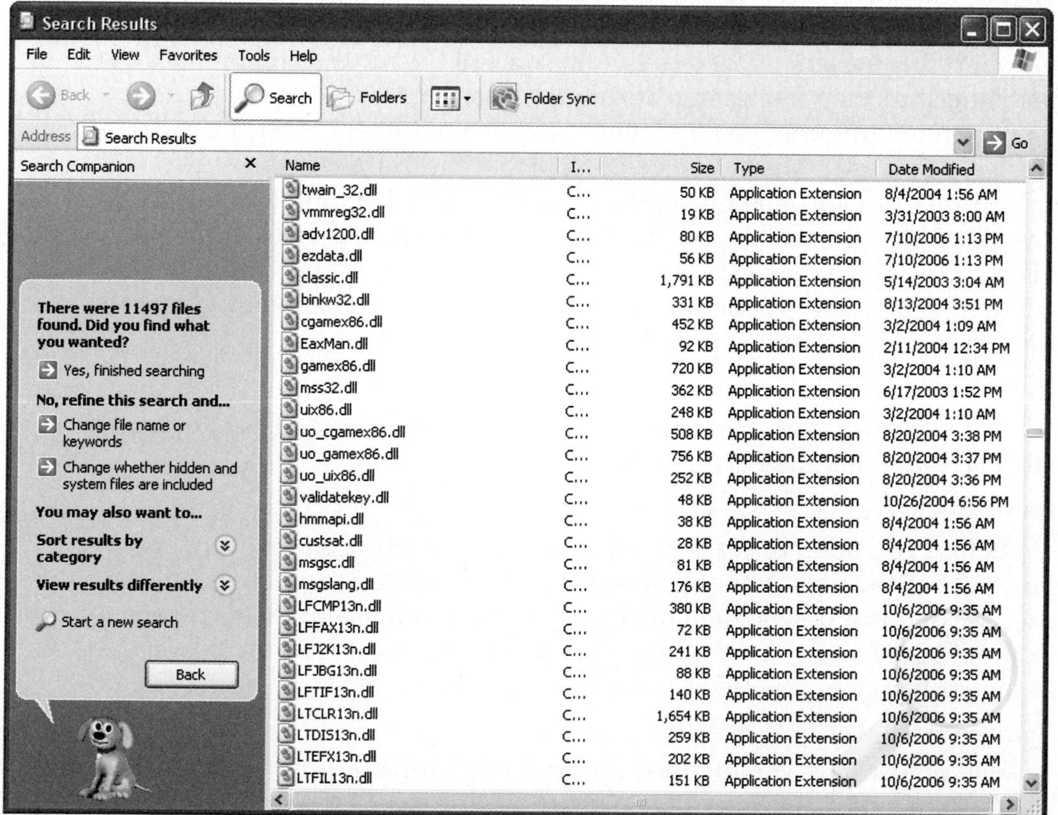

Figure 15-3. DLL files are called by software applications to perform common tasks.

The most appropriate utility for diagnosing a problem after the logon is the System Configuration Utility (msconfig.exe). This and other utilities for diagnosing problems during this stage are covered in the Recovering from a System Startup Failure and the Windows Diagnostic Utilities section.

A malicious software program (virus or worm) can attack a computer at any time, not just after the system logon. For example, if the MBR is corrupted by a virus, the computer will fail before switching from text mode to graphic mode.

Typical Startup Problems

startup problem problem that causes the computer to lock up during the boot process.

Startup problems are a tough class of computer error that you are bound to run into. A ***startup problem*** is a problem that causes the computer to lock up during the boot process. These problems occur too early in the PC operation to be solved by system diagnostic tools. This section details some of the most common and catastrophic boot problems that you will encounter while starting the PC. Each of the following problems is described as a symptom. Possible solutions are provided as a guide. The list of symptoms is condensed and centers on the problems encountered before the boot process is completed. Keep in mind that there are hundreds of possible computer symptoms. What follows are a few of the most common system hardware failures during the boot.

Think about the boot process and the steps involved. System boot failures involve the power supply, CPU, hard drive (boot device), BIOS, CMOS, system configuration, autoexec.bat file, loading of drivers, and the loading of the operating system. Now let's look at some of the most common hardware problems and their symptoms during the boot process.

When reading the list that follows, assume that there is one hard drive labeled C and a CD drive labeled D. Note that these are recommended procedures, not absolute procedures. Also, viruses can imitate some of the described symptoms. Always check for the presence of a virus and protect your disk while doing so.

Remember, always attempt the simplest tests first. Then, move on to the more complex and labor-intensive tests.

Symptom 1:

There is no power light, no fan running, and no sound of boot operation at all. It appears that the PC is completely dead.

Items to check:

Before you open the case, make sure the PC is plugged in. Next, check the power from the wall outlet or power strip or both. Be sure there is power to the unit. If you have power, then the likely problem is the computer's power supply. Open the case and test the power supply outputs. Swapping out power supplies is generally more cost effective than fixing a broken one.

Symptom 2:

The power light (LED) is on and the fan is running, but there is no activity. The system appears dead.

Items to check:

Check the power supply for a power good signal. The *power good signal* is sent back to the BIOS system to signal that the power supply is on and ready. The signal back should be approximately 5 volts. Pin 1 is usually the power good pin. Pull the connector back just far enough to check for 5 volts (+/–1 volt). If the power is very low, there may not be sufficient voltage to power up the system. The power output does not have to be completely dead to affect startup.

If the power good signal checks out, check the connection from the power supply to the motherboard. Reseat this connection. Try reseating the CPU. Sometimes the CPU is not making a good electrical contact. CPUs operate on fairly low voltages. A slight oxidation buildup on one of the CPU's pins that is operating at 3.3 volts is sufficient to render the CPU dead. Cleaning the oxidation will bring it back.

If you perform all of the listed operations and the system still fails to activate, you *probably* have a defective motherboard.

Symptom 3:

The system tries to boot. There are two or more beeps, and then nothing (no video). The fan is running, and there is a power light.

Items to check:

Make sure the monitor is plugged in correctly (both the data plug and the power cord). Check the video card. Try reseating the card. If those actions do not help, try to decode the beep error code. If you have the manual that came with the motherboard, start there. Newer manuals are often CDs as opposed to the traditional paper booklet. If there is no manual, look up the BIOS chip manufacturer on the Internet. First, copy all information from the BIOS chip or motherboard and then head to the manufacturer's Web site.

Symptom 4:

You see a setup error indicated on the screen.

Items to check:

This is probably a CMOS setup problem. Access the BIOS setup routine by using the key combination indicated on the screen. If no setup routine is given, try key combinations you are familiar with. Some popular combinations can be found in Figure 3-39 from Chapter 3—Motherboards. You can also look up the keystroke combination for accessing the BIOS at the BIOS manufacturer's Web site.

Normally, CMOS settings do not change. However, sometimes when you install a new hard drive and the drive is automatically detected, the settings change. Also, if the battery used to hold the CMOS data is going bad, you could lose the settings. The date and time not matching the true date and time is a good indication that your battery is going bad.

Be sure to write down the existing CMOS settings before you make any changes to them. This is extremely important if you are going to try something like the **Return to default settings** option. When that option is selected, many settings will change instantly, and you will not be able to tell which settings have changed or what they changed from. Check the manufacturer's Web site for the correct CMOS settings for your particular model of PC.

Sometimes people get curious and go into the BIOS setup to see what it looks like. They also make changes either intentionally or accidentally. What makes it worse is they generally deny going into the setup program.

Symptom 5:

The PC powers on, but there is no drive activity.

Items to check:

Check the system CMOS settings. Make sure the drive is identified. The drive should be identified in the setup program as far as the number of cylinders, heads, and sectors. In addition, while the PC is booting, the hard drive manufacturer followed by the hard drive model number will often flash on the screen when the BIOS finds it. If the drive is not detected during the boot, the screen will flash something similar to "No Hard Disk Drive."

You should also check the connections between the power supply and the hard drive and the motherboard and the hard drive. They should be tight.

If all that checks out, boot the system with a boot disk. From the command prompt, see if you can access the hard drive. If you can access the hard drive, change your default directory to C:\Windows. When in the Windows directory, type **win** to see if you can start Windows.

Symptom 6:

There is normal boot activity, lights and sounds, but no video.

Items to check:

Check if the monitor is plugged into the computer and that the monitor has power. Swap the monitor out for a monitor that is known to be good. If the system still fails to generate a display, you probably have a bad video adapter card. Try reseating the video adapter card. If the system will still not display, change the video adapter card.

Symptom 7:

The system crashes or reboots for no apparent reason.

Items to check:

Check the power supply and cables. Make sure they are all tight. Check for excessive heat on the CPU and memory chips. Make sure all DIMMs are seated properly. Try reseating the CPU.

If all of that hardware checks out, you likely have a defective motherboard or there is a problem with the hard drive. Swapping hard drives with one you know is working should show you where the problem lies. If the hard drive is causing the problem, check for a virus or a corrupt operating system. Always think about the last thing that occurred on the PC before the problem developed. For example, did you or your client recently install a new software program? The following section looks at hard drive failures in more detail.

Hard Drive Failures

Hard drives fail more often than would be thought. Any component that is an electronic and a mechanical combination will fail after a period of time. In addition, hard drives can fail because of software issues. A corrupt MBR can cause hard drives to be unresponsive. It is important for you to determine more than just if a hard drive is bad. You must also determine why it is bad.

A bad hard drive or a corrupt MBR will generate a screen message such as one of the following:

- ✔ Invalid partition table.
- ✔ Error loading operating system.
- ✔ Missing operating system.

If any of these three error messages appear, you most likely have a hard drive problem. To check, try booting the system from a floppy disk. If the system boots normally from the floppy, this will verify a hard drive problem.

Mechanical Hard Drive Failure

Mechanical parts wear out. A sure sign of an upcoming mechanical hard drive failure is an unusual sound coming from inside the computer when it is being accessed (a read or write operation is being done). The sound may be a high-pitched whining sound or a clanking sound. The strange sound coming from the hard drive is mechanical in origin and cannot be repaired. Swapping out the bad hard drive is the only solution.

The only guaranteed method of fully recovering from a hard drive failure is by doing regular backups of the data. You can always reinstall a collection of software when replacing a hard drive, but the data will be lost unless a recent backup has been made. Users should be instructed to back up data regularly, but it is even more important when a hard drive makes strange sounds. Data should be backed up immediately, and a technician should be called to prepare for the crash. You should have parts on hand and be prepared to replace the hard drive.

MBR Failure/Recovery

Hard drives can also fail because of corrupted files and data. The most important area of the hard disk is the master boot record (MBR). If the MBR is damaged, the hard drive will not support the booting process. However, you will still be able to boot from a bootable floppy or CD. Once you boot from the floppy or CD, try to look at the hard drive by entering the **dir C:** command at the command prompt, **Figure 15-4.** If you can view the files on the hard drive, then you are in a position to do a repair. You probably will be able to remedy the situation. As a precaution, back up all data immediately.

You will not be able to back up the files in every situation. But, if you can see files on the hard drive, you should be able to back up important data to some kind of data storage media. Generally on an older system, you will be forced to do a copy to disk. Though, on some newer systems, you may be able to access the drive via an existing network connection. A modern computer with a bootable CD-RW allows for a quicker and easier backup of system files. You can boot the PC using a system restore CD. The CD is placed in the drive and loads all necessary files to boot the PC. In addition, you may load a driver to support the CD-RW. After the drivers are loaded for the CD-RW, you can copy files that need to be backed up.

Avoid using the **fdisk/mbr** command unless it is as a last resort. The **fdisk/mbr** rewrites the boot code portion of the MBR. The last two bytes in the MBR contain partition and volume information. If the last two bytes in the MBR were deleted by a virus, all partition information will be lost when you use the **fdisk/mbr**. Two situations are made worse by this command. One situation is when you have a multiple boot system using at least two partitions. The **fdisk/mbr** command can make the second partition inaccessible as well. It overwrites the partition table,

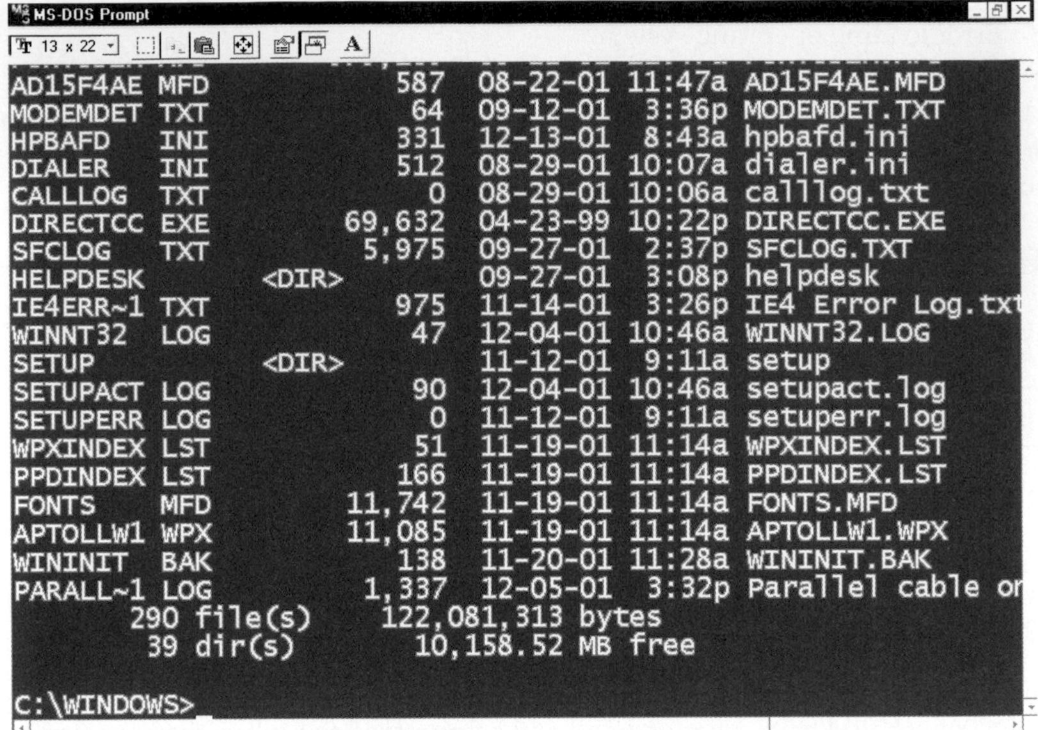

Figure 15-4. Examine your hard drive through the command prompt. If you can see your files, you should be able to repair the drive and save the data.

the boot sector, and the file allocation table. This essentially erases any record of the other partitions. The second situation affects some older computer BIOS systems that cannot access large disk drives. A third-party tool called an *overlay program* is used to remedy the large disk access problem. The **fdisk/mbr** command can overwrite the information used by the overlay program to allow large disk support. This can further complicate or compound the program.

Many third-party software systems can repair an MBR, especially if the software is installed before the problem develops. The software recovery systems make a copy of all vital information including creating a copy of the MBR. When an error occurs, the recovery software can use the copy to help recover the damaged system. In addition, third-party software systems can be used to inspect, copy, and modify bytes in each sector of the hard drive. This is a very powerful tool, but using it can be very time-consuming.

Additional Mechanical Problems

There are a number of other mechanical faults that cause problems in PCs. Boards, cards, and cables can go bad, but these occurrences are not all that common. You will find that, along with hard drive failure, most of your other mechanical problems will arise from two areas: improper hardware upgrades and accumulation of dust in the system.

Problems after Hardware Upgrades

There are many possible system failures after a hardware upgrade. The first thing to check when a system fails to boot is the power and cable connections. Many times while working inside the case, cables are pulled loose. So, the first thing to look for is free-hanging cables. However, cable problems will not always be cables that were not reconnected. Sometimes when a cable is pulled loose, the user will inadvertently replace the cable incorrectly. The cable may be off one pin, or a pin may be damaged. Data cables can also be pinched when systems are reassembled.

Another major problem occurs when mixing different generation technologies together inside the same PC. When a PC has been upgraded several times, problems do arise. An older BIOS chip may not be able to recognize certain new memory module or see the vast new hard drive that has been installed. Check the system resources for conflicts. (Use the **System Properties** dialog box or the **Microsoft System Information** utility.)

Dust Accumulation

The accumulation of dust inside a PC is typical. The type of environment in which the PC operates, as well as its age, determines how much dust has accumulated. Large amounts of dust can cause heating problems by blocking air filters and by collecting on processor heat-sink fins and fan components preventing the proper dissipation of heat. The dust acts like an insulator and holds the heat to the CPU rather than allowing the cooling fins to dissipate it. The dust can clog air filters and render a fan inoperable.

Remove dust carefully using a can of compressed air or a special vacuum cleaner designed for PC cleaning. Standard vacuum cleaners can generate a tremendous amount of static electricity, which is very dangerous to computer chips. Use only vacuum cleaners made specifically for electronic equipment.

Removing dust from a CRT can be dangerous. Do not attempt to open and remove dust from inside a CRT without special training. There are dangerous voltage levels inside a CRT case that remain even after the CRT has been disconnected from electrical power.

Recovering from System Startup Failure

Recovering from a system startup failure requires the technician to have advanced skills. Many of the utilities described in this section should not be used by the inexperienced user because they can cause additional problems if not used correctly. To become an experienced technician, you should practice using these utilities in the lab before attempting to use them on a customer's PC. You can also download extensive information about each of the utilities from the Microsoft Support Web site.

Boot Options

There are a number of different modes you can boot your computer into other than the normal mode that your PC boots into by default. The other modes are used for troubleshooting the computer. You can force your computer to boot into these other modes. They are useful if your computer has any of the following symptoms:

- ✔ System stalls for an unusually long period of time.
- ✔ Printer problems (as a last resort only).
- ✔ Video display problems.
- ✔ Computer shuts down or locks up for no apparent reason.
- ✔ Intermittent error conditions.

Pressing the [F8] key during the boot process halts the boot process and displays a menu on the screen. These choices vary somewhat depending on the operating system you are using. A typical Windows 98 operating system lists the following options:

- ✔ **Normal**.
- ✔ **Logged**.
- ✔ **Safe Mode**.
- ✔ **Safe Mode with Network Support**.
- ✔ **Step-by-Step Confirmation**.
- ✔ **Command Prompt Only**.
- ✔ **Safe Mode Command Prompt Only**.
- ✔ **Previous Version of MS-DOS**.

Normal means that you start the PC as you normally would. The second choice, **Logged**, means that a log of boot activities will be recorded in a file called bootlog.txt stored in the root directory of drive C. The log contains information about which files loaded correctly.

Safe Mode will start automatically if Windows detects a system startup failure. In safe mode, Windows uses a basic configuration. Safe mode bypasses startup files such as config.sys, autoexec.bat, the registry, high memory, and parts of the system.ini. You will likely use this very handy option on a frequent basis. In this option, only the essentials are used to start the system giving you a chance to diagnose the computer. Safe mode disables Windows device drivers and starts the display in standard VGA mode. When in safe mode, each corner of the monitor screen displays the words "Safe Mode." You can force a Windows 98 or Me system to start in safe mode by holding down the left [Ctrl] key while booting.

Step-by-Step Confirmation operates as implied. It allows you the option to carry out or reject boot process files displayed on the screen on a step-by-step basis. This allows you to disable specific drivers called for in each line in the autoexec.bat and config.sys. By disabling each line, one at a time, you can determine which files and drivers are corrupt.

Command Prompt Only allows the computer to boot to the command line interface, not to the Windows graphical user interface. The command interpreter is loaded. A command prompt appears on the screen, and you are free to issue commands from the prompt such as **scandisk**, **dir**, and **copy**. You can start Windows from the command line simply by typing **win** and then pressing [Enter].

Safe Mode Command Prompt Only starts the computer with only the essential drivers as if in safe mode. It does not load the graphical user interface. The command interpreter is loaded and the command prompt appears allowing commands to be issued.

Depending on the version of Windows you are using, not all options will be available. For example, the **Last known good configuration** option is available from safe mode of Windows 2000, XP and Vista, but not in Windows 98 or Me.

Last known good configuration, when selected, uses the last set of registry data before the system failed. This selection assumes that a change occurred in the configuration of the computer system, which resulted in the system failure.

Windows Vista uses the [F8] function key to launch the **Advance Boot Options** menu. This menu is slightly different in appearance when compared to the menu of previous versions. **Figure 15-5** shows the **Advanced Boot Options** menu.

System Restore

System Restore can be used to restore a system to a previous working state. System Restore first became available in Windows Me. Restore points, which are backups of system settings and configurations, make it possible for a computer to revert to an earlier time when the computer system was working properly.

Look at **Figure 15-6.** When System Restore first opens, it provides two options: **Create a restore point** and **Restore my computer to an earlier time.** Although System Restore automatically creates restore points daily and before a software program is installed, the **Create a restore point** option allows the user to make a backup of the existing system. Creating a restore point manually should always be performed before changing configurations, adding hardware,

```
                         Advanced Boot Options

Choose Advanced Options for: Microsoft Windows
(Use the arrow keys to highlight your choice.)

        Safe Mode
        Safe Mode with Networking
        Safe Mode with Command Prompt

        Enable Boot Logging
        Enable low-resolution video (640 x 480)
        Last Known Good Configuration
        Directory Services Restore Mode
        Debugging Mode
        Disable automatic restart on system failure
        Disable Driver Signature Enforcement

Start Windows Normally

Description: Start Windows with only the core drivers and services. Use
             when you cannot boot after installing a new device or driver.

ENTER = Choose        ESC = Cancel
```

Figure 15-5. Windows Vista **Advanced Boot Options** menu.

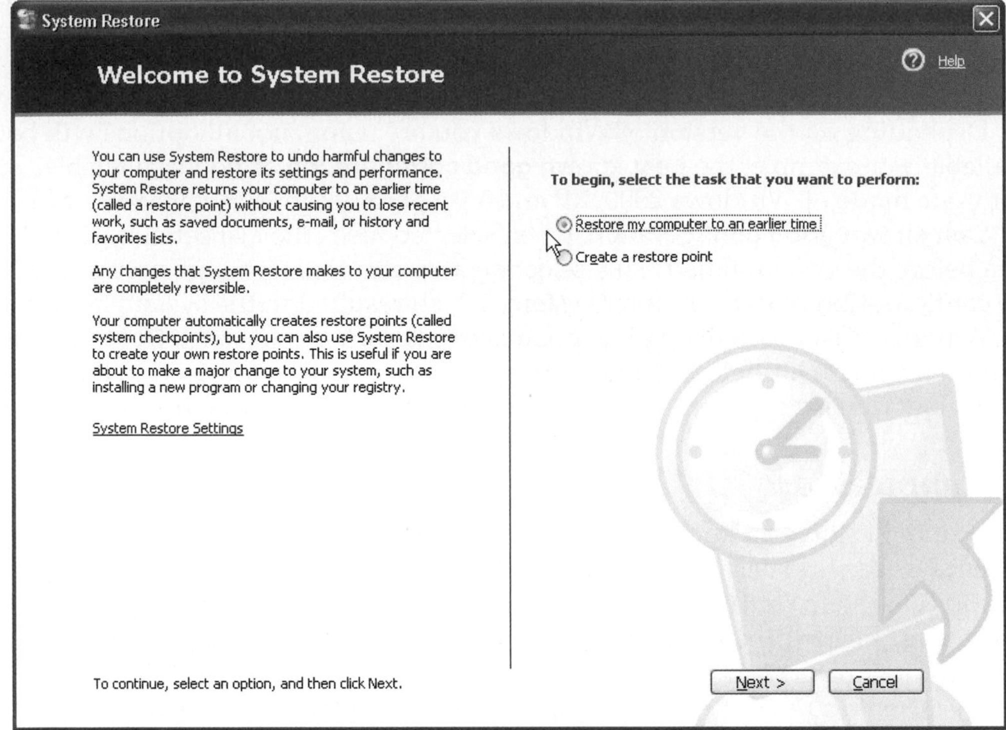

Figure 15-6. System Restore gives the option to restore the computer's system settings and performance to a previous point in time or to create a restore point.

or installing software. If something is done to the system that results in improper operation, the System Restore feature can be used to return the system to its previous state. This is done by selecting **Restore my computer to an earlier time** from the opening screen. System Restore displays a calendar of restore points from which the user can choose, **Figure 15-7.**

Microsoft Windows XP and Vista make an automatic backup of all registry files when you create a system restore point. You can create a system restore point by following the path **Start | All Programs |Accessories | System Tools | System Restore**. The path is the same for Windows XP and Windows Vista.

Recovery Console

The Recovery Console is a last resort recovery utility available in Windows 2000 and XP. Recovery Console is also referred to as "command console" and "repair console." The Recovery Console is used when the problem is so severe, you cannot access the safe mode startup option. Recovery Console is not a GUI utility. It is a text-based command line utility. Commands are issued at the Recovery Console command line prompt. The commands are very similar to the old style DOS commands issued at the DOS prompt. Many of the commands you are probably already familiar with, but there are some new ones. Look at the chart in **Figure 15-8.** The chart is a partial listing of the many commands available in Recovery Console.

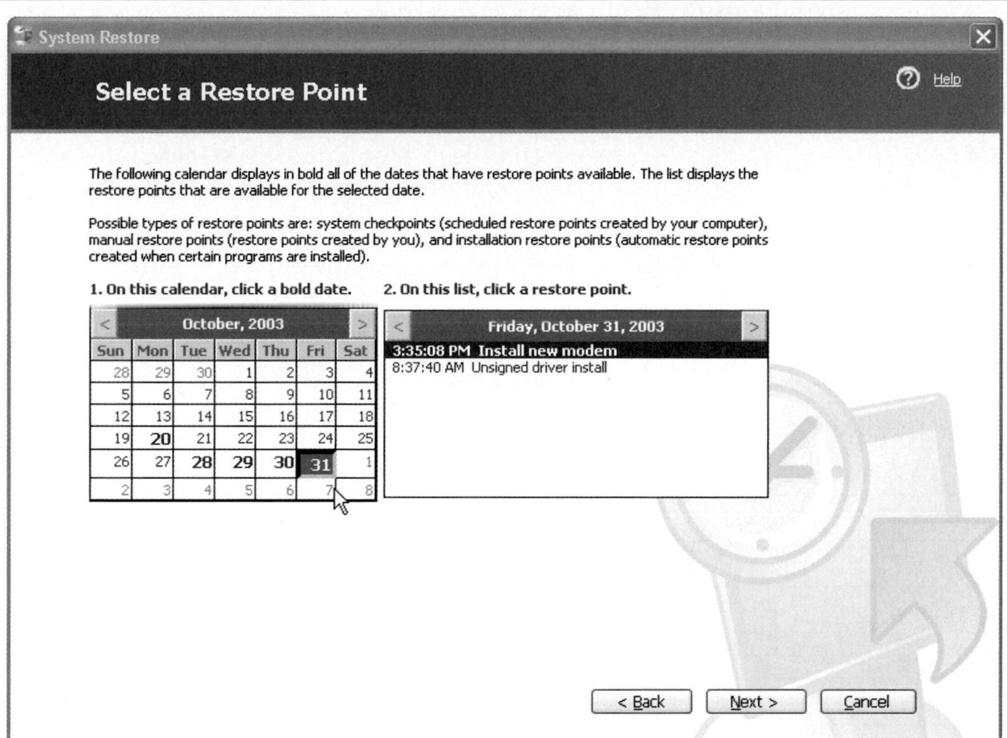

Figure 15-7.
Several restore points may be available in a single day. These include scheduled restore points created by the computer and restore points created by the user.

Recovery Console looks very much like the Windows command interpreter, but it is not the same. Recovery Console is not installed by default. Unless the computer system has been previously configured to run Recovery Console from the hard disk drive, you must use the installation CD to start the Recovery Console. To do this, insert the installation CD into a bootable CD-ROM drive. You may need to configure the BIOS settings to allow the CD-ROM drive to be the first device in the boot sequence.

When the PC boots to the installation program, select *R* to repair the system and *C* to enter Recovery Console. Selecting *R* will command the Recovery Console to perform an automatic recovery of the system similar to the **Last known good configuration** option. Choosing *C* displays the Recovery Console command prompt. You can issue commands from the command prompt or copy a missing file from a floppy disk to the operating system directory. The Recovery Console is a last resort utility and should only be used by technicians with advanced troubleshooting experience. Windows Vista has redesigned the Recovery Console into a much more sophisticated utility called the Windows Recovery Environment. It is discussed in the following section.

Windows Recovery Environment

The Windows Recovery Environment (WinRE) is a vast improvement over earlier startup repair utilities developed by Microsoft for their operating systems. It is launched by booting to the Windows Vista installation DVD. A dialog box will prompt you to select the keyboard layout and regional preferences, such as language. The next screen presents an option to perform a system repair and looks similar to that in **Figure 15-9.**

Figure 15-8. Text-based commands available in Recovery Console.

Command	Description
attrib	Clears or sets file attributes.
bootcfg	Used to recover multiboot system failures and to reconfigure the boot.ini file.
cd or **chdir**	Changes directories or folder location.
chkdsk	Checks for and may repair bad disk sectors and checks the surface of the disk.
copy	Copies a file.
del or **delete**	Deletes a file.
dir	Displays the contents of a directory.
disable	Disables a service or driver.
diskpart	Manages the partitions on a disk.
enable	Enables a service or file.
exit	Closes the Recovery Console.
expand	Extracts a compressed file known as a cab file.
fixboot	Writes a new boot sector on a partition.
fixmbr	Repairs the master boot record.
format	Formats a partition, volume, or logical drive.
help	Displays a list of Recovery Console commands.
listsvc	Lists all available services and drivers.
logon	Lists all Windows 2000 and XP systems and lets you log on to one particular system.
md or **mkdir**	Creates a directory or folder.
rd or **rmdir**	Removes a directory or folder.
ren or **rename**	Renames a file.

Look closely in the lower left-hand side of the dialog box and you will see an option to **Repair your computer**. The letter *R* is underlined, which represents the fact that you can simply press the letter *R* on the keyboard to start the repair process. This feature is a standard option in repair scenarios because the mouse might not be working, and you may only have use of the keyboard.

The first dialog box to appear requests you to identify the correct drive or partition to repair. Look at the screen capture in **Figure 15-10** to see the first dialog box as it appears in a repair scenario. The second dialog box to appear prompts you to select the type of repair, as shown in **Figure 15-11.** The five options are as follows:

- ✔ **Startup Repair**.
- ✔ **System Restore**.
- ✔ **Windows Complete PC Restore**.
- ✔ **Windows Memory Diagnostics Tool**.
- ✔ **Command Prompt**.

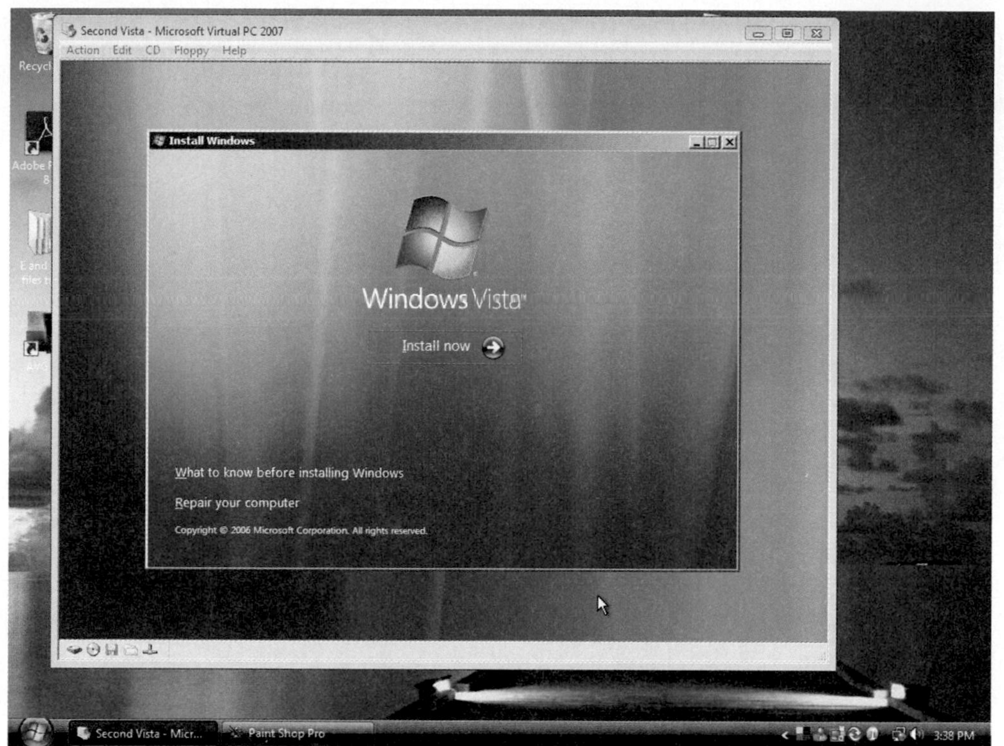

Figure 15-9. The Windows Recovery Console is accessed by booting to the Windows Vista installation DVD and selecting **Repair your computer**.

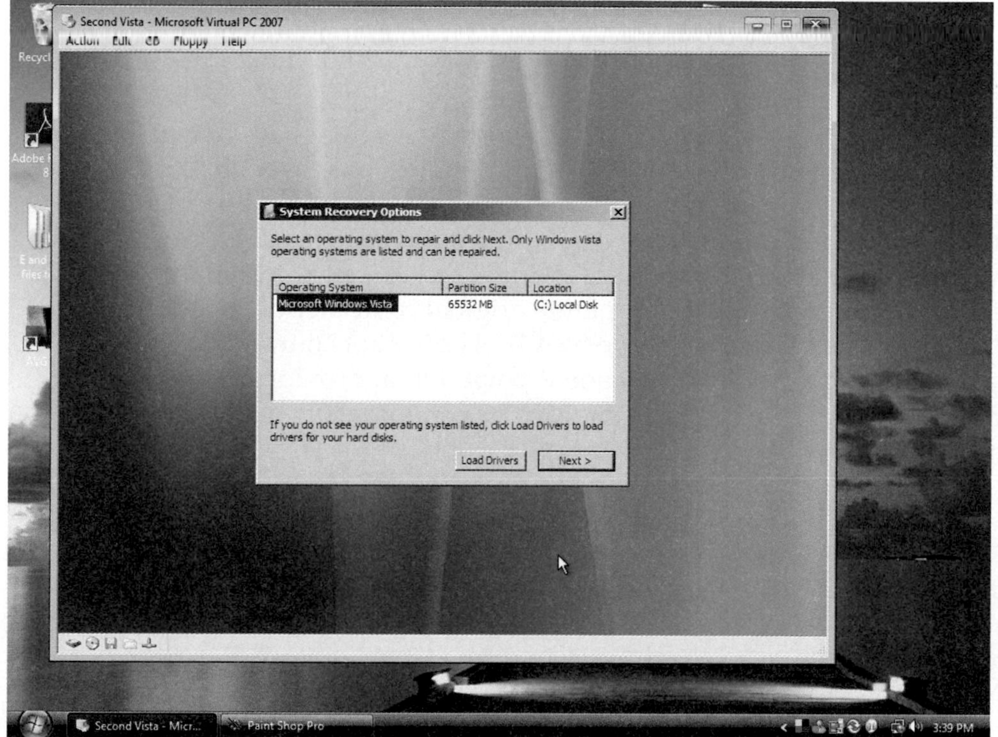

Figure 15-10. Windows Recovery Environment prompts for the operating system to repair.

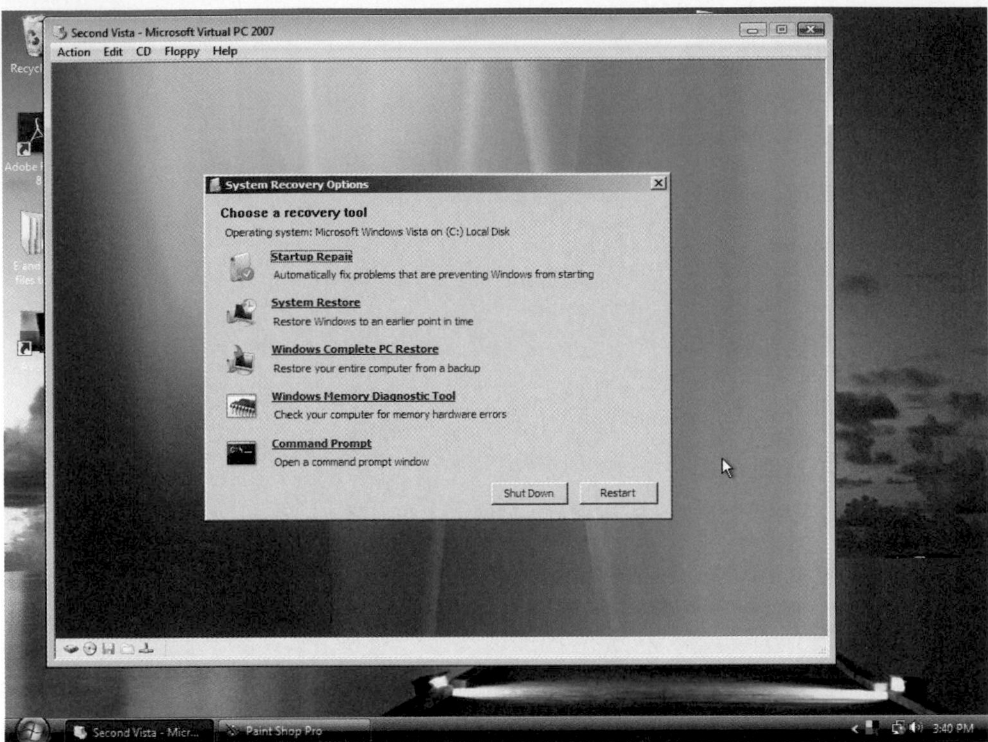

Figure 15-11. Windows Recovery Environment tools.

The **Startup Repair** option searches for and replaces corrupt or missing system files. **System Restore** provides access to the System Restore utility from which you can restore the system to a point in time that the system was working. The **Windows Complete PC Restore** option makes an image of the hard disk drive including files such as the MBR, which normally cannot be accessed or copied without the use of third-party tools. This option is only available in Windows Vista Business, Ultimate, and Enterprise editions. It is not available in the Home versions. It is the most complete restoration option. It replaces the entire collection of operating system files as well as all data. You can even restore the complete system to a brand new computer if the original computer cannot be recovered.

The **Windows Memory Diagnostics Tool** option, of course, loads the Memory Diagnostics Tool, and the **Command Prompt** option provides access to the command prompt from which you can use command line utilities to repair the system.

Some computer manufacturers pre-install System Recovery Tools. To access System Recovery Tools in a pre-installed system you would press [F8] during the boot process and then select **Repair Your Computer** from the **Advanced Boot Options** menu.

Automated System Recovery

The Automated System Recovery (ASR) utility is new with Windows XP. ASR is designed to replace the **Emergency Repair Disk** option used in Windows NT and 2000. The ASR utility automatically restores critical files that were backed up by the Backup utility. The ASR wizard can be accessed through the menu options of the Backup utility and through many third-party troubleshooting utilities.

When ASR is used in conjunction with the Backup utility, it is possible to restore critical system files and data files. The Backup utility is available through **Start | All Programs | Accessories | System Tools | Backup**. The Backup utility can also be accessed by running **NTbackup** from the **Run** dialog box.

Windows Vista continues to offer system backups through the Backup and Restore Center. However, it does not use the acronym ASR when referring to the newest backup and restore system. Be aware that there is a difference between the backup features of the Windows Vista editions. Windows Vista Home Basic and Windows Vista Home Premium do not provide a feature for performing a complete PC backup image. Windows Vista Home basic and Home Premium does include a feature for backing up personal files.

Microsoft System Configuration Utility

With the Microsoft System Configuration Utility (msconfig.exe), also referred to as Msconfig, you can perform a diagnostic startup or select specific services and applications not to load. Using the process of elimination, you can determine which service or application is causing the problem. The System Configuration Utility is used to eliminate items that can cause a problem during the startup of the computer system and after the user logon. This is one of the most common and useful troubleshooting utilities provided by Microsoft as part of the operating system.

Figure 15-12 shows the latest version of the System Configuration Utility used in Windows Vista. When used in troubleshooting startup problems, you can select the **Diagnostic startup** option, which loads only the basic devices and services necessary to start the operating system. You can also select the **Selective startup** option, which provides a more selective diagnostic startup. It allows you to choose between system services and startup items. For a very detailed selection of which services and applications to allow to load and run on the system, additional tabs are provided, such as **Boot**, **Services**, and **Startup**.

This utility is slightly different, depending on the exact operating system and the features associated with that particular operating system. For example, the Windows 95 and 98 System Configuration Utility has tabs named **Win.ini** or **System.ini** to accommodate the win.ini and system.ini files that were used in

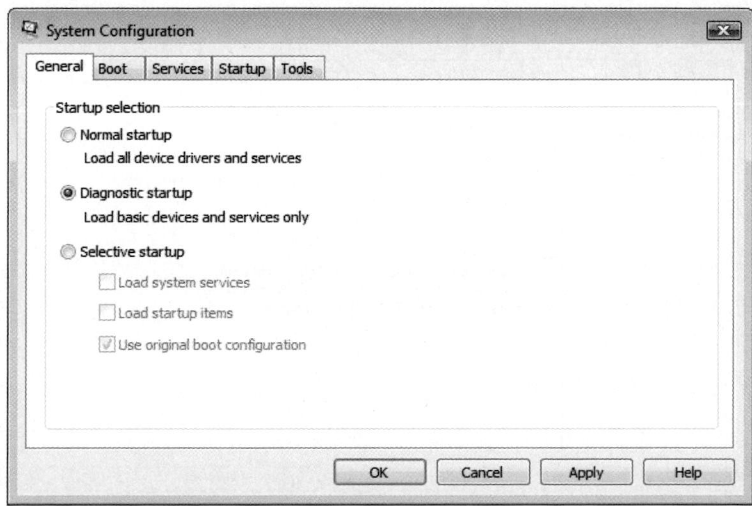

Figure 15-12. Windows Vista System Configuration.

those operating systems, **Figure 15-13.** The Windows Vista System Configuration Utility has several enhancements over previous versions of this utility. For example, the **Tools** tab provides a central and convenient location for some popular tools, such as Event Viewer, Security Center, and Task Manager.

Microsoft System Information

Windows boot problems can be very difficult to diagnose, especially if they are intermittent problems. An extremely useful utility found in the Windows 98 and later versions of the operating system is Microsoft System Information (msinfo32.exe). Microsoft System Information displays detailed information about the hardware and software in the system. **Figure 15-14** shows the window that is displayed after running msinfo32.exe. You can activate it from **Start | Programs | Accessories | System Tools | System Information**, or by typing **msinfo32** at the **Run** prompt.

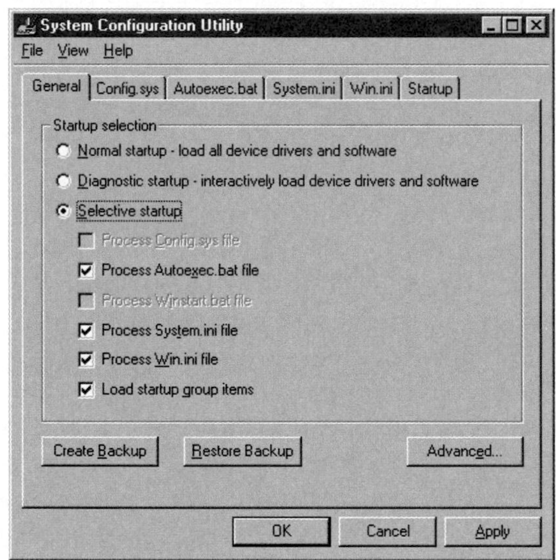

Figure 15-13. Windows XP System Configuration.

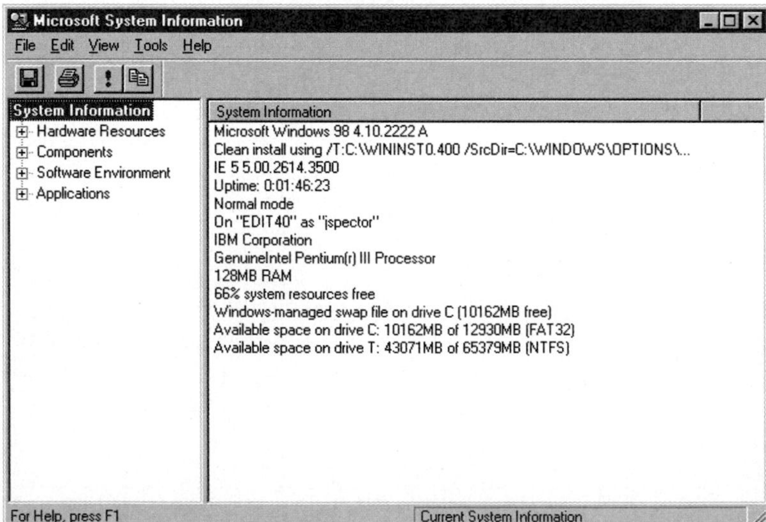

Figure 15-14. Microsoft System Information can be used to find boot problems and other conflicts.

Note that Windows NT does not respond to msinfo32exe. Windows NT is an older operating system and used a set of three emergency recovery disks when problems occurred.

Hardware devices, system resources, software, and Internet program settings can be displayed from this location. You can readily determine conflicts in system resources, as well as most startup problems. There is also an online help program. This can assist you when you need to know more about your diagnostics utilities. There are several troubleshooting utilities available through this window. The essentials of some of these utilities will be covered in the next section.

Reinstall the Operating System

If you cannot repair the system using the utilities provided, you will need to reinstall the operating system. This is the very last resort to recovering from a system startup failure. When reinstalling the operating system, first try to perform a system upgrade. This will allow you to retain the data files that reside on the hard drive. Performing a new installation rather than a system upgrade wipes out all existing files on the hard drive, thus losing all data files.

Some problems can be intermittent and be a hardware problem related to a loose connection or excessive heat. For example, heat could slowly build up inside a computer caused by partially blocked airflow path, resulting in over heating the memory modules. Once the memory module has overheated, the system locks up. Always be aware of "What happened last" when troubleshooting a computer.

Windows Diagnostic Utilities

Most Microsoft operating systems carry the same troubleshooting utilities. You need to become familiar with these utilities to save time when troubleshooting a system problem. Let's see how they might be helpful.

Dr. Watson

Dr. Watson is a standard Microsoft troubleshooting utility that is used to diagnose software fault problems. Dr. Watson collects information about the computer system during and just before a software application fault. It tracks down the program that caused the fault and reports the part of the memory and the program in which it occurred. This information can be used when contacting product support.

Dr. Watson does not load automatically. To activate Dr. Watson, click **Start | Run**, type **drwatson**, and then click **OK**. The Dr. Watson diagnostic program will appear as an icon in the system tray (bottom right taskbar area). You can then right-click the icon to open it. You can also access Dr. Watson, as mentioned earlier, through **Start | Programs | Accessories | System Tools | System Information**, click on the **Tools** menu, and then choose **Dr. Watson**.

By accessing **View** from the menu and selecting **Advanced View**, you can view the drivers, startup programs, and many more items, **Figure 15-15.** Dr. Watson can also write to a log to save errors and the descriptions of faults. These descriptions can be used when contacting support. Dr. Watson cannot diagnose a system hang or lockup condition. Starting with Windows Vista, Dr. Watson has been replaced with Problem Reports and Solutions. This utility is discussed later in this section.

DirectX Diagnostic Tool

DirectX is a software development tool used for multimedia applications. It allows programmers to directly access many of the built-in features of Windows. A poorly written program using DirectX can cause severe system hangs or crashes. The DirectX Diagnostic Tool looks at every DirectX program file on the computer, **Figure 15-16.** You can look for non-Microsoft approved program labels here. If it is Microsoft approved, you should not have a problem. That cannot be said for other programmers' tools. DirectX program files are abundant. They are used for game development and all types of multimedia programs. The Directx Diagnostic Tool is still incorporated into Windows Vista, but it is much more sophisticated than earlier versions.

System File Checker

The System File Checker (sfc.exe) can be run to check for corrupt, changed, or missing files from Windows-based applications. See **Figure 15-17.** It can also be used to restore system files. To start the System File Checker program in Windows versions earlier than Windows XP, select it from the **Tools** menu in the **Microsoft System Information** utility, or type **sfc** in the **Run** dialog box. In Windows XP, you can access the system file checker by typing **sfc** at the command prompt. The responsibilities of System File Checker are incorporated directly into the Windows Vista Resource Checker, but it can still be run from the command prompt with administrator rights using the **sfc** command.

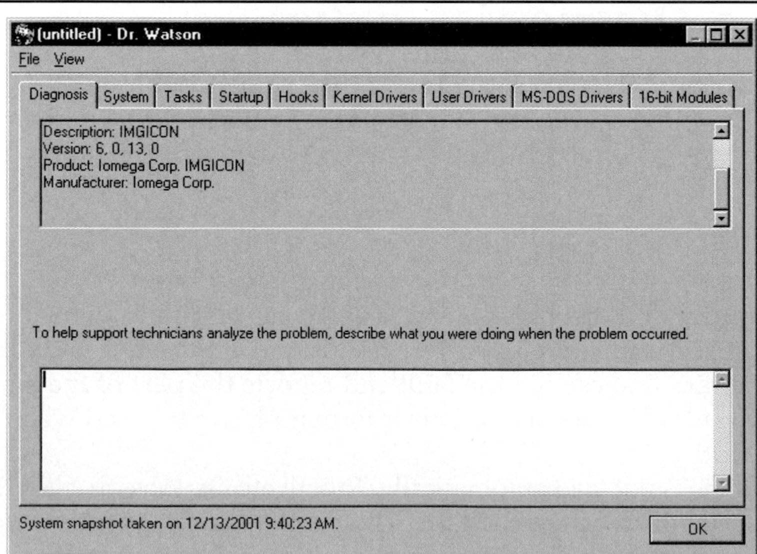

Figure 15-15. The advanced view in Dr. Watson can be shown by selecting the **View** menu and selecting **Advanced View**. Running Dr. Watson places an icon in the system tray. You can activate the program from there.

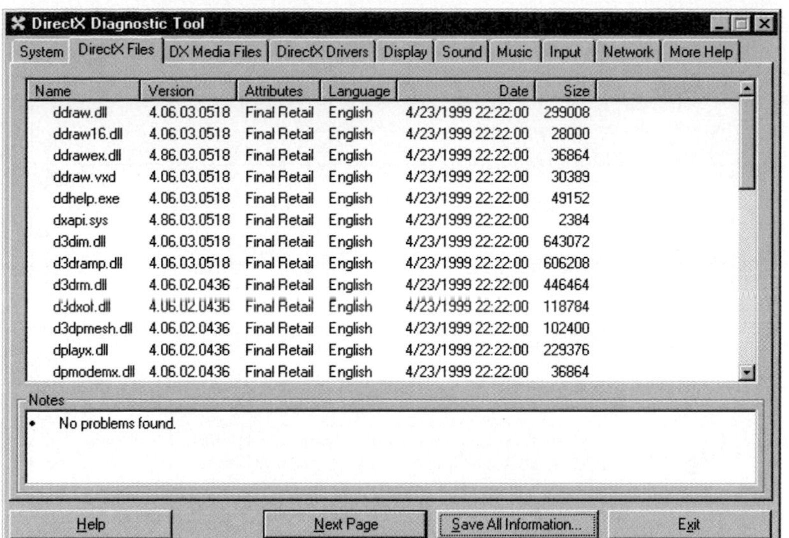

Figure 15-16. The DirectX Diagnostic Tool checks for problems with DirectX files. This check shows no problems.

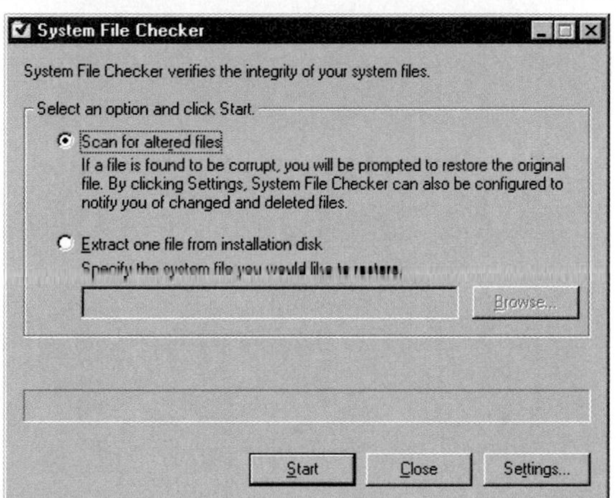

Figure 15-17. System File Checker can by used to check the integrity of system files.

Windows Report Tool

The Windows Report Tool is a utility that allows the PC system settings to be copied and sent to technical support for evaluation. Of course, a modem connection is needed and the system must be bootable. **Figure 15-18** shows the **Windows Report Tool** dialog box as it appears in Windows 98 and Me. Text box areas are provided for you to report information about the error.

Figure 15-19 shows the **Error Reporting** dialog box available in Windows XP. In Windows XP, you can choose to report errors generated by the Windows operating system or by other programs installed on the computer. Some programs may generate an error report each time they are launched or closed. If you find the automatic generation of an error report annoying, there is an option to disable it. The Error Reporting utility can be accessed through the **System Properties** dialog box in Windows XP, **Figure 15-20.** The complete path to the Error Reporting utility is **Start | Settings | Control Panel | System | Advanced | Error Reporting**.

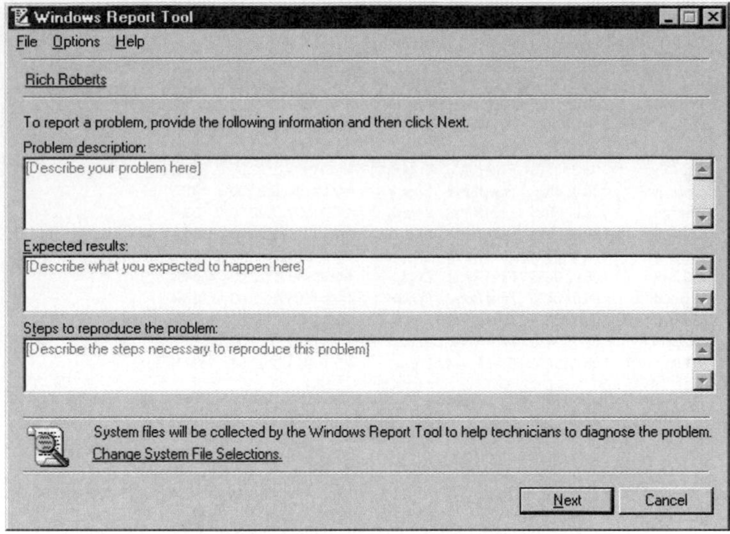

Figure 15-18. Windows Report Tool as it appears in Windows Me. Pay particular attention to the text box areas that allow user input describing the problem.

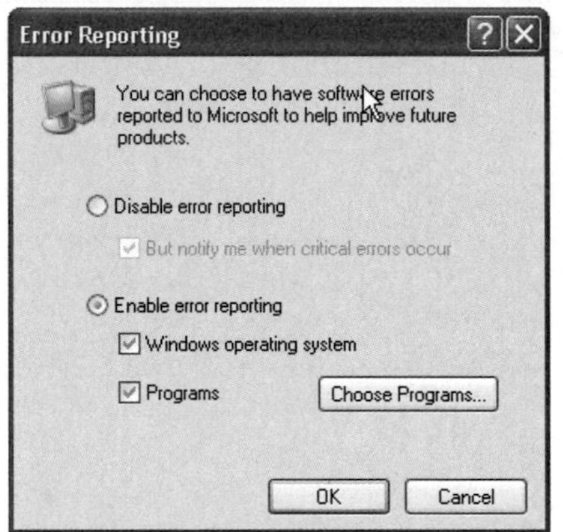

Figure 15-19. An example of the **Error Reporting** dialog box in Windows XP.

Figure 15-20. Look at the **Error Reporting** button in the lower-right area of the **System Properties** dialog box. This is used to access the **Error Reporting** dialog box in Windows XP.

Windows Vista uses the Problem Reports and Solutions feature to serve as the same function as Windows Report Tool. It is discussed later in this section.

Registry Editor

You can also manually view and modify registry contents manually by running either regedit.exe or regedt32.exe. Regedit.exe is a 16-bit version of the registry editor and regedt32.exe is the 32-bit version. Windows Vista does have a version of both available. Windows XP will run either editor, but the preferred registry editor to make changes is regedt32.exe.

Microsoft states that, in general, you should not edit or modify the contents of the system registry. There are times when Microsoft provides step-by-step instructions as to how to modify the contents of the registry using these utilities to repair a problem. Never simply use trial and error methods when working with a registry. The contents of the registry are critical. An improper modification can disable the computer operating system requiring a complete reinstallation of the system files and possible loss of important data. Microsoft has an extensive article on registry editing and recovery at the following Web site links:

- ✔ http://support.microsoft.com/kb/256986.
- ✔ http://support.microsoft/kb/322756.
- ✔ http://support.microsoft.com/kb/307545.

You should never attempt to repair the registry files directly. An error made in the registry files can render the computer system inoperable. You may have to completely reinstall the system onto a clean hard drive. Simply loading the software over the corrupt registry would do no good. The new installation would inherit the previous corrupt settings.

Event Viewer

The Event Viewer in Windows 2000 and XP allows you to view the application, security, and system log files. These log files are named AppEvent.Evt, SecEvent.Evt, and AppEvent.Evt and are only viewable through the Event Viewer program. Each log can be viewed in chronological order or by categories such as event and user. Since the Event Viewer log files retain a history of events that have occurred on the PC, it can be a very valuable troubleshooting tool. For example, users typically will not want to reveal information about installed software such as games, especially if gaming software is against company policy. A technician can quickly view a list of software changes and obtain objective data that can be used to identify possible causes of system problems.

Further enhancements were developed for Event Viewer in Windows Vista. Look at **Figure 15-21.** The Event Viewer is a centralized depository of various logs that were kept separate in early versions of Windows operating systems. Event logs relating to system setup and configuration, applications, security, and more can be accessed and grouped into summaries such as Error, Warning, Information, and Audit success. You can use the mouse to select specific types of event and expand the list. You can then select individual events and look at them in detail, as shown in **Figure 15-22.** Notice that more information about the event

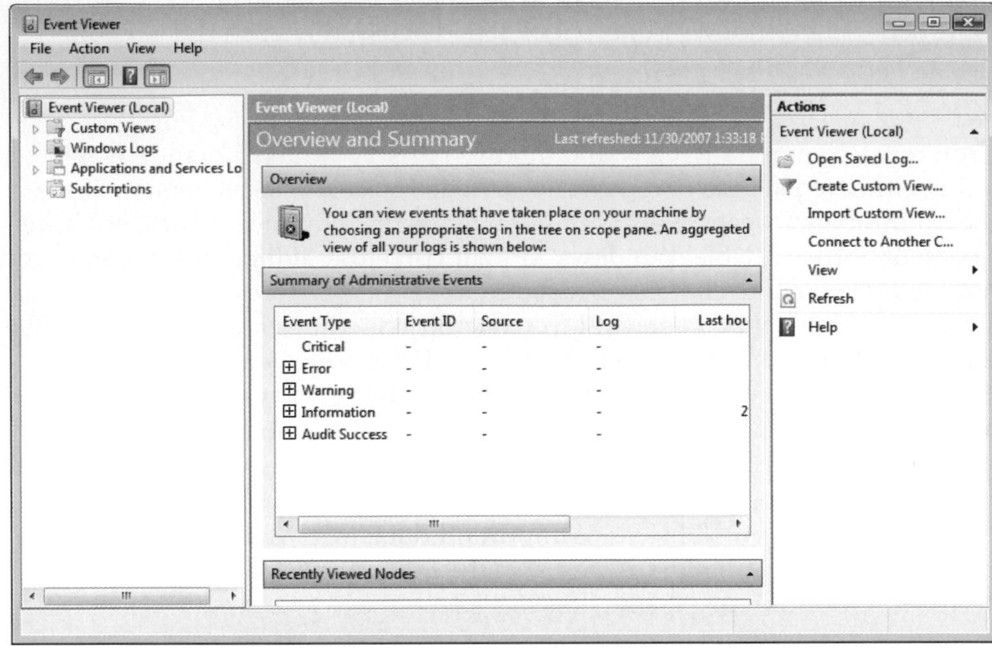

Figure 15-21. Windows Vista Event Viewer.

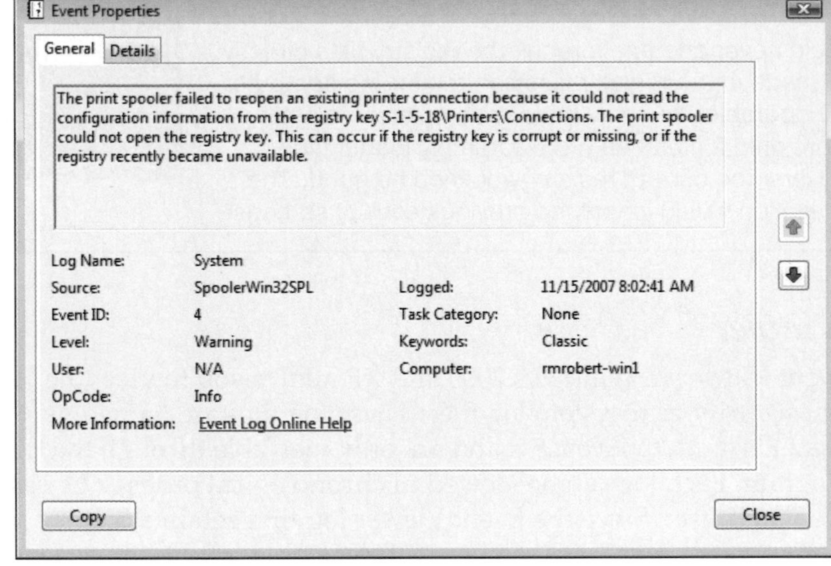

Figure 15-22. Detailed information about an event is shown in the **Event Properties** dialog box and is accessed by double-clicking the event.

can be accessed through the **Event Log Online Help** option. To find more about the extensive capabilities of the Windows Vista Event Viewer use Windows Vista Help and Support.

Log files are created as ASCII text files. They are used to record events that take place or to collect information about hardware and software systems. There can be many different log files on a computer system, not just the ones discussed in this section. These logs are created because many software and hardware manufacturers write their own log file collection programs to assist them (and you) in determining problems that may have occurred during the installation of their hardware or software package. The log files can also be used to relay information to technical support personnel by e-mail or telephone. Sometimes these files can also be accessed remotely by technical support personnel.

Remote Assistance

Remote Assistance was introduced with Windows XP. It allows a user to invite another user to access their computer and assist them in repair. The user needing help sends an e-mail invitation to another person, such as a technical support person. Technical support can then repair the system while they chat with the user.

Remote Assistance should not be confused with Remote Desktop. Remote Desktop allows a user to connect directly to their computer from another location. For example, a user could connect to their office computer from their home computer. The user would have complete control over their office computer just as if they were sitting at its keyboard. Remote Assistance is a temporary connection, and a person must be present at both locations.

Figure 15-23 shows the remote connection options listed in the **System Properties** dialog box under the **Remote** tab. Both Remote Assistance and Remote Desktop are available in Windows XP Professional and Windows Vista, but only Remote Assistance is available in Windows XP Home Edition.

Windows Vista Problem Reports and Solutions

The Windows Vista Problem Reports and Solutions utility, **Figure 15-24,** identifies problems as they occur on the system and can be used to automatically find solutions. Problems are automatically reported to Microsoft via the Internet. If a solution is known, it is sent to the computer and is posted in a window as a solution. A complete history of all problems and solutions can be archived for future use and diagnostics. This is a great improvement over previous versions of error reporting utilities. The path to this utility is **Start | Maintenance | Problem Reports and Solutions**.

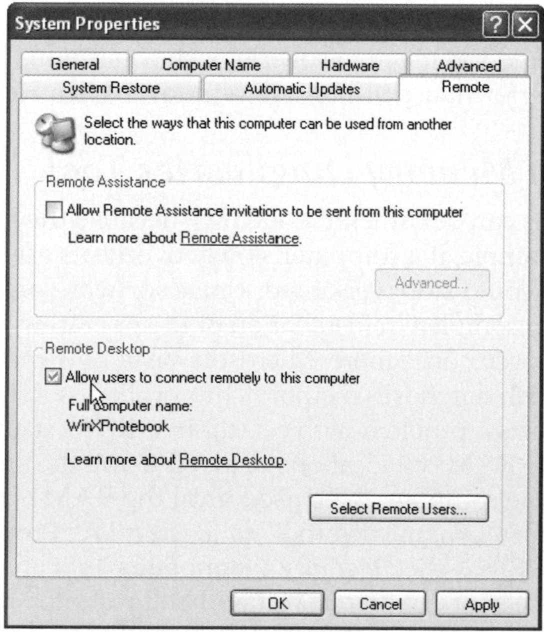

Figure 15-23.
Two remote access programs are available in Windows XP Professional: Remote Assistance and Remote Desktop. The Windows XP Home addition only includes Remote Assistance.

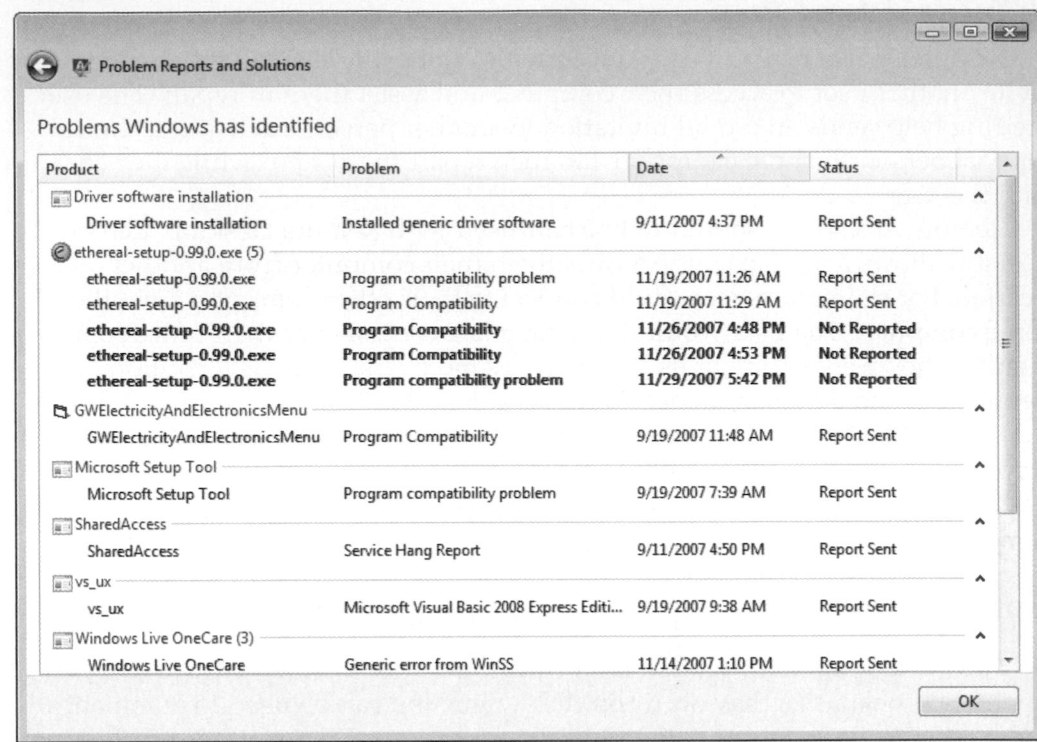

Figure 15-24. The Problem Reports and Solutions utility keeps a listing of all the problems Windows Vista has identified on the system, including a description of the problem, the date it was identified, and whether or not a report was sent to Microsoft.

Windows Vista Reliability and Performance

Windows Vista Reliability and Performance utility is a new addition to the Microsoft Computer Management console. **Figure 15-25** shows the **Reliability and Performance** option in the left-hand pane and the program in the center pane. Notice that the Reliability and Performance utility displays the current condition of the CPU, disk drive(s), network adapter, and memory. The options for this utility are extensive and too much to cover in a short section. To learn more about the Reliability and Performance utility, use Windows Vista Help and Support.

Windows Vista Memory Diagnostics Tool

Memory problems can be difficult to identify because they can occur intermittently. For example, if a computer slowly overheats after an extended period of time, RAM could stop working or cause software program errors. Often, a technician may do a complete reinstallation of the operating system only to have a random error occur once more. Microsoft Vista now includes the Memory Diagnostics Tool, which diagnoses memory chip problems. If the Memory Diagnostics Tool detects a problem with a section of RAM, it automatically restricts the use of the RAM cell locations to avoid using the defective memory section. This allows the computer to be used until the RAM is replaced.

To start the Memory Diagnostics Tool, go to **Start | All Programs | Administrative Tools**. Right-click **Memory Diagnostics Tool** and select **Run as administrator** from the shortcut menu. You will be prompted that Windows needs your permission to continue. Click **Continue** to grant permission.

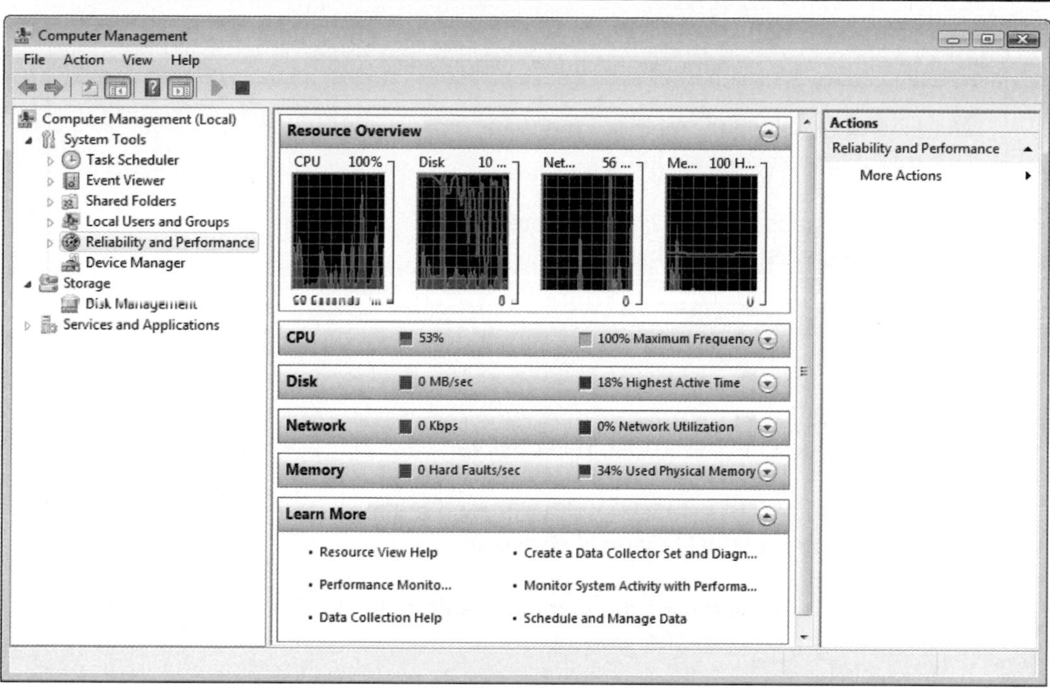

Figure 15-25. Windows Vista Reliability and Performance utility.

You can also start the Memory Diagnostics Tool from the command line. To do this, right-click **Command Prompt** in the **Start menu**. Select **Run as administrator** from the shortcut menu. You will be prompted that Windows needs your permission to continue. Click **Continue**. Enter **mdsched** at the command prompt.

Figure 15-26 shows the **Windows Memory Diagnostics Tool** dialog box. Notice that the test can be performed immediately or scheduled to run the next time the computer is started. The **Windows Memory Diagnostics Tool** in progress looks similar to that in **Figure 15-27.** Notice that the status of the memory diagnostics appears on the screen in text mode, not graphic mode. The progress of the tests is presented as a bar graph and as a numerical percentage. Any problems identified are also presented on the screen.

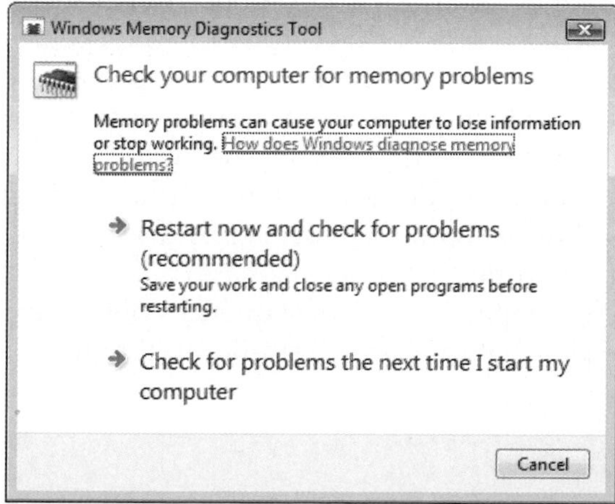

Figure 15-26. The Windows Memory Diagnostics Tool is a new utility introduced with Windows Vista.

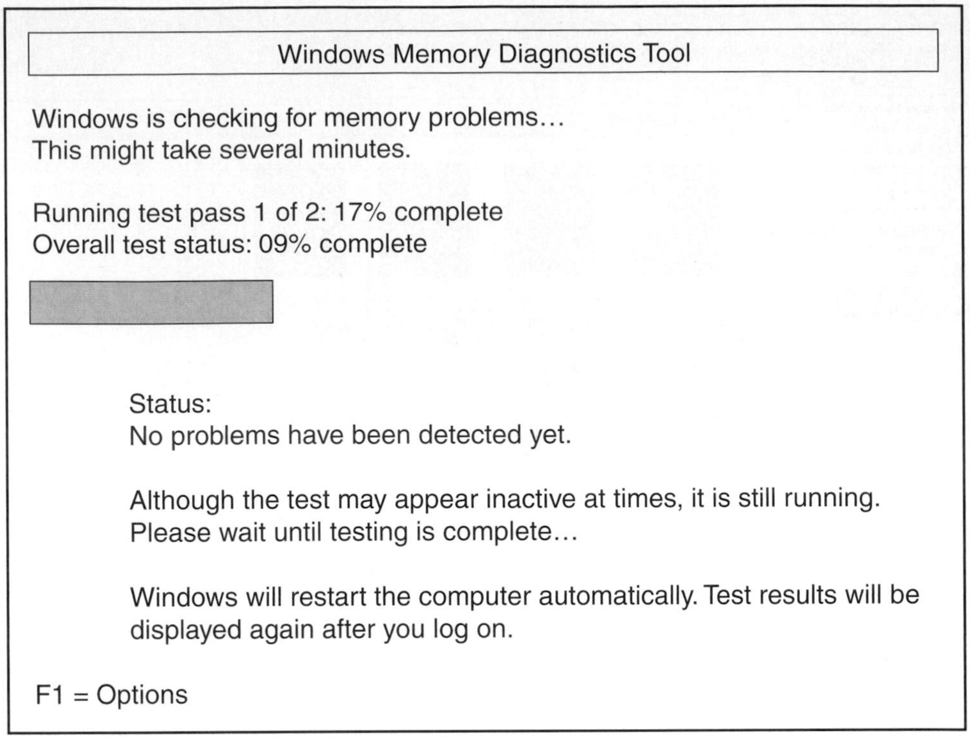

Figure 15-27.
A recreation of the Windows Memory Diagnostics Tool in progress.

```
Windows Memory Diagnostics Tool

Windows is checking for memory problems...
This might take several minutes.

Running test pass 1 of 2: 17% complete
Overall test status: 09% complete

        Status:
        No problems have been detected yet.

        Although the test may appear inactive at times, it is still running.
        Please wait until testing is complete...

        Windows will restart the computer automatically. Test results will be
        displayed again after you log on.

F1 = Options
```

The Windows Memory Diagnostics Tool can also be run from the **Memory Diagnostics Tool** option on the Windows Vista installation DVD.

Boot Sequences

The computer boot sequence is very similar in all the Windows NT-based operating systems (Windows 2000 and Windows XP) and Windows Vista. However, the boot sequence of these operating systems is very different from Windows 98 and earlier operating systems. A good understanding of the startup process is an essential part of troubleshooting. It is, therefore, imperative that you study the boot sequence of all standard operating systems and compare the differences. One way to accomplish this is to study the programs associated with the boot disk created for each system. The boot disk contains the files necessary to boot the computer as well as some of the various enhancement files. Not all files on a boot disk are necessary for booting the system. Information about a system boot sequence and boot files are usually contained in the readme.txt file of the installation discs. Always read the readme.txt files of the operating system you are installing for the first time.

The following table compares the boot sequences of the various Windows operating systems. Notice that they are all similar in that they begin with the POST.

Windows 95, 98, and Me	Windows 2000 and XP	Windows Vista
POST	POST	POST
io.sys	Initial startup phase	Initial startup phase
msdos.sys	Boot loader phase	Windows Boot Manager phase
config.sys	Detect and configure hardware phase	Windows Boot Loader phase
command.com	Kernel loading phase	Kernel loading phase
autoexec.bat	Logon phase	Logon phase

Power-On-Self-Test (POST)

When a computer has power first applied to the motherboard by pressing the on power switch, the BIOS or EFI will start the boot process by performing a quick check of hardware components and verifying that all hardware devices listed in the BIOS configuration database are present and appear to be in working order. The BIOS configuration settings are typically automatically detected or manually modified when the computer is first assembled and started the very first time. The BIOS typically has a default configuration that will usually start most computers without a problem, but not always. Some BIOS configurations require technician modification. The hard disk drive is automatically detected and configured by the BIOS and typically does not need to be modified by the technician. All configuration data is then stored in the CMOS memory.

The BIOS is independent from the operating system. All systems today use either BIOS or EFI as the first computer software routine to run on the computer. Since the POST is independent of the operating system, it is safe to assume that you have a hardware problem if the computer fails during the POST or the POST generates an error message or a series of beeps. You can research the error message or beep codes at the BIOS or motherboard manufacturer Web site. You can also do an Internet search using the contents of the error message as the key terms. The following is a partial list of the system hardware checked during the POST:

- ✔ CPU system clock.
- ✔ CPU registers.
- ✔ Keyboard controller.
- ✔ Video controller.
- ✔ RAM.
- ✔ Disk controllers.
- ✔ Motherboard bus.
- ✔ Adapter card ROM.

The POST can only display error messages after the video has been tested and verified. The system can fail or lock up before the video has been verified and thus give no screen error message.

When POST is complete, some adapters such as video cards or hard disk drives may carry out their own firmware diagnostics routine that is built into the device. This is independent from BIOS diagnostics.

The Extensible Firmware Interface (EFI) is a new approach to the BIOS system. The original BIOS program was first developed in the late 1970s. Before BIOS, each computer manufacturer had to have a matching operating system designed especially for that computer. After the BIOS was developed, you could run a variety of operating systems on the same computer. The BIOS was responsible for linking the communications between the operating system and the PC hardware. EFI was first introduced by Intel, but now a large group of computer hardware manufacturers are involved with creating a set of standards of design for EFI. The group organization is the United EFI (UEFI). EFI can be installed to work directly with BIOS or as a replacement for BIOS. EFI is required on computers that wish to use a new file system directory structure referred to as GUID. In the future, EFI is expected to replace BIOS.

EFI was not supported by the Windows Vista operating system at the time of Windows Vista's original release. However, the Windows Vista service pack 1 does include support for EFI system. Apple MAC OS X first started support of EFI in 2006. EFI is also supported by various Linux systems such as Red Hat and Novell SUSE. The Intel Itanium processor is designed to support EFI as well. Microsoft Windows Server 2003 was the first Microsoft operating system to support EFI. Hewlett Packard (HP) also supports EFI on their HP-UX servers, which are Unix-based systems.

Traditional BIOS is limited in size and typically has less than 1 MB of ROM. It also uses 16-bit drivers. EFI is not limited in size and can load 32-bit and 64-bit drivers before the operating system is loaded. EFI can also load and run applications during the POST without the loading of an operating system. For example, a diagnostic utility or disaster recovery tool, or even a virus check program, can be run before the operating system is actually loaded. This is an extreme difference when comparing BIOS- to EFI- based systems.

BIOS is not governed by any collective organization, and there is no one set of standards controlling the design of BIOS code. The United EFI (UEFI) organization has designed the EFI to be totally vender neutral. This means no one operating system or no one BIOS manufacturer can control the firmware coding. All source code is open and shared so that all software and hardware designers have full access to the EFI coding. Expect the transition from BIOS to EFI to be gradual, not abrupt. EFI motherboards also support traditional BIOS.

Initial Startup Phase

In the initial startup phase, the POST completes and then looks for the boot device where the master boot record (MBR) is stored. The BIOS configuration determines the order for the computer system to locate the next boot device. The boot device could be the floppy drive, the hard disk drive, the CD or DVD drive, or the USB Flash drive. The exact order can be changed in the BIOS Setup program and stored in the CMOS memory. In general, the computer uses the hard disk drive as the boot device. Exceptions are when a floppy is used to startup the computer or when an installation CD or DVD is used to install an operating system or for system recovery.

After identifying the location of the MBR, the BIOS loads the MBR into RAM. For Windows 95, 98, and Me, the BIOS then loads the io.sys file into RAM. You should recall that the io.sys file contains generic drivers necessary for communicating with hardware devices such as the monitor, floppy drive, hard drive, and keyboard. This io.sys file then loads the file allocation table (FAT) into RAM. The FAT is a table of all the files on the hard drive along with their attributes and locations. For Windows 2000 and XP, the BIOS loads the ntldr file into RAM, and for Windows Vista, it loads the Windows Boot Manager (bootmgr).

Keep in mind, you cannot use a non-bootable CD, DVD, or floppy to start the computer. When a non-bootable media is encountered during the boot sequence, an error message will appear on the screen. Some possible errors include the following:

- ✔ Non system disk.
- ✔ Missing Ntloader (ntldr).
- ✔ Hard disk errors.

In an EFI system, a GUID Partition Table (GPT) is used instead of an MBR to locate partitions on a physical disk(s). This table overcomes the partition limitations imposed by the MBR. Before GPT, Microsoft operating system partitioning was based on the limitations of the MBR. Partitions could consist of four primary partitions or three primary partitions and one extended partition subdivided into logical partitions. This is an archaic partitioning system, which evolved from the DOS file system. The maximum number of partitions that can be supported by the Microsoft operating systems is 128. Since the GPT does not have the same limitations of MBR-based partitions, you can have almost an unlimited number of partitions using GPT. EFI does not require a GPT partition and can be used with a partition system based on MBR. Also, EFI can use a disk system that contains both GPT and MBR partitions.

Since the rest of the boot sequence is different for each of the three types of operating systems, the rest of this section is organized by operating system. Each operating system boot sequence discussion continues from the initial startup phase to the last phase for that particular operating system.

Windows 95, 98, and Me

In the previous stage, the io.sys file was loaded into memory, and the io.sys file loaded the FAT into memory. With the FAT in memory, the io.sys file can locate the msdos.sys file. The msdos.sys file is a text file that contains references to items such as where the Windows files are located and options for displaying the boot menu.

The io.sys file then processes the config.sys, command.com, autoexec.bat and win.com files. The Windows startup process only loads the config.sys file and then the autoexec.bat file, if they are required for support of legacy programs. With these operating systems, Microsoft started moving away from the use of config.sys, autoexec.bat, and the win.ini and system.ini files. The win.ini and system.ini files were used with earlier versions of Windows and stored hardware and software information. These files were replaced with the system registry. The system registry is a database that stores information about the hardware and software systems. The registry is continually referenced by the operating system and software programs. The autoexec.bat, config.sys, command.com, and io.sys have been renamed for Windows 98 by changing the file extensions to .dos. For example, io.sys in Windows 98 is now called io.dos.

The config.sys and autoexec.bat files are not required for Windows 95, 98, and Me but are still available to maintain downward compatibility with legacy software programs and drivers.

After autoexec.bat loads, the win.com file loads. Win.com then loads the Windows kernel (krnl386.exe), the graphic device interface (gdi.exe), and user.exe. The krnl386.exe is the kernel file or core program of the operating system. (There is also a krnl286.exe, which was used with earlier models of the operating system.) It manages the processor functions and system resources such as memory DMA channels, IRQs, and port functions. It also loads programs, schedules processor events, and controls the actions of the CPU. The user.exe file is designed to allow the user to manipulate the icons, windows, and elements that make up the user interface. The gdi.exe is the graphic device interface. It is responsible for displaying the screen images used as the interface between the user and the operating system. All three files are located in the directory structure under **Windows | System**.

After these three program files are processed, the logon window appears. The user logs on, and the system processes the user's individual settings.

The system registry contains two main files called system.dat and user.dat. The system.dat file contains information that is specific about the computer. The user.dat contains information about the user. A PC may have multiple users, thus there can be multiple user.dat files containing information about each specific user. Such user information would include, but not be limited to, desktop layout preferences and specific documents created by the user.

Windows 2000 and XP Boot Sequence

Windows 2000 and Windows XP are designed on the NT operating system kernel, not the traditional Windows 95/98 operating system kernel. However, their outward appearance is remarkably similar.

As with the other systems covered so far, these systems start with the POST, load the BIOS program, and look for the boot sector as well as the MBR. Then, Windows 2000 and XP follow the NT system. Once the BIOS has loaded the ntldr file into RAM, it turns control over to it for the boot loader phase. During this phase, ntldr loads the program startup files from the boot sector. Part of loading the startup files is the detection of the preferred operating system. This information is stored in the boot.ini file. Windows 2000 and XP, like NT, allow for the existence of more than one operating system. They will coexist with Windows 95, Windows 98, Windows NT, MS-DOS, and OS/2.

Note that in a BIOS-based system, the operating system provides a boot manager to select which operating system to boot to after the POST has been completed. Often there are compatibility issues when multiple operating systems reside on the same computer and use a boot manager designed by one of the operating system, such as Microsoft or Linux. The EFI has designed and implemented a boot manager that allows the selection of the operating system to load during the POST period. This will hopefully prevent incompatibility issues caused by the operating system designing the boot manager rather than the EFI standard implementing the operating system boot manager.

Once Windows 2000 or XP is selected as the operating system, ntldr calls the ntdetect.com file. This file detects the hardware in the PC system. After the hardware detection is complete, the boot process loads the operating system kernel called ntoskrnl.exe and the hal.dll. The hal.dll is the hardware abstraction layer. The Windows 2000 and XP operating systems do not allow software programs to gain direct access to the system hardware the way that traditional Windows programs allow. The hal.dll is a machine language program that serves as the go-between for software and hardware. The hal.dll makes it possible for the computer system to be hardware and device independent. It supports many different CPU platform designs. In other words, the PC does not have to be an IBM clone. It could use a processor such as Digital's Alpha processor. The ntoskrnl.exe file is the heart of the operating system. It initializes the hardware system and drivers. It controls and oversees the entire operating system and the processing of instructions and files.

The entire boot process is not considered complete until you log on with the [Ctrl] [Alt] [Delete] key combination. Once you log on, the system turns to the user mode of operation. There are two modes of operation: user mode and kernel mode. ***Kernel mode*** oversees the system resources and processor actions. This is an automatic mode requiring no user intervention. ***User mode*** is the actual user interface with the operating system. It is very restrictive in the sense that many areas are not accessible by the user or user programs. This environment is what makes NT-based operating system such a stable system as compared to other earlier Microsoft Windows products. The stability is due to software and users not being allowed to manipulate hardware resources and features.

kernel mode
automatic Windows NT mode of operation that oversees the system resources and processor actions.

user mode
the actual user interface mode for the NT-based operation system. It is very restrictive and many areas are not accessible by the user or user program.

Windows Vista Boot Sequence

In Windows Vista, ntldr has been replaced by the Windows Boot Manager (bootmgr) and Windows Vista Boot Loader (winload.exe). Ntdetect is incorporated into the kernel. Windows Vista also uses Boot Configuration Data (BCD) in place of the boot.ini file, which is used by previous versions of Windows. This section begins with the Boot Manager phase.

Boot Manager phase

The Boot Manager (bootmgr) is used to select which operating system to load when more than one operating system is present on a computer. If more than one operating system is installed on a computer, a screen similar to the one in **Figure 15-28** will appear. The Windows Boot Manager screen does not appear if only one operating

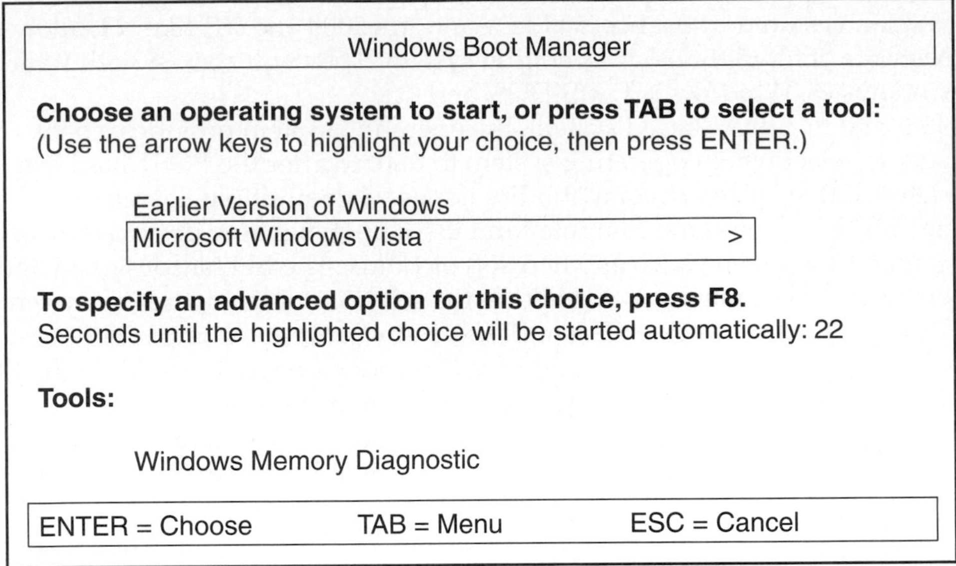

Windows Boot Manager
Choose an operating system to start, or press TAB to select a tool:
(Use the arrow keys to highlight your choice, then press ENTER.)
Earlier Version of Windows
Microsoft Windows Vista >
To specify an advanced option for this choice, press F8.
Seconds until the highlighted choice will be started automatically: 22
Tools:
Windows Memory Diagnostic
ENTER = Choose TAB = Menu ESC = Cancel

Figure 15-28. The Windows Boot Manager menu will appear by default if there are multiple operating systems on the computer.

system is installed on a computer. However, the Boot Manager still runs even if it does not appear on the display. The default for the boot manager is 30 seconds, but the delay is reduced to approximately 2 seconds when only one operating system is present. It is during this two-second interval that the [F8] key can be pressed to interrupt the boot process causing the **Advance Boot Options** menu to appear. The **Advanced Boot Options** menu is similar to the one in Figure 15-5.

If you do not press [F8] within the two seconds after completion of the POST, the operating system will quickly load the Windows Boot Loader (winload.exe), the Kernel (ntoskrnl.exe), and the Session Manager (smss.exe), which results in the familiar Windows graphical user interface. The **Advanced Boot Options** menu cannot be accessed once the computer reaches this point. You must restart the computer to access the **Advanced Boot Options** menu with the [F8] key. You may start pressing the [F8] key before POST is finished. This will usually automatically start the **Advanced Boot Options** menu. The Boot Manager then passes control to the Boot Loader.

Boot Loader phase

In this phase, the Windows Boot Loader (winload.exe) first loads the kernel (ntoskrnl.exe) into RAM, but does not execute it yet. Next, the hardware abstract layer file (hal.dll) is loaded into RAM as well as the system registry hive. Certain key services are started to support various device drivers that are required during the boot process. Lastly, the kernel (ntoskrnl.exe) is executed and takes over operation of the computer system.

Kernel loading phase

After the kernel (ntoskrnl.exe) is executed, the kernel and hardware abstract layer (hal.dll) work together to communicate with software applications, drivers, and hardware. Driver files that do not require user security clearance are typically loaded. For example, the driver and services required to minimally run the printer is loaded at this time.

Now the kernel and hardware abstract layer work together to process information stored in the registry which will be required to complete the boot process. The kernel creates a new registry key which contains information about the drivers and devices loaded so far and through the rest of the boot operation. This information is used for the **Last known good configuration** boot option when troubleshooting the system or attempting to recover from a system failure. The kernel then loads the Session Manager (smss.exe).

Session Manager phase

In this phase, the boot process switches from text mode to graphic mode. A progress bar appears at the bottom of the screen. The session manager continues to run in the background until the computer is shut down.

The Session Manager starts and runs an abbreviated version of Chkdsk and determines if the system volumes and partitions are in working order. The Session Manager is also responsible for loading the page file or virtual memory. The page file supplements the amount of RAM installed on the computer.

Microsoft does not allow third-party venders' software applications to directly access hardware and certain operating system files. But when access is needed by the third-party software applications, the Session Manager manages the activities. If the startup process fails here, you will see a Microsoft system blue screen error. Recall that a blue screen error is a full-screen text message describing the error on a plain, blue background. There will be a cryptic error code that can be used to conduct a search at the Microsoft Web site to find the most likely cause. Microsoft has a very extensive collection of troubleshooting information at their TechNet Web site. The last phase of the startup process is called the *logon phase.*

Logon phase

In this phase, the windows logon file (winlogon.exe) is executed, and the Windows Logon dialog box appears. A user typically enters his or her logon name and password to proceed to the operating system desktop.

After a successful logon, the lsass.exe file loads and runs. This file is the Local Security Authority (LSA). Then, the service subsystem file, services.exe loads and runs. The exact services loaded and started is determined by the computer's configuration and the user's credentials. Only the services the user is allowed to access will start. If there is only one default user and the computer is not connected to a network with a server, the user will be able to access and run all services for the computer. If a user has a limited account, they will only be able to run services allocated by the system administrator.

Startup programs are loaded and run at this point. Any problems such as the computer freezing up or a very long delayed appearance of the user desktop are associated with the startup files and services. If a computer user installs many programs over a period of time, the appearance of the desktop after completing logon will take more time.

After a successful logon, the boot process is considered a success. The registry is updated and will become the registry reference for the "Last known good configuration." A failure of the system after logon is usually a sign of a failed service or a software startup application.

One of the best utilities for analyzing failures after logon is the System Configuration Utility (msconfig.exe). You can select and isolate services and software applications that might be causing the problem.

Linux Boot Sequence

Some common versions of Linux are SUSE, Xandros, Red Hat, Caldera, and Debian. All have graphical user interfaces available and appear similar to the Windows screen display.

Linux is similar to the other systems in that a POST is performed and a BIOS routine is loaded. It is common to boot from a floppy disk when using Linux, but you may also boot from the hard drive. Like any typical startup operating system, after the initial system startup, the Linux operating system takes over. Linux uses a boot manager called *lilo,* which stands for *Li*nux *lo*ader. Lilo looks at the configuration file called lilo.conf to detect operational information. The lilo boot manager allows the user to select other operating systems when more than one exists on the hard drive. Linux operating systems can coexist with Microsoft Windows operating systems. Once the Linux kernel loads, the system runs the init program. The init is the system initialization, similar to DOS or Windows. All the system processes, such as the keyboard, mouse, and network connections, require initialization.

Data Recovery Techniques

Many times data on a nonfunctioning hard drive is not actually lost, although it cannot be directly accessed. Think about the causes of failure for a hard drive. They include the electronics board mounted on the hard drive, the mechanical parts inside the drive, or simply a boot sector failure. If you can still see the drive directory on drive C when using a boot disk, chances are excellent for recovering the data.

One of the most common ways to recover data is with software. There are a number of third-party programs out there designed to read disks that show as bad. **Figure 15-29** shows a disk being accessed by Norton Disk Editor. It can examine the disk and display the sectors in your choice of ASCII, binary, or hexadecimal code. Sections can then be copied to another disk.

Mechanical and electronic repairs should be left to the specialist. Many businesses specialize in this type of data recovery. An electronic circuit board controller mounted on the drive could fail. It can be replaced, but it takes a skilled electronics technician. The circuit conductors are very fragile and easily broken. Also, disk drive platters can be removed and installed on other drives. However, it takes special tools, training, and a clean room (which is not just a room that is clean). A ***clean room*** is a room where dust and foreign particles have been completely eliminated.

clean room
a room where dust and foreign particles have been completely eliminated.

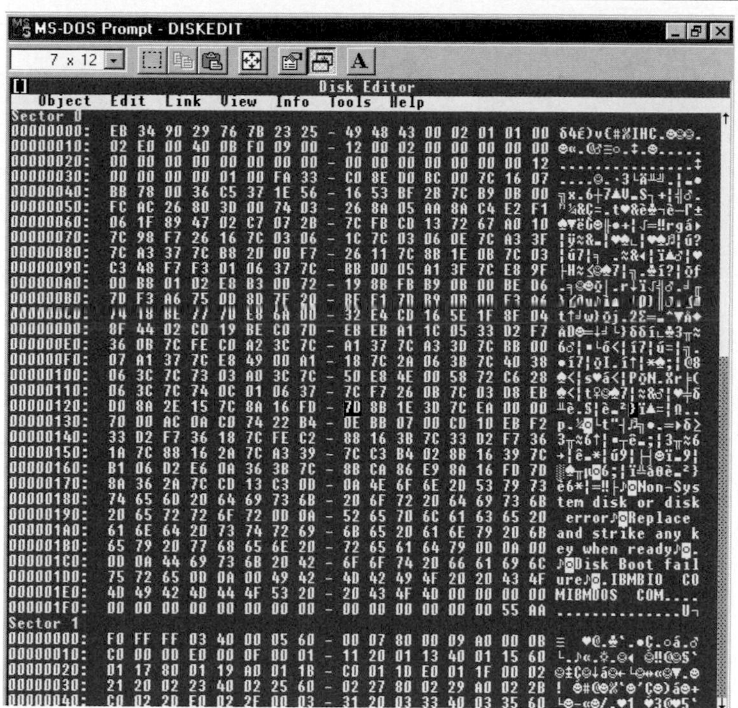

Figure 15-29. Data on a hard drive that stops working can often be accessed using special software. Here a file is being viewed in Norton's Disk Editor.

Preparation for Installing or Upgrading an Operating System

Before installing a new operating system, several appropriate practices should be followed for the ideal setup:

- ✔ Check for viruses.
- ✔ Defrag the drive.
- ✔ Read the readme.txt file.
- ✔ Check the operating system's Web site for latest updates, known installation problems, hardware compatibility lists, patches, and updates.

If you are upgrading an existing system, be sure to backup existing system data. You are probably tired of hearing "back up the system data," but it is the *only way* to rebuild a destroyed system. There are two commonly accepted methods of backing up files: *incremental* and *differential.*

incremental backup operation that backs up select files that have changed since the last backup of files. The archive bit is reset.

differential backup operation that saves files that have changed since the last full backup of all files. The archive bit is not reset.

The difference between the two is determined by the *archive bit.* The archive bit is designed to indicate if a file has been backed up or not. This issue is important on large data systems where backups are performed daily to ensure against data loss.

An ***incremental backup*** requires a disk or tape for each daily backup. When performing an incremental backup, only the changes in data since the last incremental or last full backup are copied. A copy of the last full data backup plus *each* incremental backup in sequence must be used to reconstruct an entire collection of data, **Figure 15-30.** When performing a ***differential backup,*** *all* the data changes are copied since the last full backup. Only one disk or tape is needed to perform the differential backup because it copies all changes in data since the last full backup was performed. To restore the data, you need only the last full backup and the last differential backup.

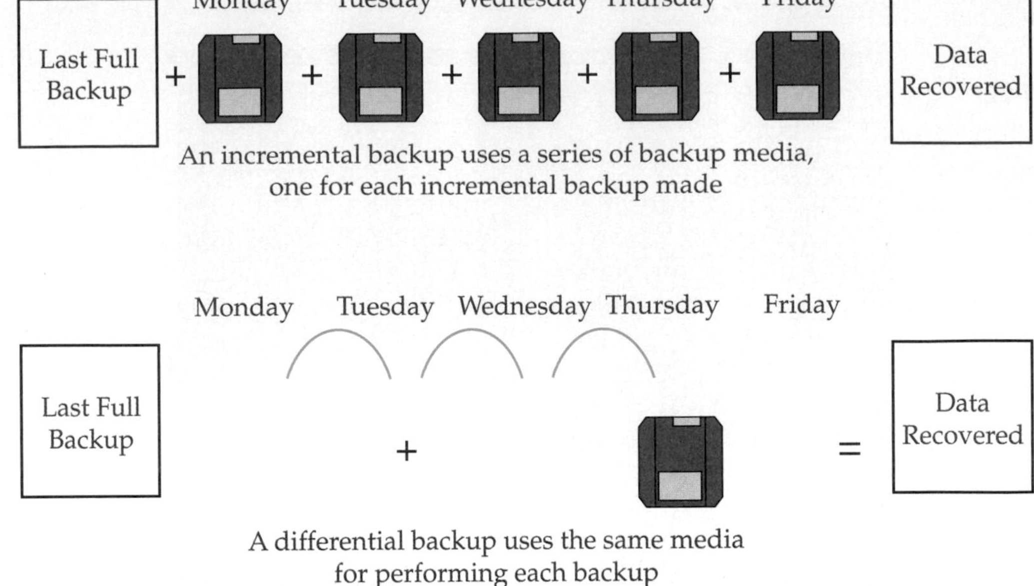

Figure 15-30. The incremental method requires the complete set of disks plus the last full backup to restore the system data. The differential method requires only the last differential backup made plus the last full backup to restore the system.

The reason for selecting an incremental or differential backup is based on the amount of time and disk space required for each type of backup. Since the incremental backup only copies changes from the last incremental backup, there is less data to copy. This results in a shorter time period required to perform the backup. A differential backup copies all data changes since the last full backup. This can require a significant amount of space and time if there is a great number of days between full backups. These differences may seem insignificant at first, but when you are talking about the large volumes of data that some corporations generate, you can be talking about significant periods of time.

Preventive Maintenance

Performing routine maintenance on the PC can help prevent future problems and improve system performance. Some of the most common but often overlooked routine maintenance items are listed in this section. Many of the items can be scheduled to perform automatically.

System Backups

Backups should be performed as part of routine system maintenance. You may not be able to repair a failed computer system, but you can at least restore critical data after installing a clean copy of the operating system. If the system has been configured to perform automatic backups, check if the backups are being performed. The automatic backup configuration may have been turned off or has been corrupted. You can verify that the backup job has run at the scheduled time and that the backup was successful by checking the backup log. Most backup programs keep a backup log, which is accessible through the program's main menu. You should occasionally verify that the data could be read and restored from the backup tape. If you have installed a patch, however, you should verify that you could still restore data. Microsoft has many problems with their DLL files. A DLL file used in the restore process could develop a problem after a system patch is installed.

Disk Cleanup Utility

The Disk Cleanup Utility can be used to regain hard drive space such as that consumed by temporary files, files sitting in the Recycle Bin, unused Windows components, unneeded installed programs, and restore points created by the System Restore utility. Some of the temporary files that Disk Cleanup allows you to remove are downloaded program files, temporary Internet files, and offline files. The Disk Cleanup Utility performs the functions of other Windows programs, such as Recycle Bin and Add or Remove Programs. From this one utility the Recycle Bin can be emptied, saving you the extra steps of accessing Recycle Bin and clicking Empty Recycle Bin. Windows components and installed programs can be uninstalled, rather than accessing Add or Remove Programs. The Disk Cleanup Utility can be used to remove all but the most recent restore points created by the System Restore utility. System Restore automatically backs up system information. This information can be used to restore a computer to a previously operational state. Depending on factors such as how much hard drive space is available, how much hard drive space is allocated to System Restore, and the amount of activity on the hard drive, System Restore can save one to three weeks of system information in files called *restore points.*

Disk Defragmenter Utility

As you recall from Chapter 9—Magnetic Storage Devices, files can become fragmented over time by opening, closing, and deleting them and by changing their contents. These activities can result in a file being segmented and stored in various clusters across the hard drive. The Disk Defragmenter utility rearranges all files on your hard drive into a continuous series of clusters. This results in better disk performance. The Disk Defragmenter utility should be run at least once per month depending on the amount of file activity on the system, and especially run after using the Disk Cleanup Utility. Also, be aware that running Disk Defragmenter on a large disk, 80 GB or more, can take a very long time. Schedule to run the Disk Defragmenter when you will not require the use of the computer for an extended period of time.

ScanDisk and Chkdsk

Disk error checking should be performed on a regular basis. Windows 98 and Me use the ScanDisk utility, and Windows NT, 2000, XP, and Vista use the Chkdsk utility. Both programs inspect the hard disk and correct errors in the file structure, such as bad sectors, lost clusters, cross-linked files, and directory errors.

Install Patches

Check for the latest software patches for your operating system. Patches should be installed on a regular basis, especially as a matter of security. Many operating system security problems are discovered after the release of an operating system. Checking for and installing patches on a regular basis will keep the security level high on the computer system. Some patches can have adverse effects on your computer system. Be sure to back up your system files before installing a patch.

Virus Protection Updates

Virus protection software requires updates on a regular basis. Your virus protection can fail to protect your system if it does contain the latest virus definitions. Check the company Web site of your virus protection software for the latest virus information and updates.

Clean the Physical System

Routinely check and clean the cooling system on the computer. The cooling system includes the power supply fan(s) and the fans located on critical components such as the CPU, chipset, memory modules, and video cards. Also, remove dust accumulations from passive heat sinks located in the same areas. Dust should be removed using a static-free vacuum cleaner.

Also, be sure to remove dust and debris from keyboards, mouse, and the screen areas. Do not use chemicals when cleaning the plastic parts of a computer system or the screen area. First attempt to clean the plastic parts with a dry, soft, lint-free cloth. Next, try a damp cloth, and as a last resort, you may use a mild, cleaning solution. Keep water away from electronic components inside the computer and computer vents. Avoid the use of any harsh chemicals for cleaning the computer and computer components.

Two Microsoft Web sites provide extensive information that will be very valuable when troubleshooting computers. The first site, http://support.microsoft.com, is designed for the average computer user, and the second Web site, http://technet.microsoft.com, is designed for advanced technicians or IT professionals. Save both links in your Internet Browser because you will most likely be using them often to assist you with computer problems.

Summary

- ✔ Try the simple things first when troubleshooting.
- ✔ Write down changes made as you progress through the troubleshooting stages.
- ✔ A failure during the POST is hardware-related.
- ✔ The PC-Doctor POST card can be used to detect and analyze system failures during the POST.
- ✔ A failure during the loading of the required operating system files and hardware initialization is usually a sign that there is a corrupt system operating file or hardware driver file.
- ✔ A failure after logon is usually a software application or service problem.
- ✔ Hard drives have a high failure rate because mechanical systems have a higher failure rate than electronic systems.
- ✔ You can start the Windows operating system in several different modes, accessed by pressing [F8] when the Windows logo appears.
- ✔ Safe mode loads the minimum generic drivers and bypasses autoexec.bat and config.sys, if they exist.
- ✔ The System Configuration Utility (msconfig.exe) allows users to modify the system configuration.

- ✔ The System Information (msinfo32.exe) utility provides information about the system, as well as online help and access to system troubleshooting tools.
- ✔ Dr. Watson is used to collect information about the computer system before and during a software failure.
- ✔ The DirectX Diagnostic Tool checks the validity of any existing DirectX software tools and add-ons.
- ✔ The System File Checker (sfc.exe) checks for missing, changed, or corrupt system files.
- ✔ Windows XP and Windows 2000 ntdetect.com is now merged into the Windows Vista kernel.
- ✔ The two methods of backing up files are incremental and differential.
- ✔ Performing regularly scheduled maintenance can prevent future problems and improve system performance.

Review Questions

Answer the following questions on a separate sheet of paper. Please do not write in this book.

1. What are the three major fault areas?
2. What is *most likely* the cause of a failure during POST?
3. How can you tell that the system kernel has been loaded in the Windows operating system?
4. If there are no power lights and the fan is not running, which is *most likely* the cause?
   a. Power supply
   b. Motherboard
   c. Hard drive
   d. CMOS settings
5. You can start the PC in safe mode after pressing _____.
   a. [Ctrl] [Alt] [Del]
   b. [F8]
   c. [F3]
   d. [Ctrl] [Shift] [Del]
6. How does safe mode differ from a normal boot process?
7. How can you access the **Advanced Boot Options** menu in Windows Vista?
8. What troubleshooting utility is available in Windows XP that can be used when you cannot access the GUI interface or safe mode?
9. How do you start the Windows Recovery Environment in Windows Vista?
10. What are the five Windows Recovery Environment options in Windows Vista?
11. What is the Windows XP ASR utility?
12. What utility can be used to eliminate services and applications while troubleshooting a computer problem?
13. What program allows you to directly access the registry files?
14. Which four hardware resources are monitored by the Reliability and Performance utility?

15. What boot sequence step is similar to all Windows operating systems?
16. How can you change the drive search order from drive C to the DVD drive as the first drive looked at for booting purposes?
17. What is used in place of the win.ini and system.ini files to store system information?
18. What does the ntldr file do?
19. What is the gdi.exe used for in the Windows 2000 and XP operating system?
20. What is the name of the Windows 2000 and XP kernel file?
21. What is the final step to the boot process in a Windows 2000 and XP installation?
22. What are some things you should do before installing a new operating system?
23. List seven things to perform during regular system maintenance.
24. What is the difference between an incremental backup and a differential backup?

Sample A+ Exam Questions

Answer the following questions on a separate sheet of paper. Please do not write in this book.

1. How do you access safe mode in Windows XP while the system is booting?
   a. Press the [Del] key.
   b. Press the [F8] key.
   c. Press [Ctrl] [Alt] [Del].
   d. Hold down the Windows logo key.
2. Which of the following typically causes a failure during the POST?
   a. Corrupt operating system boot files.
   b. A printer driver.
   c. A critical hardware device.
   d. A software application.
3. Which two files are required to load the Windows XP operating system? (Select two.)
   a. ntldr
   b. ntoskrnl.exe
   c. autoexec.bat
   d. cmd.com
4. What is the name of the Windows XP kernel?
   a. ntldr
   b. ntoskrnl.exe
   c. ntdetect.com
   d. service.exe
5. What key combination is used to access the Windows XP logon dialog box?
   a. [Ctrl] [Esc] [Alt]
   b. [Ctrl] [Alt] [Del]
   c. [Ctrl] [Shift] [Tab]
   d. [Ctrl] [Shift] [Esc]

6. Which is the recommended way to back up the system registry files in Windows XP?
   a. Insert the Windows XP installation CD into the CD drive. Reboot the computer and then select **Backup registry** from the menu.
   b. The Windows XP registry is backed up each time the operating system is started.
   c. Open **Control Panel** and then double-click the **Registry Backup and Restore** icon.
   d. Create a restore point.
7. How do you access the System Restore feature in Windows XP?
   a. **Start | All Programs | System Restore.**
   b. **Start | All Programs | Accessories | System Tools | System Restore.**
   c. Right-click **My Computer**, select **Properties** from the shortcut menu, and then select the **System Restore** tab.
   d. **Start | All Programs | Accessibility | System Restore.**
8. What command can be run to view and manually edit the system registry in Windows XP?
   a. **msconfig**
   b. **sysconfig**
   c. **boot.ini**
   d. **regedt32**
9. What command can be issued to view the Windows XP System Configuration Utility?
   a. **sfc**
   b. **sysconfig**
   c. **msconfig**
   d. **regedit**
10. What would be used to diagnose a problem that occurs during the POST phase of the system boot operation?
    a. A POST card.
    b. A multimeter.
    c. Windows System Configuration Utility.
    d. A DOS disk.

Suggested Laboratory Activities

Do not attempt any suggested laboratory activities without your instructor's permission. Certain activities can render the PC operating system inoperable.

1. Launch **msinfo32.exe** from **Start | Run** in Windows XP or **Start | Search** in Windows Vista. View all the information related to the system.
2. Launch **msconfig.exe** from the **Start | Run** in Windows XP or **Start | Search** in Windows Vista. Look at all the options available that can be used to diagnose a system problem. Try stopping the loading of a specific software application and observe the results.
3. Access the boot options menu in both Windows XP and Windows Vista. Press the [F8] key during the boot to access the menu, and then select **Safe mode** option to observe the effect on the operating system. See what files and programs can be accessed and run during safe mode.

4. Using a specific workstation designated for experimentation by your instructor, try several of the following tests:
   - ✔ Remove the data cable from the hard disk drive and boot the system to observe any error messages.
   - ✔ Perform a complete PC backup using Windows Vista. The backup utility is located at **Start | All Programs | Maintenance | Backup and Restore Center**.
   - ✔ Run **regedt32** in Windows XP and Windows Vista and inspect the contents of the registry. Do not make any changes to any of the contents.
   - ✔ Open the **Problem Reports and Solutions** in Windows Vista located at **Start | All Programs | Maintenance | Problem Reports and Solutions**. After opening the utility, explore the features available, but be careful not to select the **Clear solution and problem history** option.
5. Visit the Microsoft TechNet Web site and look at all the available features for technicians.
6. Visit the following Web sites and look at the information about BIOS beep codes:
   - ✔ www.ami.com
   - ✔ www.phoenix.com
   - ✔ http://bioscentral.com
7. Visit the Dell Advanced Troubleshooting Web page at http://support.dell.com/support/edocs/systems/dim2300C/advanced.htm and look at the information provided to assist with troubleshooting Dell Computers.
8. Run the Windows Vista Memory Diagnostics Tool (mdsched.exe) from the command prompt.

Interesting Web Sites for More Information

http://bioscentral.com

http://support.dell.com/support/edocs/systems/dim2300C/advanced.htm

http://support.microsoft.com

www.ami.com

www.bioscentral.com/postcodes/awardbios.htm

www.computerhope.com/beep.htm

www.configsafe.com

www.pc-doctor.com

www.phoenix.com

www.sysinternals.com

www.winternals.com

Chapter 15
Laboratory Activity
Advanced Boot Options

After completing this laboratory activity, you will be able to:

✔ Access the **Advanced Boot Options** menu.

✔ Explain the purpose of each **Advanced Boot Options** menu option.

✔ Explain the purpose of the ntbtlog.txt file.

✔ Explain why the **Advanced Boot Options** menu may not be available to a technician.

Introduction

One of the most important steps in troubleshooting a PC system is accessing the Windows **Advanced Boot Options** menu. This menu is accessible only after a successful POST has been completed. If you cannot access the **Advanced Boot Options** menu, you most likely have a hardware problem and the computer did not successfully complete POST. Another reason you will not be able to access the **Advanced Boot Options** menu is because required system startup files are corrupted. If system files are corrupted, you will need to reinstall the system files.

The most common option in the **Advanced Boot Options** menu is **Safe mode**. This option allows the computer to finish the complete boot sequence, but with a minimal number of drivers and services. Drivers and services are often the cause of a computer system failing to complete the boot process. By loading only a minimal number of drivers and services, a failed computer system can be often started and repaired while in safe mode.

The **Advanced Boot Options** menu is accessed at startup by pressing the [F8] key after POST and before loading the operating system. The following table describes each menu option. Similar options are available in Windows XP.

Advanced Boot Option	Description
Safe Mode	Starts the operating system with only the minimal drivers and services required to operate the system.
Safe Mode with Networking	Includes the necessary network adapter drivers and services needed to establish a network connection.
Safe Mode with Command Prompt	Starts with the command prompt rather than the GUI. Requires fewer drivers this way.
Enable Boot Logging	Creates a log file called ntbtlog.txt, which lists all the drivers installed during the startup sequence.
Enable Low-Resolution Video (640x480)	Uses the lowest possible video resolution and a low refresh rate for minimal impact of system resources.
Last Known Good Configuration (advanced)	Starts Windows using the last set of successful registry and configuration settings.
Directory Services Restore Mode	Used for starting a domain controller for directory support.
Debugging Mode	Used for advanced troubleshooting, usually by programmers. Sends information to another computer via a serial connection.
Disable Automatic Restart on System Failure	Will not let the system automatically restart on a boot failure.
Disable Driver Signature Enforcement	Does not require drivers to have a driver signature.
Start Windows Normally	Starts Windows normally, not with any reduced drivers, services, or configuration.

As a computer repair technician, your main interest will be the following four boot options: **Safe Mode**, **Safe Mode with Networking**, **Safe Mode with Command Prompt**, and **Last Known Good Configuration**.

Safe Mode is the most commonly accessed option when troubleshooting a computer using the **Advanced Boot Options** menu. It loads only the bare minimum drivers required to run the system. Once the computer is started in safe mode, you can access other utilities such as System Restore, System Configuration Utility, Backup, other troubleshooting tools.

By selecting the **Enable Boot Logging** option, the ntbtlog.txt will be created during the system boot. The ntbtlog.txt file contains a list of all drivers loaded and not loaded during the boot. This information can help you determine what driver file the computer is having problems loading. The ntbtlog.txt file can be read using Notepad or a similar software application. The following screen capture shows an example of the ntbtlog.txt file contents. As you can see, all drivers are clearly identified as either "Loaded driver" or as "Did not load driver."

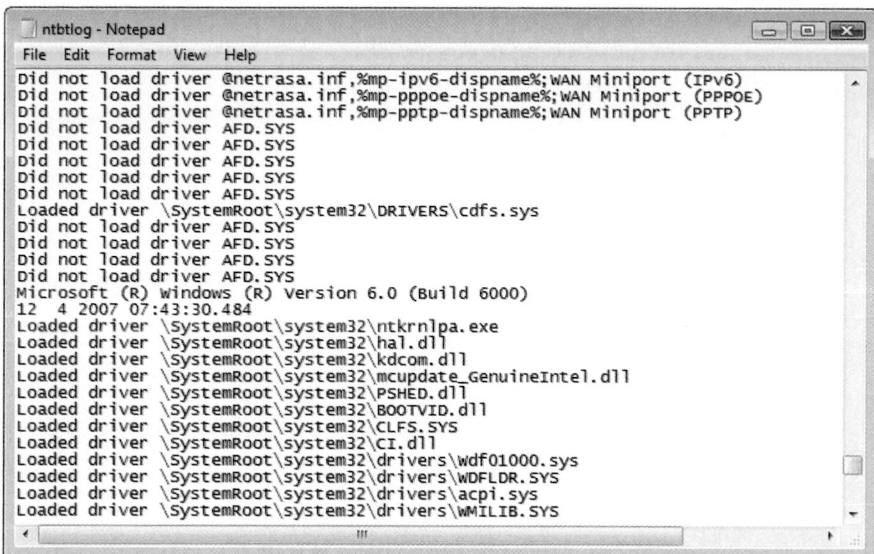

The computer will automatically start up in a modified boot menu called **Windows Error Recovery** if the computer did not shut down properly—for example, if you shut the computer down with the power switch rather than use the option from the **Start** menu. There will be only four choices to choose from: **Safe Mode**, **Safe Mode with Networking**, **Safe mode with Command Prompt**, **Start Windows Normally**. If no selection is made in approximately 30 seconds, the computer will automatically select the **Start Windows Normally** option.

Equipment and Materials

✔ PC with the Windows Vista operating system installed. (You may substitute a Windows XP system for this lab activity.)

Procedure

1. _______ Boot the computer and wait for the desktop to be displayed. This step is to ensure your system is working properly.
2. _______ Restart the PC and press [F8] during the boot sequence to access the **Advanced Boot Options** menu. At times, it is very difficult to catch the exact moment when POST ends and the loading of the operating system begins. You can try tapping the [F8] key repeatedly after the computer starts and continue until the **Advanced Boot Options** menu appears on the screen. If you cannot access the **Advanced Boot Options** menu, call your instructor for assistance.
3. _______ After the **Advanced Boot Options** menu appears, select the **Safe Mode** option.
4. _______ When the computer starts in safe mode, the words "Safe Mode" will appear in all four corners of the display. The desktop background will be black. Also, the screen resolution is reduced.
5. _______ On a separate sheet of paper, make a list of all **Advanced Boot Options** menu options.

6. _______ Copy the following list of items on a separate sheet of paper and indicate if each can be accessed during safe mode operation. Indicate each item with a "yes" or "no."
   Backup and Restore _____
   Windows Remote Assistance _____
   Command Prompt _____
   System Tools _____
   System Restore _____
   Access the Internet _____
   Event Viewer _____
   Task Manager _____
   Control Panel _____
7. _______ Now, reboot the computer and let the computer start normally. Do not press the [F8] key.
8. _______ Shut down the computer using the power on-off button. Restart the computer and see which boot options are available to you. List the available options on a separate piece of paper.
9. _______ Now, reboot the computer and select **Safe Mode with Command Prompt** from the **Advanced Boot Options** menu. Answer the following question on a separate piece of paper.

   Is the user interface text mode only or graphic user interface?
10. _______ Type and enter the **dir** command at the command prompt and observe the action.

Note:
To stop the directory command, press [Ctrl] [Pause Break].

11. _______ Type and enter **exit** at the command prompt. Then, press [Ctrl] [Alt] [Del] and click the **Shut down** button in the lower-right corner of the display. This will shut down the computer.
12. _______ Restart the computer and then use [F8] to open the **Advanced Boot Options** menu.
13. _______ Select the **Enable Boot Logging** option to create a driver status log.
14. _______ Look in the root directory and look under the Windows folder to see if the ntbtlog.txt file exists. The file is a hidden system file, so you will need to change the folder options to show hidden files. You can do this by opening an Explorer window and selecting **Tools | Folder Options | Show hidden files and folders**. You can use the **Start** menu **Search** box to assist you in locating the file. After the file is opened, look at its contents. Close the file and shut down the computer.
15. _______ Now, restart the computer and select **Safe Mode** from the **Advanced Boot Options** menu.
16. _______ After the computer enters safe mode, type **msconfig** into the **Search** box to start the System Configuration Utility. After the **System Configuration Utility** dialog box opens, select the **Services** tab to observe which services were loaded. All services should be marked "Stopped" under the "Status" column.
17. _______ Close the System Configuration Utility and then shut down the computer.

18. _______ You may spend a few minutes exploring the **Advanced Boot Options** menu at this time. If you are having difficulty opening the **Advanced Boot Options** menu, take some time to practice.

19. _______ Return the workstation to its original condition and then go on to answer the review questions.

Review Questions

Answer the following questions on a separate sheet of paper. Please do not write in this book.

1. Which function key is used to access the **Advanced Boot Options** menu?
2. Which options are available when restarting a computer after turning off the computer using the power switch?
3. Can you access Control Panel while in safe mode?
4. Can you run **msconfig** from the **Search** box while in safe mode?
5. What is contained in the ntbtlog.txt file?
6. Where is the ntbtlog.txt file located?
7. Can you run the System Configuration Utility while in safe mode?
8. What services are shown running in the System Configuration Utility during safe mode?
9. What words appear in the four corners of the display during safe mode?
10. What would cause the **Advanced Boot Options** menu or safe mode not to be available?

Disassembly of an older (or nonfunctioning) hard drive will allow you to see how the mechanical and electronic parts of a hard drive work together. Do not attempt to open any hard drive that you intend to use again for data storage. Once a hard drive case has been opened, the drive cannot be used.

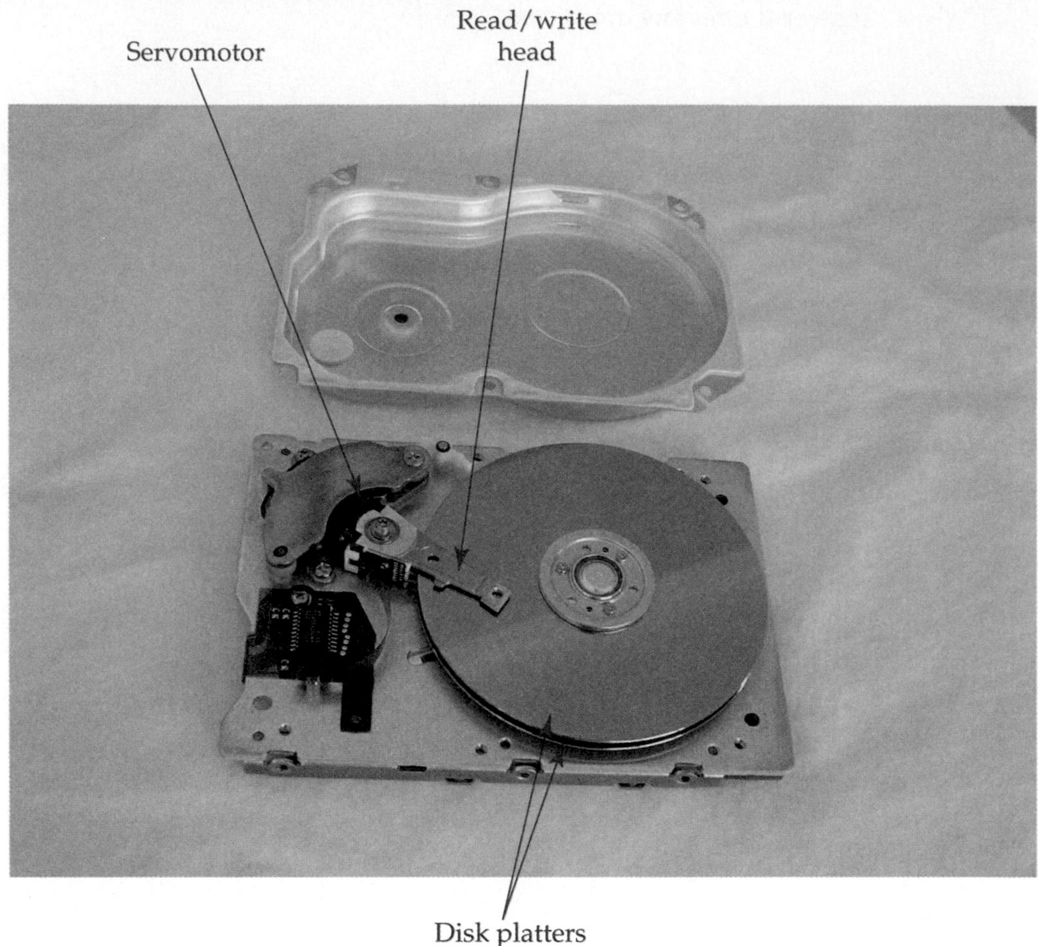

Introduction to Networking

After studying this chapter, you will be able to:

- ✔ Identify and describe network topologies.
- ✔ Describe the communication theory of a network system.
- ✔ List and describe common network systems.
- ✔ Describe the communication principles of Ethernet and Token Ring systems.
- ✔ List and describe common network protocols.
- ✔ Describe the installation of a typical network adapter.
- ✔ Identify common network cabling materials.
- ✔ Identify a network's basic hardware devices.
- ✔ List and describe the layers of the OSI model.

A+ Exam—Key Points

Be sure you can identify the layers of the OSI model and identify the various network topologies. You should be familiar with network protocols. Also, know how to use Control Panel to install a network interface card manually.

Key Words and Terms

The following words and terms will become important pieces of your computer vocabulary. Be sure you can define them.

- active hub
- backoff interval
- BNC (British Naval Connector)
- bus topology
- Carrier Sense Multiple Access with Collision Avoidance (CSMA/CA)
- Carrier Sense Multiple Access with Collision Detection (CSMA/CD)
- client/server model
- client
- coaxial cable
- cross talk
- dedicated server
- Ethernet network
- fiber-optic cable
- hub
- hybrid topology
- local area network (LAN)
- media access code (MAC) address
- mesh topology
- metropolitan area network (MAN)
- Multistation Access Unit (MAU)
- network
- network interface card (NIC)
- node
- Open Systems Interconnection (OSI)
- packet
- passive hub
- peer-to-peer network
- protocol suite
- query
- ring topology
- segment
- sequence number
- server
- star topology
- switching hub
- token
- Token Bus network
- Token Ring network
- topology
- twisted pair cable
- wide area network (WAN)
- wireless topology

The technical support of multiple computers in the home and office requires special skills. As a technician, you must have a basic understanding of the principles and operation of networked computers. This chapter and the following three chapters will introduce you to the basic knowledge required to successfully network and support a small group of computers and related equipment. All technicians will encounter some form of a network when troubleshooting a computer system. In recent years, CompTIA has increased the percentage of questions related to networking on the A+ Certification exams.

Networks—What Are They?

network
two or more computers connected together for the purpose of sharing data and resources.

A computer ***network*** consists of two or more computers connected together for the purpose of sharing data and resources. Networked computers can share data, hardware, programs, and provide a means of e-mail communications and video conferencing. See **Figure 16-1.**

In the illustration, there are several computers connected to a server. A server is usually the most powerful computer in the network system. It contains the network operating system (NOS) on its hard drive. The server also controls network security and communications. There are many benefits to using

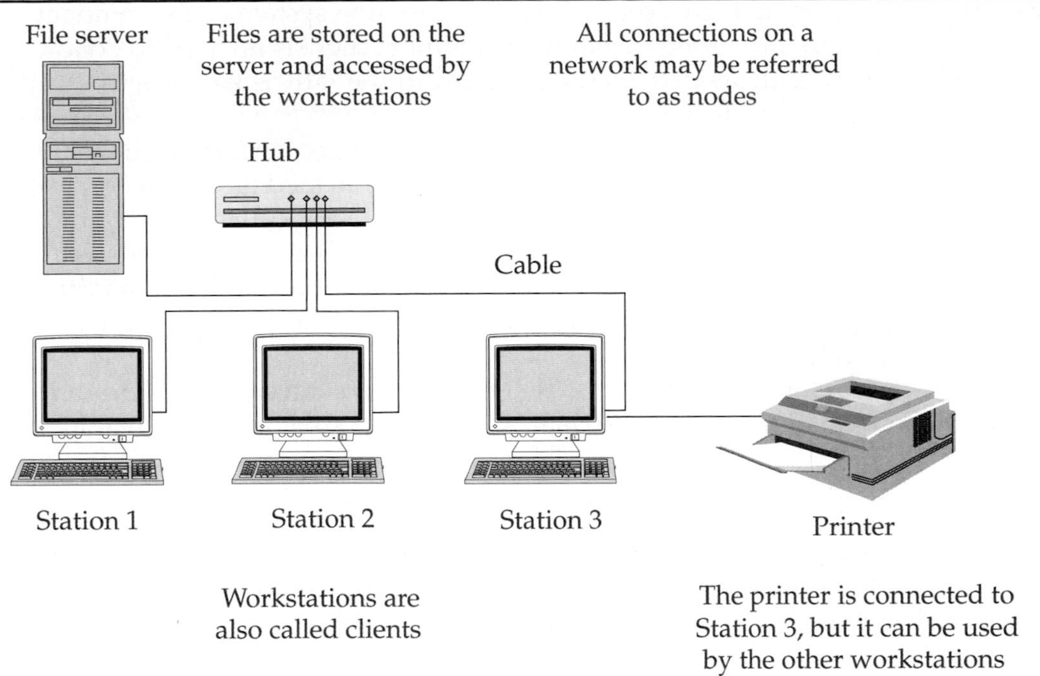
File server
Files are stored on the server and accessed by the workstations
All connections on a network may be referred to as nodes
Hub
Cable
Station 1
Station 2
Station 3
Printer
Workstations are also called clients
The printer is connected to Station 3, but it can be used by the other workstations

Figure 16-1. A simple client/server network.

networks. Networks often increase the productivity, cost effectiveness, and security of an institution because they allow different parties to interact and share data quickly. These benefits are worth looking at more closely.

Shared Resources

Networks provide an economical solution for sharing hardware such as printers. Look again at Figure 16-1. A printer is connected to one of the computers. When connected as a network device, the printer can be accessed by any of the computers connected to the network. Through this arrangement, all the computers on the network share a common printer instead of each having its own expensive printer.

Shared Data

The main reason for installing a network system is to simultaneously share data among a large group of computer users. For example, a company that sells computer parts has sales, supply, distribution, and accounting departments. If the company did not have a network, daily operation would depend on written or verbal communication between these departments. The various departments would have to work very closely and carefully to organize complex tasks such as ordering inventory for projected seasonal sales trends or reducing sales discounts to slow paying customers.

Before computer networks, this system required a large quantity of paperwork, such as customer order forms, inventory forms, and customer invoices. The completion of these forms consumed personnel time and the exchange of information could take days or even weeks depending on the size of the company. A network system alleviates the lag time required to match customer orders to warehouse inventory and distribution. The sales department has immediate access to the warehouse and distribution system of the company. Customer orders are processed instantly. In addition, there is no need to do a physical inventory of the warehouse because a running tally is kept electronically for each item in the inventory.

As soon as the sales force enters an order, the products can be pulled from the warehouse, sent to distribution, and put in the mail or loaded on a delivery truck. The invoice can be generated at the same time and automatically mailed to the customer. If the inventory levels drop below predetermined limits, the items are automatically reordered or manufactured to replenish the inventory. In addition to the above steps, a customer's information is added to the customer list, which can be used for catalog distribution.

This speed can only be achieved with a network. The inventory, billing, and distribution information is stored on the file server and shared by all who require it.

Computer System Management

A network can make the management of a large number of computers much easier. For example, distribution of new software or upgrades can be handled quicker using a network than individual computers. Think of a large corporate network consisting of hundreds or even thousands of computers. If the word-processing application used by the company's personnel is installed in one central location and accessed by all users, it is relatively easy to upgrade or swap with a new software package. In contrast, loading software onto hundreds of computers can be very time-consuming.

Productivity

A folder of information such as a client list containing telephone numbers, addresses, and e-mail addresses can be easily and instantly shared by users on a network. A business's inventory can be constantly updated as orders are placed. Shipping can be made automatic.

Cost Effective

A network system is usually expensive, but when compared to the cost of individual computers needed to accomplish the same scope of work, networks can actually save money. Savings are realized through the sharing of expensive equipment and reduced labor costs.

Security

Security is a major issue in the world. A network can limit data access to only authorized personnel. Network operating system software can determine who can read, copy, or erase the contents of a file. The network can also keep a log of all files accessed, who accessed them, and from which workstation they were accessed. The hours and days of the week that a user is authorized to use the network can be controlled. The network administrator can control the appearance of a workstation display and the programs and information the user can access.

Network Administrative Models

There are two main networking models: client/server and peer-to-peer. We will look at both models and compare them.

Client/Server

The ***client/server model*** is an architecture in which the network is made up of computers that are either clients or servers. A ***server*** is a more powerful computer used to manage network resources and provide services such as security and file sharing. A ***client*** is an individual PC or workstation that accesses a server's resources and shared files. The client/server model provides a method for centralized administration of the network.

A network administrator controls the operation of the file server, which in turn controls the workstations' access to the files located on the server. The network operating system software located on the file server also controls how each workstation interacts with other workstations, printers, and any devices connected to the network. A device connected to the network is often referred to as a ***node.*** Nodes are connected together by a device called a *hub.* A ***hub*** is used to provide a quick and easy method of connecting network equipment together by cables. The cables simply plug into the hub. A typical client/server network is represented in Figure 16-1.

client/server model
networking model in which the network is made up of computers that are either clients or servers.

server
powerful computer used to manage network resources and provide services such as security and file sharing.

client
individual PC or workstation that accesses a server's resources and shared files.

node
device connected to a client/server network.

hub
device used to provide a quick and easy method of connecting network equipment together by cables.

Servers

The server is very similar to the standard PC in design. In fact, early versions of servers were simply PCs designated as servers. Today, many small networks still use a typical PC for the network server. For large network systems, the server is an enhanced, more powerful PC. It may contain two, four, or more CPUs and ten times the amount of RAM normally found on a typical PC. The additional RAM and CPUs allow faster processing of information when connected to many workstations. The server is usually equipped with several hard drives. The server may also have a duplicate set of hard drives used to back up the data saved on the first set of hard drives. Backup systems for servers will be covered in greater depth later in the textbook.

A network system may consist of one or more servers, each having a special function. A server with special functions is referred to as a ***dedicated server.*** Some types of dedicated servers are file servers, print servers, database servers, Web page servers, and administrative servers. A file server is used to store data files that can be accessed by individual workstations. A printer server coordinates printing activities between PCs and network printers. An administrative server may be used to administer network security and activities. A database server contains data files and software programs that query the data. ***Query*** is a term used to describe locating and extracting data from a database. A common server software system, Microsoft SQL server, is a typical database query software package.

dedicated server
server with special functions, such as file servers, print servers, database servers, Web page servers, and administrative servers.

query
locating and extracting data from a database system.

Clients

Clients are computers connected to the client/server network and access network resources controlled by the server. The term *client* is also used to define the software program that runs on a computer and accesses the resources on the network. For example, an e-mail client is used to send and receive e-mail stored on the network mail server. Clients are also cross-platform. For example, you can connect a client running a Microsoft Windows operating system, such as Windows XP, to a server running Novell NetWare, UNIX, or Linux.

Peer-to-Peer

peer-to-peer network
network administration model in which all the PCs connected together are considered equal.

Another type of network administration model is the ***peer-to-peer network.*** As the name implies, all the PCs connected together on this type of network are considered equal, or peers. A typical peer-to-peer network is represented in **Figure 16-2.** Devices on a peer-to-peer network are also connected together by a hub. On a peer-to-peer network, the workstations are typically standard PCs.

Since a peer-to-peer network has no centralized administration, each workstation has equal administrative powers over the network. A workstation must grant permission to the other workstations before they can access its files or use its hardware. This model is usually used on very small networks of less than 25 workstations. It is very difficult to keep an organized administration of this type of network. For example, if all the workstations had to access a database of the company customers, each user would have to be aware of the file location, as well as any other files or software that they may need. The advantages of a peer-to-peer network is that they are inexpensive to install and simple to administer as long as they remain small. Unlike the client/server model, a peer-to-peer network requires no costly network-specific software. You can build a simple peer-to-peer network using only Windows 95 or later and minimal hardware.

Approximately 45% of all networks used in the world are composed of fewer than 25 computers. This number does not include home networks.

Figure 16-2.
A simple peer-to-peer network.

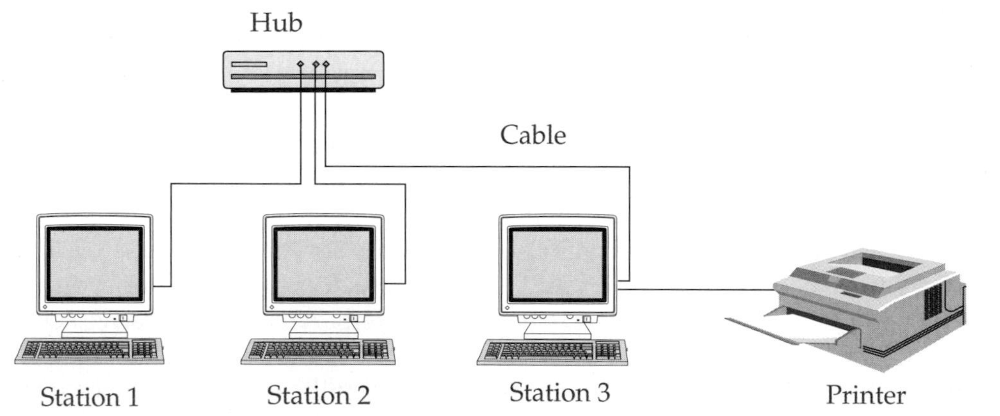

Network Classifications—LAN, MAN, WAN

Networks are classified into three major categories. The categories are used to describe the size and complexity of the system. The three major categories of networks are the local area network (LAN), metropolitan area network (MAN), and wide area network (WAN). These classifications are based on the physical size, management, and use of a telecommunication system, such as the telephone network.

A ***local area network (LAN)*** is a small network of computers contained in a relatively small area, such as an office building. It operates under a single management. An example of a LAN would be the computer network in a small business office.

A ***metropolitan area network (MAN)*** is a group of two or more interconnected LANs operating under a single management. An example of a MAN would be a network system on a university campus. It consists of a group of LANs but is limited to the campus area.

The ***wide area network (WAN)*** is typically a large number of computers, spread over a large geographic area and under the control of a centrally located administrator. The communication over the large area is made possible by the world's telecommunication network. The Internet is a good example of a WAN. It consists of millions of PCs spread across the entire world. A WAN is usually composed of a group of LANs interconnected through a telecommunication network. See **Figure 16-3.**

local area network (LAN)
a small network of computers contained in a relatively small area, such as an office building.

metropolitan area network (MAN)
a group of two or more interconnected LANs operating under a single management.

wide area network (WAN)
a large number of computers, spread over a large geographic area and under control of a centrally located administrator.

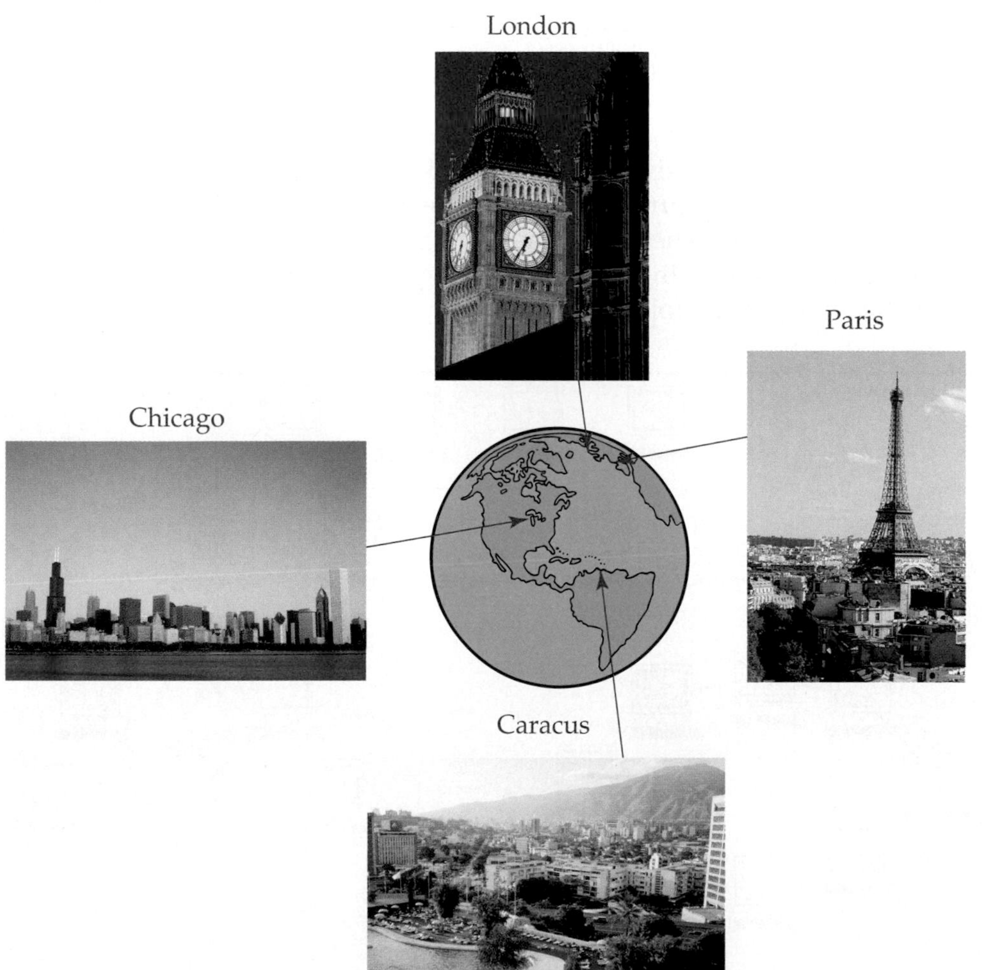

Figure 16-3.
A WAN can be used to connect smaller networks around the globe.

Topologies—Bus, Ring, Star, Hybrid, Mesh, Wireless

topology
the physical arrangement of hardware and cabling in a network system.

The physical arrangement of hardware and cabling in a network system is referred to as the ***topology.*** The most distinctive identifier of topology is the computer cable arrangement. The three major topologies are the bus, ring, and star. See **Figure 16-4.**

Bus Topology

bus topology
a network topology in which a single conductor connects to all the computers on the network.

In a ***bus topology,*** a single conductor connects to all the computers on the network, Figure 16-4A. A bus topology uses less cable than the other cabled topologies and requires a 50-ohm terminating resistor at each end of the cable. The resistor absorbs the transmitted signals when they reach the end of the bus. Without the terminating resistors, some of the signals being transmitted would be reflected back through the cables, distorting the data being transmitted.

In a bus topology, the single conductor which connects all computers to the network is often referred to as the trunk or backbone.

ring topology
a network topology in which a single cable runs continuously from computer to computer.

Ring Topology

The ***ring topology*** consists of a single cable that runs continuously from computer to computer, Figure 16-4B. The cable begins and ends at the first computer in the system. The ring must remain unbroken. Depending on the type of equipment and cable being used, a ring topology can resemble a star topology, which is discussed in the following section.

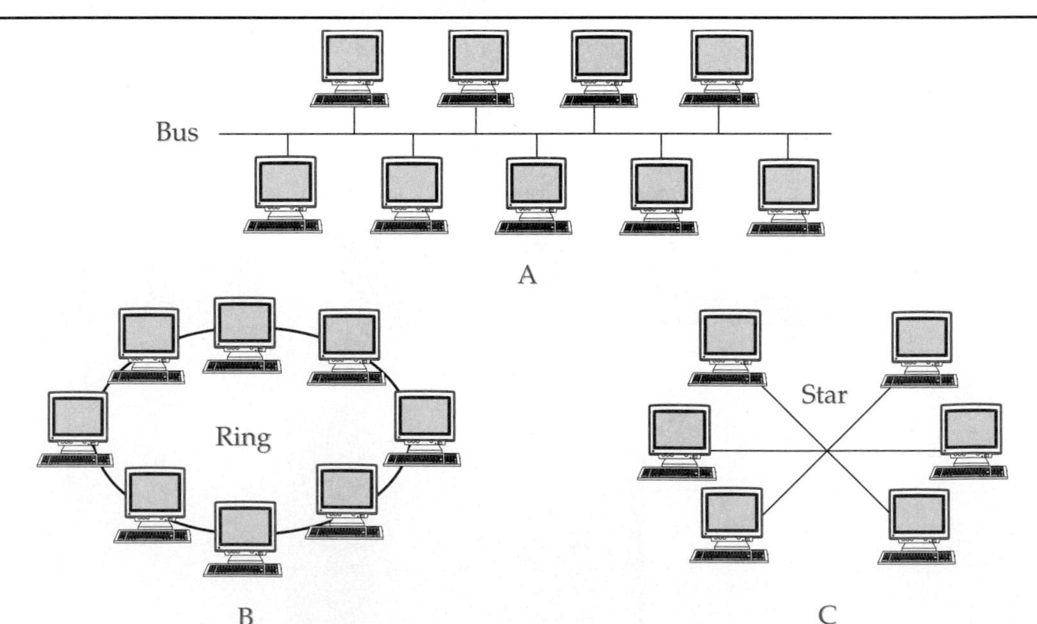

Figure 16-4.
A—An example of bus topology. All workstations are connected to a single conductor known as a backbone. B—An example of ring topology. All workstations are connected in series, forming a closed loop. C—An example of star topology. All workstations are connected to a center point, known as a hub or concentrator.

When laid out in star form, each computer is wired directly to a central location called a ***Multistation Access Unit (MAU).*** A MAU resembles a hub, but functions differently. A MAU allows quick connection and disconnection of Token Ring cables while maintaining the integrity of the ring topology. The ring's integrity is maintained at the MAU by the use of switches at the access ports. The unused ports act as closed switches, completing the circuit. When a cable is plugged into the access port, the switch is opened. The circuit is completed by the pair of wires running from the PC to the MAU. A MAU is sometimes referred to as MSAU. See **Figure 16-5.**

Multistation Access Unit (MAU) a hub-like device that physically connects computers in a star arrangement while maintaining a ring structure.

star topology a network topology in which a cable runs from each computer to a single point, forming a star.

passive hub acts as a connection point in the star topology. Transmitted digital signals from one computer are passed to all computers connected to the passive hub and through the hub to other network sections.

active hub has a source of power connected to it. When a signal is received by an active hub, it is regenerated.

switching hub enhanced active hub. It can determine whether a signal should remain in the isolated section of the network or be passed through the hub to other parts of the network.

Star Topology

The ***star topology*** is a network in which cables run from each computer to a single point, forming a star, Figure 16-4C. The center of the star is usually a device known as a hub or concentrator. Cables from the network's computers plug into the hub, and it provides a common electrical connection to all the computers in the network.

Hubs are classified as either active or passive hubs. A ***passive hub*** simply acts as a connection point in the star topology. Transmitted digital signals from one computer are passed to all computers connected to the passive hub and through the hub to other network sections. An ***active hub*** has a source of power connected to it. When a signal is received by an active hub, it is regenerated. The active hub can be used to extend the range of a signal transmission. The passive hub does not extend the range of the transmission signal.

Some hubs are referred to as switching hubs, or intelligent hubs. A ***switching hub*** is an enhanced active hub. It can determine whether a signal should remain in the isolated section of the network or be passed through the hub to another section of the network. For this reason, switching hubs are used to divide LANs into different segments.

A+ Note:

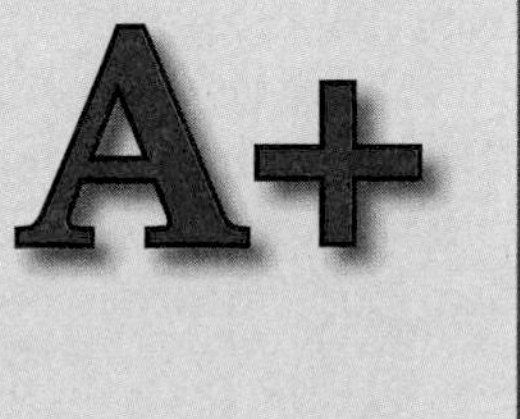

Switching hubs and switches are very similar. In the A+ Certification exams, references to hubs will usually be limited to active and passive hubs, not switching hubs. Switches are referred to as a separate network device, not as a hub. Switches are used to divide networks to make them operate more efficiently. Switches forward network packets based on the packet's destination address.

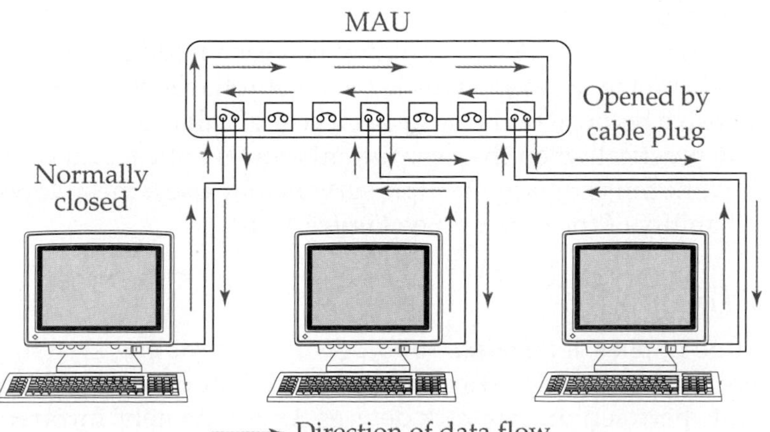

Figure 16-5. A MAU maintains ring integrity while cables are connected to or disconnected from the network.

Figure 16-6. Switching, or intelligent, hubs are used to segment the network, reducing unnecessary data traffic.

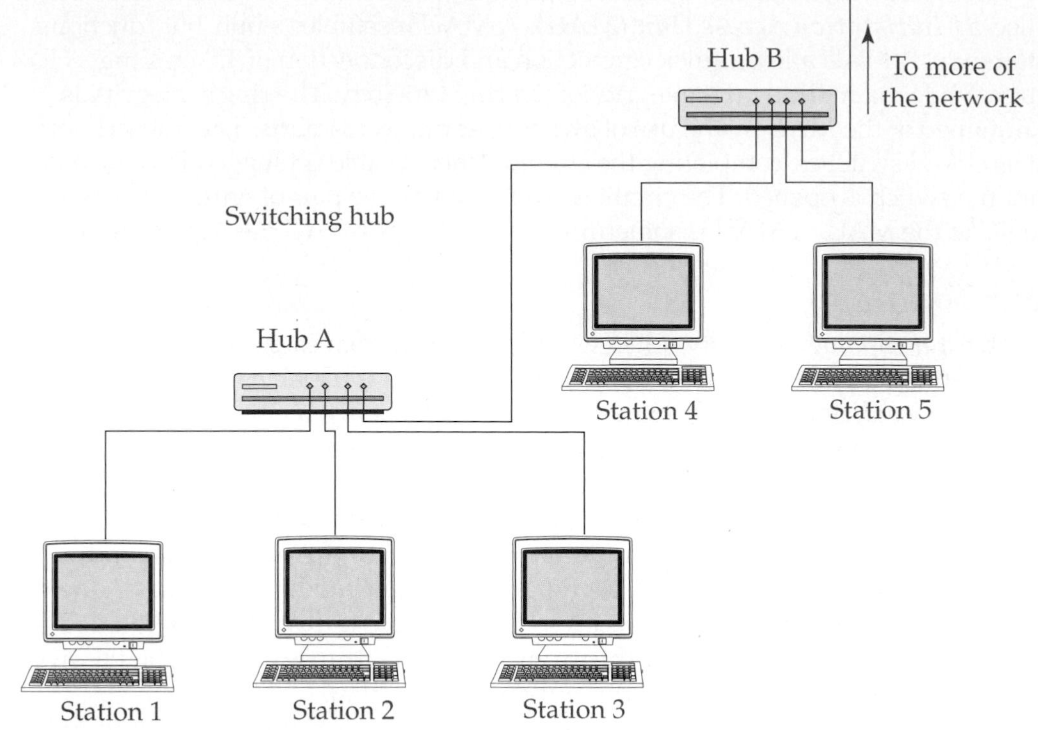

Examine **Figure 16-6.** Imagine Station 3 is attempting to communicate with Station 1. The switching hub will not allow the data frame to be transmitted through the hub to other parts of the network. The hub directs the frame directly to Station 1. Switching hubs are used to reduce excessive data transmissions on a network. A network with an excessive number of collisions can be broken into segments by adding switching hubs. This can reduce the amount of frames being transmitted over the entire network. This will only reduce the traffic if there are a significant number of transmissions between computers on the same network segment.

hybrid topology a mixture of star, bus, and ring topologies.

mesh topology a network topology in which each node connects directly to every other node on the network.

wireless topology a network topology that uses no cabling system between the computers. It uses either infrared light or radio transmission to communicate between the network devices.

Hybrid Topology

A ***hybrid topology*** is simply a mixture of star, bus, and ring topologies. Look at **Figure 16-7.** Notice the different sections of the network in the example.

Mesh Topology

Mesh topology is a network design in which each node connects directly to every other node on the network. This is the most reliable network system and the most expensive because of the additional cost of cabling and equipment. A mesh is only practical when the network mission is critical and cost is not a barrier. A network consisting of multiple servers may use a mesh topology to ensure the reliability of the servers. See **Figure 16-8.**

Wireless Topology

As the name implies, a ***wireless topology*** uses no cabling system between the computers, **Figure 16-9.** It uses either infrared light or radio transmission to communicate between the network devices. Unfortunately, infrared

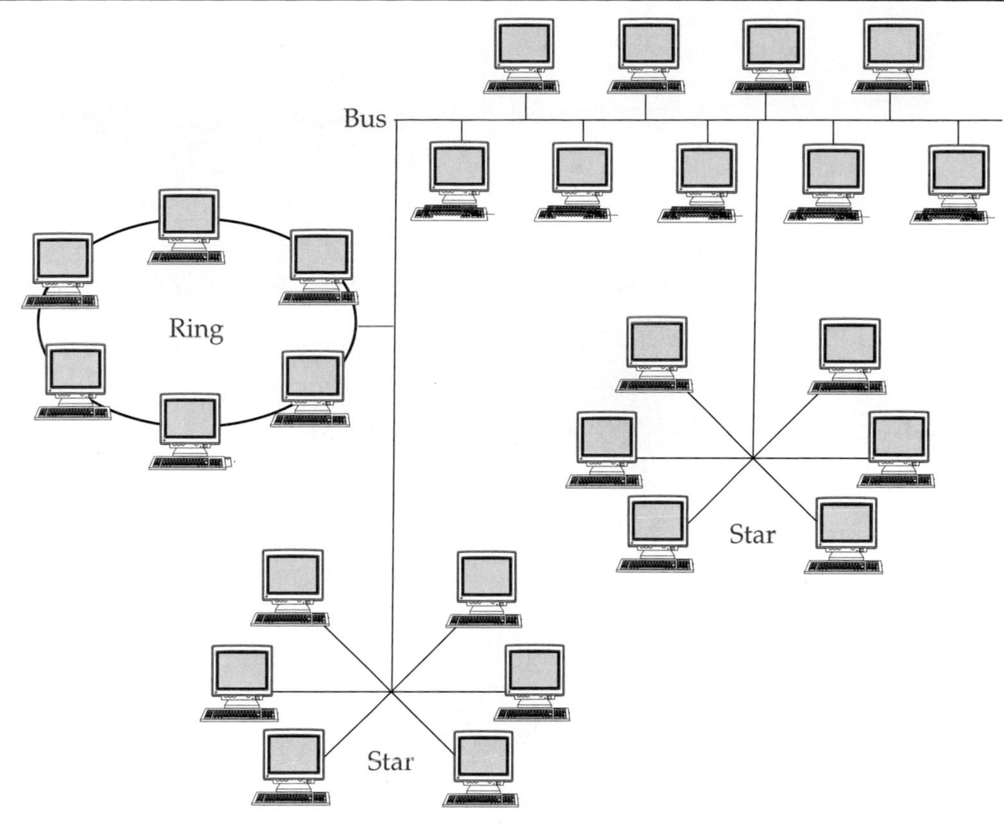

Figure 16-7. Any mixture of topology types, even if it is only two different types, is known as hybrid topology. Shown here is a network consisting of all four topology types.

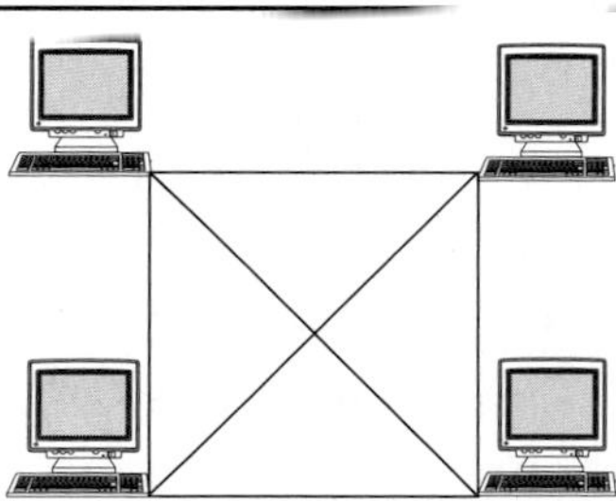

Figure 16-8. Mesh topology connects each workstation to every other workstation on the network.

transmissions require an unobstructed line of sight between devices to establish connections. This means that nothing can be placed between the computers that would block the light beam used for communication. Radio transmission systems don't need a line of sight. However, they can experience difficulties caused by the building structure and other interference generated by a variety of electrical equipment, such as radios, motors, welders, and microwaves.

There are many reasons to use wireless topologies. Wireless topology can be used to connect vehicles to a network. The transmission can originate from a building antenna or even from a satellite, Figure 16-9A. Wireless technology may be used in place of conventional network cabling to bridge a gap between two buildings separated by a wide metropolitan street or a river, Figure 16-9B. Connecting two buildings with cable could be more expensive and time-consuming than installing transmitters and receivers. A wireless system can provide a quick way to reconfigure a computer arrangement, Figure 16-9C. Moving cables to rearrange computers may not be as easy.

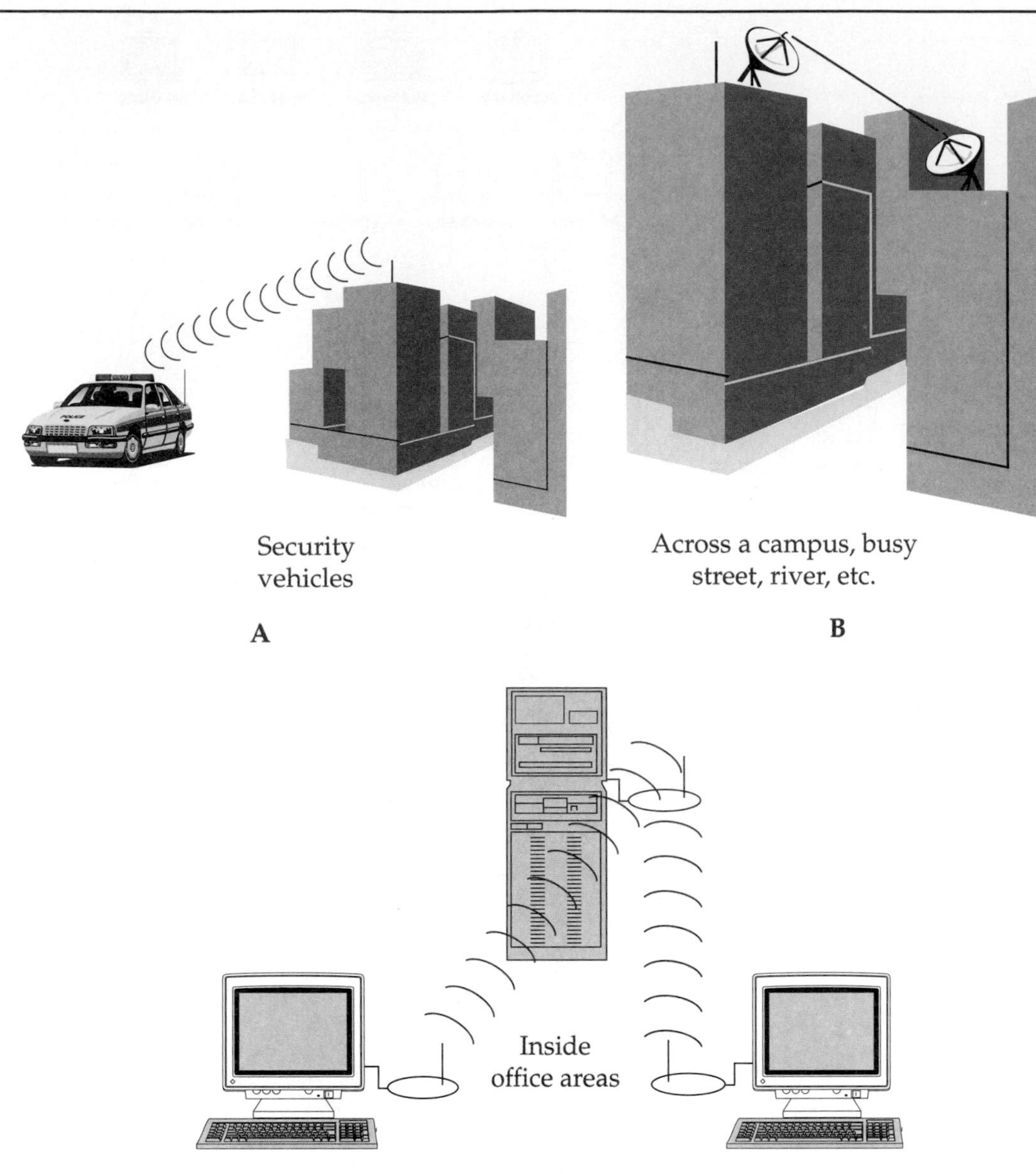

Figure 16-9. A—Wireless topology can be used to connect mobile computers, as found in many police cars, to a stationary network. B—Wireless topology can bridge a gap between buildings where cable connection is impractical. C—A wireless topology can also be used to connect workstations to a server.

Segments

segment a section of cable between two network devices. Also, a portion of a network that shares a common collision or token passing domain.

The term ***segment*** can be applied to a physical portion of a network or to a logical portion of a network, **Figure 16-10.** In the physical sense, a segment is a section of cable between two network devices. It can be the backbone or drop cables in a bus topology, the cables between nodes and hubs or hubs and hubs in a star topology, or a single cable in a ring topology, Figure 16-10A.

In a logical sense, a segment is a portion of a network that shares a collision or token passing domain. It is often bounded by routers and switches. This definition will become clearer to you when you learn about how networks communicate.

A logical segment varies according to the type of topology to which the term is applied. In a bus topology, a segment is the complete section of backbone and nodes. In a ring topology, it is the complete ring. In a star topology, it is the complete star. See Figure 16-10B.

Figure 16-10.
A—Examples of physical segments in various topologies. B—Examples of logical segments in various topologies.

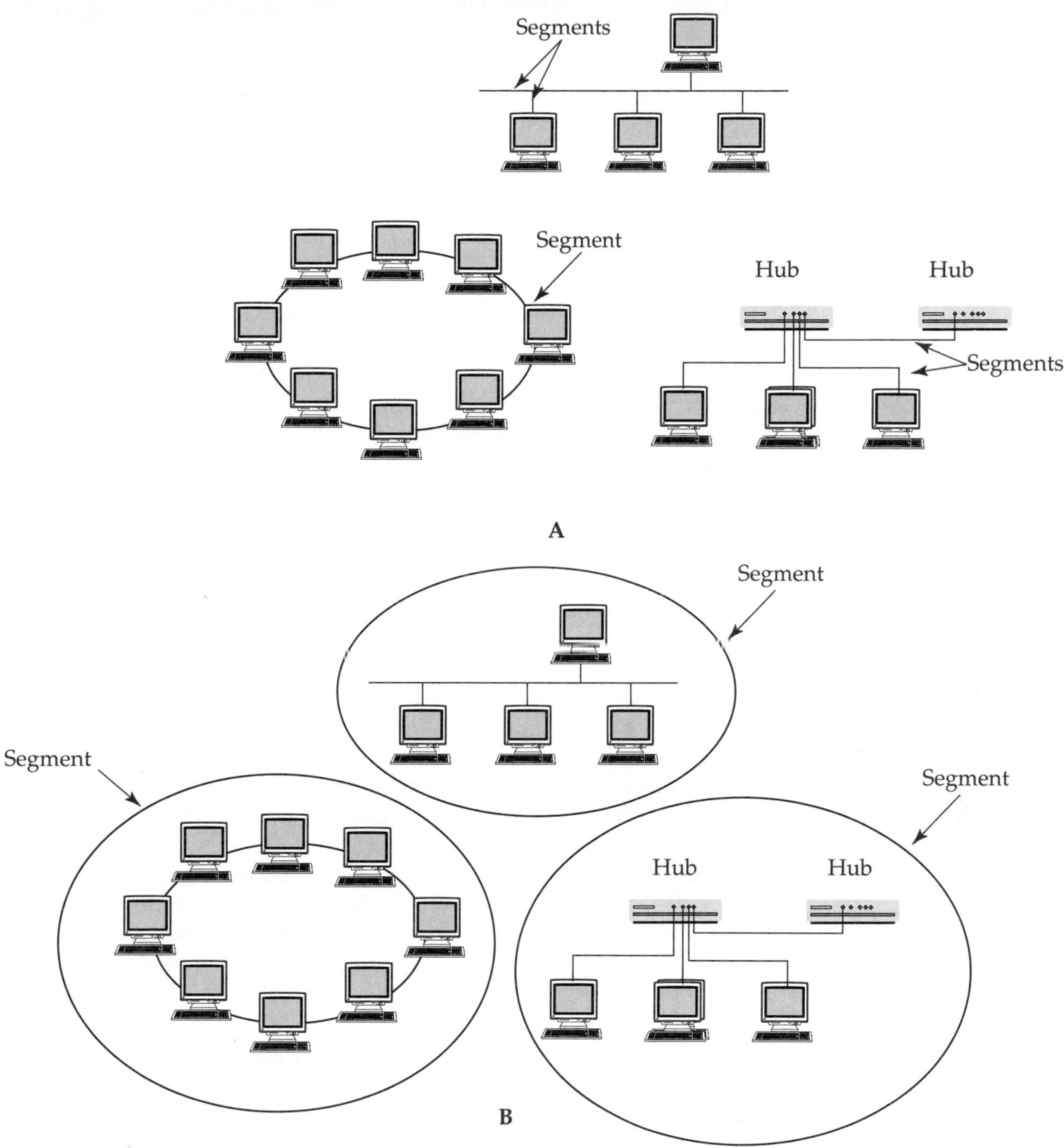

How Networks Communicate

For two or more computers to communicate, they must use the same system of identification and data transfer. There are two main communications schemes used by networks: Ethernet and Token Ring. In each of these types, data is divided into smaller units called *packets* or *frames* before it is transmitted across the network. Like an envelope going through the mail system, each ***packet*** contains the address of the sender and the intended recipient. When all of the packets have arrived at their destination, they are reassembled to form a complete message or file.

packet
small unit of data into which larger amounts are divided for passage through a network.

How Data Is Packaged

Data is sent across a network in the form of digital pulses, or rapidly changing levels of voltages. For data to be sent across a network from node to node, a common data-packaging scheme must be used. The sequence and length of the information is the key to coding and decoding the data frames.

The digital pulses represent binary and hexadecimal codes, which in turn represent the data that is being transmitted. Different network operating systems use different encoding schemes for transmitting their data. In a typical data frame, the first six bytes represent the *network interface card (NIC)* to which the data is being sent. The NIC is identified by its *media access code (MAC) address.* NICs and MAC addresses are discussed more thoroughly later in this chapter.

The second six bytes represent the NIC that is transmitting the data. Again, the MAC address of the sending NIC is used. Additional blocks of encoded data may contain information such as the length of the particular packet being sent, a sequence number for the packet, and an error checking code. Error checking is incorporated into the packet to ensure the data was not corrupted during transmission. A frame of data has a maximum length, usually approximately 1500 bytes.

A ***sequence number*** is attached to each packet of data. The sequence number ensures the data will be reassembled in the exact order it was transmitted. Some network systems, such as the Internet, are very complex. The various packets of information that make up a message may not be routed through the same path and may not arrive at their destination in the same order they were sent. Packets of information arriving at different times would be garbled when reassembled.

sequence number
attached to each packet of data being transmitted, ensuring that the data will be reassembled in the exact order it was transmitted.

The amount of time it takes data to arrive at its destination is influenced by three major factors:

- ✔ Length of route taken.
- ✔ Type of media and equipment used to route the data.
- ✔ Amount of data traffic on that particular route.

Protocols

For computers to be capable of communicating with each other, they must use the same protocol. A protocol is a set of rules for formatting the data stream transmission between two computers or devices and for describing how to transmit data, usually across a network. Data can be transmitted between two computers in small packets or as a steady stream of data. The protocol determines the size of the packets. It also compresses the information to allow for faster transmission rates, verifies that the information transmitted is complete, and reassembles the information packets when they are received. The protocol usually has some error-checking capabilities. The following is a list of common protocols:

- ✔ NetBEUI (NetBIOS Enhanced User Interface).
- ✔ TCP/IP (Transmission Control Protocol/Internet Protocol).
- ✔ FIP (Fast Infrared Protocol).
- ✔ IPX/SPX (Internet Packet Exchange/Sequenced Packet Exchange).
- ✔ ATM (Asynchronous Transfer Mode).
- ✔ VoIP (Voice over IP).

Protocol Suites

A ***protocol suite*** is a combination of individual protocols, each designed for specific purposes. TCP/IP and IPX/SPX are examples of a protocol suite. While TCP/IP and IPX/SPX consist of two major protocols (separated by the slash, "/"), they both combine many more protocols to offer a vast array of services to the end user.

protocol suite combination of individual protocols each designed for specific purposes.

Some protocols within a suite guarantee delivery of a data packet, while others do not. For example, if a command is issued from one computer on a local network to another on the same local network, delivery is almost guaranteed. No method of checking for delivery is absolutely necessary. If one computer is sending a message to another across the United States, a method needs to be used to verify delivery.

As technology progresses, newer protocols must be added to existing suites. For example, when transmitting a collection of data, such as a large document, there is no requirement that the individual packets that represent the entire document arrive at the destination in proper sequence or with extraordinary speed. The document can be reassembled at the final destination in a reasonable amount of time. However, when transferring data such as sound or video, data must be received in proper sequence in a short period of time. A telephone conversation that is broken into packets and received out of order sounds garbled. Protocols constantly evolve and grow as new technologies emerge.

NetBEUI

NetBIOS is software that provides basic services for the transfer of data between nodes, allowing a computer to communicate with many other computers. NetBEUI is an enhanced version of NetBIOS. IBM and Microsoft jointly developed the NetBIOS Enhanced User Interface (NetBEUI) protocol. This simple protocol is used for small network systems of 100 or fewer computers. The ideal small computer network system for NetBEUI consists of 25 computers or fewer. If more than 25 computers are installed on a network using the NetBEUI protocol, the system starts to slow down significantly because of user activity.

NetBEUI is now obsolete as a network protocol. Windows Vista does not provide support for NetBEUI or IPX/SPX. Windows XP supports NetBEUI, but does not install it by default.

TCP/IP

Transmission Control Protocol/Internet Protocol (TCP/IP) is the standard default Internet protocol. It was developed for UNIX to communicate over the Internet. TCP/IP is the combination of two different protocols: transmission control protocol (TCP) and Internet protocol (IP). TCP is designed to guarantee delivery of all packets. It simply delivers packets and assumes they are received. TCP/IP is the default protocol installed in a Windows operating environment.

FIP

Fast Infrared Protocol (FIP) is used for transmitting data from laptop computers to desktop PCs without the use of cables. This protocol governs the transmission of data by infrared light.

IPX/SPX

Internet Packet Exchange/Sequenced Packet Exchange (IPX/SPX) is the standard protocol suite of Novell NetWare. IPX/SPX controls how packets of data are delivered and routed between nodes and LANS. The IPX protocol does not guarantee the delivery of a complete message, but SPX does.

ATM

Asynchronous Transfer Mode (ATM) is a protocol used for transmitting data, voice, and video simultaneously over the same line. It rearranges the packets in such a way that the quality of the voice or video will not be degraded when transmitted. Data is broken into packets containing 53 bytes each, which are switched between any two nodes in the system at rates ranging from 1.5 Mbps to 622 Mbps.

VoIP

Voice over IP (VoIP) is not just one protocol, but rather a suite of protocols. VoIP is designed to support voice communications over an existing network system. Originally, networks were designed to exchange text-based information. Text-based information does not require high-speed network systems. As network systems evolved, network media and equipment were designed to meet the requirements for high-resolution images, movies, and music. With the increase in network bandwidth, it became possible to move telephone communications to existing networks, rather than to keep separate lines—one for networking and one for telephone conversations.

Telephone companies first combined telephone and network media before making VoIP available for residential users. Today, telephone service and movie service is combined with Internet access. These services are provided by networks designed by service providers.

The big problem that service providers needed to overcome was providing telephone conversations in real time. A delay cannot be tolerated when exchanging network packets containing voice messages. Text, movie, and television downloading does not require real-time packet transfers like telephone conversations. A movie or television show can be downloaded over a long period of time and then played back. A telephone conversation must exchange voice messages instantly without a delay between network packets.

VoIP was first introduced as an alternative telephone system for overseas calls because it was approximately half the cost of a traditional telephone connection. Later it become very cost effective to use as an everyday service, especially when combined by a service provider with other services, such as television and movies.

To accomplish real-time voice packet exchange, a new set of telephone protocols had to be developed that would ensure quality of service. The protocol developed was named Quality of Service (QoS). This protocol assigns a higher priority to packets that contain time-sensitive information, such as voice, than less time-sensitive packets, such as e-mail.

Figure 16-11 shows a typical Windows XP **Local Area Connection Properties** dialog box. Notice that the QoS Packet Scheduler has been installed by default. Also, notice that the Internet Protocol (TCP/IP) is also installed by default. These two protocols combine to provide telephone service through a computer for users with an Internet connection. To learn more about VoIP, visit the government Web site located at www.fcc.gov/voip.

Ethernet

An ***Ethernet network*** communicates by broadcasting information to all the computers on the network. This is similar to a room full of people talking and one person yelling, "Bob, do you hear me?" Everyone in the room hears Bob's name being called, but only Bob will reply if he is in the room.

Ethernet network network that communicates by broadcasting information to all the computers on the network.

In an Ethernet system, each computer on the network is given a unique name; no two computers can have the same name. A computer name can be most anything you desire, such as Station 1, Accounting 3, or even WildBill. Each computer in the system also has a unique hexadecimal address programmed into the network card inside the computer. The hexadecimal address is six bytes long. For example, C0 0B 08 1A 2D 2F is a hexadecimal address. See **Figure 16-12.** No other computer on the network has the same number. Using the hexadecimal number system to communicate would be difficult for humans. Therefore, a database automatically corresponds the unique number of the network card to the unique name given to the computer.

A typical session on an Ethernet network goes something like this. Bob wants to send a message to Sue using the network. Bob uses Station 1 to send data to Sue at computer Station 4. When Bob sends the message to Sue, he is actually sending the message to all computers on the network. However, only Sue's computer accepts the message. See **Figure 16-13.** Let's take a closer look to see how this happens.

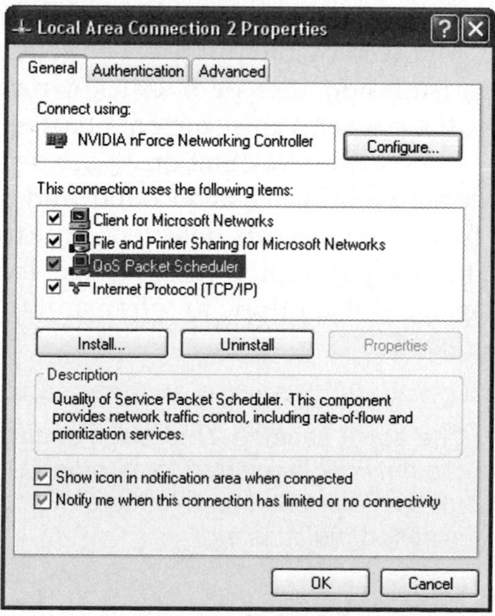

Figure 16-11. The **Local Area Connections Properties** dialog box displays the protocols and services for which a network adapter is configured. Notice that the QoS Packet Scheduler has been installed.

Figure 16-12. Close-up of a network interface card MAC address.

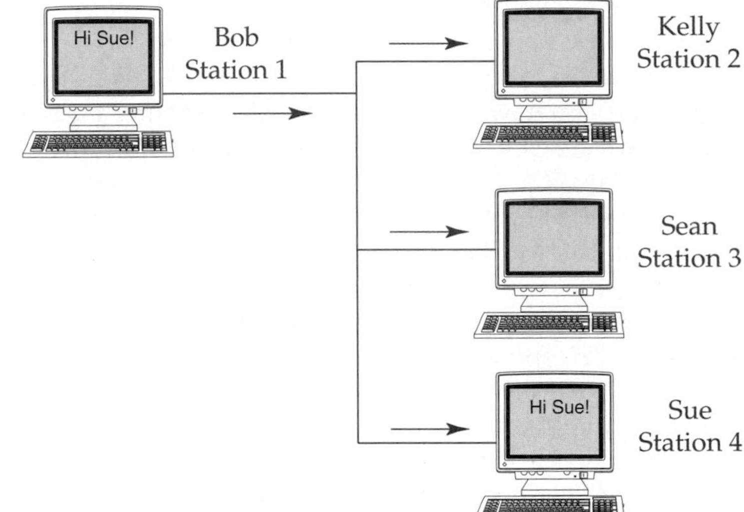

Figure 16-13. Bob transmits to all the computers on the network, but only Sue's address can accept the message.

Bob's computer transmits the first six bytes of data, the address of the target computer. Next, six more bytes are sent, the address of Bob's computer. Then the message data is sent, followed by the frame check sequence. When Sue's computer receives the transmission, it recognizes its own address in the first six bytes of data and accepts the packet. When the data packet is accepted, the next six bytes, which identify the sending PC (Station 1), are decoded and stored for a return message. Next, the actual message is decoded, and then the transmission is checked for errors. If there are no errors detected, a return message is transmitted to Bob's PC to verify receipt of the message. If Bob's PC does not receive the return message, it will continue to retransmit the data packets until the return message is received.

The act of sending a message or command to all nodes on the network is referred to as *broadcasting.* Sending a message or command to more than one, but not all nodes, is called *multicasting.*

CSMA/CD

One inherent problem with Ethernet communications is the collision of data being transmitted across the network. When two data packets collide on the network, they both become corrupted and cannot be delivered. Ethernet networks use a protocol called ***Carrier Sense Multiple Access with Collision Detection (CSMA/CD)*** to control and ensure the delivery of data.

The following passage describes how CSMA/CD works. A workstation listens for data traffic on the network before transmitting data. When the network is silent, the workstation transmits data to another workstation. However, another station may choose the same lull in activity to transmit data also. If the data packets from the two stations collide on the network, each station waits a random period of time, known as the ***backoff interval,*** before trying to retransmit the data. The random period is a very small fraction of a second. A typical network can transmit thousands of data packets in one second. Collisions do not usually noticeably affect the performance of a properly installed network. However, a poorly designed network may operate very slowly due to excessive collisions.

Carrier Sense Multiple Access with Collision Detection (CSMA/CD)
protocol used by Ethernet networks to control and ensure the delivery of data.

backoff interval
period of time two network stations wait before trying to retransmit data after data packets from the two stations collide.

CSMA/CA

Wireless communication uses another type of network access called ***Carrier Sense Multiple Access with Collision Avoidance (CSMA/CA).*** This access method is different than CSMA/CD in that it does not detect collisions; it avoids them. There are times when wireless networks cannot detect collisions, so the Ethernet method cannot be used as a media access method.

Look at **Figure 16-14.** In the drawing, an access point and two computers with wireless adapter cards are connected to a cabled network. The limited range of the wireless network cards does not allow the two computers to communicate directly with each other. They can only communicate with the access point. To prevent both computers from communicating with the access point at the same time, which would cause collisions, each computer must ask permission first. A wireless network card sends a very small packet requesting permission to transmit before it sends larger packets to the access point. If the access point is not busy communicating with the other computer on the wireless network, it responds by giving permission for communication. The access point controls all communication. When a wireless network uses a wireless access point to control communications, the wireless network is referred to as an *infrastructure design.* The wireless access point creates a communications bridge between the cable network and the wireless network.

Carrier Sense Multiple Access with Collision Avoidance (CSMA/CA)
protocol used by wireless networks to control and ensure the delivery of data.

Token Ring

A ***Token Ring network*** is a highly organized system in which each computer must wait its turn to transmit data. A ***token*** is a short binary code generated by the network software and passed from one computer to the next along a ring topology and in some bus topologies. Before a computer can transmit information over the network, it must seize the token to take control of the network. Unlike the Ethernet design, the Token Ring network was designed to prevent collisions. The data transmission on a Token Ring is organized around the computer that possesses the token.

A computer or node must possess the token before it can transmit a message or data across the network. Once a computer has control of the token, it attaches a data frame to the token. The token is then passed sequentially to each computer

Token Ring network
a highly organized system in which each computer must wait its turn to transmit data.

token
a short binary code generated by the network software that is passed from one computer to the next along a ring topology and in some bus topologies.

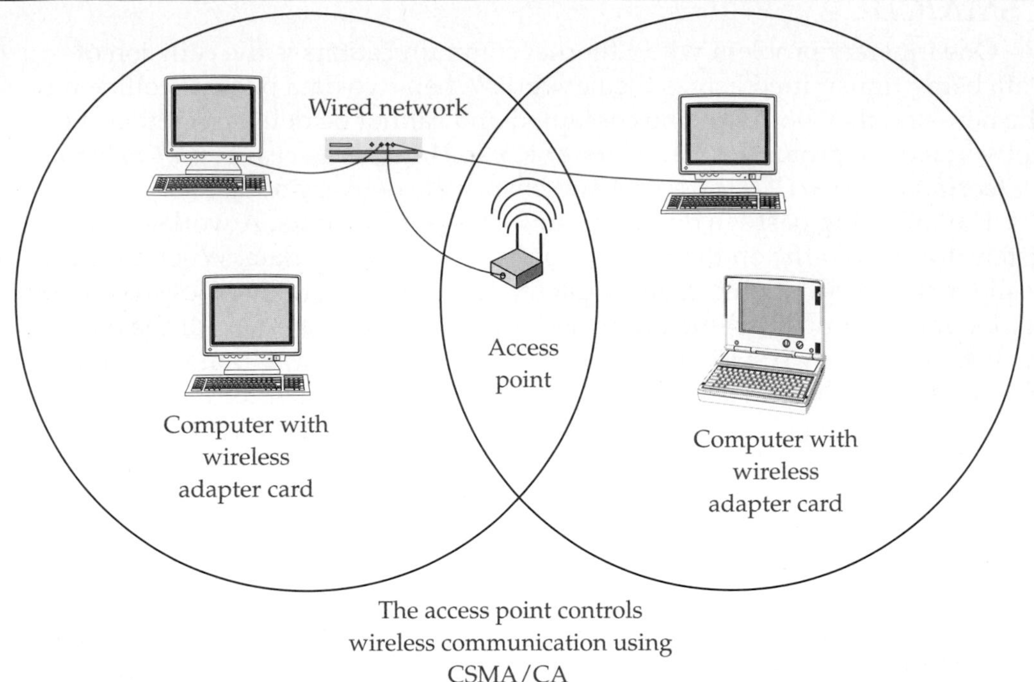

Figure 16-14. Wireless systems use collision avoidance to control communication.

on the network. Each computer checks the destination address in the token. If the destination address does not match the NIC's address, the NIC does not accept the token and it is passed along to the next computer. If the network card's address matches the token's destination address, the token is accepted and its information is transferred to the NIC's RAM to be processed by the computer. The computer that accepted the token then passes the token on to the next computer and the process is repeated. When the token returns to the originating computer, it is deleted and a new token is created.

By using this scheme, only one computer can control the flow of data at any given time. Although this method may seem time-consuming, you must remember that the process only takes a few milliseconds. One computer can control the token for up to 10 milliseconds. After that time, the computer must relinquish its control over the token and wait its turn to resume the data transfer. This prevents one station from dominating the network.

When comparing a Token Ring and an Ethernet network of equal throughput, the Token Ring will process packets faster under heavy traffic conditions than an Ethernet network. This is because Token Ring does not permit packet collisions. As traffic increases in an Ethernet system, so does the number of collisions. When there are an increased number of collisions, the transfer rate slows.

Token Bus

Token Bus network network that uses a token passing system with a bus-type topology.

A ***Token Bus network*** operates similarly to a Token Ring network. However, a different method is used to pass the token from node to node. In a typical Token Ring network, the token is passed to the next physical location on the ring. Since the token bus network uses a bus rather than a ring, a variation of token passing must be used. A list of nodes is created in a database. Each node is identified by a MAC address and computer name. A sequential list of addresses is generated, which becomes the sequence for the token to follow when passing from computer to computer.

The token bus topology is rarely encountered today and is no longer recognized as a standard by the IEEE. Token bus can be considered obsolete.

Network Media

Network media is the means by which an electronic signal is transmitted. An electronic signal can be transmitted via cable-based media or wireless media. Generally, there are three types of cable-based media from which to choose: coaxial, twisted pair, and fiber optic. There are also two types of wireless media: infrared and radio transmission.

Coaxial Cable

Coaxial cable, or "coax," consists of a core conductor surrounded by an insulator. The insulator is covered with a shield of either a solid foil or a braided wire layer. The shield protects the cable core from stray electromagnetic interference, which would corrupt the data being transmitted. See **Figure 16-15.** Coaxial cable is difficult to work with and relatively expensive when compared to some of the other wiring media.

coaxial cable a core conductor surrounded by an insulator.

BNC (British Naval Connector) connector used with coaxial cable.

The connector type used with coaxial cable is called ***BNC (British Naval Connector).*** **Figure 16-16** shows a typical BNC T-connector, a BNC straight connector, and a terminating resistor. **Figure 17-17** shows an exploded diagram of a BNC coaxial cable connector.

The true origin of the BNC acronym is a mystery. The terms *British Naval Connectors*, *Bayonet Nut Connectors*, *Bayonet-Neill Concelman*, *Baby N Connector*, and *BayoNet Connectors* all refer to BNCS.

The IBM Data Connector (IDC) and Universal Data Connector (UDC) connectors were developed by IBM to be used on their Token Ring networks. These connectors are rarely encountered today. Token Ring now commonly uses twisted pair and shielded twisted pair.

There are several classifications of network coaxial cable. Coaxial cable use for television is not acceptable for use as a network cable. Its characteristics work well for television transmission but will cause problems if used for computer networks.

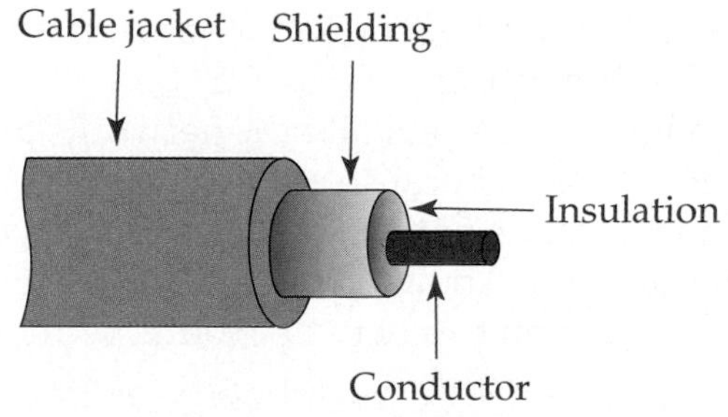

Figure 16-15. The structure of typical coaxial cable is shown here.

Figure 16-16. A BNC straight connector (left), a BNC T-connector (middle), and a terminating resistor (right).

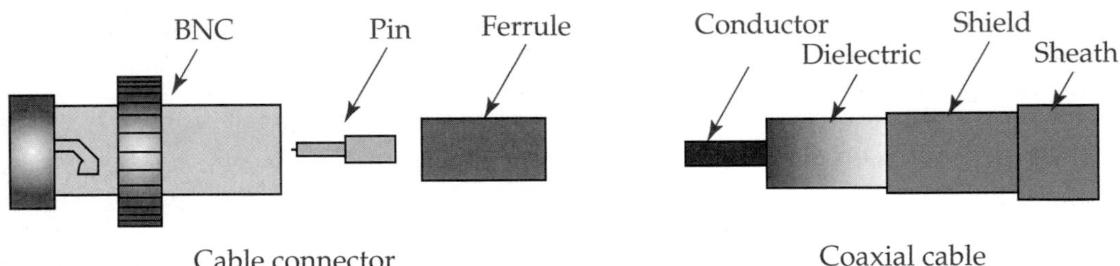

Figure 16-17. Exploded view of a standard coaxial cable connector.

The earliest coaxial cable used as network media was thick coaxial cable (10base5), also known as RG-8 or RG-11, or thicknet. Later, thin coaxial cable (10base2), also known as RG-58, or thinnet, was introduced to overcome some of the difficulty associated with the physical attributes of thick coaxial cable. As the name implies, thinnet is much smaller in diameter than thicknet. Thick coaxial cable is difficult to install when compared to thin coaxial cable. Thinnet is more flexible but does not provide the transmission distance that thicknet can provide. Thicknet supports transmissions up to 500 meters per segment while thinnet is limited to 185 meters.

Computer applications require that the coaxial cable have a 50-ohm rating. RG-8, RG-11, and RG-58 each have the required 50-ohm rating. The coaxial cable used for cable TV has a 75-ohm rating.

Coaxial cable is no longer used to install new networks and is considered obsolete. You may still encounter it because once a system is installed and it remains working, a customer tends not to replace it. Coaxial cable is still used for television cable and satellite cable. You will encounter coaxial cable running from a satellite disk or Cable connection to a network router or modem, which is used for Internet access.

A+ Note:

Do not confuse the RG-11 coaxial cable with the RJ-11 connector. They are distinctly different. If an exam question asks about the connector used for a phone jack, don't be confused if RG-11 appears as a possible answer.

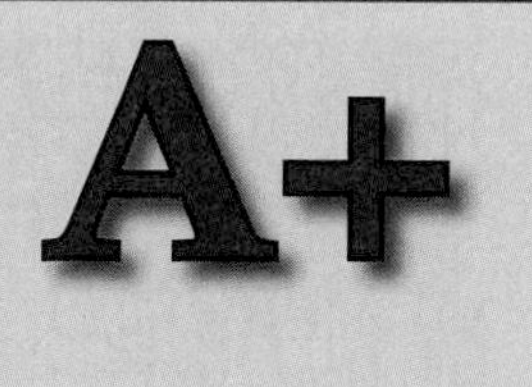

The RG prefix is an acronym for Radio Guide. The coaxial cable series was developed primarily as a radio frequency guide (path) for radio signals. Later it was used for video applications, and then much later it was used as a computer signal path.

Twisted Pair Cable

Twisted pair cable has been available for many years and was first used to carry voice transmissions by telephone companies. Today, twisted pair is the most common choice for network wiring. It consists of four pairs of conductors twisted around each other.

twisted pair cable
the most common choice for network wiring. It consists of four pairs of conductors twisted around each other.

The common Ethernet network uses only two of the pairs in the cable. Duplex Ethernet uses all four pairs. In a typical standard Ethernet installation, the extra two pairs can be thought of as spares. When only two pairs are used for the network, the remaining two pairs are often used for telephone communication.

The twists in the pairs are necessary to eliminate cross talk between the conductors. ***Cross talk*** is the imposition of a signal on one pair of conductors by another pair of conductors that runs parallel to it. Twisting each pair inside the cable greatly reduces the effect of cross talk. This occurs because, when twisted, the two pairs are no longer parallel to each other.

cross talk
the imposition of a signal on one pair of conductors by another pair of conductors that runs parallel to it.

Wire sizes range from #18 AWG to #26 AWG, with #24 AWG used most often. AWG stands for American Wire Gage, a standard method for sizing wire. There are two major classifications of twisted pair cable: unshielded twisted pair (UTP) and shielded twisted pair (STP). The categories or classifications of cable that follow are based on the physical design of the cable. The chart in **Figure 16-18** summarizes the maximum frequency and maximum speed of the most used twisted pair cable types.

Category 1

Category 1 cable consists of two twisted pairs. While this design was sufficient for electrical signals representing voice transmission, it is entirely inadequate for computer networks.

Category 2

Category 2 cable consists of four twisted pairs. This design again is not acceptable for today's networking systems. It was used in some early applications that were limited to 4 Mbps. Today's networks run at a minimum of 10 Mbps.

Figure 16-18. Common twisted pair cable types and their maximum frequency and speed (bandwidth) ratings.

Category	Maximum Frequency	Maximum Speed
Cat 3	16 MHz	16 Mbps
Cat 4	20 MHz	20 Mbps
Cat 5	100 MHz	100 Mbps
Cat 5e	100 MHz	100 Mbps
Cat 6	250 MHz	1000 Mbps / 1 Gbps
Cat 7	650 MHz	1 Ghz+

Category 3

Category 3 cable consists of four twisted pairs, three twists per foot. This can be found on existing networks usually rated at 10 Mbps and 16 Mbps. This is found in many existing telephone installations.

Category 4

Category 4 cable consists of four twisted pairs. This cable handles 20 Mbps and is only a slight improvement over category 3 cable. It reduced the amount of cross talk generated as well as cable signal loss.

Category 5

Category 5 cable consists of four twisted pairs and offers a transmission speed of 100 Mbps. It is found commonly in 10baseT and 100baseT installations.

Category 5e

The *e* in Cat 5e represents *enhanced*. Cat 5e is an enhanced version of the Cat 5 standard that provides a little less cable loss. It is designed for fast Ethernet and gigaspeed Ethernet transmissions. The Cat 5e standard is actually an addendum to the existing standard to expand the qualities of existing Cat 5 cable.

Not all Cat 5 cable can reach the Cat 5e standard, but much of it can. The real difference is in the amount of cross talk permitted for Cat 5e when compared to Cat 5. The difference is only slight.

Category 6

Category 6 cable supports frequencies as high as 250 MHz and data throughput of 1 Gbps. The high data throughput is achieved by using all four twisted pairs of wiring.

Category 7

Category 7 cable provides data transmission speeds to 650 MHz. It uses a different construction technique to achieve the higher transmission speeds. Category 7 is constructed of four pairs of twisted conductors with a protective coating of foil or an electrical conductive braided coating surrounding each pair. In addition to the individual pair protective covering, there is an overall protective foil or conductive braiding surrounding the complete assembly. See Figure **16-19.**

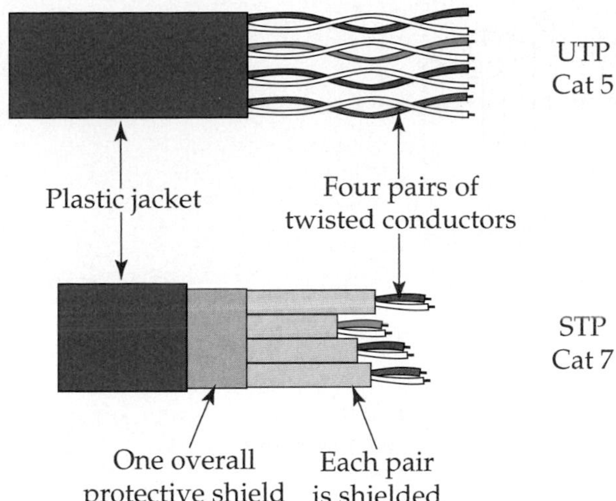

Figure 16-19.
Cat 5 is constructed of four pairs of twisted conductors. Cat 6 is similar in construction to Cat 5. Unlike Cat 5 and Cat 6, Cat 7 has individual shielding over each conductive pair, and an overall shield between the plastic outer jacket and the individual-pair shielding.

Fiber-Optic Cable

fiber-optic cable cable that contains a glass or plastic center used to carry light.

Fiber-optic cable, often referred to as fiber, contains a glass or plastic center used to carry light. The electronic signals transmitted from the computer are converted to a signal consisting of a fluctuating beam of light. The fiber-optic cable carries the light signal to its destination where it is converted back to an electrical signal. The use of fiber optics has many advantages over conventional copper wire systems. The advantages include increased security, greater resistance to corrosion, immunity to lightning strikes, longer transmission distances per segment, and decreased weight. Its biggest disadvantages are greater expense and the increased difficulty of field installations. It is ideal for network backbones.

There are many different fiber-optic cable connectors in use, but there are six common fiber-optic connectors you need to become familiar with. The six fiber-optic cable connector styles are ST, SC, FC, LC, and MT-RJ. Look at the **Figure 16-20** to see the general shape of each type of connector.

The ST connector must be pushed directly in and then twisted to the right to lock in place. The SC connector pushes directly in and then snaps into place. Both connectors offer a quick way to connect and disconnect a fiber-optic cable. The FC style is designed with screw threads. The FC connector offers superior connection strength when compared to the other connectors in Figure 16-20.

The LC style of connector is relatively new. It has a smaller form factor when compared to SC, ST, and FC styles. The LC is designed for a single cable but can be modified to an LC duplex connector to accommodate two cables. The pair of LC connectors are held together using a clip and thus form a duplex connection.

The MT-RJ style connector is similar to the shape of a copper cable RJ connector. The MJ-RJ is unique in the fact that it incorporates two fiber cables into one assembly without the use of a clip. The MT-RJ has a small form factor and is considered a duplex connector like the LC duplex. To learn more about network cables and connectors visit www.blackbox.com.

Figure 16-20. Fiber-optic cable connectors. A—ST and SC connectors. B—FC connector. C—LC connectors. D—MT-RJ connector.

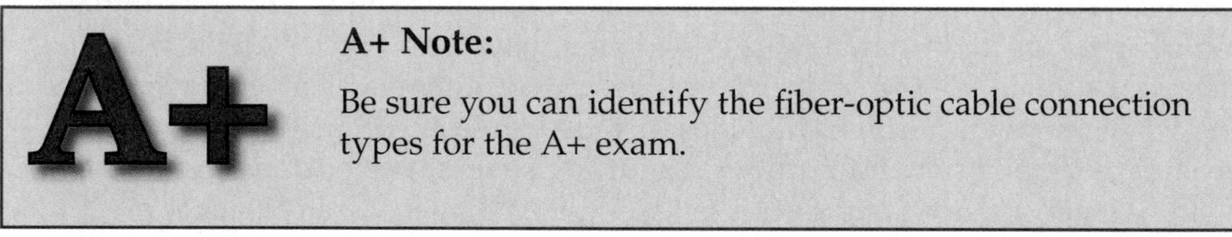

A+ Note:

Be sure you can identify the fiber-optic cable connection types for the A+ exam.

Wireless

Wireless media for local area networks are based on the IEEE 802.11 standard. The two common wireless network topologies, which are referred to as wireless modes, are ad-hoc and infrastructure. *Ad-hoc* is a peer-to-peer configuration where all wireless devices can connect directly to each other. The most common ad-hoc arrangement is when a wireless laptop connects directly to a desktop that has a wireless device installed. A *wireless infrastructure* requires an access point. An access point is used to control the flow of data between each wireless device in the network. An access point is also used to provide a connection to and from a wireless network to a wired network system. The wireless media is assigned specific radio frequencies as listed in the following table.

IEEE Standard	Radio Frequency	Frequency Range	Max. Data Rate	Approx. Range	Comments
802.11a	5 GHz	5.15 GHz–5.825 GHz	54 Mbps	50 m	Basically obsolete
802.11b	2.4 GHz	2.4 GHz–2.4835 GHz	11 Mbps	100 m	
802.11g	2.4 GHz	2.4 GHz–2.4835 GHz	54 Mbps	50 m	Compatible with 802.11b
802.11n	2.4 GHz 5 GHz	2.4 GHz–2.4835 GHz 5.15 GHz–5.85 GHz	248 Mbps	200 m	Compatible with 802.11a, 802.11b, and 802.11g

Note at the time of this writing IEEE 802.11n is still in draft form and has not been officially adopted by the IEEE organization, even though products have been released designed to match the draft standard.

Be aware that some wireless network card manufacturers exceed the standard data rate set by the IEEE organization. For example, NETGEAR offers an IEEE 802.11g network card called *Super G* that has a data rate of 108 Mbps, which is twice the IEEE standard for 802.11g.

Also, be aware that the IEEE standard does not express distances for wireless cards. The actual distance is a direct reflection of the output power of the wireless adapter expressed in watts. Distances are subject to many factors such as physical objects and sources of radio interference. Some examples of physical objects are building walls, partitions, metal storage cabinets, and especially metal buildings. Some common sources of radio interference in close proximity of the wireless network are microwave ovens, electric welding machines, cordless phones, electrical power lines, radio transmitters, portable radio equipment, baby monitors, wireless surveillance equipment such as cameras and garage door openers.

A+ Note:

The new certification exams have many questions requiring knowledge about wireless networking, both ad-hoc and infrastructure. Be sure to memorize the data rates and assigned frequency for each of the IEEE wireless standards.

Network Cable Classifications

The Institute of Electrical and Electronic Engineers (IEEE) has classified network cables according to their abilities and physical description. Network cables are classified with a short description such as 10BaseT. The "10" represents the speed of transmission—in this case, 10 megabits per second. Note that the speed is rated in bits not bytes. The "Base" refers to baseband, which means data travels across the network one message at a time rather than in multiple simultaneous messages. When a number is used as the last character(s) in the description of coaxial cable, it represents the approximate maximum distance the cable can be used in hundreds of meters. When the last character is a letter, it provides specific information about the cable used. For example, when the last letter is a *T*, the name denotes twisted pair with a maximum distance of 100 meters. An *F* represents fiber-optic cable. The chart in **Figure 16-21** lists the specifications of some common cables. Note that the 10Base2 maximum distance is 185 meters, not 200. However, the 2 serves as a good memory aid.

network interface card (NIC) connects the network communication media, usually twisted pair, to the individual network devices such as workstations, file servers, and printers.

Network Interface Cards

A ***network interface card (NIC),*** also called a ***network adapter card,*** connects the network media, usually twisted pair, to the individual network devices such as workstations, file servers, and printers. The network interface card must be selected to match the motherboard slot type and the network cable styles such as coaxial cable or unshielded twisted pair. See **Figure 16-22.** The card shown in the illustration is equipped with three styles of cable adapter: BNC, RJ-45, and AUI.

Figure 16-21. Specifications table for common cable classifications. Note that 100 meters = 328 feet.

Classification	Maximum segment distance in meters	Minimum segment distance in meters	Speed in Mbps	Description
10Base2	185	0.5	10	Thin coaxial cable
10Base5	500	2.5	10	Thick coaxial cable
10BaseT	100	0.6	10	UTP
10BaseT4	100	0.6	100	UTP
100BaseTX	100	0.6	100	Two pair of UTP
100BaseFX	2500	1	100	Fiber optic
100BaseVG	100	0.6	100	Four pair of UTP
1000BaseT	100	0.6	1000	UTP
1000BaseSX	500	1	1000	Fiber optic
1000BaseLH	5000	1	1000	Fiber optic

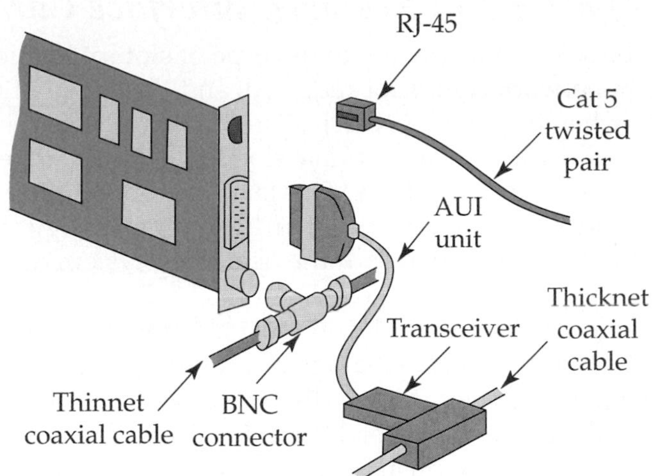

Figure 16-22. The network interface card shown here is equipped with three connector types. The BNC connector is used to connect to coaxial cable. The DB-15, or AUI, connector is used to connect to thick coaxial cable. The RJ-45 connector is used to connect to twisted pair cable.

The BNC is used to connect to coaxial cable. The DB-15, or AUI, is used to connect to thick coax, and the RJ-45 is used to connect twisted pair. A BIOS chip can be inserted into the ROM socket, allowing the computer to become a diskless station. Diskless stations are covered later in this chapter.

MAC

As discussed earlier, each NIC has a unique ***media access code (MAC) address.*** A MAC address is a hexadecimal number programmed into the card's chip. Refer to Figure 16-12. The address is composed of twelve digits divided into two equal sections. The first six digits identify the card's manufacturer. The second six-digit sequence is a number assigned by the manufacturer and is different on every card produced. No two NIC cards can have the same MAC address on the same network. The network uses the MAC address to identify the different nodes on the network. If two cards match, the network cannot communicate properly with either card. The MAC address functions like telephone numbers in a telephone system. If two people had the same telephone number, each one would receive calls that were unintended for them.

media access code (MAC) address a hexadecimal number programmed into the network interface card's chip. The first six digits identify the card's manufacturer. The second six-digit sequence is assigned by the manufacturer and is different on every card produced.

The MAC address is often referred to as the *physical address* because it is physically burned into the card. Names used to identify computers or network nodes are referred to as the *logical address.* A typical PC has both a physical address assigned through the network adapter card and a logical address assigned by the technician when the NIC is installed. For example, a computer may have a physical address of 0020AF012AB3 and a logical address such as Station 12.

The MAC address is also referred to as the Data Link Control (DLC) identifier. In the IEEE 802 standard, the Data Link Layer of the OSI model is subdivided into the Logical Link Control (LLC) layer and the Media Access Control (MAC) layer. The MAC layer communicates directly with the network while the LLC layer uses a protocol such as Address Resolution Protocol (ARP). ARP is part of the TCP/IP protocol suite. The ARP resolves the MAC address to a computer name, such as Station 1. Using the computer name Station 1 is more convenient than trying to remember the hexadecimal code number for the node.

Installation of a Typical Network Interface Card

The NIC must be selected according to the type of slot into which it will be inserted, the type of network connector required, and the speed of the network. Care must be used when handling a NIC, just as with any static-sensitive device.

Firmly push the NIC into the appropriate slot. After it is installed, boot the computer. If you are using Windows 95 or later, the operating system will probably automatically detect the new hardware item, assign the system resources, and install the proper driver. If the operating system does not detect the card automatically, you will have to install it manually.

When manually installing the card, you must also identify the NIC card from a list provided in the **Select a Device** dialog box. You may need to have the driver disc that was packaged with the card. If a disc with the driver files did not come with the card, you will need to download the appropriate driver from the Internet. To avoid a conflict, you must assign the proper IRQ and memory address. By now, you should be very familiar with the proper procedures for assigning IRQ and memory addresses. If not, go back and review Chapter 3—Motherboards. Installing a network adapter card is covered in great detail in your lab activity manual.

Diskless Workstations

A diskless workstation is just as the name implies, a workstation that runs without a floppy or hard disk. Some do have small hard drives, but they are used solely as a cache rather than for data storage. The diskless workstation relies on the file server's hard drive for application software and data storage. As you know from previous study, the hard drive contains the bootstrap program needed to boot the workstation. A diskless workstation is booted from the interaction of the NIC and the file server. The NIC is equipped with a BIOS ROM chip, which contains the boot code needed to boot the workstation and connect to the network file server.

There are some very strong advantages to diskless workstations. Diskless workstations provide extremely good security. Without a disk system for employees to use, there is no way for data files such as customer lists or account numbers to be electronically duplicated at the workstation. In addition, diskless systems eliminate the possibility of introduction of viruses from floppy disks.

Another consideration is the overall cost of installation. By eliminating the cost of hard drives, floppy drives, and CD drives, there can be substantial savings, especially when installing several hundred or thousands of PCs in an enterprise system. Another real advantage is administration of the PCs. Because all workstations are dependent on the file server for their application software, thousands of diskless workstations can be upgraded at the same time. This results in a tremendous savings in man-hour costs of installing software on individual computers. The only real disadvantage is, when the network is down, all workstations are affected.

Hubs

A hub is a device that connects network equipment of a network together quickly and easily. See **Figure 16-23.** The hub in this figure has eight RJ-45 ports for quick connection of twisted pair cable. It may also be equipped with a BNC and AUI connector for coaxial cable.

Hubs may be cascaded to provide more connections or to segment a network (as with switching hubs). See **Figure 16-24.** Compare the daisy chain arrangement to the cascading arrangement. When a network is expanded, the daisy chain arrangement can be used to add additional computers to the network. The problem is that most systems are limited to only four hubs connected in this manner. After four hubs, the signal is degraded and data may have to be retransmitted many times before it can be received at its destination. The regeneration of data causes a delay in the delivery of the packets. If the delay is too long, the packet is discarded.

The preferred arrangement is the cascading style. By connecting the hubs in a cascading arrangement as in the illustration, the number of hubs the signal travels through is limited to two. The cascade arrangement allows a greater number of PCs to be connected without traveling through four hubs.

When hubs are cascaded, a crossover cable may be needed. This particular hub is equipped with a selector switch that eliminates the need for a crossover cable. By changing the selector switch to the uplink position, port eight is reconfigured as the uplink port for a cascading hub configuration.

Network Operating Systems (NOS)

The most common network operating systems today are SUSE Linux Enterprise Server, Microsoft 2000 Server, Windows 2003 Server, and Mac OS X Server. The network operating system (NOS) provides communications between the computers, printers, and other intelligent hardware on the network. A network need not consist of a single brand of hardware or software. For example, a network may consist of a Linux server and a Windows server and client operating systems, such as Windows XP, Windows Vista, and SUSE Linux Enterprise Desktop sharing and accessing resources on the network. The NOS is also composed of software programs that provide security, user identity, remote access, and sharing for printers and other devices. Without the NOS, a network would just be a useless collection of parts.

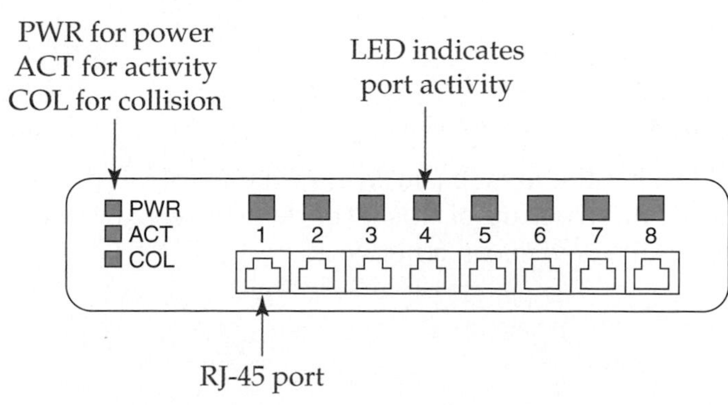

Figure 16-23. A typical hub. The RJ-45 ports allow twisted pair to be connected. Various LEDs make the hub's current status visible at a glance.

Figure 16-24.
By arranging the network in a cascading hub configuration, data must pass through a maximum of two hubs to reach its destination. With the daisy chain configuration, data may have to pass through as many as four hubs to reach its destination.

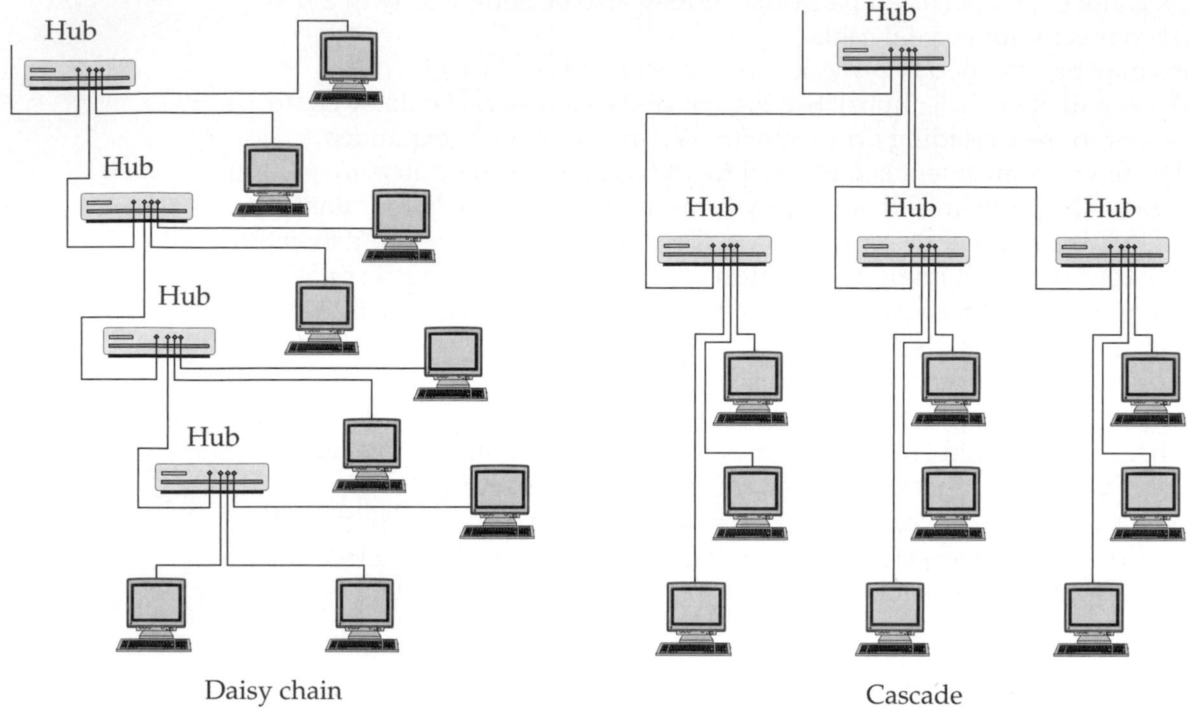

OSI Model

Open Systems Interconnection (OSI) seven-layer reference model that describes how hardware and software should work together to form a network communication system.

The ***Open Systems Interconnection (OSI)*** reference model was a joint effort of international members to standardize network communication systems. The OSI model describes how hardware and software should work together to form a network communication system. The OSI model consists of seven layers:

- ✔ Layer 7—Application.
- ✔ Layer 6—Presentation.
- ✔ Layer 5—Session.
- ✔ Layer 4—Transport.
- ✔ Layer 3—Network.
- ✔ Layer 2—Data.
- ✔ Layer 1—Physical.

Physical Layer

The physical layer is the most basic layer of the model. It consists of the cable and adapter cards. The structure of this layer determines how electrical signals are carried between the devices on a network.

Data Link Layer

The data link layer describes the network's level of operation at which the raw data is packaged for transfer from one network card to another network card. It packages binary numbers (1s and 0s) together into frames or packets for transmission between nodes.

Network Layer

The network layer is responsible for routing packets of data from one card to another across a large network. Routing provides a means of preventing or limiting congestion on large networks. It can also prioritize the transmission of data. As data is transmitted from one computer to another, several different routes may be used. If the equipment senses too much traffic along one cable section, the data can be transmitted along a different route to avoid the congestion.

Transport Layer

The transport layer's main responsibility is to ensure the data received from a transmission is reliable. It sequences the packets of data and reassembles them in their correct order. The individual data packets that compose a single file or message may arrive by very different routes when transmitted over many miles. Also, the packets of data may not arrive in the same sequence in which they were transmitted, requiring reassembly into the correct order. This correct reassembly is especially important in the transmission of graphic images.

Session Layer

The session layer is the layer at which a connection is established between two different computers. This layer also provides system security based on computer and user name recognition. The session layer and transport layers are sometimes combined. The session layer also resolves compatibility problems between dissimilar systems, such as a PC and a Macintosh or a mainframe.

Presentation Layer

The presentation layer ensures character code recognition. It is responsible for converting the character codes from the originating computer to another form that can be recognized by the receiving computer. An example would be converting ASCII codes to EBCDIC codes. Extended Binary Coded Decimal Interchange Code (EBCDIC) is a character code widely used on mainframe computers while most PCs use the American Standard Code for Information Interchange (ASCII) character code.

Application Layer

The application layer is at the top of the OSI model. The application layer manages network processes such as file transfer, mail service, and file-server database access. Thus far in your study of PCs, when you hear the term *application* you think of application software, such as word processing, spreadsheets, and graphic programs. These are not the same applications being illustrated in the

OSI model. In the OSI model, the application layer strictly is referring to network applications, such as Web browser and e-mail software. The application is designed as a communication interface for the user. Think of the application layer as a network browser.

The OSI model clearly illustrates the complexity of transmitting data from one computer to another and should be used as a model for a well-designed protocol. Not all software companies follow the strict guidelines of the OSI model. Many systems were already in place long before the model was developed and adopted. Some protocol systems combine two or more layers into a single unit. It is important to remember that the OSI model is simply a guide for future protocol development.

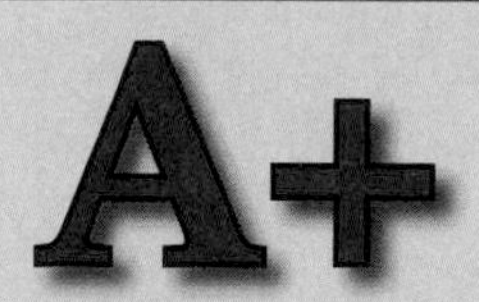

A+ Note:

A+ Certification exams will require some knowledge of the OSI model.

IEEE 802 Standards

The Institute of Electrical and Electronic Engineers (IEEE—pronounced *I triple E*) is a professional organization that continually develops standards for the networking and communication industry. The organization consists of scientists, students, commercial vendors, and other interested professionals within the industry. The IEEE's network standards are identified with an 802 prefix. Specific standards are listed here:

- ✔ 802.1—Bridging and Management.
- ✔ 802.2—Logical Link Control and Media Access Control.
- ✔ 802.3—CSMA/CD Access Method (Ethernet).
- ✔ 802.4—Token Bus.
- ✔ 802.5—DQDB Access Method (Token Ring).
- ✔ 802.6—Metropolitan Area Networks.
- ✔ 802.7—Broadband Local Area Networks.
- ✔ 802.8—Fiber Optic.
- ✔ 802.9—Isochronous LANs.
- ✔ 802.10—Security.
- ✔ 802.11—Wireless Local Area Network (WLAN).
- ✔ 802.12—Demand Priority Access.
- ✔ 802.15—Wireless Personal Area Network (WPAN).
- ✔ 802.16—Wireless Metropolitan Area Network (WMAN).

The specifications outlined in the 802 standards are not to be thought of as laws. They are a set of recommended practices that are designed to ensure the quality of a network system. However, if a contract to install a network system refers to the IEEE 802 standards, they should be thought of as law. If a new network is required to meet the IEEE 802 standards and problems arise because the standards were not followed, the installation contractor or designer of the network system can be held liable. The 802 standards will be referred to constantly throughout your studies of network systems. The most up-to-date information on the IEEE 802 standards can be obtained at www.standards.ieee.org/getieee802/portfolio.html.

Summary

- ✔ Networks provide a way to share data and hardware.
- ✔ The two most common network administration models are peer-to-peer and client/server.
- ✔ The client/server model is centrally administered; the peer-to-peer model is not.
- ✔ The three classifications of networks are LAN, MAN, and WAN.
- ✔ The three common cable topologies are star, ring, and bus.
- ✔ Data transmitted on a network is broken down into packets or frames.
- ✔ A data frame contains the address of the PC sending the data, the address of the intended recipient, an error-checking program, and a sequence number.
- ✔ A protocol is a set of programs that determines the rules for communication between two nodes.
- ✔ In general, two computers need to use the same protocol to communicate with each other.
- ✔ On an Ethernet network there are many data collisions, which require the data to be retransmitted, resulting in increased traffic on the network.
- ✔ Data transmission in an Ethernet network is chaotic.
- ✔ Ethernet uses CSMA/CD to ensure the delivery of data.
- ✔ The primary choice of topology for Ethernet is the star.
- ✔ The primary choice of cable for Ethernet is Cat 5 and Cat 5e, using RJ-45 connectors.
- ✔ Ethernet is inexpensive and easy to install.
- ✔ Wireless communications use CSMA/CA to ensure the delivery of data.
- ✔ On a Token Ring network, only one node may control the token at any one moment.
- ✔ The Token Ring network uses a ring topology.
- ✔ Data transmission in a Token Ring network is organized and predictable.
- ✔ A Token Ring network is usually expensive and difficult to install.
- ✔ The OSI model serves as a guide for troubleshooting and design of network systems.

Review Questions

Answer the following questions on a separate sheet of paper. Please do not write in this book.

1. What are the advantages of using a computer network system?
2. How does a large network server differ from a typical PC?
3. Name three types of dedicated servers.
4. What are the three major classifications of networks used to describe the size and complexity of a network system?
5. The Internet would be best described as a _____.
   a. LAN
   b. MAN
   c. WAN
   d. PAN
6. Six computers connected together in your classroom would *most likely* be classified as a _____-to-_____ network.
7. Your instructor has a computer that is connected to a powerful computer in another building. This would *most likely* be a _____/_____ network.
8. Which type of network administrative model has a centralized administration?
9. Rank LAN, MAN, and WAN by their typical sizes, from smallest to largest.
10. What are the three major classifications of network topologies?
11. A bus topology segment is often called a _____.
12. Define a segment for a typical ring and a typical star topology.
13. What does a typical frame of data contain?
14. What three things affect the time it takes for data to arrive at its destination?
15. Describe, compare, and contrast Ethernet and Token Ring network communication.
16. Which operating system no longer supports NetBEUI?
17. What is the purpose of the QoS protocol?
18. What network media is no longer installed for new networks?
19. What are the major advantages of fiber-optic cable systems?
20. What are the major disadvantages of fiber-optic cable systems?
21. Name three types of network connectors found on NICs.

22. Convert the following acronyms to complete words and capitalize the letter of the word used to construct the acronym. Example: CPU = Central Processing Unit.
    a. MAU =
    b. LAN =
    c. MAN =
    d. WAN =
    e. ATM =
    f. IPX/SPX =
    g. TCP/IP =
    h. IEEE =
    i. CSMA/CD =
    j. FIP =
    k. NIC =
23. Which layer of the OSI model is mainly concerned with network cables and connectors?
    a. Application
    b. Session
    c. Transport
    d. Physical

Sample A+ Exam Questions

Answer the following questions on a separate sheet of paper. Please do not write in this book.

1. Which of the following statements best defines a peer-to-peer network?
    a. A group of computers in which each has control of their own resources.
    b. A group of computers controlled by one central computer.
    c. A group of computers in which one is designated the control unit and the rest are defined as peers.
    d. A group of computers in which each computer has the ability to remove any other computer from the group.
2. A network limited to one particular floor of an office building would *most likely* be classified as a ______.
    a. LAN
    b. MAN
    c. WAN
    d. CAN
3. From the list of answers, choose the one that is *not* a network topology.
    a. Star
    b. Bus
    c. Ray
    d. Mesh

4. Which of the following protocols is commonly associated with Internet communication?
   a. TCP/CPS
   b. IPX/NEX
   c. TCP/IP
   d. TCP/POP3
5. CSMA/CD is closely associated with which type of network?
   a. Token Ring
   b. Ethernet
   c. ARCnet
   d. Subnet
6. The unintentional transfer of data between individual wires inside a network cable, such as Cat 5, is called _____.
   a. impedance
   b. attenuation
   c. cross talk
   d. broadcast storm
7. Which of the following best represents a network card MAC address?
   a. 123.202.16.24
   b. 1673452
   c. 00 A1 23 12 C2 F1
   d. CF12D
8. A Web browser program would be located at which layer of the OSI model?
   a. Presentation
   b. Application
   c. Session
   d. Network
9. Which of the following protocols is associated with transferring data using infrared light?
   a. TCP/IP
   b. PX/SPX
   c. FIP
   d. ATM
10. Cat 5e provides less signal _____ than Cat 5 cable.
    a. strength
    b. loss
    c. quality
    d. cost

Suggested Laboratory Activities

Do not attempt any suggested laboratory activities without your instructor's permission. Certain activities can render the PC operating system inoperable.

1. Construct a small peer-to-peer network using two or more PCs and an active or passive hub.
2. Make a Cat 5 cable for connecting a PC to a hub.
3. Make a crossover cable for connecting two computers.
4. Remove and then install a network card.
5. Inspect and change the various properties found in the **Properties** dialog box under the **Network** icon in **Control Panel**. Be sure to write down all the settings before making any changes. Watch the effect on the PC in the network. You can find more information about each setting at the technical support page at Microsoft's Web site.
6. Set up a network share for a hard drive of a set of files on a PC.
7. Set up a network share for a CD-drive and then access it from another PC.
8. Set up a network share for a printer. Share the printer for two or more PCs.

Note:
There is detailed information located at the Microsoft Web site that can be used to help you accomplish these experiments.

Interesting Web Sites for More Information

www.blackbox.com
www.cables-unlimited.com
www.howstuffworks.com
www.techfest.com

Chapter 16
Laboratory Activity
Installing and Configuring a PCI Network Adapter

After completing this laboratory activity, you will be able to:

- ✔ Install and configure a typical PCI Ethernet network adapter.
- ✔ Identify common problems associated with installing a network adapter.
- ✔ Use **Device Manager** to confirm proper installation of the network adapter.
- ✔ Disable or uninstall a network adapter for troubleshooting purposes.
- ✔ Identify system resources assigned to the network adapter.

Introduction

In this laboratory activity, you will install a typical PCI Ethernet network adapter, commonly referred to as a NIC (network interface card). While most network adapters are automatically configured through Plug and Play technology, many times a technician's intervention is required. This most commonly happens when the network adapter and the operating system are from two different eras. For example, when installing a dated network adapter into a computer with the latest operating system, a driver may need to be manually installed.

You should check the Microsoft Hardware Compatibility List (HCL) prior to purchasing a network adapter. Purchase a card that is on the list. Cards not on the HCL may present a problem during installation. When using a network adapter not previously tested and approved by Microsoft, a warning message may appear. The message will inform you that the drivers are not digitally signed and will advise you not to install the card. You may ignore the warning and continue with the installation process. Most times, the network adapter will install properly, but you will most likely need to supply the driver disk during the installation process.

All network adapters require driver software. Typically, when a Plug and Play network adapter is detected by the operating system, the driver is automatically installed and no further intervention is required from the technician. Occasionally, a network adapter driver must be installed manually. When such an instance occurs, the next step in the installation process can vary depending on how much information about the network adapter the operating system identified. For example, a newly installed device may be identified as a network adapter, but the technician must supply the driver. Or, the newly installed device may not be identified by type of device, and the network technician must identify the device as a network adapter and manually install the driver. The operating system may not detect the newly installed device at all. In such a case, the technician must start the installation from **Control Panel | Add Hardware**.

Device Manager can be used to view the status of a hardware device installed in the computer. From **Device Manager**, the technician can uninstall, disable, scan for property changes, or update the network adapter driver. **Device Manager** can also be used to view the system resource assignments of hardware devices. Network adapters use three system resources: Interrupt Request (IRQ), I/O port, and RAM memory. Some network adapters also use Direct Memory Access (DMA). **Device Manager** usually detects conflicts between devices using the same system resource.

The Windows XP operating system installs the TCP/IP protocol default when a network adapter is installed. To verify that the TCP/IP protocol is installed, issue the **ping** command at the command prompt. If TCP/IP is not installed, you will not be able to use the **ping** command.

Note:
When installing a network adapter into a computer that has a network port built into the motherboard, the motherboard network port usually needs to be disabled to prevent a conflict with the additional network adapter. The network port can be disabled through ***Device Manager.***

Equipment and Materials

- ✔ Windows XP Professional workstation. (Do not use Windows XP Home Edition for this laboratory activity.)
- ✔ Patch cable.
- ✔ Windows XP installation CD. (May be required when configuring the network adapter.)
- ✔ PCI Ethernet network adapter with driver disc.
- ✔ Manufacturer's instructions for installing the network adapter. (Your instructor may have you download the installation instructions and drivers from the manufacturer's Web site.)
- ✔ Hub.
- ✔ Screwdriver to match expansion slot screw.
- ✔ Anti-static wrist strap.

Procedure

1. _______ Gather all required materials and then report to your assigned workstation.
2. _______ Familiarize yourself with the manufacturer's installation instructions.
3. _______ Boot the computer and verify it is in working order.
4. _______ Shut down the computer and then unplug the power cord. Follow anti-static procedures as defined by your instructor.

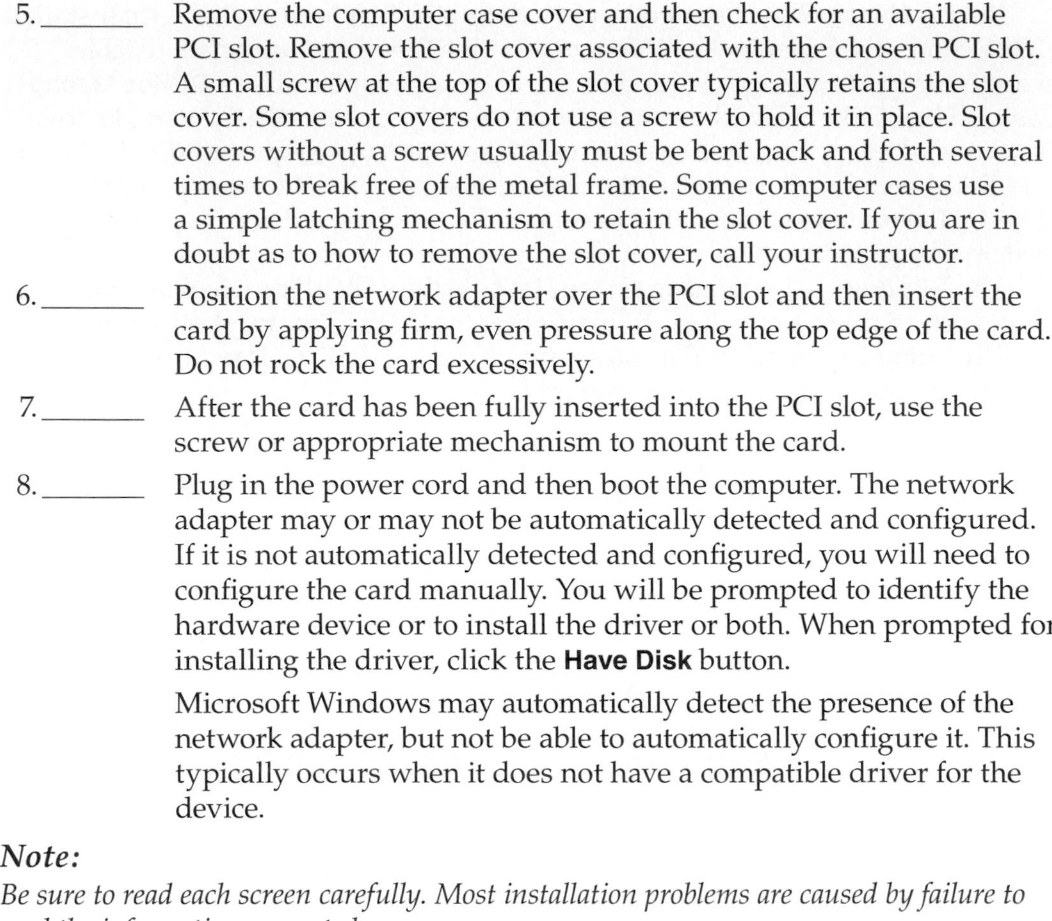

5._______ Remove the computer case cover and then check for an available PCI slot. Remove the slot cover associated with the chosen PCI slot. A small screw at the top of the slot cover typically retains the slot cover. Some slot covers do not use a screw to hold it in place. Slot covers without a screw usually must be bent back and forth several times to break free of the metal frame. Some computer cases use a simple latching mechanism to retain the slot cover. If you are in doubt as to how to remove the slot cover, call your instructor.

6._______ Position the network adapter over the PCI slot and then insert the card by applying firm, even pressure along the top edge of the card. Do not rock the card excessively.

7._______ After the card has been fully inserted into the PCI slot, use the screw or appropriate mechanism to mount the card.

8._______ Plug in the power cord and then boot the computer. The network adapter may or may not be automatically detected and configured. If it is not automatically detected and configured, you will need to configure the card manually. You will be prompted to identify the hardware device or to install the driver or both. When prompted for installing the driver, click the **Have Disk** button.

Microsoft Windows may automatically detect the presence of the network adapter, but not be able to automatically configure it. This typically occurs when it does not have a compatible driver for the device.

Note:

Be sure to read each screen carefully. Most installation problems are caused by failure to read the information presented.

9._______ After the driver is installed, open **Device Manager** to check the status of the network adapter. To access **Device Manager**, right-click **My Computer** and select **Properties** from the shortcut menu. Select the **Hardware** tab and then the **Device Manager** button. The **Device Manager** list will display.

In the **Device Manager** list, you should see **Network adapters**. Expand **Network adapters** by clicking the plus sign. Clicking the plus sign expands the device type **Network adapters** and shows all network adapters installed in the computer.

In the following screen capture, two network adapters are identified. Both are in working order. No problems are indicated. **Device Manager** indicates a hardware device problem by inserting a symbol over the device name. A red *X* indicates the device is disabled. A black exclamation mark on a yellow field indicates the device is having a problem but may still be working. A blue *i* on white field indicates that the resources for the device were manually selected.

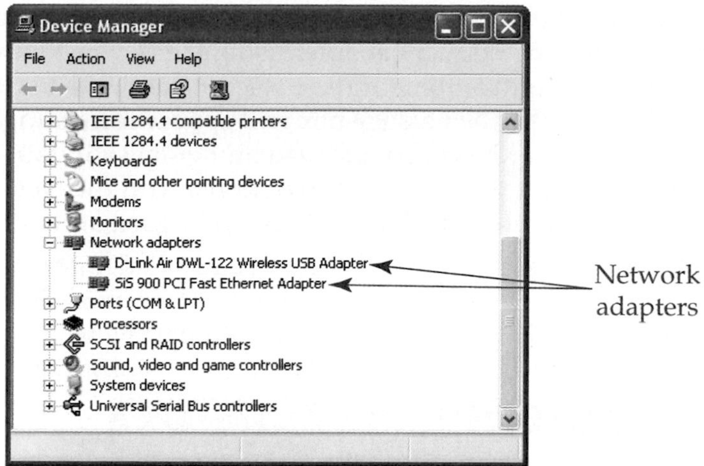

10. _______ Right-click the network adapter entry. A shortcut menu will appear with the following commands: **Update Driver**, **Disable**, **Uninstall**, **Scan for hardware changes**, and **Properties**.

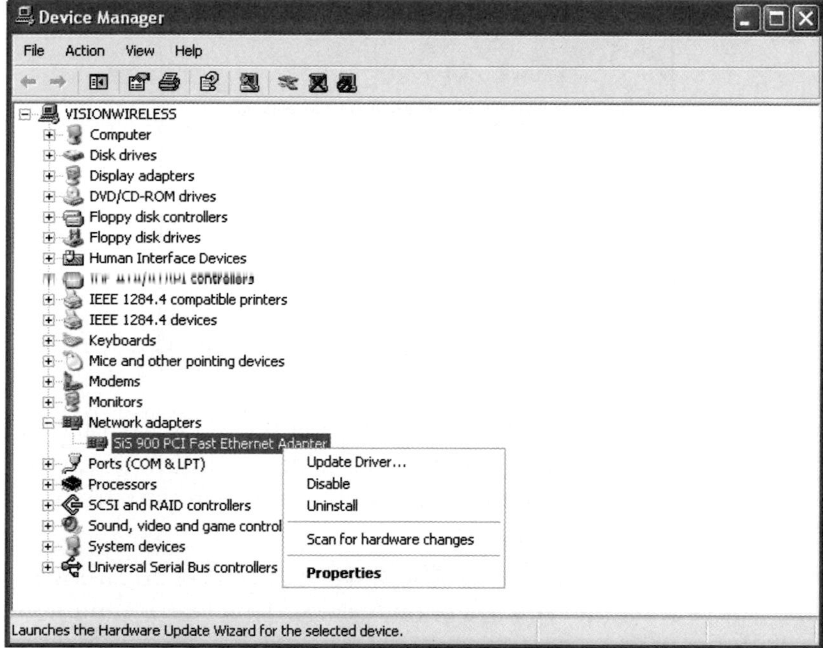

11. _______ Select **Disable** from the shortcut menu. Notice the effect on the appearance of the device. What symbol appeared over the network adapter to indicate that it is disabled? Record the answer on a separate sheet of paper.

12. _______ Enable the network adapter by right-clicking the network adapter entry and selecting **Enable** from the shortcut menu. The **Enable** option appears in the shortcut menu after the **Disable** command is selected.

13._______ Right-click the network adapter entry and select **Uninstall**. After uninstalling the network adapter using the **Device Manager**, Windows XP will automatically detect the network adapter and install the driver. A message box will appear informing you that the network adapter has been installed and will ask if you want to set up a network. It will give you an option to run the Network Setup Wizard. Do not run the Network Setup Wizard at this time.

14._______ After the network adapter has been reinstalled, open **Device Manager** and select the network adapter once more. Right-click the network adapter entry and select **Properties** from the shortcut menu. You should see a **General** dialog box similar to the following.

The **General** dialog box indicates that the network adapter is working properly. You can also enable or disable the device from here and start the automatic troubleshooter if you are having problems with the device.

15._______ Select the **Advanced** tab. The **Advanced** dialog box allows you to access a media type selection feature. This feature may be indicated with a property name such as **Media Type** or **Link Speed & Duplex** property. The property name for this feature varies with network adapter manufacturers and models.

Look at the following screen capture. The **Media Type** property is set to auto configure by default. Auto configure allows the card to automatically run a software program to detect the type of media connected to the card. You can also manually select the media type. For a small to medium network, auto configure is fine. For a large network, manually selecting the media type improves the overall performance of a large network. It prevents the card from sending out numerous packets to detect the media type and will thus reduce network traffic.

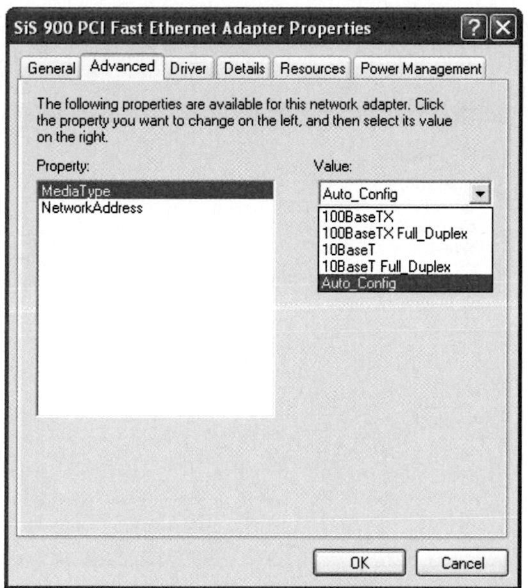

16. _______ Select the **Driver** tab. From the **Driver** dialog box, you can view driver details, update the driver, roll back the driver, and uninstall the driver. The **Driver Details** button reveals information about the manufacture, where the driver is located, and if the driver was digitally signed. A digitally signed driver means Microsoft has approved the driver. The **Roll Back Driver** option or feature removes the last installed driver for the card. You would normally use this option in place of using the System Restore feature, which rolls back all changes to the computer since the last restore point was created. Rolling back all changes since the last restore point was created can undo many changes that you wish to retain. The Roll Back Driver feature is the best choice for uninstalling a driver.

17. _______ Select the **Resources** tab. A dialog box similar to the following will appear and will display system resources assigned to the network adapter.

18. _______ Record on a separate piece of paper the resources assigned to your network adapter.
    - ✔ I/O range
    - ✔ Memory range
    - ✔ IRQ
19. _______ Select the **Power Management** tab. The **Power Management** dialog box displays several options related to power saving features available for the network adapter. Typically, you will not need to access this tab or the other tabs mentioned in this laboratory activity. Also, be aware that the type of information as well as the appearance of the information presented in a dialog box can change by card manufacturer. Manufacturers have access to Windows XP programming information. They often change the way a dialog box appears to match the capabilities of their network adapters.
20. _______ Practice accessing and opening the menu items and dialog boxes presented in this laboratory activity. After you have practiced, answer the review questions.
21. _______ Return all materials to their proper storage area.

Review Questions

Answer the following questions on a separate sheet of paper. Please do not write in this book.

1. What does the acronym NIC represent?
2. What does the acronym HCL represent?
3. What symbol is used in **Device Manager** to indicate a device is disabled?
4. What symbol is used in **Device Manager** to indicate there is a problem with a device?
5. What four options are available from the **Driver** tab?
6. Why is the Roll Back Driver feature the preferred way to remove a network adapter driver?
7. What three system resources are assigned to a network adapter?

Network Administration

After studying this chapter, you will be able to:

- ✔ Explain the difference between user-level and share-level security.
- ✔ Explain the role of the network administrator.
- ✔ Describe the characteristics of centralized and decentralized network administration.
- ✔ Describe the characteristics of a strong password.
- ✔ Describe some of the features that may be implemented to increase network security.

A+ Exam—Key Points

The A+ Certification exams do not go into great depth with networks, but they will test your basic knowledge. You should be prepared to answer questions like the following:

- ✔ What is a protocol?
- ✔ Who controls system logons?
- ✔ Who controls system security?
- ✔ How do you log on to a workstation?
- ✔ How do you set up a peer-to-peer share?

Also be prepared to explain the difference between user-level and share-level security and to identify the properties of a secure password.

Key Words and Terms

The following words and terms will become important pieces of your computer vocabulary. Be sure you can define them.

account
backup domain controllers (BDC)
domain
fault tolerance
group
network administration
permissions
primary domain controller (PDC)
RAID
rights
share-level security
share
system resources
user-level security
user

network administration the use of network software packages to manage network system operations.

Network administration is the use of network software packages to manage network system operations. The central focus of network administration is network security and coordination of shared resources on the network. In this chapter, the basics of network administration are covered. It is important to have a basic understanding of network operations when troubleshooting PCs that are connected to a network. You must be able to determine if the problem is PC-related or network-related. This chapter is not intended to prepare you for the Network+ Certification exam, but it will help you begin the process of achieving that additional certification if you desire.

Network administration in the corporate world is a vast subject requiring years of study and experience. To be competent in a single networking software package can take years. Home and small business networks are becoming more popular everyday. It is imperative that you have a basic understanding of small peer-to-peer networks. The four major network systems will also be introduced, and then the majority of the chapter will concentrate on the Windows .Net Server 2003 network operating system, also called Windows Server 2003.

Peer-to-Peer Network Administration

Peer-to-peer networks are rapidly becoming popular, especially in home and small-business offices. Small networks can be set up easily and administered to allow users to share files, printers, hardware, and Internet connections. You can set up a peer-to-peer network using Windows 98, Me, 2000, XP, and Vista. These operating systems typically limit the number of simultaneous connections to ten users. Larger networking systems require a client/server operating system.

Administrative functions in a peer-to-peer network are not highly organized and are best described as decentralized. In a decentralized administrative system, no one person controls the network. All users have equal rights on the network, and each user usually controls access to their own files and hardware.

To create a peer-to-peer network, all that is required is an operating system that supports peer-to-peer networking and a network adapter card for each PC participating in the network. Microsoft operating systems after Windows 98 are easy to configure as a peer-to-peer network. They use a wizard to ask a series of simple questions. Once the questions are answered, the network's communications are automatically set up. Networks using Windows 98 and prior operating systems require a bit more input during the setup phase.

Shares

A ***share*** is an object that is shared across the network, such as a file, hard drive, DVD drive, printer, or scanner. Shares are usually set up with some form of security system. In Windows, there are two main security levels for accessing shares on a peer-to-peer network: share-level and user-level.

Share-level security is the default security system used on Windows-based networks. Share-level security requires a password to access a share. The other security system, ***user-level security,*** identifies who may have access to a shared resource but does not require a password for accessing the share. A peer-to-peer network usually uses share-level security, while a client/server network usually uses user-level security.

share
an object that is shared across the network, such as a file, hard drive, CD-ROM drive, printer, or scanner.

share-level security
default security system used on Windows-based networks, which requires a password for access.

user-level security
security system used on Windows-based networks that identifies who may have access to a shared resource but does not require a password for accessing the share.

The owner of the share in a peer-to-peer system may choose not to require a password for accessing the share. Not requiring a password is a discouraged security practice.

In the client/server network, the client is issued a password and a security level. The clients must supply a user name and password when they log on to the network. Once they successfully log on, they will automatically have the right to access certain files, hardware, and directories.

In a peer-to-peer network, it is not necessary to log on as in a client/server network system. Shares on a peer-to-peer network are recommended to be password protected but are not required to be password protected. When shares on a peer-to-peer are password protected, a window appears which is similar in design to a typical logon window. Each share must be accessed using a specific password even though the users belong to a particular group.

There are three share-level security options for peer-to-peer access in Windows 95, 98, and Me: Read-Only, Full, and Depends on Password. In Windows XP, Vista, NT, and 2000, the share-level security options are Full Control, Change, and Read. See **Figure 17-1** for a complete description of the access level security of each type. As you can see from the figures, user access levels for shares offer varying degrees of security.

It is very important that you set passwords for shares, especially if the same workstation will be connecting to the Internet.

Setting up a Resource Share

Setting up a share for a resource is easy, but you must first allow access to your files and printer. By default, Windows 95, 98, and Me operating systems do not allow other peer-to-peer network users access to your files, printers, and other hardware. Therefore, a share must be created before other users on the network can access your files and hardware. You can use the **Network** dialog box to change your file- and print-sharing settings. See **Figure 17-2.**

Figure 17-1.
A—Access levels available for shares in Windows 95, 98, and Me and the difference between those levels.
B—Access levels available for shares in Windows XP, Vista, NT, and 2000.

Windows 95, 98, and Me

User Access Level	Description
Read-Only	A user can read and copy the file but not delete or modify a file.
Full	A user can read, copy, modify, delete, move, erase and take ownership of a file or directory.
Depends on Password	A combination of Read-Only and Full access. Each access level has its own password.

A

Windows XP, Vista NT, and 2000

User Access Level	Description
Full Control	A user can read, copy, modify, delete, move, erase, and take ownership of a file or directory.
Change	A user can read, create, write, or delete a file.
Read	A user can read and copy a file but not delete or modify a file.

B

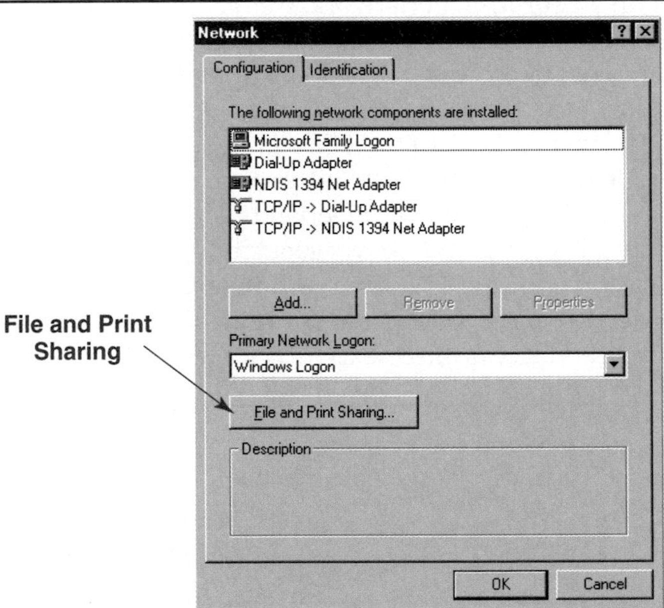

Figure 17-2.
Click the ***File and Print Sharing*** button in the **Network** dialog box to set up a share.

To change your file and print-sharing settings in Windows 95, 98, and Me open the **Network** dialog box located at **Start | Settings | Control Panel | Network**. Next, click **File and Print Sharing** and enable the appropriate options. The first option is **I want to be able to give others access to my files**. Enabling this option allows you to set up a share for your drives. See **Figure 17-3.** The second option is **I want to be able to allow others to print to my printer(s)**. Placing a check mark in this box allows you to set up a share for your printer.

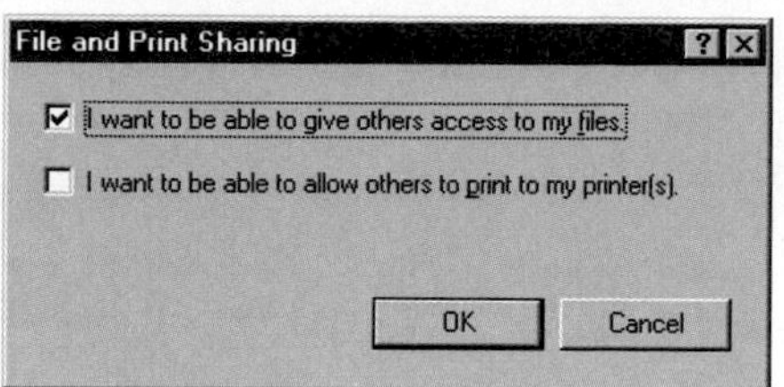

Figure 17-3. Click the appropriate box to share your files or printer.

File and print sharing capabilities are automatically enabled in Windows NT, Vista, and 2000.

To complete the share for disk drives, open **My Computer** and right-click on the icon of the item you wish to share. Select **Sharing** from the shortcut menu. Enable the **Shared As** option and then enter the name of the share in the **Share Name** text box. Click the **Add** button beneath the **Name** text box, and select the users you wish to share with from the left-hand side of the **Add Users** dialog box. Next, select one of the three center buttons to grant the selected user access to your drives. Each button corresponds to one of the access levels described in the previous section. Click the **OK** button in the **Add User** dialog box, and then click the **OK** button in the device's **Properties** dialog box to complete the share. If the share has been successful, the share icon replaces the original icon in the **My Computer** window. See **Figure 17-4.**

To create a shared folder or drive in a peer-to-peer network using Windows XP, locate the file or drive using Windows Explorer. Right-click the file or drive you wish to share and then select **Sharing and Security** from the shortcut menu, **Figure 17-5.** To create a shared folder or drive in a peer-to-peer network using Windows NT or 2000, locate the file or drive using Windows Explorer. Right-click the file or drive you wish to share and then select **Sharing** from the shortcut menu.

A Windows dialog box similar to the one in **Figure 17-6** will appear. You can configure share properties such as a share name, number of users (maximum of ten), permissions, and caching. You can also use this dialog box to remove a share. **Figure 17-7** shows the permissions for drive C given to the group Everyone.

Creating a printer share in Windows 95, 98, and Me is similar to creating a disk drive or file share in those operating systems. First, the **I want to be able to allow others to print to my printer(s)** option must be selected in the **File and Print Sharing** dialog box. To complete the share, access the **Printers** folder by choosing

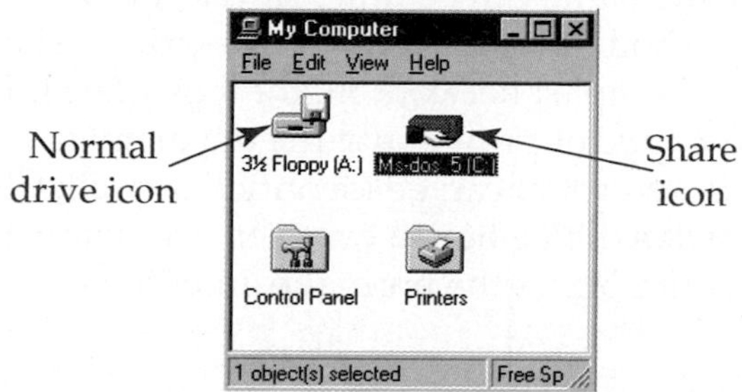

Figure 17-4. After a share has been set up, the drive's normal icon is replaced with the share icon.

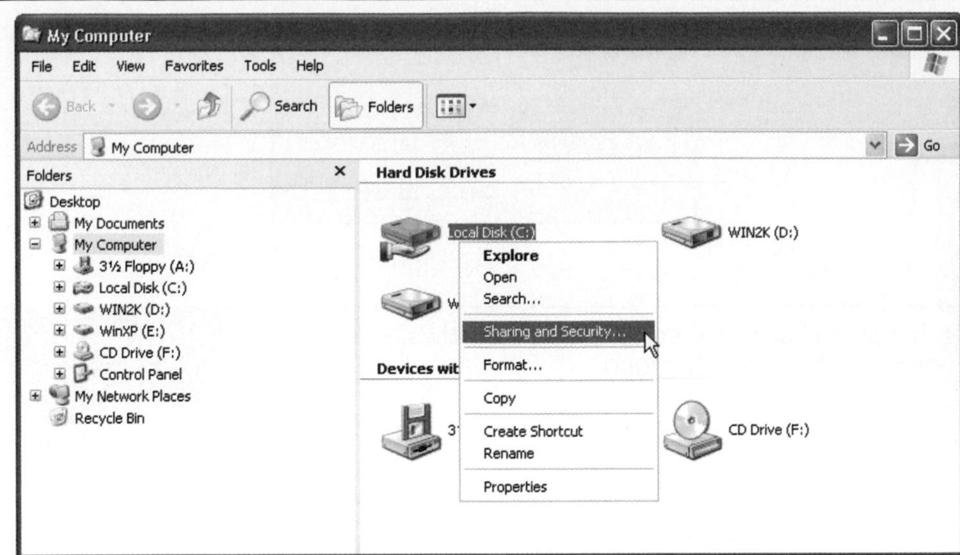

Figure 17-5. File and print sharing are enabled by default in Windows XP, NT and 2000. To set up sharing, simply right-click the file or drive you wish to share and select **Sharing and Security** from the shortcut menu.

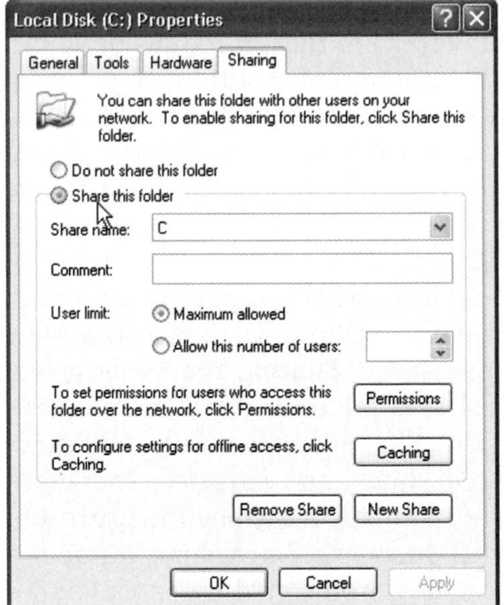

Figure 17-6. Windows XP **Sharing** dialog box.

Start | Settings | Printers. Right-click the name of the printer you wish to share. A shortcut menu will appear, and one of the choices will be **Sharing**. Selecting this option opens a dialog box similar to the one in **Figure 17-8.**

Next, enable the **Shared As** option and give the printer share a name. For a small network system, the name can be quite simple, but in a complex network environment, the name should exactly identify the printer share. An example of a printer share name on a complex network might look like HPLaser6Accounting. This name identifies the type of printer and the department in which the printer is located. The building and room can be identified as well. Click the **OK** button in your printer's **Properties** dialog box to complete the share. If the share is successful, the share icon replaces the normal printer icon.

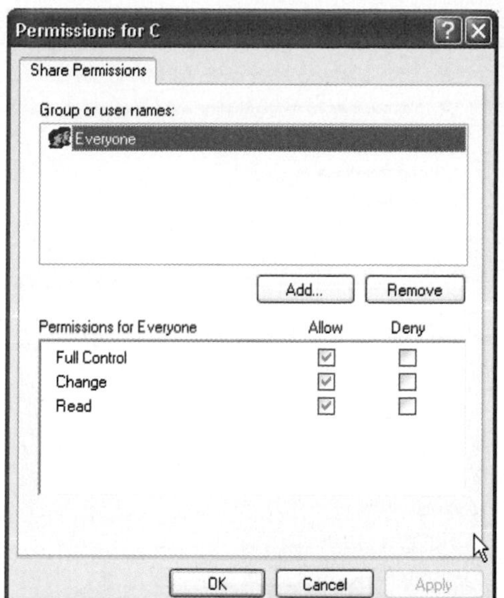

Figure 17-7.
Share Permissions dialog box. The group Everyone has been given Full Control, Change, and Read rights to drive **C**.

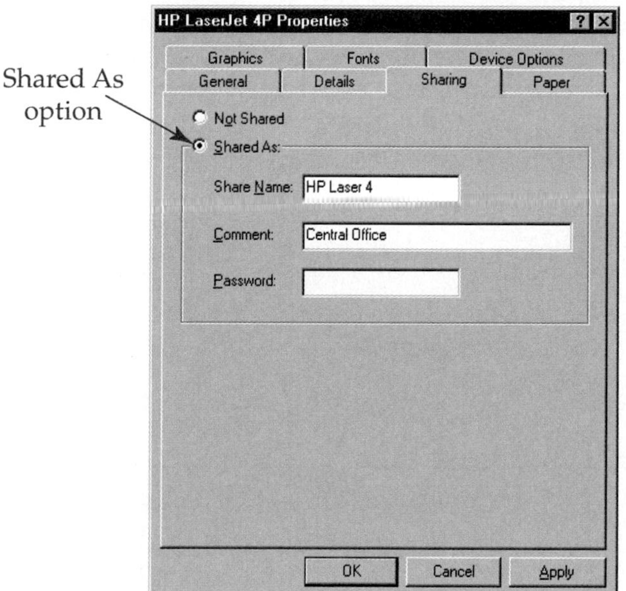

Figure 17-8.
A printer share is set up through the printer's **Properties** dialog box.

To create a printer share in Windows XP, NT, and 2000, access the **Printers** folder through **Start | Settings | Printers** (**Printers and Faxes** in XP). Right-click the name of the printer you wish to share. A shortcut menu will appear and one of the choices will be **Sharing**. Selecting this option in Windows XP will open a dialog box similar to the one in **Figure 17-9.**

Next, select **Share this printer**. Windows will automatically insert the first seven characters of the printer's name in the **Share name** text box. You may change this to a more descriptive name. There is also an option to add additional drivers for users running different versions of Windows. This will enable the correct version of the printer driver to be automatically downloaded to a user's system when they add the shared printer. If you do not choose to add the additional drivers, users will be required to provide the drivers themselves, either from the installation CD or from the Windows cab files.

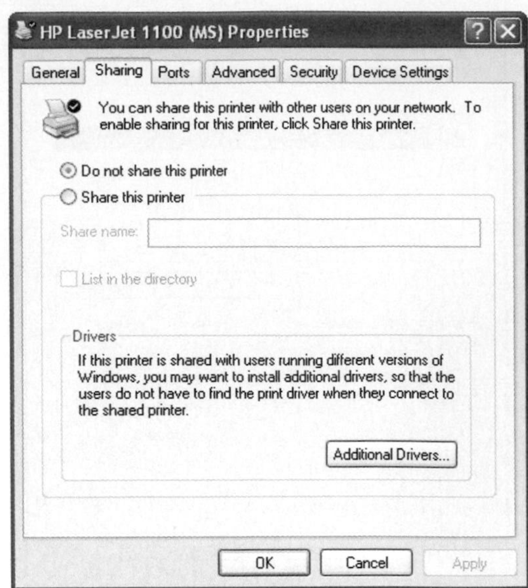

Figure 17-9. Printer **Sharing** dialog box in Windows XP.

Windows XP Simple File Sharing

Windows XP designed the Simple File Sharing feature, which creates by default a folder called Shared Documents to be shared by each user. When Simple File Sharing is enabled, **Figure 17-10,** the Shared Documents folder is automatically created. Look at **Figure 17-11** to see what the Shared Documents folder looks like in the directory. Files placed in the Shared Documents folder are automatically shared.

A+ Note:

Be sure you are familiar with how to disable Windows XP Simple File Sharing and the fact that you cannot view file share permissions when Simple File Sharing is enabled.

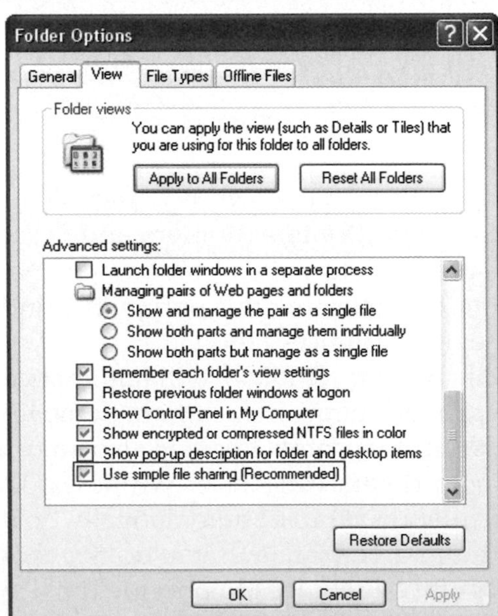

Figure 17-10. Simple File Sharing is enabled in Windows XP through the **Folder Options** dialog box.

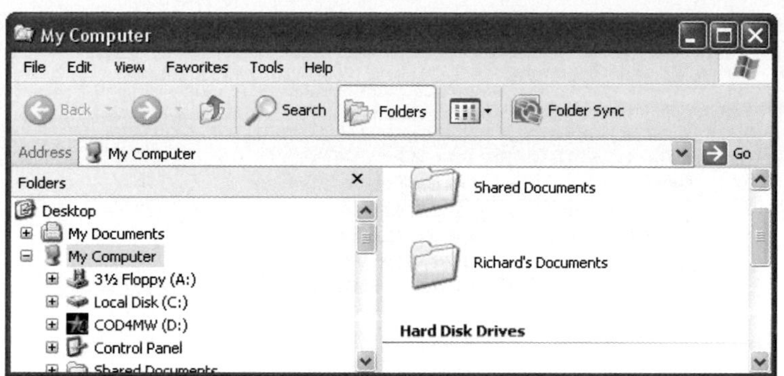

Figure 17-11. The Shared Documents folder is created when Simple File Sharing is enabled.

Windows Vista Public Folder Sharing

Windows Vista uses a similar feature to Simple File Sharing called Public folder sharing. When the Public folder sharing feature is enabled, the Public folder, located under C:\Users\ is configured as a share. Beneath the Public folder are the following subfolders:

- ✔ Public Desktop.
- ✔ Public Documents.
- ✔ Public Downloads.
- ✔ Public Music.
- ✔ Public Pictures.
- ✔ Public Videos.
- ✔ Recorded TV.

Windows Vista creates the Public folder and its subfolders by default; however, sharing is not enabled. **Figure 17-12** shows the default location of the Public folder. Notice the icon next to it. A shared folder in Windows Vista appears with a two-person icon. Earlier Windows operating systems identified a shared folder with an open hand under the folder.

Figure 17-13 shows the subfolders beneath the Public folder. Once the Public folder sharing is enabled, you can share the contents of the Public folder and its subfolders with other users of the same computer or with anyone on the local network. Public file sharing is covered in depth in Chapter 19—Small-Office/Home-Office (SOHO) Networking.

The sharing of other folders can be simplified by enabling the Sharing Wizard. The Sharing Wizard is activated when a user right-clicks a file or directory to be shared and selects **Sharing**. It guides a user through setting up the share, such as selecting the users with whom to share the file or directory and selecting the permission to assign them. The Sharing Wizard is enabled through **Windows Explorer | Tools | Folder Options** and by selecting the **Use Sharing Wizard (Recommended)** option.

Another new feature of Windows Vista is the fact that users who do not have permission to access a shared folder will no longer be able to see the folder. In previous versions of Windows, it was possible to view a shared folder even when you did not have permission to access the folder.

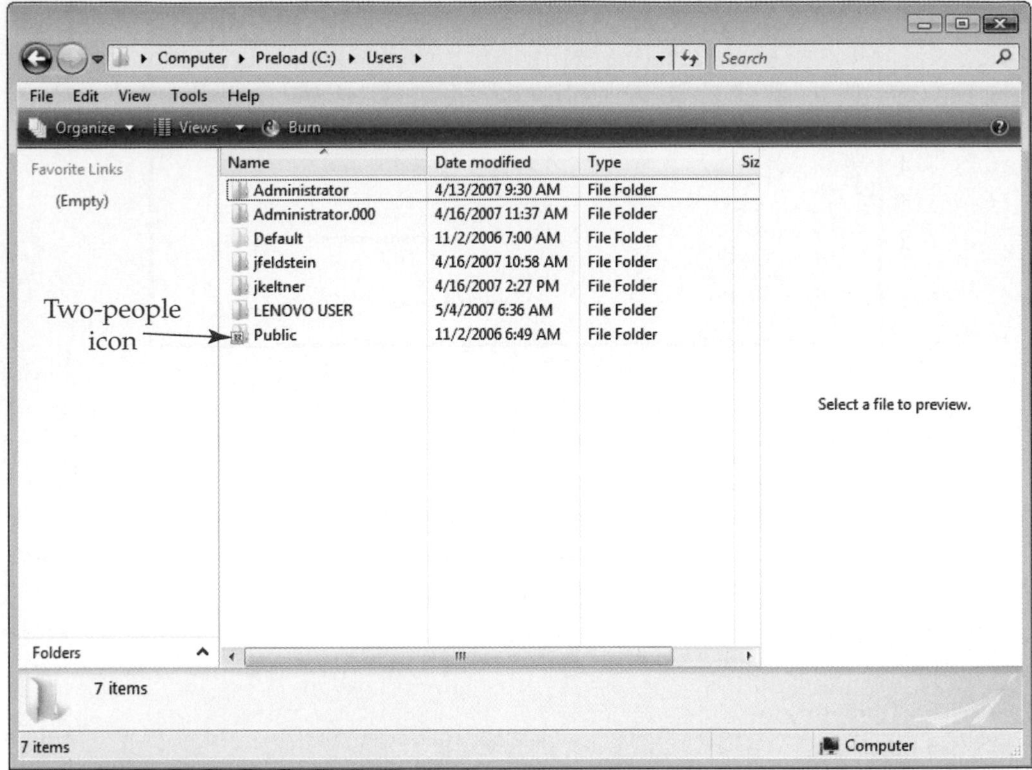

Figure 17-12. A two-people icon by a folder indicates the folder is shared.

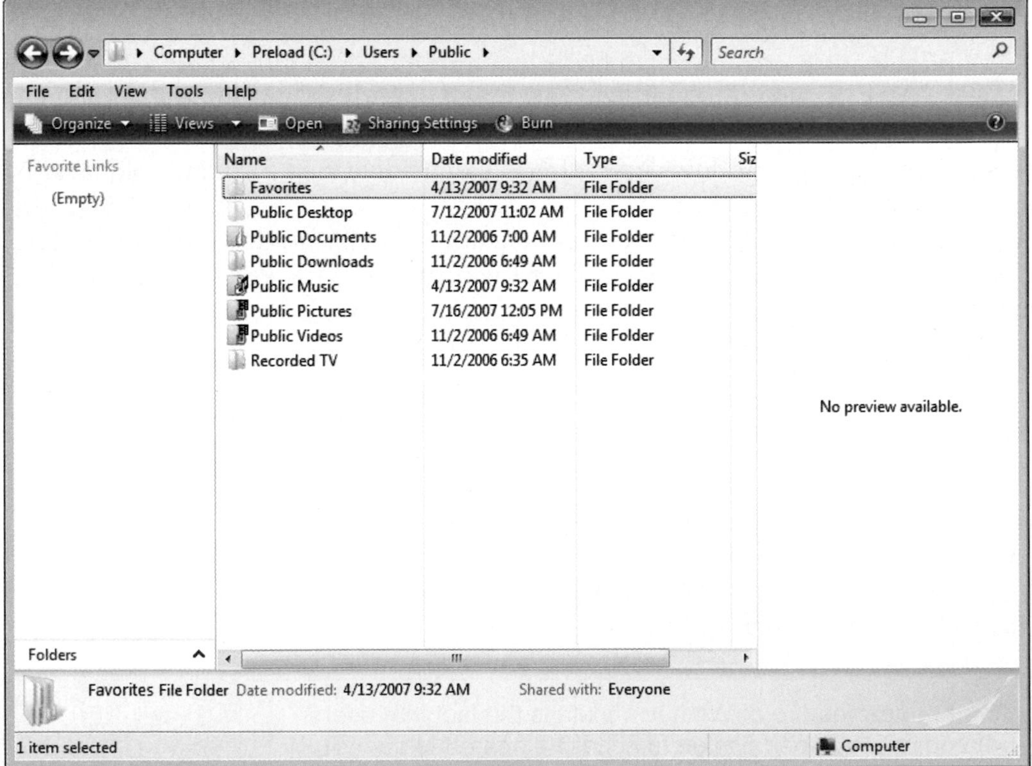

Figure 17-13. Default folders within the Public folder.

Local User Account

For added security in a peer-to-peer, or workgroup-based, network, a user account should be set up for each user on each computer that the user plans to log on and use. This type of account is called a local user account. The main characteristics of a local user account include the following:

- ✔ Associated with a peer-to-peer, or a workgroup-based, network.
- ✔ Needed to access resources at the local computer.
- ✔ Authenticated through the computer at which the account is created.
- ✔ Maintained in the computer at which the account is created.

Windows XP and Windows Vista Sharing Comparison

One of the biggest changes in Windows Vista is the way shares are handled by the operating system as compared to Windows XP. Shares can be created in the local workgroup by anyone who is an administrator or equal to the administrator. In Windows XP, when you create an account on a workstation, the account is either equal to the local computer administrator, a limited account, or a guest account. In Windows Vista, you can create an administrator account or a standard user account. The standard user account feature is new in Windows Vista.

In Windows Vista, a standard user can perform almost everything that the system administrator can but cannot make any configuration changes that affect other users. For example, a standard user cannot remove or install a software program that other users might use. This is more power than the Windows XP limited account, but not as powerful as the administrator account. A standard user account in Windows Vista can create a share. The limited account in Windows XP cannot. Look at the table in **Figure 17-14** to view a summary of the sharing features of both operating systems.

Windows XP	Windows Vista
Can only share folders, not individual files in peer-to-peer or domain network.	Can share folders or individual files in a peer-to-peer network. In a domain, you can only share folders.
Only an administrator or equal can create a share.	An administrator or standard user can create a share.
Open hand icon represents share.	A two-person icon represents a share.
File sharing is simplified through the Simple File Sharing feature, which creates the Shared Documents folder.	File sharing is simplified through the Public folder and the Sharing Wizard. The Public folder is created during the operating system installation, but is not shared by default.
Simple File Sharing feature can only be used in local workgroup, not in domain.	The Public folder can be used in a local workgroup or domain. However, if part of a domain, the Public folder cannot be password protected.
Network shares can be viewed by anyone, even when they do not have permission.	Network users cannot view shares unless they have NTFS permissions to access the share.

Figure 17-14. Comparison of Windows XP and Windows Vista sharing.

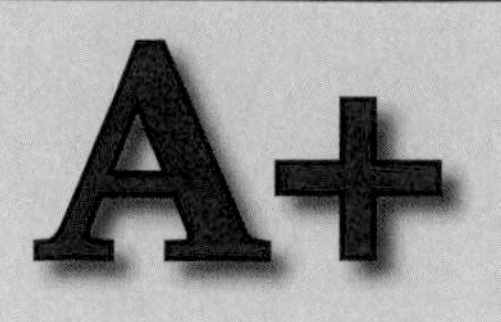

A+ Note:

CompTIA always has several questions about shares, permissions, and user accounts in the A+ Certification exams that include the Security domain.

Typical Centralized Network Administration

This part of the chapter introduces the four major network operating systems: UNIX, Novell NetWare, Microsoft Server 2003, and Linux. There are many more, but these are the most predominate systems in use.

UNIX

UNIX is the oldest of the four network operating systems. It was written in the C programming language and was mainly intended for use on minicomputers. One of the things that made it so popular was that it was not computer specific. In the early days of computers, operating systems were written specifically for certain computer types. You could only use an operating system on a specific brand and model. Today, you can run most software across the boundaries of different manufacturers with relatively few restrictions.

UNIX was adopted by IBM and became the standard operating system for their RISC-based systems. UNIX is still used on many mainframe computers and enterprise servers. The original UNIX operating system required a mainframe computer to meet the operating system hardware requirements. Early PC models did not have sufficient hardware to support the UNIX operating system. Today, many variations of UNIX exist, such as the numerous Linux versions that are designed to run on a PC. Today's PCs have more computing power than the early mainframe computers.

Novell NetWare

Novell NetWare was developed by Novell. It was a very popular network operating system in the 1980s and into the 1990s. The operating system came in several flavors, ranging from Ethernet to Token Ring.

The early versions of NetWare, equipped with a command line interface, were very complex to use. To perform functions, commands had to be typed in at the command line rather than issued by clicking an icon. Today's version incorporates a GUI interface, and you can simply point and click to access its features.

Novell's determination and progress in making it possible to share information across diverse platforms has helped NetWare to regain its popularity. In 2004, Novell acquired SUSE Linux and offers as an alternative to NetWare, the SUSE Linux Enterprise server. Novell set the standard for today's network security systems and has become a tremendously powerful and secure network operating system.

The term *platform* is often used as a synonym for operating system.

Microsoft Windows 2000 Server

The Windows 2000 and XP design is based on Windows NT technology. Windows 2000, however, was the first major change in the NT operating system. Windows 2000 introduced Active Directory, which removed many restrictions imposed by the NT domain structure and NT file system. Active Directory allowed files and information to be easily shared across large enterprise networks. Active Directory technology is based on the lightweight directory access protocol (LDAP). With the implementation of Active Directory, a user or group member can simply log on once and have complete access to resources across the entire system. In the Windows NT Server operating system, users had to be authenticated for each individual domain, and trusts relationships needed to be set up between network domains.

Windows 2000 introduced the terms *forest* and *trees* to describe the directory structure. A *tree* is a collection of domains that share a common namespace. A namespace is a name used to identify servers on the Internet, such as www.OurCompany.com. Windows NT Server did not support namespaces. A *forest* is a collection of trees. For example, a forest is a collection of Windows 2000 servers each having a unique namespace.

The Active Directory structure required a newer version of NTFS to be implemented. The newer version of NTFS was named dynamic file system by Microsoft. Other parties referred to the new file system as NTFS5.0 and the original NTFS file system as NTFS4.0. Additional changes introduced in Windows 2000 were automatic Plug and Play device detection, enhanced multimedia features, many different setup wizards to assist with common tasks, and many more features. For a complete list of additional features, visit the home page for Windows 2000 at Microsoft's Web site.

Microsoft Windows .NET Server 2003

Microsoft introduced Windows. NET Server 2003 as the next server operating system after Windows 2000 Server. Windows .NET Server 2003 continued with Active Directory as the main directory structure. Some new features included in Windows .NET Server 2003 are Automatic System Recovery, Remote Assistance, Web Interface for remote administration, improved Internet Information Service (IIS 6.0), wireless networking support, IP version 6, and more. Many of the features new for Windows .NET Server 2003 were introduced in Windows XP. One main area of development is the utilization of the Internet as a medium for accessing and administering the server. To learn more about the features in Windows .NET Server 2003, visit the Windows Server 2003 home page at Microsoft's Web site.

Windows .NET Server 2003 is now referred to as Microsoft Server 2003.

Linux

Linux is one of the latest networking operating systems to be fully developed. Because the source code is available to the public, there are many different Linux operating systems available. Linux has become very popular because its source code is readily available, and it is relatively inexpensive compared to other network operating systems.

Most software companies guard their source code and only release sufficient information about the code to allow third-party developers to write software to enhance their product. By having the complete listing of source code for the Linux operating system, programmers can write any feature they desire into the networking software. Anyone with reasonable programming skills can use the open source code to build a network operating system of their own specifications. Even though major software companies now build networking software packages based on Linux, the pricing remains very reasonable.

However, complete access to source code does have a price. In this case, it is security. If you have complete access to the source code, so does every interested hacker in the world. To abide by the Linux software copyright regulations, if you use the Linux source code to develop your software system, you must allow access to any and all modifications to the code when you market it. As far as security goes, everyone has a road map to your system's operations when the source code is freely distributed.

Many network models incorporate a Linux server together with a server of another network operating system. For example, the front-end server, the part that allows users to access the site, uses a standard high-security package such as those provided by Novell or Windows Server 2003. This provides the security that the site must have. To cut operating cost, the Linux system is used as a mail server or Web server.

System Administrator

When talking about a system administrator, or network administrator, we will be talking about the centralized model of network administration, the client/server model, rather than the peer-to-peer model. The network administrator is one person (or more) who has the highest security rating on the network. The network administrator is responsible for delegating authority all the way down to the user level. The other users on the network can exercise only the authority granted to them by the network administrator.

Delegated Administrators

The network administrator controls all aspects of the network. However, in a large organization with thousands of users spread all over the country, it would be difficult, if not impossible, for one person to perform all the duties associated with running a network. For this reason, the network administrator usually grants limited administrative powers to a middle management level of administrators. The middle management people take care of routine duties, such as adding or deleting users from the network, setting up printers to be shared, setting up specific files or programs to be shared, and doing routine data backup.

Logging on the network involves identifying the user by name and password. The user name identifies the individual and the password verifies his or her identity. The network administrator issues the user name and the user's initial password. The administrator can give permission to the user to change their logon password following the first successful logon. This is the typical password administrative scenario used.

Choosing User Names

The typical format for a user name is the user's last name followed by the underline symbol and ending in the first letter of user's first name. For example, the author's user name would likely be Roberts_R. There are many different naming styles, but once a naming style is chosen, it should remain consistent as new user accounts are added to the network. Inconsistent naming styles can easily lead to confusion.

Choosing Passwords

Passwords are used to verify that the named user is, in fact, the authorized user. Passwords should be unique and be composed of a mixture of letters (both uppercase and lowercase), numbers (*0–9*), and special symbols ($%&(){}[]+=<>). The special symbols that can be used as part of the password depend on the network operating system. There may be a maximum and minimum length for the password as well. Passwords should not be names or words found in a dictionary. Good passwords are combinations of words and other symbols that do not make sense to a typical person when used together. See **Figure 17-15.**

Letters can be replaced by symbols, such as the dollar symbol ($) for *S*, the caret symbol (^) for *A*, or the left bracket symbol ([) symbol for *C*. The use of symbols improves the security of a password. Many hackers attempt to crack passwords by using a database of dictionary words. Each entry in the database is systematically substituted for the password until the correct word is found or the database is exhausted. The use of symbols and numbers negate the use of a dictionary database as a password breaker.

Figure 17-15.
A good password combines numbers, letters, and special symbols in a way that has no meaning to a typical person. Common names, words, and phrases make poor passwords.

Good	Poor
Night$tar1	Star
Brend^01	Brenda
Dog$uper5	BigDog
Pa$$word_1	Password
Acce$$005	Access
Mountain_Blue3	Bluemountain
Rock{123}Surf	RockSurf
[h^rle$_01	Charles

Protecting Your Password

Even a secure password can be jeopardized. A password can be jeopardized by intentionally or unintentionally telling someone your password or by creating a password that is easy to guess. The following are suggestions for protecting your password:

- ✔ Never let anyone watch you enter your password.
- ✔ Never reveal your password to anyone or transmit a password in an e-mail.
- ✔ Never reveal your password to a supervisor or even the system administrator.
- ✔ Do not use a hint feature for a password such as (My dog's name).
- ✔ Do not use the "Remember Password" feature found in programs such as Outlook, Eudora, Netscape, or many Web sites.
- ✔ Never write down a password.
- ✔ Do not give your password to someone temporarily.
- ✔ Do not give your password to a PC technician.
- ✔ Change passwords often, at least every four to six months.
- ✔ Never use words found in any dictionary as a password.
- ✔ Passwords should contain numbers, special characters such as $ # & % &, and uppercase and lowercase letters.

A+ Note:

The CompTIA exam often has test items on password protection. Always select the answer that most closely conforms to the rules above.

Microsoft Server 2003 requires that the administrative password meet complexity requirements. A blank password cannot be used. The password must contain a mixture of characters—at least six—and not contain part or all of the user's name.

Network Administration Models

Each major software vender uses its own terminology to describe its network organization. They are all similar for the most part, and terminologies can be easily transferred from one system to another without losing their intended meanings. The terminology used in this chapter will be primarily based on the Microsoft network systems. Concentrating on one system in generic fashion will be less confusing than explaining different systems in one unit.

Centralized networks are organized administratively into sections. These sections are called domains, groups, and users. The ***domain*** is an organized collection of all groups and users on the network. A ***group*** is a collection of users organized together by similarities in their job tasks. A ***user*** is an individual who may use the network system resources.

domain
an organized collection of all groups and users on the network.

group
collection of users organized together by similarities in their job tasks.

user
a person who may use the network system resources.

The term *domain* has two meanings: one for the early Windows server models and another when used to discuss Internet locations. A domain in Windows NT and Windows 2000 means a collection of computers. When discussing the Internet, the term *domain* refers to a classification of a site such as .com or .org or to represent the Internet site.

Domains

The entire network organization is usually referred to as a domain. For example, ABC Inc. may be a domain. The entire organization is one whole unique network system. Inside the domain are groups of users with related tasks, such as the personnel in the accounting and sales departments. Each of these groups is composed of individual users, such as John Doe in accounting and Jane Doe in sales.

Groups

The next level in the network organization is the group. Groups are workers who share common responsibilities and can be thought of as a set. For example, the payroll, marketing, research, design, and administrative departments of a corporation could easily form five distinct groups of network users. The workers within the group usually require similar ***system resources*** (files, software, printers, etc.) to perform their jobs.

system resources
files, software, printers, and such.

Users

The individual user is at the bottom of the network organization. A user is an individual who uses the network system. Each user is assigned an account, which includes all available information about him or her. The account, which contains such information as the user's password, user name, restrictions, and the group(s) he or she belongs to, is kept in a database on the file server. Each user must have an account before he or she can use the network system. Once the user has an account, he or she can be granted full use of the network and can be given access to any area of the network by the system administrator. The individual user usually belongs to one or more groups, but may belong to no group at all.

Assigning Resources at the Group Level

If the company has several hundred or thousands of employees, the amount of time required to set up individual shares for each employee would be unreasonable. Although access to system resources can be granted to individual users, network administrators can save a great deal of time by assigning resources to groups rather than to individual users. In this case, each group can be allowed access to the normal software programs, files, and hardware required by that group. When it is necessary to add new users to the network, it is quicker and simpler to assign a new individual to an existing group than it is to authorize each individual to use specific network resources.

As you just learned, networks are organized by domains, users, and groups. These groups are often formed from the different divisions or departments in the corporate structure. Although all of these departments are part of the same company and may have many common needs, they each will likely have special needs based on their different job requirements. For example, all departments will need some sort of word-processing package but only a few would need access to the accounting software or payroll database. Each group's needs and security requirements must be determined individually.

Accounts

account contains all the security information describing a user.

primary domain controller (PDC) a file server that keeps the master record of all accounts.

backup domain controllers (BDC) a file server that keeps a backup record of all accounts in case of failure of the primary domain controller.

Even when resources are assigned at the group level, each employee must still have an account. An ***account*** can be thought of as part of the network administrative security database. The user account contains all the security information describing a user. The account usually consists of the user logon name, description, password, and other normal network necessities, such as what group they belong to and what user rights they have been assigned. A user must have an account set up before they can access a client/server network system.

In this centralized, administrative structure, all the files pertaining to the users, groups, and computers connected to the system are contained in the file server. A network may be composed of many file servers sharing the burden of the network system. In the early Windows NT system, one file server was known as the primary domain controller, and the others were called the backup domain controllers. The ***primary domain controller (PDC)*** kept the master record of all user accounts, and the ***backup domain controllers (BDC)*** kept backup copies of the user accounts. The redundancy helped to protect against losing information about the users if the primary domain controller should fail or crash. In today's systems, all servers can be configured with equal responsibilities. They no longer require the notation of primary and backup.

The terms *primary domain controller* and *backup domain controller* have become legacy terms. The newer network operating systems technologies do not require a primary domain controller or a backup domain controller.

When a user account is part of a network administrative security database, the user of that account can do the following:

- ✔ Be authenticated through the domain server.
- ✔ Access resources anywhere in the network domain.
- ✔ Log on through any computer in the domain.
- ✔ Access resources anywhere in the domain.

A Quick Tour of Windows .NET Server 2003

We will now take a quick tour of a typical Windows .NET Server 2003, which Microsoft currently refers to as Windows Server 2003. The following paragraphs illustrate differences between a simple peer-to-peer network and a much more sophisticated network system. This will be a quick tour, not an in-depth study of Windows .NET Server 2003. It is intended to introduce you to some of the capabilities of a network operating system. A complete study of Windows .NET Server 2003 would require a complete textbook of its own. Remember, a network that uses Windows .NET Server 2003 is a client/server type of network. Let's begin by looking at some of the Windows .NET Server 2003 **Start** menu selections. See **Figure 17-16.**

The Windows .NET Server 2003 **Start** menu contains many different selections not found on a typical PC running Windows 98 or earlier. However, the Windows .NET Server 2003 version does look very similar to other Windows 2000 and Windows XP workstation versions and has many of the same features.

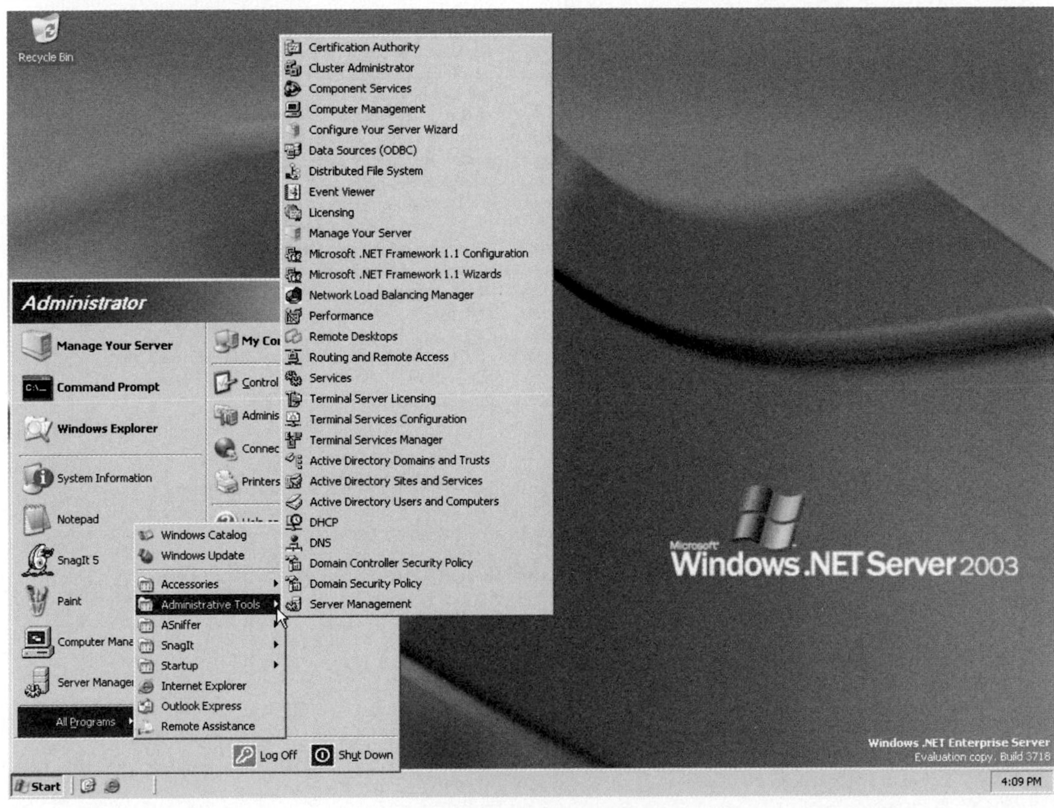

Figure 17-16. The Windows .NET Server 2003 **Start** menu is similar to previous server versions and workstations.

User Management

The Active Directory Users and Computers management utility is located at **Start | Administrative Programs | Active Directory Users and Computers**. It is used to enter or examine information about users, groups, domains, and other objects in the Active Directory structure. See **Figure 17-17.** The right-hand window contains a listing of the names and descriptions of the network's users and groups.

From the Active Directory Users and Computers window, you can add or delete users and groups. Microsoft is famous for providing software wizards to assist users with their tasks, and Microsoft Server 2003 is no exception. Microsoft provides several wizards, such as the New Object User shown in **Figure 17-18,** to assist the network administrator. This wizard helps add users to the network in a systematic way, ensuring that no important security features are inadvertently left out.

In addition to adding new user accounts, you can set up, modify, or view security levels for existing users. While the password system on a PC is quite simple, the password system for a network contains a number of added features. These features can be adjusted through the Default Domain Controller Security Settings **Password Policy** directory tree, **Figure 17-19.**

Security Features

There are many standard security features incorporated into Windows Net Server 2003. These include password, account lockout, audit, and time policies.

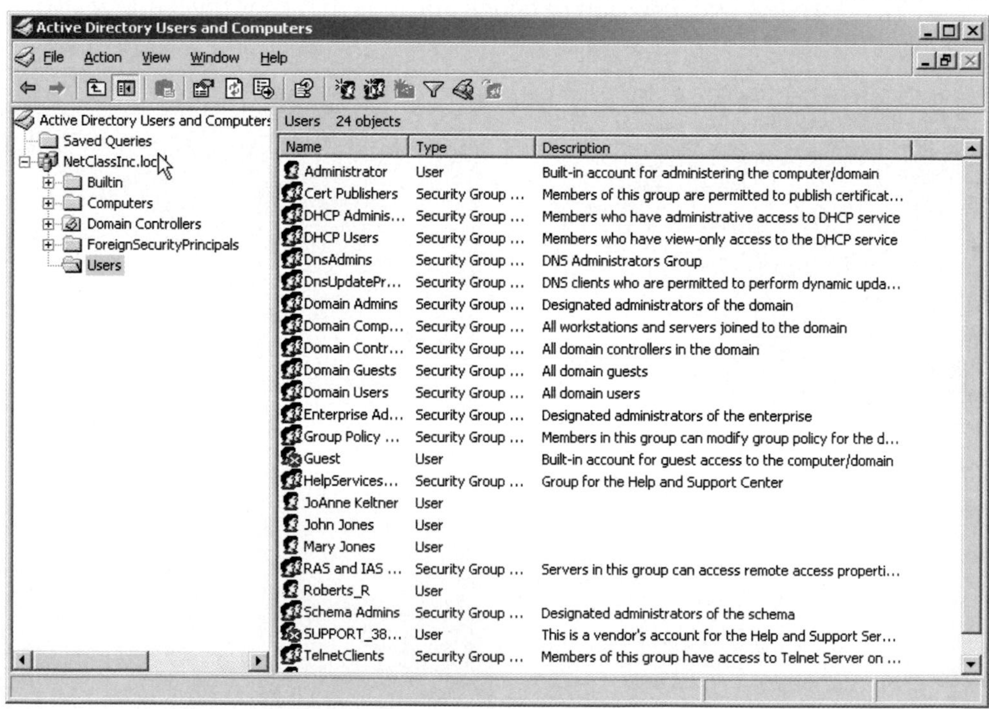

Figure 17-17. Information about groups and users can be examined or changed in the Active Directory Users and Computers utility.

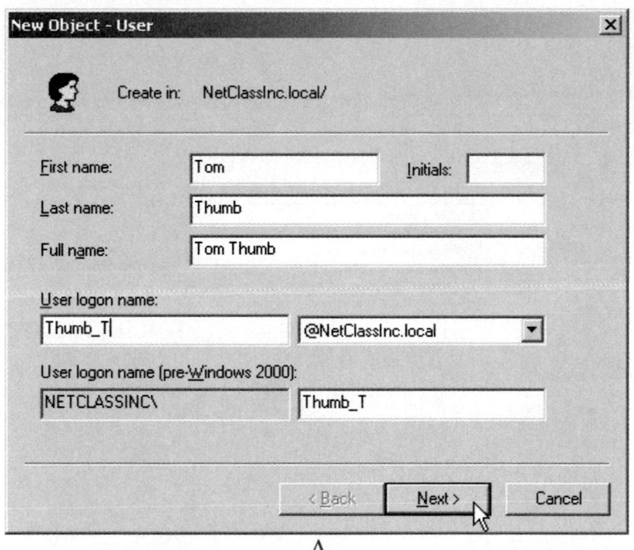

A

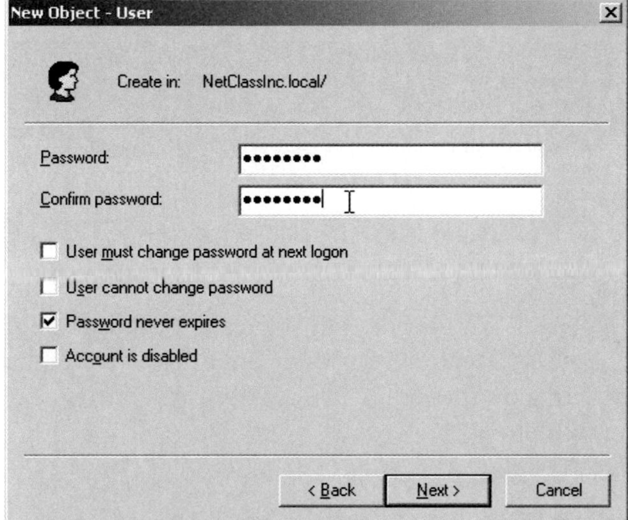

B

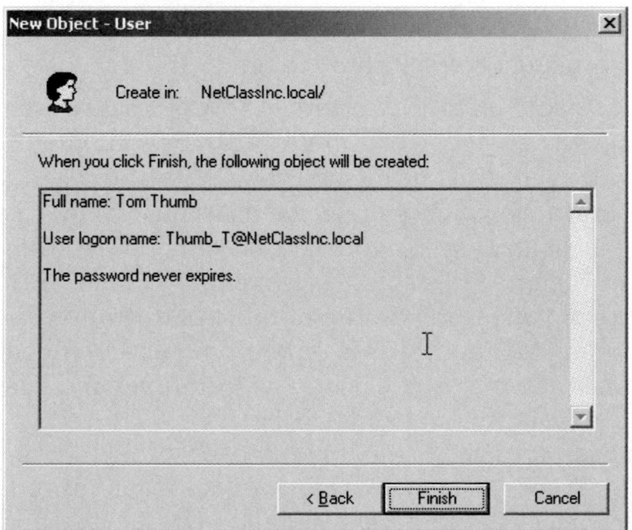

C

Figure 17-18. When adding users to the network system in Windows .NET Server 2003, the user is created using the New Object wizard. A—The first dialog box to appear during the creation of a new user in the network system. B—User password settings are entered in the second dialog box. C—The last dialog box allows you to verify the new user's settings.

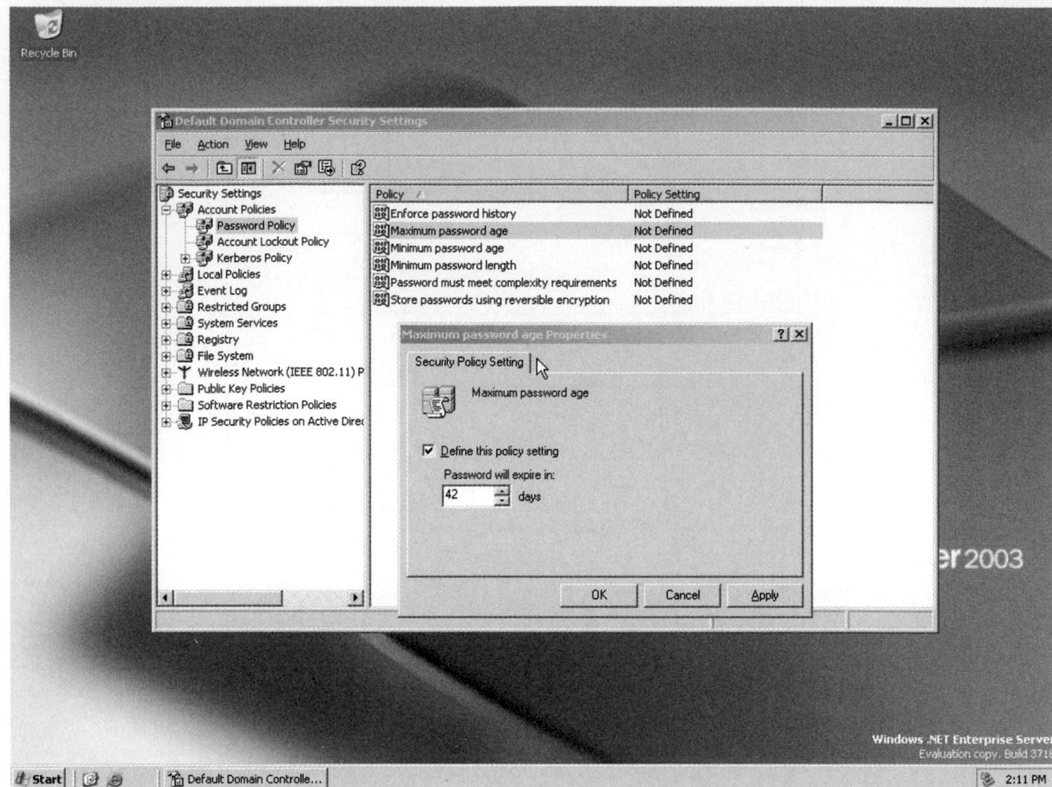

Figure 17-19. In Windows .NET Server 2003, password policies are set in the Default Domain Controller Security Settings utility. The network administrator can influence the degree of security by setting tough password restrictions.

Password policy

Look again at Figure 17-19. Notice that selecting **Password Policy** from the left window of the **Default Domain Controller Security Settings** utility reveals six password policy features on the right. The following security features are listed:

- ✔ Enforce password history.
- ✔ Maximum password age.
- ✔ Minimum password age.
- ✔ Minimum password length.
- ✔ Password must meet complexity requirements.
- ✔ Store passwords using reversible encryption.

The **Enforce password history** determines how old passwords are remembered by the system. Password controls can be set to require a user to use a different password every time he or she changes passwords. A value can be entered that determines how many times the user must change passwords before being allowed to repeat an old password. If this were not set, the user could simply flip-flop between two passwords, weakening system security.

Maximum password age is maximum number of days a password can be used before it must be changed. Passwords should be changed frequently but not so frequently it becomes a bother to the user. The recommended password age is 30 to 90 days, but the actual range is from 0 to 999 days.

The **Minimum password age** is the number of days old a password needs to be before it can be changed. **Minimum password age** is a required feature when using the password history policy. Values range from 0 to 998 and must be set at a value less than maximum. If there were no minimum password age and a value was set in **Enforce password history** that determined a user must change their password seven times before being allowed to reuse an old password, a user may change their password to meet the maximum password requirement and then immediately change their password to the original. For example, if a user's original password was "MyPassword_1," the user could create a series of passwords based on the last digit, such as "MyPassword_2," "MyPassword_3," and so on. When the password series reached the value set in **Enforce password history**, the user once more could use the original password, "MyPassword_1." Setting the minimum password age feature to as little as one day will prevent a user from cycling through all their old passwords at one sitting.

Minimum password length sets the minimum length a password can be. Enforcing passwords of six characters or more can increase security. The length of a password is directly related to the how secure the password is. The longer the password, the longer it takes to "crack." It can also, however, be more difficult to remember. The length of the password must provide a reasonable amount of security and not be too difficult or complex to use.

Microsoft and most security experts recommend a password of at least 6 characters. A longer password of at least 12 characters is not unreasonable. As the length of the password increases and if the complexity requirements of the next section are met, a lengthy password could be difficult to use. Just remember that the password must be at least 6 characters in length to be considered a minimally secure password.

The **Password must meet complexity requirements** prevents a user from choosing a password that is easily compromised by cracking tools such as dictionaries. Complex passwords require a minimum length and the use of an assortment of letters, numbers, and special symbols in the password. A complex password is extremely difficult to compromise.

Store passwords using reversible encryption hides the user password by encrypting the characters so they cannot be seen by unauthorized probes of the security database.

Account lockout policy

The Account Lockout Policy accessed through **Default Controller Security Settings | Account Policies** allows the system administrator to select a lockout duration for a set number of failed logon attempts. For example, if a person attempts three times to log on to a network system and fails, the system locks the user out for a period of time. The time can range from 0 to 99,999 minutes. The idea is to cause a reasonable delay between login failures to prevent a "dictionary attack" by an unauthorized person. Even a delay of a few minutes will ward off most attacks.

Audit policy

The Audit Policy allows a user's activities to be monitored and recorded in a log file that can be viewed by the system administrator. Audit Policy is accessed through **Default Controller Security Settings | Local Policies**. As you can see in **Figure 17-20,** selecting **Audit Policy** in the left-hand window reveals nine audit policy features on the right. The features allow the network administrator to specify certain events that are recorded in a log for later review.

Take special note of **Audit account logon events** located at the top of the right-hand window. The most common cause of a failed logon attempt is the use of a wrong password. Because the settings in the **Audit Policy** dialog box specify that failed logon attempts should be recorded, the attempted logon would appear in

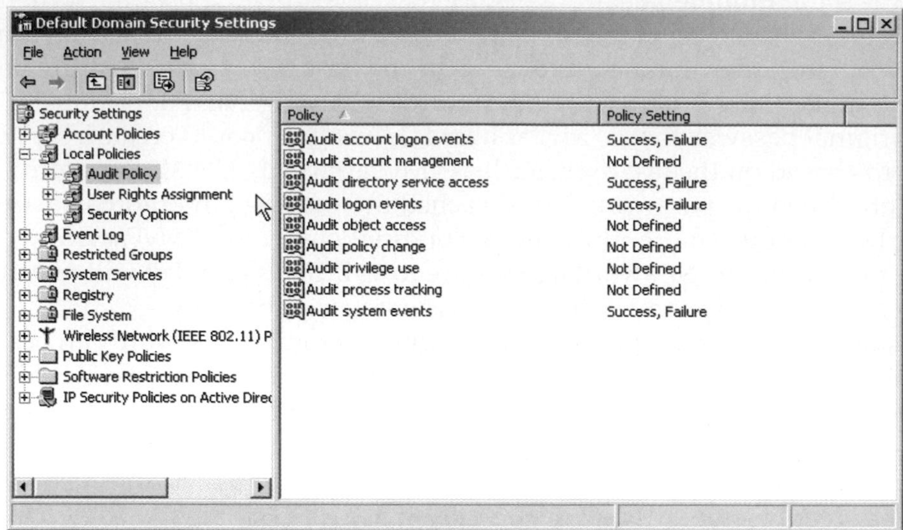

Figure 17-20. Audit policies can be set to record the success or failure of different events. This can be a valuable tool in detecting unauthorized attempts to enter the system.

the system's security log. See **Figure 17-21.** Each security event specified in the **Audit Policy** dialog box is recorded in the security log and can be viewed and saved. To see a more detailed description of the event, the administrator can simply double-click the individual event. This opens the **Event Detail** dialog box, which contains a more detailed description of the selected event. See **Figure 17-22.**

In the illustration, the event captured is the attempted logon of a user named Roberts_R. The logon was refused because of improper identification. Either the user was not an authorized user of NETCLASSINC or the user's password could not be validated. In either case, access to the server was denied. It was also recorded that the unsuccessful access attempt was made from NETCLASS-2003, at 2:33 PM on 9/18/2003. These details could be invaluable if an investigation is necessary.

Time policy

The time (days and hours) that a user may access the network can be easily controlled through an individual's **Properties** dialog box, **Figure 17-23.** In **Figure 17-24,** logon hours are configured so that the user can only access the network system from 6:00 AM to 8:00 PM Monday through Friday. At any other day or time, the user

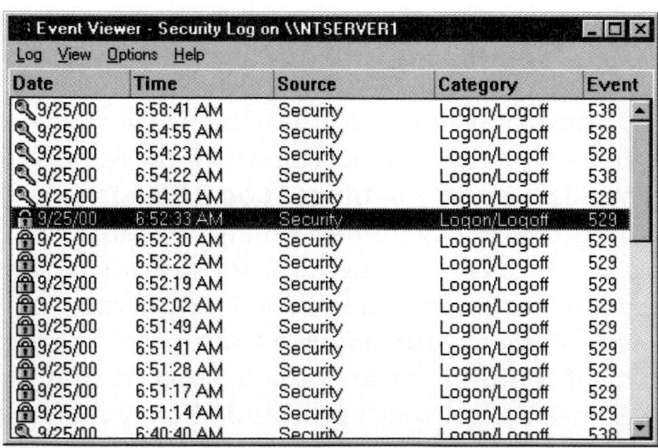

Figure 17-21. All events specified in the **Audit Policy** dialog box are recorded in the security log.

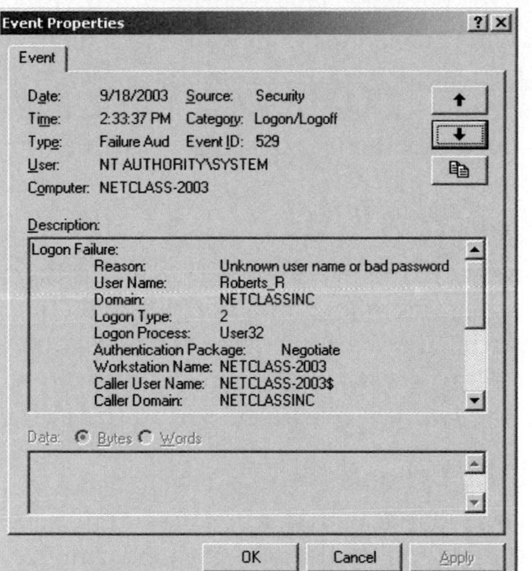

Figure 17-22.
The **Event Properties** dialog box offers greater detail about the warnings issued in Event Viewer.

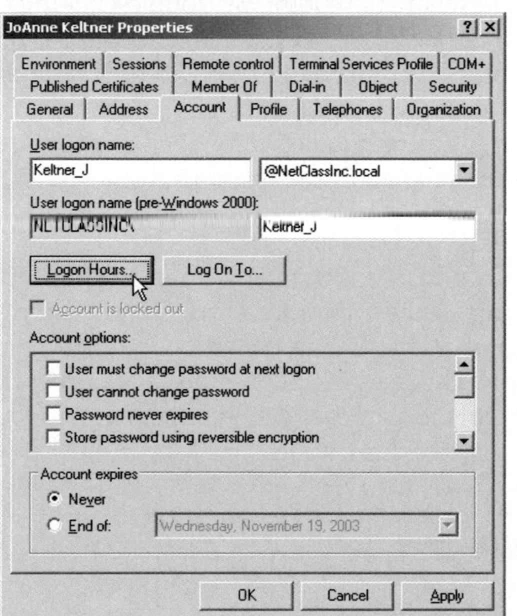

Figure 17-23.
Logon Hours is accessed through the user's **Properties** dialog box. The exact days of the week and the hours of the day a user may access the system can be restricted by the server.

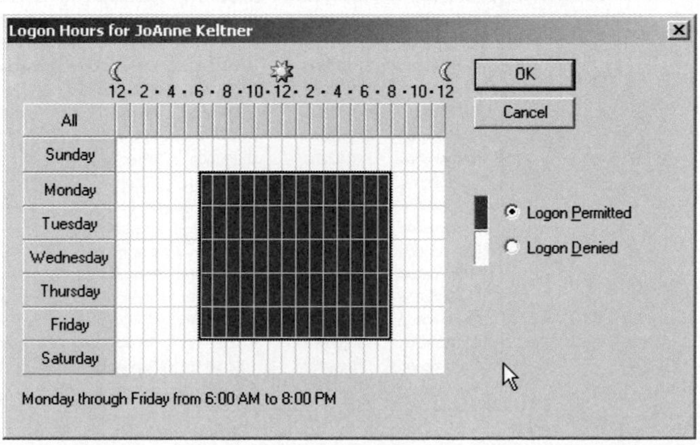

Figure 17-24.
Logon Hours dialog box. A user's access to the network can be limited to certain days of the week or hours.

will be denied access to the network. This security feature prevents someone from accessing the network with a stolen user name and password during a business's off hours. One option of this feature forces users off the system when their time expires. Another option allows them to continue (or finish) working in their current program or document but does not allow them to open any new files or services.

Monitoring the System

In addition to monitoring the users on the network, the system can monitor itself, record events in the system log, and alert the system administrator to potential problems. In addition, various other features are available in Windows .NET Server 2003 that allow the network administrator to observe and track system performance. The features are discussed in the following sections.

Event Viewer and the system log

The same Event Viewer window that is used to monitor user activity on the network can also be used to monitor the system's performance. This is accomplished by loading the system log rather than the security log. In **Figure 17-25,** the Event Viewer window has issued a warning to the administrator. A warning is indicated by the yellow circle and exclamation point. By double-clicking the warning, the administrator can open the **Event Properties** dialog box. This dialog box explains the warning in greater detail. See **Figure 17-26.** Note in the **Description** window, there is a notification that a computer was automatically configured with the IP address 169.254.0.22. As you can see, very detailed information can be captured by the system events monitor, which can help analyze system problems.

Performance Monitor

The administrator can also use the Performance Monitor utility to monitor the performance of some of the computer system components. In **Figure 17-27,** the Performance Monitor is displaying the CPU activity, memory pages, and hard disk on the same graph. The usage is expressed as a percentage from 0 to 100. The administrator can use this tool to diagnose various network problems such as network congestion or failing hardware.

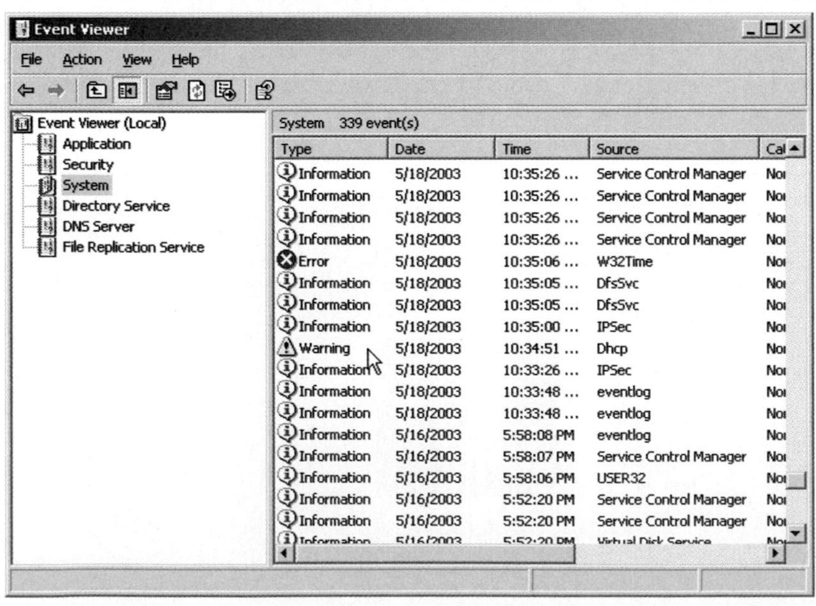

Figure 17-25.
The Event Viewer can be used to monitor system performance. Warnings are indicated by an exclamation point inside a yellow triangle.

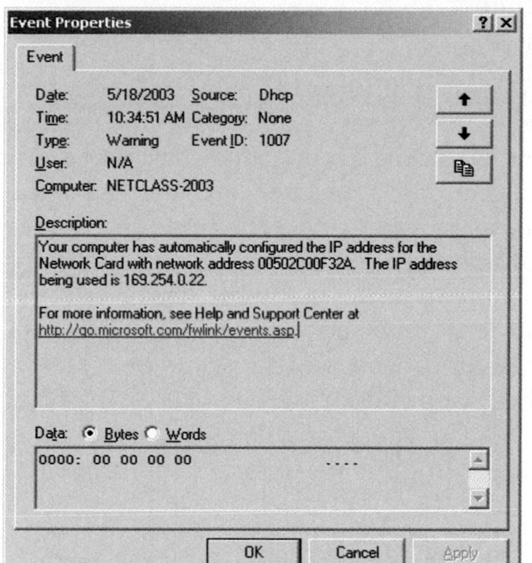

Figure 17-26. Details of a system event warning. Take a close look at the system event indicated in the screen capture. What information does it provide?

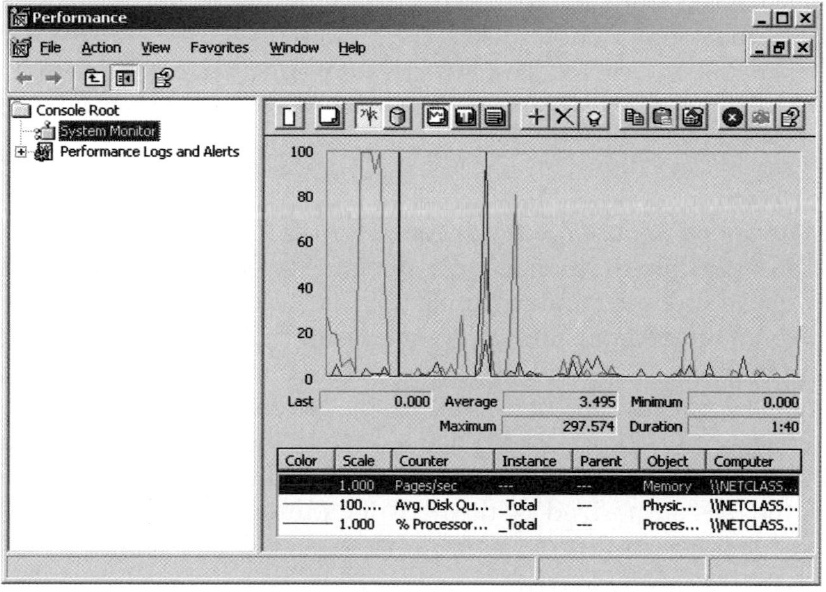

Figure 17-27. The Performance Monitor can display graphs of the system's use of certain resources.

Default Groups

Server operating systems typically have a set of default users and groups. These are the most common users and groups required in most server systems. Default users and groups save time when setting up a server.

Some of the most common users are as follows:

- ✔ Administrator
- ✔ User
- ✔ Guest

Some of the most common groups are as follows:

- ✔ Print Operators
- ✔ Backup Operators

- ✔ DHCP Administrators
- ✔ Domain Administrators

The exact title of the user or group account will vary according to the operating system used. Each group can have specific permissions set, which dictate what the members of the group can do, access, or modify. Users are simply added to each group and the users is restricted to the permissions of the group. Additional users and groups can be added to meet the needs of the environment. For example, in a school setting, a group named Teachers and another named Students can be set up on the server. A user named Teacher and a user named Student can be added to the user list. All students can log on using the user name Student. The student would be restricted according to the permissions set in the group called Students. The same scenario can be applied to the teachers. Each teacher can log on using the user name Teacher. The teacher would be restricted according the permissions set in the group named Teachers.

Rights, Properties, Profiles

A network security system maintains a database of security information on all network users. The exact terminology used to describe the individual features varies somewhat according to the network operating system software being used. The database stores information such as the group(s) the user belongs to and their access rights to files and drives. The administrator can alter, copy, delete, or simply read the contents of a profile. There are many aspects to the individual user profile.

Restrictions

In the **Advanced Security Settings for Users** dialog box, **Figure 17-28,** you can see part of the default restrictions assigned to users. Restrictions can be added or removed by selecting or deselecting each item in the list. Remove Run Command from Start Menu, Hide Network Neighborhood, and Hide Drives in My Computer are just a few of the restrictions used to limit an individual user on a Windows .NET Server 2003 network. As you can see, the network administrator can place strong limits on a user to ensure a secure network environment. The administrator can limit a user's access so that they may only run the programs and access the files authorized by the network administrator.

Rights and Permissions

rights
system control abilities that are normally reserved for the system administrator.

The **Users Properties** dialog box can give users certain abilities, or ***rights***, that are normally reserved for the system administrator, such as the ability to shut down the system or manage auditing and the security log. See **Figure 17-29.** As you can see, users can be given rights as powerful as those of the administrator, or they can have all the typical user rights taken away. There is a wide range of control over users and groups.

The process of logging on to the network as part of an assigned group either gives the user the right to access the share or not. The type of access can be limited for a share, such as read-only, full access, execute, write, delete, or no access. These access restrictions are called permissions. ***Permissions*** are the right to perform certain functions. See **Figure 17-30** for a listing of some typical additional permissions that can be assigned to users and/or groups in the Windows Net Server 2003 environment.

permissions
the right to perform certain functions.

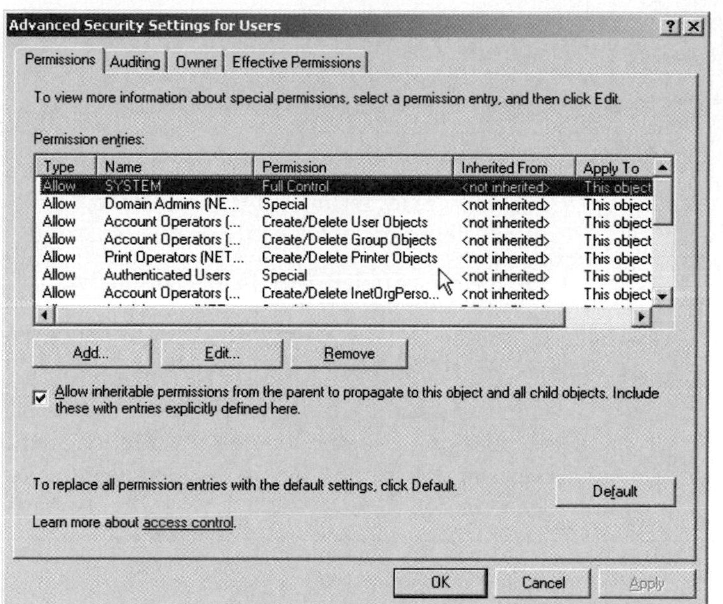

Figure 17-28.
The **Advanced Security Settings for Users** dialog box controls user permission settings. The permission settings control what the user may do based on group membership.

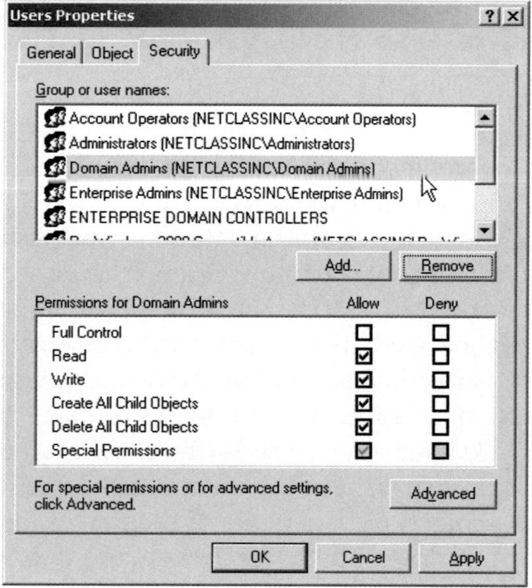

Figure 17-29.
User rights are set in the **User Properties** dialog box. Some of the permissions that can be assigned are Full Control, Read, and Write.

RAID Systems

Fault tolerance is a system's ability to recover after some sort of disaster. The hard drive could fail, the operating system could crash, a user could accidentally erase some files, and many more things could happen. Networks have the ability to recover from these types of disasters. There are many fault tolerance methods available. The two most common methods of fault tolerance are the use of RAID and the use of tape backup. In this section, we will explore common RAID configurations used with Microsoft servers.

fault tolerance
a system's ability to recover after some sort of disaster.

RAID is the acronym for Redundant Array of Inexpensive or Independent Disks. The translation of the acronym varies between the use of the word inexpensive and independent. The exact translation is not important, but the

Figure 17-30.
Typical permissions that can be assigned to users or groups.

Assigned permission	Description
Read	User can execute, read, copy, or print a file but cannot delete, change files, or add to the directory.
Execute	User may run files in shared directory.
Write	User may read, write, create, and change a file in a directory but cannot execute or delete the file.
Delete	The user may delete files from a directory.
Full Access	The user can do anything: read, write, delete, change, and execute files.
No Access	The user cannot access the file. If the user has two permissions assigned, one as an individual and one as a member of a group, the No Access setting takes precedence!

RAID
a system of several hard drive units arranged in such a way as to ensure recovery after a system disaster or to ensure data integrity during normal operation.

concept behind RAID technology is. A ***RAID*** is a system of several hard drive units arranged in such a way as to ensure recovery after a system disaster or to ensure data integrity during normal operation. There are three forms of RAID associated with Microsoft servers: Levels 0, 1, and 5. See **Figure 17-31.**

Level 0

Level 0 is called *striped without parity.* A striped set is two or more areas across two or more disks to which data is written or from which data is read. The main purpose of a striped set is to speed up the data read and write process. The data is recorded more quickly when it is being written simultaneously to multiple disks. When data is recorded in a striped set, the data is equally divided, and equal portions of the data are written to each hard disk drive.

A striped set spreads the data across two drives or volumes. Data is written alternately to each drive or volume in 64 kB blocks of data. When two separate hard drive controllers are used, one for each drive, the read and write times are faster than those of a single drive. The disadvantage to this RAID arrangement is that there is no data protection. When one of the drives fail, all data on that drive is lost. To prevent the loss of data, the arrangement for data storage must use parity. Parity, as you recall, is a technique used to ensure data is correct. See Figure 17-31A.

Level 1

The RAID level 1, or disk mirroring, configuration requires two hard drives. One drive keeps an exact copy of all data on the opposite drive. This way if one drive fails, all its data can be retrieved from its duplicate. See Figure 17-31B.

Figure 17-31.
The three forms of RAID used on a Microsoft server. A—RAID level 0 offers no data protection. It is used to speed up the read/write process. Data is spread across more than one volume in 64 kB blocks. B—RAID level 1 uses at least two volumes to store an exact duplicate of data. If one drive fails, the other still contains an exact copy of the data. C—RAID 5 is a striped set with parity. Parity is used to reconstruct data lost on any of the volumes.

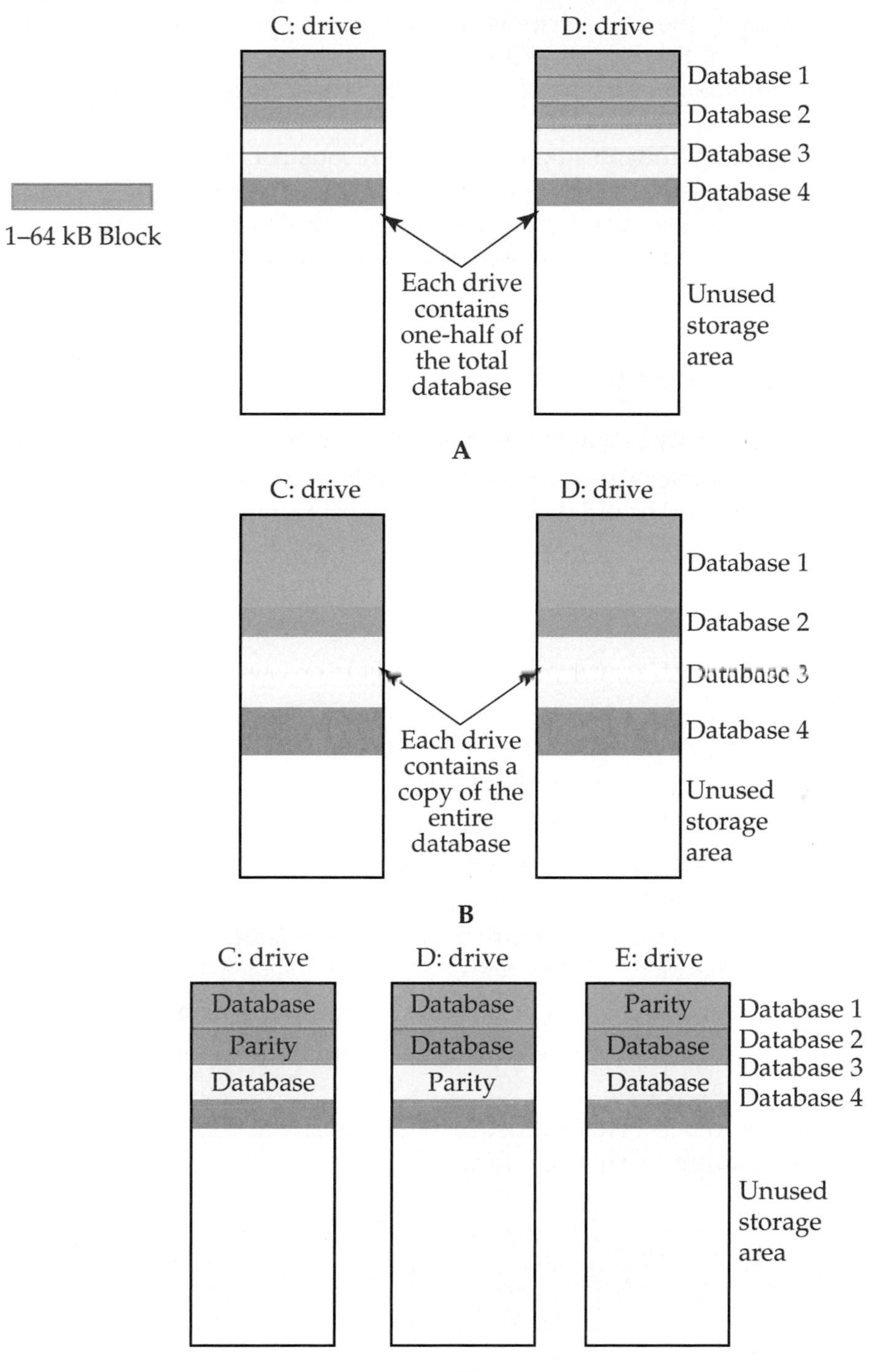

Level 5

The RAID level 5 configuration can use from three to thirty-two drives of equal partition size to form what is called *a stripe set with parity*. Parity is used to reconstruct data lost on either of the two drives that are used to store data. For example, data is duplicated on two volumes and the third is used to store the parity of the two. Parity is staggered across all drives when a minimum of three are used. See Figure 17-31C.

Remember from previous units, parity is the sum total of two bytes of data added together. The two bytes will be either odd or even. By reversing the operation, the missing data can be reconstructed using the value stored in the parity section. It is important to remember that none of the techniques discussed are infallible. Anything can happen to destroy data. Regular backups are the only way to ensure some degree of fault tolerance.

Summary

- ✔ Security is one of the main features of a network system.
- ✔ Share-level security is the default security system used on Windows-based networks, and requires a password to access a share.
- ✔ User-level security identifies who may have access to a shared resource but does not require a password for accessing the share.
- ✔ A peer-to-peer network usually uses share-level security.
- ✔ A client/server network usually uses user-level security.
- ✔ Administrative functions in a peer-to-peer network are not highly organized and are best described as decentralized.
- ✔ A centralized administration network system has a single and central network authority that controls all aspects of the network system.
- ✔ Centralized networks are organized administratively as domains, groups, and users.
- ✔ A domain is the entire network organization of all groups and users on the network.
- ✔ Users can be assigned rights and properties on a network system.
- ✔ Groups are workers who share common responsibilities and can be thought of as a set.
- ✔ RAID is a way to ensure data integrity and fault tolerance through the use of multiple drive volumes.

Review Questions

Answer the following questions on a separate sheet of paper. Please do not write in this book.

1. Who controls a peer-to-peer network?
2. Who controls the access to shares on a peer-to-peer network?
3. What is the default setting of shares when Windows 95, 98, or Me is first set up?
4. Which type of share security is usually found on a peer-to-peer network?
5. Which type of share security is usually found on a client/server network?
6. What are the responsibilities of a network administrator?
7. What are shares?
8. What are the two levels of security on a typical Windows peer-to-peer network?
9. What is the difference in the two levels of security?
10. What is a user account?
11. What is a domain?
12. What is a group?
13. What is a permission?
14. What are the three forms of RAID associated with Microsoft servers?

Sample A+ Exam Questions

Answer the following questions on a separate sheet of paper. Please do not write in this book.

1. Which of the following is the best password to use to prevent possible compromise or intrusion?
   a. secret
   b. Big$tar_5
   c. President Roosevelt
   d. Password
2. Which is *not* a typical Windows XP share permission?
   a. Read
   b. Full control
   c. Partial
   d. Change
3. What does a user need to access a network system? (Select all that apply.)
   a. User name
   b. Password
   c. Group membership
   d. A security clearance

4. Who determines a user's rights on a client/server network?
    a. Each computer user determines the user rights for their workstation.
    b. Users set their own individual rights based on their total system knowledge.
    c. The network administrator sets individual rights on the network system.
    d. All users automatically have full rights to use the entire network when they are issued an account on the network.
5. In a Windows .NET Server 2003 network, user accounts are set up in _____.
    a. Active Directory Users and Computers
    b. Performance Monitor
    c. Event Viewer
    d. User Share Setup
6. In a Windows Net Server 2003 network system, the user password is changed _____.
    a. in the **Active Directory Users and Computers** dialog box
    b. in the **Account Policy** dialog box
    c. at the user's workstation under the **Change Password** icon in **Control Panel**
    d. A user password can never be changed once it is issued.
7. Which program can be used to monitor user activity on a computer system?
    a. Event Viewer
    b. Net Monitor
    c. Performance Monitor
    d. Net Movement
8. Which program would you select to check the total amount of activity through the CPU?
    a. Net Monitor
    b. Performance Monitor
    c. CPU Monitor
    d. CPU Pole Watch
9. When using Windows .NET Server 2003, a collection of users who have similar tasks and are consequently assigned the same user rights are generally referred to as a _____.
    a. group
    b. covey
    c. pod
    d. corporate entity
10. In a centralized network, an entire business location is usually referred to as a _____.
    a. corporate entity
    b. select pod
    c. domain
    d. group

Suggested Laboratory Activities

Do not attempt any suggested laboratory activities without your instructor's permission. Certain activities can render the PC operating system inoperable.

1. Set up a client/server network. Choose one PC to be the server. All other PCs must log on through the server to gain access to the network. There is a variety of client/server software available in beta versions as well as free Linux versions. Most Linux systems that use X Windows will be remarkably similar to the Windows operating system.
2. Use an existing network to do the following:
   a. Add a new user to the network.
   b. Restrict the time of day a particular user can access the network.
   c. Set a time limit, by days, during which a user may use the network.
   d. Display a list of users and groups on the network system.
   e. Change an existing user's password.
   f. Set up a minimum password length.

Interesting Web Sites for More Information

www.dell.com
www.ibm.com
www.microsoft.com/servers/default.mspx
www.novell.com

Chapter 17
Laboratory Activity
Creating a Network Share in Windows XP

After completing this laboratory activity, you will be able to:

- ✔ Create a share on a peer-to-peer network.
- ✔ Identify the types of security associated with a peer-to-peer network.
- ✔ Enable and disable Simple File Sharing.
- ✔ Explain the affects of Simple File Sharing on the share permissions.

Introduction

Sharing files and hardware is the main purpose of a network. In this lab activity, you will set up a network share. You will share a folder with another person in your lab. You will set up a share for a variety of items such as the hard disk drive, CD/DVD drive, and a folder. You will also modify share permissions.

There are two main types of share security commonly used in network systems: share-level and user-level. Share-level security is commonly associated with peer-to-peer networks, while user-level security is associated with centrally administered networks that typically use a centralized network server. A user-level share account is configured by the domain network administrator. A share-level account is administrated by the owner/creator of the share on the local computer.

To see what folders are shared on your computer, you can use the Computer Management console. To open **Computer Management**, right-click **My Computer**, and then select **Manage** from the shortcut menu.

In this lab activity, you will be creating shared folders, files, and devices. Please be sure you return the system to its original configuration before ending this lab activity. This is especially true if other students use the assigned workstation.

Note:
This is a two-workstation lab activity.

Equipment and Materials

- ✔ Two PCs each running Windows XP and configured as a peer-to-peer network.

Note:
The partition should be formatted as NTFS not FAT32 for the lab activity to work properly.

Procedure

1. _______ Report to your assigned workstation(s) and power on the PC(s).
2. _______ Open **Windows Explorer** and create a folder named ShareTestFolder.
3. _______ Right-click ShareTestFolder and then select **Sharing and Security** from the shortcut menu. The **Properties** dialog box for that folder will display and will be open to the **Sharing** page like the following:

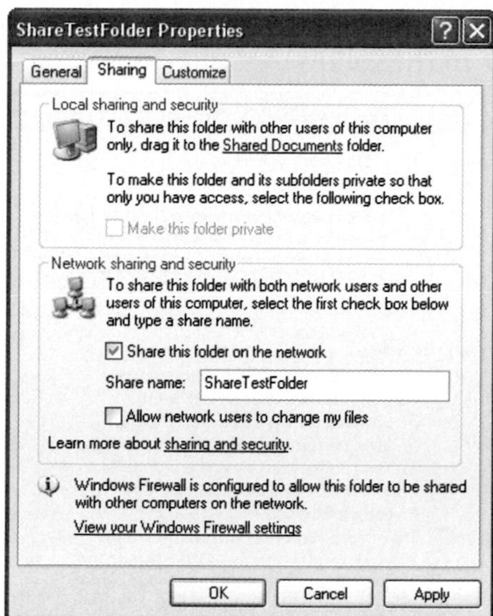

4. _______ Enable the **Share this folder on the network** option, which is located in the **Network sharing and security** section. The default name for the share will be the name already assigned to the folder. Click **Apply**. The folder is now configured as a share on the local network.
5. _______ Open the **Computer Management** console to view all shares available on the workstation. To open **Computer Management**, right-click **My Computer**, and then select **Manage** from the shortcut menu. In the left-hand pane, **click Shared Folders** and then click **Shares**. The shares on the computer will appear, similar to those in the following screen capture.

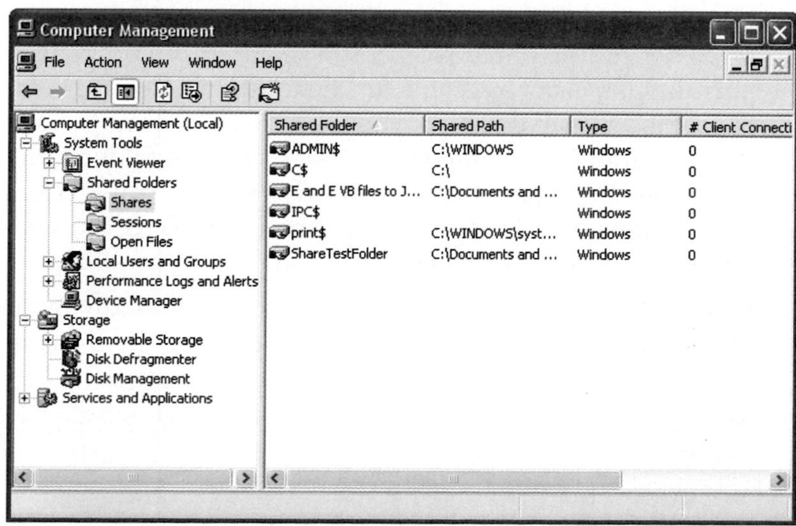

Notice that all administrative shares have a dollar sign in the folder name. User shares do not have the dollar sign. You should see the folder called ShareTestFolder at the bottom of the list. If not, call your instructor for assistance.

6. ________ Close the **Computer Management** console.

7. ________ To enable the Simple File Sharing feature, open **My Documents**, select **Tools** from the menu, and then select **Folder Options**. The **Folder Options** dialog box will display. Select the **View** tab. A dialog box similar to the following will display.

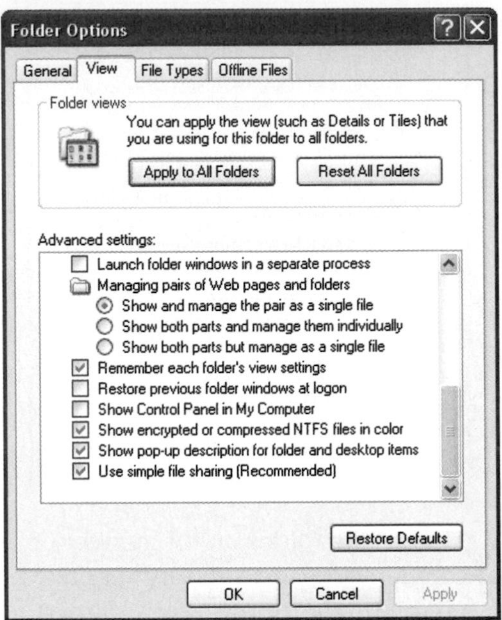

Scroll down the list until you see the **Use simple file sharing (Recommended)** option. If you do not find this option, call your instructor for assistance.

8. ________ You will now experiment with the effects of the Simple File Sharing feature on the shared folder you created earlier. Take time now to enable and disable Simple File Sharing. Compare the effects that enabling and disabling Simple File Sharing has on folder permissions. You should see that the complete set of permissions is not available for the folder when Simple File Sharing is enabled. When disabled, you should see options to various configurations of detailed permissions for the folder. Open the **Computer Management** console and see if you can access the share permissions when simple file sharing is enabled. You will be asked about viewing the permissions in the review questions.

9. ________ Before moving on, disable the Simple File Sharing feature.

10. ________ Now, you will create a shared CD/DVD drive. To create a shared CD/DVD drive in Windows XP, simply right-click the drive while in Windows Explorer. You will see a dialog box similar to the following.

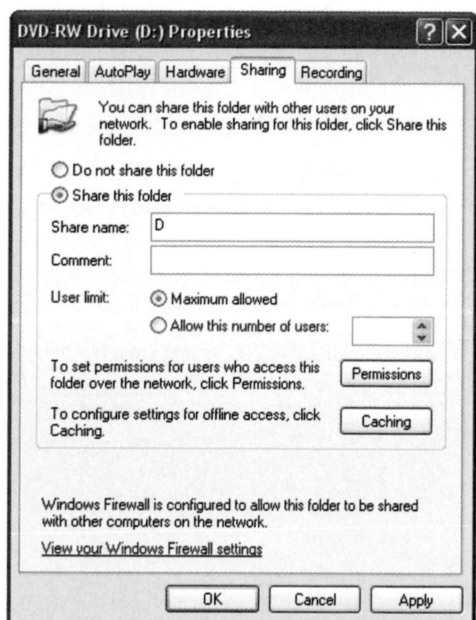

Select the **Share this folder** option. The share always has a default name of the existing drive. You can rename the drive or folder when shared. Also, you can control the number of users who can access the share. The maximum number of users is 10 by default. Go ahead and create the shared CD or DVD drive by clicking the **Apply** button.

11. ______ After sharing the CD/DVD drive, open **Windows Explorer** and view the appearance of the drive. Test the access of the drive from the other computer. If you cannot access the shared drive from the other computer, call your instructor for assistance.

12. ______ Now, reverse the share on the CD/DVD by repeating the previous steps. Start by right-clicking the shared CD/DVD drive, and then unselecting the **Do not share this folder** option.

13. ______ Repeat the file sharing exercise for folders and devices until you are sure you can create and disable a share without the assistance of this lab activity sheet.

14. ______ Now, create a shared folder and place a file, such as a short text document, inside the shared folder. You can use Microsoft Word or Notepad to create the text document.

15. ______ Right-click the folder and look at the available properties and permissions for the folder. The permissions are located under the **Security** tab in the **Properties** dialog box. Look at the following screen captures.

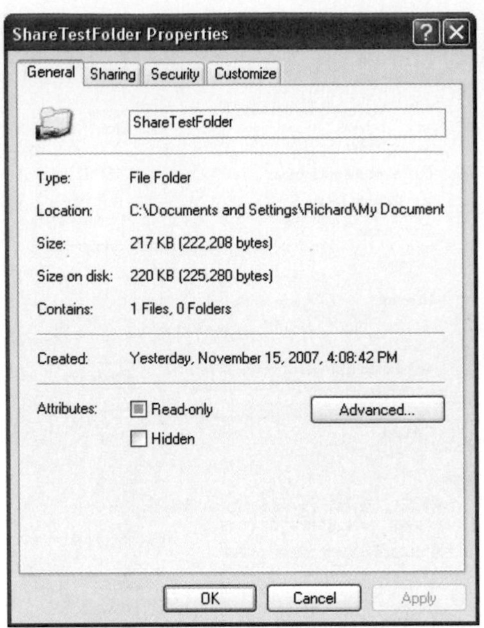

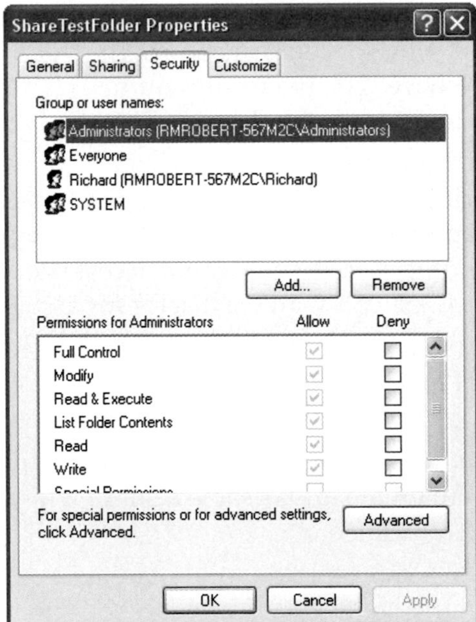

Notice that the folder's **Properties** dialog box provides access to set up a share for the folder and to security features, such as who can access the folder and what permissions are configured for that particular user.

The folder **Security** tab exposes various permissions available for the folder. You can also add or delete users or groups to keep them from accessing the share.

16. _______ Now, right-click the document file inside the folder and view the permissions available to be used with the file. The permissions are located under the **Security** tab.
17. _______ Take a few minutes to repeat the above steps and familiarize yourself with the many different permissions.
18. _______ Be sure to return all shares and folder permissions to their previous condition before completing the lab activity review questions.

Review Questions

Answer the following questions on a separate sheet of paper. Please do not write in this book.

1. How do you create a shared folder in Windows XP?
2. What effect does Simple File Sharing have on folder permissions?
3. How is a folder identified as a share in Windows XP?
4. How do you create a shared DVD or CD drive?
5. What are the two types of share security?
6. A user creates a shared folder on their local computer to be shared with other people in the local peer-to-peer network. What type of share security are they using?
7. Who is responsible for creating and administrating user-level security for shares?
8. How do you access the Computer Management console to view the shares available on a computer?
9. You use Computer Management console to view the shares on a local computer; however, you cannot view a shared folder's permissions. What is *most likely* the problem?

Computers installed in classrooms and school labs have created a need for network administrators in the school system.

WAN

After studying this chapter, you will be able to:

- ✔ Explain the difference between a LAN and a WAN.
- ✔ Explain how IP addresses are used.
- ✔ Explain DNS, WINS, and DHCP services.
- ✔ Explain the use of common diagnostic utilities associated with networks.
- ✔ Describe the physical structure and evolution of the Internet.
- ✔ Identify equipment associated with a WAN.
- ✔ Describe the function of several common network troubleshooting software commands.
- ✔ Explain how to set up an e-mail account.
- ✔ Describe the common features associated with e-mail.

A+ Exam—Key Points

A+

The A+ Certification exams require knowledge of the basic operation of network systems. As a technician, you must know where your responsibility for the repair of a PC ends and where the responsibility of the network administrator begins.

Be sure you are able to distinguish between DNS, WINS, and DHCP services. You may also be asked to identify an example of an IP address and a subnet mask.

Key Words and Terms

The following words and terms will become important pieces of your computer vocabulary. Be sure you can define them.

- Archie
- Automatic Private IP Address (APIPA)
- bridge
- brouter
- Class A network
- Class B network
- Class C network
- Domain Name Service (DNS)
- dynamic addressing
- Dynamic Host Configuration Protocol (DHCP)
- File Transfer Protocol (FTP)
- firewall
- gateway
- Gopher
- host
- Hypertext Markup Language (HTML)
- Hypertext Transfer Protocol (HTTP)
- Internet
- InterNIC
- IP address
- IP switch
- Multipurpose Internet Mail Extensions (MIME)
- octet
- Packet Internet Groper (PING)
- proxy server
- registrar
- repeater
- router
- subnet mask
- switch
- Telnet
- time to live (TTL)
- tracert
- Uniform Resource Locators (URLs)
- Windows Internet Naming Service (WINS)

Wide area networks (WANs) are network systems that cover a wide geographical area. Wide area networks require additional networking equipment and different protocols than local area networks (LANs). WANs use routers, bridges, hubs, brouters, and more. The types of equipment, protocols, and techniques required by a WAN are examined in this chapter. This will provide you with an overview of how data is delivered over the Internet, the world's largest WAN. Some of the subjects in this section are vast enough to fill textbooks of their own. The purpose of this chapter is to provide you with a basic understanding of how a WAN operates and to explain some of the technical terminology associated with wide area networks, including the Internet.

When you think about wide area networks, you must think globally. Many corporations include thousands of computers in their networked system. These systems often stretch across countries or even continents. The networks used by organizations like the United States Postal Service, the combined armed forces, an international bank, and a state school system, are all examples of wide area networks. Many of these networks are connected to the Internet.

You may wonder how the Internet or WAN handles the volume of data packets generated by all those users. It may seem like all the traffic would slow the Internet down to a snail's pace, since there are packets of information being sent everywhere.

In this chapter, the basic concepts of wide area network operation are introduced along with the technologies that make WANs possible. You will also learn how e-mail gets to its destination and how your Web browser can locate a particular Web page in the Internet's endless tangle of cables, routers, and computers. Remember, many of the topics discussed in this chapter could fill textbooks of their own. This is only an introduction.

TCP/IP Addressing

The TCP/IP protocol is the secret to communicating over the Internet and over other WANs. The TCP/IP protocol was designed for the Internet and is the dominant protocol for data exchange on a typical LAN, MAN, or WAN. TCP/IP addressing is a method of identification used to identify every node or host on a network. The terms ***host*** and ***node*** are used interchangeably to identify individual PCs, printers, and network equipment that may require an address. *TCP/IP addressing* and *IP addressing* are also interchangeable terms.

host
a computer or other piece of equipment connected to a TCP/IP network that requires an address; used interchangeably with the term *node*.

InterNIC

In a previous chapter, we discussed how data packets are delivered to the correct computer through various routes. The key to the process is the protocol. The Internet uses TCP/IP protocol to route data packets all over the world. Every network has a unique ***IP address*** assigned to it. IP addresses are regulated and assigned through the organization known as ***InterNIC.***

IP address
identifying address used for a PC or other equipment on a TCP/IP network.

InterNIC operates under the direction of the Department of Commerce. It is responsible for regulating the Internet, overseeing the issue of domain names, and assigning IP addresses to them. A user does not directly contact InterNIC for an IP address or domain name. The user places an application through a private sector company, called a ***registrar,*** which is regulated by InterNIC (www.internic.org). InterNIC allocates IP addresses much like the way the government issues telephone area codes to long distance carriers and telephone companies. IP addresses must be similarly regulated or there would be chaos in the computer world.

InterNIC
a branch of the United States government under the direction of the Department of Commerce. It is responsible for regulating the Internet, overseeing the issue of domain names, and assigning IP addresses to them.

The Internet Corporation for Assigned Names and Numbers (ICANN), under the supervision of the Department of Commerce, has assumed the name and responsibilities of InterNIC.

registrar
private sector company, regulated by InterNIC, to whom users apply for an IP address or domain name.

IP Addresses

An Internet Protocol (IP) address is assigned to nodes on a network for identification purpose. The term *host* or *node* represents network equipment that require an IP address for communication. Examples of hosts are computers, servers, network printers, routers, and gateways. The IP address was designed originally for Internet access and communications between Internet connected devices. Networks did not always access the Internet. Originally, very few computers accessed the Internet and IP addresses were not required. Instead, local area networks used the MAC address.

Today, a computer that does not access the Internet is rare. By default, all computers are automatically configured to use an IP address. Local area networks use the IP address and the MAC address for identification purposes.

There are two versions of IP address: Internet Protocol version 4 (IPv4) and Internet Protocol version 6 (IPv6). The IPv4 was introduced in 1981 and has been used to identify computers in large networks such as a WAN. With the rapid expansion of the Internet in the 1990s, there were too many computers and network devices requiring an IP address. Therefore, the IPv6 address standard was introduced to provide a larger pool of IP addresses to accommodate the increasing number of computers. An IPv5 was under development, but it was abandoned and never accepted as an alternative to IPv4.

octet
an eight-bit series of numbers.

IPv4 consists of four sets of decimal numbers. Each set, referred to as an ***octet,*** contains a set of decimal numbers in the range of 0 to 255. An example of an IP address is 183.24.202.17. An IPv6 address consists of eight groups of hexadecimal numbers. Each set is in the range of 0 to FFFF. An example of an IPv6 address is ef12:c21d:bc23:acf4:578:34da:f0b2:dc56. The IPv4 format is X.X.X.X where the *X* represents decimal numbers in the range of 0 to 255. The IPv6 format is X:X:X:X:X:X:X:X where the *X* represents hexadecimal numbers in the range from 0000 to FFFF. Look at **Figure 18-1** to see both IPv4 and IPv6 address assigned to the same network adapter in Windows Vista.

Notice that each set of IP address decimal numbers in the IPv4 address is separated by a period. In the IPv6 address, each set of hexadecimal numbers is separated by a colon. A double colon is used in an IPv6 address as an abbreviated form of an all zeros entry in an address. For example, the IPv6 address Fe12:0:0:0;ac32:0:0:ffe4 can be written as fe12::ac32::ffe4. Also notice that each network card has an assigned MAC address as well as an IPv4 and IPv6 address.

Windows Vista is the first operating system to assign to a computer both the IPv4 and IPv6 address by default. Earlier operating systems used only the IPv4 address with the MAC address. Windows XP was the first operating system that would allow you to assign an IPv6 address to a network adapter.

IPv4 provides a total of 4,294,967,296 possible addresses, while IPv6 provides a total of 340,282,366,920,938,463,374, 607,431,768,211,456 possible IP addresses.

For more information about IPv6, visit the Microsoft Web site, www.microsoft.com/technet/network/ipv6/ipv6faq.mspx. This site has a frequently asked questions (FAQ) section for IPv6. The following Microsoft Web site is completely dedicated to IPv6: http://technet.microsoft.com/en-us/network/bb530961.aspx.

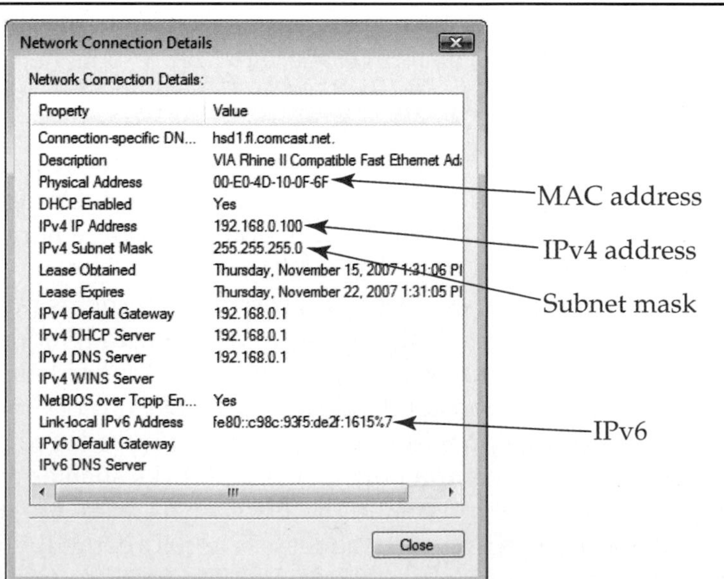

Figure 18-1.
By default, Windows Vista assigns both the IPv4 and IPv6 addresses to a network card.

Network Class

For the purpose of assigning IP addresses, networks are divided into three classifications: Class A, Class B, and Class C. Large networks are assigned a Class A classification. A ***Class A network*** can support up to 16 million hosts on each of 127 networks. Medium-sized networks are assigned Class B status. A ***Class B network*** supports up to 65,000 hosts on each of 16,000 networks. Small networks are assigned a Class C classification. A ***Class C network*** supports 254 hosts on each of 2,000,000 networks. Networks are assigned an IP address based on their network classification. Look at **Figure 18-2.**

In the table, you can see that the class of the network determines the numeric value of the first octet in its IP address. The range for a Class A network is from 1 to 127; the range for a Class B network is from 128 to 191; and the range for a Class C network is from 192 to 223. IP addresses for Class A networks use only the first octet as the network address. The remaining three octets define hosts on the network. The first two octets of a Class B network's IP address identify the network. The remaining two octets identify hosts on the network. A Class C network uses the first three octets to identify the network and the last octet to identify the individual hosts. A typical Class C network might have a TCP/IP address of 201.100.100.12. The network is identified by 201.100.100, and the host is identified as 12.

Class A network
large networks that can support up to 16 million hosts on each of 127 networks.

Class B network
medium-size networks that can support up to 65,000 hosts on each of 16,000 networks.

Class C network
small networks that can support up to 254 hosts on each of 2,000,000 networks.

subnet mask
a mask that is used to determine what subnet a particular IP address refers to.

Subnet Mask

An organizational network may be divided into several smaller networks. These networks within networks are known as subnets. A ***subnet mask*** is used to determine what subnet a particular IP address refers to.

Figure 18-2.
The attributes of networks are listed here by class. The *Format* row lists which octets in the network's IP address are used to define the network and which are used to define the host. The *Range of 1st Octet* row lists the range of numbers that will appear in the first octet of each class's IP addresses. The *Total Hosts per Network* row lists the number of hosts that each network can have. The *Total Number of Networks* row lists the total number of networks that can be supported by a class. The *Typical Address* row lists typical addresses for the three classes.

Table of TCP/IP Classes

	Class A	Class B	Class C
Format	net.host.host.host	net.net.host.host	net.net.net.host
Subnet	255.000.000.000	255.255.000.000	255.255.255.000
Range of 1st Octet	1–127	128–191	192–223
Total Hosts per Network	16,777,214	65,534	254
Total Number of Networks	127	16,384	2,097,152
Typical Address	122.57.103.147	135.200.137.102	198.45.103.67

When the subnet mask is encountered, it is usually viewed in decimal form in a series of four three-digit numbers. At first glance, a subnet mask may appear identical to an IP address. However, a subnet mask is distinguishable from an IP address because it begins with one or more octets of 255. An IP address cannot begin with 255. The subnet mask can be used to identify the class of network, but is really intended to allow the network address to be broken down into smaller subnetworks.

The octets of a subnet mask correspond to octets in the IP address. The actual numbers found in a subnet mask depend on the class of the network and the number of subnetworks it is divided into. The subnet mask is combined with the IP address using the bitwise "AND" operation, the details of which are beyond the scope of this text. The resulting address is the subnet address. For now, just remember that the subnet mask is used to identify any subnetworks at a network address. IPv6 does not require the use of a subnet mask.

Running IPCONFIG

Information about the computer IP address, MAC address, and network adapter can be obtained by running the **ipconfig** command from the command prompt. **Figure 18-3** shows the results of running **ipconfig** from the Windows Vista command prompt.

Windows NT, XP, and Vista support the **ipconfig** command. Windows Me, Windows 98, and Windows 95 use the **winipcfg** command to reveal similar information.

A+ Note:

Be sure you know which operating system uses the **ipconfig** command and which uses the **winipcfg** command. Also, be sure you know what information is revealed by the commands.

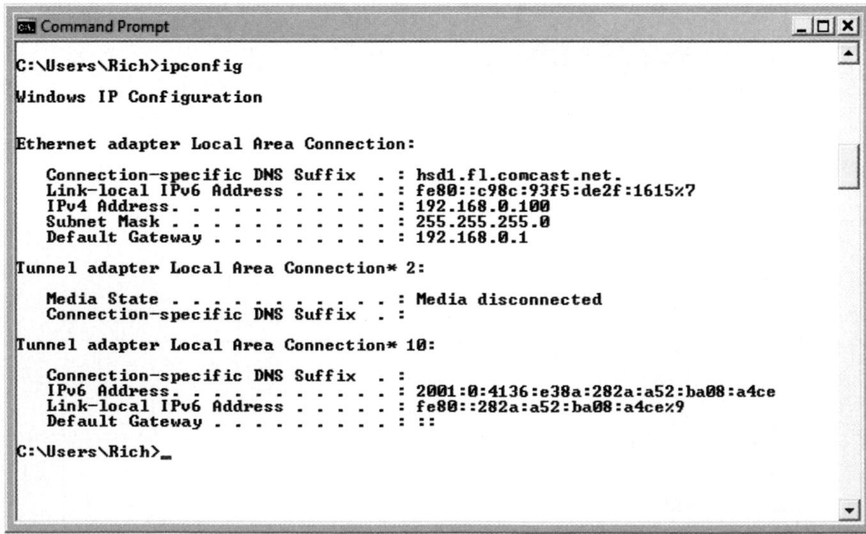

Figure 18-3. The results of issuing the **ipconfig** command at the command prompt.

DHCP

Originally, computers on a network had to have their IP addresses assigned manually as part of the routine to get a PC ready to communicate on a network and over the Internet. When IP addresses are assigned manually, the process is referred to as static IP addressing. This is a time-consuming operation if hundreds or even thousands of hosts are on a network. A log of computer names, locations, MAC addresses, and the assigned IP addresses must be recorded. IP addresses on each host must be unique. Using the same IP address on more than one host causes communication conflicts, and thus erratic behavior.

Dynamic Host Configuration Protocol (DHCP) was written to replace the manual setup of IP addresses on a network. When a server runs DHCP, the IP addresses are assigned automatically to the hosts. The act of automatically assigning IP addresses is known as ***dynamic addressing.*** The DHCP server is given a pool, or list, of IP addresses. Each host is assigned an address from the pool as it logs on to the network. The IP address is issued to each host temporarily. The address is released after a period of time and may be reissued to another host later.

Dynamic Host Configuration Protocol (DHCP) a protocol written to replace the manual setup of IP addresses on a network by assigning IP addresses dynamically (automatically) to the host PCs.

dynamic addressing the act of automatically assigning IP addresses.

WINS

On a typical Windows network, each computer has its own name, such as "Station1" or "BillC." The ***Windows Internet Naming Service (WINS)*** resolves the computer name to the equivalent IP address on the network. DHCP servers assign IP addresses to hosts from a pool of IP addresses. The same host may have a new IP address each time it logs on to the local network. To correlate a computer name to its current IP address, WINS works closely with the DHCP server.

Windows Internet Naming Service (WINS) resolves the computer name to the equivalent IP address on the network.

DNS

The ***Domain Name Service (DNS)*** is similar to WINS, but instead of translating computer names to IP addresses in the network, DNS translates domain names to IP addresses used on the Internet. The DNS service is used across the Internet, assisting computers in identifying and talking to each other.

Domain names are easier to remember than actual IP addresses. When a domain name is typed in, the DNS service searches its database for the matching IP address and connects the user to that address. Web addresses are entered manually and then passed and copied throughout the Internet by routers. Once a domain is located, the server retains a copy in a database.

Domain Name Service (DNS) translates domain names to IP addresses used on the Internet.

A+ Note:

One or more questions are always asked about DHCP and DNS. WINS is often used as a distractor.

Special WAN Equipment

A typical WAN must connect many different and diverse pieces of equipment and handle a tremendous amount of packet traffic. To accomplish this, some special equipment must be used to handle the routing of data to and from hosts all over the network system. Certain pieces of equipment are used in a network environment when all the hosts are using the same protocol to communicate. Other types of equipment are used when a mixture of protocols are being used. For example, an IP address consists of four octets that each range from 0 to 255. IPX uses an eight digit hexadecimal number, using addresses such as A11CA112. AppleTalk (used for Apple computer networks) uses a combination of alphanumeric characters, such as ArtDesign123. Look at **Figure 18-4.**

In the illustration, you see a mixture of different networking protocols. These are only naming convention differences; the data packets created by each system also differ. For the many different protocols to communicate with each other, special hardware and software must be used. This section covers the major types of equipment and briefly explains the function of each in a network environment.

Repeater

repeater
a piece of equipment that regenerates a weak digital signal.

A ***repeater*** is a piece of equipment that regenerates a weak digital signal. As you know from earlier chapters, there is a maximum length of cable run permissible for transmitting data. To send data across many miles, a repeater is

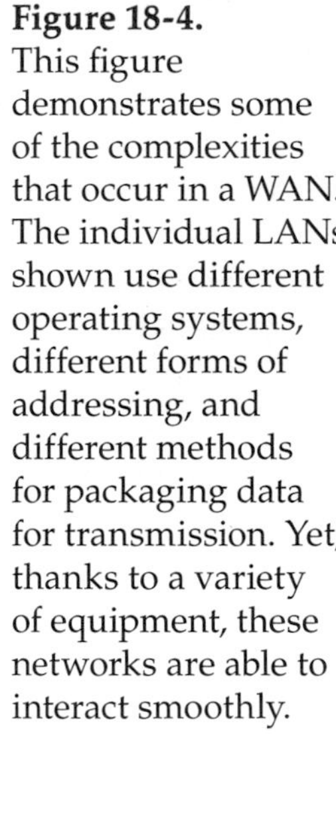
Figure 18-4.
This figure demonstrates some of the complexities that occur in a WAN. The individual LANs shown use different operating systems, different forms of addressing, and different methods for packaging data for transmission. Yet, thanks to a variety of equipment, these networks are able to interact smoothly.

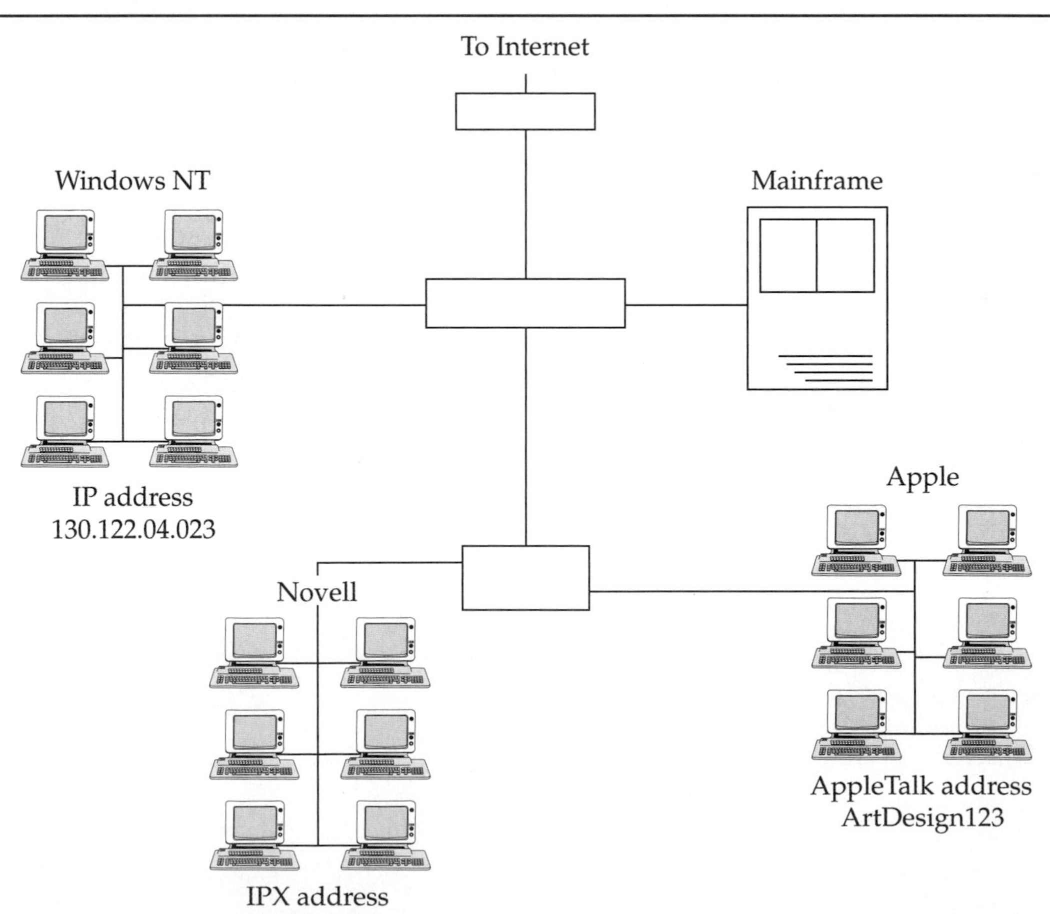

required. A repeater receives a signal, reshapes it to its original form, and sends it on along the cable. Look at **Figure 18-5.**

As a digital signal travels farther from its source, it degrades, eventually becoming unintelligible. At great distances, a network adapter cannot distinguish between the 0s and 1s transmitted through the cable. A repeater receives the degraded digital signal and reshapes it to its original form.

A+ Note:

A repeater is often referred to as an amplifier. Technically speaking, an amplifier increases the original signal strength rather than reshaping the signal to its original form. On the A+ Certification exams, the only correct answer may equate a repeater with an amplifier. In this case, choose the answer that implies that a repeater works like an amplifier.

Bridge

A ***bridge*** is a piece of equipment used to join two dissimilar network segments. For example, you may use a bridge to connect an Ethernet to a Token Ring network. The bridge simply allows the passing of packets from one system to the other regardless of the protocol being used. The bridge maintains a list of MAC addresses that are connected to it so it can filter out data packets. For example, if two network segments are connected by a bridge, the bridge can be programmed to pass only data packets that match the MAC address of hosts on the other side of the bridge. By doing this, data traffic is minimized. See **Figure 18-6.**

bridge
a piece of network equipment that is used to join two dissimilar network segments together such as a wireless and an Ethernet 100BaseT network.

Figure 18-5.
A—Digital signal is transmitted. The only values in the signal are 1s and 0s. B—As the signal approaches it's maximum transmission distance, the shoulders of the signal are slumped, creating graduated values (analog) in the transmission. Also note that the crests of the signal are no longer at maximum height. C—The repeater restores the signal to its original strength and shape.

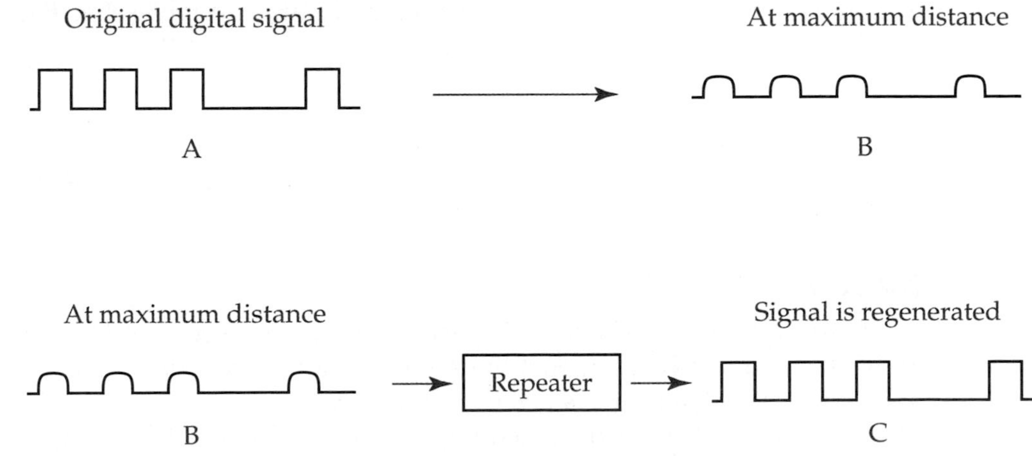

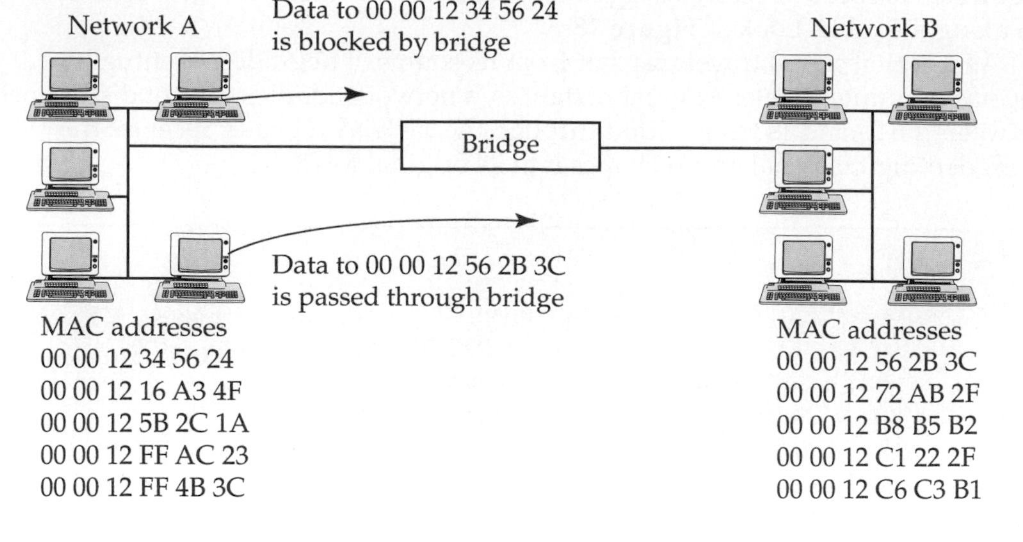

Figure 18-6. A bridge limits the number of hosts affected by data broadcasts. The bridge passes or blocks data, based on the MAC address in the destination address in the packet header. If a large network were constructed without bridge techniques, the constant broadcast of data packets would slow the entire network.

Router

router used to control the flow of data to different networks based on IP addresses.

A ***router*** is used to connect networks together and to control the flow of exchanged data packets. The term *routing* means moving a packet of data from a source to a destination. A router performs much more complex tasks than a bridge. A router not only connects hosts together on a WAN, it also determines the best route to use. The router actually calculates the cost of a number of different ways to connect the hosts together and uses the least expensive method. The cost is based on the use of leased lines and equipment, the time to transmit, and the distance.

Look at **Figure 18-7.** In the illustration, you can see that the function of the router is to determine the least expensive route from one host to another. A router adds information to the data frame surrounding the data packet. The information expands the identification of the packet's origin, its destination, and its route.

Routers are available in two styles: static and dynamic. A static router is programmed with a database of IP addresses, subnet masks, and network IDs. It does not broadcast information on a constant basis. A dynamic router communicates with other routers on the network. Dynamic routers constantly exchange data about each other's location and database tables. See **Figure 18-8** for a quick comparison of bridging and routing.

Brouter

brouter a combination router and bridge.

A ***brouter*** is a combination router and bridge. A brouter applies the best characteristics of both systems.

Switch

switch filters and forwards packets of data between network segments based on MAC addresses.

A ***switch*** filters and forwards packets of data between network segments. Switches are usually intelligent hubs, which means they can determine on which side of the switch a packet's destination is located.

There are two types of switching communication used for computer networks: packet switching and circuit switching. Packet switching divides data into packets, which can take a variety of routes to get to their destination. Circuit

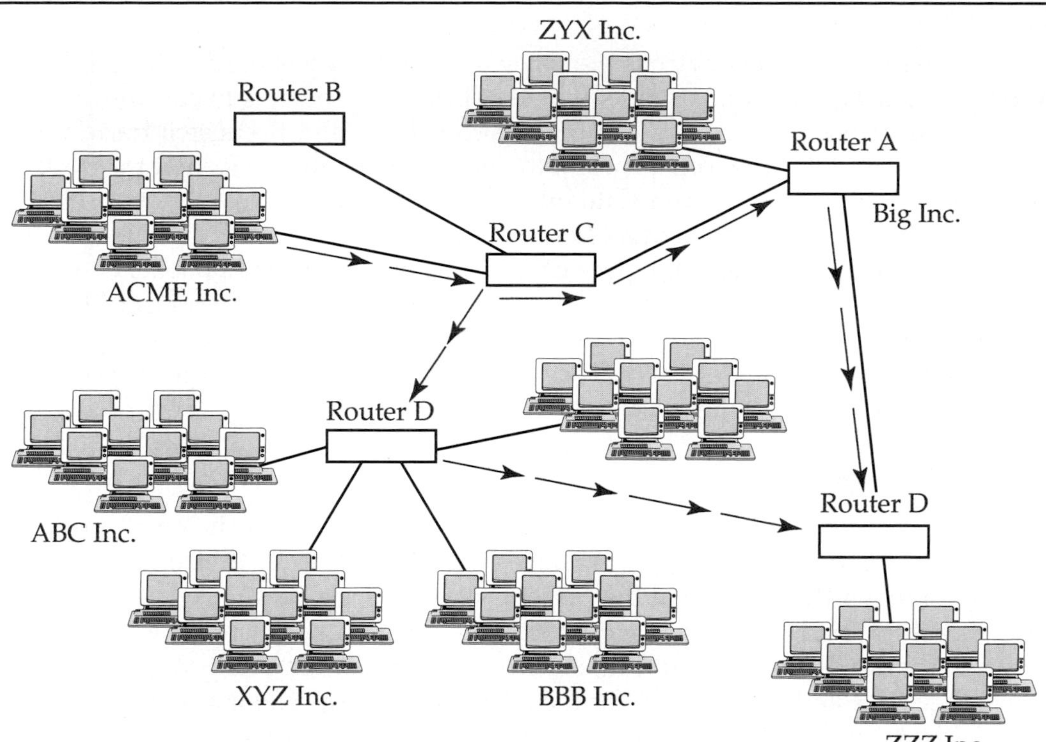

Figure 18-7. Routers route data traffic across the entire world. They also select the least expensive route to use. As you can see, there are several routes that can be chosen to send a data packet from ACME, Inc. to ZZZ, Inc.

Bridge	Router
Forwards broadcast traffic	Blocks broadcast traffic
Uses MAC addresses	Uses network addresses
Does not add to packet information	Adds to packet information
Forwards packets to unknown addresses	Blocks packets to unknown addresses

Figure 18-8. This table offers a short comparison between routers and bridges.

switching makes a permanent connection for the duration of the transmission, and data is transmitted in a steady stream. For example, when you make a dial-up connection with a modem, a circuit switch is closed to keep the modem in constant connection on the telephone line. On the network, the packet switching method is used rather than a permanent connection for the duration of the call.

IP Switch

The ***IP switch,*** introduced by Ipsilon Networks, Inc., is designed to pass ATM protocol packets. It is faster than traditional routers, but until ATM is fully implemented, TCP/IP will still be used. As you recall, ATM is a high-speed network system that allows a mixture of voice, video, and data to be transmitted on the same line. To maintain the data flow rate in an ATM system, IP switches, rather than conventional routers, must be used in the network.

IP switch designed to pass ATM protocol packets.

Gateways

gateway
translates information between two LANs using different protocols.

Another networking device is the gateway. A ***gateway*** is used to translate information between two networks that use different protocols to communicate. You can think of a gateway as a communications translator because it translates commands and data from one protocol to another, or from one format to another. For example, a gateway can translate information between a Novell network using the IPX/SPX protocol and a Microsoft network using the TCP/IP protocol.

A gateway may be a special piece of equipment or a software package loaded onto a server or a router. It is important to understand that a network server can provide more than one service. A computer can serve as a gateway, a proxy server, a firewall, and a file server. The exact name used for the server is relative to the network service being discussed.

Proxy Server

proxy server
designed to hide all the PCs in the LAN from direct connection from PCs outside of the LAN. It relays the requested information for the client, leaving the client anonymous outside the network.

When dealing with network Internet service, you may hear the term ***proxy server.*** Proxy servers are designed to hide all the PCs in the LAN from direct connection from PCs outside of the LAN. This provides a better security service than if each PC had direct access to outside the LAN. The server acts as a go-between for the distant sites and the user behind the server. The proxy server relays the requested information for the client, leaving the client anonymous outside the network. Users on the outside of the network see only the proxy server and not the client. Also, only one modem is required for a telephone connection, but more can be added to the same server.

The proxy server makes accessing the Web more efficient for the network clients by caching frequently requested Web pages. By caching the frequently accessed Web information, the process of accessing distant pages is sped up.

Firewalls

firewall
a barrier that prevents direct contact between computers outside the organization and computers inside the organization.

The term ***firewall*** refers to a barrier that prevents direct contact between computers outside the organization and computers inside the organization. A firewall can be strictly software or a combination software and hardware. All data communications to and from the organization are routed through the proxy server, and the firewall software decides whether to forward the data.

Network Diagnostic Utilities

Standard utility programs are very handy when troubleshooting networked PCs. PING and tracert are the most common.

PING

Packet Internet Groper (PING)
a utility program that is often used as a troubleshooting tool to verify network connections to Web sites.

The ***Packet Internet Groper (PING)*** is a utility that is often used as a troubleshooting tool to verify network connections to Web sites. The PING utility sends a packet to a distant site and then waits for a reply. Ping is executed as a command from the command prompt. At the prompt, you simply type **ping** followed by the IP address or its URL name, such as www.yahoo.com. **Figure 18-9** shows the results of issuing a **ping** command to the Yahoo Web site. If you are on a network with a firewall, this test may not work. The **ping** command may be blocked by the firewall. Check with the network administrator.

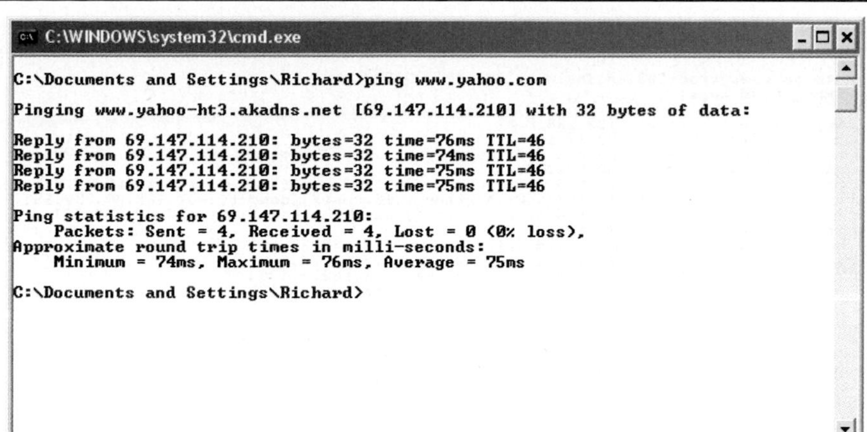

Figure 18-9. A ping performed on www.yahoo.com.

When the Yahoo site was pinged, the name "Yahoo" was automatically resolved to an IP address. You can see the IP address listed as 69.147.114.210. After the IP address was determined, four packets with 32 bytes of data were sent to that address. The site echoed back with four replies. The average round trip to the site and back was 75 milliseconds.

The ***time to live (TTL)*** is the length of time the data in a packet is valid. Packets are transmitted with the TTL setting recorded in the packet's header. This tells the network to disregard the packet after the set TTL time. There are a number of switches that can be used with the **ping** command to modify it. The additional switches for the **ping** command can be viewed by using **ping** with the help switch or by just typing and entering **ping**.

time to live (TTL) the length of time the data in a packet is valid.

A handy way of checking the network card to see if it is responding to TCP/IP transmissions is to ping the card. Simply type the **ping** command at the command prompt with 127.0.0.1 as the IP address. As an alternative, you may enter **ping localhost** at the command prompt. Either method will execute a ping to the local host. The name "localhost" refers to the computer you are using.

Tracert

The utility program ***tracert*** is short for trace route. Tracert is more advanced than the PING utility. Like PING , it sends a packet out and waits for a reply. In addition to the information that PING provides, tracert also displays information about the route that was taken to the destination. See **Figure 18-10.** As with the **ping** command, depending on how the firewall is configured, this test may not work on a network.

tracert utility program that sends a packet out and waits for a reply. It also displays information about the route that was taken to the destination.

The **tracert** command is issued from the command prompt. In Figure 18-10, the **tracert** command revealed the actual route taken by the data packet. Among the information provided is the name of the router at comcast.net and of routers at various cities and the names of the different telephone carriers. The utility also displays the time it takes each packet to reach its destination. This feature is extremely useful in locating bottlenecks along the route.

Many third-party software developers offer utilities that further enhance the tracert function. NeoTrace is a commercial product developed and distributed by NeoWorx, Inc. It is a powerful diagnostic and investigation tool. The program traces the route to any destination over the Internet and returns information about the hosts on the route taken. The information includes registered details

Figure 18-10. The tracert utility being used to trace the network path to www.yahoo.com.

```
C:\WINDOWS\system32\cmd.exe

Tracing route to www.yahoo-ht3.akadns.net [209.191.93.52]
over a maximum of 30 hops:

  1    <1 ms    <1 ms    <1 ms  192.168.0.1
  2     6 ms     8 ms     7 ms  73.17.116.1
  3    10 ms     7 ms     *     ge-2-2-sr01.sebring.fl.westfl.comcast.net [68.86.199.77]
  4     8 ms     8 ms     *     68.87.238.105
  5    11 ms     7 ms     8 ms  te-9-4-ur01.portcharlott.fl.westfl.comcast.net [68.87.238.101]
  6    11 ms    10 ms     9 ms  te-8-2-ur01.northport.fl.westfl.comcast.net [68.87.238.65]
  7     9 ms    10 ms     *     te-8-4-ar02.venice.fl.westfl.comcast.net [68.87.238.25]
  8    16 ms    18 ms    15 ms  12.124.91.37
  9    46 ms    43 ms    45 ms  tbr1.ormfl.ip.att.net [12.123.33.10]
 10    45 ms    53 ms    44 ms  tbr1.hs1tx.ip.att.net [12.122.4.101]
 11    44 ms    43 ms    42 ms  tbr2.hs1tx.ip.att.net [12.122.9.170]
 12    42 ms    42 ms    45 ms  tbr1.dlstx.ip.att.net [12.122.10.129]
 13    44 ms    45 ms    45 ms  gar8.dlstx.ip.att.net [12.122.100.21]
 14    44 ms    44 ms    43 ms  12.86.20.18
 15    46 ms    50 ms    44 ms  ge-0-1-0-p100.msr1.mud.yahoo.com [216.115.104.97]
 16    45 ms    45 ms    44 ms  te-8-1.bas-c2.mud.yahoo.com [68.142.193.7]
 17    46 ms    51 ms    46 ms  f1.www.vip.mud.yahoo.com [209.191.93.52]

Trace complete.

C:\Documents and Settings\Richard>_
```

of each host along the route, such as address, telephone number, e-mail address, and IP address. See **Figure 18-11.** The information can be displayed as a detailed listing similar to a spreadsheet and a graphical display in which the route is displayed on a map.

Pathping

The pathping utility is an enhanced combination of the ping and tracert utilities. When issued from the command prompt, it performs in a similar fashion to tracert, but with additional information. Look at **Figure 18-12.**

After pinging the path to the destination and displaying the results similar to tracert, pathping continues to ping the destination with additional test packets. After 400 seconds, the additional information is displayed, indicating what percent of the additional test packets reached the destination. This test is much more thorough than tracert because it tests the connectivity to the final destination over a longer period of time. Some network problems are intermittent and may not be revealed by a simple ping or a tracert.

After completing a trace of the route from the source computer to the destination, the pathping utility continues to send diagnostic packets. A series of additional packets are continuously sent for a period indicated at the end of the original tracert. In Figure 18-12, the time value is 450 seconds, or approximately 7 1/2 minutes. Pathping is used to detect intermittent connection problems or bottlenecks in the traffic flow. This is the main advantage the pathping utility has over the tracert utility.

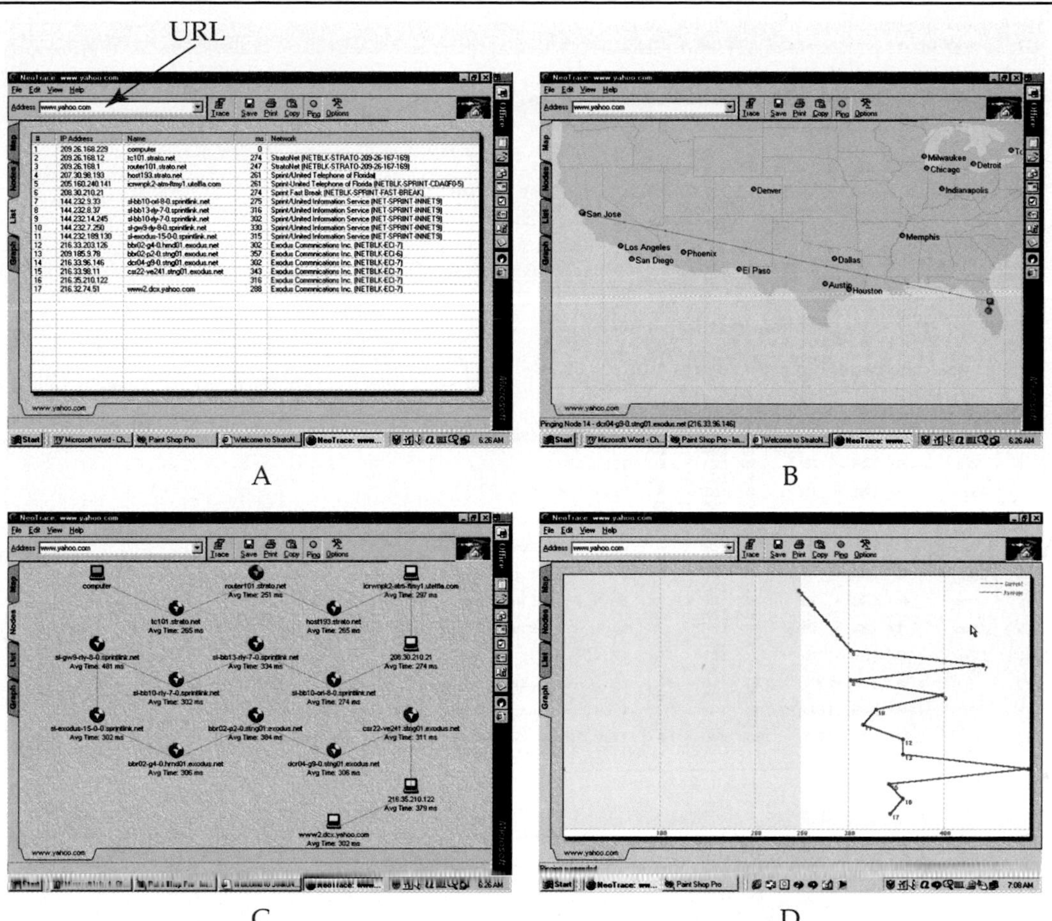

Figure 18-11. A—The network path to www.yahoo.com displayed in NeoTrace using the **List** tab. B—The network path to www.yahoo.com displayed using NeoTrace's **Map** tab. C—The network path to www.yahoo.com displayed using Neotrace's **Nodes** tab. D—The network path displayed using NeoTrace's **Graph** tab.

Nslookup

The nslookup utility is used to diagnose Domain Name Service (DNS) server problems. In the command line, you can use either the IP address or the URL of the domain being tested. The **nslookup** command queries the nearest DNS server and displays the information contained in its DNS database for the corresponding IP address. **Figure 18-13** shows the nslookup utility resolving the IP address, 66.94.234.13. Notice that Yahoo is matched to the IP address. You can also perform an nslookup on the name of a server and obtain a reply of the assigned IP address.

Net Diagnostics Utility

A utility developed by Microsoft and first introduced in Windows XP is Net Diagnostics. Net Diagnostics is easily accessed by running **msinfo32.exe** from the **Run** dialog box at the **Start** menu. Once the **System Information** dialog box opens, select **Tools** from the main menu and then **Net Diagnostics**. Another way to access Net Diagnostics is through **Help and Support**.

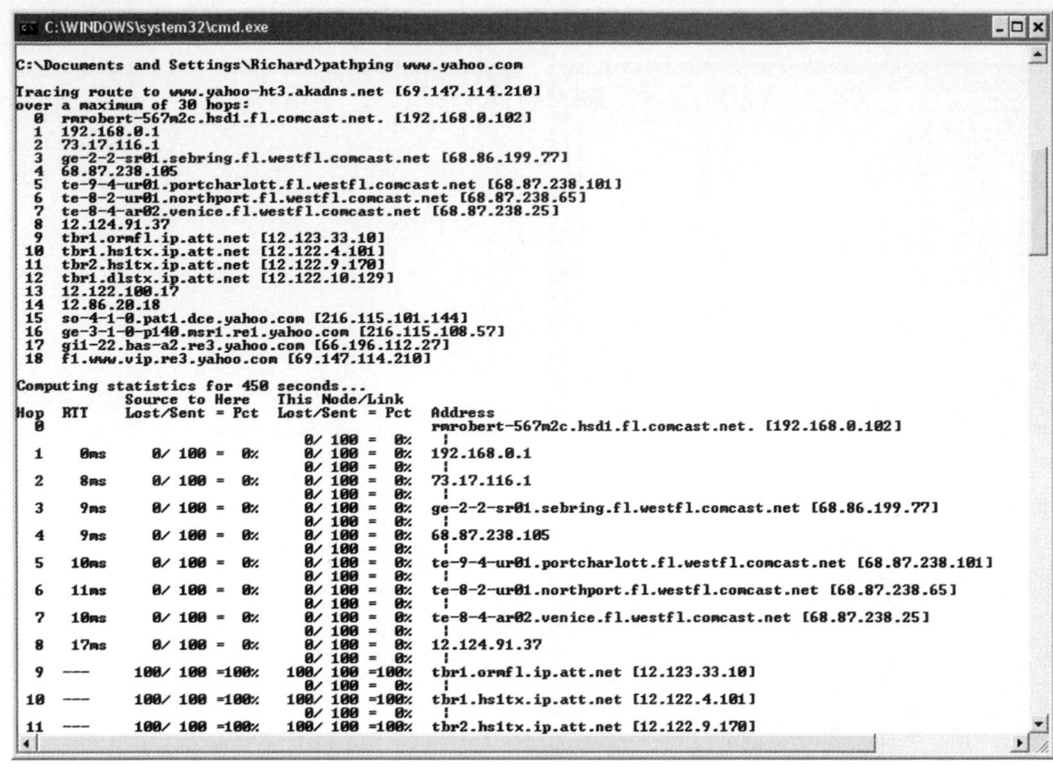

Figure 18-12. The pathping utility used on www.yahoo.com.

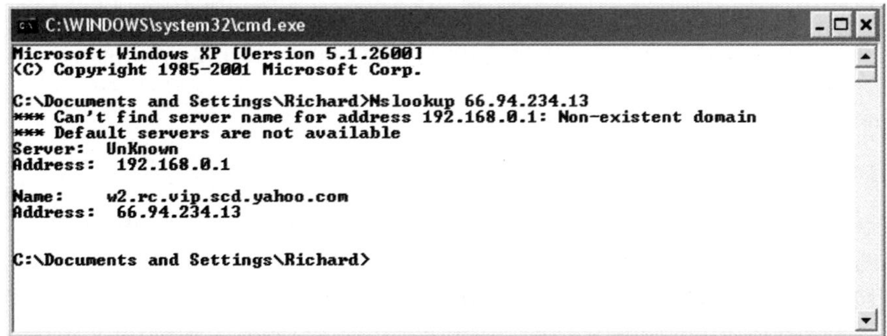

Figure 18-13. The nslookup utility resolving the IP address, 66.94.234.13.

Once the Net Diagnostics tool is run, it displays information about the network system. In **Figure 18-14,** you can see items that fail tests are displayed in red as "FAILED," and items that pass tests are displayed in green as "PASSED." Critical items are automatically tested, and information can be revealed such as the MAC address, IP address, DNS host name, and WINS server. The Net Diagnostics utility combines the PING, tracert, and other utilities into one tool.

The Internet Structure

Internet
a very large, global, decentralized network.

No discussion about WAN systems would be complete without a discussion of the largest WAN in the world, the ***Internet.*** This section will give you a brief historical background of the Internet and its development, and it will make you aware of how complex the Internet really is.

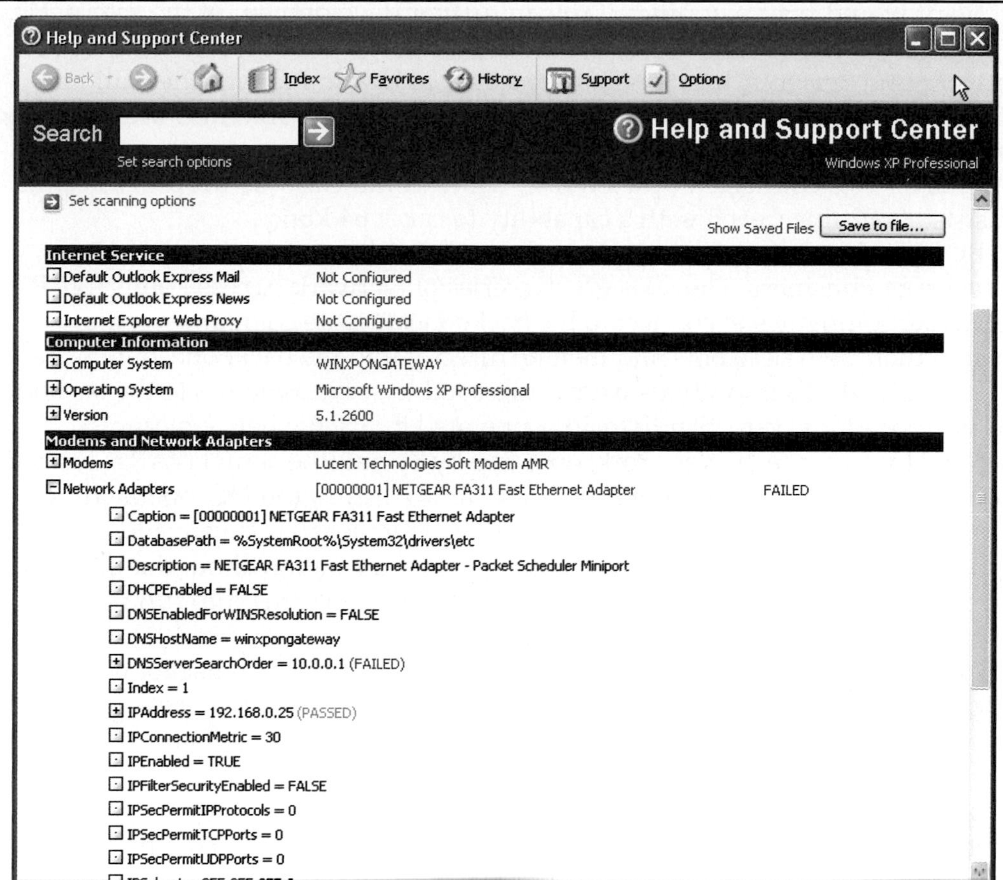

Figure 18-14. Net Diagnostics utility.

Development of the Internet

The Internet has actually been in existence since the 1960s and grew from a simple project of the Advanced Research Project Agency (ARPA). The project was designed to test the feasibility of communication between computers over telephone lines. The first experiments were very simple but also very impressive. The original experiments contained only four hosts; today there are millions.

Later ARPA was absorbed by the United States military, renamed DARPA, and operated by the U.S. Department of Defense. As the network grew, the National Science Foundation became involved by awarding grants to many different universities and private companies to develop a communications model for what is now called the *Internet.*

In 1985, some of the centers connected by the DARPA network's 56 kbps backbone included Cornell University, the National Center for Supercomputing Application at the University of Illinois, the Pittsburgh Supercomputing Center in Pittsburgh, the University of California in San Diego, and Princeton University in New Jersey. This backbone is viewed by many people as the true beginning of what was to become known as the Internet. Over the next several years, many more universities, private companies, and research centers connected to the line. Within three years, the increased traffic forced the original 56 kbps backbone to be replaced with a T-1 line that could carry 1.544 Mbps. The new line connected six diverse regional networks in the United States, including: the National Center of Atmospheric Research in Colorado, the original computer centers previously listed, and the Merit site at the University of Michigan.

Merit would play a significant role in further development of the Internet. In 1990, Merit, IBM, and MCI started a nonprofit organization called Advanced Network and Services, Inc. (ANS). Its major goal was to manage the National Science Foundation backbone and continue to upgrade it. IBM and MCI both contributed four million dollars to the venture. The backbone was expanded to 16 major sites connected by a T-3 line, which could carry 43 Mbps. A T-3 line consists of 672 lines, each with a capability to carry 64 kbps.

By 1993, the National Science Foundation bowed out of the Internet management business. They designed a series of Network Access Points (NAPs) for private companies to connect to the backbone. Private companies could develop their own networks and then tie directly into the backbone, but only at a NAP. Originally, four locations were designated to serve as access to the backbone. The four locations were: San Francisco, operated by Pacific Bell; Chicago, operated by Ameritech; New York, operated by Sprint (the actual NAP is located in Pennsauken, New Jersey, not New York); and Washington DC, operated by Metropolitan Fiber Systems. As demand grew, more locations were added.

Merit was chosen to maintain a database of information about the Internet and act as the arbitrator for disputes. The Internet then came into full power, based on the original ARPA backbone project.

Private communications companies constructed their own backbones as well. Some companies constructed MANs in large metropolitan areas. The MANs were designed to allow businesses to have access to high-speed backbone systems spanning the US. Growth has continued at an astounding rate. The Internet consists of fiber-optic and copper cables, wireless devices, infrared devices, satellites, and millions of miles of old telephone lines. The Internet grows so fast and is so diverse, there is no map of all the lines and connections in existence. Individual companies do have information regarding connection and traffic lines, but they only have what is limited to their direct control. There are over 4500 companies making changes to the Internet daily, making it impossible to create an up-to-date and all-inclusive map of the Internet.

The diversity arises from the Internet's practice of sending data along the shortest route between two points. Most Internet providers have agreements allowing each to access the other's backbones and parts of their individually constructed networks. If these agreements were not arranged, the access to the Internet would be very limited.

For example, one customer may use ABC as their Internet provider and another customer may use XYZ as their Internet provider. The two companies are located across the street from each other. However, if it were not for mutually beneficial agreements set up between the two companies, the data sent by one customer to the other customer might very well be routed hundreds or even thousands of miles to a national backbone before making a return trip back on the other provider's lines.

There are thousands of agreements in place between providers to lease line access from one another. In this manner, the route taken by data is considerably shortened. This is one of the main reasons there are so many routers used on the Internet. The routers are constantly updated either manually or automatically to find the least expensive route between two points on the Internet. In short, the Internet is a network of networks that are all interconnected forming a huge spider web of communication circuits.

You might want to conduct an experiment to see how the lines in your own geographic area are accessed. Use the tracert utility to trace the route to some point close by, such as a local business' Web site. You may be surprised to see exactly how far the data must travel. The NeoTrace utility will map the exact route for you.

Domain Names and URLS

InterNIC was the government agency first responsible for issuing uniform resource locator addresses and domain names. ***Uniform Resource Locators (URLs)*** are the global address for Web sites all over the Internet. The first part of the URL identifies the protocol used and the second part identifies the domain name.

Uniform Resource Locators (URLs) the global address for sites all over the Internet. The first part of the URL identifies the protocol used and the second part identifies the domain name.

Many people confuse domain names with URLs because they appear so similar. The domain name is an alphanumeric name that identifies one or more IP addresses. The domain name is combined with the protocol type to form the URL. For example, for the URL ftp://www.download.com/freestuff.exe, download.com is the domain. The file freestuff.exe is located at that domain and can be accessed using the FTP protocol. For the URL http://www.ace.com/index.html, the domain is ace.com. The file, index.html, is a Web page that is accessed using the HTTP protocol.

The Domain Name System (DNS), as mentioned earlier, is a system used to identify domain names of sites on the Internet and resolve them to their IP addresses. When you enter a URL in your Web browser, a query is sent to a local resolver, a database of domain names and matching IP addresses. The query requests a matching IP address for the domain name that you entered. The resolver transmits the requested IP address to your computer, and you are then seamlessly connected to the requested site. If the resolver's database does not contain the requested IP address, it forwards the query to the next resolver in the network. This continues until the IP address is located and you are connected to the requested site, or all of the resolvers are searched without success, resulting in an error message.

Originally and until 1995, InterNIC issued domain names and matching IP addresses. Then the InterNIC commercialized the system, turning it over to the private sector. Today, InterNIC retains the control of the system. However, it has delegated the responsibility of dealing with the public to private sector companies. You can access a list of authorized domain name registration companies from the InterNIC site. Domain name suffixes are assigned according to the domain's function. **Figure 18-15** lists some common suffixes found in domain names.

E-mail Communications

E-mail has become one of the most popular uses of the Internet. You can send messages anywhere in the world via the Internet. Originally, e-mail was little more than a system to exchange ASCII text files. It is now a complete communication system that allows not only text-based messages but also attached files. Any type of file can be attached, including reports, spreadsheets, database information, photos, illustrations, animations, and sound. There are numerous e-mail software packages available. The e-mail software packages wrap themselves around the available Internet e-mail protocols and greatly enhance the user interface.

Figure 18-15. This top portion of the table lists common domain suffixes and the types of organizations that use them. The bottom portion of the table contains some of the latest domain suffixes and the types of organizations that use them.

Domain	Type of Organization
.com	Commercial business
.edu	Educational
.gov	Government
.mil	Military
.net	Host or gateway
.org	Organizations usually, but not necessarily, nonprofit
.aero	Global aviation authority
.arts	Art and culture
.asia	Pan-Asia and Asian Pacific region
.biz	Restricted to business
.info	Information services
.info	Information
.jobs	Human resources management community
.mobi	Mobile products
.museum	Museums and related areas
.name	Individual personal names
.nom	Individuals
.pro	Reserved for licensed professionals
.rec	Recreational and entertainment
.store	Merchants
.travel	Travel industry
.web	Web activities

To set up an e-mail account, you must have certain information. First, you need to know your user name and password. You also need to know the name and type of mail server being used for incoming and outgoing messages. Common e-mail protocols include Post Office Protocol (POP3), Internet Message Access Protocol (IMAP), Hypertext Markup Language (HTML), and Simple Mail Transport Protocol (SMTP). A protocol is required to communicate with a mail server that is hosting the e-mail software and the Internet connection.

Your Internet Service Provider (ISP) will provide your user name, password, and e-mail server name. Providers usually have this information on an automatic installation CD. If they do not, you can contact them to get the information. Once the account is established, there are many features you need to understand.

The e-mail server usually stores all e-mail communications until the user retrieves them. In a strict network environment, e-mails can be delivered directly to the individual PCs. Once you log on to your ISP, you can open your e-mail account, which is stored on the server, and access your personal e-mail.

To send e-mail, you must type in the address of the recipient, such as jsmith@acme.net. See **Figure 18-16.** Each e-mail user has a unique address. Two or more users can have the same alpha name on the same network, but they are usually given a numeric extension to maintain the uniqueness of the address, such as

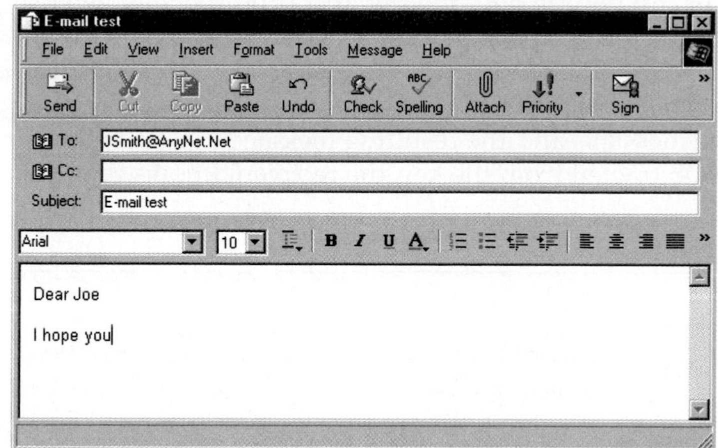

Figure 18-16. The three most important pieces of information to enter when creating an e-mail are the recipient's e-mail address, the subject of the e-mail, and the message.

jsmith23@acme.net. A message is then typed into the letter space and the **Send** button is clicked, sending the e-mail to its destination. The menus provide the user with many options, including delete and save. There are some options that are unique to e-mail, such as reply, reply to all, resend, and attach file.

MIME and S/MIME

When a non-text file is attached to an e-mail message, it must be converted to a form that can be handled by text-oriented e-mail protocols. The ***Multipurpose Internet Mail Extensions (MIME)*** standard is a specification for formatting non-text-based files for transmission over the Internet. MIME is used for graphics, audio, and video.

Multipurpose Internet Mail Extensions (MIME) a specification for formating non-text-based files for transmission over the Internet.

A newer version of MIME is S/MIME. The *S* stands for secure. S/MIME allows the sent message to be encrypted and signed with a digital signature, or certificate. Methods used to ensure S/MIME security are discussed in the following section.

Digital Signatures and Encryption/Decryption Keys

You obtain a digital ID from a third-party software vendor. You make an application using e-mail, and then the certifying authority verifies your identity. Your digital ID provides you with two digital keys. One key is a private key, which you keep entirely to yourself. The private key can be used to sign your e-mail and also encrypt messages. The receiving party will be warned if a signed message has been tampered with. It also verifies your identity to the recipient. The other key is a public key, which you distribute to people you wish to communicate with. The public key allows others to decode messages encoded with your private key. It also allows them to encode messages that can only be decoded by your private key.

There are three components required to electronically sign and encrypt a message: a public key, a private key, and the appropriate encoding software. When you digitally sign an e-mail, software compresses the message contents to a few lines of text known as a *message digest.* The message digest is then encoded using the sender's private key. The resulting data is the sender's *digital signature.* The digital signature is then added to the end of the message.

The receiver can decode both the signature and the message using the sender's public key. When the signature is decoded, it results in the same message digest used to create it. When the message is decoded, it results in the same data used to create the message digest, and therefore the signature. If the receiver compresses the message, and the resulting message digest does not match the message digest extracted from the key, the recipient knows that the message has been altered.

> **A+ Note:**
>
> CompTIA always has several questions about e-mail protocols. Remember, SMTP sends e-mail to a mail server. POP3 and IMAP download e-mail from the mail server.

Internet Protocols

Hundreds of protocols have been developed over the years. Protocols began as simple programs that carried out commands and transported plain ASCII text files but have evolved into sophisticated programs. In the strictest sense, protocols are software programs that establish a set of rules to allow two entities to communicate. As protocols evolve, they take on the appearance of application software and are classified as such. As technology evolves, there will always be new protocols, usually built on top of the older protocols to keep the downward compatibility of the system. The following are a few of the most common protocols used in Internet communications.

HTTP

Hypertext Transfer Protocol (HTTP) protocol that transports Web pages across the Internet.

Hypertext Markup Language (HTML) programming language used to create Web pages.

Hypertext Transfer Protocol (HTTP) is used to transport Web pages across the Internet. ***Hypertext Markup Language (HTML)*** is a programming language used to create Web pages and is often confused with HTTP. HTTP is the mechanism for delivery of HTML pages as well as Web pages developed using other languages. HTTP is not a secure protocol. In fact, the contents of the Web pages it transports can be easily viewed using a protocol analyzer. HTTP was never intended to be used for transmitting secure information such as business transactions involving personal identification and money. Secure Sockets Layer (SSL) was developed by Netscape Navigator to make HTTP-based Internet business transactions secure. When SSL is incorporated with HTTP, the HTTP protocol in the window at the top of the Web browser becomes HTTPS. The *S* indicates that it is a secure transaction. SSL can be used with any protocol in the TCP/IP suite, not just with HTTP.

FTP

File Transfer Protocol (FTP) is a protocol used for transmitting files across the Internet. A special FTP is called *anonymous FTP*. Many sites accept anonymous FTP, which simply means you can access the files for downloading without using a secret password and identity.

File Transfer Protocol (FTP)
a protocol used for transmitting files across the Internet.

Telnet

Telnet is a protocol that allows you to log on to a remote computer and download or upload files. It is often referred to as a terminal emulation protocol because it causes a PC to act as though it is a terminal connected to a mainframe computer. Telnet is part of an entire suite of protocols inside the TCP/IP protocol. It is often used to connect two dissimilar systems, such as a PC running Microsoft Windows and a UNIX mainframe. Telnet is commonly used to program remote routers on wide area networks. It can also be used to control other computer operations remotely.

Telnet
a protocol that allows you to log on to a remote computer and download or upload files.

Gopher

Gopher was an early Internet protocol designed to search and retrieve documents from distant computers. Gopher was created at the University of Minnesota, the home of the Golden Gophers, hence the name of the protocol. Gopher was originally designed for access only to the computer on the university campus. It was such a success, it grew and was soon used all over the country. All that was needed was a telephone modem. Gopher not only provided access, but also organized information into directories such as images, programs, and documents.

Gopher
an early Internet protocol designed to search and retrieve documents from distant computers.

Archie

Archie is similar to Gopher and is maintained by McGill University in Montreal. Archie is a program that allows you to search for information on the Internet by filename.

Archie
an Internet protocol, maintained by McGill University in Montreal, that allows you to search for information on the Internet by filename.

Network Troubleshooting

Remember the basics of networking. To create a network you need cable, a properly configured adapter card, and software support for the network. Most networking problems are simple problems, such as loose connections. When there are network system problems, check the connections first. The next step is to ping the adapter card (127.0.0.1) to verify that it is communicating the TCP/IP protocol. Finally, try to connect to a known URL using the **ping** command. You will not get any results from pinging a distant host if the modem is not connecting to the Internet service provider.

Adapter settings can be accidentally changed, especially while exploring the network setup dialog boxes. If you are accessing the network by modem, you will have to check the modem setup. You may want to review the chapter on modems. Problems can also be created by loading certain Internet-related software programs. Some software packages automatically load from the CD and can change system settings, such as the default protocol and the system configuration. These settings need to be checked closely and are often the root of the problem.

For example, you receive a magazine that includes several software programs, utilities, and games. You place the CD into the CD drive, and it automatically loads. During the installation process, the software attempts to change settings relating to the network. The system may fail, leaving you without access to the network, or the system may begin experiencing recurring problems. In this case, the network settings will have to be verified and reset as necessary.

Another common problem associated with a network is difficulty logging in. Often, the user is incorrectly entering his or her name and password or is attempting to use an expired password. As a technician, you will have your own access name and password and will be capable of easily determining if the network is accessible.

Most problems you will be expected to handle as a PC technician are simple in nature. More complex issues may require the assistance of the network administrator. With experience, you will soon be able to determine when you need to consult the network administrator or the Internet service provider.

Automatic Private IP Address (APIPA) an IP address that is automatically issued to a computer when a DHCP address cannot issue an IP address.

Most network adapters are configured for DHCP. Whenever a DHCP problem occurs, the computer will automatically issue itself an ***Automatic Private IP Address (APIPA).*** The APIPA range is from 169.254.0.1 to 169.254.255.254. A computer requires an IP address to communicate even on a local area network. When a DHCP address cannot be issued to the computer, the computer automatically issues an Automatic Private IP Address to itself so that it can communicate with other computers and equipment on the local network. When the DHCP problem is resolved, the computer drops the Automatic Private IP Address, and the DHCP server automatically issues the computer an IP address. These actions are automatic and transparent to the user. The user is never aware of what is happening. Typically, the user cannot access the Internet until the problem is solved with the DHCP server.

Summary

- ✔ Navigation across WAN systems is enabled by network devices, such as bridges, routers, brouters, gateways, and switches.
- ✔ IPv4 uses four octets containing decimal numbers; each set of numbers is in the range of 0 to 255.
- ✔ IPv6 uses eight sets of hexadecimal numbers; each set of numbers is in the range of 000 to ffff.
- ✔ The **winipcfg** command is used by Windows 98 and Windows Me to reveal IP and MAC address assignments for a network adapter.
- ✔ The **ipconfig** command is used by Windows 2000, XP, and Vista to reveal IP and MAC address assignments for the network adapter.
- ✔ Routers connect hosts across network systems using the most economical route.
- ✔ A router communicates by network addresses rather than by MAC address.
- ✔ Bridges are used to connect devices by their MAC address.

- ✔ Brouters combine the best features of a router and a bridge.
- ✔ A gateway translates information between two LANs that use different protocols.
- ✔ A proxy server acts as a go-between for the distant Web site and the user behind the server.
- ✔ TCP/IP is the most common protocol used for the Internet.
- ✔ PING and tracert are common diagnostic tools used to check if the network circuit is intact.
- ✔ Pingpath is an enhanced version of the combination of the PING and tracert utilities.
- ✔ Nslookup is used to display the assigned domain name and corresponding IP address.
- ✔ Tracert provides more information than PING.
- ✔ The Net Diagnostics utility gathers information about the network setup of the workstation.
- ✔ HTTPS displayed in a Web browser URL window indicates that HTTP is using SSL for securing the transaction.
- ✔ The Automatic Private IP Address (APIPA) feature is used to issue a computer a private IP address when a problem occurs with the DHCP server.
- ✔ APIPA is an IP address in the range of 169.254.0.1 to 169.254.255.254.

Review Questions

Answer the following questions on a separate sheet of paper. Please do not write in this book.

1. What protocol is predominately used for exchanging data on the Internet?
2. What is InterNIC?
3. What is an octet?
4. What is an octet's numeric range expressed in decimal fashion?
5. How does the TCP/IP protocol identify individual networks on the Internet?
6. Identify the class to which a network with an address of 128.204.19.103 belongs.
7. What is a subnet mask?
8. What is the difference between an IPv4 and IPv6 address?
9. Which operating system was first to assign by default an IPv4 and an IPv6 address to each network adapter?
10. What does the **ipconfig** command reveal about a PC connected to a network?
11. What does a DHCP server do?
12. What does DNS do?
13. What is the difference between DNS and WINS?
14. What device extends the maximum length of a network cable run?
15. What is the purpose of a proxy server?

16. What is a firewall?
17. What is the purpose of a ping?
18. What utility reveals the most information about a network system during troubleshooting?
19. What three components are required to send an S/MIME encoded e-mail?
20. What is a digital signature?
21. What does the acronym APIPA represent?
22. When does APIPA occur?
23. What is the range of APIPA addresses?

Sample A+ Exam Questions

Answer the following questions on a separate sheet of paper. Please do not write in this book.

1. Which is an example of a typical IP address?
   a. 168.23.145.25
   b. 10 2D C4 56 DE FF
   c. JohnH@netcom.org
   d. 255.255.255.000
2. What command issued at the command prompt allows you to inspect the IP address on a Windows NT system?
   a. winipconfig
   b. winipcfg
   c. ipconfig
   d. configip
3. Which of the following services automatically issues an IP address to a PC when it boots?
   a. WINS
   b. DHCP
   c. IPSETUP
   d. DNS
4. Which of the following services is responsible for resolving domain names to IP addresses?
   a. WINS
   b. DHCP
   c. IPSETUP
   d. DNS
5. Which of the following pieces of equipment is used primarily to extend the length of a network cable run?
   a. Repeater
   b. Hub
   c. Gateway
   d. Router

6. What command can be used as a quick test to see if a network card is functioning?
   a. **ping 127.0.0.1**
   b. **tracert 128.10.10.285**
   c. **cardTest**
   d. **NICset**
7. Which of the following is an example of a URL?
   a. JoeB@AcmeNet.Gov
   b. www.g-w.com
   c. 127.34.002.145
   d. BlakeManufacturing@setpoint.com
8. Which command would you use to check cable connectivity between a workstation named Station12 and a file server named Ntserver? (Note that the command is being issued from Station12.)
   a. **ping station12 via ntserver**
   b. **ping ntserver**
   c. **ping ntserver/station12**
   d. **ping station12/ntserver**
9. An IP address consists of _____.
   a. four octets
   b. 24 binary numbers separated by three colons
   c. a group of 24 hexadecimal numbers
   d. four three-digit decimal numbers ranging from 000 to 999
10. Which is an example of a Class C subnet mask?
    a. 255.255.000.255
    b. 255.255.000.000
    c. 000.255.255.255
    d. 255.255.255.000

Suggested Laboratory Activities

Do not attempt any suggested laboratory activities without your instructor's permission. Certain activities can render the PC operating system inoperable.

1. Install a modem and set up Internet access with an ISP.
2. Inspect the TCP/IP assignment for a PC actively connected to the Internet. Use **winipcfg** for Windows 95 or 98. Type **ipconfig** at the DOS prompt for Windows NT-based systems.
3. Set up a PC to be remotely accessed by another PC through a modem line.
4. Use the Windows Help and Support to see how to set up an Internet connection.
5. Use the Windows Help and Support to see how to share an Internet connection between two or more computers.
6. Use Windows Help and Support to set up a Virtual Private Network.
7. Set up two PCs and share a game connection. (Instructor's permission is definitely required.)

8. Set up a game connection between two PCs and enable voice chat. This allows two people to talk while sharing a game. Note: Not all games support voice chat. (Again, you must have the instructor's permission.)

Interesting Web Sites for More Information

www.cisco.com
www.domainregistry.com
www.learntcpip.com/OSIModel/OSIModel.html
www.linux.com
www.microsoft.com
www.novell.com
www.pacbell.com
www.unix.com
www.youdzone.com/signature.html

Chapter 18
Laboratory Activity
IP Address Verification with Ipconfig

After completing this laboratory activity, you will be able to:

- ✔ Inspect the assigned IP address of a workstation using the **ipconfig** command.
- ✔ Explain the purpose of a DHCP server.
- ✔ Explain the purpose of APIPA.

Introduction

One of the most commonly used utilities for diagnosing a network problem is ipconfig. Ipconfig is run from the command prompt in Windows 2000, XP and Vista. It is not supported by Windows Me or Windows 98. When the **ipconfig** command is run, you should see the DNS server connection name, assigned IP address, subnet mask, and default gateway address.

When run with the **all** switch, you should see additional information such as the host name, MAC or physical address, if DHCP is enabled, the default gateway address, the address DHCP server address, and the DNS server. You will also see a lease period if the IP address has been issued dynamically.

An IP address can be configured statically or dynamically. *Statically* means that the IP address is assigned to the computer manually. *Dynamically* means that the computer is issued an IP address automatically by a DHCP server. The Windows XP and Windows Vista operating system is configured by default to receive a dynamic IP address from a DHCP server. A computer must have an IP address to be able to communicate on a network, even on a small local peer-to-peer network. If the DHCP server is not available, the computer is issued an Automatic Private IP Address (APIPA) so that the computer can still communicate with other computers in the network. The computer will generate its own APIPA in the range from 168.254.0.1 to 169.254.255.254 and a subnet mask of 255.255.000.000. If you see an IP address that starts with 169.254, you will know the computer has a problem obtaining an IP address from the DHCP server.

The operating system will request an IP address from the DHCP server every few minutes. If the problem with the DHCP server is fixed, the Automatic Private IP Address will be dropped and an IP address will once again be issued from the DHCP server. Look at the following screen capture to see the results of the **ipconfig** command and then of the **ipconfig/all** command.

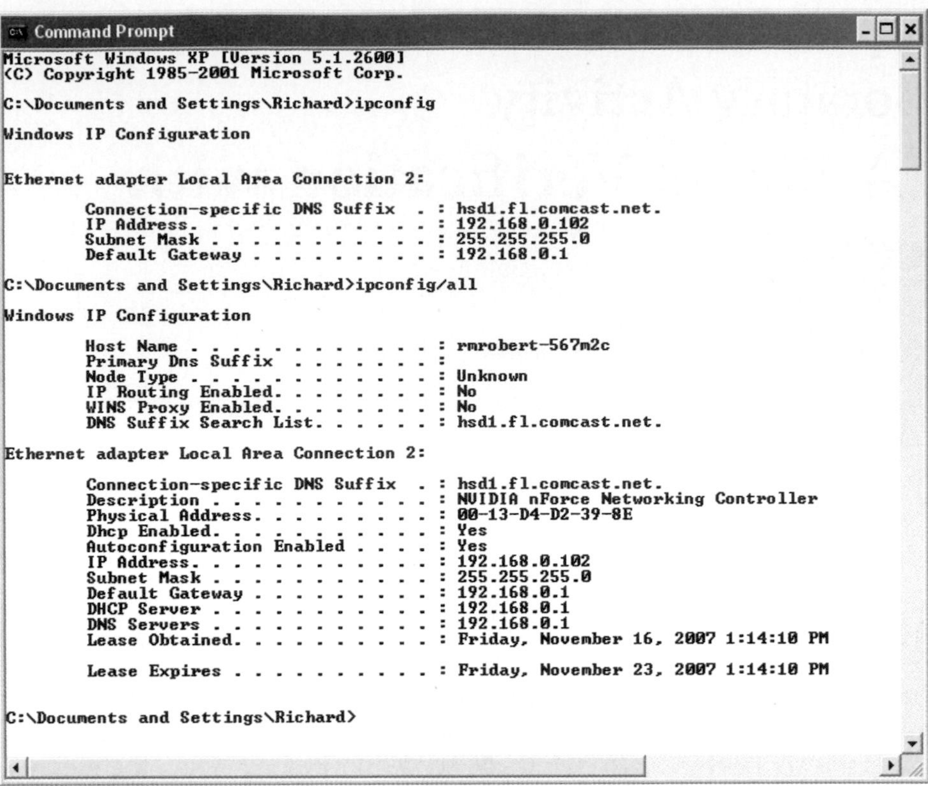

The information in the response of **ipconfig** or **ipconfig/all** will verify the assigned IP address and help you troubleshoot the network problem. The following are some switches commonly used that you should be aware of:

✔ **ipconfig/release**—Removes the IP address and displays 0.0.0.0 for the IP address.

✔ **ipconfig/renew**—Issues a new DHCP IP address. It may be the same as the last IP address used by the computer.

Equipment and Materials

✔ A workstation running Windows 2000, XP, or Vista. (You cannot use Windows 95, 98, or Me for this lab activity.)

Procedure

1. _______ Report to your assigned workstation.
2. _______ Boot the computer and verify it is in working order.
3. _______ Access the command prompt and issue the **ipconfig** command.
4. _______ On a separate sheet of paper, record the assigned IP address, the subnet mask, and the default gateway IP address.
5. _______ Now, issue the **ipconfig/all** command.
6. _______ On a separate sheet of paper, record the MAC address (physical address), the host name, whether or not the DHCP enabled, the DHCP server IP address, and the lease period. Answers will vary.

7. _______ Disconnect the network cable and record on a separate sheet of paper the message that appears on the screen after running **ipconfig**.
8. _______ Reconnect the network cable and run **ipconfig** once more. You should have the original IP address once more. If not, check the network cable connector to see that it is properly installed. If you cannot obtain an IP address, call your instructor for assistance.
9. _______ Now use the **ipconfig/release** command and record on a separate sheet of paper the results for the IP address, the subnet mask, and the default gateway.
10. _______ Now issue the **ipconfig/renew** command and record on a separate sheet of paper the results for the IP address, subnet mask, and default gateway.
11. _______ Now issue the **ipconfig/?** command and review the other available switches.
12. _______ Return the computer to its original configuration and then answer the review questions.

Review Questions

Answer the following questions on a separate sheet of paper. Please do not write in this book.

1. Which operating systems support the **ipconfig** command?
2. Which operating systems support the **winipcfg** command?
3. What does the acronym APIPA represent?
4. What does the acronym DHCP represent?
5. What two ways are IP addresses normally issued to a computer?
6. What is the purpose of a DHCP server?
7. What IP address will a computer have after issuing the **ipconfig/release** command?
8. What is the range of APIPA IP addresses?
9. What message appeared when you ran the **ipconfig** command with the network cable disconnected?
10. What does it mean when you see an IP address of 169.254.1.122 assigned to an adapter that is configured for DHCP?

Many metropolitan area networks (MANs) can exist within the same city, interconnecting businesses and college campuses that are under a common management.

Small-Office/Home-Office (SOHO) Networking

After completing this chapter, you will be able to:

- ✔ Determine the best media for use in a SOHO network based on cost and building structure.
- ✔ Determine an appropriate Internet access configuration based on the number of PCs and the type of network media used in a SOHO network.
- ✔ Design a SOHO network based on the media, the number of PCs, and the type of Internet access that will be used.
- ✔ Determine an appropriate level of administration for a SOHO network.
- ✔ Identify methods to secure a SOHO network.
- ✔ Use the Network Setup Wizard to set up Internet Connection Sharing (ICS) on a host PC.
- ✔ Use the Network Setup Wizard to allow a client access to the Internet through a host PC.
- ✔ Explain the networking features in Windows Vista.
- ✔ Explain how Network Discovery works in Windows Vista.
- ✔ Identify common problems that can occur in a new SOHO network installation.

A+ Exam—Key Points

The A+ Certification exams have increased the percentage of questions asked pertaining to networking. This is due to the growing number of small office and home networks. You need to be familiar with all aspects of home- and small-office networking. It is vital that you have some hands-on experience setting up a small network system with shared Internet access using a variety of media and equipment. The configuration for setting up Internet Connection Sharing (ICS) will most likely be covered in the exams. Be prepared to answer questions concerning shared folders and shared printers.

Key Words and Terms

The following words and terms will become important pieces of your computer vocabulary. Be sure you can define them.

gateway router
Home Phoneline Networking Alliance (HomePNA) technology
HomePNA adapter
Internet Connection Firewall (ICF)
Network Setup Wizard
packet sniffer
powerline communications (PLC)
small-office/home-office (SOHO) network
Universal Naming Convention (UNC)
virtual private network (VPN)

Installing a network in a home or small office is one of the most common tasks for a computer technician. This chapter prepares you for that task by applying many of the concepts presented earlier in the textbook to the installation, configuration, and support of the small-office/home-office (SOHO) network. You will learn how to use the Network Setup Wizard to configure a SOHO network and how to troubleshoot the common problems that can occur in a SOHO network. You will also learn about the many factors that determine SOHO network design.

Designing the SOHO Network

small-office/home-office (SOHO) network
a simple peer-to-peer LAN that is used to share resources and data in a home- or small-office environment.

The ***small-office/home-office (SOHO) network*** is a simple peer-to-peer LAN that is used to share resources and data in a home- or small-office environment. Although any computer hardware connected to the SOHO network can be shared, printers and Internet access devices are the most commonly shared.

As a computer technician, you may be called on to design and configure a SOHO network. There are several factors to consider in its design. These factors include the following:

- ✔ Type of media that will be used to connect the PCs together.
- ✔ Manner in which the networked PCs will access the Internet.
- ✔ Level of administration that will be used to secure resources and data.
- ✔ Method of security that will be used to protect the network from intruders.

This section examines each of these factors as it introduces the configurations and technologies commonly used in a SOHO network.

SOHO Media

The four common choices of networking media for SOHO networks are copper cable (Cat 5e and Cat 6), wireless, existing home telephone lines, and existing power lines. The choice is based on cost, building construction, and user or installer preference. For example, copper cable is inexpensive, but the building structure may prove difficult for installing the cables. This is especially true in buildings with open spaces, high ceilings, and concrete floors. Wireless technology is easy to install, but it has some security issues. Existing telephone lines are economical and convenient but may not be suitable for an office environment. Using existing power lines is inexpensive but undesirable to many people who do not like the idea of connecting the network to 120 volts of ac power.

There are many variables to consider when determining the type of network media to use. The following sections explore each of these variables and also look at implementing a mixed network environment and using a prewired home system.

Copper cable

Copper cable has been the choice for many years. However, the main objection to using copper cable is that it is often difficult to run the cable through the walls. To overcome this difficulty, copper cable can be used in one room and another form of network media can be used in a different room. For example, you can use copper cable in one room and wireless technology in the other. This type of network configuration is known as a hybrid, or a mixed network environment, and is discussed later in this chapter.

Wireless

Wireless is a popular choice of SOHO media. It is quick to install, and the location of the networked PCs can be easily changed. It is the ideal solution for a building that is difficult to cable. However, be aware that when using a wireless NIC to access the network, the default settings allow the network to be compromised by an intruder. The default setup configuration uses a default network group name and no data encryption. It is not difficult, though, to change the default network group name and to configure all packets to be encrypted. Doing so increases network security, **Figure 19-1.**

Existing phone lines

Home Phoneline Networking Alliance (HomePNA) technology allows existing home telephone lines to be used for the network media. Any telephone jack can be used as a connection point for the network system. Network cables and a hub are not required for making the connections. All that is needed is a ***HomePNA adapter.*** When a HomePNA adapter is installed, every telephone jack is part of the network. Some HomePNA adapters, like the one in **Figure 19-2,** include two RJ-11 ports. One RJ-11 port is used to connect to the telephone jack and the other is used to connect to either a telephone or to cascade to another HomePNA device, **Figure 19-3.** Cascading HomePNA adapters is useful when there is not an adequate amount of telephone jacks for each PC.

Home Phoneline Networking Alliance (HomePNA) technology
a technology that allows existing home telephone lines to be used for the network media.

HomePNA adapter
a networking device that allows every telephone jack that is connected together physically in a building to be part of the network.

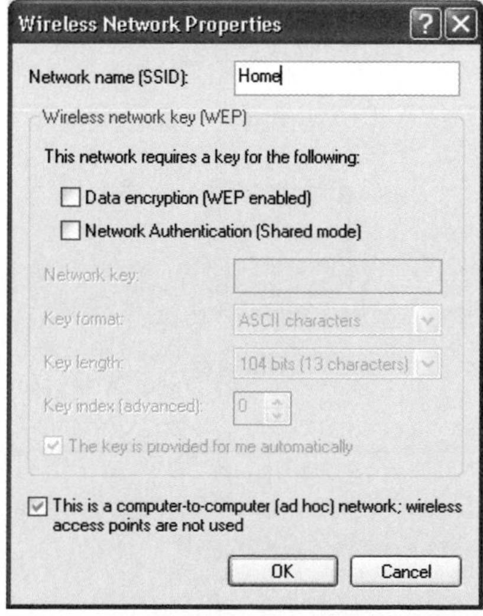

Figure 19-1.
The **Wireless Network Properties** dialog box provides information about such features as the name used for the wireless network, the type of security, and if the network is ad hoc or uses an access point.

Figure 19-2.
A—This HomePNA adapter connects to a PC with a USB cable. (Courtesy of Linksys) B—Back of HomePNA adapter. This adapter includes two RJ-11 jacks: a phone port to connect to a telephone or to another HomePNA adapter and a wall port to connect to the telephone line.

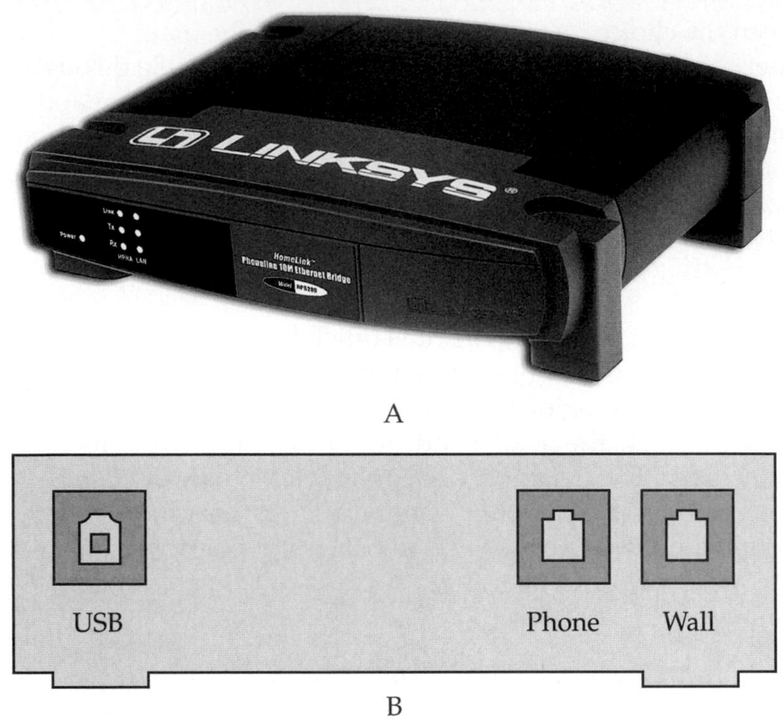

Figure 19-3.
A—PCs connected directly to separate telephone jacks through HomePNA adapters. Telephone jacks must share the same telephone line. B—PCs connected to the same telephone jack through cascading HomePNA adapters.

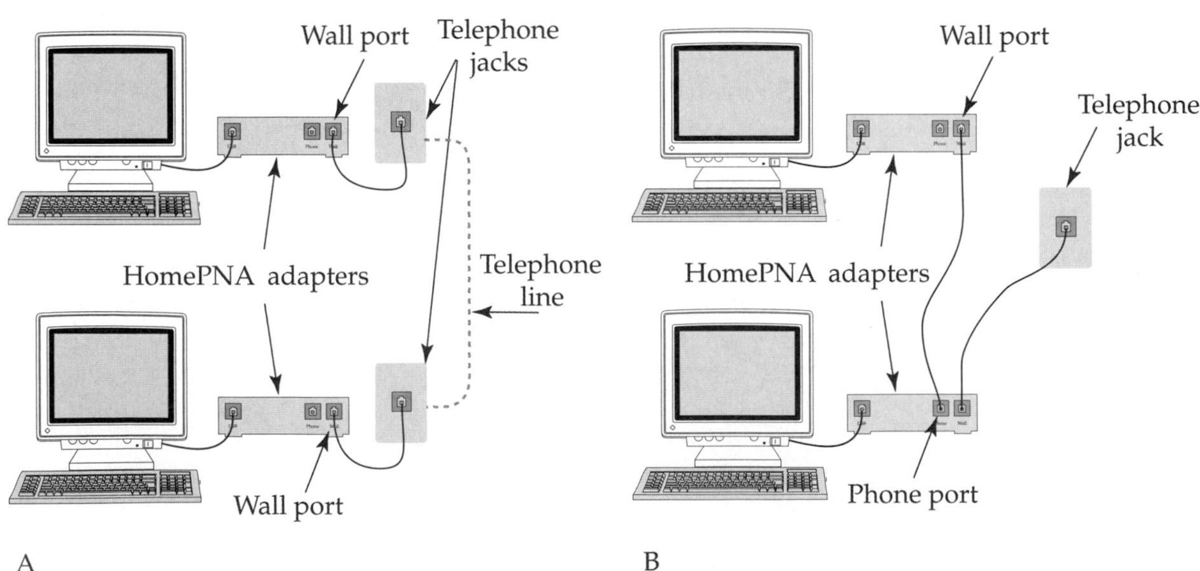

Using existing telephone lines as network media does not interfere with telephone calls. Typical voice and sound data transmitted on a residential telephone system are of relatively low frequencies, usually between 0 Hz and 4 kHz. The HomePNA adapter uses a frequency higher than 4 kHz to transmit data across the existing telephone line. The two frequencies do not interfere with each other.

While HomePNA technology is a practical solution for homes and for some businesses, it is not recommend for commercial buildings. Most corporate offices use a private branch exchange (PBX) as the centralized point of the telephone system. Because the telephone lines for a typical PBX system run directly from each telephone jack to the PBX, a complete network circuit cannot be established. The telephone lines in a home, however, typically run in a daisy-chain fashion from one telephone jack to the next, making a complete loop throughout the house.

Existing power lines

Powerline communications (PLC) technology allows existing power lines to be used as network media. A PLC adapter connects a PC to the 120-volt ac outlet, **Figure 19-4.** When a PLC network is implemented, two separate systems can operate over the same media at the same time: a 120-volt ac power source and an Ethernet network. PLC works in the same fashion as HomePNA technology by transmitting data at a higher frequency than the existing system. Data transmission on the PLC network operates at frequencies much higher than the 60 Hz of the 120-volt ac outlet.

powerline communications (PLC)
a technology that allows existing power lines to be used as network media.

Existing power lines have been used as a network media for some time in Europe, but have been slowly accepted in the United States. The main reason is that people have a natural fear of electricity. The idea of plugging their network equipment directly into a 120-volt ac outlet leaves them somewhat concerned. However, plugging in a PLC device into a 120-volt ac outlet is no more dangerous than plugging in any other electrical device. All electrical and electronic equipment used in the United States is tested for safety by the Underwriters Laboratories (UL). Any equipment designed to plug directly into the power outlet of a home is safe. After all, even the PC plugs directly into the 120-volt ac outlet, and it is safe to use.

Figure 19-4.
This PLC adapter plugs directly into an ac outlet. Some PLC adapters have a separate power cable. (Courtesy of Linksys)

PLC has some advantages over HomePNA technology. Typically a room is limited to one telephone jack or possibly two, but power outlets are spaced more conveniently throughout a building. With PLC, there is a connection point for the network just about anywhere in the building.

Mixed network environment

It is not uncommon to have a mixed network environment. For example, a home- or small-office network may use Cat 5e cable in one room and wireless technology in other rooms. When converting from one network media to another, a network bridge is required. A bridge connects dissimilar network media while making no decisions about packet contents, destination, or filtering. Bridges use MAC addresses to communicate. This allows all packets to pass through the bridge, no matter which protocol is used. (Bridges are covered in Chapter 18—WAN.)

Connecting a wireless network to another type of network always requires a wireless bridge. The wireless bridge is referred to as an *access point*, **Figure 19-5.** When a router is used to combine different media and to provide an Internet connection, it is often referred to as a ***gateway router.*** The exact terminology used can vary between different vendors.

gateway router a router that combines different media and provides an Internet connection.

Home prewired systems

New homes are often prewired for all types of low-voltage communications systems, such as telephone, audio, television, and computer network systems. Communication equipment suppliers manufacture cabinets to make telephone, television, sound, and computer network system installation simple and convenient. The cabinet shown in **Figure 19-6** provides a common connection point for each home communications system. The cabinet is designed to quickly configure network cables together as needed.

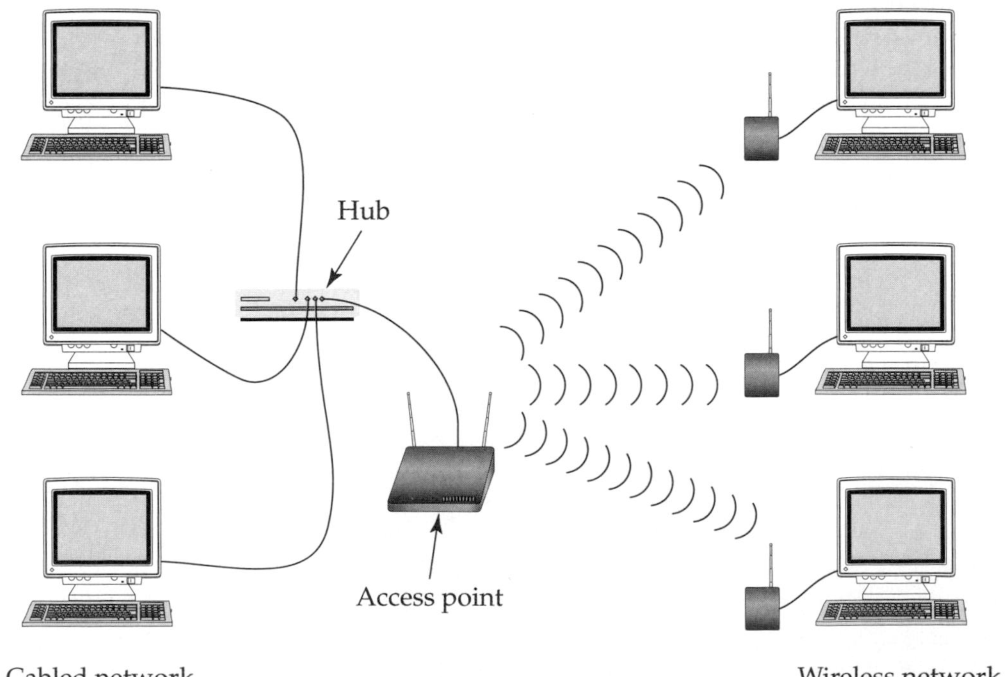

Figure 19-5. An access point functions as a bridge connecting a cabled network to a wireless network.

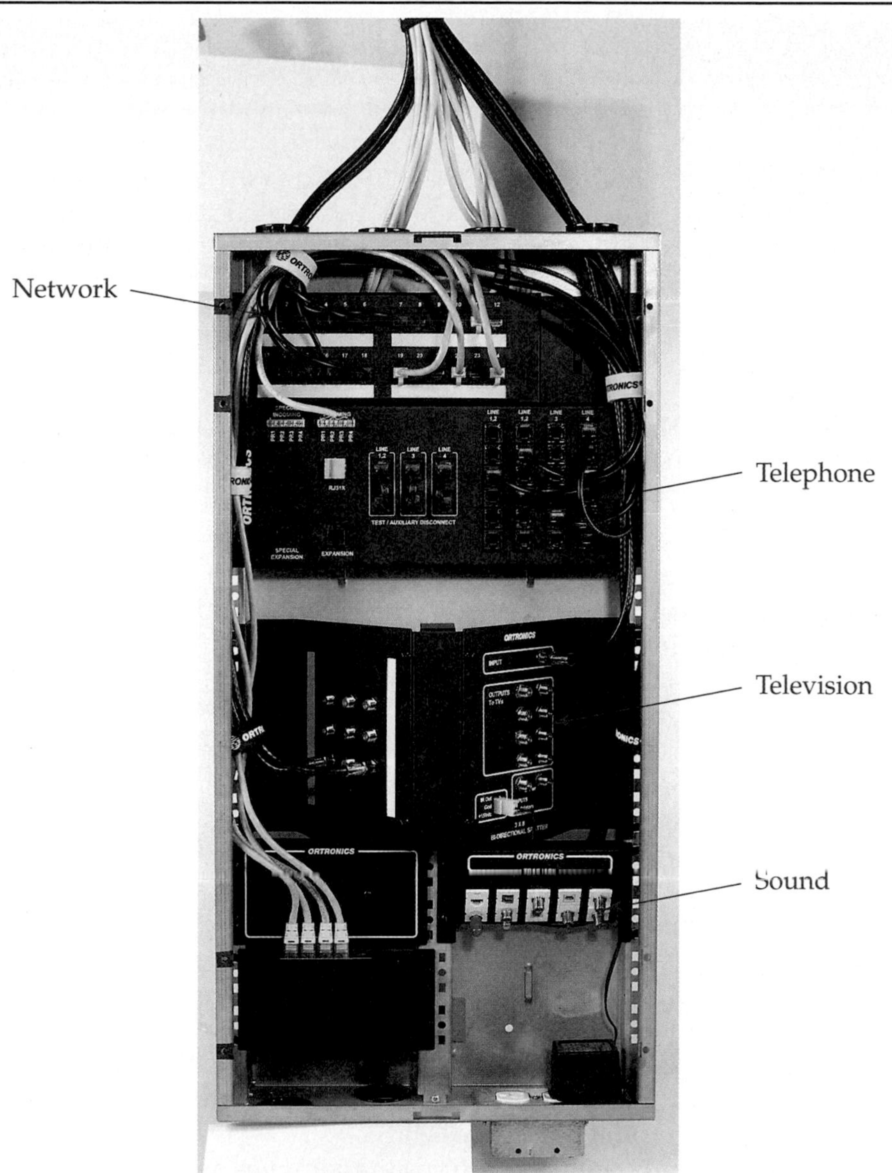

Figure 19-6. A communications cabinet provides a common connection point for home communications systems such as telephone, television, sound, and a computer network. (Courtesy of Ortronics)

Data transfer rates

A comparison of data transfer rates will also help in selecting the best media for the network. The table in **Figure 19-7** compares commonly used media in a SOHO network. As indicated in the table, copper cable has the only predictable data rate. Wireless, existing power lines, and existing telephone line data throughputs vary greatly. Often, vendors emphasize the maximum achievable throughput for these media, but this is not the normal throughput. Actual throughput varies because of environmental conditions. For example, a wireless network may advertise a throughput of 100+ Mbps but can only achieve that if the wireless network devices are at a close proximity, without radio interference or partitions between the transmitter and receiver. The farther apart the transmitter and receiver, the more the throughput rate drops. If wireless devices must transmit through walls, the transmission rate also drops, especially if the walls are constructed of a dense material such as concrete.

Figure 19-7.
Data rate comparison for various SOHO network media.

Media	Maximum Data Rate	Remarks
Copper Cable	10 Mbps or 100 Mbps	Predictable data rates.
Wireless (802.11a, b, g, and n)	100 Mbps or higher	Data rate is drastically affected by distance, building materials, and interference. Rates below 10 Mbps are not uncommon.
Existing Power Lines (PLC)	No standard	Advertised as 75 Mbps, but in reality is 4 Mbps–10 Mbps.
Existing Phone Lines (HomePNA)	No standard	Advertised as high as 32 Mbps, but in reality is 4 Mbps–10 Mbps.

PLC technology has a limited throughput because power line conductors are not designed for data transmission. Also, power line conductors may be connected to sources of interference such as electric motors. Since interference on the power line corrupts packets, the packets have to be retransmitted, thus reducing the actual system throughput.

Using the existing telephone lines is unpredictable because the older generation lines were not designed to carry high frequencies. The length of the telephone cable also reduces throughput. Cable signal losses known as attenuation increase directly with cable length. As cable length increases, the digital signal strength deteriorates which results in corrupt data packets. Each packet that is corrupt must be retransmitted. The loss of data packets and the need to retransmit each lost packet causes the loss of effective bandwidth. The length of the cable will finally reach a point where all data packets are corrupt.

Another cable length factor is cross talk. Older style telephone cable was not designed with twisted pairs. Thus, older cable is much more likely to produce cross talk even on a very short length of cable. The twists in the cable pairs is designed to counter the production of cross talk.

As you can see, the only predictable transmission rates are with traditional network cable. However, the need for a network media that overcomes building structure limitations may outweigh the disadvantages of the lower and unpredictable rates. It is, therefore, the choice of the network user or installer as to the best media to use for the SOHO network.

Internet Access and SOHO Design

There are several typical Internet access configurations that can be used in SOHO networks. The exact configuration depends on the building's environment and the type of Internet access device selected. The common choices of Internet access devices in a SOHO network are the telephone modem, DSL modem, and Cable modem. This section covers various network configurations that use a telephone, DSL, or Cable modem to access the Internet.

Telephone modem Internet access

When using a telephone modem as the Internet access device, the configuration varies depending on the number of PCs that are networked. A two-PC network may be connected directly from PC to PC without the use of a hub. **Figure 19-8** shows a two-PC network that uses a telephone modem to connect to the Internet. In this configuration, the two PCs are connected directly from NIC to NIC with a crossover cable. This is the simplest way of connecting PCs together in a SOHO network. Other ways of connecting two PCs can be with a null modem cable, a USB cable, a parallel cable, or infrared hardware.

A NIC is generally incorporated in most motherboards today, which means you may not need to purchase them for your network.

Notice that the PC with the internal telephone modem in **Figure 19-9** is designated as the host. It is the *host* because it provides the Internet connection for both PCs. For the host to provide Internet access, Internet Connection Sharing (ICS) must be established. ICS is Microsoft's simple application of the network address translation (NAT) standard. The NAT standard was developed by the Internet Engineering Task Force (IETF) and is described in detail in RFC 1631. NAT was specifically designed as a standard for sharing a single Internet connection and providing a type of firewall protection. NAT can support more clients than ICS and is more versatile than ICS.

The host in a typical ICS configuration is always assigned the IP address 192.168.000.001, and the clients are assigned IP addresses in sequence starting at 192.168.000.002. A PC that accesses the Internet through the host is called a *client*. Setting up an ICS is covered in this chapter under SOHO Administration.

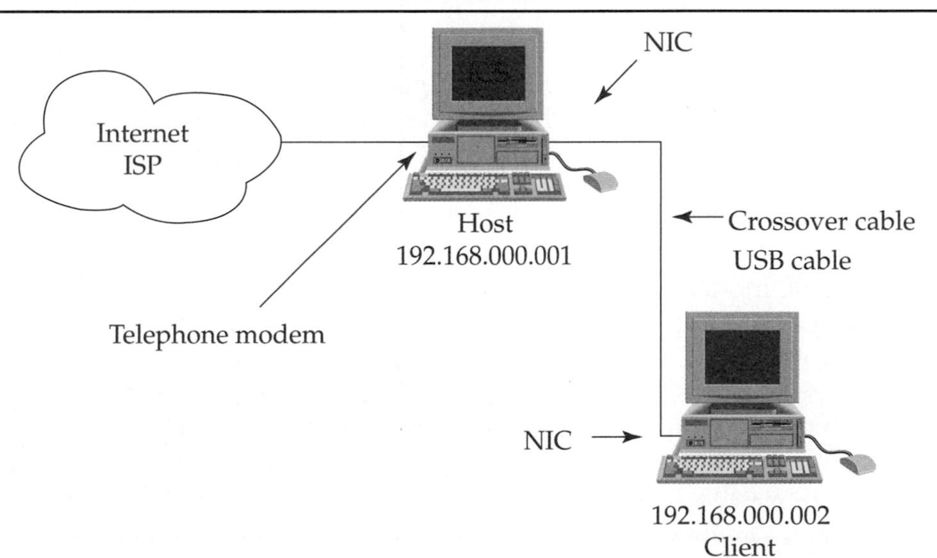

Figure 19-8. A two-PC network with Internet access via a modem. PCs are connected together with a crossover cable.

Figure 19-9.
A three-PC network with Internet access via a modem. A hub is needed in this configuration to connect the PCs together.

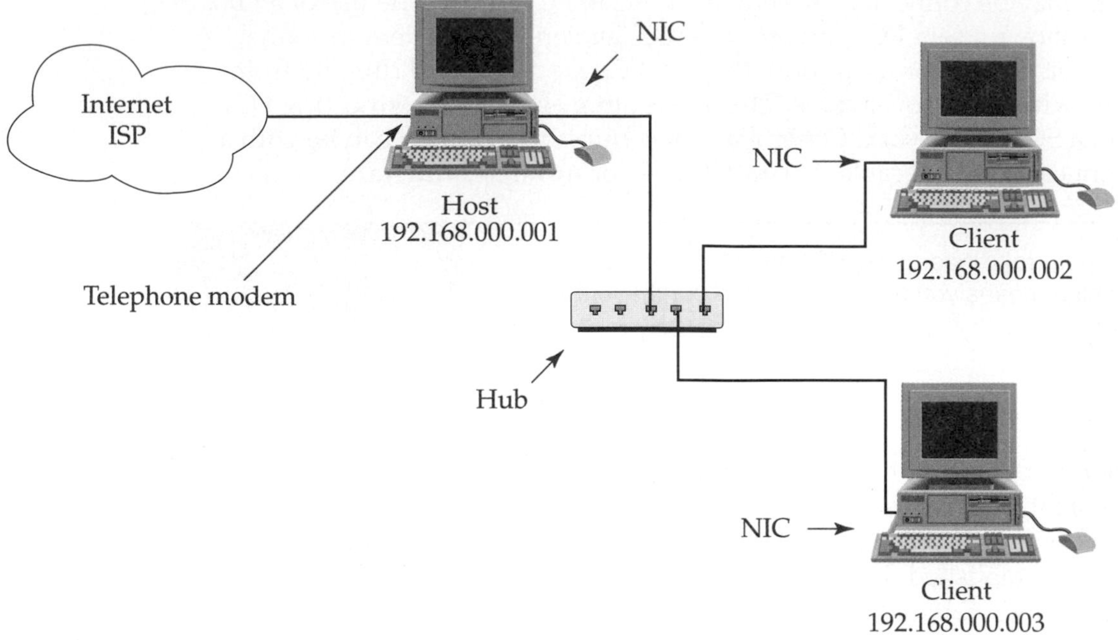

In general, the term *host* describes any computer that provides a service. The term *client* describes a computer that uses the service provided by the host. In the example of an ICS system, the host provides Internet access to the client computers that wish to connect to the Internet.

Note that the three PCs in Figure 19-9 are connected together using a hub. This is a typical copper cable arrangement. Again, note that the PC connected to the Internet is the host, while the other two are considered clients. When a client sends a request to access the Internet, the host automatically connects to the ISP. The host must be turned on for the clients to access the Internet.

DSL or Cable modem Internet access

A typical DSL modem has several types of connectors with which you need to be familiar. Look at **Figure 19-10.** An RJ-11 jack provides a connection to the DSL service provider. A DSL modem may also have a swapper connection. A *swapper connection* "swaps" the telephone line pairs so that the DSL modem can connect to the DSL signal. This feature is useful in case the DSL service was installed on the nonstandard pair. Cable pairs are often switched by mistake when new cable installers are running cable in a new dwelling during construction. The installer's mistake will go undetected until that particular pair is actually needed. Locating the switched pair using a multimeter or other test equipment could be very time consuming. It is much more convenient to simply use the swapper connection. Some DSL modems have this feature built in rather than offering a second connection point.

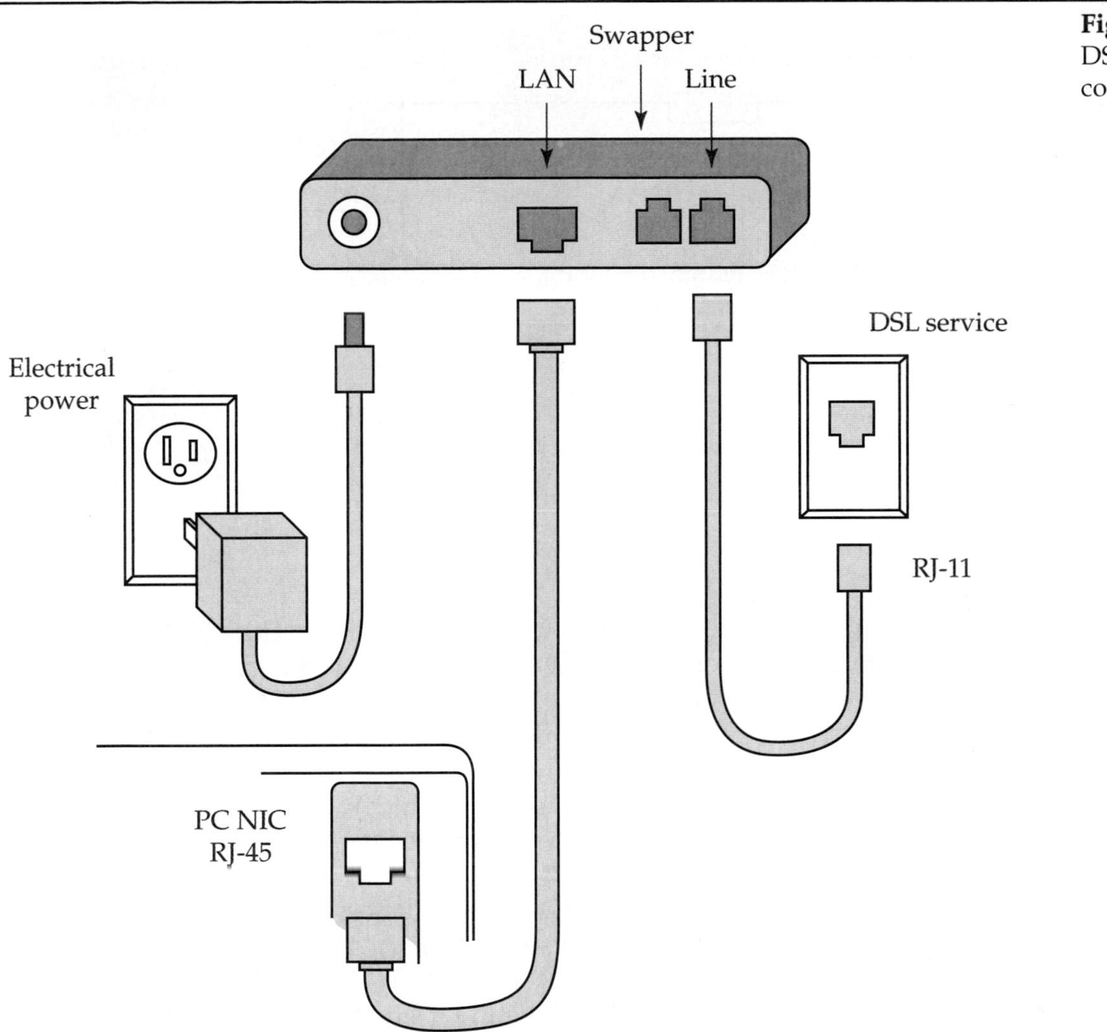

Figure 19-10. DSL modem connections.

The DSL modem is also equipped with a LAN connector. This is an RJ-45 jack that connects directly to the PC or to another network device, such as a router. The DSL modem also requires an electrical power supply. It typically connects to a standard 120-volt ac outlet and then converts the voltage level to approximately 12-volt dc through an inline adapter.

A Cable modem is installed in a similar fashion as the DSL modem. The main difference is that the Cable modem connects to the Cable television provider through the use of a coaxial cable F connector rather than an RJ-11 jack. A two-way cable splitter may be required to split the cable connection between the Cable modem and the televisions in the dwelling. Software setup is basically the same for DSL and Cable modems.

In **Figure 19-11,** a DSL modem is incorporated into a SOHO network. Here the host PC is required to have two NICs installed. One is used to make the connection to the DSL modem, and the other is used to connect to the hub. The network card can be a USB Plug and Play type rather than a PCI type.

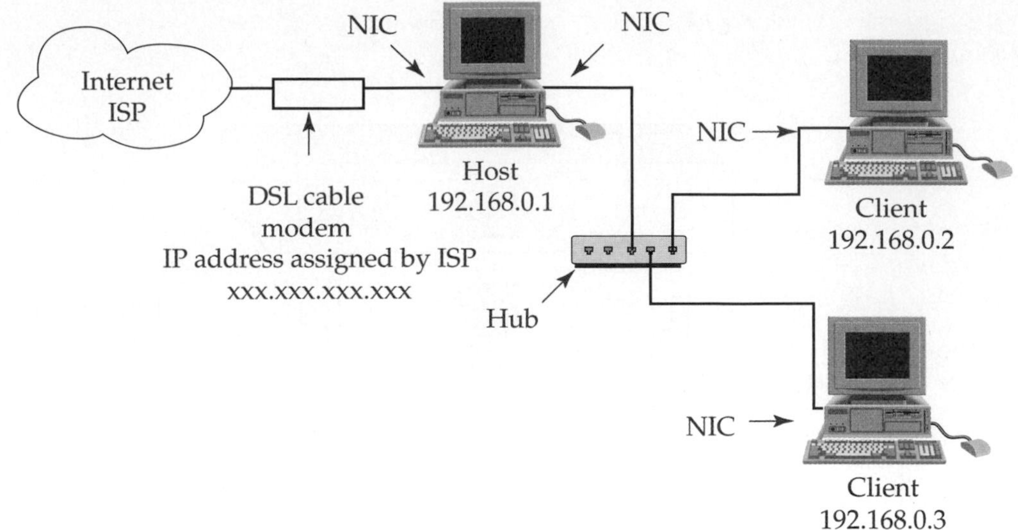

Figure 19-11. A three-PC network with Internet access via a DSL modem. The host PC contains two network cards—one to connect to the hub and the other to connect to the DSL or cable modem.

To eliminate the need for an extra NIC in the host PC, a router can be incorporated into the network, **Figure 19-12.** A router can configure the SOHO IP addresses independently. A host PC, like the one used in the ICS configuration, is not needed. When using a router to share and control network access, all computers become clients and the router becomes the host. The router controls all access to the Internet and is typically more flexible than a Windows ICS host. Most routers not only supply software wizards to automatically configure the SOHO network, but also incorporate security features such as a firewall. A router can be configured to control all port addresses, whereas a Windows XP host is limited to the most common port addresses. A router can also be configured to allow a computer in the network to connect directly to the Internet on the public side of the router and avoid port-filtering techniques. This would be useful for situations such as online Internet gaming between one of the SOHO stations and another across the Internet.

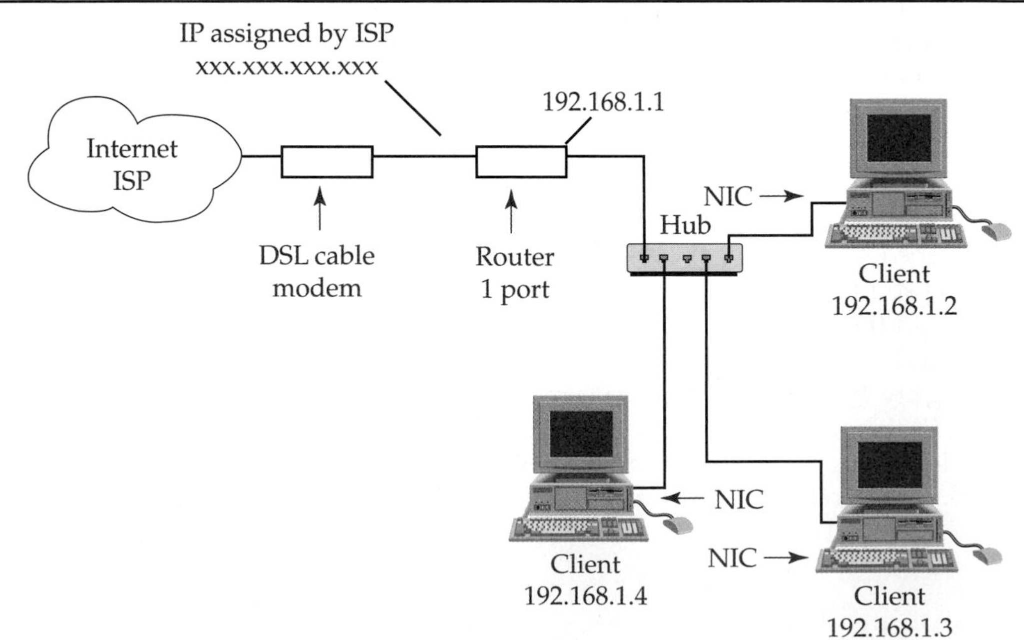

Figure 19-12. The router in this configuration has only one port, so a hub must be used.

The router is a complete small computer system. It contains a CPU, memory, and software.

A router can be purchased with one or more LAN connections. When a router with several LAN connectors is used, the hub can be eliminated from the network, **Figure 19-13.** Routers can serve the same function as a hub. The router can incorporate other features, such as firewall protection and VPN support. (Firewalls and VPNs are covered in this chapter under SOHO Security.) When the router serves both purposes, it reduces the overall complexity of the system. Always check the router specifications to be sure of all the features that are available.

A SOHO network can consist of several different technologies. Remember that when installing a mixture of technologies, a bridge or gateway router is required to connect the different technologies together. The SOHO network in **Figure 19-14** incorporates a DSL modem, router, copper cable, wireless, and HomePNA. This is a perfect example of how various network media can be combined to overcome building structure limitations. This type of SOHO network setup, however, can be challenging when the network devices come from different manufacturers. There can also be some difficulties when mixing media from various manufacturers. It is best to select equipment from the same manufacturer.

An example of a very robust router is the Motorola wireless broadband router model number WR850G. It is a combination cable and wireless router. It incorporates four 10/100BaseT RJ-45 connections and an antenna. This device is especially designed for offices that require mixed media types.

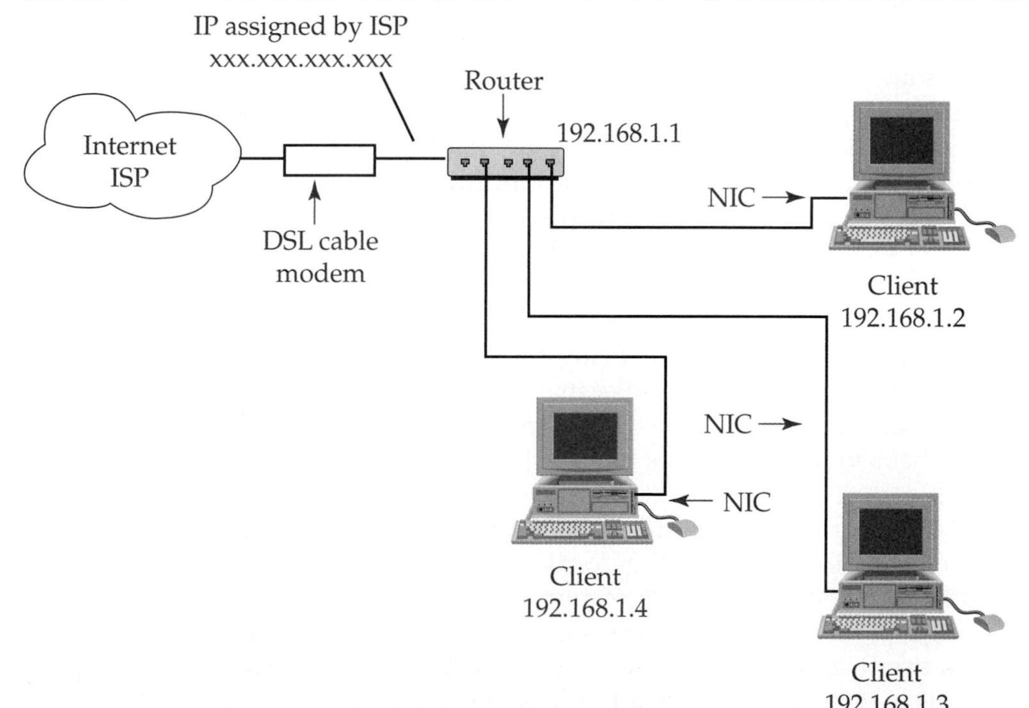

Figure 19-13.
In this example, the router has multiple LAN connections, so it functions as a hub.

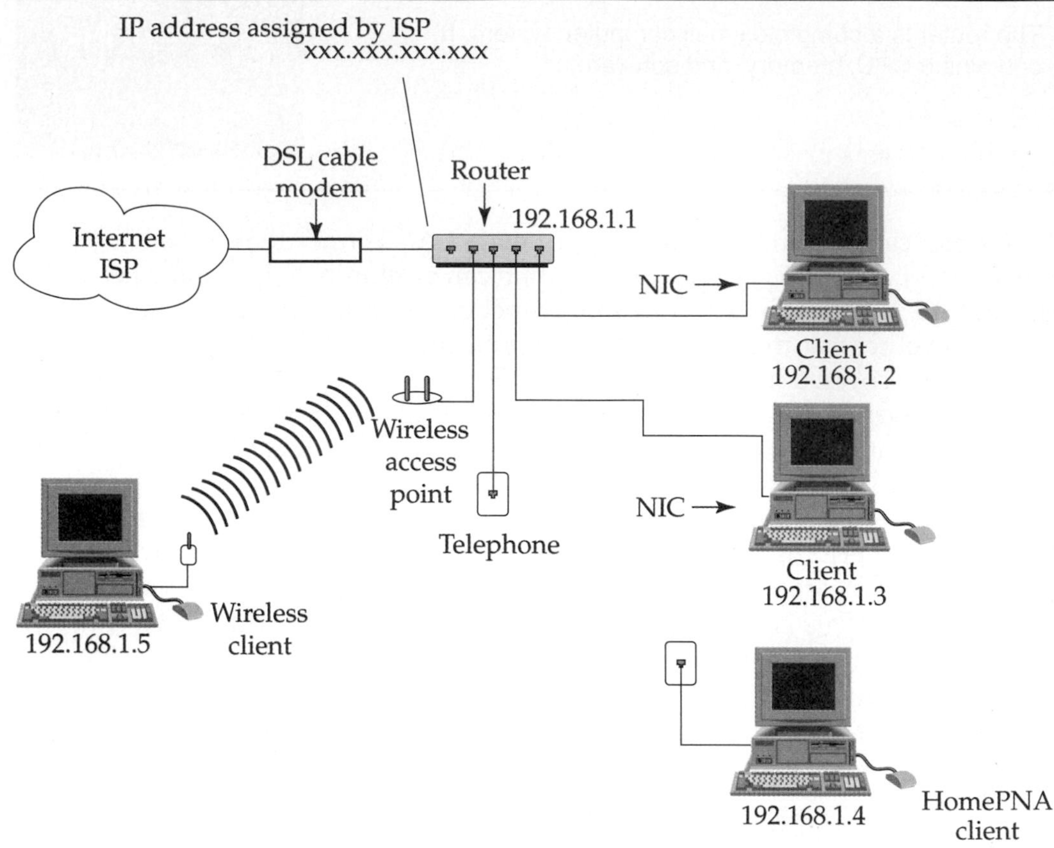

Figure 19-14. This SOHO network incorporates cable, wireless, and existing telephone lines as its network media.

SOHO Administration

SOHO network administration can be as simple or as complex as you wish to make it. Since the SOHO is a peer-to-peer network, you need not have any real administrative hierarchy. Everyone using the network can have equal access to all files and programs on the network. However, this can be disastrous. With everyone having equal access, anyone can change the properties of any PC in the network. A better scenario would be to have a single administrator with limited authority delegated to other users. The administrator can determine how much control other users have over hardware and software by setting up local and share-level security. (See Chapter 17—Network Administration for a complete discussion of local and share-level security.)

Local security is implemented by creating a local user account on each PC. The local user account allows the user to log on to a single computer where the user account has been created. Remember that a peer-to-peer network uses the workgroup model of security. This model of security maintains a security list at each PC and requires that a local user account be set up at every PC the user will access locally.

Local security protects system settings on a PC. Any changes the user makes to the desktop or to a program is stored in the user's personal settings on that PC. These changes do not affect other local users.

Share-level security protects resources accessed from across the network by requiring a password to access the share or by limiting its access. For example, a network user may only have read-only access to files on another PC, or they may not be able to access the files at all unless they know the password.

Even in a home network, local and share-level security should be implemented to avoid disastrous situations. To reinforce how important security is, let's look at a typical home network in which no security has been implemented.

In the network shown in **Figure 19-15,** two parents use one of the PCs and two children, ages 10 and 16, use the other. Each PC has been set up with a single user account. A color printer is attached to the parent's PC and is shared to allow the children to print to it from their computer. Drive C on the parent's computer is also shared and allows full access to all files. Both of the parents use their PC for work-related activities and for writing checks.

The children use their PC for school assignments and use the color printer to print their school assignments and the graphics they find on the Internet. They also use their PC for their favorite pastime, computer games. The children are constantly downloading sample gaming software and exchanging software games with their friends. The children often need to use the PC at the same time. When this happens, one of them uses the parent's PC.

As you are probably sensing, there are bound to be severe problems because of this lax setup. With everyone using the same local user account, anyone using a PC can make changes on it. For instance, the children could delete important files on their parent's PC, such as banking information. They could even delete important files from across the network if share-level security has not been set up on the parent's local hard drive. Also, one of the children can download a game on their parent's PC and then change the PC's default settings to optimize the game. Or, by simply installing the computer game, a DLL file or some other file can possibly be overwritten. This would lock up, or crash, the PC.

A better scenario would be to secure the network as in **Figure 19-16.** In this configuration, a user account for each family member has been set up on the parent's PC. This ensures that personal settings or files will not be changed or deleted. Also, drive C is no longer shared. The children cannot access it from

Figure 19-15.
A home network with no security.

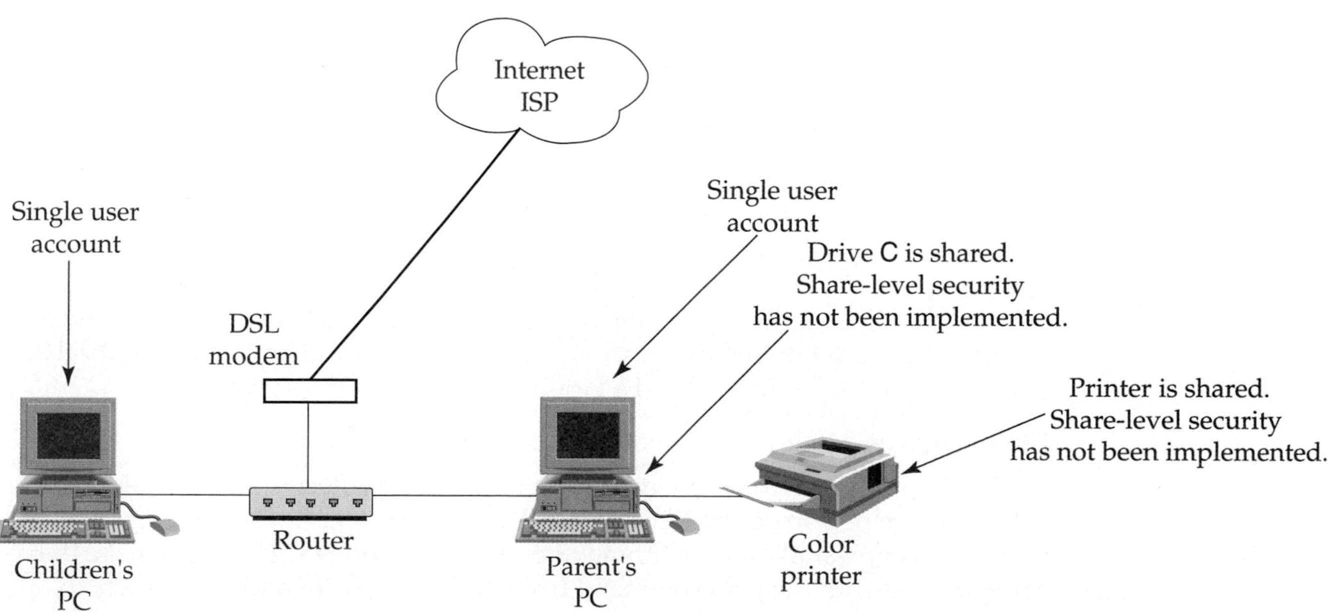

Figure 19-16.
A home network with security.

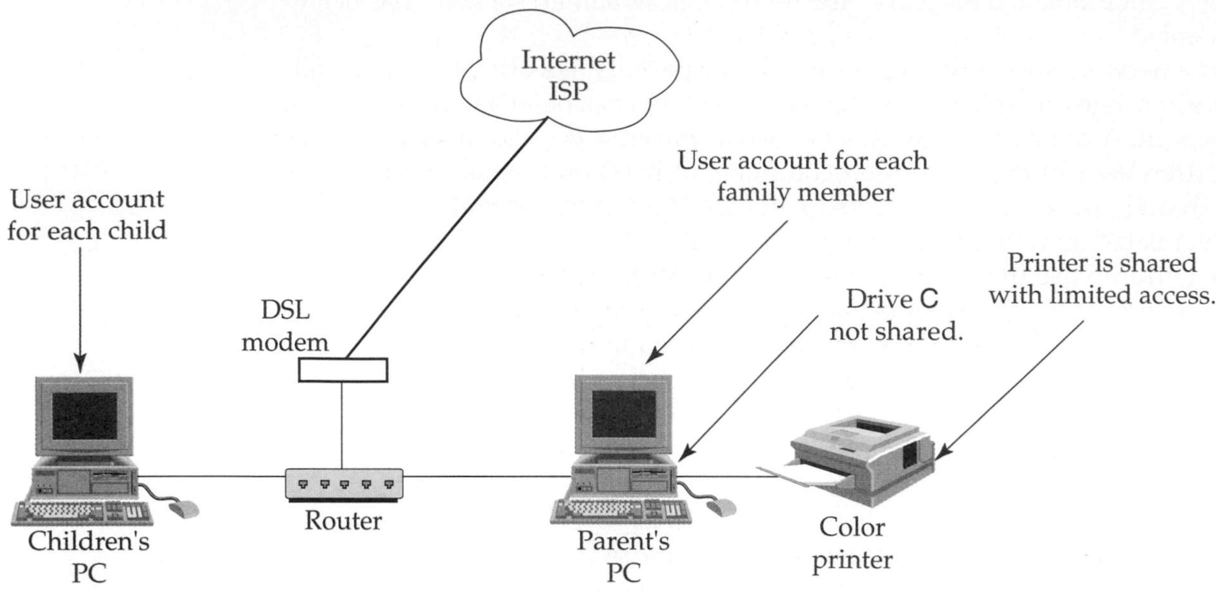

their own PC and delete important files. The printer is shared with limited access that allows the children to print through it but not change the printer's settings. As you can see, a certain level of security can lessen the opportunity for a problem to occur.

Other security practices to keep in mind are to use passwords that are complex, containing uppercase and lowercase letters, numbers, and special symbols. *Never* use a password that matches any word found in a dictionary or a person's name. *Never* leave the password blank. *Always* encrypt important data so even if it is accessed, it will be of little use to the intruder.

SOHO Security

PCs in a SOHO network are vulnerable to attacks from outside the LAN if the LAN is connected to the Internet. The Internet is a "public" media. Users from anywhere in the world could access a networked PC through the Internet connection or intercept a PC's message content. There are several ways to set up security to protect the SOHO network from intruders and to protect data as it travels across the Internet. Two common security implementations that should be configured for the SOHO network are a firewall and a virtual private network (VPN).

Firewall

In Chapter 18—WAN, you learned that a firewall protects a LAN by blocking access to specific ports or by filtering out IP addresses, packet contents, services, and protocols. For example, a firewall can filter out echo requests. This stops a site that is being probed with the **ping** command from displaying its IP address via echo.

There are times when you may need to block a specific port or open a port. For example, a firewall is set up to block all ports that are not absolutely essential. A person wishes to participate in a game online. The game "Rainbow Six" requires the use of TCP ports 2346, 2347, and 2348 for Internet gaming. These ports can be opened by entering their numbers in the firewall service properties dialog box. Opening these ports allows data to pass through the firewall, allowing two computers to communicate freely during a gaming session. You can view the Microsoft Knowledge Base Article 307554 online to see other port addresses associated with common games and services.

Windows XP comes with a standard firewall called the ***Internet Connection Firewall (ICF)***, which can be configured to keep unauthorized users from accessing the network. There are also many third-party utilities that can be used to increase SOHO security. Using the Network Setup Wizard to install ICF is covered later in this chapter.

Internet Connection Firewall (ICF) software included in Windows XP that can be configured to keep unauthorized users from accessing the network.

Remember that a firewall should only be installed on the host PC. Installing a firewall on more than one PC in the SOHO network adversely affects shares, thus preventing the network's main purpose. Also, do not implement a firewall and a VPN at the same time. The two security systems will conflict.

Virtual private network (VPN)

A ***virtual private network (VPN)*** ensures that data sent across the Internet is not intercepted, read, or modified. It does this by creating a private tunnel between the destination and source PC and encrypting packet contents. As the term *tunnel* implies, all the messages are exchanged privately as though they traveled through the public space of the Internet encapsulated in a security tunnel that no one else can see into or access, **Figure 19-17.**

virtual private network (VPN) a security configuration that ensures data sent across the Internet is not read or modified. It does this by creating a private tunnel between the destination and source PC and encrypting packet contents.

A VPN should be created to ensure security when communicating across the Internet through an ISP. A VPN can also be created if you are permanently connected to the Internet via a Cable modem or DSL modem.

Normally, because data is encoded in plain ASCII text, the content of a typical packet is completely viewable through a packet sniffer. A ***packet sniffer*** is a utility that captures packets on a network and displays their entire contents. When a VPN connection is made, all the contents of the packet are encrypted except for the destination address. The destination address remains readable so that it can travel across a series of Internet routers to reach its final destination. The VPN is transparent to users at the destination and the source.

packet sniffer a utility that captures packets on a network and displays their entire contents.

The two main security connection protocols associated with a VPN connection are Point-to-Point Tunneling Protocol (PPTP) and Layer-Two-Tunneling Protocol (L2TP). These protocols also incorporate other protocols, such as IPsec, IKE, and CHAP, to further enhance their security features.

Be aware that many ISPs do not allow VPN connections through their system. The ISP filters out protocols associated with VPNs. To determine if you can use a VPN, check with the ISP. Some ISPs advertise the use of VPN connections to recruit users. Also, since the establishment of a VPN tunnel depends on the destination and source having a unique IP address, using an ISP that assigns IP addresses from a pool of numbers can also create a problem. The VPN will only work with a SOHO network that has a permanently assigned IP address.

There can be problems implementing a VPN connection in a network that uses a firewall or ICS. Microsoft recommends that you do not use the VPN feature at the same time you are using a firewall or ICS. To connect from a SOHO network to a work site using a laptop that is implementing a VPN, it may be

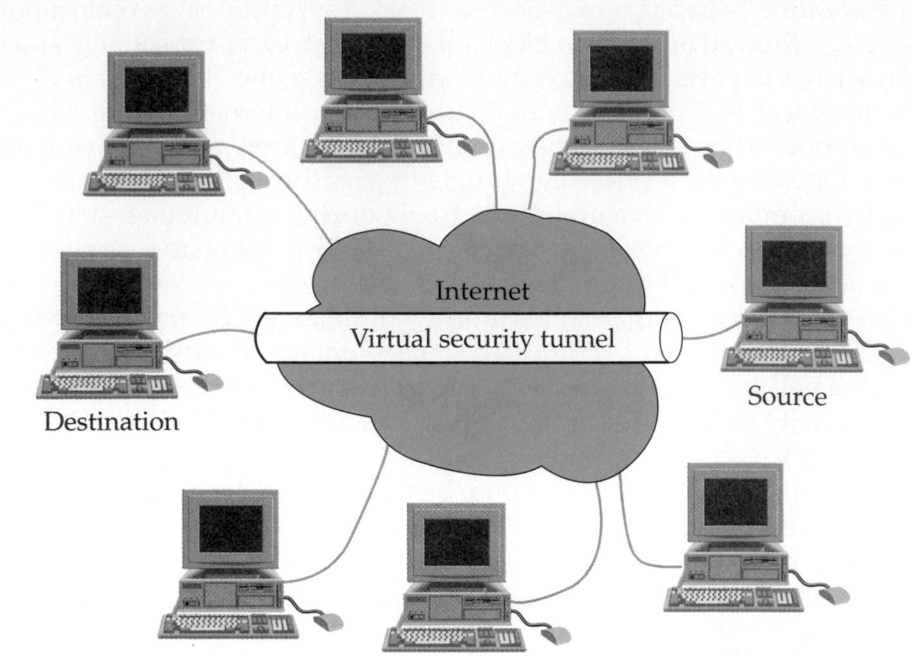

Figure 19-17. A virtual private network (VPN) creates a private tunnel between the destination and source PC. The data flowing between the two PCs cannot be interpreted by other computers on the Internet.

best to configure the laptop for an Internet connection separate from the SOHO network. In **Figure 19-18,** a laptop makes a direct connection to the Internet through the DSL modem via a hub. This avoids conflicts between the VPN on the laptop and the firewall in the router. There are third-party vendors, though, who market security software and hardware that allow both the firewall and the VPN to run on the same SOHO network.

Configuring the SOHO Network with Windows XP

Ideally, all PCs in the SOHO network would use the latest operating system. This would provide for the easiest installation. Unfortunately, this is not always the case. Many SOHO networks are constructed with various operating systems and equipment. Incorporating legacy computer systems with modern ones can be challenging but can be done if carefully thought out.

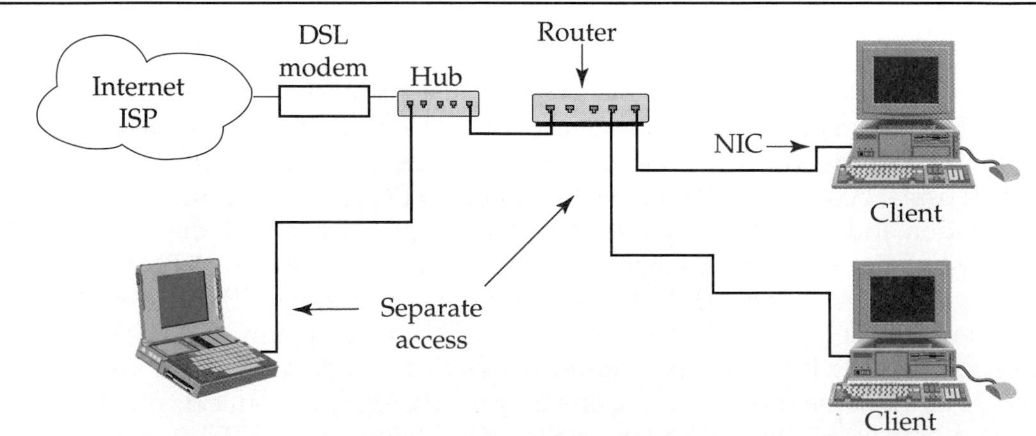

Figure 19-18. Connecting a laptop directly to the Internet access rather than to the network avoids conflicts between the laptop's VPN and the network's firewall.

Remember to use the PC with the latest or most up-to-date operating system as the host or as the computer that will share other resources, such as a printer. Typically, the latest operating system will have the technology available to support older operating systems. They will also have a wizard that assists in configuring the network. For example, Microsoft Windows XP has the Network Setup Wizard.

The ***Network Setup Wizard*** makes it easy to set up a SOHO network. It includes a series of dialog boxes that ask for information about the network. The wizard can be accessed through **Start | Settings | Control Panel | Network Connections | Setup a home or small office network**. **Figure 19-19** shows the first dialog box of the Network Setup Wizard. The Network Setup Wizard helps you to share an Internet connection, enable the Internet Connection Firewall (ICF), and enable file and printer sharing.

Network Setup Wizard a Windows XP wizard that makes setting up a network easy by including a series of dialog boxes that ask for information about the network.

The Network Setup Wizard is easy to use if you are familiar with networking hardware and terminology. However, if you have never set up a network before, it is easy to provide the wrong information. As an aid, the Network Setup Wizard includes a checklist, **Figure 19-20,** which assists in setting up a SOHO network. The checklist can be printed and carried with you until you become comfortable with setting up networks.

Share an Internet Connection

One of the main tasks of configuring a SOHO network with Internet access is setting up ICS. ICS can be configured manually or automatically. When configured automatically, choose from the Network Setup Wizard menu "This computer connects directly to the Internet. The other computers on my network connect to the Internet through this computer." See **Figure 19-21.** When activated, a series of prompts appear on the screen. Answer the series of questions presented in the dialog boxes.

Using the Network Setup Wizard is by far the easiest method for setting up an Internet connection share. Even a novice can usually configure ICS by responding to the series of dialog boxes. A technician will also use the wizard to set up ICS, but they must know how to configure the same connection manually to be able to perform and understand the results of troubleshooting ICS installation.

Figure 19-19. Network Setup Wizard welcome screen.

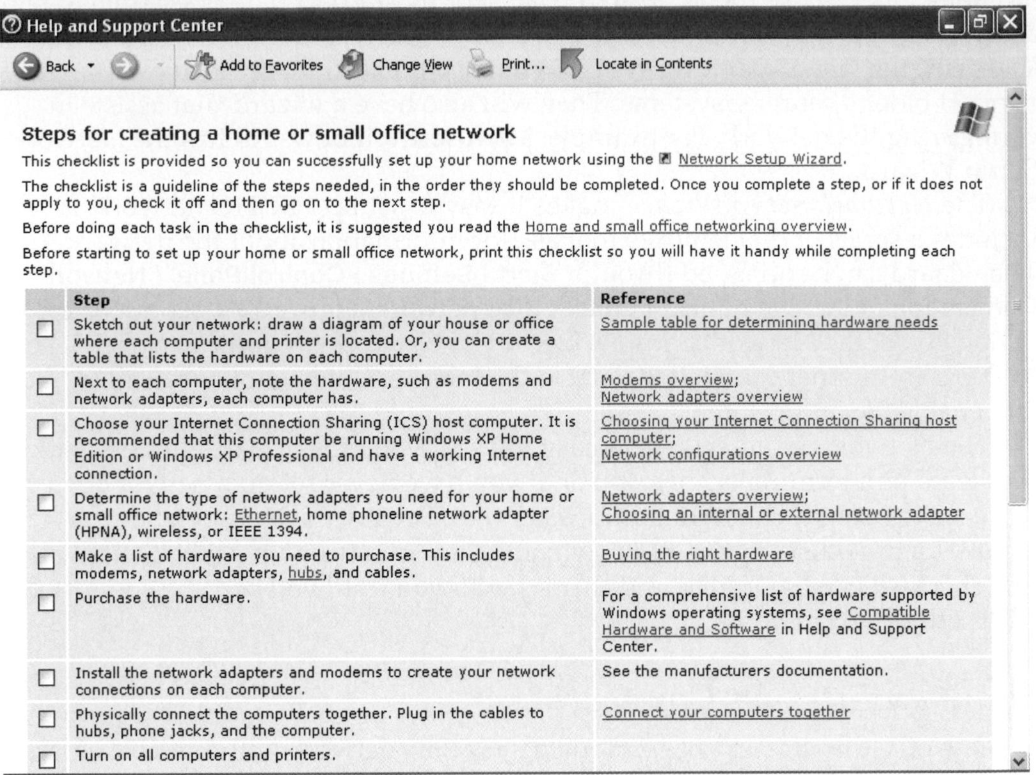

Figure 19-20. This checklist, provided by Windows XP, is a valuable aid for setting up a SOHO network.

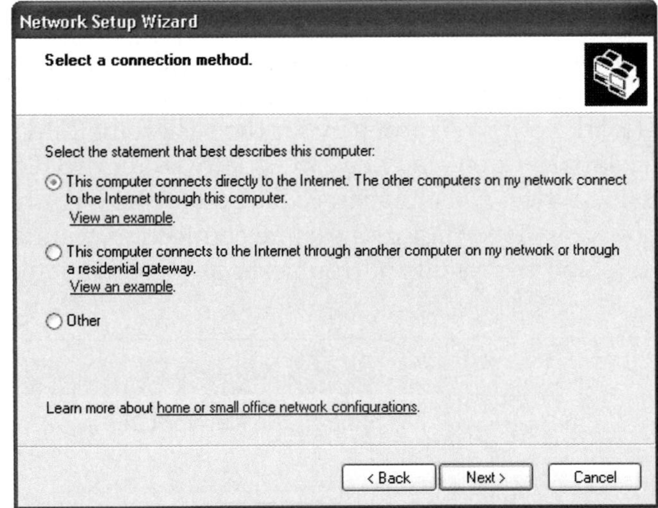

Figure 19-21. The Network Setup Wizard prompts you for a connection method.

After the computer sharing the Internet connection has been set up and configured, you can make a disk that will automatically set up the clients for you. You can make the client disks by simply inserting the Windows XP installation CD. When the first screen appears, select **Additional tasks** from the menu and follow the prompts. A client disk will be made on a floppy, which can be inserted into each client PC. It will automatically configure the client with the appropriate IP address and protocols necessary. If, however, the clients are running Windows XP, you may, as an alternative, run the Network Setup Wizard on those computers and choose **This computer connects to the Internet through another computer on my network or through a residential gateway**. The wizard will automatically configure the client with the appropriate IP address and protocols.

Set Up Internet Connection Firewall

The Internet Connection Firewall (ICF) is automatically enabled on the computer that connects directly to the Internet or has ICS installed. When ICF is enabled, it not only protects the computer on which it is configured, but also the other computers on the network. The ICF monitors all communications from the Internet by inspecting the source and destination of each packet sent to the network. The combination of port number and IP address determines if the packet may pass to the network or be discarded. The firewall can also filter packets based on services. Services are identified by port numbers.

Once ICF is enabled, it can be configured manually by accessing the **Network Connection** folder, right-clicking the firewall-enabled connection, and selecting **Properties**. From the **Properties** dialog box, select the **Advanced** tab and then click the **Settings** button. A dialog box like that in **Figure 19-22** will appear, displaying a list of services that can be filtered by the firewall. To select a service, click in the box next to the service. A check mark will appear in the box. If the service exists on another computer in the network, you must enter that computer's name or IP address in the **Service Settings** dialog box, **Figure 19-23.** To access the **Service Settings** dialog box, highlight the service to be configured and click the **Edit** button.

In Figure 19-23, the computer hosting the POP3 service is identified by its name, "infinity-soyo." Notice how the POP3 e-mail service corresponds with port 110 indicated in the text box. Port 110 is the default port number for the POP3 service.

A service that is not listed in the **Advanced Settings** may be added by clicking the **Add** button. In this case, the description of the service, the name or IP number of the computer hosting the service, and the external and internal port number for the service must be added.

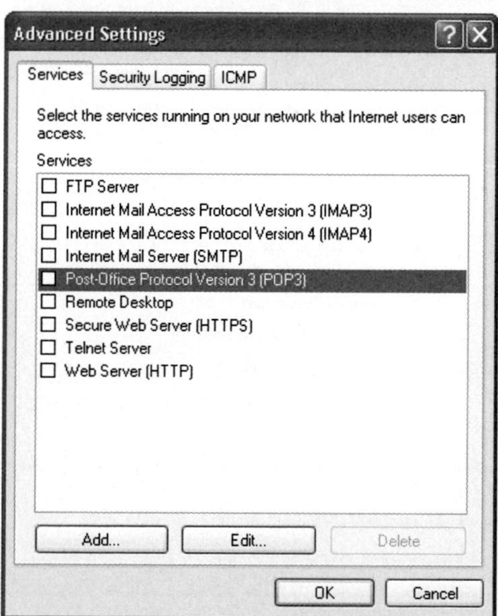

Figure 19-22. Various common network services can be filtered for added security.

Figure 19-23.
Service Settings dialog box set to filter the POP3 service on a computer named "infinity-soyo."

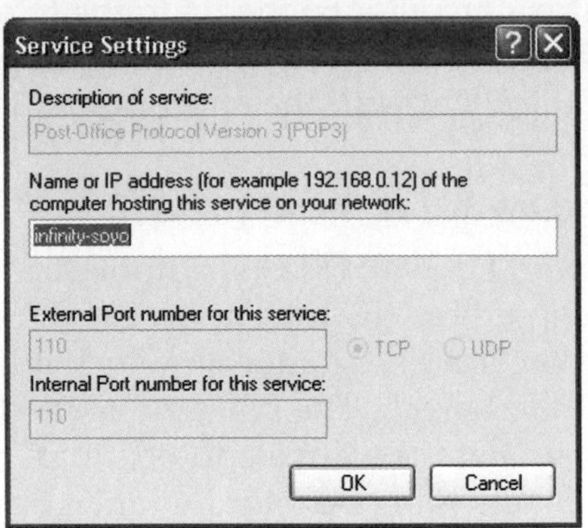

Share Files and Folders

Folders and files can be easily shared on a small peer-to-peer network. **Figure 19-24** shows a dialog box that appears on a Windows XP system after right-clicking **My Documents** and selecting **Sharing and Security**.

The dialog box gives you two main choices: **Local sharing and security** and **Network sharing and security**. The **Local sharing and security** selection allows a folder to be shared with other users on this computer. Remember that Windows XP allows for local user accounts. In this way, a user's personal files can be protected. If another user logs on to the computer with their own user account name, they will not be able to access the other user's files or folders unless the other user chooses to share them. For a user to share their files and folders locally with other users on the system, a user can simply drag their folder into the shared Documents folder.

Network sharing and security provides access to users connected to the network. To share a folder on the network, click the box next to **Share this folder on the network**. To allow users to make changes to the files, click the box next to **Allow network users to change my files**.

Figure 19-24.
The Windows XP **Shared Documents Properties** dialog box allows you to easily configure a network share.

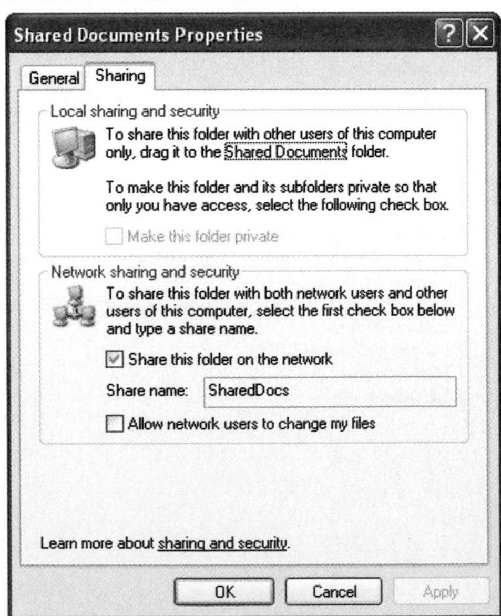

Share a Printer

Sharing a printer on a local network is similar to sharing a folder. If the printer is already installed, access the **Printers and Faxes** folder through **Start | Settings | Printers and Faxes** and right-click the printer. Select **Sharing**.

In the **Sharing** dialog box, select **Share** this printer. The first eight characters of the printer's name will automatically display in the **Share** name box. You may change this to a more descriptive name. You may also add additional drivers for users running different versions of Windows. This will enable the correct version of the printer driver to be automatically downloaded to a user's system when they add the shared printer. If you do not choose to add the additional drivers, users will be required to provide the drivers themselves, either from the installation CD or from the Windows cab files.

You can also set up user privileges on network to determine who may reconfigure the network printer. To assign printer privileges, you must be logged on as the network administrator.

To connect a computer to a networked printer, access the **Printers and Faxes** folder through **Start | Settings | Printers and Faxes**. You can then use the Add Printer Wizard to add a printer to the local computer or connect to a printer in the network, **Figure 19-25.**

The next screen in the wizard, **Figure 19-26,** displays two choices: **Local printer attached to this computer** and **A network printer, or a printer attached to another computer**. The first choice is for connecting a printer directly to the PC. When a printer connects directly to the PC it is referred to as the "local" printer. The second choice is for connecting the PC to a printer located on another PC using a network connection. Select the second choice, **A network printer, or a printer attached to another computer**. A dialog box will appear similar to the one in **Figure 19-27.**

You now have three choices: **Browse for a printer, Connect to this printer**, and **Connect to a printer on the Internet or on a home or office network**. Pay particular attention to the way the printer path is displayed in the examples in Figure 19-27. The first example, under **Connect to this printer**, uses the ***Universal Naming Convention (UNC).*** A UNC identifies the server and the share and uses backslashes to separate the server name from the share name. The second

Universal Naming Convention (UNC) a path format that identifies a server and its share and uses backslashes to separate the server name from the share name.

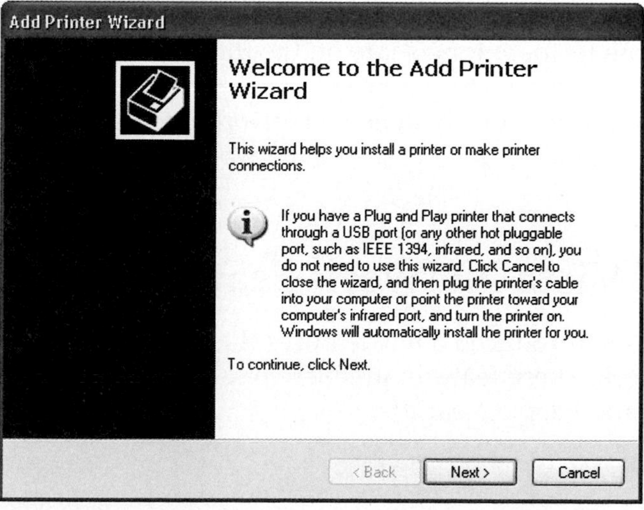

Figure 19-25. Add Printer Wizard welcome screen.

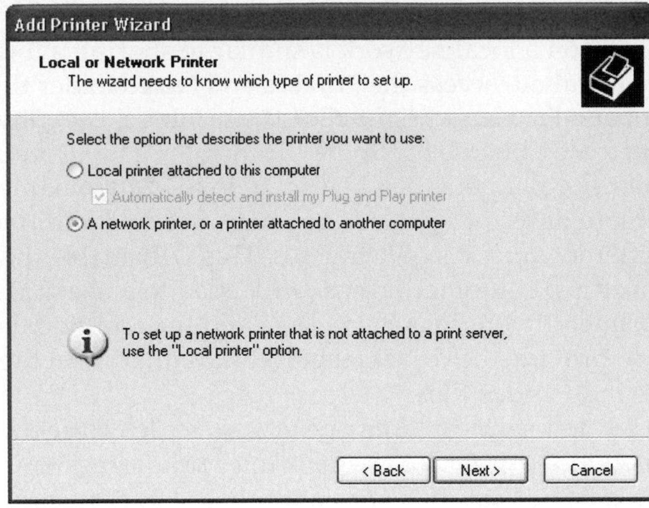

Figure 19-26. To set up access to a network printer, select **A network printer, or a printer attached to another computer**.

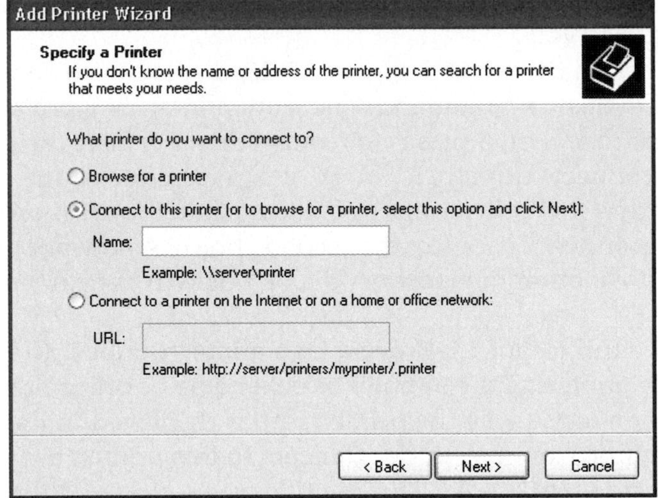

Figure 19-27. To specify a network printer, you may browse the network for it, enter its UNC path, or enter its URL path.

example, under **Connect to a printer on the Internet or on a home or office network**, uses a URL to indicate the path. A URL uses forward slashes and must be used to indicate the path for a share on the Internet or on a network using Active Directory as the directory service.

For extensive information about home networking, visit the Microsoft Web site at www.microsoft.com/windowsxp/using/networking/getstarted/default.mspx.

Windows Vista Network Features

Windows Vista introduced a few features that make it easier than ever to set up a small network. These features are Network Discovery, the Network and Sharing Center, and People Near Me.

Network Discovery

Previous versions of Windows used a network browser service based on NetBIOS broadcasts to locate other computers and resources on the local area network. Windows Vista still uses NetBIOS broadcasts but also has an enhanced feature known as Network Discovery. Network Discovery is based on the Link-Layer Topology Discovery (LLTD) protocol. It allows the Network Explorer to display devices, even if they do not yet have an IP address assigned. As its name implies, the protocol works at the data link layer of the OSI model. The data link layer is the second layer of the OSI model. It is related to the network adapter communicating MAC address information. LLTD was developed by Microsoft and was first introduced in Windows Vista. It is similar to the Link-Layer Discovery Protocol (LLDP), a vender-neutral protocol described in the IEEE 802.1AB specification.

Windows Vista lists two new components in the **Local Area Connection Properties** dialog box: Link-Layer Topology Discovery (LLTD) Mapper I/O Driver and the Link-Layer Topology Discovery (LLTD) Responder. These protocols allow for sending and receiving Network Discovery broadcasts. The LLTD Mapper I/O Driver is used to receive broadcast information from other network devices, and the LLTD Responder is responsible for sending out informational broadcast to other devices.

You can enable or disable each of these components in the **Local Area Connection Properties** dialog box by simply adding or removing the check mark in its corresponding box. These components can also be enabled or disabled when you run a networking wizard or when you see a dialog box asking if the network you are connecting to is private or public. Private networks like a home-office network automatically enable Network Discovery. Public network configurations, such as a wireless connection in a café or airport, are considered public. Network Discovery is disabled by default. This helps secure your laptop or computer system. When you configure the computer to join a domain network, the LLTD is disabled by default.

Be aware that the Network Discovery feature can be used to locate a special device such as an Xbox 360.

Network and Sharing Center

The Network and Sharing Center displays in one centralized location all aspects concerning the local area network, **Figure 19-28.** This feature allows you to view the local area network and configure sharing options as well as control the Network Discovery feature. The Network and Sharing Center is located at **Start | Control Panel | Network and Internet | Network and Sharing Center**. You can also simply right-click **Network** in the **Start** menu and then select **Properties** from the shortcut menu.

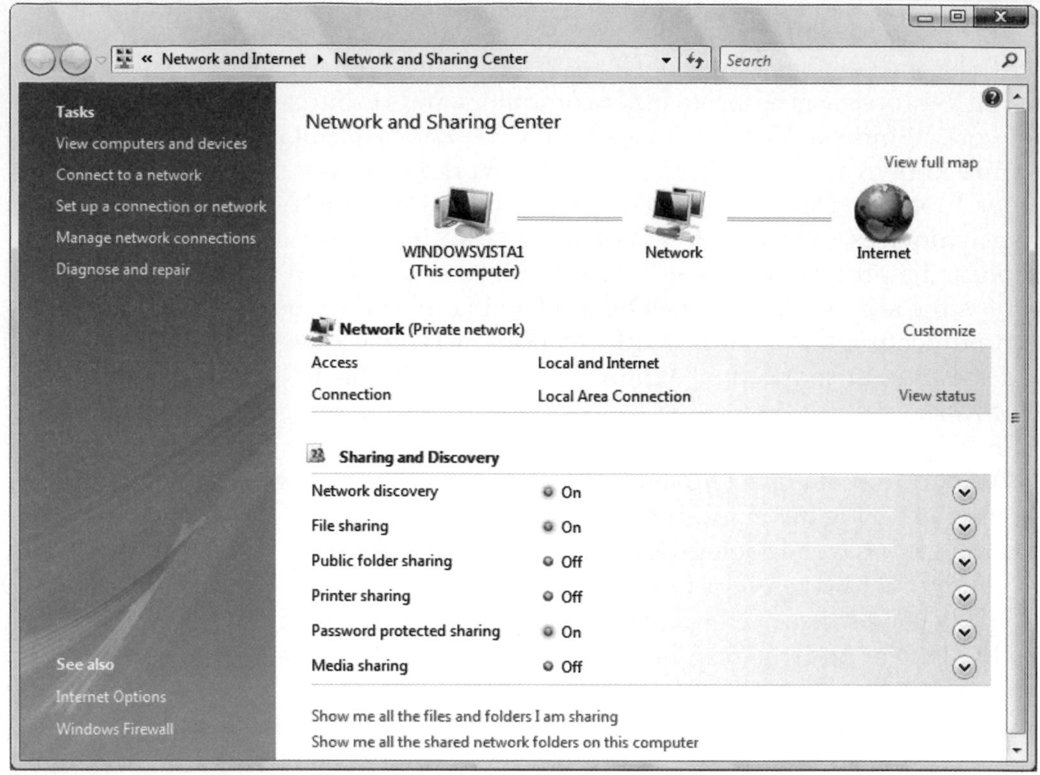

Figure 19-28. In the Windows Vista Network and Sharing Center, you can perform network related tasks such as view all computers and devices on the network and diagnose and repair the network connection.

Viewing a full network map

By selecting the **View full map** option, which is located at the top of the **Network and Sharing Center**, a detailed topology of the network and all attached devices is presented. Look at **Figure 19-29** to see an example of a full map of a peer-to-peer network.

The two workstations connected to the hub are running Windows Vista and are connected by cat 5 to the hub. The AcerLapTop is also running Windows Vista but is wirelessly connected to the gateway named Default. Notice that cable connections are illustrated with a solid line and wireless connections are illustrated with a dashed line.

At the bottom of the screen is computer RMRoberts-567, which is not illustrated in the network topology. The computer is running Windows XP, not Windows Vista. As you can see, the Windows Vista network map will not necessarily correctly identify all parts of the local network. Also, be aware that network mapping is disabled by default when the computer is connected to a domain.

Problems can occur when viewing a full map. Usually computers may not show up properly are because the LLTD protocol is disabled or is not installed, a firewall is enabled, or the device simply does not support LLTD. The RMRoberts-567 computer is running Windows XP and is connected to the network using cat 5 cable, but it is not identified in the network map because it is not running the LLTD protocol. A version of LLTD Responder for Windows XP can be downloaded from the Microsoft download Web site. After installing the LLTD Responder for Windows XP, the computer will show up correctly in the network map. There will be more about the LLTD protocol later in this section.

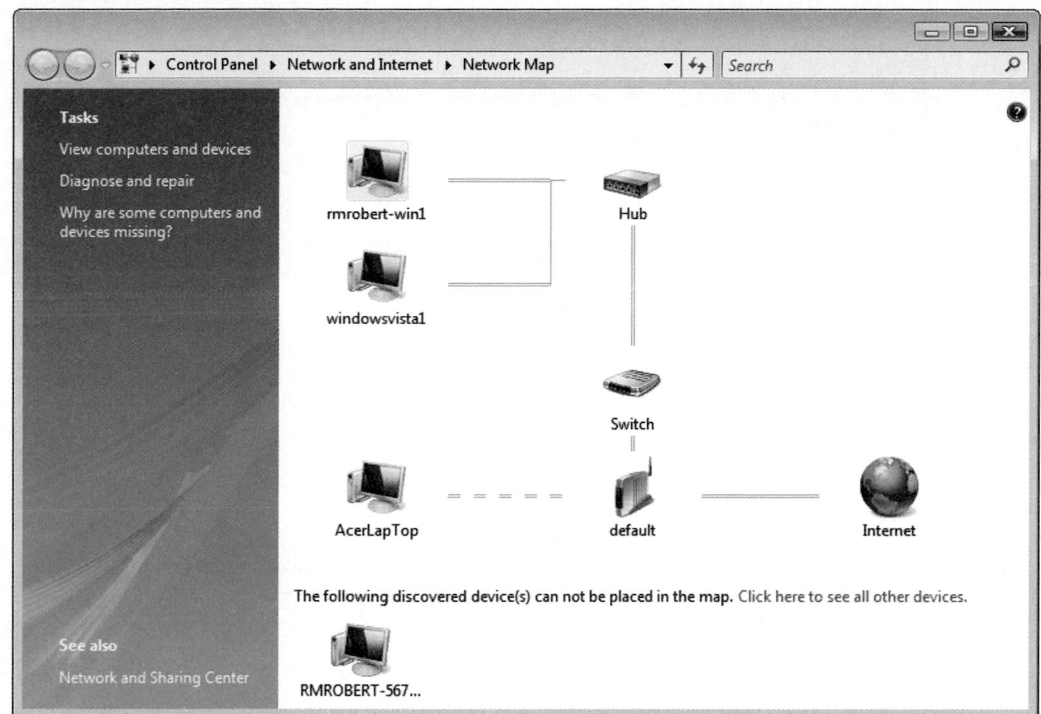

Figure 19-29. The **View full map** option in the **Network and Sharing Center** reveals a detailed topology of the network and all attached devices.

Setting the network location

Windows Vista has three classifications of network locations: home, work, and public. The home and work locations refer to a peer-to-peer network that is "hidden" or protected from the Internet by a gateway. The public location is any location where the computer would have a direct connection with the Internet, such as in a café, library, hotel, or airport.

These locations are associated with two Windows security settings: public and private. The security settings automatically change the security features associated with Network Discovery, the way shares are accessed, and the status of the firewall. They are selected through the **Set Network Location** dialog box which is accessed through the **Customize** option in the **Network and Sharing Center**. See **Figure 19-30.**

Another Windows security setting is called *domain*. It is used for a computer that is connected to a network in which access and security is controlled by a domain controller. This setting is not listed in the **Set Network Location** dialog box. This is because if the computer were part of a domain-based network, the computer simply could not be configured for the public or private setting. The following summarizes each security setting.

- ✔ **Public**—Used for a computer that connects to a public network, such as in areas with wireless hot spots such as cafés, libraries, hotels and airports. It is associated with the public location. Network Discovery is disabled by default when connecting to a public network. The firewall is enabled.
- ✔ **Private**—Used for a computer that connects to a local area network that does not use a domain controller to control network access, such as at work or in a home-office. It is associated with the home and work locations. Network Discovery is enabled by default. The firewall can be enabled or disabled.

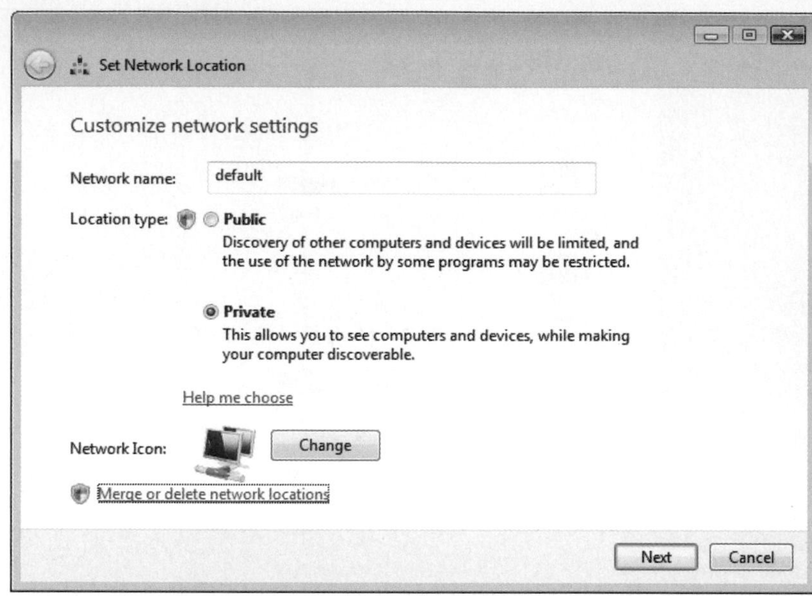

Figure 19-30.
The **Customize** option in the **Network and Sharing Center** allows you to configure the security setting for the type of network the computer belongs to.

- ✔ **Domain**—Used for a computer that connects to a network where the access is controlled by a domain controller, such as a network that uses a server to control access and set up user accounts. Network Discovery and the firewall are disabled by default.

You can only join a domain network using Windows Vista Business edition or Windows Vista Ultimate edition.

Viewing the network adapter card status

Selecting the **View status** option in **Network and Sharing Center** reveals information about the network adapter, such as connection status, connection speed, number of bytes sent and received, and more. This feature in Windows Vista is very similar to the Windows XP **Local Area Connection Status** dialog box. Look at **Figure 19-31** to see the Windows Vista **Local Area Connection Status** dialog box.

Selecting the **Details** button in the **Local Area Connection Status** dialog box reveals details about the connection. Look at **Figure 19-32** to see an example of the details of a typical network connection. Again, this is a similar feature found in Windows XP.

Notice that the **Network Connection Details** dialog box displays all technical information about the network adapter such as the IPv4 address, IPv6 address, physical or MAC address, DNS suffix, and more. You are already familiar with these details from the previous chapter.

Selecting the **Properties** button on the **Local Area Connection Status** dialog box reveals the familiar **Local Area Connections Properties** dialog box which is similar to the one designed for Windows XP and earlier operating system.

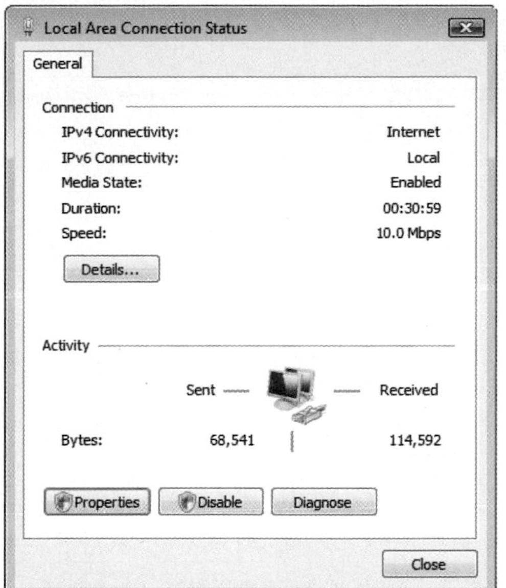

Figure 19-31. The Windows Vista **Local Area Connection Status** dialog box reveals information about the computer's local area connection.

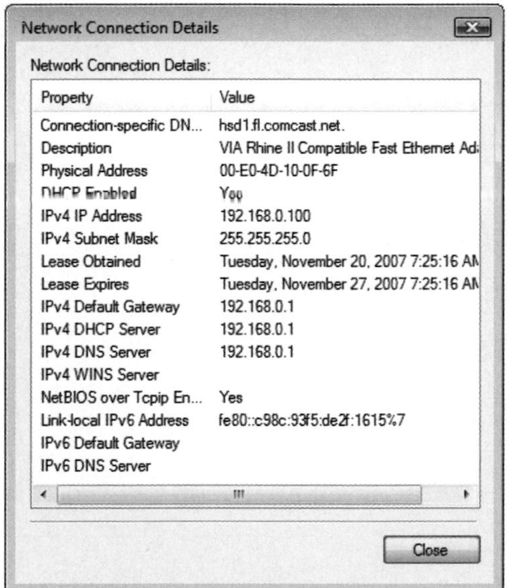

Figure 19-32. Clicking the **Details** button in the **Local Area Connection Status** dialog box opens the **Network Connection Details** dialog box.

See **Figure 19-33** for an example of the Windows Vista **Local Area Connection Properties** dialog box. Notice the Link-Layer Topology Discovery (LLTD) Mapper I/O Driver and Link-Layer Topology Discovery (LLTD) Responder listed under the **This connection uses the following items** section.

Windows Vista networking wizards

There are several networking wizards available in Windows Vista. To start the networking wizards, select the **Setup a connection or network** option from tasks list in the left-hand pane of the **Network and Sharing Center**. A **Set up a connection or network** dialog box will appear similar to that in **Figure 19-34.** As you can see, there are four main choices. Each selection starts a wizard. Everything concerning networking has been designed to be very simple in Windows Vista. Minimal technical skills are required for most tasks.

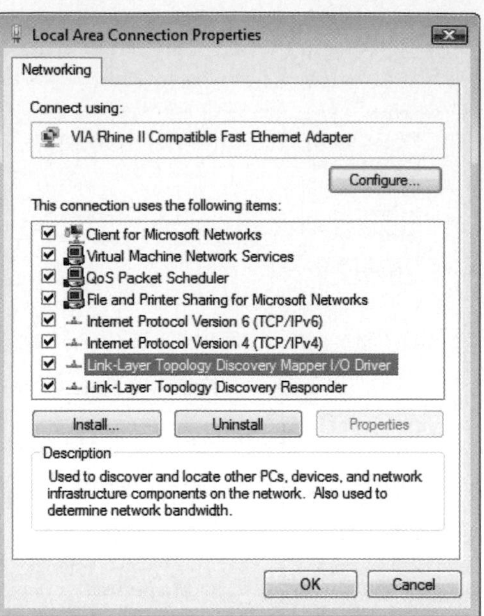

Figure 19-33. The Windows Vista **Local Area Connection Properties** dialog box.

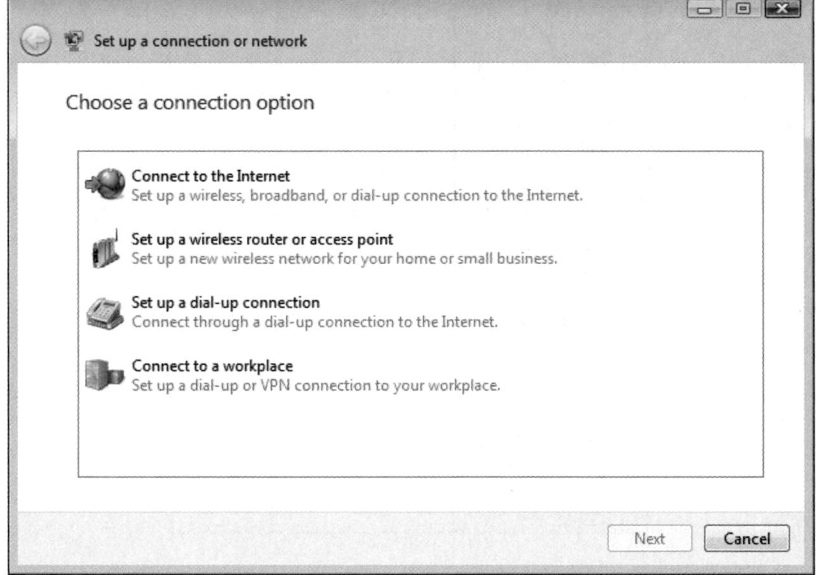

Figure 19-34. From the **Set up a connection or network** dialog box, you can launch several different networking wizards.

Sharing

Sharing in Windows Vista has been made very simple for local area network. Again, the Windows Vista Network and Sharing Center provides an easy way to manage shared folders, files, and printers. You simply open the **Network and Sharing Center**, and then select the corresponding feature you wish to enable or disable. Look again at Figure 19-28 and examine the **Sharing and Discovery** section. The following is a description of each sharing option available through the Network and Sharing Center.

- ✔ **File sharing**—Used to enable and disable file sharing.
- ✔ **Public folder sharing**—Used to automatically configure the Public folder for sharing on the network or disable it.

- **Printer sharing**—Used to enable and disable printer sharing.
- **Password protected sharing**—When password protection is enabled, a user must have a local user account on the local computer and a password to access the Public folder, files, and printer attached to the local computer. When the password-protected share is disabled, all people have access to the shared file, Public folder, and printer.
- **Media sharing**—Used to provide devices and people access to shared music, pictures, and videos on the local computer. It also allows the computer to locate the same types of resources from other locations on the local area network.

At the bottom of the **Network and Sharing Center**, there are two options: **Show me all the files and folders I am sharing** and **Show me all the shared network folders on this computer**. These options are very handy when you need to identify which resources are shared. It might seem strange, but all too often it is difficult to determine which resources are shared and which are not.

People Near Me

People Near Me is a new feature introduced in Windows Vista. When enabled, the People Near Me feature dynamically discovers when other users are on the local area network. You can send an invitation to join a user in Windows Meeting Space to have a collaboration activity. Look at **Figure 19-35** to see the **People Near Me** dialog box. Notice that under the **User Information** section, you enter the name as you want it to appear. You can also make a picture of yourself available. In the **Options** section, you can allow Windows to automatically sign you in when Windows starts.

On the **Sign in** page, **Figure 19-36,** you can sign in or out of People Near Me. Notice that the privacy information states that your name, the computer name, and IP address are made visible by default to all people in the local area network.

After the People Near Me feature is enabled, you use a utility such as Windows Meeting Space to hold a social or business collaboration meeting. Look at the **Figure 19-37** of the Windows Meeting Space utility. With this utility, you

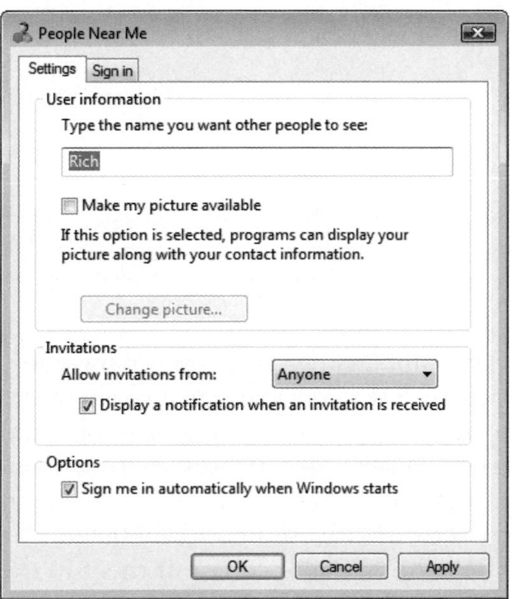

Figure 19-35.
The People Near Me feature allows you to make yourself available for a meeting or other collaborative activity over the network.

Figure 19-36. The **Sign in** page of the **People Near Me** dialog box allows you to sign in and out of People Near Me.

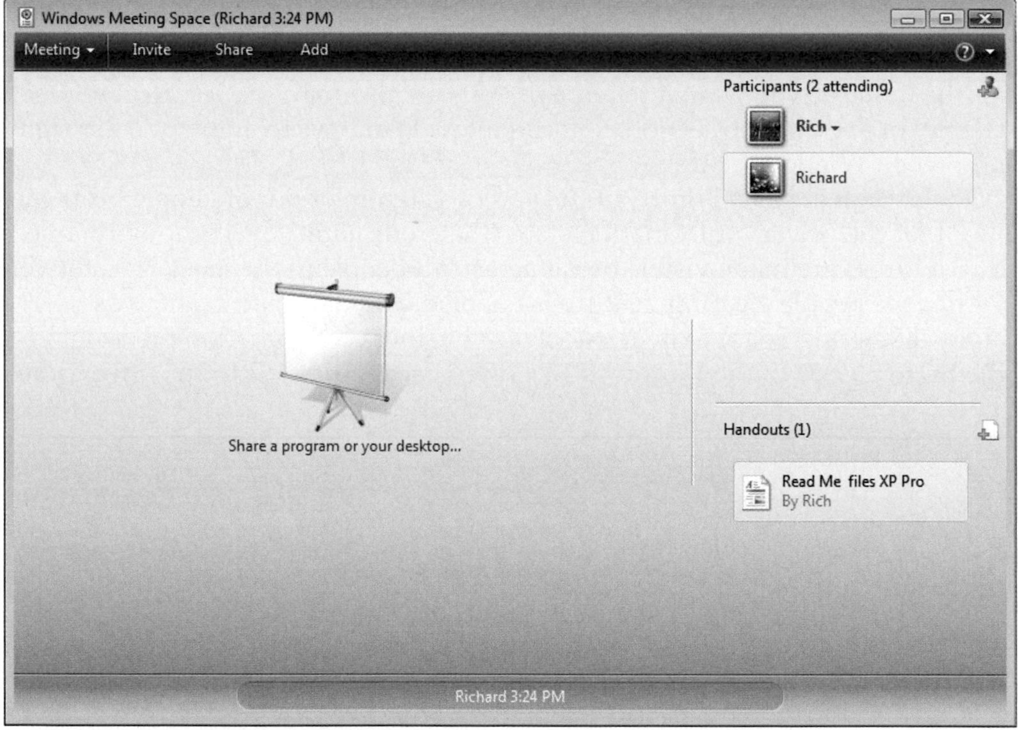

Figure 19-37. The Windows Meeting Space utility allows you to conduct meetings over the network.

can see the features available for the meeting. You can include handouts which are actual files on your computer. It is a way to create a temporary share on your computer limited to the people in your meeting. You do not need to set up permissions or shares in the traditional way. This is a very user-friendly sharing method.

You control who can be part of the meeting by sending out an invitation. People in the local area network are automatically listed. Placing a check mark in the box beside their name will automatically put them in the list of invitations. Requiring a password to join the meeting is optional.

You can also share your entire desktop in the meeting. When the desktop is shared, the desktop background will appear black on the host computer. This will make it obvious to you that your desktop is being shared. Look at **Figure 19-38** to see an example of how the desktop appears when shared for a meeting.

You can end the meeting at any time or stop the sharing at any time during the meeting. Both of these features are standard in all versions of Windows Vista except Windows Vista Home Basic.

As you can see, everything concerning networking in Windows Vista is centralized and redesigned for an average user with limited technical skills. Windows Vista makes networking and collaboration much easier than previous operating systems.

Troubleshooting the SOHO Network

Once you have installed and configured your SOHO network, you may find that you cannot access certain resources or that access is slow. This section covers the most common problems that can occur with a new SOHO network installation. These problems involve firewall installation, VPN and firewall conflicts, improper ICS host configuration, and hardware and software incompatibilities.

Internet Access Is Sluggish

The shared Internet connection can be extremely slow or sluggish if someone on the network is downloading pictures or sound files. Files containing graphics or sound clips are excessively large when compared to text files. Since the

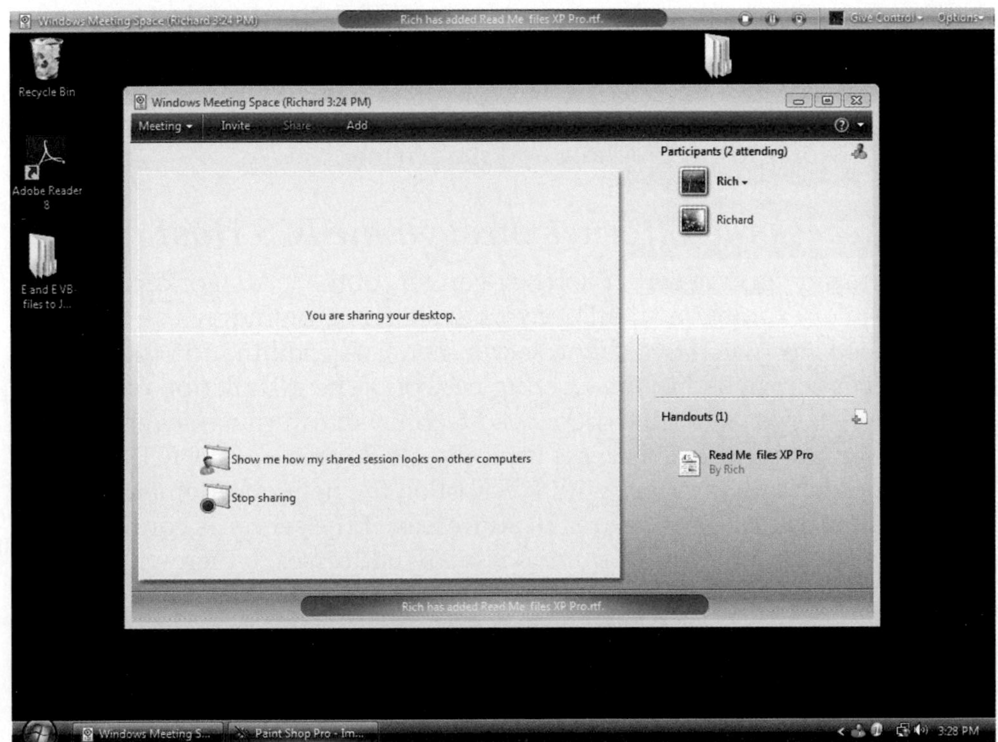

Figure 19-38. During a meeting, a black desktop indicates the desktop is shared.

bandwidth of the local network is shared by everyone connected to the network, large file transfers can reduce the network response time for everyone connected. This problem can be eliminated by blocking the ports associated with the large file transfers. For example, the music download site Napster uses TCP port 6699. If excessive use of Napster is reducing network performance, simply filter out port 6699.

Cannot Access Resources on the Network

Installing ICF on a computer that is not the ICS host can cause communications problems by blocking transmissions. Users will not be able to share a file with other PCs on the network or access the shared Internet connection on the ICS host. To solve this problem, only configure ICF on the ICS host.

A firewall and VPN on the same SOHO network can also cause access problems. Microsoft does not recommend a firewall and VPN on the same SOHO network. Use one at a time, not both at the same time. An ISP typically assigns only one IP address to a user location. If a computer is configured as a VPN, all other computers in the network will be blocked from accessing the Internet. If the Internet connection is already made to the ICS, the VPN computer will not be able to access the Internet and complete its connection to the VPN destination.

Some routers will perform multiple duties and support several functions or services simultaneously. For example, a router can provide shared Internet access and support a VPN connection at the same time. This is another example of the superiority of a router used in a small network system. Otherwise, you will need to separate the computer using the VPN from the rest of the network.

Setting up a PC with a different protocol than the other PCs on the network will prevent that PC from accessing resources on the network. This can often happen when the network is set up with a mixture of old and new computers. The older computers may be configured by default with the NetBEUI protocol while the newer computers are configured with TCP/IP by default. There may also be a conflict in the names of computers in a network of mixed operating systems. NetBIOS only allows 15 characters in the name. Windows 2000 and XP can use longer names. The first thing to check on a new network is the correct spelling of the workgroup, computer, and share name.

Cannot Access the Internet through the ICS Host

Do not use any form of server software on any of the local workgroup workstations. For example, a small network system is growing in size and eventually needs to switch to a client/server model. A combination file server and Web server is installed in the existing network. The installation of the server and Web server by an inexperienced technician can cause severe network communication problems. A server is typically configured as a DHCP server or DNS server, which will interfere with ICS host on the network. Remember, the ICS wizard automatically configures IP addresses. If the server is configured for DHCP or DNS, it will also attempt to issue IP addresses, which will cause intermittent access problems or even complete failure of the ICS feature.

Incompatible Hardware/Software

Incompatibility can be a real problem. Check the hardware compatibility list before setting up a SOHO network. If a device that is not on the hardware compatibility list is installed and it is incompatible, any unexpected occurrence might happen. The device may try to constantly broadcast, or simply communicate in only one direction. It might respond to text-based commands such as **ping** and **tracert** but not communicate at a higher level. If a network is composed of mixed computers (computers with various types of hardware and operating systems), some of the computers may support communication with the odd device and some will not. Anything might happen when using devices that have not been thoroughly tested.

Not all devices not listed on the HCL will cause problems. Many function perfectly.

Summary

- ✔ A small-office/home-office (SOHO) network is a simple peer-to-peer LAN.
- ✔ Typical media used in a SOHO network are copper cable, wireless, existing phone lines, and existing power lines.
- ✔ Home Phoneline Networking Alliance (HomePNA) technology uses a frequency higher than the telephone to transmit data over existing telephone lines.
- ✔ HomePNA technology is not recommended for use in buildings that use a private branch exchange (PBX) as the centralized point of the telephone system.
- ✔ Powerline communications (PLC) technology uses a much higher frequency than 60 Hz to transmit data over existing power lines.
- ✔ A mixed network environment requires a bridge to connect dissimilar network media.
- ✔ Home communications systems include telephone, sound, television, and computer network systems.
- ✔ Copper cabling has the only predictable transmission rate out of all SOHO network media.
- ✔ A wireless bridge is referred to as an access point.
- ✔ A gateway router is a router that combines different media and provides an Internet connection.
- ✔ Common choices of Internet access devices in a SOHO network are the telephone modem, DSL modem, and Cable modem.
- ✔ A PC that provides access to the Internet is called a *host*. A PC that accesses the Internet through the host is called a *client*.

- ✔ The host in a typical ICS configuration is always assigned the IP address 192.168.000.1, and the clients are assigned IP addresses in sequence starting with 192.168.000.002.
- ✔ When a DSL or Cable modem only provides one RJ-45 connection, an additional NIC can be installed on the host PC or a router can be added to the network to support the other computer workstations.
- ✔ A router can function as a firewall and a gateway and can provide internet connection sharing.
- ✔ Some routers incorporate other features, such as firewall protection and VPN support.
- ✔ When a router contains extra LAN connections, a hub is generally not needed on the network.
- ✔ In a peer-to-peer network, a local user account needs to be set up on each PC the user plans to access locally.
- ✔ A firewall should be used to secure an ICS host from unauthorized users.
- ✔ A virtual private network (VPN) ensures that data sent across the Internet is not intercepted, read, or modified.
- ✔ There are many wizards available to help install and automatically configure a SOHO network. Microsoft Windows XP includes the Network Setup Wizard.
- ✔ The Windows Vista Network Discovery feature is made possible by the Link-Layer Topology Discovery (LLTD) protocol.
- ✔ The Link-Layer Topology Discovery protocol allows the Network Explorer to display devices, even if they do not yet have an IP address assigned.
- ✔ The Link-Layer Topology Discovery Mapper I/O Driver and Link-Layer Topology Discovery Responder components are new in Windows Vista.
- ✔ Windows Vista has three classifications of network location: home, work, and public.

Review Questions

Answer the following questions on a separate sheet of paper. Please do not write in this book.

1. Explain some of the limitations associated with each of the SOHO network media.
2. Why may the use of telephone lines as a means of networking an office not work?
3. List the ways two PCs can be connected together in a two-PC network.
4. What is the name of a network device that connects two different types of network media?
5. What Internet access devices are commonly used for a SOHO installation?
6. Draw three possible designs of a SOHO network that has three PCs and will use a DSL modem for Internet access. Include the appropriate network devices for each design.

7. List the benefits of implementing local security and share-level security in a SOHO network.
8. Describe two instances of when a VPN should be created.
9. Windows XP includes the _____ to assist in the configuration of a SOHO network.
10. What is the path to Network and Sharing Center?
11. What does the acronym LLTD represent?
12. What are the three Windows Vista network classifications?
13. Which Windows Vista security classification (public, private, or domain) would be associated with a coffee shop that has a wireless access point provided to customers for free?
14. When is network mapping disabled by default?
15. What is the default condition of the firewall when a Windows Vista computer is connected to a domain?
16. What is the default condition of the firewall when Windows Vista is connected to a public network?
17. Which Link-Layer Topology Discovery component is used to receive broadcast information from other network devices?
18. Which Link-Layer Topology Discovery component is responsible for sending out informational broadcast to other devices?
19. What are some of the problems you may encounter in a new SOHO network installation?

Sample A+ Exam Questions

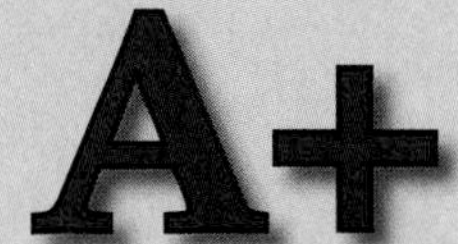

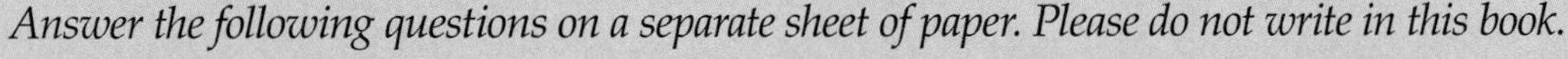

Answer the following questions on a separate sheet of paper. Please do not write in this book.

1. Which technology would provide the best protection against unauthorized access from the Internet?
   a. A standard V92 modem
   b. A firewall
   c. A good Internet access password for modem access
   d. Antivirus program
2. Which technology typically will *not* provide a persistent Internet connection?
   a. DSL
   b. ISDN
   c. Direct cable
   d. Telephone modem
3. What is the typical IP address assigned to an ICS host?
   a. 123.145.000.001
   b. 192.168.000.1
   c. 127.000.000.1
   d. 255.255.255.255

4. A small SOHO network has been set up in a local insurance company, which consists of four Windows XP Professional workstations. Jim has successfully created a local user account on Workstation_1 for his own use. All workstations belong to the same workgroup. Jim is unsuccessful at logging on to the other workstations. What is *most likely* the problem?
   a. Jim does not have a local user account set up on Workstations_2 through Workstation_4.
   b. The network cabling has been disconnected from Workstations_2 through Workstation_4.
   c. Share-level security must be configured on Workstations_2 through Workstation_4.
   d. A user on a peer-to-peer network may not log on to more than one PC at a time.
5. Jim is working late at the office. The office consists of eight computers configured as a peer-to-peer network. The office manager's computer is an ICS host and has a telephone modem installed to access the ISP. The system was installed two months ago and has worked well. Everyone has shut down their computer and has gone home except Jim. Jim attempts to access his e-mail before leaving but finds he cannot access the Internet. What is *most likely* the problem?
   a. The IP address supplied to the ICS host by the ISP has changed.
   b. The connection cannot be established because the ICS host has been shut down.
   c. The Internet Connection Firewall is configured to prevent Jim from accessing the Internet port 110.
   d. The ISP does not provide telephone support after 6 p.m.
6. Which technology allows existing power lines to be used as network media?
   a. VPN
   b. PLC
   c. ICS
   d. HomePNA
7. A(n) _____ ensures that data sent across the Internet is not intercepted, read, or tampered with.
   a. PLC
   b. firewall
   c. ICS
   d. VPN
8. A router that is used to combine different media and to provide an Internet connection is often referred to as a(n) _____ router.
   a. bridge
   b. access
   c. Internet
   d. gateway

A+

9. A SOHO network is a simple _____ LAN.
   a. client/server
   b. client/host
   c. peer-to-peer
   d. wireless
10. The HomePNA adapter uses a higher frequency than _____ to transmit data across the existing telephone line
    a. 4 kHz
    b. 10 kHz
    c. 2 kHz
    d. 15 kHz

Suggested Laboratory Activities

Do not attempt any suggested laboratory activities without your instructor's permission. Certain activities can render the PC operating system inoperable.

1. Set up a SOHO network with a shared Internet connection.
2. Configure a printer share on the SOHO network you set up in activity 1.
3. Configure a firewall for the SOHO network. Experiment with various firewall port settings to see how they affect the workstations in the network. Also, attempt to access the SOHO network from outside the immediate network. (Requires at least two modems and two private telephone lines.)
4. Configure a VPN across a peer-to-peer network. Use a packet sniffer to see if it can view the contents of the data packets flowing through the VPN.
5. Design a SOHO network for an existing home that consists of three bedrooms, an office, and a game room. Each bedroom will have one PC and the office and game room will each have a printer. There will be one Internet access point located in the office area. The access point is a DSL line. Make a drawing of the layout. Make a list of materials and costs based on current prices.

Interesting Web Sites for More Information

www.2wire.com
www.3com.com
www.microsoft.com

Chapter 19
Laboratory Activity
Using the Windows XP Network Setup Wizard

After completing this laboratory activity, you will be able to:

- ✔ Set up a SOHO network using the Windows XP Network Setup Wizard.
- ✔ Explain three ways to access the Network Setup Wizard.
- ✔ Explain the various options available through the Network Setup Wizard.

Introduction

One of the many nice features of Windows XP is the different wizards available that make life easier for not only the novice but also the experienced technician. It is very easy to forget something important when performing tasks such as setting up a small network. A wizard is comparable to an automated list of important steps needed to complete a task. While all wizards will not solve every installation problem, they can make installation easier.

Remember, wizards aren't foolproof. Plenty of things do go wrong even when using them on a small network. The advantage of using Windows XP Network Setup Wizard is it is easy to use and requires only a minimum knowledge of networking. The disadvantage is you may leave security holes by relying on the default settings. Security is often left nonexistent, especially by novice users. If you are setting up a share using TCP/IP, keep in mind that not only can all computers in the workgroup see each other's computers, computer outside the workgroup can access all the computers in the workgroup. Be sure to put the proper security in place by doing things such as configuring the firewall or incorporating a gateway.

The Network Setup Wizard is designed for small-office/home-office (SOHO) networks. It is not intended to use on large complicated networks because of the IP addresses that are assigned automatically by the wizard. The Network Setup Wizard typically assigns nonregistered IP addresses as identified by the Internet authority.

Nonregistered IP Address Ranges

10.0.0.0—10.255.255.255

172.16.0.0—172.16.255.255

192.168.0.0—192.168.255.255

When running the Network Setup Wizard, a series of step-by-step dialog boxes appear on the screen. Be sure to read carefully each screen presentation to avoid missing any important information and making an improper selection. Some installers rapidly go through a wizard clicking "Next" without reading the dialog options or explanations. Default selections do not always work for every possible network configuration. That's why choices are presented in the first place.

Networking wizards are available through a number of operating systems. Most of the wizards generate a disk when you run the wizard for the first time on a network. The disk contains configuration data to be used on other computers in the network. Using the wizard eliminates the need to manually assign IP addresses, the DHCP server location, and WINS server location.

The Network Setup Wizard gives you an option to generate a floppy disk to set up other computers in the SOHO network. The disk generated during the wizard installation contains configuration data identifying the PC with the Internet connection, the workgroup name, and a list of IP addresses that have already been issued. This prevents issuing the same IP address to two or more PCs. Duplicate IP addresses will cause problems in the network. Only one of the PCs among those with the same IP address will be able to communicate on the network.

If all the computers in the peer-to-peer network are using Windows XP, you do not need to use the generated disk. You can use the Network Setup Wizard at these computers. When the Network Setup Wizard is run, it accesses the host PC for the configuration data. Remember that a computer that connects directly to the Internet is referred to as the host and will share the connection with the computers referred to as clients. For the host to provide Internet access, Internet Connection Sharing (ICS) must be established on the host PC. *Always* set up the host first and then configure the clients.

Equipment and Materials

- ✔ A minimum of two computers: one with Windows XP and Internet access through a dial-up connection and the other with Windows 98, Me, or XP installed. (Do not use Windows NT, 2000, or Vista for this laboratory activity.)
- ✔ 1–3 1/2″ floppy disk.

Note:

You will need to have "Administrator" privileges on each of the workstations to complete this lab activity. A dial-up Internet connection is not an absolute necessity for this lab activity. This activity can be completed without any type of Internet connection or by using another form of Internet connection. If your lab has a security software system installed, you may have some problems with the lab activity. In such cases, set up a small peer-to-peer network without a connection to the Internet or the regular network system.

Procedure

1. _______ Report to your assigned workstation with required materials.
2. _______ Boot the PC to be sure it is in working order. If not, get the instructors attention before proceeding further.
3. _______ Access the **Network Setup Wizard** by opening **Control Panel** and double-clicking **Network Connections**.
4. _______ From the **Network Tasks** menu on the left side of the screen, select **Set up a home or small office network**.
5. _______ Close the **Network Setup Wizard** and access the wizard by going through the Start menu: **Start | All Programs | Accessories | Communications | Network Setup Wizard**.

6. ______ Close the **Network Setup Wizard** and access the wizard once more by right-clicking **My Network Places** and selecting **Properties**.

7. ______ From the **Network Tasks** menu on the left side of the screen, select **Set up a home or small office network**.

8. ______ Repeat the three access methods indicated in steps 3 through 7 as many times as necessary to be able to remember them in the future before going on.

9. ______ Open the **Network Setup Wizard** by using any one of the three methods. The "Welcome to the Network Setup Wizard" screen will display.

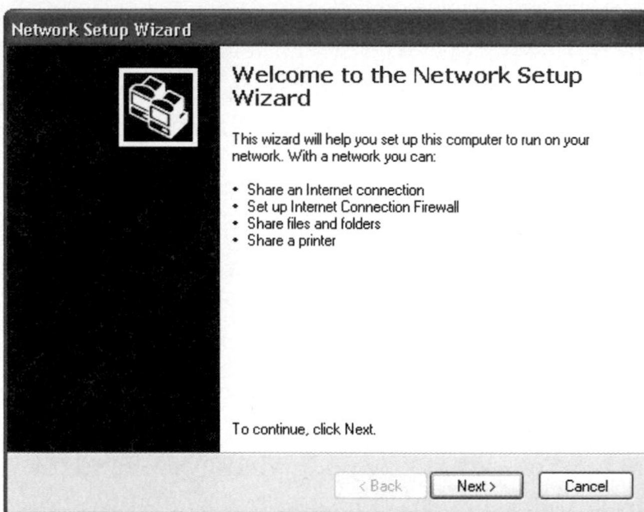

On a separate sheet of paper, list the four things that can be accomplished with the Network Setup Wizard.

10. ______ Click the **Next** button. The **Before you continue** dialog box will display. Near the top of the dialog box, you are prompted to review the checklist for creating a network. *Do not* click **checklist for creating a network** at this time. Instead, on a separate sheet of paper, list the three steps that should be completed.

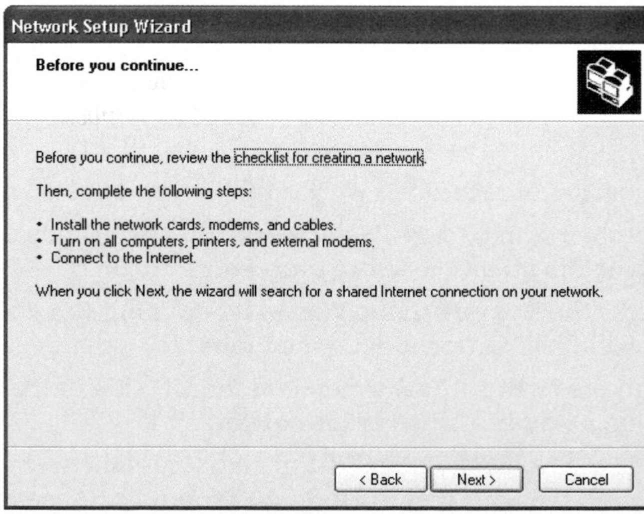

11._______ Now, click the **checklist for creating a network**. An extensive listing will appear in a dialog box titled "Help and Support" similar to the one below. The same information provided here can be also accessed through **Start | Help and Support** at any time.

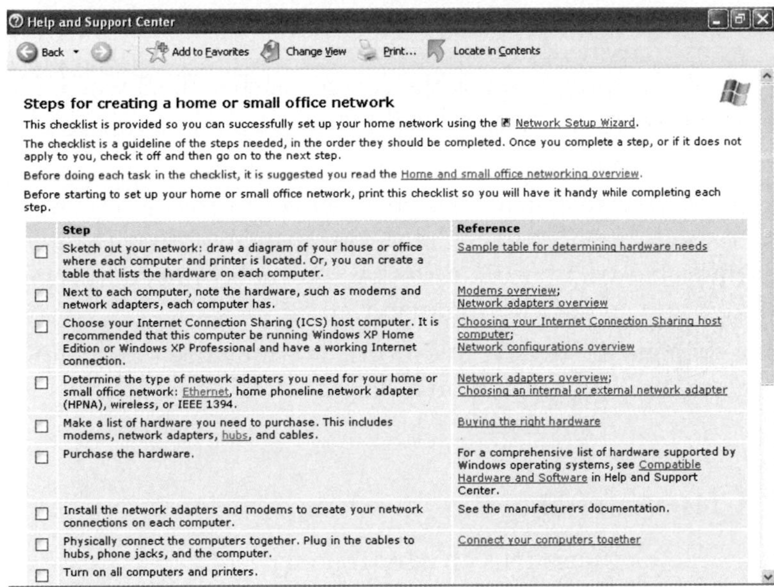

12._______ Scroll down the listing to see what type of information is available. You may wish to minimize the Help and Support dialog box before moving on so that it can be referenced at any time during the installation process.

13._______ Click the **Next** button. The **Select a connection method** dialog box will appear. You are prompted to select the statement that best describes the computer on which you are running the Network Setup Wizard. Write these three statements on a separate sheet of paper.

14._______ Select the appropriate statement and click **Next**.

Note:
*The series of screens and selections after the **Select a connection method** dialog box will vary according to the choice made in this step. Follow the series of screen prompts until the host computer and the clients are all configured. Remember, you can use the 3 1/2" floppy to create a disk that will assist in setting up the clients.*

15._______ Test the connection to the Internet from each workstation. Be sure you can connect to the Internet. If you experience problems connecting, be sure of the following:

- ✔ The host is connected to the Internet. No other workstations will be able to access the Internet unless the host is connected.
- ✔ There is no firewall protection activated on any workstation except the one making a direct connection to the Internet.
- ✔ Each workstation uses a unique name.
- ✔ Each workstation is using the same workgroup name.
- ✔ Each workstation is using the same subnet mask.

16. _______ Set up a shared directory on one of the networked computers. Create a short text file and save it in the shared directory. The text file content can be anything. On a separate sheet of paper, write the complete directory path to the shared file.
17. _______ Set up a shared printer on one of the networked computers. On a separate sheet of paper, write the complete path for the printer share. Be careful to use the correct slashes (backward, forward) when writing down the path name.
18. _______ Have your instructor inspect your project.
19. _______ After your instructor has checked your project, return all materials to their proper storage area. Your instructor may want you to repeat this lab activity using different Internet connection types as well as a variety of networking materials.
20. _______ Complete the review questions. You may use the "Help and Support" files located on a Windows XP computer.

Review Questions

Answer the following questions on a separate sheet of paper. Please do not write in this book.

1. What are the three ranges of non-registered IP addresses?
2. What does the acronym SOHO represent?
3. List several ways the Network Setup Wizard can be accessed.
4. What does the acronym ICS represent?
5. Which computer is identified as the host in an ICS configuration?
6. What is the name of the file that starts the network setup 3 1/2" floppy?
7. What symbols are not allowed as part of the computer name? (See Windows Help and Support.)
8. What is the maximum number of characters permitted in a computer name?
9. Can spaces be left in the name—for example, "Station 12"?
10. Is it best to leave the workgroup name the same as the computer name?

Customer Support, Communication, and Professionalism

After studying this chapter, you will be able to:

- ✔ Explain the difference between a help desk and a call center.
- ✔ Describe the three levels of technical support.
- ✔ Identify desirable communications skills.
- ✔ Explain how body language influences customer and client perceptions.
- ✔ Identify the traits that exhibit a professional image.
- ✔ Identify strategies for dealing with difficult customers and clients.
- ✔ Explain the importance of performing a follow-up in customer relations.

A+ Exam—Key Points

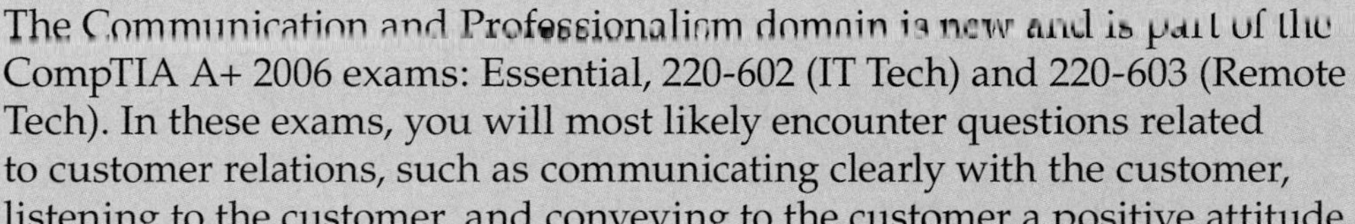
The Communication and Professionalism domain is new and is part of the CompTIA A+ 2006 exams: Essential, 220-602 (IT Tech) and 220-603 (Remote Tech). In these exams, you will most likely encounter questions related to customer relations, such as communicating clearly with the customer, listening to the customer, and conveying to the customer a positive attitude.

Key Words and Terms

The following words and terms will become important pieces of your computer vocabulary. Be sure you can define them.

call center
customer support
depot technician
emoticons
help desk
live support
professionalism
teamwork

This chapter covers the basic skills necessary to function in a customer- or client-related environment. Not all computer jobs require you to meet and work with customers and clients. However, most jobs do require working with customers and clients on a regular basis. You probably assume you already know how to deal with people. There are some specific skills required to keep customers and clients happy that you may not be aware of.

In this chapter, you will be introduced to specific customer- and client-support scenarios. You will learn about the forms of conduct that have been accepted as an industry standard. You may be the most skilled technician in the company, but if you do not deal with people in a professional and courteous manner, you will most likely lose your job or be banned from dealing with customers and clients. You will also never be raised to a position of leadership or management, and all other career options may become limited. The importance of learning the skills in this chapter cannot be emphasized enough. Reading, understanding, and being able to put into practice the skills covered in this chapter may determine your future in a computer-related career.

Customer Support

customer support the delivery of customer assistance, customer training, and customer services.

Simply put, ***customer support*** is the delivery of customer assistance, customer training, and customer services. This section provides an overview of customer support. In it, you are given the big picture of how the organization models work together to resolve customer and client computer problems. You will learn how different levels of support can be distributed across these models and will be made aware of the level of customer interaction typical of each model.

Customer Support Organization Models

There are several customer support organization models that are recognized as standard. Some of these models are help desk, call center, small business, service counter, depot technician, and corporate enterprise support. The exact model of your company and how you fit within that model depends on three main factors:

- ✔ The number of people requiring support.
- ✔ The product being supported.
- ✔ The customer location (local or global).

Some organizations are a combination of several models working together as a team. For example, a help desk service may be outsourced to a foreign country such as India. This help desk may work closely with an organization in the USA that performs the actual physical work. In the following sections, several of the most common support organization models are presented.

Help desk

help desk a central point of contact that provides technical support to clients. The clients may be company employees or customers.

A ***help desk*** is a central point of contact that provides technical support to clients. The clients may be company employees or customers. The usual method of contact is by telephone or e-mail. Examples of organizations that typically provide help desk support are Internet Service Providers (ISPs), hardware and software manufacturers, corporate businesses, and educational and government institutions.

The help desk is the first level of support used to resolve common computer hardware and software problems. In most instances, a service request and repair ticket is generated from the first moment of contact with a client.

The help desk can be a dedicated, single location or part of a larger organization, such as a call center, **Figure 20-1**. For example, a large enterprise, such as Dell, could outsource their first level of support to a call center. If the call

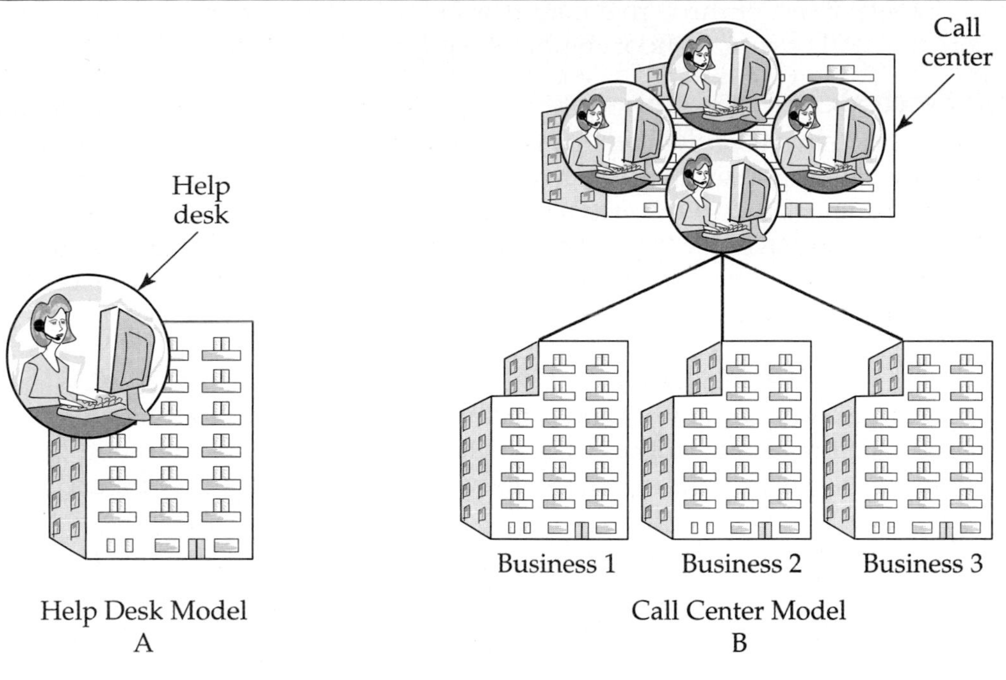

Figure 20-1. Help desk model and call center model. A—In the help desk model, the help desk is part of the company. B—In the call center model, the help desk is a part of a call center. The call center provides support to many different businesses.

center cannot immediately resolve the problem, the support request is forwarded to the next level of support, which may be a technician located at Dell. The technician is trained to handle more difficult problems that require intervention by a person with much more expertise.

Call center

A ***call center*** is typically a large collection of support people located in a common facility equipped with telephones and computer network support. Many call centers provide support for more than one company or product. The center may be located anywhere in the world.

call center a large collection of support people located in a common facility equipped with telephones and computer network support. A call center can provide support for more than one company or product.

Call center employees do not necessarily have technical skills required for repairing computer-related problems. They are more likely trained to read prepared scripts correlated to the most common general problems. If they cannot adequately fix the problem, the support request is forwarded to the next level of repair technician. This repair technician is usually located at the company who manufactures the equipment or writes the software.

Small business service counter

Small businesses are the backbone of the American economy. Over half of all American employment opportunities are in small businesses. You will very likely start your career in a small business environment. You may even start your own small business. In the small business environment, you will meet face to face with customers on a regular basis. Good customer relation skills are a key factor to your success.

The customer may be at the counter to make a purchase, request assistance in a purchase, or solicit technical support for an item purchased at the vendor location. In the small business environment, a service technician will most likely fulfill multiple roles for their employer. They may be responsible for selling computer hardware and software and related materials. They may also be responsible for technical support and for answering customer questions in person, by telephone, or through e-mail. They may be dispatched to a customer location to install or troubleshoot computer equipment or provide training.

Depot technician

depot technician a technician that performs repair work, usually covered by warranty, and has very limited customer contact or no customer contact at all.

The main job of a ***depot technician*** is to perform repair work usually covered by warranty. The depot technician receives the hardware item after the client has contacted customer support through a call center or help desk or if the problem is not immediately resolved by the first contact. Once the equipment arrives at the depot, it is assigned to a technician for inspection and for repair or replacement. A depot technician has very limited customer contact or no customer contact at all.

Corporate enterprise support

In the large corporate environment, technical support services can be composed of many people working as a team. Typically, an employee contacts a help desk. The help desk technician generates a repair or incident ticket, **Figure 20-2**. If the help desk technician fails to assist the fellow employee to make the necessary adjustments to the item, the ticket is then assigned to a technician who will report to the employee's location.

At the location, the technician will either repair or replace the piece of equipment in question. This organizational model is found where there are sufficient numbers of computers and related equipment to justify the cost of a full-time staff dedicated to this function.

Support Software

There are many different software packages designed to keep track of service requests and the final results. This is typically how service is organized and tracked. For example, when a customer or client first contacts the help desk with a service request, the call is logged, **Figure 20-3**. This includes adding the date and time and a description of the problem. The software will typically generate a repair ticket.

The help desk technician may resolve the problem immediately or may dispatch a technician to the client's location. The copy of the repair ticket is distributed to the technician who will report to the physical location of the problem.

On resolving the problem, the technician completes the ticket by adding the procedure used to resolve the problem. Any hardware or software that needs to be provided or has been provided to remedy the problem is also listed. A follow-up of the incident can be reviewed at the end of the day to ensure all problems have been resolved and that no incident has been left unresolved.

Levels of Support

There are typically three levels of support within an organization, **Figure 20-4**. Level-one support is the initial technical support contact. This is typically made with technical support from a help desk, Web site, or call center. Most problems can be corrected at this level.

Level-two support is when the problem is elevated to a person with more experience or expertise than the first person contacted. While level-one support handles most problems, the person at level one typically answers technical support questions from queue cards or a software program that has answers

Repair Ticket

Job Request Number: ____________

Contact Information

Name: ________________________ Initial contact date: ____________

Department: ________________________ Phone number: ____________

Equipment information

Brand: ____________ Model: ____________ SN: ____________

Equipment description (CPU, amount of RAM, etc.): ____________

____

Operating system (if applicable): ____________

Problem description: ____________

____

____

____

Repair Information

Service date: ____________ Service technician: ____________

Diagnosis: ____________

____

____

____

Actions taken: ____________

____

____

____

____

____

____

Parts used:

____

____

____

____

Date repair completed: ____________

Contact signature: ________________________ Date: ____________

Technician signature: ________________________ Date: ____________

Figure 20-2. Example of a repair ticket for the corporate environment.

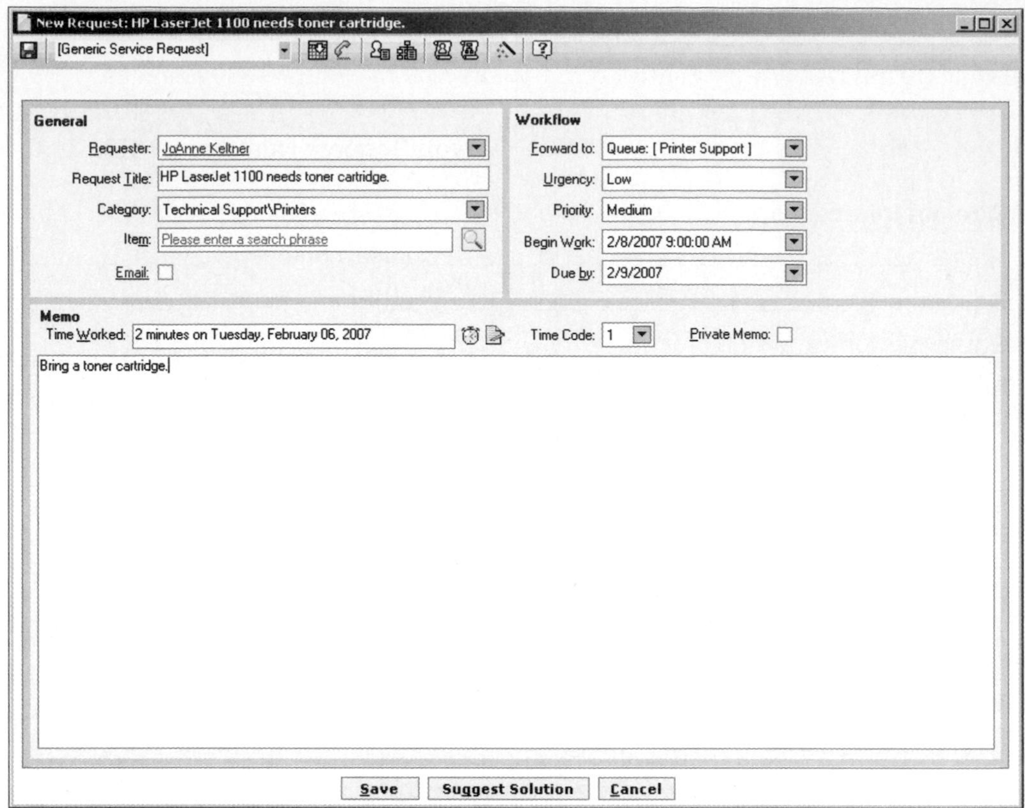

Figure 20-3. HelpStar service request. (Help Desk Technology International Corporation)

Figure 20-4. The levels of support through which a problem can flow.

Support Level	Description
Level one	Help desk, Web site, or call center.
Level two	Supervisor over the level-one response team.
Level three	Supervisor (level two) working with third-party support from a larger company.

available for the most common customer problems and questions. Level-two support is provided for problems that are much less commonly encountered or more unique in nature. For example, a new software application that has just been released to the public may be conflicting with another software application. The problem is so new that there is no or very limited information. The level-two support technician works closely with the customer to solve the problem. The technician may need to recreate the problem before being able to find a procedure for correcting the problem.

Level-three support is typically provided outside the immediate technical support location. For example, a third-party company, such as Microsoft and IBM, provides level-three support when a problem cannot be solved locally by level-one or level-two support. This is often a combined effort to solve a customer problem and is coordinated by the original support team member who is a level-two member at the home company. Level-three support may involve software programmers and engineers. Consumers are generally never involved with level-three support personnel.

Most level-one technical support is free, at least for a limited time. The highest level of support is typically not free and is set up on a cost per incident basis or through a service contract. It may also be based on a specific number of incidents or minutes of live support. ***Live support*** is when you actually talk to support personnel rather than using e-mail as a means of technical support.

live support support in which a customer or client talks directly to support personnel rather than using e-mail or FAQs.

Outsourcing

Customer support is often outsourced to a company that specializes in technical support. The outsource company may reside in the United States or be located overseas. The main reason for outsourcing is cost of the support service, of which the major cost is employee wages. It is often less expensive for a company to use a call center located in a foreign country because the wages may be far less than if the same service was provided locally.

A software or hardware company may find it more cost effective to outsource level-one support and opt to provide level-two support on a local basis. All common or routine problems encountered by customers or clients can be answered by the outsource service. Problems requiring a level-two technician are reserved for the company at the local location or authorized service centers scattered across the United States and world.

For example, the ABC Laptop manufacturer has all client and customer support requests directed to a 1-800-number or to e-mail support. The first level of support is provided by the outsource company XYZ Corporation located in Bombay, India but authorized to represent the ABC Laptop manufacturer company in the United States. The XYZ Corporation handles all routine calls and provides help to customers. They cover the basic problems that may be encountered and talk customers through such items as verifying the following:

- ✔ Power LEDs are lit.
- ✔ All cables are connected.
- ✔ Memory has been reset.

They may also talk the customer through the procedures for using the support CD to reinstall the operating system and through other basic tasks. If the problem cannot be resolved, the outsource support company forwards the problem to the ABC Laptop manufacturer. This is when more sophisticated troubleshooting diagnostics are required or the actual physical replacement of hardware items. The customer is provided an address to send the laptop to or a pickup ticket for FedEx, UPS, or similar service. The laptop is then sent to the ABC Laptop manufacturer for diagnostics and repair.

Frequently Asked Questions (FAQs)

Most businesses have a Frequently Asked Questions (FAQs) section posted on their Web site. The FAQ section is designed as the name implies, to answer the most commonly asked customer questions and inquiries. This is a very valuable tool that can help save many hours of customer support. It is especially valuable if the company or business does not have a technical staff available 24/7. Large companies typically have a very extensive FAQ section on their Web site. One such company is Dell.

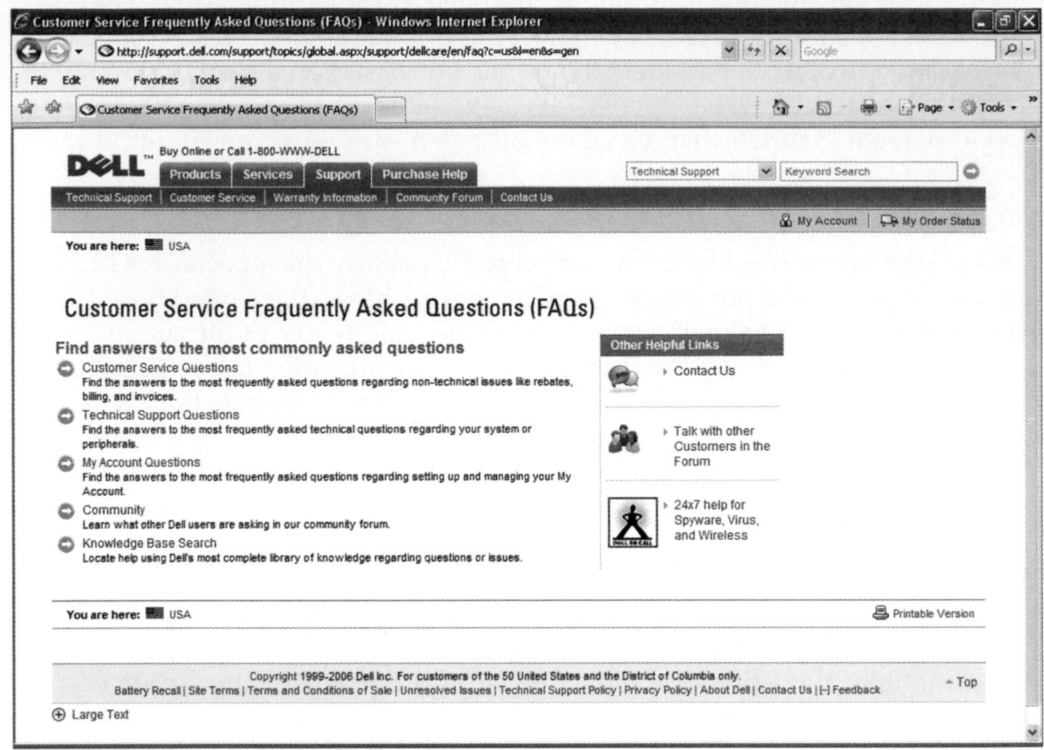

Figure 20-5. Dell provides on their Web site (www.dell.com) a FAQ for customer service questions, technical support questions, and account questions.

Dell has set up a comprehensive customer support Web page using the most commonly asked customer support questions, **Figure 20-5**. The major FAQ topic areas are customer support questions, technical support questions, and my account questions. **Figure 20-6** shows the Dell Web page for the most frequently asked topics concerning Internet security. After selecting a topic, such as,"How Do I Clear My Temporary Internet Files, Cookies, and History in Internet Explorer?", step-by-step instructions appear similar to those in **Figure 20-7.**

Dell saves thousands of dollars in manpower by posting answers to the most commonly asked customer questions. They also satisfy customer needs all around the globe by providing customer support 24/7. It is interesting to note that Dell provides the very same information that could be found on the Microsoft Technical Support Web site; however, Dell has personalized the information for their customers.

Communication Skills

Communication skills are an area of customer support in which computer technicians will most likely have the greatest room for improvement. Communication with a customer is not limited to just the actual conversation. It includes other aspects, such as body language and attitude. Although both of these communication skills are unspoken, they present a clear message to the customer about your level of willingness and concern for fixing their problem. This section discusses various aspects of communication—specifically verbal communication, body language, attitude, listening skills, telephone skills, writing skills, and e-mail.

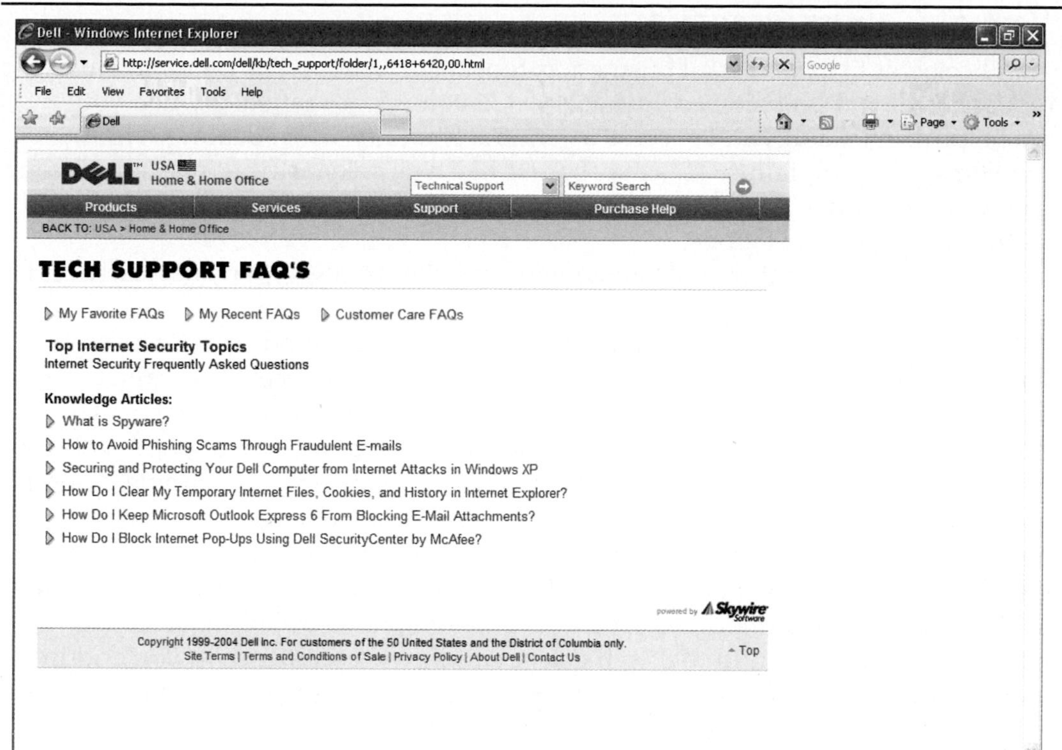

Figure 20-6. This Dell Tech Support FAQ lists the top Internet security topics.

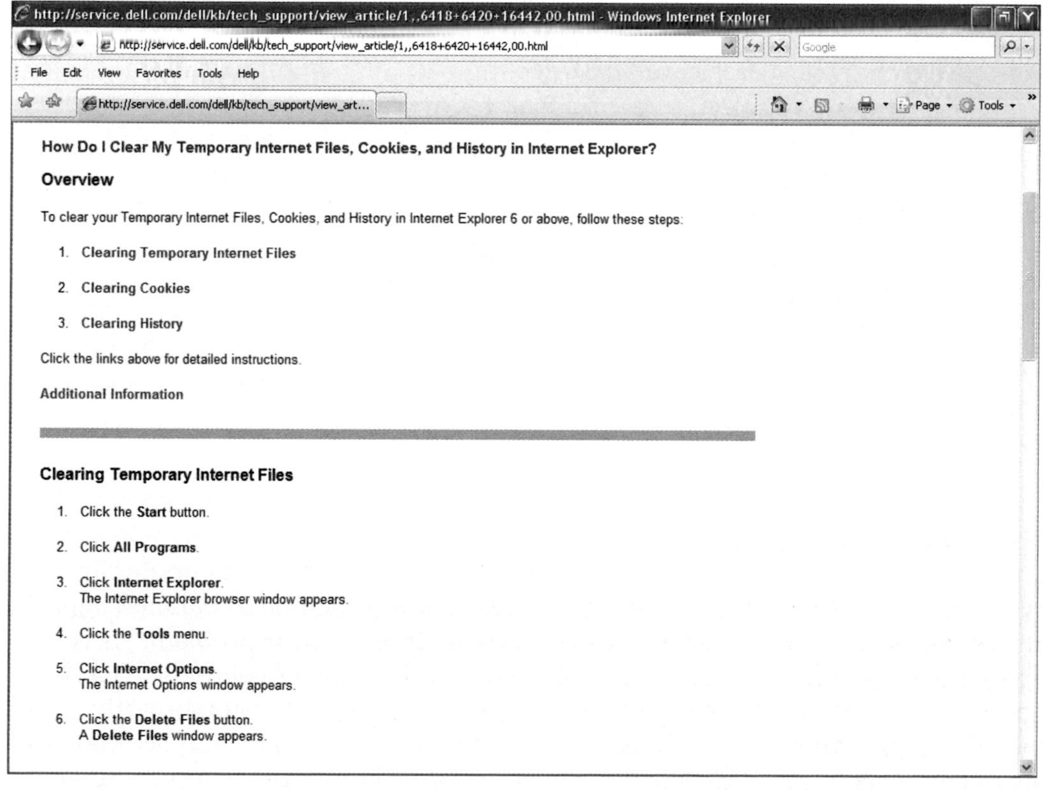

Figure 20-7. Dell provides procedures for "How do I" type questions.

Verbal Communication

The secret to a successful business is repeat customers. The secret to having repeat customers is customer satisfaction. Customers are satisfied when you are helpful, courteous, and express a genuine sincerity when dealing with their problems and complaints. This may sound like a simple task, but one slip of your tongue while you are frustrated could mean the difference between success and failure in customer relations.

When communicating with customers and clients, always speak clearly and concisely. Never use computer and network jargon and acronyms if you can avoid it. You may think that using such language makes you sound smarter or more knowledgeable. In reality, it makes the customer or client "feel" less valuable and stupid. It breaks down their confidence even further than it already must be. The customer or client should feel comfortable while engaged in a conversation with you.

Always begin your conversation with a warm greeting. For example, "Good morning, what can I do to be of service to you?" While engaged in conversation with a customer or client, use positive words to establish a "Can do!" attitude. Use reinforcing statements, such as, "Don't worry, I'll have this fixed in no time," or "This is a very common problem. Lots of people have trouble at first." Do whatever you can to build their self-esteem and their confidence in you and in your company. The following are some good and bad examples of statements used when communicating with a customer or client:

Good examples:

"Yes, we can fix that."

"No problem, we can handle that."

"Yes, we fix that type of problem all the time."

"If you have any more problems, don't hesitate to call."

"You are no bother. This is what I am here for."

Bad examples:

"I hope we can help you."

"I've never fixed that type of problem before."

"I don't know, but I'll try."

"I'll be busy later, so lets get this finished now."

Body Language

Body language and mannerisms can say more than the spoken word and reveal your true feelings. For example, as an employee you may say, "How may I help you?" However, if you continue to work on a customer's computer and avoid eye contact with the customer, you are sending the nonverbal message, "I am very busy right now and really do not have time for your problem." If you greet a person with open arms or hands, you warmly say nonverbally, "I am open to your problem." On the other hand, if you greet the customer with arms folded across your chest and a scowl on your face, you are sending the nonverbal message, "Keep out." The following are some body language key points to keep in mind:

- ✔ Smile.
- ✔ Maintain eye contact with the customer while listening, **Figure 20-8.**

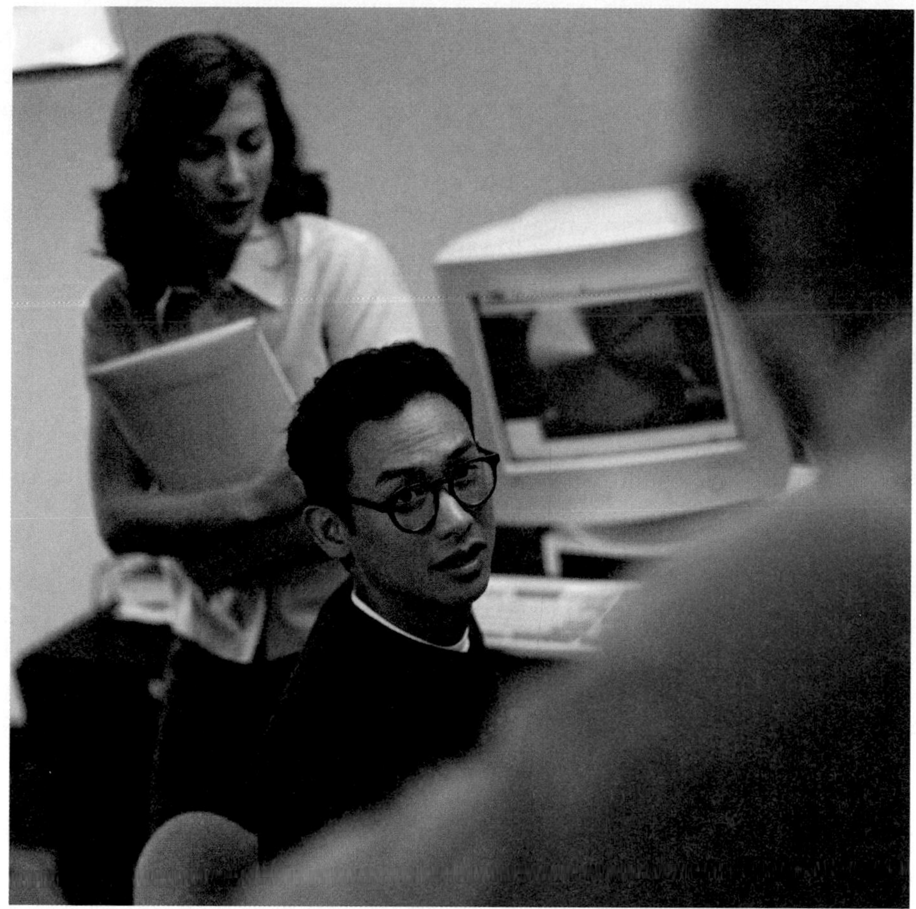

Figure 20-8.
By maintaining eye contact with the customer while listening, you tell that customer you are truly interested in helping him or her with their problem.

- ✔ Face the customer squarely.
- ✔ Never look away from the customer or stare off at a distant point while conversing.
- ✔ Do not fold your arms across your chest or take a defensive posture.

Always face people directly and squarely. Do not turn away while addressing a person or engage in other activities when you should be giving your complete attention to the customer. If you are alone in a shop and must answer a phone, always apologize and ask if you can return their call at a better time. All customers appreciate that they are being given fair attention. If you do ask to return a call at a better time because you are helping another customer, return the call.

Attitude

Attitude is easily perceived by a customer but is very hard to define in objective terms. Everyone knows a "good" attitude or a "bad" attitude when they experience it. It is critical to your success to always maintain a positive attitude while working with people. Without it, you may not have a job. It doesn't take long to earn a reputation for your attitude—good or bad.

For this chapter, the best definition of *attitude* is a subjective judgment of character made by the customer based on the perception of how the technician presents himself or herself and meets the customers' needs.

Show the customer that their problem is your main concern. You do this by asking probing questions such as, "How long have you had this problem?" Never be judgmental or indicate that the customer caused the problem, even if they did. You will use training techniques and suggestions to help them avoid the problem in the future.

Avoid distractions. A customer or fellow worker will feel you are not interested if you do not give them your full attention. For example, when working on a project, always stop your work to talk to a customer. This will give the customer a feeling of importance and show that you care about their problem. It will also keep you from making an error on your project because you are distracted. In making a customer feel important, you will gain their confidence.

Listening Skills

Listening skills are the most important trait listed by employers in recent surveys conducted to identify the trait most desired in customer support. They all agree that employees who work with clients and customers must have excellent listening skills. It seems like listening is such a simple task. So why do not all people have good listening skills? Many people, especially the type of personalities that gravitate toward the computer field, are often bright and articulate and may already be thinking ahead of the customer. Avoiding this habit will keep your customers from feeling "small" and inadequate. The following are a list of guidelines to put into practice:

- ✔ Always maintain eye contact while listening.
- ✔ Avoid distractions while listening. Do not try to perform other tasks while the customer or client is talking to you. Focus on the speaker.
- ✔ Never eat or drink while talking with a customer.
- ✔ Always allow the customer or client to complete his or her sentence. Never cut off or interrupt them, anticipating what they are going to say.
- ✔ Restate the problem to the customer or client. This will ensure that you know what they are saying or describing to you is the problem.

Check out www.listen.org, a Web site dedicated to listening skills. There you will find many interesting facts, such as only 7% of the meaning in a conversation is transmitted by actual words.

Telephone Skills

Many of the same skills used in face-to-face communication also apply to telephone support. Always speak clearly and concisely and avoid trade jargon, slang, and acronyms.

Never engage in other activities while talking to the customer or client. A person can always tell when someone is not focused on his or her conversation. When you are engaged in another activity, like working on a computer while talking to the customer on the telephone, the customer will be able to tell you are not fully engaged with their conversation. This will generate a feeling that you are not truly concerned with their problem or need and will probably irritate the customer.

Always avoid talking on a speakerphone, as this only confirms that you are not paying attention to the caller. You are a technician. If you must be "hands free," get a headset. At least this way, the customer will feel that they are the focus of your conversation. Unless it is necessary to use the keyboard or remotely access the customer's computer, keep your hands off the keyboard. Customers can hear that you are using the keyboard and will nearly always conclude that it does not have to do with their problem.

Smile while on the phone, **Figure 20-9.** It might sound crazy, but it actually works. A person on the other end of the telephone conversation can actually perceive when a person is happy on the telephone. This is interpreted as a feeling that the support person is pleased to hear from the customer and wants to help them. A good idea is to hang a mirror near the telephone with a sign that says "Smile!"

Again, do not use acronyms, jargon, or sophisticated technical terminology. Customers are not typically sophisticated computer users and are frequently intimidated by your conversation. Always use language that anyone can understand, no matter what his or her technical background. You do not impress customers with technical terms. If you want to impress a customer, use terms that express your sincere desire to help them with their problem.

Writing Skills

Writing is a part of all customer support technician duties. As a customer support person, you will either write by hand on repair tickets or enter into a computer the specifics about a repair. Content typically consists of a description of the problem and the repair procedure used to fix the problem. Often, your writing and documentation of specific problems and the method used to fix the problem will become valuable company information for problems encountered in the future.

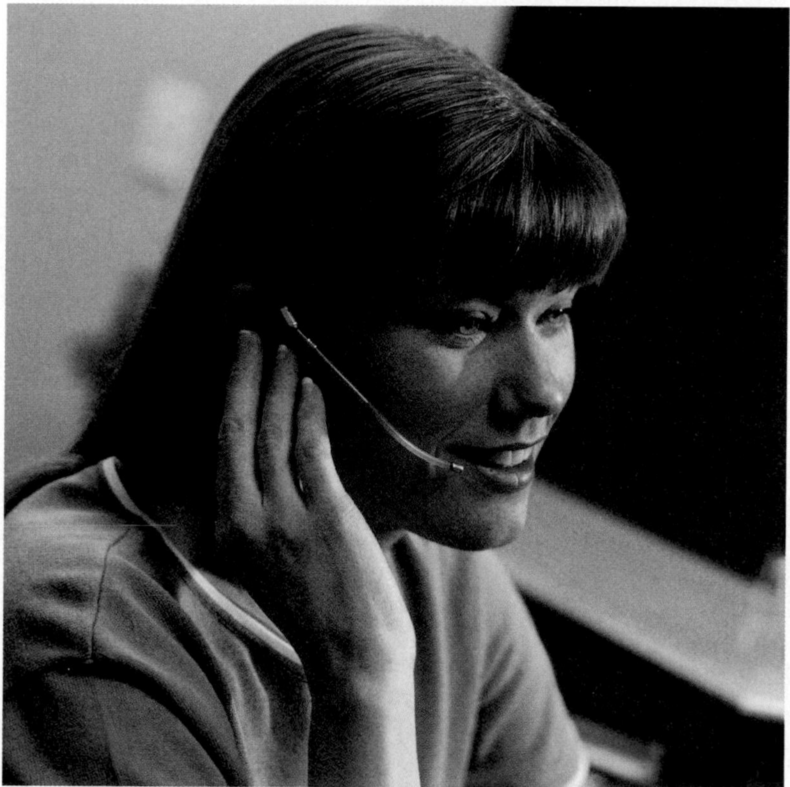

Figure 20-9. Smiling while on the telephone can help you convey that you are pleased to hear from the customer and want to help them.

When creating written communications, always use appropriate grammar and correct spelling. All word processing packages and software programs that require written responses have spell checkers and usually grammar checkers. Use them! Do not disable them or ignore them. When writing, use sentences limited to 15 to 20 words. Avoid long, run-on sentences.

Always be polite in your correspondence, and never use sarcasm. Sarcasm is always inappropriate because the customer or client may very well misinterpret your intent. Sarcasm is based on familiar personalities, and you are not familiar with all who might read your correspondence.

Many help desk support software packages contain sections to support e-mail directly from within the software package. You will need to respond to customer and client e-mails. E-mail correspondence is covered in the next section.

Another function of customer support may involve writing training manuals or a set of procedures for a company. Often, part of a contract of installing computer equipment and software involves training the customers on how to use the equipment. Many times technical support personnel must write training packages to support the customer. You may very well find yourself responsible for part of the written package.

E-Mail

Customer support may require a great deal of time answering e-mails from customers and clients. When writing e-mails to customers and clients, avoid computer jargon, acronyms, and abbreviations, just as you would in spoken language. Communicating in writing with other technicians is not the same as communicating in writing with customers and clients. While it might be perfectly all right to use an acronym or abbreviation on a customer repair ticket, you should avoid acronyms and abbreviations when communicating with customers.

E-mail auto responders

Using an e-mail auto responder can show a customer or client that you care about them and their problem. E-mail auto responders are e-mail programs provided by e-mail service providers that create an automatic response to a received e-mail. The auto responder gives the illusion that someone has just read the e-mail sent by the customer or client and that they will be answering the request very soon. The auto responder allows for an instant reply 24 hours a day, seven days a week. An auto responder can also be used to notify customers that you are out of the office for a brief time. Some mail client software, such as Microsoft Outlook, will allow you to set up an auto response, **Figure 20-10.**

E-mail acronyms and emoticons

E-mail acronyms are very popular with all of the electronic communications devices, but they are never to be used in customer support e-mail. E-mail acronyms became especially popular when phone text messaging started because they save a lot of keystrokes. You may receive e-mail acronyms or emoticons from customers, but you should never respond in these terms. The following are some e-mail acronyms:

- ✔ **LOL:** Laugh out loud.
- ✔ **BTW:** By the way.
- ✔ **TIA:** Thanks in advance.
- ✔ **IOW:** In other words.

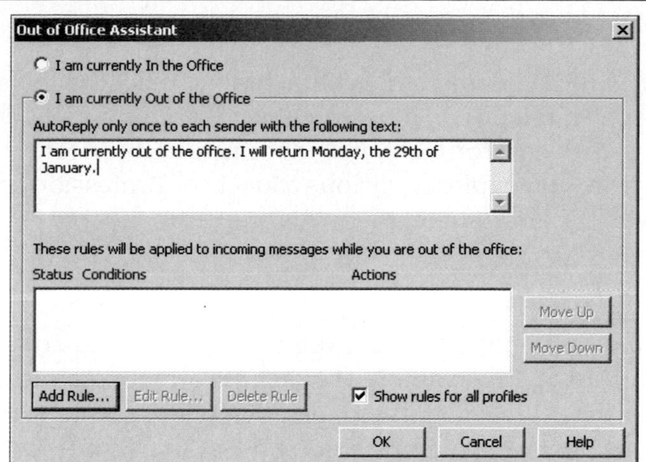

Figure 20-10. Microsoft Outlook has a tool called the Out of Office Assistant, which is used to send an auto reply to senders.

Emoticons are cartoon face characters made from keyboard symbols to express emotions in e-mails, letters, and text messaging. The following table lists some common emoticons.

emoticons cartoon face characters made from keyboard symbols to express emotions in e-mails, letters, and text messaging.

Emoticon	Emotion
:)	Smile or happy.
:o	Shock.
:(	Frown.
;)	Wink.

If you have trouble communicating with customers using e-mail, practice regularly in a business format. Try sending a few e-mails every day to friends and relatives. Writing e-mail messages daily will sharpen your skills. Use the principles previously mentioned. The following is a list of key points you should always remember when communicating through e-mail with customers and clients:

- ✔ Check your e-mail regularly.
- ✔ Keep the e-mail brief.
- ✔ Do not use e-mail emoticons.
- ✔ Limit the size of file attachments. This is especially true if the customer is using a 56 k telephone modem.
- ✔ Never use all capital letters in an e-mail to emphasize a word or phrase. If you must emphasize a word or phrase, use italics or an asterisk, for example, *this is very important.* Do not use bold or underline. This can be misinterpreted as a link.
- ✔ Never ever send sensitive or inappropriate information in e-mail.
- ✔ Do not send personal greetings, jokes, or other materials that are not suitable for the work environment.

Professionalism

professionalism a businesslike characteristic reflected in a person and work environment.

Professionalism is a businesslike characteristic reflected in a person and work environment. In relation to a person, it is identified in a person's attitude and dress. In the work environment, it is identified in its décor and general atmosphere. This section explores various aspects of professionalism in an employee and work environment.

Professional Image

Businesses and their employees are often judged by a customer's or client's first impression of them. For example, if a technician looks professional, the customer feels confident in them. If the technician looks sloppy, dirty, unkempt, or bizarre, the customer or client might have a less than confident feeling about the technician.

Dressing appropriately means dressing professionally. In the work environment, there are two distinct types of acceptable dress: formal business and business casual. Formal business typically means a suit coat or sport coat with a collared shirt and tie (or just a collared shirt and tie) and a pair of dress slacks and leather shoes, **Figure 20-11.** Business casual generally means a polo shirt (often with a company logo) or collared shirt with no tie, dress or casual slacks, leather shoes, and in rare cases, tennis shoes, **Figure 20-12.** Some computer technicians believe that they are entitled to wear torn or tattered blue jeans, T-shirts, tennis shoes, flip-flops, or sandals. These are never acceptable forms of business attire. Remember that your casual attire may reflect a casual attitude and not one that is serious about getting the job done. You are a trained professional; dress like one.

Figure 20-11. This IT person is wearing formal attire.

Figure 20-12. This IT person is wearing casual business attire.

Many businesses provide shirts for their support staff. When shirts are provided, the dress code is clearly stated to the employees. If the dress code is not clearly stated, then it is assumed. When working in the area of customer support, a polo shirt is most appropriate, but be aware that some companies require a dress shirt and tie to be worn when dealing with customers and clients at their locations.

As a computer technician, you will likely be crawling on the floor or reaching behind desks. Unisex (the same for both men and women) dress is typically the best and safest choice. Women should never wear short dresses or revealing clothing if they have to work in this environment. The following are some well-thought-out tips that should become a part of your own professional image:

- ✔ Dress professionally. Clean, neat slacks and a shirt with a collar is much more appropriate than a T-shirt with a slogan. This is especially true if the T-shirt has a controversial slogan or image printed on it.
- ✔ Hair should be neat and clean. Hair with spikes or wild colors might be cool to you, but it is entirely unprofessional in the workplace.
- ✔ Speak to customers in a professional manner. Never use curse words or inappropriate language or terms, even as a way to emphasize certain points.
- ✔ Do not eat, drink, or smoke while dealing with a customer.

Many students feel that if they have exceptional technical skills, they will never be fired. Nothing could be further from the truth. More employees have lost their jobs because of their unprofessional manner than from technical incompetence. An employer will tolerate an employee with average technical skills, but will not tolerate an employee who conducts himself or herself in an unprofessional manner. When employers contact other professionals for hiring recommendations, they typically request someone who can work well with people rather than request the "smartest" or most technically able person. The most important thing to the employer is an employee's image and personality. Employers rarely, if ever, call a second time if a nonprofessional person comes in for an interview.

Work Environment

The store or work location image is also critical, and is often a direct result of the employees' efforts to maintain a professional image. The work environment must represent a professional atmosphere. If the work environment is to be visited by customers and other employees, it should be maintained so as not to be offensive to others. For example, you may enjoy a particular style of music while you are working; however, it may not be the choice of many customers. The customer should not be offended by loud music of any generation. You should avoid music in the work environment where customers may be present, except for soft, neutral background music.

Also, be aware that listening to an MP3 player or other device through earphones is offensive to many people. You should be concentrating on the customer or client. This also applies to working at a client's workstation and in the corporate environment as a whole. The following are some tips to help you maintain a professional environment in your workplace:

- ✔ Keep your location and workstation clean and well organized.
- ✔ Never keep food containers, cups, and general trash on counters or work areas.
- ✔ Do not play music that is not in the mainstream or blast music of any kind.
- ✔ Do not let friends "hang out" around the store or workspace. The workplace is not a social club.
- ✔ Do not display inappropriate posters, pictures, or signs. You may think they are fun or entertaining, but not all customers share your view.

Handling Difficult Situations

When a client is angry and upset, they will vent their emotions toward the person who represents the company or problem. Dealing with difficult people requires patience and composure. Do not take complaints personally. Never react to a difficult customer, but rather listen and respond with empathy. *Empathy* means that you show by your words that you understand the other person's feelings and their situation. There is likely always a situation that would warrant a statement like, "I can understand how this problem is frustrating you."

A coworker or other customer might normally be very pleasant and fun to be around until a situation causes them to be very angry. While in an angry state, they say things that they normally would never say to another person. Arguing back at an upset person will only make things worse.

Your job is to defuse the situation by letting the client vent. When responding to the client, use a calm assuring voice. What you want the customer to do is stop yelling at you and begin to talk with you. At an opportune time, simply say, "Let's see what I can do to resolve this problem." When you start to work on the problem, or to tell them what you are planning to do, check if it is all right with them.

If the customer continues to vent, find out what will make them happy. For example, a customer may have brought their computer to the shop several times for the same problem. It may or may not be the same problem, but that is their perception. Find out what will make them happy by asking, "What do you think it will take to make you satisfied?"

They may want their bill adjusted or to not be charged for the present repair. If you are not authorized to waive the costs, simply say, "I'll see what we can do for you," and then check with your supervisor. If a person is upset, it will only become worse if they think that they are not being taken seriously.

Is the Customer Always Right?

There is a very old business saying: "The customer is always right." Well, this is true most of the time, but there are times when this motto just doesn't apply. When the customer or client wishes you to do something unethical or illegal, they are wrong. For example, a customer may request you write a receipt for more value than the actual cost of the repair. Or, a customer may ask you to violate some copyright law. Do not do it.

How about when a customer uses foul language in a loud tone and threatens you? Can you really make that person happy? You never need to fear for your life or bodily harm. If the customer threatens you, you should politely ask the person to leave, and if they will not, call the police or security. What if the customer is intoxicated and becomes abusive? Again, this customer should be asked to leave, and if they refuse, call the police. An intoxicated or violent customer is not only a threat to you and the business, they are also a threat to any other people who enter or are present at the business.

Follow-Up

A follow-up helps to build a good relationship with the customer or client. Perform a follow-up after you have had a break in contact with the customer or contact. For example, after a customer's problem has been fixed, follow up a few days after completing the repair to see if they are satisfied and all went well. This technique improves service and builds a client's trust. Customers and clients love the fact that someone is checking if their problem was handled in a timely fashion and that they were dealt with professionally.

Your Word

One of the most important assets you have is your word, and it costs you nothing. Your word or promise can make or break your client relationship. Be a person of your word. Your word should be your bond. Suppose you tell a customer you will contact them with a repair estimate the next day, but you run into a problem with a vendor. The vendor does not respond to your inquiry, so, in turn, you do not have the customer estimate ready. If you told the customer you would call the next morning, do so, even if it is to say you do not have the estimate yet. It is important that you be a person of your word.

Keep your promises. If you say you will be there in the morning, be there. The client may have rearranged their schedule to accommodate you. If you have a problem, call ahead, and always apologize. How often have you been given a date and been required to sit home all day to have a service done. Do not allow this type of behavior to become your business signature.

Contracts

If a company is large, it may be necessary to create a written document or contract to be sure everyone has the same expectations. The contract should contain a description of the work to be performed, the estimated or actual cost, and other terms agreed on. By having a customer signature prior to work, you always protect yourself against a misinterpretation of expectations. A client or customer should always receive exactly what they agreed to—maybe more, but never less.

Teamwork

teamwork two or more people working toward a common goal.

Teamwork is two or more people working toward a common goal. For example, the goal of customer support is customer satisfaction. When you work as part of a team, you place the common goal of the team "customer satisfaction" above your own individual goals(s), such as recognition and promotion. Teamwork is an essential component of a successful business.

As a team member, you must be willing to help other team members and to share your own expertise and knowledge with others. For example, a customer calls and asks about the status of their computer. If the person assigned to repair the computer is out of work that day, you should check the job ticket to review the status of the repair. It could be ready for pickup or awaiting parts. You should try to help the customer even if it is not your assigned repair. Make a note of the customer call and record your actions. For example, you might write a note on the ticket such as "Customer called and asked the status of the repair. I informed him it was awaiting parts and should be ready in a day or two." Then, sign the note.

When working as a member of a team, you should be willing to share your knowledge with other team members. Knowledge is not just limited to technical issues. It also covers company procedures or any other bit of knowledge that might help another team member perform their duties.

Job protection attitude

A common, yet unattractive trait in the business world occurs when a person will not share their individual knowledge with another team member. The concept is referred to as "job protection." This happens, for example, if one person is the only person that knows how to perform specific tasks and they are not willing to share this information or train another person. They feel they are secure in their position with the company if they are the only person who knows how to perform that task.

In reality, this type of person is actually jeopardizing their position with the company. The company management or owner will not like the fact that an employee is not willing to share their knowledge for the good of the company. If the person is unwilling to share their knowledge or to help other team members, they will most likely find themselves looking for other employment. Remember that working as a team requires supporting other team members, especially by sharing knowledge and reinforcing good work products. If you are not willing to function as a team member, then you will most likely not be a member of the team very long.

Helping team members

You must be willing to do more than just what you have been assigned. For example, a collection of repair tickets might be divided between team members. Each member is assigned four tickets each. If you finish your repairs before anyone else, you should not assume that you are done for that day. You should see if you could help someone else with his or her assigned work.

Employers do not like to see employees that are doing just enough to get by or wasting company time. Employers love to see employees going above and beyond their assigned duties. When you finish your assigned tasks, you should immediately inform your supervisor and volunteer to help other team members with their assigned duties. This will impress your employer and also be appreciated by fellow team members. Remember, the company goal is to repair all the customers' computers, not just the ones assigned to you that particular day.

Summary

- ✔ A help desk or call center is usually the first contact point for service.
- ✔ A help desk can belong to a single company or be part of a call center.
- ✔ A call center typically provides support for more than one company or product.
- ✔ Level-one support is the initial contact with technical support.
- ✔ Level-two support is support provided by a person with more expertise than someone in level one.
- ✔ Level-three support is typically provided by a company outside the level-one and level-two location.
- ✔ Avoid using computer jargon or computer acronyms when talking to customers.
- ✔ Body language says more to a customer than the actual spoken words.
- ✔ Smile when dealing with customers, even when on the phone.
- ✔ Always maintain good eye contact with a customer and avoid distractions.
- ✔ A customer makes an attitude judgment of your character based on their perception of how you meet their needs.
- ✔ Listening is the most important communication skill listed by employers.
- ✔ Sarcasm is never appropriate when working with customers.
- ✔ Keep e-mail messages short and to the point.
- ✔ Never send inappropriate material in e-mail.
- ✔ Avoid large e-mail attachments.
- ✔ Keep the work environment professional.
- ✔ When handling angry customers, allow them to vent.
- ✔ Respond to angry customers with a calm, reassuring voice.

Review Questions

Answer the following questions on a separate sheet of paper. Please do not write in this book.

1. What is customer support?
2. Explain the difference between the help desk model and call center model.
3. Which level of support is provided when the problem is elevated to person with more experience or expertise than the first person contacted?
4. Is it permissible to use acronyms when communicating with customers?
5. What is attitude?
6. What are the key points of body language you should use?
7. Why is sarcasm inappropriate in communications?
8. What are emoticons?
9. What are the key points in writing an effective e-mail message?
10. What two elements are required to deal with difficult people?
11. Why is it important to perform a follow-up?
12. What is the goal of the customer support team?

Sample A+ Exam Questions

Answer the following questions on a separate sheet of paper. Please do not write in this book.

1. Which is an example of level-one support?
   a. A software engineer at Microsoft.
   b. A hardware engineer at Apple.
   c. The FAQ section of a customer support Web site.
   d. A live conversation with a level-one supervisor.
2. It is 9:00 AM and you are repairing a customer's computer that must be ready by 3:00 PM because it was promised to the customer. The phone suddenly rings, and you answer to find that it is a new customer calling about a problem with their computer. Which is the best way to deal with customer support on the telephone?
   a. Do nothing except focus on the customer and their problem. You should write down key points during the conversation, starting with their name.
   b. You should continue to work on the computer repair while listening to the customer. This is the most efficient use of time and your supervisor will be pleased.
   c. Have the customer call back later after another employee comes into the shop.
   d. Tell the customer you are in the middle of an important repair and that you will return their call later in the day. Take down their name and telephone number.
3. Which is the most expensive element of customer service?
   a. Employee wages.
   b. Support software.
   c. Support hardware.
   d. Technical support articles and Web site access.

4. The company you work for performs computer system repairs in addition to selling new computers and hardware. A repair ticket is completed at the time of repair. The status of the repair is also recorded on the ticket. Some items that may be recorded on the ticket are when the repair was completed or when parts were ordered for the repair. Mr. Smith dropped his computer off at your company computer shop three days ago. The repair was assigned to Joe and he is not in at the moment. You answer the phone and find Mr. Smith is calling to find out the status of the repair of his computer. What is the most appropriate response to Mr. Smith's inquiry?
   a. Tell Mr. Smith that his computer is being worked on by Joe who is not in today and that Joe will call him back when he returns.
   b. Tell Mr. Smith to hold for a minute while you check the status of the repair ticket.
   c. Tell Mr. Smith that you are not the one that has been assigned to his repair and to call back later.
   d. Tell Mr. Smith to come by the shop and pick up the computer. The computer is most likely repaired, but if it isn't, you can have it repaired before he gets there.
5. Match the body language image with the conveyed meaning.
   a. It's really good to hear from you!
   b. How may I help you?
   c. I don't have time for your problem.
   d. I'm open to your problem.

6. When is it proper to use all uppercase letters in an e-mail?
   a. When emphasizing an important point.
   b. When making a list of steps in sequential order.
   c. When listing parts in an e-mail.
   d. Uppercase is never appropriate in an e-mail.
7. A customer calls and starts yelling about how she brought her computer home to find it has the same problem it had before she brought it in for repair. What is the first thing you should do?
   a. Smile so that the customer will sense your willingness to help her.
   b. Let the customer finish speaking and venting her anger.
   c. Interrupt her by asking her what it will take to make her satisfied.
   d. Hang up, and hope she will call back when she is in a better mood.

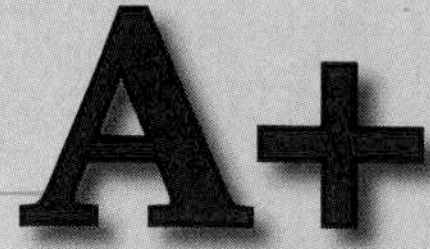

8. A customer brings into the shop a computer exhibiting a problem you have never encountered before. Which of the following responses would be appropriate?
   a. Yes, we can fix that.
   b. Yes, we fix that type of problem all the time.
   c. I've never fixed that type of problem before.
   d. I don't know if I can fix it, but I'll try.
9. You need to explain the cause of a boot failure to a customer. Which of the following explanations would build the customer's confidence in your company?
   a. A virus corrupted the MBR.
   b. A virus corrupted the master boot record.
   c. A virus corrupted the boot sector, which stores partition information.
   d. A virus corrupted an area of the hard drive that is required for startup.
10. A customer uses foul language because you will not write a receipt for more value than the actual cost of the repair. You can tell that the customer is intoxicated. What is the first thing you should do?
    a. Write the receipt for the amount he specifies.
    b. Politely ask him to leave.
    c. Call the police.
    d. Respond with empathy.

Suggested Laboratory Activities

Do not attempt any suggested laboratory activities without your instructor's permission. Certain activities can render the PC operating system inoperable.

1. Check out the FAQ sections of the Dell, IBM, and Sony Web sites.
2. Write a step-by-step procedure for checking the IP address of a Windows 2000, Windows XP, and Windows Vista computer. This step-by-step procedure would be used for customer support when, for example, a customer calls an ISP for a connection problem. Through the procedure, the customer should be able to check if they have an appropriate IP address assignment, not one such as 0.0.0.0 or 169.254.12.34. (IP address 0.0.0.0 means that a connection has not been established. IP address 169.254.xxx.xxx means that the Automatic Private IP Addressing (APIPA) feature has assigned the IP address, instead of a DHCP server.) Make the procedure as clear as possible.
3. Write the step-by-step procedure to have a customer ping a server located at www.helpdesk1.com. Include what to do next if the ping is successful or unsuccessful.
4. Write a step-by-step procedure for using System Restore on a Windows XP and Windows Vista computer.

Interesting Web Sites for More Information

http://oneorzero.com
http://technet.microsoft.com/en-us/default.aspx
www.helpstar.com
www.microsoft.com/smallbusiness/resources/management/customer.mspx
www.troubleticketexpress.com/open-source-software.html
www.unbf.ca/its/faculty/help/level1.htm

CompTIA A+ Certification Exams Preparation

After studying this chapter, you will be able to:

- ✔ Explain the format of the CompTIA A+ Certification exams.
- ✔ Explain eligibility for taking the CompTIA A+ Certification exams.
- ✔ Identify strategies for preparing for the CompTIA A+ Certification exams.
- ✔ Evaluate your readiness for the A+ Certification exams.

A+ Exam—Key Points

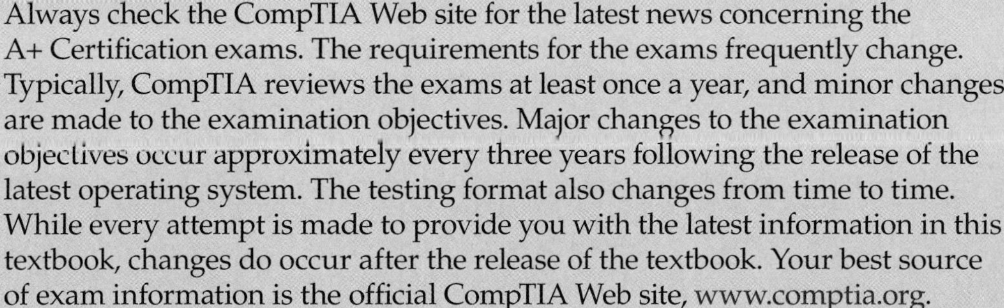

Always check the CompTIA Web site for the latest news concerning the A+ Certification exams. The requirements for the exams frequently change. Typically, CompTIA reviews the exams at least once a year, and minor changes are made to the examination objectives. Major changes to the examination objectives occur approximately every three years following the release of the latest operating system. The testing format also changes from time to time. While every attempt is made to provide you with the latest information in this textbook, changes do occur after the release of the textbook. Your best source of exam information is the official CompTIA Web site, www.comptia.org.

You can also check www.RMRoberts.com for additional information about the CompTIA A+ Certification exams and to download additional free practice exams.

Key Words and Terms

The following words and terms will become important pieces of your computer vocabulary. Be sure you can define them.

CompTIA A+ Certification exams	examination objectives
domains	weighted

If you are reading this chapter, you are probably near the completion of your course. You have gained a basic knowledge of computer service and repair and have acquired many skills by performing the lab activities. You have certainly reached a milestone in your education in computer service and repair. Your next step, should you decide to make computer service and repair a career, is to become certified. Certification proves to a potential employer that you have the knowledge and skills needed to perform the typical job duties and tasks of a PC service technician.

A+ Certification Exams

The CompTIA organization has revised the testing format for the A+ Certification exams starting in late 2006. The older exams were retired in July 2007. The new ***CompTIA A+ Certification exams*** require passing two exams. The first exam you must pass is called CompTIA A+ Essentials. After passing this exam, you must pass one of three additional exams. The other three exams are referred to by number, not by name. The three exams are CompTIA A+ 220-602, CompTIA A+ 220-603, and CompTIA A+ 220-604. Each of the three exams emphasizes skills directly related to various types of information technology jobs. For example, the CompTIA A+ 220-602 relates directly to the skills of an IT technician, the CompTIA A+ 220-603 to the skills of a remote support technician, and the CompTIA A+ 220-604 to the skills of a depot technician.

CompTIA provides examination objectives on its Web site, www.comptia.org. The ***examination objectives*** are derived from industry surveys that determine the actual job requirements of a PC service technician and are categorized according to ***domains***, or topic areas.

The following table lists the domains tested for on each exam and the percentage of which they are tested. For example, the domain PC Components makes up approximately 21% of the CompTIA A+ Essentials exam, 18% of the CompTIA A+ 220-602 exam, 15% of the CompTIA A+ 220-603 exam, and 45% of the CompTIA A+ 220-604 exam. Domains that are not required as part of an exam are labeled with the letters "NA," which represents not applicable. As you can see, the domain Communications and Professionalism is not required for the CompTIA A+ 220-604 exam.

CompTIA A+ Certification exams certification awarded by CompTIA for those who pass the CompTIA A+ Essentials exam and one of the following exams: CompTIA A+ 220-602, CompTIA A+ 220-603, and CompTIA A+ 220-604.

examination objectives test objectives that are derived from industry surveys that determine actual common job requirements needed by industry.

domains topic areas into which examination objectives are divided.

Domain	Percentage of Exam			
	Essentials (220-601)	IT Technician (CompTIA A+ 220-602)	Remote Support Technician (CompTIA A+ 220-603)	Depot Technician (CompTIA A+ 220-604)
Personal Computer Components	21	18	15	45
Laptop and Portable Devices	11	9	NA	20
Operating Systems	21	20	29	NA
Printers and Scanners	9	14	10	20
Networks	12	11	11	NA
Security	11	8	15	5
Safety and Environmental Issues	10	5	NA	10
Communication and Professionalism	5	15	20	NA
Percent Totals	100	100	100	100
Exams Required	Required	One additional exam		

The biggest single difference in the latest version of the exam and previous versions is the addition of the "Communication and Professionalism" domain. This domain measures your ability to work with customers and clients or as a computer support technician. The CompTIA A+ Essentials exam is a required exam that should be taken first by all persons seeking A+ Certification. After successfully passing the CompTIA A+ Essentials exam, you may go on to take any one of the three remaining exams. The following sections describe each CompTIA A+ exam.

CompTIA A+ Essentials

The CompTIA A+ Essentials exam is required as the first of two tests you must take to earn the A+ Certification. The exam covers necessary competencies required for entry-level technicians in all fields. The competency measured by CompTIA is equal to 500 hours of experience with lab and classroom activities in an instructional environment or experience in the field. Competencies cover all basic operating system and hardware technologies associated with the PC as well as the newest domain, Communication and Professionalism. CompTIA wants to verify that you not only have basic hardware and software skills, but also basic people skills.

CompTIA A+ 220-602

You must pass the CompTIA A+ Essentials exam before you can take the CompTIA A+ 220-602. This exam is designed to measure a candidate's ability to work in a corporate environment face-to-face with employees of the corporation while performing duties as a service technician. Typical job titles associated with the CompTIA A+ 220-602 are IT administrator, field service technician, and PC technician.

This certification appears to be a compromise between the CompTIA A+ 220-603, which emphasizes people skills, and CompTIA A+ 220-604, which emphasizes hardware skills. This will become more apparent after learning more about the other exams and reviewing the previous table covering the exams and domains.

CompTIA A+ 220-603

Again, you must pass the A+ Essentials exam before taking the CompTIA A+ 220-603 exam. This exam measures the skills of persons who work in a remote-based environment. This person typically provides telephone support as a help desk or call center specialist. The Communication and Professionalism domain is 20% of the exam—the highest of all exams. The Operating Systems and Security domain also has the highest percentage when compared to all the other exams. The PC Component domain has the lowest percentage. This means a person working in a remote-based environment need not know the hardware system as much as required by the other exams. In short, the person taking the CompTIA A+ 220-603 exam should know the PC operating system very well and be able to talk someone through a repair over the telephone.

The Laptop and Portable Devices domain and the Safety and Environmental Issues domains are not part of the CompTIA 220-603 exam. It is interesting to note that laptop computer knowledge is not required for help desk or call center support.

CompTIA A+ 220-604

The CompTIA A+ 220-604 is designed for a candidate that intends to work in an environment in which they will have very limited contact with customers or other people. A person who works in this environment will spend most of their time making hardware repairs or upgrading PCs. They will most likely work in a computer repair shop performing warranty repair work and building custom computer systems. In this situation, they will have limited customer contact. This certification requires the most extensive hardware knowledge, as indicated by the domains covered. Notice that the Operating Systems, Networks, and Communication and Professionalism domains are not covered on this exam.

The table in **Figure 21-1** summarizes the skills measured in each of the additional exams. As you can see, the highest people or face-to-face skills are measured in the CompTIA A+ 220-603 exam. The highest hardware skills and lowest people skills are measured in the CompTIA A+ 220-604 exam. The CompTIA A+ 220-602 is a compromise between people skills and hardware skills. It is best suited for an all-around technician who can work with people, perform hardware and operating system repairs, and provide support.

Details about each exam can be found at the CompTIA Web site, www.comptia.org. As an Internet assignment, you should download a copy of the current CompTIA A+ Examination Objectives for each exam. Use the objectives to learn more about each exam and its required knowledge.

A+ Note:

Always check the CompTIA Web site for the very latest information on the A+ Certification exam.

A+ Certification Exam Requirements

CompTIA recommends that a test candidate have at least 500 hours of work experience. The 500 hours is a recommendation, not a requirement. In fact, anyone is eligible to take an A+ Certification exam. There are no prerequisites. However, work experience alone does not ensure that a candidate will pass the exam. Formal training provides the best opportunity for passing the A+ Certification exams.

Figure 21-1. Summary of the skills measured in each of the additional CompTIA A+ exams.

CompTIA A+ 220-602	CompTIA A+ 220-603	CompTIA A+ 220-604
Average people and hardware skills. Covers all domains.	Highest people skills and lowest hardware skills. Does not require the following two domains: Laptop and Portable Devices and Safety and Environmental Issues.	Highest hardware skills and lowest people skills. Does not require the following domains: Operating Systems and Communication and Professionalism.

There are some candidates who do pass the exams by using self-study techniques, but this is rare. Your best preparation for passing the exams is a combination of structured classroom-related experiences and hands-on laboratory activities that reinforce classroom training and textbook studies.

When you feel you are ready to take an A+ Certification exam, you must make an appointment to test at a registered testing center. When reporting to the testing center, you must show two proofs of identification. One is typically a photo ID and the other is a document with your signature, such as a credit card. Always check the requirements for identification before reporting to the testing center. After proving your identity, you will be assigned a workstation in the testing area at which you will take your exam. You will not be allowed to bring any reference material into the testing area. You are provided with scrap paper on which you may want to do a quick "brain dump" of I/O port numbers, IRQs, and other material you think you may have problems remembering during the exam. Do *not* waste your time by writing down exam questions to share with others who are studying for the exam. You must turn this paper over to the proctor (exam attendant) before you leave the testing center.

Exam questions are not scored, or ***weighted,*** equally. This means that exam questions are worth different amounts of points. It is impossible to determine the exact weight of a question because CompTIA does not reveal it. However, the weight of one question compared to another is often rather obvious. A question that asks you to identify a component carries less weight than a question that asks you to apply analytical thinking. For example, a question that asks which component on a motherboard is responsible for processing instructions carries less weight than a question that asks you to identify the order of the Windows XP boot process.

weighted
a method of applying a measure or score to an individual question.

A+ Note:

The A+ Certification exams are graded on a scale from 100 to 900. A minimum score of 675 is needed to pass the A+ Essentials exam, and a minimum score of 700 is needed to pass any of the other three exams. Because each question is weighted, it is difficult to translate these passing scores into a percentage.

The number of questions on an A+ Certification exam can vary because CompTIA sometimes adds a few extra questions that do not count toward the score. The additional exam questions are field-test questions. By answering them, you are helping CompTIA develop new exam questions. Field-testing ensures that the question has been clearly written and the correct answer is clearly indicated in the list of answers. If an experimental exam question is too difficult to understand or does not have a clear, correct answer, it is evident to CompTIA by a higher than average number of incorrect responses to the question. These questions are rewritten and tested again before becoming a valid exam question.

Exam Preparation

To successfully prepare for an A+ Certification exam you must design an exam preparation strategy. A few possible strategies are presented. Using them will increase your chances of passing an A+ Certification exam on your first attempt.

Establish a Study Schedule

Establish a realistic study schedule. Use a calendar and write in the dates and times for study. You will know best how much time to allocate. You can also ask your instructor for input on how many hours of additional study you might need before taking the exam. Having a planned schedule for study allows you to set times for other things such as movies, dates, family plans, and television. If you have a set study schedule, you will most likely think twice about those other activities and will schedule your study time around them.

Get Hands-On Experience

Hands-on experience provides you with many of the required skills that are tested on in the A+ Certification exams. You should spend as much time as possible practicing many of the skills that are tested. For example, you should practice setting up and formatting partitions on a hard drive, rather than just reading and memorizing procedures. For many of the skills tested, there is no substitute for hands-on experience. The series of lab activities designed to accompany this textbook should provide you with many of those skills. It is highly recommended you practice performing the lab activities and review the questions at the end of each lab. Many of the lab review questions are designed to prepare you for an A+ Certification exam. Begin your review at the beginning of the lab manual. Often, students forget the basics that were covered early in the course.

Read a Variety of Computer-Related Material

It is helpful to read a variety of computer-related material. Sometimes reading the same topic in a different book or manual can illuminate the information in a new way or can commit better to memory. Some material you should read, besides this textbook, are installation manuals, Readme files, and instructional Web pages and Web sites.

Textbook material

Review the textbook material covered in the course. Just as it was suggested for the lab activities, start your review at the beginning of the textbook. Do you still remember the definition of multitasking? Review all tests, end of chapter Review Questions, pop quizzes, and classroom handouts.

Installation manuals

Installation manuals are vast sources of excellent study material. Seagate, Maxwell, Sony, Samsung, 3COM, Microsoft, and many other manufacturers have a lot of valuable information directly related to the exam in their installation manuals. You can learn by reading the installation manual for a hard drive, a network adapter card, or a multimedia card. An installation manual for a motherboard will contain a lot of valuable information, especially for setting up the BIOS configuration and for BIOS terminology which you may encounter on the test. Download at least one Intel and one ASUS motherboard manual. An installation manual reinforces what you have already learned in the course by showing you how that knowledge is applied. Most of these manuals can be downloaded from the Internet. Simply go to the manufacturer's support page on their Web site, locate the desired manual, and download the PDF file.

Readme files

The Readme files that accompany an operating system installation CD-ROM contain valuable study material. Search the operating system installation disc for the document containing the installation information. Also, check the operating system's Web site for information about the installation. Many exam content items have been derived directly from this source of information.

Instructional Web pages and Web sites

There are hundreds of Web pages available to assist you in learning more about computer technology. Seeing the same material presented in a different format by a different writer can be extremely helpful, especially when learning difficult concepts. For example, if you have difficulty learning the differences in RAID types, you could search the Internet for "RAID" or "RAID types." You will find many sources about RAID, including short tutorials.

Create a Study Guide

A great technique to use in preparing for the A+ Certification exams and reviewing for the course is to make your own study guide. Teacher handouts are convenient, but are seldom studied in-depth by the average student. There are also many study guides located on the Internet. Some are free, and some are costly. Some commercial and free study guides contain material that is no longer required for the exam or is not included in the examination objectives. To increase your retention of the subject matter, it is recommended that you make your own study guide. One suggested method of creating a study guide is to list the examination objectives on a sheet of paper, leaving ample space in which to write your own notes between the content items.

A better way to copy the examination objectives is to use a word processor. Add an ample amount of space between the content items listed. When studying, write in by hand the information you have collected about each objective and content item. See **Figure 21-2.** Using this method will not only give you a set of notes matching the exact exam objectives, it will serve as an excellent study tool.

When filling in your study guide, be aware that many content items are listed under more than one objective. When you see a content item that is listed more than once, look for key words in the related objective that identify the desired information for that content item. For example, if a USB port is listed under more than one objective, one occurrence may be under an objective that is concerned with the USB port's identification and characteristics and the other occurrence may be concerned with troubleshooting. Write your notes about the content item according to the specifics of each objective.

Figure 21-2.
Sample study guide.

My Study Guide

1.5 Identify the names, purposes, and performance characteristics of standardized/common peripheral ports, associated cabling, and their connectors. Recognize ports, cabling, and connectors by sight.

Content may include the following:

Port types:

Serial

Parallel

USB ports

IEEE 1394/FireWire

Infrared

Join or Form a Study Group

A group formed of individuals that are serious about preparing for the A+ Certification exams can be an excellent way to prepare. Here are some general guidelines to follow:

- ✔ Stay on task.
- ✔ Set a regular schedule of dates, times, and duration. (Every day is best, but not always possible.)
- ✔ Write practice exam questions for each other.
- ✔ Share resources such as sample exams or Web sites that support your studies.

A study group can make exam preparation a little more fun and provide you with the additional motivation you need to study. The members of the study group help keep one another on task. For example, you may plan to study every night for the next two weeks for three hours each night. However, when it comes to executing the plan, you may easily find a reason not to study. When two or more of you plan to study together, each member feels more obligated to meet at the established time.

The study group can also share some of the burden of exam preparation. Each member of the study group can take a particular area covered on the exam and write a set of questions for the other members. When you meet at your regularly scheduled time, you can exchange the questions. You can also share resources such as sample exams or Web sites that you have found helpful in your personal studies.

One word of caution, though, is to make sure the study group functions as a study group and not as a social group. A group of friends gathered for study can quickly get off track and spend a lot of time discussing football, movies, and other events. It is critical that the study group remains focused on the task at hand—exam preparation.

Take Practice Exams

Practice exams are an excellent way to determine your test readiness and to identify weak areas. You may discover that you do not know the printing process as well as you thought. Practice exams are an important ingredient to your exam preparation strategy. You can use the practice exams to design the content for your review sessions. After taking a practice exam, identify the topics you feel you need more help in. Make a list, and then review materials covering those topics.

There are numerous Web sites offering free on-line or downloadable practice exams. While many are quite reputable, some are rather questionable. There are hundreds of sample exams located throughout the Internet. These exams provide only a sampling of a full test bank. Some have been found to be flawed, misleading, and definitely designed to have the test taker fail. The marketing idea is to show the student how little they know about the subject so that the student may be lured into purchasing the full test bank of questions. You may take the free sample exams because they still have many good questions, but do not consider them a true measure of your ability to pass the exam. The following are some Web sites that contain free practice exams and that are at an appropriate level:

- ✔ www.learnthat.com—This site also contains links to free on-line courses and tutorials.
- ✔ www.RMRoberts.com—This site contains practice exams, textbook updates, and other student and teacher resources.

- ✔ www.proprofs.com—This site contains a lot of practice tests items, study guides, and a forum for discussing the test. To access all parts of the Web site, you must join and provide an e-mail address. However, the Web site's resources are free.

The next two Web sites are also good sources of free practice exams. Since they have occasionally changed their address, they are listed here according to their Web site name. Use the name of the Web site in a Google search to find it.

- ✔ Aplus Omega—Aplus Omega has A+ and Network+ sample exams.
- ✔ Pagesbydave A+ Test Prep—Pagesbydave has both A+ and Network+ sample exams.

Many students want to score a 100% on their A+ Certification exam. They constantly take practice exams and may continuously achieve a score that is less than 100%. Because of this, they never feel prepared for an A+ Certification exam. While scoring a 100% on a practice exam is a worthy goal, it is unrealistic for many students. To determine if you are prepared to take an A+ Certification exam, consider a passing score of 80% on a practice exam as a good indication. Remember that a student who does pass the exam on the very first attempt is well prepared and confident. A student who fails an A+ Certification exam is obviously not prepared and has not been committed to a set study schedule.

Schedule a Test Date

Scheduling a test date is an excellent component to add to the established study schedule. As soon as you think you know the amount of preparation you will need, set a time and date for the exam. Do not wait until you know the material 100%. Chances are you will most likely never feel you know the material 100%. Procrastinating setting a test date will quickly put you out of date with the material you have studied. Set a date to give yourself a deadline for preparation.

A+ Note:

The CompTIA exam often included questions about items not specifically listed in the exam objectives. For example, there may be a question about the OSI model as related to networking. The CompTIA exam objectives serve the purpose as a general guide and are not all-inclusive of the exam parameters. Be prepared for possible topics not precisely identified by the objective outline.

Sample CompTIA A+ Essentials Exam

The following is a practice exam intended to simulate the type and depth of questions commonly encountered on the CompTIA A+ Essentials exam. The exam is divided by domain. Each group of exam questions for a domain is preceded by a copy of the CompTIA A+ Essential exam objectives. Always check the CompTIA Web site for the very latest list of objectives. The objective contents can change at any time.

Domain 1.0—Personal Computer Components

1.1 Identify the fundamental principles of using personal computers.

- ✔ Identify the names, purposes and characteristics of storage devices. Some of the items to be covered include floppy disk drives, hard disk drives, CD/CD-RW/DVD drives, tape drives, Flash drives, and SD cards.
- ✔ Identify the names, purposes, and characteristics of motherboards. Some of the items to be covered include form factor (e.g., ATX/BTX and micro ATX/NLX), integrated I/O (e.g., sound, video, USB, serial, IEEE 1394/FireWire, parallel, NIC, and modem), memory slots (e.g., RIMM and DIMM), processor sockets, external cache memory, bus architecture, bus slots (e.g., PCI, AGP, PCIe, AMR, and CNR), EIDE/PATA, SATA, SCSI technology, chipsets, BIOS/CMOS/firmware, riser cards, and daughter boards.
- ✔ Identify the names, purposes, and characteristics of power supplies. Some of the items covered include AC adapter, ATX, proprietary, and voltage.
- ✔ Identify the names, purposes, and characteristics of CPUs. Some items covered include CPU chips (e.g., AMD and Intel), CPU technologies, HyperThreading, dual core, throttling, micro code (MMX), overclocking, cache, VRM, speed (real vs. actual), and 32 bit vs. 64 bit.
- ✔ Identify the names, purposes, and characteristics of memory. Some of the items covered include types of memory (e.g., DRAM, SRAM, SDRAM, DDR/DDR2, and RAMBUS), operational characteristics, memory chips (8, 16, and 32), parity vs. non-parity, ECC vs. non-ECC, single-sided vs. double-sided.
- ✔ Identify the names, purposes, and characteristics of display devices. Some of the items covered include projectors, CRTs, LCDs, connector types (e.g., VGA, DVI, HDMi, S-Video, and Component Video/RGB), and settings (e.g., V-hold, refresh rate, and resolution).
- ✔ Identify the names, purposes, and characteristics of input devices. Some of the items covered include mouse, keyboard, bar code reader, multimedia (e.g., Web and digital cameras, MIDI, and microphones), biometric devices, and touch screens.
- ✔ Identify the names, purposes, and characteristics of adapter cards. Some of the items covered include PCI, PCIe, and AGP video; multimedia; I/O (e.g., SCSI, serial, USB, and Parallel); and communications, including network and modem.
- ✔ Identify the names, purposes, and characteristics of ports and cables. Some of the items covered include USB 1.1 and 2.0, parallel, serial, IEEE 1394/FireWire, RJ-45, RJ-11, PS/2, mini-DIN, Centronics (e.g., mini and 36), and multimedia (e.g., 1/8 connector, MIDI coaxial, and SPDIF).
- ✔ Identify the names, purposes, and characteristics of cooling systems. Some of the items covered include heat sinks, CPU and case fans, liquid cooling systems, and thermal compound.

1.2 Install, configure, optimize and upgrade personal computer components.

- ✔ Add, remove, and configure internal and external storage devices. Some of the items covered include drive preparation of internal storage devices, format/file systems, and imaging technology.
- ✔ Install display devices.

- ✔ Add, remove, and configure basic input and multimedia devices.

1.3 Identify tools, diagnostic procedures, and troubleshooting techniques for personal computer components.

- ✔ Recognize the basic aspects of troubleshooting theory. Some of the items covered include performing backups before making changes; assessing a problem systematically and dividing large problems into smaller components to be analyzed individually; verifying even the obvious; determining whether the problem is something simple and making no assumptions; researching ideas and establishing priorities; and documenting findings, actions, and outcomes.
- ✔ Identify and apply basic diagnostic procedures and troubleshooting techniques. Some of the items covered include identifying the problem, including questioning the user and identifying user changes to computer; analyzing the problem, including potential causes and making an initial determination of software and hardware problems; testing related components, including inspection, connections, hardware/software configurations, Device Manager and consulting vendor documentation; evaluating results and taking additional steps if needed such as consultation, using alternate resources, manuals; and documenting activities and outcomes.
- ✔ Recognize and isolate issues with display, power, basic input devices, storage, memory, thermal, and POST errors (e.g., BIOS and hardware).
- ✔ Apply basic troubleshooting techniques to check for problems (e.g., thermal issues, error codes, power, and connections including cables and pins, compatibility, functionality, and software/drivers) with components such as motherboards, power supplies, CPUs, memory, display devices, input devices, and adapter cards.
- ✔ Recognize the names, purposes, characteristics, and appropriate application of tools. Some of the items covered include BIOS, self-test, hard drive self-test, and software diagnostics test.

1.4 Perform preventive maintenance on personal computer components.

- ✔ Identify and apply basic aspects of preventive maintenance theory. Some of the items covered include visual/audio inspection, driver/firmware updates, scheduling preventive maintenance, the use of appropriate repair tools and cleaning materials, and ensuring proper environment.
- ✔ Identify and apply common preventive maintenance techniques for devices such as input devices and batteries.

Domain 1.0—Practice Exam Questions 1–21

1. Which computer component normally contains firmware required to start the computer boot operation?
   a. Hard disk drive
   b. RAM
   c. BIOS
   d. CPU
2. An ATX12V motherboard typically has a _____-pin power connector.
   a. 12
   b. 24
   c. 16
   d. 32
3. What name is used to describe the physical shape of a motherboard?
   a. Outline
   b. Frame size
   c. Case factor
   d. Form factor
4. Which slot type provides the highest data transfer rate?
   a. PCI
   b. ISA
   c. PCIe
   d. PCI-X
5. What is the theoretical top data transfer rate of IEEE 802.11b?
   a. 1 Mbps
   b. 5 Mbps
   c. 11 Mbps
   d. 54 Mbps
6. Which type of connection is *not* associated with a keyboard?
   a. PS/2
   b. USB
   c. Bluetooth
   d. Fiber-optic
7. The purpose of CPU cache is to _____.
   a. temporarily store data
   b. create the digital clock signal used by the CPU
   c. synchronize IRQ signals with other motherboard components
   d. store BIOS setup configuration data
8. Which two port types are used to connect to an internal HDD? (Select two.)
   a. SATA
   b. PATA
   c. USB
   d. FireWire
9. What is another name for FireWire?
   a. RS-232
   b. RJ-45
   c. BNC
   d. IEEE-1394

10. What two things should you do before performing an operating system upgrade? (Select two.)
    a. Format the active partition.
    b. Disable the antivirus program.
    c. Backup all system files and important data.
    d. Disable the system boot.ini file.
11. What should be applied between a new CPU and the CPU heat sink?
    a. A thin film of lightweight oil.
    b. A thermal compound paste.
    c. Ceramic glue to ensure a tight fit.
    d. The surface area must remain absolutely clean; nothing should be applied to the surface of a CPU.
12. Which type of memory is most appropriate for desktop RAM?
    a. DDR3
    b. EPROM
    c. EEPROM
    d. Flash
13. Which file system is associated with CD technologies?
    a. FAT12
    b. FAT16
    c. FAT32
    d. UDF
14. Which socket would *most likely* be used for an Intel Core 2 Duo 2.66 GHz CPU?
    a. Socket 775
    b. Socket 8
    c. Socket AM2D
    d. Socket 370
15. Which set of voltage levels are associated with a standard ATX power supply?
    a. 3.3, 5, 12
    b. 6, 12, 18
    c. 3.3, 6.6, 18.8
    d. 3.3, 12, 24
16. Which is the correct sequence for installing a new hard disk drive?
    a. Install the hard drive into the drive bay, set the selection jumper to slave or master, format the hard disk drive, create a primary partition.
    b. Partition the hard drive, format the hard drive, set the selection jumper to slave or master, install the hard drive into the drive bay.
    c. Set the selection jumper to slave or master, install the hard drive into the hard drive bay, partition the drive, format the partition.
    d. Install the hard disk drive into the hard drive bay, format the hard disk drive, partition the drive, set the selection jumper to slave or master.
17. Which port is commonly used to support Flash drives?
    a. PS/2
    b. USB
    c. IEEE 1394
    d. DB-15

18. Which printer connection type would provide the highest data throughput rate?
    a. RS-232
    b. Serial
    c. USB 2.0
    d. Bluetooth
19. Which two devices would normally be found connected to a SCSI cable? (Select two.)
    a. Hard disk drive
    b. Tape drive
    c. Monitor
    d. Keyboard
20. A customer wants to ensure their data is protected from loss caused by a power failure and they also want to protect their data from loss caused by a hard disk drive failure. Which solution would you recommend?
    a. Install a UPS and a RAID 1 system.
    b. Install a tape backup unit and a power strip with surge protection.
    c. Install a UPS and a DVD writer, which can be used to perform daily backups.
    d. Install a dual power supply and a RAID 0 system.
21. Which of the following hard drive parameters can be viewed in the BIOS CMOS settings? (Select four.)
    a. Master and Slave IDE locations
    b. Drive speed
    c. Number of heads
    d. Number of cylinders
    e. Drive capacity
    f. Boot sector address

Domain 2.0—Laptop and Portable Devices

2.1 Identify the fundamental principles of using laptops and portable devices.

✔ Identify names, purposes, and characteristics of laptop-specific form factors (e.g., memory and hard drives), peripherals (e.g., docking station, port replicator, and media/accessory bay), expansion slots (e.g., PCMCIA I, II, and III and ExpressCard bus), ports (e.g. mini PCI slot), communication connections (e.g., Bluetooth, infrared, cellular WAN, and Ethernet), power and electrical input devices (e.g., auto-switching and fixed-input power supplies, batteries), LCD technologies (e.g., active and passive matrix; resolution such as XGA, SXGA+, UXGA, WUXGA; contrast ratio; and native resolution), input devices (e.g., stylus/digitizer, function [Fn] keys, and pointing devices such as touch pad, point stick/track point).

✔ Identify and distinguish between mobile and desktop motherboards and processors, including throttling, power management, and WiFi.

2.2 Install, configure, optimize, and upgrade laptops and portable devices.

✔ Configure power management, for example, identify the features of BIOS-ACPI and identify the difference between suspend, hibernate, and standby.

✔ Demonstrate safe removal of laptop-specific hardware such as peripherals, hot-swappable devices, and non-hot-swappable devices.

2.3 Identify tools, basic diagnostic procedures, and troubleshooting techniques for laptops and portable devices.

✔ Use procedures and techniques to diagnose power conditions and video, keyboard, pointer, and wireless card issues, for example, verifying AC power (e.g., LEDs and swap AC adapter), verifying DC power, removing unneeded peripherals, plugging in external monitor, toggling [Fn] keys, checking LCD cutoff switch, and verifying backlight functionality and pixilation. Other items covered include stylus issues (e.g., digitizer problems), unique laptop keypad issues, and antenna wires.

2.4 Perform preventive maintenance on laptops and portable devices.

✔ Identify and apply common preventive maintenance techniques for laptops and portable devices, for example, cooling devices, hardware and video cleaning materials, and operating environments, including temperature and air quality, storage, transportation, and shipping.

Domain 2.0—Practice Exam Questions 22–32

22. Which LCD resolution closely matches WUXGA?
    a. 640 × 480
    b. 1280 × 720
    c. 1920 × 1200
    d. 2560 × 1600
23. Which device is commonly used to allow a laptop computer to use a full-size video monitor, full-size mouse, and an automatic network connection and to keep the battery charged at the same time?
    a. Network hub
    b. Docking station
    c. Gateway
    d. Port expander
24. A new laptop user calls for support. The user says that while using her laptop, she often loses the sound. It happens most often when she is typing a document. Sometimes the sound returns for no apparent reason. What is *most likely* the problem?
    a. The user is accidentally striking the function key combination hitting the [Fn] key and the sound mute key.
    b. The video card is about to fail.
    c. As the battery drains, the sound volume is reduced or muted automatically to conserve energy.
    d. This is a typical laptop motherboard issue, and the laptop should be returned to the manufacturer for repair.
25. Which energy conservation mode saves the current work to hard drive and takes the longest amount of time to recover from?
    a. Standby
    b. Hibernate
    c. Suspend
    d. Sleep

26. Which laptop component does *not* support hot-swap technology?
    a. USB drive
    b. ExpressCard
    c. PCMCIA card
    d. IDE device
27. Which technology is designed to provide automatic energy-saving options for a laptop computer?
    a. DMA
    b. ATAPI
    c. ACPI
    d. PCMCIA
28. What function is provided by an LCD inverter?
    a. Convert ac to dc required for the backlight.
    b. Lower frequency for dimming the backlight
    c. Convert dc to ac required for the backlight.
    d. Convert dc voltage to a lower dc voltage required by the backlight.
29. A laptop appears dead. No LEDs are lit anywhere on the laptop. What would you do first?
    a. Replace the laptop power supply.
    b. Replace the ac adapter and power cord.
    c. Replace the laptop battery.
    d. Toggle the display brightness function key and observe the results.
30. You are troubleshooting erratic behavior of a laptop computer. You open the performance monitor and notice the maximum CPU frequency is fluctuating. What is *most likely* the problem?
    a. Fluctuating CPU frequency is most likely caused by a heat problem.
    b. The video card memory is most likely failing, causing strain on the CPU.
    c. The battery is almost depleted, causing the CPU frequency to fluctuate to levels above normal.
    d. A fluctuating laptop CPU frequency is normal by design.
31. What is the major limitation of infrared technology?
    a. It is not immune to radio interference.
    b. It is limited to only two devices.
    c. It often produces an overload on the power supply.
    d. It can only be used in a relatively dark environment.
32. Which type of memory is used most often in a laptop computer?
    a. RIMM
    b. SO-DIMM
    c. PCMCIA
    d. SIMM

Domain 3.0—Operating Systems

Unless otherwise noted, operating systems include Microsoft Windows 2000, XP Professional, XP Home, and Media Center.

3.1 Identify the fundamentals of using operating systems.

- ✔ Identify differences between operating systems (e.g., Mac, Windows, and Linux) and describe operating system revision levels, including GUI, system requirements, and application and hardware compatibility.
- ✔ Identify names, purposes, and characteristics of the primary operating system components including registry, virtual memory, and file system.
- ✔ Describe features of operating system interfaces. Some of the items covered include Windows Explorer, My Computer, Control Panel, Command Prompt, My Network Places, taskbar, system tray, and Start menu.
- ✔ Identify the names, locations, purposes, and characteristics of operating system files. Some of the items covered include boot.ini, ntdlr, ntdetect.com, ntbootdd.sys, and registry data files.
- ✔ Identify concepts and procedures for creating, viewing, and managing disks, directories, and files in operating systems. Some of the items covered include disks (e.g., active, primary, extended, and logical partitions), file systems (e.g., FAT32 and NTFS), directory structures (e.g., create folders and navigate directory structures), and files (e.g., creation, extensions, attributes, and permissions).

3.2 Install, configure, optimize, and upgrade operating systems. References to upgrading from Windows 95 and NT may be made.

- ✔ Identify procedures for installing operating systems, including verification of hardware compatibility and minimum requirements, installation methods (e.g., boot media such as CD, floppy or USB, network installation, and drive imaging), operating system installation options (e.g., attended/unattended, file system type, and network configuration), disk preparation order (e.g., start installation, partition drive, and format drive), device driver configuration (e.g., install and upload device drivers), and verification of installation.
- ✔ Identify procedures for upgrading operating systems, including upgrade considerations (e.g., hardware and application and network compatibility), and implementation (e.g., back up data and install additional Windows components).
- ✔ Install/add a device, including loading and adding device drivers and required software. Some items covered include determining whether permissions are adequate for performing the task, installing device drivers (e.g., automated and manual search and installation of device drivers), using unsigned drivers (e.g., driver signing), and verifying installation of the driver (e.g., device manager and functionality).
- ✔ Identify procedures and utilities used to optimize operating systems, for example, virtual memory, hard drives, temporary files, service, startup, and applications.

3.3 Identify tools, diagnostic procedures, and troubleshooting techniques for operating systems.

- ✔ Identify basic boot sequences and methods and utilities for recovering operating systems. Some items covered include boot methods (e.g., safe mode, Recovery Console, boot to Restore Point), Automated System Recovery (ASR), and Emergency Repair Disk (ERD).
- ✔ Identify and apply diagnostic procedures and troubleshooting techniques, for example, identifying the problem by questioning the user and identifying user changes to the computer; analyzing the problem, including potential causes and initial determination of software or hardware problem; testing related components, including connections, hardware/software configurations, Device Manager, and consulting vendor documentation; evaluating results and taking additional steps if needed, such as consultation and alternate resources and manuals; documenting activities and outcomes.
- ✔ Recognize and resolve common operational issues such as bluescreen; system lock-up; input/output device; application install, start, or load; and Windows-specific printing problems (e.g., print spool stalled and incorrect/incompatible driver for print).
- ✔ Explain common error messages and codes. Some items covered include boot (e.g., invalid boot disk, inaccessible boot drive, and missing ntdlr); startup (e.g., device/service failed to start and device/program in registry not found); Event Viewer, registry, and Windows reporting.
- ✔ Identify the names, locations, purposes, and characteristics of operating system utilities. Some items covered include disk management tools (e.g., Disk Defragmenter, NTBackup, Chkdsk, Format), system management tools (e.g., Device Manager, Task Manager, System Configuration Utility (msconfig.exe)), and file management tools (e.g., Windows Explorer and attrib.exe).

3.4 Perform preventive maintenance on operating systems.

- ✔ Describe common utilities for performing preventive maintenance on operating systems, for example, software and Windows updates (e.g., service packs), scheduled backups/restore, and restore points.

Domain 3.0—Practice Exam Questions 33–53

33. You are performing a clean install of Windows XP. The Windows XP CD is in the CD drive. Every time you boot the computer, a message is displayed saying the operating system is not found. What should you do next?
    a. Replace the CD drive with a DVD drive.
    b. Upgrade the BIOS.
    c. Replace the Windows XP installation CD.
    d. Check the BIOS configuration to ensure the CD/DVD drive is first boot device.
34. Which system file contains a list of all operating systems installed on the computer?
    a. ntuser.dat
    b. boot.ini
    c. autoexec.bat
    d. command.com

35. Which command will allow you to view the contents of the Windows XP system registry?
    a. **sysedit**
    b. **regedit/xp**
    c. **regedt32**
    d. **restore/xp**
36. Which files are required to boot Windows XP? (Select two.)
    a. ntldr
    b. autoexec.bat
    c. ntoskernl.exe
    d. command.com
37. Which Windows XP file contains the operating system kernel?
    a. ntldr
    b. boot.ini
    c. ntoskernl
    d. ntbootdd.sys
38. Which Windows XP file is required for supporting SCSI drives?
    a. ntdetect
    b. ntbootdd.sys
    c. boot.ini
    d. cmd.exe
39. Which command will make the file called mydata a read only file?
    a. **attrib mydata +r**
    b. **mydata/r**
    c. **attrib mydata/r**
    d. **set mydata attribute r**
40. A hard disk drive contains an active partition, a primary partition, an extended partition, and a logical partition. Which drive partition must be removed first?
    a. Primary partition
    b. Active partition
    c. Extended partition
    d. Logical partition
41. Which is the correct command to convert a FAT32 file system to NTFS from the command prompt?
    a. **convert c: /fs:ntfs**
    b. **change c:fat32 *.* c:ntfs**
    c. **convert c:fat32/ntfs**
    d. **format c: /ntfs**
42. When is a PC hardware check first performed?
    a. Immediately after loading ntloadr.
    b. Immediately after loading ntdetect.
    c. During the POST.
    d. After reading sector 0 on the HDD.

43. Which program is used in Windows XP to inspect the hard disk drive for errors?
    a. Chkdsk
    b. Defrag
    c. Fdisk
    d. Diskpart
44. Which key or combination of keys is used to access Windows XP Task Manager?
    a. [Ctrl] [Alt] [Esc]
    b. [Ctrl] [Alt] [Del]
    c. [F8]
    d. [Shift] [Esc]
45. Which items should be performed on a regular basis as a preventive maintenance measure for a desktop PC? (Select three.)
    a. Remove Temporary files.
    b. Defragment the HDD.
    c. Run Fdisk.
    d. Run Chkdsk.
46. Which type of device is directly affected by the Microsoft DirectX program?
    a. Video display
    b. HDD
    c. Keyboard
    d. Mouse
47. You are performing a clean install of Windows XP. When would you install the hardware device drivers?
    a. Before the operating system files are installed.
    b. Immediately after formatting the primary partition.
    c. Immediately after installing the antivirus program.
    d. Immediately after or during the installation process of the new operating system.
48. Which event viewer file in Windows XP would you look at to determine if someone has tried to make unauthorized access to a computer?
    a. Application log
    b. Security log
    c. System log
    d. Logon Activities log
49. Which three items are commonly associated with the "blue screen of death"? (Select three.)
    a. Faulty memory
    b. Corrupt DLL file
    c. Incorrect IRQ setting
    d. Corrupt registry
50. How do you access "safe mode" when using a Windows XP operating system?
    a. Press the [Del] key during system startup.
    b. Press the [F8] key after POST but before loading the operating system.
    c. Press [Ctrl] [Alt] [Del] after the operating system is loaded.
    d. Press [Ctrl] [Alt] [Del] when the system logon dialog box appears on the screen.

51. When would you install Microsoft service pack for Windows XP?
    a. Before installing the operating system.
    b. During the normal Windows XP operating system installation process and before the first logon.
    c. Only after installing the antivirus program because service packs have been known to be corrupt.
    d. After completing the Windows XP operating system installation.
52. How do you access Windows XP Task Manager?
    a. Right-click an empty space on the taskbar and then select **Task Manager**.
    b. Press [Del] during logon and then select **Task Manager**.
    c. Right-click **My Computer** and then select **Manage**.
    d. Insert the Windows XP installation CD, reboot the computer, and then select **Other**.
53. Which two methods will launch the command prompt in Windows XP? (Select two.)
    a. Right-click the taskbar and then select **cmd** from the shortcut menu.
    b. Type and enter **cmd** in the **Run** dialog box.
    c. Open **Start | All Programs | Accessories** and then select **Command Prompt**.
    d. Open **Start | Control Panel | Maintenance | System** and then select **Command Prompt**.

Domain 4.0—Printers and Scanners

4.1 Identify the fundamental principles of using printers and scanners.

✔ Identify differences between types of printer and scanner technologies (e.g., laser, inkjet, thermal, solid ink, and impact).

✔ Identify names, purposes, and characteristics of printer and scanner components (e.g., memory, driver, and firmware) and consumables (e.g., toner, ink cartridge, and paper).

✔ Identify the names, purposes, and characteristics of interfaces used by printers and scanners, including port and cable types. Some items covered include parallel, network (e.g., NIC and print servers), USB, serial, IEEE 1394/FireWire, wireless (e.g., Bluetooth, 802.11, and infrared), and SCSI.

4.2 Identify basic concepts of installing, configuring, optimizing, and upgrading printers and scanners.

✔ Install and configure printers and scanners, for example, power and connect the device using local or network port; install and update device drivers and calibrate the device; configure options and default settings; and print a test page.

✔ Optimize printer performance, for example, printer settings such as tray switching, print spool settings, device calibration, media types, and paper orientation.

4.3 Identify tools, basic diagnostic procedures, and troubleshooting techniques for printers and scanners.

- ✔ Gather information about printer and scanner problems, for example, identify symptom; review device error codes, computer error messages, and history (e.g., event log and user reports); print or scan test page; and use appropriate generic or vendor-specific diagnostic tools including Web-based utilities.
- ✔ Review and analyze collected data, for example, establish probable causes, review service documentation, review knowledge base, and define and isolate the problem (e.g., software vs. hardware, driver, connectivity, and printer).
- ✔ Identify solutions to identified printer and scanner problems, for example, define specific cause and apply fix, replace consumables as needed, verify functionality, and get user acceptance of problem fix.

Domain 4.0—Practice Exam Questions 54–62

54. Which type of printer uses a drum to transfer and image?
    a. Inkjet
    b. Laser
    c. Impact
    d. Thermo
55. What is the last step you should perform when installing a printer?
    a. Check Device Manager for driver version.
    b. Check that no print jobs were left in the spool when the printer was assembled and tested at the manufacturer.
    c. Access the **Printer Properties** dialog box for the printer and print a test page.
    d. Update the computer BIOS so that it will automatically recognize the printer device.
56. How do you print a test page?
    a. Open **Control Panel** and click the **Test Printer** icon.
    b. Open the **Printer Properties** dialog box and click the **Print Test Page** button.
    c. Open **Device Manager**, select the **Hardware** tab, and then click the **Test** button.
    d. Open **Command Prompt** and enter **Print Test**, followed by the printer name.
57. What is the proper way to remove a scanner from a PC?
    a. Open **Device Manager**, right-click the scanner device, and then select **Uninstall** from the shortcut menu. Then, unplug the scanner from the computer.
    b. Insert the Windows Setup disk and then unplug the scanner. When Windows prompts you for the scanner driver disc, insert it into the drive and follow the prompts.
    c. Run the **System Configuration Utility** (msconfig.exe) and then select the **Device** tab. Uncheck the box in front of the scanner device and then unplug the scanner from the computer.
    d. Run the **System Configuration Utility** (msconfig.exe) and then select the **Scan remove** option from the hardware menu.

58. What type of port is generally used to connect a network printer to a network hub?
    a. RS-232
    b. USB
    c. RJ-45
    d. Serial
59. A client calls you and says that his printer was working fine before lunch, but when he returned, he can no longer print any documents? What would you request the user to do next?
    a. Try reinstalling the printer drivers.
    b. Reboot the computer and try to print a document after the computer is running.
    c. Remove the printer cable and then reinstall the cable, but switch the ends this time.
    d. Open the printer, remove and then reinsert the printer toner cartridge. Then, try the printer once more.
60. A client reports that laser printer documents suddenly have started to smear when touched. What is *most likely* the cause of the problem?
    a. The wrong toner type has been installed in the printer.
    b. The paper pickup pads are worn.
    c. The laser cleaner pad needs replacing.
    d. The laser printer fuser unit is defective.
61. A network printer is connected locally to a Windows XP computer. The printer has suddenly stopped working and an error code 54 has been displayed in the printer LCD display. What is the next logical step?
    a. Conduct a search on the Microsoft TechNet Web site using the error code as the main keyword.
    b. Conduct a search on the Internet using the key words "error 54."
    c. Research the printer manufacturer's Web site for error codes for that particular printer model.
    d. Open the computer BIOS configuration and see if the BIOS has detected the printer.
62. You have just installed a scanner that is connected to a Windows XP computer. Where would you *most likely* locate the very latest driver for the scanner?
    a. The Windows XP driver section of the Microsoft Web site.
    b. On the installation CD that came with the scanner.
    c. Through a Google search using the key words "scanner driver Windows XP."
    d. On the scanner manufacturer's Web site.

Domain 5.0—Networks

5.1 Identify the fundamental principles of networks.

✔ Describe basic networking concepts. Some items covered include addressing, bandwidth, status indicators, protocols (e.g., TCP/IP, classful subnet, and IPX/SPX, including NWLink, NetBEUI, and NetBIOS), full-duplex, half-duplex, cabling (e.g., twisted pair, coaxial cable, fiber-optic, RS-232, USB, and IEEE-1394/FireWire), and networking models, including peer-to-peer and client/server.

- ✔ Identify names, purposes, and characteristics of the common network cables. Some items covered include plenum/PVC, UTP (e.g., Cat 3, Cat 5, Cat 5e, and Cat 6), STP, and fiber-optic (e.g., single-mode and multimode).
- ✔ Identify names, purposes, and characteristics of network connectors (e.g., RJ-45, RJ-11, ST, SC, LC, and MT-RJ).
- ✔ Identify names, purposes, and characteristics (e.g., definition, speed, and connections) of technologies for establishing connectivity. Some items covered include LAN/WAN, ISDN, Broadband (e.g., DSL, Cable, and satellite), dial-up, wireless (all 802.11), infrared, Bluetooth, cellular, and VoIP.

5.2 Install, configure, optimize, and upgrade networks.

- ✔ Install and configure network cards (physical address).
- ✔ Install, identify, and obtain wired and wireless connection.

5.3 Identify tools, diagnostic procedures, and troubleshooting techniques for networks.

- ✔ Explain status indicators, for example, speed, connection and activity lights, and wireless signal strength.

Domain 5.0—Practice Exam Questions 63–74

63. You are connecting a desktop computer to an Ethernet 10/100/1000 switch in a small office configuration using Cat 6 cable. What type of cable connector would be found on the Ethernet switch?
    a. RS-232
    b. RJ-45
    c. BNC
    d. IEEE-1394
64. Which protocol is used to send e-mail to a mail server?
    a. POP3
    b. FTP
    c. SMTP
    d. IMAP
65. A customer wants to install the fastest Internet connection service at their home at a reasonable cost. Which Internet access type would you recommend?
    a. V92 modem
    b. ISDN
    c. DSL
    d. T1

66. A wireless SOHO network consists of two different PCs, each located in a different room approximately 60′ apart. The system is using IEEE 802.11b wireless standard devices. You open the **Wireless Network Connection Status** dialog box on one of the two computers and see that the indicated connection speed is less than 5 Mbps. What does a speed of less than 5 Mbps indicate?
    a. The 802.11b adapter is configured for 802.11a.
    b. There is an excessive amount of data being exchanged between the two computers, causing the speed to be reduced.
    c. The computer BIOS needs to be upgraded to accommodate the 802.11 b device.
    d. This is a normal connection speed for this scenario.
67. Which is the default protocol associated with Internet communications?
    a. IPX/SPX
    b. NWLink
    c. NetBEUI
    d. TCP/IP
68. Which network technology uses the CSMA/CD method to access the network media?
    a. Ethernet
    b. Token Ring
    c. Wireless 802.11g
    d. All network systems use CSMA/CD.
69. Which network media type supports the highest data throughput rate?
    a. Cat 5
    b. Cat 5e
    c. Cat 6
    d. Fiber-optic
70. Which command is used to reveal a workstation assigned IP address, subnet mask, and gateway?
    a. **nslookup**
    b. **ping**
    c. **ipconfig**
    d. **wins**
71. Which tool or utility is commonly used to determine an assigned URL and a matching IP address?
    a. Nslookup
    b. FTP
    c. IMAP
    d. SNMP
72. Which service is responsible for automatically issuing IP addresses to computers as needed?
    a. DNS
    b. WINS
    c. DHCP
    d. FTP

73. Which protocol is associated with a shared Internet connection?
    a. FTP
    b. SMTP
    c. NAT
    d. HTTPS
74. Which is the loopback address associated with a network adapter card?
    a. 255.255.255.255
    b. 192.168.0.1
    c. 127.0.0.1
    d. 255.0.0.0

Domain 6.0—Security

6.1 Identify the fundamental principles of security.

✔ Identify names, purposes, and characteristics of hardware and software security. Some items covered include hardware deconstruction/recycling, smart cards/biometrics (e.g., key fobs, cards, chips, and scans), authentication technologies (e.g., user name, password, biometrics, and smart cards), malicious software protection (e.g., viruses, Trojans, worms, spam, spyware, adware, and grayware), software firewalls, and file system security (e.g., FAT32 and NTFS).

✔ Identify names, purposes, and characteristics of wireless security. Some items covered include wireless encryption (e.g., WEP.x and WPA.x) and client configuration, access points (e.g., disable DHCP/use static IP, change SSID from default, disable SSID broadcast, MAC filtering, change default username and password, update firmware, and firewall).

✔ Identify names, purposes, and characteristics of data and physical security. Some items covered include data access (basic local security policy), encryption technologies, backups, data migration, data/remnant removal, password management, and locking workstation (e.g., hardware and operating system).

✔ Describe importance and process of incidence reporting.

✔ Recognize and respond appropriately to social engineering situations.

6.2 Install, configure, upgrade, and optimize security.

✔ Install, configure, upgrade, and optimize hardware, software, and data security. Some items covered include BIOS, smart cards, authentication technologies, malicious software protection, data access (basic local security policy), backup procedures, access to backups, data migration, and data/ remnant removal.

6.3 Identify tool, diagnostic procedures, and troubleshooting techniques for security.

✔ Diagnose and troubleshoot hardware, software, and data security. Some items covered include BIOS, smart cards, biometrics, authentication technologies, malicious software, file system (e.g., FAT32 and NTFS), data access (e.g., basic local security policy), backup, and data migration.

6.4 Perform preventive maintenance for computer security.

✔ Implement software security preventive maintenance techniques such as installing service packs and patches and training users about malicious software prevention technologies.

Domain 6.0—Practice Exam Questions 75–85

75. A small office located in a shopping mall uses IEEE 802.11b as the media for connecting its peer-to-peer network. Files are often shared, and the owner wants to make sure the files cannot be accessed or viewed by other businesses in the shopping mall. What can be done to secure the office network from unauthorized access?
    a. WEP enable all computers in the office.
    b. Require a logon password for each computer's local account.
    c. Install the HTTPS protocol on the network.
    d. Restrict all shared system files by enabling the hidden attribute on each file so that the exact name of the file must be known to access it.
76. An office manager is worried about unauthorized access to office computers workstations. All users are required to have a user account which requires user names and passwords. What else can be done to prevent unauthorized access?
    a. Encrypt the contents of all sensitive data files.
    b. Add a biometric security device to each workstation.
    c. Enable time restrictions for logon activities in the work area.
    d. Require special characters to be use in each user password.
77. An apartment building owner has set up a peer-to-peer wireless network in her apartment office. The owner is worried that the building tenants may be able to access her wireless network and use the Internet connection, thus compromising the system. What is the best recommendation for preventing access to the wireless network? (Select two.)
    a. WEP enable the wireless network.
    b. Use MAC filtering to prevent unauthorized access to the network gateway/router.
    c. Set up local user accounts on each computer in the wireless network.
    d. Establish and enable group policies for the wireless network.
78. Which malicious program would *most likely* be used to gain information about a computer system, such as user passwords?
    a. Grayware
    b. Trojan
    c. Spam
    d. Adware

79. A home owner has a single computer running Windows XP with Internet access. The computer is shared by all members of the home. The home owner wants to restrict his children from adding any new hardware devices or software programs to the computer but allow them to use the Internet and e-mail service. What is the best way to meet the home owner's request?
    a. Configure the computer to require a password to log on.
    b. Configure the computer so that the home owner must boot the computer before anyone else can use it.
    c. Set up accounts on the computer giving the children guest accounts.
    d. Install Active Directory an create an administrative account for the home owner.
80. What is the best way to prevent virus infections from e-mail attachments?
    a. Install an antivirus software suite.
    b. Install a software program to screen adware.
    c. Install a software program that screens spam.
    d. Do not open e-mail from people you do not know.
81. An e-mail states that a security problem has occurred at eBay and that eBay needs to verify the user's account information, such as the user name and password. The e-mail looks official because it looks like other eBay e-mails they have received in the past. Which two terms closely match the e-mail request? (Select two.)
    a. Session hacking
    b. Account hijacking
    c. Phishing
    d. Social engineering
82. Which is the best method of protecting valuable data on your computer's hard drive?
    a. Install an antivirus program.
    b. Never connect to the Internet.
    c. Perform daily or automatic data backups.
    d. Use an antivirus suite that includes a spam filter.
83. A person calls tech support to report that their default home page has suddenly changed and they cannot configure their computer for the original default home page. Which term best describes this scenario?
    a. Browser tracking
    b. Browser hijacking
    c. Phishing
    d. Session hijacking
84. Which term best describes a joke program that imitates a virus program?
    a. Spyware
    b. Grayware
    c. Adware
    d. Pharming
85. Which permission allows a person to view the contents of a folder but not add any content to that folder?
    a. Read Only
    b. Write Limited
    c. Guest
    d. Limited User

Domain 7.0—Safety and Environmental Issues

7.1 Describe the aspects and importance of safety and environmental issues.

- ✔ Identify potential safety hazards and take preventive action.
- ✔ Use Material Safety Data Sheets (MSDS) or equivalent documentation and appropriate equipment documentation.
- ✔ Use appropriate repair tools.
- ✔ Describe methods to handle environmental and human accidents (e.g., electrical, chemical, and physical), including incident reporting.

7.2 Identify potential hazards and implement proper safety procedures, including ESD precautions and procedures, safe work environment, and equipment handling.

7.3 Identify proper disposal procedures for batteries, display devices, and chemical solvents and cans.

Domain 7.0—Practice Exam Questions 86–95

86. What is the purpose of an MSDS?
    a. To increase processor performance and prevent overheating.
    b. To provide safety and health information.
    c. To provide recycling information.
    d. To increase the storage capacity of a computer system.
87. Which part of a laser printer is *most likely* to cause severe burns when touched by a technician?
    a. The fuser.
    b. The laser.
    c. The toner cartridge.
    d. The drum.
88. Which two conditions are *most likely* to enhance the probability of ESD? (Select two.)
    a. Improper grounding
    b. High humidity
    c. High temperatures
    d. Low humidity
89. Which method provides the best protection from damage to a CMOS device?
    a. Properly cleaning your hands with soap and water before handling a CMOS device.
    b. Standing on a well-grounded conducive mat before touching a CMOS device.
    c. Using an antistatic wrist strap while handling a CMOS device.
    d. There are no special requirements for handling CMOS devices, only BIOS devices.
90. Which device should always be recycled?
    a. CRT
    b. Toner cartridge
    c. Motherboard
    d. All computer devices should be recycled.

91. Which device would provide the best protection from electrical brownout conditions?
    a. Surge protector
    b. Multi-outlet power strip
    c. UPS
    d. A power strip with a surge protector installed in the base.
92. Which item would present the highest possible voltage potential with the case removed?
    a. CRT
    b. Power supply unit
    c. UPS
    d. Laser printer
93. Which class of fire extinguisher should be used for electronic equipment such as computers and servers?
    a. Class A
    b. Class B
    c. Class C
    d. Class A or Class B
94. Which would *most likely* generate EMI and disrupt unshielded cable electrical signals?
    a. Low humidity
    b. UPS with wrong batteries installed
    c. A cable with the wrong type of insulation
    d. An electric arc welder
95. You have found in a rusty metal container a very powerful solvent that you are not very familiar with. The chemical is no longer permitted to be used by any employee. What should you do next to properly dispose of the chemical?
    a. Consult the chemical solvent MSDS to see the proper procedures for handling and disposing of the product.
    b. Dilute the chemical in distilled water at an approximate ratio of 20 to 1. Then pour the chemical down any approved industrial drain system.
    c. Dilute the chemical with tap water at a ratio of 50 to 1. Prepare the container for pickup and have the post office return the chemical to the producer at their cost.
    d. Because the container is rusty, the chemical while still in the container must be taken to the nearest facility approved by OSHA to be incinerated. Your company must absorb the cost.

Domain 8.0—Communication and Professionalism

8.1 Use good communication skills, including listening, tact, and discretion when communicating with customers and colleagues.

- ✔ Use clear, concise, and direct statements.
- ✔ Allow the customer to complete statements—avoid interrupting.
- ✔ Clarify customer statements—ask pertinent questions.
- ✔ Avoid using jargon, abbreviations, and acronyms.
- ✔ Listen to customers.

8.2 Use job-related professional behavior, including notation of privacy, confidentiality, and respect for the customer and customers' property.

- ✔ Behavior. Some items covered include maintaining a positive attitude and tone of voice; avoiding arguing with customers or becoming defensive; not minimizing customers' problems; avoiding being judgmental or insulting or calling the customer names; avoiding distractions and interruptions when talking with customers.
- ✔ Property. Some items covered include telephone, laptop, desktop computer, printer, and monitor.

Domain 8.0—Practice Exam Questions 96–100

96. You are an employee of a small independent repair shop. A customer has brought in her computer for repair. What should you do next?
    a. Have the customer fill out a repair ticket while you open the case and look for possible damage.
    b. Inspect the outside of the computer case to verify any scratches or dents with the customer before proceeding.
    c. Ask the customer probing questions using novice terminology so you can narrow the scope of the repair.
    d. Verify that the computer was purchased at your location. A dated sales receipt will be required.
97. You are the only person in the repair shop and are in the middle of installing an operating system on a customer's computer. A customer walks in with his computer in need of repair. What should you do?
    a. Ask the customer to wait because you are in the middle of a repair job that can't be interrupted.
    b. Continue working on the repair while you also talk to the customer. This will always impress the customer.
    c. Keep concentrating on the job at hand. You can gesture to the customer to wait using your hands. You need not make eye contact. Keep your focus on the screen so that you do not miss an important step in the setup process.
    d. Stop what you are doing and focus all your attention on the client.
98. When dealing with an upset customer, what is the best course of action?
    a. Listen patiently and be attentive. Let the customer air their complaint and let them know you are concerned about their problem.
    b. Turn away from the irate customer and use the passive-aggressive tactic so that the problem doesn't escalate.
    c. When a customer first starts appearing upset, call your supervisor immediately. Your supervisor is a professional when dealing with difficult customers. This is not the job of a technician.
    d. You can stop the customer by maintaining eye contact with the customer. Never look away. They will break away from your stare when the confrontation has ended.

99. You are at a client's worksite. You have just finished and corrected the problem as presented on the work ticket. An employee stops and asks you to look at her printer. She has been having a problem printing documents. What is the best course of action?
    a. Inform the employee you are not authorized to fix the printer and tell her to report the problem to her supervisor.
    b. Go directly to the employee's workstation and make the repair as requested. Later, make out a work ticket and submit it to your supervisor.
    c. Tell her that you will be glad to perform the work, but first she will need to get authorization for the repair.
    d. Tell the employee that you are sincerely sorry, but you cannot make a repair without a repair ticket, and then leave the area immediately.
100. Which is the best method of dealing directly with clients at a service desk?
    a. Avoid using too simplistic terminology because this can make you sound condescending to the customer.
    b. Use technical jargon when discussing the client's problem because it will impress the client.
    c. Try to complete other work at the same time you are discussing the problem with the client. This will impress the client and show how you save time by performing two tasks at the same time.
    d. Use simple terminology and look directly at the client giving the client your full attention. This is the most commonly accepted business procedure for dealing with clients.

Scoring the Exam

Copy the following table onto a separate sheet of paper. Use the table to determine your readiness to take the CompTIA A+ Essentials exam. Simply record in the appropriate column the number of questions you answered correctly. Then, place a *P* for "pass" in the "Pass or Fail" column if the number of questions you answered correctly is equal to or exceeds the number indicated in the "Number of Correctly Answered Questions Needed to Pass" column. Place an *F* for "fail" in the "Pass or Fail" column if the number of questions you answered correctly is less than the number indicated in the "Number of Correctly Answered Questions Needed to Pass" column. Please do not write in this book.

Domain	Number of Questions	Number of Correctly Answered Questions Needed to Pass	Number of Correctly Answered Questions	Pass or Fail
Personal Computer Components	21	14		
Laptop and Portable Devices	11	7		
Operating Systems	21	14		
Printers and Scanners	9	6		
Networks	12	8		
Security	11	7		
Safety and Environmental Issues	10	7		
Communications and Professionalism	5	4		
Total	100	67		

Remember, the actual exam pass or fail status is not expressed as a percentage. The exam uses a weighted calculation to determine a score from 100 to 900. A test with weighted questions means that not all questions have equal value. Some questions are worth more than others and have a special numerical value assigned to each. The exact numeric value is used to derive at the weighted score between 100 minimum and 900 maximum. You need to achieve a weighted score of 675 to pass the CompTIA A+ Essentials exam. A percentage score of 67 is approximately equal to obtaining a weighted score of 675. I have indicated a score of 67 in the table as needed for the minimum passing for the practice exam.

A score of 80 or better indicates you are well prepared and ready to take the real CompTIA A+ Essentials exam. A passing score below 80 is considered marginal and indicates that you should do some additional preparation before taking the real exam. A score below 70 means you are not well prepared and should most definitely perform additional study.

You can look at the table and the scores you recorded to determine the areas you need most review. I have found many students perform poorly in the areas they are least interested in. For example, I have found many students perform poorly on safety and environmental issues, printers and scanners, and security for the simple reason they spend little time studying this area and would rather concentrate on areas of more interest, such as personal computer components and operating systems.

After completing some additional study in each deficient area, take another A+ Essentials practice test. Check www.rmroberts.com for additional A+ Essentials practice. Also, check with your instructor for recommended sites for practice tests.

A+ Note:

Never give up if you fail the exam. If you apply yourself and work hard toward your goal, you will surely accomplish the task at hand.

Summary

- ✔ The requirements for the A+ Certification exams change frequently. Always check the CompTIA Web site for the latest news concerning the A+ Certification exams.
- ✔ The examination objectives are categorized according to domains and are based on industry surveys that correlate exam content to actual job requirements.
- ✔ CompTIA recommends that a test candidate have at least 500 hours of work experience. This is not a requirement.
- ✔ When reporting to the testing center, you must typically show two proofs of identification. Always check the requirements for identification before reporting to the testing center.
- ✔ The A+ Certification exams are multiple-choice tests.
- ✔ To ensure success on an A+ Certification exam, establish a realistic study schedule and stick to it.
- ✔ Hands-on experience provides you with many of the required skills that are tested on the A+ Certification exams.
- ✔ Additional study resources include installation manuals, Readme files, and instructional Web pages and Web sites.
- ✔ Creating your own study guide will improve your overall retention of the subject matter.
- ✔ A group formed of individuals that are serious about preparing for an A+ Certification exam can be an excellent way to prepare.
- ✔ Taking practice exams helps evaluate your weak areas.

Review Questions

Answer the following questions on a separate sheet of paper. Please do not write in this book.

1. How many tests must a candidate pass to earn the CompTIA A+ certification?
2. Which exam must be taken by all candidates and should be taken first?
3. After passing the CompTIA A+ Essentials, which test would *most likely* meet the needs of a candidate who intends to perform computer repair work with limited or no contact with customers or clients?
4. After passing the A+ Essentials exam, which exam would *most likely* meet the needs of a computer tech working in a corporate environment where he or she would work with desktop computers and laptops, thus working closely with employees?
5. In addition to the CompTIA A+ Essential exam, which test would best measure the skills required to work as a help desk or call center technician?
6. What percentage of the CompTIA A+ Essentials exam is representative of the Communications and Professionalism domain?
7. Which exam does not require knowledge in the Laptop and Portable Devices domain?
8. Which exam does not require knowledge in the Safety and Environmental Issues domain?
9. Which domain is not covered on the CompTIA A+ Essentials exam?
10. Which exam requires the most knowledge about networks?

Suggested Lab Activities

1. Form a study group of students who are serious about preparing for the A+ Certification exams.
2. Make a date to take an exam and construct a schedule of study times and dates.
3. Write practice exams for other members in your study group.
4. Make 3 × 5 flash cards with A+ Certification exam questions. Include the answers on the opposite side. Use the cards to test your knowledge.
5. Create your own study guide using the examination objectives provided by CompTIA.
6. Write your own exam questions using the examination objectives provided by CompTIA. If you have formed a study group, you can try the exam questions out on each other. You will be surprised how many questions written by you will be similar to ones found on the A+ Certification exams.

Employment and Advanced Education

After studying this chapter, you will be able to:

- ✔ Conduct a job search.
- ✔ Identify appropriate interview skills.
- ✔ Discuss a variety of computer careers and the associated educational requirements.
- ✔ Define entrepreneur and entrepreneurship.
- ✔ Identify career information sources.
- ✔ Identify advanced training options.
- ✔ List the elements of a successful resume.
- ✔ Outline ideas for a successful job search.

This unit discusses ways to gain employment and ways to advance your career in the future. Because the world of technology is constantly advancing, careers in the computer technology field require continuing education. New ideas become reality every day. To keep up with the rapid changes in technology, you must form an action plan. Your plan must include strategies for keeping up-to-date with the changes in technology and using that newfound knowledge to create career advancement opportunities. See **Figure 22-1.**

Employment issues are discussed in this chapter. Although you may already be employed in a computer repair or related job, this chapter can help you better define your career goals. First, let's look at some of the many job titles found in the computer industry.

A Career Working with Computers

By successfully reaching this point in the textbook, you have probably decided whether or not to pursue a career working with computers. If you have the interest, desire, and ability, you can find a very rewarding career in the computer technology field. By completing this course, you have attained the first level of expertise. You may elect to go on for additional training in a more advanced field of computer technology. PC technician is only one broad area in a field rich in choices.

Some of the many other fields from which you can choose are:

- ✔ Network installation and support.
- ✔ Network administration.
- ✔ Digital electronics.
- ✔ System analysis.

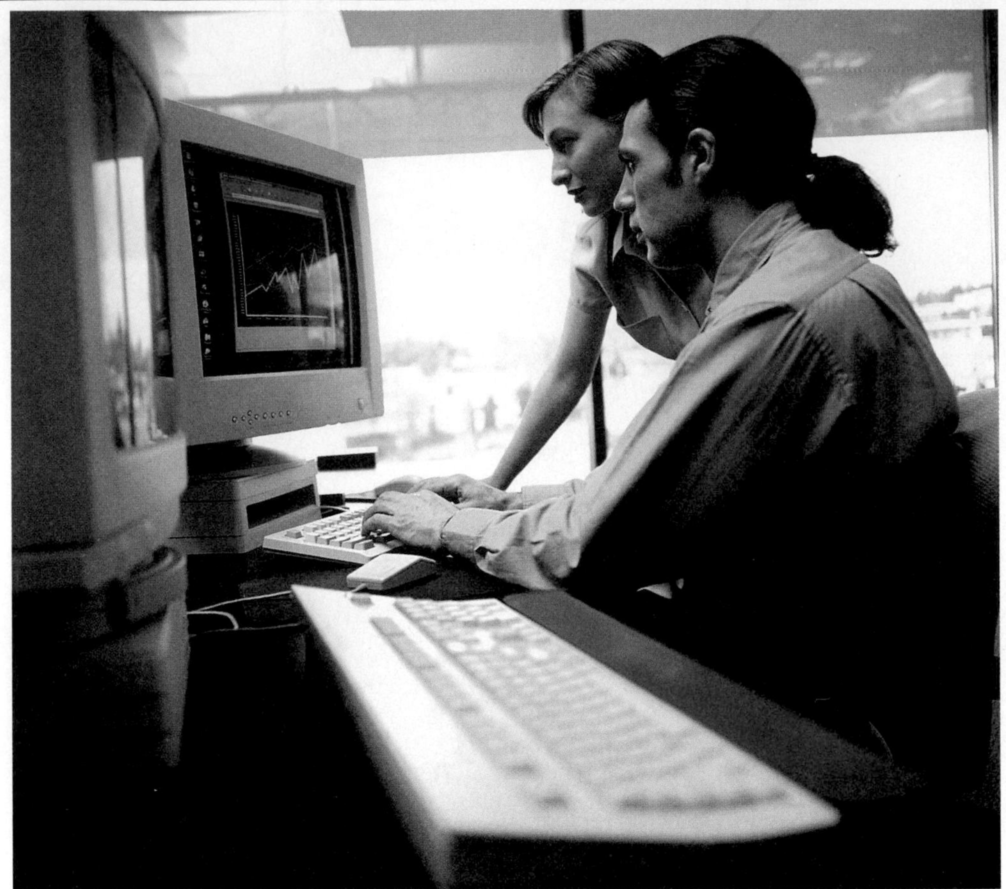

Figure 22-1. Once you land a job in the information technology field, you must continue to learn about new software and hardware or your skills will quickly become obsolete.

- ✔ Technical sales.
- ✔ Help desk support.
- ✔ Web support.
- ✔ Computer programming.
- ✔ Computer engineering.

Because the tools of the trade are constantly changing, a PC technician must continuously learn new software, operating systems, and hardware. You can expand your knowledge to make yourself even more valuable as a PC technician or just to satisfy your own curiosity. There are no limits to your education in the field of computer technology. In fact, if you stop learning, the entire technology will soon pass you by. It would only take a few years before you would feel as obsolete as some of the equipment on which you may work.

Some possible career positions are as follows:

- ✔ Entry-level help desk operator.
- ✔ PC support professional.
- ✔ Technical sales and marketing professional.
- ✔ Technical writer.
- ✔ Application developer.
- ✔ Customer service representative.
- ✔ Security specialist.

- ✔ Internet Web site developer.
- ✔ Internet systems administrator.
- ✔ Database specialist.
- ✔ Network hardware specialist.
- ✔ Network engineer.
- ✔ Systems engineer.
- ✔ Software engineer.
- ✔ Programmer.
- ✔ Analyst.
- ✔ Chief information officer.
- ✔ Telecommunications data specialist.
- ✔ Voice-over IP engineer.
- ✔ Data communications engineer.
- ✔ ATM engineer.
- ✔ Web master.
- ✔ Web developer.
- ✔ Industrial control engineer.
- ✔ IT consultant.
- ✔ PC support.
- ✔ Service/help desk technician.
- ✔ PC installation.
- ✔ Network support.
- ✔ Software programming specialist.
- ✔ Network security specialist.
- ✔ Training specialist.

You may be considering a career that requires a college-level education. There are many outstanding career opportunities for persons who earn a computer science or related degree, **Figure 22-2.** Some college level training programs offer specialized degrees in many of the areas listed. Some colleges award credit based on technical certifications or work experience.

If you are interested in science and math in high school, you would probably enjoy studying computer science at a four-year college. Mathematics is a large part of computer-related college education. If you do not like mathematics and still want a good career, you may choose to pursue an alternative educational path.

One alternative path you may consider is the training offered in the armed forces. The various branches of the military offer many specialized areas of study in the computer technology field. The opportunities for education are very good in the military services, and valuable work experiences are gained along the way.

Another alternative educational path might be the completion of a special technical program offered at a local school, college, or technical center. These programs typically consist of advanced courses leading to certifications that are recognized worldwide. For example, Novell, Microsoft, Cisco Systems, and many other companies offer certification examinations in many advanced fields of study. One of the most demanding certifications offered by Microsoft is called the

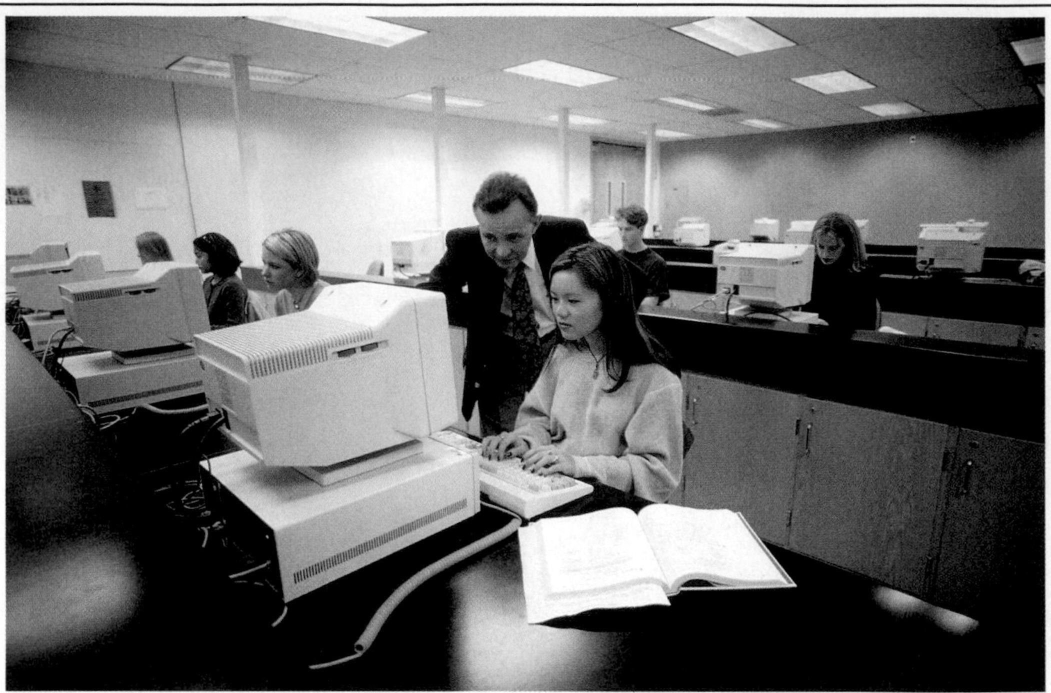

Figure 22-2. Many universities offer an extensive information technologies curriculum.

Microsoft Certified Systems Engineer (MCSE). To receive certification you must pass a series of examinations designed to test your knowledge and competency. It can easily take one or two years of study to pass all the different examinations required for the certification.

Each person must ask himself or herself several questions before going further into the computer arena. Have you enjoyed this PC textbook and the laboratory activities? The fact that you are studying the PC is a good indicator of an interest in this area. Have you taken other classes in computer technology? Did you like them? Did you do well? Give serious thought to the questions before responding. Your answers may provide you with the insight you need to choose a rewarding career.

Careers in the Information Technology Industry

As we have noted, there are a wide variety of career options in the information technology (IT) industry. Computers, communications, and information systems play a major role in our daily life. Think of all the things that depend on computer systems today. For example, our communication systems—telephone, television, and radio—are all linked to computers. Hollywood studios use advanced computer graphics software to create special effects that were impossible before the advent of the computer, **Figure 22-3.**

The manufacturing industry uses computer-controlled robots and automated assembly lines. In the business world, computers tie a company's sales department to its accounting and shipping departments for seamless transactions. The entire banking industry relies on computers to track money exchanges, post records of interest and earnings, and compile mortgage statistics. Computer technology has also saturated the field of medicine. Surgeons can now perform computer-assisted surgeries. Patient medical records are all computerized, **Figure 22-4.** MRI scans can be transmitted instantly across a network to a specialist in a distant city for expert evaluation.

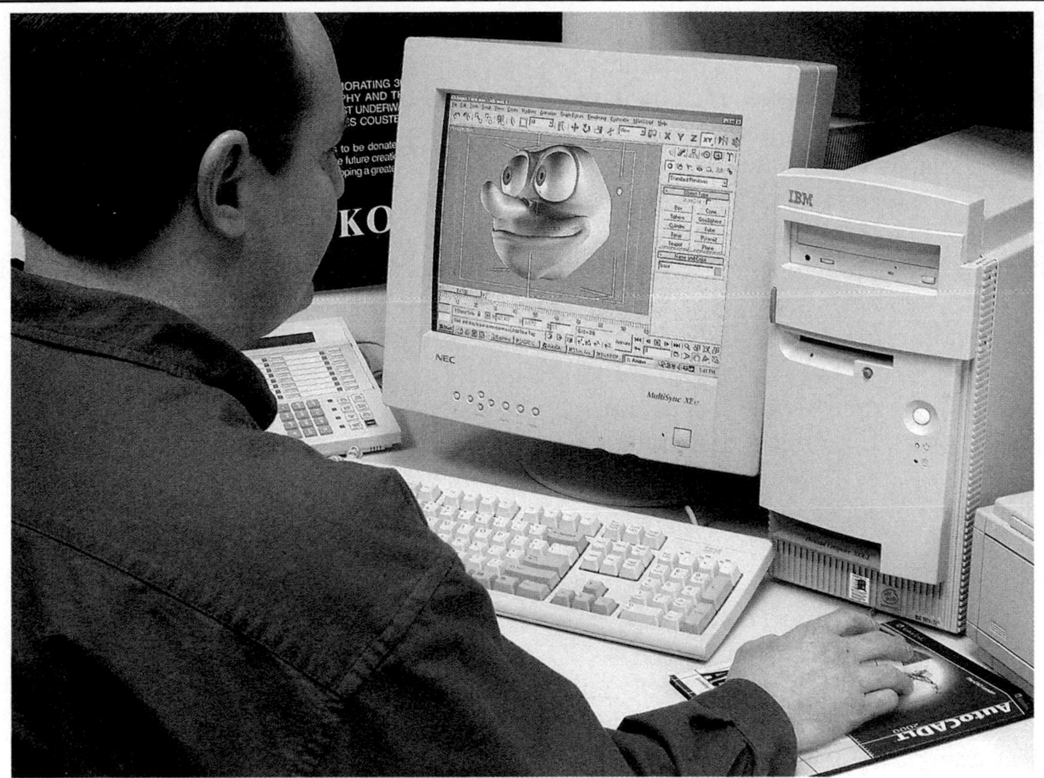

Figure 22-3. Computer-generated animation has become very popular in Hollywood.

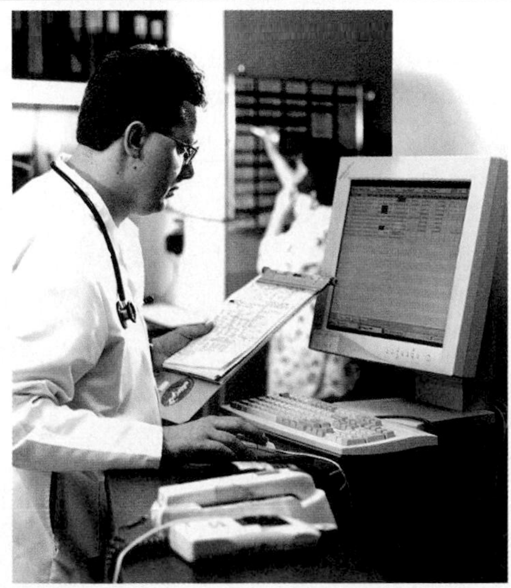

Figure 22-4. Medical records are computerized, allowing for immediate access in case of emergency, automated scheduling, and a reduced risk of misplacement.

With development of each new application for the computer, many highly skilled technicians must be trained to maintain and service it. The need for people with PC technology training will continue to grow rapidly into the next century. Law enforcement, the military, and other governmental units rely a great deal on computers. Architects and engineers use computers to design structures. With computers, they cannot only design the structure but also get a realistic first-person view of the design as they take a virtual stroll through its corridors. As computer technology integrates into every aspect of our world, the need for highly trained and skilled technicians grows.

Entrepreneurs

Entrepreneurs own and operate their own businesses. These small businesses make up 97% of businesses in the United States. They also provide 58% of the jobs in America. Entrepreneurs usually start with an idea for filling a gap in the marketplace, perhaps where a new product or service is needed. Typically, a business plan is produced before a group or individual decides to open a private business. A business plan will always be required if financial support is being sought to open a business. This plan outlines goals for the business, an action plan, and a timetable for meeting those goals. A business plan is vital if the business is to succeed.

In addition to a sound business plan, a successful entrepreneur possesses a good knowledge of his or her business, industry, service, or product. This knowledge allows the owner to make smart business decisions. The successful entrepreneur also has sound management skills. These skills allow the owner to successfully manage money, time, and employees. Management of each of these is critical to success, and poor management in any of these areas leads to certain failure.

Entrepreneurial skills, or the ability to think and move creatively and wisely, are also very important for the successful entrepreneur. These skills allow the business owner to control the business and move it in the right direction. Entrepreneurial opportunities are vast in the information technology industry. The tremendous growth in the PC market has triggered a similar growth in the demand for computer services. These highly demanded services include PC maintenance and repair, training, and Internet services.

Consulting is yet another growing business in the information technology industry, **Figure 22-5.** Consultants work for clients on special or individual projects. The specific job they do often depends on what work is needed. Clients pay a consultant for his or her expertise. When the job is completed, the consultant is free to move on to a new job and client.

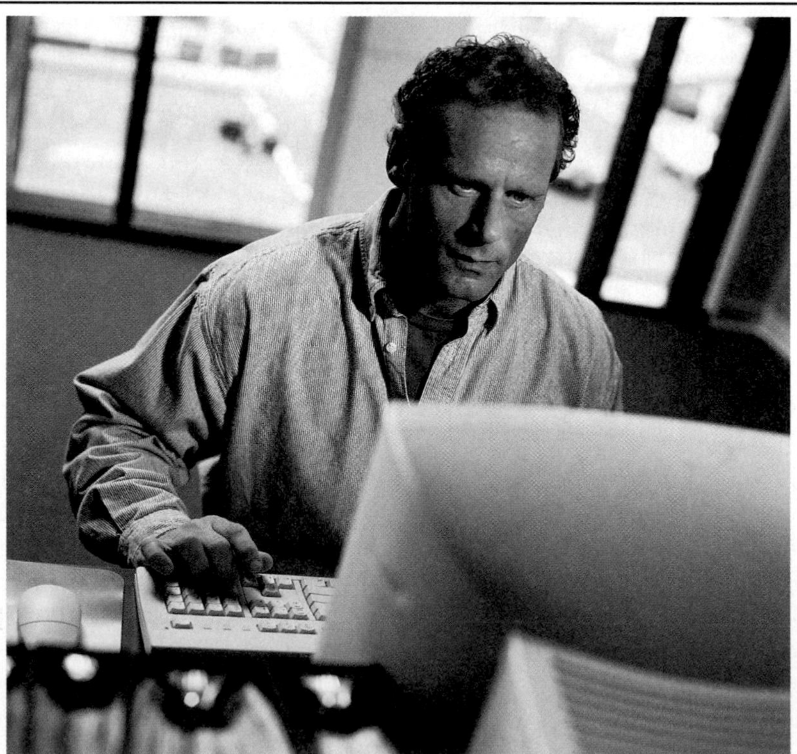

Figure 22-5. Consultants are computer experts who offer their services on a per job basis.

Career Information Sources

The Occupational Outlook Handbook offers information on careers in many industries. It is published by the United States Department of Labor and the Bureau of Statistics. Most high school, community college, university, and public libraries have copies of this book. It can also be viewed online at www.bls.gov/oco.

School guidance counselors, local labor markets, and one-stop offices are other outstanding sources of career information. They can help you find information on particular careers, colleges, and other programs that offer training in areas that you are interested in. These people are typically well-informed and ready to help in your search for jobs or training. Many colleges offer job information and placement services as well.

The Internet also contains a great amount of career and training information. Many private company sites list employment opportunities. Usually the listing includes the required skills and educational levels and a brief job description with a list of duties.

Education

The educational requirements for jobs in the information technology industry vary. However, a minimum of a high school education is a solid foundation on which to build. Some high school graduates enter industry directly and receive specialized education in employer sponsored training programs. However, many of these workers do not stop at this point. They continue to study to keep abreast of all the changes and new technologies that develop in the industry.

As discussed, specialized training can also be found in colleges, technical schools, or the military. Advanced degrees are becoming more commonplace as a means of moving ahead. Many state and private universities offer engineering and computer science degrees. Talk with your school counselor to learn locations and entry requirements.

Advanced Certification

Often, people who work in the field of computer technology have minimal certification. They must study at night for the certification exams, while working during the day in a related job. They most likely work under the supervision of another person who already has the certification. This can limit their career advancement.

Certification is a way to advance your knowledge and career in the information technology industry. Certification combined with work experience is a way to prove your abilities to a potential employer. It is also a way to advance within a company and gain job security. As an IT professional, you will be learning the rest of your life. The knowledge base of the computer industry is ever expanding. Part of what you know now may very well be obsolete in a few years. If you did not learn another thing from this point forward, your skills would be very weak in just a few short years.

Obtaining your A+ Certification should be just the beginning for you. You should immediately start advancing toward another area of certification. The Network+ Certification is a good place to continue. This area will serve as a springboard to other more advanced certificates.

You may choose to not pursue another certification, and this decision is acceptable as long as you keep your skills up-to-date. Subscribe to and read professional journals in your area of work. Take as many courses as you can, such as digital electronics, to enhance your PC repair skills.

Home-study groups and courses are becoming commonplace. A student simply signs up from home and takes courses online. Gateway offers many such programs, but there are many other sources as well. Unfortunately, this type of study takes a lot of self-discipline. Most people do not have the drive needed to stick with this type of schooling. Another drawback is the lack of hands-on activities, which are essential to be successful in technical areas of study. Without the hands-on application, simple memorization of facts is useless. If you are already employed in a technology field and do not have time to attend school on a regular basis, home study may be best for you. You will not be looked down on for earning your certification through home study. The place you study and the method you use to learn your skills are not indicated on your certificate.

After you enter the workforce at an entry-level position, you will want to consider further developing your technical skills. If you feel you have a future with the company, you should match the certification route to the company's needs. For example, if the company network system is based on Microsoft 2000, you should pursue the Microsoft line of certificates. If the company uses a system such as Novell, UNIX, or Linux, you should seek certification in one of these areas.

The time required to earn any certification depends on the individual's abilities. Some people are able to complete certification within a year; others lack the necessary aptitude and will never earn their certification. A good rule of thumb is at least two years experience and one year of study before attempting most advanced certifications.

Let's look at some other certifications you may wish to obtain.

CompTIA Certifications

The CompTIA organization offers certification by examination in many areas. Receiving an A+ Certification from CompTIA is just the beginning. They offer advanced certificates that you may elect to pursue, such as CDIA+, Network+, Server+, Linux+ and Convergence+. The CompTIA certifications discussed in this section are limited to what an A+ student might actually consider. Visit CompTIA's Web site (www.comptia.org/certification) for more detailed information about the various certifications.

CDIA+

The CDIA+ (Certified Document Imaging Architect) is a good, advanced certification. Today, there is a great demand for persons with expertise in computer imaging. The CDIA+ examination tests your knowledge of imaging systems, including scanners, displays, printers, graphic file types, file conversion, and image enhancement. Typical questions include those about storage systems, transition speeds across networks, and PC performance, as they relate to imaging. There is a tremendous need for technicians who can quickly and efficiently convert text pages and illustrations into formats recognized by computer systems.

Network+

The Network+ Certification is designed to test knowledge of small and large network systems. The ideal candidate should have 18 to 24 months of networking experience. Experience alone, however, will not prepare you for the examination. You need to prepare for the test by taking an instructor-led course, a distance-learning course, or a self-study program. The test is not vendor specific. This means that the test is not based solely on Windows NT, Windows 2000, Novell, or any other brand name of software or hardware. The examination tests knowledge of the universal concepts of network systems.

Although you need to know the basics of network administration to pass the Network+ Certification exam, the knowledge is only intended as a foundation before going on to network administration certification. The Network+ Certification is required prior to many advanced certificates. For example, the Network+ Certification can be used toward Novell's Certified Engineer (CNE) program and Lotus's CLP Domino Messaging Administrator R4 certification, among others.

The A+, Network+, and Server+ Certifications count as electives toward the MCSA Certification.

Server+

The Server+ Certification is designed to test a person's knowledge about network server hardware and software. The candidate will be tested on installation, configuration, and diagnosis of network server hardware and network operating systems. The examination requires an in-depth knowledge of protocols, backup system standards, and system security.

Linux+

The Linux+ Certification covers the installation, configuration, and troubleshooting of the Linux operating system for the single PC as well as the network server. The Linux operating system is similar to the operating systems you have studied thus far. However, there are enough significant differences to warrant a separate certification. This is not unusual. In fact, Microsoft has offered separate certifications for their different systems, such as Windows 2000 and Windows 2003, even though they are similar in design and presentation.

Security+

The CompTIA Security+ Certification measures the candidate's mastery of general security concepts. Areas covered include communications, infrastructure, cryptography, and organizational security. Candidates are recommended to have at least two years experience in networking, a good knowledge of TCP/IP, some experience in related network security, and possess the Network+ certification. While these are recommended, they are not required before taking the exam.

It has rapidly become recognized internationally as an excellent verification of basic security principles and application. The CompTIA Security+ Certificate can be used to award credit toward other certifications offered by companies such as Microsoft, Novell, and Symantec. You should consider the Security+ Certification if you plan to stay in information technology as a career.

Convergence+

The Convergence+ Certification is one of CompTIA's newest certifications. The term *convergence* as it relates to technology means a combination of different technologies incorporated into one IP-based network media. In the case of the Convergence+ Certification, it means combining communications such as telephone (VoIP), video, multimedia, and data across a common network media.

The Convergence+ Certification covers all skills associated with communications technologies, such as Voice over IP (VoIP), video and multimedia broadcasts, telephony as directly related to computers, servers, and networks. The test measures a candidate's ability to design, implement, and manage both data and VoIP networks. Candidates are recommended to have 18 to 24 months experience in data networking and VoIP and other closely-related convergence technologies. The introduction of the Convergence+ exam objectives recommends that the candidate also have an A+ and Network+ Certification or at least equivalent knowledge.

The certification is vender neutral, but the biggest corporate backer of the CompTIA Convergence+ Certification is the Avaya Corporation, a leader in VoIP communications. The certificate is an exact match for the basic competencies they desire in an employee.

PDI+

PDI+ is another new CompTIA certification. PDI stands for Printing and Document Imaging. The PDI+ Certification is recommended for persons associated with printer, scanner, copier, fax, and multifunctional machines at the entry level or at the basic level one for support personnel. The PDI+ Certification validates a candidate's abilities to install, maintain, and troubleshoot software and hardware associated with the document printing industry. The test items cover the printing process and components, scanner process and components, basic electronic components and tools, color theory, and network connectivity. Many of the same skills measured in the CompTIA A+ Essentials exam are on the PDI+ exam. The biggest difference is the objectives that cover electronic components, such as electrical relays, solenoids, motors, sensors, and switches. A student that has achieved an A+ Certification and has had some basic electronics training is a good candidate for this certification. Check CompTIA's Web site for the very latest information concerning certification credit.

Microsoft Certification Areas

Microsoft has a rich offering of various certifications such as MOS, MCDST, MCSE, MCSA, MCSD, MCDBA, MCTS, and MCITP. The series of Microsoft certifications are designed to support the Microsoft family of products. These individual certifications usually require two or more separate examinations. In addition to the certification offered for specialized areas, Microsoft offers examinations and certification for their operating systems, such as Windows 2000 and Windows XP. Visit the Microsoft Training Web page (www.microsoft.com/learning/training) for more details on all certification areas.

MOS

The Microsoft Office Specialist (MOS) certification process tests knowledge of Microsoft Office software such as Word, Excel, Access, PowerPoint, Project, and Outlook. There are presently three levels of certification: Master, Expert, and Specialist.

To earn a Specialist certification, the user must demonstrate the ability to use the software's basic features, such as cut, copy, and paste. To earn an Expert certification, the user must be able to use all of the features included in the Specialist certification, plus more advanced features. For Microsoft Word, these features would include modifying the contents of tables, setting up automatic calculations for tables, and embedding worksheets. To earn a Master certification, you must demonstrate expert-level skill in five Office products. You must also be able to embed in and freely exchange information between the five products.

As a technician and not a secretary, why would you want to learn these products in detail? When you become a technical support person for a large or small company, people automatically think of you as somewhat of an expert in all areas of computers and system information. Automatically, they feel you are qualified to advise them about software, monitors, and even Internet service providers. For example, a person may want to know how to perform a mail merge in Word. After all, you are supposed to be the expert on computers. If you are unable to answer the question, the customer may perceive you as being poorly trained, even if the question falls outside the scope of your job.

A good way to increase your value to a company is to master popular software, such as Word, Access, Excel, and PowerPoint. You will probably be asked more questions about these products than questions about hardware, operating systems, or drivers.

MCDST

The Microsoft Certified Desktop Support Technician (MCDST) measures the skills necessary to support end users and troubleshoot Microsoft desktop environments. The certification consists of two core examinations. One exam centers on a Microsoft desktop operating system and the other on Microsoft desktop applications. A candidate must pass both exams to become an MCDST. This is a certification you may wish to obtain after finishing this course. It is a likely certification step toward a job as a help desk specialist or as part of a network support team in a corporate environment. Many of the skills learned for PC support are directly related to the skills required for the MCDST.

MCSE

The Microsoft Certified Systems Engineer (MCSE) is a certification based on the ability of the candidate to design, implement, maintain, upgrade, troubleshoot, and administer a network system based on the Microsoft's Windows 2000 and 2003 platform. Some job titles requiring this certification are systems engineer, technical support engineer, systems analysts, network analysts, and technical consultant. It is not unusual for a person seeking this certificate to dedicate one to two years of constant study.

There is not one test but a series of examinations leading to certification. A typical candidate is a person who has been working with large network systems of between 200 and 26,000 users spread over 5 to 150 physical locations. This certification requires expertise in a desktop operating system, network design, and administration. Requirements are constantly changing. Check the Microsoft Web site for up-to-date information.

MCSA

The Microsoft Certified Systems Administrator (MCSA) certificate is designed to prove competency and skills required to implement, administer, and troubleshoot a Windows 2000 or 2003 network system. This certification is designed for a person who wishes to specialize in network support and administration. MCSA certification is not as difficult to obtain as MCSE certification. It requires a less intense series of exams. The MCSA can be obtained while working toward the MCSE. Many of the required series of examinations are the same as those required to receive MCSE certification.

If you choose to earn several CompTIA certifications, it can help you earn an MCSA certificate. The A+ Certification in combination with the Network+ or Server+ Certification will count toward this particular Microsoft certification. Always check the Microsoft and CompTIA Web sites for the very latest information about reciprocal certification agreements.

MCSD

The Microsoft Certified Solution Developer (MCSD) certificate is awarded to individuals who prove they have the ability to design, implement, and administer business solutions using Microsoft Office or BackOffice products. In other words, they can set up a network system for a business based on the individual business needs, select the appropriate software packages, design the hardware requirements or specifications, and install and maintain the system. This certification area would be most appropriate for persons who work in sales and promotion of specific office products rather than a technician.

MCDBA

The Microsoft Certified Database Administrator (MCDBA) certificate is earned by proving expertise in creating, maintaining, optimizing, installing, and managing the SQL databases server (a Microsoft database server design). Database technology is used extensively by business, government, educational, and research institutions.

MCTS

Microsoft Certified Technology Specialist (MCTS) is a relatively new Microsoft certification that can be earned by proving in-depth competency in one of 19 different software systems. Most of the MCTS certifications center on one particular Microsoft product. For example, some of the certification areas are as follows:

- ✔ Windows Vista, Configuration.
- ✔ Windows Vista and Microsoft Office 2007 Microsoft System Desktops, Deploying and Maintaining.
- ✔ .Net Framework 2.0 Web Applications.
- ✔ SQL Server 2005.
- ✔ Microsoft Office Live Communications Server 2005.
- ✔ Microsoft Exchange Server 2007.
- ✔ Microsoft Office SharePoint Server 2007, Configuration.

MCITP

Microsoft Certified IT Professional (MCITP) is a more advanced certification than the MCTS. The Microsoft Certified Technology Specialist (MCTS) requires only one exam, but MCITP typically requires two or more exams. For example, the Microsoft Desktop Support Technician (MCDST) requires two exams and is considered an MCITP certification.

There are many other Microsoft certifications available that are based on programming skills or administrative IT skills, such as job planning, job coordination, and instructor skills. You may want to visit the Microsoft Certification Web site to see the many different certifications available.

Novell Certification Areas

Novell offers several certifications, such as CNA , CNE, CLP, and CLE. The certifications are tied directly to Novell software products such as NetWare 6. The Novell certifications are similar to the Microsoft certifications. However, they prove knowledge of Novell network products rather than Microsoft products. You can learn more detailed information about the Novell certifications by visiting Novell's Web site (www.novell.com/training/certinfo/).

CNA

The Novell Certified Network Administrator (CNA) certificate is awarded for skills necessary to set up and manage user stations and manage network system resources such as files, printers, and software. It requires that the person understand how to monitor network performance, provide remote access to the network, and possess various other network skills. Novell recommends that a CNA candidate have a CompTIA Network+ certification.

CNE

The Certified Network Engineer (CNE) certificate proves expertise in a wider range of network applications than the CNA. You must prove expertise in WAN and LAN design, development, implementation, support, and troubleshooting. The CNE may specialize in one particular area of network software such as NetWare 5 or NetWare 6.

CLP

Novell Certified Linux Professional (CLP) is designed to prove expertise as an administrator for Novell SUSE Enterprise Server. The test is a practicum. A practicum is a hands-on type demonstration of skills.

CLE

Novell Certified Linux Engineer (CLE) is the next step above CLP. You must earn the CLP before acquiring the CLE. The CLP is designed for administrating the operating system. The CLE adds the elements of design to the administrative certification. Typically, two Novell courses are required before taking the CLE after acquiring the CLP.

In summary, the Novell CNA and CNE are based on the Novell Netware operating systems, while the CLP and CLE are based on the Novell SUSE Linux system.

Cisco Training and Certificates

Cisco Corporation provides training opportunities at high schools and colleges all over the United States. The Cisco sites are referred to as networking academies. These academies emphasize network design, implementation, and troubleshooting using Cisco products. Cisco products are widely used for network communications. The academy courses are designed as a combination of lecture, textbook, on-line learning, and hands-on laboratory activities.

Some of the certificates available through Cisco are Cisco Certified Network Associate (CCNA), Cisco Certified Design Associate (CCDA), Cisco Certified Network Professional (CCNP), Cisco Certified Design Professional (CCDP), and Cisco Certified Internet Expert (CCIE). The certificates are obtained by passing specific Cisco examinations. You can learn more about the certifications offered and locate the Cisco academy nearest you by going to the Cisco Web site (www.cisco.com).

Other Certifications

Many other companies have certification programs as well as the ones outlined in these sections. These companies include 3-Com, Corel, Nortel Networks, Compaq, Red Hat Linux, and Oracle. Check the related Web sites for in-depth information about the exams including exam outlines, study materials, schools and training available, and prerequisites.

Job Search Ideas

Finding a job can be a time-consuming and difficult task. The Occupational Outlook Handbook has excellent tips for conducting a job search. Start by talking to your parents, neighbors, teachers, and guidance counselors. These people may know of job openings that have not been advertised. Read the classified ads in the newspaper, especially the Sunday editions. Look through the Yellow Pages to generate a list of local companies, their addresses, and phone numbers. Companies are grouped according to industry in the Yellow Pages. You may see companies to contact.

City, county, and state employment services may also provide useful job leads. Private employment agencies might also provide leads, but they often charge a fee for a job placement.

The Internet is a valuable source of job information. Almost every computer-related site has a section devoted to job opportunities. You can often complete an application online. There are also many Web sites that will allow you to post a resume.

Job Interviews

The three most important factors that determine your ability to land a job are your work history, technical expertise, and the job interview. A work history tells the employer a lot about you as a future employee, even if the job experiences are unrelated to the job you are applying for. You may just be entering the IT profession, but a solid recommendation from a past employer can make the difference. A recommendation from a former employer shows that you have been a valuable and dependable employee. A person with no work history is a gamble in most employers' eyes.

Prior technical experiences can prove to be a real asset, whether they are past jobs or formal training. Other applicants may have no technical employment history or technical training. They may have simple, informal experience helping friends with their home computer and now believe they can handle the job. This is where your training and work history puts you ahead of others.

The job interview is the major factor in determining if an applicant gets the job. The job interview gives the employer a chance to evaluate the applicant through a series of questions. The way a question is answered is at times more important than the answer itself. For example, if an employer asks, "What would you do if you could not fix a PC problem?" The way you answer the question may tell the employer about your character, your confidence, and your ability to work with others. The employer is looking for certain traits in the individual he or she is about to hire. Some common traits are honesty, confidence, dependability, and the ability to work well as a team member. While your physical attractiveness may not be important to an employer, your neat and clean appearance shows that you take pride in yourself and your work. Even if the job is a "backroom" position, dress well for the interview. Blue jeans and a T-shirt are never appropriate.

Employers may not ask the same questions of all applicants and will not usually be direct about the qualities they are seeking. The employer will ask questions to probe for the character and job-related qualities they want. For example, an employer may ask you to describe a time you had a problem with a fellow employee. How was it resolved? The answer to this question can tell an experienced interviewer a lot about the character of the applicant. Once you have secured an interview, it is important to be prepared for it. Read the following tips for a successful interview.

Preparation for the Interview

An interview is perhaps the most critical stage in a job search, and a process that you can control to a great extent. A good interview can cause an employer to overlook a lack of experience or education. On the other hand, a poor interview can cause even the most qualified candidate to be passed over. The following are a few tips to help you prepare for your interview.

✔ Always learn about the prospective employer and the position. Many times this information is available on their Web site. This preparation lets the employer know you are truly interested in the company and that you possess the personal initiative to research and learn.

✔ Have a specific job or jobs in mind, generally at an entry level. Most companies do not begin a new employee in a high level job until they have proven their worth to the company.

✔ Review your qualifications for the job. Make sure your qualifications match those desired by the employer. Do not waste their time or yours by interviewing for a job that is far beyond your level.

- ✔ Prepare to answer broad questions about yourself. It is wise to practice interviewing with someone who has knowledge about job interviews. A family member or friend who regularly does hiring for a company can be a great help, even if they do not work in the field you are seeking. Practicing the interview will help you learn to control your natural nervousness and become more relaxed for the real thing.
- ✔ A quality resume can make a favorable impression on an employer. Use a good quality paper and a cover sheet. Make sure you have produced an original copy that they may keep.
- ✔ Arrive at least 15 minutes prior to the scheduled time of your interview, **Figure 22-6.** Showing up late for your interview does not enhance your prospects for the job. It displays a lack of care for the job, the company, and your interview person or committee. Locate the building in advance and figure how much time it will take to get there. Consider the traffic conditions for that time of day. Do a practice run so that you will know exactly how to get to the interview and the length of time it will take you to arrive.
- ✔ If you really want that job, have a backup plan in case you have difficulty with your transportation.

Personal Appearance

The first impression you make on an employer is critical. People are summarily judged on their outward appearance. If you look and act professional, you will make a favorable impression on your interviewer and future coworkers.

- ✔ Dress appropriately and be well groomed.
- ✔ Blue jeans and a T-shirt are never appropriate. Regardless of the job conditions, men and women should always dress up rather than down for an interview. Do not dress for a party. Dress for a formal business setting.

Figure 22-6. Arrive fifteen minutes early for your interview. Make a practice run to the location of your interview a day or two before the actual interview. This will help you predict how long it will take you to arrive at the interview site.

- ✔ Smile and use a firm handshake when you introduce yourself. This shows your confidence, **Figure 22-7.**
- ✔ Do not chew gum, eat candy, or smoke at any time when you are on the company premises. This is not a social visit, and you may likely encounter your prospective supervisor on the property prior to your interview.

The Interview

Once the interview begins, your responses to questions are being actively evaluated. The interviewer is trying to determine your work ethic, attitude, intelligence, and competency based on your answers and body language. The following are tips to help you avoid creating the wrong impression on the interviewer.

- ✔ Answer all questions to the best of your ability, and if you do not know the answer, simply say so. Do not try to make up an answer. Express your willingness to learn any new topics with which you may not be familiar. The person conducting the interview is an expert. You will not fool them by trying to invent an answer. Admit your limitations, and you will find they will most likely respect your honesty.
- ✔ Use proper English and avoid slang. Speak slowly and concisely. Never use foul language, even in a joking manner.
- ✔ Use good manners. Always address the persons who are conducting the interview as "Sir" and "Ma'am." Even if you are personally acquainted with your prospective employer, treat them with polite formality. Do not become complacent or presume you have the job.
- ✔ Convey a sense of cooperation and enthusiasm. Your body language will convey a lot about your personality. Keep smiling. Have a look of confidence. Sit up straight and look the interviewer directly in the eyes. Do not slump or look away as you talk.
- ✔ You can ask questions about the position and the organization, but limit your questions to operations or conditions that you do not understand. Much information regarding a job can be obtained prior to the interview, especially if the information was posted. Unless it has not been covered in a job posting, uncovered through your research, or discussed by your prospective employer during the interview, do not ask questions regarding salary.

Figure 22-7. A neat appearance, good posture, and a firm handshake demonstrate self-confidence.

- ✔ Remember that the interview has not ended when you start asking questions. As a matter of fact, your questions can reveal even more to the employer. Asking how many breaks you will get during a day will send an undesirable message to the employer. It is not required that you ask questions, especially if the interview has been thorough, but do not hesitate if you believe that there is pertinent information that you must know.
- ✔ Remember that there will be additional time to make any clarifications or salary negotiations after you are offered the job.

Employer Testing

Employer testing is very common today as part of the job interview process. An employer can tell a lot about your technical knowledge and communications skills through a test, especially if handwritten answers are required. Written responses reveal a lot about an interviewee, **Figure 22-8.**

- ✔ Be sure you understand all written test directions. If you are unclear about the instructions, verbally confirm them before you begin the test.
- ✔ Read each question carefully.
- ✔ Write legibly and clearly. Printing helps if your handwriting is poor.
- ✔ Budget your time wisely and don't dwell on one question.

Information to Bring to an Interview

The common information required at an interview is social security number, driver's license number, and a copy of your resume. On your resume, make a complete and chronological list of your education and training. List all of your past employment in sequence, and do not leave blank dates. If you stopped your employment to go to school, note the dates. This ensures that your potential

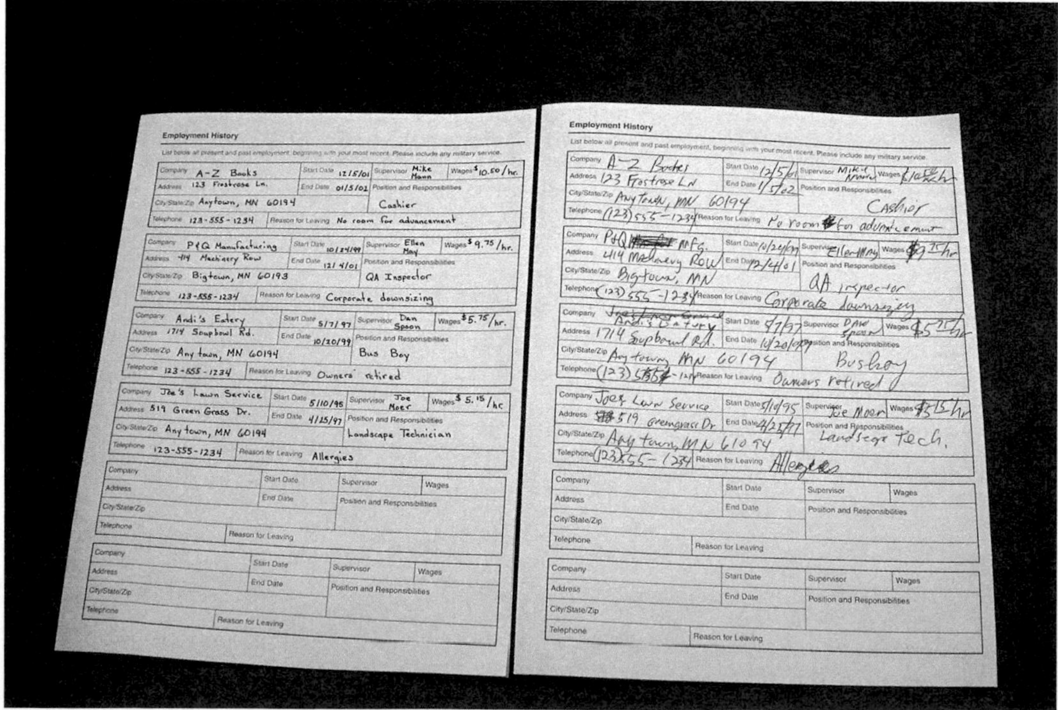

Figure 22-8. Write neatly (application on left) when filling out employment applications or taking tests. Poor penmanship (application on the right) can make a bad impression on a prospective employer.

employer does not think you are trying to leave out an employer who may not give you a good reference. List the reasons for any breaks in your employment history.

You may wish to include copies of training and award certificates, transcripts, and letters of reference with your resume. Typically, these will be verified anyway if listed on your resume. Including copies with your resume may speed up the verification procedure.

Three References

It is customary to provide references for a job. The quality of your references can mean a great deal to the employer. Some good reference people are teachers, past employers, supervisors, and fellow employees. Friends, family, and your clergy are not considered good references. Get permission from people before using them as a reference. For each reference, provide name, address, telephone number, and occupation. Also, note if the person was a past supervisor.

Summary

- ✔ An information technology (IT) position requires continuous education.
- ✔ A recognized certification is a way of proving your expertise in a computer technology specialty.
- ✔ An entrepreneur owns and operates a private business.
- ✔ CompTIA offers examinations for A+, CDIA, Network+, Server+, Linux+, and Convergence+ certification.
- ✔ After gaining A+ Certification, Network+ is a good next step in your career advancement.
- ✔ Microsoft, Novell, Cisco, and many other companies also offer certifications based on examinations.
- ✔ Arrive early or on time for your interview.
- ✔ Smile and show a sense of cooperation and enthusiasm during the interviewing process.
- ✔ If tested by the prospective employer, be sure you understand instructions for the examination.
- ✔ When you are interviewing for a new job, be sure to take your social security card, driver's license, and a quality resume.
- ✔ Be able to produce a list of at least three references, including addresses and phone numbers. List only people who have agreed to be references.

Review Questions

Answer the following questions on a separate sheet of paper. Please do not write in this book.

1. Why is continuing education required for an employee in the IT industry?
2. What is an entrepreneur?
3. What items should you take to a job interview?
4. What information must be provided in your list of references?

For Discussion

1. What type of career would you like to have? How much training and education will this career require?
2. What traits do you think are required of successful entrepreneurs?
3. What professional goals do you hope to accomplish in the next five years? The next ten years?

Suggested Laboratory Activities

1. Download the requirements for a Microsoft System Engineer Certificate and a Microsoft System Administrator Certificate. Go to Microsoft's Web site for the latest list of requirements and exams that must be taken.
2. Download the test information for a Windows 2003 exam.
3. Download the test information for MCDST certification.
4. Go to Novell's Web site and download the requirements for Novell CNA and CNE.
5. Do a search to see what colleges will give degree credit for certifications. See how much credit can be obtained and under what conditions.
6. Locate the Cisco Academy nearest you. How much does it cost, and how long does it last?

Appendix A

List of Acronyms

A

ac	alternating current
ACK	acknowledge
ACPI	Advanced Configuration and Power Interface
ADSL	asymmetrical digital subscriber line
AGP	Accelerated Graphics Port
AI	artificial intelligence
AIFF	Audio Interchange File Format
ALU	arithmetic logic unit
AM	amplitude modulation
AMD	Active Matrix Display, *also* Advanced Micro Devices
ANSI	American National Standards Institute
AOL	America Online
APC	American Power Conversion
API	application program interface
APM	Advanced Power Management
ARCnet	Attached Resource Computer network
ARP	Address Resolution Protocol
ARPANET	Advanced Research Project Agency Network
ASCII	American Standard Code for Information Interchange
ASP	application service provider
ASPI	Advanced SCSI Programming Interface
ASR	Automated System Recovery
ATA	AT Attachment
ATAPI	AT Attachment Packet Interface
ATM	Asynchronous Transfer Mode
AUI	Attachment Unit Interface
A/V	audio/video
AWG	American Wire Gauge

B

BASIC	Beginner's All-purpose Symbolic Instruction Code
BAT	batch file
BBS	bulletin board system
BCC	blind carbon copy
BCD	binary coded decimal
BCU	Bus Controller Unit, *also* BIOS Configuration Utility
BDC	backup domain controller
BEDO DRAM	Burst EDO Dynamic Random Access Memory
BFT	Binary File Transfer
BGP	Border Gateway Protocol
BIOS	basic input/output system
BIT	binary digit
BIU	Bus Interface Unit
BMP	bitmap
BNC	British Naval Connector, *or* Bayonet Nut Connector, *or* Bayonet-Neill Concelman
BOOTP	Bootstrap Protocol
bps	bits per second
Bps	bytes per second
BRI	Basic-Rate Interface
BSD	Berkeley Software Distribution UNIX

C

CA — Certificate Authority
CAD — computer-aided design, *or* computer-aided drafting
CAD/CAM — computer-aided design/computer-aided manufacturing
CAL — Client Access License, *also* Computer-Assisted Learning, *also* Computer-Aided Logistics
CAM — computer-aided manufacturing
CAS — Column Address Select
CAV — constant linear velocity
CBT — computer-based training
CCD — charge-coupled device
CCITT — Comité Consultatif International Téléphonique et Télégraphique
CD — carrier detect, *also* compact disc, *also* collision detect
CDFS — CD-ROM File System
CD-R — Compact Disc Recordable
CD-ROM — Compact Disc Read Only Memory
CD-RW — Compact Disc Rewriteable
CD-WO — Compact Disc, Write-Once
CD-WORM — Compact Disc, Write-Once Read-Many
CGA — color/graphics adapter
CGM — Computer Graphics Metafile
CHAP — Challenge Handshake Authentication Protocol
CHS — Cylinder, Head, Sector
CID — Certified ID, *also* Caller Identification
CIDR — Classless Inter-Domain Routing
CIFS — Common Internet File System
CISC — complex instruction set computer
CLV — constant linear velocity
CMOS — complementary metal oxide semiconductor
CMTS — Cable Modem Termination System
CMYK — cyan, magenta, yellow, black
CNA — Certified Netware Administrator, *also* Cisco Networking Academies
COA — Certificate of Authority
COBOL — common business oriented language
codec — compressor/decompressor
cpi — characters per inch
cps — characters per second, *also* cycles per second
CPU — central processing unit
CRC — cyclic redundancy check
CRT — cathode ray tube
CSMA/CA — Carrier Sense Multiple Access with Collision Avoidance
CSMA/CD — Carrier Sense Multiple Access with Collision Detection
CSU/DSU — Channel Service Unit/Data Service Unit
CTS — clear to send

D

DAC — digital-to-analog converter
daemon — Disk and Execution Monitor
DARPA — Defense Advanced Research Projects Agency
DAT — digital audio tape
dB — decibel
dc — direct current
DCC — Direct Cable Connection
DDL — Dynamic Data Link, *also* Document Description Language, *also* Data Definition Language
DDR — Double Data Rate, *also* Dynamic Desktop Router
DDR-SDRAM — Double Data Rate Synchronous Dynamic Random Access Memory
DEC — Digital Equipment Corporation
DEK — Data Encryption Key
DHCP — Dynamic Host Configuration Protocol
DHTML — Dynamic HTML
DIB — Dual Independent Bus
DIMM — dual in-line memory module
DIN — Deutsche Industrie Norm (connector)
DIP — dual in-line package

DLC	Data Link Control
DLL	Dynamic Link Library
DMA	direct memory access
DNS	Domain Name System, *or* Domain Name Service
DOCSIS	Data Over Cable Service Interface Specification
DoD ARPA	Department of Defense's Advanced Research Project Agency
DoS	denial of services
DOS	disk operating system
dpi	dots per inch
DRAM	dynamic random access memory
DRDRAM	Direct Rambus Dynamic Random Access Memory
DSIMM	dual single in-line memory module
DSL	digital subscriber line
DSR	data set ready
DSS	digital satellite system
DTE	Data Terminal Equipment
DTR	data terminal ready
DUN	Dial-Up Networking
DVB	Digital Video Broadcasting
DVD	Digital Versatile Disc, *or* Digital Video Disc
DVDR	Digital Video Disc Recordable
DVI	Digital Video Interactive
DVM	Data/Voice Multiplexer

E

EBCDIC	Extended Binary-Coded Decimal Interchange Code
ECC	error code correction
ECMA	European Computer Manufacturers Association
ECP	Enhanced Capabilities Port
EDO	Extended Data Output
EDO DRAM	Enhanced Data Output Dynamic Random Access Memory
EDSI	Enhanced Small Devices Interface
EEPROM	electrically erasable programmable read only memory
EFS	encrypted file system
EGA	enhanced graphics adapter
EHF	extreme high frequency
EIA	Electronics Industries Association
EIDE	Enhanced IDE
EIGRP	Enhanced Interior Gateway Routing Protocol
EISA	Extended Industry Standard Architecture
EMI	electromagnetic interference
EMM	Expanded Memory Manager
EMP	Electromagnetic Pulse
EMS	expanded memory standard
ENIAC	Electronic Numerical Integrator Analyzer and Calculator
EOF	end of file
EOT	end of transmission, *or* end of text, *or* end of table
EP	electrophotographic process
EPA	Environmental Protection Agency
EPP	Enhanced Parallel Port
EPROM	erasable programmable read only memory
EPS	Encapsulated PostScript
ERD	Emergency Repair Disk
ESC	escape
ESD	electrostatic discharge
ESDI	Enhanced Small Device Interface
ESDRAM	Enhanced Synchronous Dynamic Random Access Memory
ESMTP	Extended Simple Mail Transfer Protocol
ESP	Encapsulated Security Payload, *also* Enhanced Serial Port
ETSI	European Telecommunications Standards Institute
EXT	external

F

FAQ	frequently asked questions
FAT	file allocation table

FC fiber channel
FCC Federal Communications Commission
FCPGA Flip Chip Pin Grid Array
FDD floppy disk drive
FDDI Fiber Distributed Data Interface
FDHD floppy drive, high-density
FDI flat display, *also* floppy drive, *also* floppy disk, *also* full duplex
FDM Frequency Division Multiplexing
FF form feed
FIFO first in first out
FLOPS floating-point operations per second
FM frequency modulation
FORTRAN formula translator
FPM Fast Page Mode
FPU floating-point unit
FRU field replaceable unit
FSB front side bus
FTP File Transfer Protocol, *or* File Transport Protocol

G

Gb gigabit
GB gigabyte
GDI Graphical Device Interface
GHz gigahertz
GIF graphics interchange format
GUI graphical user interface

H

HCL Hardware Compatibility List
HD hard disk, *also* high density
HDD hard disk drive
HDSL High bit-rate Digital Subscriber Line
HDTV High-Definition Television
HMA high memory area
HP Hewlett-Packard
HPFS High Performance File System
HTML Hypertext Markup Language
HTTP Hypertext Transfer Protocol
Hz Hertz

I

IANA Internet Assigned Numbers Authority
IBM International Business Machines
IC integrated circuit
ICANN Internet Corporation for Assigned Names and Numbers
ICF Internet Connection Firewall
ICMP Internet Control Message Protocol
ICS Internet Connection Sharing
ID Identification
IDE Integrated Development Environment, *also* Integrated Drive Electronics, *or* Intelligent Drive Electronics
IDN Integrated Digital Network
IDSL ISDN Subscriber Line
IE Internet Explorer
IEEE Institute of Electrical and Electronics Engineers
IETF Internet Engineering Task Force
IIS Internet Information Server
IMAP Internet Message Access Protocol
I/O input/output
IP Internet Protocol
IPX Internet Packet Exchange
IR infrared
IRC Internet Relay Chat
IrDA Infrared Data Association
IRQ interrupt request line
ISA Industry Standard Architecture
ISDN integrated services digital network
ISO International Organization for Standardization
ISP Internet Service Provider
IT Information Technology
ITSP Internet Telephony Service Provider
ITU International Telecommunications Union

J

JPEG	Joint Photographic Experts Group

K

kbps	kilobits per second
kBps	kilobytes per second
kHz	kilohertz

L

LAN	local area network
LBA	logical block addressing
LCD	liquid crystal display
LCN	Logical Cluster Number
LDAP	Lightweight Directory Access Protocol
LEC	local exchange carrier
LED	light emitting diode
Li-ion	lithium-ion
LLC	Logical Link Control
LPT	line printer terminal
LQ	letter quality
LSB	least significant bit
LSI	large-scale integration
LUN	logical unit number

M

MAC	media access code, *also* media access control
MAN	metropolitan area network
MAPI	Message Application Programming Interface
MAU	Media Attachment Unit, *also* Media Access Unit, *or* Multistation Access Unit
MB	megabytes, *also* motherboard
Mb	megabit
MBps	megabytes per second
Mbps	megabits per second
MBR	Master Boot Record
MCA	Micro Channel Architecture
MCGA	multicolor/graphics array, *or* multicolor/graphics adapter
MDRAM	Multibank Dynamic Random Access Memory
Me	Millennium Edition (Windows)
MFT	Master File Table
MHz	megahertz
MIDI	musical instrument digital interface
MIME	Multipurpose Internet Mail Extensions
MIPS	million instructions per second
MO	magneto-optical
MODEM	modulator-demodulator
MOV	metal oxide varistor
MPEG	Moving Picture Experts Group
MSB	most significant bit
MS-DOS	Microsoft Disk Operating System
MZR	multiple zone recording

N

NAK	negative acknowledge, *or* not acknowledged
NAP	Network Access Point
NAS	Network Access Server, *also* network attached storage
NAT	Network Address Translation
NBT	NetBIOS on TCP/IP
NDS	Netware Directory Services, *or* Novell Directory Services
NetBEUI	NetBIOS Enhanced User Interface
NetBIOS	Network Basic Input/Output System
NFS	Network File System
NIC	network interface card
NiCad	nickel-cadmium
NiCd	nickel-cadmium
NiMH	nickel-metal hydride
NOS	network operating system
NSP	Network Service Provider
NT	New Technology (Windows), *also* Network Terminator

NTFS New Technology File System
NVRAM Non-Volatile Random Access Memory

O

OC Optical Carrier
OCR optical character recognition
OCX OLE Custom Control, *or* OLE Control Extension
OEM original equipment manufacturer
OLE Object Linking and Embedding
OOP object-oriented programming
OOPL object-oriented programming language
OS operating system
OSI Open Systems Interconnection
OSPF Open Shortest Path First
OSR 2 OEM Service Release 2 (Windows 95)
OTDR Optical Time Domain Reflectometer

P

P2P peer-to-peer, *also* point-to-point
PAP Password Authentication Protocol
PBX private branch exchange
PC personal computer, *also* printed circuit
PCI Peripheral Component Interconnect
PCMCIA Personal Computer Memory Card International Association
PDA personal digital assistant
PDC primary domain controller
PDF Portable Document Format
PDL Page Description Language
PDU Protocol Data Unit, *or* Packet Data Unit
PEL Picture Element
Perl Practical Extraction and Report Language
PGA pin grid array, *also* Professional Graphics Adapter
PGP Pretty Good Privacy
PIC Lotus Picture
PIF Program Information File
PIN personal identification number
PING Packet Internet Groper
PIO Programmed Input/Output, *or* Programmable Input/Output
pixel Picture Element
PLC powerline communications
PLD Programmable Logical Device
PnP Plug and Play
PoP Point of Presence
POP Post Office Protocol
POP3 Post Office Protocol version 3
POSIX Portable Operating System Interface for UNIX
POST power-on self-test
POTS plain old telephone service
PPGA Plastic Pin Grid Array
ppm page(s) per minute
PPP Point-to-Point Protocol
PPTP Point-to-Point Tunneling Protocol
PRI Primary Rate Interface
PROM programmable read only memory
PS/2 Personal System 2
PSTN Public Switched Telephone Network
PVC permanent virtual circuit

Q

QIC Quarter-Inch Cartridge
QoS quality of service

R

RAID Redundant Array of Independent Disks, *or* Redundant Array of Inexpensive Disks
RAM random access memory
RAS Remote Access Server, *also* Remote Access Service, *also* Row Address Selection
RD receive data
RDRAM Rambus Dynamic Random Access Memory

RF radio frequency

RFC Request for Comments

RGB red, green, blue

RIMM Rambus In-line Memory Modules

RIP raster image processor, *also* Routing Information Protocol

RISC reduced instruction set computer

RJ-11/12/45 Registered Jacks

RLE run-length encoding

ROM read only memory

RS (RS-232) recommended standard

RTF rich text format

RTS request to send

S

SAM Security Accounts Manager

SANS System Administration, Networking and Security Institute

SAP Service Advertising Protocol

SAP Serial Attached SCSI

SCSI Small Computer System Interface

SDRAM Synchronous Dynamic Random Access Memory

SDSL Symmetric Digital Subscriber Line

SEC Single Edge Contact

SET Secure Electronic Transaction

SGML Standard Generalized Markup Language

SGRAM Synchronous Graphic Random Access Memory

SIMM single in-line memory module

SIP single in-line package

SLDRAM Sync Link Dynamic Random Access Memory

SLIP Serial Line Internet Protocol

SMB Server Message Block

SMM System Management Mode

SMTP Simple Mail Transfer Protocol

SNA Systems Network Architecture

SNMP Simple Network Management Protocol

SOHO small-office/home-office

SOM Start of Message, *also* System Object Model

SONET Synchronous Optical Network

SPARC Scalable Processor Architecture

SPD serial presence detect

SPX Sequenced Packet Exchange

SQL structured query language

SRAM static random access memory

SSD Solid State Disk, *or* Solid State Drive

SSL Secure Sockets Layer

STP shielded twisted pair, *also* Secure Transfer Protocol

SVC switched virtual circuit

SVG Scalable Vector Graphics

SVGA super video graphics array

T

TAPI Telephony Application Programming Interface

TB terabytes

TCO Total Cost of Ownership

TCP Transmission Control Protocol

TCP/IP Transmission Control Protocol/Internet Protocol

TDM Time Division Multiplexing

TDR Time Domain Reflectometer

TFT thin film transistor

TFT-LCD thin film transistor liquid crystal display

TFTP Trivial File Transfer Protocol

TI Texas Instruments

TIFF Tagged Image File Format

TLD top-level domain

TPI tracks per inch

TSR terminate and stay resident

TTF TrueType Font

TTL time to live, *also* transistor-transistor logic

TTY teletypewriter

TWAIN Technology without an Interesting Name, *or* Toolkit without an Interesting Name

U

UART	universal asynchronous receiver-transmitter
UCS	universal character set
UDF	Universal Disk Format
UDMA	Ultra Direct Memory Access
UDP	User Datagram Protocol
UHF	ultrahigh frequency
ULSI	ultra large scale integration
UMB	Upper Memory Block
UNC	Universal Naming Convention, *or* Uniform Naming Convention
UPI	universal peripheral interface
UPS	uninterruptible power supply
URI	Universal Resource Identifier
URL	Uniform Resource Locator
USB	Universal Serial Bus
UTP	Unshielded Twisted Pair
UWB	ultra-wideband
WUSB	Wireless USB

V

VAR	value-added reseller
VB	Visual Basic
VC	Virtual Circuit
VCN	Virtual Cluster Number
VDSL	very high data-rate digital subscriber line
VDT	video display terminal
VESA	Video Electronics Standards Association
VFAT	virtual file allocation table
VGA	video graphics array
VHF	very high frequency
VLAN	virtual local area network
VLB	Video Electronics Standards Association (VESA) local bus
VLSI	Very Large-Scale Integration
VMM	Virtual Memory Manager
VMS	Virtual Memory System
VoIP	Voice over Internet Protocol
VOM	volt-ohmmeter, *also* volt-ohm milliameter
VPN	virtual private network
VR	virtual reality
VRAM	video random access memory
VxD	virtual device driver

W

W3C	World Wide Web Consortium
WAN	wide area network
WATS	wide area telephone service
WINS	Windows Internet Naming Service
WLAN	wireless local area network
WMF	Windows Metafile Format
WORM	write once, read many
WRAM	Windows Random Access Memory
WWW	World Wide Web
WYSIWYG	what you see is what you get

X

XGA	extended graphics array
XML	Extensible Markup Language
XMS	extended memory system

Y

Y2K	the year 2000

Z

ZIF	zero insertion force

Appendix B

Binary Math

Binary math accurately represents digital circuitry. In digital electronics, a circuit is either on or off or a voltage condition is high or low. For example, a digital circuit may have two distinct conditions: 5 volts present or 0 volts present.

Binary math uses only 2 numbers, 1 and 0, to represent an infinite range of numbers. The binary number system accomplishes this in basically the same way the decimal number system does, by placing numbers into discrete digit positions. The decimal number system fills these digits with values 0 through 9. The first digit position is commonly referred to as the 1s. The maximum value that can be entered here is 9. The second digit position must therefore be the 10s. If the maximum value of 9 is entered in both the 10s position and the 1s position, the resulting number is 99. The third position must therefore be the 100s position, and so on. Notice in **Figure B-1** that each of the positions can be expressed as an exponent of the base 10.

Digit Positions	1s	10s	100s	1,000s	10,000s	100,000s
Exponent	10^0	10^1	10^2	10^3	10^4	10^5
Range	0–9	10–99	100–999	1000–9999	10,000–99,999	100,000–999,999

Figure B-1

Note:

The Range row indicates the range of number for which the selected digit position would be the leftmost digit, not the range of number that could contain that digit position.

Look at the number 2753. It contains the following:

2-1000s	2000
7-100s	700
5-10s	50
3-1s	3
Total	2753

Add the values together for a total of 2753.

Binary numbers are expressed in similar fashion. However, instead of each digit position being 10 times greater than the position before it, the value of each position is double that of the position before it. See **Figure B-2.**

Digit Positions	1s	2s	4s	8s	16s	32s	64s	128s
Exponent	2^0	2^1	2^2	2^3	2^4	2^5	2^6	2^7
Range	0–1	2–3	4–7	8–15	16–31	32–63	64–127	128–255

Figure B-2

Look at the binary number 101011000001 for example. It contains the following:

1-2048s	2048
0-1024s	0
1-512s	512
0-256s	0
1-128s	128
1-64s	64
0-32s	0
0-16s	0
0-8s	0
0-4s	0
0-2s	0
1-1s	1
Total	2753

As you can see, 101011000001 is the binary equivalent of 2753, **Figure B-3.**

2048s	1024s	512s	256s	128s	64s	32s	16s	8s	4s	2s	1s
1	0	1	0	1	1	0	0	0	0	0	1

Figure B-3

To convert the binary number to a decimal number, simply insert the value assigned to the location when a binary number 1 is in the location and then add the decimal numbers together. See **Figure B-4.**

32s	16s	8s	4s	2s	1s
1	0	1	1	0	1
32	+	8 +	4	+	1 = 45

Figure B-4

When converting a decimal number to a binary number, you simply reverse the previous operation. For example, to convert the decimal number 178 to a binary number, you must divide it by a series of "powers of 2." The "powers of 2" are 1, 2, 4, 8, 16, 32, 64, 128, 256, 512, 1024, 2048, and so on.

To convert the decimal number 178 to binary, start by finding the largest "power of 2" that does not exceed 178. The largest "power of 2" value that does not exceed 178 is 128 (2^7). Place a 1 in the binary number position that represents 128. See **Figure B-5.**

Powers of 2	128	64	32	16	8	4	2	1
Binary Digit	1							

Figure B-5

Subtracting 128 from 178 leaves 50. Fifty is less than 64 (2^6), the next smaller "power of 2." Therefore, you must insert a 0 in the 64s position, as seen in **Figure B-6.**

Powers of 2	128	64	32	16	8	4	2	1
Binary Digit	1	0						

Figure B-6

Next, 50 is larger than 32 (2^5), so place a 1 in the 32s position. See **Figure B-7.**

Powers of 2	128	64	32	16	8	4	2	1
Binary Digit	1	0	1					

Figure B-7

Next, subtract 32 from 50 and the difference is 18. The 18 is larger than 16 (2^4), so place a 1 in the 16s position. See **Figure B-8.**

Powers of 2	128	64	32	16	8	4	2	1
Binary Digit	1	0	1	1				

Figure B-8

Subtracting 16 from 18, leaves 2. The 2 is smaller than the next two "powers of 2," 8 (2^3) and 4 (2^2). That means the next two positions in the binary number are both 0s. See **Figure B-9.**

Powers of 2	128	64	32	16	8	4	2	1
Binary Digit	1	0	1	1	0	0		

Figure B-9

The next "power of 2" is 2 (2^1), and the number remaining from the last step is also 2. Therefore, a 1 goes into the 2s position. See **Figure B-10.**

Powers of 2	128	64	32	16	8	4	2	1
Binary Digit	1	0	1	1	0	0	1	

Figure B-10

There are no decimal numbers remaining, so the ls position should be filled with a 0. The binary equivalent of the decimal number 178 is 10110010, **Figure B-11.**

Powers of 2	128	64	32	16	8	4	2	1
Binary Digit	1	0	1	1	0	0	1	0

Figure B-11

Appendix C

Number Conversion Table			
Decimal	Binary	Octal	Hexadecimal
0	000000	0	0
1	000001	1	1
2	000010	2	2
3	000011	3	3
4	000100	4	4
5	000101	5	5
6	000110	6	6
7	000111	7	7
8	001000	10	8
9	001001	11	9
10	001010	12	A
11	001011	13	B
12	001100	14	C
13	001101	15	D
14	001110	16	E
15	001111	17	F
16	010000	20	10
17	010001	21	11
18	010010	22	12
19	010011	23	13
20	010100	24	14
21	010101	25	15
22	010110	26	16
23	010111	27	17
24	011000	30	18
25	011001	31	19
26	011010	32	1A
27	011011	33	1B
28	011100	34	1C
29	011101	35	1D
30	011110	36	1E

Number Conversion Table (continued)			
Decimal	Binary	Octal	Hexadecimal
31	011111	37	1F
32	100000	40	20
33	100001	41	21
34	100010	42	22
35	100011	43	23
36	100100	44	24
37	100101	45	25
38	100110	46	26
39	100111	47	27
40	101000	50	28
41	101001	51	29
42	101010	52	2A
43	101011	53	2B
44	101100	54	2C
45	101101	55	2D
46	101110	56	2E
47	101111	57	2F
48	110000	60	30
49	110001	61	31
50	110010	62	32
51	110011	63	33
52	110100	64	34
53	110101	65	35
54	110110	66	36
55	110111	67	37
56	111000	70	38
57	111001	71	39
58	111010	72	3A
59	111011	73	3B
60	111100	74	3C
61	111101	75	3D
62	111110	76	3E
63	111111	77	3F

Appendix D

Table of Standard ASCII Characters		
0	NUL	Null
1	SOH	Start of header
2	STX	Start of text
3	ETX	End of text
4	EOT	End of transmission
5	ENQ	Enquiry
6	ACK	Acknowledgment
7	BEL	Bell
8	BS	Backspace
9	HT	Horizontal tab
10	LF	Line feed
11	VT	Vertical tab
12	FF	Form feed
13	CR	Carriage return
14	SO	Shift out
15	SI	Shift in
16	DLE	Data link escape
17	DC1	Device control 1
18	DC2	Device control 2
19	DC3	Device control 3
20	DC4	Device control 4
21	NAK	Negative acknowledgment
22	SYN	Synchronous idle
23	ETB	End of transmit block
24	CAN	Cancel
25	EM	End of medium
26	SUB	Substitute
27	ESC	Escape
28	FS	File separator
29	GS	Group separator
30	RS	Record separator
31	US	Unit separator
32	SP	Space
33	!	
34	"	
35	#	
36	$	
37	%	
38	&	
39	'	
40	(	
41	)	
42	*	

(Continued)	
43	+
44	,
45	-
46	.
47	/
48	0
49	1
50	2
51	3
52	4
53	5
54	6
55	7
56	8
57	9
58	:
59	;
60	<
61	=
62	>
63	?
64	@
65	A
66	B
67	C
68	D
69	E
70	F
71	G
72	H
73	I
74	J
75	K
76	L
77	M
78	N
79	O
80	P
81	Q
82	R
83	S
84	T
85	U

(Continued)	
86	V
87	W
88	X
89	Y
90	Z
91	[
92	\
93	]
94	^
95	_
96	`
97	a
98	b
99	c
100	d
101	e
102	f
103	g
104	h
105	i
106	j
107	k
108	l
109	m
110	n
111	o
112	p
113	q
114	r
115	s
116	t
117	u
118	v
119	w
120	x
121	y
122	z
123	{
124	|
125	}
126	~
127	DEL

Glossary

A

A+ Certification: certification awarded on successful completion of the CompTIA A+ exams.

Accelerated Graphics Port (AGP): a bus designed exclusively for the video card. It supports data transfer of 32 bits at 254.3 MBps, 508.6 MBps, 1.017 GBps, and 2.034 GBps.

access time: the amount of time that passes between the issue of the read command and when the first data bit is read from the CD.

account: contains all the security information describing a user.

active hub: a network device that has a source of power connected to it. When a signal is received by an active hub, it is regenerated.

active partition: the designated boot disk for the system.

active-matrix display: an LCD display in which each individual cell in the grid has its own individual transistor.

actuator arm: the device that moves the read/write head over the disk.

address bus: a bus system that connects the CPU with the main memory module. It identifies memory locations where data is to be stored or retrieved.

ad-hoc network: a wireless network formed between two or more wireless devices such as a full-size PC and a notebook PC.

Advanced Configuration and Power Management (ACPM): an open industry power management standard for desktops, laptops, and servers. ACPM allows the operating system to control the power management features.

Advanced Power Management (APM): power management standard that allows the BIOS to control power management features of the computer system. APM is configured in the BIOS Setup program and determines the amount of time before the display and hard disk drive are turned off.

Advanced SCSI Programming Interface (ASPI): an interface that allows CD devices to communicate with SCSI system components.

alkaline battery: a common battery found in small devices such as TV remote controls and some palmtops.

alternating current (ac): electrical current that reverses direction cyclically.

alternating-frame rendering: a method of sharing the video workload in which each card is responsible for rendering every other frame. For example, if four cards are used, then each card is responsible for the fourth frame image.

American Standard Code for Information Interchange (ASCII): the first attempt to standardize computer character codes among the varieties of hardware and software.

amperes (A): a scale used in measuring the volume of electron flow in a circuit.

analog: a system using a continuous, infinite range of values.

anti-static wrist strap: a strap, typically worn around the wrist, that connects the technician to ground and bleeds off any electrostatic charge.

application service provider (ASP): provides software applications to a personal digital assistant (PDA) or palmtop by downloading the application from a provider as needed.

application software: software designed for a specific purpose, such as creating databases or spreadsheets, word processing, producing graphics, or just for entertainment.

Archie: an Internet protocol, maintained by McGill University in Montreal, that allows you to search for information on the Internet by filename.

arithmetic logic unit (ALU): a CPU component that performs mathematical functions on data stored in the register area.

aspect ratio: ratio of a display area's height and width.

assembly language: a low-level language in which a CPU's instruction set is written.

AT Attachment (ATA): a standard for disk drive interface that integrates the controller into the disk drive. Often referred to as IDE or EIDE.

AT Attachment Packet Interface (ATAPI): the interface used for standard IBM PC AT and compatible systems for accessing CD devices.

Automatic Private IP Address (APIPA): an IP address that is automatically issued to a computer when a DHCP address cannot issue an IP address.

B

backfeed: a type of ohmmeter reading in which the resistance is measured through the circuit components even though the circuit is open.

backoff interval: period of time two network stations wait before trying to retransmit data after data packets from the two stations collide.

backplane: a circuit board with an abundance of slots along the length of the board.

backup domain controllers (BDC): a file server that keeps a backup record of all accounts in case of failure of the primary domain controller.

bandwidth: the range of frequencies that an electronic cable or component is designed to carry.

bar code reader: a device that converts bar code images into data.

basic disk: the traditional FAT16, FAT32, and NTFS file storage systems.

basic input/output system (BIOS): special firmware that permits the compatibility between the CPU and devices such as the hard drive, CD-ROM drive, and monitor.

battery: the component that supplies voltage to the CMOS chip. Without the battery, the information stored in the CMOS chip would be lost every time the computer was shut off.

baud rate: analog frequency rate of modem transmission.

benchmark tests: performance tests used to compare different hardware and software.

binary number system: a system in which all numbers are expressed as combinations of 0 and 1. Also known as the base 2 number system.

biometrics: the science of using the unique physical features of a person to confirm their identity for authentication purposes.

bit: short for binary digit. A bit is a single binary unit of one or zero.

bitmap (.bmp): a graphics standard for uncompressed encoding of images.

blue screen error: a blue screen that appears with an error code and then freezes the system. Also refered to by Microsoft as fatal error, stop error, and stop error message.

Bluetooth: royalty-free standard developed for short-range radio links between portable computers, mobile phones, and other portable devices so that major manufacturers could develop compatible equipment.

BNC (British Naval Connector): connector used with coaxial cable.

boot sequence: the process of starting the computer and loading the operating system.

bootstrap program: a short program that runs the POST, searches for the Master Boot Record (MBR), loads into memory some basic files, and then turns the boot operation over to the operating system.

bridge: a piece of network equipment that is used to join two dissimilar network segments together such as a wireless and an Ethernet 100BaseT network.

brouter: a combination router and bridge.

bubble jet printers: an inkjet printer.

buffer: an area to temporarily store data before transferring it to a device.

buffering: a technique used to play a downloaded file without skips or quiet spots during playback.

bugs: errors in programming.

bus: a collection of conductors that connect multiple components, allowing them to work together for a specific purpose.

bus mastering: a feature of some buses that allows data to be transferred directly between two devices without the intervention of the CPU.

bus topology: a network topology in which a single conductor connects to all the computers on the network.

bus unit: the network of circuitry that connects all the other major components together, accepts data, and sends data through the input and output bus sections.

byte: equal to eight bits.

cabinet (cab) files: compressed files that contain the operating system software.

C

Cable modem: transceiver similar to a DSL modem that allows existing Cable television coaxial cable to be used for Internet access.

cache: a small temporary memory area that is used to separate and store incoming data and instructions.

call center: a large collection of support people located in a common facility equipped with telephones and computer network support. A call center can provide support for more than one company or product.

carpal tunnel syndrome: an inflammation of the tendons in the hands and wrists.

Carrier Sense Multiple Access with Collision Avoidance (CSMA/CA): protocol used by wireless networks to control and ensure the delivery of data.

Carrier Sense Multiple Access with Collision Detection (CSMA/CD): protocol used by Ethernet networks to control and ensure the delivery of data.

cathode ray tube (CRT): a picture tube in which a beam of electrons sweeps across the glass tube, exciting phosphorous dots in the screen.

CD-ROM File System (CDFS): another name used for ISO 9660.

central processing unit (CPU): the brain of the computer. Most of the computer's calculating takes place in the central processing unit. In PCs, the central processing functions are carried out by a single chip, which is called a *microprocessor*.

chipset: handles data manipulation that would otherwise need to be performed by the CPU. Chipsets also handle such things as connecting motherboard buses together that run at different frequencies and connecting ports of various speeds, such as USB, FireWire, and PS/2, to the motherboard buses.

Class A network: large networks that can support up to 16 million hosts on each of 127 networks.

Class B network: medium-size networks that can support up to 65,000 hosts on each of 16,000 networks.

Class C network: small networks that can support up to 254 hosts on each of 2,000,000 networks.

clean room: a room where dust and foreign particles have been completely eliminated.

client: individual PC or workstation that accesses a server's resources and shared files.

client/server model: networking model in which the network is made up of computers that are either clients or servers.

clock doubling: running the CPU at a multiple of the bus frequency.

cluster: One or more sectors of a disk storage device. The smallest unit in which a file will be stored. Also referred to as allocation units.

CMOS Setup (or BIOS Setup) program: a program that allows you to identify the type of hard drive and other storage systems in the PC, set up a password for accessing the PC and the CMOS Setup program, select certain power management features, and select the boot order of bootable devices.

CMYK: standard combination of colors (cyan, magenta, yellow, and black) used by color inkjet printers.

coaxial cable: a core conductor surrounded by an insulator.

codec: any hardware, software, or combination of hardware and software that can compress and decompress data.

cold boot: when the electrical power switch is used to turn on the computer.

color palette: a collection of possible different colors that can be displayed on a monitor.

color thermal printer: printer that applies color by heating a special ribbon that is coated with wax-like material.

color/graphics adapter (CGA): a video standard that features two resolutions: 320 × 200 in four colors and a higher resolution of 640 × 200 in two colors.

colored books: the set of books that outline disc system specifications.

Column Address Select (CAS): describes the time it takes to access the exact column location in the memory matrix after RAS.

Compact Disc Read Only Memory (CD-ROM): an optical disc able to store very large amounts of data.

Compact Disc-Recordable (CD-R): an optical storage media that uses photosensitive reflective dye to simulate the pits and lands of a standard CD.

Compact Disc-ReWritable (CD-RW): an improvement over the CD-R technology, featuring special discs that can be erased and rerecorded.

compiler: a special program that translates the higher-level language into machine language based on the CPU's instruction set.

complementary metal oxide semiconductor (CMOS): the chip that stores the BIOS Setup program data.

complex instruction set computer (CISC): a CPU with a complex instruction set.

CompTIA: a not-for-profit vendor-neutral organization that certifies the competency level of computer service technicians.

computer: an assemblage of electronic modules that interact with software to create, modify, transmit, store, and display data.

configuration file: a file that contains information about the system hardware and software.

constant angular velocity (CAV): a method of reading data from a CD where the drive maintains the same RPM regardless of the data location.

constant linear velocity (CLV): a method of reading data from a CD where the speed of the CD drive adjusts so that points on the inside and outside of the disc are read at a constant linear velocity.

continuity: a state of connectedness. In electronics, an unbroken circuit is said to have continuity.

contrast ratio: a numeric expression in the form of a ratio that describes the amount of contrast between the darkest and lightest pixel in the image.

control bus: a bus that delivers command signals from the processor to devices.

control unit: A CPU component that controls the overall operation of the CPU.

conventional memory: the first 640 kB of a PC's RAM.

cooling fan: a fan that supplies a constant stream of air across the computer components.

cooperative multitasking: one program dominating the operating system but allowing another program to run while it is idle.

cross talk: the imposition of a signal on one pair of conductors by another pair of conductors that runs parallel to it.

current: the electron flow in a circuit.

customer support: the delivery of customer assistance, customer training, and customer services.

cycle: the completed sequence of flow, first in one direction and then in the other.

cylinder: a vertical collection of one set of tracks.

D

data: information, which can be presented in alpha/numeric form (such as ABC or 123), visual form (pictures), and audible form (music or voices).

data bus: a bus used to move data between components.

Data Over Cable Service Interface Specification (DOCSIS): standard for Cable modems that allows any DOCSIS Cable modem to communicate with any other DOCSIS Cable modem.

data transfer rate: a measurement of how much data can be transferred from a CD to RAM in a set period of time.

decode unit: a CPU component that decodes instructions and data and transmits the data to other areas in an understandable format.

dedicated circuit: a circuit installed in an electrical power distribution system that is designed to serve only computer equipment.

dedicated server: server with special functions, such as file servers, print servers, database servers, Web page servers, and administrative servers.

deflection yoke: the electromagnets used to deflect the electron beam in a CRT.

defragment: rearranging clusters on the disk so each file is stored in consecutive clusters.

deport technician: a technician who performs repair work, usually covered by warranty, and has very limited customer contact or no customer contact.

device bay: a drive bay designed to accommodate the easy hot swap of devices such as hard disk drives, tape drives, CD-RW drives, and DVD drives.

differential backup: operation that saves files that have changed since the last full backup of all files. The archive bit is not reset.

digital: a system that uses discrete values.

digital camera: a type of camera that captures and stores images as digital data instead of on photographic film.

digital subscriber lines (DSL): provides high-speed Internet access over telephone lines. A DSL can provide a constant connection to the Internet and can send both voice and data over the same line.

Digital Versatile Disc (DVD): the highest storage capacity of all laser-based CD storage types. Also called *digital video disc.*

digital-to-analog converter (DAC): a chip that converts the digital signal from the computer to an analog signal that is displayed on the computer's monitor.

digitizer pad: a pointing device consisting of a tablet and a puck or pen-like stylus.

direct current (dc): electrical current that flows in one direction.

direct memory access (DMA): a combination of software and hardware that allows certain system devices direct access to the RAM.

directories: a file used to group other files together in a hierarchical file structure. It is analogous to a file folder in a conventional, paper filing system. Directories are referred to as *folders* in many operating systems.

disk operating system (DOS): an operating system typically requiring the user to issue text line commands to perform operations.

docking station: an electronic cradle that provides power for a laptop, allowing users to turn the laptop into a full-size PC.

domain: an organized collection of all groups and users on the network. Also, topic areas into which examination objectives are divided.

Domain Name Service (DNS): translates domain names to IP addresses used on the Internet.

DOS system boot disk: a floppy disk that contains the files necessary to run a computer with DOS.

dot matrix printer: printer that uses a pattern of very small dots to create text and images.

dot pitch: the distance between two color dots on the screen, measured in millimeters.

drivers: software that enables proper communication between the computer and peripheral devices.

DSL modem: transceiver that allows for high-speed Internet access over existing phone lines.

dual-boot system: a computer with two operating systems installed.

Dual Independent Bus (DIB): a bus system architecture in which one bus connects to the main memory and the other connects with the L2 cache.

dual in-line memory module (DIMM): a memory module in which the edge connectors are located directly across the circuit board from each other and do not connect electrically.

dual in-line package (DIP): a memory chip that has two rows of connections, one row per side of the chip.

dye-sublimation printers: printer that produces near photo quality printed images by vaporizing inks, which then solidify on paper.

dynamic addressing: the act of automatically assigning IP addresses.

dynamic disk: an improved version of the NTFS file system.

dynamic execution: a term coined by Intel to describe the enhanced, the superscalar, and the multiple branch prediction features associated with the Pentium II processor.

Dynamic Host Configuration Protocol (DHCP): a protocol written to replace the manual setup of IP addresses on a network by assigning IP addresses dynamically (automatically) to the host PCs.

dynamic RAM: a type of integrated circuit that utilizes capacitors to assist in storing data in the transistors.

E

electrically erasable programmable read only memory (EEPROM): read only memory that can be erased electrically and written to more than once.

electron guns: the components that produce the electron beam, which sweeps across the inside of the screen.

electrophotographic process (EP): a photographic process that uses a combination of static electricity, light, dry chemical compound, pressure, and heat.

electrostatic discharge (ESD): a release of energy (electrical current), created when an object with an electrostatic charge makes contact with a conductor.

emoticons: cartoon face characters made from keyboard symbols to express emotions in e-mails, letters, and text messaging.

encrypted file system (EFS): an NTFS native encryption system that uses a file encryption key (FEK) to encrypt and decrypt the file contents.

encryption: method of encoding data that must be converted back to meaningful words by using an encryption key. The encryption key is a mathematical formula for substituting values in strings of data.

enhanced graphics adapter (EGA): a video standard that improved on the resolutions and color capabilities of the CGA standard.

Enhanced Integrated Drive Electronics (EIDE): an enhanced version of the IDE disk drive controller standard. The term is commonly used when referring to the AT Attachment.

Enhanced Parallel Port (EPP): a parallel port standard that allows a throughput as high as 2 Mbps. The EPP is also referred to as the IEEE-1284 standard.

erasable programmable read only memory (EPROM): read only memory that can be erased with an ultraviolet light and written to more than once.

error code correction (ECC): an alternative form of data-integrity checking.

Ethernet network: network that communicates by broadcasting information to all the computers on the network.

even parity checking: a data integrity checking method in which every time the number of bits counted is even, an extra bit of data is transmitted as a one to indicate even.

examination objectives: objectives that are tested for on an exam and are derived from an industry survey that determines actual job requirements.

expanded memory standard (EMS): an early method to move past the 1 MB memory barrier.

expansion card slots: connectors that allow devices to be quickly and easily plugged into the bus system.

expansion cards: a board that can be easily installed in a computer to enhance or expand its capabilities.

ExpressCard: card that is used to add memory or expand a portable PC. It is designed to connect internally to either the USB 2.0 bus or the PCIe bus.

Extended Capabilities Port (ECP): a parallel port standard that provides for bidirectional communication and has extended capabilities to support multiple devices.

extended graphics array (XGA): a video standard that supports a resolution of 640 × 480 with 65,536 colors, or 1024 × 768 with 256 colors.

Extended Industry Standard Architecture (EISA): an I/O (expansion) bus with a 32-bit data bus. Designed in response to IBM's MCA bus system. EISA buses are backward compatible with ISA cards. This means that an ISA card can fit and function in an EISA expansion slot.

extended memory system (XMS): all of the PC's memory beyond the first 1 MB when the CPU is running in real mode.

extension: the second part of a filename. An extension is typically three characters long and indicates the function of the file.

external commands: individual executable files that extend DOS's functionality beyond the limits of its internal commands.

F

fake parity: when the parity bit is always set to one regardless of the true number of ones contained in the byte.

FAT16: a file system in which file storage information is recorded with 16 bits of data.

FAT32: a file system in which file storage information is recorded with 32 bits of data.

fault tolerance: a system's ability to recover after some sort of disaster.

fiber-optic cable: cable that contains a glass or plastic center used to carry light.

field: a complete sweep of the entire video display area orientation.

field replacement unit (FRU): any major part of a computer system that could be completely replaced on site rather than repaired.

file: a program or collection of data that forms a single unit.

file allocation table (FAT): a table used by the operating system to record and recall the locations of files on the disk.

File Transfer Protocol (FTP): a protocol used for transmitting files across the Internet.

firewall: a barrier that prevents direct contact between computers outside the organization with computers inside the organization.

FireWire (IEEE 1394): a bus system that provides a high rate of data transfer (speeds of 400 Mbps). A single IEEE 1394 port can serve up to 63 external devices in daisy-chain fashion.

Flash BIOS: BIOS that is stored on a reprogrammable chip, allowing for easy upgrades.

Flash memory: memory type that stores data but does not require a power source to retain the data.

Flash ROM: ROM that can be erased in blocks using a high voltage.

floppy disks: soft magnetic disks used for storing small amounts of information.

floppy drive: a device that reads and writes to floppy disks.

font: a design for a set of symbols, usually text and number characters. A font describes characteristics associated with a symbol such as the typeface, size, pitch, and spacing between symbols.

form factor: the physical shape or outline of a motherboard and the location of the mounting holes. Also called a *footprint*.

formatting: preparing a disk to receive data in a systematic, organized manner.

fragmented: stored in nonconsecutive clusters on the disk.

front side bus (FSB): another term for local bus.

fuse: an inexpensive, passive component that is engineered to burn open at a predetermined amperage, protecting the rest of the circuit from overload.

G

gas-plasma displays: a display that operates on the principle of electroluminescence.

gateway: translates information between two LANs using different protocols.

gateway router: a router that combines different media and provides an Internet connection.

Gopher: an early Internet protocol designed to search and retrieve documents from distant computers.

graphical user interface (GUI): an operating system interface that allows the user to perform functions by selecting on-screen icons rather than by issuing text line commands.

group: collection of users organized together by similarities in their job tasks.

H

hard drive: a magnetic storage media consisting of a set of magnetic disks and read/write heads housed inside a hard case.

heap: how Windows refers to the entire memory.

help desk: a central point of contact that provides technical support to clients. The clients may be company employees or customers.

hexadecimal number system: a system in which all numbers are expressed in combinations of 16 alphanumeric characters (0–F). Also know as the base 16 system.

high memory area (HMA): the first 64 kB of the extended memory area.

High Performance File System (HPFS): file system developed for IBM PCs to overcome the limitations of DOS.

High Sierra format: a standard for compact discs that was created so that CDs could be read on any CD device.

high-level format: a process that prepares the disk for file storage.

Home Phoneline Networking Alliance (HomePNA) technology: a technology that allows existing home telephone lines to be used for the network media.

HomePNA adapter: a networking device that allows every telephone jack that is connected together physically in a building to be part of the network.

host: a computer or other piece of equipment connected to a TCP/IP network that requires an address; used interchangeably with the term *node*.

hot swap: a technology that allows a computer device to be plugged into or unplugged from a computer while the computer is running. Also, the act of plugging and unplugging a device from a computer while the computer is running.

hub: device used to provide a quick and easy method of connecting network equipment together by cables.

hybrid topology: a mixture of star, bus, and ring topologies.

Hypertext Markup Language (HTML): programming language used to create Web pages.

Hypertext Transfer Protocol (HTTP): protocol that transports Web pages across the Internet.

I

I/O bus: a bus that connects the processor to the expansion slots.

I/O port address: a memory address expressed in hexadecimal notation, which is used to identify a computer device such as a video card.

incremental backup: operation that backs up select files that have changed since the last backup of files. The archive bit is reset.

Industry Standard Architecture (ISA): an I/O (expansion) bus system featuring a 16-bit data bus.

infrastructure network: a wireless network that contains a wireless access point.

inkjet printer: printer that uses specially designed cartridges that spray a fine mist of ink as they move horizontally in front of a sheet of paper.

input devices: equipment that provides the computer with data.

instructions: commands given to the processor.

instruction set: a set of basic commands that control the processor.

integrated circuit (IC): a collection of transistors, resistors, and other electronic components reduced to an extremely small size.

Integrated Drive Electronics (IDE): an early standard for a disk drive interface that integrated the controller into the disk drive. The term is still commonly used when referring to the AT attachment.

integrated services digital network (ISDN): standard that allows a completely digital connection from one PC to another.

interleave factor: describes how the sectors are laid out on a disk surface to optimize a hard drive's data access rate.

internal bus: part of the integrated circuit inside the CPU.

internal commands: a set of programs that are wholly contained within the command processor program (command.com or cmd.exe).

Internet: a very large, global, decentralized network.

Internet Connection Firewall (ICF): software included in Windows XP that can be configured to keep unauthorized users from accessing the network.

Internet Service Provider (ISP): provides a connection to the Internet and to other services.

InterNIC: a branch of the United States government under the direction of the Department of Commerce. It is responsible for regulating the Internet, overseeing the issue of domain names, and assigning IP addresses to them.

IP address: identifying address used for a PC or other equipment on a TCP/IP network.

IP switch: designed to pass ATM protocol packets.

IRQ: an acronym for "interrupt request." An IRQ is a signal that interrupts the processes taking place in the CPU and requests that the processor pay attention to a specific device.

ISO 9660: the file system standard that CD-ROMs use, which is an update on the High Sierra format.

ISO image: an image that is the exact copy of data. It is made by copying all sectors containing data and ignoring the file system used.

K

kernel: the core of the operating system.

kernel mode: automatic Windows NT mode of operation that oversees the system resources and processor actions.

L

L1 cache: a cache contained within the processor that is designed to run at the processor's speed.

L2 cache: a cache mounted outside of the processor. (Note: The Pentium III incorporates the L2 cache in the processor.)

L3 cache: the cache mounted on the motherboard when L1 and L2 caches are incorporated into the CPU.

lands: the flat areas between the pits in a compact disc.

laptop: a lightweight, portable computer with the monitor, motherboard, processor, disk drives, keyboard, and mouse molded into one unit.

light pens: input devices that interact with the light beam that creates the image on the monitor.

liquid crystal display (LCD): a type of monitor that uses polarized light passing through liquid crystal to create an image on screen.

lithium-ion (Li-ion) battery: rechargeable battery found in most new portable computers. Has no problem with memory effect and holds a charge longer than NiCad and NiMH batteries.

live support: support in which a customer or client talks directly to support personnel rather than using e-mail or FAQs.

local area network (LAN): a small network of computers contained in a relatively small area, such as an office building.

local bus: a bus system that connects directly to the CPU and provides communications to high-speed devices mounted closely to the CPU.

local printer: printer that connects directly to a specific PC.

logical drives: separate storage areas on a single drive that simulate separate drives. Also referred to as partitions.

logical unit numbers (LUN): an identifier used with SCSI extenders to distinguish between (up to) eight devices on the same SCSI ID number.

low-level format: a process that determines the type of encoding to be done on the disk platter and the sequence in which the read/write heads will access stored data.

LS-120 drive: a very high capacity disk drive that is able to store 120 MB of data on a single disk.

M

Magneto-optical (MO) drives: disk drives that combine magnetic and optical principles to store and retrieve data.

Master Boot Record (MBR): an area of the hard disk that contains information about the physical characteristics of the drive, the disk partitions, and the boot procedure. Also referred to as the boot sector.

master: the primary drive on an IDE channel.

math coprocessor: a component of the CPU that improves the processor's ability to perform advanced mathematical calculations.

media access code (MAC) address: a hexadecimal number programmed into the network interface card's chip. The first six digits identify the card's manufacturer. The second six-digit sequence is assigned by the manufacturer and is different on every card produced.

memory address range: an assigned section of memory used as a temporary storage area for data before it is transferred.

memory bus: a bus that connects the processor to the memory.

mesh topology: a network topology in which each node connects directly to every other node on the network.

metal oxide varistor (MOV): a gate in a surge suppressor that becomes conductive at a given voltage, causing current to bypass the equipment plugged into the suppressor.

metropolitan area network (MAN): a group of two or more interconnected LANs operating under a single management.

Micro Channel Architecture (MCA): an I/O (expansion) bus system featuring a 32-bit data bus. MCA and ISA cards and slots are not physically compatible.

Microsoft Dynamic Link Library (DLL): an executable file that can be called and run by Microsoft software applications or by third-party software programs.

mini connector: a two-pin connector that delivers a +5 volt signal from the power supply. A variation of this connector has four wires and delivers both +12-volt and +5-volt signals.

MMX processor: a processor with an additional 56 commands that enhance its abilities to support multimedia technology.

modem: electronic device that is used to convert serial data from a computer to an audio signal for transmission over telephone lines and vice versa.

Molex connector: a four-wire, D-shaped connector that delivers +12-volt and +5-volt signals from the power supply.

monochrome: a monitor type that displays only a single color, usually amber or green.

motherboard: a circuit board covered by a maze of conductors that provide electrical current to the computer components and expansion slots. Also used to refer to the main circuit board and all of its electronic components (chipset).

Motion Picture Experts Group (MPEG): a standard format for recording motion picture video and sound.

mouse: a computer pointing device used to manipulate an onscreen pointer.

multicolor/graphics array (MCGA): a video standard that supported CGA and also provided up to 64 shades of gray.

multimedia: incorporating sound or video.

multiple-boot system: a computer with more than two operating systems installed.

multiple branch prediction: a technique that predicts what data element will be needed next, rather than waiting for the next command to be issued.

multiple zone recording (MZR): a method of sectoring tracks so there are twice as many sectors in the outermost tracks as there are in the innermost tracks.

Multipurpose Internet Mail Extensions (MIME): a specification for formatting non-text-based files for transmission over the Internet.

Multistation Access Unit (MAU): a hub-like device that physically connects computers in a star arrangement while maintaining a ring structure.

multitasking: the ability of an operating system to support two or more programs running at the same time.

musical instrument digital interface (MIDI): a file standard developed for music synthesizers.

N

nanosecond (ns): equal to one billionth of a second.

native resolution: the resolution that matches the pixel design of the display.

network: two or more computers connected together for the purpose of sharing data and resources.

network administration: the use of network software packages to manage network system operations.

network interface card (NIC): connects the network communication media, usually twisted pair, to the individual network devices such as workstations, file servers, and printers.

Network Setup Wizard: a Windows XP wizard that makes setting up a network easy by including a series of dialog boxes that ask for information about the network.

New Technology File System (NTFS): a file system found in Windows NT and Windows 2000. NTFS features improve security and storage capacity and are compatible with FAT16.

nickel-cadmium (NiCd) battery: rechargeable battery used in early portable computers. Has a problem with memory effect.

nickel-metal hydride (NiMH) battery: second generation of rechargeable battery used for portable computers. Has no problem with memory effect and holds a charge longer than the NiCad battery.

node: device connected to a client/server network.

north bridge: the portion of the chipset that controls higher data speed systems such as graphics and DVD hardware.

notebook: lightweight, portable computer with the monitor, motherboard, processor, disk drives, keyboard, and mouse molded into one unit. It is slightly smaller than a laptop.

O

octet: an eight-bit series of numbers.

odd parity checking: a data integrity checking method in which every time the number of bits counted is odd, an extra bit of data is transmitted as a one to indicate odd.

Open Systems Interconnection (OSI): seven-layer reference model that describes how hardware and software should work together to form a network communication system.

operating system (OS): software that provides a computer user with a file system structure and with a means of communicating with the computer hardware.

optical character recognition (OCR): a type of software that is able to distinguish between the various letters, numbers, and symbols in a scanned image.

overclocking: forcing a processor to operate faster than its approved speed.

P

packet: small unit of data into which larger amounts are divided for passage through a network.

Packet Internet Groper (PING): a utility program that is often used as a troubleshooting tool to verify network connections to Web sites.

packet sniffer: a utility that captures packets on a network and displays their entire contents.

packet writing: records data in small blocks similar to the way hard drives store data.

page file: a file that is located on a special section of the hard disk drive used to supplement RAM.

palmtop: portable computer that can rest in the palm of the hand.

paper jams: when a printer pulls one or more sheets through its mechanism and the paper becomes wedged inside.

paper train: the route the paper follows through the printer.

parallel: side-by-side. In parallel transfer, more than one bit of data is transferred at a time.

parity: the counting of either odd or even bits being transmitted.

partitions: areas on a hard drive that simulate separate drives. Also referred to as logical drives.

passive hub: acts as a connection point in the star topology. Transmitted digital signals from one computer are passed to all computers connected to the passive hub and through the hub to other network sections.

passive-matrix display: an LCD display in which a grid of semitransparent conductors is run to each of the crystals that make up the individual pixels.

pathname: a string of characters used to identify a file's location in the directory structure.

PCMCIA card: card designed by the Personal Computer Memory Card International Association (PCMCIA) to add memory or expand a portable PC. The PCMCIA card is often referred to as simply a "PCM" or "PC" card.

peer-to-peer network: network administration model in which all the PCs connected together are considered equal.

Peripheral Components Interface (PCI): a bus system featuring a 32-bit data bus that provides a high-speed bus structure needed for faster CPUs.

peripherals: optional equipment used to input or output data.

permissions: the right to perform certain functions.

persistence: the continuation of the glow after the electron beam ceases to strike the phosphor areas.

personal digital assistant (PDA): portable computer comparable in size to a palmtop. Has a limited amount of memory and is used mostly to retain to-do lists, store personal data, connect to the Internet, and send and receive e-mail.

photocell: an electronic component that changes light energy into electrical energy.

pin grid array (PGA): the pattern of pins on a CPU.

pitch: unit of measure for the width of a font.

pits: the holes etched into a compact disc in order to record data.

pixel: the smallest unit of color in a screen display.

pixel pitch: the distance between two same color pixels on the display area.

Plug and Play (PnP): a BIOS function that enables the automatic detection and configuration of new hardware components. Also, the automatic assignment of system resources such as DMA channels, interrupts, memory, and port assignments.

points: unit of measure for the height of a font. Each point is equal to 1/72 of an inch.

polarized light: light energy composed of light beams with a matching wave angle.

port replicator: an external computer device that provides additional ports to be used by a computer system.

power: the amount of electrical energy provided or used by equipment.

power bus: a bus system that sends electrical power for small consumption devices, such as speakers, lights, and switches.

power good signal: a signal sent from the power supply to the motherboard that verifies the power supply is working properly.

powerline communications (PLC): a technology that allows existing power lines to be used as network media.

preemptive multitasking: multiple programs sharing control of the operating system. It is sometimes referred to as *time slicing.*

primary domain controller (PDC): a file server that keeps the master record of all accounts.

printer: an electromechanical device that converts computer data into text or graphic images printed to paper or other presentation media.

processor affinity: the ability to select the number of CPU cores to apply to a software application.

processor throttling: controlling processor frequency to conserve battery life and produce less heat.

professionalism: a businesslike characteristic reflected in a person and work environment.

programmable read only memory (PROM): read only memory that can be written to only once.

protected mode: an operating mode that supports multitasking and allows access to memory beyond the first 1 MB.

protocol: set of rules for formatting the data stream transmission between two computers or devices and for describing how to transmit data, usually across a network.

protocol suite: combination of individual protocols each designed for specific purposes.

proxy server: designed to hide all the PCs in the LAN from direct connection from PCs outside of the LAN. It relays the requested information for the client, leaving the client anonymous outside the network.

Q

query: locating and extracting data from a database system.

queue: list of print jobs waiting to be completed and their status.

R

RAID: a system of several hard drive units arranged in such a way as to ensure recovery after a system disaster or to ensure data integrity during normal operation.

rails: the conductor paths inside the metal power supply case of an ATX12V power supply. There is one rail for each voltage level. Each rail then supplies the electrical voltage level to all connectors that require that specific voltage.

random access memory (RAM): a volatile memory system into which programs are loaded. When the computer's power is shut off, all data stored in RAM is lost.

raster: the sweep of the electron beam.

read only memory (ROM): memory that stores information permanently.

read/write head: the mechanism that records information to and reads information from a magnetic medium.

real mode: an operating mode in which only the first 1 MB of a system's RAM can be accessed. Also, an operating mode in which the 286 or later processor emulates an 8088 or 8086 processor.

reduced instruction set computer (RISC): a type of CPU architecture that is designed with a fewer number of transistors and commands.

refresh rate: the rate at which the electron beam sweeps across the screen.

register unit: a CPU component containing many separate, smaller storage units known as registers.

registered memory: a memory module that incorporates driver and synchronizing electronics as part of the unit.

registers: small pockets of memory within the processor that are used to temporarily store data being processed by the CPU.

registrar: private sector company, regulated by InterNIC, to whom users apply for an IP address or domain name.

registry: a database that stores configuration information.

repeater: a piece of equipment that regenerates a weak digital signal.

reserved memory: another term for upper memory.

resistance: the opposition to the flow of electrical energy.

resolution: the amount of detail a monitor is capable of displaying.

response time: the amount of time it takes a TFT pixel to display after a signal is sent to the transistor controlling that pixel.

rights: system control abilities that are normally reserved for the system administrator.

ring topology: a network topology in which a single cable runs continuously from computer to computer.

root directory: the top of the directory structure. A root directory is analogous to a file cabinet drawer in a conventional, paper filing system. A root directory is also referred to as the *root*.

router: a device used to control the flow of data to different networks based on IP addresses.

Row Address Selection (RAS): describes the time it takes to start a memory read or write to the row location in the memory matrix. RAS is the first step of a memory access operation.

run-length encoding (RLE): a graphics compression format that reduces image file size by recording strings of identical pixels.

S

safe mode: mode that boots the computer with minimum required drivers and programs to allow for troubleshooting.

sampling: measuring an analog signal at regular intervals.

scan code: a data signal created from electrical signals sent by an input device.

ScanDisk: a program included in Windows operating systems that is used to inspect the surface of a disk and identify bad and lost clusters.

scanner: a device that digitizes printed images and text.

SCSI ID number: a unique number assigned to a device on a SCSI chain and used to identify that device.

sectors: subdivisions of tracks, usually about 512 bytes in size.

segment: a section of cable between two network devices. Also, a portion of a network that shares a common collision or token passing domain.

sequence number: attached to each packet of data being transmitted, ensuring that the data will be reassembled in the exact order it was transmitted.

serial: occurring one at a time. In serial transfer, data is transmitted one bit at a time.

Serial Attached SCSI (SAS): A SCSI device that transfers data in serial fashion rather than in parallel. The SAS design allows 128 devices to be attached directly and can be expanded to as many as 4,032 storage devices.

serial presence detect (SPD): a technology used to identify the type of RAM installed on a computer. It involves the presence of an extra chip on the memory module that contains technical information about the RAM module.

server: powerful computer used to manage network resources and provide services such as security and file sharing.

shadow mask: a metal mesh with triangular holes that a CRT's electron beam passes through, creating a crisper image.

share: an object that is shared across the network, such as a file, hard drive, CD-ROM drive, printer, or scanner.

share-level security: default security system used on Windows-based networks, which requires a password for access.

simultaneous threading: executing two or more threads at the same time.

Single Edge Contact (SEC): a processor configuration in which the CPU is mounted on a circuit board and the edge of the circuit board inserts into the motherboard socket.

single in-line memory module (SIMM): a memory module containing a row of DIP memory chips mounted on a circuit board.

single in-line package (SIP): a memory chip containing a single row of connections, which run along the length of the chip.

slave: a secondary drive on an IDE channel.

Small Computer System Interface (SCSI): the standard that allows up to 7 or 15 devices to be connected to a SCSI adapter board.

small-office/home-office (SOHO) network: a simple peer-to-peer LAN that is used to share resources and data in a home- or small-office environment.

smart card: credit card-like device with a chip embedded in the plastic. The chip allows the card to be used for a variety of purposes.

soft power: another term for the features provided by a standby power connection.

solid ink printer: printer that uses solid ink cartridges similar to wax.

Solid State Disk (SSD): a storage system designed with no moving parts and consisting entirely of DRAM chips. The SSD is also referred to as a RAM drive.

Solid State Drive (SSD): a storage device that uses Flash memory chips.

source code: the programming code used to make the operating system.

south bridge: the portion of the chipset that controls the slower devices associated with the PCI and ISA buses.

split-frame rendering: a method of sharing the video workload in which each card is responsible for an equal part of the frame image. For example, if four cards are used, each card is responsible for one fourth of each image.

spooling: a technique that stores data to be printed in memory so that printing operations can be completed in the background while other tasks are performed by the PC.

standby power connection: provides power to reactivate or wake up a system in standby mode.

star topology: a network topology in which a cable runs from each computer to a single point, forming a star.

startup problem: problem that causes the computer to lock up during the boot process.

static RAM: an integrated circuit using digital flip-flop components.

subdirectories: A file that subdivides the contents of a directory. A subdirectory is analogous to a folder within a folder in a conventional, paper filing system. Subdirectories are referred to as *subfolders* in many operating systems.

subnet mask: a mask that is used to determine what subnet a particular IP address refers to.

Super VGA (SVGA): a video standard that supports 16 million colors and various resolutions up to 1600×1200.

superscalar: processing multiple instructions simultaneously.

switch: filters and forwards packets of data between network segments based on MAC addresses.

switching hub: enhanced active hub. It can determine whether a signal should remain in the isolated section of the network or be passed through the hub to other parts of the network.

synchronous: data transferred on the same timing as the computer.

System Management Mode (SMM): a standby mode developed for laptop computers to save electrical energy when using a battery.

system resources: items such as files, software, and printers that can be shared in a network environment.

T

T-carrier lines: lines designed to carry voice and data at a much higher rate than traditional phone lines.

teamwork: two or more people working toward a common goal.

telephone jack: where the telephone line connects to the cabling. This is a standard connection used to attach devices such as modems and telephones to the wiring system.

Telnet: a protocol that allows you to log on to a remote computer and download or upload files.

text line command: commands issued by typing in text at a command prompt.

thin film transistor liquid crystal display (TFT-LCD): a display that consists of a matrix of thin film transistors, in which each transistor controls a single pixel.

thread: part of a software program that can be executed independently of the entire program.

time to live (TTL): the length of time the data in a packet is valid.

token: a short binary code generated by the network software that is passed from one computer to the next along a ring topology and in some bus topologies.

Token Bus network: network that uses a token passing system with a bus-type topology.

Token Ring network: a highly organized system in which each computer must wait its turn to transmit data.

topology: the physical arrangement of hardware and cabling in a network system.

touch screen displays: computer display that is modified to accept input by touch.

tracert: utility program that sends a packet out and waits for a reply. It also displays information about the route that was taken to the destination.

track ball: a pointing device similar to a mouse that is operated upside down.

tracks: the concentric circles of data storage areas on a disk.

twisted pair cable: the most common choice for network wiring. It consists of four pairs of conductors twisted around each other.

U

Ultra-Wideband (UWB): a short distance (10 meter) radio communication standard developed by the WiMedia Alliance.

Uniform Resource Locators (URLs): the global address for sites all over the Internet. The first part of the URL identifies the protocol used and the second part identifies the domain name.

uninterruptible power supply (UPS): a power supply that ensures a constant supply of quality electrical power to the computer system.

universal asynchronous receiver-transmitter (UART): main chip in a modem that changes parallel data to serial data and vice versa.

Universal Disk Format (UDF): the file system standard accepted for CD-RW, magneto-optical disc, and DVD technology.

Universal Naming Convention (UNC): a path format that identifies a server and its share and uses backslashes to separate the server name from the share name.

universal peripheral interface (UPI): a chip on the motherboard that directs communications between the CPU and the input device.

Universal Serial Bus (USB): a bus system designed to replace the function of expansion slots with a data transfer rate as high as 480 Mbps. The USB is accessed by plugging a USB device into the bus at a port opening in the case. Additional devices (up to 127) can be connected to the bus in a daisy-chain configuration.

upper memory: term for a PC's memory range between 640 kB and 1 MB.

user: a person who may use the network system resources.

user-level security: security system used on Windows-based networks that identifies who may have access to a shared resource but does not require a password for accessing the share.

user mode: the actual user interface mode for the NT operation system. It is very restrictive and many areas are not accessible by the user or user program.

V

vector graphics: a graphic standard based on a series of mathematical formulas that can be converted into geometric shapes representing the image to be displayed.

Video Electronics Standards Association (VESA) local bus: a bus system that could handle a higher data transfer rate than MCA or EISA. The VL-Bus was developed by a consortium of video adapter and monitor manufacturers.

video graphics array (VGA): the minimum standard for video adapters, that displays at a resolution of 640 × 480 with 16 colors or 320 × 200 with 256 colors.

viewing angle: a measurement of the angle at which a person can adequately see an image on a display without it looking excessively distorted.

virtual file allocation table (VFAT): a method of programming the FAT16 file system to allow long file capabilities similar to FAT32.

virtual machine: a computer on which more than one operating system can be executed at the same time.

virtual memory: a section of the hard disk drive reserved to supplement RAM.

virtual mode: an operational mode in which the processor can operate several real mode programs at once and access memory higher than the first 1 MB.

virtual private network (VPN): a security configuration that ensures data sent across the Internet is not read or modified. It does this by creating a private tunnel between the destination and source PC and encrypting packet contents.

voltage: the amount of electrical pressure present in a circuit or power source.

volt-amperes (VA): an alternative scale for measuring electrical power.

volts (V): a scale used in measuring electrical pressure (electromotive force).

volume mount points: allow a volume or additional hard drive to be attached to a directory structure. Volume mount points can be used to integrate a dissimilar file system into a logical file system.

W

warm boot: using the reset button or key combination [Ctrl], [Alt], and [Delete] to restart a computer that is already running. A warm boot can also be initiated by a software program as part of a typical installation such as installing a game.

watts (w): a scale used in measuring electrical power.

weighted: a method of applying a measure or score to an individual question.

wide area network (WAN): a large number of computers spread over a large geographic area and under control of a centrally located administrator.

Wi-Fi: the registered trademark of the Wi-Fi Alliance organization that applies to any IEEE 802.11 wireless device that conforms to the Wi-Fi Alliance standard.

Windows CE: version of Windows designed for less-powerful devices, such as PDAs or smart appliances.

Windows Internet Naming Service (WINS): resolves the computer name to the equivalent IP address on the network.

Windows system disk: a disk containing all the files necessary to start the Windows-based computer and load the operating system.

wireless access point: a device used to support communications between wireless devices and a hard-wired network system.

wireless topology: a network topology that uses no cabling system between the computers. It uses either infrared light or radio transmission to communicate between the network devices.

Wireless USB (WUSB): the specification for USB wireless devices that use the radio frequencies between 3.1 GHz to 10.6 GHz.

word: the total amount of bytes a computer can process at one time.

Z

zero insertion force (ZIF) socket: a processor socket equipped with a lever to assist in the installation of the CPU.

Zip disk: a form of removable computer data storage that can contain over 200 MB of data.

Index

C

D

G

H

I

J

K

L

M

Q

R

S

T

U

V

W

X

Z